D1452124

Enhancing Qualitative and Mixed Methods Research with Technology

Shalin Hai-Jew
Kansas State University, USA

A volume in the Advances in Knowledge
Acquisition, Transfer, and Management (AKATM)
Book Series

Managing Director:	Lindsay Johnston
Acquisitions Editor:	Kayla Wolfe
Production Editor:	Christina Henning
Development Editor:	Erin O'Dea
Typesetter:	Kaitlyn Kulp
Cover Design:	Jason Mull

Published in the United States of America by
Information Science Reference (an imprint of IGI Global)
701 E. Chocolate Avenue
Hershey PA, USA 17033
Tel: 717-533-8845
Fax: 717-533-8661
E-mail: cust@igi-global.com
Web site: http://www.igi-global.com

Library of Congress Cataloging-in-Publication Data

Enhancing qualitative and mixed methods research with technology / Shalin Hai-Jew, editor.
     pages cm
  Includes bibliographical references and index.
  Summary: "This book explores the integration of new digital tools into the research process, including current information on data visualization, research design, information capture, as well as social media analysis"-- Provided by publisher.
  ISBN 978-1-4666-6493-7 (hardcover) -- ISBN 978-1-4666-6494-4 (ebook) -- ISBN 978-1-4666-6496-8 (print & perpetual access) 1. Information visualization. 2. Social media. 3. Qualitative research. I. Hai-Jew, Shalin.
  QA76.9.I52E54 2015
  001.4'226--dc23
                                        2014026481

This book is published in the IGI Global book series Advances in Knowledge Acquisition, Transfer, and Management (AKATM) (ISSN: 2326-7607; eISSN: 2326-7615)

British Cataloguing in Publication Data
A Cataloguing in Publication record for this book is available from the British Library.

For electronic access to this publication, please contact: eresources@igi-global.com.

Advances in Knowledge Acquisition, Transfer, and Management (AKATM) Book Series

Murray E. Jennex
San Diego State University, USA

ISSN: 2326-7607
EISSN: 2326-7615

MISSION

Organizations and businesses continue to utilize knowledge management practices in order to streamline processes and procedures. The emergence of web technologies has provided new methods of information usage and knowledge sharing.

The **Advances in Knowledge Acquisition, Transfer, and Management (AKATM) Book Series** brings together research on emerging technologies and their effect on information systems as well as the knowledge society.AKATM will provide researchers, students, practitioners, and industry leaders with research highlights surrounding the knowledge management discipline, including technology support issues and knowledge representation.

COVERAGE

- Cognitive Theories
- Cultural Impacts
- Information and Communication Systems
- Knowledge Acquisition and Transfer Processes
- Knowledge Management Strategy
- Knowledge Sharing
- Organizational Learning
- Organizational Memory
- Small and Medium Enterprises
- Virtual Communities

IGI Global is currently accepting manuscripts for publication within this series. To submit a proposal for a volume in this series, please contact our Acquisition Editors at Acquisitions@igi-global.com or visit: http://www.igi-global.com/publish/.

Titles in this Series

For a list of additional titles in this series, please visit: www.igi-global.com

Knowledge Management Practice in Organizations The View from Inside
Ulla de Stricker (de Stricker Associates, Canada)
Information Science Reference • copyright 2014 • 318pp • H/C (ISBN: 9781466651869) • US $205.00 (our price)

Knowledge Discovery, Transfer, and Management in the Information Age
Murray E. Jennex (San Diego State University, USA)
Information Science Reference • copyright 2014 • 302pp • H/C (ISBN: 9781466647114) • US $175.00 (our price)

Harnessing Dynamic Knowledge Principles in the Technology-Driven World
Mark Nissen (Royal Oaks, USA)
Information Science Reference • copyright 2014 • 291pp • H/C (ISBN: 9781466647275) • US $175.00 (our price)

Emerging Pedagogies in the Networked Knowledge Society Practices Integrating Social Media and Globalization
Marohang Limbu (Michigan State University, USA) and Binod Gurung (New Mexico State University, USA)
Information Science Reference • copyright 2014 • 352pp • H/C (ISBN: 9781466647572) • US $175.00 (our price)

Knowledge Management and Competitive Advantage: Issues and Potential Solutions
Michael A. Chilton (Kansas State University, USA) and James M. Bloodgood (Kansas State University, USA)
Information Science Reference • copyright 2014 • 387pp • H/C (ISBN: 9781466646797) • US $175.00 (our price)

Ontology-Based Applications for Enterprise Systems and Knowledge Management
Mohammad Nazir Ahmad (Universiti Teknologi Malaysia, Malaysia) Robert M. Colomb (University of Queensland, Australia) and Mohd Syazwan Abdullah (Universiti Utara Malaysia, Malaysia)
Information Science Reference • copyright 2013 • 423pp • H/C (ISBN: 9781466619937) • US $175.00 (our price)

Knowledge Management and Drivers of Innovation in Services Industries
Patricia Ordóñez de Pablos (Universidad de Oviedo, Spain) and Miltiadis D. Lytras (The American College of Greece, Greece)
Information Science Reference • copyright 2012 • 349pp • H/C (ISBN: 9781466609488) • US $175.00 (our price)

Customer-Centric Knowledge Management Concepts and Applications
Minwir Al-Shammari (University of Bahrain, Bahrain)
Information Science Reference • copyright 2012 • 315pp • H/C (ISBN: 9781613500897) • US $175.00 (our price)

www.igi-global.com

701 E. Chocolate Ave., Hershey, PA 17033
Order online at www.igi-global.com or call 717-533-8845 x100
To place a standing order for titles released in this series, contact: cust@igi-global.com
Mon-Fri 8:00 am - 5:00 pm (est) or fax 24 hours a day 717-533-8661

This is for R. Max.

Editorial Advisory Board

Table of Contents

Section 1
Setting the Parameters for Technology Use: Qualitative and Mixed Methods Theories and Models

Section 2
All-Environments Information Collection

Section 3
**Technology-Enhanced Data Management, Data Processing, Data Visualization, and
Human-Machine Analysis**

Section 4
Data Acquisition and Extraction from Social Media Platforms

Section 5
Cases of Technology-Enhanced Qualitative and Mixed Methods Research (and the Converse)

Detailed Table of Contents

Section 1
Setting the Parameters for Technology Use: Qualitative and Mixed Methods Theories and Models

This first section sets a basic understanding of the roles of technologies and new methodologies in qualitative and mixed methods research. It features some of the strongest analysts and writers working in this area of qualitative and mixed methods research with applied technologies. The assumption is that readers already have a fairly solid understanding of some of the related research theories and methodologies, so the works here highlight some understandings in approaching technology-enhanced research.

Chapter 1

Kakali Bhattacharya, Kansas State University, USA

Current discourses in qualitative research, especially those situated in postmodernism, represent coding and the technology that assists with coding as reductive, lacking complexity, and detached from theory. In this chapter, the author presents a counter-narrative to this dominant discourse in qualitative research. The author argues that coding is not necessarily devoid of theory, nor does the use of software for data management and analysis automatically render scholarship theoretically lightweight or barren. A lack of deep analytical insight is a consequence not of software but of epistemology. Using examples informed by interpretive and critical approaches, the author demonstrates how NVivo can provide an effective tool for data management and analysis. The author also highlights ideas for critical and deconstructive approaches in qualitative inquiry while using NVivo. By troubling the positivist discourse of coding, the author seeks to create dialogic spaces that integrate theory with technology-driven data management and analysis, while maintaining the depth and rigor of qualitative research.

The overall aim of this chapter is to provide a better understanding of how a specific technique of online research methodology, online focus groups, has been theoretically conceptualized and practically utilized in order to examine its advantages and disadvantages to improve future applications of this technique in qualitative and mixed methods research. The chapter offers an overview of qualitative and mixed methods empirical research using online focus groups in different disciplines and outlines the strengths and weaknesses of this data collection technique. In addition, based on the review of empirical and theoretical research, the current and emerging practices in and characteristics of using online focus groups for data collection are outlined and used to suggest future trends in using this data collection technique in qualitative and mixed methods research.

### Chapter 3

In qualitative and mixed methods research, the researcher and/or research team are critical elements in the research. Given perceptual, cognitive, and memory limitations, human researchers can often bring these shortcomings to their research and decision-making. To combat such tendencies, researcher reflection, self-awareness, and self-critique are seen as some research controls, as are various standardizations in research to control for bias and to provide for multiple points-of-view. One tool that has long been used for researcher reflection to promote research quality has been the research journal. Research journals are field texts created by the researcher or a research team to make sense of the research work; these are professional forms of narrative analyses or narrative inquiries to enhance researcher self-consciousness of their work, their reasoning, their decision-making, and their conclusions. A contemporaneous electronic version of the qualitative or mixed methods research journal is multimedia-based (including visuals, audio, and video) and may be built in data management software programs, shared cloud-based work sites, or simple folders or digital objects. Guided research e-journals may be structured for the elicitation and capture of specific information to ensure researcher attentiveness, awareness, mindfulness, and thoroughness. Guided electronic journaling (used prior to, during, and post-research) may be used to enhance research quality. This chapter proposes a partial typology of guided structures for research journaling and suggests channels for publishing and distributing research e-journals.

Section 2
All-Environments Information Collection

Whether the research occurs in physical space or online, or both, technologies enable high-fidelity information capture. The work of data acquisition in its various forms is an important part of research. Information and Communication Technology (ICT), broadly speaking, is important for information recording in real spaces and intercommunications, surveying, and data extraction in cyber spaces. Section 2 addresses some creative ways technologies are used for information collection and reporting for practical uses and data research.

In this chapter, the author describes the technologies she employed while conducting an Ethnography of Communication on Eloqi (pseudonym), a for-profit start-up company that built and operated a proprietary Web-based, voice-enabled platform connecting English language learners in China with trainers in the United States. While Eloqi existed, its unique platform not only connected trainers and students for short one-to-one English conversation lessons but also brought together the company admins, trainers, and students in a virtual community. This chapter describes the technologies that the author used to carry out the qualitative study from start to finish, including the steps of online participant observations, online and offline interviews, qualitative coding, and qualitative data analysis. Because the author studied a virtual community, technologies played a critical role in how she collected, managed, and analyzed the dataset, which was completely electronic. The chapter concludes with tips and advice for fellow researchers using technologies to support qualitative studies of communication, whether online or offline.

In broadest terms, ecology is the scientific study of interactions among organisms and their environment, and ecosystem defines a community of living organisms in conjunction with the nonliving components of their environment interacting as a system. At present, both terms are references of many studies including education; various authors and studies investigating distance education with an ecological perspective refer to the ecosystem concept as frameworks for defining the operational components and processes. Among all these contributions, the concept of "waste," one of the key concerns of sustainability, seems to be vaguely discussed. Having this as a standpoint, an online Delphi study was carried out in a research project at Anadolu University, Turkey, aiming to define a sustainable distance education ecosystem including the explanation of "waste" with reference to ecosystem definitions. The study was processed online and is explained by both presenting the results and discussing the benefits and also difficulties encountered.

This chapter synthesizes the literature on real-time, synchronous, video interviews as a qualitative data collection method. The authors specifically focus on the advantages and disadvantages of this method in social science research and offer conceptual themes, practical techniques, and recommendations for using video-interviews. The growing popularity of computer-mediated communication indicates that a wider audience will be willing and able to participate in research using this method; therefore, online video-conferencing could be considered a viable option for qualitative data collection.

Chapter 7

Tianxing Cai, Lamar University, USA

Industrial and environmental research will always involve the study of the cause-effect relationship between emissions and the surrounding environment. Qualitative and mixed methods researchers have employed a variety of Information and Communication Technology (ICT) tools, simulated or virtual environments, information systems, information devices, and data analysis tools in this field. With the collection and representation of information in a range of ways, software tools have been created to manage and store this data. This data management enables more efficient searching ability of various types of electronic and digitized information. Various technologies have made the work of research more efficient. The results of the qualitative or mixed methods research may be integrated to reach the research target. Right now, a lot of software tools are available for analysis to identify patterns and represent new meanings. The programs extend the capabilities of the researcher in terms of information coding and meaning-making. Machine-enhanced analytics has enabled the identification of aspects of interest such as correlations and anomalies from large datasets. Chemical facilities, where large amounts of chemicals and fuels are processed, manufactured, and housed, have high risks to originate air emission events, such as intensive flaring and toxic gas release caused by various uncertainties like equipment failure, false operation, nature disaster, or terrorist attack. Based on an available air-quality monitoring network, the data integration technologies are applied to identify the scenarios of the possible emission source and the dynamic pollutant monitor result, so as to timely and effectively support diagnostic and prognostic decisions. In this chapter, several systematic methodologies and preliminary data integration system designs for such applications are developed according to the real application purpose. It includes two stages of modeling and optimization work: 1) the determination of background normal emission rates from multiple emission sources and 2) single-objective or multi-objective optimization for impact scenario identification and quantification. They have the capability of identifying the potential emission profile and spatial-temporal characterization of pollutant dispersion for a specific region, including reverse estimation of air quality issues. The chapter provides valuable information for accidental investigations and root cause analysis for an emission event, and it helps evaluate the regional air quality impact caused by such an emission event as well. Case studies are employed to demonstrate the efficacy of the developed methodology.

Section 3
Technology-Enhanced Data Management, Data Processing, Data Visualization, and
Human-Machine Analysis

It stands to reason that technologies that enable the archival and coding of data for qualitative and mixed media research should be able to accommodate and store a variety of multimedia file types: audio, video, imagery, text, and others. Further, such technologies surely complement human analytical capabilities with a range of analytical tools and data visualizations. Section 3 addresses various uses of technology for data management, data visualization, and human-machine analysis.

The purpose of this chapter is to illustrate how Computer-Assisted Qualitative Data Analysis Software (CAQDAS) packages, such as ATLAS.ti or Transana, can be used to support the transcription and data analysis process of large interactional data sets – specifically data analyzed from a discourse analysis perspective. Drawing from a larger ethnographic study, in this chapter the author illustrates how carrying out the transcription and analysis process within a CAQDAS package (in this case, Transana and ATLAS. ti) allows for an increase in transparency within the transcription and data analysis process, while also meeting the particular needs of the discourse analyst. By using one particular case/research study, the author demonstrates how CAQDAS packages might function to support a researcher in generating a more systematic and transparent analytical process, specifically during the early stages of the analysis process. The author gives particular attention to interactional data (i.e., 300 hours of video and audio recordings of therapy sessions) collected in a larger study and demonstrates the potential benefits of working across two CAQDAS packages, specifically Transana and ATLAS.ti, to support both the nuanced transcription process and the larger data analysis process.

The purpose of this chapter is to explain the effective use of digital tools to display and analyze mixed methods data and to identify the challenges and possibilities of doing a qualitatively driven mixed methods study of technology use in education. To frame this chapter, examples from a qualitatively driven mixed methods study of doctoral students, which explored how the use of mobile technology affected engagement in the class experience, are presented. Additionally, the authors discuss the limits, implications, and possibilities of inductively driven mixed methods, while dealing with issues of academic rigor and trustworthiness using Morse and Niehaus's (2009) guidelines for mixed methods research design and the ways in which digital tools enhance rigor and trustworthiness.

This chapter introduces a guide to transcribing qualitative research interviews assisted by digital transcription software. It also provides practical advice on transcribing methods, conventions, and options. It is useful in its exploration of the challenges involved with transcribing, while it offers detailed solutions and advice for the novice researcher. The chapter also addresses key concerns, like the time it takes to transcribe, transcription tools, and digital versus analogue recordings. As a method chapter based on experiences from a case, it takes on a practical approach by demonstrating the benefits of data analysis software packages with examples and screenshots on how to specifically use the software package Express Scribe. The pros and cons of using a transcriptionist are also discussed. A real transcript is presented in the chapter, and the steps involved with developing and formatting it are offered in detail. The guidelines suggested in this chapter are concentrated on the pragmatic hands-on experience of a researcher with examples from a real life large-scale qualitative study based on in-depth interviews. The significance of transcribing within the analytical process and the methodological insights of using Express Scribe eventually emerge as a developing concept from this work.

### Chapter 11

Understanding Web network structures may offer insights on various organizations and individuals. These structures are often latent and invisible without special software tools; the interrelationships between various websites may not be apparent with a surface perusal of the publicly accessible Web pages. Three publicly available tools may be "chained" (combined in sequence) in a data extraction sequence to enable visualization of various aspects of http network structures in an enriched way (with more detailed insights about the composition of such networks, given their heterogeneous and multimodal contents). Maltego Tungsten™, a penetration-testing tool, enables the mapping of Web networks, which are enriched with a variety of information: the technological understructure and tools used to build the network, some linked individuals (digital profiles), some linked documents, linked images, related emails, some related geographical data, and even the in-degree of the various nodes. NCapture with NVivo enables the extraction of public social media platform data and some basic analysis of these captures. The Network Overview, Discovery, and Exploration for Excel (NodeXL) tool enables the extraction of social media platform data and various evocative data visualizations and analyses. With the size of the Web growing exponentially and new domains (like .ventures, .guru, .education, .company, and others), the ability to map widely will offer a broad competitive advantage to those who would exploit this approach to enhance knowledge.

Section 4
Data Acquisition and Extraction from Social Media Platforms

The congregation of billions of people around the world on various social media sites—social networking sites, social media platforms, content-sharing sites, microblogging sites, Web logs, wikis, immersive online games, virtual worlds, and others—has provided a lot of potential for social computational, online ethnography, and other types of research. The thought is that understanding electronic presences may illuminate the cyber-physical confluence—or the reality of people's lives in physical space. While some suggest that electronic communications have changed how people interact and socialize, many also observe that there are continuing patterns of social relations from the real to the virtual. To conduct such research, researchers use a variety of software tools to extract information from various sites and socio-technical spaces and then to visualize and analyze the data. Big data analysis advancements suggest that there may well be more effective ways of extrapolating value from this information; these new methods may well upend current methods of hypothesis-based research and enable nearly pure discovery based on correlations.

This case study uses multiple qualitative methods to examine cultural meanings of virtual goods in a virtual world or Massively Multiplayer Online Game (MMOG) with consumer marketing promotions. Through participant observation, avatar hair emerged as a key virtual good. Symbolic displays in social interaction showed different meanings and uses for types of hair available to users, including high-status rare hair, and versions aligned with marketing promotions and real-world brands. Study of online artifacts examined user-generated content, such as user forums and machinima. The long interview method subsequently was employed to gather insight from users. Findings demonstrate how different data from these online methods provide rich meanings for avatar hair related to symbolic interactionism and self-presentation. Methods explore co-production among users, platform, and marketing efforts. Cultural meanings, user self-displays, and corporate influences related to avatar hair are presented. Avatar hair emerged as a status artifact that often revealed levels of social skills or wealth in this virtual culture, at times connected with marketing promotions relevant outside of the virtual world. Methodological implications are explored for avatar-based participation, artifacts from social networking and other technologies, and ethical approaches.

A lifetime collection of microblogging messages captured from a microblogging account may be extracted from Twitter using NCapture (an add-on to Chrome and Internet Explorer); these short messages may be analyzed through NVivo and other data analysis and visualization software tools in order to highlight compressed-time gists (essences) of Twitter accounts for rapid assessment. This chapter provides an overview of how this work may be done and how the resulting word clouds, word trees, and tree maps may be analyzed for latent insights. This research approach may be applied to a range of social media platforms using the same software tools here (or using others that are publicly available). This chapter concludes with ideas for how to extend these methods.

### Chapter 14

The broad popularity of social content-sharing sites like Flickr and YouTube have enabled the public to access a variety of photographs and videos on a wide range of topics. In addition to these resources, some new capabilities in multiple software programs enable the extraction of related tags networks from these collections. Related tags networks are relational contents built on the descriptive metadata created by the creators of the digital contents. This chapter offers some insights on how to understand public sentiment (inferentially and analytically) from related tags and content networks from social media platforms. This indirect approach contributes to Open-Source Intelligence (OSINT) with nuanced information (and some pretty tight limits about assertions and generalizability). The software tools explored for related tags data extractions include Network Overview, Discovery, and Exploration for Excel (NodeXL) (an open-source graph visualization tool which is an add-in to Microsoft Excel), NCapture in NVivo 10 (a commercial qualitative data analysis tool), and Maltego Tungsten (a commercial penetration-testing Internet-network-extraction tool formerly known as Maltego Radium).

Section 5
Cases of Technology-Enhanced Qualitative and Mixed Methods Research (and the Converse)

In the same way that surveys and interviews may wrap with a catch-all category, a section on cases may be seen as a broad category of unique applications of the book's topic. It is one thing to conceptualize possibilities, but it is more difficult to actualize the work in real world and online settings. By their example, these cases illuminate potentials for others in their respective contexts. Case studies have intrinsic value in terms of the action research learning. Section 5 highlights researchers' applied uses of technologies for qualitative and mixed methods research and the converse, their applied methods in analyzing technologies, and their implications for their research and/or other applications. These cases affirm the variety of approaches that may be taken with technology-enhanced qualitative and mixed methods research.

This chapter presents an overview of process research and places a particular emphasis on reviewing the process method. Some insights into the nature of process are presented. The purpose of this chapter is to describe the process method in detail. Some of the methodological challenges involved in conducting process-oriented inquiry are highlighted. Appropriateness of the method to study strategy-related issues is presented which interlocks well with its suitability to investigate issues of interest in relation to IT strategy-making. Application of the process method cycle of research steps is recommended to distil rigorous and relevant theory. Alternative process research sense-making strategies are revealed at a very high-level only. Narrative analysis is presented as a viable sense-making approach to theorize process data and key features of this analytical strategy are revealed. Emerging issues and opportunities that intersect with the IT strategy-making construct are discussed.

Contributing to the ongoing debate in research on sensitive issues such as business ethics, this chapter provides a discussion of mixed methods research design, examining the processes and challenges of developing and deploying an online survey tool using technology within an interpretive mixed methods design. This chapter provides pointers on how to deploy this approach through technology to research business ethics using the example of researching ethical mindsets and its components, including spirituality and aesthetics. It is found that mixed methods research is an effective approach because it allows often sensitive issues (i.e. business ethics, aesthetics, spirituality) relating to questioning individuals' inner values and ethical propensities, which are usually subtle and difficult to measure and analyze constructs. While this tool was developed in the Australian context, it has the potential to form a foundation for wider examination and research in business ethics. The chapter contributes to the collective discussion of research methods using a framework that has both practical relevance and theoretical rigor.

Interactions with external peers have been identified in the Information Systems (IS) management literature as being one of the most influential sources of contact for the Chief Information Officer (CIO), supporting them in their role as the most senior IS executive in the organisation. Today, due to the strategic importance of IS to the operations and competitive position of many organisations, the CIO often operates as a key member of the top management team. At the centre of this role, the literature suggests, is the ability of the CIO to identify relevant strategic IS knowledge in the external technological marketplace, via their external boundary spanning activities, that can impact the organisation's strategic positioning and overall success. However, whilst the IS management literature identifies interactions with external peers as being one of the most influential sources of contact available to CIOs, it fails to identify why they are such an important support to the CIO, or for that matter, how CIOs actually interact with such external peers. Similarly, a review of the wider management literature, whilst confirming the reasons why top management executives, such as the CIO, favour interactions with external peers, it again fails to clarify how such executives, in fact, actually interact with external peers, via contacts in external networks. Consequently, this has led to a clear gap in our knowledge and understanding relating to one of the key activities of the modern day CIO. For that reason, this research study set out to explore how CIOs, in fact, interact with external peers via network connections. As no previous theory existed, the Grounded Theory (GT) methodology was adopted, within an interpretivist perspective, to develop new theory. The research setting chosen was the Irish Private Sector, with a specific focus on organisations in the finance, hi-tech, telecoms, and airline industries. The purpose of this chapter is to draw into sharp focus the nature of GT as applied in this study, rather than the findings from the study itself, and to consider the use of appropriate technology tools to support this application.

This chapter examines the integration of process inquiry and the case method in the study of Information Systems (IS) failure. Having acknowledged the prevalence of IS failure and the need for continued inquiry in this domain, the two predominant methods of inquiry, factor and process studies, are described along with the utility of both methods. The chapter then examines the nature of process inquiry and notes its utility and prevalence in the study of IS phenomena, and its potential applicability for inquiry into IS failure. The case study method is then briefly described along with its potential contribution when combined with process inquiry. The chapter then describes how the case method can provide an overall framework for the conduct of a process inquiry and presents an iterative six-stage research process model based on the case method to assist with the planning, design, preparation, data collection, data analysis, and reporting of findings.

This chapter develops an innovative focus group method—the Discount Focus Subgroup (DFSG)—through its application in research aimed at identifying the ethical and social concerns of using an emerging technology, called near field communication, for mobile payments. The DFSG method was needed to address the challenges encountered when this research was conducted, such as limited financial research resources, the emergent nature of the research topic, and the challenges of gathering and analyzing qualitative data. This chapter illustrates when and how to use the DFSG method. It provides the methodological steps for its application, which can be followed while researching emerging topics in the Information Systems (IS) field. The chapter also discusses why DFSG is an innovative method and reflects on its application.

Section 6
Technologies for Presenting the Results of Qualitative and Mixed Methods Research

A critical aspect of qualitative and mixed methods research has been to share the methods and findings with not only colleagues and peers but also the broad public. Over the years, there have been a number of ways that research has been "packaged" and shared: through parametric and non-parametric data visualizations, narrations, and writing structures. At present, there are even more tools that enable presentations. Some offer data visualizations of big data and macro trends. Others offer creative mapping for accessing and understanding locational data. Many of these presentational methods are Web-enabled, so that consumers of that information may actually interact with the research findings.

If qualitative and mixed methods researchers have a tradition of gleaning information from all possible sources, they may well find the Google Books Ngram Viewer and its repository of tens of millions of digitized books yet another promising data stream. This free cloud service enables easy access to big data in terms of querying the word frequency counts of a range of terms and numerical sequences (and languages) from 1500 – 2000, a 500-year span of book publishing, with new books being added continually. The data queries that may be made with this tool are virtually unanswerable otherwise. The word frequency counts provide a lagging indicator of both instances and trends, related to language usage, cultural phenomena, popularity, technological innovations, and a wide range of other insights. The text corpuses contain de-contextualized words used by the educated literati of the day sharing their knowledge in formalized texts. The enablements of the Google Books Ngram Viewer provide complementary information sourcing for designed research questions as well as free-form discovery. This tool allows downloading of the "shadowed" (masked or de-identified) extracted data for further analyses and visualizations. This chapter provides both a basic and advanced look at how to extract information from the Google Books Ngram Viewer for light research.

Chapter 21

Virtually every subject area depicted in a learning object could conceivably involve a space-time element. Theoretically, every event may be mapped geospatially, and in time, these spatialized event maps may be overlaid with combined data (locations of particular natural and human-made objects, demographics, and other phenomena) to enable the identification and analysis of time-space patterns and interrelationships. They enable hypothesis formations, hunches, and the asking and answering of important research questions. The ability to integrate time-space insights into research work is enhanced by the wide availability of multiple new sources of free geospatial data: open data from governments and organizations (as part of Gov 2.0), locative information from social media platforms (as part of Web 2.0), and self-created geospatial datasets from multiple sources. The resulting maps and data visualizations, imbued with a time context and the potential sequencing of maps over time, enable fresh insights and increased understandings. In addition to the wide availability of validated geospatial data, Tableau Public is a free and open cloud-based tool that enables the mapping of various data sets for visualizations that are pushed out onto a public gallery for public consumption. The interactive dashboard enables users to explore the data and discover insights and patterns. Tableau Public is a tool that enables enhanced visual- and interaction-based knowing, through interactive Web-friendly maps, panel charts, and data dashboards. With virtually zero computational or hosting costs (for the user), Tableau Public enables the integration of geospatial mapping and analysis stands to benefit research work, data exploration and discovery and analysis, and learning.

Foreword

by William H. Hsu

A TAKE ON INFORMATICS AND KNOWING

It is my pleasure to introduce this volume edited by Dr. Hai-Jew, whose previous books I have served twice on as a contributor: one on open-source technologies for education and one on techniques for the presentation of digital information, including information visualization. This foreword briefly outlines the convergence of technologies and user needs that makes the present book timely and useful.

DATA SCIENCE OF, BY, AND FOR HUMANS

The field of qualitative and mixed methods for data analysis has expanded significantly in the past decade due to an influx of contributions from researchers working at the interfaces of informatics, especially between the humanities and data science. This includes both fields traditionally classified as digital humanities, such as digital ethnography, and applications of quantitative (especially statistical) computational methods to problems that involve a "human in the loop" and intrinsically subjective elements, such as user experience.

There is a fine line between these two aspects of qualitative data analysis as a result of technological convergence, but the primary distinguishing characteristic of the first category is that it involves data science and other information technology as assistive tools for activities that are traditionally carried out using analog media. For example, dialogue and discourse analysis are aspects of the theory of communication that originate from linguistics, anthropology, and sociology, pre-dating computer-mediated communication and electronic representation of text. By contrast, the second category involves tasks that have always been defined within a computing context but admit an irreducible aspect of individual aesthetics and qualitative judgment.

That is, both types of problems are defined of, by, and for humans, but the difference lies in the motivation for and direction of synthesis: introducing new informatics tools for a study of human culture, especially natural language communication, or incorporating subjectivity into "hard" data science. In the intersection of these categories lie tasks subjectivity, sentiment, and discourse analysis from text, traditionally considered the purview of soft computing. As a topic of knowledge representation and automated reasoning, soft computing comprises uncertain reasoning using probability and other representations cf. fuzzy logic and vague domains.

Meanwhile, subjective topics such as human factors and ergonomics have traditionally been treated using the methods of quantitative science or qualitative study, rather than the empirical synthesis that underlies many of the chapters of this book. This is especially relevant to applied areas of the study of User Experience (UX) that have undergone rapid growth, such as user modeling, adaptive hypermedia, and personalization of user interfaces.

THE NEW DATA ANALYTICS: RELEVANCE AND SCOPE

"Big data" and qualitative data analytics are two highly popular terms that do not seem to mix very much or very well at the time of this writing. The term "big data" refers to size and complexity at a minimum of upper terascale to lower petascale as of 2014, while qualitative methods such as field notes and human-produced annotations, except for digital video and other high-volume media, represent bandwidth use that is at least several orders of magnitude below this in scale. Thus, the conventional wisdom is that qualitative and mixed methods simply do not constitute big data at present and will not do so for the foreseeable future.

Some evidence runs counter to this notion: namely, the global scale of social networks and media and the explosion in development of new media. The observed growth rate of digital hypermedia such as the Web and post-Web environments (dynamic content and data grid services *aka* Web 2.0, the semantic Web *aka* Web 3.0), even during the worldwide recession of the past decade, indicates a demand for UX technology that matches that for physical and natural sciences.

Beyond simple considerations of scale and bandwidth, however, there are some basic trends in methodology to observe. The first of these is an accelerating convergence of information visualization as an area of data science and engineering with the social science of applied analytics. This brings together machine learning and data mining, which are themselves also motivated by performance elements such as Decision Support Systems (DSS), Business Intelligence (BI), Customer Relationship Management (CRM), and the above-mentioned UX areas of personalization and user modeling, with a powerful delivery mechanism that we are continuing to understand in terms of graphical design principles. The second of these is organic growth of the search engine industry in service to existing and emergent user needs: ubiquitous computing in the form of new user interfaces (e.g., wearable computing devices and augmented reality systems) and resources for analytics such as the gigaword parallel corpora developed primarily for research in machine translation and multi-lingual text mining. The third is the parallel convergence of assistive and augmentative technologies, such as Unmanned Aerial Vehicles (UAVs) for videography, 3-D printing, medical devices, and cyber-physical systems. These are technologies that serve humans in new ways but are based on underlying principles that have been studied for much longer than the new synthesis.

THE FUTURE OF QUALITATIVE AND MIXED METHODS: AN INFORMATICS PERSPECTIVE

Informatics is a broad academic field encompassing information science and technology, algorithms, specific areas of applied mathematics, digital foundations in the humanities and social sciences, and applications of computation to many other disciplines, particularly the natural sciences and engineering. It describes computational, mathematical, and statistical tools for data integration, analytics, and information retrieval. Drawing on theory and research from systems, information processing, simulation and modeling, visualization, machine learning, data mining, and databases, informatics is a pervasive, crosscutting theme.

Some of the desiderata of qualitative and mixed methods for data science are identical or similar to those for quantitative methods: reproducibility and general applicability to previously unseen domains. This is a hallmark of informatics as an area of research and development – it is intrinsically applied but rooted in the needs of empirical science. Most areas of informatics that serve scientists as purveyors and users of data resources are furthermore subject to the same challenges of usability, validation, and adaptivity as other areas of UX for users in general.

The interrelated fields of predictive analytics, Computational Information and Knowledge Management (CIKM), and scientific, data, and information visualization continue to be recombined in significant ways through developments in fundamental theory and methodology. It is to be hoped that volumes such as this one will help to guide the way to realizing fielded systems from these advances.

William H. Hsu
Kansas State University, USA

William H. Hsu *is an associate professor of Computing and Information Sciences at Kansas State University. He received a BS in Mathematical Sciences and Computer Science and an MSEng in Computer Science from Johns Hopkins University in 1993, and a PhD in Computer Science from the University of Illinois at Urbana-Champaign in 1998. His dissertation explored the optimization of inductive bias in supervised machine learning for predictive analytics. At the National Center for Supercomputing Applications (NCSA), he was a co-recipient of an Industrial Grand Challenge Award for visual analytics of text corpora. His research interests include machine learning, probabilistic reasoning, and information visualization, with applications to cybersecurity, education, digital humanities, geoinformatics, and biomedical informatics. Current work in his lab deals with: spatiotemporal mapping of opinions, crimes, and other events; data mining and visualization in education research; graphical models of probability and utility for information security; analysis of heterogeneous information networks; and domain-adaptive models of large natural language corpora and social media for text mining, link mining, sentiment analysis, and recommender systems. Dr. Hsu is editor of the forthcoming book Emerging Methods in Predictive Analytics, and has over 50 refereed publications in conferences, journals, and books, plus over 35 additional publications.*

Foreword
by Robert Gibson

A TAKE ON MIXED METHODS

Traditionally, *Mixed Methods (MM) Research* design, also called *Compatibility Thesis* and *Multimethodology*, is defined as a procedure for collecting, analyzing, and blending both quantitative and qualitative research methods into a single study in order to understand a research problem. The term *Mixed Methods*, however, is a relatively recent naming convention that is primarily associated with research in the social sciences. It has gained particular prominence since the 1980s. Mixed-Method Research is increasingly becoming more clearly defined, associated with empirical research practice, and often recognized as the third major research paradigm which provides better triangulation of data results because both qualitative and quantitative research methods are engaged. *Quantitative Research* is considered postpositivist in nature – being singular in reality, objective, and deductive. Data collection methodologies can include performance tests, personality measures, closed-ended questionnaires, and content analysis. *Qualitative research*, on the other hand, relies primarily on the views of participants; asks broad, general questions; collects data consisting largely of words (or text) from participants; describes and analyzes these words for themes; and conducts the inquiry in a subjective, biased manner. It is constructivist in nature – based on multiple realities and inductive in its approach. Data collection strategies typically include interviews, open-ended questions, direct observations, content and data analysis, direct participation, and focus groups.

The utilization of technology in both qualitative research and more recently Mixed Method data collection has a relatively long history – dating back to the mid-20th century. Gibbs, Friese, and Mangabiera (2002) indicated that researchers transitioned from hand written notes to analog tape recorders in early field studies more than 50 years ago. This was especially useful in the disciplines of anthropology, psychology, and other social sciences where transcription was critical. This transition inadvertently led to several positive research effects, including contribution to new ways of thinking about data and the analytical ideas of the researcher, and improved data analysis that would only be possible if accurate records of the event were captured at the moment of data collection. Rather than spending valuable time transcribing aural communication into notes, the researcher was instead able focus on the questions and responses of the study participants and/or the research event.

Advances in technology in the latter half of the last century have provided more opportunities for researchers to effectively collect both qualitative and Mixed-Method research feedback from multiple data points. As the ubiquity and capability of technology increased and the cost simultaneously decreased, so too did opportunities for researchers to engage a variety of media in their research efforts. For example, Kanstrup (2002) successfully utilized still analog photography and observational data in collecting data regarding teachers' work practices. Koch and Zumbach (2002) utilized analog video and field notes when studying small group interaction communication patterns. While these media were non-digital format technologies at the time, they provided additional data collection opportunities that expanded the field and improved the accuracy of research.

More recently, advances in digital media technologies have provided additional capabilities to support Mixed-Method and qualitative data collection. That is, textual, visual, aural, spatial, and temporal information. New means of processing digital video data have led to a rapid growth of video analysis. Digital tools for supporting and partially automating content analyses have become increasingly common. The archived interactions in Internet chats and forums, for example, have provided new options for qualitative research with a broader research audience.

Granted, many of these technologies were developed for purposes other than research and data collection, so there is much to learn about their efficacy. However, examples abound regarding the use of both established and emerging technologies in a variety of research scenarios:

- Secrist, Koeyer, Bell, and Fogel (2002) effectively utilized digital video software to study mother-infant relationships. After capturing the video footage, the researchers were then able to sequence the digital data chronologically in order to study developmental changes over a period of time.
- Kimbler, Moore, Schladen, Sowers, and Synder (2013) presented a variety of emerging technology tools that are commonly used in qualitative data collection, including a blend of mobile device recording and transcription applications; learner interaction software to study virtual patients; and Web conferencing technologies to collect verbal and non-verbal interview data.
- Young and Jaganath (2012) successfully utilized social networking technologies in HIV prevention research among African American and Latino participants.
- Morse conducted facial analysis using video cameras on patients in emergency rooms to link behavioral indices of the transition between enduring and suffering in patient care experiences (Spiers, 2004).
- Rutledge successfully used digital video to study interpretive phenomenology in modern dance (Spiers, 2004).
- Wu, Rossos, Quan, Reeves, Lo, Wong, Cheung, and Morra (2011) were able to demonstrate effective use of smartphones in a Mixed Method research study involving healthcare clinicians. These researchers found that use of smartphones improved the quality of communication and reduced the quantity of extraneous contact when dealing with patient care. Their study found that the technology improved interpersonal relationships and professionalism, while balancing efficiency and reducing interruptions.
- Dimond, Fiesler, DiSalvo, Pelc, and Bruckman (n.d.) found that while telephone conversations yielded four times as many words on average when compared to instant message and Email data collection, there was no significant difference in the number of unique qualitative codes expressed between any of the technologies. This indicates that any of these technologies was equally effective in qualitative and Mixed Method research.

I have had the opportunity to conduct Mixed Method Research when exploring the efficacy of lecture capture in the context of rehabilitation and mental health counseling education. In those studies, a faculty co-investigator and I were able to review qualitative evidence using captured sessions from actual clients in a Master's degree program. We were then able to triangulate the effectiveness of the technology by reviewing the number and duration of recorded sessions conducted by each student. In this study, we were afforded access to recorded sessions, which were captured during actual client-student interactions. We were able to determine the quality of the interviews and the client-interaction by replaying a sample set of sessions and by reviewing the interactive notations made by the students regarding the session. In this type of study, quantitative data alone does not provide a clear indication of how effective the technology was in promoting improved client interactions. However, when combined with a qualitative analysis of the sessions and of the student notations, we found that the technology not only provided the researchers a more accurate representation of the session quality, but allowed us to review multiple sessions from multiple students long after the sessions had concluded. The quality of the student notations also provided evidence as to the efficacy of using this technology in the context of counseling education.

The future trends for enhancing Mixed Method and qualitative research methodologies using technology are quite optimistic. Increasingly, mobile devices and online technologies are providing a variety of rich technology opportunities for capturing and recording research data and phenomenology. Advances in mobile software applications (Apps) provide a variety of data collection opportunities including digital video, voice annotation, text input, and even certain kinesthetic and haptic (sense of touch) input options. Other research opportunities can leverage built-in device spatial and location recognition, virtual and augmented reality, instantaneous data transmission and analysis, image recognition, and facial and expression analysis. Software tools on devices can provide instant access to social networks and data sets, providing real-time data reporting and knowledge base access. A subject's mood or activities can be combined into time stamped diary information and instantly uploaded to databases to provide an overview of the respondent's behavior and well-being.

The advantages of using technology in Mixed-Method and qualitative research include:

- Ease of use,
- Better file transferability,
- Improved data quality,
- Accurate speech to text and transcription accuracy,
- Reduced cost,
- Immediacy and social cues,
- Codification of non-verbal behaviors,
- Data analysis,
- Content richness.

The future use of technology in Mixed Method and qualitative research is intriguing. Increasingly, researchers are engaging a variety of mobile, Internet-enabled technologies in their research. The plethora of mobile applications (Apps) provides a variety of data collection strategies, including:

- Managing files,
- Managing research references,
- Accessing databases,
- File backups,

- Journaling and note taking,
- Conducting live webinars,
- Video and audio capture.

Advantages of using technology—especially Internet-capable technology in Mixed Method and qualitative research—include the following:

- Mobile and compact size supports data collection in a variety of research locations.
- Devices often include a variety of applications combined into a single, small form factor platform.
- Data can be synchronized across a variety of devices.
- Supports multi-modal data (auditory, visual, kinesthetic, etc.)
- Data can be uploaded and stored in the cloud, allowing for access from nearly any location.
- Data can be managed remotely – including encryption and deletion.

However, there are disadvantages in relying on digital, Internet-based technologies for research purposes as well. While many research environments support ubiquitous, fast Internet access and data transmission, not every environment has the requisite support and infrastructure:

- Unless the technology supports offline utilization, the researcher is dependent upon Internet connectivity, which can be limited in many locations.
- Confidentiality and ethical concerns can emerge when using institutionally owned technologies and devices.
- Some academics do not perceive emerging technologies as a valid research and data collection tool.
- Technology can introduce research collection bias.
- Technology can introduce the Hawthorne Effect, which affects respondents' feedback patterns. Rather than responding to research prompts, the respondents may offer feedback that placates the researcher simply based on the presence of the technology.

Furthermore, Biber and Johnson (2013) indicated that disciplinary concerns reside when interfacing Mixed Methods Research with newly emergent technologies for data analysis and collection.

Despite these concerns, there are significant advantages in using both established and emerging technology in Mixed Method and qualitative research. Not only do technologies provide increased richness in data but also the researcher can leverage these technologies to expedite the collection and analysis of data, compare data sets, and provide additional dimensions of data collection. For example, researchers at Emporia State University are planning to conduct a study of the efficacy of Google Glass in library information search and data retrieval processes using Mixed Methods and qualitative research. Researchers plan to construct a Mixed Method Research study that investigates the use of this technology to locate information in the context of an academic library. Qualitatively, they plan to explore the type and quality of information I am able to access and locate using Glass. Quantitatively, they plan to investigate the number of journals and academic resources that are available to a prospective patron who may be utilizing the technology within the library. They will also be able to determine the time required to locate resources when using these technologies vs. asking a reference librarian. The technology will allow researchers to record my interactions and data collection methods during a series of visits to the library, and then later review those sessions to determine how effective wearable technologies are in information retrieval. This type of Mixed Methods research may have a profound effect on how libraries support information retrieval using wearable technologies in the future.

Robert Gibson
Emporia State University, USA

Robert Gibson *is the Director of Learning Technologies at Emporia State University. In this role, he and his team provide a variety of learning technology support for faculty, staff, and students, including the Learning Management System; video production; Web/video conferencing; lecture capture; instructional design services; training and development; classroom support services; research support; and other related services. He has served in this capacity since 2008. Robert has worked in higher education since 1988. He began his career at the University of Wyoming working with early distance education systems that utilized analog phone lines to send graphics and data from Laramie, Wyoming to students located 45 miles away in Cheyenne, Wyoming. After completing his first Master's degree, he accepted a position at Wichita State University where he served as the instructional designer for a television-based distance education system in the early 1990s. In 1995—the dawn of Web browsers—Rob and a Nursing Informatics faculty member designed and developed what is thought to be the first online course in Kansas – well before course management systems. He later worked for Friends University in Wichita, KS before accepting a position at CU Online located at the University of Colorado-Denver and Health Sciences Center. He has published numerous peer-reviewed articles and book chapters, and presents nationally at a variety of conferences. He actively promotes instructional technology through a variety of social media outlets. Robert holds a BS in Business Administration; a BFA and BA in Graphic Design; a MS in Instructional Technology and Design; an MBA in Information Technology and Project Management; and an EdD in Instructional Technology and Distance Education. An early champion of online course delivery, Rob elected to pursue his doctoral degree in the late 1990s when online and hybrid programs were still an exception rather than a norm. His dissertation research investigated the effectiveness of various faculty development programs regarding online learning. Rob has been an early and consistent champion of emerging technologies that have the potential to shape education. His research interests include gesture-based computing, augmented reality, usability analysis, online learning, psychometrics, instructional systems design, learning theory, and competency-based learning. Rob serves on several product advisory boards and has been the recipient of outstanding course development awards. He is also holds multiple certifications from Quality Matters and Google, and is currently pursuing the CPLP and PMP certifications.*

REFERENCES

Dimond, J., Fiesler, C., DiSalvo, B., Pelc, J., & Bruckman, A. (n.d.). *Qualitative data collective technologies: A comparison of instant messaging, email, and phone.* Retrieved March, 2014 from http://jilldimond.com/wp-content/uploads/2010/10/group115-dimond.pdf

Gibbs, G. R., Friese, S., & Mangabeira, W. C. (2002). The use of new technology in qualitative research. *Forum: Qualitative Social Research.* Retrieved March, 2014 from http://www.qualitative-research.net/index.php/fqs/article/view/847/1840

Hess-Biber, S., & Johnson, R. B. (2013). Coming at things differently: Future directions of possible engagement with mixed methods research. *Journal of Mixed Methods Research*. Retrieved March, 2014 from http://mmr.sagepub.com/content/7/2/103.full.pdf+html

Kanstrup, A. M. (2002). Picture the practice – Using photography to explore use of technology within teachers work practices. *Forum: Qualitative Social Research*. Retrieved March, 2014 from http://www.qualitative-research.net/index.php/fqs/article/view/856

Kimbler, J., Moore, D., Maitland-Schladen, M., Sowers, B., & Snyder, M. (2013). *Emerging technology tools for qualitative data collection*. Nova Southeastern University. Retrieved March 2014 from http://www.nova.edu/ssss/QR/TQR2013/Kimbler_etal_TQRHandout.pdf

Koch, S. C., & Zumbach, J. (2002). The use of video analysis software in behavior observation research: Interaction patterns in task-orientation small groups. *Forum: Qualitative Social Research*. Retrieved March, 2014 from http://www.qualitative-research.net/index.php/fqs/article/view/857

Secrist, C., Lise de Koeyer, H. B., & Fogel, A. (2002). Combining digital video technology and narrative methods for understanding infant development. *Forum: Qualitative Social Research*. Retrieved March, 2014 from http://www.qualitative-research.net/index.php/fqs/article/view/863/1874

Spiers, J. A. (2004). Tech tips: Using video management/ analysis technology in qualitative research. *International Journal of Qualitative Methods, 3*(1), Article 5. Retrieved March, 2014 from http://www.ualberta.ca/~iiqm/backissues/3_1/pdf/spiersvideo.pdf

Wu, R., Rossos, P., Quan, S., Reeves, S., Lo, V., Wong, B., et al. (2011). *Works citing "an evaluation of the use of smartphones to communicate between clinicians: A mixed-methods study"*. Paper presented at the World Congress on Social Media, Mobile Apps, Internet/Web 2.0. Retrieved March 2014 from http://www.jmir.org/article/citations/1655

Young, S. D., & Jaganath, D. (2012). Using social networking technologies for mixed methods HIV prevention research. *Journal of Mobile Technology in Medicine*. Retrieved from http://www.journalmtm.com/2012/using-social-networking-technologies-for-mixed-methods-hiv-prevention-research/

Foreword
by Nancy Hays

A TAKE ON BROADENING RANGES OF RESEARCH POTENTIALS

Over the 25-plus years I've worked with peer review of technology-supported research, the technologies from which researchers can choose have become more specialized and sophisticated in some cases (statistical analysis, geographical information system software) and more generic and easy to use in others (spreadsheets and online surveys). Technology allows researchers to collaborate across continents and time zones, taking advantage not only of the expertise of their international colleagues but also of expensive equipment (telescopes, supercomputers) otherwise beyond their budgets and research subject communities not otherwise accessible to them (to determine culture-specific responses vs. biology-controlled responses, for example). When investigators complete their research and analysis, the reports of their work reach wider audiences than ever before thanks to technology-supported distribution methods. This can spur further research along the same lines and often invitations to collaborate with scientists doing similar or related work. It also allows others in the same field, whether professionals, students, or interested amateurs, to keep up with current research and join in evaluations and discussions of the methods, analyses, and results of research, either to critique, suggest alternatives, or share their own insights. Technology thus facilitates research from initial planning to dissemination of new results and genesis of continuing efforts and new ideas. It connects people and ideas around the world to further advances in human knowledge.

The biggest effect of improvements in technology to support research is the increased pace of exploration possible, from small projects conducted by single researchers using online surveys and free analysis software to massive research groups funded by governments and large international corporations. Even high school students have conducted sophisticated research that has won science prizes and recognition, giving them a jumpstart not only on college but also on successful careers.

For the first time in history, people anywhere in the world can work with senior scientists using large telescopes, massive centrifuges, or virtual worlds to conduct their research—or they can compete as scattered individuals or small groups in contests (to develop new encryption methods or a new drug), share their individual resources in a large endeavor (think of SETI), or come together as a community (to research worldwide issues such as bird migrations). Anyone with an interest can access basic technologies by going online to learn about their chosen field, connect with other interested people and groups, and participate in data collection, surveys, knowledge dissemination—research.

The opportunity for anyone with access to the Internet to participate in and contribute to research marks a new stage in human development. Research in recent decades has already pushed the boundaries of our knowledge further in a few generations than in all the generations that preceded us. The new element fueling this progress is technology. Whether it continues to support human endeavors to discover new knowledge or takes over the job for us, technology will keep its central role in research. Whether that turns out to be good or bad depends on the wisdom we apply to its implementations. All of us can influence the future of research and where it leads us—with technology as a tool.

Nancy Hays
EDUCAUSE, USA

Nancy Hays *is editor and manager, Publishing, for EDUCAUSE, a nonprofit association and the foremost community of IT leaders and professionals committed to advancing higher education. She joined EDUCAUSE in 2000 to manage the editorial and peer-review process for EDUCAUSE Quarterly, which moved entirely online in 2009 and merged with EDUCAUSE Review and the EDUCAUSE Multimedia programs in 2012 as the association's flagship publication. As editor for EDUCAUSE, Hays works with the editorial, content, and executive teams to determine important trends in the field of higher education information technology, solicit appropriate authors to write on different topics, and develop ideas for publication online. She also runs the peer-review committee and process and oversees the editorial and production teams for EDUCAUSE publications, from conference programs to books. Prior to joining EDUCAUSE, Hays was group managing editor for the IEEE Computer Society, where she started as an assistant editor in 1985. As group managing editor, she supervised editorial and production teams and worked with the editors-in-chief and editorial boards for IEEE Computer Graphics and Applications, IEEE Multimedia, IEEE Micro, IEEE Design and Test, and the Annals of the History of Computing. From 1980 to 1985, she held editorial jobs in technology and medical publishing. Hays earned a Master's degree in English literature from UCLA in 1980 and three bachelor's degrees from Oregon State University in 1977 (English, Economics, and Liberal Studies).*

Preface

ENHANCING QUALITATIVE AND MIXED METHODS RESEARCH WITH TECHNOLOGY

Introduction

The evolution to qualitative and mixed methods research in a number of fields was initially built on the understructure of experimental research in the "hard sciences," with the sense of the simple pre-condition, a test intervention, and a post-condition, as compared to the control condition. Researchers in the social sciences and other areas started to ask ambitious questions that could not be answered by experimental research because of research ethics, costs, and complexity. They were left with having to go with non-experimental research achieved by deep empirical observations of the world. The research tools would have to be humans. With their limited perception and limited cognition and their many subjectivities, they would be studying a world that they were part of and immersed in. In this sense, humans are both the researcher and the subject of study, with complex interrelationships and situated contexts in which the research is conducted. How could they create insights that would have relevance and transferability? How could they avoid falling for spurious effects and reified ideas without equivalencies in the real world? How could they know they were on the right path and not on a blind alley?

At this juncture, researchers asked how they could instill rigor in a messy process where certain phenomena would have to be abstracted and isolated from a complex context, analyzed, generalized, and then reinstated in a complex world to have meaning. Early scientists focused on universal and transferable laws that could be abstracted from the Newtonian world but later moved to lesser and more modest forms of knowing. There would not be the pursuit of the once-and-for-all sorts of knowledge. There would be no power of the absolute last word. All findings would be couched, to some degree, in specific space-time. Readings of theorists in the 20th century show applications of mathematical reasoning and formal logic and syllogisms to express hypotheses and their tests based on empirically acquired evidence; they show the core importance of deeply specified language (and nuanced uses of qualifiers and limitations) and defined terminology to limit inexactitude and minimize error. Certain assumptions of the research were defined, with some relegated to metaphysics (such as the assumption of the existence or non-existence of causal relationships in the world) and others to the unknowable. Initial theorizing, not surprisingly, offered purist approaches: qualitative research with a relativist worldview vs. quantitative research with a positivist worldview.

Theorizing has always been a critical part of research. Whatever the inspiration—an observation of the world (in vivo) or the lab (in vitro), a hunch, interpretations of published works—theories proposed ways to understand particular phenomena in the world. Researchers would create methods to test their ideas in the real with experiments, empirical observations, and other data. Researchers pit competing interpretations against each other to see which theories had the most potent explanatory power for a complex world. In qualitative and mixed methods research, there is high importance put to deep thinking about particular phenomena in the world. There is hypercritical analysis of the definitions of terms, the descriptions of mechanisms in a model, the implications of theorizing (to second- and third-order effects, and beyond), and the design and application of research methodologies. Theories imbue the definitions of variables. They inform understandings of what comprise "facts" and even how phenomena are "measured." In a qualitative sensibility, everything is relativistic and affected by the subjective human observer, even empiricism which involves observations of the world. All observations are distortative and under-represent reality.

In the past several decades, since Miles and Huberman's classic work on qualitative data analysis, there has been progress in honing and advancing qualitative research methods. These methods include action research, portraiture, ethnography, oral history, experience sampling/ecological momentary assessment, autoethnography, interviews, surveys, Delphi studies (including modified Delphi and modified e-Delphi studies), case studies, hermeneutics (text interpretation), qualitative meta-analyses, and other research techniques. These and other qualitative methods originated from human engagements with a complex world. After all, in some domains, qualitative and mixed methods research are the only ways to query the world because experimentation may be infeasible or excessively expensive. Further, theorizing in a range of fields rejects a positivist, measureable, universalist, and objectivist approach to the world.

While qualitative or quantitative purists (absolutists) would suggest that there are only certain ways to pursue particular research (what one leading researcher calls "methodological strings attached"), the maintenance of purely one approach or another has been blurring in practice. While qualitative approaches tend to be more inductive and quantitative ones more deductive, the practices that have evolved from professional engagement with the world, reflection, and theorizing tend to blur such artificial lines. For all the power of pure theorizing, at some level, all research has some degree of interface with the world and application for knowing and decision-making. Qualitative research does not only exist in a relativist realm; some qualitative approaches are very much in the realist school of research and suggest some sense of ground truth. Mixed methods are synthesized theoretical and methodological approaches which require both intertwined qualitative and quantitative research streams to address particular research questions; one method may be more predominant with the other more supportive or supplementary. Multi-methodology involves the integration of multiple research methods to attain research-based understandings.

The thinking now is that qualitative and quantitative approaches—melded broadly as "mixed methods" or "multimethodology"—are complementary and often integrated. Clean lines of logic from theory to practice are merely conceptual. In the real world with complex ways of discovery and learning, by necessity, there have to be mixed techniques without artificial constraints. This is not to say that research methodologies are any less contested than they have ever been. Some argue that the mere existence of particular research methods involve meta-critique of other approaches. Indeed, professional reputations are built on methodologies and discoveries. Whether research gets funded or a draft article or chapter makes it into publication depends in large part on the quality (rigor and significance) of the research work. The methodology may make or break the research and even the researcher (professionally speaking) or research team. While research approaches fall in and out of favor, sparkling exemplars of research work changes, and the "right mixes" of idealized senses of appropriate amounts of theory and research may be debated, it may seem that research work into the future will be a broad mix of theorizing and various methodologies based on efficacy and results.

Regardless of the approach, the researcher(s) has to justify it. Even if initial conceptualizations of the research methodology and the research methods may resonate on paper, researchers often will engage in much lead-up work before solidifying a full approach: exhaustive literature reviews, key informant consultations, pilot testing, instrumentation testing, and other angles. The research process itself may be highly emergent and informed by realizations as they occur. The research shapes the researcher, and vice versa. Why all this attention to method? Research methodology and method, in a sense, is the thread that can unravel all.

Figure 1 shows word frequency occurrences in tens of millions of digitized books. Among the terms "qualitative research," "quantitative research," "multimethodology," and "mixed methods research," the most popular term in 2000 is "qualitative research" followed by "quantitative research." The syncretic terms are much less popular and seem to have about the same number of mentions. In general, Google Book's Ngram Viewer works as a lagging indicator of ideas as they percolate through society and are memorialized in the formal processes of book publishing.

In qualitative and mixed method research, the researcher himself or herself (or themselves) is trained to be an effective research tool, designed to function in various immersive "in vivo" ("within the living") situations. For many, personal obsessions and interests drive the work, which can take many decades to fully actualize. The human imagination itself is a critical research tool to ponder questions,

Figure 1. Popularity of research terms in (digitized) books historically and of late (Google Book's Ngram Viewer)

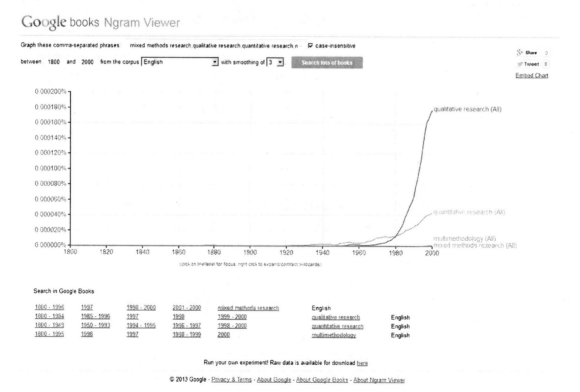

consider research approaches (with full human cunning but also the restraints of ethics and professional standards), brainstorm counterfactuals (alternative worlds if certain antecedent events were different), and ultimately bring together masses of information into a coherent and provocative vision. This is an imagination bounded by rules of engagement and enhanced and constrained through techniques (modeling, theorizing, and mathematical applications) and technologies.

Qualitative and mixed method researchers are trained to use themselves as research tools. As such, they need to build a large skill set in terms of how they engage others and also in how they discipline themselves. They instill rigor in their work through various means: explicit theorizing and specification, triangulating data, research saturation, sampling broadly and/or in depth and/or with maximum variation, applying a range of analytical tools, applying deep self-awareness about their own biases, documenting thoroughly through field notes/video-recording/audio recording, long-term immersions in related settings or among particular communities, and other methods. Researchers interact with their colleagues in research discourses about their respective work and methods. Their engagement with languages is intimate and hyper-precise. This mixed methods work results in a rich range of parametric and non-parametric data, and while they strive for reliability and validity, their data often cannot be generalized broadly across similar types as in quantitative research. Qualitative research is used in a variety of fields, typically, in the social sciences, including anthropology, sociology, political science, education, and other areas. In recent years, a number of technologies have come online to enhance the work of qualitative and mixed methods researchers.

Over time, as researchers conducted their work in the field and human behavior labs, they would draw from both qualitative and quantitative traditions for mixed methods research. While they blurred theories, they were able to combine practices that were more insightful and nuanced. They were able to apply abductive logic by using the world as informant to define "black box" models with relational mechanisms. They could apply coding insights attained through deep immersions in field and from their readings of the secondary research literature.

It may be that people come at qualitative and mixed methods research simply, through a small project with a simple question. This may be in the context of graduate school or a workplace. Anyone who has trained in qualitative and mixed methods research but has not been immersed in it for the past few years will likely be surprised at the changes in the thinking and the practices. My sense is that most researchers are deep experts in some aspects of this research but likely lack total knowledge of other aspects. As with most things in life, while one has been focused on other aspects of life, the world has moved on. To engage a complex world, researchers in various domains and disciplines have contributed new research techniques, technologies, and theories; they have combined and recombined various research approaches and capabilities in new ways. Anyone starting work in qualitative and mixed methods research today likely will find the work even more complex and overwhelming, in part because of the overwhelming mixes of strategies and research methods that may be applied and then the complexities of analysis.

Online ethnography, the study of human communities and cultures, is one major. This research involves the usage of a range of social media platforms on the WWW and Internet, including social networking sites, microblogging sites, Web logs, wikis, immersive virtual worlds, learning management systems, immersive games, content-sharing social sites, and others. This work involves usage of a broad range of technologies and fresh applied techniques (like network analysis, electronic social network analysis, sociometry, and others). The data captures often result in high-dimensional multivariate data.

Enhancing Qualitative and Mixed Methods Research with Technology is not set up to debate various research methods since these vary deeply across fields and domains, and they are hotly contested. This book does not suggest that the rigors of technologies justify any qualitative or mixed methods work that is not sufficiently well conceptualized and executed. The technologies described here complement, and in some cases enable, qualitative and mixed methods research.

This brief overview was provided only to provide a light sense of the context for the uses of technologies. In this text, the focus is on how contemporary technologies enhance the work of researchers using qualitative and mixed methods theories and approaches. The technologies are foregrounded. One more caveat: This text does not assert that the presented technologies are exclusively designed for the portrayed uses. All have functionalities well beyond this particular general "use case."

Some Contemporary Integration of Technologies in Qualitative/Mixed Research Work

The uses of contemporary technologies (beyond the technologies of pencil and paper) for research are itself contested. There are traditionalists who prefer mostly manual methods to their analysis. Researchers do form habits in how they like to think and process what they perceive. Technology, though, may be used in a range of ways—as "ego extenders" to broaden human capabilities of observation, data collection, analysis, data visualization, and presentation. Some types of information today may only be accessed using a range of technologies such as mass-scale queries of large data sets or targeted large-scale data extractions from websites. Technologies are not seen as replacing human researchers in any sense, but their role as complementary to human capabilities is an important one. There are superb researchers who eschew technologies as there are mediocre ones who use technologies. The competitive advantage for researchers comes from their thinking, knowledge, research execution, intellectual style, professionalism, and ultimate insights, among others.

In the past few decades, there have been a number of advancements in technologies used to enhance qualitative and mixed methods research. While some of these capabilities often required access to high-end computing systems (including those in the cloud) and access to specialized talent sets and specialized programs, many software tools have become available to the broad public in the common marketplace (and using commercially available computers). The learning curve for many of these tools have become less steep. Developers have encapsulated some of the complexity of the analytical tools behind easier-to-use interfaces. These recent innovations have expanded human knowing and the breadth of what is knowable.

Technologies may be integrated with the qualitative and mixed methods research process at any point in the work. The fluent uses of these tools, with clear understandings of what may or may not be asserted from the data and visualizations, are a critical part of the contemporary researcher repertoire. It could be argued that computational research is a necessary part of the researcher skill set. Some have argued that the knowledge of coding (to customized open-source tools and to even create "feral" ones) is important for research capabilities.

While the individual chapters of this text highlight tools that are specific to qualitative and mixed methods research (or general tools that are used in a targeted way for such research), the following overview will be inclusive of tools used during any of the phases of qualitative and mixed methods research. This broader summary view, which is not comprehensive by any means, is more accurate to how various technologies are being used.

Figure 2 depicts these technologies in four main categories relevant to different phases of qualitative and mixed methods research. Broadly speaking, there is the initial secondary information collection, then primary information capture and collection, then data and information management systems, and

Figure 2. Four main areas of technology used to support qualitative and mixed methods research

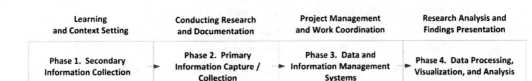

finally the "data processing, visualization, and analysis" category. In a more colloquial sense, Phase 1 is related to the learning and context setting. Phase 2 relates to the actual conducting of the research and documentation. Phase 3 relates to project management and work coordination through the management of relevant information. Phase 4 refers to the work of research analysis and presentation of the findings. While the arrows and structure might suggest a linear approach, this is conceptualized as recursive. Research may be inspired at any phase of the process. In addition, while the visual seems to show a condensed process, as many who read the literature know, there may be a long time span spent in especially Phases 2 and 4 (think decades in some cases). There may also be a separation between the research analysis and the presentation of the findings, but those elements were condensed because data visualizations used in analyses are in accessible form for presentations in most cases. While there is still a lot of work that exists between when research has been conducted and data analyzed and when a work is in final presentation form, in terms of the technologies used, the move to the presentation phase is often a small one technologically. (Very little post-processing is required although contextualizing the visualizations to be informative to a general audience may be non-trivial.)

Figure 2 is a generalized and over-simplified typology based on practical and necessary research functions. These are not mutually exclusive categories, and in the real world, there are some software tools that cover several of these groupings. These categories are also not necessarily unique to qualitative and mixed methods research; they could apply to any sort of original research. The four main areas are presented as general phases of research: 1) Secondary Information Collection, 2) Primary Information Capture/Collection, 3) Data and Information Management Systems, and 4) Data Processing, Visualization, and Analysis.

1. **Secondary Information Collection with Publication (and Data) Repositories, Electronic Publications, Referatories, and Bibliographic Data Management Systems:** The capture of secondary research and metadata (such as for literature reviews) has been enhanced with the wide access to a broad range of information in online libraries, databases, referatories, repositories, and the wilds of the Web and Internet. Published works are currently more accessible than ever. There is also much more "grey literature" (less formally published works) available as well as a lot of crowd-sourced information. Publication repositories are databases that make a wide variety of prior published works available to a broad audience; electronic publications are periodicals which offer directly published work; referatories are annotated collections of content-related metadata and links that point to resources hosted elsewhere; bibliographic data management systems enable mass downloads of articles along with their metadata (often in various formal citation formats).

There have been discussions about the publishing of qualitative and mixed methods data sets to the public to further the value of the research and to extend further exploitation of the original data set by other researchers. Because of potential challenges to the privacy and confidentiality of research participants (through re-identification possibilities) and issues with copyright protections (of the secondary research that may be included in full data sets), this phenomena of releasing qualitative and mixed methods datasets for public consumption likely will not occur until some of these issues have been addressed. However, the release of quantitative datasets linked to social research is laying a strong path for something similar.

2. **Primary Information Capture/Collection with Inter-Communications, Recording, Sensor, and Data Extraction Tools:** These include software programs that enable data extraction and acquisition and mapping from electronic sources, such as understandings of various network ties on the Internet. There are open-source and proprietary tools that enable the extraction of social network and other information from a wide range of social media platforms. There has been dynamic network mapping and analysis by using humans in social networks as "sensors." One well-known approach has been the machine capture and analysis of microblogging messages across various geographies and time zones in order to understand unfolding events. The structure or "topology" of social networks may be analyzed to understand social power dynamics, respective roles, organizational features, and other features. Various case studies surrounding human interactions and learning have emerged in immersive virtual worlds and simulation environments. Online surveys have been deployed to capture both parametric and non-parametric information. Various mobile devices have been deployed to support the collection of research data—whether automated sensor data or human-submitted information. Eye-tracking programs enable the capture of eye-movements as human test subjects engage visuals on a computer screen to illuminate insights about human perception and attention. Web conferencing has been used to bring together various researchers with their research subjects. Various technologies may be used to collect primary information. There are intercommunications tools like Web conferencing tools, Voice Over IP (VOIP), shared virtual worlds, and other dedicated spaces. There are a variety of recording devices such as camcorders, screen recording tools, digital audio recording devices, and others to enhance qualitative and mixed methods research. There are mobile sensors that people may wear for various types of recording, such as mobile devices with digital journaling capabilities. There are also data extraction tools that enable the capture of social networking data from social media platforms (such as for online ethnography and social computing). The nature of qualitative and mixed methods research suggests that the human researcher or researcher team have to be honed along with the other research tools—and there are technologies that enable researcher brainstorming and journaling to enhance the work of shaping the researcher.

3. **Data and Information Management Systems:** With the collection and representation of information in a range of digital and analogic ways, a range of software tools have been created to manage and store this data. This data management enables more efficient searchability and findability of various types of electronic and digitized information. A simpler version of this may include various folder structures for data archival. These newer integrated systems enable metadata annotation, cross-referencing of resources, and other data analysis tools. Indeed, various technology-based systems supporting research blur the lines and boundaries of various research tool types. These systems often provide ways for researchers to organize and visualize the data in various structures.

4. **Data Processing, Visualization, and Analysis:** Researchers have a number of technology tools that enable them to process their data. Machine transcription of live or recorded speech has improved for easier text rendering for rough-copy text. Network graphing tools provide analysis of

large data sets of relational data and offer rich 2D and 3D visualizations of that data. Geographic Information Systems (GIS) enable rich uses of geographical data and its mapping. A variety of statistical analysis tools enable ways to query the data and to report out the findings in visuals.

Texts are a core aspect of qualitative research. There are quite a few software tools available for the analysis of textual data to identify patterns and represent new meanings (through text frequency counts, word searches and word trees, cluster analysis, and others). There are tools that enable the searching of vast book corpora for first mentions of particular terms and phrases (decontextualized ngrams). There are tools that enable stylometry, or the understanding of individual writing "tells" and "fists." There are software programs that serve as ego-extenders, tools that extend the capabilities of the researcher in terms of information coding and meaning-making.

"Noisy" datasets may be used with greater clarity with cleaned data. Large heterogeneous (unstructured) datasets may be reduced through clustering and other forms of data reduction. Machine-enhanced analytics have enabled the identification of aspects of interest (such as pattern recognition, themes, correlations, and anomalies) from "big data" (represented as having an "N of all" or massive datasets with millions to billions of records). "Big data" datasets are queried for pattern recognition and anomalies. Human analysis is brought into play with hypotheses of causation and causes-and-effects (beyond the correlations). It is now no longer unusual to read of datasets with tens of millions of records and to see coherent analysis of the data using data visualizations and cogent descriptions and analyses. The "datafication" of information (the transformation of some data point in the world into electronic information) in machine-analyzable ways has also enabled richer ways of analyzing data. The broad collection of sensor data from a range of equipment, mobile devices, and wearable computing is feeding the so-called Internet of Things.

Researchers may run models or simulations out simplified systems and inter-relationships over time. Models are created, tested against real-world data, and re-calibrated, over many cycles. Decision-making processes are specified and actualized in neural networks, which are then compared to real-world outcomes.

Various software tools enable data visualizations: word clouds, two-dimensional and three-dimensional relational graphs, mind maps, spatialized mapping, and other methods of depicting the data. These visualizations not only inform the analysis by showing relational features, trendlines, and entity features, but also highlighting anomalies. Data visualizations are often published out through interactive displays on the Web for user learning and further potential discoveries.

An Overview of the Book's Contents

Enhancing Qualitative and Mixed Methods Research with Technology opens with three original forewords by three accomplished individuals, all of whom served on the Editorial Advisory Board for this work. Each of the three forewords was written without an overview of the text, which was still in development while these were written. As such, they reflect the thinking of the three, who have variant areas of professional expertise and high accomplishments in their respective fields. It was in my interest to protect the originality of their perspectives and voices. I am appreciative of the prefatory writings of Dr. William H. Hsu, Dr. Rob Gibson, and Nancy Hays.

The body of the text is broken into six sections:

Section 1: Setting the Parameters for Technology Use: Qualitative and Mixed Methods Theories and Models.

Section 2: All-Environments Information Collection.

Section 3: Technology-Enhanced Data Management, Data Processing, Data Visualization, and Human-Machine Analysis.

Section 4: Data Acquisition and Extraction from Social Media Platforms.

Section 5: Cases of Technology-Enhanced Qualitative and Mixed Methods Research (and the Converse).

Section 6: Technologies for Presenting the Results of Qualitative and Mixed Methods Research.

Section 1 offers foundational thinking about technology use in qualitative and mixed methods research work. Section 2 highlights technology used in information collection for research in "all environments." Section 3 focuses on the uses of technology for data management, data processing, data visualization, and human-machine analysis. Section 4 addresses issues of data acquisition and extraction from social media platforms, given the wide availability of publicly released data in social spaces. Section 5 offers a range of real-world cases of technology-enhanced research and/or high-method-based qualitative or mixed methods research applied to technology questions (and those arising in technology environments). Section 6 introduces technologies used for presenting the results of qualitative and mixed methods research.

Section 1, "Setting the Parameters for Technology Use: Qualitative and Mixed Methods Theories and Models," consists of three chapters that help set a baseline for understanding the potential roles of technology in contemporary research. Kakali Bhattacharya takes on the resistance to the uses of technology for qualitative and mixed methods research with her opening chapter, "Coding is Not a Dirty Word: Theory-Driven Data Analysis using NVivo." As a theoretical heavyweight and qualitative researcher par excellence, Bhattacharya applies a leading qualitative and mixed methods data analysis tool to explore where theory, technology, and insightful research interact. In Chapter 2, "Online Focus Groups: Lessons Learned from 15 Years of Implementation," Oksana Parylo explores the role of technology-mediated and geographically distributed focus groups in research for data collection. Then, Shalin Hai-Jew explores the work of research e-journaling as a method for mixed methods research rigor in Chapter 3, "Research E-Journaling to Enhance Qualitative and Mixed Methods Research: Mitigating Human Limits in Perception, Cognition, and Decision-Making." This is a work that takes into account recent findings in human tendencies toward perceptual shortcomings and cognitive illusions and the reality that all research is ultimately conducted, framed, and interpreted by people.

Section 2, "All-Environments Information Collection," sheds light on the importance of technologies for data collection in both physical and cyber spaces. Tabitha Hart's "Technologies for Conducting an Online Ethnography of Communication: The Case of Eloqi" describes a unique training platform for foreign language learning and virtual community that was used for a qualitative study. In Chapter 5, co-authors M. Banu Gundogan, Gulsun Eby, and T. Volkan Yuzer describe their use of an online Delphi study for capturing public definitions to aid in the development of a sustainable distance education ecosystem, in "Capturing Definitions for a Sustainable Distance Education Ecosystem through an Online Delphi Study." In "Video-Conferencing Interviews as a Data Collection Method" (Chapter 6), co-authors Kimberly Nehls, Brandy D. Smith, and Holly A. Schneider study the application of real-time synchronous video interviews for social sciences research. Then, Tianxing Cai describes "Data Integration Technology for Industrial and Environmental Research via Air Quality Monitoring Network" in Chapter 7.

Section 3, "Technology-Enhanced Data Management, Data Processing, Data Visualization, and Human-Machine Analysis," features four chapters that describe a range of technologies used for data management, processing, visualization, and analysis in qualitative and mixed methods research. Jessica Lester illustrates applied Computer-Assisted Qualitative Data Analysis Software (CAQDAS) applications in her uses of multiple technologies for transcription and data analysis for an ethnographic study in Chapter 8, "Leveraging Two Computer-Assisted Qualitative Data Analysis Software Packages to Support Discourse Analysis." Nancy J. Smith and Kakali Bhattacharya, in "Practical Wisdom of Tool and Task: Meeting the Demands of the Method with Digital Tools in Qualitatively Driven Mixed Methods Studies," explore the effective use of software to manage qualitative and mixed methods data. In Chapter 10, Taghreed Justinia describes her technology-supported transcription of interviews for her qualitative research in "Software Assisted Transcribing for Qualitative Interviews: Practical Guidelines." Hai-Jew describes a workflow for capturing "enriched knowledge" of Web network structures through a sequence of data extractions and network-based analyses in Chapter 11, "Exploiting Enriched Knowledge of Web Network Structures: Chaining Maltego Tungsten, NCapture and NVivo, and NodeXL."

Section 4, "Data Acquisition and Extraction from Social Media Platforms," provides deeper insights into the capture and usage of data from Web 2.0 social media sites. In Chapter 12, Sara Steele Hansen offers a riveting chapter on the study of the cultural meanings of virtual hair in a (now-defunct) virtual world, in "Trendy Avatars and their Hair: Studying a Symbolic Cultural Artifact with Multiple Qualitative Methods." Hers is a chapter about the uses of an immersive virtual space for cultural studies research. "Tweet Portraiture: Understanding the Gist of Electronic Identities through Microblogged Messaging in Social Media using NCapture and NVivo 10" (Chapter 13), by Hai-Jew, addresses the uses of Tweet streams to understand electronic identities through self-expression. Further, "Sampling Public Sentiment using Related Tags (and User-Created Content) Networks from Social Media Platforms" (Chapter 14) describes a functionality that enables the association of various tags based on co-usage (expressed as proximity or clustering) in social media content platforms.

Section 5, "Cases of Technology-Enhanced Qualitative and Mixed Methods Research (and the Converse)," consists of chapters which both address unique cases of application of technologies on qualitative and mixed methods research, and the converse, the application of qualitative and mixed methods research on Information Science (IS) applications. Eamonn Caffrey and Joseph McDonagh explore "The Theory and Application of Process Research to the Study of IT Strategy-Making" in Chapter 15. Theodora Issa and David Pick, in Chapter 16, "Mixed Methods Research Online: Problems and Potential in Business Ethics Research," explore the nuanced challenges of applying online survey research to business ethics. Brian Davis and Joseph McDonagh, in "Applying Grounded Theory to a Qualitative Study of CIO Interactions with External Peer Networks" (Chapter 17), introduce the uses of grounded research to the enhancement of CIO knowledge especially in relation to professional peers. Authors Brian Dempsey and Joseph McDonagh focus on the causes of information systems failure through the application of creative research methods in "Integrating Process Inquiry and the Case Method in the Study of IS Failure" (Chapter 18). In Chapter 19, Mohanad Halaweh describes the fresh "Discount Focus Subgroup Method: An Innovative Focus Group Method used for Researching an Emerging Technology" study of near-field communications and its implications through structured discussions with convenience-sample focus groups.

Section 6, "Technologies for Presenting the Results of Qualitative and Mixed Methods Research," is the final section. The two chapters here introduce two tools. In Chapter 20, "Querying Google Books Ngram Viewer's Big Data Text Corpuses to Complement Research," Hai-Jew describes the use of the Ngram Viewer for mixed methods research. In Chapter 21, "Expressing Data, Space, and Time with Tableau Public™: Harnessing Open Data to Enhance Visual Learning through Interactive Maps and Dashboards," Hai-Jew describes the use of a publicly accessible tool that enables the visualization of spatialized data on interactive maps.

Text Objectives and Target Audience

This edited book updates the state-of-the-art of technologies used in qualitative and mixed methods research, with practical and applied insights. As every other text, this one is also limited in its focus given the affordances of the development process in this time. The scope of technologies used in qualitative and mixed methods research is broad, and their ranges of applications make the topic practically infinite. The ambition of this work then is to provide a broad and real-world sampler. The intended readers for *Enhancing Qualitative and Mixed Methods Research with Technology* are faculty members, research practitioners, graduate students, technologists, and software developers. It is hoped that this book will encourage others to experiment with various tools to enhance their work. Too often, graduate students are imprinted in graduate school about how to engage technologies, and if they did not acquire some fundamental skills then, many are prematurely satisfied with their skill set. It is non-trivial to learn how to use technologies in research work, but I am hopeful that researchers of all stripes carry their lifelong learning into everything, including the application of technologies into their respective field research and labs. These tools are eminently learnable and applicable to research, and they stand to benefit work in a wide range of fields. I also see the intended audience as those in the future who may look back at this time for understandings of technology-augmented (and technology-based) qualitative and mixed methods research work.

One more note. While the images here are rendered in the highest quality possible, the b/w print production means that there is some loss of information and quality. Please refer to the electronic versions for the optimal quality.

Shalin Hai-Jew
Kansas State University, USA

Acknowledgment

From the outside, editorial work seems easy and easeful, and I can attest that in general it is neither. However, if there is any such thing as a book that just sort of comes together without excessive strain, then this may well be it. Out of all the projects I've worked on, this one had the smoothest work process and surprisingly came in healthily under deadline. This is not to say that the work of research and writing was easy, and the double-blind peer critiques were likely fairly tough and grueling for some of the respective authors. The meld between academia and technology is not always smooth, and expectations of published works vary.

My deep gratitude goes to the authors who contributed to this text. Their hard work and generosity have made this text possible. The topics that obsess me and that fuel the work are almost always non-mainstream and "hard fun." It's pretty tough finding others who may have the same compulsions, and I am deeply grateful that there are others out there who share some of my same interests. In addition, virtually all the authors provided double-blind peer critique for several chapters each—for which I am grateful. This may seem like extraneous work, but it's so critical to the ultimate quality of the text.

In the past several years, I've been taking graduate-level courses related to qualitative and mixed methods research, and I am grateful to my professors. The Editorial Advisory Board deserves special mention for their willingness to lend their names and hard work to this effort. In particular, prefatory comments were offered by William H. Hsu, Rob Gibson, and Nancy Hays. The three offered rich and original forewords. Even though all are busy professionals, Nancy, Rob, and Ya-Chun generously critiqued a number of draft chapters, which enhanced the respective works. Brent A. Anders generously spent time on a few draft chapter critiques.

In addition, I am grateful to Erin O'Dea and the many at IGI Global who invested much effort in this project. This manuscript was partially used to beta-test a book management tool at the publisher, and I am grateful to have been part of that effort. Thanks to Austin DeMarco for support in that effort. I am grateful for the supportiveness of the team that has made this book processing tool and their friendly outreach and support to the users. The marketing team at IGI-Global has always been highly supportive and professional. The typography and image layout were especially challenging in this text, and I am grateful to Kaitlyn Kulp and the others who brought together the book's layout. A book is very much a collaborative endeavor that requires a wide skill set from people of good will.

Shalin Hai-Jew
Kansas State University, USA

Section 1
Setting the Parameters for Technology Use:
Qualitative and Mixed Methods Theories and Models

This first section sets a basic understanding of the roles of technologies and new methodologies in qualitative and mixed methods research. It features some of the strongest analysts and writers working in this area of qualitative and mixed methods research with applied technologies. The assumption is that readers already have a fairly solid understanding of some of the related research theories and methodologies, so the works here highlight some understandings in approaching technology-enhanced research.

Chapter 1
Coding is Not a Dirty Word:
Theory–Driven Data Analysis Using NVivo

Kakali Bhattacharya
Kansas State University, USA

ABSTRACT

Current discourses in qualitative research, especially those situated in postmodernism, represent coding and the technology that assists with coding as reductive, lacking complexity, and detached from theory. In this chapter, the author presents a counter-narrative to this dominant discourse in qualitative research. The author argues that coding is not necessarily devoid of theory, nor does the use of software for data management and analysis automatically render scholarship theoretically lightweight or barren. A lack of deep analytical insight is a consequence not of software but of epistemology. Using examples informed by interpretive and critical approaches, the author demonstrates how NVivo can provide an effective tool for data management and analysis. The author also highlights ideas for critical and deconstructive approaches in qualitative inquiry while using NVivo. By troubling the positivist discourse of coding, the author seeks to create dialogic spaces that integrate theory with technology-driven data management and analysis, while maintaining the depth and rigor of qualitative research.

INTRODUCTION

Since the National Research Council (NRC) released its report on scientific research (Feuer, Towne, & Shavelson, 2002; Shavelson & Towne, 2002) outlining what counts as evidence, especially fundable scientific evidence, qualitative researchers have been extremely concerned about how this discourse limits the practice and theorization of qualitative inquiry (Cannella & Lincoln, 2004; Popkewitz, 2004; St. Pierre, 2002). To the disappointment of many qualitative scholars,

the American Educational Research Association (AERA) used the NRC report to construct a definition of *scientific research* (AERA, 2009). The ensuing discussion addressed questions of accountability, what good research in qualitative inquiry might look like, and how one might weigh the merits of evidence presented in qualitative inquiry (Freeman, deMarrais, Preissle, Roulston, & St. Pierre, 2007; Slavin, 2007).

Qualitative researchers argued that discourses of accountability and expectations of evidence driven by positivist paradigms were not only

DOI: 10.4018/978-1-4666-6493-7.ch001

limiting but also dangerous and uninformed, marginalizing multiple epistemological ways in which knowledge could be constructed (Lather, 2004). On the heels of these discussions, a healthy amount of skepticism arose whenever the call for accountability was introduced, or when scholars claimed that using qualitative data management software allowed them to preserve some accountability, conduct systematic reviews, and document a trail of their data management and analysis (MacLure, 2007).

Qualitative researchers presented multiple panels at various conferences, such as the International Congress of Qualitative Inquiry and AERA, to invite the authors of the NRC Report to engage in dialogue and find common ground across differences. However, while these discussions were productive, the report remained the same; thus, the fundability of research continued to privilege experimental or other quantitative studies. This prompted a move in qualitative research to emphasize theory-driven discussions and to infiltrate several discursive spaces, such as top tier qualitative research journals, national and international conferences with strong qualitative presence to demonstrate the importance of theory to any other aspect of data management and analysis (St. Pierre, 2013; Pierre & Jackson, In Press).

In these discussions, criticism was aimed at various aspects of data management and analysis, particularly coding and those who use software to manage and analyze data. Theory-based data analysis continued to claim the academic high ground (St. Pierre, 2013; 2011), and coding became a dirty word. People chuckled at conferences at those who still utilized coding, and those who used software were viewed by those who did not as theoretically light.

In this chapter, I problematize this narrow and limited conceptualization of coding and the role of software, and address the accusations of a theoretical void aimed at those who use coding and software. Specifically, I argue that software

itself cannot create a theoretical void, because software cannot conduct data analysis without a human operator who drives the thinking, writing, and in-depth inquiry. Similarly, I deconstruct the notion that coding in and of itself is positivist, limiting, and critique such essentialist understandings of coding.

Using a broad theoretical approach, I demonstrate how NVivo can allow for powerful data management and analysis. Although a more extended discussion is beyond the scope of this chapter, I address briefly the ways in which theory-driven data analysis can be integrated with NVivo in conducting critical and deconstructive work. Moreover, I highlight the depth of inquiry and analysis that can be achieved using software with efficient processes such as clustering, connecting, interrogating data, and visualizing results while using various data sources such as YouTube videos, Twitter feeds, Facebook conversations, and Web-based articles. Please note that this chapter is not about advocating for the use of NVivo as the only tool for data management and analysis. There are many tools in the market that can assist with qualitative data management and analysis. However, this chapter demonstrates how using NVivo contributed towards a theory-driven research experience for me.

BACKGROUND: SITUATING THEORETICAL APPROACHES

While there are many ways in which qualitative researchers think of and categorize theoretical perspectives (Creswell, 2007; Flick, 2006; Strauss & Corbin, 1998), I find Patti Lather's categorization especially helpful (Lather, 1991; 2008). Lather describes the terrain of qualitative research from three broad theoretical perspectives: interpretive, critical, and deconstructive. The purpose of interpretive approaches is to understand human experiences or phenomena through an in-depth interpretation of their context-rich environments. Such inquiries produce ethnographies, case studies, grounded theory studies, phenomenological studies, narrative inquiry, or studies informed by symbolic interactionism and hermeneutics (Crotty, 1998). Methodologically, these studies draw on the deep analytical insights of the researcher to produce rich, thick contextual descriptions.

In this chapter, I provide an example of the use of NVivo in a qualitative study informed by symbolic interactionism. Symbolic interactionism relies on three fundamental assumptions: 1) human beings act towards things based on the meanings those things have for them; 2) the meanings of things arise from people's social interactions with others; and 3) any meanings made are constantly modified and remodified based on an interpretive process carried out by people making meaning of the things they encounter (Blumer 1986).

Critical theory, the second theoretical perspective identified by Lather (1991; 2008), is grounded in the assumption that society is hierarchically organized, thereby benefitting some people more than others (Bernal, 2002; Giroux, 2003). Critical theory is used in qualitative research to interrogate the social structure of inequities. Critical theory encompasses such specific theoretical perspectives as feminism, Marxism, critical race theory, queer theory, and disability theory, and other theories grounded in interrogating various means of social stratification.

Central to these perspectives is the assumption that our experiences are not value neutral but instead result from the social structures of inequality that play out in our daily lives. Critical theory informs perspectives that interrogate these social structures, highlight the various ways in which people's lives are affected, and where possible suggest actions to be taken to ease or erase inequities. Methodologies informed by these perspectives include, but are not limited to, critical ethnography, autoethnography, arts-based approaches, critical incident studies, critical case

studies, and so on. In this chapter, I provide a brief discussion of how NVivo may be used when the researcher employs a critical perspective.

The third category identified by Lather (1991, 2008) is the deconstructive perspective. Qualitative scholars have long debated whether deconstructive approaches constitute theoretical perspectives or whether they are simply critiques of existing theoretical perspectives (St. Pierre & Pillow, 2000; St. Pierre, 2000). Because the theoretical perspectives within this category primarily challenge strongly held assumptions that maintain power structures in our society, they often become critique of certain structures, breaking apart foundational assumptions and leaving only broken pieces behind. With these remaining pieces, agentic readers of such work can create something else, identifying the potential for multiple possibilities, none of which are stable in their truth or meaning.

Scholars working from deconstructive perspectives operate on the assumption that there is no stable truth, reality, or meaning. If something appears to be so, that appearance rests on multiple power-imbalanced structures connected with deep-rooted assumptions. For example, gender roles reflecting society's understanding of masculinity and femininity represent quite strongly held assumptions that deconstructive feminist scholars seek continuously to challenge.

The purpose of deconstructive perspectives is to break things apart--to deconstruct, as the name suggests. Deconstructive perspectives are informed by postmodernism, poststructuralism, and postcolonialism, amongst other theoretical and philosophical perspectives. Postmodernism critiques the assumptions of modernism; poststructuralism critiques the assumptions of structuralism; and postcolonialism critiques the effects and assumptions of colonialism (Hutcheon, 1987; Lather, 1993; Loomba, 1998/2002; Peters, 1998). Key to deconstructive approaches is the belief that there should be no grand narrative as the prime directive for understanding discourses, actions, social order, or other issues of equity. If such a grand narrative can be discovered, it must be deconstructed and its power relations analyzed to identify how knowledge is produced and privileged, and how particular "truths" are promoted as stable and absolute.

Another tenet of deconstructive perspectives is the need to identify binary relationships such as *us versus them* and *First World versus Third World* and analyze the assumptions that construct and uphold these relationships. Typically, inequities in power, knowledge, economic mobility, class, and social visibility (and much more) exist between the two groups in a binary relationship. Deconstructionists seek to demonstrate how easily binary relationships are destabilized once the assumptions upholding those relationship are broken apart.

Deconstructive scholars also challenge the notion of stability in meaning. They argue that meaning cannot be found in one object, concept, or idea. Instead, like power, meaning too exists in relationships, and thus is fluid rather than static. Specifically, several deconstructive scholars subscribe to Bové's (1990) recommendation to ask questions about how discourses function instead of seeking to identify the meaning of discourses.

There is no prescribed research design, data collection procedure, approach to data analysis, or method of data representation for scholars who align with deconstructivism. This is because no matter which path of inquiry such scholars choose, their approach requires deconstructing the very path itself, by conducting a process and problematizing it simultaneously (Jones, 2004). This group of scholars is thus highly averse to coding as a process of data analysis, regarding it as rigid, restrictive, contained, and theoretically oversimplified. Such scholars prefer non-linear approaches to inquiry, data analysis, and representation. They value research that keeps ideas

in play and highlights uncertainties, ambiguities, tensions, and contradictions, without allowing any easy settling to denote stable reality, truth, or meaning (Lather, 1996; St. Pierre & Pillow, 2000).

This chapter presents a brief discussion of how NVivo can be used to conduct research informed by de/colonizing perspectives. Fundamentally, de/colonizing perspectives critique colonizing discourses and their effects on people's daily lives (Smith, 1999/2012). It is important to note that despite the discussion above, which presents interpretive, critical, and deconstructive approaches in terms of distinctive theoretical and methodological boundaries, in practice the lines between these perspectives are often blurred. As a result, such work may be informed by feminist postmodernism, for example, or hermeneutic phenomenology. In the following section, I argue for a broader understanding of data management and data analysis than is highlighted by the current postmodern discourses in qualitative research.

SITUATING SELF, METHODOLOGICAL UNDERSTANDINGS, AND NVIVO

Many qualitative researchers ground their work epistemologically in constructivism (Crotty, 1998). Such a foundation situates researchers as actively constructing the meaning of the qualitative data they gather based on their prior knowledge, personal, socio-cultural history, and the social discourses with which they identify. For this reason, claims that researchers are somehow separate from that which they research and that they can be value neutral are intellectually inaccurate. Instead, qualitative researchers situate themselves in relation to their study and document how their beliefs, values, and assumptions intersect with what they produce as knowledge. There is no claim of researcher neutrality in qualitative research, because such a claim would require the impossible: the capacity to divorce one's values, beliefs, assumptions, and connections from one's understanding and processing of the world and the subject of study.

Situating Self, Situating Subjectivities

Peshkin (1988) suggests that qualitative researchers address their subjectivities meaningfully instead of making a generic assertion that everyone has subjectivities. *Subjectivities* encompass the various subject positions with which a researcher identifies--such as woman, student, mother, sister, person of color, person of a certain nationality, person of certain socioeconomic status, person of certain religious background, person of certain disability, sexuality, and a professional being--and the ways in which those subject positions inform the researcher's values, beliefs, and assumptions. Meaningful engagement with a researcher's subjectivities provides readers with insight into the researcher's ways of thinking, processing information, and drawing conclusions. Readers then can situate the study within the researcher's subjectivities, to understand the paths the researcher took in conducting the study and reporting its conclusions. This expression of subjectivities creates intellectual honesty in one's work and thereby lends credibility to readers who value such things. Thus, I present my subjectivities below in relation to the knowledge produced in this chapter.

I am a qualitative research methodologist who has served for the past eight years as a dissertation supervisor and methodologist for qualitative and qualitatively driven mixed methods dissertations. My training as a qualitative methodologist at the University of Georgia provided me with a deep methodological understanding grounded in multiple theoretical perspectives, enabling me to effectively mentor students with diverse theoretical preferences. I situate my work in de/colonizing epistemological and methodological perspectives. Theoretically, my work is driven by transnational feminism. I focus on race, class, and gender issues in higher education and on technology-integrated learning and social spaces in higher education. I incorporate various forms of representation in my work, including thematic narratives, ethnodrama, and poetic representations.

I value methodological rigor and open-mindedness in the pursuit of knowledge. I have been especially troubled by recent discussions about theory, coding, and critique of coding that have occurred at various qualitative conferences of national and international prominence and in top-tier refereed journals. I am concerned that those who do not or rarely collect empirical data are privileging theory that is divorced from rigorous pragmatic approaches. Often, postmodernist scholars who critique coding or software-driven qualitative data management and analysis do not collect large amounts of qualitative data. Instead, many pursue autoethnographic work or undertake deep analysis of one empirical study over the course of 10 years. Of course, taking a portion of textual data and analyzing it deeply through various theoretical discourses can be accomplished without software, and with much depth as well. However, that approach should not be privileged and software use marginalized as theoretically and methodologically shallow. A quick review of special issues published in the between 2011 and 2014 by *Qualitative Inquiry, International Journal of Qualitative Studies in Education,* and *Cultural Studies <=> Critical Methodologies,* and of the proceedings of *International Congress of Qualitative Inquiry*, reveals an ongoing methodological critique of coding and accompanying accusations of methodological simplicity lacking theoretical influence.

Recently, veteran qualitative research scholar Johnny Saldaña expressed his frustration at the reductive discourse that promotes a narrow understanding of what a code is and how codes function in qualitative research. Rejecting the binary discourse created through methodological elitism and oversimplification, Saldaña (2014) published an article entitled, "Blue-Collar Qualitative Research: A Rant" in *Qualitative Inquiry,* a top-tier qualitative research journal. Writing "like a redneck 'cause that's what's in my blue-collar soul," Saldaña presents a "redneck manifesto" (Saldaña, 2014, p. 2) in response to the theoretical and methodological elitism of postmodern scholars.

Saldaña (2014) observes that while qualitative research may be complicated, it cannot be so complicated that research questions can never be answered in some way, even with tensions and contradictions. He reflects, "If alls there is these days is ambiguity, uncertainty, unresolved complexity, and unanswered questions, then Jesus Christ, what's it all for? Let's just pack up and go home" (Saldaña, 2014, p. 3). While research is complicated, it falls on us, as qualitative researchers, to explain how we arrived at a conclusion, whatever that conclusion is. If our research is so complicated that we cannot answer the research questions we pose, then we relegate ourselves to the sidelines of our own game, leaving the playing field to those who--lacking an understanding of the complex, multilayered, non-linear, contradictory nature of qualitative research--conduct oversimplified qualitative research.

I admire the courage it took for Saldaña (2014) to identify and "rant" against the marginalization engendered by the very scholars who pride themselves on deconstructing dominant narratives. Nevertheless, I have chosen to invest my efforts in tangible ways by initiating and engaging in discussions that offer another perspective on data management and software-assisted analysis. I invite anyone interested in the various ways in which theory can be integrated into data management and software-assisted analysis to join in this discussion.

Methodological Understandings: Situating and Expanding Discourses

As should be expected in qualitative inquiry, there is no fixed definition of *coding*. Researchers have offered a variety of understandings of coding and of the functionality of various forms of coding (Charmaz, 2006; LeCompte & Preissle, 1993; Miles & Huberman, 1994; Saldana, 2009/2013; Spradley, 1980; Strauss & Corbin, 1990). On the one hand, a code can be a basic semantic unit of meaning comprised of data sources that represent a single word or a phrase. On the other hand, a code can encompass large chunks of paragraphs, visual images, songs, and so forth.

Broadly speaking, coding is a process of data management. A qualitative researcher who collects volumes of data that may include interview transcripts, expanded field notes from observations, and archived documents must find some way to manage the data in order to engage in an in-depth analysis that aligns with the researcher's theoretical perspective, research questions and purpose, epistemology, and ontology. While no one prescribes how this data management process should be conducted by a given qualitative researcher, and certainly one is free to choose one's process of data management, scholars often seek to manage data by "chunking" it into smaller pieces for deeper exploration and insight. These chunks may be reduced to a word, a phrase, a sentence, a paragraph, or a page.

Some methodological perspectives do offer guiding paths for data analysis, whereas others encourage researchers to identify and justify their own processes. Most qualitative scholars do not claim that the meanings they identify through iterative analysis of these data chunks are fixed or absolute, do not vary, do not occupy multiple spaces, and are free of tensions and contradictions. Qualitative researchers often discuss the ambiguities and messiness of their work and how they learn to work with such uncertainties.

Well-trained qualitative scholars know that regardless of their approach to data management and analysis, they are not in the business of capturing, predicting, and generalizing "truth," as such an approach to knowledge building rests on a positivism that is incompatible with qualitative inquiry. I am therefore confused by the criticism lobbied from some postmodern quarters. St. Pierre (2013), for example, claims:

Conventional qualitative inquiry that uses a positivist ontology—even when it claims to be interpretive—treats qualitative data, words, as brute, existing independent of an interpretive frame, waiting to be "collected" by a human. However, a Deleuzo-Guattarian ontology that does not assume the subject/object binary might not think the concept data at all. The author resists recuperating data in the collapse of the old empiricism and is content to pause in the curious possibilities of a normative ontology that imagines a superior, affirmative, and experimental empiricism in which all concepts, including data, must be re-thought. (p. 223)

I have been unable to determine whom St. Pierre (2013) has in mind when she refers to those who, employing "conventional qualitative inquiry," conduct positivist qualitative work based on subject/object binary assumptions. Such researchers, she argues, view data as existing outside an interpretive frame, independent of the observer, as if in some Vienna Circle's logical positivist paradise (Stadler, 2001). In her article, St. Pierre (2013) references nameless researchers who conduct qualitative inquiry as follows:

Following interpretivism, qualitative researchers diligently, carefully, and accurately textualize in written words in interview transcripts and fieldnotes what people tell them and what they observe. In other words, they make texts to interpret. One would assume they would then use some interpretive theory—feminism, critical race theory, neo-Marxist theory—to make meaning of, to interpret, the written texts they've created. Not so. Their epistemology, ontology, and methodology cease to align at that point. (p. 225)

It would surely be a problem if qualitative researchers suddenly misaligned or divorced themselves from their theoretical, epistemic, and ontological positions. However, St. Pierre (2013) fails to identify who these deviant qualitative researchers are or how someone other than the researcher can determine exactly what happens when one codes, since the process is personal, non-linear, and inherently destabilizing, inviting the researcher to return repeatedly to the data to re-view the ways in which the researcher engages with the data. What St. Pierre accomplishes instead is to create a binary discourse of *us versus them*, where *us* encompasses methodologically complex postmodern researchers, who despite their stated mission create their own grand narrative through the citational privileging of the works of respected French authors such as Gilles Deleuze, Félix Guattari, Michel Foucault, and Jacques Derrida.

I am certainly not advocating for poorly conducted qualitative research, and indeed in all fields there are scholars who are vigilant about their research processes and those who are not. This is not an issue unique to the field of qualitative inquiry. However, St. Pierre's (2013) critique is aimed not at a marginal group of poorly equipped qualitative researchers, but at a group of unidentified qualitative researchers (*them* in the above-mentioned binary) who just cannot seem to get it right theoretically, epistemically, ontologically, or methodologically.

It is difficult to respond to such claims in a meaningful way when the targets of the critique are unidentified, leaving readers unable to determine for themselves whether such a key misalignment does characterize this research. In contrast, I can identify a number of qualitative researchers whose use of coding aligns with particular theoretical, epistemic, and ontological perspectives, such as the postmodern dissertation of Violet Jones (2004), the critical race work of Gloria Ladson-Billings (2009), the ethnographic work of Sarah Lamb (2000), and the grounded practical theory dissertation of Amy Mathews-Perez (Mathews-Perez, 2013). Such work demonstrates that coding does not in itself reflect a narrowly empirical state of mind. Given this acknowledgment, I would like to engage in a discussion not of "who is doing it right" or "who is doing it wrong," but rather of what the process of coding might look like when it is informed by theoretical perspectives.

In fact, a researcher drawing on logical positivism in her approach to coding is not misaligned with or divorced from her epistemology, ontology, or theoretical framework. On the contrary, she is reflecting *exactly* her epistemic, ontologic, theoretical framework of logical positivism. Such an individual is, however, a mismatch for qualitative inquiry and should investigate paradigms of inquiry other than qualitative research. One's own orientation to the world and to research informs the researcher's data management and analysis process. In other words, someone who understands the world through feminism will inevitably see her data through a feminist lens. Hence, the researcher's epistemology and ontology drive the data management and analysis process. It is thus crucial for researchers to engage reflexively in their own processes to identify how they orient themselves to their research and how this orientation aligns with their theoretical perspective.

A researcher, who does not demonstrate a connection to theory in any stage of the research process including design, data collection, analysis, or representation, probably could benefit from being exposed to the critical role of theoretical perspectives in qualitative research.

Such a researcher is not necessarily a logical positivist hiding in the qualitative realm with the intention of converting word data into pseudo numbers, charts, and graphs (St. Pierre, 2013) using software like NVivo. Genuinely closed-minded researchers will remain closed minded; they are unlikely to read St. Pierre's (2013) article and, even if they do, they are equally unlikely to feel a need to change their manner of conducting research.

However, many other qualitative researchers have simply lacked access to the rich theoretical training necessary to understand how to incorporate theory into data management and analysis. Moreover, many researchers are not aligned or even conversant with postmodern, poststructural, or postcolonial perspectives. Researchers who want to learn more about theory but lack an affinity for deconstructive perspectives need an alternative approach that reflects their own ways of knowing the world, and their own states of being, to align their work more effectively with a suitable theoretical perspective. In the following section, I describe my process of aligning my work through theoretical perspectives while conducting qualitative inquiry and using NVivo for data management and analysis.

THEORY-DRIVEN DATA MANAGEMENT AND ANALYSIS IN NVIVO

NVivo is software created by QSR International and used by qualitative researchers for data management and analysis. NVivo does not manage or analyze my data; it cannot conduct data management or analysis on its own, independent of its user. Users select options in NVivo to assist with data management and analysis in ways that are appropriate for their projects.

NVivo is not, in itself, positivist or linear. Positivist researchers use NVivo in ways that align with linear, unproblematic, absolute, positivist thinking. However, NVivo can no more be described as positivist in nature than can Microsoft Word. If I use Word to write a chapter praising the merits of positivism, this does not indicate that Word is a positivist word processing tool. It indicates only that I have used Word as a tool to produce my work in a manner that reflects my positivist epistemology. Similarly, if I am drawn to postmodernism and I write a non-linear, problematizing, deconstructive paper in Word, this does not make Word postmodern software. The thinking, ideas, connections, and textual representations were efforts that I made using Word as a tool.

Granted, NVivo initially became popular with many grounded theorists because one of its creators, Lyn Richards, is a grounded theorist who highlighted all the features in NVivo that could be used to conduct grounded theory work. However, this does not indicate that NVivo supports only linear thinking, provides a platform primarily for grounded theory work, or specifically creates a space in which only logical positivism and attempts to quantify non-numerical data will thrive. While NVivo may be used to support positivist views of the world, it may just as readily be used to support other epistemologies.

Symbolic Interactionism and NVivo

In this section I offer an example of how NVivo may be used to support a symbolic interactionist perspective. IRB stipulations prevent me from sharing raw data from my own studies for this discussion. Instead, I have used publicly available information to create a research scenario that enables me to highlight key issues related to theory, methodology, and technology integration in data management and analysis.

Symbolic interactionism provides a lens for understanding how we create and modify the meanings of the objects, events, and people in our lives with which we interact. What is symbolic could be something tangible or abstract. My example draws on public reactions to the crowning of Nina Davuluri, a woman of Indian descent born and raised in the U.S., as Miss America 2014. My

research question will be: How did people who disapproved of Nina Davuluri's selection express their understanding of her win?

Here, the symbolic aspect around which the interaction occurs is the winning of the title "Miss America 2014" by a woman of Indian descent who was born and raised in the U.S. To investigate the understandings of people who disapproved of Davuluri's win, I would gather information from Web pages, Twitter, Facebook, and YouTube. I will not assume any fixed meaning in any of the data I gather. Instead, I assume that meaning is transient, and what is said in social media appears stable if the pattern that I identify can be connected to various data sources. In other words, if a pattern can be identified in various data sources, one should not assume that the pattern is stable, generalizable, or the absolute truth. Rather, the perceived stability of the pattern could trigger a fertile ground for inquiry exploring what holds the pattern stable in multiple data sources.

However, I recognize that any understanding I achieve of people's reaction to Davuluri's win is interpreted through my filters and subjectivities, as well as my understanding of symbolic interactionism.

I started the project keeping the three broad tenets of symbolic interactionism in mind in relation to the research question. These tenets include:

1. Human beings act towards things on the basis of the meanings those things have for them.
2. These meanings arise out of the interaction of the individual with others.
3. An interpretive process is used by the person in each instance in which he must deal with things in his environment (Blumer, 1969, p. 2).

In my example, human beings are responding to Davuluri's win based on their constructed meaning of this win. Additionally, such meanings are constructed through interactions with people, discourses, and events, and these interactions are constantly undergoing an interpretive process of understanding, which might be in various states of modification based on how people were handling the meanings they made of Davuluri's win.

When I opened up NVivo, I created a document titled *focal document,* indicating that the document would maintain the focus on the research purpose and questions while I am managing and analyzing the data (see Figure 1). In the focal document I recorded the theoretical tenets of symbolic inter-actionism and the research question. This step reflected a process I used prior to being introduced to NVivo. I would have my research questions and theoretical tenets printed on separate pieces of paper that I posted on the walls of my home office. If I was traveling I would have smaller versions of the text printed on pieces of paper that I taped to my laptop. That way, while I analyzed the data, wrote about the data, and explored connections, I would be reminded to work in the theory with my management and analytic processes.

After creating the focal document, I began to collect data sources from public spaces on the Internet documenting people's reactions to the crowning of Nina Davuluri as Miss America, 2014. Once I found appropriate sources with material to analyze further, I began capturing the information to import into NVivo as sources. This process is accomplished through a feature on the browser called NCapture. NCapture can be downloaded into most browsers as a service pack from QSR, allowing the use of Internet Explorer or Google Chrome to capture relevant web-based sources (see Figure 2).

It is important to keep in mind that I wanted to capture information from Twitter as a dataset, a choice available when the user clicks on the NCapture button to capture the source for import-ing into NVivo. Using the dataset option, I was able to further sort information based on various attributes of Twitter users, such as gender, loca-tion, time, and frequency of posts. I also had the option of cross-referencing information about the user with the comments made and with the frequency of words used, if that was relevant

Figure 1. Focal document for symbolic interactionism

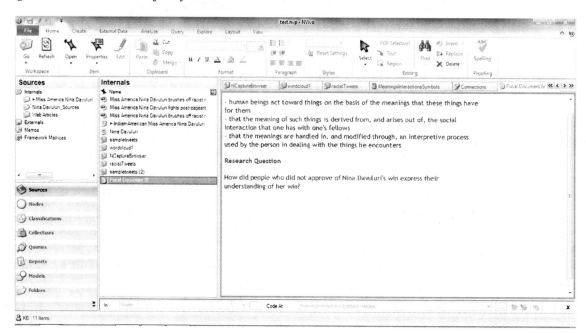

Figure 2. NCapture option marked on the top line of the browser

to my research. At the time, I was not sure if it would be, but I wanted to reserve the option for possible future use.

Once I imported all my web-based sources into NVivo, I created a list of memos. Memos are placeholders through which I could document my thoughts, hunches, guesses, connections I make with readings, data sources in NVivo, or anything else outside of NVivo. They also provided a free writing space to explore my theoretical and methodological insights. NVivo allows for each memo to be linked to only one element within its program at one time. Therefore if one memo was linked to an interview, it cannot be linked to my observation notes, or to a photo, or to anything else. My memos fell roughly into two categories (see Figure 3).

The first category of memos was directly connected to thoughts associated with each source of data. This meant that for every source that I considered to be a source of information, I had a memo associated with that particular source. This kind of memo attachment allowed me to write around the source with theoretical and methodological reflections, and with any other

connection I was making to whatever that seemed relevant. The second category of memo was really just one general memo that reflected my thoughts for all data sources. I titled the memo in this category as *MeaningInteractionsSymbol* as this was a reminder to me that I am documenting overall theoretical, methodological, and substantive reflections around my entire study in whatever dis/orderly way I chose to do so. Since the memos in the first category were connected to individual data sources, I wanted to find a way to have this general memo connect to multiple data sources, which was impossible to do if I kept this memo as a memo. NVivo allows a memo to be converted into a node, so I converted this memo to a node and labeled the node the same as what I labeled the memo (see Figure 4).

Nodes in NVivo are placeholders that can be used as codes, categories, and themes while conducting inductive analysis of data. Nodes can be arranged visually in a tree structure where a broad idea can be subdivided into smaller ideas. The broad undivided tree is called parent node and the subdivided smaller ideas are called child nodes in NVivo. However, please note, even though

Figure 3. Memo list linked to other elements in NVivo

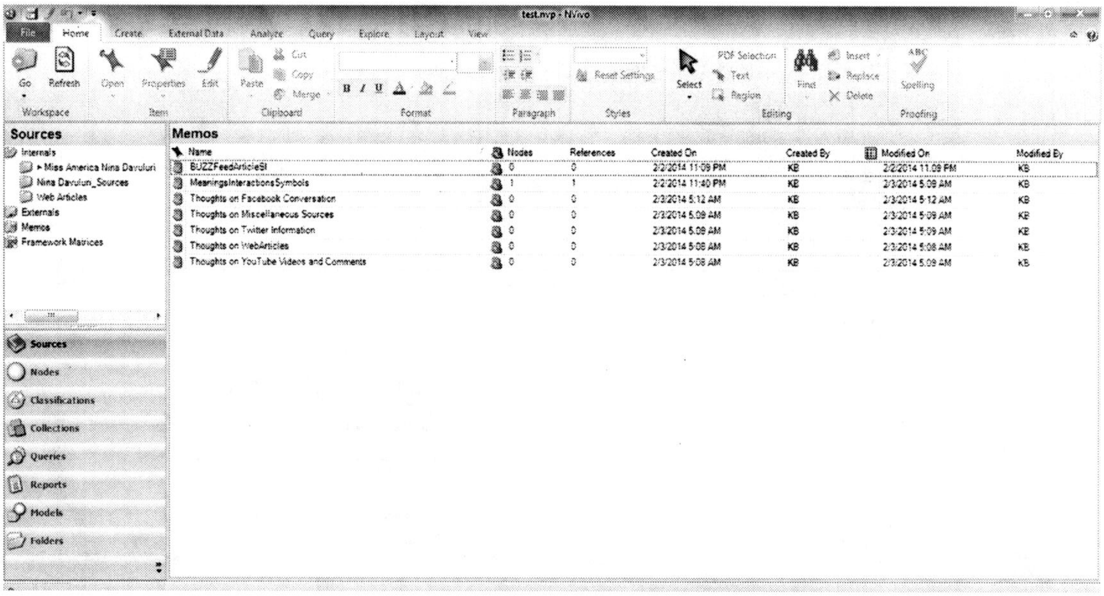

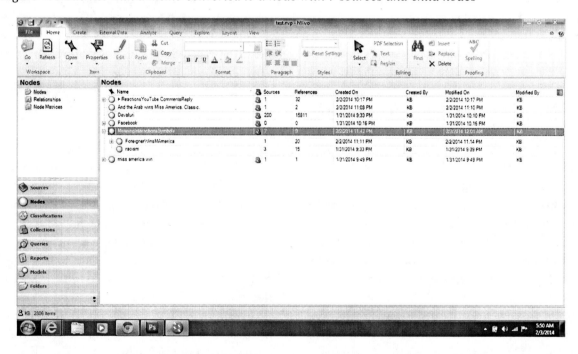

Figure 4. Node list with a memo converted to a node with 7 sources and child nodes

the tree structure is visually linear and hierarchical, unless one is prone to thinking linearly and hierarchically, these structures could be utilized in non-linear, clustered ways, as I describe below.

NVivo allows multiple sources of information to be connected to a node as child nodes or just be contained as labeled information sources within the parent node itself. Therefore, converting my general memo into a node allowed me to connect my overall reflections to as many information sources I liked, any way I liked it. This memo node was no longer a hierarchical symbol for me. Rather it became a cluster, a placeholder for connections, iteratively developed and modified continuously (see Figure 5).

In Figure 5, on the right hand side, the rectangular box encompasses all the data sources I connected to while reflecting on the symbolic interaction tenets played out in these data sources. Creating a node out of a memo allowed me to continuously update the memo and aggregate many different thoughts together in one node. Thus, the meaning of this one node was not fixed to a word, category, or some absolute truth.

Additionally, as I began to review other data sources, I could "code" them at this cluster node. This allowed me to assign the label of this cluster node *MeaningInteractionsSymbols* to various data sources. Because a node is a placeholder, a "bucket" of information, NVivo allows many things to be coded at a node. Thus, I could bring in other nodes, pictures, PDF files, and YouTube

videos to the single location of my cluster node, which is in fact a memo, enabling me to continuously update my thoughts without needing to adhere to one meaning and allowing me reflect on the contradictions, tensions, and ambiguities I may discover in my data sources. It is important to note that *data sources* in NVivo are conceptualized broadly, as virtually anything could be deemed a source: tangible documents imported from the Internet or one's computer files, audio, video, pictures, or something the researcher creates internally in NVivo, all constitute data sources.

This process of "coding" might look different from more traditional understandings of coding as including only particular words or phrases associated with certain parts of textual or multimedia data. However, as discussed above, one's epistemology drives the ways in which one pursues knowledge. Therefore, shuttling between a need to organize and a tendency toward non-linear thinking, my process reflects how I am chunking, categorizing, reflecting, processing, connecting, and arriving at a deeper understanding of the data. Further, to ensure that I was working with

Figure 5. Expanded cluster node connected to multiple sources highlighted on right

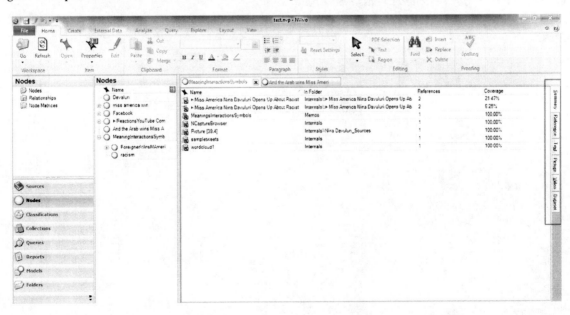

theory as I analyzed the data, I used the *See Also* link in NVivo in my cluster memo node to remain focused on the theoretical tenets and the research question (see Figure 6).

While I could have executed the same operations manually, without the software, the process would have filled my home office, dining room table, and computer desk with papers, sticky notes, folders, and index cards. This would have created a level of chaos and non-linear thinking that my brain could not handle, requiring organization of all this information to allow me to move more readily between various parts of my data in order to make connections. Using NVivo allows me to have a clean house, and, more importantly, having digitally stored my data sources allows me to be mobile and take my project anywhere for analysis, instead of being bound to the location where all my data sources are physically located.

Another advantage, for me, of using NVivo was the chance to interrogate the data quickly while having access to all data sources at once. The manual process of interrogating data takes much longer, even when I am extremely organized with my data, because I am manually sorting, reading,

placing, resorting, searching, connecting amongst hundreds of pages of raw data. As I started to manage the process of noding, memo writing, connecting elements within NVivo to various parts of the data sources, and writing around the data sources, keeping the tenets of symbolic interactions as my primary focus, I wanted to visualize my data sources in another format to reflect on them in ways that I might not have thus far. NVivo can create Word Clouds based on various options for conducting queries on the data. A query of the data sources allows me to see where certain terms appear in content, how frequently the terms appear in content, how I might have coded the term in my data sources, and the relationships that exist between various types of coding content. And this kind of query made and the results returned could be done within a matter of one to two minutes, which is more efficient than conducting the query manually.

Given the high volume of text drawn from articles, tweets, Facebook conversations, and YouTube comments, I wanted to investigate word frequencies in my content and the context in which the most frequent words occured. Some

Figure 6. See Also link attached to cluster memo node

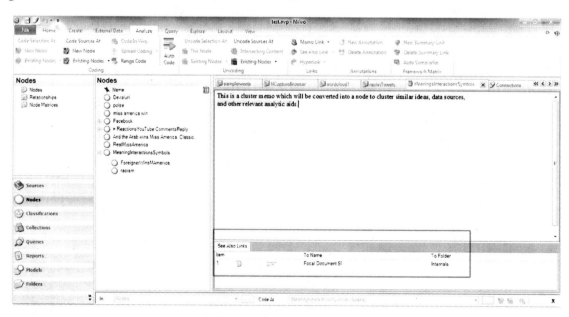

of the queries were informed by the content in a number of tweets surrounding Davuluri's win (see Figure 7).

I conducted several queries, which are listed in Figure 8. Once a query is conducted, the results could be displayed in various visual forms: as clustered relationships, a chart, a table, or a word cloud. I chose to look at word cloud representations of several queries, one of which I present in Figure 9.

I chose the word cloud because not only does this option present a data visualization of frequently used words from a variety of sources, but it also enables me to see other terms in relation to the most frequently used words. Additionally, NVivo creates a "live" word cloud, which means I can click on any word in the word cloud and it will create a condensed report showing the source and context of that word, with the option of broadening the context of the word's occurrence if I need more information.

The results of the word cloud prompted me to explore the context of the occurrence of *proud people, hate,* and *pretty* further. I clicked on these links and began to code the word cloud picture and the specific words and phrases I explored under the cluster memo node *MeaningInteractionsSymbols*. This allowed me to see how my thoughts on different data sources were coming together as I worked with theory. Normally I use the model feature of NVivo for further visualization, but in this case I did not need to. My cluster memo became a placeholder for writing around the sources and for exploring my understanding

Figure 7. Sample tweets about Davuluri's win

When her win was announced, Twitter immediately exploded with hateful tweets, with people calling her Arab.

POOKIE.   Follow
@Granvil_Colt

And the Arab wins Miss America. Classic.

10:58 PM - 15 Sep 13   Reply Retweet Favorite

Jake Amick   Follow
@jakeamick5

How the fuck does a foreigner win miss America? She is a Arab! #idiots

10:58 PM - 15 Sep 13   Reply Retweet Favorite

Logan VanVoorhis   Follow
@LrVanVoo0741

Miss Arab wins Miss America and the score of the Seattle/SanFran game is 5-0 at the half? What is life?

11:03 PM - 15 Sep 13   Reply Retweet Favorite

Figure 8. Query list

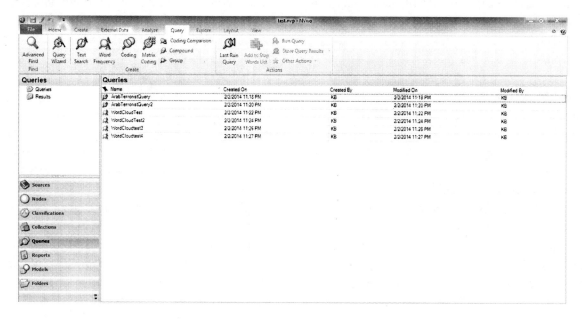

Figure 9. Word cloud result

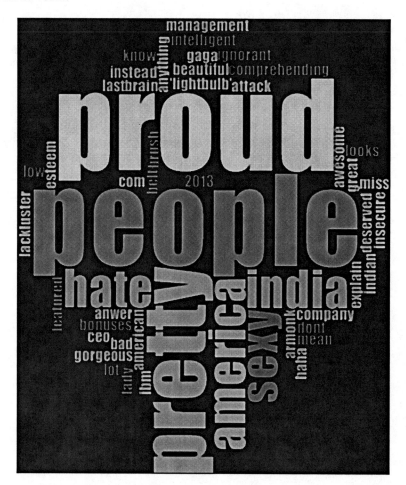

of the connections with no word limit, which is a restrictive feature in any mind mapping options, whether in NVivo or elsewhere.

These processes of clustering, writing around various data sources, re-reading, revisiting various data sources, and connecting my thoughts while interacting with other data sources guided me to the following insights, documented in a portion of my cluster memo node. I have included below, in quotation marks, a portion of text I had in the cluster memo node. Additionally, I am including my *See Also* connections as *See Figures*, to offer the reader a sense of how I was connecting to other sources in my reflections. Because it would be too awkward to read through the screen captures, I have copied and pasted the elements in MS Word below.

"People who reacted negatively to Nina's win did so based on the meanings they had for Miss America. Miss America is a representative figure to these people. The representative figure cannot come in a brown body because Brown = Arab = Terrorist (see Figure 10).

Not only did they have a problem with a Brown skinned woman being an American, let alone an American representative who is not a terrorist, their disapproval demonstrated the meanings they derived about Brown skin based on the discourses arising out of the 9/11 events (see Figure 11).

It did not matter that Nina Davuluri was born in the U.S., because she was seen through the lens as someone who did not deserve to be a representative when there was Miss Kansas, who was seen to be the real Miss America because she loved hunting, loved her country, loved tattoos. Discourses about how neither the current President nor the current Miss America is from America came to the forefront (see Figure 12).

It was becoming clear to me that the meaning of who is the real Miss America was grounded in various post-9/11 race- and ethnicity-based discourses. Not only were these beliefs pervasive in the U.S., they were also widely shared through social interactions in various spaces on the Inter-net, thereby strengthening the assumption that *Brown* must mean terrorist and non-citizen in an automatized manner. It was surprising, however, that the equation of Brown with terrorism was so strong that it had not been modified to reflect the Brown people on this globe who are not terrorists. Instead, what had taken a strong hold was the notion that "Americans" are *proud people* who hunt, who are war friendly, who take down terrorists, and who love their country, as part of the dialogue in Twitter, Facebook, and other spaces on the Internet." The preceding quoted portion is direct copy paste of the text in my cluster memo node with connections made to other elements in NVivo.

Seeing that I was beginning to form a theory-driven narrative reflecting the tenets of symbolic interactionism, I then identified the kind of representation I thought was best suited for this study. Having done some free writing in a memo to explore what I wanted to include in my representation, I decided the best way to integrate multimedia as well as text-based sources was through a hyperlinked article, like a web-based news article, with a theme or overarching pattern providing the headline for the article.

I began to brainstorm in my cluster memo, writing out terms from the word cloud and connecting them to thoughts I had documented in various memos to identify what the broad theme might be. Among the many possibilities this process generated, one that stood out was *Patriotism Meets Racism*. I liked this as a thematic heading because it captured the tension of patriotism leading to blind hatred of an entire group of people. The theme also gave me a chance to reflect on the irony of hating an entire group of people who are part of the country the patriot professes to love. The tension between love and hate does not allow this theme to stand fixed in meaning, because it is difficult to demonize someone who loves so deeply yet it is simultaneously difficult to see the merit of blind hatred. In this space of ambiguity, I can then construct my thematic narrative by con-

Figure 10. Miss America is a terrorist

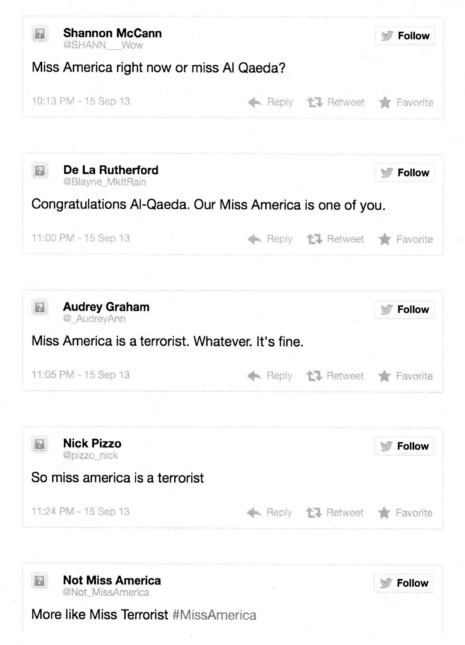

necting to various data sources, investigating the contradictions and tensions within the findings, and reflecting on the insecurities many feel in response to non-White people holding positions of power and visibility, and being put forth as role models, in the country they profess to love.

In this section I have offered a detailed example of the processes I used to conduct theory-driven data management and analysis in NVivo. I have demonstrated that codes or nodes in NVivo are not necessarily fixed or positivist unless one enters the space with a positivist epistemology. I have

Figure 11. Discursive effects of 9/11

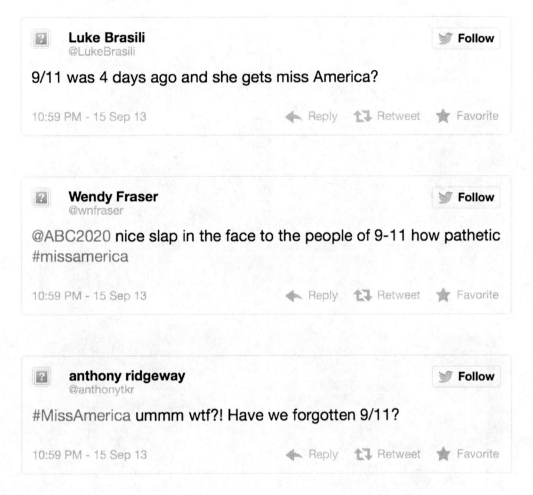

also illustrated how nodes may be used in open-ended ways, connecting to multiple data sources and providing opportunities to write around each data source as well as to write broadly to connect all data sources. I have highlighted as well the need to conduct every analysis with one's theoretical perspective and research question continuously in focus.

To that end, I have discussed ways to enhance the influence of theoretical tenets and the research question using NVivo. I presented the process through which a theory-driven narrative was constructed and the ease of connecting to various data sources with help from the software, a process that would have been difficult, time consuming, and unwieldy for me to undertake manually. Finally, I shared the steps through which I began to identify a thematic pattern, why that pattern resonated with me, and why such a pattern does not capture any fixed meaning or position, but instead illuminates the tensions and contradictions present in the various ways people author themselves, informed by multiple, conflicting discourses. In the next section I discuss some ways in which research informed by critical and deconstructive perspectives may be managed and analyzed using NVivo.

Figure 12. The real Miss America

Critical and Deconstructive Perspectives and NVivo

Due to space limitations, I will not discuss NVivo's use for critical and deconstructive frameworks in as much detail as I did for symbolic interactionism. However, I will provide an example to help the reader understand my process of using NVivo with critical/deconstructive perspectives. The example is drawn from my dissertation, and IRB confidentiality stipulations prevent me from sharing NVivo screenshots of raw data from this work. However, this should not be a disadvantage as this discussion centers on the conceptual use of NVivo for these examples, and the primary NVivo functions used in my dissertation involved creating nodes, memos, and links, which were discussed and demonstrated with screenshots in the previous example.

Because I operate from de/colonizing transnational feminist perspectives, my work falls simultaneously in the critical and deconstructive realms. It falls in the critical realm because I look at how people's global movements reflect local and global structures of inequity. My work is also deconstructive because it challenges various dominant discourses, destabilizes binary relationships, and problematizes power relations that favor one group of people over another. As stated previously, the boundaries between what clearly distinguishes one theoretical perspective from another often blur and it falls on researchers to situate and defend their work.

I am also extremely drawn to arts-based approaches to educational research (Barone & Eisner, 2006; Barone & Eisner, 2012), which integrate tenets from the creative arts into scholarly work. Such approaches are particularly effective in expressing the multiplicity of lived experiences in nuanced, complex ways while also remaining accessible and evoking emotional connections. Arts-based approaches thus offer valuable ways of knowing, analyzing, and representing data. In the discussion below, I describe how I integrate theoretical perspectives with arts-based approaches while using NVivo.

My dissertation explored the experiences of two female Indian graduate students during their first year of school in the U.S. I used a case study approach, but eventually my representation became an ethnodrama of a series of interconnected front- and back-stage plays. In ethnodramas (Saldaña, 2005), the researcher produces information shared by the participants in a dramatic format as a means of engaging with nuanced aspects of participants' lived experiences. Findings may be demonstrated through either a written format or a live, in-person performance. Ethnodramas are written with dialogues, scenes, and stage direction, so if they are ever performed the relevant details will be present. Some scholars intend only for their plays to be read, not performed, and in such cases they state this intention at the outset.

The process of data management and analysis for this research project was completely non-linear and multidirectional, and I was grateful to have a tool like NVivo to assist with the 1200 pages of raw data I collected. Epistemologically, my study was informed by de/colonizing perspectives that called into question the ways in which colonizing discourses and social structures create inequities. Theoretically my study was grounded in transnational feminism, allowing me to explore the ways in which women with migratory histories negotiate their experiences while maintaining connections to more than one nation.

When I started the data management and analysis process, I created a folder for each type of data source in NVivo. Conversations went into one folder, observation notes into another, and photo-elicitations and object-elicitations each had their own folders. I asked the participants to collect pictures and store anything they would like in a memorabilia box I gave them. When we met, the participants shared their reasons for selecting various pictures and objects for the memorabilia box; thus, these conversations were elicited by the pictures and objects. Because my perspective was informed by feminism, I was mindful of power sharing, so I abandoned the traditional interview format and engaged in more conversational dialogues. In these interactions participants were free to ask me questions, and often did, so the information flow was bidirectional.

At the time of this study, I was using an earlier version of NVivo with different features from the current version. I created a document in the program to serve as a project log, where I documented every analytical step I took as I chunked, managed, and analyzed data. This was a key step for me because each time I returned to work on NVivo, I was able to revisit where I was in my thinking procedurally, theoretically, and methodologically. I used the link function to connect to relevant elements in NVivo as I logged my activities. This exercise served me incredibly well when I had to document my process for the methodology chapter of my dissertation. I was able not only to demonstrate the paths I took and how I made my connections, but also to speak about how I worked theory and how theory worked for me.

For example, one of my theoretical reflections was based on the performative aspect of gender, which for these participants meant drawing on discourses of what a "proper Indian woman" and an "alien graduate student" should be and performing accordingly in various formal and informal social and academic spaces during their first year of graduate school in the U.S. I ended up creating a parent node called *performance*. Within this node, I included child nodes for each example I found of a performance or performative behavior. The "chunks" I put in the child node were not words, sentences, or paragraphs; often they were entire narratives of critical incidents. I would code the narrative with some theoretical label of performance, then move to the next turn in the conversation to code the next critical incident relayed. I would then write a memo about what I coded to further explore my thoughts and connect to the appropriate node. As I began to examine my node tree, I realized the participants were indeed performing in one way in a certain space and in another way in another space.

Eventually, reflecting on the performative elements in the participants' accounts led me to decide on an ethnodrama approach, which also fit my interest in arts-based research. I divided my nodes into two parent nodes titled *Frontstage* and *Backstage*. Theoretically, this move aligned with Goffman's (1959) dramaturgical notion of front and back stages on which individuals perform differently based on their audience. In back stage performances people are able to step out of character without fear of punishment, indicating that power relations in front stage performances

are more unbalanced than those on the back stage. This approach provided yet another connection between my methodology and theory, as it linked performance, dramaturgy, and the broad idea of inequities based on power relations that feminism addresses. I modified Goffman's (1959) front and back stage metaphor to suit my study, using a concept of "back stage" that incorporated an audience, but one comprised of individuals with similar backgrounds and experience as the participants.

Additionally, I linked multiple front and back stage performances together, arguing that participants draw on various discourses simultaneously. Notably, nowhere in this process of exploration, analysis, and insight did I keep any meaning stable or any reality firm. Instead, I explored how power relations produced different performances in different spaces. This meant that any meanings created from the experiences in various spaces reflected the functioning of power relations in those spaces, similar to the postmodern affinity for the types of questions that could be asked of discourse as posed by Bové (1990), such as how discourse functions in certain spaces instead of the meaning of discourse.

After establishing the two parent nodes *Frontstage* and *Backstage,* I then created child nodes of *scenography, character, visual, sound effects, dialogue, conflict, stage direction, and props.* These ideas were gathered from Saldaña's (2003) primer, in which he offers tangible suggestions on how to dramatize data collected in qualitative research. I subsequently returned to the information in my performative node and placed the nodes of *scenography, character, visual, sound effects, dialogue, conflict, stage direction, and props* as child nodes underneath the *Frontstage* and *Backstage* nodes. Table 1 shows how the front and backstage were conceptualized for one participant, Neerada.

The first column presents the name of the play depicting the participant's performance. The second and third columns reflect the spaces in which

Table 1. Front and back stage performances for Neerada

Play	Front Stage	Back Stage
Me, an international student: What are my rights?	Formal academia	*Adda* space with researcher
I AM a student!	Formal academia	Informal academia
What kind of an Indian/Asian are you?	Informal academia	Hickory Towers
A divided department	Informal academia (time based)	Informal academia (time based)
Mini-India - Familiar but modified	Hickory Towers	Alternate communities
Worshipping religion, culture	Non-resident Indian in the U.S.	Indian in the U.S.

the play was occurring differently. After populating the parent and child nodes of *Frontstage* and *Backstage*, I started another sorting process in which I compiled related information to create a specific scene and titled the play using something the participant said, coded in-vivo. My nodes now comprised the following structure, with pertinent information populating relevant nodes.

- Name of Play.
  - Front stage.
    - Scenography.
    - Dialogue.
    - Characters.
    - Stage direction.
    - Sound effects.
    - Conflict.
    - Props.
  - Back stage.
    - Scenography.
    - Dialogue.
    - Characters.
    - Stage direction.
    - Sound effects.
    - Conflict.
    - Props.

Following Table 1, I have included a boxed excerpt from my dissertation (Box 1) to demonstrate how the parent and child nodes of ethnodrama were transformed into a scene of a one-act play. The scene presented incorporates scenography, which

is the description at the beginning of the scene, as well as characters, dialogue, conflict, and props.

As is evident in these examples, my use of NVivo was continuously informed by critical/deconstructive perspectives, while also maintaining some connections to an interpretive approach. First, I remained focused on the theoretical tenets and research questions guiding my study. Second, I wrote intensively around the ways in which I was chunking my data with substantive, theoretical, and methodological insights. Third, a node did not represent a stable place for me, but a placeholder for incorporating multiple types of data—data that might be used in multiple nodes. Thus, not only was the meaning of a source not captured in a node, but the sources themselves were not stable enough to belong to one space.

Fourth, I used methodological literature, in this case Saldaña's (2003) primer for dramatizing data, to add organizational structure. Fifth, I continuously incorporated more than textual data in my analysis. Human experiences are embodied and multilayered; thus documenting human experience requires more than presenting an existence in text, analyzed through literary and theoretical lenses. My understanding of arts-based research enabled me to incorporate multiple data sources to render a representation of my findings in an artistic format.

None of the approaches described above reflect reductive, positivist thinking or detach theory from the process of managing and analyzing data.

Box 1.

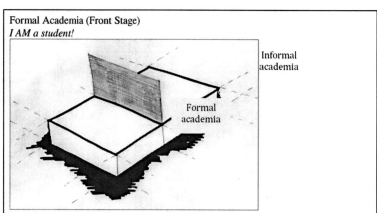

Formal Academia (Front Stage)
I AM a student!

Informal academia

Formal academia

Act 1, Scene 1 (Time: Late August 2004)
Scenography: Neerada is in the office of a White professor in his early 30s. His office
contains a tall chair for the professor and a shorter chair for the visitor.
Neerada: Dr. Baxter, I have been struggling with the readings in biotechnology from
our text. The British author of the text writes very densely and I don't understand all of
it. Could you please recommend another book?
Dr. Baxter: What seems to be the problem? It is written in English. Don't you know
English? See, A, B, C, D . . . (recites the English alphabet in a mocking tone).
Neerada (appears stunned, gulps): Yes, I do, but I cannot understand the text. Actually
I did not have to take this course in India so this is my first time with this material. Can
I read something in addition to the text?
Dr. Baxter (reaches for his bookshelf and pulls down a book): Try this one. It is a basic
level book that can bring you up to speed with the rest of us.

Note: From Bhattacharya (2005), *Border crossings and imagined nations: A case study
of socio-cultural negotiations of two female Indian graduate students in the U.S.,* p. 167.

Instead, these examples reinforce the argument that epistemology, not software, drives a researcher's way of knowing and of creating knowledge. A positivist-minded researcher will code in ways that reflect this epistemology. Scholars who are not positivists will seek approaches to data management and analysis that are reflective of their epistemologies. This could include, but not limited to, creative, expansive, decentered, non-linear, reflective approaches to data management and analysis.

Possibilities and Recommendations

I offer possibilities and recommendations in this section both to provide a counter-narrative and to offer ideas for those seeking to integrate theory into the data management and analysis process. I have not labeled this section "Solutions and Recommendations" because my role is not to identify solutions for others. I offer suggestions based on my knowledge and experience, but others must judge whether they provide solutions for their own situation.

First, qualitative researchers stand to benefit from a strong foundational understanding of positivist, post-positivist, interpretive, and critical theoretical perspectives. It is not necessary for researchers to incorporate all of these approaches. However, a working knowledge of when which approach is suitable will help in proper alignment with various elements of research design, data management, analysis, and representation. Second, once a researcher identifies a theoretical perspective, it is important to know the historical background, and how the theoretical perspective has been taken up in various discursive spaces. This could help researchers determine whether they can apply the tenets as originally conceived, or whether they will have to modify some aspects of the framework based on the particulars of the study, as I had to do with Goffman's (1959) work.

Third, it is important to find a methodological approach and develop a set of well-composed research questions that align with one's theory. These alignments make a study cohesive, with one part feeding into another and each part reinforcing the others, yielding an enriching analysis. Fourth, because data representation comprises another layer of data analysis, researchers who can think with theory and align the representation to the theoretical tenets are more likely to produce representations that are complex and multilayered.

NVivo is simply a tool, and as such it is most useful for researchers to utilize it in the context of a strong understanding of epistemology, theory, research purpose, research questions, methodology, and data representation. Without such a foundation, NVivo can be overwhelming, the learning curve may seem steep, and one might be tempted to click on all the options without reference to a guiding theoretical or methodological focus. For this reason, in my qualitative research methods classes I wait to introduce NVivo until after students have learned to analyze data without technology using multiple analytic approaches. This allows students to identify their own processes, to discover what resonates with them, and to develop their own methods of achieving deep insights.

My own process is first to establish an overarching organizational structure so I can see everything in one space. My kitchen table would fill up rapidly with index cards, scraps of paper, and sticky notes if I conducted data management and analysis manually. I therefore construct an overarching structure in NVivo, using memos or documents to create project logs and constructing one broad organizing document as a space holder, to which I return repeatedly to record thoughts,

hunches, and theoretical and methodological insights, and to connect with various data sources and analytic elements.

Next, I need the freedom to spread out without linearity, hierarchy, or other limiting structures. I need to be able to do anything I want with any portion of the data in whatever ways I choose. Translated to NVivo, this means creating many memos, writing around various parts of the data, chunking and re-chunking data, connecting parts of the data to other elements in NVivo, seeing how multiple connections inform my understanding of the topic, and writing around those connections. I ask a lot of questions of my data, needing to know "What is going on?" and then further, "What *else* is going on?" In NVivo, I satisfy this curiosity through various types of queries.

Because I am a visual person, I need to visualize my findings, as evidenced by my actions prior to using NVivo. When conducting analyses manually, I would move my sticky notes and index cards around on my kitchen table in many different ways to explore relationships. With NVivo, I use the word cloud and modeling features, when relevant, to explore my analyses visually. The visual depiction in NVivo functions as a management system for the ideas and analytical moves I have made. I then write around the visual or interrogate the visual further to deepen my analysis.

For example, in the word cloud rendering, clicking on any word generates a report on where that word is used in all the elements in NVivo. The user has the option of broadening the context to see the paragraph, surrounding paragraphs, or entire document within which the word appears--again demonstrating that meaning or truth is not fixed to one word or label but can change when viewed in varying contexts. When I expanded the context, I started writing again, using linking heavily to connect to relevant elements in the program. I returned to the overarching structural memo repeatedly to avoid feeling lost or scattered, which is an easy space to get into when digging into the details of data analysis.

In summary, having a solid theoretical and methodological foundation and a knowledge of one's own process with keen reflexivity allows for a robust data management and analysis process while using NVivo. For researchers who are intentional in using NVivo in a manner driven by epistemic, theoretical, or methodological needs, NVivo provides a powerful tool.

FUTURE RESEARCH DIRECTIONS

Given the explosion of social media, one of the most attractive features of NVivo 10 is its NCapture feature. Our discourses in social media shape public opinion, build connections, inform decision-making, and highlight various social structures of inequity in tangible ways. Thus, the availability of such a feature in NVivo has implications that have yet to be imagined for research on public discourse from a variety of theoretical perspectives. Even for an autoethnographic study, incorporating some data management, reflection, and analysis with this system can only strengthen the study. It is therefore important for researchers who want to get intimate with their data, interrogate the data, create visualizations, and document their processes to explore the potential of NVivo to aid their thinking, processing, and reflection. More documentation is needed on how theory-driven data analyses may be supported or strengthened using NVivo, to challenge with evidence the perception of NVivo and other computer-aided data analysis as superficially descriptive and inherently reductive.

The goal of this chapter is to enhance qualitative and mixed methods research with knowledge gained from using state-of-the-art technology. Although this chapter focuses specifically on the use of NVivo for qualitative research, the software is also beneficial for mixed methods studies. It is vital for researchers to continue to discuss not only the uses of technology, but also how to integrate technology meaningfully into the research process. As connectivity continues to explode in multiple, decentered ways, such dialogue will shape the future of qualitative research, engaging scholars in the ongoing task of discovering research methods suitable for an expanding, technology-integrated global village.

CONCLUSION

The purpose of this chapter was to offer a counter-narrative to the critique that characterizes coding processes and data analysis software in qualitative research as theoretically void. I highlighted the theoretical elitism underlying such claims, which emerges mostly from the postmodern and poststructural quarters of qualitative research. I offered a deconstructive critique of this theoretical posturing, arguing that positivist research results from positivist epistemology, not from the use of coding or software.

I noted further the binary discourse of *us versus them* created by postmodern theorists, in which *us* refers to theoretically complex researchers influenced primarily by Foucault, Derrida, and Deleuze and Guattari, and *them* refers to those who do not read or use the same theory as the postmodern researchers and are consequently labeled theoretically void, simple, wrong, or positivist. Problematizing this binary discourse, I observed that it is futile to argue against post-modernists who fail to identify the theoretical simpletons conducting such inferior research, as many qualitative researchers produce scholarship that is nuanced, multilayered, and highlights the complexities of lived experience.

Instead of seeking to contradict such arguments, I focused on providing examples that demonstrate theory-driven data management and analysis using NVivo. Specifically, I demonstrated the use of NVivo for conducting data management and analysis informed by symbolic interactionism. I also provided conceptual examples of NVivo's use with critical and deconstructive perspectives. The possibilities and recommendations I presented called for possessing a solid theoretical and methodological foundation before using NVivo, so the user is not seduced by the software's many options and remains adequately focused.

Qualitative research is a complex process to conduct, manage, and document. If there are ways in which this process and the product delivered can be enriched, we ought to explore these possibilities in a meaningful way, rather than refusing to engage with them based on a limited understanding of the functionalities of technology or technology-integrated learning environments. There may be a genuine need for more theory-driven analysis and research design in qualitative inquiry, with or without technology integration. Such a need, however, only reinforces the importance of opening the dialogic space to discuss how researchers think with theory while conducting their research.

Finally, because theory may seem abstract to many, initiating more conversations about how scholars can make theory a tangible part of their research may encourage qualitative researchers to engage with theory in more deep, rich, and meaningful ways. However, theory and understandings of theory should not focus on a set of grand narratives occupying a specialized area in academic discourses, as such a focus excludes recognition of the theorizing that occurs regularly in other forms and other spaces, including informal spaces outside academia. Our practice and pursuit of knowledge should be open and inclusive instead of rigid and exclusive, privileging only the ideas of those scholars who have read what we have read. Engaging, with epistemologies unlike our own, without dismissing them, is important for dialoging across differences. Else, we stand to talk to ourselves, a niche group of people who cite each other, who understand each other, who exclude those who do not pledge allegiance to certain ways of thinking, and strangely we start to look like the very same positivists we critiqued when we opened up our spaces for multiplicity in research.

REFERENCES

AERA. (2009). *Definition of scientifically based research.* Retrieved from http://aera.net/opportunities/?id=6790

Barone, T., & Eisner, E. (2006). Arts-based educational research. In J. Green, G. Camilli, & P. Elmore (Eds.), *Handbook of Complementary Methods in Education Research* (pp. 93–107). New York: Lawrence Erlbaum.

Barone, T., & Eisner, E. W. (2012). *Arts-based research.* Thousand Oaks, CA: Sage.

Bernal, D. D. (2002). Critical Race Theory, Latino Critical Theory, and Critical Raced-Gendered Epistemologies: Recognizing Students of Color as Holders and Creators of Knowledge. *Qualitative Inquiry, 8*(1), 105–126. doi:10.1177/107780040200800107

Bhattacharya, K. (2005). *Border Crossings and Imagined Nations: A case study of socio-cultural negotiations of two female Indian graduate students in the U.S.* (Ph.D. Dissertation). University of Georgia, Athens, GA.

Blumer, H. (1969). *Symbolic interactionism: Perspective and method.* Prentice Hall.

Bové, P. (1990). Discourse. In F. Lentricchia, & T. Mclaughlin (Eds.), *Critical terms for literary study* (pp. 50–65). Chicago: University of Chicago Press.

Cannella, G. S., & Lincoln, Y. S. (2004). Dangerous discourses II: Comprehending and countering the redeployment of discourses (and resources) in the generation of liberatory inquiry. *Qualitative Inquiry, 10*(2), 165–174. doi:10.1177/1077800404262988

Charmaz, K. (2006). *Coding in grounded theory practice. In Constructing Grounded Theory: A Practical Guide through Qualitative Analysis* (pp. 42–73). Thousand Oaks, CA: Sage.

Creswell, J. W. (2007). *Qualitative inquiry and research design: Choosing among five approaches* (2nd ed.). Thousand Oaks, CA: Sage Publications.

Crotty, M. (1998). *The foundations of social research: Meaning and perspective in the research process*. Thousand Oaks, CA: Sage Publications.

Feuer, M. J., Towne, L., & Shavelson, R. J. (2002). Scientific Culture and Educational Research. *Educational Researcher, 31*(8), 4–14. doi:10.3102/0013189X031008004

Flick, U. (2006). *An introduction to qualitative research*. Thousand Oaks, CA: Sage Publications.

Freeman, M., deMarrais, K., Preissle, J., Roulston, K., & St. Pierre, E. A. (2007). Standards of Evidence in Qualitative Research: An Incitement to Discourse. *Educational Researcher, 36*(1), 25–32. doi:10.3102/0013189X06298009

Giroux, H. (2003). Public pedagogy and the politics of resistance: Notes on a critical theory of educational struggle. *Educational Philosophy and Theory, 35*(1), 6–16. doi:10.1111/1469-5812.00002

Goffman, E. (1959). *The presentation of self in everyday life*. New York, NY: Anchor Books.

Hutcheon, L. (1987). Beginning to theorize postmodernism. *Textual Practice, 1*(1), 10–31.

Jones, V. (2004). *Race is a verb: An effective history of young adults subjected to racial violence.* (Dissertation). Athens, GA.

Ladson-Billings, G. (2009). *The dreamkeepers: Successful teachers of African American children.* San Francisco, CA: Josey-Bass.

Lamb, S. (2000). *White Saris and Sweet Mangoes*. Los Angeles, CA: University of California Press.

Lather, P. (1991). *Getting smart: Feminist research pedagogy with/in the postmodern.* New York: Routledge.

Lather, P. (1993). Fertile obsession: Validity after poststructuralism. *The Sociological Quarterly, 34*(4), 673–693. doi:10.1111/j.1533-8525.1993.tb00112.x

Lather, P. (1996). Troubling clarity: The politics of accessible language. *Harvard Educational Review, 66*(3), 525–545.

Lather, P. (2004). This IS Your Father's Paradigm: Government Intrusion and the Case of Qualitative Research in Education. *Qualitative Inquiry, 10*(1), 15–34. doi:10.1177/1077800403256154

Lather, P. (2008). (Post)Feminist methodology: Getting lost or a scientificity we can bear to learn from. *International Review of Qualitative Research, 1*(1), 55–64.

LeCompte, M. D., & Preissle, J. (1993). Analysis and interpretation of qualitative data. In Ethnography and qualitative research design in educational research (2nd ed., pp. 234-278). San Diego, CA: Academic Press, Inc.

Loomba, A. (1998/2002). *Colonialism/Postcolonialism.* London: Routledge.

MacLure, M. (2007). Clarity bordering on stupidity: Where's the quality in systematic review? In B. Somekh & T. A. Schwandt (Eds.), Knowledge production: Research work in interesting times (pp. 45-70). Abdingdon, UK: Routledge.

Mathews-Perez, A. (2013). *Speak, review, change, repeat: An analysis of discourse surrounding dilemmas At admission, review and dismissal meetings.* (Dissertation). Texas A & M University, Corpus Christi, TX.

Miles, M. B., & Huberman, A. M. (1994). *An Expanded Sourcebook: Qualitative Data Analysis* (2nd ed.). Thousand Oaks, CA: Sage.

Peshkin, A. (1988). In search of subjectivity- One's own. *Educational Researcher, 17*(7), 17–22.

Peters, M. (1998). *Naming the multiple: Poststructuralism and education.* Westport, CT: Bergin & Garvey.

Pierre, E. A. S. (2013). The appearance of data. *Cultural Studies, Critical Methodologies, 13*(4), 223-227.

Pierre, E. A. S. (2013). *Post Qualitative Research: The Critique and the Coming After.* Paper presented at the Ninth International Congress of Qualitative Inquiry. Champaign/Urbana, IL.

Pierre, E. A. S., & Jackson, A. (in press). Introduction: Qualitative data analysis after coding. *Qualitative Inquiry.*

Popkewitz, T. S. (2004). Is the National Research Council Committee's Report on Scientific Research in Education Scientific? On Trusting the Manifesto. *Qualitative Inquiry, 10*(1), 62–78. doi:10.1177/1077800403259493

Saldaña, J. (2003). Dramatizing data: A primer. *Qualitative Inquiry, 9*(2), 218–236. doi:10.1177/1077800402250932

Saldaña, J. (Ed.). (2005). *Ethnodrama: An anthology of reality theatre* (Vol. 5). Walnut Creek, CA: AltaMira Press.

Saldaña, J. (2009/2013). *The Coding Manual for Qualitative Researchers* (2nd ed.). Thousand Oaks, CA: Sage.

Saldaña, J. (2014). Blue-collar qualitative research: A rant. *Qualitative Inquiry.* doi:10.1177/1077800413513739

Shavelson, R. J., & Towne, L. (2002). *Scientific research in education.* Washington, DC: National Academy Press.

Slavin, R. E. (2007). *Educational research: In an age of accountability.* Boston: Pearson Education, Inc.

Smith, L. T. (1999/2012). *Decolonizing methodologies: Research and indigenous peoples* (2nd ed.). London, UK: Zed Books.

Spradley, J. P. (1980). *Step seven: Making a taxonomic analysis. In Participant Observation* (pp. 112–116). Wadsworth Thomson Learning.

St. Pierre, E. A. (2000). Poststructural feminism in education: An overview. *International Journal of Qualitative Studies in Education, 13*(5), 4677–5150. doi:10.1080/09518390050156422

St. Pierre, E. A. (2002). "Science" rejects postmodernism. *Educational Researcher, 31*(8), 25–27. doi:10.3102/0013189X031008025

St. Pierre, E. A. (2011). *Data analysis after coding in qualitative research.* Paper presented at the Seventh International Congress of Qualitative Inquiry. Champaign/Urbana, IL.

St. Pierre, E. A. (2013). The appearance of data. *Cultural Studies, Critical Methodologies, 13*(4), 223-227. doi: 10.1177/1532708613487862

St. Pierre, E. A., & Pillow, W. S. (2000). *Working the ruins: feminist poststructural theory and methods in education.* New York: Routledge.

Stadler, F. (2001). The Vienna Circle (C. Nielsen, J. Golb, S. Schmidt & T. Ernst, Trans.). Vienna, Austria: Springer-Verlag/Wien.

Strauss, A., & Corbin, J. (1990). Open coding. In A. Strauss, & J. Corbin (Eds.), *Basics of qualitative research: Grounded theory procedures and techniques* (2nd ed., pp. 101–121). Thousand Oaks, CA: Sage.

Strauss, A., & Corbin, J. (1998). *Basics of qualitative research: Techniques and procedures for developing grounded theory* (2nd ed.). Thousand Oaks, CA: Sage Publications.

KEY TERMS AND DEFINITIONS

Coding: A way to manage data through providing some semantic structure on data. The semantic structure on data varies based on the researcher's epistemology, theoretical and analytical frameworks. Semantic units could include, words, phrases, paragraphs, or even larger chunks of data.

Interrogating Data: Asking questions of data and querying for answers.

NCapture: A function in NVivo that allows for capturing of information on webpages, YouTube, Twitter, and Facebook, which can be imported to NVivo for further analysis.

Non-Linear Connection: Connection made without any linear sequencing.

NVivo: A data management software by QSR International that can be used for qualitative and mixed methods research.

Qualitative Inquiry: A reflexive form of inquiry that explores in-depth understanding of contexts in which truths are perceived and meanings are constructed. This form of inquiry intersects with various social discourses and how such discourses shape the ways in which people navigate their daily lives.

Theory-Driven Analysis: Data analysis that is driven primarily through the tenets of one's theoretical connection.

Visualizing Data: Creating visual representations that allow the researcher to "see" the data management or analysis in a visual format.

Writing with Data: Using parts of the data to become prompts for writing, leading to deep introspective insights.

Chapter 2
Online Focus Groups:
Lessons Learned from 15 Years of Implementation

Oksana Parylo
Katholieke Universiteit Leuven, Belgium

ABSTRACT

The overall aim of this chapter is to provide a better understanding of how a specific technique of online research methodology, online focus groups, has been theoretically conceptualized and practically utilized in order to examine its advantages and disadvantages to improve future applications of this technique in qualitative and mixed methods research. The chapter offers an overview of qualitative and mixed methods empirical research using online focus groups in different disciplines and outlines the strengths and weaknesses of this data collection technique. In addition, based on the review of empirical and theoretical research, the current and emerging practices in and characteristics of using online focus groups for data collection are outlined and used to suggest future trends in using this data collection technique in qualitative and mixed methods research.

INTRODUCTION

As a research medium, the Internet has become widely used in the recent decades. Not only did the Internet provide the base for enhanced secondary research (e.g., online databases, repositories, etc.), it also offered a new ground for primary research (e.g., adapting traditional methods and developing new methods to capture data for original research) to be carried out in a virtual environment (Hewson & Laurent, 2008). Known as online research, web-based research, or Internet-mediated research (Hewson, Yule, Laurent, & Vogel, 2003), it is a relatively new direction that is quickly growing in popularity and applications.

The innovations in technology allow researchers to consider new types of data collection, analysis, and preservation, thus pushing the boundaries of what research process has meant traditionally. In addition to new forms and directions in conducting research, the Internet medium offers significant advantages for researchers (e.g., decreased cost and data collection time; reduced geographical limitations: the ability to reach more

DOI: 10.4018/978-1-4666-6493-7.ch002

participants and remote populations; and higher methodological rigor and data accuracy) and for participants (e.g., higher participant anonymity and control over the input, convenience, easy to use format) (Ahern, 2005). Along with the advantages, researchers point out new challenges and methodological considerations pertaining to web-based research, emphasizing the need to review and adapt traditional research approaches to be effective in the online environment (Duffy, 2002; Cantrell & Lupinacci, 2007). In addition, researching online necessitates the revision of research ethics and related concerns such as anonymity, privacy, and data protection (Eynon, Fry, & Schroeder, 2008). Therefore, researchers have developed guidelines for conducting research online that accounted for peculiarities in participant recruitment, obtaining informed consent, ensuring participant anonymity, data collection, and data storage and retrieval while conducting online research (e.g., Klein, 2002; Lakeman, 1997).

In spite of the concerns and shortcomings, web-based research is here to stay. Even though it is hard to make predictions about the future directions and developments in research, it is save to assert that with time, the use of the Internet medium in research will be increasing, taking new forms, and adapting traditional approaches. Therefore, a "strong grasp of the technologies, techniques, and procedures of online research methodology is one means within our reach to ensure that, whatever the state of the online world in general, its research dimension will be as securely founded as possible" (Lee, Fielding, & Blank, 2008, p. 19). Thus, the overall aim of this book chapter is to provide a better understanding of how a specific technique of online research methodology (i.e., online focus group) has been theoretically conceptualized and practically utilized in order to examine its advantages and disadvantages to improve future applications of online focus groups in qualitative and mixed methods research.

Specifically, this book chapter examines online focus groups as a technology-enabled method of data collection for qualitative and mixed methods studies. Even though online focus groups were first used in research in the mid-1990s (Miller & Walkowski, 2004), now, almost 20 years later, there is still little consensus among researchers about this technique (e.g., Graffigna & Bosio, 2006). Furthermore, a broad search for empirical studies across major databases not limited to a specific discipline yielded surprisingly low number of studies that used online focus groups (more details provided later in the chapter). These findings suggest the need to further examine the literature on online focus groups, paying special attention to how online focus groups have been used in recently published empirical research. Specific purposes of the chapter are threefold: (1) to provide a brief overview of the history and uses of online focus groups; (2) to report the results of a systematic review of research on online focus groups (both theoretical/methodological articles and empirical studies); and, based on the literature and research review, (3) to outline advantages and disadvantages of online focus groups and to provide recommendations for using this form of data collection.

BACKGROUND

Since its introduction in the middle of the 20th century, focus groups have been frequently used in qualitative and mixed methods research in different disciplines. Traditionally, face-to-face focus groups bring together 6-8 people for 30 minutes to 2 hours to discuss or debate the topic of interest and can be used at different stages of the research process (Patton, 2002). Focus group discussions are typically guided by a question guide (interview guide) developed in advance based on the literature and researcher experience (Krueger, 2000).

As a data collection method, focus group is a versatile instrument that can be used individually or complementary to other methods (e.g., surveys, individual interviews, observations) to elicit the viewpoints of a group of carefully selected participants on a topic of interest. Focus groups also allow evaluating ideas in the process of group interaction (Gaiser, 2008), shifting the focus from an individual point of view to the meaning obtained as a result of group discussion and/or debate. However, some researchers question the assertion that the findings of the focus group discussion equally represent the opinions of all participants (e.g., Duggleby, 2000) and caution about interpreting these data. Yet, regardless of these critiques, focus groups continue to be used in the traditional (face-to-face) as well as innovative (virtual) formats.

From the late 1990s, virtual data collection methods have been adopted and adapted by social scientists (Graffigna & Bosio, 2006). With the ever-increasing use of the Internet, online focus groups (also known as virtual focus groups) have been gaining popularity in academic research and marketing, becoming "the most commonly employed data-gathering method found in the online research setting" (Graffigna & Bosio, 2006, p. 57). Because different forms of online focus groups (OFGs) have been developed, researchers do not agree on one definition for this method (Graffigna & Bosio, 2006). However, generally, an online focus group is used to describe "a selected group of individuals who have volunteered to participate in a moderated, structured, online discussion in order to explore a particular topic for the purpose of research" (Peacock, Robertson, Williams, & Clausen, 2009, p. 119). Online setting of the focus group predefines three characteristics that set this form apart from the traditional face-to-face focus group: (1) communication is based solely on text, excluding the non-verbal cues; (2) participant anonymity; and (3) increased destructive behaviors of participants (Graffigna & Bosio, 2006).

Virtual vs. Traditional Focus Groups

The original application of a focus group in an online setting was characterized by an attempt to carry out the online discussion as close as possible to the face-to-face discussion (Graffigna & Bosio, 2006). For example, in an early article on using virtual focus groups in qualitative research, Murray (1997) suggested selecting 6-8 participants for each online focus group discussion, mirroring the accepted standards for the traditional focus group. However, more recent publications emphasize that the ability of online focus group to engage a higher number of participants is a notable advantage over the traditional face-to-face format (Oringderff, 2004). Furthermore, the "online environment can furnish new levels and types of group interactivity, highlighting its potential as a legitimate addition to qualitative methodologies" (Mann & Stewart, 2000, p. 125).

Over time, researchers have embraced the advantages offered by the online settings, moving online focus group further from its traditional applications and characteristics. This shift has led to the academic debate about the validity and reliability of this type of data collection. While some researchers questioned whether online focus group that is not conducted in real time (asynchronous) could be considered a true focus group method (Bloor, Frankland, Thomas, & Robson, 2001), others assert that online focus groups are superior to the traditional form (e.g., Murray, 1997; Williams et al., 2012). Yet, other researchers position online focus groups separately from their traditional counterparts because "in the case of focus groups, online qualitative research cannot be considered a reproduction of traditional techniques on the Internet but is a different set of tools, with its own peculiar advantages and limitations" (Graffigna & Bosio, 2006, p. 12). This point of view represents the stance some researchers take describing online focus group as a distinct research instrument that should be assessed differently from its traditional predecessor (e.g., Gaiser, 1997; Im & Chee, 2004).

Participant Recruitment for Online Focus Groups

While online focus groups allow the researcher to bring together participants located in different geographical settings and time zones, they also make sampling and recruitment process more challenging. Recruitment for participation in online focus groups may combine traditional approaches (e.g., random sampling, reputational sampling, membership lists) and online means of contacting potential participants such as chat rooms, virtual conference rooms, and listservs (Mann & Stewart, 2000). Furthermore, online settings for conducting research present a new set of ethical risks and considerations about the respondents' truthfulness (Gaiser, 2008; Reinharz, 1992). Therefore, recruitment and informed consent for participating in an online focus group should be carefully considered in advance to minimize potential threats and limit self-selection and disproportionate representation (Gaiser, 2008).

Moderating Online Focus Groups

It is acknowledged that the success of traditional focus groups largely depends on the skills of a moderator (e.g., Feig, 1989). Due to the peculiarities of doing research online, the importance of a skillful moderator is even more pronounced. It is moderator's responsibility to monitor participant dynamics, balance uneven participation, and resolve potential virtual group conflict (Mann & Stewart, 2000). Given that it is easy to sidetrack and to get distracted in an online discussion, the "moderator's task is to remain attentive, keep the group focused, and maintain a professional demeanor, while also gently reminding participants

of the central purpose of the group's interaction" (Gaiser, 2008, p. 297). While moderators' styles differ depending on the situation (Krueger, 2000), the tasks listed by Gaiser (2008) appear to be generally representative of successful online focus group moderation.

Types of Online Focus Groups

Generally, researchers distinguish between two major types of online focus groups based on the timing: synchronous and asynchronous. Synchronous online focus groups occur in real time with all participants contributing to the ongoing discussion scheduled within a pre-set timeframe. Although the ways of carrying out synchronous online focus groups have changed along with the technological developments, currently synchronous online focus groups are conducted in online chat rooms, instant messaging programs, conferencing software, and other shareware and freeware applications (Gaiser, 2008; Liamputtong, 2011). In comparison, asynchronous online focus groups are not set in real time and occur over a period of time (several days, weeks, or even months), allowing participants to contribute to online discussions at the time convenient for them. Asynchronous online focus groups can be conducted via email exchanges, email subscription lists, forums, or discussion boards (Graffigna & Bosio, 2006; Liamputtong, 2011).

While synchronous online focus groups are more interactive, facilitating immediate exchange of thoughts and ideas among participants (Mann & Stewart, 2000), asynchronous focus groups provide more flexibility and control for participants by letting them choose convenient time to contribute to online discussions and to think through, revise and polish their contributions before sharing them with the group (Graffigna & Bosio, 2006). Furthermore, additional time allows for deeper and richer participant contributions (Oringderff, 2004). Due to these advantages, asynchronous online focus groups are more commonly used in academic research (Graffigna & Bosio, 2006).

It is also worth noting that some researchers supplement the two major types of online focus groups with a mixed category that combines synchronous and asynchronous computer-mediated communication (Graffigna & Bosio, 2006) and an online focus group that supplements the textual exchange with the use of 3D graphics (Liamputtong, 2011; Mann & Stewart, 2000). In addition, latest developments in technology have led researchers to consider facilitating video-mediated online focus groups, although this approach has additional ethical considerations (e.g., privacy, confidentiality) to take into account. In summary, although these novel approaches are present and are experimented with, they are less frequently used than the two major types of online focus groups—synchronous and asynchronous.

Advantages

Notably, the Internet offers notable advantages to conducting focus groups such as reducing the cost, including participants located in different countries or in remote parts of the country, reducing researcher bias, enhancing participant anonymity, and recording the meeting for future references and analysis (Gaiser, 2008; Liamputtong, 2011; Mann & Stewart 2000; Oringderff, 2004). In addition, online focus groups have the potential to reach the participants who would not be willing or able to participate in traditional face-to-face focus groups (Williams et al., 2012). Furthermore, online settings free interactions from social factors that may inhibit face-to-face debates and opinion exchange (Galimberti, Ignazi, Vercesi, & Riva, 2001), providing the safety net of 'social equalization' (Oringderff, 2004). Finally, online focus groups do not have traditional time constrains and may include larger groups of participants than traditional face-to-face focus groups (Oringderff, 2004).

Disadvantages

As any research instrument, online focus groups are not without shortcomings. More specifically, researchers have voiced concerns regarding participant recruitment and obtaining informed consent, setting an appropriate environment, moderating online discussions, technical issues, and ensuring rigor, validity, reliability and generalizability in online focus groups (Bloor et al., 2001; Gaiser, 2008; Mann & Stewart, 2000; Oringderff, 2004). Online focus groups require careful advance planning and a skillful moderator, able to overcome the disadvantages of the absence of non-verbal cues and disruptive behavior of some participants (Oringderff, 2004).

In summary, peculiarities, strengths, and limitations of online focus groups have been debated and detailed accounts of them are provided in numerous previously published books and book chapters (see, for example, Bloor et al., 2001; Gaiser, 2008; Liamputtong, 2011; Mann & Stewart, 2000). This chapter aims to add to the discussion on the use of online focus groups in research by examining how this method has been used in empirical studies in the recent years.

PRACTICAL APPLICATIONS OF ONLINE FOCUS GROUPS IN EMPIRICAL RESEARCH

Methods

To examine the uses of online focus groups, the systematic review of published research on online focus groups was conducted. A broad online database search using a sensitive search strategy ("online focus group*") was undertaken with no limit set for the date of publication or a specific discipline. The search was limited to articles published in peer-reviewed journals (excluding dissertations, technical reports, and conference presentations) and to manuscripts in English; thus, it is possible that relevant manuscripts were excluded if they did not appear in a journal. Both qualitative and mixed methods studies were included. The choice of these inclusion criteria was purposeful to limit the examined manuscripts to peer-reviewed empirical studies, but sufficiently broad to include different disciplines, years of publication, and research methodologies.

Supporting researchers' assertion about the origins of online focus groups in the 1990s, this search retrieved papers from the last 15 years (1999-2013), suggesting the possible growth in popularity of this technique in the recent years due to the increasing use of technology in research. Databases searched included: ERIC, EBSCO, ProQuest, OVID, Francis, PsycInfo, JSTOR, Web of Science, Sage Journals Online, Science Direct, and Academic Search Elite (see Table 1). The originally identified 462 articles were included at the screening stage that was based on the detailed review of abstracts and, where necessary, full text (based on the inclusion criteria detailed above). Subsequently, 76 studies met inclusion criteria and were used at the appraisal stage. From these,

Table 1. Data sources

Database	Number of Initially Generated Queries (Including Duplicates)
ERIC (ProQuest, EBSCO, OVID, ESDE)	72
Francis	2
PsycINFO	60
Sage Journals Online	27
Web of Science (5 databases)	59
JSTOR	17
Science Direct	97
Academic Search Elite	59
ProQuest (14 databases)	33
Total	462

6 were excluded as duplicates; 2 were excluded because they did not report an empirical article; 5 were omitted as not relevant to this analysis, and 4 were excluded because they used online focus groups data in quantitative analyses. Remaining articles (N=59) were then sorted into two major groups: (1) empirical (n=44) and (2) theoretical (n=15) papers.

The empirical papers were examined for eight aspects pertaining to how researchers have used online focus groups to collect data:

1. Topic;
2. Research design (qualitative or mixed methods);
3. Participants (number and age);
4. Session(s) number and length;
5. OFG type (synchronous or asynchronous);
6. Technology used to facilitate OFGs;
7. Reason(s) for using online focus groups; and,
8. Solo method of data collection or used in combination with other methods (both in qualitative and in mixed methods studies).

The findings of the analysis were then summarized in a table format and detailed in a written summary. In addition, if offered by the authors, the advantages and disadvantages of using online focus groups in qualitative and mixed methods studies were noted and used to supplement the major findings of theoretical studies.

Then, theoretical, methodological and conceptual papers were examined to distill the current and emerging practices in and characteristics of using online focus groups for data collection. Specifically, the benefits and limitations of online focus groups and their characteristics in comparison with traditional face-to-face format were outlined and used to suggest future trends in using this data collection technique in qualitative and mixed methods research.

Findings: Empirical Papers

Given the broad search with few limitations, the low number of empirical studies using online focus groups to collect data was a somewhat surprising finding. However, there was an increase in the number of articles in the recent years (the vast majority of the articles included were published between 2009 and 2013), indicating the likelihood of the increasing use of this instrument in the future. This finding also suggests that online focus groups have gained popularity as a data collection method in qualitative and mixed methods inquiry. Notably, the amount of qualitative studies was much higher (n=30) than the number of mixed methods studies (n=14) in the sample. Given that the field of mixed methods inquiry is much younger compared to qualitative research, there is a potential for online focus groups and other forms of virtual data collection to be incorporated as the field further develops and grows.

In the mixed methods designs, authors used online focus groups alongside surveys and document data. Furthermore, 21 qualitative studies used online focus groups as a solo method of data collection, while 9 supplemented it with individual interviews, observations, or face-to-face focus group data. Most of these studies relied on some form of thematic analysis (mainly inductive); however, 3 articles used online focus groups for program evaluation purposes; 3 studies used phenomenological analysis; and 5 studies applied grounded theory to examine focus group data. The summary of the analysis of all empirical papers that were identified is offered in a graphical format (see Table 2).

The identified articles examined different subject matter and came from different disciplines such as healthcare, education, and marketing. Notably, the largest subgroup of the articles examined came from the field of medicine and healthcare. Interestingly (although not altogether unexpected), several studies used OFGs to study topics related to using Internet in various field of daily and professional life such as online teaching and learning (e.g., Armstrong, 2011; Monolescu & Schifter, 1999; Sinclair, 2009) and various aspects of Internet use habits (e.g., Yang, Chiu, & Chen 2011; Yu, Taverner, & Madden, 2011). Another expected finding was that numerous studies used online focus groups to gather online data from traditionally stigmatized, marginalized, or hard-to-reach populations such as lesbian and gay young people or ill people (e.g., Hillier, Mitchell, & Ybarra, 2012; Horvath et al., 2012; Williams & Reid, 2012).

When it comes to online focus groups' population, participants ranged from teenagers to older adults. To be able to contribute to online focus group discussions, participants had to have access to the computer, to the Internet, and also have a certain level of technological skills and computer literacy. Some authors (e.g., Aguilar, Boerema, & Harrison, 2011; Kenny & Duckett, 2005) have specified this as a disadvantage of this form of data collection because it limited potential participants to those meeting the aforementioned criteria, while others used this characteristic to their advantage because they specifically focused on online settings and studied active users of online forums, discussion boards, or videogames (e.g., Horvath et al., 2012; Yang et al., 2011).

Mainly due to the freedom of choosing appropriate time to contribute, more than half of the studies (n=25) used asynchronous online focus groups. In addition, 15 articles featured synchronous virtual focus groups; 1 study (Wilkerson et al., 2012) combined synchronous and asynchronous online focus groups; and 3 articles did not specify the type of online focus groups they used. Finally, there was a range in the technology used by researchers to facilitate online focus groups. In addition to a commonly used option of online learning management systems hosted by the universities of researchers' affiliation (e.g., E-Learning Commons, WebCT), authors also used commercial (e.g., Adobe Connect Pro chat; Phorum Software program) and non-commercial

Table 2. Examination of empirical articles using online focus groups

#	Author(s), Year	Topic	Research Design (Type of Analysis Used)	Participants	Session Number and Lengths	OFG Type	Technology Used	Reason(s) for Using OFG	Solo Data Collection Method?
1	Adams, Rodham, & Gavin (2005)	Deliberate self-harm	Qualitative (interpretive phenomeno-logical analysis)	22 focus group participants and additional 4 interview participants Age: 16 -26 years old	2 online focus groups Length not specified	Not specified	Public message boards of an online Web site	Topic connected to the Internet use (online self-expression)	No, along with 4 individual e-mail interviews
2	Aguilar, Boerema, & Harrison (2011)	Older adults' computer use	Qualitative (interpretive phenomenological analysis)	9 participants Age: 65 -82 years old	2 online focus groups Length: 10 days	Asynchro-nous	Online focus groups run through the University of South Australia's Information Technology System	Mirrored the natural setting being studied; overcame distance and time barriers	Yes
3	Armstrong (2011)	Students' perceptions of online learning	Qualitative (thematic analysis)	16 students; 8 of them participated in OFG Age: mid-20s	Not specified	Not specified	Not specified	To serve as an additional data source	No, along with interviews (main method) and observations
4	Barratt (2009)	Video-recorded clinical examinations in nurse practitioner education	Qualitative (thematic content analysis)	16 students; 8 in a traditional focus group; 8 in an online focus group Age not specified	1 traditional and 1 online focus group Length: 1 hour each	Synchro-nous	Discussion board hosted by the university	This data collection methods was previously used in this field; a convenient way to collect data from people sharing similar experiences	No, along with face-to-face focus groups
5	Bernhardt, Zayac, & Pyeritz (2011)	Barriers to genetic screening for autosomal dominant disorders	Mixed methods	246 survey participants; 204 focus group participants Age: 25-80 years old	12 sessions Length: 1 hour	Synchro-nous	Log-in enabled (by invitation only) discussion group	To have input from a large number of participants from a wide geographical area	No, along with a survey

continued on following page

Table 2. Continued

#	Author(s), Year	Topic	Research Design (Type of Analysis Used)	Participants	Session Number and Lengths	OFG Type	Technology Used	Reason(s) for Using OFG	Solo Data Collection Method?
6	Blue Bird Jernigan & Lorig (2010)	Internet diabetes self-management workshop for American Indians and Alaska Natives	Mixed methods (thematic analysis of focus group data)	54 participants Age not specified	1 focus group Length: 1 week	Asynchro-nous	Online listserv discussion	Suitable to the context (online focus group was used after the online workshop was offered)	No, along with questionnaires, blood test data; and process evaluation data
7	Boman et al. (2013)	Fathers' experiences with support from pediatric diabetes team	Qualitative (grounded theory)	11 fathers: 6 fathers in an OFG; 8 in an individual interview (3 fathers participated in both) Age: 37-47	4 focus groups Length: 20 days	Asynchro-nous	Virtual group rooms in Fronter	No geographical limits; potential to generate more unique ideas than do face-to-face focus groups	No, along with an individual interview
8	Boshoff, Atlant, & May (2005)	Challenges in early intervention service delivery	Mixed methods	14 managers Age not specified	1 session Length: 1 week	Asynchro-nous	Online forum	Offering an option of a conversation at a convenient time	No, along with the questionnaires
9	Bramlett, Mayer, & Harrison (2012)	Public health	Qualitative (formative program evaluation)	38 college students Age not specified	4 sessions Length not specified	Synchro-nous	Chat rooms on E-Learning Commons (hosted by the university)	Low cost; previously used for formative program evaluation	Yes
10	Bruening & Dixon (2007)	Work-family conflict	Qualitative (deductive and inductive analyses)	41 mothers Age: 29-40 years old	5 online focus groups Length: 18 weeks	Asynchro-nous	Log-in enabled site (WebCt)	Ability to engage a group of participants who would not be able to meet face-to-face	Yes (but had to fill in a short biographical survey before the focus group meeting)

continued on following page

Table 2. Continued

#	Author(s), Year	Topic	Research Design (Type of Analysis Used)	Participants	Session Number and Lengths	OFG Type	Technology Used	Reason(s) for Using OFG	Solo Data Collection Method?
11	Burnett et al. (2007)	Student satisfaction with online learning	Mixed methods (content analysis used to analyze focus group data)	14 students Age not specified	1 face-to-face session; 1 online session Length not specified	Not specified, likely synchronous	Online chat (platform not specified)	Not specified	No, online focus group was supplemented by a face-to-face focus group and the analysis of bulletin boards' messages of 8 online courses offered in 1 semester
12	Cameron et al. (2005)	Adolescence	Qualitative (formative, scoping research for a larger study)	40 teenagers Age: 14-17 years old	4 sessions Length: 1-1.5 hour	Synchro-nous	Web-based focus group interface (similar to chat rooms)	Not specified	Yes
13	Dattillo et al. (2008)	Perceptions of leisure of adults with cerebral palsy	Qualitative (thematic analysis)	8 adults Age: 27-44 years old	1 session Length: 8 weeks	Asynchro-nous	Phorum software program	Online focus groups have been previously used in this research area	Yes
14	De Jong et al. (2012)	Feelings of children with unilateral congenital below elbow deficiency	Qualitative (thematic analysis)	42 youth (8-20 years old); 16 parents; 19 health care professionals Age not specified	5 online focus groups Length: 7 days	Asynchro-nous	Specially designed website	Not specified	Yes
15	Dilworth et al. (2013)	Health promotion	Mixed methods (evaluation of the health unit)	72 survey respondents; 11 online focus group participants Age not specified	1 session Length not specified	Synchro-nous	An interactive web forum	Not specified	No, along with a survey and analysis of previous evaluations
16	Dixon & Bruening (2007)	Work-family conflict	Qualitative (deductive and inductive analyses)	41 mothers Age: 29-40 years old	5 online focus groups Length: 18 weeks	Asynchro-nous	Log-in enabled site (WebCt)	Ability to engage a group of participants separated geographically	Yes (but had to fill in a short biographical survey before the focus group meeting)

continued on following page

Table 2. Continued

#	Author(s), Year	Topic	Research Design (Type of Analysis Used)	Participants	Session Number and Lengths	OFG Type	Technology Used	Reason(s) for Using OFG	Solo Data Collection Method?
17	Finke, McNaughton, & Drager (2009)	Teachers' perspectives on the inclusion of children with autism	Qualitative (thematic analysis)	5 female elementary school teachers Age: 26-35 years old	1 session Length: 15 weeks	Asynchro-nous	Phorum software program	Appropriate to explore a new topic; interest in the meanings developed through interactions	Yes
18	Fox, Morris, & Rumsey (2007)	Young people with psoriasis	Qualitative (grounded theory)	8 participants Age: 11-18 years old	3 online focus groups Length: 1 hour	Synchro-nous	Secure online forum hosted by the university website	Less threatening alternative to the face-to-face option for participants with visible psoriasis	Yes
19	Garde-Hansen & Calvert (2007)	Students' collaborative project-based learning at the university level	Qualitative (descriptive, thematic analysis)	Not specified	Not specified; likely 1 Length not specified	Asynchro-nous	Not specified	Not specified	Not specified
20	Garrett & Cutting (2012)	Social media in promoting international student partnerships	Mixed methods (focus groups used for evaluation purposes and analyzed using content analysis)	19 students participated in focus groups; 20 students filled in the questionnaire Age not specified	1 online focus group Length not specified	Synchro-nous	Web-based tele-conference	To reach students from 2 universities in different countries	No; along with a questionnaire, web analytics
21	Goby (2011)	Intrafamilial computer-mediated communication	Qualitative (grounded theory)	48 participants (unmarried college students) Age: 20-24 years old	5 online focus groups Length: 1 hour each	Synchro-nous	Instant messaging program ICQ	Higher participant anonymity	Yes
22	Greaney et al. (2009)	Students' healthful weight management	Mixed methods	115 college students Age: 18-24 years old	16 online focus groups Length not specified	Synchro-nous	WebCT chat program	Protecting participant anonymity and promoting frank discussions	No, supplemented with a survey

continued on following page

Table 2. Continued

#	Author(s), Year	Topic	Research Design (Type of Analysis Used)	Participants	Session Number and Lengths	OFG Type	Technology Used	Reason(s) for Using OFG	Solo Data Collection Method?
23	Hillier, Mitchell, & Ybarra (2012)	Internet use of LGB and non-LGB youth	Qualitative (thematic, comparative analysis)	33 LGB young people and 26 non-LGB youngsters Age: 13-18 years old	3 sessions: 2 with LGB youth; 1 with non-LGB youth Length: 3 days	Asynchro-nous	Online bulletin board format focus groups software by Harris International	To reach participants from different regions and income levels; sensitive topic	Yes
24	Hoffman et al. (2009)	Teaching mathematics	Mixed methods	10 award-winning teachers participated in a focus group Number of survey participants not reported	1 session Length: 2 weeks	Asynchro-nous	E-mail focus group	Ability to reach and include teachers from all over the country	No, preceded by a survey
25	Horvath et al. (2012)	Online social networking by people with HIV	Mixed methods	312 survey participants; 22 online focus group participants (English-speaking, self-reported HIV-positive status) Age: 18 years or older	2 sessions Length: 90 minutes	Synchro-nous	Online chat room (platform not specified)	To provide more detailed data following the survey results (specific questions developed based on the responses to the open-ended survey questions)	No, along with the survey; focus group provided supplemen-tary data
26	Kenny & Duckett (2005)	Australian enrolled nurse conversion	Qualitative (thematic analysis)	38 nurses Age not specified	1 session Length: 2 month	Asynchro-nous	WebCT software for closed online discussion	Non-threatening medium for participants	Yes

continued on following page

Table 2. Continued

#	Author(s), Year	Topic	Research Design (Type of Analysis Used)	Participants	Session Number and Lengths	OFG Type	Technology Used	Reason(s) for Using OFG	Solo Data Collection Method?
27	Lagan, Sinclair, & Kernohan (2011)	Impact of internet on decision making during pregnancy	Qualitative (deductive analysis)	92 women Age not specified	13 sessions (4-11 participants each) Length: over 3 months	Asynchro-nous	Online discussion forum	Ability to include difficult-to-reach participants; asynchro-nous format assisted participants living in different time zones and those with lower levels of computer literacy	Yes
28	Lim et al. (2011)	Adult sport participation	Qualitative (thematic analysis)	122 participants Age: 20 years old or older	18 focus groups (6 sessions in each participa-ting country) Length: 6-8 weeks	Asynchro-nous	Simple Machines Forum	Ability to include participants from 3 countries	Yes
29	Lloyd & Larsen (2001)	Veterinary practice management	Qualitative (inductive analysis)	21 consultants and 14 teachers Age not specified	2 online focus groups Length: 1 week	Asynchro-nous	Bulletin boards	Ability to reach and include experts from across the country	Yes
30	Monolescu & Schifter (1999)	Online learning (students' perspectives)	Qualitative (pilot study on using OFG to evaluate students' online course experiences)	8 students Age not specified	1 focus group Length: 15 days	Asynchro-nous	Focus group discussion hosted by the university server	To use asynchro-nous OFG to evaluate an online course	No, along with the Delphi technique

continued on following page

Table 2. Continued

#	Author(s), Year	Topic	Research Design (Type of Analysis Used)	Participants	Session Number and Lengths	OFG Type	Technology Used	Reason(s) for Using OFG	Solo Data Collection Method?
31	Pittenger et al. (2010)	Pharmacy students' knowledge and opinions about managed care pharmacy	Mixed methods (constant comparative approach to analyze focus group data)	332 survey participants; 5 face-to-face focus group participants; 4 online focus group participants Age: 18 years old and older	1 face-to-face focus group; 1 online focus group Length not specified	Asynchro-nous	Not specified	To obtain more detailed responses based on the survey findings	No, along with the survey and face-to-face focus group
32	Riesch et al. (2013)	Public opinion and understanding of carbon capture and storage in two countries	Qualitative (thematic analysis)	60 adults (30 from each participating country) Age not specified	2 online focus groups Length: 2 days	Asynchro-nous	Specially developed online forum	Allowed to bring together participants from different countries	Yes
33	Schmitz Weiss & de Macedo Higgins Joyce (2009)	Online journalism and digital occupation	Qualitative exploratory (grounded theory)	16 journalists from 7 countries Age not specified	3 focus groups Length: 1 hour each	Synchro-nous	Chat room of Tapped In organization	Real-time interaction among participants in different countries	Yes
34	Sinclair (2009)	Online learning (teachers' perspectives)	Qualitative (descriptive case study)	40 participants (teachers studying at the university); 20 of them participated in a focus group Age not specified	1 session Length: 2 weeks	Asynchro-nous	Not specified	Distance (easier to reach with online methods); online nature of the program	No, along with a questionnaire (supplemen-tary data source)
35	Thomas, Wootten, & Robinson (2013)	Experiences of gay and bisexual men with prostate cancer	Qualitative (thematic analysis)	10 men Age not specified	1 online focus group Length: 4 weeks	Asynchro-nous	Online forum on the Cancer Council Victoria website	Used to encourage self-disclosure on sensitive topics	Yes

continued on following page

Table 2. Continued

#	Author(s), Year	Topic	Research Design (Type of Analysis Used)	Participants	Session Number and Lengths	OFG Type	Technology Used	Reason(s) for Using OFG	Solo Data Collection Method?
36	Vasluian et al. (2013)	Opinions regarding prosthetic use and rehabilitation treatment	Qualitative (framework approach to data analysis)	42 youth (age: 8-20 years old); 17 parents; 19 health care professionals	5 online focus groups Length: 1 week	Asynchro-nous	Password-protected online forum	Enhances anonymity; decreases social pressure; provides comfortable environment	Yes
37	Walsh, White, & Greaney (2009)	Healthy weight management in college men	Mixed methods (focus group data analyzed using grounded theory approach)	47 male students Age: 18-24 years old	6 focus groups: 3 online and 3 face-to-face Length: 90 minutes	Synchro-nous	WebCT chat forum available through the university	Not specified	No, along with a questionnaire and face-to-face focus groups
38	Wilkerson et al. (2012)	Sexual and relationship therapy	Qualitative (thematic analysis with subsequent conceptual model development)	79 men in synchronous FGs; 66 of them participated in an asynchronous focus group Age not specified	13 synchro-nous sessions; Length: 90 minutes 1 asynchro-nous session; Length: 48 hours	Synchro-nous and asynchro-nous	Chat using Adobe Connect Pro	Ability to reach participants in different areas	Yes
39	Williams & Reid (2012)	Anorexia nervosa and its relation to the self	Qualitative (interpretative phenomenological analysis)	4 focus group participants; 10 interview participants Age not specified	1 session Length: 4 weeks	Asynchro-nous	WebCT's discussion board	Ability to include participants from different countries	No; some participated in an email interview

continued on following page

Table 2. Continued

#	Author(s), Year	Topic	Research Design (Type of Analysis Used)	Participants	Session Number and Lengths	OFG Type	Technology Used	Reason(s) for Using OFG	Solo Data Collection Method?
40	Wolfinbarger & Gilly (2002)	Etail quality (marketing)	Mixed methods; (specific qualitative analysis not stated)	64 online buyers. Age not specified	9 focus groups (7 online; 2 offline) Length: 90-120 minutes	Synchro-nous	Not specified	Focus groups were used to generate data about consumer perceptions of online shopping quality	No, along with a survey and offline focus group
41	Wouters et al. (2013)	Breast cancer patients' perceptions about endocrine therapy	Mixed methods (qualitative data from OFGs was quantified)	37 patients: 31 of them participated in online focus groups. Age not specified	2 online focus groups Length: 2 weeks	Asynchro-nous	Not specified	Not specified	No, along with individual interviews and a questionnaire
42	Yang, Chiu, & Chen (2011)	Social influence on college students who play online games	Mixed methods	College students: 10 participants in a focus group; 280 participants in a survey. Age not specified	1 focus group session Length: 2 hours	Synchro-nous	Skype	Not specified	No, along with a survey
43	Yu, Taverner, & Madden (2011)	Sharing health-related stories online by young people	Qualitative (thematic analysis)	13 young people. Age: 16-19 years old	1 session Length: 3 weeks	Asynchro-nous	Online forum hosted by Ning, a free social networking site	Ability to reach people in different areas	Yes
44	Zhang & Kramarae (2012)	Talk of young Chinese women	Qualitative (thematic analysis)	16 undergraduate college students. Age not specified	3 sessions (1 with women, 1 with men, 1 mixed) Length: 2 hours	Synchro-nous	QQ – synchronous instant messaging groups popular in China	Students are used to communica-ting online; they are used to this specific chat program	No, along with an individual interview (supplemen-tary)

(e.g., QQ messaging; ICQ messaging) online chats, bulletin boards, and instant messaging programs. To limit interferences, most authors opted for password-protected chat options, available to participants by invitation only.

In summary, empirical studies examined here ranged greatly in their subject matter, technology used, and session number and length. The participants were computer-literate adolescents or adults with an Internet access. Qualitative research design was much more common than mixed methods; while some qualitative studies relied solely on the online focus groups' data, other qualitative and all mixed methods studies supplied OFG data with data collected by other instruments. Finally, the common reasons for using online focus groups to collect data included low cost (Bramlett Mayer, & Harrison, 2005; Lloyd & Larsen, 2001); ability to reach participants from different geographical areas (Boman et al., 2013; Hillier et al, 2012; Riesch et al., 2013; Wilkerson et al., 2012; Williams & Reid, 2012); mirroring the natural setting studied such as participants' Internet use or online learning (Adams, Rodham, & Gavin, 2005; Aguilar et al., 2011); and choosing OFG as a safer setting for

participants to promote frank opinion exchanges and to provide higher participant anonymity (Fox, Morris, & Rumsey, 2007; Greaney at al., 2009; Kenny & Duckett, 2005)

Current and Emerging Practices in Conducting Online Focus Groups

Empirical and theoretical research on online focus groups is limited. Although the increasing number of papers on this topic in the recent years suggests the growing interest in the application of this research technique in qualitative and mixed methods research, the empirical and methodological base underlying this research technique needs further development and examination. While describing current and emerging practices in conducting online focus groups, researchers typically outline benefits and limitations of this form of data collection (see Table 3 for comparison of advantages and disadvantages).

Overall, the Internet medium is described as providing a safer environment for participation and an easier way out if the participant chooses to withdraw from the study. Coupled with higher

Table 3. Benefits and limitations of online focus groups

Benefits	Limitations
• Greater anonymity (Nicholas et al., 2010; Reid & Reid, 2005; Terrell, 2011; Walker, 2013). • More appropriate to study sensitive topics (Burton & Bruening, 2003; Chase & Alvarez, 2000). • Ability to include participants that were previously hard to reach (Nicholas et al., 2010; Schneider et al., 2002; Stewart & Williams, 2005; Tates et al., 2009; Underhill & Olmstead, 2003; Walker, 2013). • Lower cost (Kenny, 2005; Klein, Tellefsen, & Herskovitz, 2007; Nicholas et al., 2010; Reid & Reid, 2005; Schneider et al., 2002; Underhill & Olmstead, 2003). • Ability to overcome time and location constraints (Reid & Reid, 2005; Tates et al., 2009; Underhill & Olmstead, 2003). • Easier to reach youngsters (Chase & Alvarez, 2000; Fox, Morris, & Rumsey, 2007). • Safe, more comfortable environment of the Internet (Burton & Bruening, 2003; Kenny, 2005). • Easier for participants to withdraw (Kenny, 2005).	• Software limitations and technological challenges (Chase & Alvarez, 2000; Nicholas et al., 2010). • Need for technological proficiency/knowledge level (Kenny, 2005; Klein, Tellefsen, & Herskovitz, 2007; Stewart & Williams, 2005; Tates et al., 2009; Terrell, 2011). • Need of Internet access (Burton & Bruening, 2003; Schneider et al., 2002). • Higher disruptive behavior (Reid & Reid, 2005). • Higher no-show rates (Burton & Bruening, 2003; Schneider et al., 2002). • Selection bias (Klein, Tellefsen, & Herskovitz, 2007; Tates et al., 2009). • Shorter, abbreviated responses (Burton & Bruening, 2003; Hughes & Lang, 2004). • Lack of non-verbal cues (Hughes & Lang, 2004). • Additional ethical considerations (Stewart & Williams, 2005; Walker, 2013).

anonymity, Internet-based research has a potential to be more effective in studying sensitive topics and in attracting participants that were hard to reach before (e.g., youth, people with disabilities, sick people, etc.). At the same time, characteristics of online environment lead to a different dynamics of focus group, with multiple participants commenting at the same time, thus leading to numerous discussion threads developing at the same time (especially in the asynchronous online focus groups). Thus, moderator is important to handle these multi-threaded conversations. When it comes to participants, OFGs work better reaching out to the online communities of users, thus failing to include those without Internet access or with limited technological abilities. These considerations, along with the common practice of self-selection, diminish external validity of the data and generalizability of findings.

When compared to face-to-face focus groups, online focus groups may be regarded as an extension of the traditional format or as an entirely new approach to collecting data. While both face-to-face and online focus groups require a moderator, a skillset of a good moderator is different in these types of focus groups when compared to the traditional version (Chase & Alvarez, 2000). Moreover, OFGs have to consider ethical challenges related to researching online in addition to the general ethical code of research conduct (Stewart & Williams, 2005). Like in the case of traditional focus groups, ethical considerations should be accounted for at all stages of conducting research. When it comes to participation, OFGs seems to promote more even involvement (Schneider, Kerwin, Frechtling, & Vivari, 2002); a dominant participant is more likely to emerge in the face-to-face format. However, it is possible that the online participant who types faster may skew the online discussion (Fox, Rumsey, & Morris, 2007). Furthermore, online responses are usually shorter and (especially in the asynchronous format)

carefully proofed and edited before submission. Overall, online focus groups are believed to generate comparable (Underhill & Olmstead, 2003) or even better quality data (Easton, Easton, & Belch, 2003) than do traditional focus groups, thus earning their place among data collection techniques used in qualitative and mixed methods studies.

Future Trends in Conducting Online Focus Groups

As Internet growth in popularity, demand, and use across the world, online data collection methods will be more frequently used. This is true for online focus groups – as evidenced by the growing number of papers from the recent years that use this approach to gather data for qualitative and mixed methods studies. The studies in the sample used mainly traditional methodologies and data analysis techniques (e.g., grounded theory, phenomenology, thematic analysis). There is a range of other methods, especially those that were recently suggested that may (and, in the future, will) benefit from using data from online focus groups. A special place in this discussion is reserved for mixed methods approaches that continue to develop. Adjusting to the new developments and trends, mixed methods studies are bound to rely more on online data collection in the future. Due to their versatility and the ability to be used at different stages of the research process, online focus groups are likely to be among the novel techniques to be integrated into the mixed methods realm.

One of the major limitations of online focus groups is connected to technological requirements—not only does Internet access predetermine possible participants, but also technological literacy is required from a moderator and participants to ensure that an OFG is successfully conducted. However, as the Internet communications are becoming more widely used as time passes, this limitation may not be applicable in the near future. Moreover, it is likely that in the future, technological innovations may provide researchers an automated version of an OFG moderator. Similarly, it is likely that new types of technology will be used to conduct OFGs.

It is unlikely that online focus groups with replace traditional format entirely; rather, these types of data collection will be used to gather data from different participant populations. Furthermore, with the new developments in technology, online focus groups will also be changing, adapting to the new possibilities offered by technological innovations. Possible directions include combining textual contributions with graphics and using online environments to choose an avatar to role-play different situations pertaining to the topic. Finally, it is likely that both synchronous and asynchronous online focus groups will continue to exist; however, asynchronous model has more appeal for future studies attempting to include participants from different countries—an important characteristic in the world that is growing more interconnected and interdependent with each passing year.

CONCLUSION

In summary, online focus group is a relatively new method that has been actively developing over the last 15 years. With the growing acceptance of researching online, this data collection technique has been gaining popularity in both qualitative and mixed methods designs. Like other novel approaches and techniques, online focus groups are constantly evolving to better meet the needs of researchers. In spite of some early criticisms, online focus groups have become more popular and have been used in different disciplines with considerable increase in the number of studies in the recent years. These findings indicate the potential for the growing use of this technique in the future as researchers further explore and embrace online research medium.

REFERENCES

Adams, J., Rodham, K., & Gavin, J. (2005). Investigating the "self" in deliberate self-harm. *Qualitative Health Research*, *15*(10), 1293–1309. doi:10.1177/1049732305281761 PMID:16263913

Aguilar, A., Boerema, C., & Harrison, J. (2010). Meanings attributed by older adults to computer use. *Journal of Occupational Science*, *17*(1), 27–33. doi:10.1080/14427591.2010.9686669

Ahern, N. R. (2005). Using the Internet to conduct research. *Nurse Researcher*, *13*(2), 55–69. doi:10.7748/nr2005.10.13.2.55.c5968 PMID:16416980

Armstrong, D. A. (2011). Students' perceptions of online learning and instructional tools: A qualitative study of undergraduate students' use of online tools. *TOJET: The Turkish Online Journal of Educational Technology*, *10*(3), 222–226.

Barratt, J. (2010). A focus group study of the use of video-recorded stimulated objective structured clinical examinations in nurse practitioner education. *Nurse Education in Practice*, *10*(3), 170–175. doi:10.1016/j.nepr.2009.06.004 PMID:20202909

Bernhardt, B. A., Zayac, C., & Pyeritz, R. E. (2011). Why is genetic screening for autosomal dominant disorders underused in families? The case of hereditary hemorrhagic telangiectasia. *Genetics in Medicine*, *13*(9), 812–820. doi:10.1097/GIM.0b013e31821d2e6d PMID:21637104

Bloor, M., Frankland, J., Thomas, M., & Robson, K. (2001). *Focus groups in social research*. London, UK: Sage.

Blue Bird Jernigan, V., & Lorig, K. (2011). The Internet diabetes self-management workshop for American Indians and Alaska natives. *Health Promotion Practice*, *12*(2), 261–270. doi:10.1177/1524839909335178 PMID:20534807

Boman, A., Povlsen, L., Dahlborg-Lyckhage, E., Hanas, R., & Borup, I. (2013). Fathers' encounter of support from paediatric diabetes team; the tension between general recommendations and personal experience. *Health & Social Care in the Community, 21*(3), 263–270. doi:10.1111/hsc.12013 PMID:23190009

Boshoff, K., Atlant, E., & May, E. (2005). Occupational therapy managers' perceptions of challenges faced in early intervention service delivery in South Australia. *Australian Occupational Therapy Journal, 52*(3), 232–242. doi:10.1111/j.1440-1630.2005.00495.x

Bramlett Mayer, A., & Harrison, J. A. (2012). The use of online focus groups to design an online food safety education intervention. *Journal of Food Science Education, 11*(4), 47–51. doi:10.1111/j.1541-4329.2012.00145.x

Bruening, J. E., & Dixon, M. A. (2007). Work-family conflict in coaching II: Managing role conflict. *Journal of Sport Management, 21*, 471–496.

Burnett, K., Bonnici, L. J., Miksa, S. D., & Kim, J. (2007). Frequency, intensity and topicality in online learning: An exploration of the interaction dimensions that contribute to student satisfaction in online learning. *Journal of Education for Library and Information Science, 48*(1), 21–35.

Burton, L. J., & Bruening, J. E. (2003). Technology and method intersect in the online focus group. *Quest, 55*(4), 315–327. doi:10.1080/00336297.2003.10491807

Cameron, K., Salazar, L., Bernhardt, J., Burgess-Whitman, N., Wingood, G., & DiClemente, R. (2005). Adolescents' experience with sex on the web: Results from online focus groups. *Journal of Adolescence, 28*(4), 535–540. doi:10.1016/j.adolescence.2004.10.006 PMID:16022887

Cantrell, M. A., & Lupinacci, P. (2007). Methodological issues in online data collection. *Journal of Advanced Nursing, 60*(5), 544–549. doi:10.1111/j.1365-2648.2007.04448.x PMID:17973718

Chase, L., & Alvarez, J. (2000). Internet research: The role of the focus group. *Library & Information Science Research, 22*(4), 357–369. doi:10.1016/S0740-8188(00)00050-5

Dattilo, J., Estrella, G., Estrella, L. J., Light, J., McNaughton, D., & Seabury, M. (2008). "I have chosen to live life abundantly": Perceptions of leisure by adults who use augmentative and alternative communication. *Augmentative and Alternative Communication, 24*(1), 16–28. doi:10.1080/07434610701390558 PMID:18938755

De Jong, I., Reinders-Messelink, H., Janssen, W., Poelma, M., van Wijk, I., & van der Sluis, C. K. (2012). Mixed feelings of children and adolescents with congenital below-elbow deficiency: An online focus group study. *PLoS ONE, 7*(6), e37099. doi:10.1371/journal.pone.0037099 PMID:22715362

Dilworth, K., Tao, M., Shapiro, S., & Timmings, C. (2013). Making health promotion evidence-informed: An organizational priority. *Health Promotion Practice, 14*(1), 139–145. doi:10.1177/1524839912461274 PMID:23099658

Dixon, M. A., & Bruening, J. E. (2007). Work-family conflict in coaching I: A top-down perspective. *Journal of Sport Management, 21*, 377–406.

Duffy, M. E. (2002). Methodological issues in web-based research. *Journal of Nursing Scholarship, 34*(10), 83–88. doi:10.1111/j.1547-5069.2002.00083.x PMID:11901974

Duggleby, W. (2000). What about focus group interaction data? *Qualitative Health Research, 15*(6), 832–840. doi:10.1177/1049732304273916 PMID:15961879

Easton, G., Easton, A., & Belch, M. (2003). An experimental investigation of electronic focus groups. *Information & Management, 40*(8), 717–727. doi:10.1016/S0378-7206(02)00098-8

Eynon, R., Fry, J., & Schroeder, R. (2008). The ethics of Internet research. In N. Fielding, R. M. Lee, & G. Blank (Eds.), *The SAGE handbook of online research methods* (pp. 23–41). Thousand Oaks, CA: Sage. doi:10.4135/9780857020055.n2

Feig, B. (1989). How to run a focus group. *American Demographics, 11*(December), 36–37.

Finke, E. H., McNaughton, D. B., & Drager, K. D. R. (2009). "All children can and should have the opportunity to learn": General education teachers' perspectives on including children with autism spectrum disorder who require AAC. *Augmentative and Alternative Communication, 25*(2), 110–122. doi:10.1080/07434610902886206 PMID:19444682

Fox, F. E., Morris, M., & Rumsey, N. (2007). Doing synchronous online focus groups with young people: Methodological reflections. *Qualitative Health Research, 17*(4), 539–547. doi:10.1177/1049732306298754 PMID:17416707

Fox, F. E., Rumsey, N., & Morris, M. (2007). "Ur skin is the thing that everyone sees and you cant change it!": Exploring the appearance-related concerns of young people with psoriasis. *Developmental Neurorehabilitation, 10*(2), 133–141. doi:10.1080/13638490701217594 PMID:17687986

Gaiser, T. (2008). Online focus groups. In N. Fielding, R. M. Lee, & G. Blank (Eds.), *The SAGE handbook of online research methods* (pp. 290–306). Thousand Oaks, CA: Sage. doi:10.4135/9780857020055.n16

Gaiser, T. J. (1997). Conducting on-line focus group: A methodological discussion. *Social Science Computer Review, 15*(2), 135–144. doi:10.1177/089443939701500202

Galimberti, C., Ignazi, S., Vercesi, P., & Riva, G. (2001). Communication and cooperation in networked environments: An experimental analysis. *Cyberpsychology & Behavior, 4*(1), 131–146. doi:10.1089/10949310151088514 PMID:11709902

Garde-Hansen, J., & Calvert, B. (2007). Developing a research culture in the undergraduate curriculum. *Active Learning in Higher Education, 8*(2), 105–116. doi:10.1177/1469787407077984

Garrett, B. M., & Cutting, R. (2012). Using social media to promote international student partnerships. *Nurse Education in Practice, 12*(6), 340–345. doi:10.1016/j.nepr.2012.04.003 PMID:22595660

Goby, V. P. (2011). Psychological underpinnings of intrafamilial computer-mediated communication: A preliminary exploration of CMC uptake with parents and siblings. *Cyberpsychology, Behavior, and Social Networking, 14*(6), 365–370. doi:10.1089/cyber.2010.0289 PMID:21114409

Graffigna, G., & Bosio, A. C. (2006). The influence of setting on findings produced in qualitative health research: A comparison between face-to-face and online discussion groups about HIV/AIDS. *International Journal of Qualitative Methods, 5*(3), 1–16.

Greaney, M. L., Less, F. D., White, A. A., Dayton, S. F., Riebe, D., & Blissmer, B. et al. (2009). College students' barriers and enablers for healthful weight management: A qualitative study. *Journal of Nutrition Education and Behavior*, *41*(4), 281–286. doi:10.1016/j.jneb.2008.04.354 PMID:19508934

Hewson, C., & Laurent, D. (2008). Research design and tools for Internet research. In N. Fielding, R. M. Lee, & G. Blank (Eds.), *The SAGE handbook of online research methods* (pp. 58–78). Thousand Oaks, CA: Sage. doi:10.4135/9780857020055.n4

Hewson, C. M., Yule, P., Laurent, D., & Vogel, C. M. (2003). *Internet research methods: A practical guide for the social and behavioral sciences*. London, UK: Sage.

Hillier, L., Mitchell, K., & Ybarra, M. (2012). The Internet as a safety net: Findings from a series of online focus groups with LGB and non-LGB young people in the United States. *Journal of LGBT Youth*, *9*(3), 225–246. doi:10.1080/19361 653.2012.684642

Hoffman, E. S., Caniglia, J., Knott, L., & Evitts, T. A. (2009). In their own words: Good mathematics teachers in the era of NCLB. *Mathematics Teacher*, *10*(6), 468–473.

Horvath, K., Danilenko, G., Williams, M., Simoni, J., Rivet Amico, K., Oakes, J. M., & Rosser, S. (2012). Technology use and reasons to participate in social networking health websites among people living with HIV in the US. *AIDS and Behavior*, *16*(4), 900–910. doi:10.1007/s10461-012-0164-7 PMID:22350832

Hughes, J., & Lang, K. R. (2004). Issues in online focus groups: Lessons learned from an empirical study of peer-to-peer filesharing system users. *Electronic Journal of Business Research Methods*, *2*(2), 95–110.

Im, E., & Chee, W. (2004). Issues in Internet survey research among cancer patients. *Cancer Nursing*, *27*(1), 34–44. doi:10.1097/00002820-200401000-00005 PMID:15108950

Kenny, A. J. (2005). Interactions in cyberspace: An online focus group. *Journal of Advanced Nursing*, *49*(4), 414–422. doi:10.1111/j.1365-2648.2004.03305.x PMID:15701156

Kenny, A. J., & Duckett, S. (2005). An online study of Australian enrolled nurse convention. *Journal of Advanced Nursing*, *49*(4), 423–431. doi:10.1111/j.1365-2648.2004.03306.x PMID:15701157

Klein, E. E., Tellefsen, T., & Herskovitz, P. J. (2007). The use of group support systems in focus groups: Information technology meets qualitative research. *Computers in Human Behavior*, *23*(5), 2113–2132. doi:10.1016/j.chb.2006.02.007

Klein, J. (2002). Issues surrounding the use of Internet for data collection. *American Journal of Occupational Health*, *56*(3), 340–343. doi:10.5014/ajot.56.3.340 PMID:12058524

Krueger, R. (2000). *Focus groups: A practical guide for applied research* (3rd ed.). Thousand Oaks, CA: Sage. doi:10.1037/10518-189

Lagan, B., Sinclair, M., & Kernohan, G. (2011). What is the impact of the Internet on decision-making in pregnancy? A global study. *Birth Issues in Perinatal Care*, *38*(4), 336–345. doi:10.1111/j.1523-536X.2011.00488.x PMID:22112334

Lakeman, R. (1997). Using the Internet for data collection in nursing research. *Computers in Nursing*, *15*(5), 269–275. PMID:9329228

Lee, R. M., Fielding, N., & Blank, G. (2008). The Internet as a research medium: An editorial introduction to *The SAGE handbook of online research methods*. In N. Fielding, R. M. Lee, & G. Blank (Eds.), *The SAGE handbook of online research methods* (pp. 3–20). Thousand Oaks, CA: Sage. doi:10.4135/9780857020055.n1

Liamputtong, P. (2011). *Focus group methodology: Principles and practice*. Thousand Oaks, CA: Sage.

Lim, S., Warner, S., Dixon, M., Berg, B., Kim, C., & Newhouse-Bailey, M. (2011). Sport participation across national contexts: A multilevel investigation of individual and systemic influences on adult sport participation. *European Sport Management Quarterly, 11*(3), 197–224. doi:10.1080/16184742.2011.579993

Lloyd, J. W., & Larsen, E. R. (2001). Veterinary practice management: Teaching needs as viewed by consultants and teachers. *Journal of Veterinary Medical Education, 28*(1), 16–21. doi:10.3138/jvme.28.1.16 PMID:11548770

Mann, C., & Stewart, F. (2000). *Internet communication in qualitative research: A handbook for researching online*. London, UK: Sage.

Miller, T. W., & Walkowski, J. (2004). *Qualitative research online*. Milton Keynes, UK: Research Publisher LLC.

Monolescu, D., & Schifter, C. (1999). Online focus group: A tool to evaluate online students' course experience. *The Internet and Higher Education, 2*(2-3), 171–176. doi:10.1016/S1096-7516(00)00018-X

Murray, P. J. (1997). Using focus groups in qualitative research. *Qualitative Health Research, 7*(4), 542–549. doi:10.1177/104973239700700408

Nicholas, D. B., Lach, L., King, G., & Scott, M. et al. (2010). Contrasting Internet and face-to-face focus groups for children with chronic health conditions: Outcomes and participant experiences. *International Journal of Qualitative Methods, 9*(1), 105–121.

Oringderff, J. (2004). "My Way": Piloting an online focus group. *International Journal of Qualitative Methods, 3*(3). Article 5. Retrieved December 28, 2013 from http://www.ualberta.ca/~iiqm/backissues/3_3/html/oringderff.html

Patton. (2002). *Qualitative research and evaluation methods* (3rd ed.). Newbury Park, CA: Sage.

Peacock, S., Robertson, A., Williams, S., & Clausen, M. (2009). The role of learning technologists in supporting e-research. *ALT-J, 17*(2), 115–129. doi:10.1080/09687760903033041

Pittenger, A. L., Starner, C., Thompson, K., & Gleason, P. B. (2010). Pharmacy students' views of managed care pharmacy and PBMs: Should there be more exposure to managed care in the pharmacy curriculum? *Journal of Managed Care Pharmacy, 16*(5), 346–354. PMID:20518587

Reid, D. J., & Reid, F. J. M. (2005). Online focus groups: An in-depth comparison of computer-mediated and conventional focus group discussions. *International Journal of Market Research, 47*(2), 131–162.

Reinharz, S. (1992). *Feminist methods in social research*. New York, NY: Oxford University Press.

Riesch, H., Oltra, C., Lis, A., Upham, P., & Pol, M. (2013). Internet-based public debate of CCS: Lessons from online focus groups in Poland and Spain. *Energy Policy, 56*, 693–702. doi:10.1016/j.enpol.2013.01.029

Schmitz Weiss, A., & de Macedo Higgins Joyce, V. (2009). Compressed dimensions in digital media occupations: Journalists in transformation. *Journalism, 10*(5), 587–603. doi:10.1177/1464884909106534

Schneider, S. J., Kerwin, J., Frechtling, J., & Vivari, B. (2002). Characteristics of the discussion in the online and face-to-face focus groups. *Social Science Computer Review, 20*(1), 31–42. doi:10.1177/089443930202000104

Sinclair, A. (2009). Provocative pedagogies in e-Learning: Making the invisible visible. *International Journal of Teaching and Learning in Higher Education, 21*(2), 197–209.

Stewart, K., & Williams, M. (2005). Researching online populations: The use of online focus groups in social research. *Qualitative Research, 5*(4), 395–416. doi:10.1177/1468794105056916

Tates, K., Zwaanswijk, M., Otten, R., & van Dulmen, S. et al. (2009). Online focus groups as a tool to collect data in hard-to-include populations: Examples from paediatric oncology. *BMC Medical Research Methodology, 9*(15). Available from http://www.biomedcentral.com/1471-2288/9/15 PMID:19257883

Terrell, S. R. (2011). Face-to-face in writing: My first attempt at conducting a text-based online focus group. *Qualitative Report, 16*(1), 2860291.

Thomas, C., Wootten, A., & Robinson, P. (2013). The experiences of gay and bisexual men diagnosed with prostate cancer: Results from an online focus group. *European Journal of Cancer Care, 22*(4), 522–529. doi:10.1111/ecc.12058 PMID:23730947

Underhill, C., & Olmsted, M. G. (2003). An experimental comparison of computer-mediated and face-to-face focus groups. *Social Science Computer Review, 21*(4), 506–512. doi:10.1177/0894439303256541

Vasluian, E., de Jong, I., Janssen, W., Poelma, M., van Wijk, I., Reinders-Messelink, H. A., & van der Sluis, C. K. (2013). Opinions of youngsters with congenital below-elbow deficiency, and those of their parents and professionals concerning prosthetic use and rehabilitation treatment. *PLoS ONE, 8*(6), e67101. doi:10.1371/journal.pone.0067101 PMID:23826203

Walker, D. (2013). The Internet as a medium for health services research. Part 2. *Nurse Researcher, 20*(5), 33–37. doi:10.7748/nr2013.05.20.5.33.e295 PMID:23687847

Walsh, J. R., White, A. A., & Greaney, M. L. (2009). Using focus groups to identify factors affecting healthy weight maintenance in college men. *Nutrition Research (New York, N.Y.), 29*(6), 371–378. doi:10.1016/j.nutres.2009.04.002 PMID:19628102

Wilkerson, J. M., Iantaffi, A., Smolenski, D., Brady, S., Horvath, K., Grey, J., & Rosser, S. (2012). The SEM risk behavior (SRB) model: A new conceptual model of how pornography influences the sexual intentions and HIV risk behavior of MSM. *Sexual and Relationship Therapy, 27*(3), 217–230. doi:10.1080/14681994.2012.734605 PMID:23185126

Williams, S., Clausen, M., Robertson, A., Peacock, S., & McPherson, K. (2012). Methodological reflections on the use of asynchronous online focus groups in health research. *International Journal of Qualitative Methods, 11*(4), 368–383.

Williams, S., & Reid, M. (2012). 'It's like there are two people in my head': A phenomenological exploration of anorexia nervosa and its relationship to the self. *Psychology & Health, 27*(7), 798–815. doi:10.1080/08870446.2011.595488 PMID:21736500

Wolfinbarger, M., & Gilly, M. C. (2003). eTailQ: Dimensionalizing, measuring and predicting etail quality. *Journal of Retailing*, *79*(3), 183–198. doi:10.1016/S0022-4359(03)00034-4

Wouters, H., van Geffen, E., Baas-Thijssen, M., Krol-Warmerdam, E., Stiggelbout, A. M., & Belitser, S. et al. (2013). Disentangling breast cancer patients' perceptions and experiences with regard to endocrine therapy: Nature and relevance for non-adherence. *The Breast*, *22*(5), 661–666. doi:10.1016/j.breast.2013.05.005 PMID:23770134

Yang, D.-J., Chiu, J.-Z., & Chen, Y.-K. (2011). Examining the social influence on college students for playing online games: Gender differences and implications. *TOJET: The Turkish Online Journal of Educational Technology*, *10*(3), 115–122.

Yu, J., Taverner, N., & Madden, K. (2011). Young people's views on sharing health-related stories on the Internet. *Health & Social Care in the Community*, *19*(3), 326–334. doi:10.1111/j.1365-2524.2010.00987.x PMID:21288270

Zhang, W., & Kramarae, C. (2012). Are Chinese women turning sharp-tongued? *Discourse & Society*, *23*(6), 749–770. doi:10.1177/0957926512455376

KEY TERMS AND DEFINITIONS

Asynchronous Online Focus Group: Lasts from several days to several months and does not require participants to be online at the same time, allowing them to contribute to online discussions at their convenient time.

Focus Group: A group of people recruited to participate in a guided discussion about a specific issue, product, or service. In a brief period of time (typically 1-2 hours), participants are invited to share their experiences of, beliefs, and perceptions about the topic.

Online Focus Group: A type of a focus group allowing participants to meet online to discuss the topic of interest during the predetermined time.

Synchronous Online Focus Group: Occurs in real time with all participants contributing to the ongoing discussion scheduled within a pre-set timeframe (typically, 1-2 hours).

Chapter 3
Research E-Journaling to Enhance Qualitative and Mixed Methods Research:
Mitigating Human Limits in Perception, Cognition, and Decision-Making

Shalin Hai-Jew
Kansas State University, USA

ABSTRACT

In qualitative and mixed methods research, the researcher and/or research team are critical elements in the research. Given perceptual, cognitive, and memory limitations, human researchers can often bring these shortcomings to their research and decision-making. To combat such tendencies, researcher reflection, self-awareness, and self-critique are seen as some research controls, as are various standardizations in research to control for bias and to provide for multiple points-of-view. One tool that has long been used for researcher reflection to promote research quality has been the research journal. Research journals are field texts created by the researcher or a research team to make sense of the research work; these are professional forms of narrative analyses or narrative inquiries to enhance researcher self-consciousness of their work, their reasoning, their decision-making, and their conclusions. A contemporaneous electronic version of the qualitative or mixed methods research journal is multimedia-based (including visuals, audio, and video) and may be built in data management software programs, shared cloud-based work sites, or simple folders or digital objects. Guided research e-journals may be structured for the elicitation and capture of specific information to ensure researcher attentiveness, awareness, mindfulness, and thoroughness. Guided electronic journaling (used prior to, during, and post-research) may be used to enhance research quality. This chapter proposes a partial typology of guided structures for research journaling and suggests channels for publishing and distributing research e-journals.

DOI: 10.4018/978-1-4666-6493-7.ch003

INTRODUCTION

Errāre hūmānum est (To err is human).

If quantitative research is about random samples, valid (accurate) instrumentation, statistical significance, reliability (the repeatability of results), and objective or dispassionate analysis, it may be said that qualitative research is about human insights achieved through in-depth and selective case sampling, data triangulation, analysis of human-created artifacts and texts, and deep researcher immersion in the subject matter. Qualitative and mixed methods research, while they are built on a substructure of relativism (vs. positivism) and based on an interpretive lens (based on various inter-subjectivities), involve high standards of rigor and meticulous double-checks to achieve ground truth. There are several dozen research methods that have been described under the qualitative research umbrella. This qualitative approach enables changes in methodological strategies mid-stream during the research based on learning during the work. It involves the study of social realities as described in people's lived experiences often expressed in language (such as in oral histories, surveys, interviews, documents, texts, and other forms). In a mixed methods approach, which uses elements from both quantitative and qualitative research, there are even wider methodological options for customized research, even if there are potentially contrasting (and even conflicting) epistemological approaches. Such methods evolved to address ways of knowing that were not possible through quantitative means and with objectivist and positivist (Newtonian) assumptions of the world. For example, qualitative research is used to elicit opinions and experiences; they are used to understand scenarios; they are used to understand cultures. Qualitative research is often paired with quantitative research for the combined strengths of mixed methods research—to capture statistically grounded data with the color of detail-rich qualitative research.

Defining research quality depends on a variety of factors: the research context, the research methodology, the technologies used, the data types and methods of analysis, and the application of the knowledge (generalizability and transferability). Research should generally be based on evidence (and empirics where possible). It should be focused on the proper unit of analysis: focused out too broadly (at the macro level), over-generalizations may occur without sufficient nuance and detail; focused in too specifically, larger trends may be missed. Research should generally be couched in relevant theory. Research relevance should be bounded—in time, in space, in applicability, and in contexts—to avoid the risks of over-generalization (and misapplication). In virtually all research contexts, people are in a limited or incomplete information context. It should be ethically and legally conducted. It should be original. In qualitative research which involves people, there has to be appropriate professional distance even while engagements with others may be close, in-depth, and relatively long-term (measured in years, for example). Most environments in which research is conducted are dynamic, complex, and changing. The world contains immense irreducible complexity:

Many phenomena have stymied the reductionist program: the seemingly irreducible unpredictability of weather and climate; the intricacies and adaptive nature of living organisms and the diseases that threaten them; the economic, political, and cultural behavior of societies; the growth and effects of modern technology and communications networks; and the nature of intelligence and the prospect for creating it in computers. The antireductionist catch-phrase, 'the whole is more than the sum of its parts,' takes on increasing significance as new sciences such as chaos, systems biology, evolutionary economics, and network theory move beyond reductionism to explain how complex behavior can arise from large collections of simpler components (Mitchell, 2009, p. x).

The human element is a critical and unavoidable factor from the very initial stages of problematizing the issue and designing the research. Contemporary research requires researchers to face ill-structured puzzles or problems in dynamic environments and within a thicket of laws, policies, and ethics. Research methodologies are applied to capture limited quanta of information, from which they have to extract understandings. The research may involve single or multi-stages; it may involve various uses of methods and technologies. Researchers apply their knowledge and savvy to analyzing the data in order to cull what is knowable, and they also work to understand how this new learning may apply to future research and to practical applications. At any point in this process, error may be introduced into the work; the effects of continuing errors compound, potentially

resulting in work which is unsupportable and irrelevant. Even minute degrees of error can lead to researcher misunderstandings and misjudgments. It is with this awareness that researchers ask, "What observables could show my hypothesis to be erroneous or misdirected?" and then to pursue all disconfirming evidence possible in order to better achieve their work. Evidence is seen to confirm, disconfirm, or qualify their hypotheses.

In terms of research outcomes, clearly, research data and information should be factual and accurate; they should adequately reflect real-world realities. The information should provide deeper understandings to people and enhance decision-making and pragmatic ensuing actions. In some cases, the research information should offer some level of prediction to the future. Applications of the new learning should be practical to a workplace or other practical context. Figure 1, "The Centrality of the Qualitative / Mixed Methods Researcher," shows a simple conceptualization of the centrality of the researcher—in an environment where limited raw data is collected in an information asymmetric environment and where processed information entails some prior interpretive skew (which must be corrected for for accuracy). Even

Figure 1. The centrality of the qualitative / mixed methods researcher

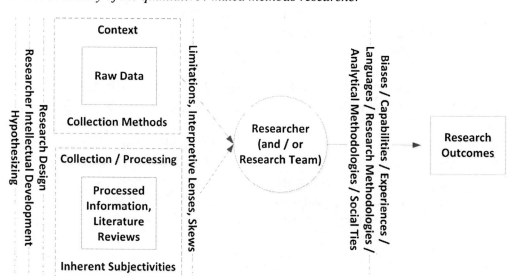

if data is captured using computing machines and sensors, and various computations are run on the data, a human being is always part of the final interpretive loop. A human being stands in to make decisions from that information.

Tools that may enhance performance do not have to be necessarily complex or expensive. Ideally, tools to enhance work would be fairly easy and low-cost to deploy but have outsized effects, such as checklists used for complex tasks (Gawande, 2009). In that spirit, electronic journaling (e-journaling)—and particularly structured or guided electronic journaling—may provide advantages to researchers in a number of ways that may ultimately enhance the research quality. Research journals draw from professional journal traditions. Contemporaneous electronic journaling stems from advancements in software tools, low-cost digital recording equipment, and cloud-based services. The culture of sharing of digital and multimedia artifacts--including visuals (such as photos, digital drawings, diagrams, and art), audio, and video—stems in part from the Web 2.0 ethos of the Social Web. (Indeed, there are streams of research on visual journaling, video journaling, and others.) Personal journals themselves have been used for adult self-development, problem-solving, self-expression, health, and learning (Hiemstra, 2002) for over four decades now. Journaling has been linked to increasing individual controls over their own affective domains (Pomfret & Medford, 2007). The work of mentally simulating what led up to certain problems has been found to enhance the ability to conceptualize ways to solve those problems; mental reviewing of skills has also enhanced performance of those skills (Heath & Heath, 2007, pp. 210 – 214).

Writing is an activity that supports "learning and thinking" (Lai & Land, 2009, p. 142); it enhances people's ability to learn from their experiences. This tool helps calibrate the qualitative and mixed methods researcher as a honed research tool. Combined with the knowledge of human limits in cognition and analysis, a journal may help a researcher consider a broader range of research sources, methodologies, and data interpretations. For some researchers, they see their research journals as private and limited to their own consumption. One rationale is that such an approach will limit self-monitoring and self-censoring since the journal is only for the researcher. Depending on how a research e-journal is approached, it may serve as a catharsis for researcher frustrations and other emotions; it may reinforce proper practices and standards for work; it may serve as documentation of the work. An electronic journal leaves an artifact that may be revisited later for deeper understandings and to review hypotheses, ideas, and research methods—whether accepted or discarded in the formal work.

There may be valuable insights beyond the researcher purview. There may be a value for posterity as well, to show the provenance of work; historians seeking to understand research advancements may be able to extract themes and insights from archived research journals. A researcher or research team may be able to prove the provenance of their work with the documentation in research journals; this may be an artifact of authentication, in both legal and other contexts. Research journals may be studied as field texts that may offer insights about particular researchers, research teams, projects, domains, and mixed domains. There are not just releases of research journals retroactive to the publication of the research work. Some research journals are created with the idea that they will be publicly shared and published contemporaneous to or shortly after the release of the research. Some thinking in this regard refers to the value in the transparency of research (achieved through explicit specification of all assumptions, all methods, and other details). Along with core datasets, research journals may be released broadly as peripheral sources to advance the field and support colleagues in the particular domain.

REVIEW OF THE LITERATURE

In qualitative, quantitative, and mixed methods research, there are a number of explicit standards and checks and double-checks to ensure quality: defined ethics, oversight by regulatory offices, common practices, and peer- / editor- / grant funder- / public oversight. There are explicit methodologies in place to mitigate human limits:

Scientific work is supposed to be described explicitly in detail, with terms and methods defined to permit the work to be repeated exactly in its entirety by anyone else. This is the key guard against untruth: repeating work to see whether the same results emerge (Trivers, 2011, p. 305).

One little-mentioned tool to enhance research is the unprepossessing research journal. The affordances of technologies enable the inclusion of a variety of multimedia for such journaling, such as through digital imagery, figures, audio, video, slideshows, and other forms; the packaging of such multimedia and multimodal journals may more accurately be described as research e-portfolios. Technologies enable project team journaling, to advance and document projects. Finally, they also enable the potential broad sharing of research journals via the cloud. To understand the potential value of electronic research journals, though, it helps to consider some limits to people in their roles as researchers. The centrality of the researcher in all research makes human limits a real concern.

Studies about human capabilities and limits stem from work in psychology, neuroscience, and economics. A core assertion in classic economics theories about people as rational utility maximizers was a paradigm used for many years until more contemporaneous research found various ways

that people's systems of perception, cognition, and decision-making could be manipulated through priming (various methods of using stimuli to condition a human memory response in a subsequent exposure to a stimulus). Further, there have been findings that people make decisions based on emotions and impressions more than pure logic, in many cases. People tend towards emotions, "partisanship," and other so-called "idols of the mind" (Bendix, 1984). These findings resulted in a revision and the idea that people make decisions based on "bounded logic" or limited logic. The mapping of known human limits enables ways to institutionalize countermeasures, to shore up human perception, cognition, and decision-making.

Human Limitations

"Human factors" refers to human capabilities (such as perception, cognition, physical, and others), particularly limits, that inform the design of technological systems. In the same way, human factors considerations may inform the design of research e-journals. The very limits of people stem from the way the brain has evolved and how it processes information and arrives at decisions. Psychologist and winner of a Nobel Prize in Economics, Daniel Kahneman posits that the brain works as two mental systems. System 1 is automatic and fast, with the capturing of impressionistic judgments and often-erroneous intuitions created in milli-seconds. This system tends to capture the gist of a situation, without accuracy, in a complex world. It is the de facto system of perception and cognition. This system is associative and impressionistic. It tends to be hyper-suggestible based on nuanced information from the world, without the conscious mind being aware that it is being triggered or manipulated by subliminal cues. System 2 is the executive control system which allocates human attention purposefully; it is the center of human discipline and self-control. It uses plenty of resources in effortful mental activities. This is the system used for complex and logical computations, planning, comparisons, and deliberative decision-making. System 2 accesses long-term memory. It is used for reflective thought. Kahneman suggests that the human brain tends towards efficiency and laziness; it will run on heuristics, stereotypes, and shortcuts, and it will not engage the executive System 2 unless there is some indication that more in-depth analysis is needed. In a complex and uncertain world, the engagement of the incorrect system may lead to deeply erroneous choices. (These concepts of System 1 and System 2 seem to align generally with what Daniel Goleman calls the "low road" and the "high road.")

Rationality must ultimately trump "inbred propensities" and irrational consistencies of behavior that have consistently shown up in models of human behavior in order to bring value to human thinking. To work well as a strong researcher, individuals require "a firm command of logic" that is so well learned that it seems "hardwired" (Abbott, 2004, p. 215). If the logic of an author is impeachable, the work itself will contain the seeds for its own destruction. In one context, economics, Alan Greenspan (2013) writes about the risks of (John Maynard) Keynesian "animal spirits" affecting markets—which return to rationality because of this dimension of human rationality:

All such (animal) spirits, as I observe later, are tempered by reason to a greater or lesser degree, and hence I more formally choose to describe such marketplace behavior as 'propensities.' The technologies that have driven productivity since the Enlightenment were, at root, reasoned insights. Random irrationality produces nothing. If reason were not ultimately prevailing, we could not explain the dramatic improvements in standards of living that the world has achieved in the past two centuries (p. 16).

In the economic context, "irrational exuberance" leads to extremes in buying behavior which lead to economic bubbles, which ultimately break with prices returning to values closer to reality or even below actual values.

In qualitative research, reification (the act of turning an abstraction like an idea into something perceived as real; the turning of the ephemeral and imaginary into something substantive and real) is to be avoided; this occurs when people's illusions of a reality result in the apparent creation of such a reality. Here, the act of naming an observed phenomena gives this an outsized sense of reality, which may not be actual. Taken to the extreme, reification becomes an act of "fetishizing," or irrationally obsessing over a concept or approach. Over-adherence to a particular school or thought or approach may mean closing off possibilities for other insights. On the other hand, classic works in qualitative and mixed methods research have brought to consciousness latent and non-obvious phenomena—that have informed knowledge, decision-making, and policies. Some insights are so fragile that they shimmer with other interpretations of reality. Researchers then are walking a fine line.

Human Perceptual Systems

The human body has a range of perception systems which help the individual interact with the environment and others in the environment. These include sight, hearing, smell, taste, touch, and proprioception. The "far senses" refer to sight and sound; the near senses refer to touch, smell, taste, and proprioception. People's sensory organs enable them to perceive energy in the environment: light wave energy through sight, air dislocation through hearing, pressure and temperature through touch, molecules through taste and smell, and combined internal and external signals through proprioception (the physical experience of being within a physical body). Much of the world's energy is beyond the range of unaided human perception. Perceptual stimuli stem from both exogenous and endogenous sources: in other words, they come from both the external environment and from within the brain and human body (synaptic firing may occur in the brain and cause sensations which are not from the environment). "Dark light" or "intrinsic light" refers to brain activities that result in perceived visual sensations; "spontaneous emissions" and "phantom tones" refer to sound signals that occur without any external sound wave. Hallucinations may stem from a number of brain states as well. Physical duress—like hypoxia or insufficient oxygen to the brain—may also affect human perception. For example, Pete Takeda (2006) writes of how inherent stressors in mountain climbing tend to "exacerbate psychosis and exploit emotional fractures" (p. 203). Takeda elaborates:

Altitude, namely its accompanying hypoxia, does funny things to the mind. The physiological change, combined with the deprivation of distractions like television, Internet, alcohol, career, and whatever static fills our heads often dredges up of all types of buried experiences, memories, and unmanaged emotions. Having been on more than my share of trips like this, I'm used to it. I've also seen more than one apparently well-adjusted climber, flip out and leave the expedition or become so antsy, he can't maintain the emotional resiliency and energy required to carry on with the program (2006, pp. 214-215).

Fieldwork in some locales can be highly stress inducing even if the settings are not those that physically tax the human body and mind. Perception is non-veridical, which means it does not match the world's inputs in either full accuracy or magnitude. Further, the world itself does not offer clear or non-conflicting signaling; the existence of metamers is one example of visual stimuli that may add confusion to human visual perception.

The brain processes various sensory inputs through defined channels and specialized cells. There are specific locales in the brain for process-

ing certain types of sensory information. Some of the brain's receptors are polysensory, which means that they accept and integrate multisensory types of information. There is cortical magnification of particular signals. The perceptual signals are prone to amplification or suppression, with some signals made stronger and others made dimmer—based on the importance of that signal to human survival, functioning, and decision-making. What is perceived is affected by human attention. People pay attention to what evokes emotional reactions and what is perceived as salient or relevant; the brain also tends to follow movement and color. Human perception may be enhanced by "ego extenders" which are technologies that serve as intermediaries in capturing information.

According to the direct perception/ecological model of perception, the world offers sufficient information for full perception—as long as people sample the environment sufficiently. In this concept, each animal—based on its affordances and constraints—will perceive the environment differently. There is a mutuality or synergy between the animal and the environment (Michaels & Carello, 1981). Memory and awareness themselves are not required for perception. In terms of indirect perception/constructivism, the world does not provide sufficient information. The brain has to augment the sensory experience with prior experiences and analysis in sense meaning and context. In this latter conceptualization, the human brain interpolates information by filling in informational gaps, usually with whatever interpretation is mentally closest at hand.

Personality affects how much an individual engages the world. An inhibited personality can be overwhelmed by exposures to a number of sensory information and shut down due to hyper-arousal (Goleman, 2006). Individuals who prefer high volumes of sensory details may handle such feedback better without being overwhelmed. Individual temperament will affect how much individuals expose themselves to the world as well, which will affect what they have access to in terms of perceptual information. Along the same lines, Andrew Abbott (2004) describes the importance of a person's "intellectual personality" which is built on "everyday character" and which informs his or her research: "The strengths and weaknesses of your intellectual character decisively influence the way you evaluate ideas and, indeed, everything about the way you think," he writes (p. 234).

The human brain is thought to work on both a primitive or lower-order level and an executive or higher-order level. Lower-order brain processes capture sensory information at the detail level; the more evolved parts of the brain contain higher levels of color perception, depth perception, and visual sensitivity. The higher-order brain processes organize perceptual information, direct human attention, support decision-making, and support action. The higher order mind analyzes new information and integrates it into memory. Memory is not coded in a purely objective way; rather, the brain is a highly subjective organ that rewrites and reinterprets. Memory is highly mutable and constructed; it is revisable. Memory is selective and incomplete; it is fallible. While there is a learning curve to acquire new knowledge into memory, there is also a forgetting curve through which knowledge and memory may dissipate per Hermann Ebbinghaus (Aiden & Michel, 2013, pp. 154 – 157). Goleman (2006) writes:

Our memories are in part reconstructions. Whenever we retrieve a memory, the brain rewrites it a bit, updating the past according to our present concerns and understanding…Thus each time we bring a memory to mind, we adjust its very chemistry: the next time we retrieve it, that memory will come up as we last modified it. The specifics of the new consolidation depend on what we learn as we recall it. (p. 78)

The higher-order mind also controls interacting systems in the body for a "coalition" of aspects to promote perception and action in an integrated way. People also bring their imaginations into play by considering a range of possible counterfactuals (alternate possibilities to what actually happened) in a situation. Counterfactual conditionals are based on antecedent events that may lead to particular outcomes based on causal relationships. One type of narrative heuristic, counterfactuals are "what-ifs" based on latent potentials. These are often built based on a historical sense of circumstances but for which an antecedent agent may be changed for different outcomes; other ahistorical factors may be introduced into the context. These "mutated" historical alternatives are mental constructs about what might have been if other antecedents or precursor factors had been present. (In organizations where a wide range of possibilities have been considered, there are "red cell" groups trained to propose and think through ideas that are beyond far-fetched to be as inclusive as possible of long-tail possibilities, in order not to be caught up short by a failure of the imagination.) Counterfactuals range from the wholly imaginary to the possible, and they are typically judged on analytical insights in some cases and real-world plausibility in others. Researchers have observed that counterfactual thinking may affect causality judgments "by changing beliefs about the probabilities of possible alternatives to what actually happened, thereby changing beliefs as to whether a cause and effect actually co-vary (Spellman & Mandel, 1999, p. 120). With counterfactual thoughts, people tend to be goal directed. They tend towards normalizing extreme negative events (in upwards counterfactuals which conceptualize a better outcome) and exceptionalizing other counterfactuals (upwards) based on the "optimality of the counterfactual outcome" (Dixon & Byrne, 2011, p. 1317). The "temporality effect" highlights the tendency for people to reverse more recent events in a sequence of independent events and accepting earlier ones as "givens".

The executive functions of the human mind may limit what is perceived as well. "Change blindness" describes how people's attention focused on one thing may mean that they may miss some glaringly obvious other information. An over-focus on a particular issue will mean less attention for other aspects of the environment or context. When people are under stress, they tend to experience tunnel vision and notice even less. A trained and broad curiosity may enhance a person's capability to observe and glean opportunities from the environment (Johansson, 2012). There is empirical research showing that certain mixes of sensory stimuli trigger concurrent "time-shared" attentional resource competition in a task allocation / high demand situation (leading to overload and decrements in performance) (Wickens, 2002). Examples of such competition may be when a person tries to visually read multiple sources simultaneously or tries to listen to multiple speakers while attending to them equally. People's affective states affect perception and may emphasize particular features of the perceptual landscape over others; for example, phobias or "looming maladaptive style" often result in a world experienced as threatening because of the emotional overlay or filter (Herbert, 2010, p. 33). A person's physical state may also affect their perception of task difficulties and features of the natural world (Herbert, 2010, p. 34); an individual's sense of social support and self concept also affects sensory perception and ultimately their resilience in engaging the world. Herbert (2010) explains that people's reception of sensory signals from the environment is mixed with "all sorts of mental and emotional baggage" (p. 37).

People have been observed to "depersonalize" when they are under extreme anxiety or pressure (Fine, 2006). This has been described colloquially as an "out of body" experience, in which the individual seems separate from his or her own thoughts and feelings, and the world seems unreal.

In situations where people have been under duress and were approaching the "limit physiology" of survivability, some have reported instances of the sense of a presence of another being, an "illusory shadow person" who is accompanying them on their travails (Geiger, 2005, p. 42). This experience has been termed spiritual by some, but other thinkers suggest that this is a sign of the brain's hallucinatory coping with duress and a core indicator of the human need for company, so imagining the other. Some have suggested that the imagined other is maybe an adult version of children's imaginary playmates (Geiger, 2005, p. 130). This phenomenon has been termed "the third man effect" by Geiger, who shows that this sense of another's presence generally dissipates once a person is out of extreme danger and duress. In some cases, this "third man" illusion state may provide impetus for individuals to find internal reserves to get themselves out of difficult situations, but in other cases, duress-based hallucinations have resulted in counter-productive decision-making and actions, which have resulted in documented cases of severe injury or death. Varki and Brower (2013) highlight the challenges of evolutionary human denial in the face of threats, which could lead to paralyzing anxieties; in such conditions, people may suppress awareness of information that may be so terror-inducing that it may hinder human action and ultimately survivability. In this shared evolutionary theory, denial evolved (psychological evolution along with physiological evolution) in the complex human brain in order to enhance survival of the species. However, when this denialism is applied to a complex analytical situation with a known set of facts, this may lead to highly skewed analysis and decision-making. Another individual-based bias may involve other skews, including paranoia, depression, mania, and other mental states that affect the intake of sensory signals as perceptual information.

In human interactions with each other, people may erroneously project their own internal realities on others; this is a severe limitation of interpretation because the researcher is applying internal signals to incorrectly interpret external ones. This transference is often applied by those who are self-absorbed (Goleman, 2006, p. 115). People may be sparked to mass actions through rumor chains alone, with many suspending their senses of disbelief if the source is someone within their close social network (Herriman, 2010). Often, people observe others' behaviors and emulate; they are often more influenced by social networks than any built-in rationality based on insights from "social physics" research (Pentland, 2014).

Research Countermeasures against Perceptual Illusions

One of the most effective ways to mitigate human perceptual limits involves the uses of "ego extenders" for research. These are tools which further the capabilities of the individual in terms of perception and memory. These may be digital cameras to videotape interactions or interviews or field research sites. These may be digital recording devices to capture interactions. Such recording enables the researcher or researchers to review the materials multiple times to capture information. In terms of coding the recorded data, whether there are single or multiple coders, it may help to standardize the observations in order to ensure consistency in coding. Some norming training among multiple coders would be helpful for the quality of the coding. Qualitative researchers train to increase their abilities of observation and memory. For the latter, they train in various memory devices, including mnemonics, cryptic in-field note-taking, and other memory triggers (Berg & Lune, 2012, pp. 232 – 233).

In a live setting (with or without the ability to use technologies), it may help to have multiple observers engaging the scene. Because fatigue can detract from insightful observations, particularly of elusive or subtle phenomena, it may help for the researcher or researchers to be refreshed and well-rested. Tiredness may detract during interviews and other types of information collection—by preventing researchers from asking the hard questions or pursuing previously unplanned but relevant lines of questioning.

Since perception is heightened for issues considered salient or important to the observer, it would be important to prepare for the perception by pre-training the observer on what to observe. In other words, it's important to identify what is salient in the particular circumstance, so he or she could use the executive functions of the mind to direct attention.

Perception research has shown that different strategies should be used for capturing different types of information. A generalized scanning is more useful to capture anomalies in an environment than in-depth focus on particular parts of a scene. While humans may capture the gist of a situation in milliseconds, closer study of a scene requires clear focal visual attention. Peripheral observations are notoriously inaccurate.

In situations of duress and high risk, there are a range of designed trainings to mitigate human perceptual, cognitive, and decision-making limits during crises—for the most optimal assessment, choice-making, and follow-through. There are preparations that individuals and groups may take. There are also various types of rehearsals that may be engaged. To address issues of psychological projection or transference, researchers need to be self-aware and other-aware. The ability to apply such complex meta-awarenesses requires intense training and notation and recording for post-interaction analysis.

Confirmation Bias

People fall into a range of what Kahneman calls "cognitive illusions." Based on pre-conceived notions, people pursue, focus on, and better remember information that supports their pre-existing mental models or worldviews; they show a "confirmation bias." Of particular concern are monological worldviews that are self-sustaining because they are untested and unquestioned; by contrast, dialogical worldviews at least engage the environment in a dialogue about the validity of that mental model or framework. A dialogical view is questioned and interrogated for validity. One major rationale for maintaining value neutrality towards an issue and for maintaining self-awareness while conducting research is the human tendency towards confirmation bias or seeing what they want to see. The human tendency to go with a "fixation of thought" has been noted for decades (Luchins, 1942, as cited in Bilalić, McLeod, & Gobet, 2008, p. 653), sometimes to their detriment. The *Einstellung* (set) effect is described as "an instance of the negative impact of previous knowledge" (p. 653). In familiar situations, habitual mental tracks are brought into play. Said another way, systematizing understandings can blur understandings and discourage a focus on details. Pariser (2011) writes:

Understanding the rules that govern a messy, complex world makes it intelligible and navigable. But systematizing inevitably involves a trade-off—rules give you some control, but you lose nuance and texture, a sense of deeper connection. And when a strict systematizing sensibility entirely shapes social space (as it often does online), the results aren't always pretty. (p. 173)

In research, this confirmation bias may mean a preference for data that confirms the original research hypothesis and a tendency to ignore data that disconfirms this hypothesis. For many researchers, they disallow the falsification of their hypothesis—both in research design (which does not seek disconfirming information and in practice, such as in data analysis, when data is collected and analyzed). This approach may mean that researchers stop asking the hard questions once they have some evidence for what they expect to find. New incremental information by its piecemeal processing may enable the holding of an erroneous mental model because the information is not looked at as a whole (Heuer, 1999, p. 15). This selectivity of information may result in

highly biased research that skews away from reality rather than towards it. (Or this selectivity may play a role in the analysis of the research, with some details foregrounded or given pre-eminence and others backgrounded, ignored, or even forgotten.) Cognitive dissonance (the discomfort with holding two mutually contradictory ideas simultaneously) is often resolved with individuals going with the more familiar concepts and discarding those that are less familiar. People may rationalize away the importance of opposing evidence or arguments, based on the well-documented phenomena of self-deception, where individuals may maintain a position that they know to be false or unsupportable in the face of incontrovertible evidence through untruths, equivocations, denial, or concealment. Self-deception has come about as an adaptation of human (and animal) evolution and is used to convince others of a particular untruth by self-believing in the untruth; further, humans engage in self-deceptions when they emotionally commit to an idea which is important for them to maintain (Trivers, 2011). One of the most common self-deceptions involves self-inflation as a kind of ego protection. Fine (2006) describes the ubiquity of the "vain brain" that self-aggrandizes individuals and excuses faults and failures and helps people think that they are "invincible, invulnerable, and omnipotent" (p. 4). This tendency may lead to a lack of acknowledgment of mistakes or misunderstandings; it may lead to exaggerated over-estimations of individual capabilities and denials of personal limits. Self-deceptions may be conscious or unconscious (sublimated). While Trivers points to evolutionary advantages to self-deception (suppressing potentially paralyzing fears or anxieties), this characteristic does not come without cost—namely "the misapprehension of reality, especially social, and an inefficient, fragmented mental system" (Trivers, 2011, p. 28). In terms of research in academic disciplines, "… self-deception may deform the structure of intellectual disciplines" and decrease progress in the field (Trivers, 2011, p. 319).

Another cognitive illusion stems from the "availability heuristic": what comes to mind easily or with little effort is often perceived as the correct answer to a question. This happens so quickly that many people do not realize that they may have offered a non-thinking response that may have conflated a state-of-mind for a well-thought-out-answer. What exacerbates the availability heuristic is the speed with which people will weave narratives from limited information, without considering potential alternative understandings. As Kahneman has noted, people tend to be rarely stumped and to have ready answers for a range of issues, whether or not they are particularly informed. This tendency to go with what comes to mind first may be seen in the phenomenon of "anchoring and adjusting" (Herbert, 2010, p. 127), a phenomena in which people fix on an idea or a measure and adjust their assessments around that anchor; this may be a fine cognitive tool except that the fixing of the initial anchor may be triggered randomly, subliminally, or even artificially planted, in ways that do not effectively reflect reality.

Those who over-use System 1 believe in premonitions and assume that the world is more predictable than it is. The human mind finds it easier to create coherent stories when they know little. As they know more, coherent stories are harder to create or "fit" to a particular coherent narrative. (In research, this may appear as an interpretation of causation instead of correlation, or there may be a relationship seen when the null hypothesis has not been rejected.) A number of studies have shown how people tend to sense-make and create patterns even where none exist; the human brain is "designed to perceive order instead of randomness" (Johansson, 2012, pp. 71 - 72). Research on priming people shows that subtle signals may affect subsequent human decision-making based on human hyper-suggestibility; this priming influence is often not obvious to the person's conscious mind. In reputational considerations, innuendos may be highly effective in creating impressions

(Fine, 2006, p. 122). Priming is thought to work because the human brain may maintain a cascade of ideas in a way that is associatively coherent even if the ideas and emotions are not accurate to the world; many ideas are activated simultaneously in associative memory. Even exposure to pictures that are shown in milliseconds and which do not rise to the level of the conscious mind is sufficient to affect people's subsequent decision-making. Further, exposure to ideas has been shown to have an ideomotor effect as well, with ideas affecting physical actions, and physical actions reciprocally affecting thinking. Researchers have been able to plant memories through suggestion and evoke a false familiarity with an issue by exposing research participants to stories; human memory is malleable and suggestible.

People also have been found to maintain a "halo effect," using one early impression of an individual and generalizing that across other characteristics of that individual. A halo effect may be either positive or negative. In any case, it's a stereotype and is unfounded.

There is a popular term for how a certain type of misinformation, taken as received wisdom, may propagate in academia. The "Woozle effect" ("evidence by citation" or "pseudo facts") is about information sourcing and information provenance that leads back to an assertion that has sprung up *ex nihilo* and without basis. In academia, researchers tend to daisy-chain research, without fully tracking sources to their original source and then checking the validity of that source. Pseudo-facts, if accepted as truth, "have a way of inducing pseudo-problems" (Merton, 1959: xv, as cited in Merton, 1987, pp. 3 – 4). This trust in colleagues' work is a matter of both mutual academic respect (be that as it may) and efficiency. What this means is that a number of publications may cite particular information that gains credence without actually being valid at core. The rules of evidence are not followed. This may lead to widespread misconceptions. Due diligence would suggest that it is important to pursue original sources where possible. One thinker has criticized the confining limits of going with prior published research and known data (Taleb, 2012), in lieu of broader thinking; in his conceptualization, more effective ideas may be arrived at through purely original thinking.

Another type of bias may stem from subjective human relationships. Closeness with subjects in a research project may result in skewed observations and interpretations. This is why qualitative and mixed methods researchers work hard to maintain professionalism and some distance in relationships, in order to maintain research-based objectivity. Qualitative researchers have to maintain multiple roles. Berg and Lune (2012) describe a continuum of covert-to-overt qualitative researcher roles in the field—from a complete participant who is covert and fully immersed (totally unannounced) to "participant as observer" (with an announced role as a researcher) to "observer as participant" (with "the overt role as an investigator") and "complete observer" (a passive non-participatory role) (pp. 83 – 84).

Research Countermeasures against Confirmatory Bias

If a person's bias may be seen by what he or she chooses to believe, and such beliefs are often kept unchallenged in an internal mindset, then there has to be some researcher responsibility for questioning beliefs (particularly before these are shared in the broad light-of-day with other researchers). To combat the confirmatory bias, then, researchers need to seek falsifying or discrediting information (what some call "lines of falsification inquiry" to actively try to disconfirm a favored hypothesis); they need to search as hard for data that would show their hypothesis false as they would that would show their hypothesis as true. The human tendency to see what they expect means that it will require more information to recognize "unexpected phenomena" (Heuer, 1999, p. 8). They

need to consider a range of alternate hypotheses and assess their explanatory power based on the body of evidence. Researchers need to be aware of their own mental models and biases. They have to be aware of their tendencies and what ideas they protect. Then, they need to correct for their own biases: if their tendency is to pattern a particular way or take a particular approach, they need to work hard to go against those initial tendencies. They need to exercise deep skepticism about what information they are seeing and how they are interpreting it. They have to know where the information comes from and if the sourcing is valid. They need to use a wide aperture to collecting information; they have to get over their inherent intellectual laziness and the laziness of the efficient mental systems (that try to run on heuristics or generalized rules of thumb). People have to nullify some of the influences of their own hard-wired mental shortcuts and pre-conceptions.

To combat the availability heuristic, Kahneman suggests that people need to give an explanation for the fluency of the retrieval—which weakens the "availability heuristic" effect. That explanation helps individuals not attribute the fluidity of the retrieval (from memory) with the veracity of the information. This way, individuals may focus on the validity of the actual contents without any mistaken effects from ease-of-retrieval. [Wray Herbert refers to this as a "familiarity heuristic" (2010, p. 4).]

They need to use a broad sensibility to interpret the information and not to lock in early on particular understandings. To this end, researchers suggest that it may help to legitimize doubts. The introduction of "disfluency" may break the mental cycle of going along with an existing individual paradigm (the "default heuristic" or "dominant logic") and cause reconsideration and reinterpretation of the known facts. Disfluencies may come from new facts and new interpretations (including imaginary and counterfactual ones).

By promoting metacognitive difficulty, disfluency can lead to deeper processing of the information and less reliance on heuristic modes of processing. In contrast, the ease that is facilitated by fluency leads to greater use of heuristic reasoning, and sometimes more errors in judgment (Hernandez, 2013, p. 178).

Disfluency may be triggered with something as light as the readability of font types (Herbert, 2010, p. 54). Heuristics are generalized rules that are applied to generally familiar situations in an unthinking way. This is also known as "low-information rationality" or "frugal reasoning," a form of cognitive short-cut. A disfluency experience breaks the illusion of familiarity, and it causes the individual to reconsider and re-evaluate. In terms of decision-making, there are cognitive limits here, too. A trained individual may be aware that he or she is relying on a heuristic for particular decision-making and resist this impulse of premature closure by mentally considering the relevant factors to that decision. (Structured decision-trees may be used in more formal organizational settings to ensure that the relevant details are being considered. Checklists may offer another way to systematize this process definition.) Another aspect of disfluency involves maintaining multiple counter arguments to the preferred argument (Huang, Hsu, & Ku, 2012, p. 443). This different narrative, along with the highlighting of discomfirming information, may provide the mental space to consider a wider range of possibilities. To head off confirmation bias in terms of holding opinions or deciding on options, it is important to hold opinions lightly. Further, it is important to avoid premature commitments or "option fixation" (Sieck, Merckle, & Van Zandt, 2007). On the other hand, people may react irrationally to unfamiliar objects, even if the objects are only slightly different; one study found that people devaluated a $2 bill and preferred two $1 bills simply because the first was atypical (Herbert, 2010, pp. 57- 58); in the same way, unfamiliar

names were seen as not as "cognitively palatable as more familiar names and resulted in the latter being treated more favorably at least initially (p. 58). Of course, disfluencies may trigger over-thinking in situations where that behavior may be counter-productive. There are times when letting the System 1 brain function would be appropriate. The executive mind has to help individuals decide when a closer reading of facts makes sense or not. It may also help to define gaps in knowledge in a systematic way because such gaps encourage further seeking per Loewenstein's "gap theory of interest" (1994, as cited in Heath & Heath, 2007, pp. 94–95). This theory found increased curiosity for additional investigation and learning from those who know a lot about a topic already; there was not a decrease in curiosity for those who already knew a lot about a topic (Heath & Heath, 2007, pp. 89–90). One way to motivate people to learn more about a particular topic may be to salt their knowledge with some basic information, from which they may start to build further knowledge.

To combat the halo effect, researchers need to be aware of this phenomenon. If they have to assess an individual, they need to have standardized and factual questions to get rid of any halo effect. There should not be over-generalizing of one characteristic to others. For example, higher education should not be unthinkingly conflated with any other characteristics; rather, there should be independent streams of evidence to show these other characteristics.

To combat the Woozle effect, researchers need to be fastidious about source validity. They need to check understandings of others' ideas. They need to track information to its source and test the validity of that source. They cannot rely on reputation of the individual professing trust or belief in information in lieu of actual tests of source validity for that information.

Ironically, people who have fallen into certain mistakes in the past and have been found to have been erroneous may over-balance against making that same mistake and introduce yet another type of bias or skew. To avoid such over-weighting against a particular kind of error (and thus risk other types), researchers have to work against past failures in order to focus on the present.

The various professional domains should encourage the publication of findings even if they are diametrically opposite to the hypothesized results. There should be recognition that there is informational value in the research findings (assuming they are solid) even if (or especially if) conventional expectations of results are confounded or contradicted. New findings may be grounds for new understandings or paradigm shifts.

Over-Confidence in Limited Information

Abbott (2004) suggests the importance of creative rashness in thinking new ideas to contribute to the qualitative research field; sometimes, research work does benefit from audacity of thinking, puzzle-making, research, and analysis. Audacity, as Abbott notes, stems from earned self-confidence and Kahneman coined the acronym "WYSIATI," which means "what you see is all there is"; this is another cognitive illusion with powerful limiting implications on human decision-making. When people make decisions, they only have partial information—in an environment of uncertainty and informational asymmetries (people having different amounts and types of information). WYSIATI is a problem of having insufficient information to decide an issue but still being over-confident about making that decision. Various experiments with sequential revelations of information have shown how new details can so easily affect people's cognition, understandings, and assessments of a situation and lead to broad swings in analyses and decision-making. Limited information can lead to some serious misapprehensions. Another term for this may be "naïve realism," the belief that the world is as it seems. In terms of online research, the "filter bubble" of personalization of Web browsing, email systems, social media platforms, and other online portals may mean

further distortions, narrowing, and intensification of information (Pariser, 2011). Technologies may introduce invisible filtering through complex algorithms which are impenetrable black boxes to a majority of its users. Specific details, even if they are unrelated to a particular decision, by their mere existence, can mislead people by encouraging them to think that an assertion as more validity than otherwise (Heath & Heath, 2007, pp. 138 – 139).

Research Countermeasures against Over-Confidence in Decision-Making from Limited or Wrong Information

During the information collection phase, researchers need to collect sufficient information without artificial limits. They need to spark their "foraging heuristic" (Herbert, 2010) to spark a wide and exploratory search. They need to engage serendipity in their search to allow chance effects to broaden what they may collect and see. While cognitive styles are seen to inform how foraging occurs, some persisting and some merely satisficing (going for "good enough" only), people do have capacities for both types of foraging. This is only possible, of course, within the limits of time and other factors that may constrain a project. Researchers often do well to collect the most relevant information, too, by strategizing what needs to be known for an informed decision (instead of taking a scattershot approach). Then, they may use an information-ful approach to the work. Pariser (2011) highlights research that shows that exposure to different people, access to multiple languages, exposures to different cultures and ideas, and other approaches help promote open-mindedness in how people engage the world (pp. 100 – 101).

Researchers need to know where their information has come from in terms of the original source. What standards were used for the collection of that information? How much trust may be placed on the data? They have to understand that information without the distorting lenses of media, people, or the human mind (Pariser, 2011, p. 82). Information may be raw data; it may be synthesized and packaged through many layers of processing. A strong researcher has to be aware of the state of the information being used and how the state may affect validity or accuracy. In terms of analysis, they need to consider all possible interpretations of the information at hand instead of forming a preconception (like a schema or framework) and then fitting information into that preconception (Heuer, 1999, p. 62). It is critical to revisit information and to analyze it holistically as well to see if a change to a pre-existing mental model is necessary for accuracy—in a dynamic environment.

Likewise, in models, all variables have to be defined in depth and clarity for fuller understanding of how models are operationalized. Finally, when it comes time to make decisions, it's critical that the decisions made are sufficiently understood and informed, without an artificial sense of what is knowable or unknowable. The tendency to take certain ideas on faith—adherence to fideism (the concept that knowledge depends on revelation)—may prematurely quell further investigation or exploration.

Another important approach to countering over-confidence involves de-constructing approaches in order to understand the assumptions being made at every step of the informational, analytical, and decision-making process. Assumptions and frameworks which go un-analyzed may remain invisible and unaddressed; they may ultimately sway decision-making in negative ways. Long-held conclusions or paradigms, likewise, may seem invisible. All analyses (and conclusions) are predicated on particular understandings; defining those assumptions and testing their validity will be critical for solid analysis.

An important element of understanding comes from proper semantics or understandings of the varied meanings of terminology as defined by various researchers; a slippage of meaning from one researcher to another may lead to misunderstandings that may move the researcher far from the original intended meanings of the secondary (or even primary) sources. One aspect of precision in language involves ensuring that what is asserted is properly qualified for clear understandings. Assertions should not just be made in the larger context without as clear an understanding as possible for those receiving the research information.

Finally, it is critical to accept the occasional reality of indeterminacy (as a corrective against a misleading sense of determinism), the lack of knowability in certain contexts, with the available information. Research should be properly qualified to clarify what is or is not knowable.

Assumptions of Predictivity

People are informed by a distorted sense of "hindsight bias," which leads them to assume that they knew what would happen all along with 20/20 hindsight (or post-hoc rationalization). They tend to use outcome knowledge to influence their interpretation of the past for an unjustifiable reasoning backwards in time. Research findings may seem self-evident once others have paved the way through challenging research. The human mind has a tendency towards the pretense of orderliness. Some "hindcasts" may have been brought about by people's expectations, which may lead to self-fulfilling prophecies (Ball, 2004, pp. 235 - 236). This delusional approach may lead to a sense of fatedness or inevitability, even if other alternate versions of the past may be possible and even imaginable. People tend to (mis)remember what they predicted prior to an event in a selective way, and they often forget what they mis-judged. This tendency leads to an over-estimation of the amount of control they have over a situation, called the "illusion of control" (Fine, 2006, p. 20). In this state, people miss the capricious randomness of the world. Johansson (2012) further suggests that people are "simply not wired to handle the idea that the world is random, despite the fact that it is" (p. 77). This hindsight bias creates a sense of the past as if it were pre-determined, fixed, fated, and immutable. An over-focus on a fixed past (in terms of reasoning forward in time) means that researchers are using an archaic mental model to address modern or contemporary issues; their point-of-reference may no longer apply. Tetlock and Belkin write, "The cognitive perspective also leads us to be suspicious of people's capacity to transcend (avoid contamination by) outcome knowledge" given their tendency to sense-make by connecting an event to prior knowledge structures (1996, p. 34). Richard Ned Lebow (2009) suggests that "the very nature of the scholarly enterprise encourages the illusion of hindsight bias with researchers and thinkers fitting events into particular theories *ex post facto* (p. 59).

Another human tendency is to over-rate themselves, by seeing themselves as above average (Fine, 2006). They tend to over-value what they own based on "the endowment effect" instead of going to more objective market valuations. They tend to dismiss others' failures and assume that they can do what others have not been able to. People tend to have preferred sense of the world and their own prescience:

If an event had actually occurred, people exaggerated the probability that they had assigned to it earlier. If the possible event had not come to pass, the participants erroneously recalled that they had always considered it unlikely. Further experiments showed that people were driven to overstate the accuracy not only of their original predictions but also of those made by others (Kahneman, 2011, p. 203).

In terms of estimating probabilities, they are often misled by stereotypes and representations instead of going with known statistical base rates. Even with known information, people often do not do the simple math to understand probabilities; they neglect the base rate (what is called "denominator neglect"). They will assume that some exceptionalism is at play, and the odds will not apply to them. There are multiple names for the

human tendency to inflate their own sense of capability, including the Dunning-Kruger effect or the "inside view" (a term coined by Daniel Kahneman) or "the human tendency to predict success in novel endeavors—and the timing of success—as derived from a statistically insignificant reference class, namely one's personal experience" (Tucker, 2014, p. 36). Influenced by their egos, people will play long odds (what is known as a "dominated strategy" in game theory). To analyze effectively, people need to evaluate what is actually relevant and then know how to weight that information. There may be situations of irreflexivity or "intransitive relation" where there is no dominant or preferred strategy. Kahneman suggests the application of Bayesian probability (a calculation of probabilities of future outcomes given a particular indicator to inform present-moment decision-making, based on Bayes Theorem or

$$P(A \mid B) = P(B \mid A)\frac{P(A)}{P(B)}$$

in its common form read as: the probability of A given B equals the probability of B given A multiplied by the probability of A divided by the probability of B) to evaluate probabilities of certain outcomes against a base rate. One example that the author uses to show the benefit of base rates is the assessment of risk in new and large projects. A very human tendency is to under-estimate risk in new projects because of their assumption of best case scenarios and their own exceptionalism and (delusional) sense of significance, in what Kahneman calls the "planning fallacy," a typical underestimation about the amounts of work required to achieve particular aims This phenomenon may be seen in people's consistent underestimations about the amounts of work that it will take to successfully complete work but also in their ego-protecting blame-shifting to other factors when they fail (Fine, 2006). To achieve a more realistic sense of project requirements, costs, and timelines, people need to compare reference cases of similar projects.

Another challenge to the accuracy of human predictiveness involves misattribution of causes. The more extreme a performance is, the greater the likelihood that chance will result in regression to the mean; this phenomena suggests that if a first measure is extreme or outlying, then the next measure of it will likely be closer to average. The converse would also be true. If a variable is extreme on a second measure, it is more likely to have been closer to average on the first. Regression effects, which tend towards the average or mean, tend to be ubiquitous and to occur with statistical regularity.

Certain cognitive styles are more effective for the work of prediction. Philip Tetlock, a psychologist and political scientist, analyzed predictions made in political science and categorized individuals based on their performance. Few did better than chance (a 50-50 coin toss). This researcher then applied personality tests to the various political science experts and classified them on a spectrum between hedgehogs and foxes. Based on an Isaiah Berlin essay (which borrowed the idea from the Greek poet Archilochus), hedgehogs pursue big ideas or governing principles; foxes are scrappy and use multiple approaches to problems; they chase little ideas. Hedgehogs tend to pursue big ideas within their own domains; foxes draw from a range of disciplines. "They tend to be more tolerant of nuance, uncertainty, complexity, and dissenting opinion. If hedgehogs are hunters, always looking out for the big kill, then foxes are gatherers," writes statistician Nate Silver (2012, pp. 53-54). Between the two, the foxes are more accurate at prediction; they do not pursue big claims but pursue cautious ones that are qualified. Where hedgehogs suffer a theory-induced blindness, foxes pay attention to the world more as it is than what they might want it to be. Johansson (2012) calls this multi-disciplinary approach "intersectoral thinking" (p. 132). (As a side note: Theorizing itself is critical for research in general because theories help frame the work; further, theories may help researchers collect the proper theoretically relevant data to test hypotheses. The ability to theorize well includes the capability to understand complex definitions and associated facts.)

Empirics are critical to decision-making in order to provide the most informed decision-making based on the real world. In many contexts, though, precedence (history) is only partially informative; in many cases, it may be highly misleading, particularly if the naïve assumption is that the future will be a linear expression of the past. The sense of a bell curve normalcy may mask the potential occurrences of rare and highly disruptive "black swan" events that do not fit in a bell curve (Taleb, 2010). Apparent stability may belie an upcoming phase transition or paradigm shift. Chaos theory, as originated by physicists T.Y. Li and James Yorke, suggest that very small differences early on may result in highly divergent trajectories in time. The initial conditions of a small change in a nonlinear or complex system (with elusive discontinuities) may lead to very large differences at a later state in the future; there is a sensitive dependency on initial conditions. This phenomena of non-linearities, observed in various systems like the weather and climate, suggest that perfect predictivity is likely impossible.

In short, the presence of chaos in a system implies that perfect prediction a la Laplace is impossible not only in practice but also in principle, since we can never know x_0 to infinitely many decimal places. This is a profound negative result that, along with quantum mechanics, helped wipe out the optimistic nineteenth-century view of a clockwork Newtonian universe that ticked along its predictable path (Mitchell, 2009, p. 33).

Another limitation of human predictivity is the tendency to only consider near-impacts or simple after-effects and not second- and third-order effects. This human limitation has been informally called "the law of unintended consequences," which is considered inevitable. Policies may be instituted and implemented without understanding of broader impacts or perverse incentives (unintended consequences of the new incentive structures). Policies that are put into play to solve one issue may have unintended and unforeseen repercussions well beyond the expectations of policy proponents. This is why academic and professional practice encourages a broad range of research approaches and tools (to act as distributed sensors to the effects of policies).

Subjective desires for certain outcomes (what Fine calls "wishful thinking") are also seen to influence estimates of the likelihoods of certain outcomes: "We think it will be so, simply because we would prefer it to be so, the research suggests" (Fine, 2006, pp. 21 – 22). The stronger the yearning, "the greater the confidence" (Fine, 2006, p. 23). This is a subjective human sense of "mind over matter," with the idea that if they want something with sufficient passion that they will make the dream real.

Research Countermeasures against Inaccurate Predictivity

To break out of hindsight bias, Herbert (2010) proposes the consideration of if-then possibilities (or counterfactuals or subjunctive conditionals) to break up the sense of the inevitability of occurrences (p. 48). It helps to understand that human predictivity itself is highly inaccurate, even in the best of circumstances. In a complex world, a researcher with limited access to information will have very limited ability to predict the future. Further, if researchers are influenced by particular favored ideologies, they need to tamp down the influence of such ideologies and pursue "fox" strategies of learning broadly and across disciplines and breaking the influence of ideologies on their thinking and work. Tetlock and Belkin (1996) describe other methods that researchers have discussed to counter hindsight bias:

Sideshadowing calls attention to what could have happened, thereby locating what did happen in the context of a range of possibilities that might, with equal or even greater likelihood, have taken place instead. Sideshadowing serves as a valuable check on foreshadowing (the tendency, in extreme form, to reduce all past events to harbingers of the future) and backshadowing (the even more insidious tendency to judge historical actors as though they too should have known what was to come. (p. 15)

Sideshadowing helps break the illusions created by hindsight bias-informed "foreshadowing"—or that sense of predictivity that is often illusory. In the same way, when people use models, they need to understand the underlying assumptions of those models. After all, models are necessarily parsimonious and austere in order to be functional, and thus, they leave out information. They may tend towards overfitting or having too many parameters than indicated by the data. They may tend towards underfitting or having too few parameters than indicated by the data. They may leave out relevant but unseen data. When they use software for computational research, they need to understand the back-end functions and algorithms (generally speaking) to understand and describe what is occurring. There is some tradeoff between rigorous specifications of variables and relationships versus the higher level abstraction necessary to make a model projectable to other contexts (and cases). Figure 2, "Overfitting and Underfitting Models to the Data," shows some of these dynamics and implies various adjustments to get models better aligned to the real-world data.

To head off potential unintended consequences of new policies or actions, it may help to go through exercises to anticipate first-, second-, third- and additional orders of effects on various aspects of the environment or context. After all, once a decision has been made and actions taken, the world does not stop; rather, even if *ceteris*

Figure 2. Overfitting and underfitting models to the data

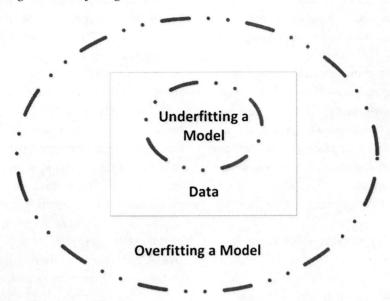

paribus is assumed, there are a range of factors in constant and dynamic change. It may help to explore who the direct and indirect stakeholders may be to particular policies or actions. If metrics or measurements may be attained to measure effects, it may help to capture a range of these effects to understand actual implications. Also, predictivity is actually only generally accurate for a limited near-future; oftentimes, accuracy dissipates into the mid- and far-futures because of a range of factors in complex environments.

Cognitive Overload

Systematic errors in judgments and decision-making may be exacerbated when the individual is experiencing overload in emotional and mental systems. Cognitive busyness or distraction may lead to more superficial judgments. The over-loaded state may result from stress on physical systems such as through a lack of sleep, hunger, or tiredness; having a few drinks may contribute to the overload. Emotional stressors may be brought on by anxiety, conflict, multi-tasking, a sense of

hurry, or other pressures. They experience lowered stamina for their endeavors. They may engage in impulsive behaviors or react aggressively to provocations; self-control requires sufficient executive control, attention, and effort. They may be seeing the world with "tunnel vision" without realizing it. People have limited cognitive loads for perception and information processing; they have limited capabilities in both short- and long-term memory. Given these limits and the expense of cognition, they need to dole out their attention and processing. Attention is somewhat zero-sum: intense focus on some issues means inattention on others. "Change blindness" describes how people miss major elements in their environments while their attention is focused on something else.

Research Countermeasures against Cognitive Overload

To combat the limiting factors related to cognitive overload, people need to be sufficiently self-aware to recognize their limited mental bandwidth and state of ego depletion. They need to compensate for that ego depletion with increased attentiveness and structured analysis, if they cannot avoid the situation of mental, emotional, and / or physical overload.

The limitations mentioned above address limits to individuals in terms of perception, cognition, and decision-making. There are similar challenges of such phenomena at group levels of sensing, awareness, and decision-making, which have been studied at length. With this awareness, there should be mitigations of that ego depletion for more stable decision-making.

Limits to Human Decision-Making

As noted above, people are informed in their decision-making based on a range of factors, including biased perceptions and irrational cognition. People's decision-making is also informed by personality traits, which are described on a number of facets. One critical one in decision-making involves impulsivity (or low self-control, a tendency to act without forethought). On a continuum, those who are low-impulsivity tend to be risk-averse and focused on security; they may be fairly inert in taking risks and may consider a range of factors before making a decision. On the other polar extreme are those who are high-risk-taking and novelty-seeking; they engage in extremes of behavior that may end up in self-harm, particularly when they are "boundary blind". Statistically, it is generally estimated that three-fourths of people are low-impulsivity, and a fourth are high-impulsivity. To make progress in a work field, people have to innovate; they have to be sufficiently strong to go against select social norms; otherwise, they just maintain the *status quo*. One irony of risk-taking emerges with the phenomenon of "risk homeostasis," which suggests that people have differing levels of comfort with risk; when one area of risk is lessened, the individual increases risk-taking in other areas and behaviors (Johansson, 2012, pp. 146 – 147).

Decision-making changes to varying degrees based on human emotional states. People may differ immensely between a sitting "cold state" of non-arousal versus how they perceive, think, and act in a "hot state" of emotional arousal (Loewenstein, 2005), such as impassioned states of anger, pain, fear, or physical attraction. Emotions, though, do play critical rules in virtually all decisions. Somatic markers or emotional tags (conceptualized as mental associations between stimuli that induce a physiological affective state—such as skin conductance or increased heart rate) are thought to play a critical role in inducing humans to make decisions that may have strategic impacts on their lives. Cold-state objectivity may be a better state-of-being for important decision-making. Other research has shown that irrelevant uncertainty can hinder or even paralyze decision-making because of people's preference for the "sure-thing" (Heath & Heath, 2007, pp. 35 – 36). An excess of choices can also befuddle choice-making (Heath & Heath, 2007, pp. 36 – 37), especially for those without articulated standards for prioritization.

The efficacy of decision-making may also depend on training, the amount of information that is available to the decision-maker. Expert decision-makers are seen to use a broader store of information to their analyses and to apply more relevant heuristics than novice or amateur decision-makers. The conceptual models of experts are more inclusive and complex than the mental models of the non-experts. Experts, though, may benefit from the insights of a broad range of novices and other practitioners through the restructuring of their expert attention through the sharing of others' areas of micro-expertise and insights (Nielsen, 2012). Individuals may benefit from collective (crowd-sourced) insights, in particular semi-structured or structured circumstances.

There are a range of known logical fallacies that have been applied to arguments to test their logical clarity or fallaciousness. For example, an analogy may be used to artificially describe a real-world situation—when in fact—that analogy or extended comparison does not particularly apply or describe the real-world situation with accuracy. A slippery slope fallacy suggests that there is a necessary following of one event after another, even though there may be no such deterministic link. A "genetic fallacy" suggests that a particular origin necessarily determines a particular character or nature. A circular argument is a closed one, with the assertion restated instead of any evidence given. An either-or fallacy limits the scope of thinking to one possibility or another and suggests that those are the only possibilities when there may be a range of possibilities. An ad hominem attack focuses on critiquing the character of an individual instead of his or her arguments directly. An ad populum attack focuses on a call to emotion instead of analytical thinking. A red herring diverts attention from the key issues of argument and rather addresses a side issue. A "straw man" argument misrepresents and simplifies counter-arguments in order to better argue against them. Moral equivalence fallacies mis-weigh smaller misdeeds with major ones. There are a range of deductive logical fallacies, too, which are tested in syllogisms; some are tested based on the veracity of their premises.

Fine (2006) reviews a range of research that shows the human "moral backbone" is quite breakable based on what she calls 'the immoral brain." In a context of human rationalizations and ego-protective excuses making, a majority of people are quite willing to engage in behaviors that may be considered universally morally questionable: causing harm to others, engaging in dishonesty, acting selfishly without consideration for others, and other actions. Another very human short-coming involves the problem of accurate understanding of possible implications of certain choices, which require consideration of a wide range of dispassionate analysis of potentialities and implications—not only for direct effects but

also second- and third-order effects. People tend to be fairly poor at predictivity, particularly in complex real-world environments.

Research Countermeasures against Limits in Decision-Making

Nick Tasler (2008) suggests that high impulsivity individuals need to make sure that they are directionally correct when apply their impulsivity to new directions. They have to logically think through their direction. They have to empirically test their decisions and strategies to see if these are constructively effective in the world. Their hypotheses have to be testable and falsifiable—not general and abstract. "Functionally impulsive people are generally only antisocial to the extent that they aren't afraid to stand alone…But that decisive trait becomes dysfunctional when quick thinking is accompanied by a lack of planning and a complete disregard for consequences," Tasler writes (2008, p. 46). High-impulsivity individuals need to assess the world accurately, and they must be aware of their own limitations—in order to counterbalance their own weaknesses. In other words, they must temper their impulsivity with mental executive control. The insights here show that there can be too much smart rumination without action as there can be too much action without empirical-based rumination.

Johansson (2012) provides a range of from-life examples of innovators and others experiencing extreme luck and success in business that was unexpected and even logic-defying. Their focus, intentions, and thinking were distinctly elsewhere; in other words, for many, their success was unpredictable and surprising. For some of the author's sources, he used interviews of the principals prior to their success to capture their ideas and frame-of-mind at the time, which controls for the hindsight bias. He suggests that those working in fields where people can rewrite the rules, there is an advantage in happening into ideas and practices that can suddenly catch fire and gain popularity; he emphasizes the importance of launching many tries to attain the right mix of factors for success. Because rules are always changing in a complex environment, serendipity and randomness may be assumed in various contexts. Even if randomness is the dominant and most advantageous strategy for success in a context, though, people have a difficult time following through on such a strategy because "people are terrible at using randomness as a rationale" (Johansson, 2012, p. 79). While it may seem that the number of tries (or iterations) is an overly simplistic way to attempt to achieve objectives, increasing attempts (but with smaller and "affordable" risks) may be an effective approach (Johansson, 2012, pp. 153 – 172). Those who achieved success in his book were positioned for achievement though by being able to engage the market in relevant ways. (For example, prototyping and market testing are common ways of testing ideas, albeit at different ends of the development cycle.)

Controlling for "hot state" decision-making is important to exert executive control over such decision-making. Individuals need to be aware of their emotional state, the possible triggers that led to that emotional state, and how to come off the "hot state" for more cool-headed decision-making. In research, method and technique have to trump impulsive or uninformed on-the-fly decision-making. This phenomenon has implications in a converse state, when the researcher is in a cold state but the research subjects are in a hot state. In an emotional "cold state," individuals may not as effectively and empathetically relate to those in a "hot state" (Loewenstein, 2005). This has implications on research which relies on understanding others' in-depth.

Attaining actual expertise in a discipline and those in peripheral domain fields may enhance decision-making in those areas. This assumes that people hold their ideas lightly and do not overcommit to the point that they exclude new information.

It is critical to adhere to proper professional ethical and moral guidelines in all work. In this, it is critical to have external regulatory oversight. Given human tendencies to consider issues in an egocentric and self-serving way, it may help to also have a range of advisers who provide initial and ongoing oversight on work.

Thought experiments enable researchers to deeply explore social phenomena and to place competing explanatory theories of that phenomena in "crucial experiments" to see which hypotheses have more support from in-world observations. These ruminative experiments help researchers identify strategic research materials that may shed light on particular events or phenomena. At times, the thought work of these experiments may be sufficient to answer particular research questions and preclude some actual research; insights from thought experiments may hone and further hone the precision of designed research.

Group Decision-Making Factors Challenges

Groupthink refers to alignment of group members around a consensus because of individuals' desires to conform socially, without adequate consideration of alternatives. There is plenty of research showing individuals engaging in various forms of conscious and unconscious mimicry (emulation) and mirroring of others' body language and communications; the individuals engaging in the copying of another's actions is seen as the "submissive" to the other's "alpha," with the first eager to impress the latter. The power of homophily—people preferring those who are like themselves—is a major factor in such conformance. Such dynamics may be exacerbated by the so-called spiral-of-silence in which dissenting opinions are discouraged and only a predominant view holds. The pressure to conform may force an early decision and close off consideration of other possibilities. Once there is a commitment to a decision or direction, people tend to fall in line behind that decision and not accept conflicting information. There are other forms of groupthink. The "bandwagon effect" results in a follow-the-leader phenomenon in which people copy those who are influential. The "Abilene paradox" refers to a phenomenon in which a collective decision is made against the actual preferences of many of the members of the group because the individual members assume that their preference is in the minority. People are prone to social and emotional contagions (and convergences) and unthinking acceptance of the ideas of those who are influential in their lives; such dynamics may lead to faddish herd behavior. People may follow unthinking "anti-patterns" that have developed in an organization and become common practice, even though it may be counterproductive or inefficient. This following of anti-patterns in unthinking ways occurs because people tend to withdraw attention once something becomes familiar. There is the tendency for people to believe even absurd propositions if they "are sustained by a community of like-minded believers" (Kahneman, 2011, p. 217). There are paradoxes, too, in terms of "moral licensing," in which groups may psychologically "bank" pro-social behavior in order to allow themselves later license in terms of socially irresponsible behaviors; further, many use an in-group relativist set of ethics to anchor their ethical norms (Ormiston & Wong, 2013). Researchers have found many contexts in which people engage in dubious moral self-licensing in which they give themselves a pass for dubious moral behaviors once they've established their own moral credentials of virtues (Merritt, Effron, & Monin, 2010).

Social interactions invariably involve transfers of feelings, with people's attunements and rapport to each other considered critical for successful human interchanges (Goleman, 2006). If people's natural interactive non-verbal synchrony is off, people will perceive this disjuncture and will experience a sense of awkwardness. To interact socially, people need sensitivity to others' "thoughts,

feelings and intentions" (Goleman, 2006, p. 84); they need empathic accuracy to actually understand each other (p. 89); those who are unable to socially synchronize may suffer from dyssemia or "a deficit in reading—and so acting on—the nonverbal signs that guide smooth interactions" (p. 91). Power and influence can affect others' emotions as well (Goleman, 2006); this would suggest that leaders will have outsized effects on group dynamics whether the leaders are right or wrong. Goleman (2006) writes:

The feelings that pass through a group can bias how all the group members process information and hence the decisions they make. This suggests that in coming to a decision together, any group would do well to attend not just to what's being said, but to the shared emotions in the room as well. (p. 49)

Feelings are connected with expressiveness (signaling) and actions. Fine (2006) describes emotions as merely the state of arousal combined with emotional thoughts (p. 38); the state of arousal is physiologically the same no matter what emotions accompany it, she observes. The feeling of "*any* emotion stirs the related urge to act," observes Goleman (2006, p. 61). Those feelings also express facially through unconscious and fleeting micro-expressions that may offer "tells" to other people who are interacting with an individual. As such, people influence each other with their own emotional states. Positive feelings like happiness have been connected with more expansive views and creativity but may result in erring on the side of rosy predictiveness. Negative feelings like sadness have been connected with more limited views but also more accurate predictiveness in a situation.

Beyond the interpersonal relations in a group, at a larger unit of analysis, organizations and institutions are built around shared cultural values and behaviors. These values and behaviors may incline the organization to evaluate information a certain way, make decisions a certain way, and respond in certain ways at certain decision junctures. These tendencies may be selected to the exclusion of other approaches. Institutions have varying capacities to adapt and change as necessary to deal with particular issues. The agents of an organization may be so enculturated that they cannot see the cultural understandings and assumptions.

Research Countermeasures against Group Decision-Making Factors Challenges

How groups make decisions has been studied for many years. The nature of group decision-making differs from individual decision-making. Committees tend to "be more prone to inertia, caution, and compromise than most individuals," writes Pollack (2013, p. 18). Understanding structural constraints in decision-making may inform analysis of potential decision-making outcomes.

The psychology literature suggests that there is a constant tension between the need for people to socially belong and to individuate. Essentially, to break dynamics of groupthink, it is important to have work and social places that are less hierarchical and socially flatter. There needs to be wide awareness of the various types of limits to group assessment and decision-making. Organizations often benefit from heterophilous work groups with diverse personalities and skill sets, along with an appreciation for diversity. The culture has to encourage a broad range of ideas and alternative interpretations (and counterfactuals), which are given their due. Philip E. Tetlock and Aaron Belkin cite Kahneman's 1995 research about the value of conducting mental simulations

...by revealing previously unnoticed tensions between explicit, conscious beliefs and implicit, unconscious ones. In this sense, people discover aspects of themselves in mental simulations that *would otherwise have gone undiscovered. We find it useful to distinguish three specific ways in which mental simulations can yield insights into our own thought processes: by revealing double standards in moral judgment, contradictory causal beliefs, and the influence of unwanted biases such as certainty of hindsight (Tetlock & Belkin, 1996, p. 13).*

Many professional organizations assign (or select) individuals to serve as counterpoints to argue against various points-of-views with counter-arguments and various interpretations. Their "devil's advocacy" role is to legitimize doubts. Leaders are trained to elicit a broad range of perspectives and to allow both the time and the social space to fully explore options—so as to head off precipitous commitments. Some assign exploration of a full range of possibilities, even into the highly improbable (such as "red cell" thinkers), in order not be limited by cognitive rigidity or taken by surprise by real-world events (rare events tend to be underweighted and dismissed by analysts and planners) (Henshaw, 2012). A wide range of language may be used to express concepts because how something is phrased or depicted has been shown to affect decision-making. This is true for data visualizations as well, which may emphasize particular aspects of data versus others. To understand second- and third-order effects, groups may use various practices to model the implications of particular choices or actions. Depending on the various domain fields, there are clear steps to think-through potential repercussions.

There may be other ways of knowing. In complex environments where there is a range of complex information, informed computer algorithms have been found to outperform human experts by detecting weakly valid cues and by using relevant cues consistently. Expert intuitions draw from various experiences and use observable cues (if available), but these work in environments which are not highly volatile or dynamic. Expertise may be confounded in complex environments with dynamism and noise.

To effectively harness collective intelligence, there must be strong group skills and methods to capitalize on the group intelligence. Conflicting opinions and ideas need to be elicited and addressed. Countervailing viewpoints need to be brought into play. Nielsen (2012) writes:

These and many other studies paint a bleak picture for collective intelligence. They show that groups often don't do a good job of taking advantage of their collective knowledge. Instead, they focus on knowledge they hold in common, they focus on knowledge held by high-status members of the group, and they often ignore the knowledge of low-status members of the group. Because of this, they don't manage to convert individual insight into collective insight shared by the group." (pp. 71 – 72)

All information environments are incomplete, and decision-making in complex environments run up against the limits of what is knowable. How people strive to fill in the gaps in knowledge as well as the assumptions they apply will affect what is understood and resulting preferences. Decision makers often move forward within information limits with practical undecidability as a condition of the environment.

To de-link arousal, emotions, and moods from decision-making, people can make themselves more self-aware of their emotional states and what may have triggered them. If they can understand logically what has led to certain emotional states, they can more objectively parse a decision based on relevant facts and details. Group emotional awareness also should be considered for groups making decisions. Bringing such dynamics to the team's attention may minimize the power of this influence rather than leaving it unaddressed. Being aware of moods may enable a group to

address the effects more directly; seasoned teams may potentially calibrate group emotions and their effects on decision-making in a direct way. Inaction is also a decision, and that approach will involve potential risks, costs, and benefits. Non-action at various decision junctures may result in forced choices later.

Finally, groups and organizations may do well to integrate systematic ways to consider a broad range of decisions—so as not to automatically exclude certain points-of-view. It may help to have external insights about the group's or organization's values and dynamics to surface tendencies, in order to enhance the group and organization's capabilities at evaluating research and coming to the appropriate decision-making, given the context.

Complex Data Challenges

The world offers a range of possibilities for research and information collection. Qualitative and mixed methods are used in a variety of contexts. In a number of fields (particularly in the social sciences), there may be challenges with inaccessible documentation (historical records), data sets with low N, active deception by various actors, or contexts where true experimentation or even quasi-experimentation (and data replication) are not possible. In such contexts, what is directly knowable is almost always necessarily limited because of reasons of access, legal and ethical protections, testability, and cost. This complex research context has implications for research methods, knowability, generalizability, and confidence in outcomes.

The complex nature of data may also cause challenges to research. For example, outsized effects may be observed based on limited case studies based on the so-called "law of small numbers." Small data sets do not offer sufficient data points or records to understand the nature of the subject being studied. Large datasets tend to show less extreme variance or outlier effects. "Big data," indicated as complete datasets of large-scale data, has become much more available in the present age. One researcher even suggests that the future will be a "naked" one because of the transparencies enabled by such broad proliferation of information (Tucker, 2014). Whole cities may be "data-driven" ones, with a nervous system which informs broad-scale policies (Pentland, 2014). There is much wider access to cloud computing that enable mass analysis of such data. Such datasets, though, have important features to consider. There is higher noise-to-signal ratio due to "the imperfection of the tools we use to measure, record, and analyze information" (Mayer-Schönberger & Cukier, 2013, p. 41). The parameters and protocols for data collection are much less defined with "big data" sets. Often, such data is a byproduct of other processes, such as the electronic "data exhaust "left by people's online interactions. Aiden and Michel (2013) write: "Right now, the average person's data footprint—the annual amount of data produced worldwide, per capita—is just a little short of one terabyte. That's equivalent to about eight trillion yes-or-no questions. As a collective, that means humanity produces five zettabytes of data every year: 40,000,000,000,000,000,000,000 (forty sextillion bits)" (p. 11). Data may be missing from ranges of cells; the data itself may be unstructured and multimodal. There may be false indicators of correlation where none exist simply as an artifact of the analytical methods and tools used with big data. The increased scale suggests that figures are more "probabilistic than precise" (Mayer-Schönberger & Cukier, 2013, p. 35). Causality may be inferred, but difficult to prove. Unexpected findings may be possible based on explorations of "big data". Such large sets also enable not only broad-level analysis but evaluations of single-level record data, or high levels of granularity.

It's a tradeoff: with less error from sampling we can accept more measurement error. When our ability to measure is limited, we count only the *most important things. Striving to get the exact number is appropriate...This type of thinking was a function of a 'small data' environment: with so few things to measure, we had to treat what we did bother to quantify as precisely as possible. In some ways this is obvious: a small store may count the money in the cash register at the end of the night down to a penny, but we wouldn't—indeed couldn't—do the same for a country's gross domestic product (Mayer-Schönberger & Cukier, 2013, p. 13).*

While there has been hype around the "end of theory" given big data, theorizing will likely continue to be an important part of research. Not everything in the world is datafied (rendered into quantitative data). Not all research questions will be solved with big data and its analysis (which generally involves the extraction of patterns and the identification of unexpected anomalies). Lanier (2013) observes that the rigor has not fully be designed for the proper scrutiny and analysis of big data; these would include standards for the documentation of the chain of custody of data (to ensure tamper-free data), the degree of replication of results for validity, and tests to keep "big data scientists from fooling themselves" (pp. 112-113), among others. Big data is used to check historical human assertions (Aiden & Michel, 2013).

UNGUIDED AND GUIDED ELECTRONIC RESEARCH JOURNAL STRUCTURES

At its simplest level, a research journal records the research. The recording may be in the form of simple measurements. It may be in the form of basic narrations and thoughts. Optimally, such journals should be reflective of actual processes. One researcher describes how "problem-solving experiences are fraught with failed attempts, wrong turns, and partial successes that move in fits and jerks, oscillating between periods of inactivity, stalled progress, rapid advancement, and epiphanies" (Liljedahl, 2007, p. 661); in many ways, there is a deep "discordance between process and product" in problem-solving (Liljedahl, 2007, p. 662), and the same may be said for research. Research journals may include more formal elements like field notes, interviews, imagery, and other artifacts from the field. This multimedia set helps understand individuals in a research context.

Unstructured and Self-Organizing

This section offers some proposals for structures or "guides" for electronic research journals. These are listed broadly from unstructured to structured. This shows that there are many different ways of providing angles to the journal structuring. The ultimate and varied purposes of research journals will guide their structure and evolution.

An Organic and Emergent Approach

A totally unstructured journal allows the researcher(s) the freedom to evolve a journal organically, based on whatever seems relevant at the times of the journaling. Such an approach assumes that information will emerge in a self-organizing way, and based on the conditions of the research and the approach of the researcher, there may be an emergent form or formlessness or something in-between.

In work places, people record ideas on their mobile devices, calendars and day planners, white boards, sticky notes, digital audio recorders, and other places. They may have various drafts of a presentation or chunk of writing; these may show the in-between states of evolving works. Having a research journal may enable them to single-source ideas related to their research as well as peripheral but related ideas. They may jot down ideas on how to improve their work. There may be snippets of ideas they come across in their readings that they want to revisit. They may have identified leads that they want to pursue later. They may want to

record notes on a particular issue. They may have discovered more nuanced or effective ways to use technologies, or they may have come across a glitch in the technology. All of these observations may be recorded.

They may draft out imagery that they will develop later. Research journals may be used for various purposes. Another common usage may be as a "sounding board" to engage their ideas and to use the journal for catharsis.

Technological Structuring

Another type of guidance involves technology enhanced tools that may partially guide or shape a research journal. One may be a frequency-based probe to remind researchers to update their research journals. Regular recording may better capture the immediacy of real-time work. This chronicling may capture information that is relevant only in retrospect but may have seemed mundane or banal at the moment. Retroactive journaling may miss a lot of particular details and be influenced by the research outcomes. Technologies may offer a range of tools to enable various types of information recording and captures of researchers' thoughts and work.

Some tools (based on shared work sites) may automatically capture data and record meta-data; other tools are opt-in ones that may be selected for researcher convenience. Some socio-technical spaces (STSes) may enable the sharing of team members' research documentation with others. Some STSes offer ways to structure data and to visualize the relationships between data.

There may be more ad hoc sorts of documentary structures for project sharing. Social media may offer venues for both small and large team collaborative work. These collaborations may be loosely or tightly structured. One example is Twitter™, a microblogging site. Figure 3, "The GitHub Social Coding Social Network on Twitter, is a visualization of the online members of this loosely structured community. This visualization

Figure 3. The GitHub social coding social network on Twitter

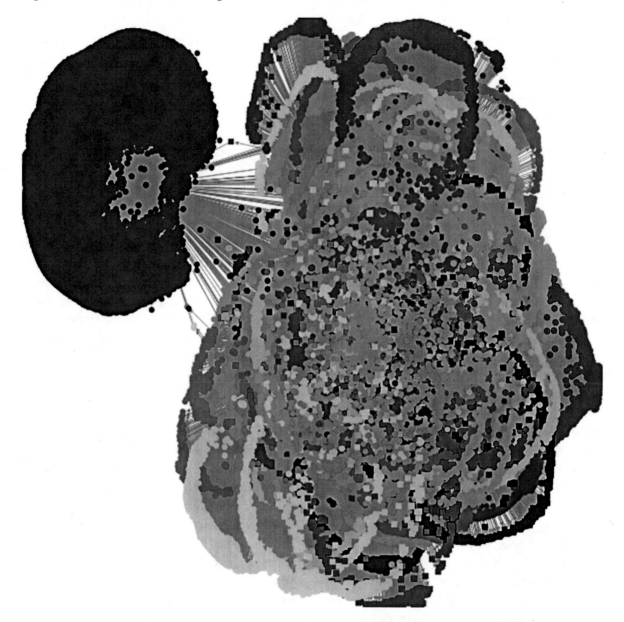

captures both some of those whom the GitHub site is following and some of its followers. At the time of this data crawl, there were 2,537 Tweets to this account, with 177 following and 151,651 followers. This directional capture was enabled by NodeXL, the Network Overview, Discovery and Exploration for Excel tool. The parameters of the capture are two degrees, with a 9,999-persons limit. Given the brevity of the microblogs (144 characters), this social media platform offers thin journaling. The GitHub site on Twitter is located at https://twitter.com/github. This social network is captured in the graph drawn from the data based on the Fruchterman-Reingold force-based layout algorithm. An extraction of the clusters found 22 clusters, with the one on the left as a central one connecting the disparate sub-cliques indicated by the various shapes and colors of the sub-networks to the right.

The graph metrics table shows 32,877 vertices (nodes), with fairly high connectivity through 53,342 unique edges (links). There were no self-loops or self-referential vertices. The diameter of the graph is 4, which suggests that any two nodes are at most three hops away (as indicated by the average geodesic distance) from the furthest other node. The graph density is 4.9, which suggests that the connectivity between vertices may be strengthened with even more inter-connectivity.

Classic Chronologies

Straight Calendar-Day Chronology

A classic approach to research journaling usually involves a straight chronology of the research. Here, researchers rely on their expertise to know what to observe or not. These generally do not have any "guided" or directed structure except time. And even then, often times, researchers may not regularly write entries into their research journal.

The affordances of software tools (like learning management systems, data analysis and management systems, and others) that enable the organization of multimedia may mean that various types of files may be intermixed for the chronological electronic journal: digital audio recordings of thoughts after an interview or at the end of the day; video podcasts of the researcher speaking into his or her mobile device or laptop; smart phone video of field work; formal videotaped interviews; text entries; digital imagery; and any number of other contents. There may be screencasts of interactions with a website or a software program. There may be datasets. There may be data extractions from various websites.

An innovation on this traditional approach is to include a pre-and post-research aspect to these research journals. The pre- and post- may cover ground not traditionally addressed in research journals. For example, the pre-research journal may include reviews of the extant literature and broad hypothesizing. The post-research journal may include a post-project assessment, ideas for new research, and other analyses.

Chronology of Research Project Phases (with Analytical Questions or To-Do Lists)

To enhance the structured journal that uses a project-based work chronology, it may help to spell out a typical project phasing—and enhance the image with questions designed to enhance research rigor. It is helpful to evaluate the phases as recursive until certain processes are locked in; however, if there are still challenges with the research, even a locked process may have to be halted for adjustments and a re-start.

Table 1. Graph metrics of the GitHub social coding social network on Twitter

Graph Metric	Value
Graph Type	Directed
Vertices	32877
Unique Edges	53342
Edges With Duplicates	4
Total Edges	53346
Self-Loops	0
Reciprocated Vertex Pair Ratio	0.03427951
Reciprocated Edge Ratio	0.066286743
Connected Components	1
Single-Vertex Connected Components	0
Maximum Vertices in a Connected Component	32877
Maximum Edges in a Connected Component	53346
Maximum Geodesic Distance (Diameter)	4
Average Geodesic Distance	2.982229
Graph Density	4.93531E-05
Modularity	Not Applicable
NodeXL Version	1.0.1.245

In Figure 4, "A Recursive Chronology of Research Project Phases for Both Single- and Team-Based Researchers," there are five basic recursive steps to the research: 1) Pre-research, 2) Literature review, instrumentation, and research, 3) data, 4) presentation, and 5) wrap-up. In addition to these steps, those working on teams (indicated below) would have to set up their teams, define their roles, develop shared understandings, and setup shared technologies. Finally, ideally, they would also have a team de-briefing during the wrap-up phase. To understand the value-added in this conceptualization, it would help to understand what questions may be considered during the journaling in each phase. The questions offered here are minimalist and generic, with the understanding that nuanced questions will be added for value.

1. Pre-Research
- What does the researcher want to know? How is this information possibly knowable?
- What research questions are being considered? Why? What would the potential relevance be of this research?

- What are some of the main findings from the pre-research literature review?
- What do professionals in the field suggest might be a rewarding line of inquiry?
- What work has been done in the field that may offer insights for research? What theories may apply?
- What are some typical research methods? What are their respective strengths and weaknesses?
- What are some unique approaches that may be taken to approach this question?
- What standards will be used for the work? (What is the basis for this authority?)
- What are possible concerns of the review board for the research? How may these issues be addressed or mitigated?
- What are the guidelines for the grant funding? What are the requirements for the research based on the funding agencies?
  - 1T. Team Setup:
    - Ideally, what skill sets would be included on the team? Which of these would be available within

Figure 4. A recursive chronology of research project phases for both single- and team-based researchers

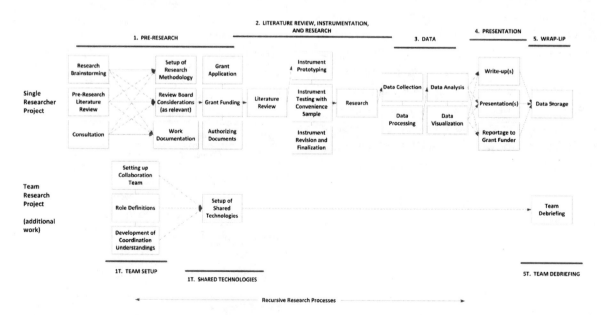

the organization, and which from outside the organization (if necessary)?

- Who would be available for the team?
- How will the team collaborate? How will they communicate?
- Will there be some redundancy in terms of skill sets? Will there be cross-trainings for greater team resilience?
- How will decisions get made?
  - 1T. Shared Technologies:
    - What technologies will be used for collaboration? Communication? Record-keeping?

2. Literature Review, Instrumentation, and Research

- Where are the various sources of relevant information (in any form) that may be collected for this research work?
- From the research, what is relevant, and what is not relevant? What is peripherally relevant and should be considered for possible inclusion?
- What must a thorough literature review include?
- What are some fresh insights related to the research?
- What themes are not appearing in the collected data?
- What information is not being collected?
- Are there ways to improve the research?
- What research methodology should be used to collect primary information?
- How will the research be bounded and delimited?
- Is this research methodology suitable for the learning context? Why or why not?
- What sort of instrumentation should be created for this research?

- Is there instrumentation that covers the same ground already? Or is there overlap in instrumentation?
- How should the instruments be designed to elicit the data needed?
- How should the instruments be designed to be as objective as possible?
- How should the instruments be designed to make data analysis as efficient as possible?
- Does the instrument enable the confirmation or disconfirmation of the hypothesis or hypotheses? If the hypothesis were false, would the instrument be able to indicate that? If the hypothesis were true, would the instrument be able to indicate that?
- What sort of testing should be done to try to validate / invalidate the instrument?
- What are the standards for validation?
- Who would comprise a convenience sample audience to test the prototype instrument?
- How can the instrument be kept secure and private until it is used and / or published (or released)?
- What revisions and adjustments need to be made to the instrument to ensure that it is valid?
- How should the research be conducted in order to be as valid and objective as possible?
- Have all possible reasonable approaches to research been considered?
- Does the team have the expertise and resources to carry the research?
- What weaknesses in the design have emerged during the actual research? Are there ways to improve the research on the fly? Or if not, are there ways to improve the research in the future?
- Are there gaps in the research? Are there gaps in the data collection?
- Are participants' interests being protected before, during, and after the research?

- Are ethical standards being followed at every step? Are there any gray areas in terms of ethics?

3. Data

- What comprise the collected data?
- Have all the data been effectively collected? Have the data been effectively analyzed?
- How complete is the collected data? If there are holes in the data, are there ways to close the gaps (such as with additional information collection or with new ways to exploit the already-collected data)?
- What is the quality of the data? How can one tell what the quality of the data is? If the data is insufficient quality, are there ways to rectify that—by including a larger sample size or making other adjustments? (Or should the findings be written to reflect the limits)?
- How relevant is the collected data? Are there ways to improve the data quality?
- What are more effective ways to gather information?
- What are effective ways to scrub the data for clearer analysis?
- What anomalous data have been discovered? How may those anomalies be addressed?
- What sorts of logic have been applied to the data? Is the logic solid?
- Have researcher biases been addressed? How so? Have these elements been sufficiently addressed?
- Do new research or analytical instruments have to be created? If so, how, and why? What features will these instruments require?
- What sorts of validation processes would these instruments have to go through, and why?
- Do existing instruments have to be revised? Why? Why not?
- How should the data be processed? Why?

- In terms of data analysis, how effective is the current approach? What are ways to improve this?
- Is every bit of informational value being exploited with the collected data?
- What sort of logic is applied to the analysis of the data? If inductive logic is applied, are the generalizations and extrapolations from the evidence warranted? If deductive logic is applied, are the syllogisms tight and accurate? Are there logical fallacies of any sort?
- Are the conclusions accurate or not? Why or why not? Are there ways to qualify the findings to be more accurate?
- Is there sufficient clarity to promote clear understandings of the data and to avoid negative learning (or misdirections)?
- What sorts of data visualizations are possible with the data? How accurate are the data visualizations? Are there ways to improve the clarity of the data visualizations?
- What do the data structures look like? What insights do these data sets offer?
- Based on the data, what are ideas for follow-on research? For new research?

4. Presentation

- What are the most salient points from the research? Why? What is not so relevant? Why?
- How does the new research relate to the extant published data in the field? Does this agree with prior work or not? In terms of nuanced differences, what are they?
- What are proper venues for the sharing of this research?
- Who are the potential audiences who might be interested in the research?
- What should be shared about the research?
- What should be held back about the research? How may the information be held back from others' exploitation, if needed?
- What may be held in reserve for future research?

- Are there ways to offer multiple perspectives on the research through multiple publication and / or presentation channels?
- Should the instrumentation be publicly shared or not? If yes, what level of sharing should be done, and what is the proper venue?
- Are there implications for new practices (in-domain, out-domain, and / or cross-domain) based on the research?
- Who should be acknowledged in the publications and presentations? Why?
- What should be reported and shared with the grant funder?
- How will the participants be notified about the release of the research data?
- How will they benefit from the work in which they participated?

5. Wrap-Up
- Where and how will the information be stored for the time limit required by professional ethics and contractual understandings?
- What are some possible future research directions?
- Were there intriguing anomalies on the periphery of the research that would bear further exploration?
- What are some possible hypotheses that may come from the research results?
- What are ways to improve the research? What are some counterfactual possibilities in the research? What could have been done differently?
  - 5T. Team Debriefing:
    - What may be learned from the research team members for future work?
    - Were there benefits for all the team members from the project? Did they advance professionally?

- What was the quality of work relationships at the end of the project?
- What new skills were acquired by the team? What new learning occurred?
- Are there possible follow-on presentations?
- Are there possible follow-on research?

This highly structured observation approach could focus on quality issues based on virtually every work facet. The questions could be reworked for various projects. Additional questions may be brought to bear.

To support these questions at the various project phases, various analytical and cognitive structure "tools" may be built into the research journal template. For example, there may be quality checklists or rubrics. To aid in decision-making between various options, there may be comparison tables. To aid in analyzing sources, there may be a structure for an annotated bibliography (with a summary and analysis of each of the sources). If there are research work sequences, there may be decision trees and timelines. There may be the uses of lists—to delineate research sources—for example. There may be spatial diagrams (like cluster charts) showing inter-relationships. The research journaler himself or herself may write tests for various aspects of the research: there could be test questions for source credibility, for example. There may also be to-do sections or lists for researchers to address. A "to-do" list is less directly analysis-based than questions, but they still may provide some prompt for the research journal entries.

Topical Structures

A topic-based structuring method for research journals may be built around categories of information. For example, there may be a collection of all materials for a literature review. This may not be linked to a particular work phrase as literature reviews may actually occur at every phase of work from the pre-research through the research and even post-research (since so many areas of study continue between projects). Another folder may contain datasets of a certain types. Another could contain various visualizations. Or topics may be various subject-based ones based on particular categories within a subject domain. There may be a folder for theories and another for practical applications. `

Maybe research journaling is done at the time each individual contributes some work to the respective folder. The journaling may just involve the inclusion of a note or metadata. The level of elaborateness to the journaling may vary based on the needs of the team (and the proclivities of the various team members).

Bureaucratic Structures

Perhaps another approach to structuring a research e-journal could be based on the bureaucratic organization based on various teams (or the various individuals by roles) and their project-based objectives. In this sense, depending on the structures of the work teams, journaling could then occur on a micro-team by micro-team basis.

A shared journal could be created in a shared socio-technical space, and the team members may be aware of each other's roles and project contributions. If there are shared problems, various members of the group could come forward and problem-solve in real time. The recorded files or information may also be used as a searchable space with information to advance the work.

Other Research E-Journal Structure Variations

In addition, the above structures may be adjusted for various research contexts. The time period of

the journaling may be one adjustable factor. Another may be the selection of elements to include or exclude.

Longitudinal and Multi-Year Research Journaling

Longitudinal and multi-year journals may be maintained over time especially about a long-running project or related multiple shorter-term projects. The power of capturing information over time may enable deeper analysis of information and comparability over time. Such journals may enhance institutional memory, so that understandings are not so "lossy" (tending to lose or forget or mis-remember information; information entropy).

A "Human Limits" and Mitigations Rumination

Another approach may involve using a general checklist of human limits to be reviewed every so often during a project, with observations recorded. A rough checklist could look like the following, based on perception, cognition, and decision-making.

Partial or Selective "Modular" Structures

Another approach to an electronic research journal may be using a journal part that is strategically or tactically useful. After all, the creation of a research journal requires energy and investment. If that work does not offer a clear benefit, then it generally should not be pursued (although those who believe in serendipity would argue that comprehensive journaling efforts may turn up surprising insights that may have been unforeseen). Approaching research journaling as a partial journal may open up the usefulness of the tool. For example, a journal may be used only to explore research methodology: its sources, its hypotheses, its design (both the one used and others considered and discarded), its data results,

Table 2. A (partial) checklist of human limits in perception, cognition, and decision-making

Human Limits	Research Countermeasures
Perception	
Perceptual illusions Human brain interpolation of sensory details Selective perception based on attention Human denial (or magical thinking) Projection and transference Others	Ego extenders (technological and otherwise) Multiple observers Training for saliency Meta-awareness Others
Cognition	
System 1 vs. System 2 thinking Logical fallacies Confirmation bias Cognitive dissonance Self-deception Ego protection Availability heuristic Subconscious anchoring Ideomotor effect Halo effect Woozle effect Premature closure Option fixation WYSIATI (what you see is all there is) Hindsight bias Denominator neglect Exceptionalism Planning fallacy Others	Training to apply System 2 thinking when necessary Logical reasoning Seeking disconfirming information Broad research Encouragement of cognitive dissonance Encouragement of disfluency Rigorous definitions of terms and variables Deploying testable hypotheses Acceptance of indeterminacy Training in counterfactual logics (and limitations) Encouragement of researcher self-doubt Training in identification of cognitive biases Sideshadowing Awareness of actual information provenance Training in breaking priming and other skewing effects Training in researcher objectivity and non-bias Maintenance of broad options (and avoidance of any early commitment or premature closure) Continual open-mindedness Understanding of contingencies through counterfactuals Expanding imagination through counterfactuals and mental or thought experiments Application of base rate analysis Restraint of human ego Applying a multiplier effect to estimating investments in projects Promoting rest and fitness to combat cognitive overload Revisiting and testing paradigms and assumptions Encouragement of creativity in theorizing, analysis, and method Others
Individual and Group Decision-Making	
Impulsivity Hot state Groupthink Mimicry Abilene paradox Anti-patterns Real-world undecidability Emotion and mood influences Others	Moving to cold-state decision-making Using non-hierarchical groups Role assignment including those serving as "devil's advocates" Eliciting feedback privately Avoiding rushes to solutions Seeing past the familiar Meta-cognition Emotional intelligence Others

its data analysis, and then a project post-mortem. The ambit of a journal may be narrow or broad or somewhere in between.

This prior listing offers a partial typology of framing or contextualizing structures that may be used in research journals. These are described in very barebones ways as a way to start readers thinking about possibilities without constraining them. Many other structural approaches exist. How these conceptual structures work out in the real will depend on the work of other researchers and organizations. Professional groups may have a role in deciding conventions for such journaling, particularly if the uses of these become common practice in research. Until there is a sufficiently broad level of access to various types of research journals (as stand-alone units-of-analysis or as parts of corpuses), which may be studied en masse, other research journal patterns (whether defined a priori, or organic or emergent) may not clearly emerge in an empirical way.

Possible Venues for E-Journal Distribution to Stakeholders

Many contemporary research journals that have been created are relegated to obscurity because they are not shared more broadly. While these journals may have impacts on the research, their effects are generally elusive. These field texts may provide contemporaneous value in a field if they can be shared more broadly and are findable (and searchable). To that end, it may be important to incentivize not only the creation of research journals across many fields but to encourage their sharing by making it part of the publication process, by rewarding that behavior with prestige, and by showing how research journals provide larger-scale benefits beyond the particular research. Figure 5, "Anticipated Stakeholders to Public Electronic Research Journals," identifies a number of stakeholder groups who could benefit from public sharing.

The core beneficiaries are conceptualized as the researcher or research team at the center because of their improved meta-cognition and application of critical thinking skills to the research. The discipline of maintaining a research journal forces a researcher or a research team to think and re-think what they are doing iteratively and in various contexts and over time. Their work stands to benefit, even if they engage in "data hoarding," which has been described as leading to "data divides". More peripherally, clockwise, the other potential beneficiaries are the following: other researchers (in-domain, out-domain, and cross-domain); innovators; students, novices, and amateurs; historians and analysts; journalists and reviewers; and instructors, teaching assistants, and research assistants.

To elaborate, researchers may acquire new research techniques or insights. Innovators may discover ideas on how to move an innovation from research into the world. Students, novices, and amateurs may acquire new field knowledge; inspiration; and directions for study and research. They may glean understandings of the many layers of policies they must adhere to as professional researchers; they may gain a sense of the messiness of data; they may understand the limits of computation; they may get a sense of the complexities of collaborating with colleagues on research; they may gain some tactics for situating their work for appropriate attention in publications and at conferences. These published research journals may be used in communities of practice to offer entre into a particular topic or to add depth to a formal research work (by offering an immersive perspective into research). Historians and analysts may be able to probe research journals for deeper understandings of researchers and their work, as well as the nuanced details and atmospherics surrounding that work. Informational value may be machine-gleaned as well, with machine-based text analysis of individual research journals, domain-level research journals, or even cross-domain journals. Journalists and reviewers may learn more about research and carry those understandings into their work to benefit the public. (Reviewers could consider factors like the writing voice, the workflow and decision junctures, research methodologies, and the power of insights.) For the broader public, they may gain clearer understandings of the nature of research work, with a

Figure 5. Anticipated stakeholders to public electronic research journals

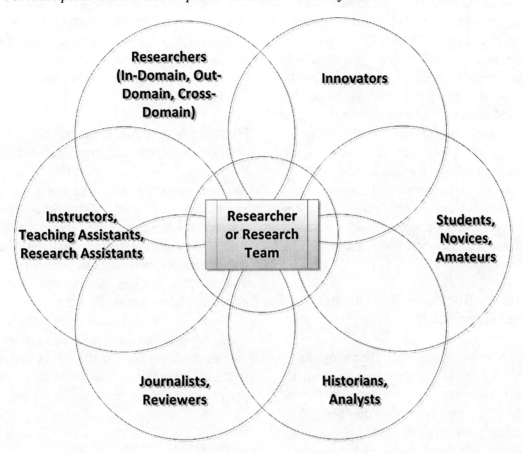

de-mythifying-of-expertise function. Instructors, teaching assistants, and research assistants may improve their instruction and curriculum development through research journal insights. If there are so many potential beneficiaries of the release of such information, what are some ways to collect and disseminate electronic research journals?

Co-Release of Research Journals with Formal Publications

In both "hard science" and "social science" fields, datasets (quantitative data, text-based corpuses, video-taped sessions, digital photo sets, and others) are often co-published or co-released to the public with the acceptance and publication of a formal research paper. Science and research are about sharing information and encouraging structured debates and variant interpretations of data through claims and counter-claims. These datasets are often lightly processed for data clarity (such as the elimination of outlier records that skew the data or the elimination of noisy data). Fellow researchers may use these data sets to verify researcher results; they may analyze the data for other insights; they may extrapolate methodological understandings from analyzing the data sets. Corpuses or sets of documents are also released as training sets to test new algorithms or software programs. Researchers are working on methods to archive and share qualitative data sets with the sufficient amount of metadata documentation for contextual depth (Cliggett, 2013, p. 2). In the same way, electronic research journals could be made available to a broad public readership at the time of formal publication. These may be considered addendums or complements to the formal publications, with value for those who are conducting similar research. Another venue for informal publication of research journals could be in the appendices of electronic publications. (Less formal artifacts from research projects are often featured on project websites, including memos, group minutes, notes, schedules, and other less formal work files.)

An Online Electronic Research Journal Repository

Another potential channel would be through dedicated repositories of electronic research journals. In the same way that journals are used for formal discourses in particular subject domains, Web-accessible repositories could offer opportunities for informal discussions of research approaches. These could offer opportunities to study research methods to various researchers, students, and amateurs. The informality of some journals may provide a lower barrier to research work than highly stylized and rigorous published papers and slideshows.

Is it possible that there could be an informal value to research journals as artifacts of the research process as field texts? Could these authentic objects benefit the novices and amateurs looking to enter a field or to participate in research? Could these be insightful resources into the minds of leading researchers in various fields? Are there ways to study the value-added from having access to research e-journals? Would these possibly find

an academic or other broader audience? Further still, is it possible to incentivize the creation of such research journals (beyond improving research quality and researcher insights) by offering a venue for research journal publication and academic sharing?

Research Journal Sharing on Individual Professional Web Sites

Another venue for sharing research e-journals may be individual professional websites, on which researchers often share publications, curriculum vitae (CVs), and datasets. An additional feature may be their publication-related research journals. The interplay between these various texts may reveal helpful work-based insights.

There are certainly other potential ways that research e-journals may be released to broader publics, both peers in the field, in peripheral fields, in unrelated fields, and then just the wider potential general audiences.

POTENTIAL CONCERNS AND LIABILITIES

Practically speaking, it is important to consider when research e-journaling makes sense because this does entail work. The core assertion of this chapter is that a research e-journal may offer a mirror to the researcher to show strengths and weaknesses; with the ideas of human tendencies in terms of perception, cognition, and decision-making, such e-journals may offer ways to highlight areas for improvement and research accuracy. The default state of not recording research insights means much useful information may be lost to both the present and to history. The creation of such journals, though, is not just about the individual maintaining a private and protected self-communication. There are benefits in releasing such research e-journals to broader publics for their learning and insights.

To summarize, the following figure engages some of the asserted pros and cons to maintaining a research e-journal—that goes into public release. Some of the "bones" go in both directions. For example, investment of effort is a cost, but it's also a pro because it enables the researcher to hone his or her skills more effectively. Likewise, having a record of the researcher's thinking and voice is both a pro and a con to reputation, depending on the contents of the research e-journal. Figure 6, "Some Potential Pros and Cons to Maintaining and Publishing a Research E-Journal (A Fishbone Diagram)" reveals some of the potential benefits and risks of publishing research e-journals.

Ownership Questions

Once a research journal has been created, it may be used for means beyond what the researcher may have initially intended. It may offer multi-use information. For example, it may be subpoenaed for court cases. Depending on the policies at various institutions of higher education and private industry, the research journals themselves

may not belong to the author. If institutions or businesses have interests in the journal contents, and they have legal standing, they may actually "own" these journals. Legal ownership may be enforced whether or not a journal is released for public consumption.

Release to the Public?

A core question for research journalers will be whether to release their work to the public or not. It's likely that journals that are released to the public will have to be redacted or revised for public consumption to align with privacy protections, intellectual property protections, and other regulations. This will mean additional work. The release of even a redacted journal may be challenging. For example, creating a journal that will eventually be released to the public may mean that the journaler may be more self-conscious and self-editing when recording the ideas in the journal. By nature, research e-journals will contain a range of issues that may include vulnerabilities to the researcher / writer: conceptual challenges, methodological struggles and paths not taken, messy data, personal struggles with learning, and difficult professional relationships. Given these vulnerabilities, the journal contents may be

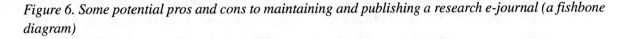

Figure 6. Some potential pros and cons to maintaining and publishing a research e-journal (a fishbone diagram)

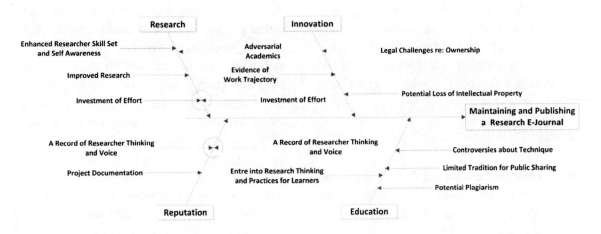

fundamentally affected with the engagement of the research journaler's inner critic, which limits what is shared publicly. Researchers will have to consider whether it is in their interests to broadly share their research journals, particularly if these contain ideas for future research or other contents. Premature release of information may result in a loss of competitive advantage. Further, for many researchers, releasing a research journal may result in unnecessary vulnerability; they are opening up a professional flank. [Similarly, "re-studies" of released datasets have occasionally challenged initial results or interpretations (Cliggett, 2013, p. 1)]. In present-day computer mediated communications, with online polylogue contexts, academic discussions may include "blunt criticism or insults," often without hedging strategies (Luzón, 2013, p. 112). The tradition of adversarial academics in which various researchers call each other out and challenge each other's research methods, findings, and data interpretations, may mean that many are disincentivized against sharing research journals. This cultural reality may require a change in academic culture at least in some parts of academia. Academic practice usually involves researchers and authors receiving critique from two sources: known and trusted professional networks and double-blind peer reviewers. Another concern of releasing research journals to a public readership involves possible interference with the creativity and independent thinking required of many researchers. Ideas may be released too soon to the public, in unformed states. Going public may dissipate the researchers' limited attention towards handling generalized public responses. To summarize: Public releases of research e-journals make sense to a degree in certain contexts about certain topics.

Limited "Defined Group" Release

Clearly, another option involves the limited release of research journals to limited audiences, in a semi-embargoed and semi-restricted state. Here, access is controlled and limited to certain individuals who are read-in the research. The rationale here is that some individuals could benefit from the information without releasing the information into the broader publics, which may create undesirable additional vulnerabilities.

FUTURE RESEARCH DIRECTIONS

This chapter proposes the use of research journaling to improve research quality by raising issues of human limitations to the awareness of the researcher throughout the research process. The research journal may be potentially more applicable in some research contexts than others—such as in contexts of the need for high research reliability. This journaling is conceptualized as a generic journal, with some factors emphasized over other elements, depending on particular research needs. It is conceptualized as a tool that may enhance the breadth of a researcher's repertoire by encouraging mindful reflection related to the work.

Very little direct research has been done on either non-structured or structured research e-journals. On a more foundational level, very little has been done on the study of research journals in any form. In terms of future research directions, a range of angles and contexts may be evaluated: the roles of research journals in particular fields of study; in particular types of quantitative, qualitative, and mixed methods research; in application by particular researchers; across various domains, and in broad-scale cross-domain studies. There may be analyses of various types of organic and designed structures that may be particularly useful for certain purposes. There may be studies of technological advancements that enhance research journaling, in computer automated, semi-automated, and non-automated ways. There may be in-depth analyses of particular research cases.

Clearly, theoretically and practically, there should be some actual beneficial value to the research journal information. Without new learning and without fresh insights, research journaling would be a waste of time. To settle the questions of whether to maintain a research e-journal and how, it would help to identify the recorded ideas that turn out to be valuable (and to whom) and to know how those ideas advanced the research (and its quality), increased efficiencies, or promoted learning (as in educational applications).

CONCLUSION

The work of qualitative and mixed methods research is continually evolving, with new methods coming online for attaining knowledge in a variety of fields. Those who would maintain a portable skill set that could apply to a variety of contexts would do well to continually learn and hone their tradecraft. For many, a way to stay reflective and sharp may involve maintaining electronic research journaling before, during, and after the research work. (Some would say that the research work never ends, and researchers live and breathe the work at every moment.) While qualitative and mixed methods work require rigor, no work is ultimately definitive; no one has the power of the last word. Truths are constantly evolving, and a one-degree change in perspective involves fresh insights.

For some, the maintenance of an electronic research journal may be considered extraneous to the work; the recorded observations may seem mundane. The focus on the minutiae of research and decision-making may seem to be an endless loop of concerns, without clear progress. However, that is not the point of a research journal. A research journal has a critical role in helping the researcher and others understand a project. If used correctly, it may enhance researcher skills and aptitude. It may increase the accountability of a researcher or of research teams to their various clients; it may dissuade researchers from self-indulgence in their mental denials and very human perceptual and analytical shortcomings. The investment in this endeavor is not to add inefficiencies to the process but to enhance the validity of the research and to increase researcher fitness, foremost, by helping researchers mitigate their ineradicable limitations in perception, cognition, and decision-making. A research journal offers ways for people to systematize the research for increased accuracy and analytical depth. It helps researchers be more aware when they should invest more effort into research or analysis instead of going with the *status quo*. Here, it is suggested that researchers in qualitative and mixed methods research would benefit from this tool because of the criticality of the researcher role in these contexts. In addition, the creation of guided or structured electronic journals may enhance their efficacy, particularly for certain projects and certain purposes. The broad publication of electronic research journals is seen to benefit the broader publics and stakeholders connected to the research domain and beyond.

Creativity is "relational" and in that aspect requires a long time for innovations to percolate through different communities of research, observes Andrew Abbott. Abbott (2004) has observed, "You can easily be too radical for an audience" (p. 111). There is a chance that the creation of research journaling to mitigate human limitations may be too radical for some fields. These endeavors may be a little too far beyond the interests of practitioners in particular areas of research or domains. Even so, the concept seems to be worth considering, and there are some benefits that may be gained from its practice.

ACKNOWLEDGMENT

This is in memory of both ASJJ, who first started me off on the path of learning, and HCJ, who taught me to go for broke. This is for R. Max, who "pressure-tests" all assumptions both professional and personal.

REFERENCES

Abbott, A. (2004). *Methods of Discovery: Heuristics for the Social Sciences.* New York: W.W. Norton & Company.

Aiden, E., & Michel, J.-B. (2013). *Uncharted: Big data as a lens on human culture.* New York: Riverhead Books, Penguin.

Ball, P. (2004). *Critical Mass: How One Thing Leads to Another.* New York: Farrar, Straus and Giroux.

Bendix, R. (1984). Rationalism and Historicism in the Social Sciences, Force, Fate, and Freedom. Berkeley, CA: University of California Press.

Berg, B. L., & Lune, H. (2012). *Qualitative Research Methods for the Social Sciences* (8th ed.). Boston: Pearson Publishers.

Bilalić, M., McLeod, P., & Gobet, F. (2008). Why good thoughts block better ones: The mechanism of the pernicious Eistellung (set) effect. *Cognition, 108*(3), 652–661. doi:10.1016/j.cognition.2008.05.005 PMID:18565505

Cliggett, L. (2013). Qualitative data archiving in the digital age: Strategies for data preservation and sharing. *Qualitative Report, 18*(1), 1–11. Retrieved from http://www.nova.edu/ssss/QR/QR18/cliggett1.pdf

Dixon, J. E., & Byrne, R. M. J. (2011). 'If only' counterfactual thoughts about exceptional actions. *Memory & Cognition, 39*(7), 1317–1331. doi:10.3758/s13421-011-0101-4 PMID:21547605

Fine, C. (2006). *A Mind of its Own: How your Brain Distorts and Deceives.* New York: W.W. Norton & Company.

Gawande, A. (2009). *The Checklist Manifesto: How to Get Things Right.* New York: Metropolitan Books.

Geiger, J. (2009). *The Third Man Factor: Surviving the Impossible.* New York: Weinstein Books.

Goleman, D. (2006). *Social Intelligence: The New Science of Human Relationships.* New York: Bantam Books.

Greenspan, A. (2013). *The Map and the Territory: Risk, Human Nature, and the Future of Forecasting.* New York: The Penguin Press.

Heath, C., & Health, D. (2007). *Made to Stick: Why Some Ideas Survive and Others Die.* New York: Random House.

Henshaw, M. (2012). *The Red Cell: Fact and Fiction.* Spycast. International Spy Museum. Retrieved Dec. 28, 2013, at http://www.spymuseum.org/multimedia/spycast/episode/the-red-cell-fact-and-fiction/

Herbert, W. (2010). *On Second Thought: Outsmarting your Mind's Hard-Wired Habits.* New York: Crown Books.

Hernandez, I., & Preston, J. L. (2013). Disfluency disrupts the confirmation bias. FlashReport. *Journal of Experimental Social Psychology, 49*(1), 178–182. doi:10.1016/j.jesp.2012.08.010

Herriman, N. (2010). The great rumor mill: Gossip, mass media, and the ninja fear. *The Journal of Asian Studies*, 69(3), 723–748. doi:10.1017/S0021911810001488

Heuer, R. J., Jr. (1999). *Psychology of Intelligence Analysis*. Center for the Study of Intelligence. CIA. Retrieved Aug. 30, 2013, at https://www.cia.gov/library/center-for-the-study-of-intelligence/csi-publications/books-and-monographs/psychology-of-intelligence-analysis/PsychofIntelNew.pdf

Hiemstra, R. (2002). Uses and benefits of journal writing. *New Directions for Adult and Continuing Learning, 2001*(90), 19 – 26. Retrieved on Aug. 9, 2013, at http://onlinelibrary.wiley.com/doi/10.1002/ace.17/abstract

Huang, H. H., Hsu, J., & Ku, C.-Y. (2012). Understanding the role of computer-mediated counter-argument in countering confirmation bias. *Decision Support Systems*, 53(3), 438–447. doi:10.1016/j.dss.2012.03.009

Johansson, F. (2012). *The Click Moment: Seizing Opportunity in an Unpredictable World*. New York: Portfolio / Penguin.

Kahneman, D. (2011). *Thinking Fast and Slow*. New York: Farrar, Straus and Giroux.

Lai, T.-L., & Land, S. M. (2009). Supporting reflection in online learning environments. In M. Orey, et al. (Eds.), Educational Media and Technology Yearbook (pp. 141 – 154). DOI 9. doi:10.1007/978-0-387-09675-9

Lanier, J. (2013). *Who Owns the Future?* New York: Simon & Schuster.

Lebow, R.N. (2009). Counterfactuals, history and fiction. *Historical Social Research / Historiche Sozialforschung*, 34(2), 57 – 73.

Liljedahl, P. (2007). Persona-based journaling: Striving for authenticity in representing the problem-solving process. *International Journal of Science and Mathematics Education*, 5(4), 661–680. doi:10.1007/s10763-007-9092-9

Loewenstein, G. (2005). Hot-cold empathy gaps and medical decision-making. *Health Psychology*, 24(4), 549–556. doi:10.1037/0278-6133.24.4.S49 PMID:16045419

Luzón, M. J. (2013). 'This is an erroneous argument': Conflict in academic blog discussions. *Discourse. Context and Media*, 2(2), 111–119. doi:10.1016/j.dcm.2013.04.005

Mayer-Schönberger, V., & Cukier, K. (2013). Big Data: A Revolution that will Transform How we Live, Work, and Think. Boston: Houghton Mifflin Harcourt.

Merritt, A. C., Effron, D. A., & Monin, B. (2010). Moral self-licensing: When being good frees us to be bad. *Social and Personality Psychology Compass*, 4/5(5), 344–357. doi:10.1111/j.1751-9004.2010.00263.x

Merton, R. K. (1987). Three fragments from a sociologist's notebooks: Establishing the phenomenon, specified ignorance, and strategic research methods. *Annual Review of Sociology*, 13(1), 1–28. doi:10.1146/annurev.so.13.080187.000245

Michaels, C. F., & Carello, C. (1981). *Direct Perception*. Englewood Cliffs, NJ: Prentice-Hall, Inc.

Mitchell, M. (2009). *Complexity: A Guided Tour*. Oxford, UK: Oxford University Press.

Nielsen, M. (2012). *Reinventing Discovery: The New Era of Networked Science*. Princeton, NJ: Princeton University Press.

Ormiston, M. E., & Wong, E. M. (2013). License to ill: The effects of corporate social responsibility and CEO moral identity on corporate social irresponsibility. *Personnel Psychology*, 66(4), 861–898. doi:10.1111/peps.12029

Pariser, E. (2011). *The Filter Bubble: What the Internet is Hiding from You*. New York: The Penguin Press.

Pentland, A. (2014). *Social Physics: How Good Ideas Spread—The Lessons from a New Science*. New York: The Penguin Press.

Pollack, K. M. (2013). *Unthinkable: Iran, the Bomb, and American Strategy*. New York: Simon & Schuster.

Pomfret, M. P., & Medford, J. L. (2007). Affective domain: Journaling. In R.J. Seidel, K.C. Perencevich, & A.L. Kett (Eds.), *From Principles of Learning to Strategies for Instruction with Workbook*. Springer. Retrieved Aug. 7, 2013, at http://link.springer.com/content/pdf/10.1007%2F978-0-387-71086-0_12.pdf

Sieck, W. R., Merkle, E. C., & Van Zandt, T. (2007). Option fixation: A cognitive contributor to overconfidence. *Organizational Behavior and Human Decision Processes*, 103(1), 68–83. doi:10.1016/j.obhdp.2006.11.001

Silver, N. (2012). *The Signal and the Noise: Why so Many Predictions Fail—but Some Don't*. New York: The Penguin Press.

Spellman, B. A., & Mandel, D. R. (1999, August). When possibility informs reality: Counterfactual thinking as a cue to causality. *Current Directions in Psychological Science*, 8(4), 120–123. doi:10.1111/1467-8721.00028

Takeda, P. (2006). *An Eye at the Top of the World: The Terrifying Legacy of the Cold War's Most Daring Operation*. New York: Avalon Publishing Group.

Taleb, N. N. (2010). *The Black Swan: The Impact of the Highly Improbable* (2nd ed.). New York: Random House.

Taleb, N. N. (2012). *Antifragile: Things that Gain from Disorder*. New York: Random House.

Tasler, N. (2008). *The Impulse Factor: Why Some of Us Play it Safe and Others Risk it All*. New York: Fireside, Simon & Schuster Publishers.

Tetlock, P. E., & Belkin, A. (1996). Counterfactual thought experiments in world politics: Logical, methodological, and psychological perspectives. Princeton, NJ: Princeton University Press.

Trivers, R. (2011). *The Folly of Fools: The Logic of Deceit and Self-Deception in Human Life*. New York: Basic Books.

Tucker, P. (2014). *The Naked Future: What Happens in a World that Anticipates Your Every Move?* New York: Current, Penguin-Random House.

Varki, A., & Brower, D. (2013). *Denial: Self-Deception, False Beliefs, and the Origins of the Human Mind*. New York: Hachette Book Group.

Wickens, C. D. (2002). Multiple resources and performance prediction. *Theoretical Issues in Ergonomics Science*, 3(2), 159–177. doi:10.1080/14639220210123806

ADDITIONAL READING

Fine, C. (2006). *A Mind of its Own: How your Brain Distorts and Deceives*. New York: W.W. Norton & Company.

Gawande, A. (2009). *The Checklist Manifesto: How to Get Things Right*. New York: Metropolitan Books.

Goleman, D. (2006). *Social Intelligence: The New Science of Human Relationships*. New York: Bantam Books.

Kahneman, D. (2011). *Thinking Fast and Slow*. New York: Farrar, Straus and Giroux.

Silver, N. (2012). *The Signal and the Noise: Why so Many Predictions Fail—but Some Don't*. New York: The Penguin Press.

Taleb, N. N. (2010). *The Black Swan: The Impact of the Highly Improbable* (2nd ed.). New York: Random House.

Taleb, N. N. (2012). *Antifragile: Things that Gain from Disorder*. New York: Random House.

Varki, A., & Brower, D. (2013). *Denial: Self-Deception, False Beliefs, and the Origins of the Human Mind*. New York: Hachette Book Group.

KEY TERMS AND DEFINITIONS

Abilene Paradox: A form of groupthink in which a group ends up going with a collaborative decision which a majority of its members individually would not have pursued, often due to the erroneous assumption by the individuals that their ideas are not shared by others.

Antifragile: A phenomena that becomes more robust in times of turmoil or chaos.

Availability Bias: The ease with which ideas come to mind (leading to the individual to assume that his or her ideas are accurate).

Backshadowing: A mental exercise in which contemporary peoples assume historical actors should have known certain historical outcomes and used those in their decision-making.

Big Data: A complete data set, an "n" of "all," large-size datasets with millions of records or more.

Ceteris Paribus: All things being equal.

Cognition: Human mental processing, including short-term and long-term memory, learning, and executive functions; System 1 and System 2 brain systems.

Cognitive Dissonance: The resulting mental or emotional discomfort while holding two or more apparently contradictory concepts.

Cognitive Illusion: A mental shortcoming in human thinking that leads to errors in judgment.

Cold State: A state of emotional non-arousal.

Confirmation Bias: The privileging or acceptance of information that tends to align with one's preconceived notions or mental models.

Corpus: Body or set of contents, data set of documents.

Counterfactual: The conceptualization of an alternate reality that is contrary to facts.

Datafication: Rendering real-world phenomena into data or information.

Denial: The unconscious suppression of threatening or painful information from the conscious mind in order to enable humanity to function; also known as "magical thinking".

Denominator Neglect: The ignoring of actual probabilities to a situation.

Disfluency: An interruption in cognitive ease due to conflicting or contradictory information through the use of language, concepts, narratives, or facts.

Dyssemia: Difficulty sending and receiving nonverbal communications cues necessary for social interactions.

Ego Depletion: A state of low self-control or will power due to limited mental resources.

Electronic Research Journal: A collection of digital files that are used to document a research project or multiple research projects.

Emotional Tag: A mental association between a stimulus and a physiological affective state though to be critical to human decision-making.

Epistemology: A philosophy-based understanding of the nature of knowledge and methods of knowing.

Fetishize: To obsess over a phenomenon; to show irrational fascination with a particular thing or concept.

Field Text: Various journals, notes, letters, interviews, and stories used to inform the understanding of human sense-making through narration.

Fox: A type of decision-maker (according to Philip Tetlock) who learns broadly and across domains and knows numerous small details (instead of just specializing in one area); this decision-maker tends to be tolerant of uncertainty and complexity and variant opinions; he or she tends to qualify claims and not to over-claim.

Groupthink: The tendency of a group to coalesce around a particular idea even without thorough vetting due to the tendency for people to want to agree.

Guided: Structured, directed.

Halo Effect: The tendency to use one impression (whether perceived as positive or negative) to inform on an unrelated other factors, a cognitive bias.

Hedgehog: A type of decision-maker who specializes and is described as one who knows only one big thing in his or her domain of expertise; this decision-maker tends to be ideological and poorer at prediction than "foxes".

Heterophily: An appreciation for differences between people.

Hindsight Bias: The illusion that the past was predictable with 20-20 hindsight.

Hot State: A state of emotional or affective arousal.

Human Factors: Cognitive, affective, physical, and other properties of people.

Impulsivity: A tendency to have low self-control, a proclivity to taking action without consideration of the consequences, a lack of self-discipline.

Instrumentation: Tools created for research measurement.

Metamer: A color that appears identical to another but which actually has a different spectral composition.

Mimicry: The act of copying another person.

Mirror: The act of near-synchronous miming others' bodily movements, expressions, tempo, and communications during a social interaction, in conscious or unconscious ways.

Mixed Methods: A research approach which combines both qualitative and quantitative research.

Narrative Analysis (Narrative Inquiry): A qualitative research approach which uses field texts including written matter from people's lives to show how they create meaning through narratives.

Overfitting (a Model): The tendency to indicate too many parameters or variables in a model as related to the empirical research.

Perception: The intake and interpretation of sensory information.

Perverse Incentive: The structuring of a policy or action that has unintended (and often counterproductive) consequences or effects.

Polylogue: Involving multiple speakers or communicators.

Portfolio: A collection of objects; variations include "digital portfolio" or "electronic portfolio" to indicate a collection of multimedia objects.

Priming: Various methods of using stimuli or cues to condition a human memory response (an unconscious sensation, thought, or attitude, for example) in a subsequent exposure to a stimulus.

Prototype: A mock-up or sample or model.

Qualitative Research: A range of research techniques based on relativist and interpretive assumptions of the world that involve the study of human experiences and decision-making; often case-based research.

Quantitative Research: Empirical study of phenomena based on both *in vivo* ("in the living" or from the world) and *in vitro* ("within the glass" or in a laboratory, usually based on the experimental method involving hypothesizing, experiment design, and pre- and post-intervention observations) studies and analysis involving statistical, mathematical, and / or computational techniques.

Reification: The making real of an abstract thing or idea based on its naming when there may be no reality or basis-in-fact of that phenomena.

Reliability: The repeatability of a study.

Satisficing: A portmanteau word of "satisfy" and "suffice" suggesting achieving satisfaction once reaching a basic (minimal) threshold.

Selective Attention: The concentration on particular details to the exclusion of others.

Sideshadowing: A mental exercise of considering what could have happened in a historical event based on a sense of plausible likelihoods (as a counter against the human bias for seeing foreshadowing in indeterminate situations).

Somatic Marker (Emotional Tag): A mental association between a stimulus and a physiological affective state, such as skin conductance or increased heart rate, thought to play an important role in human decision-making and choice-making.

Underfitting (a Model): The tendency to indicate too few parameters or variables in a model as related to empirical research.

Validity: A state of accuracy and logical soundness.

Woozle Effect ("Evidence by Citation"): The buildup of broad misunderstandings based on citations of unfounded research or other ephemera.

WYSIATI ("What You See Is All There Is"): A cognitive illusion known as "what you see is all there is," a kind of narrow framing that leads to misconceptions.

Section 2
All–Environments Information Collection

Whether the research occurs in physical space or online, or both, technologies enable high-fidelity information capture. The work of data acquisition in its various forms is an important part of research. Information and Communication Technology (ICT), broadly speaking, is important for information recording in real spaces and intercommunications, surveying, and data extraction in cyber spaces. Section 2 addresses some creative ways technologies are used for information collection and reporting for practical uses and data research.

Chapter 4
Technologies for Conducting an Online Ethnography of Communication:
The Case of Eloqi

Tabitha Hart
San Jose State University, USA

ABSTRACT

In this chapter, the author describes the technologies she employed while conducting an Ethnography of Communication on Eloqi (pseudonym), a for-profit start-up company that built and operated a proprietary Web-based, voice-enabled platform connecting English language learners in China with trainers in the United States. While Eloqi existed, its unique platform not only connected trainers and students for short one-to-one English conversation lessons but also brought together the company admins, trainers, and students in a virtual community. This chapter describes the technologies that the author used to carry out the qualitative study from start to finish, including the steps of online participant observations, online and offline interviews, qualitative coding, and qualitative data analysis. Because the author studied a virtual community, technologies played a critical role in how she collected, managed, and analyzed the dataset, which was completely electronic. The chapter concludes with tips and advice for fellow researchers using technologies to support qualitative studies of communication, whether online or offline.

INTRODUCTION

Imagine a private language school specializing in EFL (English as a Foreign Language) training. The students attending this school want to use their English language skills to change their lives, whether that means securing a place at a good university, getting a competitive job, or moving forward on their chosen career paths. The trainers want to gain instructional skills and add new experience to their portfolios, while also developing their professional network. The school founders and administrators want to attract sufficient students to turn a healthy profit, while also contributing to the educational field in innovative ways. Such was the case with Eloqi (pseudonym),

DOI: 10.4018/978-1-4666-6493-7.ch004

an EFL school that I studied. What stood Eloqi apart was the fact that it was an online environment, and its different members (admins, trainers, students) never met one another face-to-face. The Eloqi founders built a proprietary web-based, voice-enabled platform to connect students and trainers for one-to-one conversation lessons. Eloqi's only office was located in Beijing, its students were spread all over China, and the trainers were located across the continental United States. Eloqi was a *virtual community*, i.e. a group of people who are relationally involved with one another and share common (to the group) norms, rules, and practices, and who assemble and interact with one another online. (Komito, 1998; Kozinets, 2009; Rheingold, 1993) I engaged in an ethnographic study of Eloqi to learn about that community's *speech code*, or code of communicative conduct, i.e. their norms, premises, and rules for engaging in speech with one another (Philipsen, 1997; Philipsen, Coutu, & Covarrubias, 2005).

Eloqi's Chief Technology Officer, an acquaintance of mine, was interested in and supportive of my research goals. He and his business partner had recently graduated from Stanford University and were excited to build up their new company. Reasoning that my research would help them better understand their own developing company culture as well as their trainers and students, Eloqi invited me to join their team as a researcher-trainer. In my researcher-trainer role I was allowed to teach lessons, attend weekly trainer meetings, socialize with the other trainers, participate in Eloqi's trainer discussion forums, and access the company's growing archive of trainer-student lesson recordings – all online. I actively studied the Eloqi community for 10 months using qualitative methods that included online participation observation and interviews. By the end of my data collection phase I had amassed a sizable assortment of electronic data, including lesson recordings, interviews, fieldnotes, screenshots, and more.

In this chapter I will describe the technologies that I used to collect, manage, and analyze my qualitative data. I will cover the technological configurations that I assembled to support my online participant observations and hold my online and offline interviews. I will describe how I organized and managed my electronic dataset. Finally, I will explain the tools that I used for the data analysis phase, including the qualitative data analysis software that I used for coding, analysis, and reporting. My chapter will conclude with tips and advice for other researchers who are using technologies to support qualitative studies of communication, whether online or offline.

BACKGROUND

My aim in this research project was to identify the Eloqi community's system of rules, norms, and premises pertaining to communicative conduct, i.e. their speech code (Philipsen, 1975, 1992, 1997; Philipsen et al., 2005). For this purpose I employed the Ethnography of Communication (Hymes, 1962, 1972, 1977; Philipsen & Coutu, 2005). The Ethnography of Communication (EC) is a qualitative theoretical/methodological framework distinct from, but closely related to, ethnography. Ethnography, like EC, is geared towards studying human behavior and culture, and is intended to "[reveal that culture] through discerning patterns of socially shared behavior" (Wolcott, 1999, p. 67). What makes EC different is its unique combination of "ethnography, the description and analysis of culture, with linguistics, the description and analysis of language" to produce contextualized analyses of the "relationships between language and culture" (Keating, 2001, p. 285). The EC approach, particularly in combination with theoretical/methodological frameworks like Speech Codes Theory, generates nuanced reports on how members of a given community speak with one another, the rules and values guiding that speech, and the concepts of personhood and society linked with it (Philipsen & Coutu, 2005; Philipsen et al., 2005). The EC approach provides tools for contextualizing such reports with detailed information on what happens in, around, and through speech; it does not separate communication from the context in which it occurs (Philipsen & Coutu, 2005).

Many researchers have examined technology-mediated communication and the multifaceted ways in which people live, work, and socialize in online environments (Baym, 2006; Cassell & Tversky, 2005; Danet, Rudenberg-Wright, & Rosenbaum-Tamari, 1997; Donath, 1999; Miller & Slater, 2001; O'Brien, 1999; Sterne, 1999; Stone, 1995; Turkle, 1995) and there is substantial precedence for using ethnography in this work (Bennett, 2012; Boczkowski, 1999; Boellstorff, 2008; Boellstorff, Nardi, Pearce, & Taylor, 2012; Goodfellow & Lamy, 2009; Hart, 2011; Hine, 2000, 2008; Keating & Mirus, 2003; Kendall, 2002; Kozinets, 2009; Mann & Stewart, 2000; Markham, 1998; Miller & Slater, 2001; O'Connor, Madge, Shaw, & Wellens, 2008; Polson, 2013; Salmons, 2011). There is also a growing interest among communication scholars in using EC's theoretical/methodological approach to study technology-mediated communicative conduct, recently evidenced by the "Talking technology: New connections in the Ethnography of Communication and technology" symposium at the 2013 National Communication Association convention. EC type studies may focus on a number of communication phenomena in an almost unlimited number of technology-mediated spaces. For example, they may be in-depth reports on communication in one particular virtual community (Manning, 2008) or cross-cultural studies of comparable online communities (Hanna & De Nooy, 2004, 2009) They might even be studies of people in offline or hybrid (online plus offline) communities whose linguistic and sociolinguistic practices are impacted by technologies (Keating & Mirus, 2003).

What all of these qualitative studies have in common is that they address "the relationship between symbolic practices and social struc-

ture" (Lindlof & Taylor, 2002, p. 44). That is, the researchers doing this work are ultimately interested in discovering and explaining the connection between communication (in this case, technology-mediated communication) and culture. To determine this connection, these researchers engage in "systematic, comparative knowledge of phenomena and systems" and have the training and ability to make inferences, ask questions, and utilize the data to make sense of situated communication, with no pre-determined answers in mind (Hymes, 1977, p. 170). The situated, highly contextualized, richly descriptive ethnographic approach of EC is a natural fit for understanding online communities and the social interactions that members engage in.

To gather and analyze the contextualized, descriptive qualitative data required for an ethnographic study, multiple methods are very helpful (Brewer & Hunter, 1989). This is particularly true in international, intercultural, and cross-cultural projects where one's cultural assumptions can hinder analysis of the findings and extra measures may be needed to fully test and validate interpretations (Johnson & Tuttle, 1989). Multiple methods help investigators "collect rich, descriptive, contextually situated data in order to seek understanding of human experience or relationships within a system or culture" (Mann & Stewart, 2000, pp. 2-3) as well as "examine different levels of the same situation or to focus on different aspects of the same phenomenon" (Mann & Stewart, 2000, p. 95). The usefulness of multiple methods naturally applies to offline, online and hybrid research sites where fieldwork will be carried out.

Like other ethnographers, EC researchers almost always engage in some type of fieldwork (Keating, 2001; Saville-Troike, 1982) and/or close textual analysis (Coutu, 2000; Edgerly, 2011) to examine naturally occurring speech *in situ*. Fieldwork is critical to EC research because it creates opportunity to examine how contextual factors such as the features of the settings, the relationships between participants, the goals of the speech event, or norms and rules pertaining to the event, are implicated in or constitutive of the communication taking place. For EC researchers immersion in a field site is a critical means of collecting qualitative data on the community and communication in question, and typically generates a substantial, rich, and complex data set comprised of fieldnotes on observations and/or participant observations; interview transcripts; audiovisual recordings (Keating & Mirus, 2003); user-generated digital text (Manning, 2008); images and screenshots; or any combination of these (Gordon, Holland, & Lahelma, 2001; Keating, 2001; Saville-Troike, 1982; Smith, 2001; Wellin & Fine, 2001; Wolcott, 1999).

Considering the size and complexity of ethnographic – especially EC – data sets, it is very helpful to have technologies on hand to support the process of collecting, processing, and analyzing the data. Luckily, there are powerful yet simple and inexpensive tools that serve exactly this purpose, some of which I will describe in this chapter.

A NOTE ON RESEARCH ETHICS FOR INTERNET STUDIES

Studies of virtual communities require careful consideration and planning in regards to research ethics, data collection, and reporting procedures. To inform my decision-making process I used the recommendations from AoIR, the Association of Internet Researchers (Markham & Buchanan, 2012). I approached Eloqi as a private organization and its community as a private online environment because Eloqi's spaces (both physical and virtual) were only accessible to its members. Eloqi considered all interactions across its platform to be proprietary information and recorded them for quality control. The trainers and students had access to all of their own lesson recordings, and

trainers had access to additional recordings of group admin-trainer meetings. For the purposes of my study, Eloqi granted me special access to the trainer-student lesson archive and invited me to communicate with admins whenever I needed to. The Eloqi trainer community was informed that I was studying communication in the organization, and that I held dual researcher/trainer roles. I obtained informed consent for all interviews with Eloqi community members. To further protect the privacy of the community I applied pseudonyms to the company itself and all of its members. Finally, I removed all identifying information from the data so that members would be unidentifiable not only to my readers but also to one another. The University of Washington Human Subjects Division reviewed and approved my research proposal before I began data collection.

TECHNOLOGIES FOR DATA COLLECTION

Because I was approaching my study of Eloqi using the theoretical/methodological lens of EC, I was operating under the belief that the examination of speech requires the examination of socio-cultural structure as well as "pragmatic meaning" (Hymes, 1962, p. 104), i.e. meaning in *practice*, or everyday, real-life meanings attached to speech. Accounts of pragmatic meaning must necessarily look at the larger situations (of activity, of human relationships, of shared histories and experiences) in which speaking takes place. Codes of communicative conduct are not necessarily "visible", comprehensible, or verifiable in only a turn of conversation, or out of context of the interaction in which they are employed. Indeed, an ethnographic analysis of a community's speech codes is very similar to a traditional ethnography of a culture in that

*the study of culture is formulated out of the pat-
terned behavior of individuals interacting with
other individuals.... The ethnographer looks
at such instances in order to discern recurring
themes, behavior suggestive of underlying templates for action (Wolcott, 1999, p. 260).*

To this end, I engaged in a long-term ethnographic study of Eloqi's community of practice.
This allowed me to collect examples of real
communication between Eloqi's members (admins, trainers and students) and to see that real
communication in its larger context. The fact that
Eloqi was mostly an online community meant that
using certain technology-based data collection
methods was a natural and practical choice. Four
technology-enabled and/or –enhanced data collection methods that I employed were sustained
online participant observation, web-based interviews with Eloqi trainers, in-person interviews
with Eloqi students, and procuring digital audio
recordings of trainer-student lessons from the
web-based Eloqi archives.

Technology-Supported Online Participant Observation

When doing participant observation a researcher
enters the field site to both participate in and
observe social interactions, thus learning by doing. This process enables the researcher to make
better sense of situated meanings, learning more
deeply about the experience of the research participants themselves (Frey, Botan, & Kreps, 2000;
Saville-Troike, 1982; Wolcott, 1999). Regardless
of what technologies or means of communication the informants are using, the corpus for an
EC study must provide information on speaking
in context (Hymes, 1962, 1972, 1977; Lindlof
& Taylor, 2002; McDermott, Gospodinoff, &
Aron, 1978). That is, the corpus should contain
not merely transcripts of speech, but data on the
place, time, and circumstances in which that
speech took place, and its cultural, social, and

historical aspects. "[To] participate is to know
enough about the rules for interaction and movement so that movement and interaction with and
within this space is possible" (Markham, 1998,
pp. 23-24). My online participant observation at
Eloqi, which I conducted for 10 months, allowed
me to learn the appropriate rules for interaction
in this virtual space.

The *participation* component of my technology-supported ethnography was intensive,
demanding, and time-consuming. As an Eloqi
trainer I attended weekly trainer conference calls
and worked weekly shifts. During the conferences calls and shifts I actively followed the talk
going on in the trainer chat room, and I joined in
synchronous and asynchronous discussions with
other trainers by posting questions and comments.
As per my trainer duties I took regular live, one-
to-one calls from Eloqi students, during which I
used the company's lesson plans and materials
to help the students with their English conversation skills. I also stayed up to date on the Eloqi's
teaching modules, completing new ones as they
were released so that I could qualify to teach the
lessons associated with them. At the same time
that I was engaging in these activities, I was also
collecting data (notes, conversation transcripts,
screenshots) meaning that I was always multitasking, collecting and processing information while
also engaging in the routine tasks that went along
with my role as a trainer.

A typical participant observation session
for me involved two levels of technology-based
concerted work. The first level was to fulfill my
duties as a member of the Eloqi trainer team. In
this capacity, I took part in the routine activities
prescribed by my role. Once I had committed to
a shift, I made arrangements to be in a quiet place
with a stable Internet connection for the duration
of the shift. About fifteen minutes before the start
of my shift I would sit down at my laptop, switch it
on, and open up a virtual machine using VMWare.
The Eloqi platform ran on Windows but not on
MacOSX. Since I use a Mac, I needed to install

a virtual PC – essentially a computer inside a computer – on my laptop. Once inside the virtual machine I used a web browser to navigate to the Eloqi trainer portal, where I logged in using my unique username and password. Inside the portal I navigated to and entered the Eloqi chat room. Inside the chat room I could see and exchange instant messages with the supervisors on duty as well as all the other trainers working the shift. In addition to being inside the chat room, I also initiated a version of the company's special software, called the Trainer Client (TC), which I kept on my virtual desktop. The TC was the platform for the lessons between the Eloqi trainers and the students and served as the virtual classroom where the trainers and students met one another. Finally, I made sure to have word processing software (Microsoft Word) open and running for the purpose of jotting down notes and impressions. From inside the Eloqi virtual space I waited for student calls to come in. In the meantime, I followed and participated in the discussions going on in the trainer chat room.

Whenever a student call came in to me I'd accept it and proceed with the call using the lesson screen, which initiated automatically and provided a trainer script correlating with the particular lesson that the student had chosen. Like all the other trainers I taught each lesson by following the prompts and guidelines that appeared on my screen.

At the conclusion of the lesson I wrote up the required qualitative feedback for the student, closed the lesson window and returned my attention to the chat room. Finally, at the end of my shift I bade my fellow trainers goodbye, logged out of the chat room and the trainer portal and closed all related windows.

The second level of work was collecting data simultaneous to engaging in my trainer work routine. Although I could have recorded all of the activities on my laptop by using third-party

Figure 1. Desktop with Eloqi TC and chat room

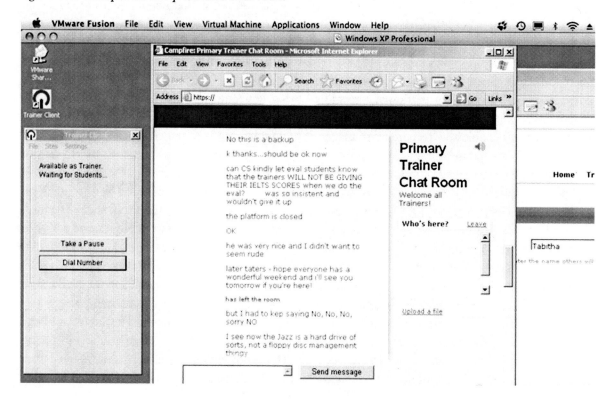

Figure 2. Eloqi lesson screen

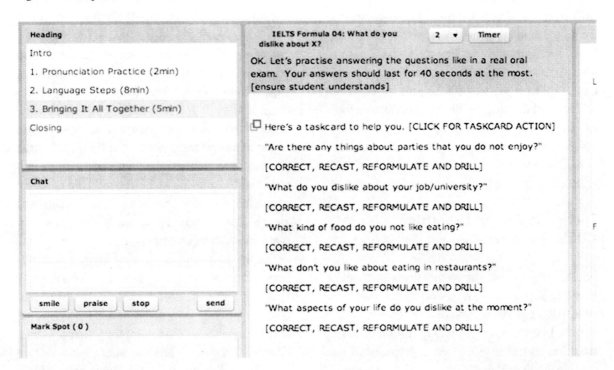

screencasting software, I was on a limited research budget and so opted to use a combination of two tools that I already had: word-processing software and screenshot capture shortcuts. It wasn't necessary for me to audio-record my lessons with the students because Eloqi did this as a matter of course with all of the trainers, and I had access to the lessons through the Eloqi cloud-based archive (more on this later).

The word-processing and screenshot tools were very easy to use. For each of my participant observation sessions I created a new blank document, which I continually kept open on my screen beside my other open windows. Into this blank document I typed notes and jottings while I was working, and pasted text from other open windows (for example, conversational turns from the trainer chat room). During my work sessions I didn't bother to format or edit this document in any way; rather, I concentrated on simply getting information into it. At the same time, I periodically created screenshots of the activities in the open

windows by using my operating system's built-in key combination. By holding down the required keys on the keyboard I created snapshots of my screen, a window, or an area that I selected. The snapshots were instantly saved as images (png files) on my desktop.

After the end of each shift I followed the guidelines of Emerson, Fretz and Shaw (1995) to expand the jottings and notes saved in the Word document into full fieldnotes. Doing this while my memory was still fresh allowed me to recall and document the maximum amount of detail and description. When it seemed important, I also embedded copies of relevant screenshots into my fieldnotes as reference. Otherwise, I simply renamed each screenshot according to the conventions I had adopted for this project (more on this later) and filed them away.

The tools that I used to document my online participant observation in this phase of the project were simple and easy to use. The challenge was actually in doing simultaneous technology-based participation and data collection. A normal trainer shift was by default an intense experience because it entailed managing multiple time-sensitive tasks in different windows. Adding on the extra component of data collection made it even more demanding. The advantage was that all activity happened on a virtual desktop enabled with effective tools for quickly and effectively capturing information. The fact that the information captured was already in electronic format was another time-saver, as I will describe later in this chapter.

Technologies for Procuring Audio Recordings

For this project it was important to procure and/or generate digital audio recordings whenever possible. Although I took copious notes during speech events, I could never accurately jot down all of what was said; even on my best days I probably lost thirty percent or more of utterances when relying only on my own note taking. What's more, my notes alone could not capture paralinguistic cues such as interviewees' volume, pitch, inflection, intensity, speed, or silence. Because such nonverbal cues can convey important meaning, it was desirable to have accurate recordings. Finally, recordings allow for the creation of transcripts, an important addition to a qualitative dataset. Since I was interacting with my research participants online and offline, and both in-person and remotely, I needed a variety of recording solutions. Ultimately I relied on three different technology-based configurations for collecting audio recordings: (1) Skype-based interviews with third-party recording software for remote interviews, (2) a portable hardware set-up for in-person interviews, and (3) downloads from the company's cloud-based archive of trainer-student lesson recordings. A description of each follows below.

Skype-Based Interviews and Third Party Recording Software

All of the Eloqi trainers worked directly from home and were spread across the continental United States. Given budgetary and time restrictions, it was not practical or even possible for me to meet the trainers in person. Luckily, because of the nature of their work with Eloqi, all of the trainers were highly skilled with web-based communication, so using an online meeting platform to conduct the interviews with them was a natural choice. Specifically, I selected Skype as the primary medium of communication.

Skype is a communication service that utilizes Voice over Internet Protocol (VoIP). VoIP is essentially a means of enabling a telephone-type experience over the Internet, whereby an Internet-enabled device (laptop, smart phone, tablet) is the phone and the Internet connection is the line (Bertolucci, 2005). When using Skype from computer-to-computer, there are no restrictions on where in the world users can be located. Skype's good sound quality is one of the features that makes it so popular (Max & Ray, 2006). Using Skype is free of charge when users are connecting computer-to-computer over the Internet. The basic software can quickly and easily downloaded from the Skype website. An additional benefit of Skype is that it includes an instant messaging (IM) function with which callers can text one other before, during, or after the voice call. Skype also supports live video (users must have a functional webcam) and file transfer (callers can send files to each other using the platform).

To use Skype computer-to-computer, each party needs to have a device on which the software is loaded (a laptop, tablet, smart phone, etc.) as well as a fast Internet connection. For most of my interviewees this wasn't a problem, since they either already had Skype installed, or were open to downloading it and using it with me. In these cases, we used the free version of Skype to connect computer-to-computer.

Some of my interviewees, however, either wanted me to call them on their phones or preferred to call me themselves. Neither of these scenarios posed a problem using Skype. To accommodate them, I subscribed to two of Skype's additional, for-cost services. First, I purchased a subscription to Skype's "Unlimited US and Canada" service, which lets you place an unlimited number of calls to landlines in the United States and Canada. With this service I could log in to Skype, select the "call phones" function, and easily call the phone number that my interviewees had given me. For those interviewees who wanted to call me themselves, I set up an online Skype number. With an online Skype number you essentially rent a phone number from Skype. The phone number can be associated with one of 25 countries. I rented a US American number, meaning that the international code of my number was "1" and I had a three-digit area code, just like any phone number in the United States. To receive calls placed to my online Skype number, I needed to have a device loaded with Skype switched on (in this case, my laptop), and I needed to be connected to the Internet with the Skype software running. If any of these conditions were not met and someone attempted to call my online number, they would not have been able to connect with me. Instead, their call would have gone to my Skype voice mail account, which came with the service.

Overall Skype proved to be a good match for interviewing the Eloqi trainers. A challenge of using technology-mediated communication tools can be the degree of computer literacy that you and your participants have (Mann & Stewart, 2000). However, since members of Eloqi's trainer pool were accustomed to using Internet-based communication tools to connect with colleagues and students, it was appropriate to conduct the interviews through similar channels. Many of the trainers were already veteran Skype users, and those who were not were already familiar with Eloqi's similar platform, which combined VoIP with interactive text. Because of this, downloading and using Skype was a simple matter for them. For those interviewees who either wanted me to call them or wanted to call me themselves, Skype became an invisible (to them) platform supporting our calls. Skype also offered flexibility in choosing our physical locations for the interviews, provided we all had a device and an Internet connection (when we used Skype for computer-to-computer calls) or at least a phone line (when we used Skype-to-phone or phone-to-Skype calls).

Using Skype was not problem-free. During peak hours (typically the late afternoons and early evenings, after people across the United States had finished work) the sound quality degraded. Skype's IM feature does allow users to exchange text messages with one another instantaneously, and these text messages are automatically recorded on a users' profile, allowing you to go back and read them (or analyze them) after the fact. However, since relying on text messages was not ideal for my purposes, when Skype's sound quality became too poor to continue I either re-established the connection using Skype-to-phone (which could also have poor sound quality) or rescheduled the interview altogether.

Despite the occasional traffic and sound quality issues, Skype proved to be a convenient and cost-effective means of conducting the trainer interviews. The greatest advantage to using Skype was that I could easily record the interviews using third-party software. For this project the additional software that I chose was Audio Hijack Pro, a program that can record any sound file that is being played on or generated by the computer on which it is loaded. There are numerous software choices for recording Skype calls, but I opted for Audio Hijack Pro because it was reasonably priced (USD $32) and, most importantly, was Mac compatible. Once Audio Hijack Pro was installed on my laptop, I simply opened it up and selected the application that I wanted to record from (in this case, Skype). During interviews I could click "record" and "pause" as with a physical recording device. At the end of each interview, the recording was saved to my hard drive as an MP3 file, which I could then play back on my laptop using VLC media player, and transcribe using Word.

Portable Hardware for In-Person Interviews

Through support from the University of Washington Graduate School and the University of Washington Department of Communication I was able to fund a trip to Beijing, during which time I conducted individual face-to-face interviews with Eloqi students. Prior to the trip Eloqi helped me in creating a suitable interviewee pool, ensuring that all of the candidates were located in Beijing and that they felt comfortable holding the interviews in English. Using email and phone calls to make arrangements, the students and I met in public places all around the city in locations convenient to them. As I quickly learned, Beijing is enormous – the city's total area is nearly 7,000 square miles – and so traveling to different parts of the city for interviews was a serious undertaking.

Given that I was carrying my own equipment and using public transportation to cover a very large territory, it was important to have portable, lightweight equipment for recording the student interviews. A smartphone or tablet with sophisticated all-in-one functionalities (audio- and video-recording, camera, note-taking) would have been perfect; at the time, however, I did not have such a device and couldn't have afforded to purchase one. Instead, I used what I had: a music player (iPod Touch) loaded with free built-in voice recording software (Apple's Voice Memo) fitted out with an inexpensive external microphone (MityMic). On the plus side, the music player was small, very portable, and had good battery life. The software was easy to use, and the digital recordings were

easily transferred to my laptop. The external microphone was small but powerful and picked up voices effectively, even with the inevitable background noise of our meeting places. The downside to this set-up was that the music player had only one audio jack, so I could either plug in the microphone *or* my earbuds, but not both. This meant that I couldn't do sound checks during the interviews. Instead, I had to record a sample, stop the recording, pull out the microphone, plug in my earbuds, play back the recording to check its quality, and then reinitiate the interview.

Downloading from the Eloqi Cloud-Based Archive

Eloqi routinely recorded each trainer-student lesson for quality assurance purposes. At the conclusion of each lesson, the platform generated an audio recording (about 2.7 megabytes each) which was instantly stored as a compressed digital audio (mpg) file in an archive on the company server. Eloqi granted me password-protected access to the archive of recordings, of which there were tens of thousands. I used the archive's search features and my selection criteria to sort through the lessons. Ultimately I downloaded 130 recordings and transcribed about half of them for final analysis.

TECHNOLOGIES FOR DATA PROCESSING AND MANAGEMENT

One advantage of building an electronic dataset is that, with careful planning and organization, it can be mined for future projects. It is therefore important to create a durable, navigable system for archiving, storing, and sorting through electronic data in their both their raw and coded formats. This section will describe the tools and technologies that I used processing and managing the qualitative Eloqi dataset.

Data Storage

By the end of the data collection phase, I had amassed a sizable collection of files, all of them digital. My first order of business was to securely store these data and to ensure that all files were neatly organized in a way that allowed me to quickly find what I needed, when I needed it. I saved everything on my laptop and backed it all up onto a portable external drive. Although I did carry my laptop with me (to work, on trips, etc.), the external drive remained safe in my home. To further enhance security I made both devices password-protected. To organize the data I developed a simple naming protocol that included the data type (interview, fieldnotes, trainer-student lesson, screenshot, etc.), the date that the lesson or observation took place, the time that the data were generated (if applicable, as with screenshots), and participant name (where relevant). Some filenames following this protocol were:

- Interview_student_20091012_Lucky.
- Interview_trainer_20091012_Jessa.
- Fieldnotes_20100122.
- Lesson_20091204_JessaLucky.
- Screenshot_20091204_0944_chatroom.

After naming files I placed them in folders by file type; i.e. all interviews stored in a file called "Interviews," all fieldnotes stored in a file called "Fieldnotes," etc. All of these files were nested under one master project data file.

Data Processing

At this point I was still working with a variety of file types, including images (png) text (Word documents), and audio recordings (MP3), so the next step was to convert all the data to a usable format. This meant transcribing the audio recordings of the interviews and trainer-student lessons, and then converting all project files to rtf or pdf for use with my qualitative data analysis software.

Transcribing Audio Recordings

At the end of my data collection phase, I had collected roughly 150 separate audio files of trainer-student lessons, trainer interviews, and student interviews. Of these I fully transcribed about 50 files comprising 30 hours of talk. There are now interesting software options on the market to support transcription by easing playback and inserting hyperlinked time codes. Inqscribe, for example, is a relatively new Mac compatible transcription program. At the time of this project, however, limited choices and funds meant that I selected software that I already had access to. For audio playback I used VLC, a free program for playing multimedia files. To type up the transcripts I simply used Microsoft Word. To create the transcripts I opened both programs and kept their two separate windows open, side by side. I played back the audio recording while simultaneously typing up the transcription. I transcribed the talk verbatim, and for some sections where it seemed important I also included Jeffersonian notations (see Atkinson & Heritage, 1984) to preserve audible paralinguistic information. While this configuration certainly eased the process, there is no way around the fact that transcribing talk is an arduous, time-consuming task, particularly when including additional notations. The one great advantage of transcribing talk from scratch is that it enables the researcher to engage in a close reading of the data, which is a useful precursor to the analysis phase of the research (Lapadat & Lindsay, 1999). To create a basic transcription without notations, I generally needed about four times the amount of actual talk time; that is, 15 minutes of talk took roughly 60 minutes to transcribe.

Converting Electronic Project Files

The final step in the data processing phase was to convert all my project files for use with the qualitative data analysis (QDA) software that I had selected: TAMS Analyzer (more on this later).

Most qualitative data analytic software programs are built to support a limited number of file types. The TAMS version that I was using (4.12b3h) allowed for coding only into rtf, pdf, and jpeg files. Audio and video files could only be used in that version of TAMS for playback – not for actual coding. My preferred format was rtf because rtf files could be edited inside TAMS.

To convert the word documents to rtf, I opened up each file one-by-one and clicked "Save as," then selected rtf as the file type. To convert files into pdfs I used Adobe Acrobat X Pro. With this software you can open any file, click "Print" and then select "PDF" or "Save as PDF." This creates a pdf copy of the original file. An important side note is that with TAMS Analyzer, as with most other qualitative software programs, the files that you import into the program are earmarked only for that program's use. That is, the files that you save and import into the program must never be opened or used again except from within that program. For this reason, it is imperative to avoid importing original documents (or the only set of documents) into QDA programs. Rather, one should always make copies of all original files and import those copies into the QDA program. Original digital files should be kept elsewhere on the hard drive and ideally on a separate device.

SOFTWARE FOR QUALITATIVE ANALYSIS: TAMS ANALYZER

Once the data processing phase was complete, my dataset contained 130 digital audio recordings and 60 transcripts of trainer-student lessons; 7 digital audio recordings and 9 transcripts of student interviews; 12 digital audio recordings and transcripts of trainer interviews; and 10 month's worth of digital fieldnotes and screenshots from my participant observations. The next step was

to import these data into the QDA program that I would use for coding and analysis: TAMS Analyzer (Weinstein, 2008).

I selected TAMS Analyzer primarily because it is free, written expressly for MacOSX, built to support the type of data (electronic text files) that I was working with, and perfectly suitable for use by a solo researcher. Had I been working with other file types, using a different operating system, or coding with other researchers I might have selected a different QDA program. Transana, for example, is highly recommended for video data, ATLAS.ti is excellent for multimedia and geospatial data (but only works on Windows), and Internet-based services like Dedoose are well suited to team projects.

Like other QDA programs, the main function of TAMS Analyzer is to support qualitative coding. Coding can be initiated in TAMS after importing data files into the program. To code you simply open a data file (transcript, fieldnotes, etc.), select a passage/excerpt, and attach a code to it. New codes or families of codes can be created on the fly, and they can be paired with descriptive information to help maintain a record of what the code means. Once codes have been created they appear alphabetically in the "Codes" library for that specific TAMS project, and they can be applied to excerpts from that moment on. Even better, TAMS supports overlapping and nested codes, so any given passage can have multiple codes attached to it as needed.

It is easy to set up *a priori* codes in TAMS, but in keeping with the EC framework, I did not do this. A priori codes are often eschewed in ethnographic studies because of the ethnographer's commitment to avoid "...preconceived categories [which] can blunt the keen edge of observation, ignoring differences important to those in the scene while giving undue importance to categories of less consequence" (Wolcott, 1999, p. 134). EC

Figure 3. TAMS Analyzer coding window with sample code list and coded data

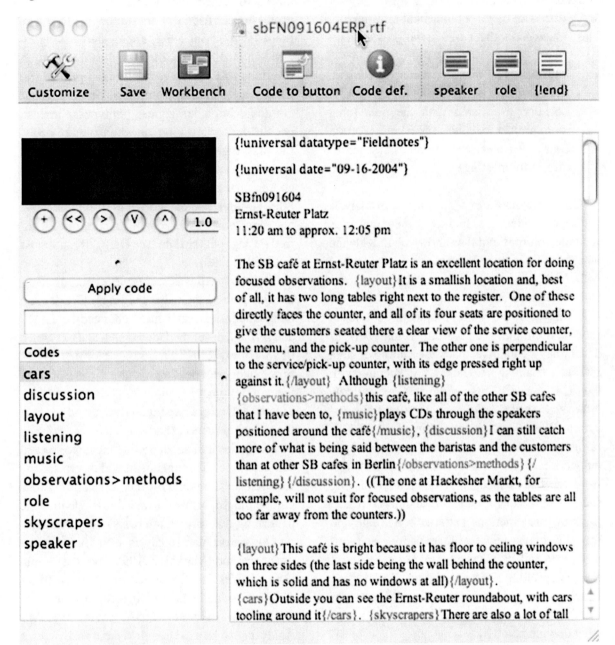

researchers do not generally test predetermined concepts. Rather, in EC studies the researcher is expected to report on the situated realities of the research participants. In other words, one should first describe the situated, contextualized communication as participants experience it (Hymes, 1962, 1972, 1977; Philipsen, 1975, 1992, 1997; Philipsen & Coutu, 2005; Wolcott, 1999).

I did use TAMS Analyzer to apply context codes to the data. Context codes, which can be applied to either excerpts or entire files, allow the user to tag data with meta- or contextual information. The context codes that I used in this project were:

- Informant's role (trainer, student, administrator).
- Location associated with the data (chat room, trainer meeting, lesson).
- Data type (interview, fieldnotes, lesson, forum, team meeting).

Context codes are extremely useful in analysis and report generation. In TAMS they appear as separate columns and thus show you at a glance what contexts your coded passages are associated with. In this way they help a researcher organize and make sense of the coded data.

Using QDA software to attach a code to an excerpt is simple – it's the intellectual work of developing qualitative codes for a complex data set that is challenging. However, in keeping with the EC framework I assumed that there would be discoverable order, or structure, in my participants' communicative activities (Philipsen, 1992). To bring this structure to light, I engaged in analytic induction, which involves "inferring meanings from the data collected, rather than imposing such meanings on the data from another source… [looking] for emerging patterns in the data and [revising one's] tentative formulations as [you] proceed to collect and analyze more data" (Frey et al., 2000, p. 281). "Emerging patterns" implies that structure is discovered organically, as it presents itself in the data and in the informants' reports on what they do and why.

For the first-level (also called open) coding phase I diligently went through each file that I had imported into TAMS Analyzer, reading and rereading the materials line by line. I scrutinized the material for high-inference categories (Lindlof & Taylor, 2002) that pertained to my research questions. As I read I created codes on the fly. These codes ran that gamut from describing specific activities (customer service, grammar, small

talk), to perceived psychological states (nervous, professional, friendly) to problems (technical breakdown, script issue, unpreparedness, tardiness) and many more, including feedback, rules, relationships, scripts, problems, procedural knowledge, self disclosure, sense of place, goals, communication strategies, politeness, impact, encouragement, asking questions, monitoring, multitasking, terminology, patience, status, and misunderstandings. By the end of the first level coding phase I had inductively developed about 80 high-inference categories of communicative behavior, which I subsequently named and identified throughout the data (see Berg, 2001; Strauss & Corbin, 1990).

The next step was second-level coding. During this phase I looked at the original codes and code categories that I had generated in TAMS and refined, developed, described, and explained them (Berg, 2001; Strauss & Corbin, 1990). Some categories dealing with multiple aspects of the same subject I combined, and others, which seemed less relevant to my study, I abandoned. At the end of this phase, I had condensed the original 80 categories into about 45 major categories and sub-categories. Throughout the coding process my research questions and my theoretical framework guided me. In this way I was able to identify the patterning that formed the basis of my findings.

Qualitative data analysis is a messy, non-linear method (Markham, 1998), but the simple yet powerful functionalities of QDA software can be extremely helpful in bringing order to this process. Like other QDA programs, TAMS Analyzer can be used to quickly and easily create codes, and also to change codes names throughout the dataset, create memos attached to codes and excerpts, link files, and view coded passages within the context of the original files. Best of all, when using TAMS you can quickly and easily run both general and specific searches, and generate reports on the search results. For example, I could search for all instances of a particular code and then further sort through, group, and/or narrow those results by data type, date, location, role, etc. Other useful functionalities of the software were the data comparison function, which allows users to examine co-occurrence of codes; the code count function, which helps you generate a list of extant codes along with the number of coded instances for each one; and code count by file, which produces counts of each code per file. In this way, a QDA program can be used to categorize data; sort through coded excerpts; identify connections between code categories; and further analyze the data for patterns and themes.

It is important to note that QDA programs like TAMS Analyzer do not do the analysis for the researcher. Rather, a researcher would use TAMS for finely navigating, sorting through, categorizing and retrieving data in large and complex digital datasets.

TECHNOLOGIES FOR REPORTING

One final point worth noting pertains to anonymizing digital data files for reporting purposes. For the final write up I wanted to use data excerpts as well as selected screenshots (jpeg and png files) in my manuscript. Before including of this data in my reports I needed to anonymize it. With the textual excerpts I needed to change the names of the participants, and with the images I needed to remove all identifying features, including names, usernames, avatars, and logos. To change the names I simply used the find and replace feature in Microsoft Word. This feature is particularly helpful because it shows at a glance how many instances of the searched-for word (or words) appear in the document. Because this information is hyperlinked you can simply click to be taken to any particular instance. To anonymize the screenshots I chose two different Mac-compatible programs: Skitch and Pixelmator. Skitch is free and works on various devices and operating

systems and has limited but useful features for adding text, colorful call-outs, and hand-drawn graphics to digital images. Pixelmator must be purchased but is specifically for MacOSX and has a broad range of sophisticated functionalities. For my purposes, the key task was to erase small portions of the screenshots and then camouflage the blank areas with matching background colors. Once the images had been appropriately edited I inserted them into the final report, which I then printed as a pdf.

REFLECTIONS AND ADVICE

In preparing this chapter I have documented the technologies and related competencies, preparation, and resources used in this particular Ethnography of Communication. The keys to using an array of different technologies to conduct such a qualitative study are mostly foresight and preparation. In this section, I offer some final points of consideration for researchers undertaking similar projects.

- **Project Arrangements:** Are you embarking on a solo project or a team project? If you're part of a research team, do you have access to a shared server where the data and data analytic tools can be stored? If not, how will you share information with one another? If you're using a QDA program, is it built to support team and/or multi-sited analysis? Before selecting any tool or platform for data collection or analysis, make sure that it will adequately support your project arrangements.
- **Data Type:** What type of data (video, audio, text, still images, maps, etc.) do you plan to collect and are your data analysis tools compatible? QDA software packages usually accommodate only certain types of

data. If you wait until after data collection to choose a QDA program, the type of data you have collected will dictate your choice.

- **Compatibility:** Before choosing any type of hardware or software, make sure that it is compatible with the machines and operating systems that you, your research team, and your research participants will be using. Not all programs have cross-platform compatibility and may be limited to particular machines or operating systems.
- **Cost:** Studies of online environments can significantly reduce or even eliminate costs associated with traveling to or living for extended periods in a field site. There are other costs, however, and these need to be anticipated. Is the software free? If not, is it something that you will purchase one time only, or is it subscription-based? Are trial versions available? Are there discounts for students or educators? Will additional hardware be needed to maximize its utility?
- **Usability:** What is the typical learning curve for the tool? Can you successfully pick it up and start using it within your time constraints? What user support (customer service center, online forums, manuals) exists? Who will you and your research participants turn to if there are any problems?
- **Security:** Protecting data is almost always a requirement for Human Subjects approval, which in turn is required for most ethnographic (whether online, offline, or hybrid) research projects. It is therefore critical to have strategies in place for keeping digital files and data secure. Rather than storing data on a personal device (particularly those that are carried into field sites) it might be preferable to have all data on external hard drives that can be locked in the researcher's home or office. At the very least, all devices that hold research data should be password protected.

- **Requirements for Functioning in the Field Site:** What technical knowledge will be required to study your chosen field site and/or engage in fieldwork there? If it's an online environment, what knowledge or skills are required to be competent there? Of course, it isn't always necessary to be competent at the outset, since a legitimate part of ethnographic research is exploring what it means to be competent in the field site, and how members develop or acquire that competency. However it can be challenging when a researcher must balance data collection with functioning productively in the environment under study.
- **Other Knowledge and Resource Requirements:** What special technical knowledge will be required of the researcher to use the array of tools and technologies selected for the project? What requirements will there be for the research participants? For those participants who are communicating via web-based channels, do they have adequately fast Internet access? Will they have to acquire additional hardware or software to participate and, if so, will it cost them anything? Do they feel knowledgeable and comfortable enough to use the proposed communication setup?
- **Reporting:** What sorts of reports (textual, visual, etc.) are needed, and does the technological configuration have the capacity to produce them? How will the data files be anonymized? This is worth thinking about early in a project when there is still flexibility in determining the type of data to collect and the format (digital, analog, image, text) to collect it in.
- **Durability:** Can the coded data files be saved or exported in a format that will be viewable and usable without the original software/tools? If you are using a subscription-based program, what will happen to

the data once the subscription is discontinued? If you switch to a different QDA program, will you be able to import your original data files and/or your coded data?

CONCLUSION

The technologies that I selected to support data collection and analysis for this Ethnography of Communication project allowed me to gain regular access to a virtual community, observe and participate in the activities there, collect information on these experiences, reach out to community members, and make sense of the data that I had collected. Technologies not only allowed for the existence of the Eloqi community, they also enabled me to study it. It was an informative – even transformative – experience that, with preparation and patience, I recommend to my fellow communication studies researchers.

REFERENCES

Atkinson, J. M., & Heritage, J. (1984). *Structures of social action: Studies in conversation analysis*. Cambridge, UK: Cambridge University Press.

Baym, N. K. (2006). Interpersonal life online. In L. A. Lievrouw, & S. Livingstone (Eds.), *The handbook of new media* (pp. 35–54). London: Sage.

Bennett, L. (2012). Music fandom online: R.E.M. fans in pursuit of the ultimate first listen. *New Media & Society, 14*(5), 748–763. doi:10.1177/1461444811422895

Berg, B. L. (2001). *Qualitative research methods for the social sciences* (4th ed.). Needham Heights, MA: Allyn & Bacon.

Bertolucci, J. (2005, September). Net phones grow up. *PC World,* 103-106.

Boczkowski, P. J. (1999). Mutual shaping of users and technologies in a national virtual community. *Journal of Communication, 49*(Spring), 86–108. doi:10.1111/j.1460-2466.1999.tb02795.x

Boellstorff, T. (2008). *Coming of age in Second Life: An anthropologist explores the virtually human*. Princeton, NJ: University Press.

Boellstorff, T., Nardi, B., Pearce, C., & Taylor, T. L. (2012). *Ethnography and virtual worlds: A handbook of method*. Princeton, NJ: Princeton University Press.

Brewer, J., & Hunter, A. (1989). *Multimethod research: A synthesis of styles*. Newbury Park, CA: Sage.

Cassell, J., & Tversky, D. (2005). The language of online intercultural community formation. *Journal of Computer-Mediated Communication, 10*(2).

Coutu, L. (2000). Communication codes of rationality and spirituality in the discourse of and about Robert S. McNamara's "In retrospect". *Research on Language and Social Interaction, 33*(2), 179–211. doi:10.1207/S15327973RLSI3302_3

Danet, B., Rudenberg-Wright, L., & Rosenbaum-Tamari, Y. (1997). Hmmm... Where's that smoke coming from? Writing, play, and performance on Internet relay chat. *Journal of Computer-Mediated Communication, 2*(4).

Donath, J. S. (1999). Identity and deception in the virtual community. In M. Smith, & P. Kollock (Eds.), *Communities in cyberspace* (pp. 29–59). New York: Routledge.

Edgerly, L. (2011). Difference and political legitimacy: Speakers' construction of ''citizen'' and ''refugee'' personae in talk about Hurricane Katrina. *Western Journal of Communication, 75*(3), 304–322. doi:10.1080/10570314.2011.571653

Emerson, R. M., Fretz, R. I., & Shaw, L. L. (1995). *Writing ethnographic fieldnotes*. Chicago, IL: The University of Chicago Press. doi:10.7208/chicago/9780226206851.001.0001

Frey, L. R., Botan, C. H., & Kreps, G. L. (2000). *Investigating communication: An introduction to research methods* (2nd ed.). Boston, MA: Allyn and Bacon.

Goodfellow, R., & Lamy, M. N. (Eds.). (2009). *Learning cultures in online education*. London: Continuum.

Gordon, T., Holland, J., & Lahelma, E. (2001). Ethnographic research in educational settings. In P. Atkinson, A. Coffey, S. Delamont, J. Lofland, & L. Lofland (Eds.), *Handbook of ethnography* (pp. 188–203). London: Sage. doi:10.4135/9781848608337.n13

Hanna, B., & De Nooy, J. (2004). Negotiating cross-cultural difference in electronic discussion. *Multilingua*, *23*(3), 257–281. doi:10.1515/mult.2004.012

Hanna, B., & De Nooy, J. (2009). *Learning language and culture via public internet discussion forums*. Houndmills, UK: Palgrave MacMillan. doi:10.1057/9780230235823

Hart, T. (2011). Speech codes theory as a framework for analyzing communication in online educational settings. In S. Kelsey, & K. St.Amant (Eds.), *Computer mediated communication: Issues and approaches in education*. Hershey, PA: IGI Global. doi:10.4018/978-1-61350-077-4.ch012

Hine, C. (2000). *Virtual ethnography*. London: Sage.

Hine, C. (2008). Virtual ethnography: Modes, varieties, affordances. In N. G. Fielding, & R. M. Lee (Eds.), *Sage handbook of online research methods* (pp. 257–270). Los Angeles, CA: Sage. doi:10.4135/9780857020055.n14

Hymes, D. (1962). The ethnography of speaking. In T. Gladwin, & W. C. Sturevant (Eds.), *Anthropology and human behavior* (pp. 13–53). Washington, DC: Anthropological Society of Washington.

Hymes, D. (1972). Models of the interaction of language and social life. In J. J. Gumperz, & D. Hymes (Eds.), *Directions in sociolinguistics: The ethnography of communication* (pp. 35–71). New York, NY: Holt, Rinehart and Winston.

Hymes, D. (1977). Qualitative/quantitative research methodologies in education: A linguistic perspective. *Anthropology & Education Quarterly*, *8*(3), 165–176. doi:10.1525/aeq.1977.8.3.05x1511c

Johnson, J. D., & Tuttle, F. (1989). Problems in intercultural research. In W. Gudykunst, & M. Asante (Eds.), *Handbook of international and intercultural communication* (pp. 461–483). Newbury Park, CA: Sage.

Keating, E. (2001). The ethnography of communication. In P. Atkinson, A. Coffey, S. Delamont, J. Lofland, & L. Lofland (Eds.), *Handbook of ethnography* (pp. 285–300). London: Sage. doi:10.4135/9781848608337.n20

Keating, E., & Mirus, G. (2003). American Sign Language in virtual space: Interactions between deaf users of computer-mediated video communication and the impact of technology on language practices. *Language in Society*, *32*(05), 693–714. doi:10.1017/S0047404503325047

Kendall, L. (2002). *Hanging out in the virtual pub: Masculinities and relationships online*. Berkeley, CA: University of California Press.

Komito, L. (1998). The Net as a foraging society: Flexible Communities. *The Information Society*, *14*(2), 97–106. doi:10.1080/019722498128908

Kozinets, R. (2009). *Netnography: Doing ethnographic research online.* London: Sage Publications Ltd.

Lapadat, J. C., & Lindsay, A. C. (1999). Transcription in research and practice: From standardization of technique to interpretive positionings. *Qualitative Inquiry, 5*(1), 64–86. doi:10.1177/107780049900500104

Lindlof, T. R., & Taylor, B. C. (2002). *Qualitative communication research methods* (2nd ed.). Thousand Oaks, CA: Sage.

Mann, C., & Stewart, F. (2000). *Internet communication and qualitative research: A handbook for researching online.* London: Sage.

Manning, P. (2008). Barista rants about stupid customers at Starbucks: What imaginary conversations can teach us about real ones. *Language & Communication, 28*(2), 101–126. doi:10.1016/j.langcom.2008.02.004

Markham, A. N. (1998). *Life online: Researching real experience in virtual space.* Walnut Creek, CA: AltaMira.

Markham, A. N., & Buchanan, E. (2012). *Ethical decision-making and internet research 2.0: Recommendations from the aoir ethics working committee.* Retrieved from http://www.aoir.org/reports/ethics2.pdf

Max, H., & Ray, T. (2006). Skype: The definitive guide. Indianapolis, IN: Que.

McDermott, R. P., Gospodinoff, K., & Aron, J. (1978). Criteria for an ethnographically adequate description of concerted activities and their contexts. *Semiotica, 24*(3/4), 245–275.

Miller, D., & Slater, D. (2001). *The Internet: An ethnographic approach.* Oxford, UK: Berg.

O'Brien, J. (1999). Writing in the body: Gender (re)production in online interaction. In M. Smith, & P. Kollock (Eds.), *Communities in cyberspace* (pp. 76–106). New York: Routledge.

O'Connor, H., Madge, C., Shaw, R., & Wellens, J. (2008). Internet-based interviewing. In N. G. Fielding, & R. M. Lee (Eds.), *Sage handbook of online research methods* (pp. 271–289). Los Angeles, CA: Sage. doi:10.4135/9780857020055.n15

Philipsen, G. (1975). Speaking 'like a man' in Teamsterville: Culture patterns of role enactment in an urban neighborhood. *The Quarterly Journal of Speech, 61*(1), 13–23. doi:10.1080/00335637509383264

Philipsen, G. (1992). *Speaking culturally: Explorations in social communication.* Albany, NY: State University of New York Press.

Philipsen, G. (1997). A theory of speech codes. In G. Philipsen, & T. L. Albrecht (Eds.), *Developing communication theories* (pp. 119–156). New York, NY: State University of New York Press.

Philipsen, G., & Coutu, L. M. (2005). The ethnography of speaking. In K. L. Fitch, & R. E. Sanders (Eds.), *Handbook of language and social interaction* (pp. 355–379). Mahwah, NJ: Lawrence Erlbaum Associates.

Philipsen, G., Coutu, L. M., & Covarrubias, P. (2005). Speech codes theory: Restatement, revisions, and response to criticisms. In W. Gudykunst (Ed.), *Theorizing about intercultural communication* (pp. 55–68). Thousand Oaks, CA: Sage.

Polson, E. (2013). A gateway to the global city: Mobile place-making practices by expats. *New Media & Society*. doi:10.1177/1461444813510135

Rheingold, H. (1993). *The virtual community: Homesteading on the electronic frontier*. Reading, MA: Addison-Wesley.

Salmons, J. (2011). *Cases in online interview research*. Thousand Oaks, CA: Sage.

Saville-Troike, M. (1982). *The ethnography of communication: An introduction*. Baltimore, MD: University Park Press.

Smith, V. (2001). Ethnographies of work and the work of ethnographers. In P. Atkinson, A. Coffey, S. Delamont, J. Lofland, & L. Lofland (Eds.), *Handbook of ethnography* (pp. 220–233). London: Sage. doi:10.4135/9781848608337.n15

Sterne, J. (1999). Thinking the Internet: Cultural studies versus the millenium. In S. Jones (Ed.), *Doing Internet research: Critical issues and methods for examining the Net* (pp. 257–288). Thousand Oaks, CA: Sage. doi:10.4135/9781452231471. n13

Stone, A. R. (1995). *The war of desire and technology at the close of the mechanical age*. Cambridge, MA: The MIT Press.

Strauss, A., & Corbin, J. (1990). *Basics of qualitative research: Grounded theory procedures and techniques*. Newbury Park, CA: Sage.

Turkle, S. (1995). *Life on the screen: Identity in the age of the Internet*. New York: Simon & Schuster.

Weinstein, M. (2008). *TAMS analyzer*. Retrieved from http://tamsys.sourceforge.net/

Wellin, C., & Fine, G. A. (2001). Ethnography as work: Career socialization, settings and problems. In P. Atkinson, A. Coffey, S. Delamont, J. Lofland, & L. Lofland (Eds.), *Handbook of ethnography* (pp. 323–338). London: Sage. doi:10.4135/9781848608337.n22

Wolcott, H. F. (1999). *Ethnography: A way of seeing*. Walnut Creek, CA: AltaMira Press.

KEY TERMS AND DEFINITIONS

Ethnography of Communication: A theoretical/methodological framework for studying communication and communication practices in the natural contexts in which they occur.

Ethnography: A theoretical/methodological framework for studying human culture and activities in the natural contexts in which they occur.

Fieldnotes: Detailed textual materials produced by researchers describing their observations and/or participant observations.

Participant Observation: A method for studying contextualized human activity; the researcher not only observes the community under study but also participates in its activities.

Qualitative Coding: An approach to analyzing qualitative data in which the researcher carefully scrutinizes the data and tags it with descriptive labels, i.e. codes. These codes are used as interpretive resources to identify recurring patterns in the data.

Speech Codes Theory: A theoretical/methodological framework for studying human communication activity and the patterned norms, premises, and rules that pertain to communication in a given community.

TAMS Analyzer: A free software program for MacOSX, used for supporting qualitative coding and analysis.

Chapter 5
Capturing Definitions for a Sustainable Distance Education Ecosystem through an Online Delphi Study

M. Banu Gundogan
Middle East Technical University, Turkey

Gulsun Eby
Anadolu University, Turkey

T. Volkan Yuzer
Anadolu University, Turkey

ABSTRACT

In broadest terms, ecology is the scientific study of interactions among organisms and their environment, and ecosystem defines a community of living organisms in conjunction with the nonliving components of their environment interacting as a system. At present, both terms are references of many studies including education; various authors and studies investigating distance education with an ecological perspective refer to the ecosystem concept as frameworks for defining the operational components and processes. Among all these contributions, the concept of "waste," one of the key concerns of sustainability, seems to be vaguely discussed. Having this as a standpoint, an online Delphi study was carried out in a research project at Anadolu University, Turkey, aiming to define a sustainable distance education ecosystem including the explanation of "waste" with reference to ecosystem definitions. The study was processed online and is explained by both presenting the results and discussing the benefits and also difficulties encountered.

INTRODUCTION

Within an ecological perspective, the ecosystem concept has been associated with education and learning by various authors (Brown, 2000; Richardson, 2002; Jones, 2008). Matching the

ecosystem definition which states that the living community and the nonliving environment function together as an ecological system or ecosystem (Odum & Barret, 2005), a learning ecosystem is described as "a collection of overlapping communities of interest (virtual), cross-

DOI: 10.4018/978-1-4666-6493-7.ch005

pollinating with each other, constantly evolving, and largely self-organizing" (Brown, 2000). In a learning ecosystem formal, social, informal and traditional learning intersect and learning "just happens" (Jones, 2008) providing the presence of diverse learning options (Brown, 2000). A learning ecosystem matrix with reference to studying, teaching, projects and exercises quadrants based on instruction delivery and navigation control is also presented (Richardson, 2002). In terms of distance education, the concept of ecology and ecosystems are referred as frameworks for defining the operational components and processes (Zachry, 2000; McCalla, 2004; Frielick, 2004; Chang & Guetl, 2007; Uden & Damiani, 2007; Dong, 2009; Pata, 2011; Reyna, 2011; Nasr, 2011; Johnson, 2012). These frameworks can be grouped as follows:

1. **The Learning Ecosystem:** Encompassing up-to-date information and content,
2. **The Teaching Ecosystem:** Encompassing complex interactions between the learner, interface, instructor and content,
3. **The Digital Ecosystem:** Focusing on the rapid growth in digital technology,
4. **The Learning Environment Ecosystem:** Covering content providers, consultants and infrastructure. Moreover, the future of distance education is mentioned to be feasible only if these ecosystems are well understood and analyzed (Dillon & Hallett, 2001) and the need for developing models that support the development and sustainability of these ecosystems are underlined (Uden & Damiani, 2007; Issa, Issa & Chang 2011).

A sustainable ecosystem is a biological environment that is able to flourish and support itself without outside influence or assistance. In ideal sustainable ecosystems, everything for the life to survive is already provided and no waste is generated. To 'sustain' is not only about keeping up, supporting or maintaining continuity but also

is about nourishing, cultivation and acknowledgement (Uden & Damiani, 2007). 21st century incentives in all fields of human endeavor have replaced sustainability measures in their plans and actions as a necessity for meeting the needs of the present and future generations. Within this framework, 'Green Engineering' and 'Green Design' perspectives and 'Life Cycle Assessment' procedures introduce valuable methodologies. 'Green Engineering' is the design, discovery, and implementation of engineering solutions for sustainability (Anastas & Zimmerman, 2006) and 'Green Design' is intended to develop more environmentally benign products and processes (Hendrickson,1999). Life Cycle Assessment, a systematic analysis of the environmental effects of a new product or process, is common to both green design and engineering perspectives. This necessitates defining a system boundary, carrying out an inventory of all the materials and energy used and assessing all the environmental discharges resulting from the product's manufacture, use, and disposal within the defined boundary. Regarding the disposal process, the design choices on recycle, reuse or beneficial disposition becomes important. Within this framework, after completing its intended usage the product or process could be an input in; *a closed-loop*, which refers to the re-use of the product or service for the same function and *an open loop*, which refers to the re-use of the product or service in a different function, typically with lower quality requirements (Hendrickson, 1999).

Distance education is also a process designed to serve actual human beings and alike every design, the process has inputs, outputs and unfortunately, produces waste. Unless managed properly, waste is harmful; to avoid possible harms and to be able to respond both to current and future demands and expectations, distance education has to include ecological and sustainable perspectives to its vision. In literature regarding distance education ecosystems, 'waste' is a concept which has not yet been adequately discussed. Believing this being an important research area, an online Delphi study was carried out in a research project at Anadolu University, Turkey, aiming to gather explanations for a sustainable distance education ecosystem including the definition of 'waste' with reference to ecosystem definitions.

The study encompasses:

1. Definition of distance education ecosystem,
2. Inputs, outputs and balance constituents within the ecosystem,
3. Waste in distance education ecosystem,
4. The life cycle analysis of the products and services within the ecosystem in which waste could be managed. The following section explains the process and results of the above mentioned Delphi study.

THE DELPHI STUDY AND THE MIXED RESEARCH MODEL

Delphi studies are considered valuable in structuring effective group communication processes when dealing with a complex problem. As qualitative research methods, they are helpful in gathering the opinions of a larger group of experts and in fields where there is not a lot of evidence about the developments and where experts often do not dare to explain their real opinion (Linstone & Turoff, 2002). The Delphi method is mainly used when long-term issues have to be assessed (Eto, 2003). The experts involved need to be selected on the basis of their knowledge and experience so that they are able to give a competent assessment. They have the opportunity to gather new information during the successive rounds of the process (Häder & Häder 1995). The study is conducted anonymously in order not to let anyone lose face in the event of a change of opinion and the methodology is designed to avoid domination by particular individuals; the goal is to achieve a degree of convergence (Cuhls, Blind & Grupp, 2002). Giving feedback and the anonymity of the Delphi survey are important characteristics. The survey is designed for two or more sessions in which, in the second and later sessions the results of the previous round are given as feedback (Cuhls, Blind & Grupp, 1998). The idea is that the respondents can learn from the views of others, without being influenced by them.

The following ten steps are described for the Delphi method (Fowles, 1978):

1. Formation of a team to undertake and monitor a Delphi on a given subject.
2. Selection of participants.
3. Development of the first session questionnaires.
4. Testing the questionnaire for proper wording (e.g., ambiguities, vagueness).
5. Transmission of the first session to participants.
6. Analysis of the first round responses.
7. Preparation of the second session questionnaires (and possible testing).
8. Transmission of the second session to participants.
9. Analysis of the second round responses (Steps 7 to 9 are reiterated as long as desired or necessary to achieve stability in the results).
10. Preparation of the report.

Since e-learning ecosystem was a novel area of study and the concept of 'waste' had not yet been adequately discussed, Delphi was decided as a convenient method for the research explained in this chapter. Moreover, aiming to gather explanations from different experts who were also geographically separated necessitated an online correspondence and this greatly met the anonymity proviso where dominance was certainly to be avoided.

Capturing definitions for a sustainable distance education ecosystem through an online Delphi study was planned with the following steps:

1. Selecting and inviting participants.
2. Planning the Sessions.
3. Designing online questionnaires.
4. Re-designing second and further sessions according to feedbacks.
5. Data collection.
6. Analyzing data.
7. Reporting.

The first session aimed to define the components of a distance education ecosystem with reference to ecosystem definitions, namely, inputs, units and outputs by answering 10 open ended questions. Due to the novelty of the subject and the experts' characteristics, diverse contributions were anticipated and for the second session inclusion of measurement scales were found to be beneficial to attain consensus regarding definitions. This led to the selection of a mixed method. Mixed methods are intended to offer the best of both worlds: the in-depth, contextualized, and natural insights of qualitative research coupled with the persuasive power of quantitative research. As Trochim states, "…qualitative and quantitative data are intimately related to each other… all quantitative data is based on qualitative judgments and all qualitative data can be described and manipulated numerically" (Trochim, 2008). Definitions received from the first session were listed and shared via Likert and numeric rating scales in the second session, enabling participants to view and rate all given answers. Since the study was processed online and participants were given the opportunity to change their opinions even after completing the first two sessions, the mixed method was valuable in obtaining consensus among diverse contribu-

tions. Although the process was time consuming both for the participants and researchers, the final value of consensus was outstanding, making all efforts worth. All the steps are explained in the following sections.

Selecting and Inviting Participants

In Delphi studies, deciding on the number of participants depend on the size, needs and the budget of the project but it is noted that each session should consist of approximately 10 to 18 members (Bourgeois, 2006). The same authors state that "Unlike traditional statistical surveying, the goal is not to select a representative sample of the population. The whole premise behind the Delphi theory is that the panel members are in fact experts in their field in order to yield more accurate results. The criteria that qualifies an individual as an expert is determined by those administering the process" (Bourgeois, 2006). Researchers compiled a list of 50 experts from different disciplines (computer education and instructional technology, sustainable computer science education, distance education, instructional design, biology (ecology) and industrial design). Experts were selected among local and international academia and distance education professionals. Personal invitations were sent by e-mails and experts were informed about the subject of the study. The sessions were briefly explained. It was made clear that all sessions would be completed online and that all respondents will be given feedback after each session. They were also informed that they would have the opportunity to view and change their opinions any time, even after completing each session. 33 approvals were received. Contribution differed from 15 to 20 for individual sessions, nevertheless, 16 experts contributed to all three sessions.

Planning the Delphi Sessions

As mentioned above, the study aiming to capture definitions for a sustainable distance education ecosystem covered the following issues:

1. Definition of distance education ecosystem,
2. Inputs, outputs and balance constituents within the ecosystem,
3. Waste in distance education ecosystem,
4. The life cycle analysis of the products and services within the ecosystem in which waste could be managed.

These issues were grouped into 3 sessions as follows:

Session 1: Participants were expected to define the components of a distance education ecosystem with reference to ecosystem definitions, namely, inputs, units and outputs by answering 10 open ended questions.

Session 2: This session consisted of 4 parts. The first part presented all the answers from the first session given as input and output constituents of the distance education ecosystem in a Likert Scale (strongly agree, agree, undecided, disagree, strongly disagree). The second part presented a rating scale ('0'- not important, '7'-of highest importance) in terms of input-output relations. The aim of using a Likert and a rating scale was to clarify answers and reach a degree of convergence. The third part aimed to gather comments on the balance within the distance education ecosystem. With reference to sustainability definitions and the former session answers given as input and output constituents, participants were asked to rate these relations ('0'- not important, '7'- of highest importance). The researchers aimed to collect exact opinions by using this scale. This also served as a triangulation for parts 1 and 2. The last part was an open

ended question, By presenting Article 6 of the Bill of Rights for the Planet declared at EXPO 2000, participants were to define the 'waste(s)' of distance education.

Session 3: This session was for analyzing the concept of 'waste'. Answers to the last part of session 2 were listed and participants were asked to match these answers with Life Cycle Assessment definitions. Since the concept of 'waste' in an distance education ecosystem has not been studied regarding sustainability principles, each and every answer showed a unique approach to be included, thus, when analyzing answers, no consensus or rating scales were used; all answers were recorded without a specific order and grouping. Figure 1 presents the Delphi sessions.

Designing Online Questionnaires

A key ingredient to the Delphi process is the anonymity of participants. The contributions need to be collected so that no participant knows the identity of the others. Only by this way a true consensus can be reached and problems arising from bias and peer influence among the participants could be eliminated (Bourgeois, 2006). In this study, the fact that participating experts were geographically separated necessitated online correspondence and designing sessions and questionnaires to be reached online met the needs for anonymity and overcame distance barriers.

Researchers designed an online questionnaire page which was labeled with the participants' name. The following e-mail was sent to each participant, explaining the session and providing the link to the web page assigned. An exemplary e-mail for the first session was as follows:

Dear Dr. Banu Gundogan, The first round of the Delphi technique aiming to gather expert views regarding the integration of ecological design principles and sustainability issues to the design

Figure 1. Delphi sessions on capturing definitions for a sustainable distance education ecosystem

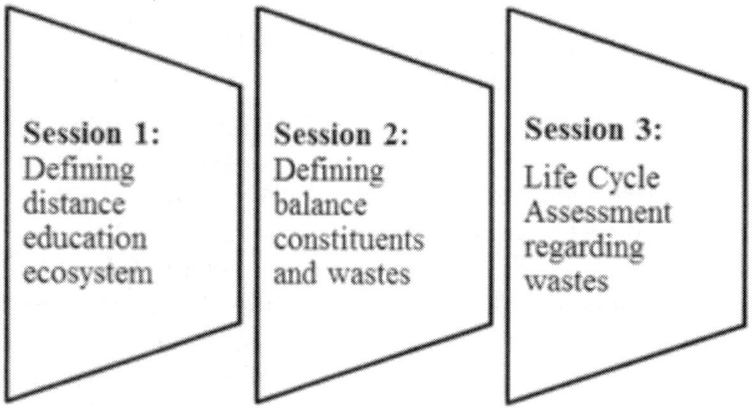

of distance education programs is available for your contributions at the following address: http://distanceeducationecology.com/DelfiTour1. php?id=xxxx. The link opens with your name and surname entered. For any comments and questions, please do not hesitate to contact me at: xxxxxxxx@ distanceeducationecology.com. Sincerely,

Upon clicking the address, the participant reached the page given in Figure 2, which ended with a 'save the answers' button.

Receiving response for questionnaires, moreover getting quality contributions is not easy and this may be common to most researchers. Participants, although having accepted to contribute, may not be motivated to spend time on an abstract guesswork with people they do not know and where their performance is unrelated to their survival (Scheele, 2002). Within the framework of this study, the whole correspondence had taken place online, including the invitation e-mails. Expecting to serve as an 'ice breaker' and to overcome the feeling of abstraction, researchers decided to put their photos on the questionnaire.

Researchers provided no time limit for contributions, but sent reminding e-mails in 2 weeks periods to the participants who had not submitted

responses. The first session was completed in 4 months; a rather long period. The reasons might have been the comparatively abstract nature of 10 open ended questions and the date it was announced; it was mid-August, a rather busy period for experts from academia.

Re-Designing Second and Further Sessions According to Feedbacks

Giving feedback is an important characteristic of the Delphi study. The survey is designed for two or more sessions in which, in the second and later sessions the results of the previous round are given as feedback (Cuhls, Blind & Grupp, 1998). As Mitroff & Turoff indicate "What distinguishes the Delphi from an ordinary polling procedure is the feedback of the information gathered from the group and the opportunity of the individuals to modify or refine their judgments based upon their reaction to the collective views of the group" (Mitroff & Turoff, 2002).

The second session, as described in the former section, was based on the results obtained in the former session. The online design was preserved with two important additions; a time limit was given, and the participants were given the chance

Figure 2. Partial screenshot of the online Delphi questionnaire for the first session. (Text obscured to protect participants).

to review their former answers and make changes if they wanted. An exemplary e-mail for the second session was as follows:

Dear Dr. Banu Gundogan, The second round of the Delphi technique aiming to gather expert views regarding the integration of ecological design principles and sustainability issues to the design of distance education programs is available for your contributions at the following address until January 23, 2012: http://distanceducatio-necology.com/DelfiTour02.php?id=xxxx. The link opens with your name and surname entered. You can also view the first round by clicking the given link and make any changes or add comments if you wish. Sincerely,

Upon clicking the address, the participant reached the page given in Figure 3, which in-

cluded a button with 'I want to view/change my answers for the first round' text on it. By clicking this button, the participant was directed to his/her previous answers. The second session was announced on December and a month later, all contributions (including excuses for incompletion) were collected.

Figure 3. Partial screenshot of the online Delphi questionnaire for the second session. (Text obscured to protect participants).

Data Collection

When each questionnaire was saved, the participants received a 'Thank You' screen and the researchers received an e-mail containing the answers listed. The answers were collected in a spreadsheet application (Figure 4). The spreadsheet contained the questions, the participants name, time of completion and text based answers.

The same procedure was followed for the following sessions. In session 2, results of the Likert and rating scales were color coded in the spreadsheet (Figure 5). In addition to numerical analysis, the color coding (tones getting darker according to number of agreements) also enabled to visualize the consensus degree the darker tones indicate.

When all three sessions were completed, the participants received the following e-mail informing about the completion of the study.

Dear Dr. Banu Gundogan, Your answers for the third round of our Delphi study have been saved. Our study is completed with this last round. Your contribution has been very valuable for our efforts on developing an ecological and sustainable distance education design vision. Once again, we thank you very much for sharing your comments and evaluations throughout the study. Sincerely,

Analyzing Data and Reporting

The whole study is reported as a project titled *Application of Ecological Design Principles to Open*

Figure 4. Partial screenshot of the spreadsheet for the first session. (Text obscured to protect participants).

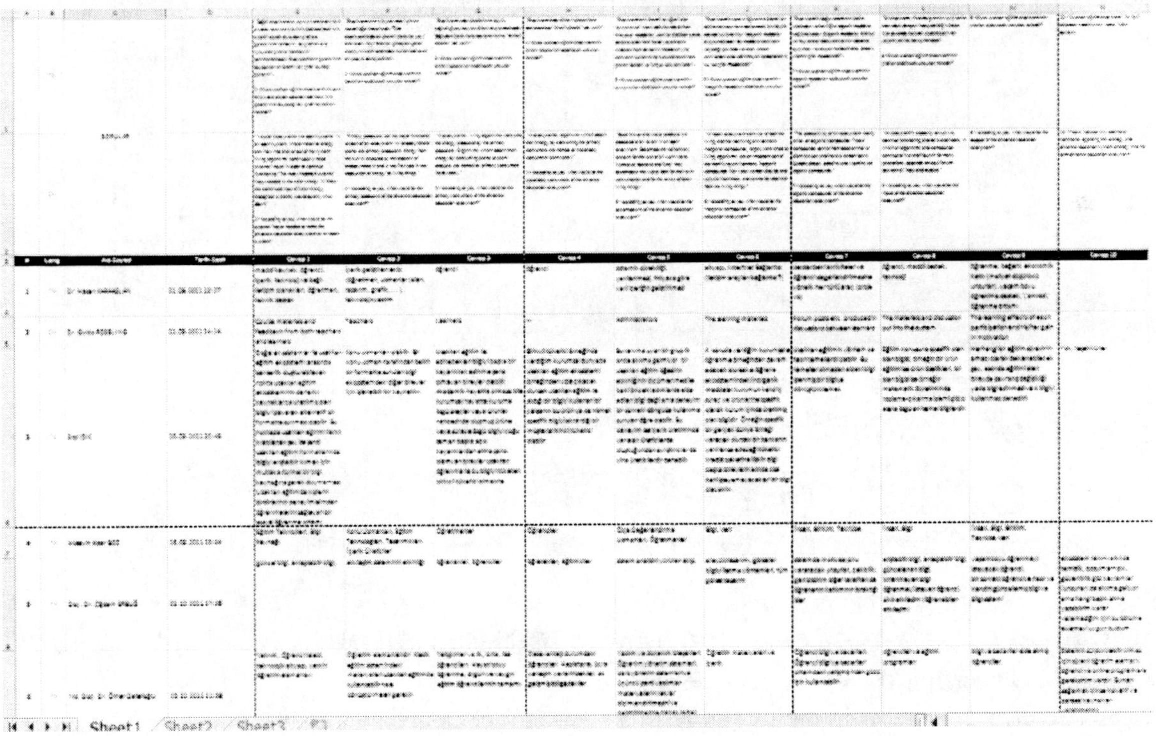

Figure 5. Partial screenshot of the spreadsheet for the second session. (Text obscured to protect participants).

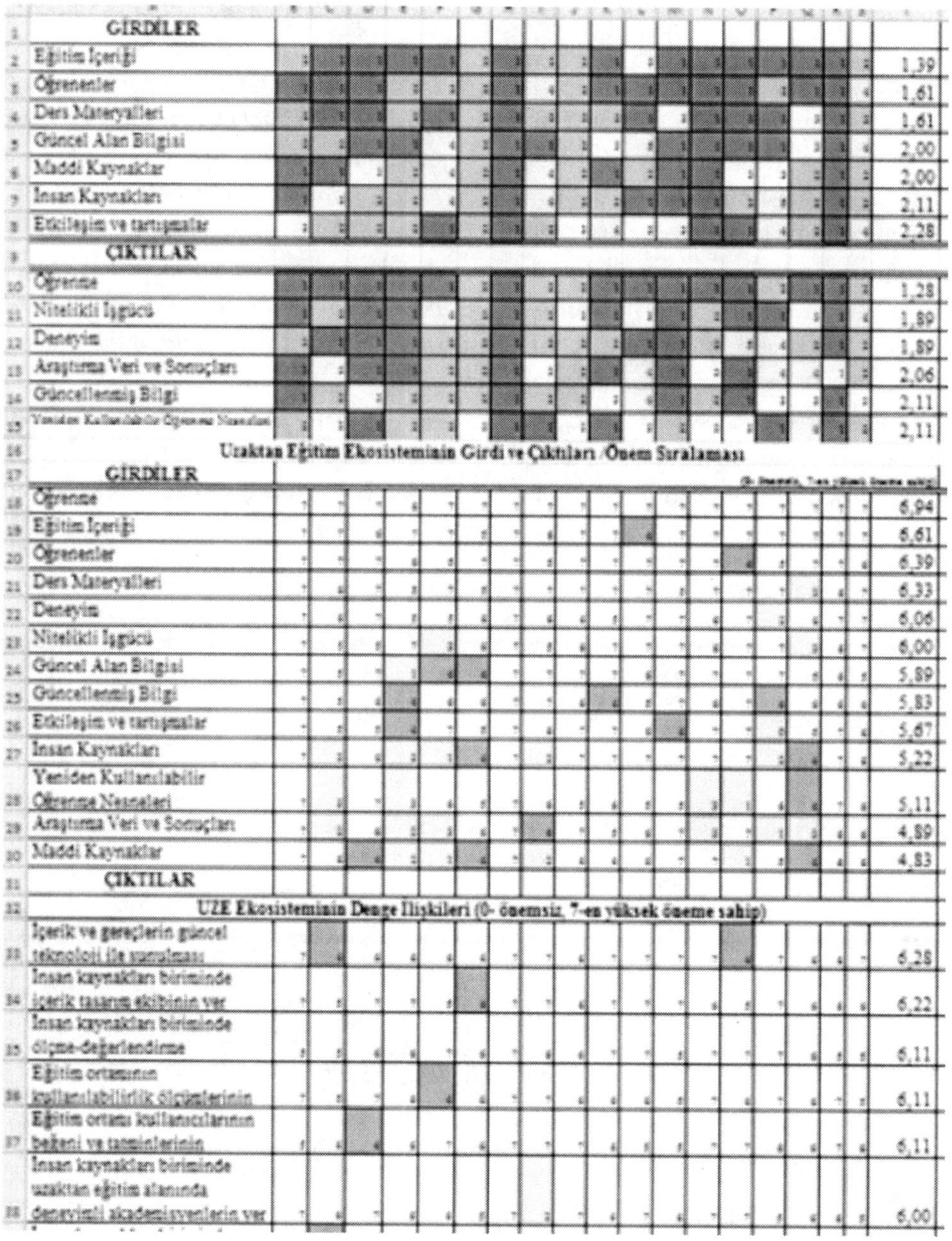

and Distance Learning (Project No: 1103E050) at Anadolu University, Turkey. To give the readers an overall view, the main topics and results (excluding session 3, the Life Cycle assessment) is presented in Table 1.

CONCLUSION

This chapter explains an online Delphi study carried out in a research project at Anadolu University, Turkey, aiming to define a sustainable distance education ecosystem. The study aimed to gather

Table 1. Partial results of the Delphi study

Topics	Results obtained from Delphi Study
Inputs of the distance education ecosystem	learners, up-to-date educational content, budget, human resources, interaction and course materials
Outputs of the distance education ecosystem	learning, qualified workforce, experience, knowledge, reusable learning objects and research results
Prioritized balance issues regarding the distance education inputs and outputs	• Planning for qualified graduates ready to enter workforce • Designing the content and materials as reusable learning objects • Matching updated content in the field of study with experience • Prioritizing the experience provisions in planning and managing financial resources • Employing professional distance education experts in human resources Measuring the user satisfaction of the distance education environment
The concept of waste in distance education	• Content which is not up-to-date or valid • Students who have gained wrong experience because of misleading information • Dropouts (students) • Technology • The uncertainty in managing / executing and auditing offered programs • Stationery / paper-work • Redeveloping learning objects/content that have already been created but not shared/reused • Unneeded mouse clicks and obstructive user interfaces wasting the learners' time • Course content and materials which do not serve the learning outcomes stated within learning objectives

explanations for a sustainable distance education ecosystem including the definition of 'waste' with reference to ecosystem definitions. 50 participants from different disciplines were invited, of which, 33 approvals were received. 16 of these contributed to all three sessions. To increase the credibility and validity of the results, both qualitative and quantitative methods were used. The study was processed online and participants had the opportunity to view and change their opinions any time, even after completing each session.

Due to the novelty of the subject and characteristics of experts, researchers anticipated that including quantitative study instruments (i.e. Likert and numeric rating scales) would be beneficial to attain consensus. This inclusion shaped the study as a mixed method study where narrated expert contributions were collected, listed, shared via feedback and then presented as scales in which all contributors needed to rate all the answers. Important characteristics of a Delphi study, namely gathering expert views, conducting multiple sessions, providing anonymity and giving feedback were followed. Presenting the sessions online was definitely an aid in overcoming time and place issues, but it is noteworthy to state that giving time limits for each session speeded up the response time and motivation. Although the process was time consuming both for the participants and researchers, the final value of consensus was outstanding, making all efforts worth.

REFERENCES

Anastas, P. T., & Zimmerman, J. B. (2006). The Twelve Principles of Green Engineering as a Foundation for Sustainability. In M. A. Abraham (Ed.), *Sustainability Science and Engineering: Defining Principles* (pp. 11–32). New York: Elsevier B.V. doi:10.1016/S1871-2711(06)80009-7

Bourgeois, J., Pugmire, L., Stevenson, K., Swanson, N., & Swanson, B. (2006). *The Delphi Method: A qualitative means to a better future*. Retrieved August 13, 2013, from http://www.freequality.org/documents/knowledge/Delphi-method.pdf

Brown, J.S. (2000, March/April). Growing up digital: How the web changes work, education, and the ways people learn. *Change Magazine*, 11-20.

Chang, V., & Guetl, C. (2007) Distance education ecosystems (ELES). In *Proceedings of the Inaugural Conference on Digital Ecosystems and Technologies*. IEEE.

Cuhls, K., Blind, K., & Grupp, H. (Eds.). (1998). Delphi '98 Umfrage: Zukunft nachgefragt: Studie zur globalen Entwicklung von Wissenschaft und Technik. Karlsruhe.

Cuhls, K., Blind, K., & Grupp, H. (2002). *Innovations for our Future. Delphi '98: New Foresight on Science and Technology*. Heidelberg: Physica. doi:10.1007/978-3-642-57472-6

Dong, B., Qinghua, Z., Jie, Y., Haifei, L., & Mu, Q. (2009). *A distance education ecosystem based on cloud computing infrastructure*. Paper presented at the 9th IEEE International Conference on Advanced Learning Technologies. Riga, Latvia.

Eto, H. (2003). The suitability of technology forecasting/ foresight methods for decision systems and strategy, A Japanese view. *Technological Forecasting and Social Change, 70*(3), 231–249. doi:10.1016/S0040-1625(02)00194-4

Fowles, J. (1978). *Handbook of futures research*. Greenwood Press.

Frielick, S. (2004). Beyond constructivism: An ecological approach to distance education: Beyond the comfort zone. In *Proceedings of the 21st ASCILITE Conference* (pp. 328-332). ASCILITE. Retrieved August 13, 2013, from http://www.ascilite.org.au/conferences/perth04/procs/frielick.html

Häder, M., & Häder, S. (1995). Delphi und Kognitionspsychologie: Ein Zugang zur theoretischen Fundierung der Delphi-Methode. *ZUMA-Nachrichten, 37*(19), 12.

Hendrickson, C., Conway-Schempf, N., Lave, L., & McMichael, F. (1999). *Introduction to Green Design*. Green Design Initiative, Carnegie Mellon University. Retrieved May 5, 2012 from http://gdi.ce.cmu.edu/gd/education/gdedintro.pdf

Issa, T., Issa, T., & Chang, V. (2011). *Green IT and sustainable development strategies: An Australian experience*. Paper presented at the 12th International Conference of the Society for Global Business & Economic Development. Singapore.

Johnson, G. M. (2012). The ecology of interactive learning environments: Situating traditional theory. *Interactive Learning Environments*. doi: 10.1080/10494820.2011.649768

Jones, K. (2008). *Creating a Learning Ecosystem – Why Blended Learning is Now Inadequate*. Retrieved August 13, 2013, from http://engagedlearning.net/post/creating-a-learning-ecosystem-why-blended-learning-is-now-inadequate/

Linstone, H. A., & Turoff, M. (Eds.). (2002). The Delphi method - Techniques and applications. Reading, MA: Addison-Wesley.

McCalla, G. (2004). The ecological approach to the design of distance education environments: Purpose-based capture and use of information about learners. *Journal of Interactive Media in Education, 2004* (7), 1-23

Mitroff, I. I., & Turoff, M. (2002). Philosophical and Methodological Foundations of Delphi. In H. A. Linstone, & M. Turoff (Eds.), *The Delphi Method - Techniques and Applications*. Reading, MA: Addison-Wesley Educational Publishers Inc.

Nasr, M., & Ouf, S. (2011). An Ecosystem in distance education Using Cloud Computing as platform and Web2.0. *The Research Bulletin of Jordan ACM, II*(1), 134–140.

Odum, E. P., & Barrett, G. W. (2005). *Fundamentals of Ecology*. Thomson Brooks.

Pata, K. (2012). *Modeling open education learning ecosystem*. Retrieved August 13, 2013, from http://tihane.wordpress.com/2012/05/08/modelling-digital-learning-ecosystem/

Reyna, J. (2011). Digital Teaching and Learning Ecosystem (DTLE): A Theoretical Approach for Online Learning Environments. In *Proceedings ASCILITE 2011*. Hobart, Australia: Concise Paper. Retrieved August 13, 2013, from http://www.ascilite.org.au/conferences/hobart11/downloads/papers/Reyna-concise.pdf

Richardson, A. (2002). *Ecology of Learning and the Role of Distance education in the Learning Environment*. Sun Microsystems Global Summit.

Scheele, D. S. (2002). Reality Construction as a Product of Delphi Interaction. In H. A. Linstone, & M. Turoff (Eds.), *The Delphi Method - Techniques and Applications*. Reading, MA: Addison-Wesley Educational Publishers Inc.

Trochim, W., Marcus, S. E., Mâsse, L. C., Moser, R. P., & Weld, P. (2008). The Evaluation of Large Research Initiatives: A Participatory Integrative Mixed-Methods Approach. *The American Journal of Evaluation, 29*(1), 1, 8–28. doi:10.1177/1098214007309280

Uden, L., & Damiani, E. (2007). The future of distance education: distance education ecosystem. In *Proceedings of Inaugural IEEE International Conference on Digital Ecosystems and Technologies*, (pp. 113-117). IEEE.

Zachry, M. (2000). The ecology of an online education site in professional communication. In Technology and Teamwork, (pp. 433-442). IEEE.

KEY TERMS AND DEFINITIONS

Delphi Study: Delphi studies are considered valuable in structuring effective group communication processes when dealing with a complex problem. As qualitative research methods, they are helpful in gathering the opinions of a larger group of experts and in fields where there is not a lot of evidence about the developments and where experts often do not dare to explain their real. The study is conducted anonymously in order not to let anyone lose face in the event of a change of opinion and the methodology is designed to avoid domination by particular individuals; the goal is to achieve a degree of convergence The survey is designed for two or more sessions in which, in the second and later sessions the results of the previous round are given as feedback so that respondents can learn from the views of others, without being influenced by them.

Digital Ecosystem: A digital ecosystem is the digital environment of networking through which cooperation, knowledge sharing and cross-disciplinary interaction are supported. Diverse digital ecosystems respond to diverse needs, in which, software, databases, applications or software services form a dynamic and interrelated ecosystem.

Distance Education Ecosystem: Distance education is a method of delivering education and instruction. Participants who are not physically present in a traditional setting such as a classroom benefit from this method. Regarding diverse backgrounds, various motivations, expectations and different teaching and learning styles, every distance education practice needs to be unique. The major objective is to cultivate efficient learning experiences and the widespread usage of communication technologies has already left the 'one size fits all' savvy behind.

Ecosystem: In broadest terms, ecology is the scientific study of interactions among organisms and their environment and ecosystem defines a community of living organisms in conjunction with the nonliving components of their environment, interacting as a system.

Learning Ecosystem: A learning ecosystem is a designed system where information navigation models simplify and support personal learning styles and provide enjoyable learning experiences with updated information and content. A learning ecosystem with up to date information and well managed learning activities is a necessity in keeping up with the rapid change in learner needs.

Life Cycle Assessment: Life Cycle Assessment is a systematic analysis of the environmental effects of a new product or process. This necessitates defining a system boundary, carrying out an inventory of all the materials and energy used and assessing all the environmental discharges resulting from the product's manufacture, use, and

disposal within the defined boundary. Regarding the disposal process, design choices on recycle, reuse and/or beneficial disposition becomes important. Within this framework, after completing its intended usage the product or process could be an input in; a closed-loop, which refers to the re-use of the product or service for the same function and an open loop, which refers to the re-use of the product or service in a different function, typically with lower quality requirements.

Sustainability in Distance Education Ecosystem: A sustainable ecosystem is a biological environment that is able to flourish and support itself without outside influence or assistance. In ideal sustainable ecosystems, everything for the life to survive is already provided and no waste is generated. To 'sustain' is not only about keeping up, supporting or maintaining continuity but also is about nourishing, cultivation and acknowledgement. Distance education is also a process designed to serve actual human beings and alike every design, the process has inputs, outputs and unfortunately, produces waste. Unless managed properly, waste is harmful; to avoid possible harms and to be able to respond both to current and future demands and expectations, distance education has to include ecological and sustainable perspectives to its vision.

Sustainability: Sustainability holds our planet and our lives as focal points by drawing attention to the risks created by the consumption of natural resources and the harm made by technology. It introduces provisions for keeping resources undamaged and renewable so that they continue to serve future generations and constitutes a precondition for the human wellbeing by defining how systems would remain diverse and productive over time. 21st century incentives in all fields of creation have placed sustainability measures in their procedures.

Teaching Ecosystem: A teaching ecosystem encompasses complex interactions between the learner, interface, instructor and content. It needs to provide a learning process which is controlled by the learner so that self-directed learners would own their responsibility for identifying their learning needs and implementing their unique learning paths. In such a teaching environment, students can actively locate, select, and initiate their learning from various sources of information and activities and this would resolve the workload of teachers. The importance of integrating experts and expert systems to the teaching ecosystem must also be considered.

Chapter 6
Video–Conferencing Interviews in Qualitative Research

Kimberly Nehls
University of Nevada – Las Vegas, USA

Brandy D. Smith
University of Nevada – Las Vegas, USA

Holly A. Schneider
University of Nevada – Las Vegas, USA

ABSTRACT

This chapter synthesizes the literature on real-time, synchronous, video interviews as a qualitative data collection method. The authors specifically focus on the advantages and disadvantages of this method in social science research and offer conceptual themes, practical techniques, and recommendations for using video-interviews. The growing popularity of computer-mediated communication indicates that a wider audience will be willing and able to participate in research using this method; therefore, online video-conferencing could be considered a viable option for qualitative data collection.

INTRODUCTION AND PURPOSE

Video-conferencing has been popular for at least a decade as a means of communicating via distance using technology. Adobe Connect, Apple's Face-Time, Wimba, Google Chat, and Skype are just some of the many options available for face-to-face communication in real time through technology. In recent years, Skype has exploded as an avenue for job interviews (e.g., Winzenburg, 2011). Now video-conferencing is gaining traction in qualitative research for video-conferencing interviews.

The purpose of this book chapter is to synthesize the literature on real-time, synchronous, video interviews, specifically focusing on the advantages and disadvantages of this method in social science research. Conceptual themes, techniques, and recommendations for this method will also be explored. This chapter was developed as a literature review and a reflection of the authors' own research experiences using this medium in their own studies. Skype interviews can and should be considered by both scholars and practitioners engaged in qualitative research as a viable option for

DOI: 10.4018/978-1-4666-6493-7.ch006

data collection. Video-conferencing environments allow real-time communication with both audio and video (Mann & Stewart, 2000). This is much like a traditional interview, except the researcher and participant are simply in different locations.

Interviews are used in almost all forms of qualitative research, but surprisingly little has been written about interviews conducted via new technological resources. Many researchers still refer to in-person, face-to-face (FTF), interviews as the "gold standard" of data collection, whereas interviews via technology have a perceived inferiority (McCoyd & Kerson, 2006). This chapter does not negate the importance or the utility of the FTF in-person method; rather, it delineates the pros and cons of a new option for qualitative researchers. Because computer-mediated communication is so commonplace, it simply makes sense to explore online data collection methods for contemporary research. Similar to Deakin and Wakefield (2013), we believe "the online interview should be treated as a viable option to the researcher rather than just as an alternative or secondary choice when face-to-face interviews cannot be achieved" (p. 3).

Video-conference interviews take place synchronously, with the participant and interviewer using a computer, tablet, or other device to communicate at the same time. Many free video-conferencing options are widely available. Skype, FaceTime, vox.io, and Veribu are several complimentary examples. In our research projects, we chose Skype because it is the most commonly used desktop video-conference application (Weinmann, Thomas, Brilmayer, Heinrich, & Radon, 2012). We also used Skype for all of our video-conferencing interviews because of ease of the technology. The name Skype comes from Sky-peer-to-peer, meaning that friends are connected "in the sky" via computers rather than in-person. Skype reported 663 million users worldwide at the end of 2010, up from 474 million just one year earlier

("Skype grows FY revenues," 2011). Therefore, the video-conferencing technology is widespread and growing. At peak times, there are as many as 30 million Skype users online at one time!

Skype interviews allow the interviewer to ask questions and interviewee respond online just like in a FTF setting. The structure of the interview depends upon the study; the exchange can last as long as need be. On average, our Skype interviews lasted between 30-60 minutes. Most of our participants were at work or home when they were being interviewed online. For the purpose of this chapter, we are also referring to one-on-one online interviews, where there was one interviewer and one participant. We recognize that there are many variations that can take place, with several participants in an online focus group setting or even multiple interviewers with multiple interviewees. However, for simplicity and because of the way we organized our online research, we are primarily approaching this chapter from the perspective of using one interviewer and one participant in an online format.

We believe this topic is an important one for discussion in qualitative and mixed-methods research for several reasons. First of all, there are very few studies that use video-conferencing interviews as a primary research method. If video-conferencing interviews are utilized, they are typically mentioned as a back-up or alternative option when more traditional methods of face-to-face or phone interviews cannot be realized. Secondly, none of the articles we found described how and when to use video-conferencing techniques such as Skype. This chapter will offer specific procedures as well as logistical considerations for researchers. Lastly, the growing popularity of video-conferencing options means that a wider audience will be amenable and able to participate in research using this method. For these reasons, we deem this chapter a timely contribution.

OVERVIEW OF CONCEPTUAL FRAMEWORKS

Qualitative research should be grounded in theoretical and empirical work (Marshall & Rossman, 2006). Prior theory can provide the rationale as well as a conceptual framework for a study. This section of the chapter briefly reviews four conceptual frameworks that may be useful for researchers seeking to use video-conferencing, or other computer-mediated communication (CMC) methods in their qualitative research. It is in no way intended to be a full treatment of theories relevant to CMC, nor advocating for the use of one model or framework in particular. Rather, a brief discussion of each is provided with specific attention given to the application of the frameworks to video-conferencing.

Psychobiological Model

A theoretical framework developed by Kock (2004) uses a psychobiological model to propose a link between the naturalness of CMC and FTF communication. Crucial to the psychobiological model is the media naturalness proposition which "states that the higher the degree of 'naturalness' of a CMC medium, the lower the 'cognitive effort' required to use it for communication" (Kock, 2004, p. 333). The degree of naturalness of a CMC, according to this proposition, is dependent on its inclusion of elements of FTF communication (p. 333). Therefore, the video interview has a high degree of naturalness since it is taking place in real-time, as synchronous communication.

In addition to media naturalness and cognitive effort, the Kock model accounts for "schema alignment" and "cognitive adaptation" which contributes to CMC interactions as well. Schema alignment describes the similarity of mental schemas between the individuals communicating, while "cognitive adaptation refers to the level of schema development associated with the use of a particular medium for communication"

(Kock, 2004, p. 341). The greater the disparity in schema alignment between individuals, the greater the required effort will be to reach a shared understanding to complete the task. Therefore, researchers considering using video-conferencing for qualitative interviews should be aware of differences between their selves and the participants they plan to interview. Further, the participant's cognitive adaptation to a particular CMC such as video-conferencing software should be taken into account by the researcher. Cognitive adaption may be reflected in the participant's prior experience with the software, as well as their perceived competence and comfort in using the medium.

Taken together, the elements discussed in Kock's (2004) psychobiological model contribute to understanding how the use of media such as video-conferencing may be a viable method of collecting data for research.

Medium Theory

Looking beyond the focus of the content of media, communication scholar Joshua Meyrowitz (1994) extended the work of prior medium theorists (e.g. Innis, 1964/1972; McLuhan, 1962/1964) that examined the features of individual medium or types of media. In particular, Meyrowitz (1994) adapts role theory into his conceptualization of media theory, highlighting the influence of new media of communication on behavior.

Social identity, Meyrowitz (1994) argues, is shaped by social networks and can also be influenced by patterns of access to information as much as the content. For example, the exclusion of students from faculty meetings provides a clear distinction in social identity. Without restricted access to the social situation, such distinction would begin to dissipate. Further, Meyrowitz makes the claim that while situations tend to be perceived as a physical place, they are "information systems." As a result, media influence information flow patterns and in turn may make roles more or less distinct. For instance, the patient that has access to the website WebMD becomes privy to information that may once have only been available by communicating directly with a doctor or health professional, hence resulting in less distinct roles between doctor and patient.

Looking at role changes across time, Meyrowitz (1994) covers three phases of culture: nomadic oral societies, literate societies, and society exposed to electronic media. Nomadic oral societies lacked boundaries, which in turn meant a lack in role distinction. Men, women, children, leaders and followers held comparatively equal roles. By the Middle Ages, literacy is used by the church to maintain a hierarchy between the literate elite and illiterate masses. As information in print gains momentum, information and roles become more segmented: "Print society depends on division of labour, separation of social spheres, segmentation of identities by class, occupation, sex, and so forth" (Meyrowitz, 1994, p. 66). However, the introduction of electronic media such as telephones, radio, television, and the internet have begun to undermine the social isolation and role segmentation brought about by the print society by providing individuals access to others where physical structures once restricted that access.

While medium theory does not distinctly make the case for the appropriateness of particular medium for research purposes, it raises awareness of the impact of media on social roles and behavior. The use of a particular medium such as video-conferencing technology adds an additional layer of positionality that the qualitative researcher must contend with. In addition to considering how study participants' behavior may be influenced by the use of such technology, the researcher should be aware of how they themselves are influenced. For example, the researcher may be well practiced in using video-conferencing technology for multiple purposes and take for granted the novelty of the technology that others may experience. The experienced user of video-conferencing technology is likely well aware of the potential glitches and malfunctions that may occur, and may be equipped

to handle these distractions with relative ease, whereas an inexperienced user faced with the same challenges may decide it is not worth the effort to troubleshoot, and decline to participate. Despite the challenges and questions associated with using video-conferencing technology, medium theory provides a useful lens for researchers to consider how the use of this media influences their participants' behavior.

Theory of Electronic Propinquity

Rooted in organizational communication research, Korzenny (1978) proposed a theory of mediated communication called electronic propinquity. Propinquity refers to nearness in place and time, and is used interchangeably with the term proximity. Electronic propinquity provides the opportunity for communication when physical proximity is not available. Korzenny (1978) presents six major propositions relevant to communicators' perceptions of nearness which are discussed hereafter.

The first major proposition, Korzenny (1978) posits, is that propinquity increases as bandwidth widens. Bandwidth permits and constrains the amount of information that may be transmitted. For example, in FTF communication, bandwidth is considered wide because any of the five senses may be utilized. Contrast that with communication via the telephone, where bandwidth is limited to one sense, the voice. Video-conferencing technology provides the capability for multiple senses to be utilized, thus increasing the available bandwidth and propinquity.

Second, Korzenny (1978) proposes that as information increases in complexity, propinquity decreases. Specifically, as the information that needs to be transmitted increases in complexity, more senses will be necessary to deliver the information. Again, video-conferencing technology appears useful in that more senses are available for communication than in other media such as the telephone or email. Third, as mutual directionality of the channel increases, so does propinquity.

Mutual directionality refers to the perception of feedback, which is required for propinquity. Therefore, the perception of nearness that is experienced using mediated forms of communication is a function of its similarity to the face-to-face interaction. Similar to FTF interactions, video-conferencing provides individuals with the opportunity to observe both verbal and non-verbal cues, lending to perceptions of feedback.

Korzenny's (1978) fourth proposition outlines that greater communication skills result in greater propinquity. A particular medium of communication is more likely to be considered to provide an adequate degree of propinquity if the person has mastered the necessary skills to communicate using that particular medium. Thus, for individuals lacking a wide range of communication skills, media providing wider bandwidth would be necessary to establish greater propinquity. Video-conferencing provides relatively wider bandwidth than other media which would allow for increased propinquity, however, researchers should ensure their participants have some mastery of the skills needed to use the video-conferencing software to ensure they establish adequate propinquity.

Fifth, propinquity is decreased as communication rules increase. Korzenny (1978) contends that observance of particular rules during communication can inhibit individuals from utilizing necessary skills. For example, Korzenny outlines how perceived rules in a phone call between subordinate and superior can inhibit the subordinate from exercising the necessary skill of redundancy for fear of insulting the superior. In the case of conducting qualitative interviews using video-conferencing, the researcher should be aware of the power structure between researcher and participant, the participant's perception of the relationship, and how that may hinder communication.

Finally, the more limited the number of channels, the greater the propinquity. Given limited choices for communication, individuals will find that selected medium satisfactory in providing propinquity because that is all that is available.

However, if more channels are available for communication, individuals are likely to select the medium requiring the least effort, or with which they have the most experience with. Once again, it is incumbent upon the researcher to understand the level of comfort their participants may have regarding the use of video-conferencing technology. Participants that have little experience with the technology or that view it as cumbersome to use may be less likely to participate in the interview.

Certainly video-conferencing is not a perfect substitute for FTF interactions, but it appears promising in providing perceived propinquity. While the use of video-conferencing has some disadvantages such as dependence on the individual's mastery of skills, the unintended influence of communication rules and the preference for the medium which requires the least effort, time will tell if the benefits outweigh these drawbacks. As the availability of video-conferencing applications becomes more wide-spread through mobile devices and people begin to use these applications for everyday purposes, the issues of skill mastery and perceived effort to use video-conferencing may become less commonplace.

Social Presence Theory

Social psychologists, Short, Williams and Christie (1976) proposed a theory of Social Presence in regards to medium of communication. They viewed Social Presence as a subjective quality of the communication medium. Social Presence represents a number of factors including verbal and non-verbal cues such as facial expressions, physical appearance, direction of eye gaze, and signals from the trunk and arms that an individual is capable of transmitting using a particular medium.

Short, et al. (1976) posited that individuals may avoid certain medium particularly if they perceive that medium does not provide the degree of Social Presence needed for the interaction. In fact, "the suitability of any given communications medium for a specified type of interaction will depend upon two things: the degree of Social Presence of the medium, and the degree of Social Presence required by the task" (Short, et al., 1976, p. 75). According to this proposition, a higher degree of Social Presence would be required of the communication medium selected for interactions that necessitate attention to the idiosyncrasies, reactions, and the personal feelings of others. Alternatively, in interactions that do not focus on personal qualities of individuals communicating (e.g. simply transferring information), the degree of Social Presence in the medium would hold less salience.

Video-conferencing provides a high degree of Social Presence with the capacity to transmit both verbal and non-verbal cues, and thus may be suitable for communications requiring a higher degree of Social Presence. There is the caveat, however, that Social Presence is defined as a subjective quality of the communication medium. Therefore, the Social Presence of video-conferencing

as a medium of communication is subject to participants' perceptions. Social Presence Theory provides another perspective on the suitability of video-conferencing as a form of data collection for research.

To summarize, the Psychobiological Model, Theory of Electronic Propinquity, and Social Presence Theory offer frameworks that may be useful to researchers in substantiating video-conferencing as a viable method of data collection for qualitative research (see Table 1 for a summary of all the models). Medium Theory, on the other hand, may be especially useful for researchers seeking to understand how video-conferencing technology influences the behaviors of specific populations. As the use of CMC continues to gain in popularity, theories such as these can aid in researchers' understanding of using different media for data collection, and perhaps with the advent of new technologies we will also see the inception of new theories to guide future research.

Table 1. A Summary of the models

Theory or Model	Psychobiological Model	Medium Theory	Theory of Electronic Propinquity	Social Presence Theory
Major points of theory or model	Links naturalness of CMC and FTF (media naturalness). Schema alignment. Cognitive adaptation.	Media or medium influence behavior. Social identity is shaped by social networks and access to information as much as content.	Propinquity = nearness in place/ time; proximity. • Bandwidth. • Complexity of information. • Mutual directionality. • Mastery of communication skills. • Communication rules. • Limited channels.	Social presence = subjective quality of the communication medium. • Verbal and non-verbal cues that an individual is capable of transmitting using a particular medium. Suitability of medium is dependent on the degree of Social Presence of the medium and the degree of Social Presence required by the task.
Application to video-conferencing	Video interview has high media naturalness. Researcher must account for differences in schema alignment and be aware of cognitive adaptation to video-conferencing software.	Researcher must be aware of the influence of media on participants' behavior as well as on their own.	Video-conferencing appears promising in providing perceived propinquity. Researcher must acknowledge participants' mastery of skills, communication rules, and preference for medium requiring least effort.	Video-conferencing provides a high degree of Social Presence. Participants' perceptions of Social Presence may differ from the researcher.

ADVANTAGES OF VIDEO-CONFERENCE INTERVIEWS

Of key importance, online video-conferencing overcomes the barrier of geography. Researchers interviewing international participants, rural populations, or colleagues located elsewhere suddenly find it an easier task thanks to online interviews. Participants are afforded flexibility because they can engage in the research at their own location. Simply put, access to a larger sample of individuals may be realized (Chapman, Uggerslev, & Webster, 2003; Deakin & Wakefield, 2013; Murthy, 2008).

Additionally, the participants may feel more comfortable when they participate online at a location of their choosing, typically from their home or office. This may put them at ease in the interview situation, more so than in a FTF interview at a random location. We further discuss this idea in the logistics section of our chapter, but note that a comfortable setting for the participant may increase willingness to talk openly and honestly. The video-conferencing interview allows the interviewee to have just as much control over location as the interviewer. Skype and online interviews may also provide an increased level of privacy. Individuals who worry about the interviewer and interviewee being seen together may seek the online interview so there is little chance of the duo being seen together.

Online video-conferencing also affords the ability to pick up on non-verbal, sensory, and emotional cues, similar to in-person interviews. Bekkering and Shim (2006) describe how the "richness of a medium depends on the availability of instant feedback, the use of multiple cues (such as facial expressions, voice inflections, and gestures), the use of natural language for conveying a broad set of concepts and ideas, and the personal focus of the medium" (p. 104). Online video-conferencing

provides such a medium, simulating a rich FTF environment. Recent studies even have described a rapport that is developed between interviewers and interviewees over online video-conferencing (Deakin & Wakefield, 2013; Sedgwick & Spiers, 2009).

It has been suggested that the quality of responses in FTF and online interviews is much the same. According to Deakin and Wakefield (2013), the occurrence of pauses and repetitions do not differ significantly between the two methods. Some researchers (e.g., Dowling, 2012) indicated that the online interviews were stronger than their FTF ones on the same topic:

Although I had not anticipated this, the fullest and richest data were obtained from the online interviews. Many of the same topics were addressed by F2F and online interviewees, but the prolonged nature of the contact with the latter meant that issues were explored in more depth... It also seemed that women interviewed online felt more able to be critical or negative about their experiences than women interviewed F2F (p. 290).

Other advantages of online interviews include low cost and convenience. Efficiency studies have confirmed online video-conferencing is indeed a cost effective means of conducting research. The low price point of online video-conferencing combined with significant travel savings make Skype and other electronic interviews an attractive option for qualitative researchers. There is also a "reduced cost of failure," meaning that if meetings were rescheduled or cancelled, the associated costs were much less than those of in-person interviews (Shore et. al., 2007, p. 834). The added convenience of online interviews results from the logistical ease of arranging compatible interview times among multiple individuals. The difficulties normally encountered in rescheduling interviews are often avoided.

DISADVANTAGES OF VIDEO-CONFERENCE INTERVIEWS

In contrast, the method is not without flaws. The biggest disadvantage of video-conference interviews is the need for substantial technology beyond just a basic computer and internet connection. Using Skype or another video-conferencing medium requires that "the researcher and all respondents have access to the required technology and the confidence to use it" (Mann & Stewart, 2000, p. 66). Video-conferencing interviews may not be easy or possible for all. The online interview presents methodological and ethical potential and versatility in research, but should not be perceived as an easy option (Deakin & Wakefield, 2013).

Video-conferencing interviews are only possible if computers are new enough to handle the software and only if both parties have high-speed internet connections, web-cams, and microphones capable of running the video-conferencing software. It is also possible to use a laptop or iPad which could have built-in webcams and microphones. Many campus buildings, especially libraries, have small group study rooms available with a computer and webcam that can be used by either the participant or the interviewer. However, in general, technology requirements may be too great to overcome by either party to make video-conferencing an option.

Additionally, participant access may be limited due to these technological requirements. The Pew Internet and American Life Project (2012) reported that, "while internet adoption and the rise of mobile connectivity have reduced many gaps in technology access over the past decade, for some groups, digital disparities still remain" (Zickuhr & Smith, p. 1). The same report, just released last year, indicated that one in five American adults does not use the internet. Senior citizens, adults with less than a high school education, individuals living in households earning less than $30,000 per year, and Spanish-speakers, are all least likely to have internet access (Zickuhr & Smith, 2012).

Clearly these demographics have implications for the type of population that would lend itself to online data collection. In particular, qualitative researchers should be mindful of studies that involve elderly individuals or persons with low socio-economic status.

Depending upon the research design, some studies would clearly not be suited to video-conferencing interviews for the data collection. Certain qualitative studies may require the interviewer to be enmeshed with the subjects and the environment, which may not be possible through real-time video. For example, for an ethnographic study about an unnamed university, Gaye Tuchman (2009) spent six years immersed in campus life and politics during which time she interviewed countless faculty members and administrators and attended meetings, convocations, presidential addresses, classes, and the like. Other qualitative studies encourage direct observation, which is also unlikely through video-conferencing alone.

TECHNIQUES FOR VIDEO-CONFERENCING AND LOGISTICS

The procedures and practices involved in online video-conferencing interviews are fairly similar to traditional face-to-face interviews in some ways, but contrasting in others. This section of the chapter discusses the logistical issues of video-conferencing interviews including recruitment of participants, preparation for the interviews, rapport with participants, the actual interview, as well as records and analysis of the data.

Recruitment

When recruiting participants for online video-conferencing interviews, it is important to mention in the initial communication with potential respondents that the means of interviewing will be through an online portal, such as Skype or Face Time (Salmons, 2010). Participants should be aware of the basic technological requirements and equipment necessary to participate in the interview from the outset. As mentioned earlier, these requirements may include an internet connection, a webcam, speakers, and a microphone. Even most smart phones or tablets with CMC applications may be sufficient to successfully conduct interviews.

Deakin and Wakefield (2013) describe that some participants may be apprehensive regarding the process of being audio- or video-recorded, therefore withdrawing early from the pool. Early notice regarding the technological nature of the interview is beneficial in finding suitably qualified replacements. In many cases, the use of online video-conferencing interviews actually serves to increase sample size. Today's vast availability of technical connections enables access to populations that may have, in the past, been unable to travel or participate for other reasons. Those who are place-bound, such as those with disabilities or familial obligations, value the opportunity to have their voices heard through this online medium (Evans, Elford, & Wiggins, 2010). Although the technology requirements may still pose an access issue to some individuals or groups, the availability of such connections is rapidly spreading. Even rural populations have been able to successfully participate in video-conferencing interviews because of advances in technology, the Internet, and connectivity (Sedgwick & Spiers, 2009). Most importantly, the sample selected must adequately represent the population and lie within the parameters of the research design.

Recruiting participants for online video-conferencing interviews may have naturally emerged during the participant selection process. It is possible that the research design began with in-person FTF interviews as the primary means of data collection but then shifted towards the online modality because of logistical issues such as time, travel, etc. This may be beneficial, as Kasmer and Xie (2008) found that allowing individuals to choose the medium actually increased their willingness to participate in the study. Allowing for participant input into the process is also a very good way to build rapport and trust between the interviewer and interviewee.

Scheduling synchronous online interviews may be easier in some ways than traditional in-person interviews, although there are still some challenges that must be addressed. Kasmer and Xie (2008) found that "scheduling can be quite complicated especially when the medium is synchronous" (p. 260). Holding face-to-face interviews over technology, as mentioned before, can reduce travel costs and increase access to individuals worldwide. In many ways, it may be more convenient to meet online, with interviews held at times and locations that are amenable to both the interviewer and interviewee. At the same time, it is essential to be cognizant of different time zones and personal schedules. Most likely, participants will maintain a daily schedule which must be worked around, regardless of whether the interview is in person or via technology. Interviewers must be flexible in order to accommodate different schedules. Consider the interview of a person located in a country across the world. If the participant is in Australia and the interviewer is in the U.S., one person will have to vary his or her schedule for the convenience of the other person, and as a matter of professionalism, that person most likely should be the researcher.

Online interviews are beneficial for both the researcher and the participant because the interview is conducted in locations that are familiar and comfortable for both individuals. Hanna (2012) describes how a "neutral yet personal location is maintained for both parties throughout the process" (p. 241). This neutrality may have a positive impact on the interview, lending to an increased willingness to talk openly and honestly.

Rapport

Building a rapport with participants, particularly those new to video-conferencing systems, is important. (Bertand & Bourdeau, 2010; Evans, et al, 2010). All communication prior to the actual online interview builds upon the participants' impressions and trust of the researcher. In-person interviews provide an opportunity for the researcher and participant to get to know each other a little bit right before the interview. In some ways, it is easy to build a foundation of trust when you can look someone directly in the eye. Online interviews fall in line second to in-person interviews, so the researcher should take care to be specific regarding all aspects of the interview. Most likely, the initial scheduling and arrangements for the online interview will be on the telephone or via email. The researcher should provide details regarding expectations of the interview, answer any and all questions that may arise, and alleviate possible apprehensions of the interviewee. In all communications, the researcher should try to build a tone of openness and approachability. Evans, et al. (2010) describe that in part, the "experience of online communication may shape the expectations of the online interview" (p. 10). Managing expectations, early with thorough open communication, is essential to laying the foundation to a successful interview.

Participants may express some apprehension regarding the confidentiality and security of an interview over an online mode. Fortunately, in some instances, certain participants may feel that the online modality is one of increased privacy, prompting additional sharing (Evans, et al., 2010). Researchers should follow all conventions regarding protection of participants, similar to in-person interviews, ensuring participants prior to starting the interview that all necessary precautions have been taken to protect the information and/or identity. Interviewees should know that all records of the interviews, including audio or video recordings, are maintained on a secure, password-protected computer system. Additional ethical considerations of online video-conferencing interviews are discussed in more depth later in the chapter.

Rapport building is not exclusively for the time leading up to an interview. It is good practice following an interview to send a quick note or email thanking each interviewee for their time and participation. This is just as important, if not more so, in online interviews since there was not an opportunity for a formal thank you in person.

Preparation

Being technically prepared for an online interview is one of the most important steps for both researchers and participants. Although voice-over-internet-protocol (VOIP) technology has been around since 1995, it may be new to some in research (Greenberg, 2013). Fortunately, in most instances, it is a rather low-cost, easily-learned option. Installing the software at least a day ahead of time is recommended. Testing the equipment and trying out the software a sufficient amount of time prior to the interview allows those in the online conversation to address any issues or glitches that may arise. You may consider video interviewing a friend, colleague, or family member and asking for feedback. Determine if the room was set up properly so that they could see you clearly. A "technical preoccupation," although quickly overcome, was described by some individuals who had to download the software and test it for the first time (Bertand & Bourdeau, 2010). We have found success in conducting a second test immediately preceding the actual interview in order to ensure the equipment, software, and internet connection are working.

Preparation also includes the consideration of presentation. Researchers want to ensure that they have appropriate attire for the interview. Even though it is from a distance, researchers still must maintain a professional appearance. This can also be extended to the background which appears on the computer screen. Interviewers should be cognizant of what the webcam picks up behind them, for it will appear on the participant's computer screen and stay in their range of sight for the duration of the conversation. The focus of the interview needs to be on the questions and responses, rather than on potentially "loud" artwork or clothing. Researchers also need to prepare for and attempt to minimize or eliminate potential distractions. If working from home, it is advisable to complete the interview in a closed room where children, pets, and other potential disruptions can be avoided. In an office setting, a "do not disturb" sign on a closed door is effective.

Researchers also need to be prepared, as with any qualitative interview, with the questions, probes, prompts, and other techniques to further the conversation. Once the interview is in process, it is the researcher's responsibility to focus on the interview itself, ensuring that the necessary data is collected in order to answer the overarching research questions. The researcher will easily be able to turn his or her attention to these matters if all proceeds well with the technology and Internet connection. On the other hand, if difficulties arise such as a spotty connection or large time lag, the researcher must be prepared to handle and adapt to the situation as necessary. Building in additional time and/or making allowances for technical delays is a strategy that potentially increases the opportunity for all of the questions to be answered thoroughly, increasing the validity of the study.

During the Interview

When the actual interview starts, as much as possible, maintain eye contact throughout the discussion. Along this line, also manage your microphone. Be conscious of how small sounds like rustling papers or rocking in a chair may be amplified through the microphone. Talk clearly and converse just like you would in person. Use facial expressions and hand gestures to emphasize points.

Active listening is very important as well. We noticed in our video interviews that the interviewee was aware if we were really listening to their answer or just prepping for the next question. Position yourself so you are centered and looking into the camera, and have the camera at eye-level, if possible, so you are not looking up or down at the interviewee. Sit up straight or lean forward slightly to help increase eye contact.

Records and Analysis

Using media such as Skype enables the researcher(s) to record both the audio and video conversations (Bertand & Bourdeau, 2010; Hanna, 2012). There are several "video call recording" plug-ins or applications that can be used with either Windows or Mac platforms, with costs being minimal or free (e.g. Pamela for Skype or Audio Hijack). As mentioned regarding the interview software, these applications should be tested thoroughly before the interview to ensure proper recording. An audio recorder and/or hand-written notes may also be recommended as backup in the event of technical difficulties. Unfortunately, there does not appear to be similar software available to easily transcribe the interviews, leaving the process of transcribing similar to that with a traditional audio recorder or Dragon software.

As with the technology making online interviews possible, qualitative analytic software programs are also advancing to meet needs of researchers. Software tools such as Atlas.ti or NVivo have features which enable coding directly in an audio/video file, potentially eliminating the need for transcription. Coding the data is only one step in analysis. Online interviews also present additional considerations for the analysis process. Salmons (2010) mentioned that the online component of an interview should not cease at the end of the discussion. Researchers need to think about the reasons for, process of, and results from the video-conferencing interview. Some questions that Salmons (2010) suggests asking include the following:

- How did the participant respond to the process as well as to the interview questions?
- Did the interview proceed as planned or were adjustments needed?
- Does the data allow the researcher to conduct the analysis and generate conclusions that achieved the purpose of the study? (p. 7).

Qualitative research is oftentimes strengthened by the inclusion of researcher perspective or worldview. Studies conducted via online data collection methods, and in this case video-conferencing interviews, are no different. Researchers' recollections of the process of online interviews can actually strengthen both the study and the field, even lending suggestions for future studies. Efforts toward reflexivity should be made, with notes and documentation collected by the researcher, throughout the process of interviews as the online setting may play a role in the answers and perceptions discerned through the video-conferencing interviews.

ETHICAL CONSIDERATIONS

In the discussions of ethics regarding online qualitative research, the primary focus of the literature remains on online asynchronous communications such as webpages, blogs, groups, etc. The protection of subjects remains equally as important in online interviews as in FTF interactions or any other online research. Institutional Review Boards (IRBs) are evolving in their interpretation of such data collection methods. Each institution is responsible for establishing offices and regulating policies regarding protection of research subjects and informed consent, all of which must meet the requirements outlined by the U.S.'s Office for Human Research Protections. It is the responsibility of researchers to work in cooperation with their IRB offices to address new, innovative data collection methodologies. As referenced in Nehls (2013), Office of Research Compliance requires that "all studies, including those using computer and Internet technologies, must (a) ensure the procedures fulfill the principles of voluntary participation and informed consent; (b) maintain the confidentiality of information obtained from or about human participants; and (c) adequately address possible risks to participants including stress and related issues" (p. 310).

In our experience, the informed consent process is slightly different in online interviews than in a FTF environment, although the documentation is the same. In a recent study, we delivered a document (Word or PDF) online via email prior to the interview to the participants. After the connection online was initiated but prior to beginning the actual interview, the statement was then reviewed by the researcher and then a verbal affirmation was given by the participant. At that time, participants were also informed of their right to stop the interview for any reason at any time during the interview. A separate statement must be included, with verbal consent given, if the interview is going to be recorded in any way. Deakin and Wakefield (2013) describe how such an informed consent process may hinder rapport-building efforts, although we argue that the process is not any more intimidating than that found in FTF interviews. Ample time must be allowed in order to answer any questions regarding the process or the interview questions throughout the time online.

LESSONS LEARNED

The experience of using video-conferencing interviews has been both interesting and fruitful for our research. Online communication is starting to become commonplace with the majority of our recent participants. The most recent video-conferencing interviews we completed did not need to include directions for installing and practicing with the Skype application. The participants were college students and/or worked for colleges and universities; therefore, most were familiar with Skype, Face Time, and other video-conferencing technologies. As these technologies are increasing in popularity, we assume that we will continue to find more and more participants willing and eager to engage in interviews via technology. They are already using it on a regular basis in their personal lives, so it is a natural extension to move into the realm of research.

That being said, technology still has its limitations. Broadband connectivity and the speed of the internet may hinder some interviews with pauses or uneven breaks in the conversation. Some people also felt that this form of communication was somewhat awkward, and they didn't know exactly where to look or place the webcam for the best shot. In one example with our interviewee in a different state, "Sally" was participating in our online interview via her smartphone in her car, which was parked at a shopping center at dusk. The interview started off really well with Sally resting her phone on the car's steering wheel. But, after a while, her arm got tired and she put the phone in her lap, which was awkward for viewing her while talking. Then the sun set and it was very dark and difficult to see her in her vehicle. Sally turned on an inside car light which slightly improved our sight of her. Sally also wanted to end the call to get into the shopping center before close, so none of these things created the ideal interview situation. All that being said, however, this FTF interview would never have even been possible had it not been for Skype. We were able to catch Sally after work (her preference) and before she started evening errands, and she was candid and fun to talk to in her car. It was also exciting

to see her in her "natural" setting, yet still in a different time zone and location, with neither of us traveling to do so.

In another online interview, we talked to "Jose" while he was on vacation and staying with cousins. Jose talked to us from the comfort of his cousins' living room, but it was in the middle of a heavy thunderstorm. Every time the lightening cracked in the background, the Skype connection briefly paused, and more distractedly, the dogs at the house barked ferociously at the noise of the storm. Again, though, we felt like this interview was only possible because of the technology. Jose would have been less likely to participate in an interview while on vacation had he not been able to set it up easily in his own space and at his convenience. The place of the online interview is more fluid.

Both of the interviews mentioned above were conducted in the evening, and many times this is not a preferable time for the FTF option for many reasons, including health and safety. However, those times were preferable for the participants mentioned above since Sally works full-time and Jose was traveling that day. It was because of the power of online interviews that we were able to conduct the interviews at all. As Deakin and Wakefield (2013) suggested, "Offering the option to be interviewed via Skype may increase participation" (p. 7). We certainly found this to be the case in many of our research projects.

In comparing telephone and video-conference interviews, we found video interviews to be superior to telephone on many levels. First of all, the FTF nature of the video-conference, even in different locations, made the entire interview seem more personal and natural. We also concluded that there was more focus during video-conference interviews. During phone interviews, individuals were able to check email, answer text messages, and even doodle while they chatted with us, which meant that we did not have their undivided attention. The video-conference interviews definitely felt more purposeful. We also experienced individuals with strong accents or different dialects were more easily understood in video-conference interviews instead of on the phone. This could have been because of social or physical cues in the online interviews.

One of our final "lessons learned" is that video-conference interviews may work well for certain studies, but they are not perfect for all types of studies. As always, the research question and method need to drive the type of data collection, and certain populations fit the video-conference interview method better than others. For example, in one recent study we conducted with college students, the population was very familiar with online technology and easily adapted to this interview format. In this instance, the Skype video-conferencing technology was a very good alternative to FTF interviews.

FUTURE TRENDS

Acceptance of CMC technologies for conducting qualitative research has grown in recent years, particularly with the use of qualitative email interviews (McCoyd & Kerson, 2006; Meho, 2006; Nehls, 2013). On the other hand, the use of synchronous video-conferencing technology for qualitative interviews is still in its infancy (Deakin & Wakefield, 2013; Matthews & Cramer, 2008; Sedgwick & Spiers, 2009). Deakin and Wakefield (2013) aptly observe, "While the literature has often discussed the logistics of online communication and interviewing, there is a lack of discussion around how telecommunication such as Skype fits within the paradigm of interviewing in a global age" (p. 10). Building on Holt's (2010) argument for telephone interviews as a viable substitute for FTF interviews, Hanna (2012) makes the case

for video-conferencing as a suitable alternative. Evans et al. (2010) note, however, that the feasibility of interviewing using video-conferencing will be dependent upon interviewees' access to the technology.

Access to video-conferencing technology for the masses has become more commonplace as a number of free video-conferencing applications have surfaced that are readily available for use on many devices. Skype is compatible with Windows, Mac and Linux operating systems, as well as multiple devices including desktops, tablets, mobile phones, smart T.V.s, the PlayStation Vita, and iPod Touch. Other free video-conferencing applications that are available across operating systems and multiple devices include Google Hangouts, Viber, and ooVoo. Meanwhile, Mac users have access to Face Time on several compatible Mac devices.

Although it has been reported that one in five American adults do not use the internet (Zickuhr & Smith, 2012), ownership of mobile devices is on the rise. A recent Pew Internet and American Life Project Report reveals that the majority, 91%, of American adults have a cell phone with more than half owning a smartphone, while nearly a quarter of Americans ages 16 and older own an e-reader, and 35% of Americans ages 16 and older own a tablet (Brenner, 2013). The same report indicates 63% of adult cell phone owners use their phones to access the internet. While only 21% reported using their phones to make video calls or video chats, there is great potential to reach people using video calls on their cellular devices. As more and more individuals begin to explore the video calling applications available to them, the possibilities for using these applications in qualitative research are still yet to be seen.

Related to the use of video-conferencing technology for qualitative research is the growing need for innovation in qualitative data analysis software that is compatible with the commonly used video-conferencing applications. For instance, Pamela for Skype software (see: http://www.pamela.biz/en/) is compatible with Skype for recording audio and video data free of charge. Additional software such as NVivo 10 (see: http://www.qsrinternational.com/) and Transana (see: http://www.transana.org/) can be purchased to aid in transcription and analysis of video content, though the ease of transfer of video from the selected applications discussed previously is not well known to the authors. Moreover, as new technologies emerge alongside the use of video-conferencing for qualitative research, there is a "research-skills gap" that will need to be addressed (Hesse-Biber & Griffin, 2013). Likewise, Palys and Atchison (2012) highlight the importance of training future scholars:

The current generation of graduate students needs to know enough about what digital possibilities are available to them to make their own choices about the extent to which they want to pursue the options the digital world opens to them, and help develop the next generation of digital tools so that they are maximally beneficial for both researchers and participants alike (p. 364).

Along with the technological possibilities that are envisioned, potential concerns must also be addressed. Palys and Atchison (2012) warn of the vulnerability of security for digitally collected data. Further, they express concern over the widespread use of cloud computing which subjects researchers and their data to the privacy policies of the company running the cloud server. Specifically, many of these companies are under the jurisdiction of the United States Patriot Act, which threatens the confidentiality of participants (Palys & Atchison, 2012). Thus, as the use of technology for research becomes more readily adopted, researchers must go to great lengths to ensure security of data and protect their participants' confidentiality. In this regard, Palys and Atchison (2012) note the ideal would be for researchers to "develop the capacity to run their own" data servers (p. 364).

The use of video-conferencing technology for qualitative research is still in its early stages. Limited research exists that has utilized video-conferencing as a method of qualitative data collection, and video-conferencing applications are continually evolving to meet consumers' needs. The landscape for future research on video-conferencing in qualitative research is wide open, and presents a gap that needs to be filled.

CONCLUSION

Collecting data through online video-conferencing is becoming a commonly accepted technique for businesses and corporations, especially when making new hires. However, it is still infrequent in qualitative research as a primary means of data collection, and we hope this chapter identifies the strengths and weaknesses of using Skype and other means of video-conferencing for interview research. Our initial efforts to incorporate this technology were primarily employed to minimize costs while increasing flexibility. Additional benefits, such as expanded access, additional convenience, and a rich FTF experience, were soon realized. On the other hand, researchers must note that technological requirements may limit the access to online video-conferencing for certain populations, an important consideration when embarking on any study or research project. The logistics of video-conferencing interviews also warranted discussion, as well as the theories lending to and the analysis resulting from FTF data collection. As this mode of qualitative research is in its infancy, researchers must be cognizant of the potential vulnerabilities, such as data security, as well as budding innovations in CMC technology and software. Over all, we believe video-conferencing interviews expand the boundaries of rich, descriptive qualitative research, in a manner that is both convenient and accessible.

REFERENCES

Bekkering, E., & Shim, J. P. (2006). i2i trust in videoconferencing. *Communications of the ACM*, *49*(7), 103–107. doi:10.1145/1139922.1139925

Bertrand, C., & Bourdeau, L. (2010). Research interviews by Skype: A new data collection method. In *Proceedings of the 9th European Conference on Research Methodology for Business and Management Studies*, (pp. 70-79). Madrid: IE Business School. Retrieved from http://books.google.co.uk/books?id=8mTywIN8EXkC&printsec=frontcover#v=onepage&q&f=false

Brenner, J. (2013). *Pew internet: Mobile.* Retrieved January 3, 2014, from http://pewinternet.org/Commentary/2012/February/Pew-Internet-Mobile.aspx

Chapman, D. S., & Rowe, P. M. (2001). The impact of videoconference technology, interview structure, and interviewer gender on interviewer evaluations in the employment interview: A field experiment. *Journal of Occupational and Organizational Psychology*, *74*(3), 279–298. doi:10.1348/096317901167361

Chapman, D. S., Uggerslev, K. L., & Webster, J. (2003). Applicant reactions to face-to-face and technology-mediated interviews: A field investigation. *The Journal of Applied Psychology*, *88*(5), 944–953. doi:10.1037/0021-9010.88.5.944 PMID:14516254

Chen, M. (2002). *Leveraging the asymmetric sensitivity of eye contact for videoconference.* Paper presented at the Special Interest Group on Computer-Human Interaction Conference on Human factors in Computing Systems. Minneapolis, MN. doi:10.1145/503384.503386

Deakin, H., & Wakefield, K. (2013). Skype interviewing: Reflections of two PhD researchers. *Qualitative Research*. DOI: .10.1177/1468794113488126

Dowling, S. (n.d.). Online asynchronous and face-to-face interviewing: Comparing methods for exploring women's experiences of breastfeeding long term. In J. Salmons (Ed.), *Cases in Online Interview Research* (pp. 277–296). London: Sage.

Evans, A., Elford, J., & Wiggins, D. (2010). Using the internet for qualitative research in psychology. In C. Willig, & W. Stainton-Rogers (Eds.), *The Sage Handbook for Qualitative Research* (pp. 315–334). London: Sage.

Greenberg, R. (2013). The history of VOIP. *The Digest.* Retrieved December 18, 2013, from http://www.thedigest.com/blog/the-history-of-voip

Hanna, P. (2012). Using internet technologies (such as Skype) as a research medium: A research note. *Qualitative Research*, *2*(2), 239–242. doi:10.1177/1468794111426607

Hesse-Biber, S., & Griffin, A. J. (2013). Internet-mediated technologies and mixed methods research: Problems and prospects. *Journal of Mixed Methods Research*, *7*(1), 43–61. doi:10.1177/1558689812451791

Holt, A. (2010). Using telephones for narrative interviewing: A research note. *Qualitative Research*, *10*(1), 113–121. doi:10.1177/1468794109348686

Innis, H. A. (1964). *The Bias of Communication.* Toronto: University of Toronto Press.

Innis, H. A. (1972). *Empire and Communications.* Toronto: University of Toronto Press.

Kazmer, M. M., & Xie, B. (2008). Qualitative interviewing in internet studies: Playing with the media, playing with the method. *Information Communication and Society*, *11*(2), 257–278. doi:10.1080/13691180801946333

Kock, N. (2004). The psychobiological model: Toward a new theory of computer-mediated communication based on Darwinian evolution. *Organization Science*, *15*(3), 327–348. doi:10.1287/orsc.1040.0071

Kock, N. (2005). Media richness or media naturalness? The evolution of our biological communication apparatus and its influence on our behavior toward e-communication tools. *IEEE Transactions on Professional Communication*, 48(2), 117–130. doi:10.1109/TPC.2005.849649

Korzenny, F. (1978). A theory of electronic propinquity: Mediated communication in organizations. *Communication Research*, 5(1), 3–24. doi:10.1177/009365027800500101

Mann, C., & Stewart, F. (2000). *Internet communication and qualitative research: A handbook for researching online*. London: Sage Publications.

Marshall, C., & Rossman, G. B. (2006). *Designing qualitative research* (4th ed.). Thousand Oaks, CA: Sage Publications.

Matthews, J., & Cramer, E. P. (2008). Using technology to enhance qualitative research with hidden populations. *Qualitative Report*, 13(2), 301–315.

McCoyd, J. L. M., & Kerson, T. S. (2006). Conducting intensive interviews using email: A serendipitous comparative opportunity. *Qualitative Social Work: Research and Practice*, 5(3), 389–406. doi:10.1177/1473325006067367

McLuhan, M. (1962). *The Gutenberg Galaxy: The Making of Typographic Man*. Toronto: University of Toronto Press.

McLuhan, M. (1964). *Understanding Media: The Extensions of Man*. New York, NY: McGraw-Hill.

Meho, L. I. (2006). E-mail interviewing in qualitative research: A methodological discussion. *Journal of the American Society for Information Science and Technology*, 57(10), 1284–1295. doi:10.1002/asi.20416

Meyrowitz, J. (1994). Medium Theory. In D. Crowley, & D. Mitchell (Eds.), *Communication Theory Today* (pp. 50–77). Stanford, CA: Stanford University Press.

Murthy, D. (2008). Digital ethnography: An examination of the use of new technologies for social research. *Sociology*, 42(5), 837–855. doi:10.1177/0038038508094565

Nehls, K. (2013). Methodological considerations of email interviews. In Advancing Research Methods with New Media Technologies (pp. 303-315). New York: IGI-Global Publishing.

Palys, T., & Atchison, C. (2012). Qualitative research in the digital era: Obstacles and opportunities. *International Journal of Qualitative Methods*, 11(4), 352–367.

Rose, G. (2007). *Visual methodologies: An introduction to the interpretation of visual materials* (2nd ed.). Thousand Oaks, CA: Sage Publications.

Salmons, J. (2010). *Online interviews in real time*. Thousand Oaks, CA: Sage.

Sedgwick, M., & Spiers, J. (2009). The use of videoconferencing as a medium for the qualitative interview. *International Journal of Qualitative Methods*, 8(1), 1–11.

Shore, J., Brooks, E., Savin, D., Manson, S., & Libby, A. (2007). An economic evaluation of telehealth data collection with rural populations. *Psychiatric Services (Washington, D.C.)*, 58(6), 830–835. doi:10.1176/appi.ps.58.6.830 PMID:17535944

Short, J., Williams, E., & Christie, B. (1976). *The Social Psychology of Telecommunications*. New York, NY: John Wiley & Sons.

Skype grows FY revenues 20%, reaches 663 million users. (2011). Retrieved April 8, 2014, from http://www.telecompaper.com/news/skype-grows-fy-revenues-20-reaches-663-mln-users--790254

Tuchman, G. (2009). *Wannabe U: Inside the Corporate University*. Chicago: University of Chicago Press. doi:10.7208/chicago/9780226815282.001.0001

Weinmann, T., Thomas, S., Brilmayer, S., Henrich, S., & Radon, K. (2012). Testing Skype as an interview method in epidemiologic research: Response and feasibility. *International Journal of Public Health, 57*(6), 959–961. doi:10.1007/s00038-012-0404-7 PMID:22945842

Winzenburg, S. (2011). How Skype is changing the interview process. *The Chronicle of Higher Education*. Retrieved April 15, 2012, from http://chronicle.com/article/How-Skype-Is-Changing-the/126529/

Zickuhr, K., & Smith, A. (2012). *Digital differences*. Pew Internet & American Life Project. Retrieved April 30, 2012, from http://pewinternet.org/Reports/2012/Digital-differences.aspx

KEY TERMS AND DEFINITIONS

Computer-Mediated Communication (CMC): Communication between individuals that is conducted via any type of computer application (e.g. e-mail, chat rooms, video-conferencing).

Medium Theory: A theory extended by Meyrowitz (1994) to examine how types of media influence communication behavior.

Psychobiological Model: A model proposed by Kock (2004) to explain the link between the naturalness of CMC and FTF communication.

Skype: A video-conferencing application that is easily downloadable for multiple communication media (e.g. PC's, tablets, mobile phones, etc.).

Social Presence Theory: Proposed by Short, Williams and Christie (1976), Social Presence Theory examines individuals' perceptions of the quality of communication media via the capacity to transmit both verbal and non-verbal cues.

Theory of Electronic Propinquity: A theory developed by Korzenny (1978) which examines individuals' perceptions of nearness when communication is mediated electronically.

Video-Conferencing: Technology that allows individuals to communicate via video and audio connection in real-time through a computer or other mobile platform (e.g. tablet or mobile phone).

Chapter 7
Data Integration Technology for Industrial and Environmental Research via Air Quality Monitoring Network

Tianxing Cai
Lamar University, USA

ABSTRACT

Industrial and environmental research will always involve the study of the cause-effect relationship between emissions and the surrounding environment. Qualitative and mixed methods researchers have employed a variety of Information and Communication Technology (ICT) tools, simulated or virtual environments, information systems, information devices, and data analysis tools in this field. With the collection and representation of information in a range of ways, software tools have been created to manage and store this data. This data management enables more efficient searching ability of various types of electronic and digitized information. Various technologies have made the work of research more efficient. The results of the qualitative or mixed methods research may be integrated to reach the research target. Right now, a lot of software tools are available for analysis to identify patterns and represent new meanings. The programs extend the capabilities of the researcher in terms of information coding and meaning-making. Machine-enhanced analytics has enabled the identification of aspects of interest such as correlations and anomalies from large datasets. Chemical facilities, where large amounts of chemicals and fuels are processed, manufactured, and housed, have high risks to originate air emission events, such as intensive flaring and toxic gas release caused by various uncertainties like equipment failure, false operation, nature disaster, or terrorist attack. Based on an available air-quality monitoring network, the data integration technologies are applied to identify the scenarios of the possible emission source and the dynamic pollutant monitor result, so as to timely and effectively support diagnostic and

DOI: 10.4018/978-1-4666-6493-7.ch007

prognostic decisions. In this chapter, several systematic methodologies and preliminary data integration system designs for such applications are developed according to the real application purpose. It includes two stages of modeling and optimization work: 1) the determination of background normal emission rates from multiple emission sources and 2) single-objective or multi-objective optimization for impact scenario identification and quantification. They have the capability of identifying the potential emission profile and spatial-temporal characterization of pollutant dispersion for a specific region, including reverse estimation of air quality issues. The chapter provides valuable information for accidental investigations and root cause analysis for an emission event, and it helps evaluate the regional air quality impact caused by such an emission event as well. Case studies are employed to demonstrate the efficacy of the developed methodology.

BACKGROUND

Data integration techniques or information and communication technologies have been intensively used in different data mining applications such as data clustering, classification, association rules mining, sequential pattern mining, outlier detection, feature selection, and information extraction in the industrial and environmental research via air quality monitoring network. A huge increase in the number of papers and citations in the area has been observed in the previous decade, which is clear evidence of the popularity of these techniques. These have included the adoption of such kind of methodologies in the research field of polarization-difference imaging for observation through scattering media (Rowe, Pugh, Tyo, & Engheta, 1995), biologically inspired self-adaptive multi-path routing in overlay networks (Leibnitz, Wakamiya, & Murata, 2006), a biologically inspired system for action recognition (Jhuang, Serre, Wolf, & Poggio, 2007), programmable self-assembly using biologically-inspired multia-gent control (Nagpal, 2002), biologically inspired growth of hydroxyapatite nanocrystals inside self-assembled collagen fibers (Roveri, Falini, Sidoti, Tampieri, Landi, Sandri, & Parma, 2003), biologically inspired cognitive radio engine model utilizing distributed genetic algorithms for secure and robust wireless communications and networking (Rieser, 2004), biomimetics of biologically inspired technologies (Bar-Cohen, 2005), biologi-

cally inspired computing (De Castro & von Zuben, 2005), and biologically inspired algorithms for financial modeling (Brabazon & O'Neill, 2006). Before we start to give the introduction of these techniques in the research field of industrial operation and environment sustainability, the brief introduction will be given for these techniques.

1. **Artificial Neural Networks:** In computer science and related fields, artificial neural networks are models are derived from animal central nervous systems (Wang & Fu, 2008). The biologically neural networks are capable of machine learning and pattern recognition. They can be regarded as systems of internally connected neurons. They can compute values from inputs by feeding information through the network (Stevens & Casillas, 2006). For example, in a neural network for image recognition, a set of input neurons may be activated by the pixels of an input image representing a shape or color. The activations of these neurons are then passed on, weighted and transformed by some function determined by the network's designer, to other neurons, etc., until finally an output neuron is activated that determines which image was recognized. Similar with other methods of machine learning, neural networks have been applied to solve a wide range of jobs which are difficult to solve using ordinary rule-

based programming (Yang & Zheng, 2009). Generally, artificial neural network handles a problem with the combination of simple processing elements which have complex global behavior. A class of statistical models will be called "neural" if they have sets of adaptive weights (numerical parameters that are tuned by a learning algorithm, and are capable of approximating non-linear functions of their inputs) (Patterson, 1998).

The adaptive weights are conceptually connection strengths between neurons. They will be activated during the period of model training and prediction. Neural networks can also perform functions collectively and in parallel by the units, which are also similar to biological neural networks. The terminology of neural network usually means the model with the integration of statistics, cognitive psychology and artificial intelligence (Sarle, 1994). They are part of theoretical neuroscience and computational neuroscience. In modern software implementations of artificial neural networks, the approach inspired by biology has been largely abandoned according to statistics and signal processing (Holler, Tam, Castro, & Benson, 1989). In some of these systems, neural networks or parts of neural networks can form components in larger systems that combine both adaptive and non-adaptive elements (Cochocki, & Unbehauen, 1993). The general approach of such systems is feasible for real-world problem solving while it has been different from the traditional artificial intelligence connectionist models, which adopt the principles of non-linear, distributed, parallel and local processing and adaptation.

2. **Fuzzy Logic System:** Fuzzy logic is a logic form of multiple values. It helps to handle the problems which are not fixed and exact. Compared to traditional binary variables, fuzzy logic variables may have a truth value that ranges in degree between 0 and 1. It can be regarded as the concept of partial truth, where the truth value may range between completely true and completely false (Perfilieva & Močkoř, 1999). The term "fuzzy logic" was introduced with the proposal of fuzzy set theory by Lotfi A. Zadeh (Zadeh, 1965; Zalta, 2003). It has been applied in many fields of control theory and artificial intelligence. A basic application might characterize subranges of a continuous variable. For instance, a temperature measurement for anti-lock brakes might have several separate membership functions defining particular temperature ranges needed to control the brakes properly. Each function maps the same temperature value to a truth value in the 0 to 1 range. These truth values can then be used to determine how the brakes should be controlled.

3. **Genetic Algorithms:** In the field of artificial intelligence, a genetic algorithm (GA) is a search heuristic with the process of natural selection. This heuristic is normally used to generate useful solutions to optimization and search problems. Genetic algorithms is one of the algorithm of evolutionary algorithms (EA) (Whitley, 1994). The evolutionary algorithm applies the evolution techniques of inheritance, mutation, selection, and crossover to generate solutions to optimization problems. It can be used in bioinformatics, computational science, engineering, economics, manufacturing, mathematics, physics, chemistry, and other fields (Goldberg & Holland, 1988). In a genetic algorithm, a population of candidate solutions to an optimization problem is evolved to better generations of solutions. Each candidate solution has a set of properties of chromosomes which can be mutated and altered. The procedures usually start from a population of randomly generated individuals. Then the iterative process will provide a new generation of population in each iteration (Vose, 1999). The fitness of

every individual in the population is evaluated in each generation. It is usually the value of the objective function in the optimization problem being minimized or maximized. The more fit individuals are selected from the current population, and each individual's genome is changed through recombination and possibly randomly mutation to form a new generation. The new generation of candidate solutions is then used in the next iteration of the algorithm. Commonly, the algorithm terminates when either a maximum number of generations has been produced, or a satisfactory fitness level has been reached for the population. A typical genetic algorithm requires: a genetic representation of the solution domain, a fitness function to evaluate the solution domain. A standard representation of each candidate solution is as an array of bits. The main property that makes these genetic representations convenient is that their parts are easily aligned due to their fixed size, which facilitates simple crossover operations. Variable length representations may also be used, but crossover implementation is more complex in this case. Tree-like representations are explored in genetic programming and graph-form representations are explored in evolutionary programming; a mix of both linear chromosomes and trees is explored in gene expression programming. When the genetic representation and the fitness function are defined, a GA proceeds to initialize a population of solutions and then to improve it through repetitive application of the mutation, crossover, inversion and selection operators. Initially many individual solutions are randomly generated to form an initial population. The population size is based on the nature of the problem, but typically contains thousands of possible solutions. Normally, the population is generated randomly in order to cover the entire range of possible solutions in the searching space.

During each successive generation, a proportion of the existing population is selected to breed a new generation. Individual solutions are selected through a fitness-based process, where fitter solutions are typically more likely to be selected. The selection methods help to rate the fitness of each solution and select the best solutions. The next step is to generate a second generation population of solutions from those selected through genetic operators: crossover and/or mutation. For each new solution to be produced, a pair of parent solutions is selected for breeding from the previously selected pool. By producing a "child" solution using the above methods of crossover and mutation, a new solution is created which typically shares many of the characteristics of its "parents". New parents are selected for each new child, and the process continues until a new population of solutions of appropriate size is generated. These processes ultimately result in the next generation population of chromosomes that is different from the initial generation. Generally the average fitness will have increased by this procedure for the population, since only the best organisms from the first generation are selected for breeding, along with a small proportion of less fit solutions. These less fit solutions ensure genetic diversity within the genetic pool of the parents and therefore ensure the genetic diversity of the subsequent generation of children. The attention should be paid to the tuning parameters such as the mutation probability, crossover probability and population size to find reasonable settings for the problem solving. There are theoretical but not yet practical upper and lower bounds for these parameters that can help guide selection through experiments. This above introduced processes are repeated until a termination condition has been reached. Common terminating conditions are the achievement of the identification of solution to satisfy criteria, fixed number of generations, allocated budget of computation time and the highest ranking solution's fitness (Deb, 2001).

4. **Ant Colony Optimization:** The ant colony optimization algorithm (ACO) is a probabilistic technique for solving computational problems which can be reduced to finding good paths through graphs (Dorigo & Di Caro, 1999). This algorithm is one of the ant colony algorithms family of swarm intelligence methods and some meta-heuristic optimizations (Dorigo, & Birattari, 2010). Ant colony optimization algorithms have been applied to many combinatorial optimization problems, ranging from quadratic assignment to protein folding or routing vehicles and a lot of derived methods have been adapted to dynamic problems in real variables, stochastic problems, multi-targets and parallel implementations. It has also been used to produce near-optimal solutions to the travelling salesman problem (Dorigo, 2007). They have an advantage over simulated annealing and genetic algorithm approaches of similar problems when the graph may change dynamically; the ant colony algorithm can be run continuously and adapt to changes in real time. This is of interest in network routing and urban transportation systems (Dorigo, 2006).

5. **Particle Swarm Optimization:** Particle swarm optimization (PSO) helps to optimize a problem by iteratively trying to improve a candidate solution with regard to a given measure of quality (Kennedy, 2010). PSO optimizes a problem by having a population of candidate solutions of dubbed particles and moving these particles around in the search-space according to simple mathematical formulae over the particle's position and velocity (Kennedy, 2010; Poli, Kennedy, & Blackwell, 2007). Each particle's movement is determined by its local best known position

and guided toward the best known positions in the search-space. They are updated as better positions found by other particles. PSO is a meta-heuristic due to its characterization with few or no assumptions about the problem being optimized and can search very large spaces of candidate solutions. However, meta-heuristics such as PSO do not guarantee an optimal solution is ever found. More specifically, PSO does not use the gradient of the problem being optimized, which means PSO does not require that the optimization problem be differentiable as is required by classic optimization methods such as gradient descent and quasi-Newton methods (Venter & Sobieszczanski-Sobieski, 2003). A basic variant of the PSO algorithm works by having a population (called a swarm) of candidate solutions (called particles). These particles are moved around in the search-space according to a few simple formulae (Clerc, 2006). The movements of the particles are guided by their own best known position in the search-space as well as the entire swarm's best known position. When improved positions are being discovered these will then come to guide the movements of the swarm. The process is repeated and by doing so it is hoped, but not guaranteed, that a satisfactory solution will eventually be discovered. PSO has also been applied to multi-objective problems, in which the objective function comparison takes Pareto dominance into account when moving the PSO particles and non-dominated solutions are stored so as to approximate the Pareto front (Lazinica, 2009).

6. **Artificial Immune System:** Artificial immune systems (AIS) are a class of computationally intelligent systems inspired by the principles and processes of the vertebrate immune system. The algorithms typically exploit the immune system's characteristics of learning and memory to solve a problem.

The field of Artificial Immune Systems (AIS) is concerned with abstracting the structure and function of the immune system to computational systems, and investigating the application of these systems towards solving computational problems from mathematics, engineering, and information technology. AIS is a sub-field of Biologically-inspired computing, and Natural computation, with interests in Machine Learning and belonging to the broader field of Artificial Intelligence. Artificial Immune Systems (AIS) are adaptive systems, inspired by theoretical immunology and observed immune functions, principles and models, which are applied to problem solving. AIS is distinct from computational immunology and theoretical biology that are concerned with simulating immunology using computational and mathematical models towards better understanding the immune system, although such models initiated the field of AIS and continue to provide a fertile ground for inspiration. Finally, the field of AIS is not concerned with the investigation of the immune system as a substrate computation, such as DNA computing. The common techniques are inspired by specific immunological theories that explain the function and behavior of the mammalian adaptive immune system (Timmis & Neal, 2001; DasGupta, 1999; Coello & Cortés, 2005; Lei, 2002; Coello & Cortés, 2002).

a. **Clonal Selection Algorithm:** A class of algorithms inspired by the clonal selection theory of acquired immunity that explains how B and T lymphocytes improve their response to antigens over time called affinity maturation. These algorithms focus on the Darwinian attributes of the theory where selection is inspired by the affinity of antigen-antibody interactions, reproduction is inspired by cell division, and variation is inspired by somatic hypermutation. Clonal selection algorithms are most commonly applied to optimization and pattern recognition domains, some of which resemble parallel hill climbing and the genetic algorithm without the recombination operator.

b. **Negative Selection Algorithm:** Inspired by the positive and negative selection processes that occur during the maturation of T cells in the thymus called T cell tolerance. Negative selection refers to the identification and deletion (apoptosis) of self-reacting cells, that is T cells that may select for and attack self tissues. This class of algorithms are typically used for classification and pattern recognition problem domains where the problem space is modeled in the complement of available knowledge. For example in the case of an anomaly detection domain the algorithm prepares a set of exemplar pattern detectors trained on normal (non-anomalous) patterns that model and detect unseen or anomalous patterns.

c. **Immune Network Algorithms:** Algorithms inspired by the idiotypic network theory proposed by Niels Kaj Jerne (Timmis & Neal, 2001; DasGupta, 1999; Coello & Cortés, 2005; Lei, 2002; Coello & Cortés, 2002) that describes the regulation of the immune system by anti-idiotypic antibodies (antibodies that select for other antibodies). This class of algorithms focus on the network graph structures involved where antibodies (or antibody producing cells) represent the nodes and the training algorithm involves growing or pruning edges between the nodes based on affinity (similarity in the problems representation space). Immune network algorithms have been used in clustering, data visualization, control, and optimization domains, and share properties with artificial neural networks.

d. **Dendritic Cell Algorithms:** The Dendritic Cell Algorithm (DCA) is an example of an immune inspired algorithm developed using a multi-scale approach. This algorithm is based on an abstract model of dendritic cells (DCs). The DCA is abstracted and implemented through a process of examining and modeling various aspects of DC function, from the molecular networks present within the cell to the behaviour exhibited by a population of cells as a whole. Within the DCA information is granulated at different layers, achieved through multi-scale processing.

7. **Culture Algorithm:** Cultural algorithms (CA) are a branch of evolutionary computation where there is a knowledge component that is called the belief space in addition to the population component (Reynolds & Sverdlik, 1994; Reynolds, 1994). In this sense, cultural algorithms can be seen as an extension to a conventional genetic algorithm (Coello Coello & Becerra, 2004). The belief space of a cultural algorithm is divided into distinct categories. These categories represent different domains of knowledge that the population has of the search space. The belief space is updated after each iteration by the best individuals of the population. The best individuals can be selected using a fitness function that assesses the performance of each individual in population much like in genetic algorithms. The population component of the cultural algorithm is approximately the same as that of the genetic algorithm. Cultural algorithms require an interface between the population and belief space (Jin & Reynolds, 1999). The best individuals of the population can update the belief space via the update function. Also, the knowledge categories of the belief space can affect the population component via the influence function. The influence function can affect population by altering the genome or the actions of the individuals (Chung & Reynolds, 1996).

MOTIVATION

The operation of chemical facilities will always handle large amounts of chemicals and fuels. The manufacturing will have the risk to cause potential air emission events. The normal emissions originate from plant normal operations. They will have a large impact on the pollution concentration profile in the surrounding region. The air emission events may also be caused by severe process upsets due to planned operations such as plant scheduled start-ups or shut downs. Therefore, it is very necessary to conduct industrial and environmental research to investigate the cause-effect relationship between the emission and the surrounding environment. Chemical plant emission events can also be caused by uncontrollable and unpredictable uncertainties such as emergency shutdown, nature disaster, or terrorist attack. For example, an oil refinery at eastern Japan exploded with huge amounts of toxic emissions due to Japan's tsunami and earthquake occurred on March 11th of 2011 (NDTV, n.d.). In another emission event on March 22nd of 2011, the blast of a carbide plant in Louisville, Kentucky, fired calcium carbide and produced a large amounts of inhalation hazardous gases (United States Chemical Safety Board, n.d.).

The air-quality impacts from chemical plant emission events can be serious to both local communities and their surrounding environments. One of the major concerns is the exposure of acute or short-term toxicity. Release of acutely toxic contaminants, such as SO_2 and chlorine, would likely be transported to a populated area and pose an immediate threat to the public health and environment quality. Generally, the plant personnel should document and report emission details in response to an emission event, so that valuable information of hazardous releasing rate, possible transportation speed and directions, and potential harmful impacts on exposed populations and ecosystems can be estimated to support responsible decision makings. Since such responsible decisions are very critical, independent supporting information such as real-time measurements from a local air-quality monitoring network is vitally needed, especially in industrial zones populated heavily by various chemical facilities.

A local air-quality monitoring network can measure and record multiple pollutant concentrations simultaneously and alarm dangerous events in a real-time fashion. Meanwhile, based on measurement data from each monitoring station, plus regional meteorological conditions during the event time period, a monitoring network could help estimate possible emission source locations or even their emission rates. This inverse characterization of abnormal emission sources is very valuable to all stake holders, including government environmental agencies, chemical plants, and residential communities.

In the bulk of previous research, inverse modeling ideas were originated by the adoption of atmospheric dispersion models, which was normally used in the forward modeling problem to determine downwind contamination concentrations with given meteorological conditions and emission rates. "Gaussian Plume Model" is an approximate analytical method for point-source emissions for calculation of air pollutant concentration in the downwind area (Bowman, 1996; Turner, Bender, Pierce, & Petersen, 1989; Griffiths, 1994; Halitsky, 1989; Slade, 1986; Seinfeld, 1986; Hanna, Briggs, & Kosker, 1982; Turner, 1979, 1994; Pasquill, 1961, 1974; Church, 1949; Goldsmith & Friberg, 1976). Even though inverse modeling methods based on Gaussian plume models have been re-

ported (Hogan, Cooper, Wagner, & Wallstrom, 2005; Jeong, Kim, Suh, Hwang, Han, & Lee, 2005; MacKay, McKee, & Mulholland, 2006), they are generally used to estimate emission rates of point sources in an average long-time period based on measurements from multiple monitoring stations. It means their emissions are assumed under steady-state conditions and their values are treated as constants. Therefore, there is still a lack of studies on the reverse modeling for abnormal emission identifications with the consideration of dynamic emission rates of point emission sources.

Based on an available air-quality monitoring network, the data integration technologies will be applied to identify the scenarios of the possible emission source and the dynamic pollutant monitor result, so as to timely and effectively support diagnostic and prognostic decisions. Qualitative and mixed methods researchers have employed a variety of information and communication technology (ICT) tools, simulated or virtual environments, information systems, information devices and data analysis tools in this field. With the collection and representation of information in a range of ways, software tools have been created to manage and store these data. This data management enables more efficient searching ability of various types of digitized information. Various technologies have made the work of research more efficient. The results of the qualitative or mixed methods research may be integrated to reach the research target. Right now, a lot of software tools are available for the analysis to identify knowledge patterns and represent new meanings. The programs extend the capabilities of the researcher in terms of information coding and meaning-making. Machine-enhanced analytics has enabled the identification of aspects of interest such as correlations and anomalies from large datasets.

In this chapter, the application of artificial neural networks for such applications have been developed according to the real application purpose. It includes two stages of modeling and optimization work: i) the determination of background normal emission rates from multiple emission sources and ii) single-objective or multi-objective optimization for impact scenario identification and quantification. They will have the capability to identify the potential emission profile and spatial-temporal characterization of pollutant dispersion for a specific region, including reversely estimation of the air quality issues. It provides valuable information for accidental investigations and root cause analysis for an emission event; meanwhile, it helps evaluate the regional air quality impact caused by such an emission event as well. Case studies are employed to demonstrate the efficacy of the developed methodology.

DATA SOURCE

The basic mission of the industrial and environment research with web service is to preserve and improve the air quality of our living environment. To accomplish this, we must be able to evaluate the status of the atmosphere as compared to clean air standards and historical information. The following are some of the topics associated with monitoring air pollution.

In USA, the Clean Air Act requires every state to establish a network of air monitoring stations for criteria pollutants, using criteria set by OAQPS for their location and operation. The monitoring stations in this network are called the State and Local Air Monitoring Stations (SLAMS). The states must provide OAQPS with an annual summary of monitoring results at each SLAMS monitor, and detailed results must be available to OAQPS upon request. To obtain more timely and detailed information about air quality in strategic locations across the nation, OAQPS established an additional network of monitors: the National Air Monitoring Stations (NAMS). NAMS sites, which are part of the SLAMS network, must meet more stringent monitor siting, equipment type,

and quality assurance criteria. NAMS monitors also must submit detailed quarterly and annual monitoring results to OAQPS.

Between the years 1900 and 1970, the emission of six principal pollutants increased significantly. These six pollutants, also called criteria pollutants, are: particulate matter, sulfur dioxide, carbon monoxide, nitrogen dioxide, ozone, and lead. In 1970, the Clean Air Act (CAA) was signed into law. The CAA and its amendments provides the framework for all pertinent organizations to protect air quality. EPA's principal responsibilities under the CAA, as amended in 1990 include:

- Setting National Air Quality Standards (NAAQS) for pollutants considered harmful to the public health and environment.
- Ensuring the air quality standards are met or attained (in cooperation with the States) through national standards and strategies to control air emission standards from sources.
- Ensuring the sources of toxic air pollutants are well controlled.
- Monitoring the effectiveness of the program.

One way to protect and assess air quality was through the development of an Ambient Air Monitoring Program. Air quality samples are generally collected for one or more of the following purposes:

- To judge compliance with and/or progress made towards meeting ambient air quality standards.
- To activate emergency control procedures that prevent or alleviate air pollution episodes.
- To observe pollution trends throughout the region, including non-urban areas.
- To provide a data base for research evaluation of effects: urban, land-use, and transportation planning; development and

evaluation of abatement strategies; and development and validation of diffusion models.

With the end use of the air quality samples as a prime consideration, the network should be designed to meet one of four basic monitoring objectives listed below:

- To determine highest concentrations expected to occur in the area covered by the network;
- To determine representative concentrations in areas of high population density;
- To determine the impact on ambient pollution levels of significant sources or source categories;
- To determine general background concentration levels.

These four objectives indicate the nature of the samples that the monitoring network will collect which must be representative of the spatial area being studied.

The EPA's ambient air quality monitoring program is carried out by State and local agencies and consists of three major categories of monitoring stations, State and Local Air Monitoring Stations (SLAMS), National Air Monitoring Stations (NAMS), and Special Purpose Monitoring Stations (SPMS), that measure the criteria pollutants. Additionally, a fourth category of a monitoring station, the Photochemical Assessment Monitoring Stations (PAMS), which measures ozone precursors (approximately 60 volatile hydrocarbons and carbonyl) has been required by the 1990 Amendments to the Clean Air Act.

State and Local Air Monitoring Stations (SLAMS)

The SLAMS consist of a network of ~ 4,000 monitoring stations whose size and distribution is largely determined by the needs of State and local air pollution control agencies to meet their respective State implementation plan (SIP) requirements.

Figure 1. State and local monitoring (SLAMS) network

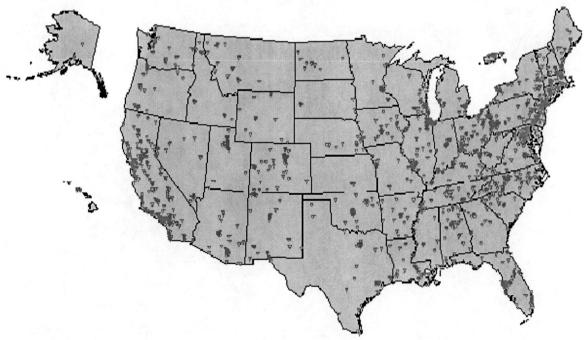

National Air Monitoring Stations (NAMS)

The NAMS (1,080 stations) are a subset of the SLAMS network with emphasis being given to urban and multi-source areas. In effect, they are key sites under SLAMS, with emphasis on areas of maximum concentrations and high population density.

Special Purpose Monitoring Stations (SPMS)

Special Purpose Monitoring Stations provide for special studies needed by the State and local agencies to support State implementation plans and other air program activities. The SPMS are not permanently established and, can be adjusted easily to accommodate changing needs and priorities. The SPMS are used to supplement the fixed monitoring network as circumstances require and resources permit. If the data from SPMS are used for SIP purposes, they must meet all QA and methodology requirements for SLAMS monitoring.

Photochemical Assessment Monitoring Stations (PAMS)

A PAMS network is required in each ozone nonattainment area that is designated serious, severe, or extreme. The required networks will have from two to five sites, depending on the population of the area. There will be a phase-in period of one site per year starting in 1994. The ultimate PAMS network could exceed 90 sites at the end of the 5-year phase-in period.

The AirData website gives you access to air quality data collected at outdoor monitors across the United States, Puerto Rico, and the U. S. Virgin Islands. The data comes primarily from the AQS (Air Quality System) database. You can choose from several ways of looking at the data:

- Download data into a file (or view it on the screen);
- Output the data into one of AirData's standard reports;
- Create graphical displays using one of the visualization tools;

Figure 2. National air monitoring (NAMS) network

Figure 3. Photochemical assessment monitoring network

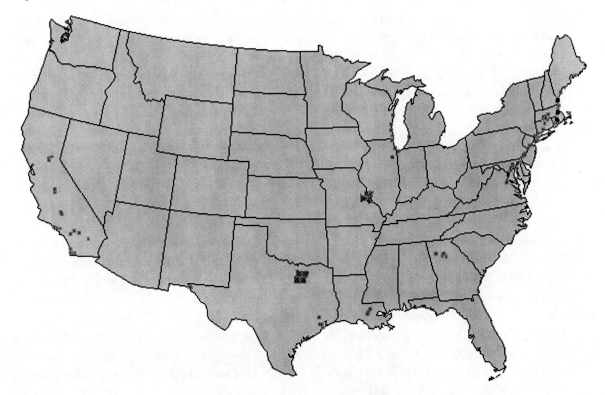

- Investigate monitor locations using an interactive map.

AirData assists a wide range of people, from the concerned citizen who wants to know how many unhealthy air quality days there were in his county last year to air quality analysts in the regulatory, academic, and health research communities who need raw data.

AirData lets you display and download monitored hourly, daily, and annual concentration data, AQI data, and speciated particle pollution data. If you need data that AirData does not have (such as emissions data) please see Other Sources of Data.

There are four main parts of the AirData website: Download Data, Reports, Visualize Data, and the Interactive Map.

Download Data

This part of the website has two query tools. The first tool provides daily summary concentrations and Air Quality Index values for the criteria pollutants for each monitoring site in the location you select. The second tool provides raw data for a specific location and time for any pollutant.

Reports

This part of the website provides a way to generate customized reports based on criteria you select (pollutant, location, etc.). The About Reports page explains exactly what is in each report, including individual column descriptions.

- **Air Quality Index (AQI) Report:** This report displays a yearly summary of AQI values in a county or city (specifically a CBSA - Core Based Statistical Area) . The summary values include maximum, 90th percentile and median AQI, the count of days in each AQI category, and the count of days when the AQI could be attributed to each criteria pollutant.

- **Air Quality Statistics Report:** This report shows yearly summaries of air pollution values for a city or county. The report shows the highest values reported during the year by all monitors in the CBSA or county. The report uses highlighted text to show values that exceed the level of an air quality standard.

- **Monitor Values Report:** This report shows a yearly summary (first through fourth maximum values, number of samples, etc.) of the measurements at individual monitors and provides descriptive information about the sites.

- **Air Quality Index Daily Values Report:** This report provides daily Air Quality Index values for the specified year and location.

Visualize Data

Sometimes "seeing" the data is the best way to understand it. AirData's visualization tools display data in unique and helpful ways.

- **AQI Plot:** Compare AQI values for multiple pollutants for a specific location and time period. This tool displays an entire year of AQI values – two pollutants at a time - and is useful for seeing how the number of unhealthy days can vary throughout the year for each pollutant.

- **Tile Plot:** Plot daily AQI values for a specific location and time period. Each square or "tile" represents one day of the year and is color-coded based on the AQI level for that day. The legend tallies the number of days in each AQI category.

- **Concentration Plot:** Generate a time series plot for a specific location and time period. This tool displays daily air quality summary statistics for the criteria pollutants by monitor. You can choose to plot all monitors in a county or CBSA, or you can select specific monitors.

- **Concentration Map:** Generate an animated series of daily concentration maps for a specific time period. Daily air quality is displayed in terms of the Air Quality Index (AQI) for the criteria pollutants, or in concentration ranges for certain PM species like organic carbon, nitrates, and sulfates. This tool may be useful for tracking an air pollution episode like a wildfire event.

- **Ozone Exceedances:** Compare 8-hour ozone "exceedances" from this year with previous years. Comparisons are presented in three ways. The first plot shows the comparisons by MONTH. The second plot shows the comparisons by DAY (for cumulative counts). The third plot shows the comparisons by YEAR.

The Interactive Map

Use the interactive map to see where air quality monitors are located, get information about the monitor, and download data from the monitor. You can select which monitoring networks to display on the map.

There are also other sources of air data about the monitoring network files and air quality data (shown in Table 1).

Table 1. Sources of air data

Name	Type of Data
AirNow	Air quality forecasts and real-time data in a visual format for public health protection.
AirCompare	AQI summaries for comparison of counties.
AirTrends	Trends of air quality and emissions.
Air Emission Sources	Emissions - national, state, and county-level summaries for criteria pollutant emissions.
The National Emissions Inventory	Emissions - a comprehensive and detailed estimate of air emissions of both Criteria and Hazardous air pollutants from all air emissions sources.
AQS Data Mart	Monitored ambient air quality data from AQS; for those who need large volumes of data.
AQS Data Page	The most requested data from the Air Quality System (AQS) are posted on this web page.
CASTNET	The Clean Air Status and Trends Network (CASTNET) is the nation's primary source for data on dry acidic deposition and rural, ground-level ozone.
Remote Sensing Information Gateway (RSIG)	Air quality monitoring, modeling, and satellite data.
Radiation Monitoring Data	Air quality and emissions; Links to databases and maps.
EPA Data Finder	Air, Water, other EPA data.
Visibility Information Exchange Web System (VIEWS)	Air quality monitoring, modeling, emissions, and satellite data.
DataFed	Air quality monitoring, modeling, emissions, and satellite data.
Data.Gov	Air, Water, other U.S. Federal Executive Branch datasets.

From the web service, below information is available.

Types of Data

- **Monitoring Data:** Ambient (outdoor) concentrations of pollutants are measured at more than 4000 monitoring stations owned and operated mainly by state environmental agencies. The agencies send hourly or daily measurements of pollutant concentrations to EPA's database called AQS (Air Quality System). AirData retrieves data from AQS.
- **Emissions Data:** EPA keeps track of the amount of pollution that comes from a variety of sources such as vehicles, power plants, and industries. The emissions data reported to EPA by state environmental agencies can be an actual reading taken at a source or an estimate made using a mathematical calculation. AirData does not contain emissions data at this time. Emissions data can be obtained from the Air Emissions Sources website (for general summaries) and the NEI browser (for detailed reports).

Types of Air Pollutants

- **Criteria Air Pollutants:** EPA sets national air quality standards for six common pollutants, also called criteria pollutants, to protect public health. Monitoring sites report data to EPA for these six criteria air pollutants:
  - Ozone (O3)
  - Particulate matter (PM10 and PM2.5)
  - Carbon monoxide (CO)
  - Nitrogen dioxide (NO2)

- ○ Sulfur dioxide (SO2)
- ○ Lead (Pb)
- ○ (PM10 includes particles less than or equal to 10 micrometers in diameter. PM2.5 includes particles less than or equal to 2.5 micrometers and is also called fine particle pollution.)
- **Hazardous Air Pollutants (HAPs)/Toxic Air Pollutants:** Hazardous air pollutants (HAPs) (also called toxic air pollutants or air toxics) are pollutants that are known or suspected to cause serious health problems such as cancer. There are 188 hazardous air pollutants. Examples of toxic air pollutants include benzene, which is found in gasoline; perchlorethlyene, which is emitted from some dry cleaning facilities; and methylene chloride, which is used as a solvent and paint stripper. Examples of other listed air toxics include dioxin, asbestos, toluene, and metals such as cadmium, mercury, chromium, and lead compounds. The National-Scale Air Toxics Assessment (NATA) is EPA's ongoing comprehensive evaluation of air toxics in the U.S.

The AQI (Air Quality Index)

AirData uses the Air Quality Index (AQI) in some of its reports and tables and to display data using the visualization tools. The AQI is an index for reporting daily air quality. It tells how clean or polluted the air is, and what associated health effects might be a concern, especially for ground-level ozone and particle pollution.

Think of the AQI as a yardstick that runs from 0 to 500. The higher the AQI value, the greater the level of air pollution and the greater the health concern. For example, an AQI value of 50 represents good air quality with little potential to affect public health, while an AQI value over 300 represents hazardous air quality.

An AQI value of 100 generally corresponds to the national air quality standard for the pollutant, which is the level EPA has set to protect public health. AQI values below 100 are generally thought of as satisfactory. When AQI values are above 100, air quality is considered to be unhealthy-at first for certain sensitive groups of people, then for everyone as AQI values get higher. The AQI is divided into six categories (shown in Table 2).

Each category corresponds to a different level of health concern. The six levels of health concern and what they mean are:

- "Good" AQI is 0 - 50. Air quality is considered satisfactory, and air pollution poses little or no risk.
- "Moderate" AQI is 51 - 100. Air quality is acceptable; however, for some pollutants there may be a moderate health concern for a very small number of people. For

Table 2.

Air Quality Index (AQI) Values	Levels of Health Concern	Colors
When the AQI is in this range:	*..air quality conditions are:*	*...as symbolized by this color:*
0-50	Good	Green
51-100	Moderate	Yellow
101-150	Unhealthy for Sensitive Groups	Orange
151 to 200	Unhealthy	Red
201 to 300	Very Unhealthy	Purple
301 to 500	Hazardous	Maroon

example, people who are unusually sensitive to ozone may experience respiratory symptoms.

- "Unhealthy for Sensitive Groups" AQI is 101 - 150. Although general public is not likely to be affected at this AQI range, people with lung disease, older adults and children are at a greater risk from exposure to ozone, whereas persons with heart and lung disease, older adults and children are at greater risk from the presence of particles in the air.
- "Unhealthy" AQI is 151 - 200. Everyone may begin to experience some adverse health effects, and members of the sensitive groups may experience more serious effects.
- "Very Unhealthy" AQI is 201 - 300. This would trigger a health alert signifying that everyone may experience more serious health effects.
- "Hazardous" AQI greater than 300. This would trigger health warnings of emergency conditions. The entire population is more likely to be affected.

METHODOLOGY AND APPLICATION

1. Temperature Prediction

Climate Prediction

The first priority and prerequisite for a region's development is appropriate climate condition because the climate can affect almost all the aspects of our life such as economy, society, culture, education, food supply or even transportation safety. For example, the frequency of traffic accident will increase definitely during the snowing or raining days; the city cannot become the economic center if it always encounter extreme weather. The city's prosperity relies heavily on the climate with high adaptation to the people who live there so

that there is no need for them to worry about the unexpected conditions the extreme meteorology condition. Therefore, it is very important for us to make a prediction on the climate change trend if we want to make a decision for municipal development plan in the future. It is very necessary to investigate the climate change trend, which will let us know whether it will have a great change in the weather condition such as temperature increase. Furthermore, such kind of climate prediction result can also become the data input for the other models such as pollutant dispersion model and flight scheduling in their further evaluation and risk assessment. Up to now a lot of professional scientists have dedicated their research to meteorology simulation and modeling and their great work has helped to provide multiple model tools in microscale, mesoscale, synoptic scale and global scale. These meteorological models rely on the application of meteorological principles (boundary layer meteorology and dynamic meteorology) and typically require powerful computers to produce output on winds, temperature, and precipitation at different horizontal locations and vertical levels in the atmosphere. The high requirement of computation hardware and professional understanding of modeling language cannot always be satisfied by the communities even though they can provide relatively more accurate result. To the majority of people, a better way for common application to predict the regional climate change is a statistical tool by data regression and analysis instead of those complex system provided by national and international research laboratories and organizations. There are two major benefits for this choice: the first benefit is data availability which means the historic climate date will always be available from websites and the second benefit is tool availability which means we can even use the common software to proceed the data mining to get the prediction results. Therefore the tool derived from this study can be used by the citizens to get more understanding of their regional climate conditions(NWS and NCEP, 2013).

As Dr. Steve Running, Climate Change Studies Program Director, and a lead author on the Nobel Prize winning Intergovernmental Panel on Climate Change said, "The climate change topic is rapidly evolving from only an earth science issue to a technological, economic and sociological issue." (Climate Change Studies Program, 2013).

Climate change describes the change trend of average pattern of weather over the long term. In the previous millions of years, the earth's climate has been warmed and cooled, even long before our appearance on the earth. Even though climate change isn't new, the study of how the climate change is. The exploration of climate change encompasses many fields of study, including physics, chemistry, biology, geology, meteorology, oceanography, and even sociology.

The scientists study natural phenomena of climate change through evidence gathering, theory test, and conclusion generating. There are several general methodologies to study the climate change: simulation experiment, historical data analog, field observation, numerical modeling and computer simulation.

- **Simulation Experiment:** The procedures in order are carried out to achieve the goal of verifying, refuting, or establishing the validity of a hypothesis of climate change. Experiments provide insight into cause-and-effect between multiple natural and anthropogenic factors and the result of climate change. For example this method is used to study the responses of grassland plants to experimentally simulated climate change depend on land use and region (Bütof, et.al., 2012).

- **Historical Data Analog:** Historical recorded data is processed to be in a form to identify its similarity of its original structure of climate change trend in the spatial and temporal distribution. It has been used to conduct multi-field analog prediction

of short-term climate fluctuations by the adoption of a climate state vector (Barnett & Preisendorfer, 1978).

- **Field Observation:** Climate field observation provides long-term or short-term, high quality, timely, observational data, information and products in support of climate and weather research communities, forecasters, and other service providers and users. It has included climate observing system according to climate monitoring principles, time-series indicators of climate variability and change. The observation result will be used to develop and maintain standard data sets for initialization and evaluation of climate forecast models, assessments of climate change, and informed risk management. It will be further used to develop informational products, diagnostics, and assessments of observed climate variability and change on different scales. This method has been used in many studies such as indirect radiative forcing of climate change through ozone effects on the land-carbon sink (Sitch, Cox, Collins, & Huntingford, 2007).

- **Numerical Modeling:** The results of a numerical model consist of numbers, which represent particular "cases" or "realizations." There are particular examples of what the (model) atmosphere can do: for example, we can "run" a numerical model to create a weather forecast, which consists of a large set of numbers. The application of numerical modeling for climate change has been introduced in a lot of books, such as atmosphere circulation, meteorology dynamics and three dimensional climate modeling (Chang, 1977; Durran, 1999; Haltiner & Williams, 1980; Kalnay, 2003; Manabe, 1985; Mesinger & Arakawa, 1976; Randall, 2000; Washington & Parkinson, 1986).

- **Computer Simulation:** It is a computer program which is run on a single computer, or a network of computers in order to simulate a particular system of climate. For example, the Weather Research and Forecasting (WRF) model(UCAR, 2010) is a specific computer program with a dual use for forecasting and research. It was created through a partnership that includes the National Oceanic and Atmospheric Administration(NOAA), the National Center for Atmospheric Research(NCAR), and more than 150 other organizations and universities in the United States and abroad(NCAR, 2006; Wikipedia, 2013; NCDC & NOAA, 2013).

The section will present the data analysis results based on the statistical processing of the historical temperature monitor results. During data analysis, several years of records have been summarized to characterize the climate so that a large data record of long time period will help to achieve a relatively stable change trend and statistical results. During the seasonal analysis, four seasons with respective to months are defined as below: spring (March ~ May), summer (June ~ August), autumn (September ~ November) and winter (December ~ February).

The section will present the linear regression for the above data analysis results of seasonal and annual average temperatures of Cincinnati. In the linear regression model, the independent variable will be the year, t and the dependent variable will be the temperature, Y_t. The linear regression will generate the linear function expression with respective to the year, t. The linear equation which is used in our regression is $Y_t = m + k * t$. The methodology of least square will be used to get the linear regression results, which is the value of coefficient of the above equations: k and m. Here, k is the slope which represents the trend rate of temperature change by time in-

terval (year or decade) and m is the intercept which is a constant term. The change tendency can be identified by the sign of slope k :if the slope k is larger than zero, there will be a rising upward trend of average temperature; if the slope k is less than zero, there will be a descending downward trend of average temperature; if the slope k is equal to zero, there will be no change trend of average temperature. The absolute value of slope k will reflect the increased or decreased degree. The linear regression model for annual average temperature is constructed based on available dataset. The trend analysis plot for annual temperature has also been provided (Figure 4).

The linear regression model for spring average temperature is constructed based on available data set. The trend analysis plot for annual temperature has also been provided (Figure 5).

The linear regression model for summer average temperature is constructed based on dataset of temperature monitor result in the summer. The trend analysis has also been plotted (Figure 6).

The linear regression model for autumn average temperature is constructed based on available data set (Figure 7). The trend analysis plot for annual temperature has also been provided.

The linear regression model for winter average temperature is constructed based on available data set (Figure 8). The trend analysis plot for annual temperature has also been provided.

2. Inverse Emission Identification

The second application is to develop a systematic methodology to reversely detect the emission conditions from a list of candidates (local chemical plants) according to the abnormal air-quality measurements from an available monitoring network, so as to support diagnostic and prognostic decisions timely and effectively. The outcome of the developed methodology should provide information of emission source location, starting time, time duration, total emission amount, and dynamic emission rate and pattern from the ab-

Figure 4. Change trend analysis for annual temperature

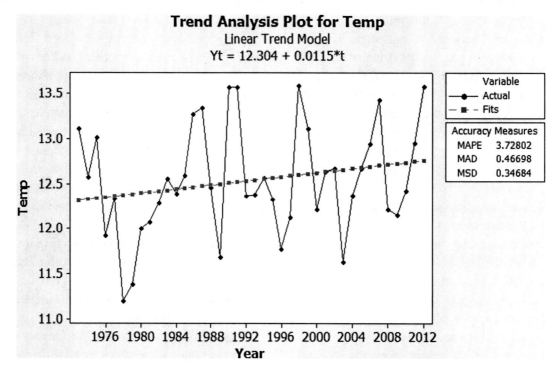

Figure 5. Change trend analysis for spring temperature

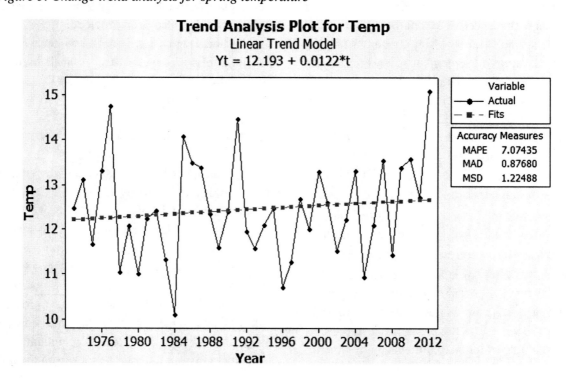

Figure 6. Change trend analysis for summer temperature

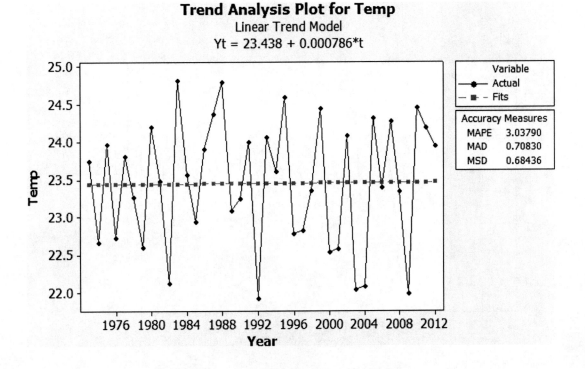

Figure 7. Change trend analysis for autumn temperature

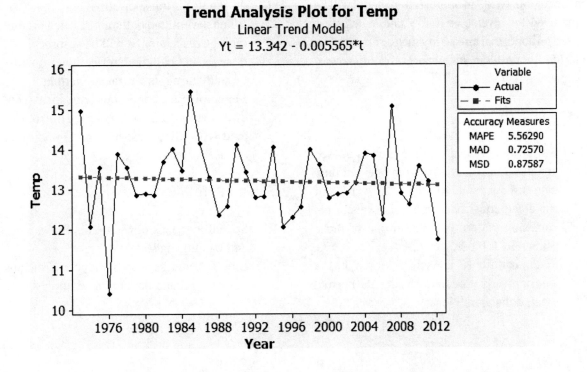

Figure 8. Change trend analysis for winter temperature

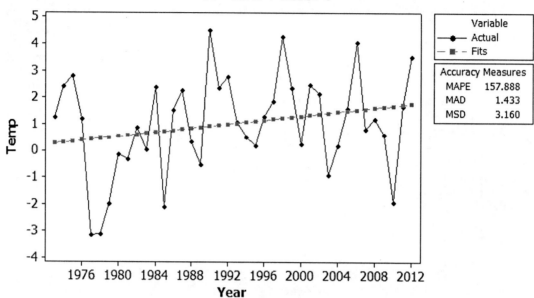

normal emission sources. The methodology will firstly determine the background normal emission rates for a given list of candidate emission sources in the region. Next, an optimization model will be employed for reverse emission source detection based on abnormal air-quality measurements. For clarity, the problem statements are summarized below.

Assumptions

1. An air-quality event in a region is caused by abnormal emissions from one and only one emission source based on a given list of candidate emission sources, whose abnormal emission pattern belongs to one of those shown in Table 3;
2. Each candidate emission source has a constant emission rate during its normal operational conditions;

3. Emission transportation follows Gaussian dispersion model and there is no secondary consumption or generation of the pollutant during its air transportation;
4. When the emitted pollutant reached ground through dispersion, it will be absorbed, i.e., there is no pollutant reflection from the ground during its air transportation;
5. Meteorological conditions (e.g., local wind direction and wind speed) during the considered scheduling time horizon are constant (or near constant) in the region.

Given Information

1. Spatial locations of each emission sources and monitoring stations;
2. Emission source stack parameters, such as stack height and outlet temperature;

Table 3. Summary of monthly mean temperature(1973-2012)

Year/Month	Jan	Feb	Mar	Apr	May	Jun	Jul	Aug	Sep	Oct	Nov	Dec
1973	0.8	1.0	10.5	11.2	15.7	23.3	24.4	23.6	21.0	15.2	8.8	2.1
1974	2.9	1.8	8.5	13.4	17.5	20.4	24.2	23.4	17.0	11.8	7.5	2.6
1975	2.6	3.0	4.9	10.3	19.8	22.8	24.1	25.0	17.8	13.5	9.5	3.0
1976	-1.4	6.4	10.4	13.0	16.6	22.3	24.0	21.9	18.0	9.9	3.4	-1.3
1977	-9.0	-0.2	9.3	14.2	20.8	21.8	26.0	23.6	21.3	11.9	8.5	-0.2
1978	-5.8	-5.9	3.8	12.8	16.6	22.8	23.9	23.1	21.5	11.3	8.0	2.4
1979	-4.4	-4.4	8.2	11.1	16.9	21.8	22.9	23.0	19.1	12.7	6.8	2.8
1980	0.3	-2.4	4.0	10.8	18.2	21.4	25.7	25.5	21.0	11.6	6.1	1.8
1981	-2.6	1.7	5.7	15.3	15.7	23.3	24.4	22.8	18.9	12.8	6.9	0.0
1982	-3.4	-0.1	6.8	10.2	20.2	20.1	24.7	21.6	18.7	13.9	8.6	6.2
1983	0.5	2.3	7.4	10.7	15.9	22.2	26.3	25.9	20.3	14.0	7.9	-2.6
1984	-3.0	4.3	2.8	11.3	16.2	24.1	23.0	23.6	18.5	16.3	5.7	5.9
1985	-3.8	-1.1	8.6	15.1	18.6	21.3	24.4	23.1	20.3	15.5	10.6	-1.4
1986	0.1	2.7	7.8	13.6	19.1	23.3	25.8	22.6	21.5	14.1	6.9	1.8
1987	0.1	3.2	7.4	12.1	20.6	23.9	24.9	24.3	20.3	10.3	9.3	3.6
1988	-1.3	0.6	6.3	12.2	18.5	23.0	25.9	25.5	19.8	9.7	7.6	1.8
1989	3.6	0.0	7.2	11.7	15.9	21.8	24.6	22.9	18.7	12.4	6.6	-5.1
1990	4.4	5.1	8.9	11.9	16.4	22.5	24.2	23.0	20.3	13.1	9.0	4.1
1991	0.3	3.2	8.1	14.1	21.3	23.7	25.0	23.3	20.0	14.2	6.2	3.6
1992	1.2	4.5	6.8	12.6	16.4	20.6	23.9	21.3	18.7	12.0	7.7	2.7
1993	2.2	-0.6	5.1	11.7	18.0	21.7	26.0	24.4	18.9	12.4	7.1	1.7
1994	-3.6	1.0	6.5	13.9	15.9	23.8	24.4	22.7	18.6	13.4	10.2	4.1
1995	0.8	0.0	7.8	12.3	17.3	22.7	25.1	26.0	18.2	13.7	4.3	-0.3
1996	-1.2	1.0	3.6	10.9	17.6	22.2	22.9	23.2	19.1	13.6	4.2	4.2
1997	-1.0	4.3	8.1	10.4	15.3	21.2	24.7	22.5	18.9	12.9	5.9	2.3
1998	4.0	4.8	7.1	11.8	19.2	22.4	23.9	23.8	21.5	13.1	7.5	4.1
1999	1.1	3.7	4.1	13.7	18.2	23.1	27.0	23.2	19.4	12.6	9.0	2.3
2000	-0.6	4.8	8.9	11.8	19.2	22.5	23.0	22.2	18.3	13.9	6.2	-3.4
2001	-0.3	3.6	5.0	14.9	17.9	20.9	23.4	23.5	17.4	12.3	8.9	4.2
2002	2.4	2.6	5.9	13.1	15.6	22.6	25.4	24.3	20.9	12.1	5.7	1.5
2003	-3.3	-1.4	7.1	12.7	16.8	19.9	23.1	23.1	18.0	12.3	9.2	2.0
2004	-1.9	1.0	7.8	12.4	19.7	21.8	23.0	21.4	19.6	13.2	8.9	1.4
2005	1.7	3.2	4.3	13.0	15.5	23.3	24.9	24.7	20.7	13.0	7.9	-0.1
2006	5.6	1.8	5.9	13.9	16.4	20.8	24.6	24.8	17.6	11.7	7.5	4.8
2007	3.1	-3.9	9.9	11.4	19.4	23.0	23.1	26.7	21.7	16.0	7.5	3.3
2008	0.3	1.3	5.7	12.8	15.8	22.8	23.9	23.3	20.5	12.6	5.6	2.1
2009	-2.3	2.7	8.9	13.2	18.1	22.5	21.3	22.1	19.1	11.0	7.8	1.4
2010	-1.8	-1.9	7.4	14.4	19.0	23.8	25.0	24.6	20.4	13.7	6.6	-2.0
2011	-2.1	2.7	7.1	14.0	17.1	22.3	26.5	23.8	18.2	12.0	9.4	4.5
2012	2.3	3.8	12.8	12.5	19.9	22.5	26.4	23.0	18.6	11.9	4.7	4.6

3. Dynamic monitoring results at each monitoring station;
4. Meteorological conditions in the studied region during the event time period.

Information to be Determined

1. Which emission source caused the investigated pollutant concentration pattern;
2. What are the emission pattern and dynamic emission rate for the identified emission source.

The input parameters at the modeling stage include geographical information (locations of every possible emission source and monitoring station), meteorological condition (e.g., wind direction, speed, and atmospheric stability), measurements at each monitoring station, and emission source data (e.g., stack height, exit diameter and outlet temperature). The next step is to map locations of candidate emission sources and monitoring stations into a rectangular coordinator system (see Appendix). Then, the firs- stage modeling aims at the determination of normal emission rates from every emission source. The task is accomplished through a regression model based on Gaussian-dispersion model to minimize the sum of squared error (SSE) between the model calculated results and monitoring results from multiple monitoring stations. Since the normal emission rate of each emission source is the background emission during plant steady-state operational conditions, it is also called steady-state emission rate.

This regression model is to identify the normal emission rate for each candidate emission source by minimizing SSE between the model predicting results and the monitoring results from multiple monitoring stations at normal emission status (without emission events).

Objective Function

$$\varphi_1 = \min_{m_i^S} \sum_{t \in T^D} \sum_{j \in J} \left(\bar{C}_j - C_{j,t}^S \right)^2 \qquad (2)$$

where j represents the index of monitoring stations grouped by set J; T^S represents a selected steady-state time set when each emission source has a normal emission rate. T^S contains multiple time instants indexed by t. $\bar{C}_j$ and $C_{j,t}^S$ respectively represents model calculated and measured pollutant concentrations at the j-th monitoring station at time t. Equation (2) suggests the objective function is to minimize SSE between $\bar{C}_j$ and $C_{j,t}^S$.

The model calculated pollutant concentration at the j-th monitoring station ($\bar{C}_j$) should be the cumulative of $\bar{C}_{i,j}$ from all the emission sources, which can be formulated by Eq. (3).

$$\bar{C}_j = \sum_{i \in I} \bar{C}_{i,j}, \; \forall \, j \in J \qquad (3)$$

Dispersion Transportation Principle

Note that $\bar{C}_{i,j}$ should be calculated by the following Eq. (4). It represents pollutant dispersion from emission sources to monitoring stations under the impact of meteorological conditions. The associated details of Eq. (4) can be referenced in the Appendix.

$$\bar{C}_{i,j} = \frac{m_i^S f\left(Z_{i,j}, H_i\right)}{2U_i \pi \sigma_{Y_{i,j}} \sigma_{Z_{i,j}}} \exp\left[-\frac{1}{2}\left(\frac{Y_{i,j}}{\sigma_{Y_{i,j}}}\right)^2 \right],$$

$$\forall \, i \in I, \, j \in J \qquad (4)$$

where $\bar{C}_{i,j}$ is the pollutant concentration at the j-th monitoring station caused by the emission from the i-th emission source; $Y_{i,j}$ is the projection of $d_{i,j}$ along Y direction (Here, X direction is the same as the wind direction; Y direction is horizontally perpendicular to X direction); $Z_{i,j}$ is the ground height difference between the i-th emission source to the j-th monitoring station; H_i is the plume height above the ground for source i; $\sigma_{Y_{i,j}}$ and $\sigma_{Z_{i,j}}$ are the standard deviations of the emission plume's probability distribution function along Y and Z directions, respectively; $f\left(Z_{i,j}, H_i\right)$ is a function with respect to $Z_{i,j}$ and H_i; m_i^s represents the constant emission rate at the i-th emission source in the normal condition.

The related equations and procedures to calculate the parameters shown in Eq. (4) has been included in the Gaussian dispersion model area (Pasquill, 1961, 1974; Turner, 1979, 1994; Hanna et al., 1982; Seinfeld, 1986; Slade, 1986; Halitsky, 1989; Griffiths, 1994; Turner et al., 1989; Bowman, 1996).

Artificial Neural Network Model

Among all the above mentioned techniques, one of the commonly used methodologies is artificial neural network. In computer science and related fields, artificial neural networks are models inspired by animal central nervous systems that are capable of machine learning and pattern recognition. They are usually presented as systems of interconnected "neurons" that can compute values from inputs by feeding information through the network. Like other machine learning methods, neural networks have been used to solve a wide variety of tasks that are hard to solve using ordinary rule-based programming, including computer vision and speech recognition.

Generally, it involves a network of simple processing elements exhibiting complex global behavior determined by the connections between the processing elements and element parameters. Commonly, though, a class of statistical models will be called "neural" if they

1. Consist of sets of adaptive weights, i.e. numerical parameters that are tuned by a learning algorithm; and
2. Are capable of approximating non-linear functions of their inputs.

The adaptive weights are conceptually connection strengths between neurons, which are activated during training and prediction.

Neural network models in artificial intelligence are usually referred to as artificial neural networks (ANNs); these are essentially simple mathematical models defining a function of $f : X \rightarrow Y$ or a distribution over X or both X and Y, but sometimes models are also intimately associated with a particular learning algorithm or learning rule. A common use of the phrase ANN model really means the definition of a class of such functions where members of the class are obtained by varying parameters, connection weights, or specifics of the architecture such as the number of neurons or their connectivity.

The word network in the term 'artificial neural network' refers to the inter–connections between the neurons in the different layers of each system. An example system has three layers. The first layer has input neurons, which send data via synapses to the second layer of neurons, and then via more synapses to the third layer of output neurons. More complex systems will have more layers of neurons with some having increased layers of input neurons and output neurons. The synapses store parameters called "weights" that manipulate the data in the calculations.

An ANN is typically defined by three types of parameters:

- The interconnection pattern between different layers of neurons.
- The learning process for updating the weights of the interconnections.
- The activation function that converts a neuron's weighted input to its output activation.

To train the artificial neural network we obtain a generalized transfer function of the values of emission rate and the pollutant concentrations which are normalized in the procedure of model preparation. The normalized features were used to give the training on the neural network with the Lavenberg - Marquardt back propagation algorithm. In mathematics and computing, the

Levenberg–Marquardt algorithm (LMA), also known as the damped least-squares (DLS) method, is used to solve non-linear least squares problems. These minimization problems arise especially in least squares curve fitting. The LMA interpolates between the Gauss–Newton algorithm (GNA) and the method of gradient descent. The LMA is more robust than the GNA, which means that in many cases it finds a solution even if it starts very far off the final minimum. For well-behaved functions and reasonable starting parameters, the LMA tends to be a bit slower than the GNA. LMA can also be viewed as Gauss–Newton using a trust region approach.

Different numbers of hidden neurons were used and we found a good approximation and

Figure 9. Percentage selection of the samples for validation and test data

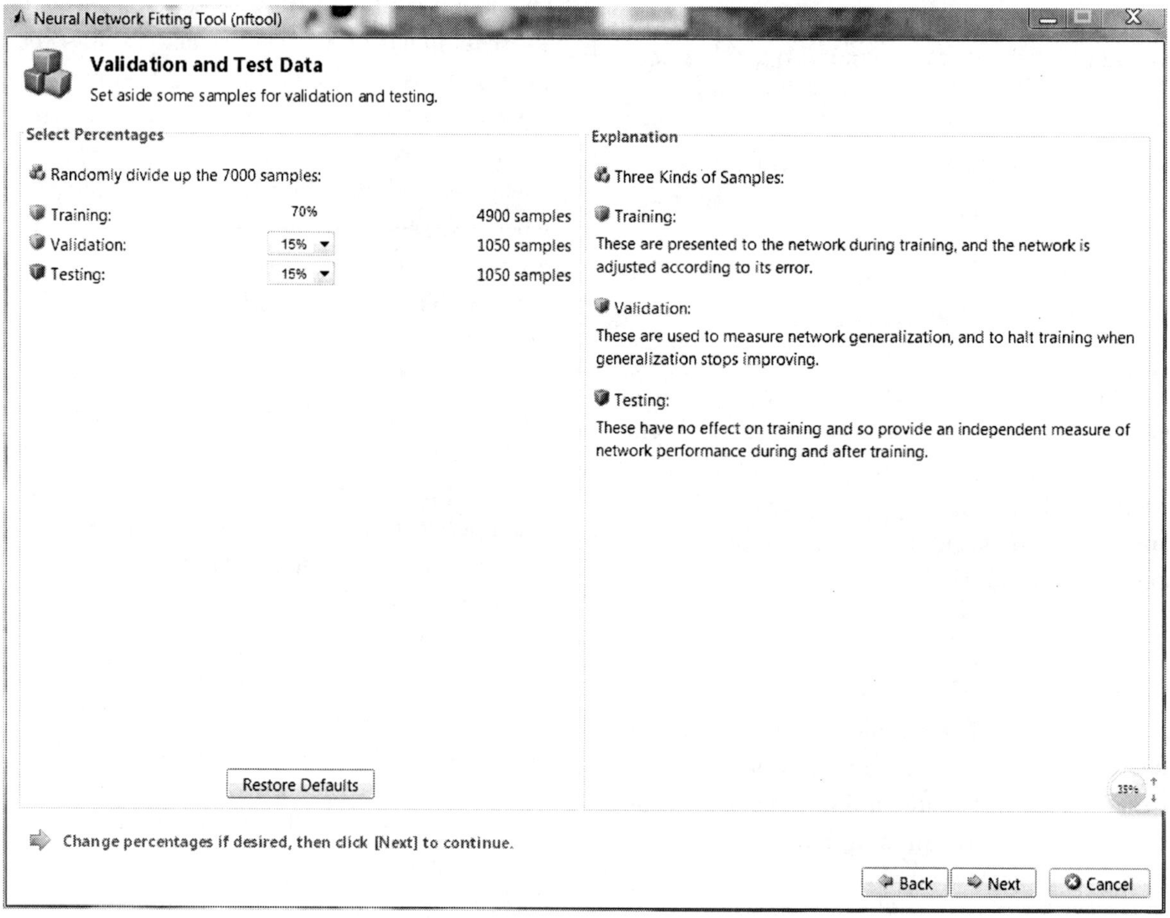

Figure 10. Setting for the hidden neurons

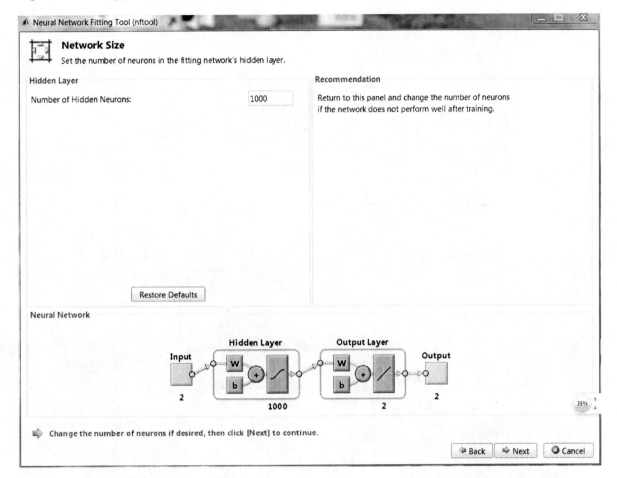

generalization with 1000 neurons. The measurement of the dynamic emission rate changes is not easy because the systolic and diastolic values are measured at different time instances. There are total 7000 samples have participated the modeling of the artificial neural network. 70% of the samples are training samples, which are presented to the network during training, and the network is adjusted according to its error. 15% of the samples are validation samples, which are used to measure network generalization, and to halt training when generalization stops improving. The rest 15% of the samples are testing samples. These have no effect on training and so provide an independent measure of network performance during and after training.

15% of the samples are validation samples, which are used to measure network generalization, and to halt training when generalization stops improving. The rest 15% of the samples are testing samples. These have no effect on training and so provide an independent measure of network performance during and after training.

Figure 11. Training neural network

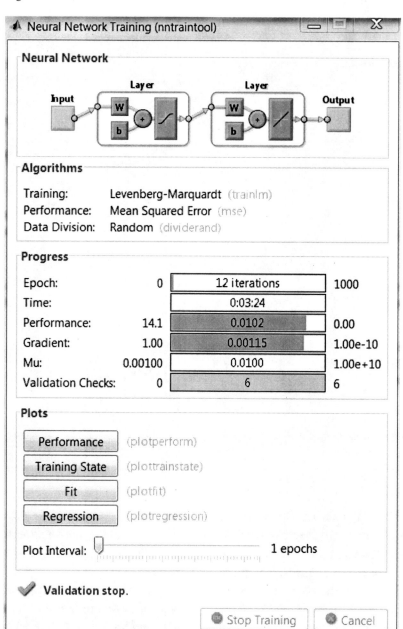

CASE STUDY

To demonstrate the efficacy of the developed systematic methodology, two case studies including the detection of a real SO_2 emission event are conducted.

As shown in Figure 4, the studied involves five chemical emission sources (E1, E2, E3, E4, and E5 represented by red dots) and four monitoring stations (S1, S2, S3, and S4 represented by green dots) distributed in a squared region (30 km×30 km). The entire region is gridded and the edge length of each gridded cell is 1 km. The surface wind blows from the southwest to northeast as shown in Figure 9. A common pollutant emitted from these five emission sources is monitored by the monitoring stations through hourly measurements.

The plume and stack parameters of the five emission sources are given in Table 4. During the event time period, the lapse rate was 4 K/km, the wind speed was 1.6m/s at 10-meter height, and the ambient temperature was 20 °C. For the investigation, the entire time period has been separated into two parts: steady-state time period and dynamic time period. The data in the steady-state has been applied to determine the normal emission rates for each emission source.

The modeling result for the developed artificial neural network has been plot in the Figure 10. It can be seen that the training has the R square value of 0.41802 while the validation and test has the R-square of 0.15516 and 0.13702 respectively. It can be seen that the R square value among the periods of training, validation and test are quite similar and the overall R square value has been 0.16433. This has shown that the artificial neural network model can give the quantitative identification of the normal emission rate. The results of m_1^s through m_5^s are identified as 10.8, 10.5, 10.1, 9.2, and 9.8 kg/h, respectively.

CONCLUSION

A local air-quality monitoring network has potentials to proactively identify abnormal emission

Figure 12. Spatial scope of case study

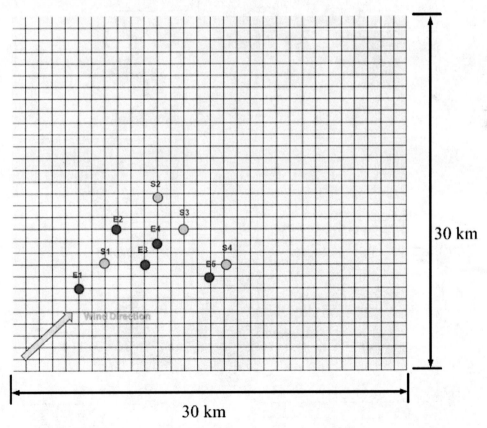

Table 4. Plume and stack parameters for each emission source

Chemical Emission Sources	E1	E2	E3	E4	E5
Stack Height H_i *(m)*	80	110	95	100	105
Stack Exit Temperature $T_{s,i}$ *(K)*	480	400	460	440	430
Stack Exit Velocity $V_{s,i}$ *(m/s)*	17.5	13.0	15.6	14.2	16.1
Stack Exit Diameter $D_{s,i}$ *(m)*	1.6	1.9	1.5	1.7	1.8

Figure 13. Regression result for training, validation and test

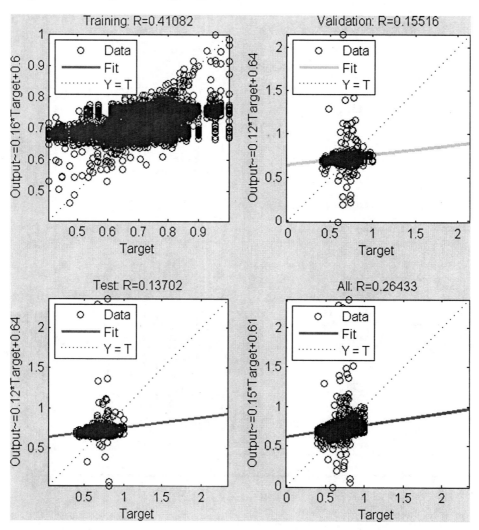

events. In this chapter, a systematic methodology for simultaneous identification of a emission source and its emission rate has been developed to conduct regression for background emission rate determination and emission source identification and quantification. The case study is employed to demonstrate the efficacy of the developed methodology. This study lays out a solid foundation for multiple stake holders on diagnostic and prognostic decisions in face of an industrial air-pollution event, including government environmental agencies, regional chemical plants, and local communities. Based on an available air-quality monitoring network, the data integration technologies will be applied to identify the scenarios of the possible emission source and the dynamic pollutant monitor result, so as to timely and effectively support diagnostic and prognostic decisions. The application of artificial neural networks for such applications have been developed according to the real application purpose.

FUTURE RESEARCH DIRECTIONS

This study can not only determine emission source location, starting time, and time duration responsible for an observed emission event, but also reversely estimate the dynamic emission rate and the total emission amount from the accidental emission source. It provides valuable information for accidental investigations and root cause analysis for an emission event; meanwhile, it helps evaluate the regional air-quality impact caused by such an emission event as well. It lays out a solid foundation for multiple stake holders on diagnostic and prognostic decisions in face of an industrial air-pollution event, including government environmental agencies, regional chemical plants, and local communities.

It is necessary to further extend the current research to be integrated into the website service of environmental protection agency. Similar case studies and applications in using technologies and fundamental theory can be applied and demonstrated in the representative service domains with the combination of e-business services, mobile services, social networking services, cloud services, legal services, healthcare services, logistics services and educational services taking into account demands from government, organization, enterprise, community, individual, customer, and citizen.

REFERENCES

Bar-Cohen, Y. (2005). *Biomimetics: biologically inspired technologies*. CRC Press.

Bowman, W. A. (1996). Maximum ground level concentrations with downwash: The urban stability mode. *Journal of the Air & Waste Management Association*, *46*(7), 615–620. doi:10.1080/10473289.1996.10467495

Brabazon, A., & O'Neill, M. (2006). *Biologically inspired algorithms for financial modelling*. Berlin: Springer.

Chung, C. J., & Reynolds, R. G. (1996, February). A Testbed for Solving Optimization Problems Using Cultural Algorithms. In Evolutionary programming (pp. 225-236). Academic Press.

Church, P. E. (1949). Dilution of Waste stack gases in the atmosphere. *Industrial & Engineering Chemistry*, *41*(12), 2753–2756. doi:10.1021/ie50480a022

Clerc, M. (2006). *Particle swarm optimization* (Vol. 243). London: ISTE. doi:10.1002/9780470612163

Cochocki, A., & Unbehauen, R. (1993). *Neural networks for optimization and signal processing*. John Wiley & Sons, Inc.

Coello, C. A. C., & Cortés, N. C. (2002, September). An approach to solve multiobjective optimization problems based on an artificial immune system. In *Proceedings of 1st International Conference on Artificial Immune Systems (ICARIS)*. University of Kent at Canterbury.

Coello, C. A. C., & Cortés, N. C. (2005). Solving multiobjective optimization problems using an artificial immune system. *Genetic Programming and Evolvable Machines*, 6(2), 163–190. doi:10.1007/s10710-005-6164-x

Coello Coello, C. A., & Becerra, R. L. (2004). Efficient evolutionary optimization through the use of a cultural algorithm. *Engineering Optimization*, 36(2), 219–236. doi:10.1080/030521504 10001647966

DasGupta, D. (1999). *An overview of artificial immune systems and their applications* (pp. 3–21). Springer. doi:10.1007/978-3-642-59901-9

De Castro, L. N., & von Zuben, F. J. (Eds.). (2005). *Recent developments in biologically inspired computing*. IGI Global.

Deb, K. (2001). Multi-objective optimization. *Multi-Objective Optimization using Evolutionary Algorithms*, 13-46.

Dorigo, M. (Ed.). (2006). *Ant Colony Optimization and Swarm Intelligence: 5th International Workshop, (Vol. 4150)*. Springer-Verlag New York Incorporated.

Dorigo, M. (2007). Ant colony optimization. *Scholarpedia*, 2(3), 1461. doi:10.4249/scholarpedia.1461

Dorigo, M., & Birattari, M. (2010). Ant colony optimization. In Encyclopedia of Machine Learning (pp. 36-39). Springer US.

Dorigo, M., & Di Caro, G. (1999). Ant colony optimization: a new meta-heuristic. In *Proceedings of Evolutionary Computation, (Vol. 2)*. IEEE.

Goldberg, D. E., & Holland, J. H. (1988). Genetic algorithms and machine learning. *Machine Learning*, 3(2), 95–99. doi:10.1023/A:1022602019183

Goldsmith, J. R., & Friberg, L. T. (1976). Effects of air pollution on human health, Air Pollution. In A. C. Stern (Ed.), *The Effects of Air Pollution* (3rd ed., Vol. 2, pp. 457–610). New York, NY: Academic Press.

Griffiths, R. F. (1994). Errors in the use of the Briggs parameterization for atmospheric dispersion coefficients. *Atmospheric Environment*, 28(17), 2861–2865. doi:10.1016/1352-2310(94)90086-8

Halitsky, J. (1989). A jet plume model for short stacks. *Journal of the Air Pollution Control Association*, 39(6), 856–858.

Hanna, S. R., Briggs, G. A., & Kosker, R. P. (1982). *Handbook on Atmospheric Diffusion*. NTIS. doi:10.2172/5591108

Hofmeyr, S. A., & Forrest, S. (2000). Architecture for an artificial immune system. *Evolutionary Computation*, 8(4), 443–473. doi:10.1162/106365600568257 PMID:11130924

Hogan, W. R., Cooper, G. F., Wagner, M. M., & Wallstrom, G. L. (2005). An inverted Gaussian Plume Model for estimating the location and amount of Release of airborne agents from downwind atmospheric concentrations. RODS Technical Report. Pittsburgh, PA: Real time Outbreak and Disease Surveillance Laboratory, University of Pittsburgh.

Holler, M., Tam, S., Castro, H., & Benson, R. (1989, June). An electrically trainable artificial neural network (etann) with 10240'floating gate'synapses. In *Proceedings of Neural Networks*, (pp. 191-196). IEEE.

Jeong, H. J., Kim, E. H., Suh, K. S., Hwang, W. T., Han, M. H., & Lee, H. K. (2005). Determination of the source rate released into the environment from a nuclear power plant. *Radiation Protection Dosimetry*, *113*(3), 308–313. doi:10.1093/rpd/nch460 PMID:15687109

Jhuang, H., Serre, T., Wolf, L., & Poggio, T. (2007, October). A biologically inspired system for action recognition. In *Proceedings of Computer Vision*, (pp. 1-8). IEEE. doi:10.1109/ICCV.2007.4408988

Jin, X., & Reynolds, R. G. (1999). Using knowledge-based evolutionary computation to solve nonlinear constraint optimization problems: a cultural algorithm approach. In *Proceedings of Evolutionary Computation*, (*Vol. 3*). IEEE.

Kennedy, J. (2010). Particle swarm optimization. In Encyclopedia of Machine Learning (pp. 760-766). Springer US.

Lazinica, A. (Ed.). (2009). *Particle swarm optimization*. InTech. doi:10.5772/109

Lei, X. R. B. W. (2002). Artificial Immune System: Principle, Models, Analysis and Perspectives. *Chinese Journal of Computers, 12.*

Leibnitz, K., Wakamiya, N., & Murata, M. (2006). Biologically inspired self-adaptive multi-path routing in overlay networks. *Communications of the ACM*, *49*(3), 62–67. doi:10.1145/1118178.1118203

MacKay, C., McKee, S., & Mulholland, A. J. (2006). Diffusion and convection of gaseous and fine particulate from a chimney. *IMA Journal of Applied Mathematics*, *71*(5), 670–691. doi:10.1093/imamat/hxl016

Nagpal, R. (2002, July). Programmable self-assembly using biologically-inspired multiagent control. In *Proceedings of the First International Joint Conference on Autonomous Agents and Multiagent Systems: Part 1* (pp. 418-425). ACM. doi:10.1145/544838.544839

NDTV. (n.d.). *Japan: Earthquake triggers oil refinery fire.* Retrieved from http://www.ndtv.com

Pasquill, F. (1961). The Estimation of the Dispersion of Windborne Material. *The Meteorological Magazine*, *90*(1063), 33–49.

Pasquill, F. (1974). *Atmospheric Diffusion* (2nd ed.). New York, NY: Halsted Press, John Wiley & Sons.

Patterson, D. W. (1998). *Artificial neural networks: theory and applications.* Prentice Hall PTR.

Perfilieva, I., & Močkoř, J. (1999). *Mathematical principles of fuzzy logic.* Springer.

Poli, R., Kennedy, J., & Blackwell, T. (2007). Particle swarm optimization. *Swarm Intelligence*, *1*(1), 33–57. doi:10.1007/s11721-007-0002-0

Reynolds, R. G. (1994, February). An introduction to cultural algorithms. In *Proceedings of the third annual conference on evolutionary programming* (pp. 131-139). World Scientific.

Reynolds, R. G., & Sverdlik, W. (1994, June). Problem solving using cultural algorithms. In *Proceedings of Evolutionary Computation*, (pp. 645-650). IEEE.

Rieser, C. J. (2004). *Biologically inspired cognitive radio engine model utilizing distributed genetic algorithms for secure and robust wireless communications and networking.* (Doctoral dissertation). Virginia Polytechnic Institute and State University, Blacksburg, VA.

Roveri, N., Falini, G., Sidoti, M. C., Tampieri, A., Landi, E., Sandri, M., & Parma, B. (2003). Biologically inspired growth of hydroxyapatite nanocrystals inside self-assembled collagen fibers. *Materials Science and Engineering C, 23*(3), 441–446. doi:10.1016/S0928-4931(02)00318-1

Rowe, M. P., Pugh, E. N. Jr, Tyo, J. S., & Engheta, N. (1995). Polarization-difference imaging: A biologically inspired technique for observation through scattering media. *Optics Letters, 20*(6), 608–610. doi:10.1364/OL.20.000608 PMID:19859271

Sarle, W. S. (1994). *Neural networks and statistical models*. Academic Press.

Seinfeld, J. H. (1986). *Atmospheric Chemistry and Physics of Air Pollution*. New York: J.Wiley.

Slade, D. H. (Ed.). (1986). *Meteorology and Atomic Energy*. Washington, DC: Atomic Energy Commission, Air Resources Laboratories, Research Laboratories, Environmental Science Services Administration, U.S Department of Commerce.

Stevens, R., & Casillas, A. (2006). *Artificial neural networks. In Automated Scoring of Complex Tasks in Computer Based Testing: An Introduction* (pp. 259–312). Mahwah, NJ: Lawrence Erlbaum.

Timmis, J., & Neal, M. (2001). A resource limited artificial immune system for data analysis. *Knowledge-Based Systems, 14*(3), 121–130. doi:10.1016/S0950-7051(01)00088-0

Timmis, J., Neal, M., & Hunt, J. (2000). An artificial immune system for data analysis. *Bio Systems, 55*(1), 143–150. doi:10.1016/S0303-2647(99)00092-1 PMID:10745118

Turner, D. B. (1979). Atmospheric Dispersion Modeling. *Journal of the Air Pollution Control Association, 29*(5), 502–519. doi:10.1080/00022 470.1979.10470821

Turner, D. B. (1994). *Workbook of Atmospheric Dispersion Estimates: An Introduction to Dispersion Modeling* (2nd ed.). Boca Raton, FL: Lewis Publishers.

Turner, D. B., Bender, L. W., Pierce, T. E., & Petersen, W. B. (1989). Air Quality Simulation Models from EPA. *Environmental Software, 4*(2), 52–61. doi:10.1016/0266-9838(89)90031-2

United States Chemical Safety Board. (n.d.). Retrieved from http://www.csb.gov

Venter, G., & Sobieszczanski-Sobieski, J. (2003). Particle swarm optimization. *AIAA Journal, 41*(8), 1583–1589. doi:10.2514/2.2111

Vose, M. D. (1999). *The simple genetic algorithm: foundations and theory* (Vol. 12). The MIT Press.

Wang, L., & Fu, K. (2008). *Artificial neural networks*. John Wiley & Sons, Inc.

Whitley, D. (1994). A genetic algorithm tutorial. *Statistics and Computing, 4*(2), 65–85. doi:10.1007/BF00175354

Yang, X., & Zheng, J. (2009). Artificial neural networks. Handbook of Research on Geoinformatics, 122.

Zadeh, L. A. (1965). Fuzzy sets. *Information and Control, 8*(3), 338–353. doi:10.1016/S0019-9958(65)90241-X

Zalta, E. N. (Ed.). (2003). Stanford encyclopedia of philosophy. Academic Press.

ADDITIONAL READING

Abrahamse, W., Steg, L., Vlek, C., & Rothengatter, T. (2005). A Review of Intervention Studies Aimed at Household Energy Conservation. *Journal of Environmental Psychology, 25*(3), 273–291. doi:10.1016/j.jenvp.2005.08.002

Banker, R., Bardhan, I., Chang, H., and Lin, S. 2006. Plant Information Systems, Manufacturing Capabilities, and Plant Performance, *MIS Quarterly* (30:2), pp. 315-337.

Barrieu, P., Sinclair-Desgagné, B., & Policies, O. P. (2006, August). On Precautionary Policies. *Management Science, 52*(8), 1145–1154. doi:10.1287/mnsc.1060.0527

Blevis, E. Sustainable interaction design: invention & disposal, renewal & reuse, *Proceedings of the SIGCHI conference on Human factors in computing systems*, April 28-May 03, 2007, San Jose, California, USA doi:10.1145/1240624.1240705

Boccaletti, G., Loffler, M., & Oppenheim, J. 2008. How IT Can Cut Carbon Emissions, *McKinsey Quarterly*, October (available online at http://www.mckinsey.com/ clientservice/ccsi/pdf/how_it_can_cut_carbon_missions.pdf)

Boudreau, M.-C., Chen, A., & Huber, M. 2007. Green IS: Building Sustainable Business Practices, in: Information Systems, Global Text Project, 2007, pp. 1-15.

Brown, T. (2008). Design Thinking. *Harvard Business Review*, (June): 84–92. PMID:18605031

Chen, C. (2001, February). Design for the Environment: A Quality-Based Model for Green Product Development. *Management Science, 47*(2), 250–263. doi:10.1287/mnsc.47.2.250.9841

Collins, C., Steg, L., and Koning, M. 2007. Customers' Values, Beliefs on Sustainable Corporate Performance, and Buying Behavior, *Psychology and Marketing* (24:6), pp. 555-577.

Corbett, C. J., and Kirsch, D. A. 2001. International Diffusion of ISO 14000 Certification, *Production and Operations Management* (10:3), pp. 327-342.

Daly, H. 1990. Toward Some Operational Principles of Sustainable Development, *Ecological Economics* (2:1), pp. 1-6.

Denzer, R., Schimak, G., & Russell, D. (Eds.). (1995). *Environmental Software Systems*. London: Chapman & Hall; URL http://cfc.crle.uoguelph.ca/isess97/

Dewan, S., & Chung-ki, M. (1997, December). The substitution of information technology for other factors of production: A Firm Level Analysis. *Management Science, 43*(12), 1660–1675. doi:10.1287/mnsc.43.12.1660

EPA. (2006). *Environmental Management Systems Benchmark Report*. Washington, D.C.: Environmental Protection Agency.

Erdmann, L., Lorenz, H., Goodman, J., & Arnfalk, P. 2004. *The Future Impact of ICTs on Environmental Sustainability*, European Commission Joint Research Centre. (available online at ftp://ftp.jrc.es/pub/EURdoc/eur21384en.pdf)

Esty, D. C. 2004. Environmental protection in the information age. *NYUL rev.*, 79, 115.

Felin, T., and Foss, N. 2005. Strategic Organization: A Field in Search of Micro-Foundations, *Strategic Organization* (3:4), pp. 441-455.

Felin, T., & Foss, N. (2006). Individuals and Organizations: Thoughts on a Micro-foundations Project for Strategic Management and Organizational Analysis. In D. J. Ketchen, & D. D. Bergh (Eds.), *Research Methodology in Strategy and Management* (pp. 253–288). Amsterdam: Elsevier Ltd. doi:10.2139/ssrn.982095

Fishbein, M., & Azjen, I. (1975). *Belief, Attitude, Intention, and Behavior: An Introduction to Theory and Research, Reading*. MA: Addison-Wesley Publishing.

Gephart, R. 1999. Paradigms and Research Methods, *Academy of Management Research Methods Forum* (4), pp. 1-12.

Gérard, P. (2000, August). Cachon, Marshall Fisher, Supply Chain Inventory Management and the Value of Shared Information. *Management Science*, *46*(8), 1032–1048. doi:10.1287/mnsc.46.8.1032.12029

Gladwin, T. N. (1993). The Meaning of Greening: A Plea for Organizational Theory. In K. Fischer, & J. Schot (Eds.), *Environmental Strategies for Industry: International Perspectives on Research Needs and Policy Implications* (pp. 37–61). Washington, DC: Island Press.

Gregor, S., and Jones, D. 2007. The Anatomy of a Design Theory, *Journal of the Association for Information Systems* (8:5), pp. 1-25.

Gunther, O., & Voisard, A. (1997). Metadata in Geographic and Environmental Data Management. In W. Klas, & A. Sheth (Eds.), *Managing Multimedia Data: Using Metadata to Integrate and Apply Digital Data*. McGraw Hill.

Heiskanen, E. (2000). Managers' Interpretations of LCA: Enlightenment and Responsibility or Confusion and Denial. *Business Strategy and the Environment*, *9*(9), 239–254. doi:10.1002/1099-0836(200007/08)9:4<239::AID-BSE250>3.0.CO;2-6

Hevner, A., March, S., and Park, J. 2004. Design Science in Information Systems Research, *MIS Quarterly* (28:1), pp. 75-105.

Section 3
Technology–Enhanced Data Management, Data Processing, Data Visualization, and Human–Machine Analysis

It stands to reason that technologies that enable the archival and coding of data for qualitative and mixed media research should be able to accommodate and store a variety of multimedia file types: audio, video, imagery, text, and others. Further, such technologies surely complement human analytical capabilities with a range of analytical tools and data visualizations. Section 3 addresses various uses of technology for data management, data visualization, and human-machine analysis.

Chapter 8
Leveraging Two Computer-Assisted Qualitative Data Analysis Software Packages to Support Discourse Analysis

Jessica Nina Lester
Indiana University, USA

ABSTRACT

The purpose of this chapter is to illustrate how Computer-Assisted Qualitative Data Analysis Software (CAQDAS) packages, such as ATLAS.ti or Transana, can be used to support the transcription and data analysis process of large interactional data sets – specifically data analyzed from a discourse analysis perspective. Drawing from a larger ethnographic study, in this chapter the author illustrates how carrying out the transcription and analysis process within a CAQDAS package (in this case, Transana and ATLAS.ti) allows for an increase in transparency within the transcription and data analysis process, while also meeting the particular needs of the discourse analyst. By using one particular case/research study, the author demonstrates how CAQDAS packages might function to support a researcher in generating a more systematic and transparent analytical process, specifically during the early stages of the analysis process. The author gives particular attention to interactional data (i.e., 300 hours of video and audio recordings of therapy sessions) collected in a larger study and demonstrates the potential benefits of working across two CAQDAS packages, specifically Transana and ATLAS.ti, to support both the nuanced transcription process and the larger data analysis process.

INTRODUCTION

The transcription process is central to the work of many discourse analysts, often being positioned as one of the first steps of the analysis process (Rapley, 2007). Discourse analysts typically position transcription as "a constructive and conventional activity" that is a critical component of the analysis process (Potter & Wetherell, 1987, p. 166). Historically, the literature base related to discourse analysis, particularly conversation analysis (Sacks, 1992), has given relatively little

DOI: 10.4018/978-1-4666-6493-7.ch008

attention to the potential uses of computer-assisted qualitative data analysis software (CAQDAS). There are exceptions (e.g., King, 2010; Ten Have, 1991, 1998), however, in which conversation analysts have examined whether and illustrated how such tools may or may not be compatible with the methodological tasks that discourse analysts pursue. MacMillan (2005) suggested that when researchers are conducting a discourse analysis, CAQDAS packages are only useful for practical tasks, such as searching for data segments. She argued that such packages offer only limited support to analysts who engage in more than "rudimentary coding", and thereby may simply "…be more time consuming than useful…" (p. 15). In contrast to this cautionary tale, in this chapter, I illustrate how CAQDAS packages, such as Transana and/or ATLAS.ti, are useful for discourse analysts throughout the data analysis process, particularly during the early stages of analysis (e.g., Jeffersonian transcription).

More specifically, the purpose of this chapter is to illustrate how CAQDAS programs, in this case Transana and ATLAS.ti (Muhr, 2004), can be used to support the early analysis and transcription of large interactional data sets – specifically data analyzed from a discourse analysis perspective (Potter & Wetherell, 1987). Drawing from a larger ethnographic study (Lester, 2012; Lester & Paulus, 2012, 2014), in this chapter, I illustrate how carrying out the transcription process within a CAQDAS program allowed for me to stay close to the data set, while increasing the transparency of the data analysis process (Paulus, Lester, & Dempster, 2014).

By using a particular case/research project, I demonstrate from the very first steps of the analysis process how I worked across two CAQDAS packages (Transana and ATLAS.ti), to support a systematic and transparent analytical process. Within the research study example of focus, data included: (1) approximately 300 hours of video and audio recordings of therapy sessions, social group sessions, office conversations, and waiting room conversations; (2) interviews with therapists and parents of children with autism labels; (3) approximately 200 hours of participant-observations; and (4) interviews with state disability advocates. In this chapter, I focus on the interactional data (i.e., 300 hours of video and audio recordings of therapy sessions), which was collected over a two-year period. Through this focus, I demonstrate how Transana was used to support the transcription process and allow for a nuanced conversation or discourse analysis of the data (Sacks, 1984), while ATLAS.ti supported my emergent understandings of the transcribed data.

Further, while I do not share step-by-step procedures for transcribing or annotating data with a particular CAQDAS package, I do offer key points to consider when engaging in the analysis process, while pointing to the affordances of the software packages. I conclude the chapter by offering suggestions for researchers working with large interactional data sets. In doing so, I demonstrate the pragmatic and technical aspects of engaging in the transcription process within the context of two CAQDAS packages.

To begin, I consider the role of CAQDAS packages in qualitative research more generally, while more specifically examining how CAQDAS might relate to the work of researchers focused on the analysis of everyday talk.

BACKGROUND

During the 1980s, qualitative researchers began developing software to support the data analysis process. Ethnograph and Non-numerical Unstructured Data Indexing Searching and Theorising (NUD*IST) were two of the first packages developed. NUD*IST was the earlier version of NVivo, which is a readily used CAQDAS package today. With the increased use of desktop computing, over time these packages became more frequently used (Fielding, 2008). In 1994, the CAQDAS Networking Project in the United Kingdom began, which became a central site for engaging in critical discussion about the uses of CAQDAS in qualitative research. The CAQDAS project was funded by the Economic and Social Research Council from 1994 until 2011. Despite the occurrence of on-going methodological conversations regarding the advantages and disadvantages of using CAQDAS, qualitative researchers have had an uncertain relationship with CADQAS.

In Davidson and di Gregorio's (2011) overview of the history of technology and qualitative research, the uneasiness between technology and qualitative research was highlighted. This uneasiness has been particularly true in relation to CAQDAS, with qualitative researchers expressing few concerns regarding the use of technologies such as digital recorders for the collection of interviews. Specifically, many qualitative researchers have expressed concern that the software 'does' the analysis for the researcher, which works against one of the main assumptions of qualitative research – the researcher is the research instrument and the primary interpreter of the data. Yet, as Gibbs, Friese, and Mangabeira (2002) noted, CAQDAS is "…just a tool for analysis, and good qualitative analysis still relies on good analytic work by a careful human researcher" (p. 9). Further, resistance surrounding the use of technology in the data analysis process has also centered on concerns that CAQDAS packages only support one type of methodology, specifically grounded theory (Lonikila, 1995). Additionally, some researchers have suggested that many of the software packages support only one analytical approach, specifically coding (Coffey, Holbrook, & Atkinson, 1996). Davidson and di Gregorio (2011) suggested that the privileging of grounded theory in the software package may be explained by the fact that grounded theory became popularized at the same time that the first CAQDAS packages were being developed.

Paulus, Lester, and Britt (2013) conducted a discourse analysis of introductory qualitative research textbooks, noting that the many of the textbook authors, most of whom were senior scholars in the field, positioned the use of technology during the data analysis stage as something to be used with caution. Similarly, discourse analysts have generally been cautious about using CAQDAS, particularly in relation to conversation analysis (MacMillan, 2005). Seale (2000), for example, stated that the "more popular CAQDAS packages are unable to support many of the things conversation analysts wish to do" (p. 165). One of the main tasks is developing detailed transcripts, using Jeffersonian transcription symbols (Jefferson, 2004). Gibbs et al. (2002) highlighted this particular concern, noting that:

…there are some forms of qualitative research where there is little use of CAQDAS. This is true of approaches like narrative, conversation analysis, biography and discourse analysis. The most likely reason is that current programs give little support to the special forms of transcription needed and/ or they poorly support the chronological dimension. (p. 13)

While new versions of many CAQDAS packages have addressed this concern to some extent, there remains hesitancy around the 'true' applicability of CAQDAS to the work of discourse analysts.

It is important to note that there are vast differences between using CAQDAS for a discourse analysis that aims at counting and coding lexical items and a discourse analysis that focuses on the function of language, with the later being more qualitative in scope. So, for many discourse analysts the question becomes: if a discourse analyst seeks to engage in a qualitatively informed study is CAQDAS useful or does it primarily meet the needs of more quantitatively oriented discourse analysis? In MacMillan's (2005) review of discourse studies using CAQDAS, she noted that of those studies that used qualitative software, the majority of researchers were doing qualitative linguistic analysis or a form of discourse analysis in conjunction with quantitative analysis. This makes evident the lack of literature highlighting how CAQDAS packages might support a discourse analysis that is both qualitative in scope and employs conversation analysis. For this reason, this chapter seeks to add to the literature base by presenting a research example of how multiple CAQDAS packages can support the work of discourse analysts, specifically the work of those who seek to produce detailed transcripts.

CAQDAS: A POSSIBLE SOLUTION

Indeed, the needs of discourse analysts are unique, often centering on particular approaches to transcription. At present, there are a plethora of technologies that can be used to support the transcription process, ranging from basic word processing systems to more robust CAQDAS packages. Some have argued that when using CAQDAS packages there is value in carrying out the entire research process within one package (Paulus & Lester, 2013), such as ATLAS.ti. Working within one package, however, does not always allow for the preferences and needs of a researcher to be fully met. This is particularly true when working with naturally-occurring data, such as talk. Quite often, the aim of a discourse analyst is to produce a detailed transcript, while also engaging in a robust analysis of the full data set. At times, this requires working across multiple CAQDAS packages, and generating an approach to analysis that is both robust and efficient. As such, I suggest here that one possible solution to the critiques mounted by discourse analysts regarding CAQDAS packages is found in flexibly moving across packages. Prior to offering a more detailed description of how Trasana and ATLAS.ti might be used in tandem to support the early stages of a discourse analysis, I offer a brief overview of both packages and then move to provide an overview of the research study example.

OVERVIEW OF ATLAS.ti AND TRANSANA

There are a growing number of CAQDAS packages available to qualitative researchers, including packages for those who engage in discourse analysis studies. While many of these packages offer similar features, they each possess some unique features. ATLAS.ti 7, MAXQDA 11, and NVivo 10 are considered the most commonly used CAQDAS packages (Paulus et al., 2014). In the research example of focus, ATLAS.ti was used, along with Transana – a package designed for researchers analyzing digital video or audio data. More specifically, ATLAS.ti was selected primarily out of convenience, rather than MAXQDA and NVivo. ATLAS.ti was both supported by my institution and the primary package that I had been trained to use. I selected to work with Transana because of its ability to support nuanced transcription processes.

In 1989 at the Technical University of Berlin, ATLAS.ti was developed. Initially, it was developed as a research project and later launched for commercial use in 1993. The most recent version, Version 7, was released in 2012 (see: http://www.atlasti.com/index.html). A mobile application was released in 2013; this application allows researchers to record audio and video data at a given research site and then immediately begin segmenting and coding the recorded data. The annotated data can then be transferred to the researcher's desktop version of ATLAS.ti, after which the researcher can access all of the features available in the full version. The newest version of ATLAS.ti also allows researchers to associate Google Earth coordinates to data sources, allowing for geodata analysis. Further, like other CAQDAS packages, ATLAS.ti allows a researcher to import survey data and supports team sharing and team analysis. In 2014, ATLAS.ti released its first iOS version. There are several rich descriptions of ATLAS.ti available, all of which walk a researcher step-by-step through the process of using the package (e.g., Friese, 2012). Such resources are invaluable for individuals who aim to take advantage of all of the features that ATLAS.ti offers.

Generally, ATLAS.ti supports researchers who analyze image, audio, and video data. An analyst can directly code data and/or transcribe files. While ATLAS.ti does allow the analyst to synchronize a transcript with a media file, it does not yet fully support any specialized approach to the transcription process. For the discourse analyst, this is a particular feature that is essential for the transcription process, as many analysts who draw upon conversation analysis desire to use Jeffersonian transcription symbols (Jefferson, 2004) and/or isolate the portions of the data they hope to transcribe in a more nuanced way. While ATLAS.ti can support the bulk of a discourse analyst's research process, the program's limitations in relation to the transcription process can be supplemented through the use of an additional CAQDAS package.

Across my discourse work, I have found Transana (Fassnacht & Woods, 2005) to be a particularly useful tool for the early stages of listening to and transcribing large sets of naturally-occurring talk. In contrast to ATLAS.ti, Transana (see: http://www.transana.org/) is an open source computer program. It can be used across platforms and was specifically designed for researchers who need to transcribe and analyze relatively large audio and video data sets, being specifically useful for the analysis of videos and images. This package allows a researcher to transcribe video or audio files in as much detail as they desire, while also working to manage potentially hundreds or thousands of audio or video recordings. Transana allows a researcher to create a synchronized transcript, using time stamps throughout, which is discussed in greater detail below. Transana also has a feature that allows an analyst to manage and organize videos into small clips that can than be searched with keywords and/or analyzed in greater detail. Specific to a discourse analyst, these clips can

in turn be transcribed in a very nuanced way, as Transana supports Jeffersonian-based transcription (as well as other forms of transcription). The transcription capabilities of Transana, then, are particularly appealing to researchers engaged in the analysis of everyday talk. Further, for researchers working together there is a multi-user version available.

RESEARCH STUDY EXAMPLE

Like many discourse analysis studies, particularly those informed by conversation analysis (Sacks, 1984), the research study example of focus involved a relatively large data set of everyday talk. This study was also informed by discursive psychology (Edwards & Potter, 1993) and focused on the everyday talk that took place at a pediatric clinic designed to support the therapeutic needs of children with disability labels. This clinic was located in the Midwestern region of the United States. The study itself involved a variety of data sources, including interviews with parents and therapists, artifacts from therapy sessions, and observational fieldnotes.

Discursive psychologists define naturally-occurring interactions as those interactions that are not necessarily fashioned by the researcher or primarily produced for the purposes of a given research study (e.g., phone conversations, talking with a friend at a party, etc.) (Edwards, 1997; Potter, 1999). In other words, such interactions would occur whether the researcher was present or not. Further, naturalistic conversations may also be institutionally structured, such as counseling sessions, an elementary school classroom lesson, or therapy sessions (O'Reilly, 2004). With my study focused on how children with autism labels and their therapists and parents interacted within a therapeutic setting, I attended primarily to both the mundane aspects of the conversations (Sacks, 1992) and how the institutional talk deviated from ordinary, day-to-day talk. Further, I sought to understand the context in which the talk was situated, hence the collection of observational data.

One of the key data sources was the 300 hours of audio and video data, which was collected over the course of two years. This naturally-occurring data included the individual therapy sessions between the participating children with disability labels and their therapists, as well as the larger social group sessions that many of the participating children attended. Within this study's analytic approach, I focused upon what the talk-in-interaction was doing, accounting for both the patterns within the corpus of data and the deviations from such patterns (Potter & Hepburn, 2008). I, thus, attended to specific discursive features of the discourse, and spent far more time analyzing the data than collecting it (Taylor, 2001). When drawing upon conversation analytic techniques, I attended to many conversational features considered fundamental to interaction, such as conversational turns, membership categories (category work), and turn-taking design, as well as other features that were made relevant in the participants' talk.

Similar to other qualitative approaches, I took an interpretive and emergent approach to analyzing the data. To analyze the data generated in this study, I attended to discursive resources and features made relevant by the participants across the data set (Rapley, 2007, Wood & Kroger, 2000). More specifically, I carried out seven broad phases of data analysis, with several sub-phases/steps included within each phase: (1) intensive listening (Wood & Kroger, 2000); (2) transcribing of the audio and video data (Potter & Wetherell, 1987); (3) repeated reading of and listening to transcripts, resulting in detailed transcription (Potter & Wetherell); (4) annotating of the Jeffersonian transcripts; (5) selecting and further analyzing of patterns across the discourse segments (i.e., episodes or segments of talk) related to the various discursive features and/or broader discourses and institutionalized practices; (6) generating explanations/interpretations; (7) reflexive and transparent sharing of findings. In the following

paragraphs, I outline how steps 1-5 were carried out across the two CAQDAS packages, supporting the particular needs of the analytical approach. I give particular attention to the transcription process and the initial stages of annotating and making sense of the larger data set.

Step 1: Intensive Listening

Within the discourse framework used in the research study example described above, the first layer of intensive analysis often begins with listening and re-listening to the audio and video recordings. Thus, for the purposes of the study of focus, I began the intensive analysis with listening and re-listening to the audio and video recordings of the entire data set after uploading and organizing the files within Transana. Rather than listening to these files in a separate program, I found it useful to organize my data within Transana and then begin the intensive listening process. These initial, repeated reviews of the data allowed me to familiarize myself with the conversations and identify initial sections that I found surprising or simply intriguing.

Most CAQDAS packages, including Transana, have navigable waveforms that help you make sense of your files as you listen and re-listen to them. In the research study example, I created waveform files for all of my data, which served to visually represent the amplitude of sound over the duration of a given audio file. The waveform was particularly useful for identifying pauses between speaker turns. Specifically, waveforms represent the intensity of the sound, and, therefore, allow a researcher to take note of how things are actually being said. Is the speech being produced quickly (represented by long vertical waves)? Is there a long absence of sound (represented by horizontal lines)? In a discourse study, in particular, these are the types of questions that are critical to consider, and packages like Transana afford a discourse analyst the opportunity to explore such analytical points of interest. Figure 1 is an example of a

Figure 1.

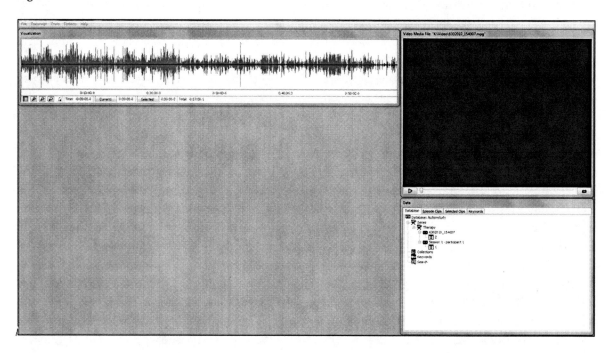

waveform from the example data set produced in Transana. In this case, there is no transcript yet developed, as the focus is on listening to the data again and again.

Throughout this first step of listening, a discourse analyst may often records notes and reflections in relation to those sections that are found to be the most striking (Rapley, 2007). During these initial listenings, I made 'notes' that captured my initial ideas related to the data and linked closely to my analytical framework. Many of these notes related to future analytic ideas. Recording thoughts in this manner served to increase the transparency of the research process and create an audit trail from the very start of the data analysis (Paulus et al., 2013). Figure 2 shows a 'note' made in relation to a particular video file.

Step 2: Transcribing of the Audio/Video Data

After the initial listening and note taking across the 300 hours of data, I created transcripts of the

data. Indeed, there are varied ways by which to approach the transcription process; each of which results in a unique transcript type related to one's analytic focus. Transcripts range from verbataim (word for word representations of data) to gisted (condensed versions of what is said) to visual (representation of meaning in images) to Jeffersonian (representations of what was said by including features of the talk beyond words) (Paulus et al., 2014). Verbatim transcripts, which include the exact words of the research participants, do not necessarily include the micro-details of the talk. Thus, many discourse analysts, particularly those that draw upon conversation analysis, return to the verbatim transcript to add additional, micro-level details to the transcript (see Appendix). How a researcher goes about transcribing their data is closely related to their methodological framework, which must always be considered when developing an approach to transcription.

I oriented to the process of transcription as an interpretive and "selective process" that reflected my theoretical "goals and definitions" (Ochs,

Figure 2.

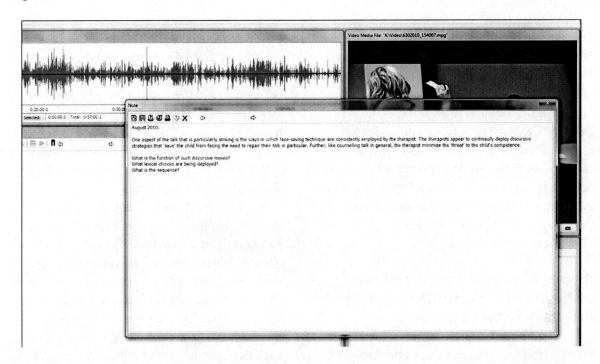

1979, p. 44). The initial transcription process inevitably occurred concurrently with the first step of analysis, as well as the data collection process.

I transcribed the therapy sessions, 14 parent interviews, eight therapist interviews, and two interviews focused on insurance and diagnosis issues. I began with an initial verbatim transcription of each recording. Figure 3 shows a verbatim transcript from the research study example.

As verbatim transcripts were created, time stamps were also added to the media files. Time stamping is a tool that allows an analyst to return

Figure 3.

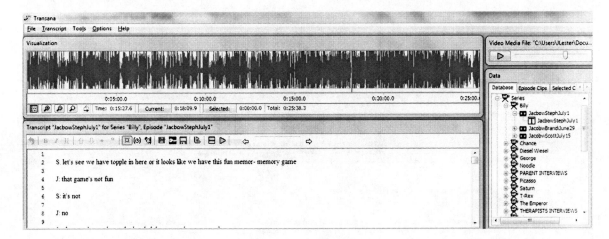

to key phrases or actions. For instance, in Figure 4, time stamps are shown. If I were to click on the time stamps, I could easily and quickly return to a portion of the actual audio or video file and listen to the interaction while reading the transcript. In other words, I bypassed the hassle of having to fast forward through large amounts of data to find an analytically meaningful segment. Further, in many ways, this tool keeps the discourse analyst close to the data, avoiding the risk of everyday talk simply turning into words on a paper. Rather, the nuanced nature of the talk remains 'alive' as the analyst spends time navigating through the synchronized transcript file.

Step 3: Repeated Reading of and Listening to Transcripts Resulting in Detailed Transcription

Third, I read and listened to all of the transcripts in their entirety, searching for and identifying patterns and conversational features (e.g., turn-taking

organization), as the following broad, discourse analytic questions sensitized the process: (1) What is the discourse doing?; (2) How is the discourse constructed to do this?; and (3) What resources are present and being used to perform this activity? (Potter, 2004; Wood & Kroger, 2000). These analytical questions informed me as I began narrowing my focus. With such a large data set, it was important to begin identifying key 'clips' to transcribe in greater detail. Transana was built to support this analytical step.

Specifically, Transana was designed around the metaphor of a 'television series'. As such, the top, organizational level consists of a 'series' with individual 'episodes'. Sections within a given 'episode' can be cut, thereby creating 'clips'. These clips can then be organized into 'collections', and further analyzed and/or more closely transcribed. In my case, 'clips' were analytically significant portions of the talk that I aimed to transcribe in greater detail. This allowed me to move from 300 hours of transcribed data to approximately 70

Figure 4.

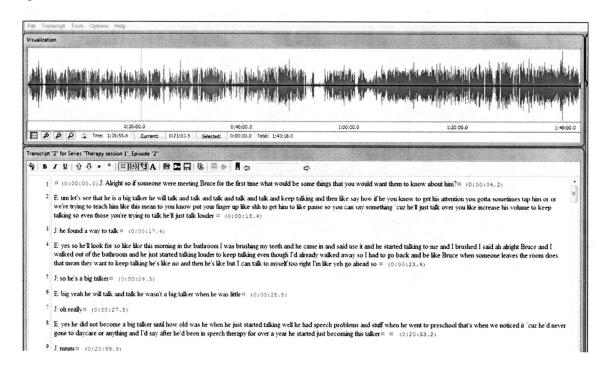

hours of data, which was transcribed in greater detail. I was then able to transcribe the 70 hours of data, using a modified version of the transcription system developed by conversation analyst Gail Jefferson (2004). While there are a variety of notation systems (e.g., Du Bois, 1991), in the research study of focus, a modified version of Jeffersonian's notation system was employed. This matched the analytical framework of the study, which was informed by conversation analysis (Sacks, 1992). Figure 5 illustrates how Transana supports specialized transcription processes, with relevant transcription symbols (e.g., whispered speech, audible breath, falling intonation, rising intonation, etc.) applied easily to a transcript via shortcuts.

The tools allow for a more detailed transcription, as conversational details (e.g., pauses, prosody, gaps, intonation, etc.) may be represented in an alternate form to sound. Recognizing that it is impossible to include all of the relevant details within a transcript, in the research study example, I added only those symbols that were relevant to the claims I made and that I believed would "provide readers with data and evidence" to determine whether "alternative interpretations" might be plausible (Hammersley, 2010, p. 566). Generally, Jeffersonian transcripts are created in rounds, with the transcriber focused on one particular conversational feature during each round (ten Have, 2007). Thus, in the research study example, I focused on one particular feature, attending to this feature throughout the 70 hours of data. Then, I completed subsequent rounds that attended to different features of the talk. For example, during the first round, I attended to pauses in the speech, particularly between the conversational turns. In the second round, I attended to rising and falling intonation.

Step 4: Annotating of the Jeffersonian Transcripts

After the Jeffersonian transcripts were completed, I spent time further reading and annotating the transcripts, using the 'note' feature to chronicle my thoughts and emergent ideas. These initial readings allowed me to become more familiar with the overall interchanges, as well as begin the initial labeling of the transcribed data set, "preparing the way for a much more intensive study of material culled through the selective coding process" (Potter & Wetherell, 1987, p. 167).

While Transana does provide a coding system, I desired to work with a system that provided more flexibility, particularly as my data set included data beyond audio and video files (e.g., artifacts from the therapy sessions). Further, I found Transana's coding system to be more 'top-down' than I desired, requiring too much to be defined a-priori. At this stage of the analysis, I desired an even more inductive coding design. Specifically, rather than broadly coding 'clips' of the data, I sought to make analytical and theoretical memos directly on the micro-segments of the short 'clips' or transcript. Further, while there were theories informing my work, I oriented to the 'coding' process as emergent and focused on the actions of the talk. Thus, memos directly connected to multiple portions of the data and a more flexible coding scheme was

Figure 5.

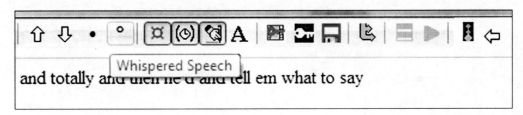

needed at this stage of the analysis. As such, I began working across two CAQDAS packages, incorporating ATLAS.ti into my analysis process. As illustrated in Figure 6, I created reports of all of the transcribed 'collections' within Transana, uploading these documents as primary data in ATLAS.ti for further analysis.

One of the limitations of this approach is that the report was no longer attached the video files; therefore, I began working with unsynchronized data. However, at this particular stage of the analysis, I found the Jeffersonian transcript alone to be analytically meaningful.

Step 5: Selecting and Further Analysis of Discursive Patterns

Concurrent to the aforementioned analytical step, I imported all of my typed observational/field notes, research journal reflections, transcripts, and documents used by the participants in the course of the

therapy sessions (e.g., PowerPoints constructed by a participating child and his therapist during a recorded therapy sessions) into ATLAS.ti (Muhr, 2004), a package that I utilized to systematize and expand the analysis process. As I read and re-read the data, I began to name or label segments of the discourse, taking note of patterns of the talk from the actual words of the participants and from concepts drawn from discourse theory, conversation analysis, and the social relational model of disability (Thomas, 2004). Taking advantage of the features available within ATLAS.ti, I systematically annotated the data, constructing detailed theoretical and analytical memos as I worked across my research journal, observational notes, and therapy-session related documents. Figure 7 provides an example of one of the 'collection' reports from Transana that was analyzed within ATLAS.ti. The memoing and coding features were applied to the Jeffersonian transcript.

Figure 6.

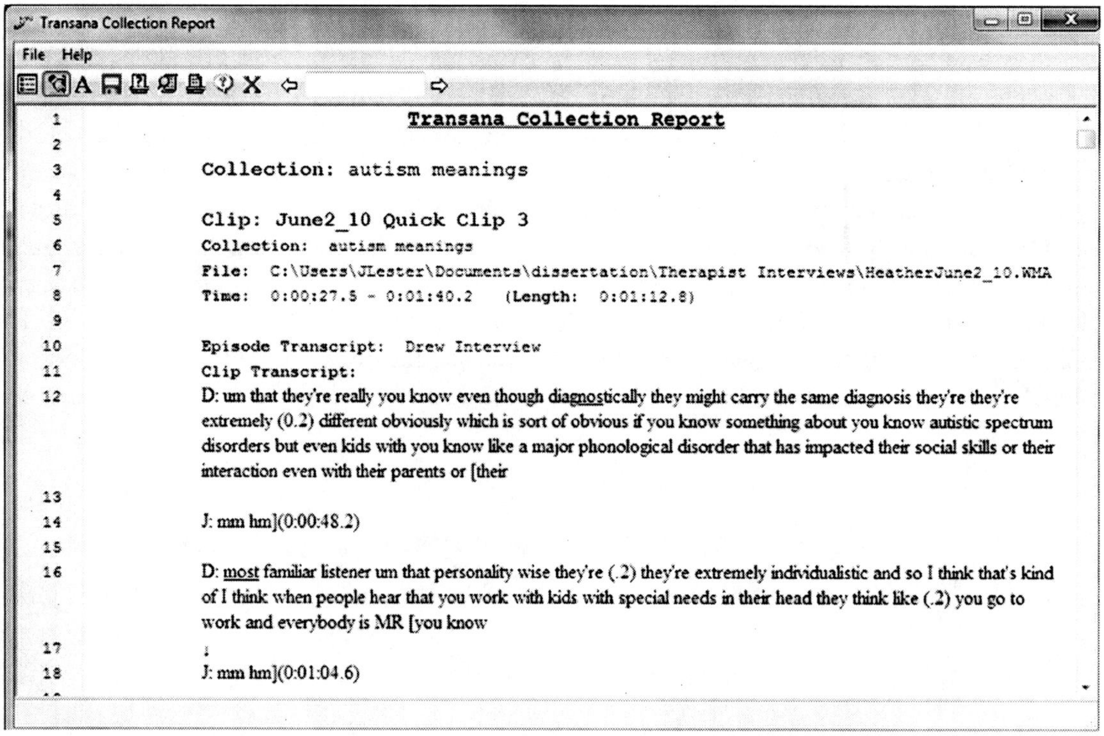

Figure 7.

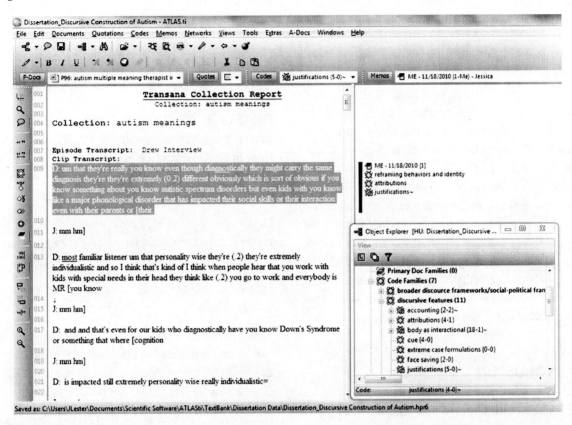

I then carried out several more rounds of analysis in ATLAS.ti, working across the interview and naturally-occurring conversational data. As I did so, I further refined and identified patterns and variability across the data. I also created extensive memos of selected excerpts, later incorporating the analysis of a given excerpt directly into the findings sections of publications.

FUTURE TRENDS

To date, many of the major CAQDAS packages support the transcription process, as well as other aspects of a robust qualitative analysis. However, there have been noted limitations for some qualitative researchers, particularly discourse analysts (Gibbs et al., 2002; MacMillan, 2005).

As CAQDAS packages continue to develop and respond to user needs, I anticipate being able to engage in the above described analysis within one package, rather than working across two packages. Further, while I was able to manipulate the packages to meet my analytical needs, in the future, CAQDAS will perhaps be designed specifically to support qualitative forms of analysis that do not use traditional forms of coding. Nonetheless, at present, analysts can leverage the features within the available packages to support the analysis process, while also providing means to increase the transparency of the research process. Rather than qualitative analyses being positioned as occurring within a black box -- hidden from others -- CAQDAS opens up the process, as each analytic decision is chronicled in detail. Such digital tools are particularly helpful when working with large sets of data and when drawing upon methodological frameworks that call for nuanced approaches to transcribing and analyzing the data.

Certainly, as new digital tools emerge and the various CAQDAS packages further develop, qualitative researchers will have to think carefully about the research process, being reflexive about how they shape new technologies and how new technologies shape the research process. As Fielding and Lee (2008) noted: "...new digital tools come with strings attached in the form of research politics, institutional expectations, and shifting boundaries around customary normal of what is and is not legitimate..." (p. 491). Thus, with the rise of new technologies, issues around methodological compatibility will certainly persist; yet, researchers will be afforded new opportunities to take advantage of the affordances of digital tools.

CONCLUSION

This chapter highlighted how discourse analysts might work across CAQDAS packages to meet their analytical needs, particularly as related to the transcription process. First, in this chapter, I highlighted the place of CAQDAS in qualitative research more generally, eventually focusing this discussion on how discourse analysts have conceptualized the uses of CAQDAS. Second, I presented a brief description of ATLAS.ti and Transana, positioning the use of both of these packages as a possible means by which to support a discourse analysis approach to data analysis. Third, I shared a brief description of the research study, which was used to illustrate the various features of the CAQDAS packages that a discourse analyst may desire to use and could access when using Transana and/or ATLAS.ti. Fourth, I provided examples of the specific analytic steps that might be used when using both Transana and ATLAS.ti to support a discourse analysis study. I concluded by highlighting the future directions of CAQDAS packages as related to discourse approaches to research.

REFERENCES

Coffey, A., Holbrook, B., & Atkinson, P. (1996). Qualitative data analysis: Technologies and representations. *Sociological Research Online*, *1*(1). doi:10.5153/sro.1

Davidson, J., & di Gregorio, S. (2011). Qualitative research and technology: In the midst of a revolution. In N. K. Denzin, & Y. S. Lincoln (Eds.), *The Sage handbook of qualitative research* (4th ed., pp. 627–643). Thousand Oaks, CA: Sage.

Du Bois, J. W. (1991). Transcription design principles for spoken discourse research. *Pragmatics*, *1*(1), 71–106.

Edwards, D. (1997). *Discourse and cognition*. London: Sage.

Edwards, D., & Potter, J. (1993). Language and causation: A discursive action model of description and attribution. *Psychological Review*, *100*(1), 23–41. doi:10.1037/0033-295X.100.1.23

Fassnacht, C., & Woods, D. (2005). *Transana v2.0x* [Computer software]. Retrieved from http://www.transana.org

Fielding, N. (2008). The role of computer-assisted qualitative data analysis: Impact on emergent methods in qualitative research. In S. Hesse-Biber, & P. Leavy (Eds.), *Handbook of emergent methods* (pp. 655–673). New York: The Guilford Press.

Fielding, N., & Lee, R. M. (2008). Qualitative e-social science/cyber-research. In N. Fielding, R. M. Lee, & G. Blank (Eds.), *The Sage handbook of online research methods* (pp. 491–506). Thousand Oaks, CA: Sage Publications. doi:10.4135/9780857020055.n26

Friese, S. (2012). *Qualitative data analysis with ATLAS.ti*. Sage.

Gibbs, G. R., Friese, S., & Mangabeira, W. C. (2002). The use of new technology in qualitative research. *Forum: Qualitative Social Research*, *3*(2), Art. 8.

Hammersley, M. (2010). Reproducing or construction? Some questions about transcription in social research. *Qualitative Research*, *10*(5), 553–569. doi:10.1177/1468794110375230

Jefferson, G. (2004). Glossary of transcript symbols with an introduction. In G. H. Lerner (Ed.), *Conversation analysis: Studies from the First Generation* (pp. 13–31). Amsterdam: John Benjamins. doi:10.1075/pbns.125.02jef

King, A. (2010). 'Membership matters': Applying membership categorization analysis (MCA) to qualitative data using computer-assisted qualitative data analysis (CAQDAS) software. *International Journal of Social Research Methodology*, *13*(1), 1–16. doi:10.1080/13645570802576575

Lester, J. N. (2012). A discourse analysis of parents' talk around their children's autism labels. *Disability Studies Quarterly, 32*(4), Art. 1.

Lester, J. N., & Paulus, T. M. (2012). Performative acts of autism. *Discourse & Society*, *12*(3), 259–273. doi:10.1177/0957926511433457

Lester, J. N., & Paulus, T. M. (2014). "That teacher takes everything badly": Discursively reframing non-normative behaviors in therapy sessions. *International Journal of Qualitative Studies in Education*, 27(5), 641-666.

Lonikila, M. (1995). Grounded theory as an emerging paradigm for computer-assisted qualitative data analysis. In U. Kelle (Ed.), *Computer-aided qualitative data analysis* (pp. 41–51). London: Sage.

MacMillan, K. (2005). More than just coding? Evaluating CAQDAS in a discourse analysis of news texts. *Forum Qualitative Sozial Forschung*, *6*(3), 25.

Muhr, T. (2004). User's manual for ATLAS.ti 5.0. Berlin: ATLAS.ti Scientific Software Development GmbH.

O'Reilly, M. (2004). *"Disabling essentialism" accountability in family therapy: Issues of disability, complaints and child abuse.* (Unpublished doctoral dissertation). Loughborough University.

Ochs, E. (1979). Transcription as theory. In E. Ochs, & B. Schieffelin (Eds.), *Developmental pragmatics* (pp. 43–72). New York: Academic Press.

Paulus, T. & Lester, J. (September 2013). *Using ATLAS.ti for a conversation/discourse analysis study of blogging in an educational context.* Paper presented at ATLAS.ti User Conference 2013: Fostering Dialog on Qualitative Methods. Berlin, Germany.

Paulus, T., Lester, J. N., & Dempster, P. (2014). *Digital tools for qualitative research*. London, UK: SAGE.

Paulus, T. M., Lester, J. N., & Britt, G. (2013). Constructing "false hopes and fears": A discourse analysis of introductory qualitative research texts. *Qualitative Inquiry*, *19*(9), 637–649. doi:10.1177/1077800413500929

Potter, J. (2004). Discourse analysis. In M. A. Hardy, & A. Bryman (Eds.), *Handbook of Data Analysis* (pp. 607–624). London: Sage. doi:10.4135/9781848608184.n27

Potter, J., & Hepburn, A. (2008). Discursive constructionism. In J. A. Holstein & J. F. Gubrium (Eds.), Handbook of constructionist research (pp. 275-293). New York: Guildford.

Potter, J., & Wetherell, M. (1987). *Discourse and social psychology*. London: Sage.

Rapley, T. (2007). *Doing conversation, discourse and document analysis*. London: Sage.

Sacks, H. (1984). Everyday activities as sociological phenomena. In J. M. Atkinson, & J. Heritage (Eds.), *Structures of social action: Studies in conversation analysis* (pp. 411–429). Cambridge, UK: Cambridge University Press.

Sacks, H. (1992). *Lectures on Conversation*. Oxford, UK: Blackwell.

Seale, C. (2000). Using computers to analyse qualitative data. In D. Silverman (Ed.), *Doing qualitative research: A practical handbook* (pp. 154–174). London, UK: Sage.

Taylor, S. (2001). Locating and conducting discourse analytic research. In M. Wetherell, S. Taylor, & S. J. Yates (Eds.), *Discourse as data: A guide for analysis* (pp. 5–48). London: Sage.

ten Have, P. (1991). User Routines for Computer Assisted Conversation Analysis. *The Discourse Analysis Research Group Newsletter, 7*(3), 3-9.

ten Have, P. (1998). *Doing conversation analysis: A practical guide*. London: Sage.

ten Have, P. (2007). *Doing conversation analysis: A practical guide* (2nd ed.). London: Sage.

Thomas, C. (2004). How is disability understood? An examination of sociological approaches. *Disability & Society, 19*(6), 569–583. doi:10.1080/0968759042000252506

Wood, L. A., & Kroger, R. O. (2000). *Doing discourse analysis: Methods for studying action in talk and text*. Thousand Oaks, CA: Sage.

KEY TERMS AND DEFINITIONS

ATLAS.ti: A qualitative data analysis software package designed to support the data analysis process.

Computer-Assisted Qualitative Data Analysis Software (CAQDAS): A term used to refer to software packages traditionally designed and used to support the analysis of qualitative data (e.g., ATLAS.ti, NVivo, MAXQDA, Transana, etc.).

Jeffersonian Transcript: A specialized form of a transcript, which draws upon conversation analysis and uses particular symbols to represent micro-features of talk.

Time Stamps: A feature within qualitative data analysis software packages that allows the analyst to synchronize the words and nonverbal actions within a transcript to the particular segment of the audio or video file where the words and nonverbal actions were actually voiced/shared.

Transana: A qualitative data analysis software packages designed to support the analysis of video and audio data.

Waveform: A visual representation of the sound patterns within a video or audio file.

APPENDIX

Transcription Conventions

The transcription conventions utilized were developed by Jefferson (2004) and adapted for use within the context of this research study.

↑: Upward arrows represent marked rise in pitch.

↓: Downward arrows represent a downward shift in pitch.

> <: Text encased in 'greater than' and 'less than' symbols is hearable as faster than the surrounding speech.

< >: When turned 'greater than' and 'less than' symbols encase speech, the speech is hearable as stretched or slower than the surrounding speech.

=: Equal signs at the end of a speaker's utterance and at the start of the next utterance represent the absence of a discernable gap.

Cu-: cut-off word or sound.

e̲: Underlining represents a sound or word(s) uttered with added emphasis.

° °:Text encased in degree symbols is quieter than surrounding speech, with double degree signs indicating whispered speech.

(laugh): Description of what can be observed and/or heard.

[ ]: Extended square brackets mark overlap between utterances.

(7): Numbers in parentheses indicate pauses timed to the nearest second. A period with no number following (.) indicates a pause which is hearable, yet too short to measure.

Chapter 9
Practical Wisdom of Tool and Task:
Meeting the Demands of the Method with Digital Tools in Qualitatively Driven Mixed Methods Studies

Nancy J Smith
Texas A&M University – Corpus Christi, USA

Kakali Bhattacharya
Kansas State University, USA

ABSTRACT

The purpose of this chapter is to explain the effective use of digital tools to display and analyze mixed methods data and to identify the challenges and possibilities of doing a qualitatively driven mixed methods study of technology use in education. To frame this chapter, examples from a qualitatively driven mixed methods study of doctoral students, which explored how the use of mobile technology affected engagement in the class experience, are presented. Additionally, the authors discuss the limits, implications, and possibilities of inductively driven mixed methods, while dealing with issues of academic rigor and trustworthiness using Morse and Niehaus's (2009) guidelines for mixed methods research design and the ways in which digital tools enhance rigor and trustworthiness.

INTRODUCTION

According to Morse and Niehaus (2009), "*Mixed method design is a name given to research practices that have actually been conducted for decades,*" but they are "often difficult to identify, as researchers tend to gloss over strategies that may be considered by reviewers to be incomplete" (p.10). And even though quantitatively driven mixed methods studies have gained attention over the past decade, qualitatively driven studies are less prominent and harder to accomplish "because mixing paradigms

DOI: 10.4018/978-1-4666-6493-7.ch009

means that the researcher is using contradictory assumptions and rules for inquiry" (p.9). Morse and Niehaus's (2009)

definition of mixed methods is that the study consists of a qualitative or quantitative core component and a supplementary component (which consists of qualitative or quantitative research strategies but is not a complete study in itself). The research question dictates the theoretical drive, as either inductive or deductive, so that the onus is on the researcher to be versatile and completely switch inductive and deductive positions according to the need of the study. (p.20)

Although a variety of terminology is used among mixed methods authorities (Creswell & Plano-Clark, 2007; Greene 2008; Tashakkori & Teddlie, 2010), Morse and Niehaus (2009) use the terms core component – represented by all caps QUAL or QUAN, and supplemental component – represented by lower case *qual* or *quan,* and combine them in a number of ways via a + sign (simultaneous) or an → symbol (sequential) to reflect the theoretical drive of the study. Using Morse and Niehaus's (2009) nomenclature, the data in this chapter are from a QUAL+*quan* study. The denotation indicates that the theoretical drive of the study was qualitative, the pacing of the components was simultaneous, data collection and analysis were independent, and results of the QUAL core component and *quan* supplemental component were fit together for analysis last, which is the point of interface.

With a possibility of eight different combinations of the core and supplemental components and "because mixing paradigms means that the researcher is using contradictory assumptions and rules for inquiry" (p.9), Morse and Niehaus (2009) stress that the researcher conduct an "armchair walkthrough" (p.35). This process is described as "deliberately envisioning your project and the alternative designs and all possible outcomes. It is imagining your project step by step, to foresee

problems and the advantages and disadvantages of conducting your project using all available alternatives" (p.35). They further emphasize that through doing this "you will be able to see how they will fit at the point of interface, and what your end product will look like. Now—diagram it!" (p.35). To support their readers, numerous flow charts are included in their book to illustrate mixed method design possibilities.

Because Morse and Niehaus (2009) caution that conducting and diagraming an armchair walkthrough is important to the conceptual design of the study and visualization process, using digital tools to illustrate, visualize, and diagram the process and section for the study of student use of mobile technology was a necessary and natural fit. Additionally, the use of the Technological Pedagogical and Content Knowledge Framework was an appropriate fit as a theoretical framework.

The framework of Technological Pedagogical and Content Knowledge (TPACK) "builds on Lee Shulman's construct of pedagogical content knowledge (PCK) to include technology knowledge" (Koehler & Mishra, 2009, p. 60). This framework details the complex interaction of content, pedagogy, and technology as bodies of knowledge that together produce "the types of flexible knowledge needed to successfully integrate technology use into teaching" (p. 60). Harris, Mishra, and Koehler (2009) defined the areas of content knowledge, pedagogical knowledge, and technological knowledge as:

- **Content Knowledge:** Knowledge about the subject matter that is to be learned or taught, including, for example, middle school science, high school history, undergraduate art history, or graduate-level astrophysics
- **Pedagogical Knowledge:** Deep knowledge about the processes and practices of teaching and learning, encompassing educational purposes, goals, values, strategies, and more
- **Technological Knowledge:** Always in a state of flux—more so than content and

pedagogical knowledge. This makes defining and acquiring it notoriously difficult. However, there are ways of thinking about and working with technology that can apply to all technological tools, regardless of when they emerged. (p. 397)

The knowledge components of content, pedagogy, and technology have three overlapping areas, in the TPACK framework, in addition to their conjunction. According to Harris, Mishra, and Koehler (2009) educators are each proficient in their own content areas and have knowledge

of the pedagogical practices necessary to deliver that content. However, what is not always effective is the manner in which they are able to use or integrate technology appropriately.

As illustrated in the following graphic, Figure 1, when technological, pedagogical, and content knowledge areas are effectively integrated there is not only an overlap between each area, but also a central blend of all three. For this combination to be successful, educators must have a sound foundation and understanding in all three areas. Harris, Mishra, and Koehler (2009) wrote, "TPACK emphasizes the connections among technologies,

Figure 1. TPACK Graphic - Components of the Technological Pedagogical and Content Knowledge (TPACK) Framework – Venn diagram depicts how knowledge increases based on the intersection of three areas. Reproduced by permission of the publisher, © 2012 by tpack.org

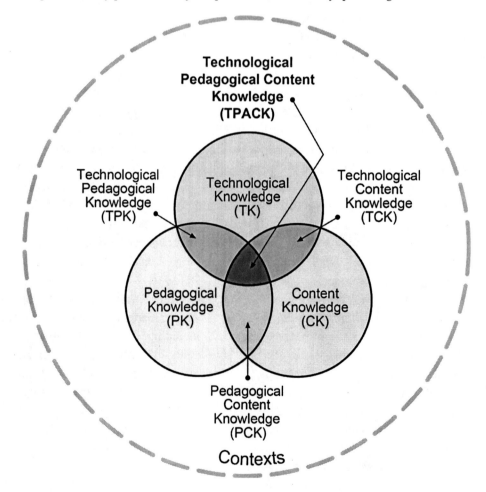

curriculum content, and specific pedagogical approaches, demonstrating how teachers' understandings of technology, pedagogy, and content can interact with one another to produce effective discipline-based teaching with educational technologies" (pp. 396-397). The overlap of the three large areas of technological knowledge, pedagogical knowledge, and content knowledge are each important to learning. However, the meat of TPACK is at the center where there is a blend of the three. Only with appropriate integration of technology can an equal and effective blend of these three areas take place.

It is important to consider the concept of technology integration in graduate level classes because adult learners encompass a wide range of age groups and many educators completed their education training before classes in technology were included in the curriculum (Croix, 2009). While many may have attended professional development in technology, these are often stand-alone classes meant to familiarize educators with specific technologies (Bracey, 2009; Gorski, 2005; Prensky, 2007). Consequently, these educators often do not "consider themselves sufficiently prepared to use technology in the classroom and often do not appreciate its value or relevance to teaching and learning" (Koehler & Mishra, 2009, p. 62). In order for teaching to change, educators need knowledge of how to use particular technologies in particular ways.

Though the TPACK framework refers to educators' use of technology in general, it was particularly useful for the integration of mobile technology, the study of which is used to illustrate examples in this chapter. Since mobile technologies are a relatively new set of tools useful to learning environments, not only do educators have a new opportunity, but also, it is even more important that digital tools be used to visualize the data collection and representation.

To frame this chapter, examples from a qualitatively driven mixed methods study of doctoral students, which explored how the use of mobile technology affected engagement in the class experience, will be presented. The chapter is grounded in insights gained from a study conducted by the two authors, includes data gained by the first author for her mixed methods doctoral dissertation (Smith, 2010). The second author of this chapter worked as a qualitative methodological guide and any use of first person in the narratives of the chapter refers to the reflections of the first author.

Through highlights of graduate student friendly softwares, the purpose of this chapter is to explain the effective use of digital tools to display and analyze mixed methods data and to identify the challenges and possibilities of doing a qualitatively driven mixed methods study of technology use in education. Additionally, the chapter includes TPACK as a framework for examining technology integration, Morse and Niehaus's (2009) guidelines for mixed methods research design, and the ways in which digital tools enhanced the study. The main body of the chapter is subdivided into two sections. The first elaborates the selection and use of tools for the QUAL component. The second subsection provides a look at the selection and use of tools for the quantitative component. Together the tools enhanced analysis, provided a clearer representation, and added deeper understanding of the combined QUAL+*quan* data at the point of interface.

BACKGROUND: ADHERING TO METHODOLOGICAL PRINCIPLES

Rapid adoption and familiarity with everyday use has become so ubiquitous that digital tools are taken for granted as a means for gathering, analyzing, and representing data in all areas of research and writing. However, these tools must allow the researcher to remain close to the data because "technology developments directly impact what we can achieve with qualitative research" (Brown, 2002, para 1), thereby affecting not only qualitative research but inductively driven mixed methods research as well. If the tool is allowed to make the decisions without question, the researcher runs the risk of not remaining close to the data in qualitative analysis and/or accepting erroneous outcomes in quantitative analysis. Brown (2002) cautions that we must pay special attention to how the researcher's choices of tools "impact upon our ontological, epistemological, and methodological standpoints" (para. 1) and how the tool may enhance rather than restrict the goals and nature of our work (para. 3). In a mixed methods research study which is QUAL+*quan*, the qualitative methodology drives the study. However, Morse and Niehaus's (2009) Principle #5 warns that the researcher must "adhere to the methodological principles of each method" (p. 25). In order to do this, the researcher must pick the right technological tool for the method, not the easiest, not the quickest, not the cheapest. If such a tool is not available, then traditional methods should trump the ubiquitous technology application we have come to expect. Practical wisdom must be employed in the choice of tool and determining its fit to the task. Practical wisdom, also known as phronesis, originated in Aristotle's *Nicomachean Ethics*. And involves a type of knowledge, which is "deliberative excellence....(and) is intimately concerned with the timely, the local, the particular, and the contingent" (Schwandt, 2007, p. 243). Therefore, practical wisdom was necessary to insure that the best tool was chosen to fit the methodological principles.

Additional challenges for mixed methods research, as pointed out by Morse and Neihaus (2009), are that the qualitative and quantitative data should never be "mixed" like a salad or a cake batter; the data must be held separate and compared. And as pointed out by Roberts and Wilson (2002), "data are fuzzy, with slippery boundaries between meanings and not ideally suited to categorization and classification using digitally based software" (p. 24). Thus, alternate forms of data visualization are necessary.

One of the greatest challenges for data representation in mixed methods research comes from what Humble (2012) describes as "intentionality." She states that researchers should take into consideration "methodology, research design, project type, and analytic approach" when choosing a software tool (p. 129). Additionally, she notes that researchers "need to be critical about how they use various software tools ... and the methodological and epistemological implications that such features have for interpretation and theorizing" (p. 122).

Since mixed methods researchers are faced with the challenges of intentionality and being able to stay close to the data, while providing trustworthiness in representing comparisons of the data, non-traditional tools should be considered. Outside of research, graphic representation tools, such as Venn diagrams, mind-maps, and digital resumes are used in classrooms and business to represent data (Hey, Tansley, & Tolle, 2009). These tools may be able to provide an additional layer of understanding and prove beneficial to a mixed methods researcher in overlaying various types of data in order to visualize and understand the meaning when comparing multiple forms of data.

A search for methods and tools for visualization of qualitative data returns results that center around computer aided data analysis tools such as NVivo and MAXQDA (Charmaz, 2009; Humble, 2012; McLellan, MacQueen, & Neidig, 2003; Richards & Morse, 2007; Roberts & Wilson, 2002;). These computer aided qualitative data analysis software (CAQDAS) tools are beneficial for storing and sorting data, and for creating codes, categories, and themes, and for their visual models of qualitative data. While CAQDAS are important tools, many of which are robust, they are often expensive. Additionally, little is found in the literature about digital tools, such as recording apps or graphics apps for collecting and representing qualitative data that may be more affordable.

Because computers are numerical machines, even less is found in the literature that elaborates their use for quantitative data representation and visualization. Studies make simple statements which name a traditional tool (e.g., SPSS was used) and move on to present the data, formatted in tables and figures. While SPSS's (Statistical Package for Social Sciences) primary output is numerical, it does have the ability to represent data in rough charts and graphs. Ultimately, both methodologies have some digital tools that support their design principles; thereby supporting the interface of a mixed method design and allowing the researcher to stay close to the data, provide trustworthiness, and adhere to the methodological principles.

In the following section, Meeting the Demands of the Method, the authors will provide examples of the use of nontraditional digital tools to collect, display, and analyze data in a mixed methods study of mobile technology use in education.

MEETING THE DEMANDS OF THE METHOD

In defining TPACK and introducing their book on the subject, Koehler and Mishra (2009) write that there is a "need for greater emphasis on the demands of subject matter" (p. 22). In other words, technology integration in science does not necessarily look the same as technology integration in art or math and we need to take this into consideration when choosing the tool or evaluating the outcome. Just as the "various affordances and constraints of technology differ by curricular subject-matter content or pedagogical approach" (Koehler & Mishra, 2009, p. 22), they also differ according to research methodology or purpose – whether data collection, analysis, or representation. Thus, the intent of this chapter is to introduce the reader to several tools for digital visualization that were chosen because of their added affordances for

each of the QUAL+*quan* parts in a mixed methods study of doctoral qualitative methods students' integration of mobile technology.

Issues, Controversies, Problems

As previously discussed, rapid adoption and familiarity with everyday use has become so ubiquitous that digital tools are taken for granted as a means for gathering, analyzing, and representing data in all areas of research and writing. However, using digital tools for data visualization presents various challenges as they must allow the researcher to enhance data representation without restricting the goals and nature of the work (Brown, 2002, para 3). Such issues are particularly important in mixed methods research as Morse and Niehaus's (2009) Principle #5 warns that the researcher must "adhere to the methodological principles of each method" (p. 25). In order to do this, the researcher must pick the right technological tool for the method, not just the easiest, the quickest, or the cheapest. If such a tool is not available, then traditional methods should trump the ubiquitous technology application we have come to expect.

The following examples use data from a study of doctoral students' use of mobile technology to illustrate the effective use of visualization for data analysis in a mixed methods study. Examples of effective use of digital tools for gathering, displaying, and analyzing mixed methods data represent data which were collected over three semesters and regarded the use of mobile technology by doctoral students who were public education professionals. Interview data were gathered via voice recording app on an iPhone and transmitted to a Wi-Fi web server then audio files were downloaded, opened in iTunes, and transcribed. Transcribed interviews were analyzed with the use of two dissimilar digital tools, the first of which was used to code and the second was used to display and outline the data for the analysis and write-up, which allowed me to use nontraditional digital tools to stay close to the data, while providing trustworthiness in representation. Quantitative data were gathered through an online survey instrument and analyzed using SPSS.

In the study used for examples this chapter, 25 doctoral students received iPod Touchs, which they were encouraged to use in their qualitative methods class, as well as their other classes and professional practice. The purpose of the study was to determine the role of using iPod Touchs on students' learning experiences, and their beliefs and attitudes towards using the iPod Touchs for coursework. Additionally, the study explored the relationship between using iPod Touchs and the students' intention to incorporate technology practices into their current and future learning and professional environments. Participants completed pre-test and post-test surveys and scales and participated in focus group and individual surveys. Adhering to Morse and Niehaus's (2009) mixed methods design, QUAL+*quan*, I collected the QUAL data separate from the *quan* and analyzed each type before analyzing the results at the QUAL+*quan* point of interface. Additionally, the substantive theoretical framework of Technological Pedagogical and Content Knowledge (TPACK) was employed to analyze both the qualitative and quantitative data. In applying TPACK as a framework to assess technology integration in pre-service teachers, researchers often use a quantitative TPACK survey. In this study, the TPACK survey was completed by doctoral students, who were in-service teachers and educational professionals, to assess their intent to integrate technology as a result of the use of mobile technology use in an educational setting. TPACK provides a graphical representation of technology integration.

As illustrated in the following sections, various digital tools were used to collect, analyze, and visualize both qualitative and quantitative data and then analyze and visualize them again at the point of interface. This process of representation gave a deeper understanding of technology, pedagogy, and content knowledge integration, as well as how those affected research skills.

Collecting Qualitative Data

Sometimes the most challenging tasks required of a researcher to carry a project to completion are finding the most effective and appropriate means of representing the findings for the reader especially ones who are not familiar with the study. Additionally, it may be challenging for the researcher who has limited technology skills and/or faculty members and graduate students who often have limited financial resources. These challenges compound the customary endeavors of gathering and analyzing data, as well as synthesizing the literature from the field, and writing up the findings. Bearing these limitations in mind, I found that the following tools effectively met the criteria of low cost, low stress, and highly appropriate for the task.

Microsoft SmartArt and Screenshot

Morse and Niehaus (2009) suggest that before a researcher attempt a mixed methods study, s/he should complete an "armchair walkthrough" (p. 79). An "armchair walkthrough" is a deliberate exercise completed by the researcher to envision the methodological fit of the components. The process examines the advantages and disadvantages in the design of the core and supplemental components and how they will interface. Diagraming the "armchair walkthrough" provided an additional layer of rigor beyond mental brainstorming or bulleted lists and assists future readers through a visual representation of the process.

To facilitate diagraming the "armchair walkthrough", Microsoft SmartArt graphics were used to visualize the process. Data from both pre-test, post-test, and qualitative interviews and focus groups were analyzed independently and then the results of the qualitative core component and quantitative supplementary component were fit together and analyzed simultaneously.

Trapezoids, created with Microsoft SmartArt, represent pacing of data collection and analysis process at *quan* (pre-test), QUAL (iPod Touch use and interviews), and *quan* (post-test). Data collection and analysis were independent. Followed by QUAL+*quan* point of interface where analysis of results of the qualitative core component and quantitative supplementary component were fit together for analysis.

Microsoft introduced SmartArt graphics in Office2007 and in spite of the fact that it can be aggravating to use and look like eye-candy, with a little help from information posts by graphic designers on the Internet and patient manipulation, it can be a useful tool to accomplish an "armchair

walkthrough." SmartArt graphics can show non-sequential information, steps in a process or timeline, a continual process, organizational components, decision trees, connections, relationships of a part to a whole, and hierarchical arrangements. Because of the variety of components available, it is useful for brainstorming and representing the direction and flow the researcher imagines the mixed methods study may take. Morse and Niehaus (2009) suggest that as part of the "armchair walkthrough" the researcher create a flowchart and conduct a self-audit because "diagramming simplifies conceptualizing your project" (p. 79). Using SmartArt tools in this study allowed the researcher to "see the project in its entirety, to discover and correct any pitfalls" (p. 80). Additionally, the SmartArt graphic acted as an introductory organizer for the reader and a reference for the researcher to aid consistency in analyzing data, writing narratives, and fitting together core and supplemental components.

Figure 2. Armchair walkthrough visualized with Microsoft SmartArt

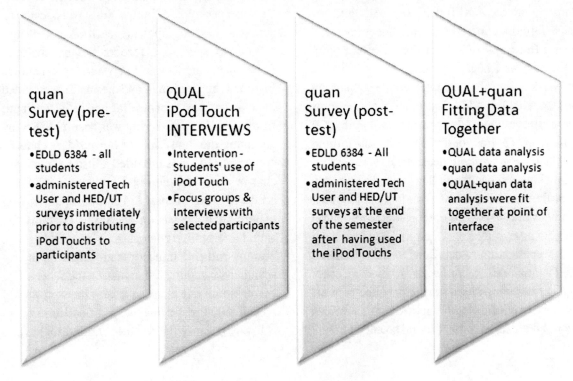

Moreover, in 2010 Microsoft quietly introduced a new twist to an old feature when it added the Screenshot tool to the Insert Ribbon. Historically, in order to capture a screenshot a series of commands such as Function+PrintScreen had to be executed, then the image had to be edited in Paint or a similar program. With the introduction of the new Screenshot variation, users are able to select Screenshot from the Insert Ribbon, and the resulting menu allows the ability to capture a screenshot of an open application or a specific area of an application window by using the screen-clipping tool. This enables the researcher to place images of any application, utility, or web browser window into their research report more easily and accurately.

HT Professional Recorder

To record interviews, I previously had used a small digital recorder and moved the mp3 files to my laptop for transcription. Because students in the introductory qualitative methods class were gathering interview data as well as becoming familiar with the iPod Touchs, one of their needs was a digital recorder. I had previously reviewed several free apps and tested them while driving in the car. As I began planning the iPod Touch study, I decided I should model mobile technology use and tried out additional voice recorder apps that were available. My criteria was (1) Free, (2) Clarity, and (3) Ease of transfer to laptop. I found that the *HT Professional Recorder* did the best job of blocking out background noise and accurately recording my voice. It was a free app and I found it relatively easy to move the recordings to my laptop with the instructions provided in the help section of the application. According to their website, *HT Professional Recorder*, is a voice recorder application, which uses speech enhancement algorithms to permit clearly captured human voices throughout a large room. I found an added bonus

when I began transcribing, the recorder allowed me to back up in 1, 5, or 10 second intervals and had variable speed playback and bookmarking capabilities. This made transcribing much easier. I modeled this recording app for students during the iPod Touch study and many used it. Recently during a class session where students who have graduated came to talk to current students, I was pleased to hear several of them suggest the *HT Professional Recorder* app as the easiest and most reliable they had found as well.

Second Life Chat Transcript

Another tool used in collecting the qualitative data for this study was *Second Life*. *Second Life* is an online virtual world, which was developed by Linden Lab in 2003. In this virtual world, users can create avatars in an infinite array of forms that are able to move among each other and interact through textual and auditory communications.

The doctoral students who participated in the study were using *Second Life* to conduct mini-ethnographies for their qualitative methods class. Because participants in this study were scattered across a wide geographical area, it was sometimes difficult to meet face to face for member checks. I found that using *Second Life* was a logical choice for scheduling meetings, and the interface provided a convenient means of meeting and gathering input from them. Data gathering was accomplished by archiving the transcripts of *Second Life* chats or conversations. This provided a history of all text chat in a conversation and transcripts could be accessed from *Second Life's* Conversation Log feature. A conversation transcript contains the actual line-by-line content of a text conversation. The log and chat transcripts are saved on the researcher's computer rather than on the *Second Life* server, so no one else can access them. It should be noted that while this means of collecting data is handy because the researcher does not have to transcribe audio tapes, as an interview tool it has its own set of characteristics and limitations that should be considered when designing the study.

Analyzing and Visualizing Qualitative Data

One of the most challenging areas for qualitative as well as mixed methods researchers is analyzing and visualizing the data as well as how to store that data once it is collected. I began by simply storing my transcribed voice recordings in Word documents, but as the transcripts began to mount up along with journal entries, diagrams, and sticky notes, I decided that I had to search for a better method. I was familiar with the conveniences of computer aided qualitative data analysis software tools, but as with the recording devices I needed one that was inexpensive and would help me clearly analyze my data, as well as store and retrieve it easily.

For the study of doctoral students' use of iPod Touch, qualitative data management involved 998

pages of both printed and digitally collected raw data. The qualitative data requiring organization and management consisted of focus group, individual, and follow-up interviews, informal observation notes, participants' *Ning* posts, researcher's journal entries and memos, and member checks, peer debriefings, and bracketing interviews. Large amounts of data, such as this study involved, require diligent organization and a reliable tool.

MAXQDA

Since the raw data included 998 pages of data, the digital copies of focus group, individual, and follow-up interview transcripts were filed in folders on the computer as well as in the computer aided qualitative data analysis software (CAQDAS) tool, MAXQDA, which acted as a database that I used to manage data. MAXQDA software allows researchers to store and organize data such as transcripts, memos, and graphics, as well as link them or add descriptive codes or comments in the margins. The software has a menu down

Figure 3. Screenshot of chat in Second Life. The chat area can be enlarged to reveal more lines.

the left side that lists all the items stored there and when an item is clicked, the complete transcript is displayed in a larger pane on the right. The transcript pane is accompanied by a margin that can be moved to the left or right side where the researcher can record notes or codes regarding selected lines of the transcript. The interface also allows the researcher to sort the results or color code for visual analysis.

My decision to use MAXQDA involved the fact that I had intentionally reviewed CAQDAS programs, looking for affordability and the ability to look at transcript codes separately so that I could adhere to the study's QUAL+*quan* methodology, which required that data be held separate until it was analyzed as a whole at the final stage. Since data were gathered from participants of three

groups over three semesters, analyzing the various sources of qualitative data separately aided trustworthiness and rigor of interpretation.

It is beyond the scope of this section to review all the different types and feature of the different CAQDAS available. Choosing an appropriate CAQDAS was primarily based on affordability and ease of use. Like MAXQDA, many CAQDAS offered a 30 day full version trial download, but in the end they were more expensive and often had to be renewed annually. Some were fairly intuitive to use, but I intentionally chose MAXQDA over other CAQDAS programs that I tested because I found it most easy to import multiple transcripts into the same project, hide codes, and navigate. I have no doubt that these others CAQDAS provide the feature I was looking for, but with time

Figure 4. Screenshot of interview transcript being coded in MAXQDA

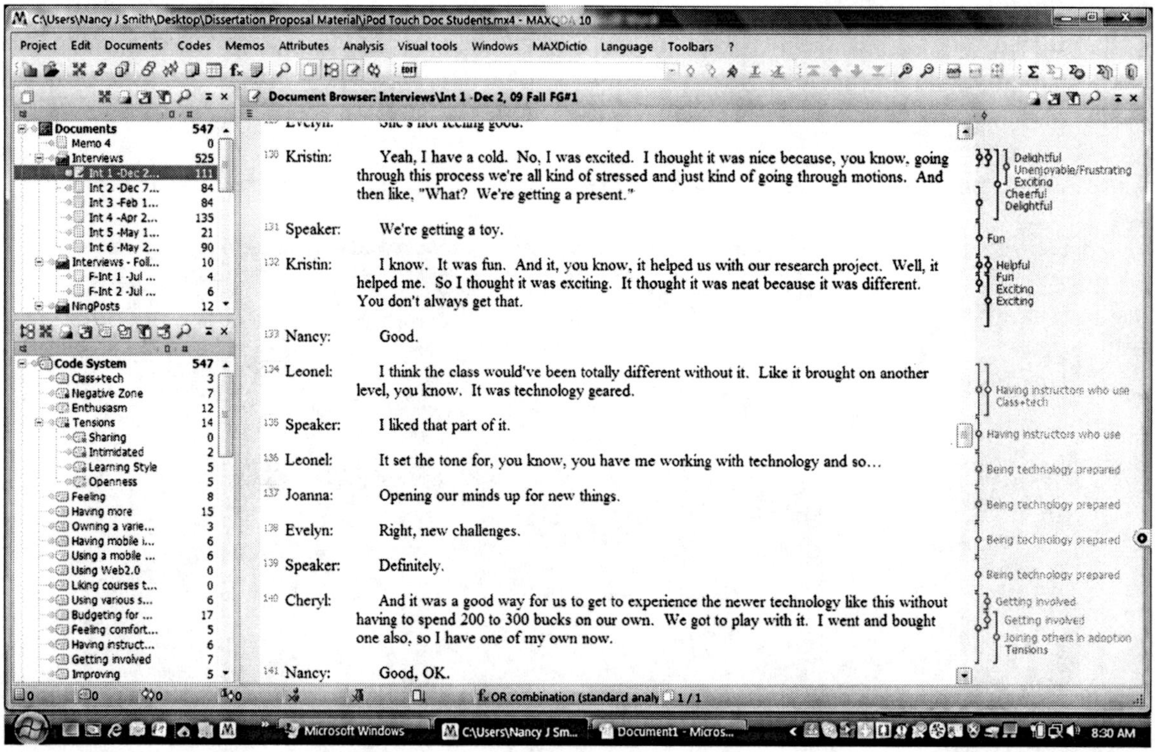

restrictions for learning the software and limited financial resources, I found that MAXQDA fit my requirements better.

Inspiration Data Visualization

Taking the lists generated from MAXQDA that contained each category and the code segments from the interviews and resorting them into groups allowed me to input this data into the software, *Inspiration,* and arrange my findings into themes. Using the *Inspiration* graphic organizer software allowed me to work back and forth between my two levels of categories from each of the data sets.

Inspiration also allowed narrative description to be tagged to each of the graphic boxes. A useful feature of *Inspiration* is its ability to convert the graphics into an outline that could be viewed or printed out in a hierarchical outline form. Looking at these resulting outlines helped form the narrative descriptions for the qualitative data analysis.

Another benefit of *Inspiration* was the ability to visualize data in multiple ways by creating new icons or simply dragging the pieces to new locations. This was significant because the process of data analysis in qualitative research is iterative. While I tried to identify a path that I employed in chunking, grouping, and theming data, the use of *Inspiration* aided the movement through each of these stages in a non-linear manner informing coding, categorizing, and theming through writing, peer debriefing, member checks, and even data collection.

Collecting Quantitative Data

The study designed to evaluate the use of iPod Touch by doctoral students in a qualitative research methods class used two instruments to gather data. The Technology User Survey was administered prior to distributing the iPod Touch to students. This survey was used to gather demographic and

Figure 5. Screenshot of Inspiration. First round of categories being created from codes.

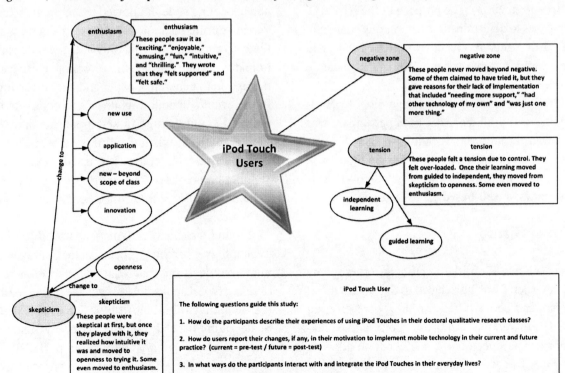

Figure 6. Final categories and themes represented with Inspiration

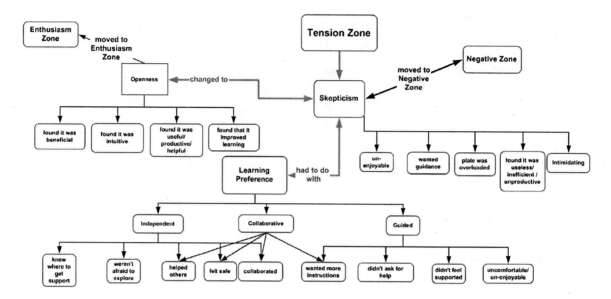

descriptive information. A pre-test and post-test survey, the Hedonic/Utilitarian Attitude Scale (HED/UT Scale), gathered information regarding the students' motivations and attitudes toward using mobile technology in class (Van der Heijden & Sørensen, 2003). The purpose of the HED/UT Scale was to determine if there was any change in the participants' motivation to use technology in their practice from the beginning of the semester to the end.

Descriptive information regarding technology use and preferences of each participant was gathered through the Technology User Survey, which was administered at the beginning of each semester. The responses were gathered via SurveyGizmo, a web-based survey site.

SurveyGizmo

SurveyGizmo allows the user to collect survey data via Internet. I was introduced to SurveyGizmo at AERA and chose it because they were offering FREE full version use to educators. The educator price has since gone to $7.99 per month with a 14 day free trial. This tool was used to gather

the demographic and descriptive data from the Technology User Survey. The survey was easily generated in the online software in one sitting. It allowed me to input several different question types and format them in a visually appropriate and appealing style. It allowed me to preview the version during the creation steps and when I was ready to publish, I was not only able to invite participants to complete an online version, I also had the option to generate a paper and pencil version in the event someone was unable to complete it online. I could then go in and input that data to merge it with the existing online data for analysis. Analysis was also convenient as SurveyGizmo supplies numerous output reports and can also be exported for use in SPSS or other data analysis softwares.

I found that SurveyGizmo was useful for the Technology User Survey because the survey had numerous questions that required multiple choice or Likert type responses. However, the scale used in the Hedonic/Utilitarian Attitude Scale (HED/UT Scale) didn't fit well with any of SurveyGizmo's formats. Consequently, data for the HED/UT Scale were collected manually via a paper based instrument that was created in Word, distributed to the participants, and manually entered into SPSS for analysis.

Analyzing and Visualizing Quantitative Data

The data were analyzed using Statistical Package for Social Sciences (SPSS) version 16.0. Descriptive statistics were used to organize the data and provide a basis for discussion. Additionally, the National Center for Educational Statistics (NCES) online chart generator was used to created graphic representations from the data to aid in visualization.

SPSS

"SPSS uses two main windows: the data editor and the viewer. The data editor has both a data view (where you input the raw scores) and a variable view (where you define variables and their properties). The viewer is a window in which any output appears, such as table, statistics and graphs" (Field, 2005, p. 61). The researcher "can code groups of people using numbers (code variables and ... rows in the data editor represent people (or cases of data) and columns represent different variables" (p. 62). The syntax window allows the researcher to enter additional codes or commands manually. SPSS also allows the researcher to open and view files.

SPSS was used to analyze the data gathered from Hedonic/Utilitarian Attitude Scale (HED/UT Scale), which was administered as a pre-test and post-test measure. To address the research question related to the quantitative supplemental component, the 17-item HED/UT Scale was administered to gain information on participants' attitudes toward the use of mobile technology in their qualitative research before and after using the iPod Touch. The scale, described in Table 1, consisted of 17 items, divided into two subscales, Hedonic and Utilitarian.

Table 1. HED/UT instrument items mapped to scales

Item Number	Item Description			Scale
1	Useless	↔	Useful	Utilitarian
2	Impractical	↔	Practical	Utilitarian
3	Unnecessary	↔	Necessary	Utilitarian
4	Unfunctional	↔	Functional	Utilitarian
5	Unhelpful	↔	Helpful	Utilitarian
6	Inefficient	↔	Efficient	Utilitarian
7	Ineffective	↔	Effective	Utilitarian
8	Harmful	↔	Beneficial	Utilitarian
9	Unproductive	↔	Productive	Utilitarian
10	Dull	↔	Exciting	Hedonic
11	Disgusting	↔	Delightful	Hedonic
12	Boring	↔	Fun	Hedonic
13	Serious	↔	Playful	Hedonic
14	Unthrilling	↔	Thrilling	Hedonic
15	Unenjoyable	↔	Enjoyable	Hedonic
16	Unamusing	↔	Amusing	Hedonic
17	Cheerless	↔	Cheerful	Hedonic

SPSS was used to conduct a series of Wilcoxon Signed Rank tests and examine practical significance of the findings by performing Z-to-r transformation (Cohen, 1988) to assess the strength of the effect size (.1 = small effect, .3 = medium effect, .5 = large effect), SPSS returned the following results (Table 2).

At the scale and subscale levels, a series of t-test for correlated samples was performed to test the difference between the pretest and post-test measures. As can be seen in Table 2, none of the differences were statistically significant. The effect sizes, as measured by Cohen's d (Cohen, 1988), ranged from .14 (small effect) to .60 (medium effect).

The lack of statistical significance in all findings could have been due to small sample size. Thus, it is important to examine the practical significance of the results carefully. This was done by using the results from SPSS and visualizing the data with the free graphing software from the National Center for Education Statistics (NCES).

Graphing: Create-a-Graph Freeware

The National Center for Education Statistics (NCES), the principle statistical agency within the U.S. Department of Education, is the primary federal government repository for collecting and analyzing data related education. This site provides

Table 2. Summary of comparison of responses to HED/UT scale pre-test and post-test items, n = 12

Item	HED/UT Pre-Test Mean[a]	HED/UT Post-Test Mean[a]	Z[b]	Asymp. Sig (2-Tailed)	Effect Size[c]
1	6.25	6.08	-0.63	0.53	0.13
2	6.08	6.08	0.00	1.00	0.00
3	5.75	5.92	0.82	0.41	0.17
4	5.83	6.33	2.12	0.03	0.43
5	6.08	6.17	0.45	0.66	0.09
6	5.75	6.00	1.34	0.18	0.27
7	6.00	6.00	0.00	1.00	0.00
8	6.42	6.17	-1.34	0.18	0.27
9	6.25	6.25	0.00	1.00	0.00
10	6.25	6.42	1.00	0.32	0.20
11	6.00	6.42	1.89	0.06	0.39
12	6.25	6.58	1.63	0.10	0.33
13	6.00	6.67	2.27	0.02	0.46
14	5.75	6.08	1.41	0.15	0.29
15	6.17	6.50	1.41	0.15	0.29
16	5.83	6.25	0.71	0.48	0.14
17	6.08	6.00	-0.58	0.56	0.12

[a]Scaling, 1 = Extremely negative, 2 = Quite negative, 3 = Slightly negative, 4 = Neutral, 5 = Slightly positive, 6 = Quite positive, 7 = Extremely positive

[b]Mean scores are reported for the ease of interpretation. Data were treated as ordinal, and Wilcoxon Signed Rank Test was used to test the differences between pre- and post measures.

[c]Effect Sizes, $r = Z / \sqrt{n}$, .1 = small effect, .3 = medium effect, .5 = large effect.

Table 3. Mean and standard deviation scores for HED/UT pre-test and post-test subscales, n = 12

Item	HED/UT Pre-Test		HED/UT Post-Test				
	Mean	SD	Mean	SD	t	p	Effect Size*
Utilitarian	6.05	.72	6.11	.99	+0.48	0.64	.14
Hedonic	6.04	.90	6.36	.60	+2.07	0.06	.60
All items	6.04	.76	6.23	.77	+1.84	0.09	.53

* Effect Sizes are computed by Cohen's *d* .2 = small effect, .5 = medium effect, .8 = large effect.

tool for data representation. In March 2013, their monthly report, *Statewide Longitudinal Data Systems (SLDS) Spotlight,* focused on data use through visualization. It stated, "Data visualizations help users focus on information that matters most, see patterns, make connections, and draw conclusions from data" ("Data Use," p.1).

Looking for patterns and trends within the quantitative data was important in this mixed methods study to explore the use of mobile technology in doctoral students because I wished to gain a deeper understanding of how participants described their use of technology over the course of semester. Data represented in a simple numeric form "may not tell a story to the untrained eye. It takes analytical skills and an understanding of the data to draw out meaningful information" ("Data Use," p.1). So that I was able to see patterns and trends in the quantitative data and subsequently compare patterns between the QUAL+*quan*, I employed NCES's visualization tools. The tool used can be found at http://nces.ed.gov/nceskids/createagraph/default.aspx.

The Create-a-Graph tool was used to visualize the responses to pre-test and post-test measures reported in Table 2, using computed the means for each participant according to each scale. Means for each participant for the hedonic scale were used to create an X coordinate and means for the utilitarian scale were used to create a Y coordinate. For example for Eduardo coordinates were pre-test (4.6, 4.5), which is indicated by a green square in that position, and post-test (5.5,

4.2), which is indicated by a purple triangle in the corresponding position. Each of these pairs were then plotted on a graph to show the change in participants attitudes toward mobile technology between pre-test and post-test use of the iPod Touch in their qualitative research methods class. Changes are shown on the graph in Figure 7.

Using the Create-a-Graph tool allowed me to visualize the data and see patterns and trends that was not only important to analysis of the quantitative data, it also allowed me to compare results of the qualitative data at the point of interface in this mixed methods study.

Solutions and Recommendations

In the previous section we provided examples of digital tools for data representation used in the study of doctoral students use of mobile technology. Because using digital tools for data visualization presents various challenges, as they must allow the researcher to enhance data representation without restricting the goals and nature of the work (Brown, 2002, para 3), such issues are particularly important in mixed methods research and must "adhere to the methodological principles of each method" (Morse & Niehaus, 2009, p. 25). In order to do this, we recommend that the researcher must spend time exploring the numerous and ever changing varieties of applications to pick the right technological tool for the method. We feel that responsible data analysis requires that we never settle for the easiest, the

Figure 7. HED/UT attitude scale score changes from pre-test to post-test

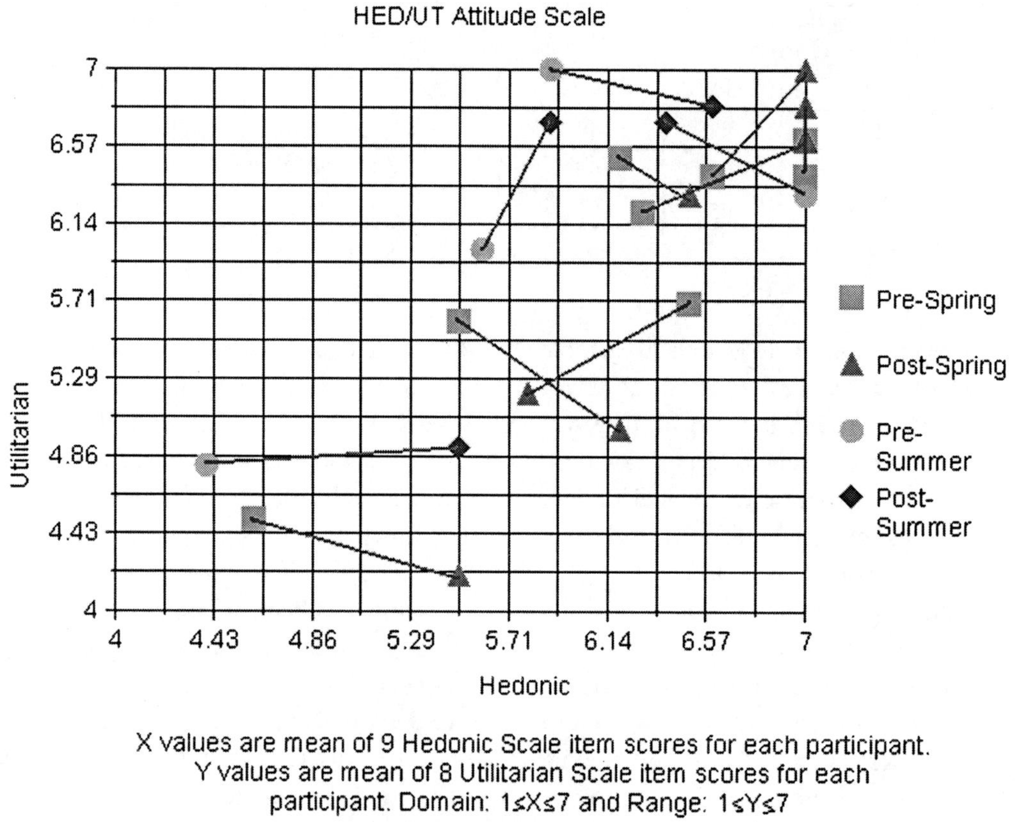

X values are mean of 9 Hedonic Scale item scores for each participant.
Y values are mean of 8 Utilitarian Scale item scores for each
participant. Domain: 1≤X≤7 and Range: 1≤Y≤7

Table 4. HED/UT values for Figure 7

Participant	Hedonic Pre-Test	Utilitarian Pre-Test	Hedonic Post-Test	Utilitarian Post-Test
Eduardo	4.6	4.5	5.5	4.2
Polly	7.0	6.4	7.0	6.8
Brianne	6.6	6.4	7.0	7.0
Herb	6.5	5.7	5.7	5.2
Priscella	5.5	5.6	6.2	5.0
Barb	6.3	6.2	7.0	6.6
Danielle	7.0	6.6	7.0	7.0
Julie	6.2	6.5	6.5	6.3
Kelsey	7.0	6.3	6.4	6.7
Stephanie	4.4	4.8	5.5	4.9
Josh	5.6	6.0	5.9	6.7
Beth	5.9	7.0	6.6	6.8

quickest, or the cheapest digital visualization too, and if a tool which accurately represents the data is not available, then traditional methods should trump the ubiquitous technology application we have come to expect. As such, the researcher must decide which tool works best for them, as well as which tool will be most easily understood by their reader or audience, while providing the most genuine representation of the QUAL+*quan* data.

FUTURE TRENDS

Future trends in data collection, analysis, and visualization in a mixed methods study of mobile technology could fill a whole chapter on their own, probably even a whole book. However, the following represent some of the possibilities highlighted recently.

A recent trend in business is the use of infographics. An infographic is a visual image such as a chart or diagram used to represent information or data that can be easily understood at a glance. Additionally, this form of representation often considered a qualitative representation of what might otherwise be quantitative data. Gerstein's (2014) site "Infographics in Educational Settings" provides numerous examples and links to other sites to create infographics for educational use.

The digital humanities is another area that is making the news. According to Parry (2014), "Computational approaches to the humanities, in existence for decades, have matured to the point where research methods once practiced by select scholars can now be taught to undergraduates in a matter of hours" (para. 3). These practices incorporate a wide range of tools for collecting, analyzing, and visualizing data.

Another future trend which requires digital technology as well as exceptional talent is conveying dissertations through comics. In other words, the comic strip repurposed as a scholarly art form. Sousanis (2014) crafts numerous pages of scholarly writing in comic strip format which reveal the evolution of this digital visualization medium. In his presentations and writing, he "looks at different forms of scholarly research, those reimagining how dissertations can be presented" and discusses the value of "talking comics and visual thinking more broadly, as a legitimate form of scholarship" (para. 2).

The Chronicle's article, "What 5 Tech Experts Expect in 2014," mentions the importance of data visualization but doesn't offer new tools. This is not bad news; in fact, it's exciting, as it leaves the playing field wide-open to researchers brave enough to repurpose favorite tools for new uses.

CONCLUSION

The preceding sections of this chapter have provided an overview of the digital tools used for visualization in a qualitatively driven mixed methods study of doctoral students' use of mobile technology. The study used Morse and Niehaus's (2009) principles of mixed methods to frame the methodology and Harris, Koehler, and Mishra's (2009) Technological Pedagogical and Content Knowledge (TPACK) framework to examine the data. TPACK is based on a quantitative profile of pre-service teachers. By applying its profile and gathering qualitative interview data, we demonstrated the ways in which a clearer picture of the participants' use of technology in general, their use of mobile technology specifically, and the perceived integration of technology in their practice both at that time and in the future was identified.

In order to illustrate the methodological and theoretical frameworks of the study, we offered examples of data and the visualization tools used. These tools were the best fit not just for the researcher, but also for alignment with the methodological principles and the tools being used. The process and application of using the chosen tools allowed meeting the challenges of a qualitatively driven mixed methods study – to stay close to the data, as well as keep the analysis of the QUAL+*quan* separate until the point of interface.

Future trends for visualization of data were also presented. We may one day see dissertations presented in infographic format or narrated through cartoons. The sure bet is that technology will continue to improve as well as frustrate writers. Time constraints, cost issues, and user friendliness will remain at the forefront of every researcher's decision making process in crafting the final product.

For the study on doctoral student use of mobile technology, using the conveniences of the chosen technology tools for data visualization made sense. The tools used varied according to whether they were used for the qualitative data analysis or representation or for the quantitative processes. Just as using a tool for science might not make sense for art, the use of a tool such as an *Inspiration* map made sense of the qualitative data and it would not have made sense for the quantitative. Likewise, a tool such as the NCES Create-a-Graph helped to visualize the shift in participants' usage seen in the quantitative data, but would have been inappropriate for representing the interview data. Using these tools for data visualization helped to adhere to the principles of the qualitative drive of the study that demanded staying close to the data, and allowed me to represent the data in a way that was more accessible for the reader, as well as helped me see how the data compared at the point of interface. In spite of the challenges of technology and the challenges of the methodology, by employing practical wisdom in their selection together these tools provided a rich array, which portrayed the consistency in fit between the qualitative and quantitative components.

REFERENCES

Bracey, G. (2009). *The Bracey report on the condition of public education*. Boulder, CO: Education and the Public Interest Center & Education Policy Research Unit.

Brown, D. (2002). Going digital and staying qualitative: Some alternative strategies for digitizing the qualitative research process. *Forum Qualitative Sozial Forschung, 3*(2), 69.

Charmaz, K. (2008). *Constructing grounded theory: A practical guide through qualitative analysis*. Thousand Oaks, CA: Sage Publications, Inc.

Cohen, J. (1988). *Statistical power analysis for the behavioral sciences*. New York: Routledge.

Creswell, J. W., & Plano Clark, V. L. (2007). *Designing and conducting mixed methods research*. Thousand Oaks, CA: Sage Publications, Inc.

Croix, W. (2007). *Adult learners and new traditions in higher education*. Retrieved from http://www.worldwidelearn.com/education-advisor/indepth/adult-learners-online.php

Data use through visualizations and narratives. (2013). *Statewide Longitudinal Data Systems Spotlight, 5*. Retrieved from http://nces.ed.gov/programs/SLDS

Field, A. (2005). *Discovering statistics using SPSS for windows: Advanced techniques for beginners* (2nd ed.). Thousand Oaks, CA: SAGE Publications, Inc.

Gerstein, J. (2014). *How to create and use infographics in educational settings*. Retrieved from http://www.scoop.it/t/infographics-in-educational-settings

Gorski, P. C. (2005). *The digital divide. In Multicultural education and the internet* (pp. 21–62). Boston: McGraw-Hill Education.

Greene, J. C. (2008). Is mixed methods social inquiry a distinctive methodology? *Journal of Mixed Methods Research*, 2(7), 17. doi:10.1177/1558689807309969

Harris, J. B., Mishra, P., & Koehler, M. (2009). Teachers' technological pedagogical content knowledge and learning activity types: Curriculum-based technology integration reframed. *Journal of Research on Technology in Education*, *41*(4), 393–416. doi:10.1080/15391523.2009.10 782536

Hey, T., Tansley, S., & Tolle, K. (2009). *The fourth paradigm: Data-intensive scientific discovery*. Redmond, WA: Microsoft.

Humble, Á. M. (2012). Qualitative data analysis software: A call for understanding, detail, intentionality, and thoughtfulness. *Journal of Family Theory & Review*, 4(2), 122–137. doi:10.1111/ j.1756-2589.2012.00125.x

Koehler, M. J., & Mishra, P. (2008). *Handbook of technological pedagogical content knowledge (TPCK) for educators*. New York: Routledge.

Koehler, M. J., & Mishra, P. (2009). What is technological pedagogical content knowledge? *Contemporary Issues in Technology & Teacher Education*, 9(1), 11.

McLellan, E., MacQueen, K. M., & Neidig, J. L. (2003). Beyond the qualitative interview: Data preparation and transcription. *Field Methods*, *15*(1), 63–84. doi:10.1177/1525822X02239573

Morse, J. M., & Niehaus, L. (2009). Mixed method design: Principles and procedures. In J. M. Morse (Ed.), Developing qualitative inquiry (Vol. 4). Walnut Creek, CA: Left Coast Press

Parry, M. (2014). How the humanities compute in the classroom. *The Chronicle of Higher Education*. Retrieved from http://chronicle.com/article/How-the-Humanities-Compute-in/143809/?cid=wc&utm_source=wc&utm_medium=en

Prensky, M. (2007). *How to teach with technology: Keeping both teachers and students comfortable in an era of exponential change*. In Emerging technologies for learning (Vol. 2, pp. 40–46). Covington, UK: Becta.

Richards, L., & Morse, J. M. (2007). *Read me first for a user's guide to qualitative methods* (2nd ed.). Thousand Oaks, CA: Sage Publications Inc.

Roberts, K. A., & Wilson, R. W. (2002). ICT and the research process: Issues around the compatibility of technology with qualitative data analysis. *Forum Qualitative Sozialforschung/Forum: Qualitative, Social Research*, 3(2), 15.

Schwandt, T. A. (2007). *The sage dictionary of qualitative inquiry* (3rd ed.). Los Angeles, CA: SAGE Publications.

Smith, N. J. (2010). *Third arm, gateway drug, or just a toy? Inductively driven mixed methods study on the use of mobile learning technologies in higher education*. (Dissertation). Texas A&M University, Corpus Christi, TX.

Sousanis, N. (2014). *Stories, MLA, & Microsoft*. Retrieved from http://www.spinweaveandcut.blogspot.com/

Tashakkori, A., & Teddlie, C. (Eds.). (2010). *Sage handbook of mixed methods in social & behavioral research*. Thousand Oaks, CA: Sage Publications Inc.

Van der Heijden, H., & Sørensen, L. S. (2003). *Measuring attitudes towards mobile information services: An empirical validation of the HED/UT scale.* Paper presented at the European Conference on Information Systems (ECIS). Naples, Italy.

What 5 tech experts expect in 2014. (2014). *The Chronicle of Higher Education.* Retrieved from http://chronicle.com/article/What-5-Tech-Experts-Expect-in/143829/?cid=wc&utm_source=wc&utm_medium=en

KEY TERMS AND DEFINITIONS

Content Knowledge: One of the three areas of the TPACK framework, which is the knowledge about the subject matter that is to be learned or taught (Harris, Mishra, & Koehler, 2009).

Digital Tools: Software applications which when chosen wisely and applied well can more effectively aid data gathering, illustration, visualization, analysis, and diagraming of processes in research.

Mixed Methods: A study consisting of a qualitative or quantitative core component plus a qualitative or quantitative supplementary component, which come together at the point of interface. It is important that both components adhere to the methodology of its own method (Morse & Niehaus, 2009).

Mobile Technology: A relatively new set of tools useful to learning environments which include smartphones, iPod Touchs, and iPads.

Pedagogical Knowledge: One of the three areas of the TPACK framework described as deep knowledge about the processes and practices of teaching and learning, encompassing educational purposes, goals, values, strategies, and more (Harris, Mishra, & Koehler, 2009).

Practical Wisdom: Also known as phronesis, originated in Aristotle's *Nicomachean Ethics.* And involves a type of knowledge, which is "deliberative excellence....(and) is intimately concerned with the timely, the local, the particular, and the contingent" (Schwandt, 2007, p. 243).

Technological Knowledge: One of the three areas of TPACK, which involves ways of thinking about and working with technology that can apply to all technological tools, regardless of when they emerged (Harris, Mishra, & Koehler, 2009).

TPACK: A framework which details the complex interaction of content, pedagogy, and technology as bodies of knowledge that together produce "the types of flexible knowledge needed to successfully integrate technology use into teaching" (Harris, Mishra, & Koehler, 2009, p. 60).

Chapter 10
Software–Assisted Transcribing for Qualitative Interviews:
Practical Guidelines

Taghreed Justinia
King Saud bin Abdulaziz University for Health Sciences, Saudi Arabia & Swansea University, UK

ABSTRACT

This chapter introduces a guide to transcribing qualitative research interviews assisted by digital transcription software. It also provides practical advice on transcribing methods, conventions, and options. It is useful in its exploration of the challenges involved with transcribing, while it offers detailed solutions and advice for the novice researcher. The chapter also addresses key concerns, like the time it takes to transcribe, transcription tools, and digital versus analogue recordings. As a method chapter based on experiences from a case, it takes on a practical approach by demonstrating the benefits of data analysis software packages with examples and screenshots on how to specifically use the software package Express Scribe. The pros and cons of using a transcriptionist are also discussed. A real transcript is presented in the chapter, and the steps involved with developing and formatting it are offered in detail. The guidelines suggested in this chapter are concentrated on the pragmatic hands-on experience of a researcher with examples from a real life large-scale qualitative study based on in-depth interviews. The significance of transcribing within the analytical process and the methodological insights of using Express Scribe eventually emerge as a developing concept from this work.

THE SIGNIFICANCE OF TRANSCRIBING

The use of audio recordings in interview studies is a popular practice that usually leads to formulating a transcript (Bowling, 2009). It is the second stage that follows the data collection (Sarangi, 2010). Transcribing the recording is therefore a significant step in qualitative research analysis, and without a transcript it would be difficult to manage the data. However, once the data collection is complete and all interviews are recorded, novice researchers might find themselves perplexed. They arrive at a stage where they have to transcribe hours and hours of recordings, usually without clear guides on how to get started. As

DOI: 10.4018/978-1-4666-6493-7.ch010

DiCicco-Bloom and Crabtree (2006) explain, "Transcribing tape-recorded interviews into text is a process that remains relatively unexplored" (318). Additionally, some of these recordings might be inaudible, or have other problems that would make them difficult to transcribe, like poor sentence structure (DiCicco-Bloom & Crabtree, 2006), weak semantics or repeated interruptions. Having experienced these concerns first hand, I have a deep sympathy for researchers at this phase of the research process. Most of the literature on the practicalities of transcribing concentrates on transcribing for discourse and conversation analysis (Ruch et al., 2007; Sarangi, 2010). These works mostly focus on language or conversation, while generally sharing a single set of detailed conventions for transcribing (Parry, 2010). The type of detailed transcription described in these studies is intimidating for someone new to research. They demonstrate techniques for phonetic verbatim transcription to methodically capture every nuance and utter. I felt undue pressure to produce similar transcripts. I then turned my focus towards examples of interview transcripts, and sought guidance on various options and approaches from similar studies and simpler guidelines (Bailey, 2008; Bird, 2005; Lapadat & Lindsay, 1999; Silverman, 2001, 2005, 2006; Tilley, 2003; Webb, 1999). I then realized that I did not need to conform to the particulars of discourse analysis techniques, allowing me to focus on how and what to transcribe. This chapter aims to provide some guidance in this area from the perspective of a qualitative researcher with hands on experience.

TRANSCRIBING QUALITATIVE INTERVIEWS

What to Transcribe

When transcribing most qualitative research interviews, it is not always be necessary to capture every utterance, pause and enunciation with the level of detail specifically required for conversation analysis research. Still, it might be useful to look at these standards as a 'rough' guide, and to apply your own techniques as needed. Decide how much detail is actually needed for the purpose of your study. Parry (2010) explains that there are different ways of structuring transcripts to meet the needs of a particular investigation. Therefore, you should not worry about having to conform to specific conventions so long as you are consistent. The resulting transcript should also be legible and formatted for analysis. As a qualitative researcher you are an interpreter and the research instrument in your study (Miles, Huberman, & Saldaña, 2014; Silverman, 2005, 2006), so your involved decisions are part of the process. It is not always necessary to record every hand gesture or vocalization, but you may feel the need to note an overly animated action. For example, you can emphasize laughter, chuckles, sighs, raised voices as well as outwardly non-verbal occurrences like hand gestures, nodding, fidgeting or other exaggerated movements. You should also think about how you want to deal with interruptions, pauses, stutters, overlapping speech, silence, muffled phrases, 'ums' and recording problems. The resulting type of transcript will also rely on decisions made during the interview. If these are not made early on, it might be too late to get the required results after the fact. Those decisions are left to the researcher depending on what type of study they are conducting and what the resulting transcript should include. As Miles and Huberman (1994) explain, "the transcription of tapes can be done in many ways that will produce rather different texts" (p. 9).

There are no concrete rules on exactly what to transcribe. Sarangi (2010) explains that "transcription has to be fit for purpose rather than just an application of a standard set of conventions" (p. 400). For example, in most ethnographic studies recording may not even be an option and researchers fully rely on field notes. Some might question the need to record the interview, or transcribe it at all. It is possible and acceptable to only take active notes during the actual interview for key points, or to revisit the recording and only make notes of important bits and transcribe selectively. That is an approach that could be taken, but it is subjective and would make it difficult to perform some types of content analysis. It would also be difficult to validate the data without a transcript to reflect the encounter. In most literature on qualitative methodology, it is considered good practice to record and transcribe interviews if possible (Bird, 2005; Justinia, 2009, 2014; May, 1998; Silverman, 2001). Having a tactile transcript in hand allows others to independently assess analytic claims by referring to excerpts from the transcript data themselves (Bryman & Hardy, 2004). Recording and transcribing would also allow the researcher to focus on the interview process and not get distracted with note taking during the interview. Ultimately, the aims of the study should inform these decisions. Conducting a pilot interview and then transcribing it could provide valuable insight that would help in making these critical decisions before actual data collection begins.

Transcribing as a Clerical Task

Some regard transcribing as "largely a clerical task that can be carried out by someone who is not a researcher" (Newell & Burnard, 2006, p. 98), while others feel they need to delegate this task because of the amount of time that needs to be committed to transcribing. If and when the task is delegated to someone else, it is recommended that the researcher treat those transcripts as rough drafts that need to be re-transcribed. Bryman and Hardy (2004) agree that transcribing large datasets is time consuming, but also explain that "so many researchers follow a two-step process in which assistants make initial 'rough' transcripts of a data corpus, which the researcher then refines in whole or in part" (p. 593).

Conversely, delegating does not always makes things easier. You must be very selective in who is entrusted with the sensitive data. Delegating

might not save much time depending on the level of accuracy achieved and how much needs to be revised by the researcher. There is also the added cost of using professional transcriptionists, on top of other issues like quality, style, and consistency. You would also need to take into account all ethical considerations of using a transcription service. Miles et al. (2014) emphasize the importance of honesty and trust with interviewees, stressing the need to consider the privacy, confidentiality and anonymity of research participants. Given that information confidentiality is a critical piece of human subjects' research; if you are seeking ethical approval for your study or going through an Institutional Review Board (IRB), you would need to verify their policies on using an external transcriptionist service, and then justify how this would be addressed within your study. This should also be disclosed to the participants who were promised confidentially. Further to that, the transcriptionist service would most likely need to sign a confidentiality agreement.

Transcribing as an Analytical Process

Transcribing is widely accepted as a key part of qualitative analysis (Bailey, 2008; Bird, 2005; Bryman & Hardy, 2004; Justinia, 2009, 2014; Tilley, 2003), where a lot of meaning and insights about the data emerge. Missing the chance to become fully engrossed with the data through this process would be a lost opportunity. When transcribing, the interview is relived many times. Not only is it an opportunity for immersion, but it is also a process where many important decisions are made. What conventions to use, what level of details is needed, what could be excluded, how to deal with an interruption, how to note non-verbal communication are best decided by someone who was there and knows the significance of omitting any of the parts. Entrusting the transcribing task with someone who cannot make the right decisions might compromise the integrity of the transcript, and any results thereafter. Therefore, deep perception is achieved during transcribing, and delegating this task might potentially lead to missing significant moments of clarity. Bryman & Hardy (2004) advise researchers to "do at least some of the transcription themselves". They explain that "often some of the most revealing analytical insights come during transcription as a consequence of the profound engagement with the material needed to produce a good transcript" (p. 615).

Similarly, transcribing is a process that could only truly be understood by someone who has experienced it first hand, and is a valuable opportunity for the researcher to become immersed in the data. Bryman & Hardy (2004) maintain that, "the transcription process itself is part of the analytical process. For this reason, it is generally recommended that researchers do at least some of their own transcribing rather than delegating the entire task to research assistants" (p. 593).

The Time It Takes to Transcribe

It is also safe to say that the amount of time required to transcribe an interview is always underestimated and never anticipated. The time required to analyse qualitative data can be roughly two to five times as long as the time required to originally collect the data (Miles et al., 2014). Many factors have a direct impact on the time it takes to transcribe a recording, like personal typing ability, transcribing tools used, recording quality, and participants' speech patterns. On average each hour of recording could take six to twelve hours to transcribe (Sarangi, 2010); and that is under normal circumstances with good quality recordings. Unclear or poor recordings could even quadruple the time needed to transcribe (Bryman & Hardy, 2004), while some recordings could take up 20 hours of transcription time (Bryman, 2004). Novice researchers regularly underestimate this

phase of their research projects and end up behind schedule, frustrated and at times sacrificing the quality of their work.

The Experience of Transcribing for the Inexperienced

For reference, a full interview transcript is appended at the end of this chapter (EA 12-12-06). This is a real transcript that was analyzed as part of a large-scale qualitative study titled: Implementing Large-scale Healthcare Implementation Systems: The Technological, Managerial and Behavioural Issues (Justinia, 2009, 2014). The recording for the interview in this sample transcript was 39 minutes long. A few of those minutes were introductions, and there were some interruptions. To record, I used a compact digital recorder with an attachable clip microphone that could be easily fixed to the participants' lapel. The recorder also has another built in microphone. This allowed me to place the recorder itself closer to me so that its built in microphone could pick up my voice (my questions also needed to be transcribed). Having the recorder at close proximity also allowed me to keep an eye on it and to make sure that the red recording light was always on (indicating that it was steadily recording, the battery was working and all was well). The participant in this interview was a non-native English speaker, but her spoken English was quite good. She spoke in clear sentences with proper grammar, and had a steady rhythm (if that makes sense). Dealing with improper grammar and run-on sentences makes it more difficult to transcribe, forcing transcribers to make judgment calls, since the insertion of a period or a comma can drastically alter the meaning of an entire sentence (DiCicco-Bloom & Crabtree, 2006).

For this particular interview, the recording quality was also good as there was no outside noise, static, microphone problems or overlapping speech. This was overall one of the better interviews. Just to show the amount of time it takes to transcribe, I dedicated a full four days to work on this transcript until it was fully transcribed. Transcribing is a very tasking job, and the labor intensive work cannot be calculated like the normal working hours of an office job. For example, you can sit in your office working an eight-hour shift and be productive, but it is impossible to get in eight hours straight of transcribing in a nine-to-five shift. When transcribing you would need frequent breaks and will usually only maintain focus for thirty minutes at a time. At the end of the thirty minutes of sheer focus and constant playback, do not be surprised that you have only transcribed 5-6 minutes of recording; and that is when you are working with a good quality recording. With problematic recordings it could take a lot longer. Seeing that I could not spend every waking hour of the day transcribing, I could personally only turn out a maximum of three hours of total transcribing time per day; usually spread out over eight hours to include breaks. I cannot stress enough how exhausting it is to keep pausing, rewinding, slowing down and typing increments of seconds in constant loops. It is not something that a non-professional finds easy to do.

From personal experience, it took me just over twelve weeks to transcribe thirty six in-depth interviews with around forty five hours of total recording time for the research project in reference. I am considered a fast typist, but the issue is not really typing speed. It has more to do with focus, listening and trying to translate what was said into a coherent transcript that reflects a conversation. Good planning and allowing enough time for transcribing is fundamental and necessary for a successful outcome.

Analogue vs. Digital Recordings

According to Bowling (2009), it is common for researchers conducting in-depth interviews to record them and later transcribe and code the content, explaining that this would allow the researcher to extract extra narratives with rich qualitative insights. Nevertheless, is it better to use analogue tapes or digital recordings to record the interviews? Analogue tapes provide better sound quality and reduced background noise. They are captured on physical tangible media that can be stored away for safekeeping. However, tapes deteriorate over time and cannot be directly transferred (in their analogue format) to a computer. Making copies comes with an added cost and is not as easy as making digital copies. Digital media on the other hand can be easily and quickly reproduced, but then again they can just as easily be deleted or corrupted. With either media, it is always recommended after each interview to immediately check the recording, back it up, make extra copies and store the master copy (and never touch it again). Always work from your copies and not the master copy.

Silverman (2006) stresses the importance of the interview recordings and transcripts explaining that the fundamental aspects of reliability in qualitative research involve selection of what is recorded, the technical quality of recordings and the adequacy of transcripts. Most experienced researchers listen to the audiotape while reading the transcriptions to ensure accuracy during interpretation (Bowling, 2009). However, once an interview is conducted, it is difficult to repeat it, so always check the venue beforehand (if possible) and think about where you want to place the recorder and microphones. You usually only have once chance to record the interview, so keep extra batteries/tapes, and if possible bring an extra recorder. Miles et al. (2014) explain that "the strength of qualitative data rest centrally on the competence with which their analysis is carried out" (p. 12), therefore no expense should be spared in ensuring that all phases of analysis; including transcribing, are done with rigor and care.

Tools to Facilitate Transcribing

There are many devices available to assist in the transcribing process, but it is up to the researcher to decide which ones to use. Getting familiar with these and understanding their functions and limitations helps in deciding. If available, it would be useful to test them. These devices might include an analogue tape recorder, digital recorder, computer, microphone, headset, Dictaphone/transcribing machine, foot pedal and digital transcription software.

Audio transcribing machines are bulky cumbersome devices that play analogue audiotapes aided by a foot pedal to start, stop/pause, and rewind the tape; freeing up the hands for typing. Many find these comfortable, but they do not allow one the mobility that could be achieved by using digital recordings and transcribing using computer software. After researching many products and devices (both analogue and digital), I finally came across 'Express Scribe Transcription Playback Software' by NHC; which is a digital transcription audio player software that is extremely useful for qualitative interview transcription (NCH Software, 2014).

HOW TO TRANSCRIBE

Trial and Error with Transcribing

Before I started to transcribe, I wanted to see what it was all about. I got permission to visit the transcriptionists at a Medical Records Department in a hospital. I had the chance to look at various transcribing machines, foot pedals, microphones, and headphones. The workers there were happy to demonstrate their online dictation system and shared some advice on transcribing. They were professionals but they transcribe for a completely different purpose. I left feeling overwhelmed and even more anxious about transcribing.

I then decided to try my hands at voice recognition software and looked at IBM's ViaVoice (later taken over by Nuance), Nuance's Dragon Dictate and even Microsoft's Speech that is built into Word. None of them were very successful for transcribing interviews by a host of different participants, because it was not possible to utilize the software's intelligent 'training' features; whereby with more use the speech recognition engine becomes more accurate. With so many respondents from various nationalities and with different dialects, I found little success with speech/voice recognition tools.

My options were narrowing but I did not want to use a 'clunky' transcribing machine, so I finally turned to Express Scribe Transcription Software by NCH Software (NCH Software, 2014). According to their website, Express Scribe is professional audio player software designed to assist the transcription of audio recordings. Express Scribe can be downloaded and installed within minutes directly from www.nch.com.au/scribe; where full details about the product features are available. It is easy to setup, is user-friendly and does not require any training. It took a lot of trial and error with different software products, but when I finally tested Express Scribe it sufficed as the best-fit technology for what I needed as a qualitative researcher. One of the best features of Express Scribe is that a working version with the essential features can be downloaded free of charge and is available for PC (Windows) or Mac. A paid version is also available and a comparison table with features of both is outlined on their website (NCH Software, 2014). I have only worked with the free version and all comments, examples and illustrations presented in this chapter are based on the free version.

Express Scribe is particularly useful for those who switch between devices with different operating systems. For instance, if you own a MacBook Air for personal use, but have a Windows PC at work, you can still upload and transcribe your recordings on either device and have the freedom to switch between them and continue your work seamlessly. Express Scribe also supports the use of a USB foot pedal and standard digital audio (MP3, WAV, WMA, AIFF, MP2, VOX) and video (AVI, MOV, WMV) file formats. It can also be used with analog or digital portable voice recorders to load recordings directly. If you do not already have a digital recorder, you can turn your iPhone or Android device into a voice recorder by downloading 'Pocket Dictate Mobile Dictation Recorder' also from NHC Software from the same website. It allows you to dictate and send recordings directly from your Android or iPhone by email (NCH Software, 2014).

Steps to Transcribing Using Express Scribe

1. Download Express Scribe from www.nch. com.au/scribe free of charge and install it on your computer.

2. Make a master copy of your recordings and store them in a safe location. You should not work from your master copy.

3. Download and save a copy of your recording onto your computer. Make sure the file format of the recording is one of the formats supported by Express Scribe (most standard formats are supported).

4. If you are using 'Pocket Dictate Mobile Dictation Recorder' then email the recordings to yourself and save them on your computer.

5. Open Express Scribe and choose 'File' then choose 'Load Dictation Files' (see Figure 1).

6. Go to the folder on your computer where you stored your recording and select it to upload it into Express Scribe (see Figure 2).

7. You will get a message from Express Scribe to notify you that you have a new dictation (see Figure 3).

Figure 1. Load dictation file

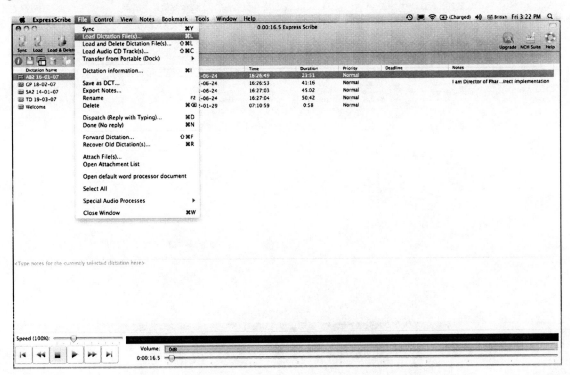

Figure 2. Upload recording

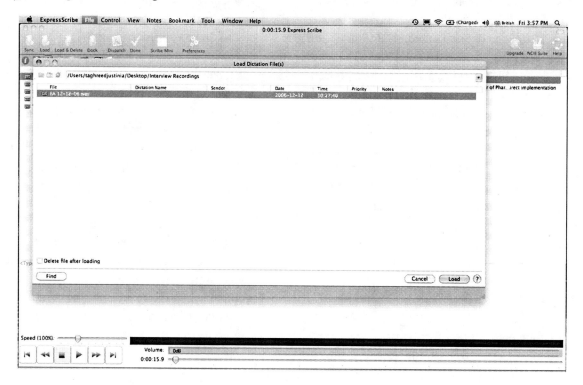

Figure 3. Message new dictation

8. You are now ready to start transcribing. If you have a foot pedal you can connect it and use it. If you do not want to use a foot pedal, you can use the default 'Hot Keys' that will make selected keyboard keys function as start, stop, rewind and fast forward buttons (including others). To view the 'Hot-Keys' go to 'Preferences' then select the tab 'Hot-Keys'. You can use the default ones, change them or add new ones (see Figure 4).

9. It is best to use headphones while listening to the recordings to minimize external noise. You can also adjust the speed of the recording at any moment and for any segment by adjusting the 'Speed' slider or changing the speed settings by selecting 'Preferences' then 'Playback' (see Figure 5).

10. You can now start writing your initial notes. Select the recording you uploaded from

within Express Scribe and it will become highlighted in purple. A section will appear with the note <type notes for the currently selected dictation here>. Click the 'Play' button. Once the recording starts playing, you can begin typing your initial notes about your recording directly in the window provided (see Figure 6).

11. You can enter a timestamp to reflect the exact segment of recording that corresponds to the text you typed. Select 'Notes' then 'Insert' and click 'Time'. The timestamp will appear where the curser is placed (see Figure 7). You can later export and save these notes as text files. This is useful for filing purposes or for initial coding, but to write the actual transcript it is better to use a Word document.

Figure 4. Hot-keys

Figure 5. Playback speed

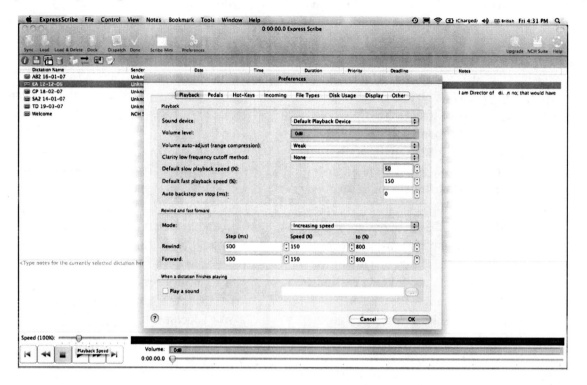

Figure 6. Type notes

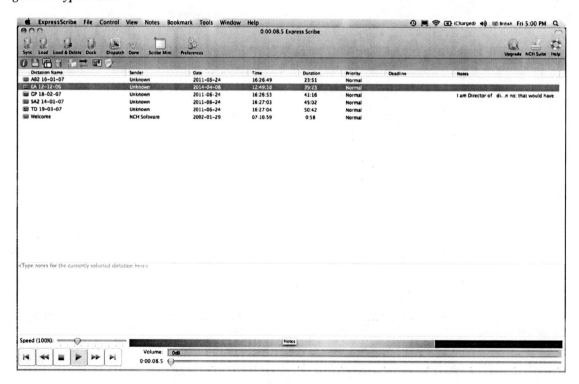

Figure 7. Insert timestamp

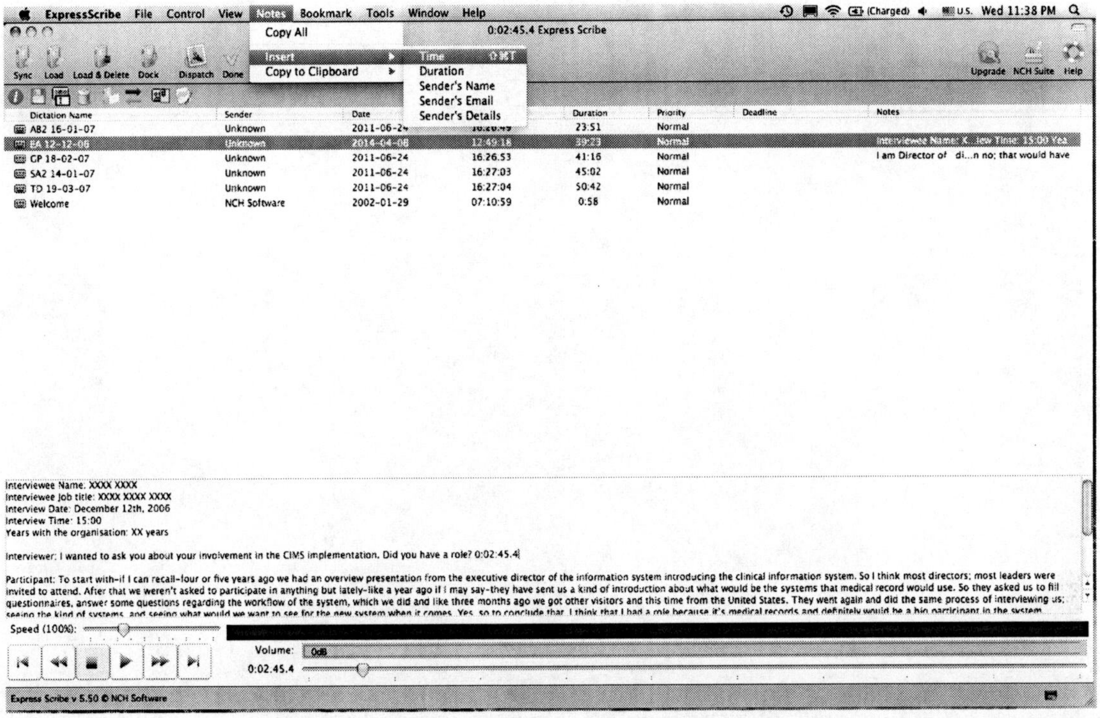

12. Go to Microsoft Word and open a new Word Document. Name it with the same name as your recording and leave it open. Make sure Express Scribe is open and press the Scribe Mini button. The Express Scribe Mini toolbox will be visible and active while you use word (see Figure 8).

The Interview Transcript

There is no precise guideline and the format of the transcript ultimately depends on personal preference. You only have to devise a format then be consistent in using it for all interviews in the same project. It is good practice to have some kind of identifier for each transcript by using a code or by devising a standard naming convention. Double spacing is recommended, but not always used (to minimize paper). Again, that comes down to personal preference. I would also recommend using

a spiral binder to bind each transcript instead of stapling them. It makes it easier to work with the transcript and to flip between pages, and minimizes the risk of a staple coming loose. If there are a lot of interviews the pages will add up, and being organized will eventually save a lot of time. Many analysts like to use 'memoing' or writing reflective notes somewhere on the transcript during initial analysis (Miles et al., 2014), so formatting the transcripts with wide margins is useful. Once your computer is ready as a transcribing machine, you can write and format your transcript.

Steps in Formatting an Interview Transcript

1. It is easier to transcribe freely first, and then format the transcript afterwards.
2. Start by writing identifying information on the transcript. If you already entered this

Figure 8. Scribe mini

information in the Express Scribe window, then copy it onto the transcript (see Figure 9). This information will be very useful later on for reference, especially when you have a large number of interviews to transcribe.

3. Start playing the recording by clicking the 'Play' button on Express Scribe Mini or use the 'Hot-Keys' and begin transcribing. You can pause, rewind and slow down the recording as needed by using the 'Hot-Keys'. You have effectively transformed your computer into a professional transcribing machine. Leave a blank line between the Interviewer and Participant dialogue. When you finish you will have what looks like a transcript, although still unformatted (see Figure 10).

4. Insert Identifiers for the Interviewer and Interviewee dialogue to differentiate between their text, like Interviewer, Question, P1, Respondent …etc (see Figure 11).

5. Wide margins are useful for taking notes and for 'memoing'. Select the 'Layout' tab in Word, and then choose 'Margins'. Set the left hand margin to 5cm and the right margin to 4 cm to allow enough space during analysis (see Figure 12).

6. Line by line numbering for the text is useful to later identify segments of text during analysis. Select the 'Layout' tab in Word, and then choose 'Line Numbers'. Tick 'Continuous'. If you want to exclude certain lines from numbering then highlight that text and tick 'Supress for Current Section' (see Figure 13).

7. Add page numbers. The transcript is now formatted and can be used for analysis. You can search for themes, highlight text, refer to specific line numbers during analysis, write notes on either margin and begin coding (see Figure 14).

Figure 9. Transcript identifying information

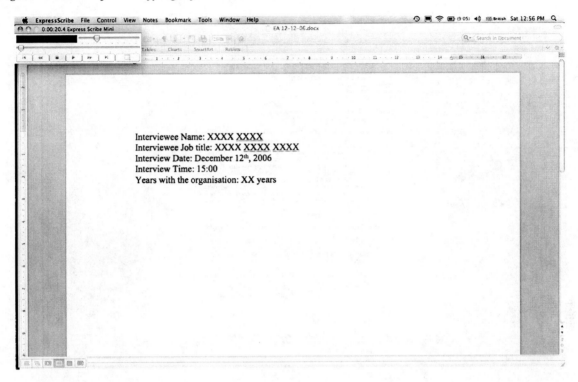

Figure 10. Unformatted transcript

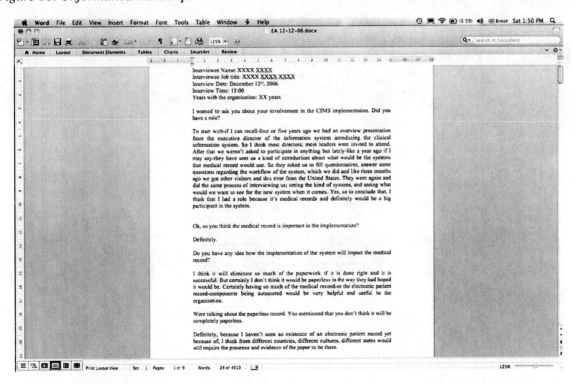

Figure 11.Interviewer and participant identifiers

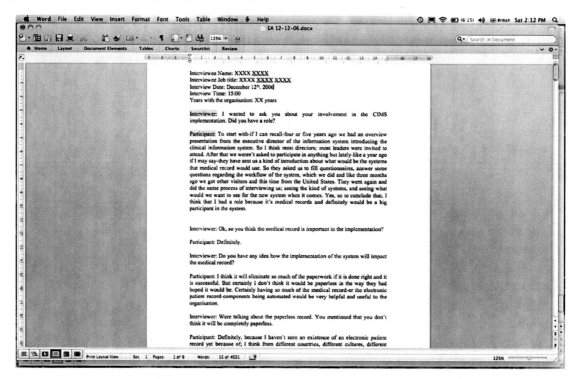

Figure 12. Wide margins

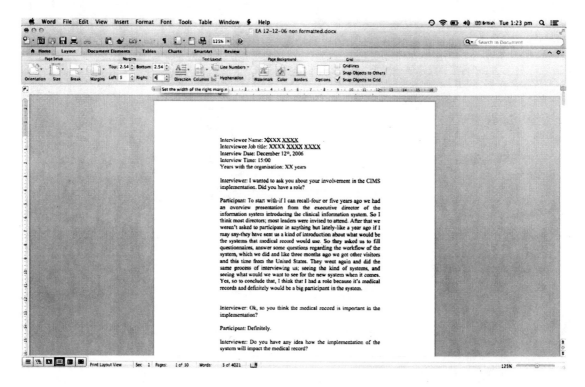

Figure 13. Line numbers

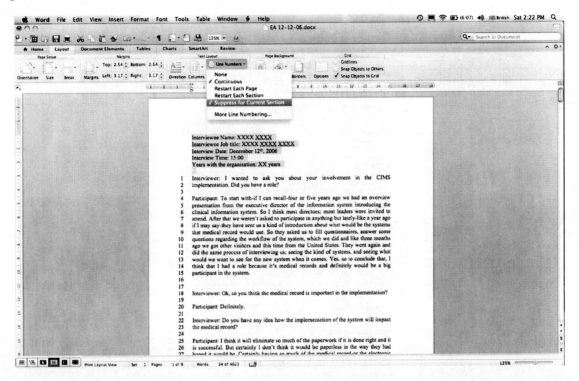

Methodological Underpinnings: ixNotes for Validity

"Transcribing tape-recorded interviews into text is a process that remains relatively unexplored" (DiCicco-Bloom & Crabtree, 2006, p. 318).

When the author engages in transcribing with Express Scribe firsthand, it allows a unique opportunity to begin analysis before transcribing begins. By using Express Scribe specifically, the researcher has the opportunity to freely listen to the recording before transcribing it word-for-word, and can then engage in making initial notes (we can call them ixNotes) directly into Express Scribe. These first instinct reactions could be saved in Express Scribe where each set of notes is directly linked to the audio recording. If enough of these notes are taken with enough thought and in an organized manner, they can create a foundation for themes or codes without having to transcribe the entire interview verbatim. This set of ixNotes

that are based on first impressions or initial instincts could be later used as a point of reference to compare against the themes/codes that emerge or are produced after methodically analyzing the transcript. If done with enough attention, these ixNotes could even be used to triangulate the findings. It would be interesting for a researcher to be able to compare between the ixNotes and the findings that are based on typed transcripts. This would also offer an opportunity to validate the research findings by comparing ixNotes with the findings of an independent analyst of the typed transcripts. The independent analyst's findings might not corroborate with the findings of the researcher (for the typed transcript), but there might appear some commonality with the ixNotes that could be grounds for validating an otherwise dismissible argument. This approach is current and original to this book, so it has not been widely used as a qualitative validity method.

Figure 14. Formatted transcript with notes

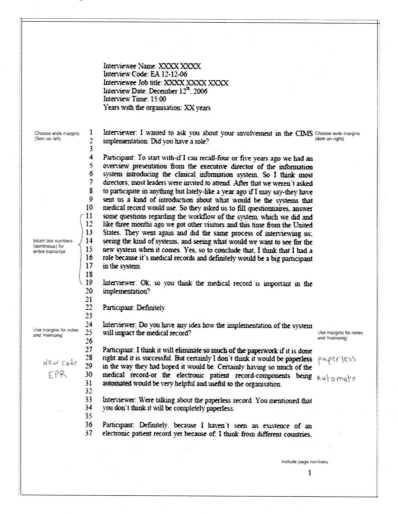

THE FUTURE: VOICE/SPEECH RECOGNITION SOFTWARE

The Future of transcribing lies in speech recognition and electronic dictation tools. Some examples of voice/speech recognition software are Nuance Dragon Naturally Speaking, and Microsoft Speech that comes bundled with Microsoft Word. Express Scribe works with Dragon Naturally Speaking to automatically convert speech to text, so that is one step in the right future direction of transcribing technology, but the technology is still developing. While it would be great to avoid the time-intensive task of transcribing interviews altogether, the technology behind voice recognition software has not yet evolved enough. These engines are best used as dictation tools rather than for transcribing pre-recorded encounters, interviews and meetings and they work better in real time. There are still too many limitations that are hindering the full replacement of transcribing with speech recognition. For example, speech recognition software has to be trained for each speaker's voice, and each speaker must speak slowly and clearly to avoid mistakes. It is best to speak into a microphone linked directly to a computer, but that is difficult in an interview situation. Moreover, since there is still no speech recognition software with 100% accuracy, one would still have to go over each transcript to make corrections. That means simultaneously listening to each recording while reading the transcript and having to pause, playback and fast forward the recording with a transcribing machine or transcription software.

Although speech recognition and dictation have achieved good levels of success, the technology is not yet at a level to fully support transcribing qualitative research interviews to a high degree of accuracy. There is still a large opportunity for growth in this area. Future research into the use of voice recognition tools specifically for qualitative data transcription is highly recommended. Research is also needed to develop the technology to automatically incorporate voice recognition software into the actual interviews.

CONCLUSION

This chapter provides a glimpse into the world of transcribing, while offering practical tools and advice along the way. Transcribing is a process dreaded by most researchers. It falls between the data collection and data analysis phases and has been the cause of frustration and unanticipated delays for many researchers. Careful time planning coupled with an understanding of the significance of this process in analysis and its impact on the reliability of the research project only makes it more tasking. However, by using the right technology, the process of transcribing can be considerably simplified. Express Scribe is a professional audio player software for PC or Mac designed to assist in the transcription of audio or video recordings. Having the option of adding a plug and play foot pedal, this software can effectively turn any computer into a professional transcribing machine. It easily works with Microsoft Word and all major word-processors allowing the researcher to immediately get started on transcripts without having to rely on external support. This chapter offers step-by-step guides

and advice for software assisted transcribing using Express Scribe and detailed guidance on formatting qualitative interview transcripts with practical examples from an actual qualitative research project.

REFERENCES

Bailey, J. (2008). First steps in qualitative data analysis: Transcribing. *Family Practice*, *25*(2), 127–131. doi:10.1093/fampra/cmn003 PMID:18304975

Bird, C. M. (2005). How I Stopped Dreading and Learned to Love Transcription. *Qualitative Inquiry*, *11*(2), 226–248. doi:10.1177/1077800404273413

Bowling, A. (2009). *Research Methods in Health: Investigating health and health services* (3rd ed.). London: Open University Press.

Bryman, A. (2004). *Social research methods* (2nd ed.). Oxford, UK: Oxford University Press.

Bryman, A., & Hardy, M. (Eds.). (2004). *Handbook of data analysis*. London: Sage.

DiCicco-Bloom, B., & Crabtree, B. F. (2006). The qualitative research interview. *Medical Education*, *40*(4), 314–321. doi:10.1111/j.1365-2929.2006.02418.x PMID:16573666

Justinia, T. (2009). *Implementing large-scale healthcare information systems: The technological, managerial and behavioural issues*. (PhD Dissertation). Swansea University, Swansea, UK.

Justinia, T. (2014). *Implementing large-scale healthcare information systems: The technological, managerial and behavioural issues*. Scholars-Press.

Lapadat, J. C., & Lindsay, A. C. (1999). Transcription in research and Practice: From Standardization of Technique to Interpretive Positionings. *Qualitative Inquiry*, *5*(1), 64–86. doi:10.1177/107780049900500104

May, C. (1998). The preparation and analysis of qualitative interview data. In R. B. & W. C. (Eds.), Research and development in clinical nursing practice. London: Whurr. doi:10.1002/9780470699270.ch5

Miles, M. B., & Huberman, A. M. (1994). *An expanded Sourcebook: Qualitative Data Analysis* (2nd ed.). London: Sage.

Miles, M. B., Huberman, A. M., & Saldaña, J. (2014). *Qualitative Data Analysis: A Methods Sourcebook* (3rd ed.). Washington, DC: Sage.

Newell, R., & Burnard, P. (2006). *Research for Evidence-Based Practice in Healthcare*. Oxford, UK: Wiley-Blackwell.

Parry, R. (2010). Video-based Conversation Analysis. In I. Bourgeault, R. Dingwall, & R. d. Vries (Eds.), *The SAGE Handbook of Qualitative Methods in Health Research* (pp. 373–396). London: Sage. doi:10.4135/9781446268247.n20

Ruch, P., Geissbuhler, A., Gobeill, J., Lisacek, F., Tbahriti, I., Veuthey, A. L., & Aronson, A. R. (2007). Using discourse analysis to improve text categorization in MEDLINE. *Studies in Health Technology and Informatics*, *129*(Pt 1), 710–715. PMID:17911809

Sarangi, S. (2010). Practicing Discourse Analysis in Healthcare Settings. In I. Bourgeault, R. Dingwall, & R. d. Vries (Eds.), *The SAGE Handbook of Qualitative Methods in Health Research* (pp. 397–416). London: Sage. doi:10.4135/9781446268247.n21

Silverman, D. (2001). *Interpreting qualitative data: methods for analysing talk, text and interaction* (2nd ed.). London: Sage.

Silverman, D. (2005). *Doing qualitative research* (2nd ed.). London: Sage.

Silverman, D. (Ed.). (2006). *Qualitative research: theory, method and practice*. London: Sage.

NCH Software. (2014). *NCH Software*. Retrieved April 2014, 2014, from http://www.nch.com.au/scribe/

Tilley, S. A. (2003). "Challenging" Research Practices: Turning a Critical Lens on the Work of Transcription. *Qualitative Inquiry*, *9*(5), 750–773. doi:10.1177/1077800403255296

Webb, C. (1999). Analysing qualitative data: Computerized and other approaches. *Journal of Advanced Nursing*, *29*(2), 323–330. doi:10.1046/j.1365-2648.1999.00892.x PMID:10197931

APPENDIX

Interviewee Name: XXXX XXXX.

Interview Code: EA 12-12-06.

Interviewee Job Title: XXXX XXXX XXXX.

Interview Date: December 12th, 2006.

Interview Time: 15:00.

Years with the Organisation: XX years.

Interviewer: I wanted to ask you about your involvement in the CIMS implementation. Did you have a role?

Participant: To start with-if I can recall-four or five years ago we had an overview presentation from the executive director of the information system introducing the clinical information system. So I think most directors; most leaders were invited to attend. After that we weren't asked to participate in anything but lately-like a year ago if I may say-they have sent us a kind of introduction about what would be the systems that medical record would use. So they asked us to fill questionnaires, answer some questions regarding the workflow of the system, which we did and like three months ago we got other visitors and this time from the United States. They went again and did the same process of interviewing us; seeing the kind of systems, and seeing what would we want to see for the new system when it comes. Yes, so to conclude that, I think that I had a role because it's medical records and definitely would be a big participant in the system.

Interviewer: Ok, so you think the medical record is important in the implementation?

Participant: Definitely.

Interviewer: Do you have any idea how the implementation of the system will impact the medical record?

Participant: I think it will eliminate so much of the paperwork if it is done right and it is successful. But certainly I don't think it would be paperless in the way they had hoped it would be. Certainly having so much of the medical record-or the electronic patient record-components being automated would be very helpful and useful to the organisation.

Interviewer: Were talking about the paperless record. You mentioned that you don't think it will be completely paperless.

Participant: Definitely, because I haven't seen an existence of an electronic patient record yet because of; I think from different countries, different cultures, different states would still require the presence and evidence of the paper to be there.

Interviewer: What about in this environment, this culture, this country?

Participant: Certainly, certainly if I may say maybe a quarter of the components of the patient record would still be papers. Like the sick-leaves, like the medical reports that go to the courts, like the birth certifications, like the death certifications...etc.

Interviewer: Why can't these be electronic?

Participant: How?

Interviewer: I don't know, I am asking you. What is the difficulty in having these documents be in electronic format, like any other document?

Participant: It can be, but still you will have to print a hard copy to the patient. You have to give a hard copy to the patient to take with them. To be accepted at the-like-Ministry of Health and for vitals statistics department (muffled).

Interviewer: So you are saying there is another issue of reporting to external=

Participant: Absolutely yeah they would, because I don't think that we have the means and the mechanism of reporting from and institute to another institute electronically.

Interviewer: So you are saying that the main problem is reporting to external [Because you still need to issue hard prints or hard copies] and you don't see this issue being overcome?

Participant: Maybe in the future if other organisations have used clinical information systems and they find a way to interact and interface and integrate it together; yeah why not? But I am seeing that not all organisations have the funds-you know-it's expensive. This is one of the obstacles I would see. Another issue not seeing complete electronic patient records is the resistance of physicians to chart everything electronically. They might be-they might be the number one issue to the failure of having an electronic patient record. If you have the culture and the awareness and the readiness for such a thing; yes.

Interviewer: So you don't think we have the culture or the awareness or the readiness? Could you elaborate on that?

Participant: Culturally; culturally we are not ready. Then there is the language barrier. Most of the Physicians; English is a second language to them. Trying to write in a computer would make them exposed to that they haven't done the documentation right from structure wise, unless it's umm customized for them in a way to make it a user friendly like sentences for them there and they can just click on an icon there and they can just copy and paste it. And then they have the training is for it. I'm seeing that, because I see it now with the hard documents and I see it when they dictate and that's really an issue; it's a painful thing for them even though they are not writing; somebody else is writing for them or transcribing for them.

Interviewer: So you see the language barrier in the medical reporting.

Participant: In our in charting, in any component such as progress reports, such as discharge summaries, such as autopsy reports; name it etc.

Interviewer: And also because of computer illiteracy?

Participant: Yeah you can say that.

Interviewer: You said there is also an issue of awareness.

Participant: Still people here are unaware of the importance of completing your documents.

Interviewer: How about readiness? You said people aren't ready.

Participant: Because we don't have these things in our culture yet.

Interviewer: Another thing I wanted to ask you about is the electronic patient record. Is there anything that has been put in electronic format so far?

Participant: There is but it's partial and it's not used as it is supposed to be, like the lab reporting [ok]. Though it is in the system, we still have to print it and get the hard copies because not every examination room has a PC so doctors can access it whenever they need whenever they see a patient and they want to look at the last investigation that was requested. The radiology reporting on the system, it's there but still people don't access it and some people don't even know it exists.

Interviewer: So that is another part of the awareness. People don't know=

Participant: They are not oriented fully about what are the automated components of the medical record that are in existence. Like the ECG report or the ACG, it's in the system.

Interviewer: And people aren't informed?

Participant: They aren't; they look at it only as hard copies; if it is there in the patient record or not. Who's aware are mostly the nurses. So whenever it's not found in the patient record they would re-print it and give it to the doctor to read it.

Interviewer: Was there resistance?

Participant: I can speak now about the culture. Unfortunately, they won't go the extra mile of completing things as perfect as they should be. So they need more awareness. They need more of measures to make them more accountable for things. Probably now with JCI the story will be different.

Interviewer: And how is that?

Participant: Because with JCI, there are certain standards; either you meet them or not. You cannot have it as 'partially met'. And because of the commitment coming from the upper management that everybody needs to do his part and his share; which-it showed really last year. There were great improvements from the physicians towards documentation, but it consumed so many hours and follow-up from upper management after those physicians. I don't know will that continue all the time?

(Interruption-overhead voice announcement-paused recording)

Interviewer: You were talking about JCI. It seems to have had a positive effect from your point of view.

Participant: We had direction. Before we didn't have direction, now we have um um we have a body that governs our practices in our hospitals which we voluntarily choose and thanks to the really the commitment of the upper management. So you cannot just pick and choose with JCI, you have to really do it right. And I think; luckily "inshallah" (meaning God willing) when we get the certificate I am sure when you earn an honor you would want always to keep it. So at least now people won't be unaccountable about documentation, but about many other issues not just documentation.

Interviewer: So to keep the certification from JCI, once it has been achieved [yes]. It seems that it had a positive effect. Do you think it had any negative effect on the implementation?

Participant: Not at all. No, I am honestly one of the people that were thrilled and happy to have it. And I have seen people who have resisted it at the beginning but now they start to see its positive outcomes. Many things have been improved in the organization and it is due to the fact that people are seeing improvements in many deficiencies we had-it has ben corrected. Any many systems we didn't have-like physical stuff-they ordered it; the departments, so=

Interviewer: I wanted to get back to one point. You were saying that one of the reasons you think would make it difficult to implement an electronic patient record is the reporting to external sources. Is the language one barrier? Do you have to report to external sources in; let's say Arabic, and then does that make it difficult or is it=

Participant: Really you got it. It could be the language because all the reports we report and we have to send for those external agencies, we use Arabic language. But I think any company could have that language as well customized for that hospital. It could have both.

Interviewer: So that's not the main reason [no]. Ok, I wanted to ask you about involvement in the implementation of the clinical system. Do you think that user involvement played a role in it? Were you involved or were you not involved?

Participant: I think you know when you are doing a system for the whole organization and when you go through a department like patient services and medical records, if you don't involve the end-users who will use the system and see what would be there needs you won't be able to minimize or will find difficulties you would face when you actually implement the system. Because you need to see the workflow of the departments in the hospital; how things really go. Because I cannot just buy a system really that was made for a culture different that us like in the United States, and you come and bring it here and you think it's going to work. You still have-you should have the room for umm modifying things to fit that particular hospital structure's needs. Even you can take that as this site and the head quarters site. Although we are two sister hospitals, we still do things differently. So you should have involved the end users to see what they can add by giving you information on how they do their work, whether you will modify things for them or you will make them understand how they can modify their work to make the system be used friendly.

Interviewer: So in your department were you involved?

Participant: Um you have to know something. The system has not yet been implemented in this site. Ok the plan is that it is going to be implemented next year. I was involved on the part of asking us about the medical record and the functions; what we currently have, what we want to have, and what their system will give us. But they are still talking theoretically and on paper it's different and using the system for real is something else.

Interviewer: Is there anything else that you would like to add about the difficulties and challenges of implementing a system; a clinical information system?

Participant: I think other than involving the people; other than understanding exactly the process of each department and how they interact with each other, your system really will be shocked with the amount of issues it will face. Of course, any company when they introduce a system to you they will tell you about their strong support for maintenance, so they should be apt to what they have promised. Meaning, they really should be committed, they should be really available when the end users use it. Usually the first year of the implementation they could overcome the anxiety and fear that comes when using something new. And even like having um an in house maintenance availability that's really useful.

Interviewer: About the delay in the implementation in this site; you said that initially they talked to you about four or five years ago, and got your overview about the implementation and until now you said that the implementation hasn't been done here yet.

Participant: I think when they talked to us about it that was the time they were introducing the system, I don't think they bought it at that time. Maybe at that time they wanted to see the reaction and decisions of the present people there, but after that I think maybe after they've interviewed many people and they've done their feasibility study and cost-benefit analysis study to see the need for having that system, they did not talk until maybe a year ago, I don't know I am not a part of that. Maybe you can exclude two years of that period. So um and I think maybe the other delay I think maybe it's due to starting with a massive, but, huge hospital like the head quarters site which they haven't really finished completely from phase one.

Interviewer: Ok, but it had nothing to do with your department's side? Anything at all or any issues to do with you?

Participant: It can't be because we haven't used it and we have not been part of the obstacles or issues. Anything they asked to do, we did it. We answered questions and did send all our policies, our system. Any information they required we sent it to them.

Interviewer: So you think the delay is [Due maybe to different factors] on the implementers' side, but not from the end users' side or from the departments?

Participant: Yes, from the implementers' side.

Interviewer: Do you see yourself as an implementer or as an end user?

Participant: No, as an end user.

Interviewer: I wanted to ask you about what you think about physicians and information systems in general.

Participant: As I told you, it's really a vision; it's a dream. You know to have a complete system. I think people are working towards achieving that dream and we have young people now. They are now very much familiar in using many of the state of the art technology; they would welcome it. It's just the reality of having the system and using it. I cannot really predict, but from literature, from visiting other hospitals, from contacting some friends, I haven't seen it %100 successful. So, but=

Interviewer: For this organisation?

Participant: Um (*then silence, I think there was an interruption here*).

Interviewer: How about nurses and information systems?

Participant: I think they would love it. It would make their life easy. Honestly it would make Medical Records' like easy (*laugh*).

Interviewer: So do you think it would be beneficial and make your job easier=

Participant: Defiantly, although it would have an impact on other functions in the department. Maybe some functions-some functions might be demolished completely; deleted. It won't be needed. You don't need to find that many hard copies. If it's um if some um maybe like %80 or %90 of the medical record component it's automated. But from the other end is the record is ready available any time for multiple users, so we don't need to worry about delivering the record on time. Um for transcriptionists it's easy. We should transcribe the report for them, they can just download it to the system and the doctors can use the electronic signature and just finish it; it's quickly. For getting records completed the dictation room staff can do that electronically as well. Doctors from any nursing station there is a PC they could look at their uncompleted components and do it. So defiantly it would have great um great impact; I mean positive. Coding; whenever a coder would need to code; if we are doing coding for money or for research; especially if we are doing it for reimbursement, most of the things I need are already in the system for me. It would make life easy for me. The legibility of the information; it's legible; it's there, I don't need to struggle so I would be able to code my files immediately even it is comes; not the whole record completed; still I would have; it would be user-friendly-easy and ease for the staff doing the coding. So for research it's easy you can just print rather than medical records just copying things for you. Record-keeping, space, I would not have to keep that big space anymore. Providing they don't do the same thing like other hospitals did. They kept a soft copy and a hard copy. So it's duplicated work.

Interviewer: How about confidentiality, security? Do you think that's an issue?

Participant: I don't think so. Because the same measures you have with the hard copy; which you cannot have %100 control and assuring confidentiality and security. Maybe it would be much better with information systems with passwords and tracking people who breeched or violated or printed part of the patient records. It would be even-I think-with information systems it would be much better. There would be more control.

Interviewer: Is there anything you can add to the regarding the electronic patient record, and the difficulties of implementing an electronic patient record?

Participant: I think for an electronic patient record, the developer of the system should really involve people participate on the hard copy. It shouldn't just be an IT person. I think-and maybe companies did that-I don't know. It should be a medical records personnel profession, should be a physician, should be a nurse, ancillary people, so they can have the overview of a hard medical record so they could tell something similar to the hard medical record. Also the use of the electronic patient record should be user friendly. He screen shouldn't be busy. I think they should think about when you are viewing the electronic patient record they should be on the reviewer of a hard copy's shoes to do it that way; to think [to get their point of view] yes [to involve the users and get their perspective; is that what you mean?] they should be aware properly about how things really exist with a hard copy so they could come up with a good electronic record and it succeeds when it is implemented.

Interviewer: So you are saying they should be familiar with [the process] with their workflow and their processes before they make it electronic? [yes] I wanted to ask you about the dictation system. I know you are involved with the project. Does this have anything to do with the clinical information systems?

Participant: Definitely, because um-you know-it's the doctors' documentation. It's a painful thing for them to do. So we have people to transcribe information for them. It could be looked at in two ways. Now we are doing an electronic patient record, so why should we transcribe for physicians? Why don't they go ahead and do their discharge summaries and other reports? The problem will be time and language barrier. Is it worth my paying a transcriptionist to do the work of a highly pad physicians rather than he spends time charting or transcribing someone else cheaper can do that for him, because physicians' time is valuable for patients' direct care. You could say that he still takes time to dictate so why doesn't he use that time to transcribe? I think speaking can consume less time than really writing. The report when it's transcribed it can be launched; downloaded to the system so the doctor can view it from any workstation in the hospital. Can it be done the same way with an email? No. with an email he read it, then what? There isn't the mechanism of having it printed on the proper format and then signing it and then sending it to Medical Records, but with electronic patient records they are already launching that report to the exact orders where it should be as the chart order of that patient record either electronically or paper.

Interviewer: So is the dictation system a step towards the electronic record or is it=

Participant: It's one of the steps it's not really a step towards because really there are other things like the lab results like I told you, the other investigations' results. There is the other ones like progress; patient progress. The flow sheets, the assessments of patients, the triage of the patient, monitoring his vital signs. When it's computerised it will be really helpful. And I think what the information system does bring better than a paper is literature of oral values of let's say you are doing an ECG report, it can guide you whether this is right or wrong with alerts; with colours. The same with nurses when they do the vital signs when something is beyond abnormality, when it's visualised.

Interviewer: Thank you for your time and participation.

end

Chapter 11

Exploiting Enriched Knowledge of Web Network Structures:
Chaining Maltego Tungsten, NCapture and NVivo, and NodeXL

Shalin Hai-Jew
Kansas State University, USA

ABSTRACT

Understanding Web network structures may offer insights on various organizations and individuals. These structures are often latent and invisible without special software tools; the interrelationships between various websites may not be apparent with a surface perusal of the publicly accessible Web pages. Three publicly available tools may be "chained" (combined in sequence) in a data extraction sequence to enable visualization of various aspects of http network structures in an enriched way (with more detailed insights about the composition of such networks, given their heterogeneous and multimodal contents). Maltego Tungsten™, a penetration-testing tool, enables the mapping of Web networks, which are enriched with a variety of information: the technological understructure and tools used to build the network, some linked individuals (digital profiles), some linked documents, linked images, related emails, some related geographical data, and even the in-degree of the various nodes. NCapture with NVivo enables the extraction of public social media platform data and some basic analysis of these captures. The Network Overview, Discovery, and Exploration for Excel (NodeXL) tool enables the extraction of social media platform data and various evocative data visualizations and analyses. With the size of the Web growing exponentially and new domains (like .ventures, .guru, .education, .company, and others), the ability to map widely will offer a broad competitive advantage to those who would exploit this approach to enhance knowledge.

DOI: 10.4018/978-1-4666-6493-7.ch011

INTRODUCTION

Since the advent of the World Wide Web (WWW) in 1991 and its popularization, researchers have been using this platform to glean publicly available information. Advancements in software tools and research methods, such as network analysis, have enabled broader publics to exploit so-called open-source (publicly available) intelligence (OSINT). The practices of network analysis borrow from math, computer science, and sociology, to depict interactive structures and power relationships in social systems based on interrelationships.

These relationships are often depicted as node-link (vertex-edge) structures, in 2D or 3D. A node (vertex) represents an entity; a link (edge or line) represents some type of relationship. If there are no line ends, the graph is an undirected one; if there are arrows on the line ends, the graph is a directed one (with an indication of the direction of the relationship and the presence or absence of reciprocity). The graph visualizations from network analysis are drawn using a dozen different layout algorithms, all with differing looks-and-feel and levels of analysis. There are some simple dynamics that apply to some classic depictions, such as the core-periphery dynamic: those in the core are often the nodes with high power influence (high in-degree and low out-degree) while those in the periphery are not as influential in that particular social network. Nodes which are pendants (those connected by only one tie) or isolates (those connected by no ties) are considered not very influential. Within networks, there may be cliques (or subclusters or islands) which are more densely connected to each other and then more sparsely connected to the rest of the network. Bridging nodes, those which connect often disparate communities, may have outsized power even if they have few ties—because of their role in connected networks which would not be in communications otherwise. There are other ways that networks are analyzed. There are a range of possible ties that are defined dyadically, triadi-

cally, quadratically, and so on, that may indicate differential power. Some networks are understood as pair-wise dyadic interactions between two nodes and then the interactions between these pairs linked into various networks; the decisions made by each node results in self-organizing or emergent (some suggest "rhizomic") behavior that may be seen as patterns at the larger social network levels. In other words, larger macro patterns of cascading behavior may be seen. One example is the phenomena of a meme "going viral" or a product or service gaining in popularity from electronic word-of-mouth percolation.

For example, a node which mediates between two other nodes which do not communicate directly has an oversized sense of power by being the go-between (in a phenomena known as "*tertius gaudens*" or "the third who benefits" or "the third who rejoices"). Motif censuses may be conducted on various networks to understand both global and node-level insights about that network, from a structural perspective. At a global level, diversity may be seen as promoting resilience but also potentially increased levels of strife. A monolithic network is seen as less robust and less adaptable but also potentially with lowered levels of strife (given the assumption of homophily or people clustering around others like themselves). A linear chain of nodes is seen to be fragile because the removal of any one node can mean a disconnection between numbers of its members. A "star" or a "wheel" (hub and spokes) is a network with an individual at the center who connects all the others; in this context, the power resides in the node at the center (the hub, not the spokes). In a mesh connection, such networks can be more resilient and robust because its members can work around the removal of a wide number of its nodes; there is not a single point-of-failure. A sparse network is thought to be less resilient than a dense (deeply inter-connected) one. This is not to say that structure is destiny. Rather, the theory is that there are interaction effects between structure and behavior, with each affecting the other.

Researchers analyze various patterns to understand real-world networks and social dynamics. They arrive at various inferences about the networks based on a range of extractable information. Based on homophily, http networks may show something of shared interests or shared clientele or audience members. Relational ties between websites may affect another site's "trust, prestige, authority, or credibility" (Kleinberg, 1999; Palmer, Bailey, & Faraj, 2000; Park, Barnett, & Nam, 2001, as cited in Park, 2003, p. 53). Others suggest that relational ties between similar organizations online may enhance their legitimacy and enhance their survival (Hannan & Carroll, 1992, as cited in Gibbons, 2004, p. 941).

In http networks, there is data about the front-end as well as the technological and data back end. Depending on the amount of overlap in the cyber-physical confluence, some aspects of real-world realities may be understood from the cyber presence. As yet, "surprising little is known about the exact relationship between real world networks and their online reflections" (Mika, 2007, p. 155). If high-indegree (numbers of nodes following the focal node relationally) with low-outdegree (numbers of out-going relationships) is seen as power for an individual node, that concept may apply to a particular web page, with various in-components and out-components (and strongly connected components as being high influence ones) in Web graphs (Serrano, Maguitman, Boguñá, Fortunato, & Vespignani, 2007, p. 10:14).

Figure 1, "A Quilt of Sample Graphs Extracted from the Web (with NodeXL)," has been included to provide a small sampling of some of the ranges of looks-and-feels of various types of social network graphs. These were all created by the author using NodeXL; the empirical data underlying the visualizations came from various social media platforms.

This chapter introduces a chaining method which integrates the usage of three stand-alone tools to reveal Web network structures and interrelationships in potentially informative ways. The three tools are the following: Paterva's Maltego Tungsten, QSR International's NVivo (with its linked browser add-in NCapture used with Google Chrome or Microsoft's Internet Explorer browsers), and the Social Media Research Foundation's Network Overview, Discovery and Exploration for Excel (NodeXL).

REVIEW OF THE LITERATURE

One method for analyzing the structures found on the Web is to conduct "hyperlink network analyses" (HNAs) (Kleftodimos & Evangelidis, 2013, p. 108), one form of Web structure mining. A hyperlink network is considered an extension of traditional communication networks (Park, 2003, p. 51). Another related term is "relational hyperlink analysis" (RHA). While these terms are fairly new, the mapping of http networks has been researched for almost two decades, with some visualizations of whole Web structures (with billions of nodes) as graphs.

Large-scale data crawls suggest that the Web follows a "small world" property with assortative mixing and preferential attachment; in this sense, there are tight clusters (connected components) of intimate networks among various sites but also a few degrees of separation between any two nodes on the Web (Serrano, Maguitman, Boguñá, Fortunato, & Vespignani, 2007, pp. 5 - 6). As such, the structure is quite robust against degeneration (except for directed attacks against highly influential nodes). The Web is also a scale-free (or inhomogeneous) network, with a handful of sites drawing the majority of traffic and then a long tail of diverse smaller sites attracting much relatively smaller audiences; in other words, the sites fall under a power law distribution, with large inequalities in terms of ties. Others have observed the "fractal" (repeating patterns at various scales) nature of the Internet" (Caldarelli, Marchetti, & Pietronero, 2000), with repeating patterns. Other researchers prefer the application of the Lorenz

Figure 1. A quilt of sample graphs extracted from the Web (with NodeXL)

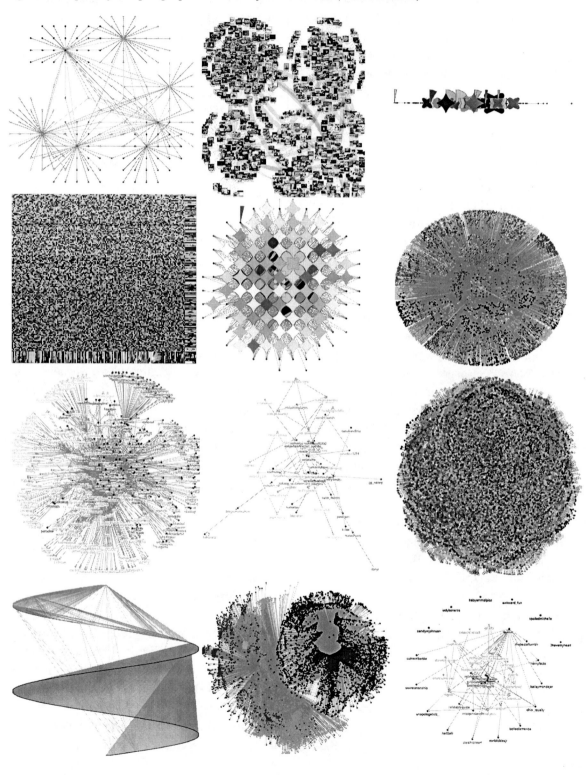

curve to depict the unequal distribution of edges or ties in part because of the assumption of an idealized or uniform proportionality of distribution of degrees (network ties) over all vertices in a network (Kunegis & Preusse, 2012). The unit of analysis may vary broadly from an N of all ("big data") to small-scale networks to individual nodes or individual relationships.

Jackson (1997) first identified the potential of using social network analysis to analyze hyperlink networks given the communicative aspects of Web structures albeit without interdependencies between sites and without labeling sites as "actors" (Lusher & Ackland, 2009, pp. 2 – 3). Researchers have worked to surface latent or non-obvious ties. For example, the study of an organization's Web network's understructure may show its global reach and regions of the world where it has more customers (based on numbers of servers in certain geographical domains). Advancements in electronic social network analysis have been extended to http (hypertext transfer protocol) networks.

Recently, a group of scholars have begun to describe websites as actors. From this perspective, an actor is a website belonging to a person, private company, public organization, city, or nation-state. These nodes are linked by their hyperlinks. Hyperlink network analysts argue that despite the Internet's brief existence, its increasing role in communication has been made possible by the continual change in the structure of the network of hyperlinks. Patterns of hyperlinks designed or modified by individuals or organizations who own websites reflect the communicative choices, agendas, or ends (Jackson, 1997) of the owners. Thus, the structural pattern of hyperlinks in their websites serves a particular social or communicative function. (Park, 2003, p. 53)

In other words, the Web is seen as a medium for direct and indirect communications between people. As an artifact of their social interactivity, it may be studied as a kind of social network, with entities (individuals, digital contents, messages, and others) in relation to each other (follower, following, commenting, tagging, mentioning, and other types of relating). This analysis will in begin with simple extractions of http networks and show how they may be enriched with a variety of other types of heterogeneous and multimodal data and other networks. *Figure 2,* "Unstructured to Structured Continuum of Network Linkage Online," provides a sense of various types of social networks on the Web as they reside along a continuum of self-organizing topology to purposive human-determined structure. Content networks, phrase networks, and hashtag conversations are considered fairly emergent, without an overarching organizing hand given the wide range of conversants and participants. On the other hand, http or Web networks, email networks, and so on, are considered fairly structured and controlled by whomever controls the organizational web presence or the email accounts.

Figure 2. Unstructured to structured continuum of network linkage online

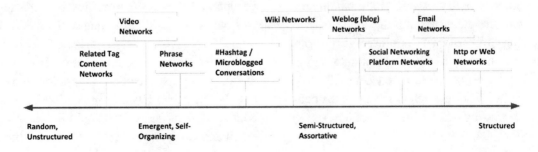

Web networks are not "emergent" in a social network sense because of the assumption of high-structure and control.

Emergence implies that any particular structure may be in various stages of existence and that the development of that structure is the result of the interaction of contextual elements. A link, in contrast, may not emerge. Links are planned and they do not change. Even sites that create Web pages dynamically are governed by static algorithms and program code. Further, the interaction of contextual elements will not affect the properties of a link. Until removed or changed by the designer, the link will continue to exist whether or not it is ever followed by a user. Nor is a link affected by changes to the Web pages that anchor that link. For as long as the designer maintains the link within the source document, any other changes can be made to either the source document or the target document, and they will not affect the link. If the URL of the target document changes, the link will be "dead," and the user will face an error message when attempting to follow the link. But a dead link reflects designer error rather than emergence. (Jackson, 1997, p. 12)

While the WWW is by definition global, the facts of local phenomena and geographical realities play important roles in network analysis. The geographical elements of networks are a critical aspect of their existence (Gastner & Newman, 2006). Per Saxenian's (1994, 1996) observations about "regional advantage," proximity to others engaged in mental work may have far reaching impacts on innovations *ceteris paribus*. Other factors come into play as well: "External threats, shared culture and ethics, similar interests, and preexisting familiarity with the other organizations further encourage collaboration within a region (Doz, Olk, & Ring, 2000, as cited in Gibbons, 2004, p. 939). The research is mixed on the benefits of increasing ties for diffusion of innovation (Gibbons, 2004, p. 939).

EXTRACTED HTTP NETWORKS

This chapter focuses on a particular "use case"—of mapping both macro and micro-level http networks through the use of three software tools: Maltego Tungsten (formerly Maltego Radium), NCapture and NVivo, and NodeXL. All three tools have much broader ranges and capabilities than what is shown here in this limited case. However, these capabilities are beyond the purview of this limited work. Maltego Tungsten is designed as a penetration testing tool to enhance the security of websites by highlighting vulnerabilities; as such, it is a tool that is often paired with exploitation tools by black hat hackers. NVivo is a qualitative and mixed methods data analysis tool. NodeXL (Network Overview, Discovery and Exploration for Excel) is a social network graphing and data visualization add-in to Excel.

Figure 3, "Chaining Enriched Web Network Capture, Visualization, and Analysis (with Maltego Tungsten, NCapture and NVivo, and NodeXL)" provides a broad overview of this process. Maltego Tungsten can provide a range of levels of domains (discrete regions of the Internet with Web addresses with a common suffix) and Web networks, including the technological understructures; it can collect up to 10,000 nodes per data extraction. It can also capture node-level data through its various "transforms" which capture data "equivalencies" across data types. This tool can capture related information but sometimes has the challenge of false positives (which require disambiguation or "pruning" of unrelated branches or links). NCapture is an add-on to Google Chrome and Microsoft's Internet Explorer browsers which enables the capturing of web pages, Tweet streams, and social media data for use in NVivo. NodeXL enables the capturing of a range of network information from social media platforms, including microblogging sites like Twitter, social networking sites like Facebook, content sharing sites like YouTube and Flickr, email accounts, and wikis and the Web (through

Figure 3. Chaining enriched web network capture, visualization, and analysis (with Maltego Tungsten, NCapture and NVivo, and NodeXL)

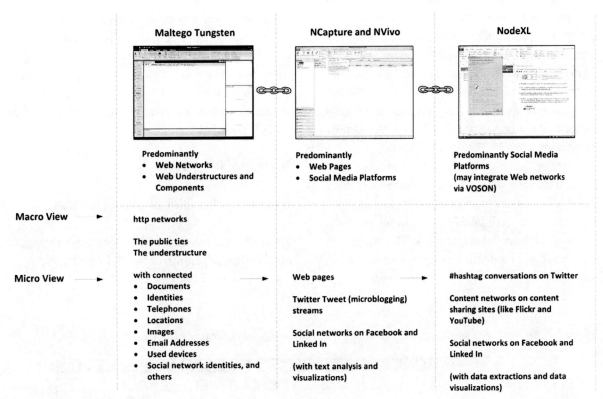

the third-party Virtual Observatory for the Study of Online Networks or "VOSON").

To simplify, in an http network, nodes are hypertext pages, and edges are hyperlinks. The research sequence here involves capturing full networks at the top level and then probing deeper as necessary.

If social networks involve the three fundamental issues, "(1) What constitutes a social tie? (2) Who are the nodes/actors? and (3) Where is the network boundary?" (Lusher & Ackland, 2009, p. 5), then it is important to define "the tie-actor-boundary triumvirate" for the various social media platforms and to understand how the various ties are weighted. On a microblogging site, "relationship" may be defined as follower / following; it may be defined as interacting around shared conversations. On a content sharing site, relationship may be defined as "replies-to." In a related tags

network, the co-occurrence of terminology may be used as relationship. A range of factors may be evaluated to understand associational ties. This approach focuses on social computing, the study of social behavior and social context in computational systems (particularly Web 2.0 ones).

What does this figure show in terms of extant technology-enhanced research capabilities? This means that researchers may access publicly available information about any named domain whether it is transnational (like .com) or national (like .us). It can map entire domain structures (like .edu or some of the newer ones like .company and .equipment). It can target micro-level structures such as company or organization networks. It can map the electronic Web structures around geographical spaces. Individuals' identities may be mapped across various online spaces and domains. A breaking online phenomena may be mapped across the World Wide Web (WWW) based on websites, identities, hashtagged microblogged conversations, and other elements. Individuals and groups may be de-aliased through maps of their presences online. Twitter streams may be mapped and machine-analyzed for their textual content. Document searches may be conducted across the Web. Images may be extracted from data crawls for more information and detail. The Web is now broadly minable by the broader public.

To show a walk-through of the process, a few data extractions were conducted (in the sequence listed) using all three software tools. The analysis was kept at a superficial level since the purpose was just to show how this might work. The "targeted" sites were selected was examples only, without any other purpose.

MACRO LEVELS

A transnational data crawl at the macro level may involve the .com domain since this cuts across various continents, regions, and countries. Maltego Tungsten has a top-level crawl of 10,000 nodes. (The increments are 12, 50, 255, and 10,000.) An L1 (Level 1) footprint was conducted for the global ".com" domain.

Maltego Tungsten

Exploring the Global .com Domain

Figure 4, "An Overview of the Global .com Domain (10,000 Results Limit) (with Maltego Tungsten)" shows a zoomed-out view of the http network from

Figure 4. An overview of the global .com domain (10,000 results limit) (with Maltego Tungsten)

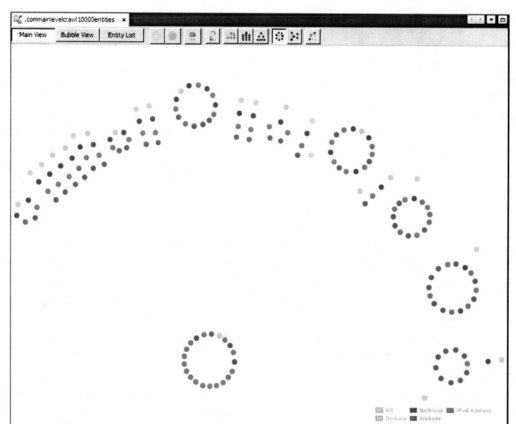

this crawl. The resulting table showed an entity list including some big-name stores; other records were indicated by IP numbers only.

There were known big-name commercial sites that did not show up on the listing at least with linked URLs, but they may have been included with their names hidden and only the IP numbers available.

Exploring the Global .com Domain

A smaller crawl of the global .com domain (at 255 records or nodes) revealed a mix of brick-and-mortar as well as online stores. The ring lattices were for the larger online spaces such as for Google

and Tumblr. There were more stand-alone branches with individual stores and commercial entities.

Figure 7, "A Large Technological Understructure to Deliver Google Images (255 Results Limit) (with Maltego Tungsten) shows a zoomed-in view of part of this http network graph, with a fairly large understructure used to deliver Google images.

Clearly, having contextual information to understand a graph is important—to understand what's there and also maybe what's not there.

Figure 8, ".com Core Surrounded by Tumblr Accounts (255 Results Limit) (with Maltego Tungsten)," shows the .com core surrounded by Tumblr accounts. Tumblr is a Yahoo-owned microblogging platform.

Figure 5. An overview of the global .com domain entity list (10,000 results limit) (with Maltego Tungsten)

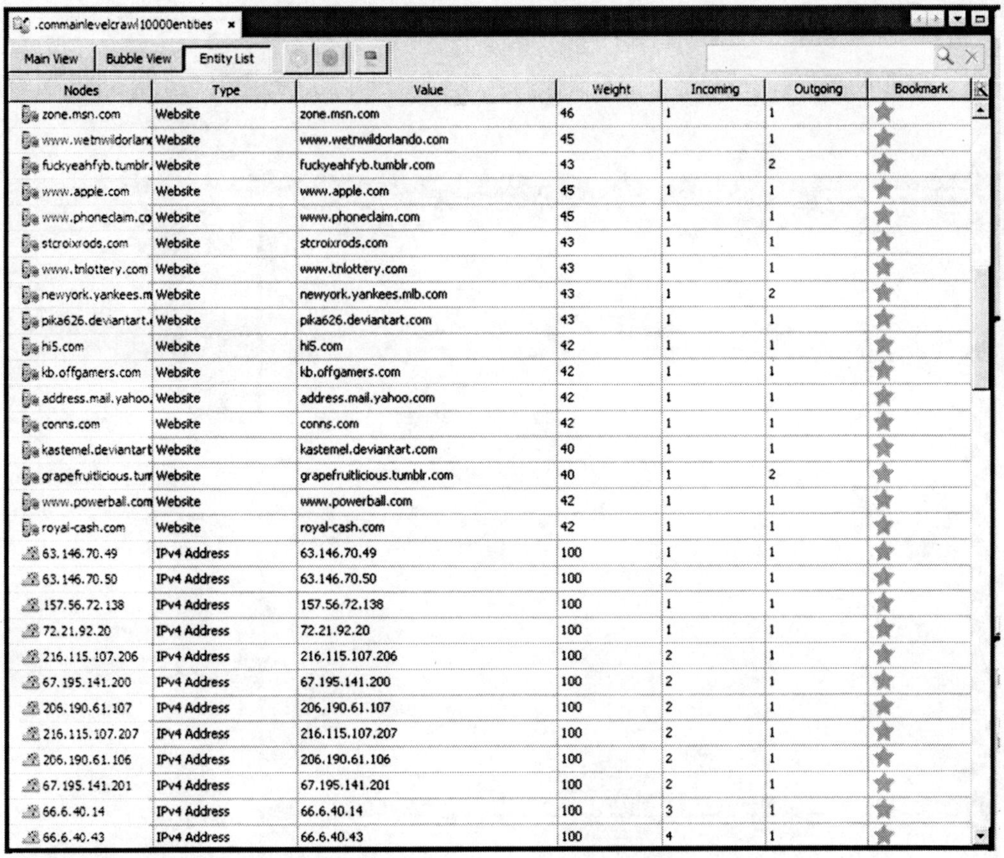

Nodes	Type	Value	Weight	Incoming	Outgoing	Bookmark
zone.msn.com	Website	zone.msn.com	46	1	1	★
www.wetnwildorland	Website	www.wetnwildorlando.com	45	1	1	★
fuckyeahfyb.tumblr.	Website	fuckyeahfyb.tumblr.com	43	1	2	★
www.apple.com	Website	www.apple.com	45	1	1	★
www.phoneclaim.co	Website	www.phoneclaim.com	45	1	1	★
stcroixrods.com	Website	stcroixrods.com	43	1	1	★
www.tnlottery.com	Website	www.tnlottery.com	43	1	1	★
newyork.yankees.m	Website	newyork.yankees.mlb.com	43	1	2	★
pika626.deviantart.	Website	pika626.deviantart.com	43	1	1	★
hi5.com	Website	hi5.com	42	1	1	★
kb.offgamers.com	Website	kb.offgamers.com	42	1	1	★
address.mail.yahoo.	Website	address.mail.yahoo.com	42	1	1	★
conns.com	Website	conns.com	42	1	1	★
kastemel.deviantart	Website	kastemel.deviantart.com	40	1	1	★
grapefruitlicious.tum	Website	grapefruitlicious.tumblr.com	40	1	2	★
www.powerball.com	Website	www.powerball.com	42	1	1	★
royal-cash.com	Website	royal-cash.com	42	1	1	★
63.146.70.49	IPv4 Address	63.146.70.49	100	1	1	★
63.146.70.50	IPv4 Address	63.146.70.50	100	2	1	★
157.56.72.138	IPv4 Address	157.56.72.138	100	1	1	★
72.21.92.20	IPv4 Address	72.21.92.20	100	1	1	★
216.115.107.206	IPv4 Address	216.115.107.206	100	2	1	★
67.195.141.200	IPv4 Address	67.195.141.200	100	2	1	★
206.190.61.107	IPv4 Address	206.190.61.107	100	2	1	★
216.115.107.207	IPv4 Address	216.115.107.207	100	2	1	★
206.190.61.106	IPv4 Address	206.190.61.106	100	2	1	★
67.195.141.201	IPv4 Address	67.195.141.201	100	2	1	★
66.6.40.14	IPv4 Address	66.6.40.14	100	3	1	★
66.6.40.43	IPv4 Address	66.6.40.43	100	4	1	★

Figure 6. An overview of the global .com domain (255 results limit) (with Maltego Tungsten)

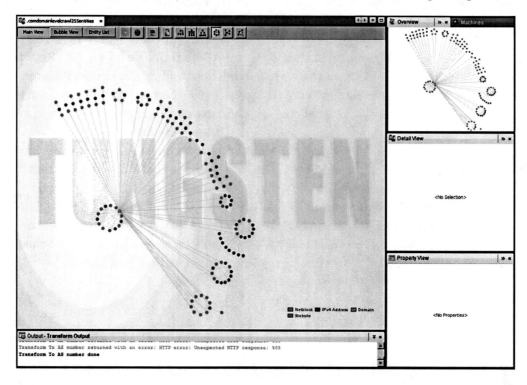

Figure 7. A large technological understructure to deliver Google images (255 results limit) (with Maltego Tungsten)

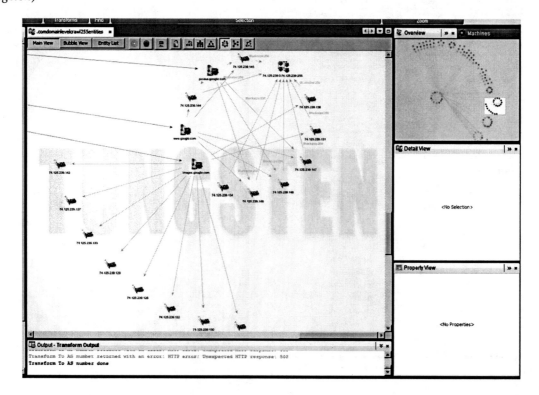

Figure 8. .com core surrounded by Tumblr accounts (255 results limit) (with Maltego Tungsten)

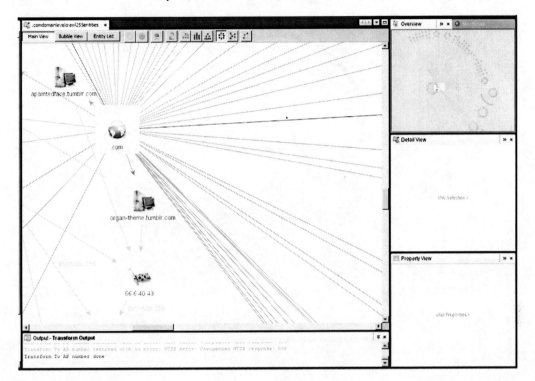

Exploring an Enriched View of the .cn Domain

A country-level domain crawl may reveal a nation's top-level http network. A recent L1 data extraction for the .cn domain (for China) with a limit of 255 results

Figure 9, "A High-Level Crawl of the .cn Domain (with Maltego Tungsten)," shows a mixture of government, educational, and commercial entities, sometimes in the same ring lattice graph. This may indicate a different sort of real-world tie between entities that is less common in countries with other forms of governance.

Figure 10, "A Zoomed-in View of Selected Websites on the .cn Domain (with Maltego

Tungsten)," shows the level of detail available. Note the "Detail View" to the right as well as the "Property View" window. Also, at the top right is an overview pane which shows which part of the http network is being highlighted.

Figure 11, "Interconnected Subcluster of Media Organizations on the .cn Domain (with Maltego Tungsten)" shows how particular connected cliques or islands in the http network may be analyzed more closely. This cluster is highlighted in the pullout at the "Overview" window inset at the top right.

The other parts of the http network (roughly from left to right) are as follows: organizations, businesses, a media organization, an educational institution and a government one, a blogging

Figure 9. A high-level crawl of the .cn domain (with Maltego Tungsten)

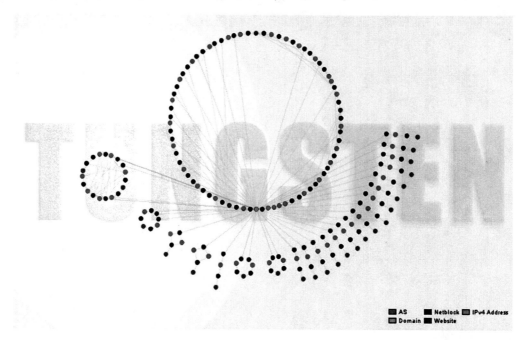

Figure 10. A zoomed-in view of selected websites on the .cn domain (with Maltego Tungsten)

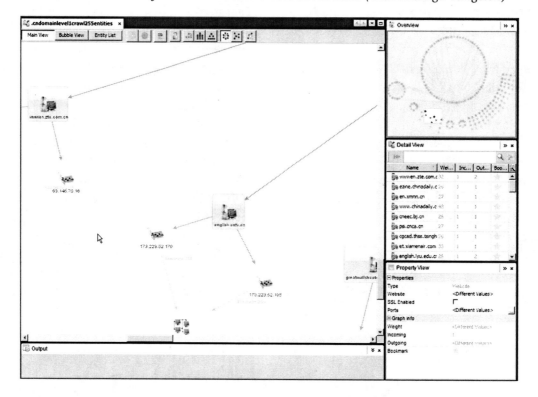

Figure 11. Interconnected subcluster of media organizations on the .cn domain (with Maltego Tungsten)

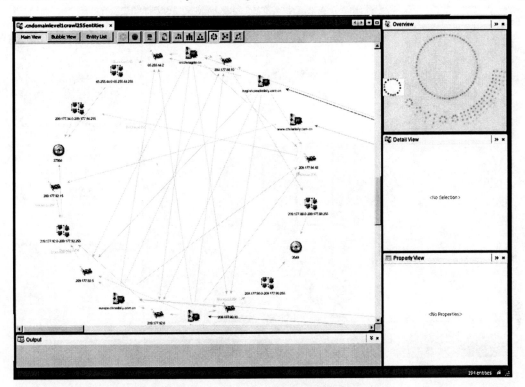

site along with a broad-based supplier site, and a range of less-linked media and commercial sites (including a shipping site, a weather site, and a local airline). These may be seen in detail at Figure 12, "Other Branches of the .cn Domain Crawl (with Maltego Tungsten)."

Contrasting a View of the .us Domain

For a simplified contrast, a 255-node L1 footprint was conducted for the .us domain. This crawl resulted in a collection of sites consisting of state agencies, educational institutions, and state and county government. No .com entities were identified.

MICRO LEVELS

At more micro levels, such as those of groups or organizations or companies, an http network extraction may start with the definition of a website's URL (uniform resource locator) and a "machine" (a sequence of automated data extractions from the Web) crawl. What follows then may be a capturing of all known "transforms" (which transform one type of online information to another type such as a Twitter entity into a linked phone number or an online document). A data extraction of the amazon.com site was made, with additional search for the linked AmazonFresh site.

Figure 12. Other branches of the .cn domain crawl (with Maltego Tungsten)

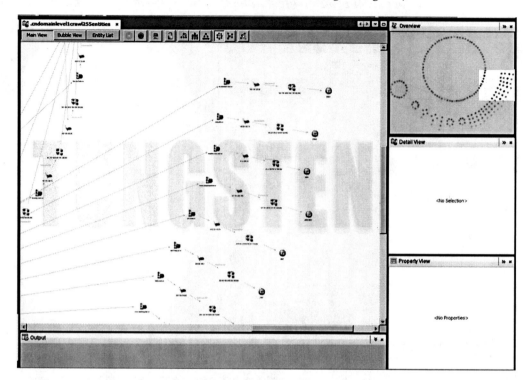

Figure 13. A high-level crawl of the .us domain (255 nodes limit) (with Maltego Tungsten)

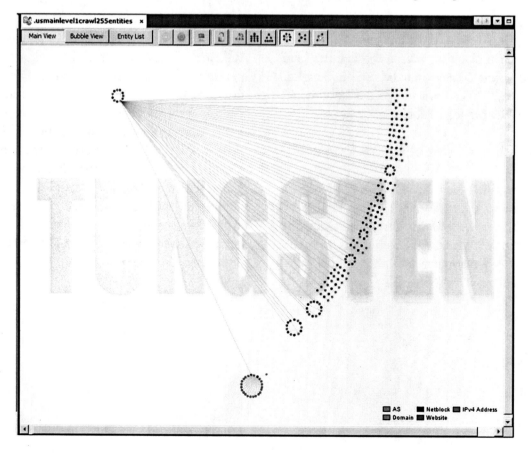

Figure 14. The .us node and cluster (255 records limit) (with Maltego Tungsten)

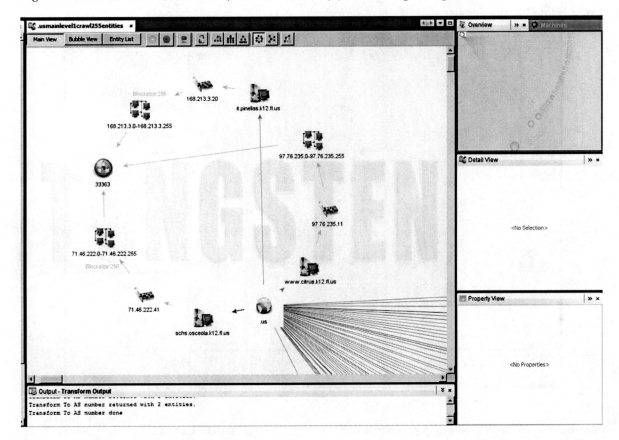

A 10,000 records search of the fresh.amazon. com site shows a range of resources and ties.

The fresh.amazon.com site may be visualized using a dynamic bubble view which simulates 3D. As such, such data extractions offer a summary view of the website and offers some promising nodes for further exploration. The various nodes suggest new ways to branch off in search of more related information for an enriched http network extraction.

For example, a researcher may put ".ru" in the search box to find all Russian Federation-domain nodes from the set and conduct various transforms or analyses of that subset. It may be possible to look at related images.

If online documents related to a site are of interest, then it's possible to run a document search linked to a particular website. In this case, AmazonFresh.com was used for a document search. (If this wasn't so specified, it would have resulted in plenty of documents about the Amazonian jungle.)

NCapture and NVivo

During the analysis, it was discovered that the AmazonFresh endeavor included a Twitter account @AmazonFresh (https://twitter.com/AmazonFresh). The account, at the time of the data extraction, had 469 Tweets, 1,915 following, and 3,243 followers. NCapture was used to extract all 469 Tweets from the Twitter stream. Those Tweets were pulled into NVivo. Figure 22, "NCapture Data of @AmazonFresh Tweets (with NVivo)" shows the NVivo workspace with the downloaded

Figure 15. amazon.com with a side branch for fresh.amazon.com (structured view) (10,000 records limit) (with Maltego Tungsten)

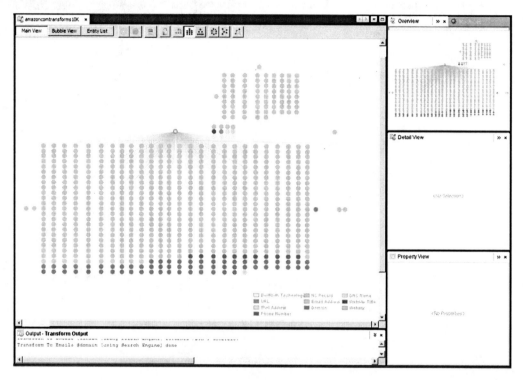

Figure 16. A close-in view of fresh.amazon.com (10,000 records limit) (with Maltego Tungsten)

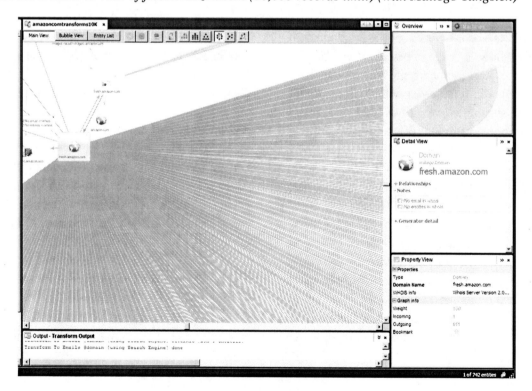

Figure 17. fresh.amazon.com in zoomed-out dynamic bubble view (with Maltego Tungsten)

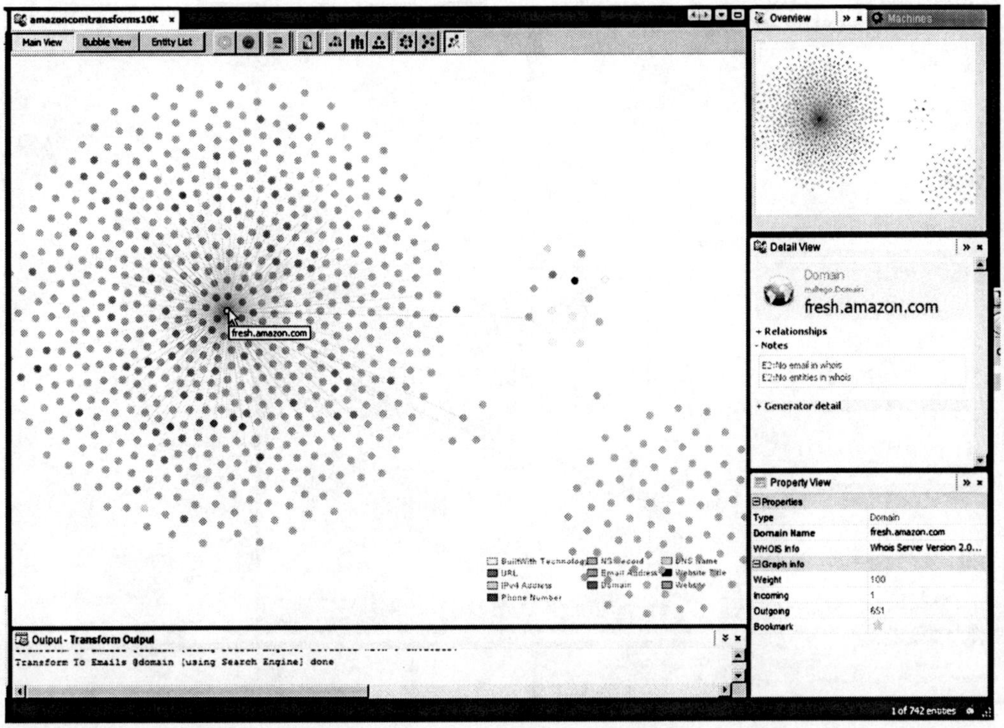

Figure 18. fresh.amazon.com zoomed-in dynamic bubble view (10,000 records) (with Maltego Tungsten)

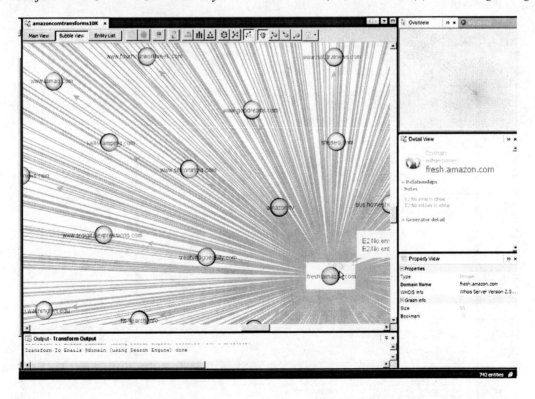

Figure 19. .ru subgroups in fresh.amazon.com (with Maltego Tungsten)

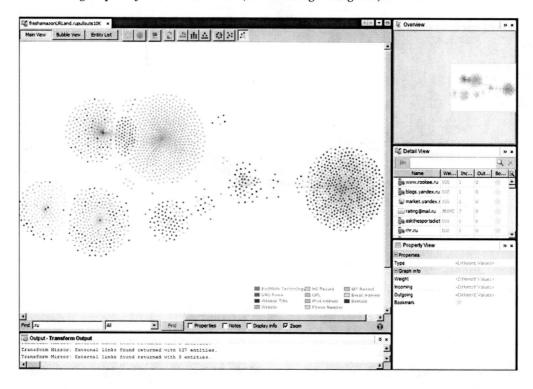

Figure 20. Setting parameters for "AmazonFresh.com" phrase ties to online documents of interest (with Maltego Tungsten)

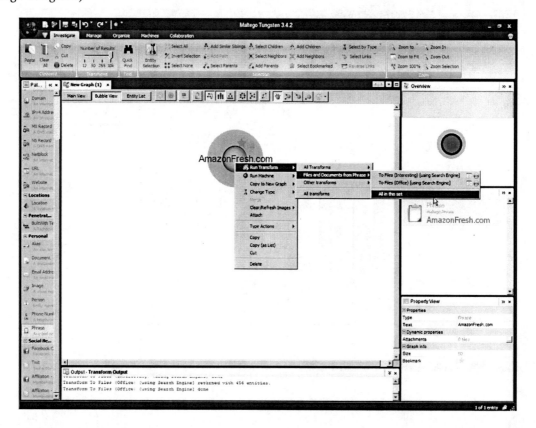

Figure 21. Results of document crawl for" AmazonFresh.com" phrase on Web (with Maltego Tungsten)

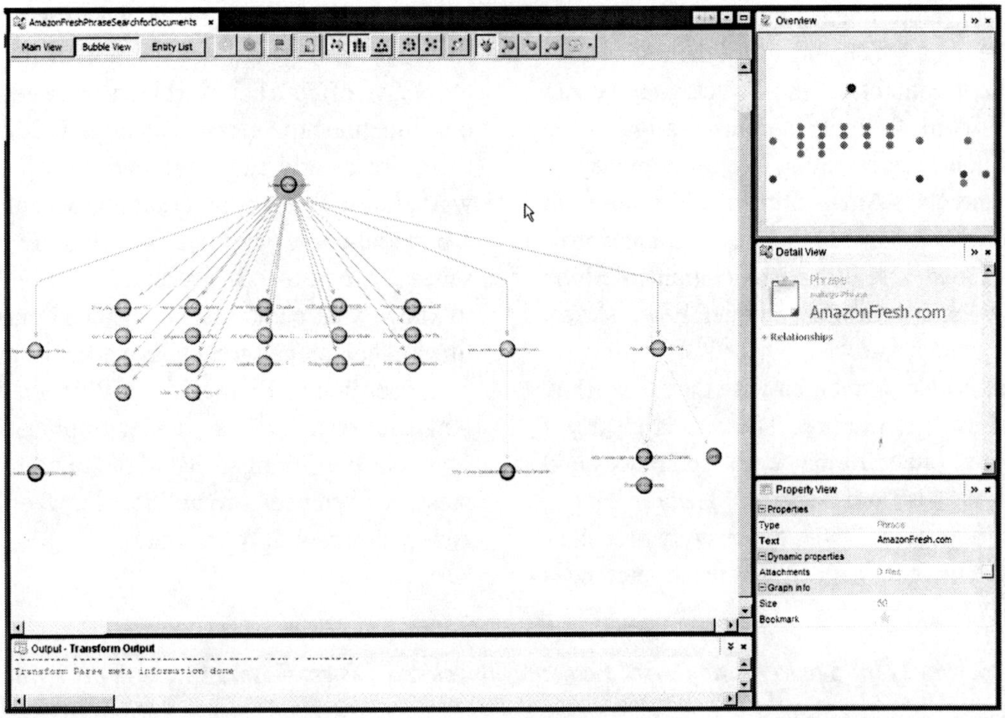

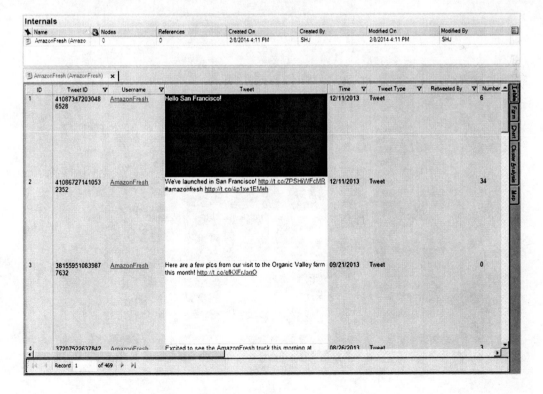

Figure 22. NCapture data of @AmazonFresh tweets (with NVivo)

Tweets. In this case, n = all Tweets, but as the numbers of microblogged messages gets higher, NCapture does not capture all of them.

The text contents of the Tweets may be run through word frequency counts. Figure 23, "Word Cloud Representing Word Frequency of Related Tweets @AmazonFresh on Twitter (with NVivo)," shows some of the predominant words. A word cloud is a data visualization in which words which appear more frequently are shown in larger typeface.

There is clear elicitation with the feedback@ amazonfresh information. The site is clearly a commercial one with the "com" references and mention of "ads" and "service." There is a lot of support for good will with the customers such as with the "customer happy". There are references

to particular specialties such as salmon, cheese, chicken, produce, and fruits. There is reference to "sorry" and "love."

NVivo offers a bar chart view of Tweets based on a timeline broken out by quarter. By this view, there are clearly two time periods when there was a lot of Tweet activity on this account (with a bimodal curve), but with a dwindling of messages in the near-term present. It may be helpful to know what occurrences happened during the times of heightened activity as well as during lulls.

According to Figure 25, "NVivo View of @ AmazonFresh Tweets in Geographical Space (with NVivo)," a majority of the microblogging messages occurred around Seattle, where AmazonFresh was first rolled out.

Figure 23. Word cloud representing word frequency of related Tweets @AmazonFresh on Twitter (with NVivo)

Figure 24. NVivo view of @AmazonFresh Tweets over time (with NCapture and NVivo)

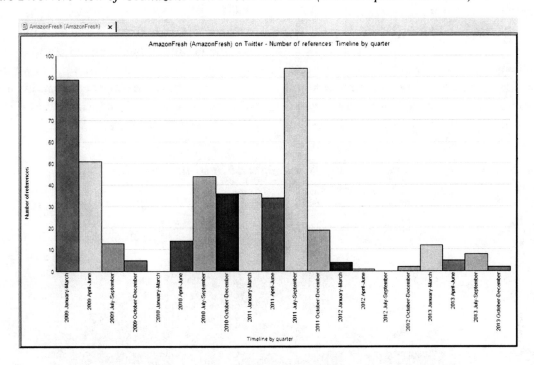

Figure 25. NVivo view of @AmazonFresh Tweets in geographical space (with NVivo)

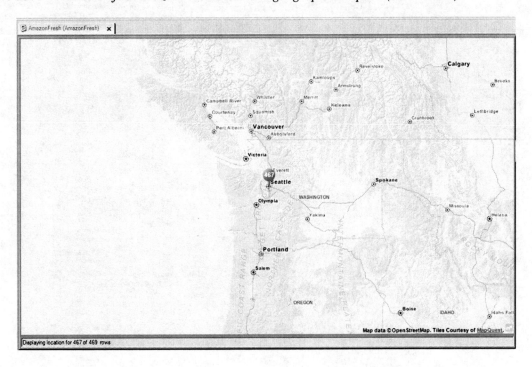

Network Overview, Discovery, and Exploration for Excel (NodeXL)

Microblogging sites are a popular way to create "buzz" for a business. To understand how much support @AmazonFresh might have on its Twitter account, it would be important to get a sense of the size of its "ego neighborhood." Here, the focal node @AmazonFresh would be at the center, and the network would only go out one-degree to its direct ties or "alters" (both following and followers). The parameters for this data extraction involved an unlimited one-degree crawl for the nearest-neighbor network.

Figure 26. A one-degree social network of @AmazonFresh on Twitter (with NodeXL)

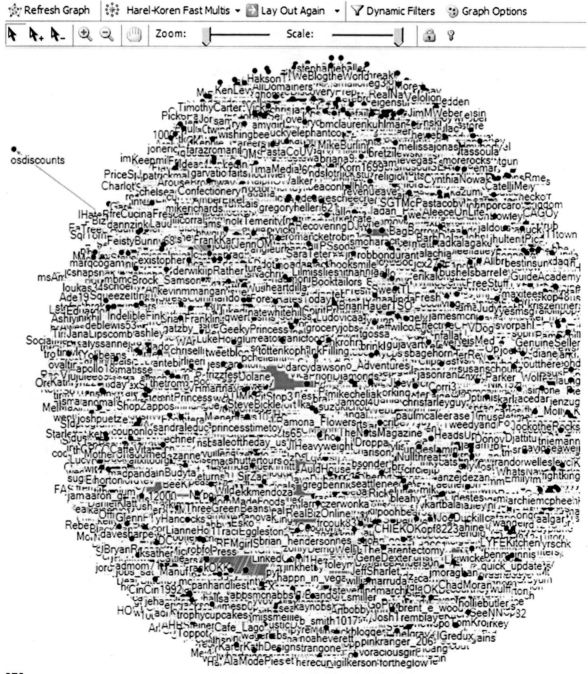

The results of this @AmazonFresh ego neighborhood was depicted using the Harel-Koren Fast Multiscale layout algorithm with all the vertices listed. This data extraction found 4,231 direct nodes linked to @AmazonFresh. Many of the names read like common individual accounts, and there are also others that are commercial-linked accounts. In this mix, there may well be accounts of humans, robots (automated Tweeters), as well as cyborgs (accounts with both human and automated information dissemination through microblogging). It would be easy to thin out the network to find those with the highest in-degree (influence) to find other accounts to map and explore.

Another way to extract information from social media is to capture content network information on social content sharing sites. To get a sense of the public mental associations linked to Amazon, a related tags network crawl was conducted on the Flickr content sharing site (images and video). A search of "AmazonFresh" and variations of that did not result in any related tags, so the author went with "Amazon". This related tags network showed a lot of references to various locales and nature but no clusters (of the 13 related tags ones) that apparently dealt with the commercial entity (the company).

The graph metrics for this network showed 738 nodes or vertices linked to "Amazon," and the co-occurrence of quite a few words that were used in relation to "Amazon" in the tagging of the digital objects put into this repository.

There were videos linked to "AmazonFresh" on YouTube. To capture a sense of the various types of videos linked to this business, there was a capture of the video network for "AmazonFresh" based on a two-degree crawl. Sample imagery was captured as well.

Table 1. Graph metrics for a one-degree social network of @AmazonFresh on Twitter (with NodeXL)

Graph Metric	Value
Graph Type	Directed
Vertices	4231
Unique Edges	5157
Edges With Duplicates	0
Total Edges	5157
Self-Loops	0
Reciprocated Vertex Pair Ratio	0.219148936
Reciprocated Edge Ratio	0.359511344
Connected Components	1
Single-Vertex Connected Components	0
Maximum Vertices in a Connected Component	4231
Maximum Edges in a Connected Component	5157
Maximum Geodesic Distance (Diameter)	2
Average Geodesic Distance	1.999055
Graph Density	0.000288147
Modularity	Not Applicable
NodeXL Version	1.0.1.251

Figure 27. A related tags network of Amazon on Flickr (with NodeXL)

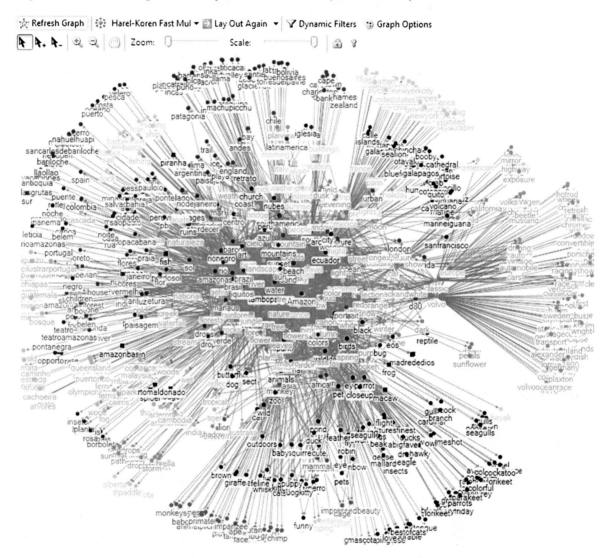

The graph depicted is based on the force-based Fruchterman-Reingold layout algorithm. There were 15 clusters of videos related to AmazonFresh. Four hundred and ninety six separate videos were identified. There were 17,407 unique edges or linkages, which suggests a high level of connectivity.

The images linked to this video network may be analyzed visually to see if there are particular themes. As such, this looks like pretty typical imagery. These clusters may be partitioned for easier analysis of the images.

It is also possible to extract #hashtag conversations about #AmazonFresh through Twitter. This captures not only the most recent microblogging messages about #AmazonFresh but also the names of those accounts engaged in the conversation, the time of the Tweet, the time zone of the account, and other data that may be helpful for those trying to understand what is being said and by whom. (A rough estimate of the location of the communications may be done by looking at the Dynamic Filters and the time zone (listed as Coordinated

Table 2. Graph metrics of a related tags network of Amazon on Flickr (with NodeXL)

Graph Metric	Value
Graph Type	Directed
Vertices	738
Unique Edges	2497
Edges With Duplicates	0
Total Edges	2497
Self-Loops	0
Reciprocated Vertex Pair Ratio	0.039117769
Reciprocated Edge Ratio	0.075290348
Connected Components	1
Single-Vertex Connected Components	0
Maximum Vertices in a Connected Component	738
Maximum Edges in a Connected Component	2497
Maximum Geodesic Distance (Diameter)	4
Average Geodesic Distance	3.228105
Graph Density	0.004590867
Modularity	Not Applicable
NodeXL Version	1.0.1.251

Universal Time / UTC) and offsetting that to look at the various regions of the world that may be engaging in particular messaging. (See Figure 31.)

Based on the Twitter API, only Tweets from the past week were included in the data extraction. In the past week (in February 2014), there were 41 accounts discussion #AmazonFresh and labeling their microblogged messages as such. There were some responses to others communications, which explains the higher level of edges (links).

The dynamic filter feature in NodeXL enables different visualizations of the graph by adjusting various sliders for a number of different variables. The screenshot in Figure 31 only highlights some of the options. Every variable captured for a particular data set may be adjusted for differing levels of information.

The prior data extractions show some functionalities of enriched Web network analysis through the use of three tools. The sequence actually could work in any number of directions, for it was presented as a general sequence from high-level to node-level for simplicity.

Delimitations

Web structure mining involves the extraction of limited amounts of information from the Web and extracting a structure from that data based on apparent interrelationships. The contents themselves may not have an obvious unifying structure prior, and the contents themselves tend to be highly diverse and heterogeneous. Based on these structures, researchers make inferences

Figure 28. A video network of AmazonFresh on YouTube (with NodeXL)

about how various organizational entities interact and the way information moves through the structures. The original extractions are necessarily partial and incomplete. Even in cases where n = all (in "big data" scenarios), the outputs from the various technologies involve data reduction and summarization; in every summarization context, data is lost. Given such limits, there may be possible sampling biases (Serrano, Maguitman, Boguñá, Fortunato, & Vespignani, 2007). While enrichment should enhance the analysis of the http network, the researcher has to decide what to

explore further (in terms of which internal nodes and which clusters, for example). Networks are often affected by external and internal events; as such, the context of networks should be studied for fuller understandings.

The method shown here uses publicly available software tools—both proprietary and open-source. Maltego Tungsten and NVivo are proprietary tools, and NodeXL is an open-source add-on to Microsoft Excel. These data extractions and network maps require some manual-intensive work and computational expense; the learning curve

Table 3. Graph metrics for a video network of AmazonFresh on YouTube (with NodeXL)

Graph Metric	Value
Graph Type	Undirected
Vertices	496
Unique Edges	17407
Edges With Duplicates	54
Total Edges	17461
Self-Loops	0
Reciprocated Vertex Pair Ratio	Not Applicable
Reciprocated Edge Ratio	Not Applicable
Connected Components	15
Single-Vertex Connected Components	0
Maximum Vertices in a Connected Component	142
Maximum Edges in a Connected Component	10012
Maximum Geodesic Distance (Diameter)	1
Average Geodesic Distance	0.985974
Graph Density	0.142016944
Modularity	Not Applicable
NodeXL Version	1.0.1.251

Table 4. Graph metrics around the online chatter about #AmazonFresh through a hashtag search on Twitter (with NodeXL)

Graph Type	Directed
Vertices	41
Unique Edges	74
Edges With Duplicates	30
Total Edges	104
Self-Loops	12
Reciprocated Vertex Pair Ratio	0.238095238
Reciprocated Edge Ratio	0.384615385
Connected Components	12
Single-Vertex Connected Components	6
Maximum Vertices in a Connected Component	25
Maximum Edges in a Connected Component	83
Maximum Geodesic Distance (Diameter)	5
Average Geodesic Distance	2.156682
Graph Density	0.047560976
Modularity	Not Applicable
NodeXL Version	1.0.1.251

Figure 29. A video network of AmazonFresh on YouTube (with vertex imagery) (with NodeXL)

is high for this work as well. Structure mining, a form of web mining, captures entities and relationships, but these structures do not reveal the contents (transmissible elements like information) moving through the networks. These captures are also static; they are non-dynamic (failing often to capture changes over time except for the discrete time phases or intervals within the time span of the initial capture). The concept of enrichment here refers to the value-added element of detailed node-level exploration made possible by all three tools. In combination, the tools offer the capability of high-level macro analysis (such as nation-state domains) all the way to single web page or single-social-network-account analysis.

Figure 30. Online chatter about #AmazonFresh through a hashtag search on Twitter (with NodeXL)

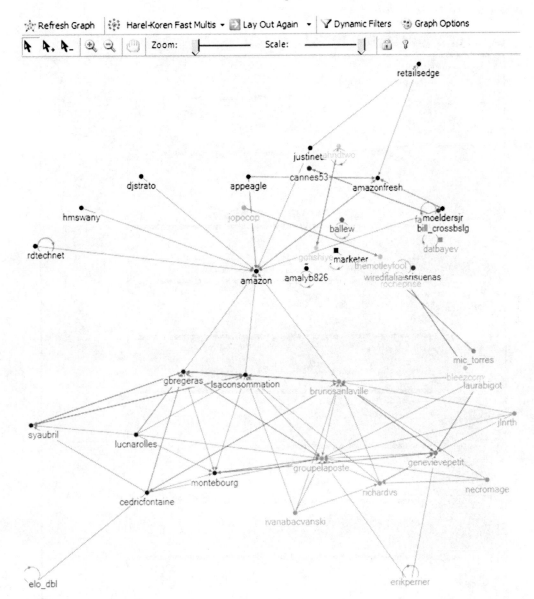

FUTURE RESEARCH DIRECTIONS

This research approach has application for a variety of fields. Researchers are examining patterns of connections and communications to understand certain types of networks—to understand if there may be revelatory "tells" of organizations that are designed for certain functions (like terrorism). Some organizational researchers have been pursuing cultural and regional differences between online interaction styles; others are studying organizational efficiencies. There are any number of types of cases that may be explored.

Figure 31. A partial dynamic filter view of the online chatter about #AmazonFresh through a hashtag search on Twitter (with NodeXL)

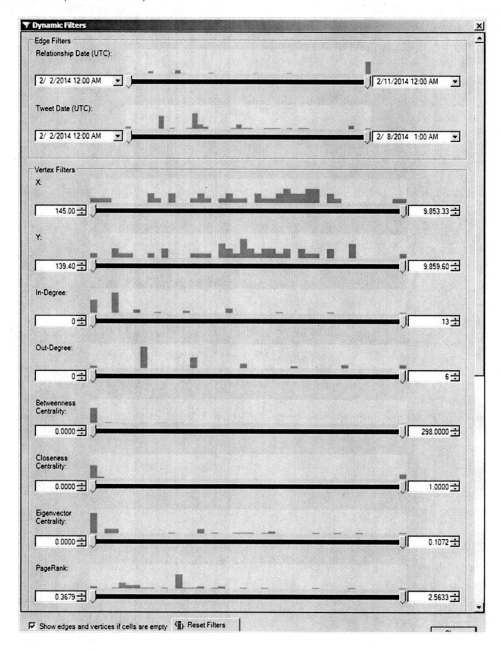

CONCLUSION

Essentially, this chapter provides a method to "chain" publicly available proprietary and free and open-source tools to acquire http networks broadly and then to dig more deeply into various nodes for multimodal data. At the heart of these data extractions are networks, which have been used in a variety of ways and at various levels: transnational http networks, national http networks, site-level http networks, Twitter account extractions and textual visualizations, Twitter account ego neighborhoods, related tags networks, video networks, and hashtag conversations based on a topic of interest. The general workflow was from the web network structure at a broadscale level down to enriched node-level analyses. With adjustments for unique research needs, it is possible to achieve sufficient expressiveness for a variety of analytical applications. Certainly, other tools may be swapped out for certain technologies in this chain. There are cloud tools available that may stand in for some of these functionalities. There are open-source tools which allow mapping of online networks with literally billions of nodes and edges, or peta-scale (a factor of 10^{15}) graphs.

Someday, it may be possible to complement such Web networks with hidden Web data (dynamically captured information). Non-English social media platforms may be integrated and mappable. This work is already fairly easily scalable with open-source tools to billions of nodes and edges.

REFERENCES

Caldarelli, G., Marchetti, R., & Pietronero, L. (2000). The fractal properties of internet. *Europhysics Letters*, 1 – 6.

Gastner, M. T., & Newman, M. E. J. (2006). The spatial structure of networks. *The European Physical Journal B*, *49*(2), 247–252. doi:10.1140/epjb/e2006-00046-8

Gibbons, D. E. (2004). Network structure and innovation ambiguity effects on diffusion in dynamic organizational fields. *Academy of Management Journal*, *47*(6), 938–951. doi:10.2307/20159633

Jackson, M. H. (1997). Assessing the structure of communication on the World Wide Web. [Wiley Library.]. *Journal of Computer-Mediated Communication*, *3*(1). doi:10.1111/j.1083-6101.1997.tb00063.x

Kleftodimos, A., & Evangelidis, G. (2013). An overview of Web mining in education. In *Proceedings of PCI 2013*. Thessaloniki, Greece: PCI. doi:10.1145/2491845.2491863

Kunegis, J., & Preusse, J. (2012). Fairness on the web: Alternatives to the power law. In *Proceedings of WebSci 2012*. Evanston, IL: WebSci.

Lusher, D. & Ackland, R. (2009). A relational hyperlink analysis of an online social movement. *Journal of Social Structure.*

Mika, P. (2007). Evaluation of web-based social network extraction. In *Mika's Social Networks and the Semantic Web*. New York: Springer Link.

Park, H. W. (2003). Hyperlink network analysis: A new method for the study of social structure on the Web. *Connections*, *25*(1), 49–61.

Saxenian, A. (1996). Regional advantage: Culture and competition in silicon valley and route 128. Cambridge, MA: Harvard University Press.

Serrano, M.A., Maguitman, A., Boguñá, M., Fortunato, S., & Vespignani, A. (2007). Decoding the structure of the WWW: A comparative analysis of web crawls. *ACM Transactions on the Web*, *1*(2), 10:1 – 10:25.

KEY TERMS AND DEFINITIONS

Document: An electronic record like an article, white paper, slide deck, or other object (structured on the conventions of a discrete piece of information).

Electronic Social Network Analysis: The study of social networks which are found on social media platforms, email systems, learning management systems, and other spaces on the World Wide Web.

Graph: A two-dimensional data visualization.

Hyperlink Network Analysis: The study of the structures formed by hyperlinked pages on the Web to understand social dynamics and other phenomena.

Image: A visual representation.

Link (Edge): A tie or line connector.

Machine: A term from Maltego Tungsten to define a series of data extractions from the WWW.

Node: An entity represented usually as an annotated circle or dot.

Node-Link Diagram: A two-dimensional figure showing entities and relationships.

Penetration Testing Tool: A software tool used to assess the penetrability or vulnerabilities of a network.

Scalability: The ability to ramp up or down in size or scale.

Social Computing: The study of socio-technical systems and human behaviors within those systems.

Social Network Analysis (SNA): The study of human interactions in groups.

Substructure: The underlying edifice or support.

Transform: A term from Maltego Tungsten to define the reconceptualization of one type of data into another.

Uniform Resource Locator (URL): A text string indicating particular locations on the WWW.

Web Network: An http network of related web pages.

Web Scale: A global macro-scale view of the Web.

Web Structure Mining: Extraction of data and information from various structures on the Web, including http networks.

Section 4
Data Acquisition and Extraction from Social Media Platforms

The congregation of billions of people around the world on various social media sites—social networking sites, social media platforms, content-sharing sites, microblogging sites, Web logs, wikis, immersive online games, virtual worlds, and others—has provided a lot of potential for social computational, online ethnography, and other types of research. The thought is that understanding electronic presences may illuminate the cyber-physical confluence—or the reality of people's lives in physical space. While some suggest that electronic communications have changed how people interact and socialize, many also observe that there are continuing patterns of social relations from the real to the virtual. To conduct such research, researchers use a variety of software tools to extract information from various sites and socio-technical spaces and then to visualize and analyze the data. Big data analysis advancements suggest that there may well be more effective ways of extrapolating value from this information; these new methods may well upend current methods of hypothesis-based research and enable nearly pure discovery based on correlations.

Chapter 12
Trendy Avatars and Their Hair:
Studying a Symbolic Cultural Artifact with Multiple Qualitative Methods

Sara Steffes Hansen
University of Wisconsin Oshkosh, USA

ABSTRACT

This case study uses multiple qualitative methods to examine cultural meanings of virtual goods in a virtual world or Massively Multiplayer Online Game (MMOG) with consumer marketing promotions. Through participant observation, avatar hair emerged as a key virtual good. Symbolic displays in social interaction showed different meanings and uses for types of hair available to users, including high-status rare hair, and versions aligned with marketing promotions and real-world brands. Study of online artifacts examined user-generated content, such as user forums and machinima. The long interview method subsequently was employed to gather insight from users. Findings demonstrate how different data from these online methods provide rich meanings for avatar hair related to symbolic interactionism and self-presentation. Methods explore co-production among users, platform, and marketing efforts. Cultural meanings, user self-displays, and corporate influences related to avatar hair are presented. Avatar hair emerged as a status artifact that often revealed levels of social skills or wealth in this virtual culture, at times connected with marketing promotions relevant outside of the virtual world. Methodological implications are explored for avatar-based participation, artifacts from social networking and other technologies, and ethical approaches.

INTRODUCTION

Researchers of virtual culture often negotiate new technologies, changing human interactions, and real-world integrations. Increasingly, commercial influences exert impact via technology platforms or user preferences. These dynamics pose chal-lenges to applying proven research methods with new phenomenon while maintaining a strong ethical approach.

This chapter will demonstrate how qualitative methods with multiple technologies provide cultural insights through user data that extends within and, importantly, outside of a virtual world

DOI: 10.4018/978-1-4666-6493-7.ch012

or massively multiplayer online game (MMOG). Cultural meanings of virtual goods were explored in Virtual MTV (VMTV), which replicated the MTV network series of *Laguna Beach* and *The Hills*. This free-to-play virtual world also served as a marketing platform for MTV and other consumer brands inserted into user experiences and activities. The objectives for this chapter are to show how multiple qualitative methods leveraged technology to explore cultural meanings for hair as an important virtual good, and how the methods enhanced findings. In this case study, findings focus on the hair's cultural status, and at times, high monetary and social value. Given user interest in avatar hair, VMTV added different hairstyles in catalogs, contests, and marketing promotions – including versions from real-world brands like Garnier and MTV series.

Avatar hair is among other virtual goods that develop cultural meanings evident through symbolic interactionism (Blumer, 1969; Solomon, 1983) and self-presentation (Goffman, 1959). Exploration for this work started with these perspectives to examine virtual goods, at times related to real brands, from which avatar hair emerged as an important cultural artifact. Methods integrated the online and offline, virtual and real worlds, and user-generated content (UGC) in various technology platforms. Ethnographic methods included participant observation with a researcher as avatar to explore social and play activities, avatar displays, and related brand promotions. The participant-as-observer acted as a researcher (Babbie, 1992) in VMTV with light user interactions to understand culture with low social disruption (Ess & the AoIR Ethics Working Committee, 2002). Screenshots in VMTV sessions and related online research were captured and edited in Microsoft Word. Hand-written observational notes from sessions in VMTV and other platforms were typed into the word processing program following sessions, along with separate writings

about researcher emotions (Bernard, 1988; Neuman, 2000). Observational data showed symbols indicating social use values – situational or due to cultural norms (Lindlof, 1995) – for hair as an important artifact. The long interview method (McCracken, 1988) was used further to gather user insights to build upon observations. Seven phone interviews, based on requests via VMTV and social network sites (SNSs), were conducted and filed with audio software. Outside of VMTV, key data were gathered through text, photo, and video content (including hundreds of machinima videos on YouTube) on SNSs, discussion forums, MTV e-mail communication, and other online sources. As such, various technology platforms were used for data gathering and documenting.

Findings exhibit how different data points supported cultural meanings for avatar hair, with enhanced validity from various methods. Hair was required for avatar creation, and was part of impression formation. Avatar hair (rare versions were valued as high as $1,400) and other virtual goods impacted social interaction, sparked user demand for new hair types from VMTV, and related to marketing promotions. Findings show how commercial and user influences unpredictably determined cultural value for hair versions. Conclusions discuss cultural meaning development within the symbolic interaction framework, enabled through the use of proven methods that integrated and enabled virtual application of techniques and technologies.

BACKGROUND

Virtual goods, including avatar hair, may serve as symbols with varied cultural meanings that may be understood in ways users interact with others. Displayed on avatars, virtual goods demonstrate a form of self-presentation. These aspects are explored in terms of the literature for development of cultural meanings, and virtual research methods that can be applied to socialization in MMOG culture.

Virtual Goods as Symbols

In virtual worlds or MMOGs, users engage in activities and social interaction. The virtual space provides default, choice-based, and achievement options (such as winning a contest) for users to represent the self in avatar displays (appearance) and virtual goods (possessions like clothing, weapons, or other objects). Researchers in these virtual, social spaces have identified virtual goods that symbolize user status, wealth, game skill, or social circles (Boellstorff, 2008; Hansen, 2013; Lehdonvirta, Wilska, & Johnson, 2009; Ludlow & Wallace, 2007; Mantymaki & Salo, 2011; Martin, 2008; Taylor, 2006).

Ways that virtual goods transpire meanings among users align with the perspective of symbolic interactionism. Within this construct, users act toward objects and others based on understood meanings, which are changing continually in an interpretive process based on social interaction (Blumer, 1969). Symbols offer a primary way of sharing meanings and responding to interactions with others (Sandstrom, Martin, & Fine, 2006). These symbols may be used as self-presentation in which people "perform" with particular appearances or actions that may reflect certain situations and audiences (Goffman, 1959). Situational identities or social roles may be performed with virtual goods as symbols supporting user activities and goals.

In consumer culture, online and offline self-displays also may incorporate brands. Brands and goods convey symbolic meaning and individual identity (McCracken, 1988a) and help people perform social roles (Solomon, 1983). Self-displays may use conspicuous consumption to show individual identity and extend the self

(Belk, 1988). People develop relationships with brands (Fournier, 1998) and advertising (Ritson & Elliott, 1999) for social uses with symbolic qualities. Brands and goods, as symbols, allow individuals to create their own social realities.

Online, users may create self-displays as an avatar that acts as a social object influenced by co-developed meanings (Fine, 1993) and show virtual consumption without real possession (Schau & Gilly, 2003). However, such self-displays may relate to offline identity and impact immersion in the virtual environment (Burbules, 2004). Indeed, co-created online artifacts may be documented outside of the online space or offline (van Dijck, 2007). For example, machinima – or UGC videos made within MMOGs or video games – shows co-creation among users as well as corporate interests providing the online space and boundaries for users to produce them (Jenkins, 2006). Further, users may create idealized avatars in self-displays that they rate more favorably than their offline selves (Bessiere, Seay, & Kiesler, 2007). Attractive avatar self-displays have supported intimate self-disclosure and interpersonal distance compared to less-attractive avatars (Yee & Bailenson, 2007).

The symbolic interactionist view shows the process that users, as avatars, may use to construct meanings for virtual goods that may stem from interactions with others, consumer culture or brands, and virtual world influences. Further, in both the online and offline contexts, uses of goods and aspects of identity may connect in contrasting ways related to self-displays. This study explores research questions focused on this intersection of user, platform, and marketing or commercial influences in cultural meaning development. Particular emphasis lies in social interaction among these influences, within and outside of VMTV, and connections to user self-displays and social roles. Importantly, virtual methods help transcend meaning development within and outside of VMTV.

Virtual Methods for Exploring Symbolic Meanings

From the symbolic interactionist perspective, direct observation provides an advantage for studying the nature of meaning development (Bauman, 1984 [1977]; Blumer, 1969; Goffman, 1959: Prus, 1996). Also, based on the literature, ethnographic methods such as in-depth interviews offer insight related to forming and negotiating symbolic meanings for virtual goods and brands (McCracken, 1988a, 1988b). Qualitative methods aid online cultural exploration and allow a view of users creating their own realities and interacting with others through communication processes mediated in virtual worlds (Williams, Rice, & Rogers, 1988). An inherent challenge in mediated environments is "because reality is jointly created, and the more dominant forces play a larger role in their action, contradictions always exist in the social world" (Williams et al., 1988, p. 42). Explorations of varied MMOGs and online user environments often leverage ethnographic methods (Boellstorff, 2008; Hine, 2000; Markham, 1998; Miller & Slater, 2000; Taylor, 2006; Turkle, 1995).

Ethnography allows meaning to be situated within one or layered contexts. During observation, it is important to see behavior as symbolic action but while it is critical to understand the symbol of the action, it is important not to define the action purely by those meanings (Geertz, 1973). The symbolic observation and its conceptual meaning should be considered within large, complex interconnected structures to provide "think description" (Geertz, 1973, p. 10). This meaning should be explored in terms of what the symbol means for users in social value in specific situations and the broader culture (Lindlof, 1995).

Virtual ethnography inherently encounters virtual manifestations of activities and relationships that blur with other online spaces and offline life. Activities in virtual spaces cannot be viewed as separate from other aspects of daily life (Miller &

Slater, 2000; Markham, 1998). In a virtual world, users may feel activities and relationships blurred or connected with other virtual- and real-world aspects (Burbules, 2004). With technology, Hine (2000) describes two views of virtual interaction among users – social interaction of users in co-presence or real-time dialogue and text as a "temporarily shifted and packaged form of interaction" (p. 50). In a virtual world, users chatting, engaging in activities, or otherwise interacting would define the former, which is ephemeral and in the moment. In terms of text, user forums, messages, machinima, and other forms of UGC separate production and consumption, and offer later reference and availability for users in the virtual world or outside of it.

Study of virtual goods as symbolic artifacts, or within larger cultural artifacts, also may be explored through multiple ethnographic methods. Hine (2000, p. 55) suggests ethnographic immersion is less of a barrier to ethnographic strangeness – to see cultural practices without distortion or taking them for granted – and more of a key competence for reflexive exploration of uses, in-depth engagement and conversations with users, and "as a way to developing an enriched reading of the practices which lead to the production and consumption of Internet artifacts." Further, the Internet as artifact could relate to the virtual world, as well as other online spaces connected to it or its users that provide insight on symbolic and cultural meanings.

An important aspect for ethics in the online research arena is in how the ethnography is conducted. Researchers should make their roles clear as users conducting research (Babbie, 1992). However, light involvement in virtual world social interaction (Ess & the AoIR Ethics Working Committee, 2002) allows for less overt disruption to daily happenings among observed users. As well, with the aid of technology, Internet artifacts offer another means to capture observations (Hine, 2000), potentially less obtrusively, of user social interactions related to symbolic meanings.

METHODS WITHIN AND OUTSIDE OF VMTV

Multiple qualitative methods of participant observation, within and outside of VMTV, and long interviews of users explored the subject area based on the literature. Methods were enhanced through multiple uses of technology. The methods aimed to describe and understand VMTV culture in terms of symbolic meanings of avatar hair among virtual goods, which at times connected to real-world brands. Observations indicated avatar hair held important status in impression formation as symbolizing a new or high-status user formed through social interaction. Displays of social interaction within VMTV, and text artifacts in online and offline spaces related to this MMOG, provide further context for research exploration and findings.

Platform and Protocol Selection

VMTV's Virtual Hills / Laguna Beach was one of only a few MMOGs with virtual goods that also served as a marketing platform with real consumer brands in 2008. VMTV was free to play with a substantial user base of more than one million users ages 16-34 (Williamson, 2007). These users could explore the virtual streets, beaches, and gathering places seen in the popular *Laguna Beach* and *The Hills* TV series. Indeed, MTV promoted the virtual world through its programming and its platform partner, There.com. Users were 85% female, at an average age of 20 (Woodson, 2007). The 3D version of VMTV closed in 2009.

The Institutional Review Board approved research methods, supported through the literature, for use of online participant-as-observer (Babbie, 1992; Ess & the AoIR Ethics Working Committee, 2002) and offline long-interview protocols (McCracken, 1988b) for adults and minors. Though considered a public space for ethnographic study, email communication with information on the research project was sent to There.com and MTV leadership. Both organizations acknowledged the project with no requests made of the researcher.

Participant Observation: Outside of VMTV

The research presence for participant observation, conducted from March to September 2008, entailed study from outside of VMTV and within the virtual world as an avatar. From the outside, observation would start as a single researcher who watched *Laguna Beach* and *The Hills*, and entered VMTV. For example, the prevalence of VMTV promotions within the television series, as well as the MTV website, encouraged fans to experience a virtual way to live the MTV life. Watching the television series helped show integrations with VMTV and familiarity with the culture of the series.

Given the expected interactions with other users in VMTV, a website was created to provide information about the research project. This website described the purpose for the research, affiliation of the researcher, and background information about the researcher including a picture and email contact information. The website URL could easily be given to other users in VMTV conversations. Making my presence clear as a researcher supported the research method and ethics for study (Babbie, 1992; Ess & the AoIR Ethics Working Committee, 2002).

Further, the periphery of the virtual world included user forums specific to VMTV, SNS postings, and MTV email communication to users. Users shared personal and technical information on user forums and SNSs. Machinima videos – or short UGC films – made in VMTV were posted on YouTube and other SNSs. Users had many options to communicate beyond VMTV with other users and without the oversight of VMTV. Research involved viewing hundreds of social networking pages posted by users. Some sites were created just with representation of the user's avatar, with no pictures or references to the offline self. Internet searches and subsequent interviews suggested that many users created SNSs just for their avatars – to limit access of personal information, create online scrapbooks of VMTV activities, or separate a user's online and offline social circles. These web pages displayed pictures and videos of avatars partying at houses, performing in dance videos, acting in dramatic or humorous videos filmed in the virtual world, getting married, and engaging in random conversations. Studying the periphery of VMTV aided cultural understanding and references among users. These observations were recorded in hand-written notes and subsequently typed into a Microsoft Word document. Online text and images were documented and printed as hard copies.

Participant Observation: Within VMTV

Participant observation also entailed in-world sessions of "playing" in VMTV at various times of day to engage in virtual world exploration, activities, and user interactions. Entering VMTV started with users downloading the virtual world to a computer for free from the VMTV website, linked from the MTV website.

A promotional video on the website suggested that users could choose avatar features to look similar or different from their offline selves. At initial log in, users created a name and selected an avatar to start from several choices featuring different hairstyles, skin tones, and clothing. Immediately upon entry at the beach, changing billboards showed things to do in VMTV, including shopping from a catalog for clothing and gear. Avatar spa treatments were ready right at the beach, to change skin tone and body features, such as body build, eye size, and head shape. All avatars were the same height.

Of course, users could just start exploring the virtual world upon entry at the beach. As avatars, they could stroll along the boardwalk by the ocean, walk up to groups of players hanging out at the beach, sit on logs near a bonfire, or teleport to places like a cinema, skatepark, club, or lounge that replicated places seen in the network series. Happenings were presented at the main page and forums, which detailed events, contests, and announcements from staff and users.

As an avatar researcher, I was disembodied from my real-world persona. This disembodiment posed opportunities, in that I could be a casual player at times but there were also challenges in providing credibility and ethical presentation as a researcher in an environment with limited self-presentation options. I identified myself as a researcher early in conversations, engaging in text chat and social actions. Data stem from observations of activities, conversations with users, interactions with platform, and participation in branded promotional events and activities. Screenshots, which are commonly made by users – at any time an avatar may be subject to another users' camera and end up in a video on YouTube – were taken. An average of 50 screenshots an hour in VMTV observation and related online research were captured, then edited and documented in Microsoft Word. Hand-written notes also were taken during participant observation. Immediately after VMTV sessions, observations were written in a Microsoft Word document, at times reaching 10 single-spaced pages for one hour of play, with separate writings about researcher emotions from each session (Bernard, 1988; Neuman, 2000). Notes from researcher emotions included a reference to hair as an important virtual good within the first month of study, a virtual good that had not been anticipated:

So, hair is important too. Hair for my avatar conveys something just like clothes... I'm also aware of the VALUE or meanings that items have – the hair, the clothing, etc. – that is expressed in the forums in last playtime. Truly telling.

These notes also reference the issue of disembodiment and credibility. Disembodiment meant having to convey the self in proper displays as a researcher. Struggles included demonstrating the right type of online persona to project in honest and authentic terms, yet not threatening as a researcher or user well above the average age in VMTV. A researcher goal was to keep it light, and fun, in order to engage with others in an authentic way within the norms experienced in VMTV:

This is so time-consuming – each session requires screenshots, editing of screenshots, notes write-up, check of notes against screenshots... I'm trying to stay authentic and honest. This is so challenging in a virtual world that is all about appearance and I can't quite be one of them.

As a new user, research notes aimed to observe everything with fresh eyes that would grow accustomed to entry views with longevity in the virtual world. Technology aided new and ongoing observation in several key ways. An ongoing challenge was to experience VMTV as a user while taking time to make screenshots and hand-written notes. It would not work well for my avatar to stare blankly at other users for no apparent reason. At times, I could leave my avatar in a paused mode but this would impede conversation with others. This reality made it important to act as a user while taking notes, and allowing time for typing notes after a VMTV session in order to improve memory.

In my early sessions as a new user, or "newb," I watched stylized avatars in clubs and at the beach wearing clothes and hairstyles that were not available in the catalog. I chatted – via typed text that appeared above my avatar's head – with other users who directed me to the Galleria, an auction marketplace for stylized clothes and accessories. At the Galleria were thousands of virtual clothes, vehicles, and goods all for sale by users. Users could sell items they own or have designed personally as UGC for sale to others for a specific price and limited time. Using my MTV dollars or virtual currency – each user starts with some MTV dollars – I purchased a few items, including a hot pink summer top and black skinny jeans. Forum postings included designers promoting their avatar clothing lines to users looking for specific items, including hair.

These stylized avatars or active users primarily wore clothes designed by others – personally created, exchanged, or purchased in Galleria. For example, in the interviews, Lars, an 18-year-old user from the U.K., and Tara, a 19-year-old user from the Eastern U.S., said they designed their own clothes to wear in the game, and also successfully sold designed clothes in the Galleria to make money. Most of these stylized or highly invested players, playing several hours a day for six months to a year or more, had valuable alpha hair – not from the catalog – to complete his or her avatar's look.

Long Interviews

Following the long-interview method (McCracken, 1988b), four steps of inquiry were used to develop the interview questionnaire for VMTV users for the broader research project. First, literature was reviewed regarding how cultural meanings may be developed and expressed related to theories for virtual spaces. Cultural categories were expanded based on this literature and researcher perspective. Then, the questions were designed based on those categories with intent for users' open responses to describe experiences in their own terms. After the interviews, data were analyzed through a five-stage approach (McCracken, 1988b). Based on observations, interview questions regarding identity and self-presentation (Table 1) included discussion of avatar hair.

Requests for telephone interviews were made through VMTV interactions and SNSs. Introductions of the researcher and the research project were aided through the website. Consent forms were sent and signed via email for users 18 years of age or older. For the one minor interviewed, an assent form was required from her and a consent form from her parent, also obtained via email. Telephone verification also was made with the minor's parent to ensure consent. The interviews lasted 90 minutes to two hours. Participants were informed of the time frame and recording of the interview, and were paid $25. Each interview was recorded through a headset connected to a laptop computer running Audacity audio software. The audio files were transcribed, each averaging about 26 single-spaced pages.

After three months of participant observation, seven users – three males and four females – were interviewed as a convenience sample. Participant observation continued during the interview time frame for another three months. Interviewees included one casual user and six serious users who were active in VMTV several times a week or daily for a six-month period or longer. Participants were 14 to 30 years of age, living in different regions of the United States, and Asia and the United Kingdom. Pseudonyms were assigned to all interviewees.

Data Analysis

Ethnographic and interview data were analyzed using the five-stage analysis of the long-interview method, based on reviewed literature and related experiences for the research focus (McCracken, 1988b). The five stages of analyses demand ethnographic observations and interview utterances listed as independent items. The five stages of analysis are: 1) treat each data item independent of other items; 2) develop observations by themselves then aligned with other findings and then per literature review; 3) examine connections between second-level observations, considering literature and culture review; 4) scrutinize this collective form to determine inter-theme consistency and contradiction; and 5) use patterns and themes displayed across findings into a final form of analysis (McCracken, 1988b).

Observations and utterances (data items) were color-coded for pertinence to questions in the Microsoft Word transcripts and documents. Highlighted items were extended for implications and possibilities with additional color-coding. During the third stage, items were expanded upon in comparison to other observations, considered separately from the transcript, and entered into an Excel spreadsheet. Highlighted items were further refined to outline themes in the fourth stage. These findings were joined to draw conclusions in the fifth stage. Patterns were sought related to the research questions and literature. Initial analyses

Table 1. Sample of interview questions regarding identity and self-presentation

Open-Ended Questions
In VMTV, how do you think other users view you?
Do you think about your avatar's "first impression"?
How do you decide to interact with other users?
Do any experiences in VMTV make you use objects, symbols, products or brands differently?
Tell me about your power or ability to control your experiences in VMTV and real life.

Note: This excerpt is from an extensive protocol for long interviews.

showed avatar hair as a virtual good with significant meaning that differed across versions, evident through social interaction and, at times, connected to marketing promotions. These analyses created a compelling choice for specific study.

FINDINGS AMONG USERS AND VMTV CULTURE

Findings from ethnographic methods show how avatar hair developed cultural meanings in social interaction. Influences among users, VMTV, and marketing promotion also are considered in terms of contributing independently and in co-creation toward meaning formation.

Avatar Hair in Social Interaction

Different kinds of hair were available for male and female users to purchase in VMTV. First, anyone could buy hair from the VMTV catalog. And during Garnier's promotions, any user could get the free, featured hair at the Garnier Rock Your Style Lounge that changed every two weeks. One Sunkist-styled hair was available for participating in activities at the Sunkist Orange Nation Club.

Further, premium members, who paid a monthly subscription fee and had voice in play, could purchase unique hairstyles from the VMAX catalog. Users who created music videos or machinima for contests were awarded *Real World* hair (named for MTV's *The Real World* series), and users who purchased the second-season DVD of *The Hills* television series, received free *Hills* Hair. Users could trade hair they owned with other users. Alpha hair, styles available during the early months of VMTV, could only be purchased through trade with other users.

Virtual world forums, related online websites, and interviews described alpha hair – the only hair available exclusively through trade – as a valuable commodity, as were other rare goods. Alpha hair could cost up to 250,000 MTV dollars,

which in virtual currency was worth about $1,400, according to long-time users. Through social interaction, alpha hair could make users popular, offer social or monetary power, affect friendships, incite jealousy, and contribute to drama. In forum postings, users requested more alpha hair from MTV for winning contests, and asked where to attain it. Dana, a 23-year-old female from Asia, said her avatar looked unique because of rare hair, clothing, and handhelds, like a candy box, teddy bear, and camera, displayed on her "avie." Some attached a social stigma of being a newb to users without alpha hair. As Louise, a 14-year-old from the Eastern U.S. who led a clique of high-status users, explains – she had a couple versions of alpha hair – it brings popularity through notoriety and friends:

Louise: Well, I was cooler. A lot of people wanted to be friends with me just because I had it. That's about it. It's just hair. But people take it really seriously and it's worth a lot.

Interviewer: So, what's up with these people who want to be your friend because of hair?

Louise: Well, they are just greedy, I guess you could say, because they know it's rare, and know everyone is going to want to be their friend if they have it. They think they've been playing so long but really, you kind of have to earn the right to own it.... You have to know how to get the connections to get it, you have to know how to get the money for it, you have to know how to trade with it and you have to have the responsibility to not cry when other people want to be your friend because you have it. ...they have to know how to deal with the challenge I guess.

Hair was important for first impressions as users interacted socially, and aided leveling up points. Louise, Tara, and Dana note that social judgments were made based on clothes, hair, and premium membership. In addition to hair, social interaction and increasing status levels in VMTV can depend on depictions of virtual goods like clothing, handhelds, and cars, and real world payment of premium membership, which is always visible on avatars. As Dana said, looks convey status and a form of wealth:

This is one of the bad things... the players judge my avatar's looks. They try to look at me if I have something expensive on me or, if like, I am holding something [a rare handheld] that's worth something.

All of the interviewed users expressed social interaction with different people as a reason for playing in VMTV. All of the users said they acted like their real-world selves in VMTV, though most said they were more outgoing in the virtual world than they were in offline social experiences. Several cited avatar displays and actions as contributing to how they decided to go up and interact with others. Todd, a 21-year-old casual user from the Midwest, said he would tend to go up to individuals instead of groups to talk, and did not focus on appearances. The female players, who all played heavily at some point, said they were aware of displays but would talk to any user in a friendly way, except for Louise. The popular 14-year-old said she would not interact with newbs, which she defines as not having premium membership with voice or alpha hair, because "they ask stupid questions, like how do you get that hair?"

Ethan, an 18-year-old, from the Midwest, had alpha hair and rare sunglasses that became his trademark. His avatar had dark, somewhat spiky hair and average build, bearing no similarity to his offline self in terms of looks, but he says his personality is the same online and offline.

Interaction among users happens in various sorts of social circles. With many different users, places, and user motivations, social interaction may be with random people or familiar faces of highly involved users, casual users, or new users – with varying backgrounds, ages, and interests.

Users said that being an overweight avatar or playing with an avatar with different looks or status – such as not being a designer or not being a premium member – usually led to negative treatment. Two female users made their avatars overweight for one day and changed back because of the annoying behavior of other users that ensued.

Certain social circles also can render harsh treatment, such as if a social norm like premium membership for highly invested players is an expectation for interaction. Dana was a highly active player who bought and sold homes, clothes, and goods; won contests; and participated in game crews and many social circles. But prior to getting premium membership, while a group of friends did become "premies" with the voice feature, she said her friends then ignored her like a lower status user. While this behavior was hurtful, she said she could easily go to other circles and make better friendships. Most of the users expressed appreciation for the ignore feature, which allowed a user to shut out another if behavior was inappropriate or hurtful. Dana was very social online and offline. But at the time of the interview, she experienced her primary social interaction in VMTV:

There was just so much drama with my real life friends.... It's just more comfortable to be away at home, designing and playing the game and at the same time being social. Even just online... I think that the reason that I really like the game is because it's like a new person or like a new start, not really like a new person, but a new start.

Interactions in social circles determined the degree of hair, clothing, and premium membership – and potentially other user attributes – being status issues. In casual play, my avatar would not have all these status markers and yet would engage in social activities like playing cards, dancing in clubs, driving cars, and hanging out to talk. Christi, a 31-year-old, played several hours everyday while a stay-at-home mom in the Western U.S., and described herself as heavily playing in VMTV for several months. She was flattered to see her avatar nickname was recognized beyond her social circles in SNSs outside of VMTV, notoriety gained without alpha hair or premium membership. She did not express the same kinds of pressure to play for status markers, instead looking to create an avatar that fit her look and personality while enjoying free attributes of VMTV.

Christi: I think my avatar looks like a confident person…. Like she's got a suit on, looks like an FBI agent. I've always thought that FBI agents were cool.

Interviewer: So, what does she look like?

Christi: She's got a black suit top on, with a tie and then I have like black jeans on. And she's got the little aviator glasses. They look like cop glasses. And then like Garnier Fructis is doing these free hairstyles. That's another reason why I go on, to get the free hairstyle of the week, or whatever. Because I like the free stuff obviously [laugh]. I don't pay for anything on these sites… yeah, so she's got brown hair like mine, wavy. She looks, I think, mostly like me."

Changing out hair and avatar attributes is common. At times in VMTV, my avatar and others would quickly change hairstyles repeatedly for fun. Similarly, other users would rapidly change clothes or run around in their underwear. I found myself most comfortable playing when my hair looked like my real hair – and not overly big like some of the hairstyles. Christi said she never had blonde avatar hair because she would never have such hair in real life. Dana said her avatar looked and acted like her real-life self most days, the only difference being blonde avatar hair. Tara switched hair and eye color frequently too with some liberties, "My avatar has bigger boobs than me [laugh]. And a bigger butt, so yeah, you kind of do a little bit of 'you wished you looked like this.'" Louise, who dresses "punky" in VMTV

but usually in a T-shirt and jeans in real life, finds the same effect, "… I wish I had the body that my avatar has and I wish that I had the clothing that I have in the game as clothing that I have in the real world. People don't realize they do it but they do it anyhow."

Impacts of Marketing Promotions

The popularity of alpha hair happened because users wanted different, rare avatar hair prior to other alternatives, which increasingly upped the value of alpha hair and perhaps impacted other forms of hair that followed from VMTV. Some users were told about a technical glitch through which they could acquire alpha hair. All of the other hair had been promoted by Garnier, for free; Sunkist, as one reward of many for creating pictures or machinima; and VMTV or an MTV series, for uploading a video, getting premium membership, or buying a DVD.

During Garnier's promotion, its presence on the VMTV main page featured the promotion every other week of new hairstyles – short, long, wavy, or full hairstyles in different colors. Users could teleport to Garnier's Rock Your Style Lounge from the main page and advertisements on the streets of VMTV, as I experienced in my many visits for newly released Garnier hairstyles:

I teleport to a few different places, ending at Laguna Cinema. From there I go to MTV Central to check out the Garnier Fructis Rock Your Style (RYS) Lounge, which I explored last week. The page has been updated in the "Current Hairstyle" section to include new his and hers hairstyles in two avatar headshots. It reads "Garnier The Perfect Body Blonde" underneath the stylish female avatar with big light blonde wavy hair and "Garnier Shaped and Flashy Blonde" underneath the stylish male blonde avatar with spiked multi-blonde textured hair. Beside the pictures, it reads: "Garnier Fructis is here to rock your virtual style! Get Garnier Shaped & Flashy Brown and Garnier

The Perfect Body Blonde hairstyle now! Be sure to check back often for the latest styles only from Garnier Fructis! Click here to go there now!"

So, I click and I'm transported to the bright green and yellow-fruit Garnier Fructis RYS Lounge. I enter and walk past the entry area and club bar with the backdrop of huge larger-than-life advertising pictures of human – not avatar – models displaying great hairstyles. In a corner of the lounge I see a handful of female players, many of which have the same big blonde hairstyle as seen in the promo. Three girls have the blonde hairstyle. One is in her underwear – white bra and underpants cover her – and she is getting asked how she got her hair from another stylized female with big dark red wavy hair who wants the blonde hair. This female is wearing a pink tank top with a heart on the top of her chest, with her tummy bare. Her tight cropped pants look like pink camouflage and she's got on pink and white athletic shoes and carries a blue cellphone. "when does the blonde come out" she asks, to which the blonde in underwear says "u press get the hair and it comes out." The redhead replies "I did but it won't let em."

These two females are standing in front of the Garnier Fructis display for the avatar hair. The display includes the same billboard type sign I had seen outside of the Refresh Spa last week, touting "Get the latest hairstyle try Garnier Fructis now!"

New hairstyle excitement in promotional events in the Garnier lounge has been documented in machinima on YouTube. And VMTV forums talk about Garnier hair by users who get paid virtual currency to promote the brand. Dana worked on a Garnier promotion crew, enjoying perks of getting the new hairstyle a week ahead of release. Usually Dana wore a *Real World* Hair, a "beautiful" hair she saw on other female players worth 20,000 MTV dollars because it was a prize for winning machinima contests. She said she stocked up on

the free Garnier hair because it was destined to be valuable someday. She sold her alpha hair because she did not think it looked "really nice" and admitted to liking Garnier hair, which she sometimes wears instead of her usual hair, saying:

Some of the guys would tease me about it, saying 'you're a premie [premium member], why are you wearing Garnier hair? It looks ugly.' And then I would … say I am a promoter of Garnier. I have to wear it.

Garnier hair is free, so its availability appeared to limit its status value at the time. As Tara explained, this hair may symbolize a newb. Again, it depends on user social circles that determine the value of the hair and its accompanying status. Tara said:

… I actually liked one of those hairstyles. And sometimes I wore it and people would say 'eee-www you look like a newb' and I'm like 'so what's your point, shut up.' Other people, when you're first on game, you know, you have to buy hair and Garnier hair is free because it's a promotional thing. People will automatically well… I think they've made a lot better hair… People, generally if they're wearing that hair [from Garnier], people consider them a newb.

The brand of Garnier, simply as a brand in world, was not of appeal to Louise. She said she did not like game advertising, "I haven't done anything with Garnier, and I'm not very active in supporting the brands like that. Most people are because they get free things out of it." Tara is aware of MTV tactics to encourage player interaction for a coveted prize:

You can buy Season Two to get Hills hair. But Real World Hair, they originally had it as a prize for the first video competition that they had… so like if you submitted a video you got a hair. … So it made people more active in game. Which was great promotional wise but now I think the big thing with the Real World Hair is that only the people that are premium can purchase it now.

In the Rock Your Style Lounge, VMTV promotions, and e-mail advertisements, users were encouraged to click for information about creating desired hairstyles for their offline selves. Calls to action to find out how to get styling tips directed users to reach the Garnier website with ideas for creating different hairstyles real world using Garnier Fructis products.

One of the users, who also worked as a staff member for events, noted others discussed purchasing Garnier products. Dana said commercials she saw in the Asia media markets advertised Garnier, with strong connections for her:

I got to watch this [television] commercial by Garnier. And I was like, oh my gosh, it's the brand that VMTV is promoting. So, in a way, constantly I remember Garnier.

CULTURAL MEANINGS AND METHODOLOGICAL ISSUES

Meanings of virtual goods, at times displayed with real-world consumer brands, developed in a co-created way among users, the virtual world platform, and marketers. The symbolic interactionism perspective helps show co-creation among these forces through social practices and interaction. Avatar hair emerges as an exemplary artifact to demonstrate both the development of cultural meanings, and ways that methods reveal values through social interaction.

Hair as Artifact with Cultural Meanings

Avatar hair is examined as one virtual good that serves as an important cultural artifact relevant to every user – in the sense that all avatars had hair.

First, as a cultural artifact, avatar hair is considered in terms of cultural meanings. Secondly, influences that shape meaning evolution are viewed through social interaction among users, and via the VMTV platform and its commercial marketing.

- **Cultural Meanings:** As with other virtual goods, hair culturally conveys status (McCracken, 1988a) through VMTV knowledge, skills, and, at times, money, necessary to acquire it. On two ends of the continuum, default hair provided for a new user required no knowledge or skills, while highly prized alpha hair conveyed instant popularity because of its rarity. In between these extremes is free Garnier hair, and versions requiring payment through the VMTV catalog or offline purchases. These various hair types saw value influenced through VMTV-determined availability and pricing, yet cultural value evolved through social uses and interactions among users (Solomon, 1983).

The type of hair itself was not enough to attain high status. As Louise noted, a user must know how to be responsible with high-status hair and its social implications due to multiple facets of social circles, market values, money, user goals, and skills (Geertz, 1973). In other words, alpha hair possession resulted from interpersonal and VMTV skills dependent ultimately on savvy social interaction. Unlike a VMTV contest that could deem a value for a virtual good, users determined alpha hair value and desire. However, VMTV allowed its existence and enforced its rarity. Though users expressed desire for high-status hair in forums and other observations, interviewees showed that whether users pursued high-status or other forms of hair partly relied on social circles. This striking contrast shows the cultural value that different circles of users assigned to avatar appearance and hair symbolization lived out through their interactions.

- **User Self-Displays:** VMTV users attached status to virtual hair that impacted interactions based on avatar depictions as seen in other MMOGs (Boellstorff, 2008; Ludlow & Wallace, 2007; Taylor, 2006). Avatar hair extends the presentation of identity as a virtual good that may bring status based on social circles and VMTV influences, or as a product helpful in engaging in social interaction (Solomon, 1983). Interview data showed users choosing avatar hair to display the self in a blurred mix of embodiment and disembodiment (Burbules, 2004). Users did not refer to their avatars as separate identities but as versions of their offline selves. Users expressed more confidence, outgoing natures, and dynamic appearances as avatars, helped by possessing symbols to extend the self through hair and other goods (Belk, 1988).

Social interaction in VMTV and UGC beyond it showed user control to create situational identities. This entailed choosing different masks or presentations of self in conversation and UGC. With this control, as seen in Christi's "confident" self-display, avatars could serve as social objects with co-developed meanings from users and VMTV (Fine, 1993). Users expressed confidence and empowerment to interact more boldly in VMTV than offline – perhaps due to avatar features (Yee & Bailenson, 2007) and idealized selves (Bessiere et al., 2007). VMTV influenced identity portrayals in avatars via videos that encouraged users to look like one's offline self or someone different, and virtual billboards that depicted stylized avatars – not the starter avatars. Social roles, such as status through hair for Louise or other gained notoriety for Christi, could be expressed through disembodied and embodied selves on SNSs outside of VMTV. Portrayals on these sites conveyed identity markers, usually with an avatar focus but some offline attributes as well.

Users expressed important meanings of avatar hair in conversations, VMTV forums, personal website displays, SNSs, and related forums outside of VMTV. Users may be emboldened to remark about virtual goods to high-status users in out-of-VMTV situations. High-status users may set a tone in VMTV about status through virtual goods like hair, clothing, and premium membership. This status can affect other social groups through social norms – reinforced by VMTV and consumer brand marketing – even for less-status-conscious groups (McCracken, 1988a).

- **Platform and Commercial Marketing:** As alpha hair became a prized virtual good, other branded versions such as *Real World* and Garnier hair entered VMTV as marketing promotions. A response to user feedback in VMTV and related Internet forums, as well as increasing virtual currency value for some forms of hair, VMTV also offered exclusive new hair versions for users engaging in machinima creation or theatrical presentations of self. Marketing interactions further allowed users to gain hair, such as Sunkist's Orange Nation requiring machinima to attain virtual goods. Users responded by interacting with these brands and posting videos outside of VMTV on YouTube and other sites. Machinima offered a way for users to create content with the help of VMTV, yet on their own terms in choices of storyline, images, and text.

This UGC intersection is one in which corporate and consumer influences may reinforce or oppose each other (Jenkins, 2006). At times, the cultural meanings that form may be aligned with either of these influences. Generally, though, this shared response showed iterative and expanding values for a virtual good and related brand (Blumer, 1969) in UGC – notably allowing attainment without purchase but with wide ability for users to display the virtual branded good in and outside of VMTV (Schau & Gilly, 2003). Users participated in VMTV- and brand-sponsored contests, which led to social interaction with others in which brands were part of the UGC in conversation, artifact creation, and social uses.

Outcomes of these intersections are unpredictable due to social interaction influences. Users referenced this virtual hair tied to a real-world consumer brand as "Garnier hair" with varied social implications (Ritson & Elliott, 1999) and outright verbal statements (Bauman, 1984 [1977]) extending out of VMTV. The Garnier name could legitimize the style with its real-world presence. Further, it added aesthetically appealing hair with constant variety in VMTV – which met oft-stated demands from users. However, it unpredictably became associated with lower-status during the first months of promotion because of its free availability. Potentially over time, older versions of Garnier hair may have attained higher status with rarity similar to alpha hair.

In terms of self-displays, VMTV contributed to the backstage/frontstage presentation of self (Goffman, 1959). At the beach, as a staging area, new users could immediately customize avatars somewhat privately before engaging with others. VMTV marketing goals – to entertain, increase revenues through premium subscription and virtual good purchase, and enhance marketing of consumer brands – were apparent. VMTV prominently featured consumer brands throughout the virtual world. Promotions included emailed newsletters with advertising, meet-celebrity events, and contests for creating machinima or pictures for virtual goods, and encouraging social interaction user to user. For example, Dana and Tara earned virtual currency for Garnier forum postings and other promotional activities. Encouraging high-status users to wear Garnier hair lessens newb connections to the brand. Likewise, offering free goods to skilled users like Christi could expand brand presence to various social groups.

A complex process of social interaction allows iterative meaning development. Status, knowledge, and achievement can be displayed through virtual goods. Users virtually possessed artifacts branded with *Hills*, *Real World*, Garnier, Sunkist, and others. These artifacts bring helpful benefits to users to leverage in advancement, engagement with others, and overall play. Corporate influences also impact user-developed meanings, and can aid in-demand artifacts like hair. Positively for marketers, insertion of a branded good with user-desired attributes further can connect users with brands, and spread brand messages peer to peer as electronic word of mouth (Hennig-Thurau, Gwinner, Walsh, & Gremler, 2004) within and outside of the virtual world. However, user perceptions of branded virtual goods may not always align with corporate-desired meanings.

Researcher's Avatar as Artifact

Key issues of researching as an avatar center on the participant observer serving as a symbolic object – a critical aspect for methods that demand interaction with users toward the research questions. Methods required using technology in navigating and exploring VMTV, studying discussions in VMTV forums, and evaluating YouTube and other SNSs to see how users were displaying the self and interacting. Without this effort, it would be difficult to understand the interactions underway around me in VMTV, and know how to present myself as an avatar that could engage adequately with others.

Researching as an avatar, displays and attitudes must fit the locale in a way that can be limiting in terms of self-displays. My self-display ideally would appeal to casual and serious users. Admittedly, viewing UGC related to VMTV and being in initial interactions with other users could be intimidating. Further, attempting to be a highly stylized avatar seemed disingenuous particularly given the consumer marketing aspect of the study that could be impacted by such emphasis. My demeanor was serious in intent and method, but easy-going in conversation and when engaging in unfamiliar virtual settings.

According to personal journal notes, it took about a month to settle into my social role in VMTV but interesting – and sometimes surprising – interactions happened continually. For example, entering a lounge could mean exploring a card game with a new friend (sure) or getting asked to "make out" with someone (no thank you). Once, a friendly conversation turned unfriendly when I was coy about my age – trying to be honest I made light of the question but my fellow user then assumed I was too young and started bullying. Fun moments included interacting at clubs and events with others, and experiencing new aspects of VMTV with other users. I encountered a fair share of negative interactions in VMTV and UGC outside of it – including helping a victimized user teleport away from an aggressor, seeing bullying among users in machinima, and watching emotional user pleas on forums when VMTV was closing.

Like Boellstorff (2008) in Second Life, I could study as a participant in VMTV with users who socially engaged and invested in this virtual culture, yet this work differs in keeping one foot outside of VMTV, so to speak, for further clarity. As Taylor (2006) noted in game culture study within EverQuest, the platform supported expanding social engagement among users beyond local proximity of character in game, online and offline. Experience as a user was combined with key artifacts emerging outside of VMTV (Hine, 2000) and also marketing intention for VMTV promotions to extend to the real world. Findings supported the blurred view participants expressed toward their virtual and real lives.

Participant observation greatly aided the long interviews, which yielded the richest data. To achieve the interviews, as seen with Markham (1998), participant observation helped adjust the interview approach to gain participants. To succeed in interviewing, researcher credibility was achieved through familiarity and interest in exploring multiple aspects of VMTV. Further, interview references to VMTV culture – such as the importance of hair and ways promotions engage users – would have been surprising without the observational basis. My own experiences reinforced and made vivid descriptions from the interviews. As well, the rigor of the long-interview method aims toward personal reflection regarding the cultural symbols in social interaction. This aspect of the method aided my view as a researching avatar – being thoughtful of my own life encounters that mimicked virtual experiences. Personal journal notes compare chatting with others in a virtual lounge in VMTV similar to casually conversing with a new acquaintance at the airport or store. As a researcher who had not played many video games, this aspect of the method improved my comfort in this new online space.

Mixing in-VMTV Artifacts with the Periphery

Issues related to the interactions outside of VMTV also raised key issues for multiple methods of research – toward clarity of seeing culture yet a yield of overwhelming data to categorize. Outside of VMTV, UGC offered extensive insight through the film-making culture that created machinima for fun and VMTV promotions. This rich display of social interaction provided further evidence to augment interview data. VMTV machinima, primarily on YouTube, showed Garnier promotional events in clubs, buggy races, romantic breakups, weddings, and many other social events referenced in interviews. Connecting all of these data items made the information more clear in terms of how practice lived in different layers (Geertz, 1973). Without all of those data points, interview findings would be limited.

When interviewing users about making machinima to win virtual goods, or ways they displayed avatar depictions outside of VMTV, I could picture promotions I experienced as a participant observer that encouraged those behaviors.

Out of game, YouTube was an immensely helpful resource. Being open as a researcher and engaging with other users was not enough to gain interviews in VMTV. Users would often suggest interviews in VMTV, which would not follow protocol. Creating a YouTube presence as a researcher, linked to the research project website, was key to reach interview participants. SNS messages led to users viewing the research site and, at times, agreeing to an interview. However, a limitation of this approach potentially was gaining interviewees as a convenience sample that included more active users.

Ethics in Self-Displays and Approach

Ethics of the researcher in terms of self-displays and approach were highly important for this project, and prevalent throughout the methodological approach. Main ethical issues focus on avatar presence as a symbolic object, public spaces and privacy protections for users, and engagement in social interaction to support the research with minimal disruption.

As noted earlier, avatar appearance had to be crafted thoughtfully to engage in VMTV toward the research goals. Reflecting on self-displays, and comparing it to artifacts outside of VMTV, helped focus this effort. Transparency as a researcher was emphasized. However, researcher self-presentation could alter interactions with users, which invites ethical questions. For example, avatars tended to be attractive human replicas – tan, thin, and wearing stylish hair, clothing, and accessories. In this mix were potentially young teenagers, for which VMTV monitored chat-logs and activities to maintain an appropriate environment. However, could a self-display with user activity, such as dancing, be deemed inappropriate in terms of young users? Could displaying the self like other users to attain research goals actually entice inappropriate behavior? At all times, this researcher mindset was key to ensure proper ethics.

VMTV was studied as a public space, with notification to the corporate interests involved. Artifacts observed also were publicly accessible on SNSs, and within VMTV. However, it was important to ensure that personal information about users in participant observation was not unwittingly broadcasted through research efforts. Any identifying aspects in text artifacts were changed in research notes, and user names were not revealed. Further, interviewee privacy also was strictly maintained with limited information about users published and no online connections made between the researcher and participants on SNSs or other places potentially visible to others.

The researcher was not a video game enthusiast with many experiences in virtual worlds. This orientation provided an opportunity to engage in VMTV with openness to experience. Yet, this orientation did not hinder experimenting with many activities in VMTV and learning how the platform operated. In time, learning about culture and aspects of platform clarified findings, as well as ensured the ethics of clearer views of social interaction underway. Further, being willing to learn independently and with users in VMTV, and using multiple methods outside of VMTV and with interviews, aided observations of social interaction with minimal disruption to the user community.

FUTURE TRENDS AND CONCLUSION

Social interaction drives user behaviors on the Internet, which may extend from MMOGs to SNSs and other online spaces. Essentially, online interactions and UGC artifacts convey cultural meanings and co-evolve with influences of users, platforms, and corporate interests. The dynamic seen in findings of social interaction, at times involving marketing promotions, in VMTV could connect with other Internet users gathering in an online space. Further, as the Internet continues its social progression, brands and marketing promotions continually will enter the mix. Co-production among these influences will dictate artifacts and symbols used in interactions. Marketing influences typically will seek outcomes related to product attitudes, brand attitudes, and purchase intentions. Further, commercial influences may affect other aspects of the user experience, such as technical features, privacy and uses of user data, and rules for social interaction. Ultimately though, in co-produced spaces, social interaction will assign cultural meanings that may or may not align with all of the producers' intentions.

This study in VMTV demonstrated how symbolic interactionism and self-presentation provided a view of cultural meaning development impactful for a key virtual good. Avatar hair intersected with user desires for self-presentation, connected to social groups, and impacted interactions based on symbolic display. Varied meanings for avatar hair versions could be seen through interview findings, further supported in participant observation within and outside of VMTV. Internet technology added depth to data while also extending demands for collection and analyses. This technology, particularly with UGC on the Internet, rounded out researcher views for VMTV to improve outcomes. These enhancements through mixed methods that leveraged technologies showed co-produced cultural meanings, and the ways social interaction aided their arrival.

REFERENCES

Babbie, E. (1992). *The practice of social research*. Belmont, CA: Wadsworth.

Bauman, R. (1984). *Verbal art as performance*. Prospect Heights, IL: Waveland Press. (Original work published 1977)

Belk, R. W. (1988). Possessions and the extended self. *The Journal of Consumer Research, 15*(2), 139–168. doi:10.1086/209154

Bernard, H. R. (1988). *Research methods in cultural anthropology*. New Berry Park, CA: Sage.

Blumer, H. (1969). *Symbolic interactionism: Perspective and method*. Englewood Cliffs, NJ: Prentice-Hall.

Boellstorff, T. (2008). *Coming of age in Second Life: An anthropologist explores the virtually human*. Princeton, NJ: Princeton University Press.

Burbules, N. C. (2004). Rethinking the virtual. *E-learning, 1*(2), 162–183. doi:10.2304/elea.2004.1.2.2

Ess, C., & the Association of Internet Researchers Ethics Working Committee. (2002). *Ethical decision-making and Internet research: Recommendations from the aoir ethics working committee*. Retrieved from http://aoir.org/reports/ethics.pdf

Fine, G. A. (1993). The sad demise, mysterious disappearance, and glorious triumph of symbolic interactionism. *Annual Review of Sociology, 19*(1), 61–87. doi:10.1146/annurev.so.19.080193.000425

Fournier, S. (1998). Consumers and their brands: Developing relationship theory in consumer research. *The Journal of Consumer Research, 24*(4), 343–373. doi:10.1086/209515

Goffman, E. (1959). *The presentation of self in everyday life*. New York: Doubleday.

Hansen, S. S. (2013). Exploring real-brand meanings and goods in virtual-world social interaction: Enhanced rewards, rarity, and realism. *Journal of Marketing Management, 29*(13-14), 1443–1461. doi:10.1080/0267257X.2013.821151

Hennig-Thurau, T., Gwinner, K. P., Walsh, G., & Gremler, D. D. (2004). Electronic word-of-mouth via consumer-opinion platforms: What motivates consumers to articulate themselves on the Internet? *Journal of Interactive Marketing, 18*(1), 38–52. doi:10.1002/dir.10073

Hewitt, J. P. (2003). Symbols, objects, and meanings. In L. T. Reynolds, & N. J. Herman-Kinney (Eds.), *Handbook of symbolic interactionism*. Walnut Creek, CA: AltaMira Press.

Hine, C. (2000). *Virtual ethnography*. London: Sage.

Jenkins, H. (2006). *Convergence culture: Where old and new media collide*. New York: New York University Press.

Lehdonvirta, V., Wilska, T.-A., & Johnson, M. (2009). Virtual consumerism: Case habbo hotel. *Information Communication and Society, 12*(7), 1059–1079. doi:10.1080/13691180802587813

Lindlof, T. R. (1995). *Qualitative communication research methods*. Thousand Oaks, CA: Sage.

Ludlow, P., & Wallace, M. (2007). *The Second Life Herald: The virtual tabloid that witnessed the dawn of the metaverse*. Cambridge, MA: MIT Press.

Mantymaki, M., & Salo, J. (2011). Teenagers in social virtual worlds: Continuous use and purchasing behavior in Habbo Hotel. *Computers in Human Behavior, 27*(6), 2088–2097. doi:10.1016/j.chb.2011.06.003

Markham, A. N. (1998). *Life online: Researching real experience in virtual space*. Walnut Creek, CA: AltaMira Press.

Martin, J. (2008). Consuming code: Use-value, exchange-value, and the role of virtual goods in Second Life. *Journal of Virtual Worlds Research, 1*(2). Retrieved from http://journals.tdl.org/jvwr/index.php/jvwr/article/view/300

McCracken, G. (1988a). *Culture and consumption*. Bloomington, IN: Indiana University Press.

McCracken, G. (1988b). *The long interview* (Vol. 13). Newbury Park, CA: Sage. doi:10.4135/9781412986229

Miller, D., & Slater, D. (2000). *The Internet: An ethnographic approach*. Oxford, UK: Berg.

Neuman, W. L. (2000). *Social research methods: Qualitative and quantitative approaches*. Boston: Allyn and Bacon.

Prus, R. (1996). *Symbolic interactionism and ethnographic research*. Albany, NY: State University of New York Press.

Ritson, M., & Elliott, R. (1999). The social uses of advertising: An ethnographic study of adolescent advertising audiences. *The Journal of Consumer Research, 26*(3), 260–277. doi:10.1086/209562

Sandstrom, K., Martin, D. D., & Fine, G. A. (2006). *Symbols, selves and social reality*. Los Angeles, CA: Roxbury Publishing Company.

Schau, H. J., & Gilly, M. C. (2003). We are what we post? Self-presentation in personal web space. *The Journal of Consumer Research, 30*(3), 385–404. doi:10.1086/378616

Solomon, M. (1983). The role of products as social stimuli: A symbolic interactionism perspective. *The Journal of Consumer Research, 10*(3), 319–328. doi:10.1086/208971

Taylor, T. L. (2006). *Play between worlds: Exploring online game culture*. Cambridge, MA: The MIT Press.

Turkle, S. (1995). *Life on the screen: Identity in the age of the internet*. New York: Touchstone.

Van Dijck, J´. (2007). *Mediated memories in the digital age*. Stanford, CA: Stanford University Press.

Williams, F., Rice, R. E., & Rogers, E. M. (1988). *Research methods and the new media*. New York: Free Press.

Williamson, D. A. (2007). *Kids and teens online: Virtual worlds open new universe*. Retrieved from http://www.emarketer.com/Reports/All/Emarketer_2000437.aspx?src=report1_home

Woodson, A. (2007, March 29). MTV to pimp "Ride" online. *Reuters*. Retrieved from http://www.reuters.com/article/industryNews/idUSN2933239120070330

Yee, N., & Bailenson, J. (2007). The proteus effect: The effect of transformed self-representation on behavior. *Human Communication Research, 33*(3), 271–290. doi:10.1111/j.1468-2958.2007.00299.x

Chapter 13

Tweet Portraiture:
Understanding the Gist of Electronic Identities through Microblogged Messaging in Social Media Using NCapture and NVivo 10

Shalin Hai-Jew
Kansas State University, USA

ABSTRACT

A lifetime collection of microblogging messages captured from a microblogging account may be extracted from Twitter using NCapture (an add-on to Chrome and Internet Explorer); these short messages may be analyzed through NVivo and other data analysis and visualization software tools in order to highlight compressed-time gists (essences) of Twitter accounts for rapid assessment. This chapter provides an overview of how this work may be done and how the resulting word clouds, word trees, and tree maps may be analyzed for latent insights. This research approach may be applied to a range of social media platforms using the same software tools here (or using others that are publicly available). This chapter concludes with ideas for how to extend these methods.

INTRODUCTION

Microblogging sites are those that aggregate and distribute short text messages between its users in private, semi-public, and public venues. If people are a sum of their actions (and habituated behaviors and thinking), then can it be said that an online account identity on a microblogging site (like Twitter) is a sum of its expressed ideas? Would 140-character microblogging messages—expressed as fleeting asides, often without the benefit

of forethought or critical mind oversight—capture an impulse-based aspect of identity that would not be seeable otherwise? Said another way, does this microblogging medium elicit communication from people that they "are less likely to express using existing technologies" (Grace, Zhao, & boyd, 2010, p. 4517). In other words, does the speed and riposte of this technology erase people's own personal filters on communications? After all, the *sine qua non* of microblogging is real-time and interactive short-form communications to capture

DOI: 10.4018/978-1-4666-6493-7.ch013

top-of-mind mental chirps. This communications medium is all about speed, brevity, and dynamic Live Web interactivity among people connecting from anywhere in the electronic environment. Would a corpus of short-message Tweets linked to an entity be able to capture a gist (or the substantive core or essence) of that entity?

This chapter explores the use of NCapture (a web browser extension) and NVivo (a qualitative and mixed methods data analysis tool) to extract the cumulative messages of a Twitter account to see what may be learned from that endeavor. While microblogs are very time-based, particularly for breaking events, this research approach will involve the extraction of cumulative messaging linked to the lifespan of the account (in an approach called "author-wise pooling" in some contexts) without an analysis of the time element except for the beginning and current date of the account (or an end date if relevant). The data are reduced from an n = all of the messaging into word clouds, text-search-based word trees, tree maps, and other data visualizations, for study. Summative content analysis "begins from existing words or phrases in the text itself (the raw data) and counts these; then the researcher extends his or her exploration to include *latent meanings* and themes that are apparent in the data…" (Berg & Lune, 2012, p. 352). Latent analysis refers to the "interpretive reading of the symbolism underlying the physical data" (Berg & Lune, 2012, p. 355). This approach will not include the analysis of inter-relationships between various accounts—although clearly such interactions may have sparked certain messaging. All these other elements—time, interrelationships, memberships, synchronous events, and linked multimedia (linked photos and videos)—are backgrounded to the focus on the text message extractions.

This approach of conducting a micro-ethnographic study (vs. macro) using a mcroblogging site may be understood as part of online ethnography (Berg & Lune, 2012, pp. 238 – 240), social-cultural research which taps into online worlds, social media, massive online games, wikis, blogs, and discussion boards. In this field research approach, collecting online information and interacting with others online are common research tools in the natural setting of immersive online spaces. These comprise online ethnography fieldwork. Intercommunications to the public are a social performance. Identifying topics of interest in Twitter users' accounts to learn about the account holders' interests is not new (Michelson & Mackassy, 2010); microblogging content may be used to profile users "according to substance, style, status, and social tendency" (Tsur & Rappoport, 2012, p. 644). What may be somewhat original is the sequencing and the application of various publicly available technologies for the analysis. This is a micro study because its unit of social analysis is an individual or group (as expressed in an account). To provide a sense of this level of analysis. Figure 1, "A Private Company's Twitter History Expressed as a Word Cloud" shows a real-world microblogging extraction depicted as a word cloud, with main words expressed by size and centrality.

At the time of the data extraction for this unnamed private company, the company had 7,507 Tweets, 192 following (accounts that this account was following), and 53,726 followers (those who followed this account). The most common term in the microblogging Tweets was "sitrep" or the shortened form for "situation report," a Western military term. The hashtagged conversations point to regions of the world which are hotspots for political strife. The words here point to extreme and timely conflictual realities. Some of the lingo for those in political leadership, military, and graduate and undergraduate students. This real-world sample word cloud points to the niche that this global intelligence company has created for itself in relation to other entities in the environment. (In a "cyber-physical confluence," the cyber does not evoke the physical world in totality; rather, there is a light overlap that highlights some aspects of the on-ground reality.) Strategically, an information

Figure 1. A private company's Twitter history expressed as a word cloud

company has to show that it has access to real-time actionable intelligence; it has to show that it can speak in the lingo of its customers.

The idea is to capture the semantic and emotional "gist" of an account in a time-static and condensed at-a-glance format; this capture represents a kind of cumulative "equilibrium state" for the account. This pseudo-manual process captures some of the affordances of various software tools with the nuance and pacing of manual work (but without the labor intensive need to directly hand-code or hand-annotate). It is hoped that this approach may highlight elusive or latent insights. As such, this research approach will be both a manual and machine-based approach as contrasted to a broad information technology (IT) literature focused on automated captures and analyses. This simple compressed-time approach is conceptualized as complementary to other research approaches like various forms of continuous or dynamic Tweet analysis (such as for trending events), the study of

bursty-ness, event graph analysis, electronic social network analysis, sentiment analysis, stylometry, and geospatial analysis. This approach may be used to complement the findings of electronic dossiers surrounding particular entities (individuals or groups / organizations).

Known colloquially as "the SMS of the Internet," Twitter is the predominant "short messaging service" microblogging site in the world, with billions of users globally representing broad geographic coverage. (Twitter, though, is only 1/8 the size of China's Sina *Weibo*.) Its hundreds of billions of microblogged messages are being archived by the U.S. Library of Congress. The generous application programming interface (API) linked to Twitter enables outside entities to query its various public holdings. Its accounts may represent individuals, groups, or combined accounts (lists) surrounding particular topics. Its accounts may be human (people sharing messages), robots (software programs collecting data and re-broadcasting), or cyborgs (a mix of people and software programs sharing messages). A perusal of account Tweets may be read in a variety of ways—as interior running monologues (accounts with few followers and even wholly private accounts), as narrow-cast messages to a pre-defined ego neighborhood of acquaintances (private accounts; semi-public accounts), and as broadcasting to a broad audience (particularly by mainline media organizations, commercial companies with global brands, non-profit organizations, and politicians).

Delimitations

Not only does the researcher's methodologies affect the quality of the data extraction and analysis, but there are many layers of socio-technological dependencies that affect the completeness of the data extraction and analysis. One important caveat is to observe the affordances and constraints of such data crawls. For example, while NCapture tends to be quite complete in its data extraction, any private messages are not capturable using this tool. Deleted Tweets disappear from users' timelines and those of their followers and so effectively disappear from Twitter searches (Almuhimedi, Wilson, Liu, Sadeh, & Acquisti, 2013, p. 898). Some discussions will be taken off-list to more private channels as necessary, especially given the inclusion of websites and email contact information for many Twitter accounts. The information captured is textual. This generally does not involve capture of imagery, audio, or video microblogging messages. How a microblogging account is used will likely affect the types of messaging which exist in its archive. A spoof account that is satirical may not read as such with just an extracted word cloud or word tree, for example. Any basic analysis must include a range of complementary (and overlapping) research. Some technologies do not enable data crawls of accounts with non-alphanumeric names or those using Latin scripts

(such as those using Arabic or Chinese). Some data extractions done during breaking events will only be able to capture some number of Tweets, not all. Ideally, a researcher would know what is going on with each technology. Another aspect is that a researcher should try to verify initial impressions. The only way to close the loop is to try to find other channels of information to verify or contradict these initial findings.

A REVIEW OF THE LITERATURE

Microblog networks, the individuals who connect around shared short message conversations, have been targeted as distributed human sensor networks which may be trolled for large-scale events like political restiveness or emergent pandemics or outbreaks of mass fandom. Researchers have conducted remote reads of people's personalities based on messaging based on zero-acquaintance and messaging alone in terms of extraversion, introversion, neuroticism, agreeableness, and conscientiousness (Qiu, Lin, Ramsay, & Yang, 2012, pp. 710 – 711); such personality revelations may be a kind of "data leakage" on the one hand but also the expression of personality on the other. Near real-time machine analysis has been critical in this mass surveillance to capture not only messaging but the locales of the messages and the sentiments. There are computer programs that can conduct sentiment analysis of people's posts to understand the general direction of opinion (expressed often as polarities like "yes" or "no"), the intensity of emotion and opinion, and other information from this sparse data; there is plenty of automated machine-based sentiment analysis of microblogging messages (Guerra, Veloso, Meira, & Almeida, 2011; Agarwal, Xie, Vovsha, Rambow, & Passonneau, 2011; Vakali, 2012). The brevity of microblogged messaging enhances the machine classifying of sentiment in microblogs (Bermingham & Smeaton, 2010).

This surveillance is conducted by governments as well as commercial entities, organizations, and individuals.

Traditionally, microblogging messages are thought to be deeply unstructured and noisy (a high ratio of noise to signal value). The severe length constraint (such as 140 characters per Tweet on Twitter) makes characters "expensive," which leads many to use informal and highly abbreviated language (Tsur & Rappoport, 2012, p. 644). Text-messaging has its own non-standard lingo including emoticons, unusual punctuation, and hashtag use to label and organize conversations with some coherence (through "Tweet pooling"). Many linguistic mannerisms have entered the mainstream from Internet argot. At the same time, microblogging messages are "expandable" posts because they link to URLs, photos, and videos, and these leads may help "reconstruct the topic space" (Deng, Xu, Zhang, Han, Zhou, & Zou, 2013, n.p.). A majority of microblogged images on Twitter tend to be accompanied by text (with 99.1% of image tweets with corresponding text, according to one study); image microblogging messages tend to be more common in the daytime (Chen, Lu, Kan, & Cui, 2013).

The online ethnographic research literature offers insights about why people participate on microblogging sites. As a core part of Social Media, such sites enable people to bond around shared issues and interests. Microblogged conversations range from the deeply personal to the social—on a wide range of issues. Such sites have been used to host discussions and organize events such as social gatherings, trips, political sit-ins, games, and flash mobs. With the very human tendency to emulate others, various forms of "memetic engineering" have occurred to support broad-scale events (including political revolutions). People have gone to Twitter to make sense of issues and to elicit information. This network is used to share news and information. There is a large commercial component to Twitter, with companies going online to burnish reputations and to move products and services. The communications on Twitter tend to be purposive (both strategic and tactical); even if impulsive, most microblog messaging shows an underlying structure and motivation. In a sense, accounts may be viewed as "influence agents" with particular agendas for "memetic engineering" (or conveying online memes to affect opinions and actions). Public-facing microblogging accounts have a seeding function in terms of sharing ideas and points-of-view.

Microblogging involves many-way messaging; people participate in order to give-and-take. In one dataset of Tweets, some 13% of those messages were questions to others. Five common information genres in Twitter include "personal updates, directed dialogue, real-time sharing, business broadcasting, and information-seeking" (Westman & Freund, 2010, p. 325). Another researcher categorized messages into various categories and then analyzed the information value of each type among users. The eight categories were the following: question to followers, information sharing, self-promotion, random thought, opinion / complaint, me now, conversation, and presence maintenance (Andre, Bernstein, & Luther, 2012, n.p.). Of these message types, followers (of accounts that they actively chose to follow) rated 36% of the Tweets as Worth Reading; 25% as Not Worth Reading, and 39% as Neutral based on a 43,000 voluntary ratings dataset on Twitter updates. Researchers found that microblog users value "information sharing and random thoughts above me-oriented or presence updates" (Andre, Bernstein, & Luther, 2012, n.p.). Readers also expressed displeasure at information that they found boring or repetitive or cryptic; there were also complaints about insufficient context for certain Tweets to be meaningful. The three most strongly disliked categories of messaging were Presence Maintenance, Conversation, and Me Now (the tweeter's current status) (Andre, Bernstein, & Luther, 2012, n.p.). The short messages that people enjoyed were those that offered information (48%) or humor (24%) in a concise way (Andre,

Bernstein, & Luther, 2012, n.p.). This sense of multi-way messaging is important because the audience then may help shape the messages made from a microblogging account based on their interests and responses to the posted messages.

GIST ANALYSIS THROUGH MICROBLOGGING DATA EXTRACTIONS

Figure 2, "An Overview of the Microblogging Data Extraction and Account Profiling Analysis," provides a multi-step overview of gist analysis from author-wise pooling of microblogging messages. To summarize, relevant accounts are identified. A capture of the data is achieved using NCapture. This data is input into NVivo, where various analytical techniques are applied to it. Finally, through a mix of machine- and human- analysis, an account is profiled through its microblogged messaging. This approach offers a path for human- and machine-mediated microblogging heuristics (discovery) in terms of electronic identity analysis. While this is a manual process, it enables the mass capture of information and its visualization for rapid analysis.

1. Identification of Twitter Account of Interest

Depending on the topic of interest, researchers may use a range of methods to identify accounts of interest. These may be identified based on mainline websites, formal publications, grey literature (informal publications), microblogged conversations, public personalities, and virtually any communications channel.

Core Memberships in Online Social Networks

One common way is to extract the ego neighborhood of a particular node of interest to find out who is in closest relationship with the target node. A straight "ego neighborhood" crawl requires a degree of 1; one that involves transitivity between the alters in the ego neighborhood requires a degree

Figure 2. An overview of the microblogging data extraction and account profiling analysis

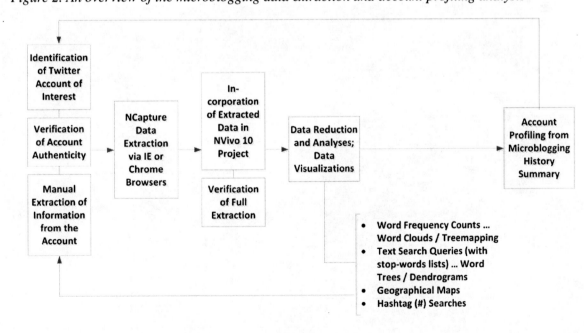

of 1.5; one that involves the ego neighborhood and the alters' ego neighborhoods involves a degree of 2. The higher degree centrality of a node in such a network, the closer it is in relationship to the target focal node. A higher degree crawl provides a larger view of connections to the focal node, but moving out too far in terms of degrees may lead to such a high level view that information may be hard to extract (at least not without the capability of focusing on sub-networks / sub-cliques / sub-graphs). Dynamic filters may also be used to sort out the important nodes from the less important ones. (The concept of homophily suggests that individuals and organizations interact closely with those with whom they are most similar.) The mapping of the social network of @AnonOps account (https://twitter.com/anonops) shows an account with 2,356 Tweets, 285,232 followers, and 2 following. Figure 3, "Accounts with an In-Degree of Two vs. an In-Degree of Five (through Dynamic Filtering" shows the clustering of the ego neighborhood close-in to the AnonOps account

(with an in-degree of at least two) but the inset highlights those with an in-degree of at least five (which suggests that these accounts are not only close to AnonOps but also are influential with a fair amount of in-degree (incoming followers) within this network. The proper ranges for the measure of popularity will differ based on the target and the target social network.

Table 1, "Graph Metrics of @AnonOps User Network on Twitter (2 deg., 9999-persons limit)" shows some 17,193 nodes connected to AnonOps, so a full representation of the network would be much larger than what was shown in the prior figure. The original crawl was for a two-degree network with a maximum of 9,999 persons. A full data crawl would not insert the artificial limit of the 9,999 persons (nodes).

The graph metrics table for @AnonOps user network on Twitter shows a sparse graph density (.0000584914 graph density), but given the size of the network, that sparseness may be understood. The density of a network involves how many con-

Figure 3. Accounts with an in-degree of two vs. an in-degree of five (through dynamic filtering)

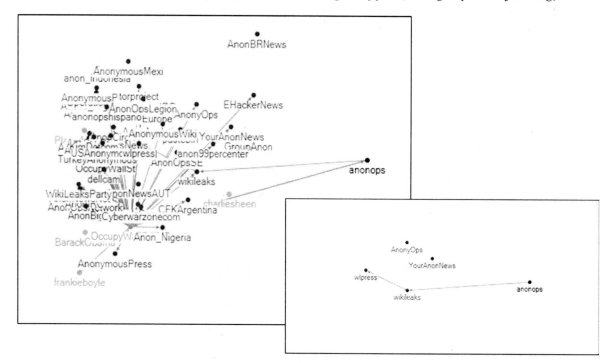

Table 1. Graph metrics of @AnonOps user network on Twitter (2 deg., 9999-persons limit)

Graph Metric	Value
Graph Type	Directed
Vertices	17193
Unique Edges	17280
Edges With Duplicates	18
Total Edges	17298
Self-Loops	0
Reciprocated Vertex Pair Ratio	5.78436E-05
Reciprocated Edge Ratio	0.00011568
Connected Components	1
Single-Vertex Connected Components	0
Maximum Vertices in a Connected Component	17193
Maximum Edges in a Connected Component	17298
Maximum Geodesic Distance (Diameter)	4
Average Geodesic Distance	2.539942
Graph Density	5.84914E-05
Modularity	Not Applicable
NodeXL Version	1.0.1.245

nections exist out of how many possible theoretical connections there may be based on the numbers of vertices in the network. (To view the full AnonOps data extraction, see the graph in the Appendix.)

Popularity or Influence

Researchers have plenty of support to make the case that the nodes that they may want to follow should be those that are popular (defined in graph theory as those with high in-degree and lower out-degree, or a large numbers of followers and much fewer following). In social media platforms, popular nodes are often authorities for certain areas of expertise. The power law distribution applies to popularity in the Twitter network, with a few who have high in-degree but a majority with low in-degree and low out-degree. When researchers created lifetime graphs based on select topics, they found that popular topics occupied the more well-connected parts of the social network; less popular topics had low network densities (few interested, with such topics moving through small isolated / disconnected clusters or sub-graphs). The authors found that a popular topic is generally discussed in a large cluster that "contains most of the users that have tweeted on that topic" (Ardon, Bagchi, Mahanti, Ruhela, Seth, Tripathy, & Triukose, 2013, p. 223); further, popular topics tend to cross regional boundaries while unpopular ones stay confined geographically (p. 220). The authors elaborate:

Twitter is a partially democratic medium in the sense that popular topics are generally nourished by users that have large numbers of followers; however, for a topic to become popular it must be taken up by users having scant followers count.

Further, regions with large number of heavily followed users dominate Twitter. (Ardon, Bagchi, Mahanti, Ruhela, Seth, Tripathy, & Triukose, 2013, p. 220)

Social network graphs, node-link diagrams that express relationships, show highly influential nodes and geographies where powerful ideas originate and then are percolated outwards. This dynamic of human influence has not been changed by new social technologies but apparently have been reinforced. Many of the core nodes in microblogging networks are traditional "news media outlets or media personalities (pop stars, politicians, writers etc.)" (Ardon, Bagchi, Mahanti, Ruhela, Seth, Tripathy, & Triukose, 2013, p. 225). They write:

There is reason to believe that despite the fact that OSN (online social network) platforms bring the world closer, older notions of proximity and community continue to contribute significantly to popularity in the way described. Our study is broad in nature and captures a coarse phenomenon that we hope will excite sociologist and invite them to tease out the finer nuances that lie within such phenomena. (Ardon, Bagchi, Mahanti, Ruhela, Seth, Tripathy, & Triukose, 2013, p. 227)

Over time, online social networks tend to cluster more deeply around popular clusters, and smaller sub-clusters or sub-cliques tend to dissipate:

Often the growth of these clusters is self-amplifying: the bigger they get, the faster they grow, because of the increase in the area of the surface on which a cluster accumulates more particles. Small clusters are doomed to disappear or be swallowed up. In physics, this is known as Ostwald ripening. It is, if you like, a case of the rich getting richer and the poor getting poorer; in the

business world it could serve as a metaphor for takeovers and globalization (Ball, 2004, p. 275)

This would suggest that a simple graphing of a social network around particular issues (such as through #hashtag searches) may show the most central or influential nodes to probe. In terms of public issues, there are many motivations for people to be vocal and to engage the public. Stealth political endeavors without individuals cultivating interest and supporting participation do not tend to win much attention or following. There usually has to be a public interface for those who are striving for social impact. To illuminate this process, this will begin with an analysis of a trending hashtag (#) conversation on Twitter. Hashtags are used to label messages based on a particular theme or thread. That thread may be pulled out and analyzed as its own set of microblog messages. Hashtags enhance the ability to "topic pool" across accounts. Some researchers suggest that hashtag adoption represents dual roles—one as a topical content label and another as "a symbol of community membership" (Yang, Sun, Zhang, & Mei, 2012, p. 261); they explain:

The community role of a hashtag presents in its functionalities to identify a community, form a community, and allow users to join a community - a role never played by traditional social tags. (Yang, Sun, Zhang, & Mei, 2012, p. 262)

Figure 4, "Extrapolating Influential Nodes in a Microblogging Conversation (#syria)" shows a social network diagram created using Network Overview, Discovery and Exploration for Excel (NodeXL) based on a recent conversation around #syria, which has been a restive country. The parameters of the Twitter search crawl were to follow all "replies-to" relationships in Tweets; "mentions" relationships; any Tweet that is not a "replies-to" or "mentions", and relationship

Figure 4. Extrapolating influential nodes in a microblogging conversation (#syria)

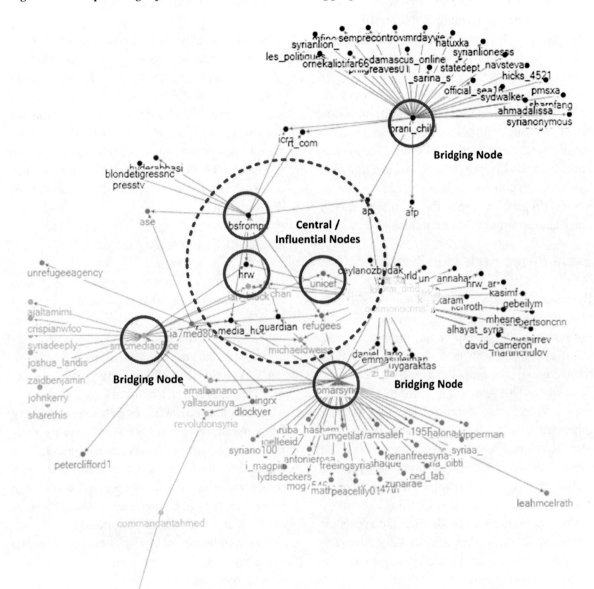

(following / follower). The limit was set at 16,000 Tweets. Given the 7-day API limit on Twitter's end, the 16,000 is the equivalent of an unlimited search. A Tweets column was added to the Edges (links) worksheet, and a statistics column were added to the Vertices (nodes) worksheet. This broad capture strives to include all facets of relationship to include not only a sense of recent conversations but some degree of potential prior connectivity. Also, a broad crawl is generally desirable because the worksheets capture information that almost invariably have additional relevance to the data visualizations. For example, sample Tweets may be explored through text analysis tools (both human and machine-based). The search was made using #syria because of the hashtag labeling of those having conversations around this topic. The metacharacter hashtag # followed by non-whitespace alphanumeric characters indicates a conversation; the "at" @ character indicates the name of the account.

Two types of nodes have been culled as benefitting from a further search. Within the dotted circle are some centralized or influential nodes in this #syria discussion community. Outside this core are some bridging nodes that are followed by important communities, and these are also of interest (in part because of their connections and reach across disparate communities).

Event-Based Node Identification

Events online tend to unfold in a semi-predictable way, depicted as a u-curve, moving from the pre-phase to the growth phase, the peak phase, the decay phase, and then the post-phase (Ardon, Bagchi, Mahanti, Ruhela, Seth, Tripathy, & Triukose, 2013, p. 222). There may be those who serve as core leaders throughout the event or others who rise in prominence certain phases. The identification of which accounts are dominant in certain phases of a breaking event may provide further motivation to research that particular account for gist and identity. Certain particularly credible accounts may be identified in events for particular identification and tracking; after all, credible accounts are critical in an online environment replete with rumors.

Snowballing to Other Nodes

Certainly, after identification of accounts of interest, there may be another strategy—of "snowballing" from original nodes outwards to their ego neighborhoods and outward further to their direct contacts, to several degrees of connectivity. There may also be broadening by identifying hashtagged conversations that are predominant in an account in order to create more leads.

Evaluating Account Quality

Some simple analysis of the node / vertex (Twitter account) would be important to assess whether it's important to explore further. Whose account is it? What sort of information access would this account have? What are some likely reasons for the sharing of information for this account? Who are the audience members for this microblogging account? What points of view may be communicated? Do these facts align with the interests of the researcher?

Avoiding Spoofed Accounts

Once accounts of interest have been identified, it is important to verify that these accounts are not faked ones. One thread of Internet expressionism and political expression involves spoofing accounts to make political statements. Oftentimes, the background data will be a giveaway about the account. Sometimes, it helps to look at the history of the account and how many followers / following it has. Spoof sites generally do not have very many followers—not as much as the genuine article—by a long shot. Many spoof sites also lack following (other accounts that the account subscribes to); spoof sites tend to be one-way tools for disseminating ideas. The actual communicated Tweets will be another set of clues. There are authentic accounts which have been discontinued; these stub accounts may look faked but are actually real (just discontinued).

2. NCapture Data Extraction via IE or Google Chrome Browsers

A data extraction from a Twitter account may be done using the NCapture download that may be used with Microsoft's Internet Explorer or Google Chrome. This work involves conducting the extraction, then opening NVivo 10 in order to bring in the data into the project. It is important to verify the number of microblogging messages listed with a Twitter account to ensure that the extraction captured all possible messages. That said, there are limits to data extractions; not all historical Tweets may be extracted. For example, the @wikileaks account listed 27,203 Tweets, 1 following, and 2,113,498 followers (https://twitter.com/wikileaks). An extraction from NCapture only captured 2,400 references. In such cases, if the extraction has been done for research, it is important to mention that only nine percent of the possible Tweets were captured and to offer the start and end dates of the extracted microblogging messages.

The word cloud that was extracted shows a range of conversations, including #snowden, #tpp, #mediastan, #postdrone, #stratfor, #sweden, and others. There are a range of locations metnioned. There are clear issues in discussion. The treemap

diagram (Figure 5, "Wikileaks Word Frequency Treemap Diagram") highlights the most important terms listed. (This data visualization was done before the "http" was put on the stop-words list. As such, this works as an illustration for why certain terms should be stop-word listed (for improved clarity of substantive semantic terms).

To illustrate the role of data tables, there was an NCapture crawl of @JulianAssange_ on Twitter (https://twitter.com/JulianAssange_). At the time of the crawl, he had 1,628 Tweets, 89 following, and 157,710 followers. This extraction resulted in the full 1,628 microblogging messages.

One impression from the word cloud of @JulianAssange_ is that although his is a powerful personality (based on media and other reports), but based on his messaging, his identity is tied in closely with the organization he founded. His name appears a fair amount in his word cloud as well,

Figure 5. @Wikileaks word frequency word cloud visualization

bu the dominant word is still "wikileaks." There are a range of assertive verbs. There are various social issues that are being debated.

The data table from NVivo shows the word frequency count from that crawl, from which the word clouds (or tag clouds) may be made.

3. Incorporation of Extracted Data in NVivo 10 Project

Political activism is a common motivation for various microblogging accounts on Twitter. @YourAnonNews on Twitter (https://twitter.com/YourAnonNews) captures the latest activism of the dispersed Anonymous hacker collective. (This account is related to youranonnews.tumblr.com, with social network accounts echoing each other's endeavors.) The Twitter account has 77,733 Tweets, 451 following, and 1,185,070 followers. From the set of known Tweets, only 3,214 messages (4 percent) were extracted using NCapture.

Even though this is related to @AnonOps, featured earlier, there are nuanced differences between these accounts' microblogged messaging.

@YourAnonNews focuses more on various types of activism (see #elsipogtog and #fracking against fracking, #blackfriday against commercialism, and others). The YourAnonNews dataset may be analyzed at a more granular level based on individual conversationalists (such as @JasonLeopold), direct and specific microblog messaging, and evolving messaging trajectories over time. (This set may be exported from NVivo in .csv, .xl, and other formats.) The captured Tweets are usually presented in reverse-order by default.

Text frequency counts are one simple application of the so-called "bag of words" profile (to broadly over-simplify), which involves the collection of words in a document or corpus and an analysis of the frequency of the words within that "bag."

Figure 6. Wikileaks word frequency treemap diagram

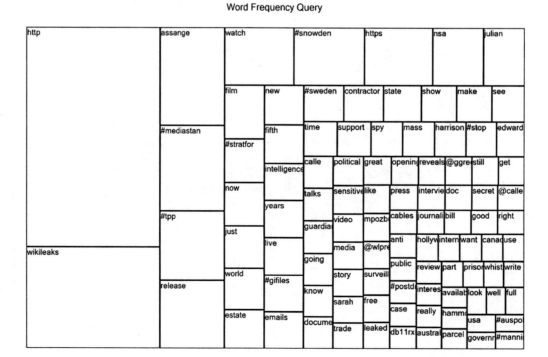

Figure 7. A word cloud of the @JulianAssange_ account on Twitter

Figure 8. The data table for @JulianAssange_ on Twitter

Word	Length	Count	Weighted Percentage (%)	Similar Words
wikileaks	9	2714	11.10	#wikileaks, @wikileaks, wikileak, wikileake, wikileaker, wikileaking, wikileaks, wikileaks', 'wikileaks', wikileaks'
news	4	1469	5.98	intelligence, news, news', words
assange	7	1210	4.95	#assange, assang, assange, assange'
breaking	8	1416	4.16	better, breach, breaking, bump, busting, check, checks, die, died', discovers, disruption, divulged, expose, exposed, exposes, exposing, failed, founder, founders, give, gives, giving, going, offended, part, recess, reveal, revealed, revealing, reveals, 'reveals, ruin, several, severed, shifts, split, stop, stopped, stops, violation, wear
bit	3	985	3.92	act, acting, bit, moment, number, second, spot, spotted, turn, turned, turns
julian	6	815	3.33	julian, 'julian, julians
yhoo	4	386	1.58	yhoo
founder	7	645	1.32	father, flop, founder, founders
release	7	400	1.09	departure', departures, dismissed, dismisses, expel, fire, fired, fires, free, 'free, going, issu, issue, issued, issues, loose, loss, outlet, outlets, passes, passing, publish, published, publisher, publishes, publishing, release, released, releases, releasing, resign, resign', resignations, resigned, resigns, secret, 'secret, secretly, secrets, spill, spilled, spilling, turn, turned, turns
chief	5	145	0.57	boss, chief, head, headed, heading, main, mains, masters
swedish	7	135	0.55	swedish
website	7	148	0.53	site, sites, websit, website, websites
new	3	103	0.42	fresh, new, newly
documents	9	144	0.40	document, documentary, documents, documents', paper, paper', papers, support, supporters, supporters'
lawyer	6	96	0.39	attorney, lawyer, lawyers
arrest	6	138	0.37	arrest, arreste, arrested, check, checks, contain, contained, get, gets, getting, halted, stay, stop, stopped, stops
sweden	6	89	0.36	sweden, sweden'
court	5	103	0.36	court, courts, formal, homage, romance, state, 'state, states, tribunal
world	5	101	0.36	#manning, creation, domain, domains, global, human, man, 'man, manning, public, publication, publications, reality, universal, world, worldwide
rape	4	84	0.33	assault, outrage, rape, 'rape', raped, violation
supporters	10	181	0.33	backup, 'confirmed', confirms, defended, defenders, defends, friend, friendly, friends, help, helped, keep, keeping, keeps, live, lives, living, stand, stands, suffers, support, supporters, supporters'
bail	4	79	0.32	bail, bond'
files	5	107	0.31	charge, charged, charges, charges', file, file', files, registered, registering, registers
order	5	114	0.31	arrangements, arranging, club, govern, government, governments, order, ordered, orderly, orders, place, put, puts, ranks, regulate, saying, society, system, tell, tells
back	4	124	0.30	back, backup, cover, fund, funding, funds, name, mount, mounting, mounts, second, staking

4. Data Reduction and Analysis; Data Visualizations

In the prior sections, there have already been some simple data reductions and analyses along with data visualizations. A text search may be done based on select terms within a dataset. In NVivo 10, a text search query was run on "government" in the @JulianAssange_ Twitter extraction dataset. Instead of exact matches, stemmed words, synonyms, and specializations were included for as broad of a capture as possible. 396 references were found. From this set, a word tree was created. This includes the words just prior to the select word and then those that follow to capture the gist of the communiation.

A geographical map may be extrapolated from the microblogged messages as well depending on if the individuals running the accounts input locational data. Broadly speaking, only one percent of Tweets in Twitter are geotagged (Carley, Pfeffer, Liu, Morstatter, & Goolsby, 2013). Since much of the data is "noisy" and unstructured, there are usually very few location indicators In the geographical map output from NVivo for the @JulianAssange_ crawl, there are only a few places marked (the Eastern U.S., Europe, and S. Africa).

5. Account Profiling from Microblogging History Summary

Finally, there is the human work of actual account profiling based on the extracted microblogging messages. Table 2, "Queries of the Microblogging Message Data Extractions" offers a beginning list of questions for consideration.

DISCUSSION

The examples so far have highlighted the electronic profiling of microblogging accounts on twitter

Figure 9. @YourAnonNews word cloud

Figure 10. A screenshot of the @YourAnonNews dataset in NVivo

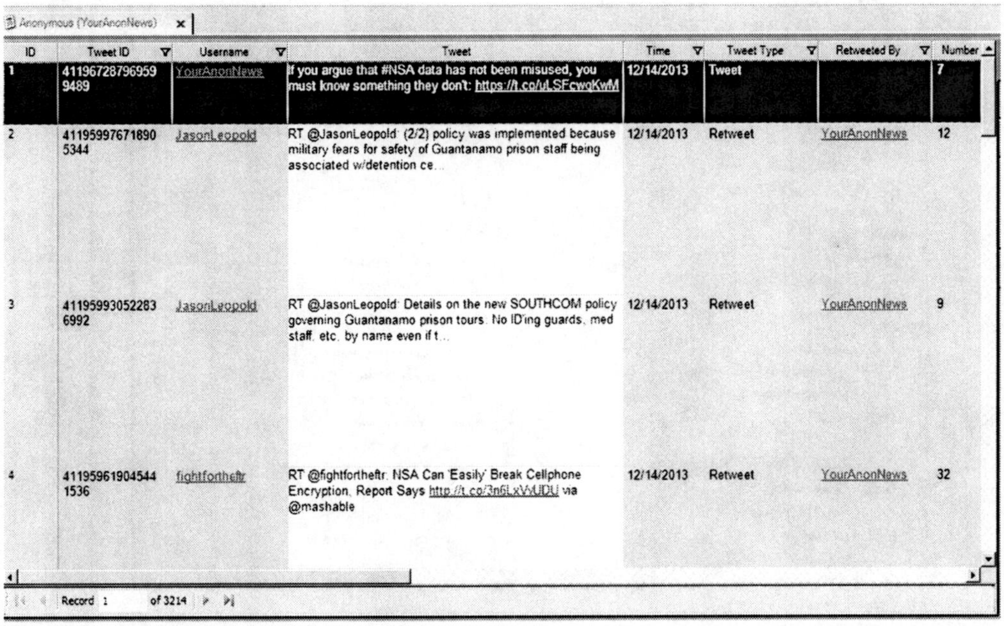

based on author-wise pooling of microblogging messages. The NCapture add-in and NVivo software may be used to extract other information from twitter, such as conversation-based networks. Conversations may be extracted as well. A cluster analysis later visualized as a lattice graph was done on a data extraction of the #cold hashtag conversation search. One thousand, eight hundred and ninety-nine Tweet records were extracted during this crawl. Clustering is based on word similarity and may provide clustering of ideas among certain members of those conversing directly or indirectly about the issue at hand.

A variety of other types of cluster visualizations are available as well, in 2D (horizontal and vertical dendrograms, circle or lattice graphs, and 2D cluster maps) and 3D (like 3D cluster maps). (The software programs listed in this chapter—NodeXL, NCapture, NVivo, and others—have a much wider capability than introduced here. The

need to focus the chapter on a particular general use case resulted in a telescoping of capabilities on a few for coherence sake.

FUTURE RESEARCH DIRECTIONS

This approach of extracting microblogging messages for textual analysis and inference-making of the account profile is not a new approach. The discovery value of such an approach is to capture a general impression or gist of the account's messaging in order to complement data extractions from other online and physical-world sources. It would be facile to only look at one channel of information—in virtually all research contexts. In a broader sense, such analysis may benefit events analysis, topics analysis, individual and group profiling, strategic communications analysis, branding, and other areas.

Figure 11. A screenshot of the "Court" word tree extracted from @JulianAssange_ microblogging messages dataset in NVivo

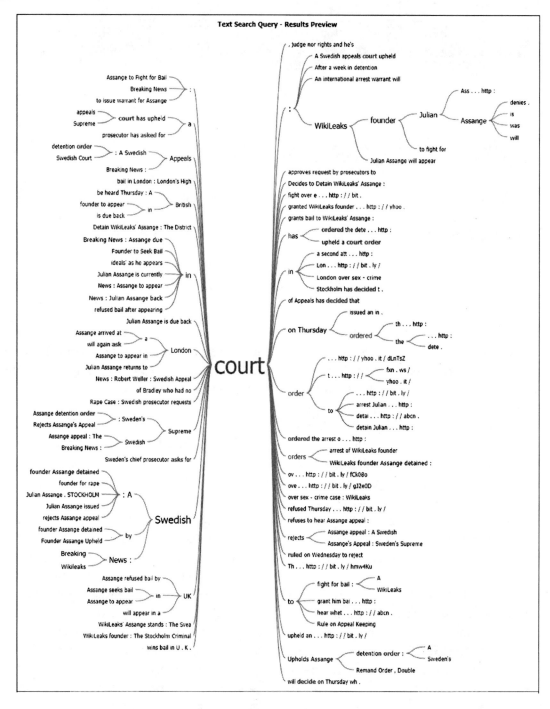

Figure 12. A geospatial map of the microblogging messages extracted from @JulianAssange_ dataset in NVivo

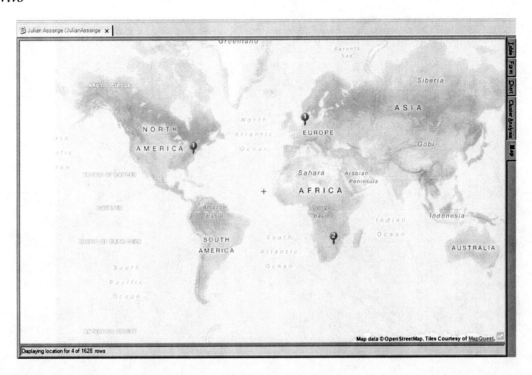

Table 2. Queries of the microblogging message data extractions

The Account	What is the account history? When did it start? How is the account self-described? The entity? How self-aware and self-referential are the words of the word cloud?
Focus	What are the main words that indicate the focus of the microblog? What are the focal issues of the account? What are some emergent ideas in the account? What is the range of focus? Is this range narrow or medium or broad? How much disparity is there between popular topics and less popular ones?
Events	What are the events that are referred to? What are the natures of these events? (Real or cyber or both? Public or private? Political or non-political?) What apparent role did this account holder / account / entity play in the event?
Interactive Conversations	What are the hashtags used to indicate conversations that are participated in? Are there collaborators or partners mentioned?
Audience Analysis	What sort of terminology is used? What does this say about the participants and audience in this microblogging account? How is the account branded? Is there a subculture among followers in this community? Are there shared values, habits, and understandings?
Calls-to-Action	Are there calls-to-actions with the microblogging messaging? If so, what? Are there information elicitations apparent?
Leads for Further Research	What are some unusual or anomalous terms or names that will require further research? What are some words which do not appear in this word cloud that should given the subject matter of the account?
Linked Multimedia	What are the images linked to the microblog corpus? What are the videos linked to the microblog corpus?
Gist	What is the main gist of the account? Why? What are ways to test the accuracy of this interpretation of "gist"?
Outsider Viewpoints	What are some outsider comments about the account? What is the account reputation from external sources?

Figure 13. #cold extraction and cluster analysis extrapolation (NCapture in NVivo)

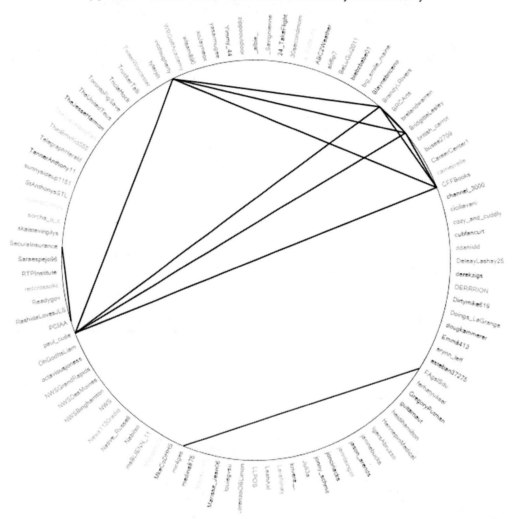

(7) Twitter ~ Search - #cold - Usernames Clustered by Word similarity

The node-level analysis of an account is understood to have value within a social network structure as well. Multiple accounts that stand in relation to each other may be analyzed to compare the differences in microblogging contents and patterns. An account's Tweet history may be studied in phases to analyze the evolution of messaging and ideas and emotions. Similar accounts may be compared for the differences in their focuses (possibly based on their respective objectives). These visualizations may highlight particular patterning, particularly when multiple accounts are compared side-by-side. Or, this approach may be used at discrete stages of an account's lifespan to understand something about the changing focuses over time. There are numerous ways to mix and match such extractions for informational value. Going beyond a simple extraction and analysis is beyond the purview of this chapter, however. Suffice it to say that the research question and its framing will affect how researchers will use the capabilities described here.

CONCLUSION

This research approach may be applied to a range of social media platforms using the same software tools here (or using others that are widely publicly available). This type of data extraction offers a way of aggregating pieces of electronic personalities and identities across multiple social media platforms and other complementary sources. This general approach applies even if the target technology is not microblogging. The microblogosphere is changing along with the rest of the Web 2.0 Social Web.

For some, there is a sense of diminishing returns in the fleeting non-relationships that are being fostered online. One author writes of a hunger for substance:

What we chase through our digital devices is instant connection and information. What we get is no more nutritious or enduringly satisfying than a sugary dessert...We don't need more bits and bytes of information, or more frequent updates about each other's modest daily accomplishments. What we need instead is more wisdom, insight, understanding and discernment—less quantity, higher quality, less breadth and more depth. (Schwartz, 2014)

With the heightened awareness of privacy compromises with the Edward Snowden revelations that have garnered global attention, there is another push for increased privacy, with many going to self-destructing or elusive messages that do not leave electronic trails.

No matter what is happening in terms of larger-level dynamics, every technology ultimately ages out and sunsets as its popularity diminishes or the felt-need for its functions disappear or another technology replaces it. Still, there are continuing human needs for connectivity. There will always be needs to reach out to various targeted or general publics. In this light, Research 2.0, built on the Social Web, is likely here to stay .

REFERENCES

Agarwal, A., Xie, B., Vovsha, I., Rambow, O., & Passonneau, R. (2011). Sentiment analysis of Twitter data. In *Proceedings of the Workshop on Language in Social Media*. Portland, OR: Association for Computational Linguistics.

Almuhimedi, H., Wilson, S., Liu, B., Sadeh, N., & Acquisti, A. (2013). Tweets are forever: A large-scale quantitative analysis of deleted Tweets. In *Proceedings of CSC@ '13*. San Antonio, TX: CSC. doi:10.1145/2441776.2441878

Andre, P., Bernstein, M. S., & Luther, K. (2012). Who gives a Tweet? Evaluating microblog content value. In *Proceedings of CSCW 12*. Seattle, WA: Association of Computing Machinery. doi:10.1145/2145204.2145277

Ardon, S., Bagchi, A., Mahanti, A., Ruhela, A., Seth, A., Tripathy, R. M., & Triukose, S. (2013). Spatio-temporal and events based analysis of topic popularity in Twitter. In *Proceedings of CIKM '13*. San Francisco, CA: Association of Computing Machinery. doi:10.1145/2505515.2505525

Ball, P. (2004). *Critical Mass: How One Thing Leads to Another*. New York: Farrar, Straus and Giroux.

Berg, B. L., & Lune, H. (2012). *Qualitative Research Methods for the Social Sciences* (8th ed.). Boston: Pearson Publishers.

Bermingham, A., & Smeaton, A. (2010). Classifying sentiment in microblogs: Is brevity an advantage? In *Proceedings of CIKM '10*. Toronto, Canada: Association of Computing Machinery.

Carley, K. M., Pfeffer, J., Liu, H., Morstatter, F., & Goolsby, R. (2013). Near real time assessment of social media using geo-temporal network analytics. In *Proceedings of IEEE/ACM International Conference on Advances in Social Networks Analysis and Mining*. Niagara, Canada: IEEE/ACM. doi:10.1145/2492517.2492561

Chen, T., Lu, D., Kan, M.-Y., & Cui, P. (2013). Understanding and classifying image Tweets. In *Proceedings of MM'13*. Barcelona, Spain: Association of Computing Machinery. doi:10.1145/2502081.2502203

Deng, L., Xu, B., Zhang, L., Han, Y., Zhou, B., & Zou, P. (2013). Tracking the evolution of public concerns in social media. In *Proceedings of ICIMCS'13*. Huangshan, ChinaL ICIMCS. doi:10.1145/2499788.2499826

Grace, J.H., Zhao, D., & boyd, d. (2010). Microblogging: What and how can we learn from it?. In *Proceedings of CHI 2010*. Association of Computing Machinery.

Guerra, P. H. C., Veloso, A., Meira, W., & Almeida, V. (2011). From bias to opinion: A transfer-learning approach to real-time sentiment analysis. In *Proceedings of KDD*. San Diego, CA: Association of Computing Machinery.

Hu, X., Tang, L., Tang, J., & Liu, H. (2013). Exploiting social relations for sentiment analysis in microblogging. In *Proceedings of WSDM '13*. Rome, Italy: Association of Computing Machinery. doi:10.1145/2433396.2433465

Michelson, M., & Macskassy, S. A. (2010). *Discovering users' topics of interest on Twitter: A first look. In Proceedings of AND '10* (pp. 73–79). Toronto, Canada: Association of Computing Machinery.

Qiu, L., Lin, H., Ramsay, J., & Yang, F. (2012). You are what you tweet: Personality expression and perception on Twitter. *Journal of Research in Personality*, 46(6), 710–718. doi:10.1016/j.jrp.2012.08.008

Schwartz, T. (2014, Jan. 17). In praise of depth. *The New York Times*.

Tsur, O., & Rappoport, A. (2012). What's in a hashtag? Content based prediction of the spread of ideas in microblogging communities. In *Proceedings of WSDM '12*. Seattle, WA: Association of Computing Machinery.

Vakali, A. (2012). Evolving social data mining and affective analysis methodologies, framework and applications. In *Proceedings of IDEAS 12*. Prague, Czech Republic: Association of Computing Machinery. doi:10.1145/2351476.2351477

Westman, S., & Freund, L. (2010). Information interaction in 140 characters or less: Genres on Twitter. In *Proceedings of IIiX 2010*. New Brunswick, NJ: Association of Computing Machinery.

Yang, L., Sun, T., Zhang, M., & Meik, Q. (2012). We know what @you #tag: Does the dual role affect hashtag adoption?. In *Proceedings of WWW'12*. Lyon, France: Association of Computing Machinery.

KEY TERMS AND DEFINITIONS

Application Programming Interface (API): Tools and resources used by developers to create software tools to interact with other computer systems (such as social media platforms).

Author-Wise Pooling: The collection of information linked to a particular identity or account.

Automated: Achieved by machine, a process which is mostly automatic.

Bag-of-Words Model: The so-called "bag-of-word model" uses a set of unordered words from a document for various types of computations; the frequency count of words may be one approach for classifying the content in a simplifying representation.

Data Crawl: An extraction of data from a website.

Dendrogram: A tree diagram.

Gist: Essence, substance, core meaning.

Graph: A diagram showing relationships between entities (such as node-link diagrams).

Grey Literature: Texts that are informally published.

Manual: Non-automated, done by hand, a process operated by hand.

Microblog: A social media platform that enables users to share short messages in near-real time.

Microblogosphere: The online environment of microblogs.

Mobile Device: A computing device that is sufficiently light and capable to be used in a variety of physical locations; a hand-held computing device.

Plug-In (Add-On or Extension): A software component that adds specific functionality to a particular software program or application.

Sense-Making: The act of understanding or applying meaning.

Sentiment: An attitude or emotion.

Stop-Words List: A listing of terms that are not included in a word search or a word cloud; literally, these are words that are stopped from inclusion (usually because they are unnecessary, informationally inert, or redundant).

Treemap Diagram: A data visualization that shows hierarchical data (including word frequency counts) based on nested rectangles.

Word Cloud: A data visualization comprised of words with the size of the word representing its frequency of appearance.

APPENDIX

Figure 14. Full @AnonOps user network on Twitter (2 deg., 9999-persons limit)

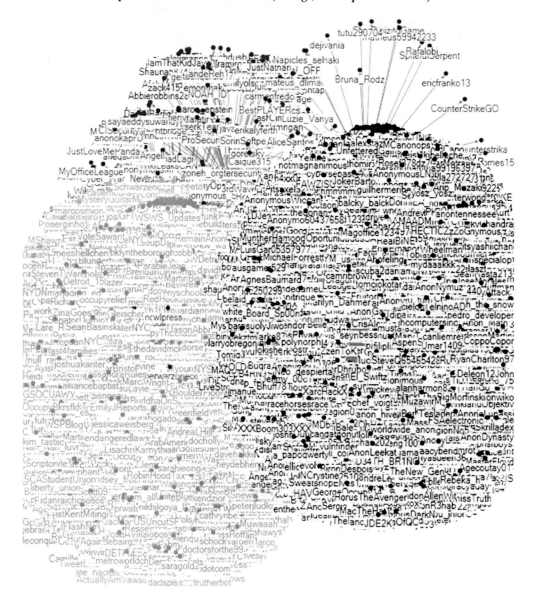

Chapter 14

Sampling Public Sentiment Using Related Tags (and User-Created Content) Networks from Social Media Platforms

Shalin Hai-Jew
Kansas State University, USA

ABSTRACT

The broad popularity of social content-sharing sites like Flickr and YouTube have enabled the public to access a variety of photographs and videos on a wide range of topics. In addition to these resources, some new capabilities in multiple software programs enable the extraction of related tags networks from these collections. Related tags networks are relational contents built on the descriptive metadata created by the creators of the digital contents. This chapter offers some insights on how to understand public sentiment (inferentially and analytically) from related tags and content networks from social media platforms. This indirect approach contributes to Open-Source Intelligence (OSINT) with nuanced information (and some pretty tight limits about assertions and generalizability). The software tools explored for related tags data extractions include Network Overview, Discovery, and Exploration for Excel (NodeXL) (an open-source graph visualization tool which is an add-in to Microsoft Excel), NCapture in NVivo 10 (a commercial qualitative data analysis tool), and Maltego Tungsten (a commercial penetration-testing Internet-network-extraction tool formerly known as Maltego Radium).

INTRODUCTION

As of late 2013, 73% of online adults used social networking sites. Forty-six percent of adult Internet users posted original photos and videos online that they created, as of August 2012. (Brenner, 2013) Social media platforms are trading cloud

space and cloud-delivered services in exchange for the partial or full use of the content of the photos and videos and labels provided by suers. Social computing through content sharing has come to the fore in a big way. The popularization of multimedia content sharing through social media platforms has resulted in the broad avail-

DOI: 10.4018/978-1-4666-6493-7.ch014

ability of billions of user-generated texts, photos, videos, and multimedia. Various content-sharing social media sites offer a heterogeneity of digital contents (multimodal contents) from a wide range of users to a wide audience. Those who created the contents will often "tag" or label this content with keywords and / or short phrases to describe the resource, which enables smoother text-based categorization and searchability for archival and sharing. Individual tagging involves the content creators labeling their own contents, with little input by others in their ego neighborhood or larger user community (such as in photo-sharing and video-sharing social media communities); collaborative tagging involves more broad-scale labeling of contents (such as in social bookmarking sites). (Some tag clouds are access-points for users to query databases and to access particular contents by clicking relevant terms.) Some authors explain:

Tags function both as content organizers and discoverers. As content organizers, tags enable tag creators to annotate and categorize a resource so that it can be retrieved subsequently with ease. Tag consumers will use those same tags to locate that resource. As content discoverers, tags could be used as a means to tap into the collective intelligence of tag creators to make serendipitous discoveries of additional relevant resources. Furthermore, through tags, a tag consumer is able to find like-minded tag creators with resources that meet his or her information needs, potentially leading to the creation of social networks (Razikin, Goh, Chua, & Lee, 2008, p. 50).

The label metadata is value-added information; they are a form of electronically-mediated social communication. These tags result in informal "folksonomies" (non-expert-created taxonomies) that are used to identify contents, enhance user searches, and increase the findability of contents. This informal indexing involves what Hotho calls "lightweight knowledge representation" (Hotho, 2010, p. 57). They are "in vivo" codes—those used

by people in the actual lived environment (even if not necessarily anything that professional archivists would use). In the attention economy of social media, having content that goes "viral" or gains exponential attention in a short time is considered grounds for bragging rights. There is empirical research that suggests that fame of contents in the photo- and video-sharing site Flickr is not generally one of exponential and sudden growth. One study found that users are able to discover new photos within hours after being uploaded and that 50% of the photo views are generated within the first two days (van Zwol, 2007, p. 184). The popularity of particular user-generated contents are a feature of social networking behavior and "photo pooling." Photos that gain a lot of attention transcend local geographical interest. The author explains that "the geographic distribution is more focussed around a geographic location for the infrequently viewed photos, than for the photos that attract a large number of views" (van Zwol, 2007, p. 184).

In terms of tag popularity (a layer of abstraction up from the contents), some researchers suggest that the more popular social tags are the more meaningful ones (Suchanek, Vojnović, & Gunawardena, 2008). Others found that the most popular tags tend to be "visually representational of contents" for photo sharing sites (Sun & Bhowmick, 2009). The growth of popularity of images in Flickr grows in "a steady linear growth of popularity over several years" (Cha, Benevenuto, Ah, & Gummadi, 2012, p. 1066); they do not tend to acquire exponential popularity. These researchers identified two factors of a social network that affect how information spreads: what they term "the burstiness of user login times" and content aging. Bursty logins refer to intervals of short and sudden episodes or groups. However, the recent-ness (freshness) of photos—those uploaded within 30 days—does play a role in the attention they get. The 30-day old photos in Flickr receive 35% of all the favorite responses in the week during the research (at just under 70,000 "favorites"); the remaining 65% of favorite markings go to older photos over a wide range of age groups (at increments past 1000 days) (Cha, Benevenuto, Ah, & Gummadi, 2012, p. 1069), in a long tail. The existence of long tails enable spaces for those with virtually every preference, even if it's a rare one; said another way, content-sharing social media may offer a space for fellow "egocentrics" (Rotman & Golbeck, 2011, pp. 229 - 230). New content has a way of displacing older contents. "While users can have multiple favorites, as the number of photos marked as favorites grows, the bookmarked photos are paged," the authors observe (Cha, Benevenuto, Ah, & Gummadi, 2012, p. 1070).

Others share social media contents for finding an audience and for professional recognition (and possible work). The tagging metadata have not only been used within the social media platforms, but they have been analyzed by researchers for insights about the respective taggers, emergent social networks, and other types of sociometry and online ethnography research. Online ethnography or virtual ethnography refers to the application of ethnographic methods to research on communities and cultures that exist from computer-mediated social interaction; this is a general term refer-ring to the study of cultural phenomena through online fieldwork. One fresh approach involves the analysis of related tags networks to sample public sentiment and understandings about par-ticular issues.

To clarify, this work does not involve machine-based text-analysis for unstructured and unsuper-vised sentiment analysis in the classic sense—of detecting polarities of opinions (up or down votes on certain brands, businesses, politicians, or events); of magnitudes of emotions based on word choices, or other direct multi-dimensional mapping of online communications. Various social media spaces including social networking sites, microblogging socio-technical spaces, and tag-ging networks have been analyzed to understand sentiment and opinion (Paltoglou & Thelwall,

2012). The approach described here is human-based analysis of machine-extracted contents to illuminate latent mental associations.

This work builds on the idea that media content is a "social nexus" (Shamma, Kennedy, & Churchill, 2012), and how people label their contents in relation to other content creators and users has informational value. "Tags" are words or phrases used of a piece to describe or categorize a particular photo or video. Freeform tags are those created by the users without more than a cursory restriction (like absolute length); they are called "freeform" because their vernacular tagging vo-cabulary is informal, uncontrolled, idiosyncratic, and not artificially delimited by the social media platform. Depending on the guidelines of the content-sharing site and user settings, tagging may be done not only by the resource owner but also by friends of that individual; some content-sharing sites allow any other members to tag contents, whether or not they have any direct tie to the user or the contents.

Folksonomies (data structures created from informal tagging) are informed by personomies— or personal tag vocabularies. Freeform tags may also be applied by friends or acquaintances of the individual who created the photos or videos (depending on the policies and practices of the social media platform) nor by any formal taxonomy (which do have controlled vocabularies and other rules for their use); they may sometimes be added by any other participant in the network. Machine-based tags are created by the computers based on machine-analysis of the image. Related tags are associated with each other based on co-relation in usage (co-occurrence); in other words, related tags are linked to each other relationally based on synonymous meaning and co-usage by informal taggers. These relationships between tags, based on semantic similarity, are expressed visually as clusters of texts (tags) or images (of user accounts or content) or partitions in a graph. Cluster analysis involves the separating out of objects with the same or similar properties and placing these in the same categories or groups (clusters). This method is a derivation of summative content analysis, in which there are counts of words and phrases in the particular corpus of data, and latent relationships are identified. Clustering may be done by division, in an *a priori* top-down manner often with pre-defined categories; clustering may be achieved by agglomeration, in a bottom-up or emergent way. Such related tags clusters for this work are created via agglomeration, with the convergence of *ad hoc* tags around shared co-appearances as labels of user-generated contents. Clusters of co-occurring tags "can help disambiguate the themes of subjects of the tagged photos" (Rodrigues & Milic-Frayling, 2011, p. 209).

Large-size clusters represent highly popular related tags; smaller ones represent less popular grouped tags. Then, at the center of each cluster are the most popular tags (expressed as centrality); at the periphery of each of the clusters are the less popular tags within that discrete cluster (expressed as periphery). This related tags analysis approach then is a form of data mining—of identifying latent patterns from tags (which themselves are a level of abstraction away from the original digital contents)—to promote new understandings; given the structure of tag networks, the more correct term is "structure mining" (or learning from interrelationships between entities). There has been research on the study of tags to understand the credibility of health contents on various websites, for example (O'Grady, Wathen, Charnaw-Burger, Betel, Shachak, Luke, Hockema, & Jadad, 2012, p. 36); others have looked at user tagging (and the tagged contents) to evaluate the expertise of the tagger. The understanding is that these tags represent the users' collective thinking and shared informal mental modeling about the core word / phrase and its meaning, based on how they tag

the mediated contents; further, this information may have value for analysis, decision-making, and action in some practical work situations or "use cases".

Social media platforms are known as "affinity spaces" where people with similar interests may find and interact with each other. There are a variety of types of human-to-human, human-to-content, content-to-content sorts of relationships on content-based social media platforms. Figure 1, "Types of Content Network Interactions on Social Media Platforms" highlights these multi-relational interrelationships and different types of connectivity. There are the people behind the various accounts who interact with each other by commenting on each other's contents, ranking them, following each other's user accounts or collections, and maintaining conversations by creating reply videos. There are event-centric tagging around events, with participants sharing their multimedia ("cultural production") from the shared experiences (Schifanella, Barrat, Cattuto, Markines, & Menczer, 2010). There are social meet-ups around social media content creation like video-making and photography. Self-organizing or emergent communities have grown up around human collaborating around shared artifacts and the work of creating collections of data around shared topics of interest, without other organizing dynamics. There are regional groupings of individuals with region-based contents. There are the contents, some held under full copyright, and others which are released to the public through various types of licensure (including Creative Commons licensing). There are private channels with only invited members to share in the contents; protected data is not available for public access or viewing, and their tags are not available for this study. In this context, tags are the labels applied to the various shared multimedia; these labels are based on vernacular literacies based around "voluntary and self-generated" activities (Barton & Lee, 2012, p. 283). The study of tagging is a small subset of these content-based social media interactions.

This approach applies a human relational semantics based on indirect communications—which are mediated through technologies, digital contents, and symbolism (including a range of language and technological multimodal literacies). "The semantics of human activity on social media sites (including Flickr and YouTube) needs to be understood as a relationship between people, actions, artifacts, and supportive contextual metadata," explain one group of researchers (Lin, Sundaram, De Choudhury & Kelliher, 2012). User networks may be extracted based on their interactions (linkages) around particular digital contents (Rodrigues & Milic-Frayling, 2011, p. 205). Even so, content networks that involve more high-investment multimedia (like slideshows and videos) tend to have less dynamism (changeover in contents) and less interactivity than microblogging sites (such as Twitter, with its 140-character Tweets). In Flickr and other shared content-based social media platforms, there tends to be "low interactivity" (Cox, 2008, p. 493), with more of a focus on the digital contents themselves. To understand this subset of analysis, then, Figure 2 offers "A Conceptualization of the Related Tags Network Extraction and Abstraction (from a Social Media Content Platform)." To the right of the image are the contents of the social media content platforms. These contents (including tags) are made available to the public through application programming interfaces (APIs) shared by the social content sharing platforms; APIs enable a range of mash-ups for Web 2.0 services. (The social media platforms do not make every data extraction possible. There are some topics and accounts which the platform will decline to offer data on, without further explanation.) The related tagging data is extrapolated through the uses of various software programs applied to various social media platforms. The extractions are necessary data reduction from potentially enormous "big data" sets. To fully understand the data extractions, it would help to understand what is going on with the data extraction software

Figure 1. Types of content network interactions on social media platforms

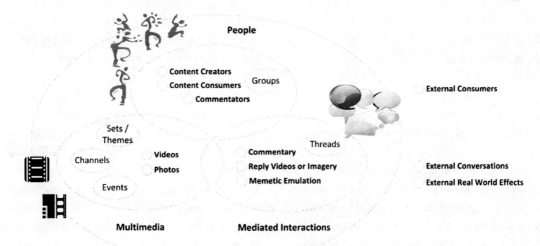

Figure 2. A conceptualization of the related tags network extraction and abstraction (from a social media content platform)

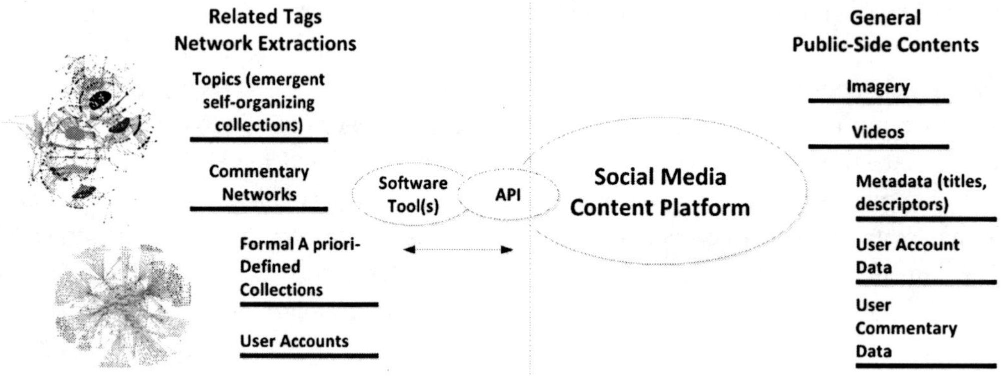

programs, the content-sharing social media sites, and the data visualization layout algorithms—but practically speaking—that complexity may be too much for most researchers to pursue.

This chapter suggests that the analysis of related tags networks may be analyzed to understand public sentiment around particular issues, particularly nuanced and latent connotations, that may affect efforts at understanding others and possibly even at strategic communications efforts like "memetic engineering" (the use of memes to activate others into desired behaviors), adversarial psychological operations (psy-ops), marketing and branding, advertising, political recruitment, and other actions using information to activate people to preferred behaviors. People themselves are homophilously drawn to others who think alike or orientate themselves to others in similar ways:

The American social psychologist Kurt Lewin argued that the kinds of attractive and repulsive interactions sketched by Horney could be broadly applied in the social sciences. He postulated in the 1950s that there might be an analogy between the forces of electromagnetism that act on particles with electrical charge and the social pressures that

determine the behavior of people. According to Lewin, individuals could be considered to 'move' in an abstract field of ideas, beliefs, habits, and notions. The field is conditioned for each person by the behavior he or she sees in others, and it pushes and pulls the person toward certain dispositions. (Ball, 2004, p. 132)

The related tags networks may show dominant ideas in a content network in terms of centrality; it may highlight which types of contents are popular based on a certain word, phrase, event, name, or other text indicator. Likewise, such graphs also indicate peripheral ideas or those on the outer edges. Such graphs may highlight the depth and shimmer of multi-meaninged words as expressed as tags of digital contents in social media sites. These may illuminate informal data ontologies to enhance knowledge and resource-seeking. This knowledge of public sentiment, in its myriad forms, may inform decision-making and actions—particularly those in terms of public communications and impression management. It is thought that this approach may have implications for a variety of fields—and some of these applications will be suggested in the examples provided here related to a variety of topics, from public health to geography to culture to political science, among others.

This approach is a form of "online ethnography" arrived at by the study of the digital contents uploaded and shared (Berg & Lune, 2012, p. 238). In cyberspace, there are many interacting cultures and subcultures with a variety of understandings, which are partially captured symbolically in language and visuals. As such, this is a rich space for exploration. This work proposes that the metadata of tags may be exploited for associations—to identify and infer information of value: misconceptions, emotions, questions, cultural tendencies, and other aspects for a deeper understanding. In that light, this chapter offers some preliminary "use cases" of the analysis of related tags networks. The data offered here are empirical and extracted from the respective social media platforms (Flickr and YouTube); a number of software tools are used for these extractions, including Network Overview, Discovery and Exploration for Excel (NodeXL), NCapture in NVivo 10, and Maltego Tungsten. Each of these tools and social media platforms involve various affordances and constraints. There are many dependencies for each of the data crawls, and the final results (many of which are depicted in this chapter) are in part a result of those interactions.

Delimitations

To clarify, the analysis of related tags networks is not definitive even as it is empirical. The individuals and groups who go online to share contents may be a particular segment of the population that has access to smart phones and digital cameras and the technological savvy and impetus to engage socially via such content-sharing social media platforms. The digerati in most societies are the relatively more well-educated and "privileged." The digital divide may be a deterrent for many to access the content-sharing social media platforms as content creators and to a lesser extent as direct

beneficiaries of the contents (generally, it costs somewhat less to merely access the contents than to actually create the contents). While certain subpopulations have an outsized voice in these realms, there are many others who are not so engaged and whose perspectives cannot be understood via related tags network analysis. (A subset of the participants who post contents in social media sites may also not be honest agents and may have a variety of motives in the sharing and tagging of work; their work may / may not show up as skew in the findings because of the magnitude of the data.) The ability to participate in such networks is not only a requirement of local access, capability, and sufficient wealth (and leisure), but it also requires a larger societal level access to Internet connectivity (and all those dependencies). There are still large areas of the planet that are not yet stably connected. In terms of content networks, there are limits to what aspects of life and human experience can be depicted in photos, screenshots, digital stills, videos, and texts. There are large areas of potential information left unaddressed. Many aspects of life not in content-sharing social media platforms.

First, the extraction process involves layers of dependencies; this process relies on the software tool used for the extraction and its interaction with the social media platform. The same data crawl done even with a split second difference would result in quite a high level of variance in the information capture in highly dynamic information spaces like microblogging and photo-sharing sites (although with less variance in video content networks, which tend to be more stable over time). While "trends" exist in content-sharing sites, usually, these are trends around singular popular items rather than an evolving mass of contents changing quickly over time. Contrast content networks to the volatile hashtag (#) conversations (on microblogs) around hot topics—which involve accruals of hundreds of millions of opinions a day when issues are running hot. (Running crawls on different machines with different processing speeds and Internet connectivity speeds can also result in differences in the dataset that is extracted.) Also, these data extractions do not enable an empirical understanding of the amount of contents that the tags are drawn from. Having some baseline data would be helpful. The data extractions are also generally static one-time analyses (one-offs). There are arguments for the fixed atemporality of such analyses because delinking a state-in-time from history may enable more in-depth focus on particular elements of the network (by excluding time as a direct study variable) (Abbott, 2004).

While sequences of data extractions may be achieved, these still fall short of dynamic and continuous temporal sampling; there may be value in understanding changes over time (short-term, mid-term, and long-term time). To gauge the amount of variance between different data crawls, it would be important to conduct an in-depth study of the algorithms and programming underlying the tools; it would be important to test for different results based on temporal issues. It may help to identify the optimal cycles for information sampling.

The parameters of a data crawl also affect the outcomes. These parameters may include the terminology chosen, the size of the data crawl, the data visualization layout algorithms, and other factors. (More about the parameters will be offered later.) The privacy protections around other accounts mean that a percentage of datasets will be "dark" or invisible to the general public. There may be language limitations to certain data crawls, with some tools enabling wide crawls in English but not so much in languages expressed in Unicode (or even in percent encoding).

As with virtually all technology systems, there is a degree of error with some of the software programs. One member of the development team for NodeXL explained that the system does not tend so much towards a false positive (falling into a Type I error of rejecting the null hypothesis when it is true; seeing an effect which does not exist) than a limited false negative (falling into a Type II error of failing to reject the null hypothesis when the null hypothesis is false); in other words, the extracted and identified relationships between nodes (entities) exist, but they may not include all such relationships in a comprehensive way. The system does not tend to identify a relationship where there is not one, but it may not capture all such relationships. Such captures are also not sufficiently fine-grained to capture so-called "orphaned tags" ("isolate nodes" or disconnected entities in a graph network) which are only assigned to a few resources; to find these, a researcher would have to conduct comprehensive tag extractions for human- and machine- analysis. One way to try to address the missing information is to conduct

Figure 3. Type I and Type II errors (in a four-celled table)

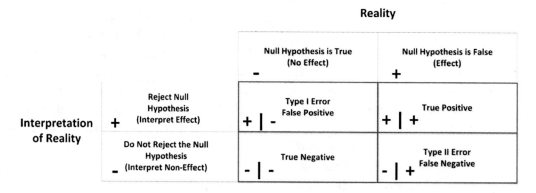

multiple data crawls with multiple software tools and at different times—for high-value queries. The positives it identifies are true, but it may not capture all of the extant relationships. The concept of the Type I and Type II errors are expressed in the variation on the classic table in Figure 3, "Type I and Type II Errors (in a Four-Celled Table)".

Another delimitation comes from the nature of related tags themselves. These tags are labels placed on digital contents by non-professional content creators, with a wide range of subjectivities and inter-subjectivities in the labeling. While professional indexers use controlled vocabularies, with explicitly described terms, in a systematic and non-redundant way, amateur taggers do not (Stvilia, Jöorgensen, & Wu, 2012, p. 100).

Language itself is polysemic, with many words with multiple denotations and even more potential connotations and localisms. The analysis of related or associated tags itself is another layer of abstraction built on top of the tags and the digital contents and the personalities behind those contents. These related tag networks comprise a low N in terms of the numbers of labels. A low ratio of labels are used to evoke a wide swath of photo and video resources on mass-scale social media platforms (hundreds of millions of artifacts from the most popular sites); with data reduction, this small subset of labels or tags is further reduced for necessary simplifications (almost like a factor analysis with encapsulation of some complexity within a simpler outer structure).

Also, power laws have been observed in tagging, which means that there is outsized condensing of attention and popularity of certain tags, and then a fast diminishing long tail of other tags. A "power law" indicates a relationship between two quantities where one varies as a power of another. This phenomena indicates a convergence of focus on certain select tags for a wide range of social media contents. This would indicate scale-free topology networks in which there are a select few tags used for a variety of contents in a network and then plenty of diversity in terms of rare or-

phaned tags used for only a few resources. Some researchers observe this phenomena:

A crucial feature of some power laws—and one that we also exploit in this work—is that they can be produced by scale-free networks. So regardless of how large the system grows, the shape of the distribution remains the same and thus stable. Researchers have observed, some casually and some more rigorously, that the distribution of tags applied to particular resources in tagging systems follows a power law distribution where there are a relatively small number of tags that are used with great frequency and a great number of tags that are used infrequently (Mathes 2004, as cited in Robu, Halpin, & Shepherd, 2009, p. 14:3).

Figure 4, "The Power Law of Social Media Content Tagging" shows the power law distribution of tagging in social media content. This distribution shows that limited tags have high degree or popularity, expressed as clustering among these tags (co-occurrence).

Each layer of abstraction, simplification, and reduction means information loss and coarser granularity (level of detail or specificity) of analysis. Yet, for all these real gaps, there is still a value in using related tags networks to summarize large datasets of information and the thinking of those who have uploaded those contents for sharing. To understand the long tail from another perspective, it is important to understand the phenomena of popularity (high-usage) of particular terms. Popularity is seen in two ways in related tags graphs. Figure 5, "'Feast' Content Network on Flickr (Unlimited) with Cluster and Node Levels of Analyses (to Differentiate Common vs. Uncommon Tags)," shows five extracted clusters of terms around the concept of a "feast" in Flickr. The top-sized graphs are the ones across the top and at bottom left. The smaller graphs are at the bottom right. At the cluster level, there is a differentiation between popular and less popular graphs. Further, in each of the graphs, there are

Figure 4. The power law of social media content tagging

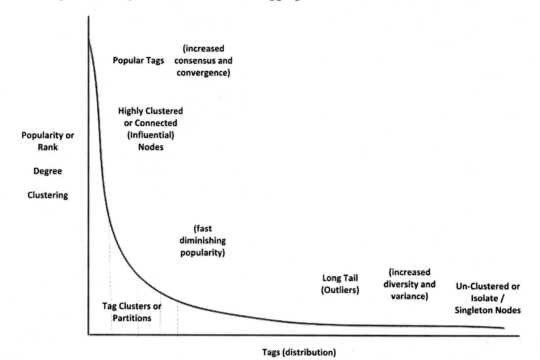

popular tags in the core…and less popular tags in the periphery; there is a core-periphery dynamic going on, too. What is not on the visualization are the orphaned tags and isolate nodes which may be part of the general "feast" related tags network but which were not used sufficiently to fit in any of the clusters and so were not listed in the visualization. In other words the popularity (left side of the power law curve) vs. lack of popularity (right side or the long tail of the power law distribution) may be expressed at both the network and cluster levels; this means that the power law dynamic has a fractal quality that carries over to both network (between clusters) and cluster (between nodes) levels of analysis. The annotations in the figure show this dynamic.

As such, this related tags network analysis is inferential and may offer nuanced shimmers of insights. They may provide a general impression or gist. The findings from such network analysis may offer leads for further research. In alignment with other information, insights from related tags network analysis may contribute to decision-making and possibly even add actionable insights. Clearly, additional work will be required to fully exploit this approach. Finally, this approach certainly does not preclude other approaches either given the complexity of social networks and content networks.

REVIEW OF THE LITERATURE

A simple contextualization of this work would place it within the realm of online ethnography and more specifically the study of digital artifacts created as part of user-created digital resource sharing on social media sites. An applicable foundational

Figure 5. "Feast" content network on Flickr (unlimited) with cluster and node levels of analyses (to differentiate common vs. uncommon tags)

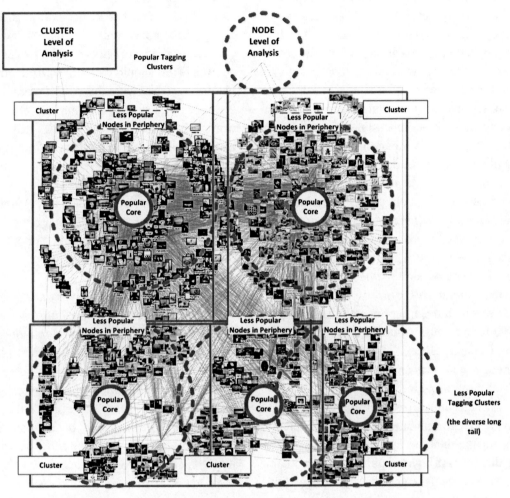

theory would be those of emergentists, who focus on the importance of the social in people's lives and their interdependence (and interaction effects) on each other. Content-sharing social media sites facilitate a variety of endeavors beyond the commercial one. The sharing of information and multimedia has supported efforts in citizen journalism, travel documentation, lifestyle sharing, social games, education, political organization, amateur photography, amateur videography, event publicizing, co-research, and other efforts. A common conceptualization is that people are both simultaneously narrow-casting the digital contents to their respective in-group friends and broad-casting to the larger Internet community.

Unstructured Tagging

Many have critiqued the challenges with unstructured tagging, or the use of everyday natural language to label digital contents. There are a range of ommon critiques. Flickr tagging is seen as part of the growing new "vernacular literacies" enabled by new technological platforms (Barton &

Lee, 2012). Tagging based on informal language learned through social interactions result in casual tagging (Barton & Lee, 2012, p. 297). Language itself is by nature imprecise: polysemy refers to the many-meaningedness aspects of words, both denotatively and connotatively; synonyms may stand in for other words with similar meanings. Word senses may require multiple readings to understand; they may be impossible to extrapolate. User-based taggers may engage in homonymy, the uses of like-sounding words in lieu of the appropriate term. Word choices to include on tags may only be weakly relevant or even irrelevant to the contents. Those uploading contents may introduce spelling mistakes given the vicissitudes of thumb typing while on-the-go. The auto-complete functions in many smart mobile devices may result in inadvertent submittal of the incorrect (but properly spelled) words; indeed, mobile applications are available for a number of devices and operating systems ("Flickr," Dec. 1, 2013). While iterative labeling (and revision) is possible, for most, the initial pass-through of a tag is the one that remains. There are differing levels of analysis in terms of categorizations. "Hypernymy" refers to the semantic relations between words that are superordinate or at a higher rank or class than other words; for example, the generic "hypernym" (or superordinate) word "money" may include other words definitionally such as "*renminbi*" or "dollar." The relative level of the work—its place in a word hierarchy—may not be parallel to those used by other taggers: words may be a generic, a speciifc, or a subjective interpretation or evocative detail. The meta-tagging annotation may refer to parts of a photo or video or page instead of the totality of the digital contents. Various social tag spaces use various strategies to deal with "syntactic variations" and other challenges (Vandic, van Dam, Fransincar, & Hogenboom, 2011, p. 1694). The word forms of informal tagging also tend not to be the same parts of speech, so there may be language mechanics issues; this is the reason why some back-end programs will use

"stemming" to identify a range of word forms to acquire the full range of meanings for the text terms. One author has identified the challenges of "syntactic constraints," asking: "How should you create tags out of phrases when spaces are not allowed? How should you deal with punctuation? How do you deal with non-ASCII words?" (Lee, 2008, p. 65). Further, amateur taggers will use words with personalized meanings that may not have any resonance with others; groups may use private languages or "codes" among themselves. Oftentimes, tagging happens quickly, with few going back to revise retroactively. Ambiguities arise also in terms of how the tagger means for the tag to relate to the contents. Simons (2008) writes of a grammar-less "Tag-elese":

Does a tag like england, for instance, mean that the tagged picture shows something from or about England, or does it simply mean that the picture has been taken in England (see Rattenbury et al., 2007)? And what about color terms? Tags like blackandwhite obviously designate stylistic features of a photo, but do tags like red, green, or blue designate properties of the photographed objects, or salient properties of the photo itself? Why is there a tag girl in Flickr's tag cloud, but not a tag boy? Problems like these do not arise from any ambiguity, polysemy or homonymy of the terms used as tags: there is nothing ambiguous about terms like england, green, or girl. [4] Rather, these ambiguities arise from the different relations these terms entertain with the tagged resources. Since these relationships are not explicitly marked by the tags, the collection of tags in Flickr's tag cloud turns out to be even messier than it already was through the known semantic ambiguities. But again, is it? It's time to try and chart these yet "unknown knowns" (Simons, 2008, n.p.).

The uses of multiple languages for tagging has resulted in yet other challenges, with computer-based translations and mono-lingual or limited-language searches resulting in limits to various data crawls. Flickr enables the uses of traditional complex Chinese, English, French, German, Indonesian, Italian, Korean, Portuguese, Spanish, and Vietnamese; however, people's contributions can be written in any language and script (Barton & Lee, 2012, p. 286). Researchers have argued for more inclusion of varied cultural perspectives in social tagging to promote diversity (Eleta & Golbeck, 2012).

On many content-sharing social media platforms, tagging also is not mandatory; it's optional. There are titles and descriptions that may be used in lieu of tags. Because of this and other factors, many digital artifacts are left untagged or only identified by geospatial tags (such as from "exchangeable image file format" or EXIF data from location-aware devices) or camera default file names. Files labeled with camera default names refer to images that were uploaded without any tags; in Flickr, these unnamed images range in the hundreds of millions (Chan, Satoh, & Yamana, 2011). Not all contents have human-applied labels but only machine-extrapolated ones.

Some Social Features of Tagging

If humans tend to be memetic or emulative of each other, this aspect of people also applies to their meta-tagging behaviors related to social media contents. The phenomenon of "social copying heuristics" has been observed in tagging, with people's social networks affecting how they tag. Empirical sets of data have been analyzed to understand the patterns found in various tagging sets, with a simple explanation:

Results indicate that simple social copying mechanisms can generate surprisingly good fits to the empirical data, with implications for the design and study of tagging systems (Lorince & Todd, 2013, p. 1).

The community aspect of tagging goes beyond the shared appreciation of particular digital contents and activities; individuals have been observed to mutually influence each other's choices of tags, particularly if they interact online. There are research efforts to identify "local interaction networks" based on users commenting on each other's photos—to understand collective tagging behavior—in order to approximate the tagging behavior of the targeted users. Underlying this approach is the understanding that those in a social network may share similar interests and vocabulary (Sawant, Datta, Li, & Wang, 2010, p. 232).

Other researchers have observed that image indexing is "a complex socio-cognitive process," which also suggests individual tagger sensory and psychological aspects (Stvilia, Jöorgensen, & Wu, 2012, p. 99). Tagging may be a genderized process. In one study of 12,000 users from six different countries, split evenly into gender identified groups, researchers found that gender identification could be achieved in an automated way from the tagged texts:

An analysis of a large user sample shows that there are significant gender determined differences of tag usage. Women and men photograph different things (to some extent) but also choose different tags for the same subjects, and analysis shows that, given a subject tag, supplementary tags added by females and males are often different (Popescu & Grefenstette, 2010, p. 14).

Adjectives are more likely to be used by females in content meta-tagging (Popescu & Grefenstette, 2010, p. 9). Image searching is "not a gender indifferent process" (p. 14). People's identities inform their preferences for tags as well. "Results show that around two thirds of participants tend to prefer image search results obtained using tag representations of their own gender and that a third of participants have a clear preference for their own gender's results" (Popescu & Grefenstette, 2010, p. 9).

Various Categories of Tags

Some researchers have extrapolated limited sets of tags from topic-based folksonomies and identified various categories—which result in a mixed lot of information. A "category model" of image tags in Flickr resulted in a broad range of inconsistent categories: adjective, compound terms, emotion, event, humor, language, living thing (plants and animals), number, person, photographic, place-general, place-name, poetic, rating, thing, time, unknown (defined as "unidentifiable terms"), and verbs (Beaudoin, 2007, p. 26). In another extrapolation, the identified themes (within which the tags resided) were the following: geographical, events, nature, style/genre, places, family, seasons, technique, people, arts, rest, and animals (in descending order) (Simons, 2008). In yet another categorization of different types of tags across multiple tagging platforms (based on music, images, videos, and other web contents), another researcher identified eight categories: topic, time, location, type, author/owner, opinion/qualities, usage context, and self reference (Krestel, 2011, Slide 16). The three prior examples are among a number that show high variances in terms of types of tags in various tagging constructs. A cursory look at Flickr's 150 most popular tags "tag cloud" (a diagram of words with their sizes indicating the word frequency of the particular term) feature provides a sense of the broad diversity of tag types ("All time most popular tags").

Informal Tagger Motivations

Various researchers have explored why people tag their shared contents. This has been of interest because of the wide diversity (on a range of demographic measures) in those who create contents for sharing on social networks. Several studies found variance in tagging results based on the ambitions for the tagging. Some authors set up an understanding of tagging motivations based on two main concepts: sociality (self or social) and function (organization and communication); tagging for self may involve organizing digital contents for later retrieval and search (organization) or for providing a context for one's memory of the contents (communication); a social approach may involve contributing to the larger group and capturing attention as well as pooling photos on a topic (organization) as well as providing content descriptions and signaling socially (communication) (Ames & Naaman, 2007, p. 976). There is often higher variance among individual taggers than those working as part of larger groups of taggers (who have an increased sense of a shared word listing). Some have used tags as part of protest strategies to publicize their dissatisfaction (Tisselli, 2010, p. 141). One core differentiation between taggers involves a general underlying motivation between "categorizing" and "describing":

Categorizers tag because they want to construct and maintain a navigational aid to the resources for later browsing. On the other hand, users who are motivated by description view tagging as a means to accurately and precisely describe resources. Describers tag because they want to produce annotations that are useful for later retrieval. This distinction has been found to be important because, for example, tags assigned by describers might be more useful for information retrieval (because these tags focus on the content of resources) as opposed to tags assigned by categorizers, which might be more useful to capture a rich variety of possible interpretations of a resource (because they focus on user-specific views on resources). (Körner, Kern, Grahsl, & Strohmaier, 2010, p. 158)

Those describing resources offered more unique details than those working to categorize contents. Those who used categorizing tags did so in order to navigate back to their own resources at a future time; those who used descriptive tags for their resources tended to be more other-focused and often used "an open set of tags, with a rather dynamic and unlimited tag vocabulary" (Strohmaier, Körner, & Kern, 2012, p. 3). The authors further found more "tag agreement" based on alignment of users' motivations for tagging (Strohmaier, Körner, & Kern, 2012, p. 2). In terms of descriptive tags, some further differentiated between objective factual descriptions and subjective evaluative ones. Taggers with more tagging experiences tend to add more tags to a resource than other participants (Stvilia, Jöorgensen, & Wu, 2012).

The debate about how much value crowd-sourced tags bring in contrast to more formal labels continues. Some researhcers suggest that the "wisdom of crowds" (per Suriowiecki's phrasing) theory might suggest that community-created tags are better than expert ones. However, these authors suggest that this assertion is debatable; further, to improve the quality of crowd-created tagging, the authors suggested improved guidelines at the social media sites (Razikin, Goh, Chua, & Lee, 2008, p. 59).

Human tagging may be further refined or complemented with machine tagging. There is the view that the automatic ingestion of tagging information "deepens the information pool and removes human error" (Beaudoin, 2007, p. 27). Human-created tags may be supplemented with machine tagging although such mixed datasets might confuse the issue of human mind sets in approaching particular topics (except where the machine tagging is on issues of geolocation only). Even recommender systems that suggest particular tags of interest may create more convergence of tag choices than might happen otherwise.

APPLICATIONS OF RELATED TAGS ANALYSIS FOR PUBLIC SENTIMENT EXTRACTION AND UNDERSTANDING

To understand how public sentiment may be extracted from related tags networks, it is important to introduce the software tools used and the targeted content-sharing social media sites. Three main software tools are used for the tagging information extractions: Network Overview, Discovery and Exploration for Excel (NodeXL), NCapture and NVivo 10, and Maltego Tungsten (formerly Radium prior to 2014). NodeXL is an open-source tool that is an add-in to Excel and is available at the CodePlex site. NCapture is an add-on tool to NVivo 10 and is used as part of NVivo 10 for data visualizations. Maltego Tungsten is a proprietary penetration testing tool that also includes the capabilities for social media data extraction and data visualization. The content-sharing social media platforms used include Flickr (an image and video-sharing site owned by Yahoo) and YouTube (a video sharing site owned by Google). Flickr was created by Ludicorp in 2004 and acquired by Yahoo in 2005. According to one media source, by March 2013, Flickr had 87 million registered users and millions of new images daily; in 2011, it already had 4 billion photos globally (Rodrigues & Milic-Frayling, 2011, p. 202). Its current terms of service offers a terabyte of storage for all users, including both photos and high-definition video. To understand what a related tags network consists of, the network that is extracted contains either directed (with arrows indicating the direction of a relationship or link) or undirected ties (without arrows and only the indicator of a relationship between two tags). The relationships between tags are a result of affiliation by semantic-based meaning and co-use in terms of the labeling of digital contents. Researchers observe:

Collectively, the Flickr community has created a large, ever-growing vocabulary of tags that is the foundation for accessing and managing content on Flickr. At the same time, the tagging mechanism depends on the social characteristics of Flickr for its effectiveness. Because tags are generated by individual users, their usefulness to other users depends on the shared understanding of the tags' meaning, which in turn is determined by the exposure of content and metadata among the users and the practices they collectively adopt (Rodrigues & Milic-Frayling, 2011, p. 202).

YouTube was started in February 2005 and was sold to Google in late 2006. As of 2013, it was said to host about 3 billion videos. A video network may be understood as the popularity of that video within a network.

Which videos are central within a category/type of videos? Which videos generate many comments, response videos, and higher ratings? These videos and users may influence the content produced in other videos and attract many relationships (i.e., subscriptions) with people who share an interest in that content. Some videos lead a specific category, whereas others are peripheral (Rotman & Golbeck, 2011, p. 230).

Videos may be linked by tagging with similar keywords, by comments between users, by video conversations (in which people offer each other reply videos).

To clarify, the software list is not a comprehensive one. There are other tools on the market that may enable some of the similar data extractions and visualizations. Likewise, there are other content-sharing social media sites that have APIs that enable the capture of tags and tag networks. However, for the purposes of introducing this approach, these elements provide sufficient breadth for the necessary examples. Figure 6, "General Related Tags Network Extraction and Analysis Workflow," provides a brief overview of the process of related tags network analysis as a general process.

Essentially, the work involves defining a relevant research question, identifying relevant search terms, and choosing a social content platform. Then, the data crawl needs to be set up and completed with the proper software. After post-processing of the data, data visualizations are output and analyzed. There may be both manual and machine-based analysis of the information. The final data may be augmented by follow-on analysis and additional research. Finally, the information is used for analysis, decision-making, or action. This process may be enhanced by selective additional information searches. Further, this is not necessarily a linear process and may involve a variety of recursion and spiraling.

What follows are some related tags network extractions from the mentioned platforms to showcase some of the types of information which may be extracted. These were all created in late 2013 and early 2014.

THEME-BASED QUERIES

A few related tags network graphs were extracted from Flickr based on health- and disease-related tags. The graphs show the various physical clusters as connected links, and then the clusters are highlighted based on certain shared colors and shared shapes. A two-degree crawl involves not only the core word (at the center), its direct ego neighborhood (the direct words that are linked to that tag), but also the ego neighborhoods of those "alters" to the original focal node. Figures 7 to 9 focus on related tag networks for "bacteria," "virus," and "disease" from the Flickr content-sharing platform. All three graphs were laid out using the Harel-Koren Fast Multiscale layout algorithm. To analyze these graphs, it's critical to examine them in depth in terms of the various types of clusters.

Figure 6. General related tags network extraction and analysis workflow

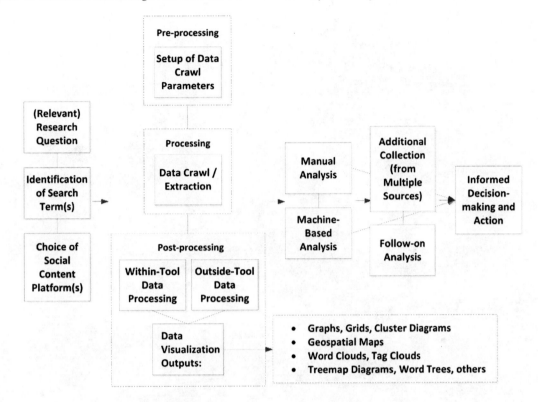

These may provide some insights on people's public sentiments and depth of knowledge towards particular aspects of health and disease.

WORD DISAMBIGUATION

To further enhance the explanation of this approach, a related tags network crawl of "book" was created to show how such a network may be used to disambiguate a term. "Book" may be a noun (she read a book) or a verb (he booked from the scene; she booked a hotel room) or adjective (a book headlamp); it has denotative and connotative meanings. This polysemic aspect of the word may be seen in the various related tags clusters, with some related to booking htoels, books for crafts, different regions and weather, photography books, books as part of the economy (book stores and

libraries), book designs, automotive books, and then a cluster based around foreign languages. This overview is a very brief cluster analysis, bit it offers a sense of how a related tags network may be viewed and queried lightly.

RELATED TAGS COMPARISONS

Another strategy involves conducting related tags network crawls for words that are semi-comparable. For example, the debate over ownership of contested islands in the East China Sea may be inferred by the word usage describing the islands—whether "Diaoyou" or "Senkaku". In this data extraction, the hashtagged conversations around these terms were crawled to see who was talking on the Twitter microblogging platform (which shares textual and image contents). The

Figure 7. "Bacteria" related tags network on Flickr (2 deg., unlimited)

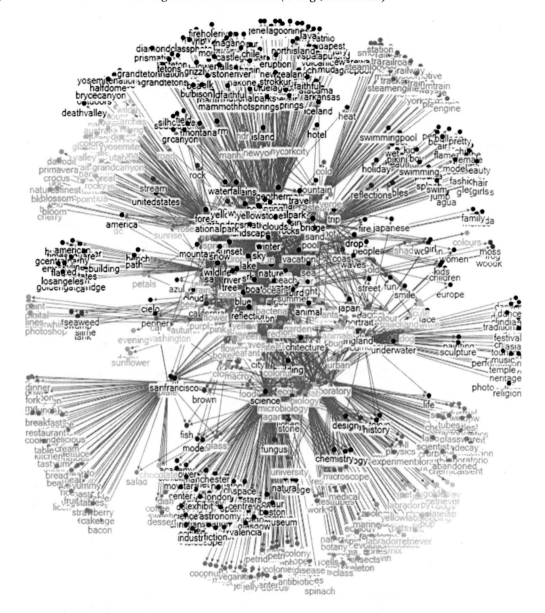

graphs show the clustering of those engaged in this conversation and their interactions with each other on the site.

Further details are available in terms of the graph metrics tables. In this slice-in-time view during a period of high tensions, this structure mining (along with sentiment, emotion, and semantic content analysis of the contents of the Tweets) may offer insights about publicly-expressed attitudes. It may be helpful to see which accounts used both terms and may be "bridging" disparate political camps or communities.

Another example involves a Twitter crawl of "North Korea" and "South Korea". It is important

Figure 8. "Virus" related tags network on Flickr (2 deg., unlimited)

to see who is talking and what is being said to understand the tensions on the Korean peninsula.

A glance at the graph metrics table shows widespread interest from the Twitter search (which only captures information for a little more than the past week). Some light assertions may be made, such as about the greater interactivity of those talking about "South Korea" and the greater relative density of their online network. Again, more meaning should be gleaned from analyzing the contents of the short textual and image-based messaging.

Figure 9. "Disease" related tags content network on Flickr (2 deg., unlimited)

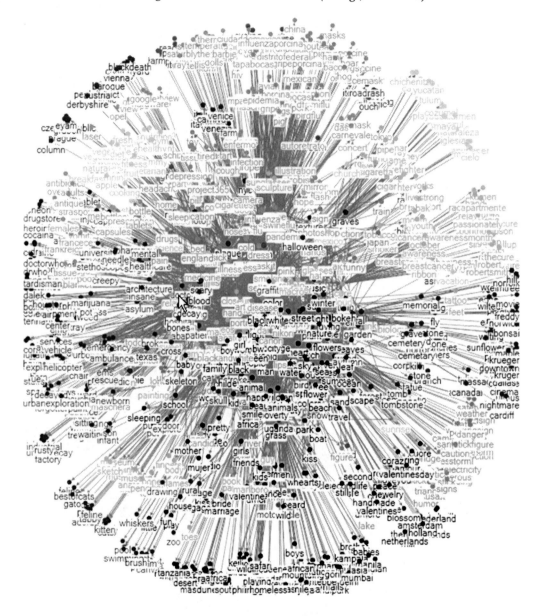

The images linked to the various user accounts used for the communications may be brought out as image-ful graphs. Figure 13, "North Korea" and "South Korea" Related Tags Graphs (with Vertex Images Extracted), may offer another layer of information in terms of the performance of identity of the various users (whose account images are shown here). This type of analysis refers to the extrapolating of image gist.

STARTING WITH GENERICS (TO INFER CULTURE OR SENSEMAKING)

Another strategy with related tags network analysis involves starting with generic words that do not, on the surface, carry heavy weighted meanings. The tags that co-occur with these generic words may highlight latent mental models or associations.

Figure 10. "book" related tags network on Flickr (2 deg., unlimited)

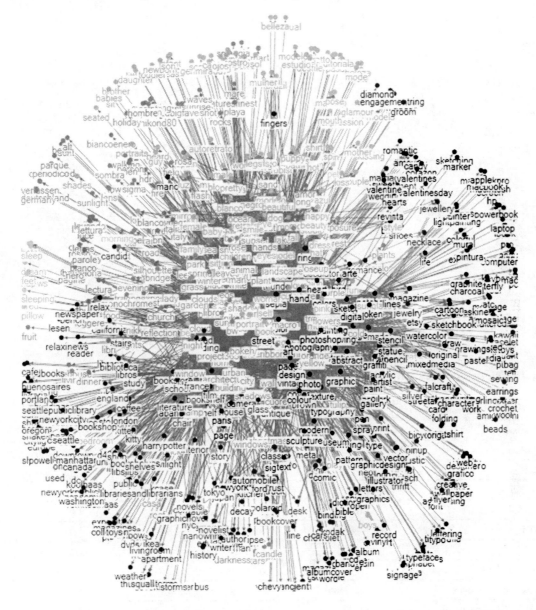

Some generics may be words like the following: male, female, children, family, people, and city. A data crawl of "male" has resulted in core clusters such as "music," "couple," "hot," and "art."

A crawl of female results in clustering around issues like "dress," "hot," "legs" "art" and oth-

ers. A search of these larger clusters and then the smaller nodes may inspire alternate search terms (and chaining of other related tags network and other social media platform crawls for meanings).

A related tags network for "children" results in references to events and pets. There are evocative

Figure 11. "Diaoyou" vs. "Senkaku" islands dispute in December 2013 (Twitter)

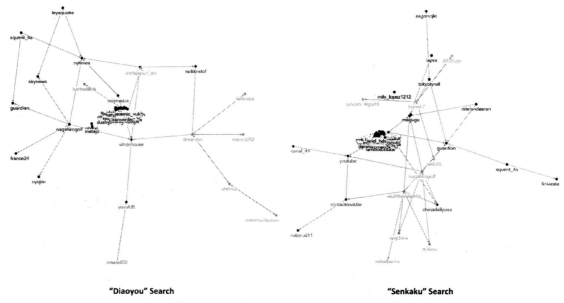

"Diaoyou" Search   **"Senkaku" Search**

"Diaoyou" vs. "Senkaku" Islands Dispute in December 2013:
Unlimited Twitter (Microblogging)Word Searches on Dec. 3, 2013

Table 1. "Diaoyou" and "Senkaku" graph metrics on Twitter

"Diaoyou"		"Senkaku"	
Graph Metric	Value	Graph Metric	Value
Graph Type	Directed	Graph Type	Directed
Vertices	112	Vertices	138
Unique Edges	29	Unique Edges	32
Edges With Duplicates	0	Edges With Duplicates	0
Total Edges	29	Total Edges	32
Self-Loops	0	Self-Loops	0
Reciprocated Vertex Pair Ratio	0.16	Reciprocated Vertex Pair Ratio	0.032258
Reciprocated Edge Ratio	0.275862	Reciprocated Edge Ratio	0.0625
Connected Components	92	Connected Components	117
Single-Vertex Connected Components	89	Single-Vertex Connected Components	115
Maximum Vertices in a Connected Component	19	Maximum Vertices in a Connected Component	19
Maximum Edges in a Connected Component	27	Maximum Edges in a Connected Component	28
Maximum Geodesic Distance (Diameter)	6	Maximum Geodesic Distance (Diameter)	5
Average Geodesic Distance	2.677507	Average Geodesic Distance	2.350133
Graph Density	0.002333	Graph Density	0.001693
Modularity	0.454816	Modularity	Not Applicable
NodeXL Version	1.0.1.245	NodeXL Version	1.0.1.245

Figure 12. "North Korea" and "South Korea" related tags graphs from Twitter

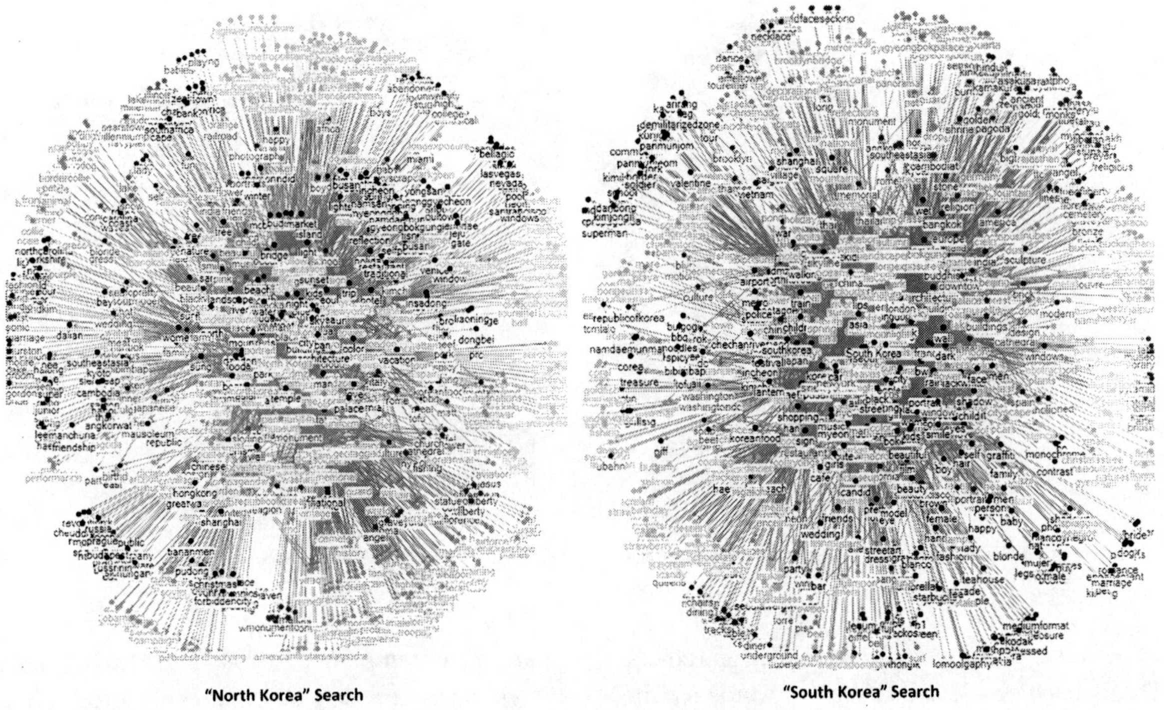

"North Korea" Search   "South Korea" Search

Table 2. "North Korea" and "South Korea" graph metrics

"North Korea"		"South Korea"	
Graph Type	Directed	**Graph Type**	Directed
Vertices	853	Vertices	856
Unique Edges	2759	Unique Edges	3948
Edges With Duplicates	0	Edges With Duplicates	0
Total Edges	2759	Total Edges	3948
Self-Loops	0	Self-Loops	0
Reciprocated Vertex Pair Ratio	0.02641369	Reciprocated Vertex Pair Ratio	0.073117695
Reciprocated Edge Ratio	0.051467923	Reciprocated Edge Ratio	0.13627153
Connected Components	1	Connected Components	1
Single-Vertex Connected Components	0	Single-Vertex Connected Components	0
Maximum Vertices in a Connected Component	853	Maximum Vertices in a Connected Component	856
Maximum Edges in a Connected Component	2759	Maximum Edges in a Connected Component	3948
Maximum Geodesic Distance (Diameter)	4	Maximum Geodesic Distance (Diameter)	4
Average Geodesic Distance	3.314266	Average Geodesic Distance	3.151187
Graph Density	0.003796322	Graph Density	0.005394327
Modularity	Not Applicable	Modularity	Not Applicable
NodeXL Version	1.0.1.245	NodeXL Version	1.0.1.245

Figure 13. "North Korea" and "South Korea" related tags graphs (with vertex images extracted)

"North Korea" Related Tags Graph in Flickr (with Image Vertices)

"South Korea" Related Tags Graph in Flickr (with Image Vertices)

words related to happiness, music, play, and others. These machine-identified hubs of words require further human analysis for meaning.

Related tags network clusters for "family" evoke life events. Specific hubs are built around the following labels: people, holiday, party, and woman.

In terms of a related tags network of "people" on Flickr, the clusters showed a more universal online culture, with references to portraits, events, human descriptors; there were references to "art" and "retrato" ("portrait" in Spanish).

The related tags network extraction of "city" from Flickr gives an intuition of the word with a focus on central regional and urban hubs. Cars, nature, and graffiti are evocations of the tagged networks, with distinctly visual aspects to the tagging.

Understanding brand. The method of contrasting related tags between a generic and a specific may be used to infer public sentiment about a

particular brand. For example, a related tags network extraction may be done for "coffee" (as a baseline) and then for "Starbucks" (as the target). "Starbucks" refers to a commercial brand of coffee and coffee bar / restaurant / cafe. Its uniqueness of terminology may mean a clearer selectivity of terminology and may be therefore more informative (more signal to noise) about people's opinions. The quality of the word clusters, the depth of the graphs, the sizes of the clusters, and those sharing contents may all provide insights about the brand.

The data extractions also involve data tables based on graph metrics. A side-by-side comparison of both the graphs and the tables may shed insight. For example, the greater number of nodes or vertices for Starbucks may show that the brand has traction. The sizes of both related tags networks are similar in terms of connectivity (diameter or maximum geodesic distance), which suggests the closeness of many of the words used for resources tagged with these terms.

Figure 14. "Male" related tags graph on Flickr

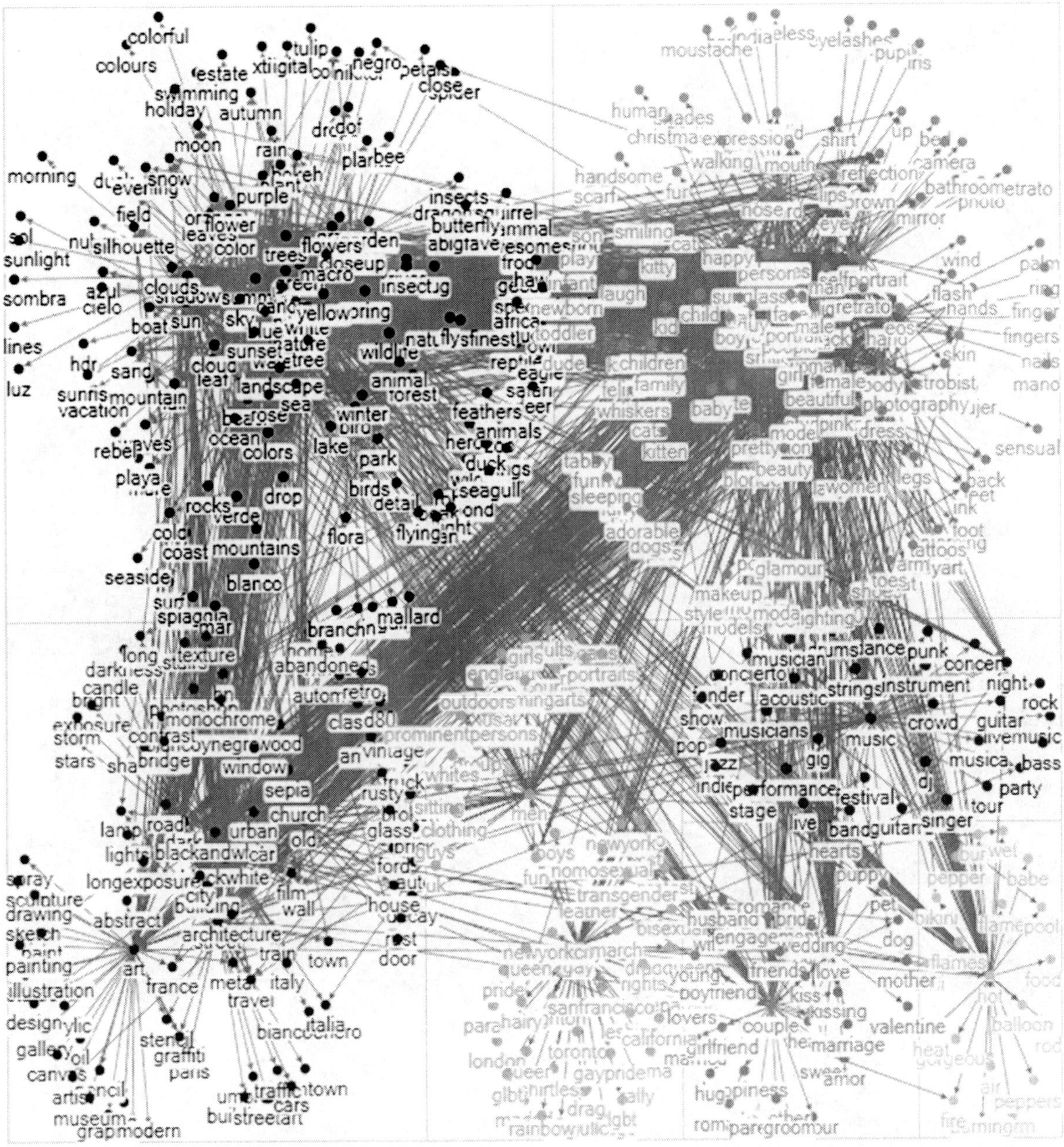

Figure 15. "Female" related tags graph on Flickr

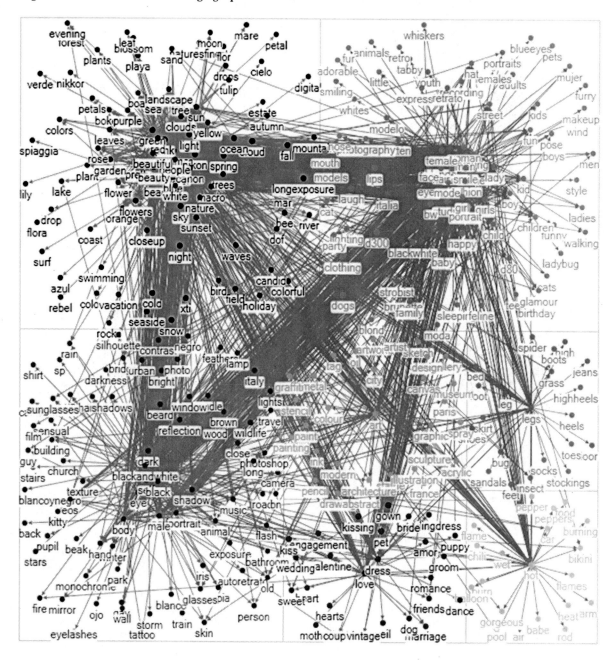

Figure 16. "Children" related tags graph on Flickr

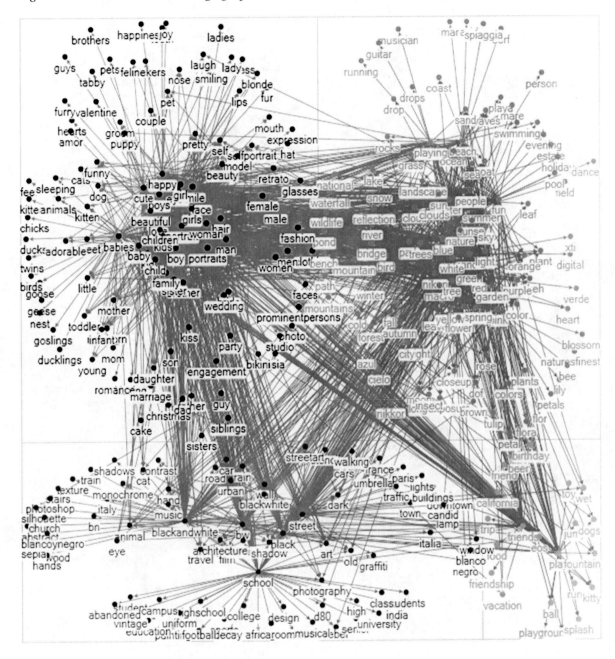

Figure 17. "Family" related tags graph on Flickr

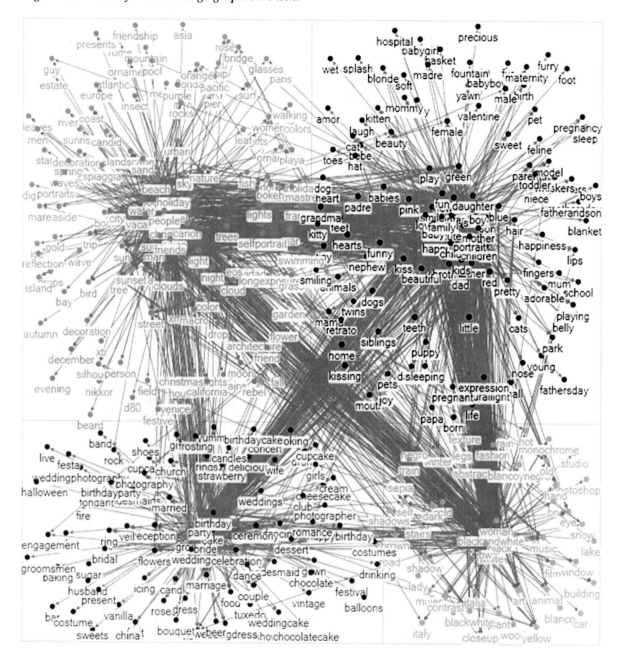

Figure 18. "People" related tags graph on Flickr

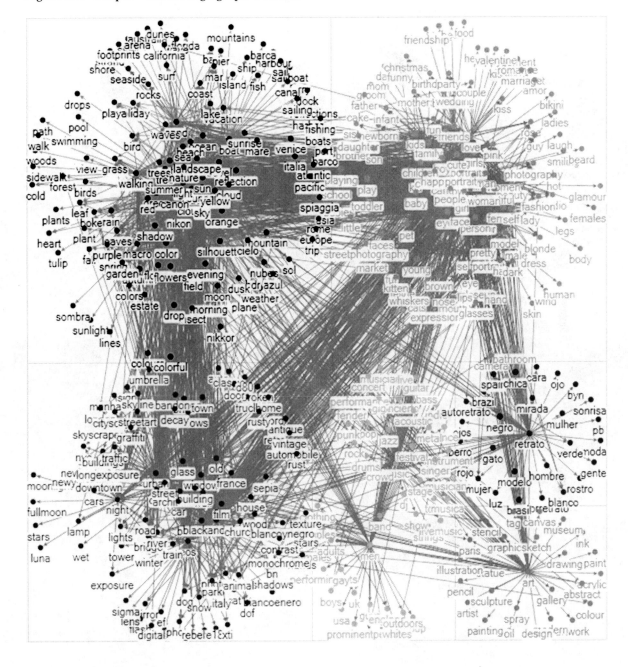

Figure 19. "City" related tags graph on Flickr

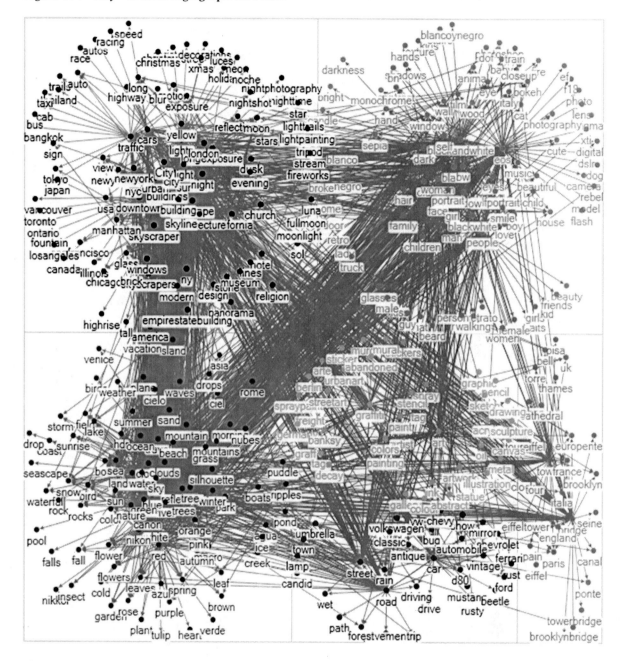

Figure 20. Comparing a generic with a brand in near-synchronous related tags data extraction from Flickr ("Coffee" vs. "Starbucks")

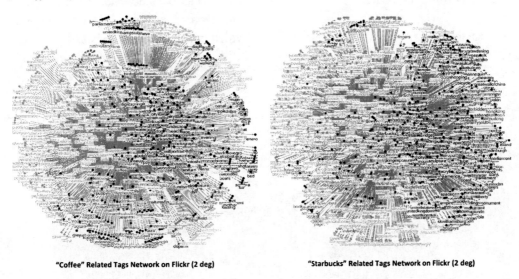

"Coffee" Related Tags Network on Flickr (2 deg)   "Starbucks" Related Tags Network on Flickr (2 deg)

Table 3. "Coffee" and "Starbucks" graph metrics

"Coffee"		"Starbucks"	
Graph Metric	Value	Graph Metric	Value
Graph Type	Directed	Graph Type	Directed
Vertices	864	Vertices	1194
Unique Edges	4520	Unique Edges	6443
Edges With Duplicates	0	Edges With Duplicates	0
Total Edges	4520	Total Edges	6443
Self-Loops	0	Self-Loops	0
Reciprocated Vertex Pair Ratio	0.07773	Reciprocated Vertex Pair Ratio	0.05295
Reciprocated Edge Ratio	0.144248	Reciprocated Edge Ratio	0.100574
Connected Components	1	Connected Components	1
Single-Vertex Connected Components	0	Single-Vertex Connected Components	0
Maximum Vertices in a Connected Component	864	Maximum Vertices in a Connected Component	1194
Maximum Edges in a Connected Component	4520	Maximum Edges in a Connected Component	6443
Maximum Geodesic Distance (Diameter)	4	Maximum Geodesic Distance (Diameter)	4
Average Geodesic Distance	3.034047	Average Geodesic Distance	3.232897
Graph Density	0.006062	Graph Density	0.004523
Modularity	Not Applicable	Modularity	Not Applicable
NodeXL Version	1.0.1.245	NodeXL Version	1.0.1.245

FREIGHTED OR CONTROVERSIAL TERMS

While generic terms start off with a sense of neutrality, there may be value in terms that are already value-laden and possibly controversial. Figures 21 to 25 involve relatively controversial words as tags.

What are the evocations around a political system that has few adherents anymore? What are content creators using around the tag of "Snowden", which may refer to "Edward Snowden," the NSA dissident/whistleblower, the music band, and other concepts? What do people co-tag with "espionage"? What about a network crawl of both "NSA" and Snowden" (using a Boolean strategy)?

Figure 21. "Communism" related tags graph on Flickr (with imagery and layout in a partition)

Figure 22. "Snowden" related tags graph on Flickr (with imagery and layout in a partition)

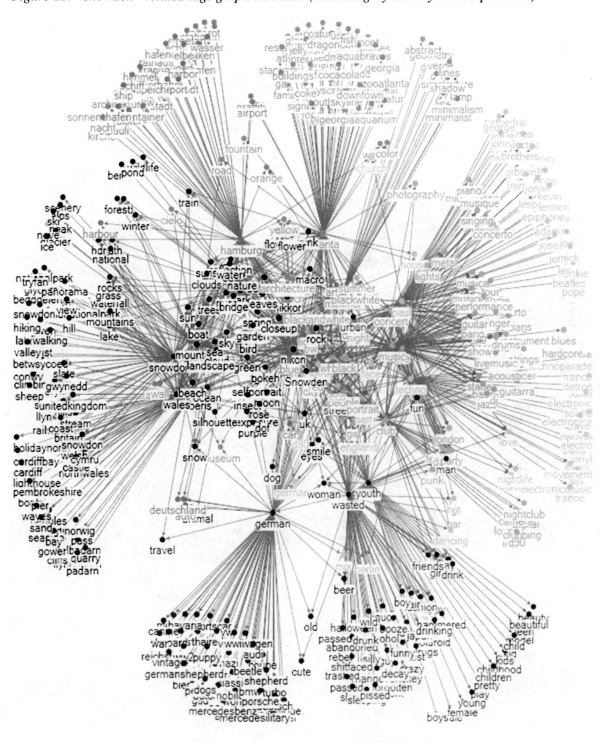

Figure 23. "Espionage" related tags graph on Flickr

Figure 24. "Espionage" related tags graph on Flickr (with imagery and partitioning)

Figure 25. "NSA" and "Snowden" network on the Internet with crossover links (with Maltego Tungsten)

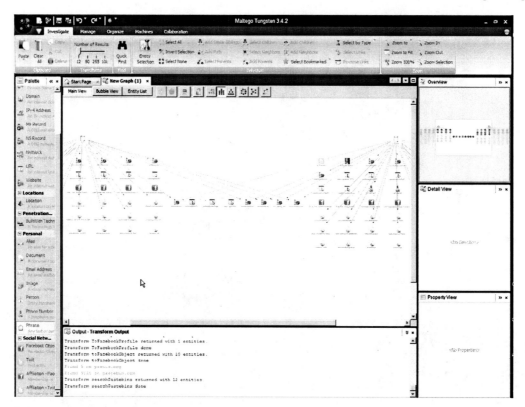

What happens with a tag that is at once both a "generic" and a "specific"—"anonymous" as the generic and as an evocation of the Anonymous hacker collective?

What about public knowledge of a potential next-generation computing machine in its infancy?

What do people think about programming? (Hint: There are evocations of computer programming, desserts, wildlife, transportation, and bookstores.) Further, a subgraph of the most popular cluster in the "programming" related tags network from Flickr may be spotlighted for more close-in analysis, as may be seen in Figure 29, "Subgraph of a 'Programming' Related Tags Network from Flickr to Understand Polysemics Dynamics (a Branch)". Note that this subgraph is taken from the top left of Figure 28, "A "Programming" Related Tags Network on Flickr to Understand Polysemics Dynamics"

ILLUMINATING GEOGRAPHICAL LOCATIONS WITH TAGS

Related tags networks of geographical locations often pull up regional spatial interests. Oftentimes, there is focus on features of the natural and human landscape. In the Flickr related tags network for "Burma," there are religious evocations of Buddhist temples. There are important celebrations and life events mentioned. Figure 30, "'Burma' Related Tags Network Graph on Flickr (in Text and Imagery)" exemplifies some of these tendencies.

Annotations were made in Figure 31, "'Ireland' Related Tags Graph on Flickr" with human-made observations of the tag clustering around natural features, alcohol-based drinks, proper names of locations, landscape features, religion-based words, floral features, and locational highlights.

Figure 26. "Anonymous" related tags graph on Flickr (with imagery and layout in a partition)

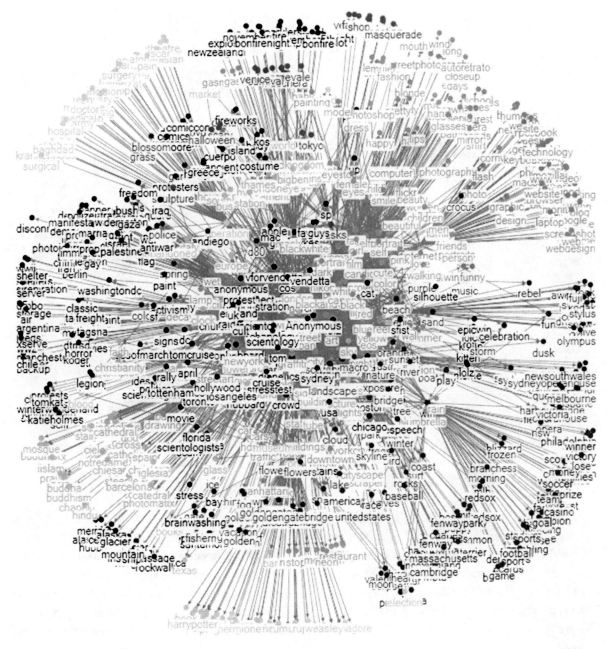

Figure 27. "QuantumComputing" video network on YouTube (with authors and related visuals)

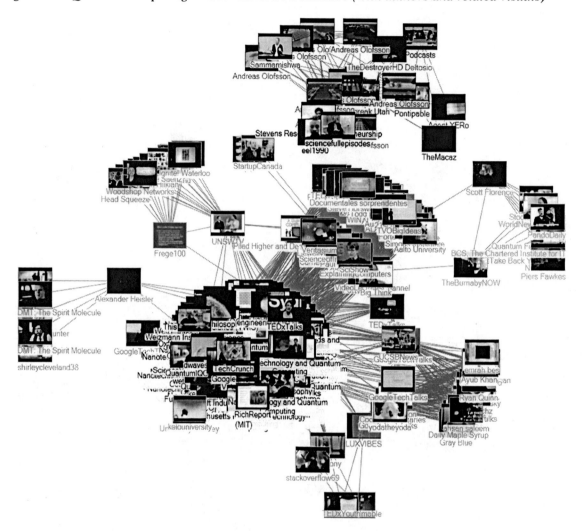

Similar manual clustering was done with Figure 32, "'Antarctica' Related Tags Graph on Flickr (with Cluster Annotations)," Figure 33, "'Bolivia' Related Tags Graph on Flickr (with Cluster Annotations)," Figure 35, "'Greenland' Related Tags Graph on Flickr (with Cluster Annotations)," Figure 36, "'Oman' Related Tags Graph on Flickr," and Figure 38, "'Papua New Guinea' Related Tags Graph on Flickr (with Cluster Annotations)". It is helpful to know that the related tags networks are multilingual.

While the technologies used in the related tags crawl determine clustering, the findings benefit from human analysis. Figure 37, "'Oman' Related Tags Graph on Flickr (with imagery)" involves the addition of an overlay of imagery from various accounts to represent particular terms. It is unclear how the social media platform selects such images or whether it is selected by the software program used for the data extraction. (It may be that this is just randomized sampling. Or it may be stratified random sampling such as selecting

Figure 28. A "Programming" related tags network on Flickr to understand polysemics dynamics

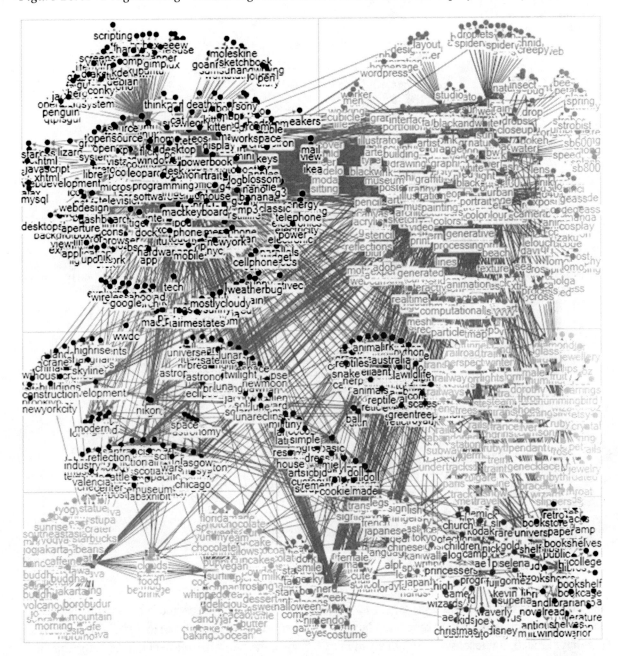

Figure 29. Subgraph of a "programming" related tags network from Flickr to understand polysemics dynamics (a branch)

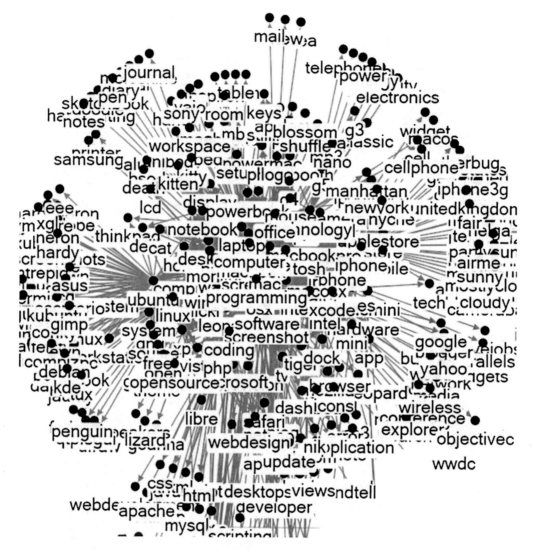

the first image identified using the tag. After all, this information is collected based on human tagging of the digital resources, with likely many thousands or more digital resources represented by those respective tags.)

The uses of imagery for the vertices (nodes) enables researchers to assess the alignment of the image with the text annotations; researchers may look for visual themes or patterns in particular sub-clusters or graphs. This analysis will likely also result in the dissonances and disparities between the images and tag contents as well as between images and other images. Sometimes, data visualizations may make better sense in sequence, with certain aspects of the related tags network highlighted at different stages; for example, the vertices may be labeled by account names first to get a sense of "who" is participating and then the overlay of images may be placed for a graphical analysis. NodeXL enables the partitioning of the respective clusters into various layout boxes as well. This partitioning enables the viewing of each

Figure 30. "Burma" related tags network graph on Flickr (in text and imagery)

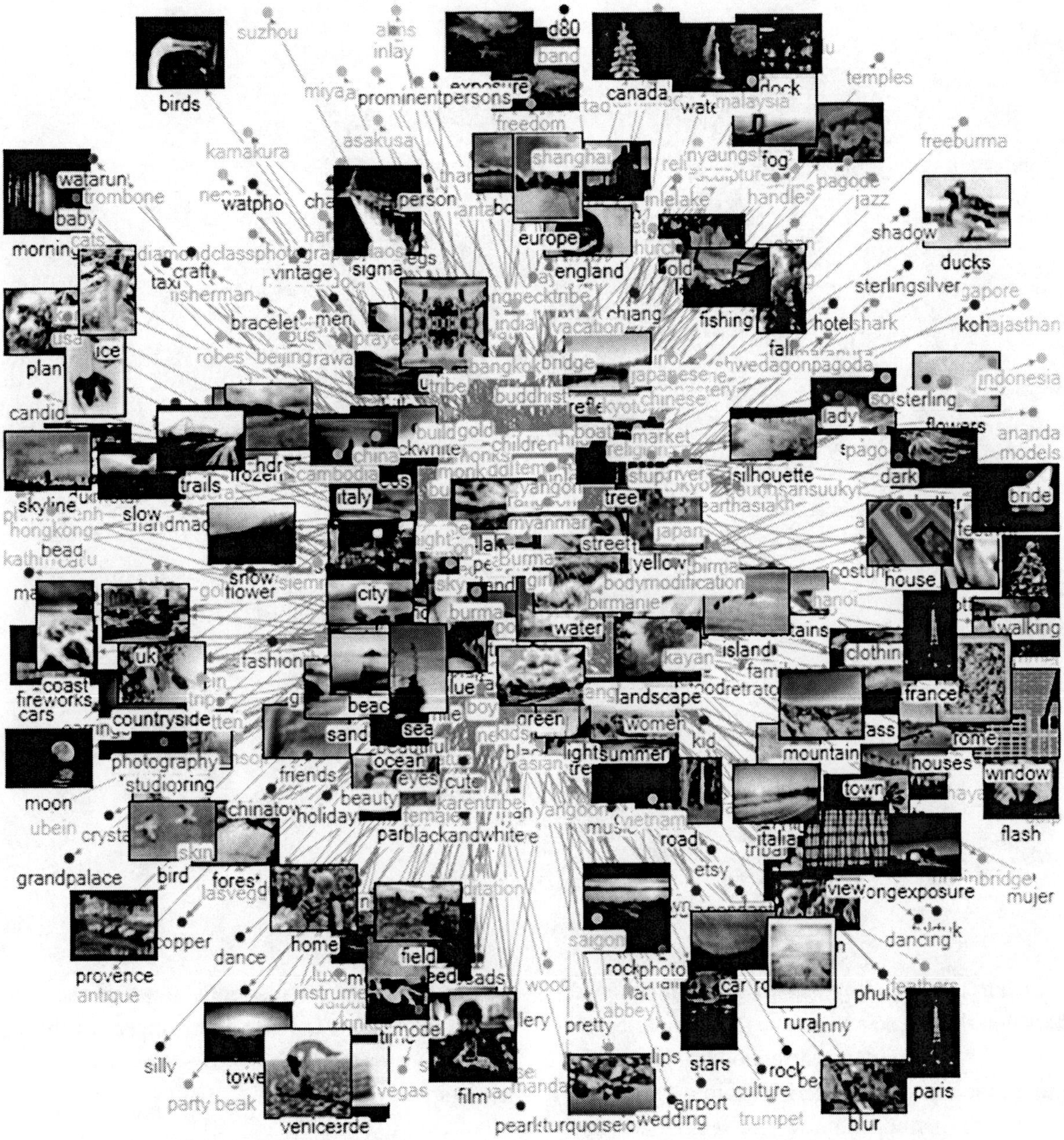

Figure 31. "Ireland" related tags graph on Flickr (with cluster annotations)

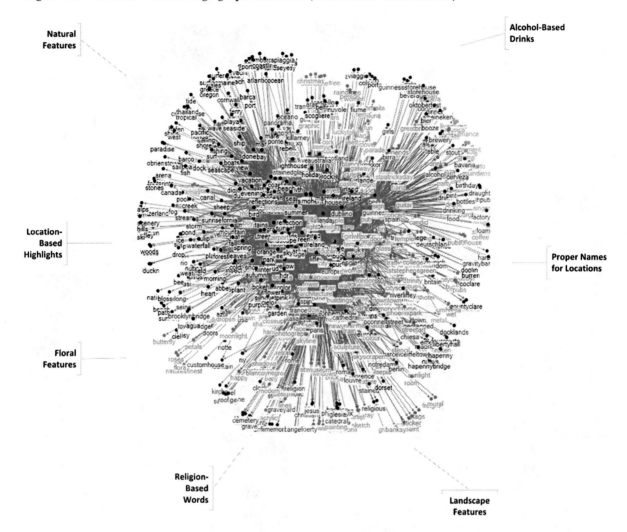

cluster as its own entity with more of a repellence between the elements (for clearer boundaries).

Some of the data extraction tools enable the extraction of information from a variety of languages, including those that require the use of Unicode for expression. Calligraphic language like 中国 may require the use of a URL decoder/encoder to create % encoded text, such as "%E4%B8%AD%E5%9B%BD" in lieu of the prior characters for China. This related tags extraction shows multiple meanings of "china"—as the country, as porcelain, and other evocations. The graph has the clusters pulled out in partitions for

easier legibility. Interestingly, some of the tag-based evocations include architecture, vacation, nation, events, regional countries, food, Christmas, and games.

GEODATA EXTRACTIONS

In Figure 42, "'Travel' Video Network Graph on YouTube," the labels here represented here as the vertices that are either an artifact of the YouTube API or the extraction tool (probably the first). The visuals evoke place. This data crawl was done to

Figure 32. "Antarctica" related tags graph on Flickr (with cluster annotations)

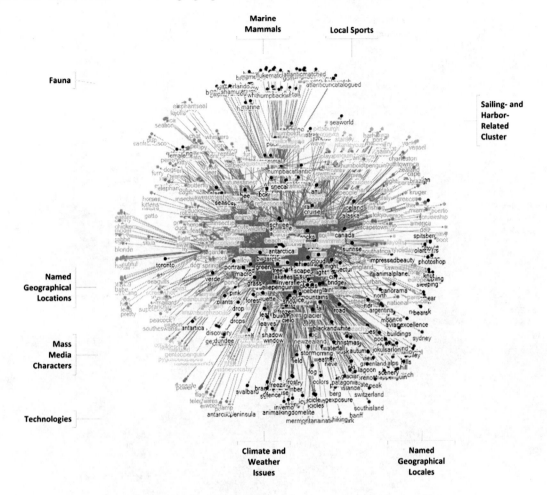

illluminate the locational column of many digital artifacts that may be extracted simultaneously with a related tags network crawl—so that information about the various accounts or the contents may be placed in geographical space.

This "Travel" video network graph network was re-visualized with the names of the videos at the various vertices in Figure 43. The capability of relabeling vertices and edges in NodeXL enables a wide range of differing visualizations.

Microblogging lists are collections of Tweets from commentators who communicate around particular topics of interest and so are corralled into a shared network (for easier following, with only the need to subscribe to the list instead of dozens of

accounts). A list focused on politics based around *The Week* (https://twitter.com/theweek/politics) is represented as a graph of a number of clusters of individuals and groups brought together by shared messaging and discussions around certain terms. Figure 44, "TheWeek/Politics" List Network on Twitter (NCapture on NVivo)," captures the names of the various user accounts in this network and offer easy ways to identify participants and their email accounts.

Finally, to illuminate spatiality, the list network on Twitter is depicted as various microbloggers from regions of the world. Figure 45, "Geo-spatial Mapping of TheWeek/Politics" List Network on Twitter (NCapture on NVivo)," shows a geo-

Figure 33. "Bolivia" related tags graph on Flickr (with cluster annotations)

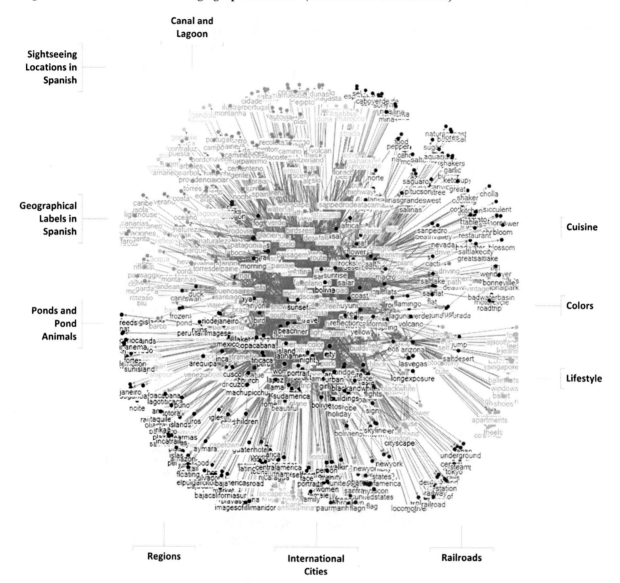

graphical map extracted from microblogged and geotagged textual and visual messages related to a user network on Twitter. The sparseness of the geospatial data reflects the rarity of spatial information in Twitter accounts for this particular network. (A look at the locational data column shows a mix of idiosyncratic labeling of location in text and numbers, with many of the labels not machine-readable. Some are "joke" locations like "outer space.") The fewer the data points, the less

informative the spatial mapping. This map shows a clustering in particular regions of the world (the U.S., mostly, with some accounts in Canada, Europe, China, the Middle East, and South Africa, as well as Central America).

To review, some strategies for how to conduct related tags extractions and analysis for public sentiment analysis may include the following: theme-based queries, word disambiguation, related tags comparisons, starting with generics,

Figure 34. "Bolivia" related tags graph on Flickr (with images)

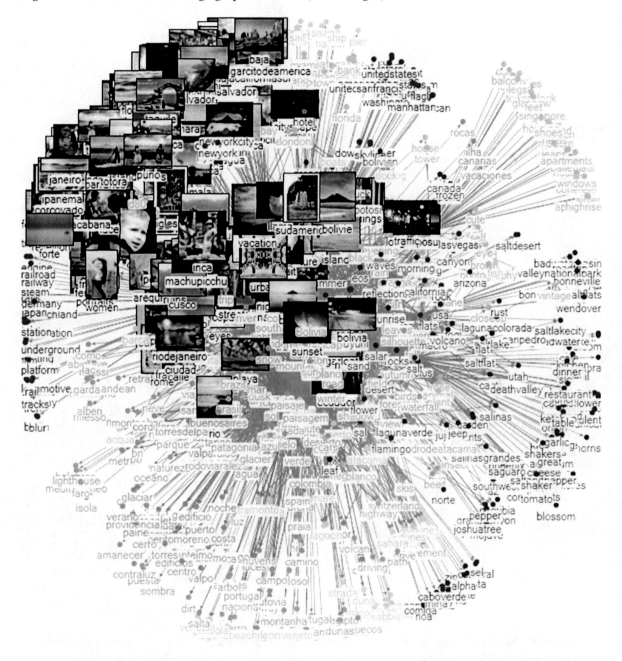

freighted or controversial terms, illuminating geographical locations, and geodata extractions. These are some simple approaches that have not been contextualized in larger research or analyses; the purpose of highlighting these is to provide some simple approaches for early and low-level queries.

Other Variations

Clearly, numerous other variations on "related tags network" queries are possible. There may be data crawls of related tags networks for a certain term or phrase sequentially over time to analyze

Figure 35. "Greenland" related tags graph on Flickr (with cluster annotations)

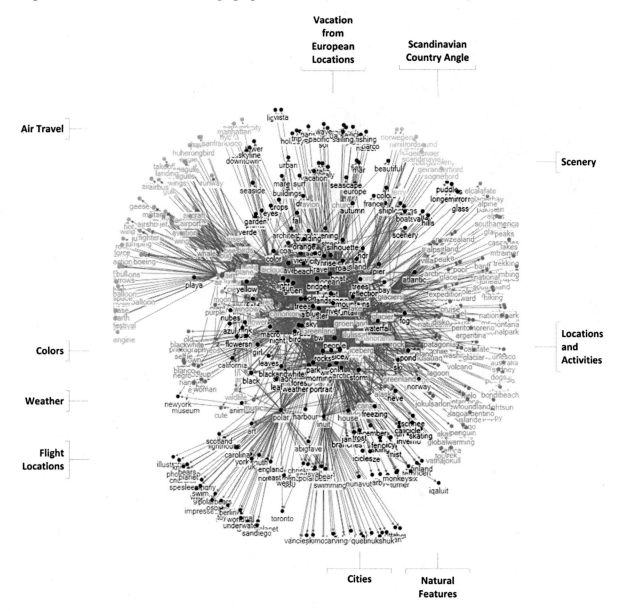

changes over time. There may be studies of how particular branches of a related tags network evolve and change and eventually stabilize or disappear. There may be synonym-antonym contrasts (analyses for differences) and comparisons (analyses for similarities). There may be analyses of foreign language variations, particularly as there are increasing capabilities for searching across multiple language sets. There may be ways to analyze related tags around particular geolocations by geolocation indicators (like latitude and longitude). There may be symbol-based searches. There may be the application of particular hashtagged conversation codes for searching. The related tags network for particular public personalities may be captured and analyzed; likewise for any number of brands or companies or organizations or political movements. Various combinations of

Figure 36. "Oman" related tags graph on Flickr (with cluster annotations)

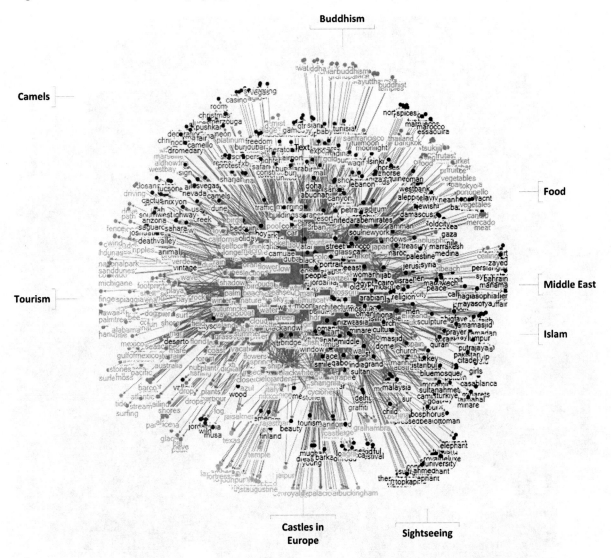

Boolean set definition search approaches may be applied (and for conjunction; or for disjunction; not for negation, and other approaches. There are a wide range of possibilities for related tags network analyses and the faint signaling that may be used for increased understandings, decision-making, and action-taking.

Strategies for Deeper Analysis

These prior examples have highlighted some obvious ways of acquiring information about public sentiment from related tags networks abstracted from content-sharing social media platforms. The assertions made here have been generally cautious, without overstating what is knowable. More in-depth analyses are possible with deeper rumination and a broader set of eyes. The human perspective is a critical element in computational research, and one major factor would be the plausibility of explanations for certain related tag clusterings and understandings.

The extracted related tags network visualizations may be manipulated to focus on particular

Figure 37. "Oman" related tags graph on Flickr (with imagery)

clusters or sub-clusters. The dynamic filtering features may enable only central parts of clusters to be revealed or only peripheral aspects. In other words, particular parts of a related tags content network may be spotlighted. Dense related tags networks may be thinned for clearer dynamics.

Machine-extracted geolocation information related to various tagged contents may be used for explorations of research leads based on geospatial data. Machine analysis of visual features of the scraped contents may also add another line of inquiry. There have been some efforts to extrapo-

Figure 38. "Papua New Guinea" related tags graph on Flickr (with cluster annotations)

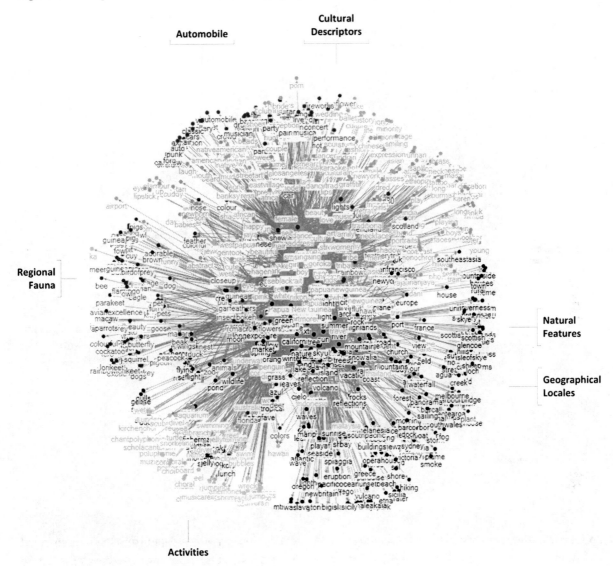

late geographical coordinates and information from just the information from Flickr tags (Van Laere, Schockaert, & Dhoedt, 2013). Specific images, microblogging messages, and video may be identified out for experiential sampling. This sort of experience would move researchers from the realm of abstract labels to the actual digital contents themselves.

One is to create a table of clustered tags (deconstructed from the related tags network graphs) in order to evaluate the actual terms in each cluster for human-based insights. While the software programs may pull the terms in a mutually exclusive way, there may be overlapping synonyms and other connections that may have been missed by the technology. A research team may analyze the clusters independent of the visualization for their own self-named clustering (as a form of data-reducing factor analysis) and for salient insights. There may be human-derived inferences

Figure 39. "Papua New Guinea" related tags graph on Flickr (with callouts, imagery, and cluster annotations)

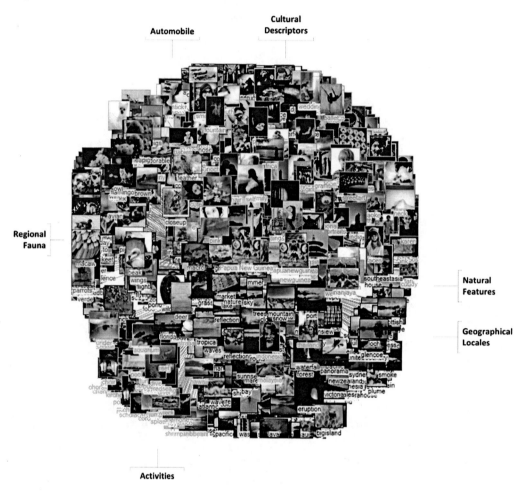

about particular word associations based on such folksonomy-based tagging. Table 4: A Table for the Analysis of Clustered Tags (from Deconstructed Related Tags Network Graphs) offers insights in this direction. Various dimensions of meanings may be analyzed across complex topics.

The datasets extracted have much more information than may be understood from the visualizations. Other methods that may offer different and deeper insights may involve word frequency analysis of particular tags (even with the use of stop-words lists) and the depiction of these counts as bubble graphs and other intuitive visualizations.

Word trees may be created from the interchanged messages around the user-created contents. These methods may be achieved semi-manually or through macros or through automated or coded methods. The informal nomenclature of tags may be compared with the formal ones; these tags may be compared across cultural milieus or language.

PURSUING RELATED LEADS

Beyond related tags network analysis, researchers offer a wide range of other ways to understand hu-

Figure 40. "Hawaii" related tags graph on Flickr (with imagery and layout in a partition)

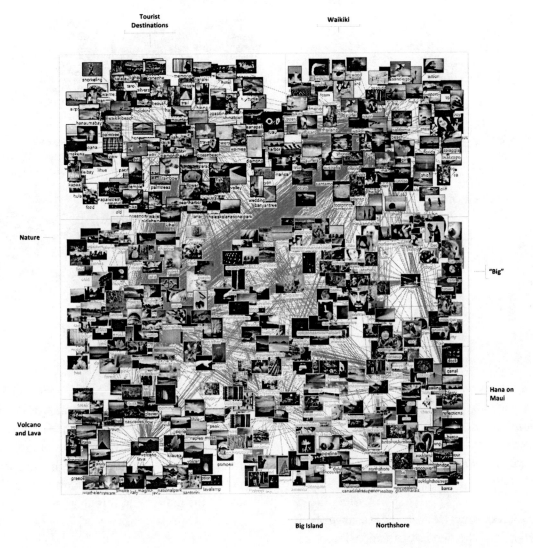

man dynamics and interactions in content-sharing social media sites—as spaces for the dissemination of information and interactivity. What are some of these research leads? The simplest ones would involve a range of explicit words and phrases to explore further to see what contents are linked to those words and to see how those contents "fit" within particular related tags networks. There may be user accounts that show dedication to particular topics, and those may be explored for their digital contents (in their content streams)

and tagging. Researchers may conduct electronic social network analysis of the various ego neighborhoods of target accounts, to understand who people are interacting with and what messages are being exchanged publicly. Some researchers offer some advice:

Looking at your network of Flickr contacts, you may wish to examine the friendship ties and see whether links are reciprocal. You probably expect a large number of reciprocal links with your friends

Figure 41. "China" related tags graph on Flickr (with imagery and layout in a partition)

**"China" Related Tags Network on Flickr
(text on left; text and imagery on right)**

who share interest and engage with you regularly by commenting on photos. Nonreciprocal connections may be of followers, distant friends, or family members who have less affinity to engage in social media (Rodrigues & Milic-Frayling, 2011, p. 209).

Social networks are analyzed in a range of ways to understand the depths of relationships—such as the frequency of interactions, the vehemence of expressed emotions, the agreement or disagreement around issues, the recentness of their interactions, the length of their interrelationships, and other factors. People and groups (related to the accounts of interest) may be contacted directly with questions and interactions—for deeper learner. Particular events may be tracked in terms of the signaling from tagging, microblogging, and contents—particularly as federated extraction tools come to the fore. Researchers may want to im-

merse in various content-sharing social networks for full immersion in these communities in order to engage in participant research. These various complementary or follow-on types of research in online and real-world spaces may be mapped out in clear workflows, but these additional trails are beyond the purview of this chapter.

FUTURE RESEARCH DIRECTIONS

A near-term follow-on to this work could involve a range of other types of "chaining" of software, social media platforms, and processes to collect and analyze related tags network data. Complementary research and data extraction endeavors could extend the informational value of related tags network analysis.

The analysis of related tags networks of social media contents offer a range of applications for

Figure 42. "Travel" video network graph on YouTube

more informed macro views of the contents, and by extension, the individuals, groups, and populations that created those. Social analysts and observers may conduct research on systematic ways to collect intelligence from particular content communities based on the tagging. They may identify ways to extrapolate gaps in content networks that may require elaboration or provisioning of digital con-

tents. They may identify other types of value-added analyses based on using related tags networks to increase the signal-to-noise ratio and also the accuracy of the collected information. There may be applications such as using such human-tagged and machine-tagged (particularly geospatial) information for fast unfolding events and disasters—in order to better strategize responses. They

Figure 43. "Travel" video network graph on YouTube (with imagery and partitions)

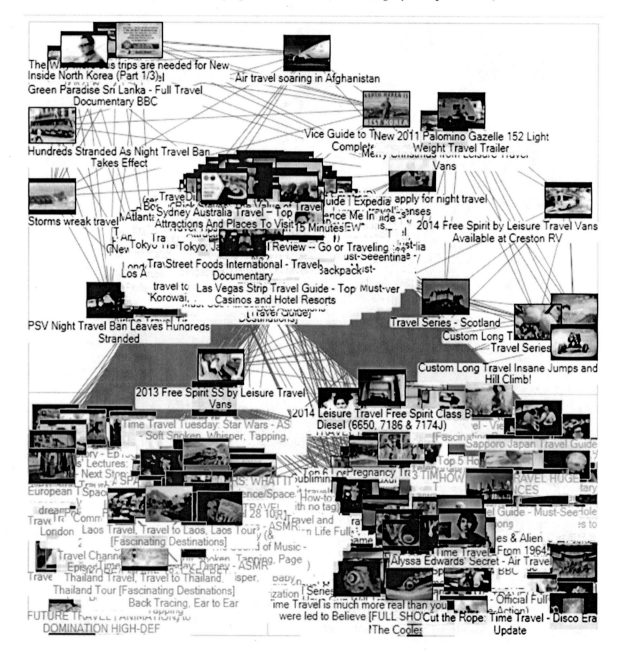

may discover new methodologies for increasing the analytical depth of the available information. They may work to infer private datasets and tags based on publicly available data.

For strategic communicators and content providers, related tags networks may offer insights on new strategies and tactics to reach various populations (and targeted individuals) with certain information, messaging, and digital contents. For those who would engage in memetic engineering, there may be new ways to harness such content-sharing social media platforms for impression

Figure 44. "TheWeek/Politics" list network on Twitter (NCapture on NVivo)

management and manipulations. Commercial strategic communicators may continue to harness such platforms for customer relationship management, advertising, and marketing. Political actors may apply this method to sample public sentiment and create outreach plans. Individuals themselves may engage more tactically and strategically in their social media self-image grooming.

From a technologist angle, future research may include explorations of various extant software tools and newly created ones—to extract more information from related tags content networks. There is need for deeper analysis of content-sharing social media platforms, their technological and social features, and other aspects.

Figure 45. Geo-spatial mapping of "TheWeek/Politics" list network on Twitter (NCapture on NVivo)

Table 4. A table for the analysis of clustered tags (from deconstructed related tags network graphs)

Cluster 1	Cluster 2	Cluster 3	Cluster 4	Cluster 5
(examples of tags)				

CONCLUSION

This chapter has offered some approaches to accessing related tags content network data to understand crowd-sourced public sentiment—so as to enhance the public mining of available information from social media platforms and expand ways of knowing through online ethnography. The learning curve is high for related tags network extraction and analysis, even as the software does the heavy lifting (at some computational expense) in terms of the information capture and data visualiza-tions. As noted, the related tags network analysis information extracted may be quite nuanced and indirect. While such information may point to latent understandings and non-obvious patterning, it makes sense to pursue other lines of query and reasoning for sufficient data for learning, decision-making, and informed action-taking. The issue of user-based tagging may be less important in the future, with impressive capabilities for machines to annotate a wide range of resources based on machine-visual analysis alone.

REFERENCES

Abbott, A. (2004). *Methods of Discovery: Heuristics for the Social Sciences*. New York: W.W. Norton & Company.

All time most popular tags. (2014, Jan. 4). *Flickr*. Retrieved at http://www.flickr.com/photos/tags/

Ames, M., & Naaman, M. (2007). Why we tag: Motivations for annotation in mobile and online media. In *Proceedings of CHI 2007*. San Jose, CA: ACM.

Ball, P. (2004). *Critical Mass: How One Thing Leads to Another*. New York: Farrar, Straus and Giroux.

Barton, D., & Lee, C. K. M. (2012). Redefining vernacular literacies in the Age of Web 2.0. *Applied Linguistics*, *33*(3), 282–298. doi:10.1093/applin/ams009

Beaudoin, J. (2007, October). Flickr image tagging: Patterns made visible. *Bulletin of the American Society for Information Science and Technology*, 26–29.

Berg, B. L., & Lune, H. (2012). *Qualitative Research Methods for the Social Sciences* (8th ed.). Boston: Pearson.

Brenner, J. (2013, Dec. 31). *Pew Internet: Social Networking (full detail)*. Pew Internet & American Life Project. Retrieved Jan. 15, 2014, at http://pewinternet.org/Commentary/2012/March/Pew-Internet-Social-Networking-full-detail.aspx

Cha, M., Benevenuto, F., Ahn, Y.-Y., & Gummadi, K. P. (2012). Delayed information cascades in Flickr: Measurement, analysis, and modeling. *Computer Networks*, *56*(3), 1066–1076. doi:10.1016/j.comnet.2011.10.020

Chan, S., Satosh, S., & Yamana, H. (2011). Increase the image search results by using Flickr tags. In *Proceedings of the DEIM Forum C1-3*. DEIM.

Cox, A. M. (2008). *Flickr: A case study of Web 2.0. In Proceedings: New Information Perspectives*. Emerald Group Publishing Limited. Doi: doi:10.1108/00012530810908210

Eleta, I., & Golbeck, J. (2012). *A study of multilingual social tagging of art images: Cultural bridges and diversity. In Proceedings of CSCW '12* (pp. 696–704). Seattle, WA: Association of Computing Machinery. doi:10.1145/2145204.2145310

Flickr. (2013, Dec. 1). *Wikipedia*. Retrieved Dec. 9, 2013, at http://en.wikipedia.org/wiki/Flickr

Hansen, D. L., Schneiderman, B., & Smith, M. A. (2011). *Analyzing Social Media Networks with NodeXL: Insights from a Connected World*. Burlington, MA: Elsevier.

Hotho, A. (2010). Data mining on folksonomies. *Intelligent Information Access*, *301*, 57–82. doi:10.1007/978-3-642-14000-6_4

Körner, C., Kern, R., Grahsl, H.-P., & Strohmaier, M. (2010). Of categorizers and describers: An evaluation of quantitative measures for tagging motivation. In *Proceedings of HT'10*. Toronto, Canada: Association of Computing Machinery.

Krestel, R. (2011). Recommendation on the Social Web: Diversification and personalization. In *Web Science—Investigating the future of information and communication*. Retrieved from http://detect.uni-koblenz.de/slides/detect11_pres.pdf

Lin, Y-R., Sundaram, H., De Choudhury, M., & Kelliher, A. (2012). Discovering multirelational structure in social media streams. *ACM Transactions in Multimedia Computing, Communications and Applications*, *8*(1), 4:1 – 4:28.

Lorince, J., & Todd, P. M. (2013). Can simple social copying heuristics explain tag popularity in a collaborative tagging system? In *Proceedings of WEbSCi '13*. Paris, France: Association of Computing Machinery. doi:10.1145/2464464.2464516

O'Grady, L., Wathen, C. N., Charnaw-Burger, J., Betel, L., Shachak, A., & Luke, R. et al. (2012). The use of tags and tag clouds to discern credible content in online health message forums. *International Journal of Medical Informatics, 81*(1), 36–44. doi:10.1016/j.ijmedinf.2011.10.001

Paltoglou, G. & Thelwall, M. (2012). Twitter, MySpace, Digg: Unsupervised sentiment analysis in social media. *ACM Transactions on Intelligent Systems and Technology, 3*(4), 66:1–66:19. DOI: .10.1145/2337542.2337551

Popescu, A., & Grefenstette, G. (2010). Image tagging and search—A gender oriented study. In Proceedings of WSM '10. Firenze, Italy: WSM.

Razikin, K., Goh, D. H-L., Chua, A.Y.K., & Lee, C.S. (2008). Can social tags help you find what you want? In *Proceedings of ECDL 2008* (LNCS) (pp. 50–61). Berlin: Springer.

Robu, V., Halpin, H., & Shepherd, H. (2009). Emergence of consensus and shared vocabularies in collaborative tagging systems. *ACM Transactions on the Web, 2*(4), 14:1–14:34.

Rodrigues, E. M., & Milic-Frayling, N. (2011). Flickr: Linking people, photos, and tags. In *Analyzing Social Media Networks with NodeXL: Insights from a Connected World*. Burlington, MA: Elsevier. doi:10.1016/B978-0-12-382229-1.00013-8

Rotman, D., & Golbeck, J. (2011). YouTube: Contrasting patterns of content, interaction, and prominence. In *Analyzing Social Media Networks with NodeXL: Insights from a Connected World*. Burlington, MA: Elsevier. doi:10.1016/B978-0-12-382229-1.00014-X

Sawant, N., Datta, R., Li, J., & Wang, J. Z. (2010). *Quest for relevant tags using local interaction networks and visual content. In Proceedings of MIR '10*. Philadelphia, PA: Association of Computing Machinery.

Schifanella, R., Barrat, A., Cattuto, C., Markines, B., & Menczer, F. (2010). Folks in folksonomies: social link prediction from shared metadata. In *Proceedings of the third ACM International Conference on Web Search and Data Mining*, (pp. 271–280). ACM. doi:10.1145/1718487.1718521

Shamma, D. A., Kennedy, L., & Churchill, E. F. (2012). Watching and talking: Media content as social nexus. In *Proceedings of ICMR '12*. Hong Kong, China: Association of Computing Machinery.

Simons, J. (2008). Tag-elese or the language of tags. *The Fibreculture Journal, 12.* Retrieved from http://twelve.fibreculturejournal.org/fcj-083-tag-elese-or-the-language-of-tags/

Strohmaier, M., Körner, C., & Kern, R. (2012). Understanding why users tag: A survey of tagging motivation literature and results from an empirical study. *Web Semantics: Science, Services, and Agents on the World Wide Web, 17,* 1–11. doi:10.1016/j.websem.2012.09.003

Stvilia, B., Jöorgensen, C., & Wu, S. (2012). Establishing the value of socially-created metadata to image indexing. *Library & Information Science Research, 34*(2), 99–109. doi:10.1016/j.lisr.2011.07.011

Suchanek, F. M., Vojnović, M., & Gunawardena, D. (2008). *Social tags: Meaning and suggestions. In Proceedings of CIKM '08*. Napa Valley, CA: Association of Computing Machinery. doi:10.1145/1458082.1458114

Sun, A. & Bhowmick, S.S. (2009, Oct. 23). Image tag clarity: In search of visual-representative tags for social images. In *Proceedings of WSIM*. Beijing, China: Association of Computing Machinery (ACM).

Tisselli, E. (2010). Thinkflickrthink: A case study on strategic tagging. *Communications of the ACM, 53*(8), 141–145. doi:10.1145/1787234.1787270

Van Laere, O., Schockaert, S., & Dhoedt, B. (2013). Georeferencing Flickr resources based on textual meta-data. *Information Sciences, 238,* 52–74. doi:10.1016/j.ins.2013.02.045

Van Zwol, R. (2007). Flickr: Who is looking? In *Proceedings of the IEEE/WIC/ACM International Conference on Web Intelligence.* (pp. 184 – 190). IEEE. DOI doi:10.1109/WI.2007.22

Vandic, D., van Dam, J.-W., Fransincar, F., & Hogenboom, F. (2011). A semantic clustering-based approach for searching and browsing tag spaces. In *Proceedings of SAC'11.* TaiChung, Taiwan: SAC. doi:10.1145/1982185.1982538

Yee, R. (2008). *Pro-Web 2.0 Mashups: Remixing Data and Web Services.* New York: Springer-Verlag.

ADDITIONAL READING

Hansen, D. L., Schneiderman, B., & Smith, M. A. (2011). *Analyzing Social Media Networks with NodeXL: Insights from a Connected World.* Burlington, MA: Elsevier.

KEY TERMS AND DEFINITIONS

Annotation: A note appended to a multimedia or other object which adds more information.

Application Programming Interface (API): A library of specifications for how to access information from a social media platform's databases for the extraction of particular types of information.

Content Network: The relationships that may be observed within a content-sharing social media platform.

Cosine Similarity: A technique for measuring similarity and cohesion within clusters.

Data Crawl: The extraction of raw information from the Web.

Data Mining: The identification of relevant, new, and useful patterns from data.

Data Visualization: The depiction of data in a graphical format (like graphs, charts, and other forms).

Degree: The amount of connectivity (in-degree and out-degree) between a node and other nodes in a network.

Emergence: The revealing or expression of latent forces in a complex system; forthcoming.

Filtering: The sifting of contents in order to access the desired information.

Folksonomy: The collaborative annotation of contents for an unstructured and informal "taxonomy" of information [a term coined by Thomas Vander Waal (2004)].

Geospatial Information: Data which pinpoints locations in geographical space or terrestrial locations.

Graph: A two-dimensional structure which depicts objects and relationships often as nodes and links (like a node-link diagram).

Image: A visual (often in two or three dimensions).

Machine Tag (in Flickr): The automatically added tags used in Flickr to add information about particular digital objects to increase informational value (such as with the inclusion of geo data).

Memetic Engineering: The work of developing memes in order to affect or change others' attitudes and behaviors (a term coined by Leveious Rolando, John Sokol and Gibran Burchett).

Metadata: Information about data.

Multimedia: Digital media that includes multiple content forms.

Open-Source Intelligence (OSINT): Publicly available information (from a broad variety of sources) exploited for informational value.

Partition: A segment or division of a graph, usually containing a cluster.

Personomy: Personal tag vocabulary; the tags used by an individual in his /her account to describe the image and/or video set.

Polysemic: Many- or multi-meaninged.

Public Sentiment: Public opinions or attitudes about a particular issue or complex of issues.

Related Tags Content Network: A graph of related tags expressed as clusters in a network with larger clusters interpreted as popular tags, and also with increased centrality in a cluster expressed as increased popularity and influence.

Repellence: A force that creates (degrees of) distance between nodes or entities.

Self-Organization: The creation of a global structure or pattern based on agent-level local interactions, choices, or actions; emergence.

Semantics: A branch of linguistics and logic dealing with meaning and sense-making.

Social Media: Socio-technical spaces that bring individuals together to interact with each other in mediated ways and around digital contents.

Social Network: A social structure of various social actors with differing inter-relationships.

Structured Tagging: Formal taxonomic labeling of digital contents.

Tag: Textual metadata labeling (structured and unstructured) of digital contents by content contributors; informal labeling of user-created contents.

Ties: Relationships or links between entities.

Unstructured Tagging: Informal folksonomy-based assigning of tags to user-generated contents.

Section 5
Cases of Technology–Enhanced Qualitative and Mixed Methods Research (and the Converse)

In the same way that surveys and interviews may wrap with a catch-all category, a section on cases may be seen as a broad category of unique applications of the book's topic. It is one thing to conceptualize possibilities, but it is more difficult to actualize the work in real world and online settings. By their example, these cases illuminate potentials for others in their respective contexts. Case studies have intrinsic value in terms of the action research learning. Section 5 highlights researchers' applied uses of technologies for qualitative and mixed methods research and the converse, their applied methods in analyzing technologies, and their implications for their research and/or other applications. These cases affirm the variety of approaches that may be taken with technology-enhanced qualitative and mixed methods research.

Chapter 15
The Theory and Application of Process Research to the Study of IT Strategy–Making

Eamonn Caffrey
Trinity College Dublin, Ireland

Joe McDonagh
Trinity College Dublin, Ireland

ABSTRACT

This chapter presents an overview of process research and places a particular emphasis on reviewing the process method. Some insights into the nature of process are presented. The purpose of this chapter is to describe the process method in detail. Some of the methodological challenges involved in conducting process-oriented inquiry are highlighted. Appropriateness of the method to study strategy-related issues is presented which interlocks well with its suitability to investigate issues of interest in relation to IT strategy-making. Application of the process method cycle of research steps is recommended to distil rigorous and relevant theory. Alternative process research sense-making strategies are revealed at a very high-level only. Narrative analysis is presented as a viable sense-making approach to theorize process data and key features of this analytical strategy are revealed. Emerging issues and opportunities that intersect with the IT strategy-making construct are discussed.

INTRODUCTION

Process research is made distinct by two types of inquiry, the variance method, and the process method. The source of process research can be traced back to the ontological distinction of how the world is organized. Democritus observed the world as being made up of stable components whereas Heraclitus perceived reality to be a world made up of meandering processes comprised of fluctuating activities that continuously evolve and bring about changing outcomes. Democritus favored the variant perspective on process. In contrast, Heraclitus saw process from an interactionist point of view; this is referred to as the process method. The chapter offers some background distinctions to make clear some key differences between the variance and process approach. This leads into the

DOI: 10.4018/978-1-4666-6493-7.ch015

main focus of the chapter which is to present our perspective on process which views reality as a dynamic state of interactional occurrence which brings us to discuss the theory of method, the process method. Embedded within the process method are many challenges that need to be considered as part of a qualitative study, particularly as it relates to studying IT strategy-making. The challenges discussed refer to: variance and process methods; complexity; context, content and process; boundaries and multiple levels; generalizability; frame of reference; vocabulary; and outcomes. One of the great strengths of the process method is that it allows us to inquire into social action such as management behavior as it relates to strategy-making. Embedded in good strategy-making are processes that unfold over time. By tracking strategy over time it is possible to trace the sequence of events and detect the generative mechanisms that shape its trajectory. It was posited by Chandler (1962) that strategy drives structure and IT is a stimulating force by which to bring about transformation through social enactment (Scott-Morton, 1991). IT strategy-making relates to the organizational perspective on the involvement in, deployment, use, and management of IT (Chen et al. 2010). Essentially, IT strategy-making reflects management's view on the role and orientation of organizational IT (Armstrong and Sambamurthy, 1999; Earl, 1989; Galliers, 2004; McLean and Soden, 1977).

If we are to truly understand the mechanisms that drive and shape IT strategy-making in terms of development and eventual outcomes; then it is necessary to inquire into the interactional nature of participant involvement to trace decision-making processes as they relate to the deployment, use, and management of organizational IT. Hence, application of the process method as a qualitative research approach is well suited to study IT strategy-making and this is explained. We then turn to the application of the method for conducting a process study and outline the process research cycle (Pettigrew, 1997). A range of sense-making strategies exist to theorize process data and these are briefly presented for completeness. In studying IT strategy-making by way of the process method, our preference is to adopt the narrative analytical technique to make sense of data. The final section is concerned with future and emerging trends that intersect with IT strategy-making and items of recent interest are discussed. Of noteworthy interest, opportunities for future research are implicitly stated. The first theme deals with the combined quantitative and qualitative multi-method approach. Additional themes of interest as they emerge or warrant further exploratory interest in relation to studying IT strategy-making include: philosophical perspective on critical realism; digital business strategy; business level implications for IT strategy-making; social capital effects on strategic IT; IT capability reputation; IT-enabled transformation – understanding and relevance; building on critical success factors for IT performance; leveraging strategic partnerships to adapt; exploring the strategic IT alignment conundrum; and finally, the opportunity to technologically advance application of the process method.

BACKGROUND

Depending on one's own ontological and epistemological point of view, this can influence and shape how process is to be identified. Much depends on how we view organizations, whether we see them as things or processes. The distinction between things and processes was traced back to the ancient past by Rescher (1996). The differing philosophies between Democritus and Heraclitus were found to distinguish in terms of whether we view reality as being made up of stable material substances or processes composed of varying and fluctuating activities. Democritus framed reality as being a stable substance that does not change but instead develops and adapts in relation to other dimensions and properties that serve only to re-order its temporal position. In contrast, Heraclitus viewed reality as not being an arbitrary formation of substances or things but rather, one of processes, produced by differing and fluctuating activities. "Process is fundamental: The river is not an object but an ever-changing flow; the sun is not a thing, but a flaming fire. Everything in nature is a matter of process, of activity, of change" (Rescher, 1996, p. 10). Arguably the view of Democritus has won out for the most part since a great many philosophers and scientists tend to see an ordered world made up of stable realities (Van de Ven and Poole, 2005). However, as Rescher (1996) pointed out, there are notable exceptions to this perspective made evident among the processual philosophies of C. S. Pierce (1839 – 1914), William James (1842 – 1910), Henri Bergson (1859 – 1941), John Dewey (1859 – 1952), and Alfred North Whitehead (1861 – 1947). From their collective perspectives, to understand the world then it is necessary to view reality as a process that evolves over time and shaped largely by a continuous process of change and creativity (Van de Ven and Poole, 2005).

The building blocks of reality, as envisioned in Whitehead's classic Process and Reality, are not substances at all but "actual occasions" – processual units rather than "things" of some sort – with human experience affording their best amalgam. Even as in conscious experience humans apprehend what goes on about them, so these actual activities "prehend" what goes on in their environment in a way that encompasses a low-grade mode of emotion, consciousness, and purpose. (Rescher, 1996, p. 20)

The underlying assumption behind process thinking is that reality is not a fixed state but a dynamic process that occurs rather than exists (Sztompka, 1991). What shapes a dynamic process was captured by Pettigrew (1997) when a workshop of scholars were asked to describe what the term process means and this is what followed: "*flow of events, chronology, mechanism, unfolding,*

two forces interacting, time, language, context, outcomes, linking things together, individuals and collectives, history, consistent story, change and long period" (p. 338). From Pettigrew's perspective, process research most often takes the form of longitudinal comparative case study research that inquires into the nature of organizational change by investigating the sequence of events and role of human conduct therein over time, set in context. Three forms of process research were described by Van de Ven (1992, p. 169): (i) as a logic used to explain a causal relationship in a variance theory; (ii) as a category of concepts that refer to activities of individuals or organizations; and (iii) as a sequence of events that describes how things change over time. The first description of process research brings us back to the philosophical debate about whether reality is a state of things or fluctuating activities and reflects the steady state perspective. The second definition considers the effect of society and role of human conduct and their activities in bringing about change vis-à-vis process. The third definition is embellished by Pettigrew strongly insofar as it is the sequence of human action and interaction and related activities (events) that lead to the temporal order of things vis-à-vis change, shaped largely through time, history, and context.

PROCESS RESEARCH

The main focus of this chapter is to explain some of the challenges associated with process research and to set out guidelines which help to make sense of process data as it relates to a qualitative approach to investigate IT strategy-making. We do this by setting out our perspective on process research next, followed by a number of known challenges which help to understand the complexities embedded within the process method. We then explain why process research is well suited to investigate matters of strategic management and its relevance and suitability to inquire into IT strategy-making.

Perspective on Process Research

Researchers with an interest in process theory and dynamic phenomena hold the philosophical belief that to truly understand how and why events occur over time, then it is necessary to investigate them directly (Mintzberg, 1979). The definition of process is given to mean a "sequence of individual and collective events, actions, and activities unfolding over time in context" (Pettigrew, 1997, p. 338). In order to capture this type of data, researchers must immerse themselves deeply into the processes, collect fine-grained qualitative data and attempt to extract theory that is accurate, parsimonious, general, and useful by working from the ground up (Bower, 1997; Langley, 1999; Pettigrew, 1992; Van de Ven, 1992). Events are at the center of any frames of reference process explanation (Peterson, 1998). Langley (1999) characterizes process research as a "sequence of events that often involve multiple levels and units of analysis that tend to be eclectic in nature drawing in phenomena such as thoughts, feelings, and interpretations" (p. 62). The underlying premise in support of process thinking is that social reality is not a steady state but a dynamic and continuous process. Pettigrew describes this as 'a process of becoming' in that human behavior occurs rather than exists. Hence, 'to catch reality in flight' (Pettigrew, 1997) becomes the underlying aim of process research.

This perspective views organizations in a world of ongoing change and flux. The organization is a reification of ongoing processes, there is always something going on of a more dynamic nature that deviates greatly from any notion of a fixed- or end-state. This is brought about by the cumulative interchange between individual and collective action (human agency); the situation within which these interactions occur (context); and its position within the sequence of events for any given process.

Challenges

This sections draws out some of the known challenges associated with conducting good process research. Distinctions between the variance and process methods are discussed. The high levels of complexity embedded in the process method are explained. The method accounts for context, content and process but too often neglects to inquire deeply into 'how' it all happens. Process research can be described as boundary-less and penetrates multiple levels; organizational processes are vast and meandering streams of activity. Versatility as it relates to the generality of process research can be rather limited or potentially all encompassing. Over time researchers and scholars form unique, but an accomplished process scholar must learn to distinguish subjective bias from objective truth. Process writing takes on a life of its own since process continuously evolves. To serve this well requires a vocabulary to display the high levels of conceptualization and analytical ability needed to reveal thematic patterns within event sequence linked to multiples levels and boundaries. The process method not only identifies patterns among processes but it must link these to outcomes. These are revealed over time and thus, at a meta-level the emphasis is on refining analysis to provide holistic explanation. Each of these challenges is considered next.

Variance and Process Methods

Process research is the method by which scholars study the nature and effects of change in organizational settings. The key difference between process scholars is usually based on the epistemological belief of how knowledge is created and best understood and subsequently gives new meaning to generate greater understanding and learning. In organizational studies, two views on the meaning of change are widely considered: (i) observable difference over time in an organizational setting on pre-selected properties; and (ii) narrative that describes the sequence of events on how development and change unfolds over time (Poole et al. 2000). The 'variance theory' (Mohr, 1982) methodology is a statistical method by which a dependent variable is taken to represent change and explained by way of measuring independent variables and subsequent impact on the dependent variable of change. The second definition is more interested to learn about event-driven sequence over time influenced by agency, history, and context and the cumulative effects these have on the outcome to explain how change and development occurs (rather than exists). This is presented in the form of an historical narrative and often associated with a 'process theory' (Abbot, 1988; Langley, 1999; Pentland, 1999; Poole et al. 2000; Tsoukas, 2005).

The variance method can be described as attempting to explain a constellation of substances and things. In contrast, process theory is concerned with explaining actual occasions. The variance method deals with a reality where things are unchanging and stable units of existence; whereas process theory views nature as continuously evolving and that all things flow (Van de Ven and Poole, 2005). It was argued by Whetten (2006) that organizations should be studied as nouns (social entities), rather than as verbs (social processes), the former being the more dominant in past and present scholarly thinking. The comparison between organizations as things or nouns is made distinct by Tsoukas (2005) when organizing is considered as a verb or process in terms of strong and weak forms of organizational change (Van de Ven and Poole, 2005). "The "weak view" treats processes as important but ultimately reducible to the action of things, while the "strong" view deems actions and things to be instantiations of process-complexities" (Chia and Langley, 2004 cited in Van de Ven and Poole, 2005, p. 1379). In this regard, the strong view embraces the characteristics of movement, change, and becoming

as being absolutely necessary, the sine qua non, of organizational life, essential to recognizing the unique nature of process. The "weak" view arguably sees the world of organizations as one where processes are characterized by changes in things. The "strong" view regards things in the social world of organizing as mere reifications of processes (Van de Ven and Poole, 2005). Fundamentally, the key distinction between the variance method and the process method of theory is the difference between scientific explanations. Variance is concerned with the causal relationship in terms of how independent variables impact the relationship with a dependent variable and this is mostly conducted through statistical modeling. The process method of theory is about story telling by way of narrative features to explain how a sequence of events unfolds and describes the temporal order. The narrative is shaped to consider social actors and associated interactions and the activities enacted as they were performed through history and situated within certain contextual conditions. It is the cumulative effect of action and interaction to relay the sequential ordering of events over time. This is important because as Pettigrew (1997) points out, 'truth is the daughter of time' and to gain access to the truth requires deep understanding of the cumulative effect of contextual irregularities that give rise to meaningful process theory. Table 1 overleaf provides a summary comparison of the variance and process method assumptions distinctive to each approach.

Under the variance method perspective, an entity is considered to be real, an existing thing by itself but composed of a fixed set of attributes that reflect the form of the entity and are responsible for any significant changes (Abbott, 1990). Each of the variant substances can potentially impact on an entity and the aim is to gain insight into the relationships among similar and different variables. Understanding of the variable factors and the consequential effects these have on an entity are complete and well known vis-à-vis causation. A variant explanation is complete when it is known

Table 1. Comparison of variance method and process method assumptions

Variance Method	Process Method
A real and existing thing by itself such as an entity is fixed in state but is composed of a fixed set of variable substances or attributes that can represent changes to the entity	A real and existing thing shaped by significant occurrences involving people and activities that impact the outcome in different ways and at different points over time – the entity can greatly influence the sequence of events
The relation between cause variables and the consequential effects on the entity are accounted for fully	Sequential ordering of events and the combined effects on developmental forces explain the entity processes whereby each causal event directs the entity towards a certain outcome
A firm grasp and understanding of what the unitary forces are, and the different kinds of cause functions that are possible	Understanding outcomes is essential to explanation and reflects the cumulative effects of attributes within the event sequence spanning the developmental process from which key patterns become observable
The generality of an entity's state is subject to validating its existence across multiple contexts to consider it 'generally' relevant in meaning	The ability of process theory to adapt to multiple situations and contexts determines the evaluative level of generalizability. This is determined by its versatility to capture a broad domain of developmental patterns (Poole et al. 2000) without change to its key formation and features.
The temporal order of variable effects will not impact on the level of outcome; time ordering of variable operationalization is not relevant	Capturing the order of event sequence is essential to explain outcomes
Causation effects are reflected in the present state of an entity insofar as 'the immediate past is perpetually producing the future' (Abbott, 1990)	Ordering of events to illustrate all process points provides insight into the event history and reveals the multi layered unfolding of cause and effect to distil an explanation for outcome; sequential ordering of events and related causal effects bring event influence to bear
Attributes retain the same meaning over time	Over time, different meaning can be prescribed to the role of entities, attributes, and events for a process

how independent variables can change the dependent variable (Mohr, 1982). Efficient causality by way of a force that represents a unit of analysis needs to be made known and explained in terms of the search to grasp its cause (Aristotle, 1941). This type of efficient causality reveals the force in terms of unitary analysis and the impact it has on the variable outcome or the consequential effects that brings about some kind of change from its previous form. Knowledge of the entity and its characteristic nature can qualify as being generally relevant once it is proven to exist across multiple contexts to validate relevance. The variance method is concerned with the collective impact of independent variables leading to an outcome regardless of the orderly operationalization of when the variable effects were triggered (Poole et al. 2000). Variance is not concerned with time ordering of the independent variables but it must

reveal a time frame that encapsulates variable operationalization to generate an outcome. The state of an entity is based on past effects but knowledge of the unique twists and turns taken to bring it to its immediate state are not of particular importance. Interest resides in causation immediacy insofar as past effects are represented in the present. It is the present form that is of interest and not necessarily a comprehensive historical account explaining the unique or particular conditions that gave rise to its present condition. Attributes retain a unitary identity over time insofar as the impact of each variable provides a uniformed response throughout the process. The underlying assumption being that entities can only remain fixed when the embodiment of attributes that forms an entity hold unitary identity and meaning over time (Poole et al. 2000).

The process method is concerned with the sequence of events pertaining to the central subject of study, the entity. Events, which can be units of social processes, can occur at multiple levels and have an impact on the entity and consequently, the entity then impacts on event occurrence. Events happen and occur brought about by the entity's participation (Abbott, 1988). These types of entity processes produce qualitative shifts that are enacted through the sequence of events and can be regarded as high level events themselves. The events are discontinuous in nature and change the shape or form of the entity under study. The entity itself may not change over time but go through a number of qualitative shifts and these developmental processes that redefine the entity are of great interest to the process narrative. The conjunction of critical events that form the entire set of forces that give rise to a particular process outcome are of great importance. The sequential ordering of these events by way of occurrence and the attribute combinations that span the changing nature thus giving rise to a newly formed entity must be made known to explain the entity processes. The process method aims to seek out the full set of causes and combinations made apparent by the sequential order and cumulative occurrence (Poole et al. 2000). To fully understand process theory then an account of the developmental path must reveal event sequence by way of the constraints and conjunctures that shape the final outcome. As pointed out by Poole et al. (2000), Aristotle distinguished between four types of causes to explain 'why' change occurs. These causes comprise of 'material, formal, efficient and final' (Aristotle, 1941). *"Respectively, they indicate that from which something was made (material cause), the pattern by which it is made (formal cause), "that from which comes the immediate origin of movement or rest" (efficient cause), and the end for which it is made (final cause) (Ross, 1949)"* (Poole et al. 2000, p. 42). Aristotle contended that all four causes were interlinked but one type may be more prominent than others. While certainly the

variance method is greatly interested in 'efficient cause', the process method aims to unlock and account for the linkage between all four causes.

Generalizability of the process method is determined by the level of versatility embedded in its suitability to fit with a broad domain of developmental patterns without deviating from its core substance (Poole et al. 2000). How well the process theory can adapt to broader domains in terms of having relevance to a range of cases, contexts, events and patterns underlines the evaluative level of generality. One of the main distinctions between the variance and process methods is often highlighted by the evaluative level to discern commonality across multiple settings and situations. The order by which events occur is critical to explaining outcomes since different event ordering can result in different outcomes. Temporal ordering is essential to event recognition because the re-ordering of events within the development path can produce entirely different results. The order and influence of events reveal both the duration and impact of the different factors that influence a developmental path towards a particular outcome. The role of events and the sequence by which they unfold over time provides insight into the unique causal history. This enables the narrative explanation to show how the entity formed to become the way it did by revealing how it happened and when it happened. The past is alive in the present because an entity's history bears influence on its current form. Capturing the multiple layers embedded deep within events such as social responses and the time endured for each sets out the ordered unfolding of key attributes that gave rise to the process trajectory that shaped the entity. A process is denoted by a developmental pathway made up of influential attributes and events. Therefore, to fully understand process it is necessary to look back in time to gain insight into entity complexity to discover the level of multilayered complexity. This is apparent when dealing with the subject of strategy; the nature of strategic enactment for a small organization is most likely to be different to that of a major corporation but as a small organization grows in size, the practice of strategy is most likely to change and thus, the relevance and meaning of events, attributes, and entities too. Nevertheless, the entity remains to be a living organization actively engaged with the real-world, but the context, content and process by which strategy is practiced to shape its developmental path, have, most likely, changed significantly, vis-à-vis qualitative shift.

Complexity

Conducting good research using the process method tends to be more complex by comparison to variance alternatives. Some of the reasons that make the process method more complex relate to: the inter-connectedness of events and attempting to link together and make relevant the significance; the varying time horizons that extend to any event-series; the eclectic nature of information sources; and the dynamic nature of processes deeply embedded in event-history methods. "Process data are messy. Making sense of them is a constant challenge" (Langley, 1999, p. 691). Langley highlights the need to consider phenomena such as experiential thoughts, feelings and interpretations, and the evolving nature of relationships. In a recent Wall Street Journal article, former U.S. Federal Chairman Alan Greenspan commented on 'What Went Wrong' in terms of the events which gave rise to the financial crisis in 2007-8. Reflecting on the crisis-driven events and how they unfolded, the following abstract from the article is relevant to the point made regarding complexity.

Studying the minutiae of the events leading to the financial crisis brought to mind some lessons from his famous friendship, from the 1950s on, with the late Objectivist philosopher Ayn Rand. He says that Rand didn't influence him politi-cally—he was always a libertarian—but she did point out tensions in his philosophy about life. "She caught me in contradictions, which shook me, and I said, 'My God, she is right,' " he says. Mr. Greenspan then believed in analysis based mainly on hard science and empirical facts. Rand told him that unless he considered human nature and its irrational side, he would "miss a very large part of how human beings behaved." At the time they weren't discussing economics, but today he realizes the full impact of emotions and instincts on markets. (Wolfe, A. (2013). "Alan Greenspan: What Went Wrong")

Alan Greenspan had up to the time of the crisis relied heavily on econometric models only, to guide prediction about future outcomes. Today he readily acknowledges that a critical oversight was made in terms of dismissing the important role of social action and human behavior and its cumulative effect on events and subsequent outcomes. Process methods are concerned with gaining insight into how things evolve over time and the embedded processes that give rise to a new temporal order by tracing the sequence of events (Van de Ven and Huber, 1990). However, "raw process data do not come quite so neatly sliced and packaged" (Langley, 1999, p. 692) as highlighted using the example shown above. Nevertheless, Greenspan's realization shows that social emotions and instincts can contribute greatly to the process in terms of reaching an outcome insofar as humans apprehend what goes on about them (Rescher, 1996).

Context, Content, and Process

The framework of context, content and process is often used in the study of organizational entities. Indeed it is very relevant and often used as part of strategic management analysis. Context is an important indicator of process methods. Pettigrew (1997) explained it well in stating that "the terrain around the stream which shapes the flow of events and is in turn shaped by them is a necessary part of the process investigation" (p. 340). In process methods, context represents the organizational life of multiple streams flowing into each other but it is uniquely shaped by the conditional settings which surround it and give it form and character. Context can be distinguished by the inner and outer contexts surrounding organizational life or institutional arrangements. Inner context refers to the internal organizing arrangements such as the structural, cultural, and political environment. Outer context is concerned with the external environment and includes political, economic, social, technological, environmental, and legal considerations along with features of the sector, industry and competitive landscape. It is the meshing together of the inner and outer contexts that shape processes hence, "processes are embedded in contexts and can only be studied as such" (Pettigrew, 1997, p. 340).

Content refers to the 'what' actually changes to the organizational interest under study. "Content studies tend to focus on the antecedents and consequences of organizational change" (Van de Ven and Poole, 2005, p. 1381) as it relates to the particular theme of exploratory interest. Fundamentally, the purpose of process methods is inextricably linked to capturing and analyzing data that provide answers to questions about the word 'how'. How does the sequence of individual and collective action, interact, and give rise to an outcome resulting in a dynamic process that is neither fixated nor steady in state. Process examines how the change comes about. Process is concerned with the sequence of events over time to identify how change unfolds and thus, affecting some aspect of organizational life (e.g. strategic management).

Context shapes and is shaped by process. Content is usually focused on what happens in relation to what. Too often process method studies overly focus on describing, analyzing and explaining the 'what' and 'why' and occasionally overlook the

important attribute of becoming or rather 'how' the process occurs in the first place. It's also worth noting that process methods are concerned with actors and time and therefore, the 'who' and 'when' form important process attributes too.

Boundaries and Multiple Levels

As an advocate of the process method it is implicitly understood that organizations are made up of organizing processes. Under this presupposition the make-up of an organization can be described as a reification of processes continuously at work to maintain its course (e.g. strategic direction) in the form of becoming. The organization is continuously structuring and managing its boundaries in a stream of other processes that re-shape the organization and its boundaries (Van de Ven and Poole, 2005). The organization form can be described as the river basin made up of inter-connected streams of processes that are continuously being constituted and reconstituted (Pettigrew, 1997; Rescher, 1996; Van de Ven and Poole, 2005). "But any researcher who has collected qualitative process data in organizations has seen how difficult it is to isolate units of analysis in an unambiguous way" (Langley, 1999, p. 692). One reason for this is the extensive boundaries aligned to organizations and the inter-dependent connections between organizations that form systematic arrangements. Where to begin and where to end collecting data when following process can be a difficult choice to make but an important one in terms of deciding what's in and what is out?! This is more complex than it sounds, the phenomena of strategy spans multiple boundaries, decision-making as part of the process involves many actors across multiple levels. Process phenomena can be complex, such as strategy, and comes with fluid qualities that are temporal in nature, spread out over time and space (Pettigrew, 1992). The need to account for context as part of the process method is avidly endorsed by Pettigrew (1990, 1992, 1997), but as Langley (1999) highlights, it only makes the analysis more complex. The process method must give consideration to the contextual settings and the inter-connected multiple levels that are not always so distinguishable by way of clear demarcation lines or structured hierarchy. Often, levels can be difficult to separate from one another.

Generalizability

Both variance and process methods make great effort to attain generality, but with the process method, generalizability depends on its aptness to readily change to adapt to different situations. The term 'versatility' is used by Poole et al. (2000) to describe this dimension of the process method as it relates to "the degree to which it can encompass a broad domain of developmental patterns without modification of its essential character" (p. 43). The capacity for a process explanation to 'shrink' or 'stretch' to match specific situations that vary in momentum and time horizon determines its level of versatility. A good example of a versatile process explanation can be found with the punctuated equilibrium model of organizational change (Gersick, 1991; Tushman and Romanelli, 1985). It can apply to varying time spans from a month to a year and also fits with different processes such as organizational change, group development, and the evolution of IT (Van de Ven and Poole, 2005). The process method is not simple, nor is it necessarily general, but it can be highly accurate within given contextual parameters. One of the many process research challenges extends to the choices made and the trade-off between generality, simplicity, and accuracy. This point is amplified by the following short statement:

Like all forms of social research, process work has its strengths and its weaknesses, its virtues and its limitations. The major contribution of process research (as characterized here) is to catch reality in flight, to explore the dynamic qualities of human conduct and organizational life and to embed such dynamics over time in the various layers of context in which streams of activity occur. The price of this dynamic analysis is the missed opportunity to see the much wider terrain in which the normally limited set of comparative cases under study are located. (Pettigrew, 1997, p. 347)

Frame of Reference

Students and scholars of the process method do not enter the field empty minded, free of assumptions and values, they come with a frame of reference. Purely events-based process methods eliminate subjectivity, subjectivity on the part of who tells the story and the researcher who narrates it. But as Pentland (1999) remarks "there is a great deal of insight to be gained from a careful analysis of the same story from multiple subjective points of view" (pp. 714-715). By eliminating subjective views and bias on the part of the researcher in terms of how an account is narrated can yield much more meaningful insights into what is actually going on beneath the surface. The example of Brown's (1998) study of software implementation is a good benchmark that reveals one way of eliminating bias both on the part of the informant and also the researcher. Brown (1998) observed that the informant groups held different perspectives shaped by the goals and values of the group e.g. technologists favored technology, whereas clinicians and medical staff emphasized patient care and convenience. In the process of Brown's (1998) analysis, he discovered that some informant groups commend certain voices while downplaying and silencing others. By focusing on the silencing effect considered largely as an act of power, it was possible to detect the chords of power among the different groups involved with the software project. Selective silencing is regarded as an unavoidable feature of narrative (Pentland, 1999) but process researchers must remain mindful of the need to display high levels of objectivity when analyzing multiple subjective points of view and not to allow their own subjective biases to tarnish analytical accuracy.

Vocabulary

The process method aims to capture the interchange between social actors and contexts by investigating the sequence of events that unfold over time. This calls for a very descriptive form of vocabulary that adequately illustrates the generating mechanisms at work in an event sequence that will lead to the development of a process theory explanation. A variable language is replaced with "*an active language of becoming, emerging, developing, transforming, and decaying*" (Pettigrew, 1997, p. 338). The language must be active insofar as it aptly reveals the evolving nature of organizational events. It must capture the emergent and transient qualities that are produced. Processes can be of a linear, directional, rational, cumulative and irreversible form, other processes can be non-linear, much less rational, even radical and transformational (Sztompka, 1993). The challenge for the process scholar is to capture the dynamic characteristics – "simultaneously telling the complete story while setting the plot is a tall order" (Langley, 1999, p. 697). Overall, the 'thick description' should convey high levels of authenticity for the process streams, observable regularities, and the linkages between them.

Outcomes

Most often the process method involves collection of large quantities of multi-faceted data. Process data comes in the form of archived records, interviews and observations. Organizational processes are typically complex. Making sense of the processes by way of distilling regularities observed in the data can be a challenging undertaking. Consequently this tends to limit the number of cases that

form part of a process study. Arguably this limits the extent of generality that can be claimed for the resultant process theory (Langley, 1999; Van de Ven and Poole, 2005). The aim of the process method is to provide a deep understanding of the organizational themes under study resulting in a 'vicarious experience' of a real world situation in all of its complex form (Lincoln and Guba, 1985). "The theorist who adopts this philosophy tries to avoid excessive data reduction and to present as completely as possible the different viewpoints of the process studied" (Langley, 1999, p. 695). Pettigrew argues quite strongly that the process method must do more than overcome the challenges of pattern recognition and analytical complexities of explanation. It must also link analyses of the process stream to location and explanation of outcomes. Explanation of outcomes can be linked to different levels such as the firm level or sector level; national or international; culture, historical and political structures, and so on. Furthermore, analysis of multiple processes at the same level must link pattern recognition and explanation to outcomes, for example, strategy and IT at the business, corporate, or network level.

Process Method and Strategy

In dealing with real world contexts vis-à-vis strategy-making, non-process situations will emerge. While process data can be used to display how events are sequenced over time, it can also be used for many other purposes. Process data can be used to develop rich descriptions of meanings, behaviors, and feelings evoked by work place situations at a given point in time (Pratt and Rafaeli, 1997). It can be used to understand an individuals' mental map of the elements in their world (Huff, 1990). Sound process research can take a variety of forms to suit the issue under study and studying processes usually involves "qualitative approaches, case-studies, observation and interviews, longitudinal and in-depth studies, the hallmarks of a different approach to studying organizations that had been central for some 20 years" (Hinings, 1997, p. 500). The application of the process method to study strategy is well suited to explore through the use of in-depth longitudinal approaches. The aim being to investigate and learn about the sequence of events as they unfold over time and to describe the conditions that influence strategic decision-making processes. In studying strategy, the process method allows us to "provide a better understanding of how and why the 'pieces of the puzzle' interact and work together to produce a participation decision" (Rowlands, 2005, p 86). The process method seeks to gain insight into the generative mechanisms discovered within event sequence and to explain the occurrence of identifiable patterns observed among them. From a strategy perspective, "these can then be made relevant for management practice by providing insight with regard to generative mechanisms and associated process trajectories of continuity and change, to allow for judgments on the favorability of the course of the process as well as the necessity to intervene or to let the process run its course" (Sminia, 2009, p. 97). The process method can enlighten us about the dynamic nature of event sequence and the complexities embedded in process situations, and therefore well suited to studying strategy insofar as strategy is complex, non-rational, and non-linear, made up of meandering processes not uniform in nature. "Strategy can best be understood by tracking it over time; by looking at behavior rather than condition; by studying 'what happens in response to what'" (Miller and Friesen, 1982, p. 1020).

The dynamism quality of the process method was ably illustrated by Pettigrew and Webb (1996) in developing a novel typology expressed in a participative language that accounted for the transient and emergent characteristics of planned and realized strategy. The authors argued that the language of business strategy had become fixated and therefore, identified more capable terms such as consolidating, internationalizing, and down-scoping, and so on. The process method

includes the study of linkages between changes in the business environment, business strategy, organizational structure, resource capabilities, and management practices (Pettigrew, 1990). Strategic impacts can penetrate linkages between organizational performance and outcomes in many different ways. Process impacts can be found to occur at the level of an individual's job, work group, organizational subunit, product or service, overall organization, or a community of organizations (Van de Ven and Poole, 2002). Strategy is concerned with developing and executing plans to bring about novel change in support of organizational priorities and long-term direction. "Novel changes entail the creation of originals, whereas routine changes involve the reproduction of copies" (Van de Ven and Poole, 2002, p. 871). Novel change is more complex and unpredictable requiring the development and execution of new change routines which often emerge from strategic plans by way of intended or emergent course of action. Suitably, the process method is well positioned to trace the patterns in a stream of action, whether intended or not.

The seminal process research to date addressing strategic management issues does not share a common underlying process theory upon which to anchor strategy-related inquiry. Henry Mintzberg had often adopted a configuration approach to study strategy; Andrew Van de Ven has sought to develop a meta-level theory that culminates in bringing together the four general process theories; and Andrew Pettigrew has relied on the dialectic model of process theory and draws support from structuration theory. Strategy researchers often adopt structuration theory to guide process studies (Pozzebon, 2004). This is done along-side gaining a good understanding of the major themes and issues as they relate to the strategic topic of interest. Under the 'strategy-as-practice' management label, often the emphasis is on tracing the interactions of strategists' themselves and the subsequent impacts on organizational performance. While differences exist among the strategy scholarly community in terms of structuration thematic choices, there is "commonality with regard to the role of agency and structure" (Sminia, 2009, p. 111). Hence, strategy-related inquiry is based upon 'structuration-like' theories to advance the process method and enables the researcher to consider both agency and structure to seek out patterns among purposeful management action and socially embedded constraints.

The role of context is an important attribute of the process method. In studying the interconnectedness between strategic social action and performance impact on structure, it was discovered that the outcome from identical action differs by context (Pettigrew, 1985). A process method that embodies a contextual approach considers both the inner and outer environments to trace its significance in relation to the sequence of events located in a specified setting. The contextual approach draws originally from the meta-theoretical framework of root metaphor, centered on the philosophical worldview of pragmatic truth (Pepper, 1942), the purpose of which is to serve practical human need (Fambrough and Comerford, 2006). The aim is to make past experience come alive again and thereby 'catch reality in flight.' A process method underpinned by a contextual approach "sees the world as a collection of events in their unique setting" and "acknowledges the local character of truth, in both time and space with corroboration taking place by way of qualitative confirmation" (Sminia, 2009, p. 104). Subsequently, strategic outcomes are a component of context, process and history (Pettigrew, 1985, 1990). Only by capturing the unique subtleties of pattern regularities can the fullness of the process be understood.

Process Method and IT Strategy-Making

Under the structuration view as it relates to the impact of IT in organizations (Orlikowski and Robey, 1991; DeSanctis and Poole, 1994), it is contended that IT and organizations continuously transform one another as new IT is implemented and the benefits leveraged. Under this perspective, Tsoukas and Chia (2002) regard change as the basic component of organizations, the process by which they transform, continuously evolving and always becoming. "The interconnected nature of people, tools, tasks, and organizational form is a well-known phenomenon" (Pentland and Feldman, 2007, p. 781). Then to see how IT and organizations are interconnected, it becomes necessary to study people performing tasks and using tools so to better understand the type of transformation resulting from strategic IT impacts on organizational processes and performance. Given that 'structuration-like' theory underpins the process method inquiring into strategy-related themes, then how does this fit with IT? "Agency produces and reproduces structure; structure constrains and enables agency" (Pentland and Feldman, 2007, p. 785) but how does IT impact on these constituents? Social action through the enactment of participants brings about structure and IT is an enabling resource for enacting structure. And even though at times it may seem that IT is pervasive and becoming institutionalized, Orlikowski (2000) reminds us that it is only stabilized for now. Furthermore, "every engagement with technology is temporally and contextually provisional, and thus there is, in every use, always the possibility of a different structure being enacted" (Orlikowski, 2000, p. 412). Accordingly, social action through the enabling resource of IT can reproduce structure vis-à-vis participant enactment but it is both contextually and temporally bounded. Participant enactment is largely concerned about the decision-making processes regarding strategic IT and management behavior as it pertains to the development and execution of strategic IT initiatives. Thus it seems, altogether fitting, to select the process method to study all aspects of strategic IT to seek out new meaning and understanding about IT-enabled transformation, particularly in relation to new structural forms and performance impacts.

Notwithstanding the reasons described above in supporting the application of the process method to study strategic IT processes, much of the extant IT literature is dominated by a variant focused mindset and thus, potentially reducing the findings to mere determinants that are fixed in state and lack the transient dynamism implicit in strategy. Positivist methods such as surveys and lab experiments account for 76% of all IT management research (Myers and Liu, 2009). And even though Ramiller and Pentland (2009) contend that a variable-centered approach to studying IT should "constitute a major platform from which our community can speak to issues of managerial interest" (p. 474), it does seem that the traditionalists do more to distance themselves from the business and IT executives that matter insofar as consideration is lacking for executive action at work. By exploring the IT strategy-making domain through the application of a process method lenses, there is the potential to discover new insights into strategic IT in related areas of interest such as: creation, development and execution of strategic IT (Chen et al. 2008); thinking processes behind major decision-making (Reich and Benbasat, 2000); management interactions (Silva and Hirschheim, 2007); interdisciplinary issues (Reich and Kaarst-Brown, 2003); events associated with strategic IT-enabled change (Tarafdar and Qrunfleh, 2009); complex contextual settings (Avison et al. 2004); and the human factors affecting strategic IT in practice (Bush et al. 2009). There are many good opportunities to further expand our understanding of strategic IT by exploring the intertwinement of processes, actors, tasks and activities, contexts, time and history.

Process Method Design

This section focuses on process method design techniques to collect and analyze data. The section is organized into three parts and presented in the following way. First, the process method research cycle as advocated by Pettigrew (1990, 1992, 1997) is outlined. Second, strategies for sense-making recommended by Langley (1999) are presently at a high-level only. Third, a typology for developing narrative as suggested by Pentland (1999) is proposed as the analytical technique to get on top of process data. Reference to narrative analysis is frequently made by Langley and Pettigrew also, but Pentland offers a good set of guidelines to structure the narrative component and serves to complement earlier reference.

Process Method Cycle

Application guidelines are recommended by Pettigrew (1990, 1992, 1997) for conducting research using the process method of inquiry. The guidelines are based on past research that inquired into strategy and organizational practice (Ferlie et al. 1996; Pettigrew, 1973, 1979, 1985; Pettigrew and McNulty, 1995; Pettigrew and Whipp, 1991, 1993; Pettigrew et al. 1992). The method distinguishes between process method inputs and outputs (Pettigrew, 1997). On the input side, choices need to be made about practical issues concerning application of method in the following areas: ethics and contracting; purpose; themes; research questions; time; and data source types. Ethics and contracting are especially important to process method studies because of the close links between researcher and the host case organization. Consideration needs to be given to issues such as respect for all persons and points of view; contracting relates to issues such as gaining organizational access and publication of findings; negotiation and agreement about matters of confidentiality, anonymity, and attribution; and the point of reciprocity, *quid pro quo* – what does the host case organization gain in return for providing access, time and information. The need for foresight about research purpose, themes, and core questions anchor the study in extant scholarly literature (e.g. IT strategy-making) and the empirical findings which follow. This approach is orientated to suit a deductive and inductive cycle of interactive analysis to follow.

On the output side, Pettigrew recommends three stages to preparing the case presentation. First, a write-up of the case history, followed next by preparing the case as an analytical chronology, with the final presentation in the form of meta-level case analysis. The case history captures preceding events that may hold antecedent conditions which could be helpful in providing explanation as part of a longitudinal case series analysis. Events of the past continuously shape the emerging future by way of what, why and how they occur and the resultant outcomes from them. Significance is dependent on when it happened within the process sequence. The historical component can provide a good foundation for the overall case structure. "For the process analyst, events and chronologies are crucial building blocks but only building blocks" (Pettigrew, 1997, p. 339). The analytical chronology begins with the search to locate patterns within the process, themes of interest that occur with regularity. Identifiable patterns between cases should be compared and distinguished in terms of unique qualities or features along with the sequential position among events. What shapes the pattern is considered to be the generative mechanism. Within the observable pattern in a process is the underlying driving force that shapes its characteristic. By embodying the 'how' aspect repeatedly into the search for process mechanisms will reveal the underlying force shaping the pattern. "The teasing out of these mechanisms in this interactive field represents one of the greatest inductive challenges for process scholars and an area of intellectual challenge which is as difficult to describe as it is to achieve and publically justify" (Pettigrew, 1997, p. 339). The next analytical phase is concerned with moving from inductively recognizing patterns in the process to deductively structuring the data sets. The research aims and related themes play a crucial role in pattern recognition within time series analyses. The final output of meta-level analysis involves moving the case study into the form of holistic explanation. This is described by Pettigrew to be the 'apotheosis'

of the process method. The attribute of time in process analysis is linked not only to studying processes over a longitudinal horizon but linking these to outcomes. The holistic ambition resides in taking the recognizable patterns of the process stream, overcoming the analytical complexities to identify the constellation of forces that shape the process under study, and link these to outcomes. "The irreducible purpose of a processual analysis remains to account for and explain the what, why and how of the links between context, processes and outcomes" (Pettigrew, 1997, p. 340). An omission in linking processes and outcomes makes any attempt at holistic explanation incomplete.

The process method is greatly interested in historical fact and contextual intricacy. The collection and analysis of historical data enables the structuring of chronological events and aids the researcher to identify key individuals of interest in the process. By assembling historical data it becomes possible to structure the core of the chronology and identify key transition points in the process under study. For example, examining a longitudinal series of strategy events in a specified context would allow the researcher to collect data about those episodes, identify key individuals involved, the timelines associated with each episode, and any transition points that may potentially represent key turning points in the process that might illustrate the occurrence of significant events. Significant findings would, during the interview process, be explored in much greater depth and ideally done so with the key individuals already linked to the strategy episodes. Building a good understanding of the contextual complexities is important too. To hold a certain level of understanding about context and the strategy processes undertaken will aid greater respect and acceptance with informants. "These individuals and the what of the chronology are then explored much more fully in the interview process whose prime purpose is to integrate information about the what, why and how of the process under investigation" (Pettigrew, 1997, p. 344). Alongside developing the pro-forma interview themes, other choices need to be made issues such as: primary unit of analysis; how context is to be refined; the need for preliminary interviews to pilot the core themes of interest with knowledgeable informants; design adjustments reflecting pilot experience; case candidate endorsement of engagement style; and determination of total study timelines. A mechanism by which to structure the approach involves the design of a case protocol. The purpose of a case protocol is to keep the researcher focused during data collection by way of general rules, procedures and information (Yin, 2003). Such a protocol can assist the researcher to remain mindful of potential problems, risks and issues that could arise during the data collection process. The protocol is considered an important instrument in longitudinal case series research that endorses the process method. However, it is difficult to accurately reflect the full level of detail required at the beginning of a research project so the protocol needs to be refreshed and revised throughout the process to reflect relevant changes to the planned process and intended aims.

Deductive structuring requires the organization of major themes and aims around the research question early on in the process. Thereafter the process becomes more open-ended to search for patterns through inductive logic. Early on in the research design, a theoretically informed interview pro-forma can help to structure the data collection process. One mechanism by which to do this in relation to strategy-related inquiry is to adopt the context, content and process analytical framework (Pettigrew, 1990). Some authors refer to this as the process, content and context framework (De Wit and Meyer, 2002, 2005). Essentially though, the aim of such a framework is to provide the underlying logic by which to conduct a study that deals with strategy-related interests. It helps to build structure into the data collection process. When it comes to analytical ability, a high level of conceptual reasoning is necessary to make sense of the data in hand. Often the level of conceptual

ability can determine the quality of research output. It is critical to inductively recognize patterns within the data and to compare and contrast these findings with that which is already known. The method entails the constant iteration of deductive and inductive reasoning to logically structure, organize and present the recognizable patterns that emerge through the creative cycle of analysis. A series of steps are recommended when conducting research using the process method and these are presented in Table 2.

Writing up of the analytical chronology is an important island of progress as part of the process method. An analytical chronology presents preliminary patterns in the data, reveals sequences across levels of analysis, and develops and presents thematic categories identified from the process of deductive and inductive analysis. The process method perceives the worldly context in terms of complexity, instability and uniqueness. By distilling the evidence presented in the form of an analytical chronology, the next step involves the deductive and inductive sighting of preliminary patterns that are taken to yield greater insights from the original data. By distilling the underlying logics in the form of dominant theme analysis, core categories become identifiable upon which to expand upon using the empirical data sets and extant scholarly literature. To develop greater insights into the core categories it can become necessary to trace and follow the themes through an iterative process involving the case accounts, interview data and extant literature. Or as Pettigrew (1990) described it, "does one stop peeling the layers from the onion only when the vapors inhibit all further sight?" (p. 272). This requires a more explicit need to interpret the narrative but to also link emerging conceptual themes inductively derived to stronger analytical themes within the data sets. "Interpretive theoretical cases move the analysis and writing beyond the analytical chronologies" (Pettigrew, 1990, p. 280). Theoretical elaboration can sometimes only be realized by linking themes with the collectible data sets and extant scholarly

Table 2. Process method research cycle

Determine subject of interest.
Identify opportunities for inquiry by way of research gaps and / or problems.
Demonstrate suitability to apply the process method to orientate the research approach.
Establish core questions of study.
Identify main themes of interest to investigate as part of the process approach.
Determine context(s) of interest to base inquiry.
Initiate early data collection by way of interviews and observation.
Seek out and recognize early patterns observable within the case data.
Write-up case history.
Confirm, verify or disconfirm facts of interest against primary and secondary sources – remove all margins of uncertainty or ambiguity.
Identify prominent themes of significant interest and craft well-meaning question(s) to explore further in more detail.
Expand investigation to collect more relevant data pertinent to new found themes and questions of interest.
Seek out recognizable patterns from across more cases.
Perform comparative pattern analysis between cases to establish core patterns of meaningful relevance to the process.
Refine the study's core research question and craft the case to reflect a meaningful process vocabulary to convey a rich narrative.

literature to build greater explanatory richness. Figure 1 illustrates the process method in terms of the continuous interplay between deductive and inductive analysis.

From this illustration we can see that meta-level themes are distilled from the data early on in the analysis. The analysis then becomes interested in discovering preliminary patterns of significance found among the meta-level themes. The preliminary themes provide a basis upon which to identify dominant analytical themes. In addition to scrutinizing the case history, this often entails reference back to the original interview pro-forma to make deeper and more meaningful connections attached to the dominant thematic points of interest. At this point the interplay between deductive and inductive drivers of analysis are intense albeit highly conceptual too. This calls for the strong enactment of creative conceptualization ability on the part of the analyst. Making apparent the connection between patterns represented by the data and that which is already known by way of

the extant literature aids the analysis and makes the findings more robust and relevant. By revealing the significance of patterns identifiable in the case data and discovering shared elements of commonality with the extant literature provides a firm basis upon which to develop credible theory. In many instances it may be necessary to consider a range of literature sets in addition to the literature set of core interest. For example, in studying strategy, it may also be relevant to consider additional topics of organization and management interest to bridge pattern analysis with theoretical knowledge, hence, the iterative interplay between analytical observation and theoretical conceptualization. Figure 1 is an example taken from a doctoral study that sought to explain the role of IT middle managers in IT strategy-making and in that particular case, role types were denoted by categories and the related role attributes and activities were shown as a set subcategories arrived at by way of inductive and deductive analysis iteratively driven. This led to a theoretical framework to explain the process

Figure 1. Application of process method to analyze and develop theory

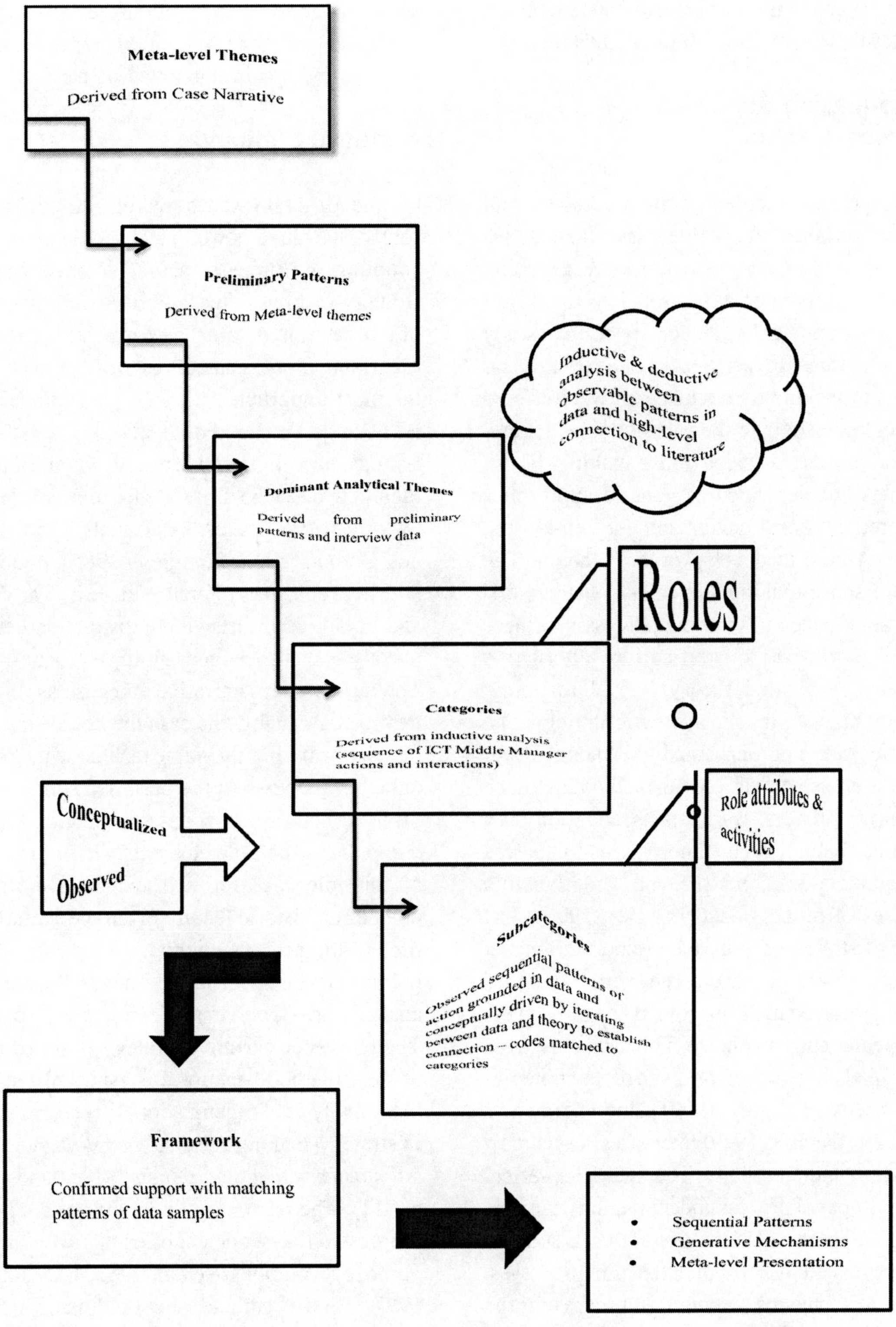

based on observable sequential patterns and the underlying generative mechanisms thus enabling a meta-level presentation of the analytical findings.

Sense-Making Strategies for Process Theory

This chapter has focused on the process method over the variance alternative. Nevertheless, the complexity of process research more generally has led scholars to offer insights into the different strategy approaches that can be used to study process. A range of sense-making heuristics and systems to tackle process research were offered by Langley (1999) in the form of seven strategies for process research sense-making. These strategies are described as generic approaches to theoretical sense-making and not step-by-step guides on how to develop process theory. The range of sense-making strategies considers different approaches to theorize process and these include: narrative; quantification; alternative templates; grounded theory; visual mapping; temporal bracketing; and synthetic strategy. The strategies are not necessarily exhaustive and can be used as part of a multi-method approach to theorize process. By focusing attention on a particular feature, each strategy aims to address the boundary-less, multi-level, and dynamic attributes of process data (Langley, 1999). The choice of strategy can have an important impact on the type of theory to emerge. Some strategies remain grounded in the original data while others offer greater abstract choice. The form of process theory likely to emerge from each of the strategies is classified by Langley (1999) using Thorngate's (1976) and Weick's (1979) categories of accuracy, generality, and simplicity. The strategies reflect different types of process understanding (Langley, 1999). The process orientation for each strategy is distinguished in terms of patterns in processes, driving mechanisms, meaning of process for the social actors involved, and prediction. The orientation for each strategy differs somewhat and the

researcher must determine the most appropriate sense-making device in terms of the type of process theory sought. Our preference is for the narrative strategy and this is elaborated on next.

Narrative Strategy

Of the different sense-making strategies presented, narrative is well suited to theorize when adopting the process method to investigate IT strategy-making. This approach tells the story of a process in detail. The narrative approach to theorizing process data is responsible for some of the most important work in organizational studies (Van de Ven and Poole, 2005). The rich story telling nature of narrative usually entails multiple themes to describe the sequence of events leading to a theory of process (Bartunek, 1984; Bartel and Garoud, 2009; Pettigrew, 1985). A point of note here concerns reference made by Van de Ven and Poole (2005) drawing a distinction between narrative histories and multiple case studies. The authors treat narrative and case as different methods. Arguably the case method is in its own unique form a highly viable technique to theorize data, but recourse to the narrative strategy most often embeds a strong case orientation that can comprise of multiple elements, either in singular or multiple case form. The narrative strategy embeds an historic feature given the centrality of time to the process method. As Langley (1999) points out the specific data needs for narrative analysis are *"one or few rich cases"* (p. 696). The choice of narrative strategy is suited to the process method because it is especially relevant to the analysis of organizational processes such as IT strategy-making because *"people do not simply tell stories – they enact them"* (Pentland, 1999, p. 711). The term narrative indicates a coherent progression or sequence of events with specific purpose (Rimmons-Kenan, 1983; Czarniawska, 1997, 1998; Pentland and Feldman, 2007). It follows then that narrative fits with the study of IT strategy-making insofar as the specific purpose of people enacting strategic processes is to execute IT-enabled initiatives to maximize organizational benefits. It is the study of strategic enactment to reveal the sequence of events and subsequent outcomes over time. Narrative is not a mere chronicling of disconnected events; it must be coherent (Abbot, 1992; Abell, 2004; White, 1981). In relation to studying the processes of strategic IT, coherence can be discovered in unity of action or purpose (Csarniawska, 1997, 1998; Pentland and Feldman, 2007). As organizational actors combine to develop and execute IT strategies, routines become embedded that unify through action, identifiable as patterns observable through event sequence and characterized by performance and outcomes.

In selecting the process method to study IT strategy-making, the aim is to discover the emergence of ongoing patterns related to strategic IT action and interaction over time. Such an approach can generate new insights into how actors enact processes concerning strategic IT to shape the organizational trajectory. In support of this, narrative strategy can be seen as *"a way of sharing meaning during strategizing activity, of constituting an overall sense of direction or purpose, of refocusing individual and organizational identities, and of enabling and constraining the activities of actors"* (Fenton and Langley, 2011, p. 1173). The purpose of narrative is to do more than merely tell a story about the sequence of organizational events over time resulting in a theoretical explanation based on the discovery of resultant outcomes. The merit of narrative is far greater for it holds the potential to become more meaningful and relevant to the organizational actors responsible for strategic enactment. It can influence the activities of actors by way of enabling or constraining actions in support of the overall direction that constitutes organizational purpose.

Turning Process Method into Narrative

Narrative has come to be viewed as a basic human strategy for coming to terms with time, process and change – a strategy that contrasts with, but not inferior to, 'scientific' modes of explanation (Herman et al. 2012). Storytelling with narrative falls within the scope of many social-scientific and humanistic disciplines in which stories can be viewed as supporting a range of cognitive and communicative activities. Narrative is often used to convey the rich contextual features that can bound a series of events (Pentland and Feldman, 2007) and provide an account of what happened to particular people, in particular situations, and offering up specific outcomes (Herman et al. 2012). Narrative is used to emphasize a set of actions or events that embodies unity of purpose (Abbott, 1992; Abell, 2004). Narrative is critical to organizational sense-making and an essential characteristic of strategy-making (Fenton and Langley, 2011). This is made explicit *"in the accounts people give of their work as strategy practitioners, and in the artefacts produced by strategizing activity"* (Fenton and Langley, 2011, p. 1171). Organizational stories as told by research informants can bring together sequential elements of the strategy process from the past into the present again (Brown, 1990).

Narrative theory presents an account by way of a story in the form of an abstract conceptual model; "it generates the mechanisms at work" (Van de Ven and Poole, 2002, p. 885) and at a minimum the story must present a description of the sequence of events. A good narrative theory, however, includes a lot more than just event progression. According to Pentland (1999, pp. 712-713), a comprehensive process narrative theory should include the following five features:

1. **Sequence in Time:** Narrative should include a clear beginning, middle and end ... Chronology is a central organizing device. The events or actions referred to in a narrative are understood to happen in a sequence.

2. **Focal Actor or Actors:** Narratives are always about someone or something ... There is a protagonist and, frequently, an antagonist as well. The character may not be developed or even identified by name, but, along with sequence, they provide a thread that ties the events in a narrative together.

3. **Identifiable Narrative Voice:** A narrative is something that someone tells (Bal, 1985), so there should always be an identifiable voice doing the narrating. That voice reflects a specific point of view (Rimmon-Kenan, 1983).

4. **"Canonical" or Evaluative Frame of Reference:** Narratives carry meaning and cultural value because they encode, implicitly or explicitly, standards against which actions of the characters can be judged ... But even without any explicit moral, narratives embody a sense of what is right and wrong, appropriate or inappropriate, and so on.

5. **Other Indicators of Content or Context:** Narrative texts typically contain more than just the bare events. In particular, they contain a variety of textual devices that are used to indicate time, place, attributes of the characters, attributes of the context, and so on. These indicators do not advance the plot, but they provide information that may be essential to the interpretation of the events (e.g. knowing that the scene is a wedding changes the significance of the utterance 'I do').

Not all features are equally relevant to every study however; too much emphasis on any single feature may unnecessarily discard attention to others. Furthermore, extending features to convey a good narrative may well increase accuracy by way of sacrificing simplicity and generality. The relationship of narrative features to theory development in organization and management studies is shown in Table 3.

Based on the features shown above in Table 3, it follows that inquiry into IT strategy-making is concerned with the strategy timeline from conception to execution and this would normally entail many years. In terms of event sequencing, two macro level events when dealing with strategy are certainly of interest: strategy formation; and strategy execution. Social actors might include the role and activities enacted by the Chief Information Officer, various IT managers at multiple levels, the involvement and interaction between IT managers, business managers and executive leaders. A principled feature would perhaps account for the level of IT structural credibility within the organization or account for the levels of exchange between IT and business executives to build mutual and shared understanding in terms of vision setting and collaboratively manifesting

Table 3. Relationship of narrative features to theory development

Narrative Feature	Device to Indicate
Time order	Event history.
Sequence of events	Recognition of the sequential ordering and patterns among events.
Social actors	Actor characteristics such as role, position, reporting structures, relationships, and demographical points of significance.
Principles	Moral features such as cultural values, assumptions and biases, beliefs and attitudes etc.
Contextual circumstances	Sector and industry settings, performance, historical facts of note etc.

the strategic agenda. Context, for example, could take note of the particular industry or sector as this can influence and impact the degree of technological capacity and capability requirements. Each feature merits strong consideration when narrating explanation for a process theory.

To become a skilled process scholar takes time, commitment to the method, and practice. Developing a robust process theory that captures the above features of method requires high levels of conceptual ability and creativity in applying methodical and reproducible analytical narration to process methods as required of social science research.

FUTURE RESEARCH DIRECTIONS

This section draws attention to a number of current topical research themes. The themes relate to the study of IT management and each intersects with IT strategy-making in one way or another. Of particular interest in terms of research methodology and in-keeping with the book's underlying theme of qualitative methods to study IT, the first theme reflects on the call to consider wider application of mixed-methods (i.e. quantitative and qualitative). Whilst positivist studies continue to dominate IT scholarly research, it is becoming more favorable among members of the research community to apply qualitative approaches to the study of IT. It is anticipated that wider application of qualitative methods will continue to rise and make valuable contributions to the field as a whole. Such contributions will provide new insights for IT itself, and also provide the basis to advance quality work of a quantitative nature. Furthermore, the theme of critical realism is gaining currency among the IT community and offers the potential to provide fresh insights which can only be a good thing for the field as a whole. The paradigmatic view of critical realism places less importance on whether the methodological approach is quantitative or qualitative. Rather,

a critical realist recognizes that both have an important contribution to make. In relation to future research directions, there is potential to explore IT strategy-making from a critically realist perspective that embeds a process-orientation to explore social and conceptual features of the construct. The themes in relation to emerging and future research directions include: mixed-methods; philosophical perspective on critical realism; digital business strategy; business level implications for IT strategy-making; social capital effects on strategic IT; IT capability reputation; IT-enabled transformation – understanding and relevance;, building on critical success factors for IT performance; leveraging strategic partnerships to adapt; exploring strategic IT alignment conundrum; and finally, technologically enabling the process method. The themes are discussed next at a very high-level only.

Mixed-Method

Research within the IT strategy-making domain can broadly be categorized into two types of methodological approach: quantitative; and qualitative. The preferred method chosen by researchers is usually determined based on their ontological and epistemological beliefs. Heretofore, the field of IT studies has been dominated by the positivist paradigmatic perspective which most often selects quantitative methods. But during the last decade there have been calls by members of the IT scholarly community to recognize qualitative methods in order to advance our understanding of IT. More recently, Venkatesh et al. (2013) advanced good reasons in support of multi-method (Mingers, 1997, 2001; Ridenour and Newman, 2008; Teddlie and Tashakkori, 2003, 2009) to strengthen IT research. Several scholars have called for a triangulation of qualitative and quantitative data in order to develop a deeper understanding of a phenomenon (Denzin, 1978; Jick, 1979; Mingers, 1997, 2001; Reichardt and Rallis, 1994) whereby such methodological combinations occur in a state of 'peaceful coexistence' (Datta, 1994; House, 1994; Ridenour and Newman, 2008; Rossi, 1994). Despite such calls to adopt a mixed-methods approach, in studying IT, the response has been minimalistic (Venkatesh et al. 2013). However, there is great hope that mixed-methods will begin to feature more prominently insofar as the need to understand and explain complex organizational and social phenomenon provides a good opportunity for IT researchers to conduct studies using such an approach (Cao et al. 2006; Mingers, 2001). A set of general guidelines to support and aid the development and validation of a mixed-methods research design is advocated by Venkatesh et al. (2013) and the authors offer some excellent advice to advance this topical theme.

Philosophical Perspective on Critical Realism

The philosophical tradition of critical realism is beginning to have real interest among IT scholars by way of forming the paradigmatic perspective to guide and conduct investigative studies (Mingers et al. 2013). The philosophical stance of critical realism contends that events occur in the world independent of our knowledge of them. It is realist in the sense that the world goes beyond that which can be empirically observed, or that understanding is reduced to our knowledge of the world in terms of what we already know. The philosophical belief prescribes to the view that our understanding of the world mediates through perception and the theoretical lenses through which we see, hence not all worldly perspectives are considered equal, hence, critical. Critical realism endorses the need for different types of knowledge and accepts the existence of physical, social and conceptual objects. Accordingly, it welcomes different methodological approaches to investigate the world around us and to study the objects within it. *"As such, it offers a robust framework for the use of a variety of methods in order to gain a better understanding of the meaning and significance of information systems in the contemporary world"* (Mingers et al. 2013, p. 795). In a recently published special issue of *MIS Quarterly*, scholarly contributions revealed different features of the critical realist paradigm including papers that addressed the themes of theory building, methods, and application. Collectively, these papers highlight the rich resources available to researchers and scholars under the critical realist paradigm and it is anticipated that greater interest in IT research under this perspective will grow.

Digital Business Strategy

The evolution of digital business strategy has provided this important theme with a firm foothold in the IT management literature and currently dominates the focus of many IT scholarly endeavors. The theme intersects with the fields of IT management, strategic management, and organizational theory. A set of critical challenges in relation to the future development of digital business strategy are set out by Bharadawaj et al. (2013). Themes of interest to the digital business strategy construct, likely to dominate research interests in this area include: senior management leadership capabilities; strategic implications of making digital market moves; future development of the digital ecosystem in terms of collaboration, processes, and infrastructure; and the shifting nature of digital value architecture (Bharadawaj et al. 2013). Digital business strategy offers many exciting opportunities for research and to re-imagine new ways of the future. The future of strategic interactions among digitally-based organizations such as fixed-wire and wireless providers, internet-based services, and TV offerings are one such opportunity deserving of scholarly inquiry. Drnevich and Croson (2013) insightfully comment on the nature of seen and unforeseen technological change in the past and query the impending challenges ahead in terms of structure, conduct and performance for these complementary digitally-based value chains.

Business Level Implications for IT Strategy-Making

A solid argument is presented by Drnevich and Croson (2013) that contends the interactional relationship between IT and strategy is maintained at the functional level only, at least in terms of extant theory, and that too little consideration is given to understand the business level implications of IT investments and subsequent business value. The authors reinforce the important role of IT in support of functional level strategy, but observe more widely, the lack of understanding about IT investment impacts at the strategic business level in terms of performance implications that have the potential to affect industry structure, and create or destroy enterprising strategic alternatives and value-creation opportunities. Essentially, too little attention has been paid to generate understanding for the business level role of IT and the IT/strategy relationship insofar as this mediates through business performance (Drenvich and Croson, 2013). What has emerged from the research findings is that although a great deal of the strategic management literature discusses key drivers of firm level performance; the level of research and discussion on the strategic role of IT on business and firm level performance is minimal. Subsequently, inquiry that seeks out ways for greater integration between the IT and strategic management fields to identify high level parallels and synergistic patterns of performance provides many good opportunities.

Social Capital Effect on Strategic IT

The role of social capital on strategic IT performance via strategic IT alignment by way of boosting organizational performance has been of interest for some time (Reich and Benbasat, 1996, 2000). Recently, Karahanna and Preston (2013) provided good insights into the effects of social capital in facilitating knowledge exchange and combination between the Chief Information Officer (CIO) and top management team (TMT). The research findings revealed that two dimensions of social capital – cognitive, and relational, can exert positively on strategic IT-business efficacy through upper echelon mediation. Enriching social capital levels between the CIO and TMT must therefore be considered an antecedent to effecting strategic IT alignment by way of organizational value creation and benefit realization. However, while it is understood to be an important theme, there is still much to do to advance and build on extant theory. For example, how are the various dimensions of social capital created and thus, extended between the CIO and TMT? We know that trust is an important relational lever in this regard but how is it shaped? What levers are used to bridge and link the CIO with the TMT in order to create greater understanding and combination and what is to be expected of the TMT in bringing this about? Essentially, even though the important role of social capital is understood in terms of bringing about shared understanding between the CIO and TMT, it is an aspect of strategic IT that will continue to dominate scholarly interest.

IT Capability Reputation

An interesting theme to emerge most recently is the concept of IT capability reputation. It is contended by Lim et al. (2013) that an organization's senior IT management team will exert themselves to foster external recognition for the IT capability. By virtue of growing an externally oriented esteemed view of the organizational IT capability, reputation will flourish and subsequently, stakeholders will view the IT structural capability favorably resulting in a potential stream of successes. The concept is built on institutional theory and it goes like this.

Senior IT managers view external legitimacy as a mechanism by which to generate greater internal recognition from the TMT and board members who in turn give greater legitimacy to the IT capability and thus, recognition is gained by way of the IT management team looking outward to gain inward. This leads to the concept of IT capability sustainability and the need for strong strategic IT leadership. It is posited that internal recognition by the TMT of IT capability reputation favorably strengthens the position of senior IT management within the organization and thus, serves to build a sustainable IT trajectory. The volatile nature of TMTs and board member recognition for IT capability from one organization to the next, does not ensure a positive IT capability reputation will steer an effective cycle of strategic IT leadership. But for those organization's where the TMT respond favorably, the likelihood to induce a sustainable path of demonstrable IT success is enhanced. Building IT capability is embedded in an organization's strategic IT leadership given that capability development is contingent on a commitment to strategic comprehension vis-à-vis maximizing business value from IT investments. Scholarly interest resides in the process of 'positive reciprocity' (Lim et al., 2013).

IT-Enabled Transformation: Understanding and Relevance

It is relatively safe to say that during the last fifty years, IT has transformed the systems and processes for organizations, markets, industries, societies, and individual lives A noble cause is being pursued by Lucas et al. (2013) based on their efforts to raise greater awareness and understanding of IT-enabled transformational effects. Recently noted in an opinion and issues article, Lucas et al. (2013) make the case that to a large extent, much of the scholarly research on

IT-enabled transformation is targeted to reach an academic audience only. In response, an argument is presented to encourage IT scholars to contribute more progressively on policy matters in relation to large-scale IT-enabled change. The intent here is to make a meaningful contribution to government policy-making and corporate practice as well as academia. The aim is to make scholarly work as it relates to IT-enabled transformation more relevant to policy and practice. This theme is not new, it has been discussed and debated for over thirty years now among organizational scholars. But the latest recommendations made by Lucas et al. (2013) add to past calls to make academic research more meaningful and relevant by informing new audiences about strategic IT enablers and constraints. Seven dimensions describe what constitutes major transformation for individuals, organizations and societies (Lucas et al. 2013). It is the authors explicit hope that scholars will act more progressively by way of advisory.

Building on Critical Success Factors for IT Performance

Building on the information systems success model (DeLone and McLean, 1992) and the related dimensions for IT success, Petter et al. (2013) conducted a comprehensive review of the extant IT literature and identified forty three specific variables deemed relevant to securing IT success. The different variables were categorized against the five dimensions of the Leavitt Diamond Model of Organizational Change (i.e. task, user, social, project, and organizational characteristics). Further analysis led to identifications of fifteen critical variables deemed to be essential factors in realizing IT success. In terms of advancing this work, Petter et al. (2013) highlight four areas that offer the potential to improve knowledge about the causes of IT success. Identification of success determinants with the potential to improve IT performance will reduce gaps in knowledge and bridge greater relevancy with practice.

Leveraging Strategic Partnerships to Adapt

A theme with potentially strong relevance to IT organizations and organizations highly reliant on an adaptive IT capability is the concept of 'adaptive strategic partnerships' (Martinez-Jerez, 2014). In relation to forming supplier-customer focused synergies, and even though traditional organizational economics literature might strongly favour vertical integration or that the management literature espouses resistance to forming supplier-customer based arrangements given that the potential for exposure to conditions lacking in specificity, verifiability, and predictability are high, an alternative option to adapt is posited by Martinez-Jerez (2014). It comes in the form of leveraging supplier-customer based arrangements to respond to complex and demanding situations that require an extension of capabilities to facilitate change towards the design and delivery of new products and services. This changing dynamic has revealed that some organizations are initiating multi-level relationships with customers and suppliers to leverage the resources and capabilities of the respective parties in an effort to design, develop and create superior products and services (Martinez-Jerez, 2014). In terms of future research directions, there is scope to inquire into how organizations successfully leverage IT management capabilities by way of strategic partnering to respond to competitive and complex market challenges. This form of strategic partnering to adapt involves a high level of collaborative activity by working more closely with both customers and suppliers. According to Martinez-Jerez (2014), organizational executives are exploring new structures to find ways of working together with customers and vendors to generate more creative solutions to

successfully overcome today's market conditions. The potential for future research here is based on exploring the degree to which organizations are adapting the IT capability via such collaborative arrangements and strategic partnering.

Exploring the Strategic IT Alignment Conundrum

The penultimate opportunity concerning future research directions relates to what has been the most persistent key issue for the field of IT management for over thirty years now. Strategic IT alignment has proven to be over a longitudinal period the top concern for IT executives and business leaders. And even though a good deal of scholarly inquiry into this particular issue has investigated many of the complex facets that make it highly elusive (Chan and Reich, 2007), it persists to be a "*long-standing pervasive conundrum*" (Luftman and Ben-Zvi, 2010, p. 265). According to Ward and Peppard (2002), the basis of the issue is a consequence of "*the inability of organizations to realize value from IS* [information systems] / *IT investments,* [and this] *is in part, due to lack of alignment between business and IS / IT strategies*" (p. 44). We define strategic IT alignment to mean: *the extent to which the IT strategy is consistent with the organizational strategy by way of supporting major business priorities and advancing the long term organizational direction based on the various business and IT management levels working congruently to generate real business value.* Based on this definition, the need for strong collaboration among business and IT executive levels is implicitly evident. This highlights an opportunity to inquire into the nature of collaborative workings between business and IT executives towards aligning business priorities with suitable IT investments. Another opportunity concerns the need for organizations to develop and cultivate strategic agility that can provide greater flexibility and innovative capability to respond to market pressures and developments. In the current competitive landscape, this could relate to how organizations respond to issues concerning social media, mobile communications, big data, privacy and security, cloud computing, enterprise architecture etc., despite many years of high IT infrastructural investment costs. To explore how IT executives' manifest strategic agility as part of the IT management agenda insofar as ensuring the organizational IT capacity and capability continues to support ever changing business priorities in a fast changing technological environment is of real interest A final note on this opportunity concerns the nature of past empirical research which has been of a highly mechanistic nature; a process method approach to explore different aspects of the construct has the potential to yield a good many meaningful insights.

Technologically-Enabling the Process Method

The purpose of this book is to present various ways for which the application of technologies can support the execution of mixed-method and qualitative approaches to research. The absence of discussion in this chapter regarding the applicability of technologies to conduct process-oriented research is not purposefully done. The lack of such discussion highlights the opportunity for the potential to develop technologies that can assist and support the conduct of a process-orientated approach. While some technologies are available and can be readily used such as EndNote for library storage, quoting and referencing, and NVivo for qualitative data analysis, there remains an apparent absence of suitable technologies designed specifically to assist and help with the conduct of a process-oriented study. This highlights the opportunity to develop technological applications designed specifically with the process method in mind.

CONCLUSION

The chapter provided an overview of process research aligned to the Heraclitus perspective that views reality as being made up of ever changing processes. Distinctions were drawn between the variance and process method of theory – 'noun vs. verb', 'thing vs. process', and 'weak vs. strong.' The underlying theory of method aligned to our view of process is focused on the sequence of individual and collective events, actions and activities and the cumulative effect, situated, over time. From an organizational interest, events are complex and meandering, made up of boundary-less processes. The interactionist nature of process adds to its complexity but can provide rich and meaningful insights into management action and interaction by capturing behavioral attributes such as feelings, thoughts, ideas, emotions, and so on; cognitive and relational responses. Time is a cornerstone of the process method. Events are traced through time to capture deep meaning to understand how they unfold; social reality is not fixated but rather, a dynamic stream of occurrences that continuously 'become.' Events are conditioned by the underlying terrain; the context, from which emanate the power of internal and external forces, that shape the condition of organizational life. The process method exhibits many fine qualities to inquire into interchanging aspects of organizational life but these also add to its dynamic form. Features such as versatility, complexity, context, content and process, boundaries and multiple levels, generalizability, frame of reference, vocabulary, and outcomes, make it characteristically eclectic.

In studying organizational strategy by way of process, the method typically acquires qualitative data in the form of longitudinal case-series through the collection of archival records, interviews and observation. In my own work recently studying the process of strategic IT alignment in public sector organizations; the first form of analysis was essentially quantitative to determine core themes of interest early on before moving to embed a process methodology to inquire into something of practical relevance. Process inquiry is flexible insofar as it can orientate a multi-method approach. The process method includes the study of linkages and this positions it suitably well for studying strategy. In studying strategy, we are interested to learn about the meaning of behavior and mental schema as it relates to the elements of an organization's world. Participative decision-making processes reveal the 'how' and 'why' aspects of the puzzle by way of 'what' and the resultant outcome that unfolds over time. Strategy is process laden shaped by the generative mechanisms at work that reveal its form. Gaining insight into these generative mechanisms, the underlying drivers and logics that determine its course is critical, and therefore, process enables the study of complex linkages and patterns detectable by studying the sequence of events. From a strategy perspective these can include structure, behavior, levels, boundaries, capabilities, capacity, resources, environment, IT, performance, and so on, and the interconnections between them. Strategy is not a means to an end, it is continuously evolving and becoming, wrapped up in processes that orientate its eventful trajectory which we as scholars attempt to make sense of and understand. IT strategy-making is an enabling force that can bring about transformation at multiple levels. The process method allows us to explore strategic IT impacts through study of the interconnections between processes, actors, tasks and activities, contexts, time and performance outcomes.

Guidelines are offered in relation to conducting inquiry. The process method research cycle (Pettigrew, 1990, 1992, 1997) provides structure to design and carry out an effective study of strategy-related interests based on inputs and outputs with the overall aim to provide holistic explanation that links pattern sequence, generative mechanisms and outcomes together in the form of meta-level analysis. Alternative sense-making strategies for process data are offered by Langley (1999). Narrative analysis reveals the sequence of events and encapsulates multiple strategic themes and their interconnectedness. Highlights of strategic IT enactment through event sequence analysis over time typically reveal complexity; the stories are rich and thick with relevant detail and meaning. Of course, consideration must be given to potential trade-offs between simplicity, accuracy and generalizability. General mechanisms are embedded deep below the surface, finding them requires methodical exertion.

Finally, a number of themes are presented that intersect with the IT strategy-making domain. These offer opportunities to advance greater understanding by way of yielding new and knowledgeable insights into areas of philosophy, digital strategy, strategic impacts, capabilities, transformation, success factors, strategic partnering, strategic IT alignment, and process-driven technologies. Strategic IT transforms worldly structures, systems and processes for individuals, business units, organizations, corporations, governments, and societies. The process method enables us to yield insight into the enabling and constraining effects realized from strategic IT; that which is considerately and meaningfully planned and executed, and that which emergently unfolds unintentionally. So often, great emphasis is placed on seeking out supporting mechanisms to understand enablement when in fact, greater insight into the mechanisms controlling constraint can reveal plenty too, particularly in terms of social action.

REFERENCES

Abbot, A. (1988). Transcending general linear reality. *Sociological Theory, 6*(2), 169–186. doi:10.2307/202114

Abbot, A. (1990). Conceptions of time and events in social science methods: Causal and narrative approaches. *Historical Methods, 23*(4), 140–150. doi:10.1080/01615440.1990.10594204

Abbot, A. (1992). From causes to events: Notes on narrative positivism. *Sociological Methods & Research, 20*(4), 428–455. doi:10.1177/0049124192020004002

Abell, P. (2004). Narrative explanation: An alternative to variable-centered explanation? *Annual Review of Sociology, 30*(1), 287–310. doi:10.1146/annurev.soc.29.010202.100113

Aristotle, . (1941). *The basic words of Aristotle* (R. McKeon, Ed.). New York: Random House.

Armstrong, C. P., & Sambamurthy, V. (1999). Information Technology Assimilation in Firms: The Influence of Senior Leadership and IT-transformation. *Information Systems Research, 10*(4), 304–327. doi:10.1287/isre.10.4.304

Avison, D., Jones, J., Powell, P., & Wilson, D. (2004). Using and validating the strategic alignment model. *The Journal of Strategic Information Systems, 13*(3), 223–246. doi:10.1016/j.jsis.2004.08.002

Bal, M. (1985). *Narratology: Introduction to the theory of narrative*. Toronto: University of Toronto Press.

Bartel, C. A., & Garud, R. (2004). The role of narratives in sustaining organizational transition. *Organization Science, 20*(1), 107–117. doi:10.1287/orsc.1080.0372

Bartunek, J. (1984). Changing interpretive schemes and organizational restructuring: The example of a religious order. *Administrative Science Quarterly, 29*(3), 355–372. doi:10.2307/2393029

Bharadwaj, A., El Sawy, O. A., Pavlou, P. A., & Venkatraman, N. (2013). Visions and Voices on Emerging Challenges in Digital Business Strategy. *Management Information Systems Quarterly, 37*(2), 633–661.

Bower, J. L. (1997). Process research on strategic decisions: A personal perspective. In V. Papadakis, & P. Barwiese (Eds.), *Strategic decisions* (pp. 17–33). Dordrecht, The Netherlands: Kluwer Academic Publishers. doi:10.1007/978-1-4615-6195-8_2

Brown, A. D. (1998). Narrative, politics and legitimacy in an IT implementation. *Journal of Management Studies, 35*(1), 35–58. doi:10.1111/1467-6486.00083

Brown, M. H. (1990). Defining stories in organizations. *Communication Yearbook, 13*, 162–190.

Bush, M., Lederer, A. L., Li, X., Palmisano, J., & Rao, S. (2009). The alignment of information systems with organizational objectives and strategies in health care. *International Journal of Medical Informatics, 78*(7), 446–456. doi:10.1016/j.ijmedinf.2009.02.004 PMID:19307148

Cao, J., Crews, J. M., Lin, M., Deokar, A. V., Burgoon, J. K., & Nunamaker, J. F. Jr. (2006). Interactions between System Evaluation and Theory Testing: A Demonstration of the Power of a Multifaceted Approach to Information Systems Research. *Journal of Management Information Systems, 22*(4), 207–235. doi:10.2753/MIS0742-1222220408

Chan, Y. E., & Reich, B. H. (2007). IT alignment: An annotated bibliography. *Journal of Information Technology, 22*(4), 316–396. doi:10.1057/palgrave.jit.2000111

Chandler, A. D. (1962). *Strategy and Structure: Chapters in the history of the American industrial enterprise*. Cambridge, MA: MIT Press.

Chen, D. Q., Mocker, M., Preston, D. S., & Teubner, A. (2010). Information Systems Strategy: Reconceptualization, Measurement and Implications. *Management Information Systems Quarterly, 34*(2), 233–259.

Chen, R. S., Sun, C. M., Helms, M. M., & Jih, W. J. K. (2008). Aligning information technology and business strategy with a dynamic capabilities perspective: A longitudinal study of a Taiwanese Semiconductor Company. *International Journal of Information Management, 28*, 366–378. doi:10.1016/j.ijinfomgt.2008.01.015

Chia, R., & Langley, A. (2004). *The First Organization Studies Summer Workshop on Theorizing Process in Organizational Research* (Call for Papers). Santorini, Greece.

Czarniawska, B. (1997). *Narrating the organization: Dramas of institutional identity*. Chicago, IL: University of Chicago Press.

Czarniawska, B. (1998). *A narrative approach to organizational studies*. Thousand Oaks, CA: Sage.

Datta, L. (1994). Paradigm Wars: A Basis for Peaceful Coexistence and Beyond. In C. S. Reichardt, & S. F. Rallis (Eds.), *The Qualitative-Quantitative Debate: New Perspectives* (pp. 53–70). San Francisco, CA: Jossey-Bass. doi:10.1002/ev.1668

De Wit, B., & Meyer, R. (2002). *Strategy: Process, Content, Context - An International Perspective* (2nd ed.). London: Thomson Learning.

De Wit, B., & Meyer, R. (2005). *Strategy synthesis: Resolving strategy paradoxes to create competitive advantage* (2nd ed.). London: Thomson Learning.

DeLone, W. H., & McLean, E. R. (1992). Information systems success: The quest for the dependent variable. *Information Systems Research, 3*(1), 60–95. doi:10.1287/isre.3.1.60

Denzin, N. K. (1978). *The research act: A theoretical introduction to sociological methods*. New York: McGraw-Hill.

DeSanctis, G., & Poole, M. S. (1994). Capturing the complexity in advanced technology use: Adaptive structuration theory. *Organization Science, 5*(2), 121–147. doi:10.1287/orsc.5.2.121

Drnevich, P. L., & Croson, D. C. (2013). Information Technology and Business-level Strategy: Toward an Integrated Theoretical Perspective. *Management Information Systems Quarterly, 37*(2), 483–509.

Earl, M. J. (1989). *Management Strategies for Information Technology*. Upper Saddle River, NJ: Prentice Hall.

Fambrough, M., & Comerford, S. (2006). The Changing Epistemological Assumptions of Group Theory. *The Journal of Applied Behavioral Science, 42*(3), 330–349. doi:10.1177/0021886306286445

Fenton, C., & Langley, A. (2011). Strategy as Practice and the Narrative Turn. *Organization Studies, 32*(9), 1171–1196. doi:10.1177/0170840611410838

Ferlie, E., Ashburner, L., Fitzgerald, L., & Pettigrew, A. M. (1996). *The New Public Management in Action*. Oxford: Oxford University Press. doi:10.1093/acprof:oso/9780198289029.001.0001

Galliers, R. D. (2004). Reflecting on Information Systems Strategizing. In C. Avgerou, C. Ciborra, & F. Land (Eds.), *The Social Study of Information and Communication Technology: Innovation, Actors, and Contexts* (pp. 231–262). Oxford, UK: Oxford University Press.

Gersick, C. J. (1991). Revolutionary change theories: A multilevel exploration of the punctuated equilibrium paradigm. *Academy of Management Review, 16*(1), 10–36.

Herman, D., Phelan, J., Rabinowitz, P. J., Richardson, B., & Warhol, R. (2012). *Narrative Theory - Core concepts and Critical debates*. Columbus, Ohio: Ohio State University Press.

Hinings, C. R. (1997). Reflections on processual research. *Scandinavian Journal of Management*, *13*(4), 493–503. doi:10.1016/S0956-5221(97)00023-7

House, E. R. (1994). Integrating the Quantitative and Qualitative. In C. S. Reichardt, & S. F. Rallis (Eds.), *The Qualitative-quantitative Debate: New Perspectives* (pp. 13–22). San Francisco, CA: Jossey-Bass.

Huff, A. (1990). *Mapping Strategic Thought*. Chichester, UK: Wiley.

Jick, T. D. (1979). Mixing Qualitative and Quantitative Methods: Triangulation in Action. *Administrative Science Quarterly*, *24*(4), 602–611. doi:10.2307/2392366

Karahanna, E., & Preston, D. S. (2013). The Effect of Social Capital of the Relationship Between the CIO and Top Management Team on Firm Performance. *Journal of Management Information Systems*, *30*(1), 15–55. doi:10.2753/MIS0742-1222300101

Langley, A. (1999). Strategies for theorizing from process data. *Academy of Management Review*, *24*, 691–710.

Lim, J. H., Stratopoulos, C., & Wirjanto, T. S. (2013). Sustainability of a Firm's Reputation for Information Technology Capability: The Role of Senior IT Executives. *Journal of Management Information Systems*, *30*(1), 57–95. doi:10.2753/MIS0742-1222300102

Lincoln, Y. S., & Guba, E. G. (1985). *Naturalistic Inquiry*. Newbury Park, CA: Sage.

Lucas, J. C. Jr, Agarwal, R., Clemons, E. K., & El Sawy, O. A. (2013). Impactful Research on Transformational Information Technology: An Opportunity to Inform New Audiences. *Management Information Systems Quarterly*, *37*(2), 371–382.

Luftman, J., & Ben-Zvi, T. (2010). Key Issues for IT Executives 2010: Judicious IT Investments Continue Post-Recession. *MIS Quarterly Executive*, *9*(4), 263–273.

Martinez-Jerez, F. A. (2014). Rewriting the Playbook for Corporate Partnerships. *MIT Sloan Management Review*, *55*(2), 63–70.

McLean, E., & Soden, J. (1977). *Strategic Planning for MIS*. New York: John Wiley & Sons.

Miller, D., & Friesen, P. (1982). The longitudinal analysis of organizations: A methodological perspective. *Management Science*, *28*(9), 1013–1034. doi:10.1287/mnsc.28.9.1013

Mingers, J. (1997). Multi-Paradigm Methodology. In J. Mingers, & A. Gill (Eds.), *Multimethodology: Theory and Practice of Combining Management Science Methodologies* (pp. 1–20). Chichester, UK: Wiley.

Mingers, J. (2001). Combining IS Research Methods: Towards a Pluralist Methodology. *Information Systems Research*, *12*(3), 240–259. doi:10.1287/isre.12.3.240.9709

Mingers, J., Mutch, A., & Willcocks, L. (2013). Critical Realism in Information Systems Research. *Management Information Systems Quarterly*, *37*(3), 795–802.

Mintzberg, H. (1979). An Emerging Strategy of Direct Research. *Administrative Science Quarterly*, *24*(4), 582–589. doi:10.2307/2392364

Mohr, L. (1982). *Explaining organizational behavior*. San Francisco, CA: Jossey-Bass.

Myers, M., & Liu, F. (2009). *What Does The Best IS Research Look Like? An Analysis Of The AIS Basket Of Top Journals*. Paper presented at the Pacific Asia Conference on Information Systems (PACIS). Tokyo, Japan.

Orlikowski, W. J. (2000). Using technology and constituting structures: A practice lens for studying technology in organizations. *Organization Science*, *11*(4), 404–428. doi:10.1287/orsc.11.4.404.14600

Orlikowski, W. J., & Robey, D. (1991). Information Technology and the Structuring of Organizations. *Information Systems Research*, *2*(2), 143–169. doi:10.1287/isre.2.2.143

Pentland, B. (1999). Building process theory with narrative: From description to explanation. *Academy of Management Review*, *24*, 711–724.

Pentland, B. T., & Feldman, M. S. (2007). Narrative Networks: Patterns of Technology and Organization. *Organization Science*, *18*(5), 781–882. doi:10.1287/orsc.1070.0283

Pepper, S. C. (1942). *World Hypothesis*. Berkeley, CA: University of California Press.

Peterson, M. F. (1998). Embedded organizational events: The units of process in organizational science. *Organization Science*, *9*(1), 16–33. doi:10.1287/orsc.9.1.16

Petter, S., DeLone, W., & McLean, E. R. (2013). Information Systems Success: The Quest for the Independent Variables. *Journal of Management Information Systems*, *29*(4), 7–61. doi:10.2753/MIS0742-1222290401

Pettigrew, A. M. (1973). *The Politics of Organizational Decision Making*. London, Assen: Tavistock /Van Gorcum.

Pettigrew, A. M. (1979). On studying organizational cultures. *Administrative Science Quarterly*, *24*(4), 570–581. doi:10.2307/2392363

Pettigrew, A. M. (1985). Context and action in the transformation of the firm. *Journal of Management Studies*, *24*(6), 649–670. doi:10.1111/j.1467-6486.1987.tb00467.x

Pettigrew, A. M. (1990). Longitudinal field research on change: Theory and practice. *Organization Science*, *1*(3), 267–292. doi:10.1287/orsc.1.3.267

Pettigrew, A. M. (1992). The character and significance of strategy process research. *Strategic Management Journal*, *13*(S2), 5–16. doi:10.1002/smj.4250130903

Pettigrew, A. M. (1997). What is a Processual Analysis? *Scandinavian Journal of Management*, *13*(4), 337–348. doi:10.1016/S0956-5221(97)00020-1

Pettigrew, A. M., Ferlie, E., & McKee, L. (1992). *Shaping Strategic Change: Making Change in Large Organizations, the Case of the NHS*. London: Sage.

Pettigrew, A. M., & McNulty, T. (1995). Power and Influence in and around the Boardroom. *Human Relations*, *48*(8), 845–873. doi:10.1177/001872679504800802

Pettigrew, A. M., & Webb, D. (1996). *Espoused business strategy and structure changes in the U.K. and German insurance industries* Paper presented at the Paper presented to the All Academy Symposium on the evolution of New Organisation Forms for the Information Age. Cincinnati, OH.

Pettigrew, A. M., & Whipp, R. (1991). *Managing Change for Competitive Success*. Oxford, UK: Basil Blackwell.

Pettigrew, A. M., & Whipp, R. (1993). Managing the twin processes of competition and change: The role of intangible assets. In P. L. Lorange, B. Chakravarthy, J. Roos, & A. Van de Ven (Eds.), *Implementing strategic processes: Change, Learning, and Co-operation* (pp. 3–42). Cambridge, MA: Blackwell Business.

Pierce, C. S. (1955). Philosophical writings of Pierce. In J. Buchler (Ed.). *New York*: Dover.

Poole, M. S., Van de Ven, A. H., Dooley, K., & Holmes, M. E. (2000). *Organizational change and innovation processes: Theory and methods for research*. New York: Oxford University Press.

Pozzebon, M. (2004). The influence of a structurationist view on strategic management research. *Journal of Management Studies*, *41*(2), 247–272. doi:10.1111/j.1467-6486.2004.00431.x

Pratt, M., & Rafaeli, A. (1997). Organizational Dress as a Symbol of Multilayered Social Identities. *Academy of Management Journal*, *40*(4), 862–898. doi:10.2307/256951

Ramiller, N. C., & Pentland, B. T. (2009). Management Implications in Information Systems Research: The Untold Story. *Journal of the Association for Information Systems*, *10*(6), 474–494.

Reich, B. H., & Benbasat, I. (1996). Measuring the Linkage Between Business and Information Technology Objectives. *Management Information Systems Quarterly*, *20*(1), 55–81. doi:10.2307/249542

Reich, B. H., & Benbasat, I. (2000). Factors that Influence the Social Dimension of Alignment between Business and Information Technology Objectives. *Management Information Systems Quarterly*, *24*(1), 81–113. doi:10.2307/3250980

Reich, B. H., & Kaarst-Brown, M. L. (2003). Creating Social and Intellectual Capital through IT Career Transitions. *The Journal of Strategic Information Systems*, *12*(2), 91–109. doi:10.1016/S0963-8687(03)00017-9

Reichardt, C. S., & Rallis, S. F. (1994). Qualitative and Quantitative Inquiries are not Incompatible: A Call for a New Partnership. In C. S. Reichardt, & S. F. Rallis (Eds.), *The Qualitative-Quantitative Debate: New Perspectives* (pp. 85–92). San Francisco, CA: Jossey-Bass. doi:10.1002/ev.1670

Rescher, N. (1996). *Process metaphysics: An introduction to process philosophy*. Albany, NY: SUNY Press.

Ridenour, C. S., & Newman, I. (2008). *Mixed Methods Research: Exploring the Interactive Continuum*. Carbondale, IL: Southern Illinois University Press.

Rimmon-Kenan, S. (1983). *Narrative fiction: Contemporary poetics*. London: Routledge. doi:10.4324/9780203426111

Ross, D. (1949). *Aristotle*. London: Methuen.

Rossi, P. H. (1994). The War between the Quals and the Quants: Is a Lasting Peace Possible? In C. S. Reichardt, & S. F. Rallis (Eds.), *The Qualitative-Quantitative Debate: New Perspectives* (pp. 23–36). San Francisco, CA: Jossey-Bass. doi:10.1002/ev.1665

Rowlands, B. H. (2005). Grounded in Practice: Using Interpretive Research to Build Theory. *Journal of Business Research Methodology*, *3*(1), 81–92.

Scott-Morton, M. S. (1991). *The Corporation of the 1990s: Informational technology and organizational transformation*. New York: Oxford Press.

Silva, L., & Hirschheim, R. (2007). Fighting Against Windmills: Strategic Information Systems and Organizational Deep Structures. *Management Information Systems Quarterly, 31*(2), 327–354.

Sminia, H. (2009). Process research in strategy formation: Theory, methodology and relevance. *International Journal of Management Reviews, 11*(1), 97–125. doi:10.1111/j.1468-2370.2008.00253.x

Sztompka, P. (1991). *Society in Action: The Theory of Social Becoming*. Chicago, IL: University of Chicago Press.

Sztompka, P. (1993). *The Sociology of Social Change*. Oxford, UK: Blackwell.

Tarafdar, M., & Qrunfleh, S. (2009). IT-Business Alignment: A Two-Level Analysis. *Information Systems Management, 26*(4), 338–349. doi:10.1080/10580530903245705

Teddlie, C., & Tashakkori, A. (2003). Major Issues and Controversies in the Use of Mixed Methods in the Social and Behavioral Sciences. In A. Tashakkori, & C. Teddlie (Eds.), *Handbook of Mixed Methods in Social and Behavioral Research* (pp. 3–50). Thousand Oaks, CA: Sage Publications.

Teddlie, C., & Tashakkori, A. (2009). *Foundations of Mixed Methods Research*. Thousand Oaks, CA: Sage Publications.

Thorngate, W. (1976). Possible limits on a science of social behaviour. In J. H. Strickland, F. E. Aboud, & K. J. Gergen (Eds.), *Social psychology in transition*. New York: Plenum. doi:10.1007/978-1-4615-8765-1_9

Tsoukas, H. (2005). *Complex knowledge: Studies in organizational epistemology*. Oxford, UK: Oxford University Press.

Tsoukas, H., & Chia, R. (2002). On organizational becoming: Rethinking organizational change. *Organization Science, 13*(5), 567–582. doi:10.1287/orsc.13.5.567.7810

Tushman, M., & Romanelli, E. (1985). Organizational evolution: A metamorphis model of convergence and reorientation. In B. Staw, & L. Cummings (Eds.), *Research in organizational behavior* (pp. 171–222). Greenwich, CT: JAI Press.

Van de Ven, A. H. (1992). Suggestions for studying strategy process: A research note. *Strategic Management Journal, 13*(S1), 169–188. doi:10.1002/smj.4250131013

Van de Ven, A. H., & Huber, G. P. (1990). Longitudinal field research methods for studying processes of organizational change. *Organization Science, 1*(3), 213–219. doi:10.1287/orsc.1.3.213

Van de Ven, A. H., & Poole, M. S. (2002). Field Research Methods. In A. C. Baum (Ed.), *Companion to Organizations* (pp. 867–888). Oxford: Blackwell Publishers.

Van de Ven, A. H., & Poole, M. S. (2005). Alternative Approaches for Studying Organizational Change. *Organization Studies, 26*(9), 1377–1404. doi:10.1177/0170840605056907

Venkatesh, V., Brown, S. A., & Bala, H. (2013). Bridging the Qualitative-Quantitative Divide: Guidelines for Conducting Mixed-Methods Research in Information Systems. *Management Information Systems Quarterly, 37*(1), 21–54.

Ward, J., & Peppard, J. (2002). *Strategic Planning for Information Systems* (3rd ed.). Chichester, UK: John Wiley and Sons.

Weick, K. (1979). *The social psychology of organizing*. Reading, MA: Addison-Wesley.

Whetten, D. A. (2006). Albert and Whetten Revisited: Strengthening the Concept of Organizational Identity. *Journal of Management Inquiry, 15*(3), 219–234. doi:10.1177/1056492606291200

White, H. (1981). The value of narrativity in the representation of reality. In W. J. T. Mitchell (Ed.), *On Narrative* (pp. 1–24). Chicago, IL: University of Chicago Press.

Wolfe, A. (2013). Alan Greenspan: What Went Wrong. *Wall Street Journal*, Retrieved October 18, 2013, from http://online.wsj.com/news/articles/SB10001424052702304410204579139900796324772

Yin, R. K. (2003). *Applications of case study research* (2nd ed.). Thousand Oaks, CA: Sage.

ADDITIONAL READING

Allen, D. K., Brown, A., Karanasios, S., & Norman, A. (2013). How Should Technology-Mediated Organizational Change Be Explained? A Comparison of the Contributions of Critical Realism and Activity Theory. *Management Information Systems Quarterly, 37*(3), 835–854.

Dionysiou, D. D., & Tsoukas, H. (2013). Understanding the (re)creation of routines from within: A symbolic interactionist perspective. *Academy of Management Review, 38*(2), 181–205. doi:10.5465/amr.2011.0215

Felin, T., Foss, N., Heimeriks, K. H., & Madsen, T. (2012). Microfoundations of routines and capabilities: Individuals, processes, and structure. *Journal of Management Studies, 49*(8), 1351–1371. doi:10.1111/j.1467-6486.2012.01052.x

Pettigrew, A. (2011). The Awakening Giant. *Continuity and Change*, ICI.

Pettigrew, A. (2011). Scholarship with Impact. *British Journal of Management, 22*(3), 347–354.

Pettigrew, A. (2012). Context and Action in the Transformation of the Firm: A Reprise. *Journal of Management Studies, 49*(7), 1304–1328. doi:10.1111/j.1467-6486.2012.01054.x

Pettigrew, A. (2013). The Conduct of Qualitative Research in Organizational Settings. *Corporate Governance: An International Review, 21*(2), 123–126. doi:10.1111/j.1467-8683.2012.00925.x

Ring, P. S., & Van de Ven, A. H. (1992). Structuring cooperative relationships between organizations. *Strategic Management Journal, 13*(7), 483–498. doi:10.1002/smj.4250130702

Salvato, C., & Rerup, C. (2011). Beyond collective entities: Multi-level research on organizational routines and capabilities. *Journal of Management, 37*(2), 468–490. doi:10.1177/0149206310371691

Van de Ven, A. H. (2007). *Engaged Scholarship: A Guide for Organizational and Social Research*. New York: Oxford University Press.

Van de Ven, A. H., Polley, D., Garud, R., & Venkatraman, S. (2008). *The Innovation Journey*. New York: Oxford University Press.

Volkoff, O., & Strong, D. M. (2013). Critical Realism and Affordances: Theorizing IT-Associated Organizational Change Processes. *Management Information Systems Quarterly, 37*(3), 819–834.

Zachariadis, M., Scott, S., & Barrett, M. (2013). Methodological Implications of Critical Realism for Mixed-Methods Research. *Management Information Systems Quarterly, 37*(3), 855–879.

KEY TERMS AND DEFINITIONS

Boundaries: Multiple theoretical views exist about the meaning of boundaries, it can relate to the perceived demarcation of an organizational social structure by way of identity, activities and rules. It can refer to organizational resources that shape the growth trajectory. It can also mean the sphere of organizational influence in terms of power and control over impacting forces located in the external environment.

Information Technology (IT): IT as it relates to a business, enterprise or organizational function is concerned with all activities associated with the development and management of computer and networking aspects of information systems.

IT Strategy: IT strategy relates to the IT plans and activities that are deemed necessary and supportive of the long-term organizational direction.

IT Strategy-Making: The deliberate and emergent processes enacted during the planning and execution of high-level organizational IT initiatives that are intended to realize performance benefits.

Narrative: A detailed written account of connected events about something of interest that happened.

Process Research: Examining the impact of dynamic phenomena such as events, actions, activities, time, history and context to understand the cumulative effects and to learn how and why entities such as organizations and strategies unfold (change, act, evolve etc.) over time.

Process: A series of actions, tasks, activities, changes, or functions performed toward achieving a particular outcome.

Strategy: In an organizational context, strategy is about planning and executing the necessary actions to achieve high-level aims aligned to its core purpose and long term direction.

Chapter 16
Mixed Methods Research Online:
Problems and Potential in Business Ethics Research

Theodora Issa
Curtin University, Australia

David Pick
Curtin University, Australia

ABSTRACT

Contributing to the ongoing debate in research on sensitive issues such as business ethics, this chapter provides a discussion of mixed methods research design, examining the processes and challenges of developing and deploying an online survey tool using technology within an interpretive mixed methods design. This chapter provides pointers on how to deploy this approach through technology to research business ethics using the example of researching ethical mindsets and its components, including spirituality and aesthetics. It is found that mixed methods research is an effective approach because it allows often sensitive issues (i.e. business ethics, aesthetics, spirituality) relating to questioning individuals' inner values and ethical propensities, which are usually subtle and difficult to measure and analyze constructs. While this tool was developed in the Australian context, it has the potential to form a foundation for wider examination and research in business ethics. The chapter contributes to the collective discussion of research methods using a framework that has both practical relevance and theoretical rigor.

INTRODUCTION

Researchers in the field of business ethics face a number of significant field-shaping challenges and questions. Challenges faced relate to difficulties in obtaining data, while the questions are particularly concerned with identifying and applying appropri-

ate research methods (Benefiel, 2003, 2005). In both cases it may be argued that realist empirical, positivist (quantitative) and interpretive (qualitative) methodologies can be employed together in a complementary way (Lee, 1999; Parry, 1998) that has become known as mixed methods see, for example (Morse & Niehaus, 2009).

DOI: 10.4018/978-1-4666-6493-7.ch016

Researching an area such as business ethics is considered difficult as it deals with sensitive issues relating to questioning your inner values and decision abilities. In his discussion on the design of research for the investigation of sensitive issues, Greener (2011) argues that research in such issues might imply some kind of neglect or other failing on the part of respondents and participants. Thus, to raise sensitive issues, a great deal of thought and care need to be taken into account to avoid giving offence or causing embarrassment. Greener (2011) highlights the need to pay great attention not only to the wording of individual questions but also to the sequence in which they appear to avoid leading respondents to particular answers. Indeed, and most importantly the method employed in research these sensitive issues as business ethics.

Debate about the application of quantitative and qualitative approaches to the study of sensitive issues in organizations has resulted in an increased valuing of qualitative approaches. Fornaciari and Lund-Dean (2001: 335), for example, challenge those researching sensitive issues and inner values in organizations to consider evidence about this phenomenon at work from the perspective of non-positivist ways of knowing. They suggest that ethno-methodological, qualitative techniques, and tradition-based stories, are more appropriate research methods than positivist methods, see also (Lund-Dean, Fornaciari, & McGee, 2003). Benefiel (2003) extends this argument claiming that qualitative methodologies should be an integral part of the researcher's toolset rather than being a 'satellite' to the quantitative paradigm. Lund-Dean et al., (2003: 389) defend the use of combined qualitative and quantitative approaches, arguing that the positivist, empiricist methodological is not only insufficient for such study, but may actually cause harm to the discipline. While Denscombe (2008) argues that the mixed methods approach has emerged as a 'third paradigm' for social research, and has developed a platform of ideas and practices that are credible and distinctive that marks the approach out as a viable alternative to quantitative and qualitative paradigms each used solely.

It is not only the techniques that are changing and challenging but also the technology we use to collect and analyze data that has been transformed over the past decade. The internet is having a profound effect on how survey research is conducted to the extent that development of online surveys is leading some to argue that they will soon replace traditional (paper-based) methods of survey data collection (Couper, 2000). Cooper's prediction is almost there in 2013 with the increased software and even organizations that have their main line of business design, collection and analysis of data online such as SurveyMonkey® and Qualtrics®. Qulatrics, established in 2002, and with the logo 'Sophisticated Research made Simple' (Qualtrics, 2013) is one company that offers such a service, which might have been impossible last century or early this century. Blasius and Brandt (2010) contend that the advantages and disadvantages of online surveys, as compared to other data collection methods, have often been extensively documented (e.g., Couper, Tourangeao, & Kenyon, 2004; Couper, Tourangeau, Conrad, & Crawford, 2004; Couper, Traugott, & Lamias, 2001; Dillman, 2000, 2007; Dillman & Bowker, 2001; Fricker & Schonlau, 2002); online surveys have the advantage of being cheaper, faster and independent in terms of time and space. The disadvantage is that they depend on the availability of internet access. However, with the ongoing technological advances this disadvantage seems to be vanishing. Certainly, the use and application of online surveys among practitioners and academics alike has been on the rise for several years (Hanna, Weinberg, Dant, & Berger, 2005); web-based surveys have become more prevalent (Greenlaw & Brown-Welty, 2009); and online surveys are becoming a promising alternative to traditional surveys with the internet (Singh, Taneja, & Mangalaraj, 2009). While acknowledging the importance of collecting data through use of technology (e.g. online surveys), Blasius and Brandt (2010) highlight a disadvantage of this method that they depend on the availability of Internet access. Indeed, conducting online surveys has its advantages; it comes with a unique set of challenges.

While nationwide face-to-face samples are considered representative for the entire population, online samples are regarded as biased, especially in terms of age, gender and education. Blasius and Brandt (2010) elaborate on this bias saying, the data can be weighted to receive a representative sample. In case of online surveys, elderly women with a low level of education receive a very high weight and young men with high education a very low one. Given this trend, it is a topic worthy of serious research attention. In this chapter the application of mixed methods research design and data collection through online surveys to spirituality and aesthetics in business ethics is examined paying particular attention to philosophical and practical issues.

BACKGROUND: METHODS IN BUSINESS ETHICS RESEARCH

Quantitative, Qualitative, and Mixed Methods Approaches

Denzin and Lincoln (2003) establish a comparison between the quantitative and qualitative techniques research outlining the implications of each of these two approaches. The word 'qualitative' implies an emphasis on the qualities of entities and on processes and meanings that are not experimentally examined or measured in terms of quantity, amount, intensity, or frequency. In contrast, quantitative studies emphasize measurement and analysis of causal relationships between variables, not processes. Denzin and Lincoln (2003) argue that the qualitative researcher stresses the socially constructed nature of reality, the intimate relationship between the researcher and what is

studied, and the situational constraints that shape inquiry. The quantitative researchers on the other hand, claim that their work is done from within a value-free framework. Krenz and Sax (1986) argue that too often, then, the link between results and 'reality' is assumed rather than systematically investigated. They contend that there are two persistent critiques of quantitative experimentalism: the lack of fit between its measures and 'reality', coupled with its failure to produce 'truths' useful to practice. This was back in the 1980s, albeit, this is continuously changing and developing.

Qualitative research methods also do not escape criticism. Denzin and Lincoln (1998) discuss how researchers cope with problems that arise from qualitative methods of research. Two schools of thought organize their discussions (Denzin & Lincoln 1998: 407). The first: 'The history of qualitative research is defined more by breaks and ruptures than by a clear evolutionary, progressive movement from one stage to the next. These breaks and ruptures move in cycles and phases, so that what is passé today may be in vogue a decade from now'. The second: 'Builds on the tensions that now define qualitative research. There is an elusive center to this contradictory, tension-riddled enterprise that seems to be moving further and further away from grand narratives and single, overarching ontological, epistemological, and methodological paradigms. This center lies in the humanistic commitment of the qualitative researcher to study the world always from the perspective of the interacting individual'.

Both qualitative and quantitative researchers 'think they know something about society that is worth telling to others, and they use a variety of forms, media and means to communicate their ideas and findings' (Denzin & Lincoln 2003: 13). They contend that qualitative research differs from quantitative research in five significant ways: (1) use of positivism and post-positivism, (2) acceptance of post-modern sensibilities, (3) capturing the individual's point of view, (4) examining the constraints of everyday life, and, (5) securing rich descriptions. These five points of difference return to the politics of research and reflect commitment to different styles of research, different epistemologies, and different forms of representation.

With regard to the quantitative method, Mc-Intyre (2005) argues that the responses to surveys need to be regarded cautiously as they are often an artefact of research design and sample construction. Romm (2006) sheds some light on Churchman's epistemological and ethical proposals, stating that Churchman's calls on those involved in inquiry endeavors, to work across disciplines and in the process to be more reflective about the possible consequences in society of their very way of framing research questions for investigation. This is because, in his view, the way of 'doing science' already delimits options for addressing issues of concern pragmatically. He proposes that individuals express a commitment to ethical thought/practice in their way of thinking/living - which he calls 'conducting ourselves properly'. Guo and Sheffield (2007) propose a framework for inquiry that supports diversity and integration through a synthesis of concepts from Churchman's way of operationalizing epistemological thinking, and Habermas the 'Habermasian Inquiring System' that has parallels with Ulrich's (1987; 2001) work. Guo and Sheffield (2007) conclude that their framework adopts a stance in describing the dynamics at the core of any representation of objective, inter-subjective and subjective realities.

In an attempt to validate the qualitative research and answer such criticisms, Cho and Trent (2006) posit that qualitative research can be more credible as long as certain techniques, methods, and/or strategies are employed during the conduct of the inquiry. In this context, Cho and Trent (2006) argue that concerns with the issues of validity in qualitative research have increased. Traditionally, validity in qualitative research involved determining the degree to which researchers' claims about knowledge corresponded to the reality (or research participants' construction of reality) be-

ing studied. However, recent trends have shown the emergence of two quite different approaches to the legitimacy question within the literature on qualitative research. While useful, Cho and Trent (2006) assert that neither the 'transactional' nor the 'transformational' approach is sufficient to meet the current needs of the field; instead, they propose a recursive process-oriented view as an alternative framework. Glaser (2003) contends that there is no 'how' to choose a methodology. Traditions in social research methodology are so fundamentally disparate that any choice between them is arbitrary and most usually are a social structurally-induced appraisal based on the methodological commitments of the researcher. With this in mind employing a mixed methods approach is an attractive alternative.

Johnson and Onwuegbuzie (2004) argue that by utilizing quantitative and qualitative techniques within the same framework, mixed methods research can incorporate the strengths of both techniques. Johnson and Onwuegbuzie (2004) contend, there are five major purposes or rationales for using mixed methods: triangulation, complementarity, initiation, development and, expansion. Johnson and Onwuegbuzie (2004) do not believe that mixed methods research is currently in a position to provide perfect solutions. Nevertheless, they are of the belief that a pragmatic approach should use a method and philosophy that attempt to combine the insights provided by qualitative and quantitative research into a workable solution.

While all research approaches have underlying philosophical assumptions that guide the inquirer, mixed methods research assumes a world view or several world views. In their book, Plano-Clark and Creswell (2008) refer to mixed methods approach as a research design with philosophical assumptions as well as quantitative and qualitative techniques. Plano-Clark and Creswell (2008: 5) define mixed methods research as '... a research design with philosophical assumptions as well as methods of inquiry'. As a methodology, it involves philosophical assumptions that guide the direction of the collection and analysis of data and the mixture of qualitative and quantitative approaches in many phases in the research process. As a method, it focuses on collecting, analyzing, and mixing both quantitative and qualitative data in a single study or series of studies. Its central premise is that the use of quantitative and qualitative approaches in combination provides a better understanding of research problems than either approach alone.

Philosophically, the mixed methods research is the 'third wave' or third research movement that moves past the paradigm debates by offering a logical and practical alternative. Philosophically, mixed research makes use of the pragmatic method and system of philosophy. Johnson and Onwuegbuzie (2004) state its logic of inquiry includes the use of induction (or discovery of patterns), deduction (testing of theories), and abduction (uncovering and relying on the best of a set of explanations for understanding one's results).

In advocating the use of mixed methods research, Johnson and Onwuegbuzie (2004) claim that they do not aim to solve the metaphysical, epistemological, axiological (e.g., ethical, normative), and methodological differences between the purist positions of quantitative or qualitative mono approaches, and they do not believe that mixed-methods research is currently in a position to provide perfect solutions. Nevertheless, they contend that mixed methods research should use a method and a philosophy that attempt to combine the insights provided by qualitative and quantitative research into a workable solution. Further, Denscombe (2008) warns that, with researchers focusing on areas of consensus within this paradigm as a genuine alternative to others, there is a danger of overlooking the complexities of the situation. Johnson and Onwuegbuzie acknowledge 'the dividing lines are much fuzzier than typically suggested in the literature' and 'positions are not nearly as 'logical' and as 'distinct' as is frequently suggested in the literature' (2007: 117). Crump and Logan (2008) demonstrated that synthesizing the

results of the data gathered from different methods (quantitative or qualitative) in one research, led to a greater understanding of outcomes. The mixed methods approach that has emerged during the past few years, and Denscombe (2008) contends that this approach had developed a platform of ideas and practices that are credible and distinctive and mark it out as a viable alternative to quantitative and qualitative paradigms. However, Denscombe (2008) warns that there are a number of variations and inconsistencies within the mixed methods approach that should not be ignored. He argues the need for a vision of research paradigm that accommodates such variations and inconsistencies. Denscombe (2008) also argues that the use of 'communities of practice' as the basis for such a research paradigm is (a) consistent with the pragmatist underpinnings of the mixed methods approach, (b) accommodates a level of diversity, and (c) has good potential for understanding the methodological choices made by those conducting mixed methods research.

Further Fassinger and Morrow (2013) contend that quantitative, qualitative, and mixed-method approaches offer different kinds of strengths in advancing research in areas such as social justice. They highlight the best practices in research for social justice in the following areas: (a) cultural competence and the role of the researcher(s), (b) formulating the focus of the research, (c) selection of the underlying paradigm and research method/design, (d) the research team: formation, process, and issues of power, (e) power and relationship with research participants, and (f) data gathering, analysis, and reporting.

Recently, Creswell (2013) posits that those undertaking qualitative studies have a baffling number of choices of approaches. Creswell provides a table that identifies some thirteen seminal works in relation the qualitative approaches and their discipline fields that range from social sciences, sociology, education, psychology and nursing. From this list it can be noticed the work of Denzin and Lincoln (1994; 2005) and that Miles and Huberman (1994) are specifically in relation to social sciences. Creswell (2013) notes that through the years some of these methods continue to be applicable as research strategies such as phenomenology and case studies with a number of narrative-related approaches with so many possibilities, however, to guide the researchers Creswell (2013) decides on five approaches which are: (i) narrative study, (ii) phenomenological study, (iii) grounded theory study, (iv) ethnographic study, and (v) case study.

Indeed, issues that needs to be considered when researching business ethics. However, the challenge is not only the selection of appropriate method, but coping with the ongoing developments in technology that is used to enhance research in business ethics.

DATA COLLECTION THROUGH ONLINE SURVEYS

Burke and James (2006) argue that a substantive literature base exists for conducting traditional survey research, while the extant literature on using online survey software is less developed. Fenlason and Suckow-Zimberg (2006) predict that future surveys will apply the internet as a complementary method of data collection to the commonly used pencil and paper surveys. While most arguments on the use of online surveys in research focus on the collection of quantitative data, Carcary (2009) discusses qualitative data collection highlighting the value of this audit trail process in confirming the findings of a qualitative study.

When considering collecting survey data online, it is not only the look and feel that matter, it is also the building of trust between respondents and researcher – something that is difficult to foster in a virtual environment. Ford (2001) highlights issues of 'authenticity' or 'true' ways of representing self that have become more apparent, given that individuals might represent themselves using technology in a variety of methods that are un-

connected to the way they appear in the everyday world. With respect to trust, Nissenbaum (2001) outlines three obstacles to developing trust in such an environment: the first relates to the relative incompleteness of identity when compared to face-to-face interviewing, the second is related to the first in that in an on-line environment, personal characteristics are hidden from view, and, thirdly the social settings for interaction are often lacking. These three obstacles tend to reduce mutual cues upon which trust may develop, and as a result caution and reserve are common. Indeed, Roberts (2000) concludes that only 'real life' face-to-face contacts will allow the formation of mutual trust and in Charles Handy's words (Handy, 1995): 'Trust needs touch'. However, the recent rapid increase in virtual communities, forums and internet sources may be rendering the arguments against online surveys less relevant. Even, there is now some debate about whether trust is less of an issue. Wharton, Hampl, Hall & Winham (2003) contend as the rate of information gathering and sharing continues to increase, new technologies have emerged to keep pace with society's demands, but are still hampered by trust issues, which echoes Koehn's (2003) argument that with the increase of internet use, many issues of trust have arisen. On the other hand, de Laat (2005) posits that such arguments are flawed theoretically and practically because trust not only applies to 'real life', but also online.

With regards to response rates, it seems that there is no conclusive evidence either way. While Crawford, Couper and Lamias (2001) argue there is little information on effective strategies for increasing response to internet-based (or online) survey, Couper et al. (2004) provide evidence suggesting that the response format used in online surveys does affect the choices made by respondents. There are also a number of studies comparing online surveys with paper and pencil or fax surveys. Cole (2005) compared responses from an online survey and those from a paper and pencil survey in terms of data quality, response rates, demographic profiles of respondents, and internal consistency of scales. While the results were inconclusive, it was clear that responses to online surveys were lower than those of the traditional approach. Further, Deutskens, Ruyter and Wetzels (2006) examined whether online and paper (mail) surveys produce convergent results finding that online and paper surveys produce equivalent results. Grava-Gubins and Scott (2008) argue that despite shortening the questionnaires, more e-mail contacts, and enhancing marketing and follow-up, no significant changes were witnessed in response rates. It is clear that more research is needed in this area to clarify how each technique compares and about strategies for achieving higher response rates.

Singh, Taneja and Mangalaraj (2009) argue, with the advent of adaptable and resourceful internet building tools, online surveys are becoming a promising alternative to traditional paper and mail-based surveys. Arguing the case of incentivized combination of postal and web-based surveys, Balajti, Darago, Adany, & Kosa (2010) conclude, a combination of mail and online surveys seems feasible in younger target groups with computer skills if supplementary measures (e.g. incentives, and reminders) are taken to increase response rate. Additionally, online surveys reduce the burden and errors related to manual data processing so their use is recommended even if at present they seem to be best used in combination with other data collection methods.

Blasius and Brandt (2010) posit that when compared to other data collection methods, online surveys have been overly acknowledged (e.g. Christian, Dillman & Smyth, 2007; Couper, Traugott & Lamias, 2001; Dillman, 2007; Dillman & Bowker, 2001). Compared to face-to-face, telephone, and mail surveys, online surveys have the advantage of being cheaper, faster and independent in terms of time and space. The disadvantage is that they depend on the availability of internet access. While nationwide face-to-face samples are considered representative for the en-

tire population, Blasius and Brandt (2010) regard online samples as biased, especially in terms of age, gender and education, providing example of minorities, uneducated and the elderly who might be left out of the equation. Nonetheless, Danielson (2010) provides two major advantages of computer survey: (1) surveys can be anonymous or pseudonymous, opening discussion of topics that named participants might avoid for various reasons, and, (2) surveys are cheap and fast, thus researchers can learn from more experimental variants. Davidov and Depner (2009) provide a wide array of advantages of this medium of data collection (i.e. asynchrony, alocality, automation, documentation flexibility, objectivity, and efficiency), arguing that the aspects and innovations of internet surveys can be illustrated by seven fundamental characteristics. While conducting online surveys has its advantages, it comes with limitations and challenges. Davidov and Depner (2009) provide a useful summary of problems (i.e. coverage, sampling, measurement, non-response, and variability of the equipment used by internet user). In their study of ten years of publication data (1999–2008) from ten leading business ethics journals, Chan, Fung and Yau (2010) examined global patterns of business ethics research and contributing institutions and scholars. Their study concluded that business ethics research output is closely linked to the missions of the institutions driven by their values or religious belief. Choi, Kim and Kim (2010) call for the globalization of the business ethics research calling for the broadening the research in business ethics to enable comparisons across business systems indifferent income levels.

Peytchev, Couper, McCabe, and Crawford (2006) and Peytchev and Crawford (2005) indicate that methodological and empirical research has not caught up with technological advancements in real-time validation of respondent input. They concede that the use of the online survey has the advantages in reducing errors in the quality of data, nonetheless, with this comes the disadvantage of higher costs. Others are of the idea that online surveys are cost effective (Kaplowitz, Hadlock and Levine, 2004; Liu, 2007), speedy with 'high response rate', an argument extended by Mc-Burney and White (2007: 245), who established comparison between online surveys and the previous techniques concluding that online surveys 'designed to provide a more dynamic interaction between respondent and questionnaire than can be achieved in e-mail or paper surveys' (Dillman, 2007: 354). Nonetheless, conducting online surveys can be difficult for people who do not have knowledge and access to the Internet. This again raises questions about whether online surveys are better than mail surveys. However, possible advantages of using online surveys might include and are not limited to time and cost savings associated with eliminating printing and mailing of a survey instrument, having returned survey data already in an electronic format, and not having problems interpreting the diverse range of handwriting styles when transforming data from completed mail surveys for analysis.

Allen and Lofferda (2006) applaud online surveys as being easier and quicker to use in that: (1) the use of online surveys saves time, enhances productivity and the impact can be measured, (2) communication has a measurable impact on behavior, and is more important than deadlines in driving behavior, (3) the initial launch communication of an initiative has the greatest impact on participation, this is echoed by research in the area (e.g., Crawford et al., 2001; Gendron, Suddaby, & Lam, 2006; Wharton et al., 2003), and (4) the audience must be primed to let them know what is coming and when it is coming. Some of the above conclusions are also supported by Liu (2007) who provided a discussion of "lessons learned" and suggestions for effectively teaching a questionnaire survey design in an Electronic Commerce design course.

To enhance advantages and lessen effect of shortcomings of this type of surveys, Davidov and Depner (2009) recommend combining internet surveys with more conventional modes of data collection. In their research on response rates and costs for online, paper and mixed-mode surveys, Greenlaw and Brown-Welty (2009) concluded that mixed-mode, while more expensive, had higher response rates. In our research in business ethics, this was dealt with by adopting a mixed methods approach applying a combination of quantitative and qualitative techniques (i.e., online surveys that allowed also the collection of qualitative data, followed by focus groups).

MAIN FOCUS OF THE CHAPTER

Researching Business Ethics

When employing mixed methods design one of the first major issues that need to be addressed is that of common method variance and common method bias. A strategy of drawing on different sources of data for key measures is an effective approach to addressing this issue (Chang, van Witteloostuijn, & Eden, 2010). Further, arguing the case of interpretivism and ethics, Greener (2011) emphasizes the need to protect the least powerful in society, and because of its nature in exploring inter-subjectivity, places a strong role on the need to achieve consent and to treat data in the most careful way possible. Research in business ethics, using the example of researching ethical mindsets, spirituality and aesthetics can be challenging. Collecting survey data about spirituality can be successfully undertaken using the work of Ashmos and Dunchon (2000), and Reave (2005). Statements relating to aesthetics can be derived from Tateosian's (2005) research and those relating to dealing with group members and others at workplaces can be drawn from Boudreau (2003).

Further issues center on the operationalization of business ethics and data interpretation. Consideration of reliability, validity and ethical conduct of the research is central to research design. To ensure validity of any research tool conducting a pilot surveys and undertake rigorous examination and iteration of instruments prior to inviting respondents to participate is necessary.

With regards to online surveys, Roy and Berger (2005) conclude there is unequivocal evidence that the reliability and validity of data collected through online surveys are as strong as those collected through any other modes, and, this approach offers additional advantages of low cost, quick turnaround and higher efficiencies. However, in an increasingly ever-changing technological environment, there is a need to continue explorations as to how the online survey can be improved as a stand-alone technique or how it can best be integrated with traditional approaches.

Measuring Spirituality and Aesthetics in Relation to Business Ethics

In the area of business, management, and organizational theory there are some attempts at developing tools to research or measure sensitive concepts such as business ethics, spirituality and aesthetics. However, these are mainly in relation to spirituality, as in fulfilment, at the work place (e.g., Altman et al. 2008) or incorporated within a dichotomy between spirituality and religion (e.g., Ashmos & Dunchon 2000 Duchon & Plowman 2005 Giacalone & Jurkiewicz 2003). While these studies concentrate on the presence of spirituality at the workplace, there seems to be confusion between spirituality and religion. Researching spirituality and meaning in the workplace, Brooke and Parker (2009) found two aspects to be problematic. One relates to the apparent ambiguity relating to the term 'spirituality' in itself and, especially, in comparison to the use of the word 'religion'. Another aspect refers to motives and drivers behind the study of workplace spirituality and the search for 'higher meaning'. Brooke and Parker (2009) conclude that the way in which 'spirituality' is conceived and constructed directly affects decisions related to methodological

choice and, ultimately, to research design itself. As for aesthetics this is mainly located within the realm of art and design. From the research that does bring aesthetics into the workplace tend to have an emphasis on information systems, web designs and in some cases office layout, and the office building (Strati & de Montoux Weggeman et al. 2007).

This survey on business ethics was developed through a series of stages beginning with a pilot paper-based design to eleven volunteers who were derived from the University's postgraduate students. With regards to design, Manfreda, Batagelj and Vehovar (2002) contend that online survey design requires special handling. They add that there are three main issues relating to the visual design of online surveys. These three issues of visual design are graphic layout, presentation of questions, and number of questions.

The pilot phase of this survey was conducted through three stages. The first stage was through a paper-based survey completed by eleven volunteers recruited from the University's postgraduate students. The second stage was an online-based pilot survey administered to thirty-three volunteers recruited via e-mail from diverse backgrounds, and different corporations and occupations. After the receipt of their approvals, e-mails introducing the 'pilot' online survey were sent with attachments. Those attachments were: (1) 'how to document' (i.e. a systematic guide to respondents) and, (2) a fact sheet (i.e. information sheet) about the research that covered issues such as: participants' rights and obligations, confidentiality, anonymity, why they need to complete this survey, and how their data will be used. Following the analysis of the pilot-study data, the survey was subject to review by a panel of experts that resulted in further refinement of the tool. The third stage involved peer review and field-testing of the tool. Based on these three pilot study stages, and especially the third stage when the expert panel examined the survey tool and the preliminary results from the first two stages of the pilot study, they recommended that the statements and questions were reduced from 115 to 97 then finally to 82. This included the sixty-six statements in four sections examining ethical mindsets, spirituality and aesthetics, and four multiple-choice questions on individuals' preferences relating to aesthetics and spirituality, with eleven demographic questions to allow the generation of descriptive data.

Online surveys are 'powerful tools for maintaining respondent interest in the survey and for encouraging completion of the instrument' (Couper, Traugott & Lamias 2001: 251). Healey (2007) argues, researchers frequently must choose between radio buttons and drop downs when collecting data using online surveys, but a strong empirical reason for favoring one format has proved elusive. Reporting on his research on the effect of response option format and input mechanism employed on data quality in online surveys (e.g. drop downs and scroll mice), Healey (2007) found that format choice did not significantly affect survey completions, number of non-substantial answers, or time to complete the survey. However, there was evidence that, at the question level, drop downs led to slightly higher non-response items and consistently longer response times. It is therefore likely that the potential for scroll mouse data entry issues will remain a concern, at least in the medium term. Indeed, especially as Healey (2007) argues, as researchers begin to experiment with emerging survey delivery channels such as portable and wireless digital devices (e.g. Couper 2005), with their proprietary browsing software and alternative input mechanisms, measurement issues may even become increasingly problematic.

The technique deployed in our research which can easily be applied to any research in business ethics was a self-administered survey involving computer-to-computer communication over the internet, asking the users to respond to the survey by clicking on radio buttons and adding additional comments in a specific area within the survey regarding the survey questions or statements. With this in mind preparation of the

survey required careful consideration. Indeed, as Crawford, Couper and Lamias (2001) cautioned, it took much longer than anticipated. However, this allowed for a variety of issues to be raised and solved, the most important being: the length of the survey, the timing of reminders, the form of access (i.e., password), progress indicator, and avoiding being labelled a 'spammer'. Further, as Porter and Whitcomb (2005) and Whitcomb and Porter (2004) argue, the design and background of e-mail prompts, reminders and 'thank you' messages are also important. With regards to surveys and e-mail reminders, Klofstad, Boulianne and Basson (2008) suggest reminder reference, when contact is first established with respondents, increases response rates to online surveys, thus increases the representativeness of findings without adversely affecting data quality, while this method was not adopted in this research, as it was prudent to assure the respondents of anonymity which is important with ethics and business ethics research, nonetheless, seems of appropriate use in research in general.

In relation to websites, and online surveys, Robins and Holmes (2008) posit that one of the factors that may influence users to stay or not is the webpage artistic features and user judgment about site credibility. They studied the possible link between page aesthetics and a user's judgment of the site's credibility. Their findings indicate that when the same content is presented using different levels of aesthetic treatment, the content with a higher aesthetic treatment was judged as having higher credibility. While planning the online survey, several designs including background, and font colors should be considered. Figure (1) provides a sample view of the layout of an effective online survey.

The Survey

In deploying an online survey it should not be assumed that there would be few problems of access to information and communications technology

Figure 1. Screenshot of part of 'Section 3D' of the online survey

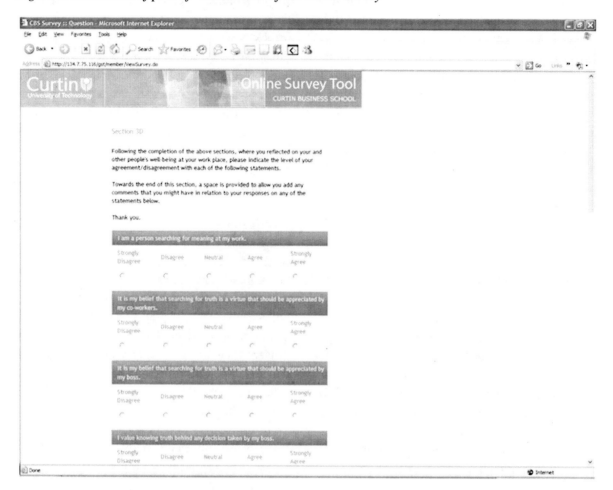

(ICT). For example, in Australia, and at the time, the Australian Bureau of Statistics (ABS) (2008), report that the proportion of businesses which use ICT varies considerably across industry sectors. The industries with the highest proportion of businesses using computers were electricity, gas and water supply, and cultural and recreational services (both 97 per cent). These industries also had the highest proportion of businesses, which used internet (both 90 per cent). Accommodation, cafes and restaurants had the lowest proportion of businesses, which used a computer (77 per cent). Internet use was then lowest in accommodation, cafes and restaurants and communication services (both 62 per cent). Web presence was highest in cultural and recreational services (50 per cent) and wholesale trade (44 per cent). Construction had the lowest proportion of businesses with a web presence of (11 per cent). Furthermore, the use of ICT by businesses in capital cities was higher than other areas for computer use, internet use and web presence. The proportions of business using computers, internet and having a web presence were 89 per cent, 78 per cent, and 29 per cent respectively for capital cities, compared with 87 per cent, 72 per cent and 22 per cent for other areas in Australia.

The most appropriate type of survey for use in the research of business ethics in the context of spirituality and aesthetics is the Likert-type.

According to Cooksey (2007), these scales are designed for measuring attitudes, beliefs, opinions, and similar psychological constructs sentiments and other sensitive issues like business ethics. In mixed methods research it is important to provide respondents with space to add comments at the end of each set of questions to amplify their responses and provide for complementarity, enhancement, illustration and clarification of responses (Burke Johnson & Onwuegbuzi, 2004). Table 1 provides examples of statements that can be used.

Demographic questions also should be included at the end of the survey to generate supporting descriptive statistics about the sample profile.

It is worthwhile to note here that and in line with the University policies, guidelines, approval from the University's ethics committee was obtained. In accordance with Curtin University's ethics approval, the collected data was analyzed using computerized quantitative and qualitative software. The data was securely stored, with access restricted to the researcher, the principal supervisor, and authorized technical support personnel who are all required to maintain confidentiality. The results could not be tracked to individuals and so anonymity was protected. Additionally all data, and documents (e.g. computer files, transcripts, disks, survey files and other data) were kept in a secured environment or password protected. Such details were passed to participants through information sheet and consent form. Participation was on a voluntary basis and participants were free to withdraw from the study at any time. Documents would be disposed of in line with the respective university policies (National Health and Medical Research Council guidelines) on information management, and electronic data will be deleted and any hard copies of any data or its analysis shredded.

Qualitative Analysis

The qualitative component to the mixed methods approach is important because the open-ended questions generated a large amount of data. Effective analysis required the employment of a qualitative analysis software package (i.e. NVivo8 ©) so that themes and categories could be identified, recorded and retrieved easily. This problem of handling the large amounts of data produced by on-line surveys echoes Danielson's (2010) findings that they often provide comments that are too numerous and difficult to aggregate. In the case of this research this issue was tackled by limiting the space for the inclusion of comments and importing the data into a qualitative analysis software package (i.e. NVivo8 ©). Nodes and Node trees were very helpful being conceptual representation of codes and logical composition of nodes into tree hierarchy that were found and conducted during the analysis of the data using NVivo8.

To test and validate the survey results it is useful to collect further qualitative data. Focus group interviews are an efficient and effective way of doing this. The data collected here may be used to triangulate, expand and dimensionalize the survey results. Examples of questions that could be are shown below (Table 2).

This stage is important because qualitative research interviews tap into human tendencies where attitudes and perceptions are developed through interaction with other people. During focus groups individuals may shift due to the influence of other comments but also attitudes may be held with certainty. In this respect, Kreuger (1988) suggests that the purpose is to obtain information of a qualitative nature from a predetermined and limited number of people (Kreuger 1988: 26).

DISCUSSION

In-house development of an online survey for the research in business ethics is a very challenging, yet rewarding task. The positive aspect is that most participants trusted the site (the survey was hosted on a University web site), and were able to

Table 1. Online survey Likert scale statements

Online Survey Item – Following Running the Frequencies and Description of the 223 Responses
Online Survey - Section 1
I feel personally responsible for my development as a person.
I feel personally responsible for my own behavior.
I believe others experience joy as a result of my work.
I fell that I make a difference to the people with whom I work.
I am aware of what is truly meaningful to me at work.
Online Survey - Section 2
I try to encourage and support a collaborative work culture.
All who work with me appreciate the consistent effort I bring to my work.
I can sense when other workers are having difficulties
At times, the constant change in information and technologies available to me interferes with my ability to get my work done. (R)
At times, I question my own competence to do my work alone. (R)
At times, I wonder about my ability to accomplish a task. (R)
Online Survey - Section 3
Section 3A
I feel hopeful about life.
I consider myself a spiritual person.
Prayer is an important part of my life.
I usually care about the well-being of my co-workers.
I feel my work gives meaning to my life.
I am able to use my gifts and talents at my work place.
At my work place, I try to empower others to succeed.
Section 3B
There is no room for spirituality in my workplace. (R)
Spiritual values are not considered important at my workplace. (R)
I am not aware of what is truly meaningful to me in my workplace (R)
Who I am, as a whole human being (i.e. body, mind, and soul), is not valued at my workplace.
I feel alienated and detached from my co-workers. (R)
I routinely compromise the quality of my work (R)
At times, I treat people as objects to be manipulated in the workplace.
Section 3C (All in the 9 components as 1ˢᵗ component)
"SUPPORT" is a value I care to see apparent in my co-workers.
"INTEGRITY" is a value I care to see apparent in my co-workers.
"COMPASSION" is a value I care to see apparent in my co-workers.
"HONESTY" is a value I care to see apparent in my co-workers.
"SUPPORT" is a value I care to see apparent in my boss.
"INTEGRITY" is a value I care to see apparent in my boss.
"COMPASSION" is a value I care to see apparent in my boss.
"HONESTY" is a value I care to see apparent in my boss.

Table 2. Questions used in the focus groups interview

Question #	Questions Asked to the Focus Groups Members
One	With the current crisis in the financial market, people would be thinking of ethics in the corporate world. When we talk about business ethics – what sorts of things come to your mind?
Two	What does spirituality mean to you?
Three	Therefore, what would be your understanding of the characteristics of a spiritual person?
Four	What does aesthetics mean to you?
Five	Therefore, what would be your understanding of the characteristics of a person who appreciates aesthetics?
Six	How would spirituality and aesthetics influence business people?
Seven	What do you think would make up an ethical mind-set?
Eight	Would it be possible to develop an ethical mind-set? How?

complete the surveys successfully, despite some technical problems (e.g. server down, especially at the early stages of data collection).

The deployment of an online survey in an interpretive mixed methods research design appears suitable for tackling a complexity of holistic, sensitive and philosophical concepts associated with examining phenomena like business ethics, through spirituality, aesthetics and ethical mind-sets. Using an online survey as the main vehicle for collecting quantitative data has the potential to enable insights to be generated into some of the key issues raised by scholars in relation to lack of empirical evidence about the appropriateness of online survey tools.

Researchers have used survey response rates as a measure of equivalency. The successful use of an online survey in this research comes in support Kieman et al.'s (2005) argument that with the increase in computer users, online surveys can be used easily and there is now the possibility that online surveys are more effective than mail surveys. Kaplowitz, Hadlock and Levine (2004) contend, due to possible advantages of cost savings associated with eliminating the printing and mailing of surveys coupled with data entry when surveys are back from respondents, the internet is increasingly becoming an important mean of surveying. Nonetheless, some might use a mixed-mode strategy (e.g., paper and online)

thus exploiting the advantages of online survey and reducing the non-response rate. However in this research it was found that despite technical difficulties, the use of these surveys is at least as efficient and effective as a mail survey.

Despite time taken in the design, preparation, testing, ultimately uploading the survey online and the collation of data it is clear that – as predicted in the literature – online surveys save time, and enhance productivity. However, in this research new issues are evident: (1) the need for ongoing follow-up on responses, (2) the need to promptly deal with comments and e-mails received from volunteer respondents, (3) it is important to have suitable software packages for collating and analysing both quantitative and qualitative data, and, (4) the need to maintain and clean up some data fields.

In more general terms it was clear that a balance had to be found between minimizing time spent by respondents to complete the survey and maximizing data collection. Therefore, care should be taken to ensure that only the most relevant questions are included. For example reverse questions should be used sparingly as they can cause confusion amongst respondents and add little to the results. It is also important to provide clear explanations about the survey, for example, a paragraph at the beginning of each section to explain the terms used in that section. However such explanations need to be precise and concise. The guidance that we included in the section of the online survey in relation to statements that deal with support, integrity, compassion, and honesty, we wrote: 'Reflecting on the above sections in relation to yours and other people's well-being at your work place, please indicate the level of your agreement/disagreement with each of the following statements. Towards the end of this section, a space is provided to allow you to add any comments that you might have in relation to your responses on any of the statements below. Thank you.' (Issa 2009: 329)

While the use of online surveys presents challenges, they do provide significant advantages, particularly in time and cost savings associated with eliminating the printing and mailing of survey instrument and having returned survey data already in an electronic format. This eliminates the need for costly transcription and removes the possibilities of data entry error. While these are clear advantages, difficulties arise with the prompting of responses, sending relevant materials and reminders, responding to participants' queries, and solving a diversity of technical difficulties.

The use of the interpretive mixed methods approach, allowed the researchers to incorporate the virtues and avoid the limitations of the sole use of either quantitative or qualitative methods and provides opportunities to access the feelings and motives of people and engage more fully with the meanings by which individuals live. These characteristics are useful for researching ethical mindsets, spirituality and aesthetics, which provided stronger inferences and the identification of a greater diversity of perspectives. Collecting data online provides valuable data for identifying important variables and relationships, while face-to-face collection of qualitative data provides a means of dimensionalizing and refining the analysis. Conway and Lance (2010) contend that, to some extent, there are perpetuated mis-

conceptions about common method bias in self-report measures, including (a) that relationships between self-reported variables are necessarily and routinely upwardly biased, (b) other-reports (or other methods) are superior to self-reports, and, (c) rating sources (e.g., self, other) constitute measurement methods. Conway and Lance (2010) argue against these misconceptions providing guidance to authors.

It is concluded here, though mixed-methods approach had assisted achieving the aims of this research, also assisted in the reduction of limitations that would attach to each of the techniques if used solely. This mixed-methods approach has had its praises sang by diverse number of scholars, it is still in the course of development, and scholars warned though it might be considered as a genuine alternative to other research methods, yet they had recently identified some shortcomings, variations and inconsistencies within, to be considered to allow further improvement to this newly developed methodology.

Some of the shortcomings that this research identified lie in the fact that the deployment of mixed-methods approach though provides vast data it is time consuming. In addition, while the employments of this approach would assist in the generation of answers to the research questions, achieving the aims. Nonetheless, this approach's limitation lies in the fact that new data is generated throughout the course of research, might not be claimed as part of this research findings. This is true especially when the qualitative data is collected following the collection of the quantitative data. Thus, this limits the generalization of generated results, raising more questions.

Certainly, this our attempt to research the sensitive issues relating to business ethics have taught us lessons about the difficulty and complexity of research business ethics, that can be made easier with the use of technology, that we endeavored to share with our readers in this chapter.

CONCLUSION

Important methodological implications and questions on research in business ethics have been identified. In particular, the importance of design and follow-up to the online survey in improving response rates giving due consideration to the need for suitable approaches to collating and analyzing both quantitative data and qualitative data to allow the research in sensitive issues such as business ethics.

A mixed methods approach that begins with a survey to collect quantitative and qualitative data collection, and focus groups coupled with the employment of ICT (i.e. online survey) was key to achieving the aims of this demanding research, especially in addressing the limitations attached to each of the techniques if used solely when researching the phenomena that was the focus of this study in the field of business ethics. The mixed methods approach has been recommended by numerous scholars, but was strengthened with the introduction of technology to data collection. However, scholars warn that although it might be considered a genuine alternative to other research methods, they have recently identified some inherent shortcomings, variations and inconsistencies. These need to be taken into consideration if there are to be any improvements made to this methodology. Nonetheless, and certainly, the outcome of this research is the development of a valid online research tool, which can be deployed in different contexts for the research in business ethics.

ACKNOWLEDGMENT

This chapter is based on a conference paper presented at EBEN Research conference held in Newcastle, UK in June 2011, and is building upon Theodora Issa's PhD thesis on ethical mindsets, which identified components of ethical mindsets including 'aesthetic spirituality' and 'religious spirituality'.

REFERENCES

Allen, E., & Lofferda, A. S. (2006). Ideas@work: Pushing response to an ethics survey. *Strategic Communication Management, 10*(3), 7.

Altman, Y., Ozbilgin, M., & Wilson, E. (2008). *'Living Spirituality in the Workplace - the Cel Way - a Study on Organisational Effectiveness Ad Well-Being at Work: Cel as a Case-Study.' U004-0108-HG, Centre for Excellence in Leadership.* Barcelona: CEL.

Ashmos, D. P., & Dunchon, D. (2000). Spirituality at Work: A Conceptualization and Measure. *Journal of Management Inquiry, 9*(2), 134–145. doi:10.1177/105649260092008

Australian Bureau of Statistics. (2008). Year Book Australia. Commonwealth of Australia.

Balajti, L., Darago, L., Adany, R., & Kosa, K. (2010). College Students' Response Rate to an Incentivized Combination of Postal and Web-Based Health Survey. *Evaluation & the Health Professions, 33*(2), 164-176.

Benefiel, M. (2003). Mapping the terrain of spirituality in organizations research. *Journal of Organizational Change Management, 16*(4), 367–377. doi:10.1108/09534810310484136

Benefiel, M. (2005). The second half of the journey: Spiritual leadership for organizational transformation. *The Leadership Quarterly, 16*(5), 723–747. doi:10.1016/j.leaqua.2005.07.005

Blasius, J., & Brandt, M. (2010). Representativeness in Online Survey through Stratified Samples. *Bulletin de Methodologie Sociologique, 107*(1), 5–21. doi:10.1177/0759106310369964

Boudreau, R. (2003). *Boudreau Burnout Questionnaire (Bbq)*. Retrieved 23rd May 2008, from http://www.cma.ca

Brooke, C. & S. Parker. (2009). Researching Spirituality and Meaning in the Workplace. *The Electronic Journal of Business Research Methods, 7*(1), 1-10.

Burke, L. A., & James, K. E. (2006). Using online surveys for primary research data collection: Lessons from the field. *International Journal of Innovation and Learning, 3*(1), 16–30. doi:10.1504/IJIL.2006.008177

Carcary, M. (2009). The Resrarch Audit Trail - Enhancing Trustworthiness in Qualitative Inquiry. *The Electronic Journal of Business Research Methods, 7*(1), 11–24.

Chang, S.-J., van Witteloostuijn, A., & Eden, L. (2010). From the Editors: Common method variance in international business research. Journal of Inernational Business Studies, 41, 178-184. doi:10.1057/jibs.2009.88

Cho, J., & Trent, A. (2006). Validity in qualitative research revisited. *Qualitative Research, 6*(3), 319–340. doi:10.1177/1468794106065006

Choi, C. J., Kim, S. W., & Kim, J. B. (2010). Globalizing Business Ethics Research and the Ethical Need. *Journal of Business Ethics, 94*(2), 299–306. doi:10.1007/s10551-009-0258-y

Christian, L. M., Dillman, D. A., & Smyth, J. D. (2007). Helping respondents get it right the first time: The influence of words, symbols, and graphics in web surveys. *Public Opinion Quarterly, 71*(1), 113–125. doi:10.1093/poq/nfl039

Cole, S. T. (2005). Comparing Mail and Web-Based Survey Distribution Methods: Results of Surveys to Leisure Travel Retailers. *Journal of Travel Research, 43*(4), 422–430. doi:10.1177/0047287505274655

Conway, J. M., & Lance, C. E. (2010). What Reviewers Should Expect from Authors Regarding Common Method Bias in Organizational Research. *Journal of Business and Psychology, 25*(3), 325–334. doi:10.1007/s10869-010-9181-6

Cooksey, R. W. (2007). Illustrating Statistical Procedures for Business, Behavioural & Social Science Research. Prahan, Australia: Tilde University Press.

Couper, M. P. (2000). Web Surveys: A Review of Issues and Approaches. *Public Opinion Quarterly, 64*(4), 464–494. doi:10.1086/318641 PMID:11171027

Couper, M. P., Tourangeao, R., & Kenyon, K. (2004). Picture This! Exploring Visual Effects in Web Surveys. *Public Opinion Quarterly, 68*(2), 255–266. doi:10.1093/poq/nfh013

Couper, M. P., Tourangeau, R., Conrad, F. G., & Crawford, S. D. (2004). What they see is what we get: Response options for web surveys. *Social Science Computer Review, 22*(1), 111–127. doi:10.1177/0894439303256555

Couper, M. P., Traugott, M. W., & Lamias, M. J. (2001). Web survey design and administration. *Public Opinion Quarterly, 65*(2), 230–253. doi:10.1086/322199 PMID:11420757

Couper, M. P., M. W. Traugott & M. J. Lamias. (2001). Web Survey Design and Administration. *Public Opinion Quarterly, 65*(2), 230-253.

Crawford, S. D., Couper, M. P., & Lamias, M. J. (2001). Web Surveys: Perceptions of Burden. *Social Science Computer Review, 19*(2), 146–162. doi:10.1177/089443930101900202

Creswell, J. W. (2013). *Qualitative Inquiry and Research Design: Choosing Among Five Approaches* (3rd ed.). Thousand Oaks, CA: Sage Publications, Inc..

Crump, B., & Logan, K. (2008). A Framework for Mixed Stakeholders and Mixed Methods. *The Electronic Journal of Business Research Methods*, 6(1), 21–28.

Danielson, P. (2010). Designing a machine to learn about the ethics of robotics: The N-reasons platform. *Ethics and Information Technology*, 12(3), 251–261. doi:10.1007/s10676-009-9214-x

Davidov, E., & Depner, F. (2009). Testing for measurement equivalence of human values across online and paper-and-pencil surveys. *Quality & Quantity*. doi:10.1007/s11135-11009-19297-11139

de Laat, P. B. (2005). Trusting virtual trust. *Ethics and Information Technology*, 7(3), 167–180. doi:10.1007/s10676-006-0002-6

Denscombe, M. (2008). Communities of Practice: A Research Paradigm for the Mixed Methods Approach. *Journal of Mixed Methods Research*, 2(3), 270–283. doi:10.1177/1558689808316807

Denzin, N., & Lincoln, Y. (1994). *The handbook of qualitative research in education*. Newbury Park, CA: Sage.

Denzin, N. K., & Lincoln, Y. S. (1998). The fifth moment. In N. K. Denzin, & Y. S. Lincoln (Eds.), *The Landscape of Qualitative Research Theories and Issues* (p. 465). Thousand Oaks, CA: Sage Publications Inc..

Denzin, N. K., & Lincoln, Y. S. (Eds.). (2003). *The Landscape of Qualitative Research: Theories and Issues*. Thousand Oaks, CA: Sage Publications, Inc..

Denzin, N. K., & Lincoln, Y. S. (2005). *The Sage handbook of qualitative research* (3rd ed.). Thousand Oaks, CA: Sage.

Deutskens, E., Ruyter, K., & Wetzels, M. (2006). An Assessment of Equivalence Between Online and Mail Surveys in Service Research. *Journal of Service Research*, 8(4), 346–355. doi:10.1177/1094670506286323

Dillman, D. A. (2000). *Mail and Internet Surveys. The Tailored Design Method*. New York: Wiley.

Dillman, D. A. (2007). *Mail and Internet Surveys "The Tailored Design Method" 2007 update with new internet, visual and mixed-mode guide* (2nd ed.). Hoboken, NJ: John Wiley & Sons Inc..

Dillman, D. A., & Bowker, D. K. (2001). The web questionnaire challenge to survey methodologies. In U. D. Reips & M. Bosnjak (Eds.), Dimensions of Internet Science (pp. 159-177). Papst: Lengerich.

Duchon, D. & D. A. Plowman. (2005). 'Nurturing the Spirit at Work: Impact on Work Unit Performance.' *The Leadership Quarterly, 16*(5), 807-833.

Fassinger, R., & Morrow, S. L. (2013). Toward Best Practices in Quantitative, Qualitative, and Mixed-Method Research: A Social Justice Perspective. *Journal for Social Action in Counseling and Psychology*, 5(2), 69–83.

Fenlason, K. J., & Suckow-Zimberg, K. (2006). Online surveys. Critical issues in using the web to conduct surveys. In A. I. Kraut (Ed.), *Getting Action from Organizational Surveys* (pp. 183–212). San Francisco: Jossey-Bass.

Ford, P. J. (2001). A further analysis of the ethics of representation in virtual reality: Multi-user environments. *Ethics and Information Technology*, 3(3), 113–121. doi:10.1023/A:1011846009390

Fornaciari, C. J., & Lund-Dean, K. (2001). Making the quantum leap Lessons from physics on studying spirituality and religion in organizations. *Journal of Organizational Change Management*, 14(4), 335–351. doi:10.1108/EUM0000000005547

Fricker, R. D. J., & Schonlau, M. (2002). Advantages and Disadvantages of Internet Research Surveys. Evidence from the Literature. *Field Methods*, *14*(4), 347–367. doi:10.1177/1525822202237725

Gendron, Y., Suddaby, R., & Lam, H. (2006). An examination of the ethical commitment of professional accountants to auditor independence. *Journal of Business Ethics*, *64*(2), 169–193. doi:10.1007/s10551-005-3095-7

Giacalone, R. A., & Jurkiewicz, C. L. (2003). *Handbook of Workplace Spirituality and Organizational Performance*. Armonk, NY: M.E. Sharpe.

Glaser, B. G. (2003). *The Grounded Theory Perspective II: Description's Remodeling of Grounded Theory Methodology*. Mill Valley: Sociology Press.

Grava-Gubins, I., & Scott, S. (2008). Effects of various methodological strategies: Survey response rates among Canadian physicians and physicians-in-training. *Canadian Family Physician Medecin de Famille Canadien*, *54*(October), 1424–1430. PMID:18854472

Greener, I. (2011). *Designing Social Research: A Guide for th bewildered*. London: SAGE Publications Ltd..

Greenlaw, C., & Brown-Welty, S. (2009). A Comparison of Web-Based and Paper-Based Survey Methods: Testing Assumptions of Survey Mode and Response Cost. *Evaluation Review*, *33*(5), 464–480. doi:10.1177/0193841X09340214 PMID:19605623

Guo, Z., & Sheffield, J. (2007). Critical Heuristics: A Contribution to Addressing the Vexed Question of So-Called Knowledge Management. *Systems Research and Behavioral Science*, *24*(6), 613–626. doi:10.1002/sres.834

Handy, C. (1995). Trust and the Virtual Organization. *Harvard Business Review*, *73*(3), 40–50.

Hanna, R. C., Weinberg, B., Dant, R. P., & Berger, P. D. (2005). Do internet-based surveys increase personal self-disclosure? *Journal of Database Marketing and Customer Strategy Management*, *12*(4), 342–356. doi:10.1057/palgrave.dbm.3240270

Healey, B., (2007). Drop Downs and Scroll Mice: The Effect of Response Option Format and Input Mechanism Employed on Data Quality in Web Surveys. *Social Science Computer Review*, *25*(1), 111-128.

Issa, T. (2009). *Ethical Mindsets, Aesthetics and Spirituality: A Mixed-Methods Approach Analysis of the Australian Services Sector*. Retrieved from http://espace.library.curtin.edu.au/R/?func=dbin-jump-full&object_id=131986&local_base=GEN01-ERA02

Johnson, B. R., & Onwuegbuzie, A. J. (2004). Mixed Methods Research: A Research Paradigm Whose Time Has Come. *Educational Researcher*, *33*(7), 14–26. doi:10.3102/0013189X033007014

Johnson, R. B., Onwuegbuzie, A. J., & Turner, L. A. (2007). Toward a definition of mixed methods research. *Journal of Mixed Methods Research*, *1*(2), 112–133. doi:10.1177/1558689806298224

Kaplowitz, M. D., Hadlock, T. D., & Levine, R. (2004). A comparison of web and mail survey response rates. *Public Opinion Quarterly*, *68*(1), 94–101. doi:10.1093/poq/nfh006

Kieman, N. E., M. Kieman, M. A. Oyler & C. Gilles. (2005). Is a Web Survey as Effective as a Mail Survey? A Field Experiment among Computer Users. *American Journal of Evaluation*, *26*(2), 245-252.

Klofstad, C. A., S. Boulianne & D. Basson. (2008). Matching the Message to the Medium: Results from an Experiment on Internet Survey Email Contacts. *Social Science Computer Review*, *26*(4), 498-509.

Koehn, D. (2003). The nature of and conditions for online trust. *Journal of Business Ethics*, *43*(1/2), 3–19. doi:10.1023/A:1022950813386

Krenz, C., & Sax, G. (1986). What Quantitative Research Is and Why It Doesn't Work. *The American Behavioral Scientist*, *30*(1), 58–69. doi:10.1177/000276486030001007

Lee, T. (1999). *Using qualitative methods in organizational research*. Thousand Oaks, CA: Sage.

Liu, C. (2007). Teaching Tip Web Survey Design in ASP.Net 2.0: A Simple Task with One Line of Code. *Journal of Information Systems Education*, *18*(1), 11–14.

Lund-Dean, K., Fornaciari, C., & McGee, J. (2003). Research in spirituality, religion, and work: Walking the line between relevance and legitimacy. *Journal of Organizational Change Management*, *16*(4), 378–395. doi:10.1108/09534810310484145

Manfreda, K. L., Batagelj, Z., & Vehovar, V. (2002, April). Design of Web Questionnaires: Three Basic Experiments. *Journal of Computer-Mediated Communication*, *7*, 3. Retrieved from http://jcmc.indiana.edu/vol7/issue3/vehovar.html

McBurney, D. H., & White, T. L. (2007). *Research Methods* (7th ed.). Thomson Learning.

McIntyre, J. (2005). Part 2: Critical Systemic Praxis to Address Fixed and Fluid Identity of Politics at the Local, National and International Level. *Systemic Practice and Action Research*, *18*(3), 223–259. doi:10.1007/s11213-005-4813-x

Miles, M. B., & Huberman, A. M. (1994). *Qualitative Data Analysis*. London: Sage Publications.

Morse, J. M., & Niehaus, L. (2009). *Mixed Method Design: Principles and Procedures*. Walnut Creek, CA: Left Coast Press Inc..

Nissenbaum, H. (2001). Securing Trust Online: Wisdom or Oxymoron? *Boston University Law Review*, *81*(3), 635–664.

Parry, K. W. (1998). Grounded theory and social process: A new direction for leadership research. *The Leadership Quarterly*, *9*(1), 85–105. doi:10.1016/S1048-9843(98)90043-1

Peytchev, A., Couper, M. P., McCabe, S. E., & Crawford, S. D. (2006). Web Survey Design. *Public Opinion Quarterly*, *70*(4), 596–607. doi:10.1093/poq/nfl028

Peytchev, A., & Crawford, S. D. (2005). A Typology of Real-Time Validations in Web-Based Surveys. *Social Science Computer Review*, *23*(2), 235–249. doi:10.1177/0894439304273272

Plano-Clark, V. L., & Creswell, J. W. (Eds.). (2008). *The Mixed Methods Reader* (Vol. 1). Thousand Oaks, CA: Sage Publications.

Porter, S. R. & M. E. Whitcomb. (2005). E-Mail Subject Lines and Their Effect on Web Survey Viewing and Response. *Social Science Computer Review, 23*(3), 380-387.

Qualtrics. (2013). *Qualtrics Website*. Retrieved 23rd November 2013, from http://qualtrics.com

Reave, L. (2005). Spiritual Values and Practices Related to Leadership Effectiveness. *The Leadership Quarterly*, *16*(5), 655–687. doi:10.1016/j.leaqua.2005.07.003

Roberts, J. (2000). From Know-How to Show-How? Questionioning the Role of Information and Communication Technologies in Knowledge Transfer. *Technology Analysis and Strategic Management*, *12*(4), 429–443. doi:10.1080/713698499

Romm, N. R. A. (2006). The Social Significance of Churchman's Epistemological Position. In J. P. Van Gigch, & J. McIntyre-Mills (Eds.), *Resucing the Enlightnment from Itself Critical and Systemic Implications for Democracy* (pp. 68–92). Springer. doi:10.1007/0-387-27589-4_6

Roy, A. & P. D Berger. (2005). E-Mail and Mixed Mode Database Surveys Revisited: Exploratory Analyses of Factors Affecting Response Rates. *Journal of Database Marketing and Customer Strategy Management, 12*(2), 153-171.

Singh, A., Taneja, A., & Mangalaraj, G. (2009). Creating Online Surveys: Some Wisdom from the Trenches Tutorial. *IEEE Transactions on Professional Communication, 52*(2), 197–212. doi:10.1109/TPC.2009.2017986

Strati, A. & P. G. de Montoux. (2002). Introduction: Organizing Aesthetics. *Human Relations, 55*(7), 755-766.

Tateosian, L. G. (2005). *Characterizing Aesthetic Visualizations.* North Carolina State University.

Ulrich, W. (1987). Critical heuristics of social systems design. *European Journal of Operational Research, 31*(3), 276–283. doi:10.1016/0377-2217(87)90036-1

Ulrich, W. (2001). The quest for competence in systemic research and practice. *Systems Research and Behavioral Science, 18*(1), 3–28. doi:10.1002/sres.366

Weggeman, M., I. Lammers & H. Akkermans. (2007). Aesthetics from a Design Perspective. *Journal of Organizational Change Management, 20*(3), 346-358.

Wharton, C. M., Hampl, J. S., Hall, R., & Winham, D. M. (2003). PCs or paper-and-pencil: Online surveys for data collection. *Journal of the American Dietetic Association, 103*(11), 1458–1459. doi:10.1016/j.jada.2003.09.004 PMID:14626248

Whitcomb, M. E., & Porter, S. R. (2004). E-Mail Contacts: A Test of Complex Graphical Designs in Survey Research. *Social Science Computer Review, 22*(3), 370-376.

ADDITIONAL READING

Alzola, M. (2011). The Reconciliation Project: Separation and Integration in business Ethics Research. *Journal of Business Ethics, 99*(1), 19–25. doi:10.1007/s10551-011-0746-8

Bergman, M. M. (Ed.). (2008). *Advances in Mixed Methods Research.* Thousand Oaks: Sage Publications.

Bryant, P. (2009). Self-regulation and moral awareness among entrepreneurs. *Journal of Business Venturing, 24*(5), 505–518. doi:10.1016/j.jbusvent.2008.04.005

Calabretta, G., Durisin, B., & Ogliengo, M. (2011). Uncovering the Intellectual Structure of Research in Business Ethics: A Journey Through the History, the Classics, and the Pillars of Journal of Business Ethics. *Journal of Business Ethics, 104*(4), 499–524. doi:10.1007/s10551-011-0924-8

Canda, E. R., Nakashima, M., & Furman, L. D. (2004). Ethical Consideration About Spirituality in Social Work: Insights From a National Qualitative Survey. *Families in Society, 85*(1), 27–35. doi:10.1606/1044-3894.256

Cho, J., & Trent, A. (2006). Validity in qualitative research revisited. *Qualitative Research, 6*(3), 319–340. doi:10.1177/1468794106065006

Coghlan, A. T., Girault, P., & Prybylski, D. (2007). Participatory and Mixed-Method Evaluation of MSM HIV/AIDS Programs in Bangladesh, Nepal and Indonesia (pp. 26). Asia: Evaluation South Asia.

Collins, K. M. T., Onwuegbuzie, A. J., & Sutton, I. L. (2006). A model incorporating the rationale and purpose for conducting mixed-methods research in special education and beyond. *Learning Disabilities (Weston, Mass.), 4*(1), 67–100.

Cragg, W. (2010). The State and Future Directions of Business Ethics Research and Practice. *Business Ethics Quarterly, 20*(4), 720–721.

Crump, B., & Logan, K. (2008). A Framework for Mixed Stakeholders and Mixed Methods. *The Electronic Journal of Business Research Methods, 6*(1), 21–28.

Gregoryk, K., & Eighmy, M. (2009). Interaction among undergraduate students: Does age matter? *College Student Journal, 43*(4), 1125–1136.

Issa, T., & Pick, D. (2010). Ethical Mindsets in the Australian Services Sector. *Asia Pacific Journal of Business and Management, 1*(1), 29–42.

Koeing, T. (2006). Compunding mixed-methods problems in frame analysis through comparative research. *Qualitative Research, 6*(1), 61–76. doi:10.1177/1468794106058874

Kolehmainen, N. (2007). Mixed Methods Research in HSR: Advantages and Challenges (pp. 32): Health Services Research Unit, University of Aberdeen.

Koury, K., Hollingsead, C., Fitzgerald, G., Miller, K., Mitchem, K., Tsai, H.-H., & Zha, S. (2009). Case-based Instruction in Different Delivery Contexts: The Impact of Time in Cases. *Journal of Interactive Learning Research, 20*(4), 445–467.

Langlois, L., & Lapointe, C. (2010). Can ethics be learned? Results from a three-year action research project. *Journal of Educational Administration, 48*(2), 147–163. doi:10.1108/09578231011027824

Martin, K., & Parmar, B. (2012). Assumption in Decision Making Scholarship: Implications for Business Ethics Research. *Journal of Business Ethics, 105*(3), 289–306. doi:10.1007/s10551-011-0965-z

Miller, H. G. (2007). *High School Athletic Eligibility Policies: A Mixed-Methods Study of the Perspectives of Public School Athletic Directors. (Doctorate)*. North Carolina: Liberty University.

Papadimitriou, A. (2010). Looking for Clues about Quality: A Multilevel Mixed Design on Quality Management in Greek Universities. *Electronic Journal of Business Research Methods, 8*(2), 85–94.

Pittaluga, F. (2007). *Using Qualitative and Mixed Methods in Livelihood systems profiling* (p. 23). FAO Fisheries Department.

Sampson, H. (2004). Navigating the waves: The usefulness of a pilot in qualitative research. *Qualitative Research, 4*(3), 383–402. doi:10.1177/1468794104047236

Scott, S. (2004). Researching Shyness: A contradiction in terms? *Qualitative Research, 4*(1), 91–105. doi:10.1177/1468794104041109

Shah, S. (2006). Sharing the world: The researcher and the researched. *Qualitative Research, 6*(2), 207–220. doi:10.1177/1468794106062710

Weber, J. (1992). Scenarios in Business Ethics Research: Review, Critical Assessment and Recommendation. *Business Ethics Quarterly, 2*(2), 137–160. doi:10.2307/3857568

Whelstone, T. J. (2003). The language of managerial excellence: Virtues as understood and applied. *Journal of Business Ethics, 44*(4), 343–357. doi:10.1023/A:1023640401539

Chapter 17
Applying Grounded Theory to a Qualitative Study of CIO Interactions with External Peer Networks

Brian Davis
Trinity College Dublin, Ireland

Joe McDonagh
Trinity College Dublin, Ireland

ABSTRACT

Interactions with external peers have been identified in the Information Systems (IS) management literature as being one of the most influential sources of contact for the Chief Information Officer (CIO), supporting them in their role as the most senior IS executive in the organisation. Today, due to the strategic importance of IS to the operations and competitive position of many organisations, the CIO often operates as a key member of the top management team. At the centre of this role, the literature suggests, is the ability of the CIO to identify relevant strategic IS knowledge in the external technological marketplace, via their external boundary spanning activities, that can impact the organisation's strategic positioning and overall success. However, whilst the IS management literature identifies interactions with external peers as being one of the most influential sources of contact available to CIOs, it fails to identify why they are such an important support to the CIO, or for that matter, how CIOs actually interact with such external peers. Similarly, a review of the wider management literature, whilst confirming the reasons why top management executives, such as the CIO, favour interactions with external peers, it again fails to clarify how such executives, in fact, actually interact with external peers, via contacts in external networks. Consequently, this has led to a clear gap in our knowledge and understanding relating to one of the key activities of the modern day CIO. For that reason, this research study set out to explore how CIOs, in fact, interact with external peers via network connections. As no previous theory existed, the Grounded Theory (GT) methodology was adopted, within an interpretivist perspective, to develop new theory. The research setting chosen was the Irish Private Sector, with a specific focus on organisations in the finance, hi-tech, telecoms, and airline industries. The purpose of this chapter is to draw into sharp focus the nature of GT as applied in this study, rather than the findings from the study itself, and to consider the use of appropriate technology tools to support this application.

DOI: 10.4018/978-1-4666-6493-7.ch017

BACKGROUND TO STUDY

The objective of this chapter is to discuss the use of grounded theory (GT) in developing theory around how CIOs interact with external peers, via contact in external networks, in the development and understanding of the ever changing IS marketplace. Specifically, the chapter will be of benefit to both researchers in the field of IS (IS) and managers and practitioners in IS today. To date, there has been a lack of empirical literature focused on addressing this key IS management issue. The chapter is made up of two main sections. The first section will address the background to why GT was deemed suitable for this inquiry. The second part will then provide some detail on the actual application of GT and supporting technology tools in practice.

FOCUS OF THE INVESTIGATION

The role of the CIO has emerged, over the last thirty years or so, to become the highest-ranking IS executive in many organisations (Smaltz, Sambamurthy, & Agarwal,. 2006, Preston, Chen, & Leider 2008). This new role was created, in the early 1980's, at a time when organisations had just begun to recognise the critical importance of IS for both their operational effectiveness and competitive positioning (Ferreira & Collins 1979, Ives & Learmonth 1984, McFarlan 1984, Porter & Millar 1985). Prior to that, the most senior role in IS had been that of the IS Manager, a functional or line departmental manager role with only limited involvement with top management (Ives & Olson 1981, Stephens 1991).

A review of the IS management literature, since the role was first envisaged, suggests that whilst still the most senior IS executive in many organisations, the focus of the role of the CIO has now widened to cover the requirement to be able to also "bridge the gap" between the organisation itself and its external technological environment (Earl 2000, Smaltz, Sambamurthy, & Agarwal, 2006, Galliers 2007, Preston, Chen, & Leider, 2008). This widening of the role of the CIO has been due to the increasing role IS now plays in many organisations today and the growing expectation of top management regarding the strategic impact of IS on their marketplace and their own competitive position (Venkatraman 2000, Sambamurthy, Bharadwaj, & Grover, 2003). To do this, the CIO must now act as an external boundary spanner(Katz & Kahn 1966, Aiken & Hage 1972, Tushman & Scanlan 1981) and interact with the external IS marketplace in order to remain up-to-date with strategic IS developments that may be relevant to their organisations (Gottschalk 2002, Smaltz, Sambamurthy, & Agarwal. 2006). Research, to date, has identified the importance of external peer networks in this regard (Watson 1990, Maier, Rainer, & Snyder, 1997, Pawlowski & Robey 2004).

However, the IS management literature fails to elaborate on how CIOs actually interact with external peers. A review of the wider literature relating to executive boundary spanning and interactions with peers in external networks, suggests that, for top management executives, such as the CIO, external interactions with peers are indeed by far the most important due to a number of key factors such as: the often equivocal or ambiguous nature of many of the strategic issues facing top management (Hambrick & Mason 1984, Daft, Lengel, & Trevino, 1987, Geletkanycz & Hambrick 1997) and therefore the need to create a shared understanding with other peers regarding the problems and issues facing them (Daft, Lengel, & Trevino,. 1987, Krauss & Fussell 1990, Wenger 1998, Carlile 2004, Malhotra & Majchrzak 2004); the dangers of delegating such sensitive inquiries to subordinates (Daft, Lengel, & Trevino, 1987); and the perceived value of face-to-face and ongoing interactions with peers in external network situations (Mintzberg 1973).

In addition, this literature also suggests that such external peer networks can often act as a support mechanism, sounding board and a barometer for gauging success (Wenger & Snyder 2000, Cross, Rice, & Parker, 2001, Ibarra & Hunter 2007). However, again this body of literature fails to clarify exactly how top management executives, such as CIOs, actually interact with peers via contacts in external networks. Therefore, this research study set out to explore how CIOs interact with external peer networks. The research setting chosen for this inquiry was the Irish Private Sector, and specifically the focus was on CIOs in the financial services, hi-tech, telecommunications and airline industries.

CHOOSING AN INTERPRETIVE RESEARCH PARADIGM

Before attempting any research inquiry, it is important that the researcher clarify their view of the nature of reality and therefore how we, as researchers, look at the world, obtain knowledge and make sense of it (Hirschheim & Klein 1992). At the core of this choice of research paradigm are the concepts of *ontology* and *epistemology* (Guba & Lincoln 1994). *Ontology* relates to the nature of reality and "what is assumed to exist", that is, the nature of the basic building blocks that make up the phenomena or objects being investigated (Iivari, Hirschheim, & Klein. 1998). Ontology questions whether the "reality" to be investigated exists external to the individual or is a product of the individual's consciousness (Burrell & Morgan 1979).

Epistemology is concerned with assumptions regarding the grounds for knowledge and about how the researcher might understand the world and communicate this as knowledge to others (Burrell & Morgan, 1979). Epistemology deals with such questions as whether knowledge can be identified objectively with precision and certitude "positivism" or whether knowledge is fashioned by the human consciousness "interpretivism" (Crotty 2003). Within the interpretivism viewpoint

social "meaning" cannot be described as being truly objective as would be the case with positivism. Social knowledge and meaning are seen to be "constructed" or interpreted by individuals based on their *frame of reference*, that is, their perceptions, experiences and understandings of the social world they occupy (Crotty 2003).

The researcher decided to choose an interpretivist research paradigm to support this research study for the following reasons: First, the aim of this research study was to explore and develop theory regarding how CIOs interact with external peer networks. Such external peer networks, by their very nature, tend to be based on a series of complex social interactions and relationships between the individual parties (Brown & Duguid 1991, Ibarra 1993, Wenger 1998, Ibarra & Hunter 2007) that tend to lead to a socially constructed worldview (Berger & Luckman 1967), local to that particular community, which reflects its shared knowledge, values, meanings, assumptions, beliefs and practices (Brown & Duguid 1991).

Therefore, the researcher has chosen an interpretivist perspective (Burrell & Morgan 1979), which seeks to make sense of such interactions and relationships, by fitting them into a "purposeful set of individual aims and a social structure of meanings" (Chua 1986, p. 614). Second, the extant literature relating to CIO interactions with external peer networks appears limited. Often an interpretivist research paradigm is a more suitable approach to take in cases where the aim of the study is the inductive development of new theory, rather than the testing of existing theories or hypotheses (Saunders, Lewis, & Thornhill, 2003, Sarantakos 2005).

Third, it has been suggested that it is not sufficient to study just the objective artefacts available from such external peer networks (Berger & Luckman, 1967, Reich & Benbasat, 2000) (such as membership lists, promotional documentation, research information, conference proceedings, and plans on evolving technologies) if one is to understand what is actually happening in these settings. One should also look to "investigate the contents of players' minds, their beliefs, attitudes and understanding of these artefacts" (Reich & Benbasat, 2000, p. 83). Consequently, it has been suggested that an interpretive research paradigm would again enable the better exploration of the underlying meanings, contexts and processes involved in such interactions (Miles & Huberman, 1984).

Fourth, whilst it has been argued that the positivist research paradigm may indeed enable a focus on the fact that individuals within a research study have interacted with each other, it often fails to consider the questions of *how* and *why* they may have interacted (Trauth 2001). However, an interpretivist research paradigm, can often better enable the researcher to gain deeper insights into what is actually happening (Kaplan & Duchon 1988, Chen & Hirschheim 2004) and thus "get at the why of the information sharing behaviour and the mechanics of how, within a particular context" (Trauth, 2001, p. 7).

Finally, it has been suggested that the personal preferences of the researcher can and should be allowed to influence the selection of a research paradigm (Creswell 1994). The background of the lead researcher, as a former CIO himself, gave him important insights into the role of the CIO and their interactions within this industry context. This, it has been suggested, can greatly assist with understanding the meanings and actions of the individuals involved by providing a rich source of contextualisation for the interpretation of the data (Klein & Myers 1999). However, that being said, the researcher also needs to recognise the responsibility to be fully aware, throughout the research process, of the implications of his/her own background and be aware of the dangers of potential biases, when undertaking such a research study (Klein & Myers 1999, Weber 2004).

CHOOSING GROUNDED THEORY

Methodology provides the link between the researcher's chosen research paradigm and the execution of the research study. Therefore, "*what* [author's emphasis] one wants to learn determines *how* [author's emphasis] one should go about learning it" (Trauth, 2001, p. 4). What was needed was a methodological approach to research which was in sympathy with an interpretivist stance and that could enable the inductive development of theory focused on understanding the specific activities of CIOs within these external peer networks. The four main methodological approaches commonly used in support of an interpretivist research paradigm within the field of IS research are: 1) Action Research; 2) Ethnography; 3) Case Study and; 4) GT. However, in reality, no single one of these approaches is appropriate in all research cases (Benbasat, Goldstein, & Mead, 1987). Therefore, before selecting GT as the appropriate research methodology, a number of specific issues in relation to the nature of the research question, needed to be addressed (Orlikowski, 1993). These include theoretical expectations of the study; focus on underlying processes; and contextual setting.

Theoretical Expectations of the Study

The primary aim of this research study was to build a theory grounded in real-world data relating to the phenomenon of how CIOs interact with external peer networks, rather than to just test or validate existing theories (Glaser & Strauss 1967, Goulding 2002, Charmaz 2006). Equally, the focus was not on the development of rich descriptions, based on the data, as would be the case for Ethnography, but the analysis and abstraction of substantive theory, related to the specifics of the research situation, where the role of the researcher is central to the interpretation of the data (Glaser & Strauss 1967, Martin & Turner 1986, Strauss & Corbin 1990, Goulding 2002, Charmaz 2006). GT, which is an inductive theory development methodology, will enable the development of new theory, that is "grounded" in the empirical data, to emerge directly from the experiences, accounts and artefacts surrounding the individual CIOs operating within these external peer networks (Glaser & Strauss 1967, Martin & Turner 1986, Goulding 2002).

In addition, GT is also often seen to be the most appropriate research methodology to adopt in such situations where little extant theory, directly relating to the area under research, already exists (Orlikowski 1993, Goulding 2002, Urquhart, Lehmann, & Myers, 2010).

Focus on Underlying Processes

At the core of these external peer networks are the operation of a series of complex social interactions, processes and relationships between the individual parties (Ibarra 1993, Wenger 1998, Ibarra & Hunter 2007). Therefore, whatever research methodology is chosen needs to be able to address the processes inherent in such interactions between CIOs. GT, as a research methodology, is well suited to "the generation of theories of process, sequence, and change pertaining to organizations, positions and social interaction" (Glaser and Strauss 1967, p. 114). In addition, GT tends to be more suitable to the exploration of micro-level processes and is therefore seen to be more suitable when used "to explore the interpretations and emotions of different individuals and groups living through the same processes" (Langley 1999, p. 700).

Contextual Setting

These external peer networks of CIOs operate within the context of the Irish IS marketplace. It

is important therefore, that the wider contextual issues relating to this particular social setting are captured in order to gain a full and holistic understanding of the phenomenon (Martin & Turner, 1986, Orlikowski, 1993). GT is particularly suited to the study of managerial processes, as it enables the capture of the contextual complexity surrounding such processes. An emergent theory is therefore able to provide both a holistic view of the processes involved and also to be of particular relevance to the practitioner community, as it is contextually based and grounded in the empirical data (Glaser, 1992; Locke, 2001).

METHODOLOGY OF GROUNDED THEORY

The concept of GT was first presented by Glaser and Strauss in their book *The Discovery of Grounded Theory* (1967), and was based on their extensive work in the fields of sociology and nursing (Goulding 2002, Urquhart & Fernandez 2013). The approach to GT was further developed by the authors in a series of subsequent publications (Glaser 1978, Strauss and Corbin 1990, Glaser 1992, Glaser 1998, Strauss and Corbin 1998, Glaser 2001, Glaser 2002, Glaser 2005). GT has its roots in symbolic interactionism (Locke 2001, Goulding 2002, Charmaz 2006). Symbolic interactionism assumes that individuals engage in a world which requires reflexive and thoughtful interaction, rather than just responses to environmental conditions. Here, people are seen to be purposeful in their actions and will act and react to environmental cues, objects and others, according to the meaning they hold for the individuals concerned (Goulding 2002).

The principle underlying symbolic interactionism is that people come to understand collective social definitions through the very process of socialisation (Goulding 2002) and therefore, "with whom, with what and how one interacts becomes a major determinant in how one perceives and defines reality" (Kendall, 1999, p. 744). The methodology of GT has been described as "a general methodology of analysis linked with data collection that uses a systematically applied set of methods to generate an inductive theory about a substantive area" (Glaser, 1992, p. 16). The emphasis within the GT approach is, therefore, on the systematic collection, recording and analysis of data, with a view to the inductive development of theory relevant to the substantive area under consideration (Charmaz 2000, Douglas 2003, Matavire & Brown 2013).

The focus within GT is on a systematic approach to data collection, handling and analysis within the research study (Douglas 2003). This systematic approach is based on a number of key concepts (Glaser and Strauss 1967) including the inductive nature of theory development; theoretical sensitivity; theoretical sampling; the constant comparison method of data analysis; theoretical saturation; and theoretical memos.

The Inductive Nature of Theory Development

The basic aim of GT is the inductive generation of theory from empirical data, rather than the verification of existing theory (Glaser & Strauss 1967). This process of theory development, within GT, is based on data being systematically collected in the field from interviews, observation and the inspection of secondary documentation sources (Goulding 2002, Douglas 2003). Strauss and Corbin suggest that the theory that develops should be based on a set of relationships within the data that offer a plausible explanation of the phenomenon under study (Strauss & Corbin 1994). Such theory, therefore, inductively "emerges" from that data, rather than being based on any *a priori* theory or perspectives (Glaser & Strauss 1967).

This emphasis on theory generation implies that the focus is not just on providing a rich description of the data, as would be the case with Ethnography (Werner & Schoepfle, 1987), but on

theory that has been developed by the conceptualisation and abstraction of theoretical concepts from the empirical data (Glaser 2001). Such theory development is not speculative in nature, but emerges and develops as part of the research process. Indeed, Glaser and Strauss (1967, p. 6) have suggested that "generating a theory from the data means that most hypotheses and concepts not only come from the data, but are systematically worked out in relation to the data during the course of the research". In addition, theories so generated are substantive in nature, in that they relate specifically to the area of research only.

Theoretical Sensitivity

Charmaz (2006, p. 135) has stated that the process of theorising involves "seeing possibilities, establishing connections and asking questions". Theoretical sensitivity refers to the ability of the researcher to think constantly about the data in conceptual terms (Douglas 2003), so that he/she "can conceptualise and formulate a theory as it emerges from the data" (Glaser & Strauss 1967, p. 46). Glaser suggests that the first step in developing theoretical sensitivity is for the researcher to enter the field with as few predetermined theoretical ideas as possible, especially logically deduced prior hypothesis, which could "contaminate" (Glaser 1992, p. 31) or restrict him/her to looking only for concepts identifiable or associated with existing theories (Glaser & Strauss 1967, Glaser 1978).

Theoretical Sampling

Under GT, the evolving process of data collection is controlled not by statistical sampling concerns, but by the requirements of the emerging theory (Glaser and Strauss 1967). Beyond the initial data collection efforts, which are focused on individuals or groups who it is believed will offer the opportunity to "maximise the possibilities of obtaining data" most relevant to the research

(Glaser 1978, p. 45), it is the emerging theory that decides or points to where further data collection efforts should be directed (Glaser & Strauss 1967). At all times, in line with the concept of constant comparison, the researcher should look to sample data that suggests both similarities and differences to the data already collected. Glaser and Strauss (1967) believe that various sources of data, such as interview, observation or documentary sources can give the researcher different views or perspectives on the emerging theory.

The Constant Comparison Method of Data Analysis

Data collection and analysis are not seen to be separate and distinct stages of theory development within GT. This is contrary to the common process seen in logico-deductive type research studies where there is a clear "linear progression from theory to data to analysis to interpretation" (Martin & Turner 1986, p. 150). In GT the process of data collection, coding and analysis is essentially non-linear in nature (Martin and Turner 1986, Pandit 1996). Glaser and Strauss (1967) have suggested that theory development is based on the constant comparison and analysis of newly gathered data with already emerging theoretical categories[1], so as to constantly build and refine these developing categories. This process of constantly comparing newly gathered data with emerging categories is continued until the core category, the category that accounts for most of the variation in the pattern of behaviour has been identified. The development of this core category is critical to the methodology of GT, as this is the category around which the emergent theory will revolve (Glaser & Strauss 1967).

Theoretical Saturation

Glaser and Strauss suggest that the researcher should continue to seek data regarding elements of the emerging theory, looking out for similarities and differences, until they reach theoretical saturation (Glaser & Strauss 1967). Theoretical saturation is defined as the point at which no new data relating to the underlying categories, or the properties of the emerging theory, can be found by the continued collection of data (Locke 2001). At this point, the individual elements of the emerging theory are seen to be "theoretically saturated", and no further data collection regarding these elements of theory is required (Glaser & Strauss 1967).

Theoretical Memos

The on-going writing of memos during the research process is a central part of the methodology of GT (Glaser, 1978). Indeed, Glaser has suggested that without using memos to record observations, insights and developing theoretical perspectives, the researcher is, in fact, not doing GT (Glaser, 1978). The process of writing memos, as data is collected and analysed, helps to clarify what is actually happening in the field (Charmaz, 2006). They are essentially a way of capturing evolving categories and ideas throughout the research process in an orderly fashion (Goulding, 2002). These evolving categories, developed via the process of the on-going writing of memos, can help direct the researcher in their theoretical sampling efforts to further the development of theory (Glaser 1978).

PRACTICAL APPLICATION OF GROUNDED THEORY

The focus of the researcher, using GT, is on the building of theory from the ground, often in an area that has received little or no attention to date (Goulding 2002). The traditional research process tends to be theory-driven and linear in nature (Flick 2002). However, with GT, theories emerge from the data, and the process of data collection, coding and analysis are undertaken in a cyclical and interconnected manner (Glaser & Strauss

1967). The cyclical nature of the process of GT, especially in relation to data collection, data ordering and data analysis, is seen to be one of the strengths of this approach, "because it forces the researcher to permanently reflect on the whole research process and on particular steps in light of the other steps" (Flick, 2002, p. 100). Pandit (1996) has identified five phases to the building of theory, via the adoption of GT. The phases include research approach; data collection; data ordering; data analysis; and literature comparison.

Research Approach

GT suggests that the researcher, whilst he/she may have formulated an overall research question, should not enter the field with any preconceived theory or hypotheses which could restrict their ability to view the emerging data or "force" the direction of such inquiry (Glaser, 1978). However, this does not mean that a researcher, adopting GT, should start with a "totally blank sheet" (Goulding, 2002, p. 55). The researcher's background assumptions and disciplinary perspectives (Charmaz, 2006) can be used to assist in developing a "partial framework of 'local' concepts" (Glaser & Strauss 1967, p. 45) to give him "a beginning foothold on his research" (Glaser & Strauss 1967, p. 45). Concepts such as "the role of the CIO", "CIO Context", "CIO Challenges" and "CIO Networking" were used in the design of the Interview Guide supporting the data collection efforts[2]. In addition, it has been suggested that such background assumptions and disciplinary perspectives can help the researcher to become "*theoretically sensitive* [authors' emphasis], so that he/she can conceptualise and formulate a theory as it emerges from the data" (Glaser & Strauss 1967, p. 46).

However, Glaser (1992) cautions the researcher against spending time undertaking prior reviews of extant literature and theories, as he believes that they can often "contaminate" the disposition of the researcher on entering the field. This view

is supported by Goulding, who in turn, has suggested that to avoid specific theories providing a "prior disposition, whether conscious of it or not, of testing such existing work rather than developing uncoloured insights specifically pertinent to the area of study" (Goulding, 2002, p. 56), the researcher should attempt to enter the field as soon as possible to start the data collection process.

Data Collection

Overall, the direction of the data collection and the sampling of data, within a GT research study, is "*controlled* [authors' emphasis] by the emerging theory" (Glaser & Strauss, 1967, p. 45). At the centre of this process of data sampling is the principle of *Theoretical Sampling* (Glaser & Strauss, 1967). Theoretical sampling is described as the "purposeful selection of a sample according to the developing categories and emerging theory" (Coyle 1997, cited in Goulding (2002, p. 66). However, in terms of starting the GT investigation, it has been suggested that the researcher should "go to the most obvious places and the most likely informants in search of information" (Goulding, 2002, p. 67), and that such candidates, where possible, should exhibit only minimal differences (Glaser & Strauss 1967).

With this in mind, the lead researcher, using his own knowledge as a former CIO, and following a review of the list of potential CIOs, identified nine CIOs for interview, as part of Phase I of the data collection and analysis stage of the research. The purpose of interviewing these CIOs was to start the process of identifying some basic categories and their properties (Goulding 2002). It was known to the researcher that many of these CIOs had active and long standing involvement in a number of the external peer networks operating in Ireland, and that therefore this might help to reflect minimal differences within the group (Glaser & Strauss 1967).

In Phase II of the data collection and analysis stage of this research study, once basic categories had begun to emerge, attempts were made to identify CIOs who might have contrasting experiences of interacting with external peer networks in Ireland. Whilst this group of seven CIOs continued to have "enough features in common" (Glaser & Strauss, 1967, p. 50) with the first group to continue to make them relevant to the study, they also had a number of important differences. Specifically, this group included a number of CIOs, such as IP01[3], IP15, IP09 and IP13 who had spent significant parts of their careers, to date, outside Ireland and were therefore potentially not as deeply integrated as many of the CIOs interviewed in Phase I, into the existing Irish based external peer networks. In addition, IP15 and IP13 held the role of CIO in conjunction with wider responsibilities for overall organisational operations as "Director of Operations".

The remaining three CIOs in Phase II were chosen based on feedback from other CIOs, who had already been interviewed, which had suggested that they could be *very interesting* and worthwhile to interview, and could potentially hold views and perspectives on external peer networks that might be different from others already interviewed. The purpose of Phase II was the theoretical saturation of the emerging categories. Theoretical saturation has been described as the point at which "gathering fresh data no longer sparks new theoretical insights, nor reveals new properties" of the emerging categories (Charmaz, 2006, p. 113).

The final stage of the data collection and analysis stage of the research study, Phase III, consisted of review meetings with four of the already interviewed CIOs. This stage was undertaken to ensure that the interpretation of the data made by the researcher had been an honest representation of the participants' accounts (Goulding, 1998), that there were no fundamental gaps in the emerging theory, and that the emerging GT did indeed have "grab" for the CIOs as practitioners (Glaser, 1978, p. 4). In essence, "grab" means that the emerging theory is seen by the practitioner to be

useful, relevant and meaningful to them in their roles (Glaser 1978). Following each of these final interviews, an e-mail was sent thanking the CIO for their time and input, and requesting sign off. In return, the CIOs replied, outlining their key thoughts relating to the emerging theoretical roles and their view on its relevance and value to them as CIOs. Equally, as each of these interviews was also taped, they were reviewed for additional comments and observations relating to the emerging theory.

Data Ordering

Researchers attempt to order their data, by way of "conceptual ordering" (Strauss & Corbin, 1990, p. 19), in an attempt to make more sense out of it, by organising it "according to their properties and dimensions and then using description to elucidate those categories" (Strauss & Corbin, 1990, p. 19). Pandit suggests that a common approach to data ordering is to order the data chronologically so as to facilitate easier analysis and examination of the underlying processes (Pandit 1996).

Data Analysis

Data collection and data analysis are not seen as being separate and distinct stages of theory development, within GT. The process of data collection and analysis is viewed as being essentially recurring and non-linear in nature (Martin & Turner 1986, Pandit 1996). Lehmann (2001) describes the process of GT as a "spiral that starts by collecting 'slices of data' in the substantive area of inquiry, which are then codified and categorised in a continuous process that moves toward saturation and results in the theoretical densification of concepts represented by the substantive theory" (cited in Fernandez 2004, p. 48). Glaser and Strauss (1967) have described these 'slices of data' as "different views or vantage points from which to understand a category and to develop its properties" (Glaser & Strauss 1967, p. 65). In the case of this research study, it was the series of interviews with the different CIOs and supporting secondary data, as described in earlier sections, which offered the opportunity to garner such 'slices of data'. At the heart of this recurring process is the concept of *constant comparison* (Glaser & Strauss 1967, Glaser 1978).

The purpose of the constant comparison approach, within GT, is constantly to compare newly acquired data with existing data and emerging categories, gradually raising the level of abstraction from descriptive levels to higher order theoretically conceptual categories, with the purpose of developing an all-encompassing supreme or 'core category' (Goulding 2002, p. 88). The core category is described by Glaser as "the 'main theme'….the main concern or problem for the people in the setting, for what sums up in a pattern of behaviour the substance of what is going on in the data" (Glaser, 1978, p. 94).

GT has its own coding techniques to help provide standardisation and structure to this analysis process. The coding techniques used within the *Glaserian* version of GT are: *Open Coding*, which is the process of breaking down or fragmenting the data into distinct units of meaning (Glaser, 1992); *Selective Coding*, which takes the conceptual categories developed by open coding and through a process of category integration and refinement, develops a central or "core category" (Glaser, 1978, p. 61); and *Theoretical Coding* which, with the assistance of "coding families" or theoretical concepts, sets out to "weave the fractured story back together again" (Glaser, 1978, p. 72), into a theory that is "grounded" in the data (Glaser and Strauss 1967). The aim of data coding and analysis is to arrive at systematically derived core category that becomes the focal concept that contributes towards theoretical development (Douglas 2003). This process of coding is undertaken, in conjunction with the literature, in order to ensure that the research remains parsimonious (Goulding 2002).

Open Coding: Open coding is the process of breaking down or "fracturing the data" (Glaser, 1978, p. 55) into distinct "units of meaning"

(Goulding 2002, p. 76) or "incidents" (Glaser & Strauss 1967, Glaser 1978). Noble describes an incident as "an event, action or participant's statement that was given emphasis by the participant through a change of voice or body language, or conveyed a sense of the participant's attitude, feeling or experience" (2002, p. 376). The first step in this process of open coding is the line-by-line analysis of text looking for "key words or phrases which connect the informant's account to the experience under investigation" (Goulding 2002, p. 76). Charmaz has suggested that through open coding you "*define* [author's emphasis] what is happening in the data and begin to grapple with what it means…..yet it is *our* [author's emphasis] view: we choose the words that constitute our codes. Thus we define what we see as significant in the data and describe what we think is happening" (2006, p. 46-47).

Such a process can result in the development of numerous "initial codes" within a piece of text. The names placed on these initial codes can be either "constructed" by the researcher (Charmaz, 2006, p. 47), based on the "imagery or meaning they evoke" (Strauss & Corbin 1998, p. 105), or can be taken directly from the interviewee's own description of the event. Such latter codes are referred to as "*in vivo codes*" (Glaser & Strauss 1967).

Shortly after the completion of each CIO interview, the tape recording was transcribed verbatim, by the researcher. Then the researcher undertook the process of open coding, by analysing the individual transcript for "initial codes". Following this, each "incident", or piece of text, with a distinct meaning, from within the transcript, was then transferred into an initial "Concept Card" and labelled with an overall descriptive title (Turner 1981, Martin & Turner 1986, Noble 2002). The use of Concept Cards in the process of the development of conceptual categories, within GT, was developed by Turner (1981) and Martin and Turner (1986). In terms of naming these concept cards, Turner (cited in Locke, 2001, p. 71) suggests that their names can be "short, fanciful or fairly long-winded. It is essential, however, that the name provide a good fit for the data incident being scrutinised".

The coding of each interview transcript was completed, and in line with the principle of the constant comparative method of data analysis (Glaser & Strauss 1967), the newly developed incidents were compared with other initial codes and incidents, recorded on existing concept cards. This process of constantly comparing the codes and incidents looking for similarities and differences (Glaser & Strauss, 1967; Glaser 1978) led, over time, to the abstraction of a number of potential basic categories and their properties from within the data (Glaser 1978). This process of abstraction (Dey, 1999) was aided by asking some fundamental questions of the data. Key amongst these questions were (Glaser, 1978, p. 57) what is this data a study of?, what category do the incidents indicate?, and what is actually happening?

The creation of these basic categories, from within the data, was supported by the development of a second set of concept cards. Each of these new concept cards was based on the incidents and initial codes associated with the developing basic category (Martin and Turner 1986), and represented "some more general phenomenon"].

Selective Coding: Selective coding[4] is the second phase in the coding process. It is the process by which the researcher starts to identify and develop the most significant and/or frequent categories in order to "synthesise and explain larger segments of the data" (Charmaz, 2006, p. 57). The researcher does this, in the first instance, by identifying the most relevant categories from within the data and attempting to theoretically saturate these categories, and then by delimiting the theory generation and identifying the overall "core category" (Dey 1999). This is the one category that "is the main concern or problem for the people in the setting" (Glaser, 1978, p. 94) and is therefore capable of pulling together "all the strands in order to offer an explanation of the behaviour under study"

(Goulding 2002, p. 88). In the case of this research study, this meant focusing on those categories that were central to the CIO's interaction with external peer networks. Therefore, as the entire interview data had been coded, some of the initial concept cards, not related to the CIOs interaction with external peer networks, were effectively dropped or "selected out" (Locke, 2001, p. 79) at this stage of the process. This approach to selective coding, based on the evolving core category of "CIO Network Activity", led to the emergence of 104 basic categories and the development of 36 higher order categories, from within the data.

Theoretical Coding: Theoretical coding is the third and final stage of the process of analysis within GT, and is focused on weaving "the fractured story back together again", by the use of a selection of "coding families" (Glaser, 1978, p. 74). These families of theoretical codes are used to conceptualise how the emerging categories may relate to each other as "hypotheses to be integrated into a theory" (Charmaz 2006, p. 63). Thus they are used to develop "possible relationships between the categories" that have developed in the selective coding process, in order that the researcher "can tell an analytic story that has coherence" (Charmaz, 2006, p. 63). The development of the underlying "analytic story" or emerging GT, is supported by the researcher reviewing and comparing the extant literature in an attempt to both assist in the conceptualisation of the developing theory (Goulding, 2002) and also to help locate the emerging GT within the existing body of knowledge and therefore to "show its contribution" (Glaser, 1992, p. 33).

Glaser (1978) originally identified eighteen "coding families" to help sensitise and assist the researcher in specifying possible relationships that might exist between the categories developed by the selective coding process, and to bring an overall coherence to the emerging theory (Charmaz, 2006). In later publications, he added further sets of theoretical codes to this list (Glaser, 1998; Glaser, 2005). The researcher can choose to use one of these "coding families" or another coding model, such as Weber's "Ideal Types" (Weber, 1962) to link the developing categories to the core category in such a way as to develop a theory that both accounts for most of the variation in behaviour and can be described in terms of a parsimonious theory (Glaser, 1978, p.61).

The researcher decided to adopt Weber's concept of "Ideal Types" (Weber 1962) to act as a theoretical coding lens to help with the construction of a typology of distinct patterns of CIO network activity. Indeed, Alasuutari has suggested that constructivist approaches to theory development should provide frames or patterns from which to view the multiple realities that can exist in any situation (1996, cited in Charmaz 2006, p. 128). Ideal types, Weber had suggested, are not so much descriptions of objects that exist in the real world, but are instruments which the social scientist creates, based on their own perspective, for the purpose of investigating the social world (Weber, 1949, p. 111, cited in Eidlin, 2006). Blaikie has also suggested that the use of the Ideal Type model enables the "social scientist to construct a hypothetical ideal type of meaning that might account for the action under consideration" (Blaikie, 2007, p. 91).

Such an approach is in sympathy with Charmaz's (2006) constructivist approach to GT, where she states "we are not passive receptacles into which data are poured" and "how you collect data affects *which* phenomena you will see, *how*, *where* and *when* you will view them, and *what* sense you will make of them [author's emphasis]" (2006, p. 15). The construction of an "Ideal Type" typology is the result of a grouping process, that, based on a number of defined properties, sets out to map the emerging categories to an overall typology of "Ideal Type" roles (Kluge, 2000).

Literature Comparison

Glaser has cautioned researchers to be careful regarding when to consult the extant literature in the "substantive area under study" (Glaser, 1992, p. 31), so that it does not contaminate their thinking and approach, or block their creativity in the early stages of the research study (Glaser & Strauss 1967; Glaser, 1978; Glaser 1992). He has suggested that such a strategy of leaving comparisons with extant literature until later in the research process "maximises the avoidance of pre-empting, preconceived concepts which may easily detract from the full freedom to generate concepts that fit and are relevant when initially coding and analysing the data as it is collected" (Glaser, 1992, p. 35). In fact, in his view, the extant literature should only be addressed "when the theory seems sufficiently grounded in the core variable and in the emerging integration of categories and properties, then the researcher may begin to review the literature in the substantive field and relate the literature to his own work" (Glaser, 1992, p. 32).

In addition, the overall approach to the literature review, presented in a GT study, "differs from the traditional model" (Locke, 2001, p. 121) in that, on the one hand, the literature is "sometimes integrated into the presentation of the model in what is usually the 'findings' section of the manuscript" (Locke, 2001, p. 121) and on the other, the set of literature selected for the literature review is presented *"in relation to your GT* [author's emphasis]" (Adam & Fitzgerald, 2000, Charmaz, 2006, p. 164), so as to "show where their ideas illuminate your theoretical categories and how your theory extends, transcends or challenges dominant ideas in your field" (Charmaz. 2006, p. 165). Therefore, the literature is used, in the

GT approach, to support the emerging data and the conceptualisation of theoretical constructs (Goulding, 2002; Heath, 2006).

CHOOSING TECHNOLOGY TOOLS TO SUPPORT GT RESEARCH

Collecting, analysing and coding efforts in support of GT research can be carried out by the researcher either manually or with the assistance of computer software, such as NVivo® or NUD*IST®. Such software packages have become common today amongst many researchers using qualitative data (Goulding, 1999; Bryman, 2004). However, their use has led to "mixed feelings" (Flick, 2002, p. 343) amongst the research community regarding their need, suitability and advantages over manual processes (Richards & Richards 1994, Saunders, Lewis, & Thornhill, 2003). Whilst undoubtedly helping to automate and speed up the coding process and providing complex ways of looking at and presenting the data, concerns have been raised around such key issues as loosing closeness with the data (Gilbert 2002); the potential for de-contextualising the data (Bryman, 2004); and the dangers of qualitative data being analysed quantitatively (Bryman, 2004).

In addition, it has been clearly noted that "the thinking, judging, deciding, interpreting etc., are still done by the researcher. The computer does not make conceptual decisions, such as which words or themes are important to focus on, or which step to take next. These intellectual tasks are still left entirely to the researcher" (Tesch, 1991, p. 25-26). Ultimately, therefore the researcher needs to be clear regarding the role such software will play in meeting their specific needs, as such software packages can often be seen as being "quite seductive and give the researcher a false impression that they are dealing with neatly packaged variables" (Mason, 2002, p. 161).

In the case of this GT study, the researcher decided to collect, analyse and code manually all the data, making use only of universally available Microsoft Office®[5] products. He used Word ® to support the all the initial collecting of transcripts, the writing of memos and the open coding efforts. Excel ® was then adopted to support the more complex coding activities of selective and theoretical coding. He adopted this pragmatic approach to the use of "appropriate" technology tools in support of GT research for two key reasons. First, he was conscious of Glaser's call for the researcher to "do his own coding" (Glaser, 1978, p. 58) no matter how "painstaking and time consuming" this process was (Glaser, 1978, p. 58). Second, as a novice researcher, he felt that the best way to really get to know the data would be to do all the coding himself manually, rather than rely on a software package that, whilst potentially helpful, may not allow him to fully get to grips with the process of data analysis.

ISSUES RELATED TO GROUNDED THEORY IN IS RESEARCH

This section sets out to look at some of the key practical issues related to the use of GT in research studies. The key observations discussed here include how to evaluate the "value" of the research produced; choosing between the different variants of GT; and the role of extant literature in GT.

Evaluating the Value of the Research Produced

It has been suggested that interpretive based GT research cannot be properly evaluated on the positivistic basis of validity, but instead should be judged on the basis of "*trustworthiness*" (Lincoln and Guba 2000). The reason put forward for this is that since the two worldviews of positivism and interpretivism are incommensurable, different sets of criteria need to be developed for addressing issues of rigour and quality (Gasson, 2004). Gasson (2004), for instance, (based on the work of Miles and Huberman (1994) and Lincoln and Guba (2000)) has suggested the following four criteria for rigour and quality which should be applied to interpretive based GT research. They include confirmability, dependability/auditability, internal consistency, and transferability.

- **Confirmability:** The findings made by any GT based research study should represent the situation being researched, rather than the beliefs, pet theories or biases of the researcher (Glaser 1978). In terms of this research study, the researcher at all times attempted to minimise the potential for his own views, experiences, assumptions and personal interests to impact on his interpretations of the data and consequent construction of the emergent theory. Indeed, it has been suggested that the best way to deal with this is for the researcher to undertake a constant, explicit process of reflexivity, where all key assumptions, biases and concepts adopted are written down, by way of memos, so that their implications on the generation of theory can be seen (Gasson 2004).

- **Dependability/Auditability:** This suggests that the way a study is conducted should be consistent across time, researchers and analysis techniques, such that another researcher, if they were to undertake a similar research study, within the same substantive area, using the same approach and procedures would potentially see the emergence of a theory that, whilst not necessarily exactly the same, would similarly reflect the underlying data. The constructivist approach to GT, advocated by the likes of Charmaz (2006), suggests that "we *construct* [author's emphasis] our grounded theories through our past and present involvements and interactions with people, perspectives, and research practices" (Charmaz 2006, p. 10) and therefore the

theory that emerges from any specific research study will reflect these experiences and dispositions.

However, Gasson (2004) suggests that a useful way of ensuring dependability is by making explicit the processes through which the theory is derived throughout the research process. With this in mind, the researcher has, at all times throughout this research study, attempted to make explicit the approach and processes adopted by him, so as to provide a clear and concise audit trail. Overall therefore, every effort was made to explain and expose the approach adopted by the researcher in this study.

- **Internal Consistency:** To achieve internal consistency, it is suggested that the researcher must explain how and from what data the theoretical constructs are derived, and also whose perspectives these constructs reflect. This involves communicating with other researchers, on an ongoing basis throughout the research study, the evolving GT process of theory development. In the case of the current study, the researcher was actively supported by a number of other GT researchers within the School. The resulting "support mechanism", he believes, helped him to ensure that his research efforts maintained internal consistency and enabled the successful development of an emerging theory, within an existing body of GT experience.

- **Transferability:** This refers to how far the researcher can make claims for the general application of the theory. It is suggested that the researcher must make explicit the extent to which the theory generated is specific to the unique area of study. The emergent theory developed within this research study is substantive rather than formal in nature, that is, it is "grounded in research on one particular substantive area" (Glaser

& Strauss, 1967, p. 79) and therefore might only apply to that particular area of inquiry. However, that is not to say that the emergent theory cannot have "important general implications and relevance" for a wider area of inquiry (Glaser & Strauss, 1967, p. 79).

Choosing between the Different Variants of Grounded Theory

Glaser believed that the more prescriptive approach to GT, advocated by Strauss and Corbin, would lead to an emphasis on deduction and verification, rather than induction, which was seen to be the original purpose of GT (Glaser 1992). Glaser argued that the role of GT was to generate hypotheses, not to test them (Dey 1999). Equally, Glaser suggested that one of the key features of GT was its ability to explain "basic social processes" (Glaser, 1978, p. 93), which he explained involved the use of the constant comparative technique of data analysis to connect categories to the emerging theory, rather than just to provide rich description for such categories (Glaser, 2001).

This split between the original authors has led to the subsequent development of two separate schools of GT implementation approaches, *"Glaserian"* and *"Straussian"* within the research community, each advocating their own separate approach to undertaking GT based research studies (Stern, 1994;' Bryant, 2009). For this reason, Urquhart (2001) has suggested that it is important for the researcher to clearly outline, up front, which version of GT they are using. For this particular research study, the Glaserian approach to the use of GT procedures was chosen by this researcher as being the most appropriate version. This decision was made on the basis of two key factors, namely the aim the research study, and the most appropriate coding and analysis approach.

As the aim of this research study was to inductively develop a new substantive theory, grounded in the empirical data, it was felt, by the researcher, that the approach to "conceptualisation offered by Glaser" was more relevant, than the emphasis on the "full description of Strauss and Corbin" (Fernandez, 2004, p. 46). Equally, it was felt by the researcher, who had had some experience of other data analysis techniques, as part of a previous role as a data modelling analyst, that the techniques, such as "axial coding" and the "conditional matrix" advocated by Strauss and Corbin, whilst providing some measure of structure by using a pre-determined model by which to connect categories and their related properties (Kendall, 1999), were, in the end, unnecessarily prescriptive in nature, and could indeed lead to the forcing of preconceived notions onto the data (Glaser 1992). Glaser had suggested that it was more important to let the conceptualisation lead the analysis "where the analysis and interpretation are assured of being grounded in that data", rather than using the axial coding paradigm where there is the danger that the researcher will only see "what will fit into a predetermined conceptual plan" (Kendall, 1999, p. 748).

In fact, the researcher did attempt to use axial coding at the start of the coding process, but found it unrewarding, formulaic and somewhat restrictive in nature (Melia 1996). Urquhart, who herself had had difficulty using the axial coding process, had stated that the axial coding approach, as outlined by Strauss and Corbin, "asks the researcher to examine the data for conditions, interactions among the actors, strategies and tactics, and consequences", but, "put simply, I found it difficult to apply the coding paradigm, and the relationships between codes and categories hard to discover" (Urquhart, 2001, p. 115). The alternative Glaserian approach, which relies on the constant comparative method as the approach adopted for constantly refining categories and developing relationships between categories, appeared to allow more freedom and flexibility to the researcher in the process of coding and conceptualisation, and therefore, in the ultimate development of theory from the empirical data (Charmaz, 2006).

As well as the differences between the two "schools" of GT outlined above, there have also been questions raised regarding the appropriate research paradigm supported by GT (Annells, 1996; Mills, Bonner, & Francis, 2006). It has been suggested that even though GT has a background in symbolic interactionism, it is inherently located within a positivist or post-positivist research paradigm (Annells, 1996; Charmaz, 2006). Indeed, the fact that the original authors talk in terms of the "discovery" of theory from the empirical data (Glaser & Strauss 1967), appears to suggest a more positivist view on the existence of such theory (Annells, 1996).

Consequently, this issue did cause some concern to the researcher when originally reviewing GT as the potential methodology of choice, as he had wished to undertake this research study from an interpretivist perspective. However, more recently, other academics with experience in GT have suggested that the positivist perspective does not necessarily have to be the case and that GT can indeed be adopted in a constructivist and interpretivist manner (Hughes & Wood-Harper 2000; Bryant 2002; Bryant 2003; Charmaz 2006). Charmaz (2006), for instance, has suggested that "neither data nor theories are discovered. Rather, we are part of the world we study and the data we collect. We *construct* [author's emphasis] our grounded theories through our past and present involvement and interactions with people, perspectives, and research practices" (Charmaz, 2006, p. 10).

Such a constructivist perspective suggests that "any theoretical rendering offers an *interpretive* [author's emphasis] portrayal of the studied world, not an exact picture of it" (Charmaz, 2006, p. 10). This constructivist viewpoint on the use of GT did appear to support the underlying theoretical perspective of the researcher. So it was decided that this research study should indeed adopt the Glaserian approach to GT, whilst at the same time, firmly locating itself within the interpretivist research paradigm, where any theory developed is recognised as an interpretation or construction of reality (Charmaz, 2006). Such an approach therefore enables the use of "basic GT guidelines with twenty-first century methodological assumptions" (Charmaz, 2006, p. 9).

The Role of Literature

The correct stage to involve the use of extant literature, relevant to the research topic, in the development of GT was also "disputed" (Charmaz 2006, p. 165). On the one hand, Glaser, advocated that "there is a need not to review any of the literature in the substantive area under study" prior to engagement in the field (Glaser, 1992, p. 31). This was, he suggested, so as not to contaminate, constrain or inhibit the researcher's analysis of the emerging theory, as he suggested that "it is hard enough to generate one's own concepts, without the added burden of contending with 'rich' derailments provided by the related literature" (Glaser, 1992, p. 31). On the other hand, Strauss and Corbin recommend that the researcher should indeed engage more proactively with the relevant literature from the beginning of the research process (Strauss & Corbin, 1990).

FUTURE DIRECTIONS

The researcher believes that it is important that future research will seek to extend and develop the current study. In particular, there are a number of further avenues of inquiry that can help to significantly develop and extend the current theoretical framework. These include extending the study to embrace other comparative groups; developing a quantitative analysis of roles; and developing a temporal process perspective.

Extending the Study to Embrace Other Comparative Groups

Extending the current study to investigate other comparative groups will help to "maximise the possibilities" (Glaser, 1978, p. 45) for obtaining similarities and differences between such comparative groups, thus deepening our understanding of how individuals interact with such external peer networks and thus enabling the theory to be further developed in a more formal manner. Specifically, two comparative groups could help to significantly extend the potential value of the extant theory. These include CIOs operating in other countries; and other senior officers operating at top management levels.

- **CIOs Operating in Other Countries:** The current study was confined to CIOs operating within Ireland, as it had been suggested that widening the research beyond a single country might only bring into play issues relating to different cultural norms and backgrounds (Preston, Karahanna, & Rowe, 2006). Indeed, feedback received from the CIOs interviewed as part of Phase III of the research did suggest that the incidence of specific roles, might differ if the study were to be carried out in a country other than Ireland. Indeed. Hofstede (2001) has suggested that cultural influences, such as the strength of the "power distance indicator" (PDI) for any nationality, can have a significant impact on how individuals perceive each other and on their relative openness to work together and build relationships. Therefore, a replication of the current research study with a similar group of CIOs and external peer networks, in another location may prove useful in further developing the extant theory in a way that clearly addresses potential cultural differences between nationalities.

- **Other Senior Officers Operating at Top Management Levels:** As stated above, external boundary spanning activities and interactions with external peers are common across a wide range of senior officers (Miles, Snow, & Pfeffer, 1974; Geletkanycz & Hambrick, 1997; McDonald & Westphal, 2003). However, again little is known about how, in fact, such groups actually interact with external peer networks. The current research has focused only on CIOs and therefore does not directly address the specific issues surrounding such other senior officers, for example, CEOs, COOs and CFO's.

The undertaking of further analysis focused on such groups of senior officers may or may not lead to a different set of roles being adopted in such external network situations. Therefore, in order to develop and extend the emergent theory beyond the bounds of the current substantive area, in a way that would make it more useful to a wider audience, it would be both beneficial and important that such a research study be replicated, in the first instance within Ireland, on groups of other senior officers, so as provide a direct comparison with the activities of CIOs.

Developing a Quantitative Analysis of Roles

The current study is focused on the development of a substantive theory relating to how CIOs interact with external peer networks. This theory has been developed within the narrow area of the current research focus, that being CIOs operating within the Irish Private Sector. Equally, the extant theory, as currently developed, does not suggest to what extent any or all of the roles are undertaken by individual CIOs. These two factors, the narrow area of the current research focus and the lack of knowledge available, to date, on any preferences between the roles, would suggest the opportunity to undertake a wider scale quantitative based study to research these issues. Such a large scale quantitative approach could help to identify differences in preferences for the roles amongst different specific groups of CIOs across different organisational types. This analysis would serve to significantly deepen our understanding of how CIOs, across a wider range of industries, actually interact with external peer networks.

Developing a Temporal Process Perspective

The current study did not adopt a temporal process perspective. Instead it adopted a cross-sectional view of the processes as currently undertaken by the CIOs operating within these external peer networks (Saunders, Lewis, & Thornhill, 2003). However, some researchers have suggested that without adopting such an orientation, there is always the danger that the researcher may have missed some of the rich historical and processual issues involved in the area of study, which have developed over time (Pettigrew, 1990). The key assumption behind a temporal process perspective is that social reality is not a steady state, but is dynamic and evolves over time. Therefore, it is only by studying process evolution over time that one can fully understand the true nature of such processes (Pettigrew, 1997). Such a temporal process perspective can help to identify and explain how contexts, incidents, activities and actions of individuals can impact on the development of specific roles over time (Pettigrew 1990).

CONCLUSION

Before deciding to adopt GT as the most suitable methodology, or for that matter, deciding to adopt an interpretivist stance to inquiry, it is important that the researcher is clear in both his/her onto-

logical and epistemological perspectives. Such views, as discussed above, should be driven both by the requirements of the research topic and by the underlying perspectives of the researcher on the world they wish to study.

This research study set out to explore how CIOs interact with external peers via network connections. Such external peer networks, by their very nature, tend to be based on a series of complex social interactions and relationships between the individual parties (Brown & Duguid, 1991; Ibarra, 1993; Wenger, 1998; Ibarra & Hunter, 2007) that tend to lead to a socially constructed worldview (Berger & Luckman 1967), local to that particular community, which reflects its shared knowledge, values, meanings, assumptions, beliefs and practices (Brown & Duguid 1991). In addition, as no previous theory existed, the methodology of GT was adopted, within an interpretivist perspective, to develop new theory. The research setting chosen was the Irish Private Sector, with a specific focus on organisations in the finance, hi-tech, telecoms and airline industries.

The chapter then went on to describe how a GT based approach to research should be carried out using a five stage approach, covering research approach, data collection, data ordering, data analysis and literature comparison. Whilst these steps were described as separate and distinct stages, in practice, there are, in fact, iterative and overlapping in nature. It is by constantly comparing and contrasting the emerging data using the coding techniques of open coding, selective coding and theoretical coding, that a theory that both accounts for the most of the variation in behaviour and can be described in terms of a parsimonious theory is developed (Glaser, 1978, p.61). In support of this theory development process, a pragmatic approach to the use of technology tools was adopted, one that enabled the researcher to both stay close to the data and to honour Glaser's call for the researcher to "do his own coding" (Glaser, 1978, p.58).

REFERENCES

Adam, F., & Fitzgerald, B. (2000). The Status of the IS Field:Historical Perspective and Practical Orientation. *Information Research, 5*(4), 13.

Aiken, M., & Hage, J. (1972). *Organizational Permeability, Boundary Spanners and Organizational Structure*. New Orleans, LA: American Sociological Association.

Alasuutari, P. (1996). Theorizing in Qualitative Research: A Cultural Studies Perspective. *Qualitative Inquiry, 2*(4), 371–384. doi:10.1177/107780049600200401

Annells, M. (1996). GTM: Philosophical Perspectives, Paradigms of Inquiry, and Postmodernism. *Qualitative Health Research, 6*(3), 379–393. doi:10.1177/104973239600600306

Benbasat, I., Goldstein, D. K., & Mead, M. (1987). The Case Research Strategy in Studies of IS. *Management Information Systems Quarterly, 11*(3), 369–386. doi:10.2307/248684

Berger, P., & Luckman, T. (1967). *The Social Construction of reality*. New York: Doubleday.

Blaikie, N. (2007). *Approaches to Social Enquiry*. Cambridge, MA: Polity Press.

Brown, J. S., & Duguid, P. (1991). Organizational Learning and Communities-of-Practice: Toward a Unified View of Working, Learning and Innovation. *Organization Science, 2*(1), 40–57. doi:10.1287/orsc.2.1.40

Bryant, A. (2002). Re-Grounding GT. *Journal of Information Technology Theory and Application, 4*(1), 25–42.

Bryant, A. (2003). "A Constructive/ist Response to Glaser" Forum Qualitative Sozialforschung/ Forum: Qualitative. *Social Research, 4*(1).

Bryant, A. (2009). "GT and Pragmatism: The Curious Case of Anselm Strauss" Forum Qualitative Sozialforschung/Forum: Qualitative. *Social Research, 10*(3).

Bryman, A. (2004). *Social Research Methods*. Oxford, UK: Oxford University Press.

Burrell, G., & Morgan, G. (1979). *Sociological Paradigms and Organisational Analysis*. London: Heinemann.

Carlile, P. (2004). Transferring, Translating, and Transforming: An Integrative Framework for Managing Knowledge across Boundaries. *Organization Science, 15*(5), 555–568. doi:10.1287/orsc.1040.0094

Charmaz, K. (2000). *GT: Objectivist and Constructivist Methods. In Handbook of Qualitative Research* (pp. 509–535). Thousand Oaks, CA: Sage.

Charmaz, K. (2006). *Constructing GT - A Practical Guide through Qualitative Analysis*. London: Sage.

Chen, W., & Hirschheim, R. (2004). A Paradigmatic and Methodological Examination of IS Research from 1991 to 2001. *IS Journal, 14*(3), 197–235.

Chua, W. F. (1986). Radical Developments in Accounting thought. *Accounting Review, 61*(4), 601–632.

Coyle, I. T. (1997). Sampling in Qualitative Research: Purposeful and Theoretical Sampling: Merging or Clear Boundaries? *Journal of Advanced Nursing*, *26*(3), 623–630. doi:10.1046/j.1365-2648.1997.t01-25-00999.x PMID:9378886

Creswell, J. W. (1994). *Research Design: Qualitative and Quantitative Approaches*. Thousand Oaks, CA: Sage.

Cross, R., Rice, R. E., & Parker, A. (2001). Information Seeking in Social Context: Structural Influences and Receipt of Information Benefits. *IEEE Transactions on Systems, Man, and Cybernetics*, *31*(4), 438–448. doi:10.1109/5326.983927

Crotty, M. (2003). *The Foundations of social Research*. London: Sage.

Daft, R., Lengel, R. H., & Trevino, L. K. (1987). Message Equivocality, Mode Selection, and Manager Performance: Implications for IS. *Management Information Systems Quarterly*, *11*(3), 355–366. doi:10.2307/248682

Dey, I. (1999). *Grounding GT: Guidelines for Qualitative Inquiry*. San Diego, CA: Academic Press.

Douglas, D. (2003). Inductive Theory Generation: A Grounded Approach to Business Inquiry. *Electronic Journal of Business Research Methods*, *2*(1), 47–54.

Earl, M. J. (2000). Perspectives - Are CIOs Obsolete? *Harvard Business Review*, *78*(2), 60.

Eidlin, F. (2006). *Ideal Types and the Problem of Reification*. Philadelphia, PA: American Political Science Association.

Fernandez, W. (2004). *The GTM and Case Study Data in IS Research: Issues and Design*. Paper presented at the 2nd Biennial IS Foundations Workshop. Canberra, Australia.

Ferreira, J., & Collins, J. F. (1979). The Changing Role of the MIS Executive. *Datamation*, *25*(13), 25.

Flick, U. (2002). *An Introduction to Qualitative Research*. London: Sage.

Galliers, R. D. (2007). *Strategizing for Agility: Confronting IS Inflexibility in Dynamic Environments. In Agile IS: Conceptualization, Construction, and Management* (pp. 1–15). London: Elsevier.

Gasson, S. (2004). *Rigor in GT Research: An Interpretive Perspective on Generating Theory from Qualitative Field Studies. In The Handbook of IS Research*. Hershey, PA: Idea Group Publishing.

Geletkanycz, M. A., & Hambrick, D. (1997). The External Ties of Top Executives: Implications for Strategic Choice and Performance. *Administrative Science Quarterly*, *42*(4), 654–681. doi:10.2307/2393653

Gilbert, L. (2002). Going the Distance: "Closeness" in Qualitative Data Alaysis Software. *International Journal of Social Research Methodology*, *5*(3), 215–228. doi:10.1080/13645570210146276

Glaser, B. G. (1978). *Theoretical Sensitivity: Advances in the Methodology of GT*. Mill Valley, CA: Sociology Press.

Glaser, B. G. (1992). *Emergence Vs Forcing: Basics of GT Analysis*. Mill Valley, CA: Sociology Press.

Glaser, B. G. (1998). *Doing GT: Issues and Discussions*. Mill Valley, CA: Sociology Press.

Glaser, B. G. (2001). *The GT Perspective: Conceptualization Contrasted with Description*. Mill Valley, CA: Sociology Press.

Glaser, B. G. (2002). Conceptualization: On Theory and Theorizing using GT. *International Journal of Qualitative Methods*, *1*(2), 1–31.

Glaser, B. G. (2005). *The GT Perspective III: Theoretical Coding. Mill Valley*, CA: Sociology Press.

Glaser, B. G., & Strauss, A. L. (1967). *The Discovery of GT: Strategies for Qualitative Research*. New York: Aldine de Guiter.

Gottschalk, P. (1999). Strategic Management of IS/IT functions: The Role of the CIO in Norwegian Organisations. *International Journal of Information Management*, *19*(5), 389–399. doi:10.1016/S0268-4012(99)00034-1

Gottschalk, P. (2000). IS Leadership Roles: An Empirical Study of Information Technology Managers. *Journal of Global Information Management*, *8*(4), 43–52. doi:10.4018/jgim.2000100104

Gottschalk, P. (2002). The Chief Information Officer: A Study of Managerial Roles in Norway. In *Proceedings of 35th Annual Hawaii International Conference on System Sciences*. IEEE. doi:10.1109/HICSS.2002.994350

Goulding, C. (1998). GT: The Missing Methodology on the Interpretivist Agenda. *Qualitative Market Research: An International Journal*, *1*(1), 50–57. doi:10.1108/13522759810197587

Goulding, C. (1999). GT: Some Reflections on Paradigm. In Procedures and Misconceptions. University of Wolverhampton.

Goulding, C. (2002). *GT: A Practical Guide for Management, Business and Market Researchers*. London: Sage.

Guba, E., & Lincoln, Y. S. (1994). *Competing Paradigms in Qualitative Research. In Handbook of Qualitative Research*. (pp. 105–117). Thousand Oaks, CA: Sage.

Hambrick, D., & Mason, P. A. (1984). Upper Echelons: The Organization as a Reflection of its Top Managers. *Academy of Management Review*, *9*(2), 193–206.

Heath, H. (2006). Exploring the Influences and Use of the Literature during a GT Study. *Journal of Research in Nursing*, *11*(6), 519–528. doi:10.1177/1744987106069338

Hickey, G. (1997). The Use of Literature in GT. *Nursing Times Research*, *2*(5), 371–378. doi:10.1177/174498719700200510

Hirschheim, R., & Klein, H. (1992). Paradigmatic Influences on IS Development Methodologies: Evolution and Conceptual Advances. *Advances in Computers*, *34*, 293–392. doi:10.1016/S0065-2458(08)60328-9

Hofstede, G. (2001). *Culture's Consequences: Comparing values, behaviours, institutions, and organisations across nations*. Thousand Oaks, CA: Sage Publications.

Hughes, J., & Wood-Harper, A. T. (2000). An Empirical Model of the IS Development Process: A Case Study of an Automotive Manufacturer. *Accounting Forum*, *24*(4), 391–406. doi:10.1111/1467-6303.00048

Ibarra, H. (1993). Personal Networks of Women and Minorities in Management: A Conceptual Framework. *Academy of Management Review*, *18*(1), 56–87.

Ibarra, H., & Hunter, M. G. (2007). How Leaders Create and Use Networks. *Harvard Business Review*, *85*(1), 40–47. PMID:17286073

Iivari, J., Hirschheim, R., & Klein, H. (1998). A Paradigmatic Analysis Contrasting IS Development Approaches and Methodologies. *IS Research, 9*(2), 164–193.

Ives, B., & Learmonth, G. P. (1984). The Information System as a Competitive Weapon. *Communications of the ACM, 27*(12), 1193–1201. doi:10.1145/2135.2137

Ives, B., & Olson, M. H. (1981). Manager or Technician? The Nature of the IS Manager's job. *Management Information Systems Quarterly, 5*(4), 49–63. doi:10.2307/249327

Kaplan, B., & Duchon, D. (1988). Combining Qualitative Methods in IS Research: A Case Study. *Management Information Systems Quarterly, 12*(4), 571–586. doi:10.2307/249133

Katz, D., & Kahn, R. (1966). *The Social Psychology of Organizations*. New York: John Wiley & Sons.

Kendall, J. (1999). Axial Coding and the GT Controversy. *Western Journal of Nursing Research, 21*(6), 743–757. doi:10.1177/01939459922044162 PMID:11512211

Klein, H., & Myers, M. D. (1999). A Set of Principles for Conducting and Evaluating Interpretive Field Studies in IS. *Management Information Systems Quarterly, 23*(1), 67–93. doi:10.2307/249410

Kluge, S. (2000). "Empirically Grounded Construction of Types and Typologies in Qualitative Research." Forum Qualitative Sozialforschung/ Forum: Qualitative. *Social Research, 1*(1).

Krauss, R., & Fussell, S. (1990). *Mutual Knowledge and Communicative Effectiveness. In Intellectual Teamwork: The Social and Technological Bases of Cooperative Work* (pp. 114–144). Hillside, NJ: Erlbaum.

Langley, A. (1999). Strategies for Theorising from Process Data. *Academy of Management Review, 24*(4), 691–710.

Lincoln, Y. S., & Guba, E. (2000). *Paradigmatic Controversies, Contradictions, and Emerging Confluences. In The Handbook of Qualitative Research* (pp. 54–76). Beverly Hills, CA: Sage.

Locke, K. (2001). *GT in Management Research*. London: Sage.

Maier, J. L., Rainer, R. K., & Snyder, C. A. (1997). Environmental Scanning for Information Technology: An Empirical Investigation. *Journal of Management IS, 14*(2), 177–200.

Malhotra, A., & Majchrzak, A. (2004). Enabling Knowledge Creation in Far-flung Teams: Best Practices for IT Support and Knowledge Sharing. *Journal of Knowledge Management, 8*(4), 75–88. doi:10.1108/13673270410548496

Martin, P. Y., & Turner, B. A. (1986). GT and Organisational Research. *The Journal of Applied Behavioral Science, 22*(2), 141–157. doi:10.1177/002188638602200207

Mason, J. (2002). *The Challenge of Qualitative Research*. London: Sage.

Matavire, R., & Brown, I. (2013). Profiling GT Approaches in IS Research. *European Journal of IS, 22*, 119–129.

McDonald, M. L., & Westphal, J. D. (2003). Getting by with the Advice of their Friends: CEO's Advice Networks and Firms' Strategic Responses to Poor Performance. *Administrative Science Quarterly, 48*(1), 1–32. doi:10.2307/3556617

McFarlan, F. W. (1984). Information Technology Changes the Way you Compete. *Harvard Business Review, 62*(3), 98–103.

Melia, K. (1996). Rediscovering Glaser. *Qualitative Health Research, 6*(3), 368–378. doi:10.1177/104973239600600305

Miles, M. B., & Huberman, A. M. (1984). *Qualitative Data Analysis - A Sourcebook of New Methods*. Thousand Oaks, CA: Sage Publications.

Miles, R. E., Snow, C. C., & Pfeffer, J. (1974). Organization-Environment: Concepts and Issues. *Industrial Relations*, *13*(3), 244–264. doi:10.1111/j.1468-232X.1974.tb00581.x

Mills, J., Bonner, A., & Francis, K. (2006). The development of Constructivist GT. *International Journal of Qualitative Methods*, *5*(1), 1–10.

Mintzberg, H. (1973). *The Nature of Managerial Work*. New York: McGraw-Hill.

Noble, G. I. (2002). *Managing Synergetic Momentum: A GT of the Management of Public-Private Partnerships*. University of Wollongong.

Orlikowski, W. J. (1993). CASE Tools as Organizational Change: Investigating Incremental and Radical changes in Systems Development. *Management Information Systems Quarterly*, *17*(3), 309–340. doi:10.2307/249774

Pandit, N. (1996). The Creation of Theory: A Recent Application of the GTM. *Qualitative Report*, *2*(4).

Pawlowski, S., & Robey, D. (2004). Bridging User Organisations: Knowledge Brokering and the Work of Information Technology Professionals. *Management Information Systems Quarterly*, *28*(4), 645–672.

Pettigrew, A. M. (1990). Longitudinal Field Research on Change: Theory and Practice. *Organization Science*, *1*(3), 267–292. doi:10.1287/orsc.1.3.267

Pettigrew, A. M. (1997). What is processual Analysis? *Scandinavian Journal of Management*, *13*(4), 337–348. doi:10.1016/S0956-5221(97)00020-1

Porter, M. E., & Millar, V. E. (1985). How Information gives you Competitive Advantage. *Harvard Business Review*, *63*(4), 149–160.

Preston, D. S., Chen, D., & Leidner, D. E. (2008). Examining the Antecedents and Consequences of CIO Strategic Decision-Making Authority: An Empirical Study. *Decision Sciences*, *39*(4), 605–638. doi:10.1111/j.1540-5915.2008.00206.x

Preston, D. S., Karahanna, E., & Rowe, F. (2006). Development of Shared Understanding between the Chief Information Officer and Top Management Team in US and French Organizations: A Cross-Cultural Comparison. *IEEE Transactions on Engineering Management*, *53*(2), 191–206. doi:10.1109/TEM.2006.872244

Reich, B. H., & Benbasat, I. (2000). Factors that Influence the Social Dimension of Alignment between Business and Information Technology Objectives. *Management Information Systems Quarterly*, *24*(1), 81–113. doi:10.2307/3250980

Richards, T. J., & Richards, L. (1994). *Using Computers in Qualitative Research. In Handbook of Qualitative Research*. Thousand Oaks, CA: Sage Publications.

Sambamurthy, V., Bharadwaj, A., & Grover, V. (2003). Shaping Agility through Digital Options: Reconceptualizing the Role of Information Technology in Contemporary Firms. *Management Information Systems Quarterly*, *27*(2), 237–263.

Sarantakos, S. (2005). *Social Research*. London: Palgrave Macmillan.

Saunders, M., Lewis, P., & Thornhill, A. (2003). *Research Methods for Business Students*. London: Prentice Hall.

Smaltz, D. H., Sambamurthy, V., & Agarwal, R. (2006). The Antecedents of CIO Role Effectiveness in Organizations: An Empirical Study in the Healthcare Sector. *IEEE Transactions on Engineering Management*, *53*(2), 207–222. doi:10.1109/TEM.2006.872248

Spiggle, S. (1994). Analysis and Interpretation of Qualitative Data in Consumer Research. *The Journal of Consumer Research, 21*(3), 491–503. doi:10.1086/209413

Stephens, C. S. (1991). *A Structured Observation of Five Chief Information Officers: The Nature of Information Technology Managerial Work.* Auburn University.

Stern, P. N. (1994). *Eroding GT. Critical Issues in Qualitative Research Methods. J. Morse* (pp. 212–223). Thousand Oaks, CA: Sage.

Strauss, A. L., & Corbin, J. (1990). *Basics of Qualitative Research: GT Procedures and Techniques.* Newbury Park, CA: Sage.

Strauss, A. L., & Corbin, J. (1994). *GTMology: An Overview. In Handbook of Qualitative Research* (pp. 273–285). Thousand Oaks, CA: Sage.

Strauss, A. L., & Corbin, J. (1998). *Basics of Qualitative Research: GT Procedures and Techniques.* Newbury Park, CA: Sage.

Tesch, R. (1991). *Software for Qualitative researchers: Analysis Needs and Program Capabilities. In Using Computers in Qualitative Research.* London: Sage.

Trauth, E. M. (2001). *The Choice of Qualitative Methods in IS Research. In Qualitative Research in IS: Issues and Trends* (pp. 1–19). London: Idea Group Publishing.

Turner, B. (1981). Some practical aspects of Qualitative Data Analysis: One way of Organising the Cognitive Processes Associated with the Generation of GT. *Quality & Quantity, 15*(3), 225–247. doi:10.1007/BF00164639

Tushman, M. L., & Scanlan, T. (1981). Boundary Spanning Individuals: Their Role in Information Transfer and Their Antecedents. *Academy of Management Journal, 24*(2), 289–305. doi:10.2307/255842

Urquhart, C. (2001). *An Encounter with GT: Tackling the Practical and Philosophical Issues. In Qualitative Research in IS: Issues and Trends* (pp. 104–140). London: Idea Group Publishing.

Urquhart, C., & Fernandez, W. (2013). Using GT Methid in IS: The researcher as a Blank Slate and Other Myths. *Journal of Information Technology, 28,* 224–236. doi:10.1057/jit.2012.34

Urquhart, C., Lehmann, H., & Myers, M. D. (2010). Putting the "Theory" back into GT: Guidelines for GT Studies in IS. *IS Journal, 20,* 357–381.

Venkatraman, N. (2000). Five Steps to a Dot-Com Strategy: How to find your footing on the Web. *MIT Sloan Management Review, 41*(3), 15–28.

Watson, R. T. (1990). Influences on the IS Manager's Perceptions of Key Issues: Information Scanning and the Relationship with the CEO. *Management Information Systems Quarterly, 14*(2), 217–231. doi:10.2307/248780

Weber, M. (1949). *The Methodology of the Social Sciences.* New York: Free Press.

Weber, M. (1962). *Basic Concepts in Sociology.* New York: The Citadel Press.

Weber, R. (2004). The Retoric of Positivism versus Interpretivism: A Personal View. *Management Information Systems Quarterly, 28*(1), 3–12.

Wenger, E. (1998). Communities of Practice: Learning as a Social System. *Systems Thinker,* 1-10. Retrieved from www.co-i-l/coil/knowledge-garden/cop/ss.shtml

Wenger, E., & Snyder, W. M. (2000). Communities of Practice: The Organizational Frontier. *Harvard Business Review, 78*(1), 139–145. PMID:11184968

Werner, O., & Schoepfle, G. M. (1987). Systematic Fieldwork. In *Foundations of Ethnography and Interviewing (vol. 1).* Thousand Oaks, CA: Sage.

KEY TERMS AND DEFINITIONS

Chief Information Officer: Most senior corporate officer with responsibility for the information systems landscape in an organisation.

External Peer Networks: Refers to the set of external networks which executive officers engage with as part of their ongoing personal and professional development.

Grounded Theory Methodology: Refers to an approach to inquiry that uses a very structured and disciplined approach to the collection and analysis of real-world data.

Information Systems Management: Refers to the most senior group of managers charged with the strategic direction and development of the information systems landscape in an organisation.

Open, Selective, and Theoretical Coding: Refers to a highly integrated system of coding data collected using the grounded theory methodology.

Theoretical Saturation: Refers to the point at which no new data relating to the underlying categories, or the properties of an emerging theory, can be found by the continued collection of data.

Theoretical Sensitivity: Refers to the ability of the researcher to think constantly about the data in conceptual terms.

Top Management: Refers to the most senior group of managers charged with the strategic direction and development of an organisation.

ENDNOTES

[1] Locke (2001, p. 39) suggests that when Glaser and Strauss (1967) talk about a "category" they use the term synonymously with the term "concept". Equally, Martin and Turner (1986, p. 147) suggest that the term "label" is also often used by GT researchers in a similar fashion. Essentially, they suggest that category, concept or label are all terms for theoretical abstractions from the underlying empirical data and can be used interchangeably. As "category" is the original term used by Glaser and Strauss in their own work, this term has been chosen for this research study (Glaser & Strauss, 1967).

[2] These "concepts" were developed from the IS management literature, analysis of secondary documentation and from the researcher's own experience as a CIO.

[3] IP02 – all direct references to CIO comments are shown in terms of the code assigned to each individual CIO in this study. At no stage are any comments from interviews directly attributed to a named CIO. This is to ensure the confidentiality of all CIOs who agreed to be part of this research study.

[4] Charmaz (2006) instead uses the term "Focused Coding" to describe this process.

[5] Microsoft Office ® products such as Word, Excel and PowerPoint were used by the researcher in this process.

Chapter 18

Integrating Process Inquiry and the Case Method in the Study of Information Systems Failure

Brian Dempsey
Trinity College Dublin, Ireland

Joe McDonagh
Trinity College Dublin, Ireland

ABSTRACT

This chapter examines the integration of process inquiry and the case method in the study of Information Systems (IS) failure. Having acknowledged the prevalence of IS failure and the need for continued inquiry in this domain, the two predominant methods of inquiry, factor and process studies, are described along with the utility of both methods. The chapter then examines the nature of process inquiry and notes its utility and prevalence in the study of IS phenomena, and its potential applicability for inquiry into IS failure. The case study method is then briefly described along with its potential contribution when combined with process inquiry. The chapter then describes how the case method can provide an overall framework for the conduct of a process inquiry and presents an iterative six-stage research process model based on the case method to assist with the planning, design, preparation, data collection, data analysis, and reporting of findings.

1. INTRODUCTION

Information systems (IS) are computer based systems that people and organisations use to collect, filter, process, create and distribute data. The failure of IS is a recurring theme in both academic and practitioner literature since the beginning of the computer age (Avots, 1969; Bostrom & Heinen, 1977a; Powers & Dickson, 1973), however despite

over 50 years of study IS failure continues to be a persistent and costly phenomenon as evidenced by both academic and practitioner studies. Studies of IS failure indicate an outright failure rate of IS projects of between 18% (Eveleens & Verhoef, 2010) and 50% (McDonagh, 2001). In addition, many projects not considered to be outright failures fall far below expectations. A study of 5,400 IS projects across a range of industries by McKinsey

DOI: 10.4018/978-1-4666-6493-7.ch018

& Company in collaboration with the University of Oxford (Bloch, et al., 2012) suggests that half of all large IT projects (defined as those with initial price tags exceeding $15 million) run 45 percent over budget and 7 percent over time, while delivering 56 percent less value than predicted.

It is impossible to place a value on the total cost of IS failure because of the lack of a definitive definition and the fact that not all IS failures get into the public domain. Gartner estimate that total global spend on IS for 2014 will be $3.8 trillion. Even a conservative estimate of the percentage of this amount that is spent on underperforming IS represents a significant figure, which is a motivation and justification for continued inquiry in this area (Drevin, 2008).

Building on Dempsey & McDonagh (2014), this paper describes the integration of process inquiry and the case method for the study of IS failure. Process inquiry is the dynamic study of behaviour in organisations, focusing on sequences of events, activities and actions, which unfold over time and in context (Hinings, 1997; Langley & Tsoukas, 2010; Pettigrew, 1997). Process inquiry takes a dynamic rather than static worldview of things in the making (Langley & Tsoukas, 2010) and therefore is particularly suited to the study of IS development and implementation because of the temporally evolving, longitudinal, and creative nature of such processes. The use of the case method in support of a process inquiry facilitates the study of IS failure in a real life setting which allows the researcher to open the 'black box' of IS projects in order to better understand the broad range of actions, interactions, and reactions amongst actors, which are subject to a range of contextual factors, and contribute to failed outcomes.

This paper first examines the nature of IS failure and the main types of inquiry into the phenomenon. Noting the utility of process inquiry for the study of IS failure (which itself is a process) the paper then examines the nature of process and the utility of process inquiry for the study of IS failure. The paper then describes the value of integrating process inquiry with the case method, and concludes with a practical six stage guide to utilising the case method for the conduct of a process inquiry.

2. THE NATURE OF IS FAILURE

Despite over 50 years of research in the domain of IS failure it remains as persistent and costly as ever as evidenced in both academic and practitioner literature. One only has to examine reports of national government audit offices to get a picture of the extent of the problem. In fact Mahaney & Lederer (1999) propose that failure has become an accepted aspect of IS implementations, an ominous proposition given the ever increasing complexity of IS (Koh et al., 2011), and its growing importance in achieving and maintaining competitive superiority (Piccoli & Ives, 2005).

The concept of IS failure has not been well defined and there is no universally agreed definition (Al-ahmad et al., 2009; Hyvari, 2006; Sauer, 1993). Based on a survey and classification of the empirical literature on IS failure Lyytinen & Herschein (1987) identified four distinct types of IS failure: (1) *Correspondence Failure:* the system does not 'co-respond' to predefined design objectives, (2) *Process Failure:* a failure to produce a system at all or failure to produce a system within planned budgets and timeframe, (3) *Interaction Failure:* failure of the system to meet the needs of its users evidenced by the level of use and the degree of user satisfaction with the system, and (4) *Expectation Failure:* the inability of an IS to meet a specific stakeholder group's expectations. Sauer (1993) expands on the model above by proposing an alternative definition of IS failure which is consistent with IS deployment as a process unfolding in a systematic web of social action. He proposes a model which he describes as a triangle of dependences among (1) the project organisation (who develop and maintain the IS); (2) the supporters (stakeholders who support the

IS in the expectation that it will serve their purposes); and (3) the IS itself. Success or failure of the system depends on the support each leg gives to the other, along with the effects of exogenous factors such as cognitive limits, the environment, organisational politics, structure, and history. In this model failure occurs when the level of dissatisfaction with a system is such that there is no longer enough support to sustain it. Failure in this case is terminal, and referred to as project abandonment (Ewusi-Mensah & Przasnyski, 1994; Pan, 2005). Sauer's approach also supports the notion that failure of an IS initiative can happen long after the system is successfully implemented.

2.1 Some Unique Features of IS and Failure

Failure is an inherent aspect of complex technological and organisational systems (Cook, 2000; Sauer, 1993) including IS (Nelson, 2007). IS are both innovative and inherently complex as they are built on conceptual rather than material constructs (Brooks, 1987), making the development of IS systems a high risk undertaking (Lyytinen & Robey, 1999). A number of reasons have been put forward for this. Firstly, the conceptual and abstract nature of software creates a difficulty of visualisation which can lead to over-ambitious aspirations, misunderstanding, and excessive perceptions of flexibility by stakeholders, and fallible decision making during specification, and design (Al-ahmad et al., 2009; Goldfinch, 2007). Secondly, the typical lifespan of an IS innovation means there is usually a degree of uncertainty about what the final outcome will be, how the process of constructing the product will progress in the face of possible unforeseen situations (Boddy et al., 2009; Sauer, 1993), and the potential for late detection of problems (Al-ahmad et al., 2009). Thirdly, the number of stakeholders affected by an IS makes it difficult to satisfy all expectations (Boddy et al., 2009; Sauer, 1993). Fourthly, the systemic nature of organisations means that the introduction of a new system in one part of the organisation has implications for others and may disturb the existing socio-technical balance (Berg, 2001; Boddy et al., 2009; Fortune & Peters, 2005; Keen, 1981; Sauer, 1993) implying the need to have a thorough understanding of not only the technology but the business processes it impacts. Lastly, the implementation of an IS requires change in the way humans work yet companies continue to inject technology without making the necessary organisational changes (Markus & Robey, 1988; Sauer, 1993). Clegg et al., (1997) and Marchland & Hykes (2006) state that IS projects are mostly technology led, and that many organisations lack an integrated approach to organisational and technical change, and often design the social system around the technology.

2.2 Factors Contributing to IS Failure

Flowers (1996) in Yeo (2002) describes the performance of IS developments as a function of managing a range of critical failure factors that may be broadly grouped as the conduct of the IS project and the organisational and people contexts within the domain of influence of the IS project (Yeo, 2002). Yeo (2002) identifies three spheres of influence over IS project outcomes as: (1) *process driven issues* such as misalignment of business/IS planning, inadequate project planning, and project management and control; (2) *content driven issues* such as complexity, inadequate business process design, poor system design, and inadequate professional knowledge and skill-sets; and (3) *context driven issues* such as organisation culture, politics, and people. These spheres of interest are broadly in line with the people, process, and project risk categories noted by Kappelman et al. (2006) and the three higher order subsystems of IS project risk (social subsystem risks, project management risks, and technical subsystem risk) identified by Wallace et al. (2004). Although different in approach each of the studies acknowledges three similar overarching spheres of influence on the outcome of an IS project. These studies therefore provide a useful framework for a detailed study of IS risk/failure as they embody the full range of project, process, people, and organisational/contextual factors that may impact on the outcome of an IS initiative. Furthermore the study by Wallace et al. (2004) found a link between all spheres of influence such that social subsystem risk influences technical subsystem risk, which in turn influences the level of project management risk, and ultimately project performance, thereby indicating a systematic connectedness among all spheres of influence.

2.3 Research in IS Failure

Sauer (1999) identifies a number of difficulties in researching IS failure. Firstly, as stated above, the concept of IS failure has not been well defined and there is no universally agreed definition (Al-ahmad et al., 2009; Hyvari, 2006; Sauer, 1993). Secondly, the study of IS failure raises a number of difficulties, including the difficulty in developing theory because of the need to combine technical, human, and organisational characteristics associated with the phenomenon, and the absence of explanatory theories of failure from other fields (Sauer, 1999).

Studies of IS failure fall broadly, although not exclusively, into two categories viz. factor analysis studies and process studies. Factor analysis studies attempt to explain, and sometimes rank in importance common factors that contribute to IS failure. Process studies examine the process by which IS have failed by examining sequences of events, activities and actions, which unfold over the duration of the process, leading to the failure outcome. Both types of study offer valuable insight into the phenomenon of IS failure.

Factor analysis studies highlight many of the important issues that have contributed to IS failure in the past, and the difficulty in addressing them (Goldfinch, 2007). Factor analysis studies fall into two main categories, those that attempt to analyse in detail a particular factor which led to failure e.g. escalation of commitment (Keil, 1995), failure to learn from failure (Lyytinen & Robey, 1999), failure of governance (Avison et al., 2006), and those that identify and attempt to prioritise lists of critical failure factors based on perceived importance (Al-ahmad et al., 2009; Kappelman et al., 2006; Schmidt, Lyytinen et al., 2001). Failure factor research has been criticised because of the lack of a standard naming convention for failure factors leading to ambiguity and difficulty in comparing studies (Al-ahmad et al., 2009), failure to capture the levels of importance of factors at different stages of the implementation process (Larsen & Myers, 1999), failure to identify relationships among the factors (Ginzberg, 1981), and a focus on project factors at the expense of broader contextual factors (Bussen & Myers, 1997; Nandhakumar, 1996).

Process studies of IS failure present an analysis of one or more failed initiatives, usually over the entire course of the initiative (Drevin, 2008). Process studies of IS failure differ from factor analysis studies because in addition to describing the causes of failure they go further by placing the causes within the context of the IS development (Sauer, 1993), and attempt to unearth the complex social and political web in which IS initiatives are undertaken (Markus & Robey, 1988), thereby offering a richer explanation in terms of both agency and context (Pettigrew, 1997). By facilitating a more incisive study of the process of failure over the entire course of the initiative process studies offer richer explanations of causal links than factor studies (Sauer, 1999), and a better explication of how IS affects, and is affected by, the people who use it (Nandhakumar, 1996). Although process research is more appropriate to the complexity of IS failure it also has limitations in terms of the complexity of analysis and theoretical foundations, and the lower amount of accumulated research when compared with factor analysis studies (Sauer, 1999). This warrants a more detailed discussion on the nature of process inquiry and in particular it's utility for inquiry into IS failure.

3. THE NATURE OF PROCESS INQUIRY

Process inquiry is the dynamic study of behaviour in organisations, focusing on sequences of events, activities and actions, which unfold over time and in context (Hinings, 1997; Langley & Tsoukas, 2010; Pettigrew, 1997). Process studies address questions about temporally evolving phenomena, that is of things not being but rather in the making (Ferlie & Mcnulty, 1997; Langley & Tsoukas, 2010).

Mohr (1982) illustrates the nature of process studies by highlighting the difference between variance models and process models. A variance model provides explanations of phenomena in terms of a deterministic causation relationship (outcome) among dependent and independent variables in which X implies Y. A process model on the other hand views outcomes as discontinuous phenomena, or changes of state, rather than variables that can take on a range of values. Thus in a process model X does not imply Y, but rather Y implies X. Process models provide explanations in terms of patterns in events, activities, and choices over time (Mohr, 1982), and unlike variance models emphasise *necessary causality* rather than *necessary and sufficient causality* because the impact of any event will depend on what precedes it, and what follows it. Thus variance models are appropriate for a static worldview whereas process models are most appropriate for a dynamic worldview of things in the making (Langley & Tsoukas, 2010).

Process models are typically multi-directional rather than linear (Tsoukas & Chia, 2002), cumulative and non-reversible (Sztompka, 1993)

in (Pettigrew, 1997), reflecting social processes which are inherently discontinuous (Markus & Robey, 1988), and open ended. Process models may incorporate several different types of effects into their explanations, including critical events and turning points, factors that influence the sequencing of events, and contextual and other factors that influence the direction of change and causal influence (Van de Ven & Poole, 2005). Process models have a lower capability to explain variance but provide richer explanations of how and why outcomes occur (Markus & Robey, 1988) by untangling the history that altered the trajectory of events (Shaw & Jarvenpaa, 1997), and identifying multiple intersecting conditions that link context and process to outcomes (Pettigrew, 1997).

3.1 The Ontological Assumptions of a Process Worldview

Sztompka (1993), in Pettigrew (1992) provides a list of ontological assumptions which are relevant for scholars of process. These are:

- **Social Reality is Not a Steady State But, Rather, a Dynamic Process:** A process orientation prioritises activity over product, change over persistence, novelty over continuity, and expression over determination (Langley & Tsoukas, 2010). Process employs the language of verbs (becoming) rather than nouns (being) to explain the origins, event sequences, and outcomes of phenomena (Pettigrew, 1987) in terms of *"What was there-then, is included in what is here-now"* (Langley & Tsoukas, 2010, p. 10). The process approach does not deny the existence of events, states, or entities, but seeks to reveal the complex activities and transactions that take place and contribute to their constitution.

- **The Social Process is Constructed:** The social process is created by human agents (individually or collectively) through their actions and interactions (Pettigrew, 1992; Sztompka, 1993; Tsoukas & Chia, 2002). Human agency is continuously influenced by rules and norms that are made relevant by the actors themselves through a dynamic process of adjustments to social conditions. In this way organisational rules are constantly adjusted, modified, or even ignored in the carrying out of actual organisational tasks (Tsoukas & Chia, 2002). This is further influenced by differences in power, knowledge, and other resources (Pettigrew, 1992). Events are also socially constructed and may be individually interpreted (Peterson, 1998), leading to different understanding and interpretation of event sequences and outcomes.

- **Social Life is a Process of Structural Emergence via Actions Which Occur in the Context of Encountered Structures:** Action occurs in the context of encountered structures, which it shapes in turn, resulting in the dual quality of structure (as both shaping and shaped) and the actors (as both producers and products) (Sztompka, 1993) in (Pettigrew, 1992), (Pettigrew, 1997; Pettigrew, 1987). Tension between actions and structures is the ultimate moving force of process (Sztompka, 1993) in (Pettigrew, 1992) which ultimately links processes to outcome (Pettigrew, 2012).
- **The Interchange of Action and Structure Occurs in Time and Is Cumulative:** Time is an integral part of a process orientation as time sets a frame of reference for what changes are seen and how those changes are explained (Pettigrew, 1987). Process models treat time as always shaping the emerging future (Pettigrew, 2012) by its location in the process sequence, and

the multiple levels of changing contexts in which the process is embedded (Langley & Tsoukas, 2010; Pettigrew, 2012).

3.2 The Use of Process Inquiry in the Study of IS Phenomena

In contrast with much of the factor analysis based IS failure studies, which focus either on a single failure factor, or present failure factors as a ranked list, process studies are particularly suited to the study of IS development and implementation because of the temporally evolving, longitudinal and creative nature of such processes (Van de Ven & Poole, 2005). Process inquiry facilitates the study of IS failure across the entire duration of the failure incorporating a broad range of complex activities and transactions undertaken by actors, which are subject to a range of contextual factors that contribute to the outcome. Unless you look at the process of IS failure it is not possible to gain an understanding of the complex interaction of actors, events, contexts and the emergent conditions that influence the trajectory over time, and their impact on the object of inquiry. The study of the process of IS failure therefore provides insight which cannot be completely explicated using variance type methodologies in a 'hands-off' fashion. Process research is seen as problem solving (Hinings, 1997) and many process studies have been motivated by a desire for a better understanding of events leading to a positive or negative outcome (Langley & Tsoukas, 2010), which confirms its appropriateness as a suitable method for the study of IS failure, and also indicates its practical relevance (Hinings, 1997; Langley & Tsoukas, 2010). Process inquiry has a strong connection with qualitative / interpretive research (Hinings, 1997; Langley & Tsoukas, 2010; Langley, 2008), and frequently employs case study investigations (Hinings, 1997; Radeke,

2010), and in particular longitudinal case studies, which facilitate inquiry over the entire duration of the IS failure (Wilson & Howcroft, 2002). In support of this Pan, et al. (2008) call for more longitudinal studies on project failures, especially those that involve in-depth case studies, in order to provide a deeper understanding of the dynamics of this phenomenon in various contexts.

The largely qualitative nature of process inquiry has raised concerns about the lack of generalisability of such studies however using only the nomothetic or scientific approach unnecessarily limits the use and applicability of any qualitative inquiry (Walsham, 2006) as a phenomenon such as IS failure may not be amenable to quantification (Bonoma, 1985), or generalisation in the nomothetic sense (Gerring, 2004; Hinings, 1997; Lee & Baskerville, 2003) as IS failure is subject to the influence of a potentially large set of precursors which interact in a systematic but nondeterministic way. Practical issues relating to all qualitative research include the need to show in a convincing manner how the data was analysed, highlighting all assumptions made, and demonstrate how the issue of bias was addressed (Shaw & Jarvenpaa, 1997). Pettigrew (1990) also highlights the sheer amount of data that can result from a process inquiry, referred to as the danger of *"death by data asphyxiation"* (p. 281), indicating a need for efficient data management throughout the inquiry. Many of the practical issues and other criticisms of process inquiry often reflect the reality of poor research planning and design, and the absence of a guiding methodology for the inquiry. Process inquiry, with an emphasis on action and events over time and in context, imposes a rigor on data collection that some other qualitative methodologies do not, however Pettigrew (1990) states that there are no fixed recipes for undertaking process studies.

Many of the practical difficulties in conducting a process inquiry can be reduced by the use of a systematic methodology to guide the conduct of the inquiry, which can also provide the necessary tools and frameworks to underpin rigor and accuracy in the research process. The use of a case study methodology is well proven for the study of phenomena related to IS and provides such a framework for the conduct of a process inquiry. The case study methodology is briefly discussed in the next section of this paper along with its appropriateness and utility for the conduct of a process inquiry.

4. THE VALUE OF INTEGRATING PROCESS INQUIRY WITH THE CASE METHODOLOGY

Yin, (2009) defines a case study as: "… an empirical enquiry that investigates a contemporary phenomenon in depth and within its real-life context, especially when the boundaries between phenomenon and context are not clearly evident" (p. 18). Case study research is the most widely used qualitative method in IS research (Darke et al., 1998), its popularity due mainly to the indivisible connection between IS and the context in which it is implemented and deployed (Benbasat, Goldstein, & Mead, 1987; Markus & Robey, 1988). Doolin (1993) states that because IS development is a complex, protean, social phenomenon the rational-technical view of systems development presented in most textbooks is a caricature, and that simple prescriptions grossly oversimplify the actual realities of systems work. Case study allows the researcher to open the 'black box' of IT focusing on the 'what', 'why', and 'how' questions which capture the dynamic changing conditions (Pare, 2004) that are appropriate for the conduct of a process inquiry.

Case studies may be longitudinal in nature (Burch, 2001; Pettigrew, 1990; Ployhart & Vandenberg, 2010), facilitating the collection and analysis of process data over time. Because the subject is studied within its real life context the researcher has access to a broad range of primary and secondary data (Kaplan & Maxwell, 2005) including documentation, archival records, other artefacts, direct observation of events and processes, and the opportunity to engage in interviews with appropriate informants. The multifaceted data collection methods as well as the use of qualitative evidence are ideal for addressing the vivid and dynamic phenomena necessary to develop complete process models (Newman & Robey, 1992), as in the case of an IS failure. The overheads of time and data volume can easily be justified in terms of the rich data and insight produced. Furthermore the richness of data sources facilitated by the case study methodology assists with triangulation (Ann Langley, 2009; Mathison, 1998), a key to confirming findings and reducing bias. Direct access to participants also provides multiple perspectives (narratives) regarding the events, situations, actions, processes, and outcomes which have, or are, taking place, and the elicitation of views and personal aspirations within this context (Kaplan & Maxwell, 2005; Walsham, 1995a, 2006) thereby adding further richness to the inquiry.

5. INTEGRATING PROCESS INQUIRY AND THE CASE STUDY METHOD IN THE STUDY OF IS FAILURE

Two clear advantages of the case study methodology for the study of IS failure are: (1) it facilitates the in-depth study of IS failure within its real life context thereby providing a real life setting within which to carry out the inquiry; and (2) the case study methodology includes a well-documented set of tools and procedures for the conduct of the case study, and for managing the resulting body of data. This unique set of features provides an ideal framework for the conduct of a process inquiry

as it provides a real life case of IS failure within which to conduct the inquiry and, if conducted correctly, forces a rigor at all stages of the inquiry, which in turn will strengthen the research findings.

A research design is a plan of the logical sequence that connects the empirical data to a study's initial research questions, and ultimately to its conclusion, such that the reader is able to follow the derivation of any evidence from initial research questions to the conclusions of the study (Wilson, 2011; Yin, 2009). The researcher must describe in detail how the research was conducted and how the results were arrived at, and present a coherent, persuasively argued point of view (Walsham, 1995b). Sufficient evidence for the research result must be presented along with consideration of alternative interpretations of the data (Benbasat et al., 1987; Dube & Pare, 2003; Walsham, 2006; Yin, 2009) and the case overall.

Yin (2009) describes case study research as a linear but iterative process with six key components which are: plan, design, prepare, collect data, analyse data, and report findings. This method, also supported by other exponents of the case method (Carroll & Swatman, 2000; Pare, 2004), may form the basis of a methodology for the conduct of a process inquiry, and is depicted in Figure 1 below:

Although depicted as six discrete steps the research process is both iterative and systematic, often requiring a return to previous stages as new data or concepts emerge. This model is congruent with the inductive-deductive cycle described by (Pettigrew, 1997) for the conduct of a process inquiry (Box 1).

The six step model is described below in the context of undertaking a process inquiry.

5.1 Stage 1: Plan

This stage is mainly concerned with deciding on the most appropriate research strategy to answer the research question(s) including an assessment

Figure 1. Case research (adapted from Yin (2009) Pare (2004) Carroll & Swatman (2000))

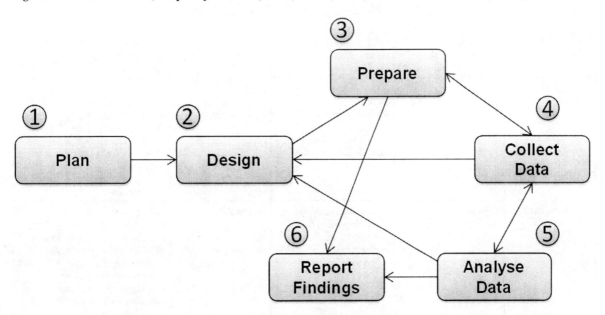

Box 1.

> research question → related themes and questions → preliminary data collection → early pattern recognition → early writing → disconfirmation and verification → elaborated themes & questions → further data collection → additional pattern recognition → more refined study vocabulary and research questions

of one's own ontological and epistemological position, and the use of any guiding theory. For the purpose of this paper it is assumed that a qualitative process inquiry has been selected and justified as the appropriate method of inquiry into an IS failure within a case based setting.

5.2 Stage 2: Design

The case study design is concerned with ensuring that the inquiry is conducted in a systematic manner which will increase the overall quality and robustness of the research findings. This stage is concerned with selecting the appropriate unit of analysis for the inquiry, selecting the appropriate case design, and addressing the issues of validity and reliability of the research.

The unit of analysis for an inquiry (Miles & Huberman, 1994; Yin, 2009) defines the boundary of what is to be studied, how the study relates to the broader body of knowledge in the research domain (Dube & Pare, 2003), and the potential generalisability of resulting theory (Pare, 2004; Yin, 2009). The unit of analysis should be a concrete real-life phenomenon rather than an abstraction (Benbasat et al., 1987; Yin, 2009), and must provide sufficient breadth and depth of data to allow the research question to be answered (Darke et al., 1998). A typical unit of analysis for inquiry in IS failure is the IS initiative which has been deemed to have failed.

A primary decision in designing the inquiry is the choice between multiple-case and single-case design. That is between the analytic and generalis-

Table 1. Application of positivist and qualitative validity and reliability criteria for the conduct of process inquiry (Adapted and expanded from Yin, 2009, Lincoln & Guba, 1985)

Validity Criteria (Yin, 2006)	Validity Criteria (Lincoln & Guba, 1985)	Case Study Tactic	Phase of Research	Relevance of Case Study Tactics to Process Inquiry
Construct Validity	N/A	• Use multiple sources of evidence. • Establish chains of evidence. • Have key informants review draft case study report.	data collection data collection composition	Multiple sources of evidence may be used to confirm actions, events, and outcomes facilitating the construction of verifiable process chains (cause and effect) using visual mapping and other techniques. Process narratives may also be used to confirm findings with informants.
Internal validity	Credibility	• Do pattern matching. • Do explanation building. • Address rival explanations. • Use logic models.	data analysis data analysis data analysis data analysis	Failure outcomes may be explained using chronological mapping to explicate the process of failure and verified by the construction of alternative explanations to test plausibility of findings. Findings may also be compared with previous research findings as a further test of credibility or novelty.
External validity	Transferability	• Use theory in single cases. • Use replication logic in multiple case studies.	research design research design	Depends on the type of inquiry and the potential for generalizing from the findings, whether a guiding theory is used for the inquiry and the number of cases. Process inquiry in IS failure often relies on a single case of IS failure because of difficulties in access to multiple cases at any one time.
Reliability	Dependability	• Use case study protocol. • Develop case study database.	data collection data collection	The case study protocol should specify how the process inquiry is to be conducted and specify how data will be stored using the case study database. Data analysis tools should also be explained including the use of any software tools.

ability benefits of replication of a multiple-case design and the depth and richness of data associated with a single-case design. Given the sensitivity that surrounds IS failure (Keil, 1995; Sauer, 1999) the researcher may seldom have the opportunity to structure a multiple case-study design, however the complex and longitudinal nature of large IS failures offers the opportunity to present an empirically rich and unbroken case narrative that is a key component of process inquiry.

Consideration must also be given to the quality of the research output in terms of validity and reliability. Yin (2009) summarises a set of tactics for increasing validity and reliability of case study case research. However Lincoln et al. (2011) assert that social scientists rely increasingly on the experiential, the personified, and the emotive qualities of human experience which contribute the narrative quality to a life. Yin's tactics have therefore been combined with Lincoln & Guba's

(1985) credibility, transferability, and dependability criteria for qualitative research, and the relevance of such criteria to process inquiry, based on the view of validity in terms of what is real, what is useful, and what has meaning (Guba & Lincoln, 2005). The resulting framework is shown in Table 1. The challenge of ensuring the quality of research must of course be continually addressed during all phases of the research (Runeson & Höst, 2009; Yin, 2009).

5.3 Stage 3: Prepare

Thorough preparation is a key precursor to the conduct of an inquiry. The preparation stage should include attention to the issues of ethical behaviour for the conduct of the inquiry, consideration of sources of bias, and the preparation of a case study protocol to guide the research process.

Considerations about ethical behaviour (harm to participants, informed consent, invasion of privacy, deception) apply to the conduct of all research. Research in IS failure however requires a particular focus on ethical behaviour because of confidentiality issues that may surround the case, non-disclosure of information, and the threat of litigation (Sauer, 1999).

Another issue which relates to all research is the question of bias. Walsham (2006) cautions that neutrality, on the part of the researcher, is not the same as unbiased therefore the researcher must ensure that sources of bias are made explicit and eliminated or reduced as far as possible. Types of bias are (1) *subject bias* whereby the subject's response is influenced due to a personal bias or external influence; and (2) *observer bias* whereby the interpretation of the research is subject to the bias of the researcher. For the study of IS failure the researcher must be particularly attentive to bias during the interview process because of the tendency of informants to rationalise their own roles, and the tendency for selective narration (Sauer, 1999).

The case study protocol is a comprehensive set of guidelines that describes the procedures for conducting the research (Maimbo, 2003; Runeson & Höst, 2009; Yin, 2009). The use of a case study protocol enforces a rigor for the conduct of the inquiry which in turn contributes to the overall quality of the research and the dependability of findings (Maimbo, 2003; Yin, 2009). For process inquiry the case study protocol can be used to specify the research instruments such as as interview guidelines, questionnaires etc., the specific types of data to be collected, and guidelines for data analysis (Maimbo, 2003; Runeson & Höst, 2009). Radeke (2010) also proposes the explication of the data collection procedure to enhance the quality of the research and dependability of findings. Explication of the data collection procedure is best achieved by the use of the case study protocol document (Yin, 2009) which states the procedures for data collection, along with general rules to be followed. Documenting the research procedures enhances the dependability of research findings.

5.4 Stage 4: Collect Data

The desired outcome of the data collection phase of a process inquiry is a well organised and categorised set of case data (Darke et al., 1998) that is relevant to the inquiry. A major strength of the case study method is the use of multiple primary and secondary data sources. This provides a rich pool of data which is particularly relevant to process inquiry. In particular the opportunity to conduct interviews with informants brings us closer than any other method to an intimate knowledge of people and their social world (Hermanowicz, 2002), and facilitates the search for meaning, intentionality, and context, all of which are major objectives of a process inquiry in general, and the study of IS failure in particular. Multiple sources of data can be cross referenced, and triangulated to corroborate findings (Mathison, 1998; Yin, 2009) and construct "converging lines of enquiry"

(Yin, 2009, p. 115) which can be used to mediate conflicting accounts (Pan & Tan, 2011), which in turn supports a more convincing narrative, and ultimately increases the quality and dependability of research findings (Dube & Pare, 2003; Kaplan & Maxwell, 2005; Yin, 2009).

Pettigrew (1990) states that for the purpose of process inquiry data collecting should be *"processual, comparative, pluralist, historical, and contextual"* (p. 277). Data collection therefore should focus on the process models' main components, viz. event sequence data, causal and consequential factors, and the identification of relationships among these components as shown in figure 2 below.

Poole et al. (2000) presents five strategies to focus data collection in a process inquiry: (1) identify events and event types; (2) characterise and classify event sequences and their properties; (3) identify dependencies in the sequences identified; (4) evaluate the data in the context of the outcome if possible; and (5) identify coherent patterns that integrate the narrative and provide explanation.

A key to management of the rich sources of data and to guard against the 'data asphyxiation' cautioned by Pettigrew is the use of the case methodology for structuring the data. This includes the use a case study database as a single repository to store, organise, and categorise the collected data, along with case study notes and other material (e.g. process maps etc…). Use of a case study database provides a single repository of case material which provides evidence supporting the case narrative and findings, which is accessible for review. The case study method also advises on constructing chains of evidence to facilitate tracing of the steps taken from the initial research question to the research conclusions, including sufficient cross-referencing to methodological procedures carried out, and the resulting evidence leading to the research findings. The construction and maintenance of chains of evidence is greatly supported by the use of the case study database, as described, with appropriate referencing, and further enhances the reliability and dependability of the research findings.

Figure 2. The components of process inquiry (Adapted from Radeke (2010))

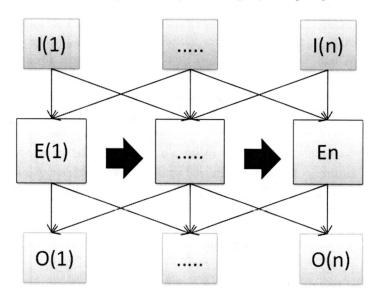

Causal factors
(antecedents, context, external constraints)

Process
(event sequence patterns)

Consequential factors
(outcomes, effects, impacts)

5.5 Stage 5: Analyse Data

The purpose of data analysis in a process inquiry is to develop or confirm theory relating to the phenomenon under investigation. Process theory describes and explains connections among phenomena (Sutton & Staw, 1995) by emphasising a dynamic view of the phenomena (Radeke, 2010) in terms of three main components: the process itself; causal factors; and consequential factors (Radeke, 2010). Process theory moves beyond a description of the components by explaining the connections among them, the underlying mechanisms that drive them, including action and context, and their relationship to certain outcomes or consequential factors (Gregor, 2006; Hinings, 1997; Radeke, 2010). Such theory has led to important new insights into phenomena related to IS (Gregor, 2006) and is therefore appropriate for the study of IS failure.

The strength of analysis is derived from the strength of the explanation of the phenomena based on the interpretation of the data (Darke et al., 1998). Eisenhardt (1989) proposes that induced theory is likely to be empirically valid when it is tightly linked to the data, a view supported by Walsham (1995a) who emphasises the importance of detailed descriptions of how findings were derived. Data analysis should be both systematic and disciplined, and should display a logical pattern of thought processes and assumptions that result in sufficient evidence for the research outcome (Walsham, 1995a), along with consideration of alternative interpretations and reasons for rejection. Carroll and Swatman (2000) note that the main difficulty when employing qualitative research is demonstrating the linkage between the data collected and conclusions drawn.

Analysis of case study evidence is one of the least developed aspects of the case study methodology (Yin, 2009) however this does not diminish its utility for the conduct of a process inquiry as a number of strategies already exist for the development of theory from process inquiry,

which are well supported by the overall case study methodology, in particular the data collection and organisation practices as described above. For example the rich sources of data available using the case study method can form the basis of the data analysis framework presented by Miles & Huberman (1994) which supports Pettigrew's description of the cycle of induction and deduction, described earlier, for the conduct of a process inquiry. In particular the case study database is an ideal repository facilitating the systematic organising and distilling of the mass of raw data collected during a case based process inquiry into some meaningful form during the first phase of analysis, referred to as the *data reduction phase*. This involves an iterative process of selecting, simplifying, abstracting, and transforming the data without diluting any of its embedded richness, leading to a set of initial categorisations which form the input to the second stage called *data display*, which involves further syntheses and summarisation of the data (presented as a combination of text and diagrams, including process charts) to produce an organised, compressed assembly of information that facilitates the final stage of *conclusion drawing and verification*. The use of a case study database facilitates the ordering and storage of data during each phase of the analysis process and the construction of chains of evidence, supported by triangulation, which facilitate the process of refinement of the data and continuous testing for plausibility of findings, which ultimately results in theory that is credible, defensible, warranted, and able to withstand alternative explanations.

The systematic collection and organisation of data as proposed by the case study methodology supports established tools for the development of theory arising from a process inquiry. This includes the construction of narratives relating to the process of IS failure as an essential first step in developing a process theory (Hirschheim & Newman, 1987; Langley, 1999) which assists with the data reduction stage of data analysis

(Miles & Huberman, 1994) by indicating patterns in the data (Pettigrew, 1997) and facilitating initial identification of key themes and categories. The deep structure of a narrative, explained by Pentland (1999), in terms of the underlying processes (generating mechanism and fabula), can be systematically categorised and depicted textually or graphically in the case study database and used in support of a description of the underlying motors (generative mechanisms) that drive the process.

Other strategies for analysing and sense making from process data as described by Langley (1999) including, quantification, alternate templates, grounded theory, visual mapping, temporal bracketing, and synthetic strategy are all supported by the conduct of an inquiry in a real life setting and the use of the data collection and storage practices recommended by the case study methodology.

5.6 Stage 6: Report Findings

There is no standard for reporting on process studies (Shaw & Jarvenpaa, 1997), however the use of well established guidelines for reporting the results of case study research (Blonk, 2003; Pratt, 2008; Yin, 2009) provide a useful template which may be applied. For example the report must contain sufficient evidence to support the research findings, and should be complemented by a case study database (Yin, 2009). To demonstrate dependability the report must describe in detail how research results were arrived at and must present a coherent and persuasively argued point of view (Walsham, 1995b). Sufficient evidence for the research results must be provided and alternative interpretations must be rejected with clear reasons (Darke et al., 1998). The dependability of the findings must also be demonstrated by providing appropriate chains of evidence along with a discussion of how bias was addressed during the inquiry process. Although reporting is depicted as the last element of the case study process it should be given explicit attention throughout the earlier phases of the study

(Yin, 2009), and should be commenced before data collection and analysis have been completed in order to facilitate continued refinement (Yin, 2009). This is consistent with Pettigrew's (1997) inductive-deductive cycle which is carried out throughout the course of the inquiry.

6. CONCLUSION

This paper has examined the nature of IS failure and the utility of process inquiry for the study of IS phenomena including IS failure. One of the striking features of process inquiry is the sheer amount and complexity of data produced which, if not managed properly, can result in *"death by data asphyxiation"* (p. 281), as described in Pettigrew (1990). Pettigrew (1990) also notes the lack of standard procedures for undertaking process inquiry. The paper notes the widespread use of the case study methodology for the conduct of research in the IS domain and proposes that this methodology is suited to the conduct of process inquiry because it specifies that the investigation be conducted within its real life context (a case of IS failure), and provides a well-documented set of tools and procedures, for the conduct of the inquiry, and for managing the resulting body of data, which are easily adaptable for process inquiry. The paper then presents a practical six stage guide to utilising the case method for the conduct of a process inquiry, which provides the benefits of a structured approach to data collection and categorisation whilst also facilitating the inductive-deductive data analysis process that is applicable for the conduct of a process inquiry.

REFERENCES

Al-ahmad, W., Al-fagih, K., & Khanfar, K. (2009). A Taxonomy of an IT Project Failure: Root Causes. *Management Review, 5*(1), 93–104.

Avison, D., Gregor, S., & Wilson, D. (2006). Managerial IT unconsciousness. *Communications of the ACM, 49*(7), 88–93. doi:10.1145/1139922.1139923

Baccarini, D., Salm, G., & Love, P. E. D. (2004). Management of risks in information technology projects. *Industrial Management & Data Systems, 104*(4), 286–295. doi:10.1108/02635570410530702

Barki, H., Rivard, S., & Talbot, J. (1993). Toward an Assessment of Software Development Risk. *Development, 10*(2), 203–225.

Benbasat, I., Goldstein, D. K., & Mead, M. (1987). The Case Research Strategy in Studies of Information Systems. *Management Information Systems Quarterly, 11*(3), 369–386. doi:10.2307/248684

Berg, M. (2001). Implementing information systems in health care organizations: Myths and challenges. *International Journal of Medical Informatics, 64*(2-3), 143–156. doi:10.1016/S1386-5056(01)00200-3 PMID:11734382

Blonk, H. (2003). Writing Case Studies in Information Systems Research. *Journal of Information Technology, 18*(1), 45–52. doi:10.1080/0268396031000077440

Boddy, D., Boonstra, A., & Kennedy, G. (2009). Managing Information Systems: Strategy and Organisation (Third Edit., p. 312). Harlow: Prentide Hall.

Brooks, F. P. (1987). No silver bullet: Essence and accidents of software engineering. *IEEE Computer, 20*(4), 10–19. doi:10.1109/MC.1987.1663532

Burch, T. K. (2001). Longituinal Research in Social Science: Some theoretical Challenges. *Canadian Studies in Population, 28*(2), 263–283.

Carroll, J. M., & Swatman, P. A. (2000). Structured-case: A methodological framework for building theory in information systems research. *European Journal of Information Systems, 9*(4), 235–242. doi:10.1057/palgrave.ejis.3000374

Clegg, C., Axtell, C., Damodaran, L., Farbey, B., Hull, R., & Lloyd-Jones, R. et al. (1997). Information technology: A study of performance and the role of human and organizational factors. *Ergonomics, 40*(9), 851–871. doi:10.1080/001401397187694

Cook, R. I. (2000). *How Complex Systems Fail* (pp. 1–5).

Darke, P., Shanks, G., & Broadbent, M. (1998). Successfully completing case study research: Combining rigour, relevance and pragmatism. *Information Systems Journal, 8*(4), 273–289. doi:10.1046/j.1365-2575.1998.00040.x

Dempsey, B., & McDonagh, J. (2014). Integrating Process Inquiry and the Case Method in the Study of IS Failure. In *Proceedings of the UKAIS, 2014.*

Doolin, B. (1993). Alternative views of case research in information systems. *Information Systems Research, 3*(2), 21–29.

Drevin, L. (2008). Making sense of information systems failures by using narrative analysis methods. In *Proceeding of the 13th and 14th CPTS Working Conference 2008.* CPTS.

Dube, L., & Pare, G. (2003). Rigor in information systems positivist case research: Current practices, trends, and recommendations. *Management Information Systems Quarterly, 27*(4), 597–636.

Eisenhardt, K. M. (1989). Building theories from case study research. *Academy of Management Review, 14*(4), 532–550.

Eveleens, J. L., & Verhoef, C. (2010). The Rise and Fall of the Chaos Report Figures. *IEEE Software, 27*(1), 30–36. doi:10.1109/MS.2009.154

Ferlie, E., & Mcnulty, T. (1997). Going to Market ": Changing Patterns in the Organisation and Character of Process Research. *Scandinavian Journal of Management, 13*(4), 367–387. doi:10.1016/S0956-5221(97)00024-9

Flowers, S. (1996). *Software Failure: Management Failure*. Chichester: John Wiley & Sons.

Fortune, J., & Peters, G. (2005). *Information Systems Achieving Success by Avoiding Failure* (p. 220). Chichester: John Wiley & Sons.

Goldfinch, S. (2007). Pessimism, computer failure, and information systems development in the public sector. *Public Administration Review, 67*(5), 917–929. doi:10.1111/j.1540-6210.2007.00778.x

Gregor, S. (2006). The nature of theory in information systems. *Management Information Systems Quarterly, 30*(3), 611–642.

Guba, E. G., & Lincoln, Y. S. (2005). Paradigmatic controversies, contradictions, and emerging confluences. In N. K. Denzin & Y. S. Lincoln (Eds.), The Sage handbook of qualitative research (3rd ed., pp. 191–215). Thousand Oaks, CA: Sage Publications.

Hermanowicz, J. (2002). The great interview: 25 strategies for studying people in bed. *Qualitative Sociology, 25*(4), 479–500. doi:10.1023/A:1021062932081

Hinings, C. R. (1997). Reflections on processual research. *Scandinavian Journal of Management, 13*(4), 493–503. doi:10.1016/S0956-5221(97)00023-7

Hirschheim, R., & Newman, M. (1987). Symbolism and Information Systems Development: Myth, Metaphor and Magic. *Information Systems Research, 2*(1), 29–62. doi:10.1287/isre.2.1.29

Hyvari, I. (2006). Success of projects in different organizational conditions. *Project Management Journal, 37*(4), 31–42.

Kaplan, B., & Maxwell, J. (2005). Qualitative research methods for evaluating computer information systems. In *Evaluating the Organizational Impact of Healthcare Information Systems* (pp. 30–55). Springer. doi:10.1007/0-387-30329-4_2

Kappelman, L., McKeeman, R., & Zhang, L. (2006). Early Warning Signs of IT Project Failure: The Dominant Dozen. *Information Systems Management, 23*(4), 31–36. doi:10.1201/1078.1 0580530/46352.23.4.20060901/95110.4

Keen, P. G. W. (1981). Information systems and organizational change. *Communications of the ACM, 24*(1), 24–33. doi:10.1145/358527.358543

Keil, M. (1995). Pulling the plug: Software project management and the problem of project escalation. *Management Information Systems Quarterly, 19*(4), 421–447. doi:10.2307/249627

Langley, A. (1999). Strategies for theorizing from process data. *Academy of Management Review, 24*(4), 691–710.

Langley, A. (2009). Studying Processes In and Around Organizations. In D. Buchanan, & A. Bryman (Eds.), *Sage Handbook of Organisational Research Methods* (Vol. 2008, p. 776). Sage Publications.

Langley, A., & Tsoukas, H. (2010). Introducing Perspectives on Process Organization Studies. In *Process, sensemaking & organizing*. Oxford University Press. doi:10.1093/acprof:o so/9780199594566.003.0001

Lincoln, E. S., & Guba, E. A. (1985). *Naturalistic Enquiry* (p. 416). Beverly Hills: Sage Publications.

Lincoln, Y. S., Lynham, S. A., & Guba, E. G. (2011). Paradigmatic controversies, contradictions, and emerging confluences, revisited. In N. K. Denzin, & Y. S. Lincoln (Eds.), *The Sage handbook of qualitative research* (pp. 97–128). Thousand Oaks, CA.

Lyytinen, K., & Herscheim, R. (1987). *Information system failures - a survey and classification of the literature. New York*. New York, NY, USA: Oxford University Press, Inc.

Lyytinen, K., & Robey, D. (1999). Learning failure in information systems development. *Information Systems Journal, 9*(2), 85–101. doi:10.1046/j.1365-2575.1999.00051.x

Maimbo, H. (2003). *Designing a Case Study Protocol for Application in IS research* (pp. 1281–1292). PACIS.

Marchland, D. A., & Hykes, A. (2006, December). Designed to Fail: Why IT-enabled Business Projects Underacheive and What To Do About Them. *Tomorrows Challenges*, 1–4.

Markus, M. L., & Robey, D. (1988). Information technology and organizational change: Causal structure in theory and research. *Management Science, 34*(5), 583–598. doi:10.1287/mnsc.34.5.583

Mathison, S. (1998). Why Triangulate ? *Educational Researcher, 17*(2), 13–17.

McDonagh, J. (2001). Not for the faint hearted: Social and organisational challenges in IT-enabled change. *Organization Development Journal, 19*(1), 11–20.

Miles, M. B., & Huberman, A. M. (1994). *Qualitative Data Analysis: A Sourcebook of New Methods.* Beverly Hills, CA: Sage Publications.

Mohr, L. B. (1982). *Explaining Organisational Behavior: The Limits and Possibilities of Theory and Research.* San Francisco, CA: Jossey-Bass.

Nelson, R. R. (2007). IT project management: Infamous failures, classic mistakes, and best practices. *MIS Quarterly Executive, 6*(2).

Newman, M., & Robey, D. (1992). A Social Process Model of User-Analyst Relationships. *Management Information Systems Quarterly, 16*(2), 249–267. doi:10.2307/249578

Pan, G., Hackney, R., & Pan, S. L. (2008). Information Systems implementation failure: Insights from prism. *International Journal of Information Management, 28*(4), 259–269. doi:10.1016/j.ijinfomgt.2007.07.001

Pan, S. L., & Tan, B. (2011). Demystifying case research: A structured–pragmatic–situational (SPS) approach to conducting case studies. *Information and Organization, 21*(3), 161–176. doi:10.1016/j.infoandorg.2011.07.001

Pare, G. (2004). Investigating information systems with positivist case study research. *Communications of the Association for Information Systems, 13*(1), 233–264.

Pentland, B. T. (1999). Building process theory with narrative: From description to explanation. *Academy of Management Review, 24*(4), 711–724.

Peterson, M. (1998). Embedded organizational events: The units of process in organization science. *Organization Science, 9*(1), 16–33. doi:10.1287/orsc.9.1.16

Pettigrew, A. (1987). Context and Action in the Transformation of the Firm. *Journal of Management Studies, 24*(6), 649–670. doi:10.1111/j.1467-6486.1987.tb00467.x

Pettigrew, A. (1990). Longitudinal field research on change: Theory and practice. *Organization Science, 1*(3), 267–292. doi:10.1287/orsc.1.3.267

Pettigrew, A. M. (1992). The character and significance of strategy process research. *Strategic Management Journal, 13*(S2), 5–16. doi:10.1002/smj.4250130903

Pettigrew, A. M. (1997). What is a processual analysis. *Scandinavian Journal of Management, 13*(4), 337–348. doi:10.1016/S0956-5221(97)00020-1

Pettigrew, A. M. (2012). JMS Context and Action in the Transformation of the Firm. *Journal of Management Studies, 49*(7), 1304–1328. doi:10.1111/j.1467-6486.2012.01054.x

Ployhart, R. E., & Vandenberg, R. J. (2010). Longitudinal Research : The Theory, Design, and Analysis of Change. *Journal of Management, 36*(1), 94–121. doi:10.1177/0149206309352110

Poole, M. S., Van de Ven, A. H., Dooley, M. E., & Holmes, K. (2000). *Organisational Change and Innovation Processes: Theory and Methods for Research* (p. 416). New York: Oxford University Press.

Pratt, M. G. (2008). Fitting Oval Pegs Into Round Holes: Tensions in Evaluating and Publishing Qualitative Rearearch in Top-Tier North American Journals. *Organizational Research Methods, 11*(3), 481–509. doi:10.1177/1094428107303349

Radeke, F. (2010). How To Rigorously Develop Process Theory Using Case Research. In Proceedings of ECIS 2010 (pp. 1–12). ECIS.

Runeson, P., & Höst, M. (2009). Guidelines for Conducting and Reporting Case Study Research in Software Engineering. *Empirical Software Engineering, 14*(2), 131–164. doi:10.1007/s10664-008-9102-8

Sauer, C. (1993). In D. E. Avison, & G. Fitzgerald (Eds.), *Why Information systems fail: A Case Study Approach* (p. 359). Henley-on-Thames: Alfred Waller Ltd.

Sauer, C. (1999). Deciding the future for IS failures: not the choice you might think. In *Re-thinking Management Information Systems* (pp. 279–309). Oxford: Oxford University Press.

Schmidt, R. C., Lyytinen, K., Keil, M., & Cule, P. (2001). Identifying software project risks: An international Delphi Study. *Journal of Management Information Systems, 17*(4), 5–36.

Shaw, T., & Jarvenpaa, S. (1997). Process Models in Information Systems. In A. S. Lee, L. J. Leibenau, & J. I. De Gross (Eds.), *Information Systems and Qualitative Research1* (pp. 70–100). London: Chapman and Hall. doi:10.1007/978-0-387-35309-8_6

Sutton, R., & Staw, B. M. (1995). ASQ Forum What Theory is Not. *Administrative Science Quarterly, 40*(3), 371–384. doi:10.2307/2393788

Sztompka, P. (1993). *The Sociology of Social Change.* Oxford: Blackwell.

Tsoukas, H., & Chia, R. (2002). On organizational becoming: Rethinking organizational change. *Organization Science, 13*(5), 567–582. doi:10.1287/orsc.13.5.567.7810

Van de Ven, A. H., & Poole, M. (2005). Alternative Approaches for Studying Organizational Change. *Organization Studies, 26*(9), 1377–1404. doi:10.1177/0170840605056907

Wallace, L., Keil, M., & Rai, A. (2004). How Software Project Risk Affects Project Performance: An Investigation of the Dimensions of Risk and an Exploratory Model. *Decision Sciences, 35*(2), 289–321. doi:10.1111/j.00117315.2004.02059.x

Walsham, G. (1995a). Interpretive case studies in IS research: Nature and method. *European Journal of Information Systems, 4*(2), 74–81. doi:10.1057/ejis.1995.9

Walsham, G. (1995b). The Emergence of Interpretivism in IS Research. *Information Systems Research, 6*(4), 376–394. doi:10.1287/isre.6.4.376

Walsham, G. (2006). Doing interpretive research. *European Journal of Information Systems, 15*(3), 320–330. doi:10.1057/palgrave.ejis.3000589

Wilson, M., & Howcroft, D. (2002). Re-conceptualising failure : Social shaping meets IS research. *Fortune, 11*, 236–250.

Wilson, V. (2011). Research Methods: Design, Methods, Case Study...oh my! *Evidence Based Library and Information Practice*, 6(3), 90–93.

Yeo, K. T. (2002). Critical failure factors in information system projects. *International Journal of Project Management*, 20(3), 241–246. doi:10.1016/S0263-7863(01)00075-8

Yin, R. K. (2009). Case Study Research Design and Methods (4th ed.). Sage Publications.

KEY TERMS AND DEFINITIONS

Case Method: Is a method of research which studies a phenomenon in a 'real life' setting.

Failure Factor: A cause of failure.

Information System (IS): Is a computer based application (system) that supports decision making and other organisational activity.

IS development: Is the process of designing, implementing and maintaining an Information System.

IS Failure: Refers to the failure of an Information System to deliver planned or expected benefits or functionality.

Methodology: A structured plan for the conduct of research.

Ontology: A position or belief about the nature of reality or being.

Process Inquiry: Is the dynamic study of behaviour focusing on sequences of events, activities and actions over time, and in context, leading to an outcome or outcomes.

Qualitative/Interpretive Research: A type of inquiry which attempts to make sense of, or interpret, phenomena in terms of the meanings people bring to them.

Theory of Failure: An explanation of how and/or why a failure occurs.

Chapter 19
Discount Focus Subgroup Method:
An Innovative Focus Group Method Used for Researching an Emerging Technology

Mohanad Halaweh
University of Dubai, UAE

ABSTRACT

This chapter develops an innovative focus group method—the Discount Focus Subgroup (DFSG)—through its application in research aimed at identifying the ethical and social concerns of using an emerging technology, called near field communication, for mobile payments. The DFSG method was needed to address the challenges encountered when this research was conducted, such as limited financial research resources, the emergent nature of the research topic, and the challenges of gathering and analyzing qualitative data. This chapter illustrates when and how to use the DFSG method. It provides the methodological steps for its application, which can be followed while researching emerging topics in the Information Systems (IS) field. The chapter also discusses why DFSG is an innovative method and reflects on its application.

INTRODUCTION AND MOTIVATION

This chapter describes the development of an innovative focus group method, called the discount focus subgroup (DFSG) method. This method was applied in research aimed at identifying the ethical and social concerns that would arise by using near field communication (NFC) technology enabled by smart phones to make mobile payments. It is worth mentioning that the focus in this chapter is on the application of the proposed method rather than the research results of the example per se. Investigating the impact of NFC technology is used in the chapter as an example of how and when to employ the proposed method, not as the motivation to write this chapter. In this section, a brief background of the research project is introduced, followed by the motivations for developing the DFSG method.

NFC can be defined as "a standards-based short-range wireless connectivity technology that makes life easier and more convenient for consum-

DOI: 10.4018/978-1-4666-6493-7.ch019

ers around the world by making it simpler to make transactions, exchange digital content, and connect electronic devices with a touch," according to the NFC forum (2014). As an emerging technology, it is still not widely used or applied for mobile payments. However, Juniper Research expects that NFC will be rapidly adopted and that one in five users worldwide will have an NFC-enabled phone by 2014 (Wilcox, 2011). Özdenizci, Aydin, Coşkun, and Ok (2010) noted that the body of literature on NFC does not include many journal articles. Nevertheless, they wrote a state-of-the-art paper after reviewing 74 academic papers from 2006 to 2010. Their findings showed that the majority of NFC research is related to NFC applications, developments, and infrastructure. Özdenizci et al. (2010) pointed out that the social and cultural issues associated with NFC represent a demanding area of investigation, as no previous research has clearly highlighted these issues.

As soon as a new technology is created, any possible ethical concerns should be highlighted immediately to use this technology so human values are protected. One should not wait until the ethical problems impede society and individuals. Ethics is an integral part of philosophy that is concerned with issues of good and bad or right and wrong acts (Stahl, 2007). One approach to studying ethics and Information Technology (IT) is through the identification and analysis of the impact of IT on human values like health, equality, opportunity, freedom, democracy, and privacy (Moor, 1985; Gotterbarn, 1991; Lucas, 2011). Sandler (2009) indicated that some people have misconceptions about ethics and emerging technology. One of these misconceptions is the belief that 'It is too soon to tell what the social and ethical issues are' (Sandler, 2009, p. 6). This is due to the narrow focus on the technology itself while neglecting broader contextual factors. Therefore, investigating the possible effects of NFC technology earlier will enable the implementation of different policies and actions to address them.

General and specific challenges arose in investigating this research (i.e., the impact of NFC technology), which led to developing the DFSG method. General challenges pertained to the limited funds available for conducting research, and there were no funds to hire research assistants to help with gathering and analyzing qualitative data. Moreover, only one researcher was involved in conducting this research. Specific challenges were related to the difficulty in finding research participants, particularly those who could provide insight and relevant information, due to the nature of this new and emerging research topic. When it comes to new technology or techniques that are not widely known or accepted, it is difficult to find participants who are familiar with them. Therefore, it is difficult to gain insight from one-on-one interviews or even focus groups with small numbers of participants, as one may conduct a focus group with four participants and find that some of them are unfamiliar with the research topic (e.g., NFC technology) or have little knowledge, as happened in the first focus group conducted by the current researcher. A third challenge concerned the analysis phase. A qualitative researcher typically spends considerable time transcribing every single recorded word—a process that may result in hundreds of pages that are not entirely insightful and useful. All of this motivated the current researcher to find new methods that would accommodate and address the above-mentioned challenges. Obviously, these challenges justify the need for DFSG, so this answers the question of when it can be applied. Although many researchers in the IS field have used the focus group method, the literature does not provide adapted methods for addressing the above-mentioned challenges.

The following two sections respectively present the literature review on the focus group method in general and in the IS field. Subsequently, a demonstration will be provided to show how the DFSG method was applied in the current research. This will be followed by a section discussing the criteria for evaluating the quality of the research that has applied the DFSG method. Finally, this chapter will discuss why DFSG is an innovative method, highlight how it solved the challenges faced in the present research, and provide reflections and limitations on its application.

Focus Group Method

The focus group is a qualitative research method that emerged amidst the social research of the 1950s (Templeton, 1992). Powell and Single (1996) defined a focus group as "a group of individuals selected and assembled by researchers to discuss and comment on, from personal experience, the topic that is the subject of the research" (p. 499). Focus groups allow researchers to obtain insight and rich data from a group discussion in a short amount of time (Morgan & Scannell, 1998). The data collected from focus groups provide profound insight into people's beliefs, opinions, and experiences. The focus groups method is most appropriate for exploratory research, but it can also be used for confirmatory research (Stewart & Shamdasani, 1990). There are several textbooks that provide detailed guidelines for planning and running focus groups (e.g., Morgan & Scannell, 1998; Puchta & Potter, 2004; Krueger & Casey, 2009), making it a method that is widely accepted and applied in different fields. According to the literature, more than one focus group meeting is needed within a study (Morgan & Scannell, 1998; Krueger, 2000). The literature also suggests that the number of focus group participants should be in the range of 4 to 12 (Jankowicz, 1995), 6 to 10 (Morgan & Scannell, 1998), 7 to 10 (Krueger, 2000) or 6 to 12 (Kelley, 1999). Participants are selected using purposive sampling, on the basis of their relevance to the research topic under investigation. Typically, focus group sessions are conducted by a moderator who should have the necessary skills to conduct the session successfully, such as allowing all participants to express their views, the ability to communicate both orally and in writing, the ability to listen, and the ability to involve all participants in the conversation (Krueger & Casey, 2000). The sessions are usually recorded with audio and/or video devices (Krueger & Casey, 2000) and then transcribed for analysis using different methods and techniques.

FOCUS GROUP METHOD IN IS RESEARCH

IS researchers have also advocated the use of the focus group method (See, e.g., O'hEocha, Wang, & Conboy, 2012; Stahl, Tremblay, & LeRouge, 2011; Burgess, 2010; Sobreperez, 2008). Despite its suitability for researching IS phenomena, it has not been used extensively in the IS field (Sobreperez, 2008; O'hEocha et al., 2010). This was confirmed by Belanger (2012), who reviewed 58 articles published in top IS journals that used the focus group method. The result of her literature review showed that quite a few published articles adopted this research method in general, and that most studies using the focus group research method have been published in recent years: 49 out of 58 studies were published between 2003 and 2011. Furthermore, she pointed out that this method is gaining acceptance for its appropriateness in IS research. An important finding was that most of the reviewed papers used the focus group method to study the new exploratory nature of IS phenomena (e.g., the critical success factors for the implementation of cloud computing). She also highlighted that focus groups can play an important role in developing theoretical models of IS phenomena to be tested.

The focus group research method has been used to study IS phenomena such as IT/IS adoption, acceptance, impact, and evaluation (See, e.g., Klaus & Blanton, 2010; Otondo, Pearson, Pearson, Shaw, & Shim, 2009; Chesney, Coyne, Logan, & Madden, 2009; Sutton, Khazanchi, Hampto, & Arnold, 2008; Weidong & Lee, 2005). However, some of the IS research using this method did not specify the number of focus groups (See, e.g., Smith et al., 1996), and some did not specify the number of participants in each group (See, e.g., Smith & McKeen, 2007; Weidong & Lee, 2005). In fact, some articles neither specified the number of focus groups in the study nor the number of participants in the focus groups (See, e.g., Wang, Lo, & Yang, 2004). In some cases, the focus group was used as the sole research method (Lee & Kwon, 2008; Campbell, Kay, & Avison, 2005), and in others, it was used in conjunction with other methods, such as a survey and/or interviews (Krasnova, Spiekermann, Koroleva, & Hildebrand, 2010; Galup, Klein, & Jiang, 2008; Weidong & Lee, 2005; Smith, Milberg, & Burke, 1996; Dickinger, Arami, & Meyer, 2008).

The focus group was also used as the method for requirement elicitation and IS development (See, e.g., O'hEocha et al., 2010; Farinha & da Silva, 2009; Le Rouge & Niederman, 2006). Stahl et al. (2011) suggested using focus groups in IS research as a critical method that can facilitate emancipation. Tremblay, Hevner, and Berndt (2010) used the focus group method as an evaluation technique for design research. However, previous IS research using the focus group method did not adapt the traditional method to clearly address the challenges mentioned in the introduction. Therefore, this chapter came to develop a new innovative focus group method that tackles those challenges.

How the Focus Group Method Was Applied in the Current Research Project

Because NFC technology is relatively new and not widely known, the focus group was an appropriate method for this research because some of the participants knew little about the research topic; this required group discussion to stimulate all the participants to make a contribution and enrich the discussion. Due to the limited resources, the researcher selected the participants from the university, that is, the researcher's work environment.

All group members were undergraduate students, and some of them were professional workers. The participants were selected purposefully. They had mobile phones (The great majority had modern ones), and some of them had NFC-enabled mobile phones.

In this research, three focus group sessions were conducted, each one lasting about 75 minutes. There were four participants in Group 1, and none of them had NFC-enabled mobile phones. The second group consisted of 16 participants, and 10 had NFC-enabled mobile phones. The third group consisted of 17 participants, but only five of them had NFC technology on their mobile phones. Some of the participants discovered during the course of the meeting that they had this technology on their mobile phones. They were neither previously aware that they had it, nor did they know the need for it. The current study used a different number of participants than that recommended by the literature. Groups 2 and 3 were larger than the group sizes suggested in the literature. However, the reason for this larger number was due to the nature of the research topic, which involved discussion and debate about emerging technology that is not widely accepted by individuals or merchants; thus, it was expected that some of the participants would be unfamiliar with this technology or have little knowledge about it. However, their contribution could still be considered effective in raising questions and enquiring into the topic, while others who were more familiar could provide answers on the basis of their opinions and experience. The first focus group comprised four participants, as suggested by the literature. However, it was found that the richness of ideas and discussion was greater in the other two groups (groups 2 and 3), which were larger.

The researcher worked as a facilitator to motivate and encourage the participants to share their opinions and beliefs freely. The researcher led the discussion by introducing the objectives of this research and providing a briefing about NFC technology. The discussions revolved around the main question: What are the ethical and social implications of using NFC technology for mobile payment? This question was rephrased for some participants who did not understand it clearly: What are the impacts of using NFC technology for mobile payment on individuals and society?

Since the number of participants in groups 2 and 3 was relatively large, the researcher divided each group into subgroups. The participants were asked to spend a few minutes writing their answers in note form and discussing them: first, with the members of each subgroup and then in open discussion among the whole group. The discussion between the members of each subgroup involved debating, joking, and sometimes reaching agreement about their opinions. The focus group session results were documented on paper by the participants themselves (See a sample in appendices A.1 and A.2), and notes were taken by the researcher during the open discussion. These results were combined into a document for analysis that focused on identifying the issues and themes. The researcher did not focus on transcribing each word spoken in the discussion; instead, the focus was on identifying the significant ideas discussed by the groups. In addition, in this research, no video or audio recordings were made; this was to avoid too much formality and the possible concern that each participant would be assessed on the basis of his or her speech. Instead, the participants themselves led the discussions, as each of the subgroups had a leader who made notes on paper. Some members of the subgroups posed the questions, while others provided the answers and opinions. This approach enabled each participant to think, speak out, and express his or her opinion freely. To ensure that no ideas were missed, each subgroup wrote its ideas on paper, and the researcher focused on writing notes during the open discussion between subgroups.

When the discussion between all subgroups was open, each one's ideas were heard in a circular manner. It was found, for example, that most of the subgroups recorded privacy as an issue. However, when the issue was raised for the first time by one subgroup, other subgroups stated their viewpoint in relation to the same issue, even when it was listed as point #4 on the sheet for another subgroup. This procedure was done to avoid repetitions of the same issues during another round of discussion. When there was open dialogue between all subgroups, the researcher got their opinions on why this is a concern (i.e., privacy) when NFC technology is used for mobile payment and how this is different from tracking credit card transactions. For example, some subgroups provided clarifications and viewpoints, and some said that it is similar to credit cards.

After collecting the papers, the researcher applied constant comparative analysis to the collected data by constantly comparing the ideas and then grouping similar ones together under one category. Constant comparative analysis is a technique used for qualitative data analysis. It was originally developed for use in a grounded theory method. Now, it is applied more widely as an independent method for analysis in qualitative research and is used outside the grounded theory method. Examples can be found in the work of Fram (2013) and O'Connor, Netting, and Thomas (2008). According to Leech and Onwuegbuzie (2007), constant comparison analysis is considered the most commonly used technique for analyzing qualitative data. The process begins by comparing incidents or pieces of data to other incidents or pieces of data during the process of coding. Leech and Onwuegbuzie (2007) elaborated on the process further by stating:

To perform a constant comparison analysis, the researcher first reads through the entire set of data (this also could be a subset of the data). After doing so, the researcher chunks the data into smaller meaningful parts. Then, the researcher labels each chunk with a descriptive title or a "code." The researcher takes pains to compare each new chunk of data with previous codes, so similar chunks will be labeled with the same code. After all the data have been coded, the codes are grouped by similarity, and a theme is identified and documented based on each grouping (p. 565).

A similar process was applied to the collected data. For example, Table 1 shows some chunks of data taken from written notes by different subgroups, which were then compared. Since they are similar, they were combined and refined under the "privacy" category. The category name reflected the data themselves. Samples of handwritten notes by the subgroups' leaders were attached in appendices A.1 and A.2. It is important to mention that the clustering process was applied before this categorization was done, and this was very important to ensure the emergence of concepts and ideas. In categorization, the researcher might have a set of predefined categories or concepts and must classify each idea according to these categories, while in clustering, the researcher tries to group a set of ideas that are similar or that have similar properties, and then a category name can be identified and assigned to them. The findings that emerged from the focus group discussions were categorized into three main ethical/social concerns as perceived by the participants: dependency and vulnerability, inequality, and privacy. These are summarized in Table 2.

HOW TO APPLY THE DFSG METHOD

DFSG can be defined as an innovative form of the focus group method that can be applied to the following: a research phenomenon that is emerging and new, research projects that have limited resources, and/or studies whose authors are seeking to economize and speed up the process of data collection and analysis.

On the basis of the demonstrated application of the focus group method in the previous section, the following five steps are generalized for applying the DFSG method:

- Utilize the limited resources available. Find participants from the work environment: in academia, including students and instructors at the university, and/or in industry, meaning staff and workers from organizations. Both have various characteristics that are suitable for a large number of research topics. For example, university students are female or male; are of different ages; come from different backgrounds, cultures, and geographical areas; and practice different religions. Some are business professionals, have mobile phones, and use the Internet.

Table 1. Codes and a category that emerged from constant comparison analysis. (Equivalent handwritten chunks of data are shown in Figure 2 in the Appendix).

Category: Privacy
Chunks (codes in italics)
Personal information privacy it will be violated
They can watch my personal information
Privacy can be violated. Not anyone can *access the information*
Companies could track the person-details used
Access to our information. Banks will easily know our location and our payment process, we can easily be *tracked*
The dilemma-*easy access to others.* Can easily violated-especially if mobile phone is stolen
Hackers *may access the information* stored in the chip and can be used in fraud transactions or purchases

Table 2. Ethical/social concerns of using NFC technology for mobile payment

Dependency and vulnerability	NFC increases people's reliance on technology, as they cannot avoid mobile phones—they have become ubiquitous. It replaces the traditional method of carrying cash in one's pocket. Losing, misplacing, or misusing a mobile phone would cause inconvenience and could get individuals into trouble, especially when the device becomes a source of money. It is not like cash or credit cards, which are kept in a safe place in one's pockets. Mobile phones are more accessible, as people hold them in their hand or place them on a table or desk. It is difficult to adopt this technology, and it will take a long time, as it requires replacing all old mobile phones with the new modern ones for which this technology is built. There is also no point to replacing a mobile phone to use this technology, as very few shops accept it as a payment method.
Inequality	NFC technology will also increase the inequality between people; it will enable individuals who have modern phones to enjoy quick payment services at sales points, whereas others who do not have this technology will have to wait longer in queues. The technology also excludes some people who cannot replace their mobile phone with an NFC-enabled mobile phone; few manufactures design mobile phones with this technology or limit this technology to expensive devices that few people can afford. Using this technology might also provoke jealousy among people who are high-tech.
Privacy	NFC-enabled mobile phones will invade people's privacy in an extreme way, as banks will know more about customers who use NFC-enabled mobile phones for payments. They will use the technology for every big or small purchase in one "wave and go" step. Banks will analyze this data to identify customers' purchase patterns and behaviors. Banks can already identify this information by tracking credit card transactions. However, the use of NFC technology might mean this might be taken to the extreme, as every payment can be tracked, whereas before NFC, there was a possibility of avoiding being tracked by paying for purchases in cash. Thus, the more data gathered, processed, and transmitted, the more privacy is violated and breached. Besides the concerns about information privacy violations, people's location is tracked.

- Divide and assign roles. Divide the participants (the larger the number, the more numerous the insights and issues that emerge from the discussion) into subgroups, and appoint one member of each subgroup as a research assistant/moderator to write notes and ideas (in the form of a list) from the subgroup discussions on papers that will later be delivered to the researcher.

- Avoid formality. Avoid using recorders and cameras to allow everyone to talk freely and spontaneously. Allow joking, debates, and fun. Avoiding formality increases participation. No one will be shy or judged by his or her speech and answers; rather, those who are unfamiliar with the topic or who have limited knowledge can pose questions and enrich the discussion. Having participants from the same environment (as indicated in step one) will facilitate the discussion and remove the formality, as the participants will know each other.

- Open the discussion, and document cross-discussions and debates among all subgroups that are not written by the subgroup leaders and that emerge from the interaction among the subgroups. Take the contribution from each subgroup in a circular manner. Start with one idea or issue from each subgroup, then do another round to take another idea or issue, and allow intervention and debate from the other subgroups.

- Consolidate and cluster lists of ideas written on paper by all subgroup leaders as well as ideas written during open discussion and debating.

By applying these steps, the data collection and analysis are carried out simultaneously as each subgroup leader writes the notes on paper in point form, and thus the researcher will not have to devote time later to transcribing each word and coding the keywords. The listed ideas from all subgroups are usually ready for clustering and categorizing.

Figure 1 shows a typical DFSG meeting. As shown in the figure, the participants in a

Figure 1. Typical DFSG meeting

big group are divided into three subgroups of seven participants each. However, the number of participants in each subgroup might be slightly different depending on the number of participants in the big group. As shown, for each subgroup, there should be one person who chairs, leads the discussion, and writes the members' viewpoint. Also, as shown there, is one document produced by each subgroup, which is delivered to the researcher at the end of session. It also shows the principal researcher who coordinates and moderates the entire session. He also writes notes or memos during the open discussion among all subgroups and through observing the subgroup members' discussions. The figure's arrow also

shows a circular direction to indicate that issues are discussed in circular manner (a unique issue is discussed once) to avoid repetition of the same issues when the open discussion occur among all subgroups.

DFSG QUALITY EVALUATION CRITERIA

After reviewing the literature, four options were considered for evaluating the proposed method. However, ultimately, one appropriately rational option was selected. Option 1, which was excluded at the outset, was to use criteria for evaluating quantitative research, such as validity and reliability. However, many qualitative researchers have deemed these criteria inappropriate for qualitative research (See, e.g., Northcote, 2012; Guba & Lincoln, 2005; Tobin & Begley, 2004; Schofield, 2002; Whittemore, Chase, & Mandle, 2001; Altheide & Johnson, 1998), because qualitative research is based on completely different epistemological and ontological assumptions compared to quantitative research. Option 2 was to use criteria/principles for evaluating interpretive research like the seven principles developed by Klein and Myers (1999). However, this option was not completely suitable and applicable to the current method, as the proposed qualitative research method can be applied using two different research paradigms, namely, the positivist and interpretive research, as Myers and Avison (2002) stated. Option 3 was to find particular criteria for evaluating the quality of the focus group research; although there is extensive literature on how to design and conduct focus group research (Morgan, 1997; Barbour, 2007; Krueger & Casey, 2009), there are very few well-defined criteria for evaluating focus group research (O'hEocha et al., 2010). It is arguably advisable to use a more holistic view of the quality of the research as a whole, rather than discuss any specific criteria to evaluate the use of the focus group method for data collection (O'hEocha et al., 2010). In the current research, to avoid ambiguity, the focus is on evaluating the quality of qualitative research in particular, rather than on generic criteria for evaluating the research in general. Hence, option 4 was to use Lincoln and Guba's (1985, 2000) criteria for evaluating qualitative research in general. These criteria are appropriate for evaluating the quality of the proposed method because it involves collecting qualitative data. These criteria are summarized in Table 3. The table also shows how these criteria are applicable and ensured when concerning the DFSG method.

DISCUSSION

This chapter developed a new, innovative focus group method. The term "innovation" has been defined in many different ways in different fields. However, one of the general definitions in Webster's New World Dictionary is that innovation is "the act or process of innovating; something newly introduced, new method, custom, device, etc.; change in the way of doing things; renew, alter." Therefore, an "innovative method" in this context means doing things in new, different ways to solve emerging problems and challenges. DFSG is considered innovative for the following three reasons.

First, more than 12 participants (the maximum number suggested in the literature) can be involved, and the method remains effective, as they are divided into subgroups. This is different from all suggestions in the literature. The more participants we have, the more insight and discussion there will be. Using subgroups in one big group is a new way of addressing a large number of participants. This is also needed for certain research topics that are new and emerging, as it is expected that some of the participants will be unfamiliar with the topic under investigation or have little knowledge, but their role is to raise questions. This, again, does not cause problems, as those participants are divided into subgroups and each is led by a leader, who plays the role of moderator or acts as a research assistant, so the session can be managed and organized.

Second, DFSG eliminates the costs of using voice/video recorders and of employing research assistants, as well as the time needed to transcribe each recorded word; instead of transcribing intensive irrelevant speech, the research can focus on issues and themes and use the participants to write the ideas. Therefore, the answers to the research questions are focused and organized, as they are written in the form of a list on paper. In addition,

Table 3. Criteria for evaluating the quality of qualitative research applied to the DFSG method

Evaluation Criteria*	Description	Application to DFSG Method
Credibility	Refers to the degree to which a study's findings are credible and represent the meanings of the research participants. Credibility is achieved by • Using triangulation. • Allowing the participants to check their dialogue transcripts and their meaning. Checks relating to the accuracy of the data may take place on the spot in the course and at the end of the data collection dialogues; here, the emphasis should be on whether the informants consider that their words match what they actually intended. • Providing thick description of the phenomenon under scrutiny.	Triangulations took several forms when the DFSG method was applied; data triangulation was achieved by (1) gathering papers, including a list of ideas discussed and written by the subgroup members; (2) notes taken by the researcher when the general discussion was opened among all subgroups; (3) close observation and listening by the researcher to each subgroup's discussion and comments. Member checks achieved on the spot and immediately by the participants, since they had written the notes, and after the members' agreements and discussions. Thick description is also a strategy to ensure transferability, so it is highlighted in the next row.
Transferability	Refers to the degree to which the findings can be applied and transferred to other contexts with similar conditions; this can be achieved by providing the reader with rich, detailed information (so-called "thick description") about the context that has been investigated.	Details on the research project, context, and participants were provided: research topic and nature, i.e., about new and emerging technology, number of focus groups, time for each focus group discussion, number of subgroups in each group, how group discussion data were collected and documented, who documented the collected data, participants' backgrounds, and events that occurred during group discussion, such as the participants picking up their mobile phones to check if they have NFC technology.
Dependability	Refers to the degree to which the research process is well-documented and can be traced and which gives documentation of the methods and approaches used in the research; this allows others outside the research project to follow the research process and involves the need for the researcher to describe the changes that occurred in the context and how these changes affected the way the researcher approached the study.	Details of the way of conducting the proposed method are provided and justified, whereby the method can be used in other similar situations in which similar challenges might be faced; see section one, three challenges that motivate adapting the focus group method, and section five, which shows how the method steps (five generalized steps) were applied, which can be followed by other IS researchers. The changes that occurred in the course of conducting the research were also documented. For example, the number of participants in the focus group was increased. The first focus group comprised four participants, but since the research topic was emergent and a small group did not produce rich information, the subsequent focus groups comprised larger numbers of participants. The decision was made to divide these large groups into subgroups.
Conformability	Refers to the degree to which the results could be confirmed or corroborated by others; this can be achieved by showing how the findings emerge from the data collected from participants, and not from preconceptions, by showing raw data and demonstrating the steps of the analysis leading to the reporting of the results and outcomes (so-called audit trail).	The participants themselves wrote their perceptions and experiences on sheets of paper, so the findings emerged naturally, as these are considered the outputs from the discussion and they were ready for clustering. Clustering was applied, first, by comparative analysis; then the categorization ensured the emergence of the concepts/categories. A sample of the notes written by the participants is attached in the appendix; attaching the sample of these notes confirms that the findings reflect the participants' meanings. (An example is also provided in section four.)

*A description of evaluation criteria and examples of strategies/techniques used to ensure quality were identified and defined from Lincoln and Guba (1985, 2000), Padgett (2008), Shenton (2004), and Venkatesh, Brown, and Bala (2013). This table provides examples of some widely used criteria for evaluating the quality of qualitative research.

the cost of finding participants is reduced, as the participants are selected from the researcher's environment, or from one that can be easily accessed (e.g., a school, university, hospital, company, etc.). Due to these economic factors, the term "discount" was added to the name of the method, which is also a new perspective that was not clearly considered by previous researchers in the context of qualitative IS research. Furthermore, the use of the term "discount" was inspired by Nielson (2009), who advocated "discount usability engineering" in the human-computer interface field as a formative technique. However, in this chapter, we use the term "discount" with the focus group method in the context of qualitative research as a formative and/or summative data collection and analysis technique involving unique and different procedures:

- Using larger groups than are typically recommended (This differs drastically from Nielson's 2009 method, which recommends testing interface designs only with five participants),
- Dividing the participants into subgroups,
- Asking participants to take notes (removing the need for transcriptions),
- Discussing unique items from each subgroup with the full group,
- Consolidating a list of ideas from all subgroup lists and full group discussion,
- Avoiding formality and recorders.

It is important to mention that the word "discount" in the method name does not mean producing lower quality research. "Discount" means reducing the research costs in a smart way, while maintaining the quality of the research, as pointed out in the previous section. That is, that the quality criteria were preserved and ensured.

Third, the application of DFSG aids in promoting awareness and learning new things (e.g., new technology and its impact). In emerging issues that are not common or widely known, it

is acceptable to have some participants who are unfamiliar with the topic under investigation. In the current research, the participants learned from the discussion about NFC, and some discovered that they have this technology on their mobile phone. The traditional focus group method does not go beyond the objective of data collection and thus does not assist in learning and spreading awareness among participants during focus group meetings.

These innovations show modifications on the traditional focus group method (e.g., involving larger number of participants, avoiding formality) or extension of the method as it delegates some of the activities (e.g., documentation, chairing the situation) to the participants themselves.

One important observation that can be noted when applying DFSG is that less data are collected compared to traditional focus groups. In fact, this is expected, since the data are already organized by the participants themselves and prepared for cross-group/subgroup analysis and clustering. Here, it is important to differentiate between the value and the amount of gathered data; it is possible that one can glean insight from a small amount of data, as was the case in the current research project, since the collected data were summarized and organized. In traditional focus groups, where audio/video is used to record every single moment of a session, it is expected that a large amount of data will be collected and will then be transcribed into tens or hundreds of pages, but not necessarily that each sentence or transcribed speech will be significant and insightful. The notion is that, by applying DFSG, the data collection and analysis processes will be shortened due to the focus on issues, ideas, and themes, as opposed to the transcription of detailed speech.

It is important to attach a sample of the notes (e.g., Appendix) written by the participants when submitting manuscripts to journals, as they increase credibility and ensure the conformability of the research findings. These might not be offered when other qualitative research methods are applied, as recorded interviews are usually transcribed in an MS Word document or in NVivo software, with no guarantee that this transcription includes exactly what the participants said or intended to say, as misunderstandings might occur when trying to convey the participants' meanings. However, it is difficult to attach audio- or video-recorded tapes with a manuscript. Therefore, providing the participants' own handwritten evidence in DFSG can be seen as an advantage over the traditional focus group and other qualitative research methods.

The proposed method is flexible; thus, it can be combined with other methods of data collection and/or analysis, such as the survey and grounded theory. For example, since a large number of participants is favored, the researcher might start by distributing a survey to all participants, so that each one can provide information on the topic under study individually. Then subgroup discussions can obtain clarifications on research issues. In addition, the researcher might apply the grounded theory coding process (open, axial, and selective coding) to the ideas that emerged from the subgroup discussions and that were written by the subgroup leaders. DFSG can also be applied in a short time at an early stage of the research, as a part or phase of a large project, with the aim of forming hypotheses that can be tested later using a survey with a large number of participants.

The DFSG method can be applied to new and emerging research areas in investigating concepts, techniques, or technology that was not researched before or was not widely known or used before. Its application is not restricted only to researching new, emerging technology, as demonstrated in this chapter. Rather, scholars from other fields can apply it to study emerging research phenomena in their fields.

Finally, this chapter discussed three main reasons for adapting the focus group method and thus developing the DFSG method. However, it is not necessary that all these conditions (i.e., limited resources, the emergent nature of the research topic, and the challenges of gathering and analyzing qualitative data) appear in any future research for a researcher to decide to use this method. A future researcher might apply the steps of this method and justify its application merely to overcome the challenges of data collection and analysis.

LIMITATIONS OF THE DFSG METHOD

Although there are advantages to using the proposed method, as indicated in the previous section, there are some limitations that need to be highlighted.

One important observation noted concerns the approach for selecting the participants from the researcher's environment. The proposed approach can help to minimize the bias in the data collection and analysis processes by involving the participants in leading the subgroups and allowing the research participants themselves to provide and document their own comments and viewpoints. In this regard, it is important to select active participants to lead the subgroups. They should have oral, written, and leadership skills. Those participants can be identified in the meeting and when the subgroups are formed. They can spontaneously volunteer to write the notes of the subgroup discussion and present them. Failing to identify those active volunteers might result in missing important ideas that are not documented. Another limitation is that some subgroups' leaders might take note of the ideas with which they agree and marginalize other ideas. Therefore, the principal researcher should observe the participants and their discussion and document those issues that are hidden or ignored by the subgroup leaders, then raise them when the discussion is opened up to all subgroups.

Another point that might be raised by researchers is that the nature of qualitative research is iterative, and thus there might be the need for another round, or several rounds, of data collection with the participants to clarify some issues collected from the first round. However, it can also be argued that, since participants wrote their notes and they were checked by each subgroup member during the meeting, the notes reflect and match the thoughts that those participants verbalized. Hence, the probability of misunderstanding or ambiguity is very minor, as things are clarified on the spot. Although another round was not conducted in the current research, this does not mean that there is no need for one at all. If there is the need and justification for more rounds of discussion, the researcher should pay careful attention to regathering the same subgroups from the first round, which is critical and might be difficult to achieve, especially when a large number of participants were involved in the first round.

CONCLUSION

This chapter contributes to IS qualitative research methods by developing an innovative focus group method and providing methodological steps for its application. The proposed DFSG method can be used to investigate emerging IS/IT research phenomena. This chapter provided evidence that the number of participants in the focus group can exceed 12 (the maximum number suggested in the literature) and still be effective, especially when the research topic is new and emergent and when the participants are not completely familiar with it (e.g., NFC). Furthermore, the DFSG method is appropriate when it is difficult to obtain relevant data from people on an individual basis or from a small focus group. In addition, the application of DFSG will reduce the financial resources required for data collection and analysis as well as assist in analyzing data in a short time. All these advantages help to address the challenges of this research.

REFERENCES

Altheide, D., & Johnson, J. M. C. (1998). Criteria for assessing interpretive validity in qualitative research. In N. K. Denzin, & Y. S. Lincoln (Eds.), *Collecting and interpreting qualitative materials.* Thousand Oaks, CA: Sage.

Barbour, R. (2007). *Doing focus groups.* London: Sage.

Belanger, F. (2012). Theorizing in Information Systems Research Using Focus Groups. *Australasian Journal of Information Systems*, *17*(2), 109–135.

Burgess, S. (2010). The Use of Focus Groups in Information Systems Research. *International Journal of Interdisciplinary Social Sciences*, *5*(2), 57–68.

Campbell, B., Kay, R., & Avison, D. (2005). Strategic Alignment: A Practitioner's Perspective. *Journal of Enterprise Information Management*, *18*(6), 653–664. doi:10.1108/17410390510628364

Chesney, T., Coyne, I., Logan, B., & Madden, N. (2009). Griefing in Virtual Worlds: Causes, Casualties, and Coping Strategies. *Information Systems Journal*, *19*(6), 525–548. doi:10.1111/j.1365-2575.2009.00330.x

Dickinger, A., Arami, M., & Meyer, D. (2008). The Role of Perceived Enjoyment and Social Norm in the Adoption of Technology with Network Externalities. *European Journal of Information Systems*, *17*(1), 1, 4–11. doi:10.1057/palgrave.ejis.3000726

Farinha, C., & da Silva, M. (2009) Focus Groups for Eliciting Requirements in Information Systems Development. In *Proceedings of UK Academy for Information Systems Conference.* Academic Press.

Fram, S. M. (2013). The constant comparative analysis method outside of grounded theory. *Qualitative Report, 18*(1), 1–25. Retrieved from http://www.nova.edu/ssss/QR/QR18/fram1.pdf

Galup, S. D., Klein, G., & Jiang, J. J. (2008). The Impacts of Job Characteristics on Employee Satisfaction: A Comparison between Permanent and Temporary Employees. *Journal of Computer Information Systems, 48*(4), 58–68.

Gotterbarn, D. (1991). Computer Ethics: Responsibility Regained, National Forum. *The Phi Beta Kappa Journal, 71*, 26-31.

Guba, E. G., & Lincoln, Y. S. (2005). Paradigmatic Controversies, Contradictions, and Emerging Confluences. In N. K. Denzin, & Y. S. Lincoln (Eds.), *The Sage Handbook of Qualitative Research* (3rd ed., pp. 191–215). Thousand Oaks, CA: Sage Publications.

Innovation. (1982). *Webster's New World Dictionary* (2nd college ed.). Webster's.

Jankowicz, A. D. (1995). *Business research projects*. London: International Thomson Business Press. doi:10.1007/978-1-4899-3386-7

Kelley, D. L. (1999). *Measurement made accessible: A research approach using qualitative, quantitative, and quality improvement methods.* London: Sage.

Klaus, T., & Blanton, J. (2010). User Resistance Determinants and the Psychological Contract in Enterprise System Implementations. *European Journal of Information Systems, 19*(6), 625–636. doi:10.1057/ejis.2010.39

Klein, H., & Myers, M. D. (1999). A Set of Principles for Conducting and Evaluating Interpretive Field Studies in Information Systems. *Management Information Systems Quarterly, 23*(1), 67–93. doi:10.2307/249410

Krasnova, H., Spiekermann, S., Koroleva, K., & Hildebrand, T. (2010). Online Social Networks: Why We Disclose. *Journal of Information Technology, 25*(2), 109–125. doi:10.1057/jit.2010.6

Krueger, R. A. (2000). *Focus Groups: A Practical Guide for Applied Research* (3rd ed.). Newbury Park, CA: Sage Publishing. doi:10.1037/10518-189

Krueger, R. A., & Casey, M. A. (2000). *Focus Groups: A Practical Guide for Applied Research* (3rd ed.). Thousand Oaks, CA: Sage Publications. doi:10.1037/10518-189

Krueger, R. A., & Casey, M. A. (2009). *Focus Groups: A Practical Guide for Applied Research.* Thousand Oaks, CA: Sage.

Le Rouge, C., & Niederman, F. (2006). Information Systems and Health Care Xi: Public Health Knowledge Management Architecture Design: A Case Study. *Communications of the Association for Information Systems, 18*, 2–54.

Lee, C. K., & Kwon, S. (2008). A Cognitive Map-Driven Avatar Design Recommendation DSS and Its Empirical Validity. *Decision Support Systems, 45*(3), 461–472. doi:10.1016/j.dss.2007.06.008

Leech, L., & Onwuegbuzie, A. J. (2007). An Array of Qualitative Data Analysis Tools: A Call for Data Analysis Triangulation. *School Psychology Quarterly, 22*(4), 557–584. doi:10.1037/1045-3830.22.4.557

Lincoln, Y. S., & Guba, E. G. (1985). *Naturalistic Inquiry.* CA: Sage.

Lincoln, Y. S., & Guba, E. G. (2000). Paradigmatic Controversies, Contradictions, and Emerging Confluences. In N. K. Denzin, & Y. S. Lincoln (Eds.), *Handbook of Qualitative Research* (pp. 163–188). Thousand Oaks, CA: Sage Publications.

Lucas, I. (2012). Phenomenological Approaches to Ethics and Information Technology. In *The Stanford Encyclopedia of Philosophy* (Summer 2011 ed.). Available at http://plato.stanford.edu/archives/sum2011/entries/ethics-it-phenomenology/

Moor, J. H. (1985). What Is Computer Ethics? *Metaphilosophy*, *16*(4), 266–275. doi:10.1111/j.1467-9973.1985.tb00173.x

Morgan, D. L. (1997). *Focus Groups as Qualitative Research*. Newbury Park, CA: Sage Publications.

Morgan, D. L., & Scannell, A. U. (1998). *Planning Focus Groups*. London: Sage. doi:10.4135/9781483328171

Myers, M., & Avison, D. (2002). *Qualitative Research Information System*. London: SAGE.

NFC Forum. (2014). *What Is NFC?*. Retrieved from http://nfc-forum.org/what-is-nfc/

Nielsen, J. (2009). *Discount Usability: 20 Years*. Retrieved from http://www.nngroup.com/articles/discount-usability-20-years/

Northcote, M. T. (2012). Selecting Criteria to Evaluate Qualitative Research. In *Education Papers and Journal Articles,* 99-110. Retrieved from http://research.avondale.edu.au/edu_papers/38

O'Connor, M. K., Netting, F. E., & Thomas, M. L. (2008). Grounded Theory: Managing the Challenge for Those Facing Institutional Review Board Oversight. *Qualitative Inquiry*, *14*(1), 28–45. doi:10.1177/1077800407308907

O'hEocha, C., Wang, X., & Conboy, K.O'hEocha C. (2012). The Use of Focus Groups in Complex and Pressurised IS Studies and Evaluation Using Klein & Myers Principles for Interpretive Research. *Information Systems Journal*, *22*(3), 235–256. doi:10.1111/j.1365-2575.2011.00387.x

Otondo, R. F., Pearson, A. W., Pearson, R. A., Shaw, J. C., & Shim, J. P. (2009). Managerial Problem-Solving in the Adoption of Radio Frequency Identification Technologies. *European Journal of Information Systems*, *18*(6), 553–569. doi:10.1057/ejis.2009.39

Özdenizci, B., Aydin, M., Coşkun, V., & Ok, K. (2010) NFC Research Framework: A Literature Review and Future Research Directions. In *Proceedings of 14th IBIMA Conference*. IBIMA.

Padgett, D. (2008). *Qualitative methods in social work research*. Los Angeles, CA: Sage Publications.

Powell, R. A., & Single, H. M. (1996). Focus groups. *International Journal for Quality in Health Care*, *8*(5), 499–504. doi:10.1093/intqhc/8.5.499 PMID:9117204

Puchta, C., & Potter, J. (2004). *Focus Group Practice*. London: Sage.

Sandler, R. (2012). *Nanotechnology: The Social and Ethical Issues*. Woodrow Wilson International Center for Scholars. Available at http://www.nanotechproject.org/process/assets/files/7060/nano_pen16_final.pdf

Schofield, J. W. (2002). Increasing the Generalisability of Qualitative Research. In A. M. Huberman, & M. B. Miles (Eds.), *The qualitative researcher's companion*. Thousand Oaks, CA: Sage Publications.

Shenton, A. (2004). Strategies for Ensuring Trustworthiness in Qualitative Research Projects. *Education for Information*, *22*, 63–75.

Smith, H. A., & McKeen, J. D. (2007). Developments in Practice Xxiv: Information Management: The Nexus of Business and IT. *Communications of the Association for Information Systems*, *19*, 34–46.

Smith, H. J., Milberg, S. J., & Burke, S. J. (1996). Information Privacy: Measuring Individuals' Concerns About Organizational Practices. *Management Information Systems Quarterly, 20*(2), 2. doi:10.2307/249477

Sobreperez, P. (2008). Using Plenary Focus Groups in Information Systems Research: More than a Collection of Interviews. *The Electronic Journal of Business Research Methods, 6*(2), 181–188.

Stahl, B., Tremblay, M., & LeRouge, C. (2011). Focus Groups and Critical Social IS Research: How the Choice of Method Can Promote Emancipation of Respondents and Researchers. *European Journal of Information Systems, 20*(4), 378–394. doi:10.1057/ejis.2011.21

Stahl, B. C. (2007). ETHICS, Morality and Critique: An Essay on Enid Mumford's Socio-Technical Approach. *Journal of the Association for Information Systems, 8*(9), 479-490.

Stewart, D. W., & Shamdasani, P. N. (1990). *Focus groups: Theory and practice.* Sage Publications Inc.

Strauss, A., & Corbin, J. (1998). *Basics of Qualitative Research, Techniques and Procedures for Developing Grounded Theory.* Thousand Oaks, CA: Sage Publication Inc.

Sutton, S. G., Khazanchi, D., Hampton, C., & Arnold, V. (2008). Risk Analysis in Extended Enterprise Environments: Identification of Critical Risk Factors in B2b E-Commerce Relationships. *Journal of the Association for Information Systems, 9*(4), 151–174.

Templeton, J. F. (1994). *The focus group: A strategic guide to organizing, conducting and analyzing the focus group interview.* New York: McGraw-Hill Professional Publishing.

Tobin, G., & Begley, C. (2004). Methodological Rigour within a Qualitative Framework. *Journal of Advanced Nursing, 48*(4), 388–396. doi:10.1111/j.1365-2648.2004.03207.x PMID:15500533

Tremblay, C. M., Hevner, A. R., & Berndt, D. J. (2010). Focus Groups for Artifact Refinement and Evaluation in Design Research. *Communications of the Association for Information Systems, 26,* 27.

Venkatesh, V., Brown, S. A., & Bala, H. (2013). Bridging the Qualitative-Quantitative Divide: Guidelines for Conducting Mixed Methods Research in Information Systems. *Management Information Systems Quarterly, 37*(1), 21–54.

Wang Y, Lo H-P, & Yang, Y (2004). An Integrated Framework for Service Quality, Customer Value, Satisfaction: Evidence from China's Telecommunication Industry. *Information Systems Frontiers, 6*(4), 325.

Weidong, X., & Lee, G. (2005). Complexity of Information Systems Development Projects: Conceptualization and Measurement Development. *Journal of Management Information Systems, 22*(1), 45–83.

Whittemore, R., Chase, S. K., & Mandle, C. L. (2001). Validity in qualitative research. *Qualitative Health Research, 11*(4), 522–537. doi:10.1177/104973201129119299 PMID:11521609

Wilcox, H. (2011). *Press Release: 1 in 5 Smartphones will have NFC by 2014, Spurred by Recent Breakthroughs: New Juniper Research Report.* Retrieved from http://www.juniperresearch.com/viewpressrelease.php?pr=239

KEY TERMS AND DEFINITIONS

Categorization: The use of predefined categories or concepts by which to organize each idea.

Clustering: The grouping of a set of similar ideas or those with similar properties in an emergent way, with a category name applied afterwards.

Code: A descriptive title.

Conformability: The degree to which research may be confirmed by others.

Constant Comparative Analysis: The analysis of collected data through comparison of the found ideas and grouping similar ones.

Credibility: The believability of the research findings.

Dependability: The sufficiency of the documentation of the research.

Dependency and Vulnerability: The sense of over-reliance on a technology.

Discount Focus Subgroup Method (DFSG): A form of the focus group method that may be applied to an emergent phenomena with limited research resources.

Emerging Technology: A technology that has just recently been deployed or is soon-to-be-deployed; a new technology.

Focus Group: A qualitative research method that involves the bringing together of selected individuals to comment on a select topic.

Grounded Theory: A qualitative research method that extracts concepts and theory through close analysis of data extracted from a real world environment.

Near Field Communication Technology (NFC): The smartphones and other devices that are radio-communication enabled through touching or close-proximity (of a few inches).

Privacy: A human right to choose when to share or not share personal information.

Transferability: The degree to which findings from one research context may be applied to another with similar conditions.

APPENDIX: SAMPLE OF NOTES WRITTEN BY THE PARTICIPANTS

Figure 2. Sample of discussion notes (chunks of data) written by subgroup leaders compared with each other

1	* Personal information privacy it will be violated.
2	4) They can watch my personal information The policy :- 1) Storing private information is out of our responsibility.
3	Companies could track the person – details used
4	⊙ Privacy can be violated. ↳ Not anyone can access the information, and if information were accessed, for example to only have prices listed, how much you paid and the date and time (without listing venue) ↳ And upon activation users must be well-informed of what information will be accessed and by who.
5	_ access to our information → bank will easily know our location and our payment processes, we can easily be tracked
6	The Dilemma – easy access to others, can be easily violated – especially if mobile is stolen
7	hackers may access the information stored in the chip and can be used in fraud transactions or purchases.

Figure 3. Sample of Some Notes Written by One Subgroup

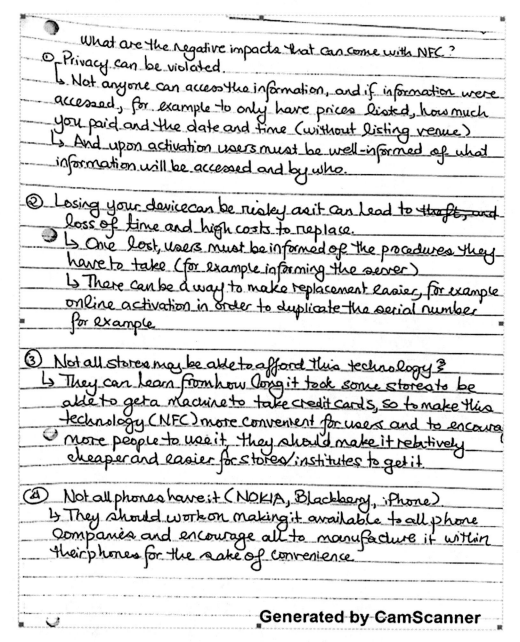

What are the negative impacts that can come with NFC?
① Privacy can be violated.
 ↳ Not anyone can access the information, and if information were accessed, for example to only have prices listed, how much you paid and the date and time (without listing venue)
 ↳ And upon activation users must be well-informed of what information will be accessed and by who.

② Losing your device can be risky as it can lead to ~~theft, and~~ loss of time and high costs to replace.
 ↳ Once lost, users must be informed of the procedures they have to take (for example informing the server)
 ↳ There can be a way to make replacement easier, for example online activation in order to duplicate the serial number for example

③ Not all stores may be able to afford this technology?
 ↳ They can learn from how long it took some stores to be able to get a machine to take credit cards, so to make this technology (NFC) more convenient for users and to encoura more people to use it, they should make it relatively cheaper and easier for stores/institutes to get it

④ Not all phones have it (NOKIA, Blackberry, iPhone)
 ↳ They should work on making it available to all phone companies and encourage all to manufacture it within their phones for the sake of convenience

Generated by CamScanner

512

Section 6
Technologies for Presenting the Results of Qualitative and Mixed Methods Research

A critical aspect of qualitative and mixed methods research has been to share the methods and findings with not only colleagues and peers but also the broad public. Over the years, there have been a number of ways that research has been "packaged" and shared: through parametric and non-parametric data visualizations, narrations, and writing structures. At present, there are even more tools that enable presentations. Some offer data visualizations of big data and macro trends. Others offer creative mapping for accessing and understanding locational data. Many of these presentational methods are Web-enabled, so that consumers of that information may actually interact with the research findings.

Chapter 20
Querying Google Books Ngram Viewer's Big Data Text Corpuses to Complement Research

Shalin Hai-Jew
Kansas State University, USA

ABSTRACT

If qualitative and mixed methods researchers have a tradition of gleaning information from all possible sources, they may well find the Google Books Ngram Viewer and its repository of tens of millions of digitized books yet another promising data stream. This free cloud service enables easy access to big data in terms of querying the word frequency counts of a range of terms and numerical sequences (and languages) from 1500 – 2000, a 500-year span of book publishing, with new books being added continually. The data queries that may be made with this tool are virtually unanswerable otherwise. The word frequency counts provide a lagging indicator of both instances and trends, related to language usage, cultural phenomena, popularity, technological innovations, and a wide range of other insights. The text corpuses contain de-contextualized words used by the educated literati of the day sharing their knowledge in formalized texts. The enablements of the Google Books Ngram Viewer provide complementary information sourcing for designed research questions as well as free-form discovery. This tool allows downloading of the "shadowed" (masked or de-identified) extracted data for further analyses and visualizations. This chapter provides both a basic and advanced look at how to extract information from the Google Books Ngram Viewer for light research.

INTRODUCTION

People have arrived to the era of Big Data, with massive amounts of digital information available for research and learning. "Big data" has been defined as an N of all, with all available data points for a data set able to be captured and analyzed; another definition has "big data" as datasets involving millions to billions of records and analysis through high performance computing. This recent development in modern life has come about for a variety of factors. One involves the prolifera-

DOI: 10.4018/978-1-4666-6493-7.ch020

tion of electronic information from the Web and Internet (such as through websites, social media platforms, and the hidden web), mobile devices, wearable cameras and Google Glasses. Much of what was analog is now digitized (transcoded into digital format) and datafied (turned into machine-readable and machine-analyzable information). This move to mass digitization is part of a global cultural paradigm of cyber-rization. The Open Data movement has swept through governments and even commercial entities, which see the "democratization of knowledge" as part of human and consumer rights. The movement for "the internet of things" or the "quantified self" will only further add to the outpouring and availability of digital information. Then, too, there have been advancements in cloud computing, which enables easier analysis of large datasets. Cheap data storage has enabled the storage of data into practical perpetuity.

Going to big data is not without controversy, particularly among researchers. In the Petabyte Age of big data, the "scientific method" and research-based hypothesizing may be irrelevant, suggests one leading thinker. With so many streams of electronic information from online social networks, sensors, digital exhaust (from commercial data streams), and communications channels, many assert that anything that people might want to know may be ascertainable by querying various databases. In a controversial article, Chris Anderson wrote: "Petabytes allow us to say: 'Correlation is enough.' We can stop looking for models. We can analyze the data without hypotheses about what it might show. We can throw the numbers into the biggest computing clusters the world has ever seen and let statistical algorithms find patterns where science cannot," in "The End of Theory: The Data Deluge Makes the Scientific Method Obsolete" (2008). The tight controls for random sampling and statistical validity in a "small data" world no longer apply in a world of big data (Mayer-Schönberger & Cukier, 2013). The authors describe a tradeoff between less sampling error in big data but a need to ac-

cept more measurement error. In a dataset with N = all, the sheer mass of data changes up the rules—even as big data may introduce spurious correlations where none may exist because of the increased "noise" in the data. Such large datasets may enable unexpected discovery, so researchers may not have to start with a hypothesis or a question or a hunch; it may be enough for them to peruse the data to see what they can find, through big data "prospecting" (Gibbs & Cohen, 2011). Mayer-Schönberger and Cukier suggest that the analysis of big data may be a necessary skill set for many in certain domains of research. In particular, big data enables researchers not only to achieve a high-level view of information but probe in depth to a very granular level (down to an individual record even if that record is one of tens or hundreds of millions of other records). In the vernacular, researchers are able to zoom-in and zoom-out of the data. Big data may not inform researchers directly about causation (because there is not an obvious way to mathematically show causality); to acquire that level of understanding may require much more additional analytical and inferential work and additional research.

Data researchers suggest that it is critical to know data intimately in order to optimize their use of the data. This includes basic information about how the data were acquired, where they were acquired from, how they were managed, and what may be extrapolated and understood from them.

The typical big dataset is a miscellany of facts and measurements, collected for no scientific purpose, using an ad hoc procedure. It is riddled with errors, and marred by numerous, frustrating gaps: missing pieces of information that any reasonable scientist would want to know. These errors and omissions are often inconsistent, even within what is thought of as a single dataset. That's because big datasets are frequently created by aggregating a vast number of smaller datasets. Invariably, some of these component datasets are more reliable than others, and each one is

515

subject to its own idiosyncrasies...Part of the job of working with big data is to come to know your data so intimately that you can reverse engineer these quirks. But how intimate can you possibly be with a petabyte? (Aiden & Michel, 2013, p. 19)

(A petabyte or *PB* is 10^{15} bytes of digital information.) While much big data is digital exhaust or information that is a byproduct of people's lived lives, there are datasets of more structured and purposive information, such as the scanned books in the Google Books digitization project. The book scans by Google Inc. have been achieved with data science standards and relatively clean data. [There have been early critiques that their scanners' optical character recognition misrepresented some less common symbols, but this issue has been addressed in newer versions. There have been concerns of repeated copies being included in the large Google Books dataset with the potential for error magnification and potential miscount (Gooding, 2013).] For millennia, books have been the repository of much of human knowledge. These are formalized works with conventions for their structuring. There are editorial gatekeepers to book publishing to ensure quality. The Google Books digitization project (formerly known as the Google Print Library Project, as an extension of the Google Print endeavor and later known as Google Book Search initiative) started in late 2004 and involved a stated ambition to digitize 15 million volumes of books in conjunction with cooperating libraries in the next decade. Now, at the decade mark, after multiple legal challenges, this project has successfully included the scanning of tens of millions of texts from the 1500s to 2000. The information from this project is partially available to the broad public through the Google Books Ngram Viewer, which debuted in 2010. This tool enables word frequency count queries to the dataset through a web-based interface and results in smoothed line graphs of the results over time in year-increments; the tool also offers some access to the raw data and actual number counts.

("Smoothing" refers to the averaging of a number of the measures on either side of a data point in order to present a clearer text frequency count line. A smoothing measure of 3 means that the placement for a data point is taken as the average of the number to the left and the one to the right and then itself. A smoothing measure of 11 would include 5 to either side and the data point itself. The higher the smoothing number, the smoother and less distinct each data point on the line is.)

In one sense, the books are reaching a much wider audience than the authors may have imagined, but in a de-contextualized form in which words and syntactical structures are extrapolated from the massive trillion-plus-word textual corpuses extrapolated from approximately a fourth of all the books published in the world. For some, there is a sense of threat to traditional research methods with the uses of large-scale digital initiatives (LSDIs) and a lack of clarity about how to integrate information from big data analyses (Gooding, 2013). Clearly, there are certain types of questions that are suited to be asked through a bibliometric lens. One writer has observed: "The Viewer is an excellent oracle for the *n*-gram data, but it answers just one kind of question: How has the frequency of a specific *n*-gram varied over time?" (Hayes, 2014)

Basic Overview of the Google Books Ngram Viewer

The name of this tool came from a term-of-art in computer science. An "n-gram" refers to a particular sequential unit of an alphanumeric string. A uni-gram (or 1-gram) refers to one single stand-alone word or number. A bi-gram (or 2-gram) refers to a two-unit contiguous sequence, such as "constructive criticism" or "they 've". There are 3-grams, 4-grams, 5-grams, and so on. The "n" refers to the number of grams in the search term sequence. The terms that register on the Ngram Viewer have to have appeared in at least 40 books to register.

The web-based interface is straightforward enough and possibly misleadingly simple (at least on initial impression). The search term or terms are input in the text window above. The user may decide whether or not the search will be case-sensitive or case-insensitive. He or she decides what the year range of the search is; the pre-sets are for 1800–2000. Another input parameter may include the selection of a particular text corpus. A recent screenshot of the dropdown menu shows the following options: American English, British English, Chinese (simplified), English, English Fiction, French, German, Hebrew, Italian, Russian, Spanish, American English (2009), British English (2009), Chinese (simplified) (2009), English (2009), English Fiction (2009), English One Million (2009), French (2009), German (2009), and Hebrew (2009). According to the Google Books site, the corpuses are books predominantly in the named language. The Google Million refers to English works from dates ranging from 1500 to 2008; further, according to their site, "No more than about 6000 books were chosen from any one year, which means that all of the scanned books from early years are present, and books from later years are randomly sampled. The random samplings reflect the subject distributions for the year (so there are more computer books in 2000 than 1980)" (Google Books Ngram Viewer, 2014). More recent corpuses include French 2012, German 2012, Hebrew 2012, Spanish 2012, Russian 2012, and Italian 2012.

The resulting two-dimensional line graph has the years on the x-axis and the percentage of the word frequencies on the y-axis (these statistics are normalized for the number of books published each year). The percentages on the vertical y-axis are often very small (within the one part per 100,000 and million word ranges because of the data corpus sizes. For example, the .0014% occurrence is read as 14 occurrences out of a set of a million words. While these are very minute counts, they may be compared to other word counts for relative frequencies as comparisons). The resulting

lines may be evaluated for long-term trends. They may show annual spikes and volatility. They may be found not to appear at all (if the term selected appears in fewer than 40 books). At the bottom of the web page are "interesting" years for the particular search terms and links to additional information about the books published in those time spans. There are also term links to resources in the Google Books project.

In Figure 1, "Using key words surrounding a contemporary issue of big data and privacy in Ngram Viewer," the query involves four comma-separated terms: "personally identifiable information, big data, privacy, anonymization", and the results show a long-term concern with privacy over hundreds of years, and with only fairly recent interest in the issues of "personally identifiable information," "big data," and "anonymization" (as a protection against privacy infringements and data leakage). The asking of the question in this data visualization forms the context. The selection of terms affects the framing. After all, what about the inclusion of "de-identification" or "crypto" or "shadowing." What are the implications of their non-inclusion? As a lagging indicator (given the historical delay of book publishing) and with access only to sources through the year 2000, Google Books Ngram Viewer (available at http://books.google.com/ngrams) itself comes with limits.

The automated parts-of-speech tagging in the most recent version of the Ngram Viewer does enable syntactic analysis and the study of the "evolution of syntax" based on twelve parts-of-speech tags (Lin, Michel, Aiden, Orwant, Brockman, & Petrov, 2012, p. 169); this tagging is a critical aspect of language disambiguation in natural language processing (p. 171). The twelve parts-of-speech included involve nouns (_NOUN), verbs (_VERB), adjectives (_ADJ), adverbs (_ADV), pronouns (_PRON), determiners and articles (_DET), prepositions and postpositions (_ADP), numerals (_NUM), conjunctions (_CONJ), particles (_PRT), punctuation marks ('.'), and a catch-all category for abbreviations

Figure 1. Using key words surrounding a contemporary issue of big data and privacy in Ngram Viewer

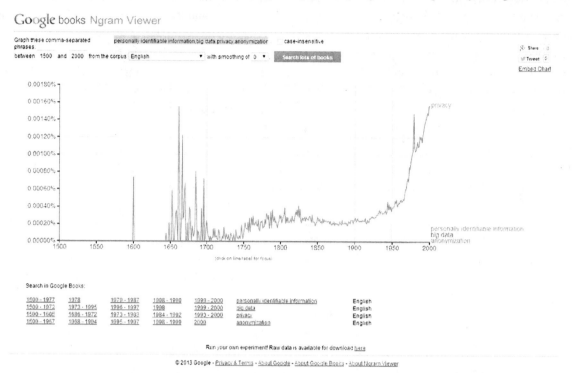

and foreign words (_X). Researchers may indicate the unidentified root of a parse tree (_ROOT) to conduct searches for which the root is initially unknown. (A "parse tree" is the syntactic structure of a string based on relationships between elements in the sentence. A _ROOT_ in a parse tree refers to what the main verb of the sentence is modifying or the main subject of the sentence. _ROOT_ stands in as a placeholder for the as-yet undetermined subject.)

If a particular search term is at the start of a sentence (_START), that may be indicated; likewise, the end of the sentence may also be indicated (_END); this is enabled through the Ngram Viewer's sentence boundary tagging. The tags may be stand-alone (_ADV_), or they may be appended to a word (fly_VERB). This syntactic annotation has been achieved for n-grams for eight languages: English, Spanish, French, German, Russian, Italian, Chinese, and Hebrew. The optical character recognition (OCR) scanning

capabilities have also improved over the years, with more accuracy for disambiguating particular symbols and terms.

Another feature involves the "dependency relations operator" (=>) in which an instance of a term or phrase or symbol is linked with another. For example, a researcher may want to know how often the term "beautiful" was linked to "sky" with the query: sky=>beautiful. This dependency relations query asks how often "beautiful" modifies "sky" as one of the descriptors used in its vicinity (even with intervening words).

Another type of query involves identifying the frequencies of a particular verb used as the main one of a sentence by using the _ROOT_ tag along with the dependency => and the target verb. The _ROOT_ serves as a placeholder for the search. The query then reads as follows within the quotation mark: "_ROOT_=>will".

Such dependency relations may be coupled with wildcard searches (*). A wildcard search

Figure 2. "sky => beautiful" dependency relations (top) vs. "beautiful sky" bigram search (bottom) on Ngram Viewer

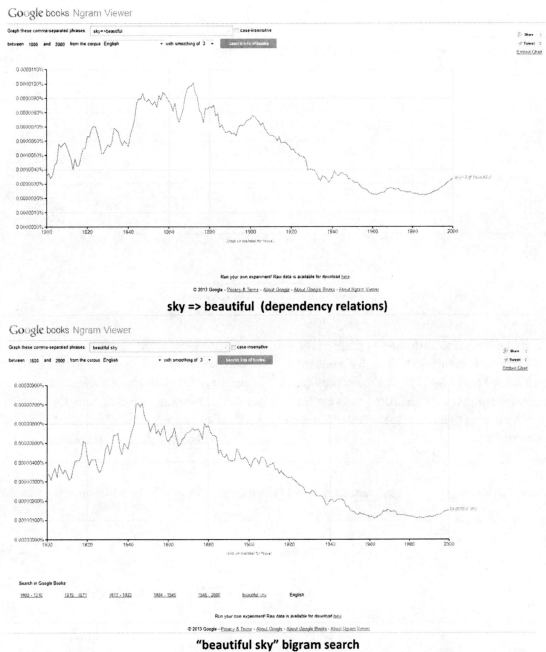

sky => beautiful (dependency relations)

"beautiful sky" bigram search

Figure 3. _ROOT_=>decide dependency relations with "decide" as the main verb of the parsed sentence (in Ngram Viewer)

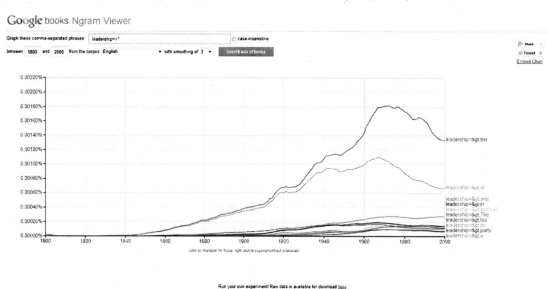

results in the top ten substitutions in place of the asterisk. The "leadership=>*" is such a wildcard query. The makers of the Ngram Viewer provide an insightful example of "*_NOUN's theorem" to acquire the top ten theorems that bear the names of their originators.

To add main word variants to a search term, researchers may conduct an "inflection search" by appending the _INF tag at the end of the search term. For example a run of win_INF results in variants of the word "win" (with various word endings (like –s, -ed, -ing, and others).

Figure 4. "leadership=>" dependency relation and wildcard query in Ngram Viewer*

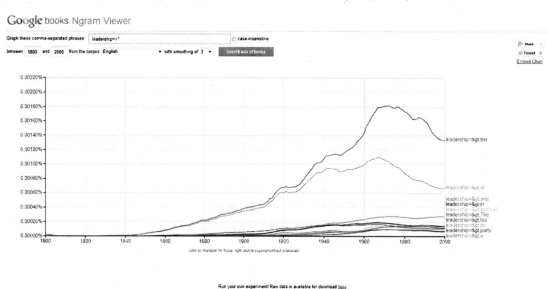

The inflection keyword may be combined with part-of-speech tags. For example, "win_VERB_ INF" is a valid query. Several appends may be used. The directions for the tools reads: "You can't freely mix wildcard searches, inflections and case-insensitive searches for one particular ngram. However, you can search with either of these features for separate ngrams in a query: "book_INF a hotel, book * hotel" is fine, but "book_INF * hotel" is not." The _INF or part-of-speech tag, the wildcard, and the case sensitivity cannot all be used simultaneously; however, two of the three may be used together.

Ngram compositions are also possible using a range of Boolean-esque operators. The + plus sign sums the expression on either side to combine multiple ngram data points. The minus – sign subtracts the expression on the right from that on the left to measure one ngram to another. (This enables the creation of a functional stop-words list.) The / serves as a division expression with the ngram on the left divided by the expression in the right—to isolate "the behavior of an ngram with respect to another." To create cumulative visualizations combining two separate ngrams, a researcher may use the following construction: (_ * _). The asterisk here combines the two terms with the number on the left multiplied by that on the right. To avoid confusing this with the wildcard search syntax, this entire string has to be within parentheses to show that composition is desired. (It can sometimes be hard to get a line reading given the smallness of the numbers.) Sometimes, a straight number is used as the multiplier in order to compare a rare occurrence with something more common (to enable the lines to interact and overlap). The colon (:) applies the ngram on the left to the corpus on the right, to compare ngrams across different corpora or text collections.

For researchers who want absolute numbers, users may set the smoothing at 0 and click the "here" link at the bottom of the site. This next

Figure 5. "win_INF" inflection wildcard query in Ngram Viewer

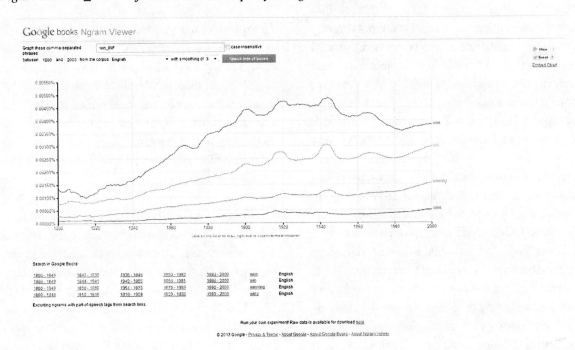

screen provides access to the number of n-grams in all corpora for all the years included in that data extraction. One author elaborates:

For 1-grams even "total counts" are given, i.e. the full number of 1-grams for each year. To obtain absolute figures, we have to read the percentage for any year off our diagram and multiply it by the number of 1-grams for that particular year. Since 1-grams are not exactly the same as words and since reading a quantity off a diagram converts analogue into digital information, the resulting figures will not be absolutely accurate, but they will give us an idea of the order of magnitude: in our period the absolute frequency of words like anger and wrath will not usually rise above two-digit figures for any one year. (Diller, 2013, p. 56)

The raw data may be downloaded as zipped compressed archive files, as in Googlebooks-ita-all-2gram-20120701-aa-gz. The datasets may be analyzed with other tools and in other ways (such as with sentiment analysis). The datasets extracted from the Ngram Viewer may be analyzed through other technological means (even if the original works related to certain numbers are not directly available). These datasets may be cross-referenced with information from other datasets and other sources and corpuses. Insights from relevant years of interest may be accessed by probing more deeply into Google Books resources. *Figure 6: A Screenshot of a Downloadable Dataset of Ngrams from a Search on the Ngram Viewer* provides a screenshot of this downloadable data screen. The data contents and visualizations are released by Google Inc. through the Creative Commons Attribution 3.0 Unported License, which allows users to share ("copy and redistribute the material in any medium or format") and adapt ("remix, transform, and build upon the material") the materials for any purpose, including commercial ones—as long as users give appropriate credit, link to the license, and reveal if changes were made (albeit without suggesting that the licensor endorses the results).

Several sources mentioned the risks of a 0% flatline with particular queries. In such cases, researchers may conduct a data extraction at a later time when the Ngram Viewer may be under less heavy load. Also, ngrams are depicted only if they appear in at least 40 books. (This artificial limit is set to enable the Ngram Viewer to conduct the necessary calculations and return results in milliseconds.) Researchers should also analyze how they structured their queries in the case of flatlines due to possible user error.

Shadow Dataset

The data that the public may access is a "shadow dataset," with a record of every word or phrase that appeared in each scanned (digitized) or digital book. The data is anonymized and decontextualized from their original sources as a feature—to protect against reverse-engineering to the original texts via "unique formulations". The data sets preserve some of the original data but filters out other information that may be mis-used. The authors on the development team explain:

Though shadowing is more art than science, it's crucial to making progress when working on big data. The wrong shadow can be ethically dubious, legally intractable, and scientifically useless. But if you choose exactly the right angle, it's possible to obscure the legally and ethically sensitive parts of the original dataset while retaining much of its extraordinary power (Aiden & Michel, 2013, pp. 60 – 61).

Strategic shadowing of datasets may minimize legal risks to the corporations that would release big data for use by public researchers and the broader public in general; they may encourage "data philanthropy," suggest Aiden & Michel (p. 63). The Ngram Viewer poses a very low cost of entry to "online data research" and engagement with big data. Both the data and the heavy computer processing are shouldered by Google

Figure 6. A Screenshot of a downloadable dataset of Ngrams from a search on the Ngram Viewer

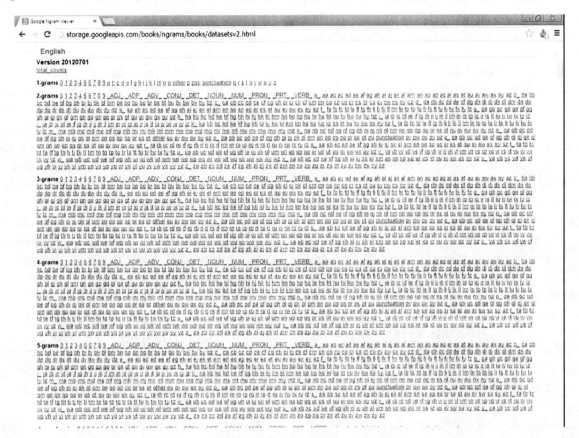

Inc. This is an early way of benefitting the larger publics with the Google Books information (beyond the text search and other benefits). In some ways, the claims that may be made from Ngram Viewer data seems somewhat indirect and rough-cut. A prevalence (high frequency) of terms (in a given year) may indicate popular awareness of a certain phenomenon, or it may mean awareness among a subset of the general population, such as the literati or the academic researcher. This approach assumes a kind of limited attention economy. Researchers are left to make sense of the text frequency lines over time based on their understanding of what is going on in the world to understand short-term fluctuations and changes, as well as longer-term trends. In a sense, researchers compare word frequency trajectories and make inferential leaps or deductive truth claims. They

may amass a range of data, including Ngram data, for inductive assertions based on real-world empirical data. Such quantitative analyses of texts may complement the acquisition of knowledge in mixed-methods and multi-methods research by offering a channel of information that would not be achievable otherwise. In the same way that much of qualitative and mixed methods research may be language-centered, Ngram Viewer data also focus intensely on language as symbol and as repository of human knowledge and meaning. This research may begin with theory and considered thinking about how texts may be used for the work through "Ngram experiments" (others would suggest "quasi-experiments"), or they may involve trial and error for discovery learning. It is helpful to review some of the research achieved using this tool.

Now that the basic tool has been introduced, it would be helpful to provide an overview of the basic research process. Researchers generally begin with a research context and questions. They formulate a strategy for the use of the Google Books NGram Viewer. They set the parameters for the data extraction; they conduct the data extraction and resultant data visualization. They conduct an analysis of that information and then decide on next steps—such as further research or finalization. Figure 7, "Basic Steps to a Google Books Ngram Viewer™ Data Extraction and Analysis" provides an overview of this process.

The potency of the Ngram Viewer stems in part from creative applications by researchers across a number of disciplines. It also flows from how people have gone to books for many generations to capture meaning and learning. While a hyper-speed computational approach to extract meaning from a big data text corpus is unprecedented at this scale, and the original book authors likely never thought their works would be consumed in this way, this Ngram Viewer tool has been used to insightful ends in a number of fields in its several years of usage.

REVIEW OF THE LITERATURE

Several new terms have been coined to describe the uses of quantitative text analysis in academic research. In the "digital humanities," a distant reading of a text may include computational analysis of the text. This approach is often combined with close reading of selected parts of the text corpus for analytical depth. Contemporary researchers are using a "combinatorial approach using both textual work and technical tools" (Gibbs & Cohen, 2011, p. 70). "Culturomics" involves the study of "human behavior and cultural trends through quantitative analysis of digitized texts" ("Culturomics," Jan. 11, 2014). Researchers may probe for particular cultural trends in particular time periods with n-grams (Klein, 2013). These ecological studies point at large-scale cultural trends over time (Greenfield, 2013). The n-gram counts of texts have been wittily termed "bit lit" (Hayes, 2014).

On first look, such an approach of quantizing text may seem "inchoate" (Gibbs & Cohen, 2011, p. 75) or haphazard. After all, this approach generally separates words from their meanings; it ignores morphology or the structure of a language's linguistic units (O'Malley, 2010). In his "denunciation" of the Ngram Viewer, O'Malley labeled this tool "an example of what Marx called 'socially unnecessary labor time'—work that takes skill and craft and time but that nobody wants or needs" (2010). Initial word frequency counts decontextualize the words and separate them from the meaning imbued by the context and the interrelationships among words in sentences and

Figure 7. Basic steps to a Google Books Ngram Viewer™ data extraction and analysis

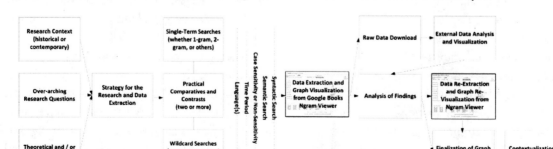

paragraphs. There may be challenges with the verifiability (and the falsifiability) of the results (Diller, 2013, p. 57), especially since such data is essentially single-sourced (even though Google is widely thought to have high standards for data inclusion and data processing). Another critique examines the limitations of both the data capture process and the inherent ambiguity in language over time:

Two are apropos here. First, digitization of text is a cumulative process, and the digitized corpus from the early years (here before 1800) are often incomplete and scant. There will be major difficulties in tracing material from the early years of publication, or even before the invention of the printing press. In addition to such logistic difficulties, there are conceptual hurdles: words are sometimes used in ways that do not convey the same single concept as the one intended in the analysis. Identical words can refer to different concepts. For example, "the first amendment" can

refer to a document different from the US Constitution. This does not pose a major problem to the profile presented in figure 8, because the Ngram Viewer search is case sensitive. Differentiating "The First Amendment" from "the first amendment" helps resolve the ambiguity. The historical corpus is growing and more and more material will be included. However, there is a limit to the extent of coverage in the sixteenth and seventeenth centuries. The issue of false referrals can also be mitigated using a combination of words that are widely known to represent a political, legal, or historical concept. For example, it is unlikely that "The French Revolution" refers to events other than The French Revolution. For words that are not as distinct, one could introduce more words to the temporal search, allowing for the discussion of a more precise topic instead of an ambiguous word (Hassanpour, 2013, p. 305).

Essentially, the functionality involves a word frequency count of large-scale databases of texts

Figure 8. "Creationism, Darwinism" paradigm shift in Ngram Viewer

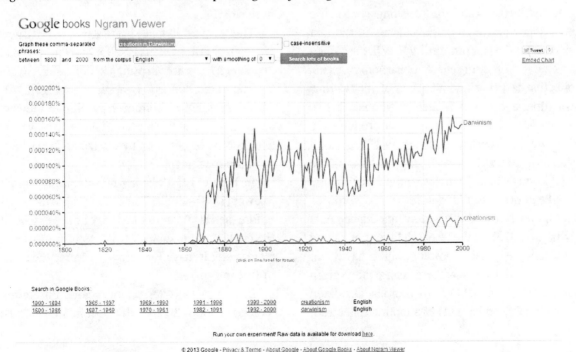

published historically. The most recent texts available are from 2000, meaning that these do not include works from the past 14 years. By its nature, the Ngram Viewer "elides context, obscuring qualitative and cultural considerations central to humanities scholarship" (Denbo & Fraistat, 2011, p. 170); in this case, the authors suggest that a close reading of the text may trump number crunching, and they suggest that a form of machine-enabled "scalable reading" may be more effective (beyond abstracting texts through word counts).

A Brief Summary of Applied Research

The Google Books Ngram Viewer has proved fruitful for various research endeavors. One project explored the problems of testing human intelligence and drawing comparisons across generations given the changes in intergenerational word usage (Roivainen, 2013). Researchers have studied the capabilities of lexicographers to capture even rare words in dictionaries of the day, the trajectories of fame and the fame curve over time, suppression of Jewish artists (and the resulting censorship and disappearance of certain names in the text corpuses) in the Nazi era during WWII, the collective human "forgetting curve" of particular events, collective learning and adoption of innovations over time, and others (Aiden & Michel, 2013). Researchers discovered changes in pronoun use over time in American books from 1960 – 2008 as an indicator of the rise of individualism in the U.S. (Twenge, Campbell, & Gentile, 2012). There have been other similar queries of text corpuses for hiphop lyrics and wedding announcements (Zimmer, 2013). In the research literature, others noted that previously unknown authors have been re-discovered by researchers using the Ngram Viewer (Barlow, 2011). This tool has also been used to analyze the points of adoption for certain

types of affective technologies (Westland, 2011). Some researchers have studied the growing awareness of particular phenomena over time as ideas proliferate in books and then surges in popularity (Percival, 2011). Still others have used this tool for implied data narratives—such as one graph that compared which came first, the chicken or the egg.

A GOOGLE BOOKS NGRAM VIEWER SAMPLER

Some Basic Google Books Ngram Viewer Querying

One way to dry-run a software tool is to run it through its paces. Some simple data visualizations have been extracted in this section to highlight some of the tool's capabilities. The earlier visualizations are based on single terms. The latter ones involve some of the more advanced operators available in the tool.

One comparison of world views shows the competition between "creationism" and "Darwinism," with the latter surpassing creationism in the 1870s.

This tool may indicate the first mention of a new idea or technology. This is so for both "robot" and "nanotech," as cases in points in Figures 9 and 10.

The same concept is applied in Figure 11, "'cloud computing' bigram on the Ngram Viewer" albeit this time with a bigram. This term may have a longer history than many realize and may have multiple meanings.

In Figure 12, "'terrorism' search on Ngram Viewer (1800 – 2000)," since the graph line starts before the 1800 year mark, it may be better to start the crawl earlier, such as 1500, to move forward from there. It may also help to examine the areas of the line spikes.

In Figure 13, "'terrorism' search on Ngram Viewer (1500 – 2000)," the Ngram Viewer also

Figure 9. "robot" search on Ngram Viewer

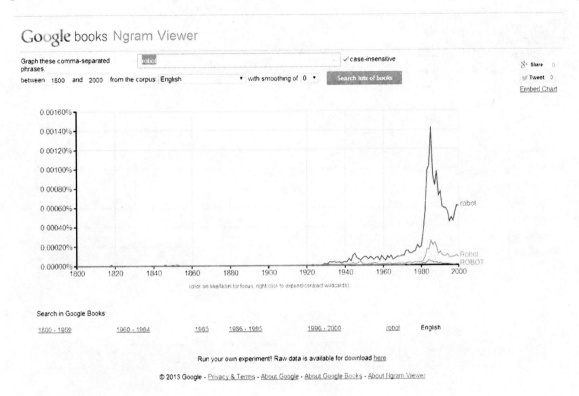

Figure 10. "nanotech" search on Ngram Viewer (1960 – 2000)

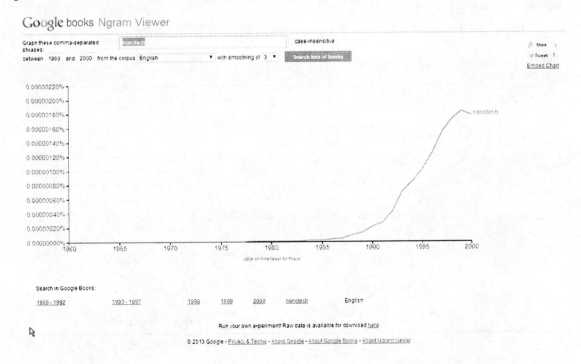

Figure 11. "cloud computing" bigram on the Ngram Viewer

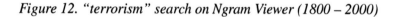

Figure 12. "terrorism" search on Ngram Viewer (1800 – 2000)

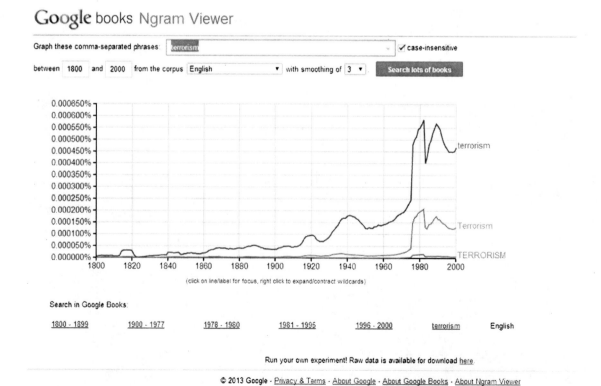

Figure 13. "terrorism" search on Ngram Viewer (1500 – 2000)

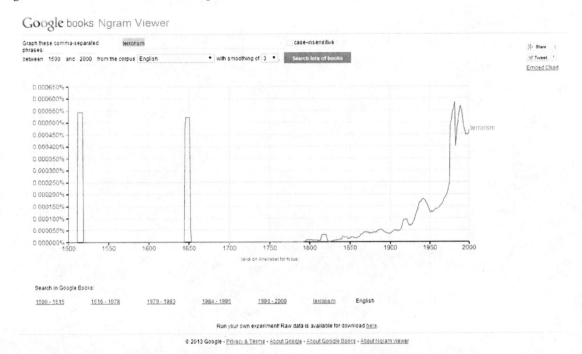

offers pull-outs of years of interest below: 1500-1515, 1516 – 1978, 1979 – 1983, 1994 – 1995, 1996 – 2000.

Figure 14, "'ceteris paribus' search on Ngram Viewer (1800 – 2000)" shows an extraction of the Latin phrase "ceteris paribus" (a 2-gram or bigram). The phrase means "with other things the same".

There can be acronym searches, such as "NTSB" (a one-gram or unigram) for the "National Transportation Safety Board".

The four-gram "Aung San Suu Kyi" follows this democracy leader's name in its appearances in books in Figure 16, " Aung San Suu Kyi (4-gram) name search on Ngram Viewer."

Practical Comparatives and Contrastives

An increased complexity may be seen in comparatives and contrastives with word pair comparisons. Clearly, there are nuances in word usages and meanings.

Figure 17, "Various forms of "pi, 3.14159, π" search on NGram Viewer," shows comparisons between various references to pi. All three run separately, but the number and the symbol are much less popular than "pi."

In Figure 18, "Various forms of "pi, 3.14159, π" and "pi+3.14159+ π" search on NGram Viewer," this new iteration of Figure #17 shows the added line of "pi+3.14159+ π".

A data extraction of a list of leading information technologies companies on the Ngram Viewer may suggest the competition between the companies and may enable inferences about each company's success, reach, and legacy. Clearly, this information may provide a lead but would need support from other data sources. (Also, popularity in the public mind may not necessarily be conflated with anything else.)

Between the acronym "PTSD" or the whole words "post-traumatic stress disorder," which is more popular in texts? The graph shows a broad usage of the acronym, which may only actually reflect the writing convention of going with

Figure 14. "ceteris paribus" search on Ngram Viewer (1800 – 2000)

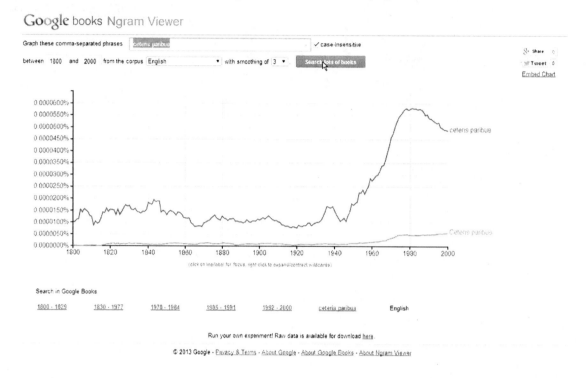

Figure 15. "NTSB" acronym search on Ngram Viewer

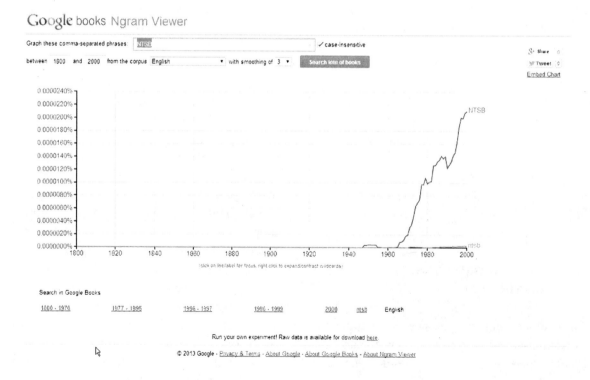

Figure 16. Aung San Suu Kyi (4-gram) name search on Ngram Viewer

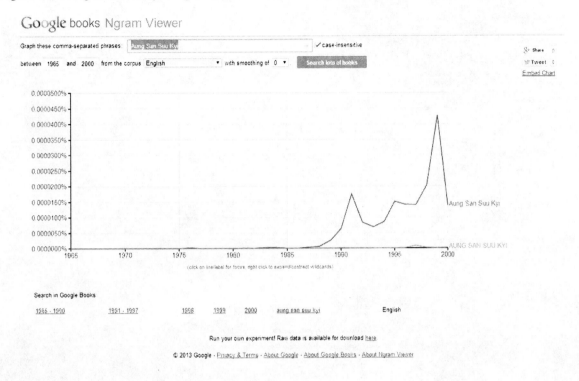

Figure 17. Various forms of "pi, 3.14159, π" search on NGram Viewer

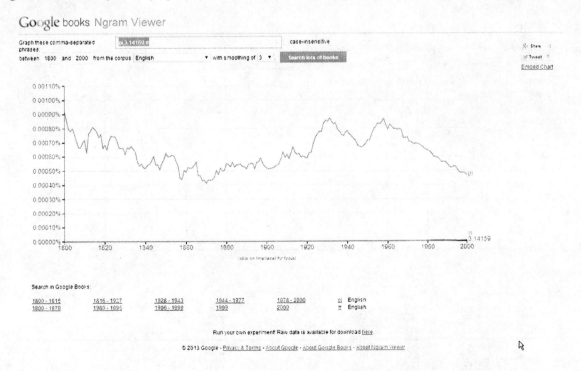

Figure 18. Various forms of "pi, 3.14159, π" and "pi+3.14159+ π" search on NGram Viewer

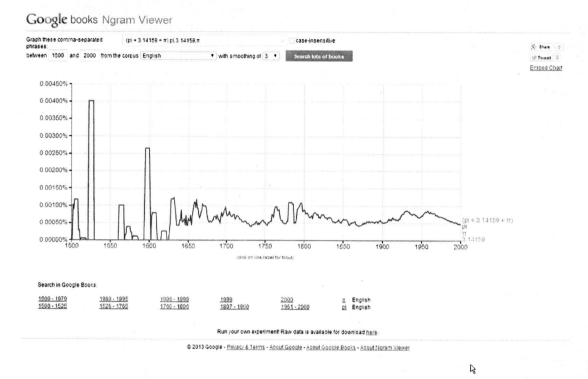

Figure 19. A leading information technologies companies search on Ngram Viewer

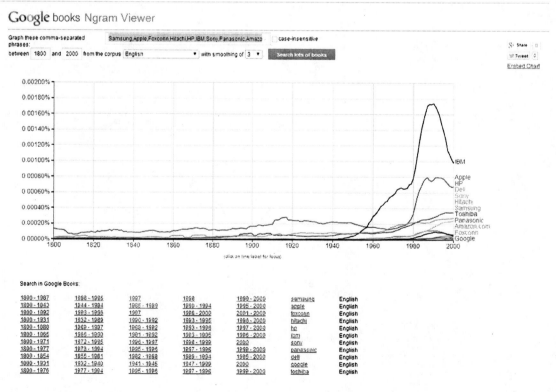

Figure 20. "PTSD" and "post traumatic stress disorder" search on Ngram Viewer

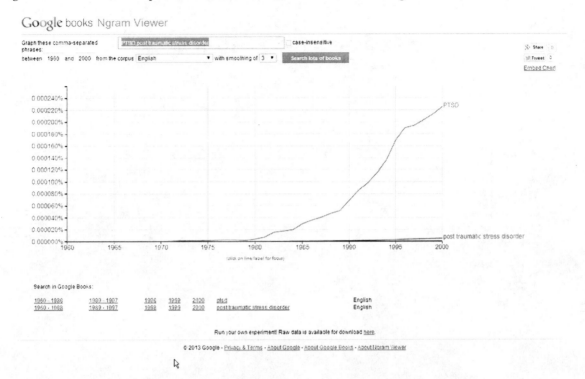

popular acronyms in the common parlance. This data crawl involved a one-gram and a four-gram.

Figure 21, "General typologies of research methods search on Ngram Viewer," involved a run of "qualitative research, quantitative research, mixed methods research, multimethod research" to surface what was most popular in the text corpuses.

The data crawl of "USSR, Soviet, Russian Federation, and Russia" shows the variations of the usages of the terms over the years based in part on political changes in Figure 22.

Figure 23, "Multiple China references search in Ngram Viewer," illuminates the relative popularity of terms with China as well in a kind of mirroring of Figure 22.

A comparative query involves the Wade-Giles and pinyin language transliteration system for Chinese. This line graph shows the rise of certain terms and the sun-setting of others—and may pinpoint the years of transition, in Figure 24.

Figure 25, "Wade-Giles" and "pinyin" comparative on Ngram Viewer (1940–2000)," offers

a close-in view of the data by limiting the years. The web tool offers insights on particular years with a mouseover at the intersections between the lines and the years.

A search of "google" in a case insensitive way shows not only the generic definition but also a recent spike in 1998 (when Google Inc. was founded in Menlo Park). This crawl results in different lines of data from title case to uncapitalized to block caps. Variances in case may differentiate meanings.

Another comparative may be the informal and formal names of a country, such as in Figure 27, "'Burma, Myanmar' comparative search on Ngram Viewer."

A more historical of the same phenomena in Figure 27 is found in Figure 28. The line for "Ho Chi Minh City" does not really appear until near the fall of Saigon. Ironically, "Saigon" remains much more popular in the text corpus through 2000.

Another list of comparatives may be the "Invisible Web, Deep Web, Hidden Web, Dark Web,"

533

Figure 21. General typologies of research methods search on Ngram Viewer

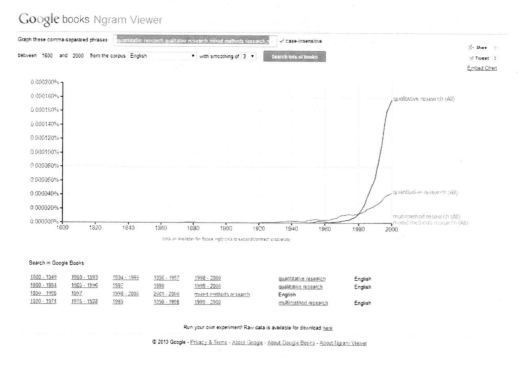

Figure 22. Multiple references to Russia on Ngram Viewer

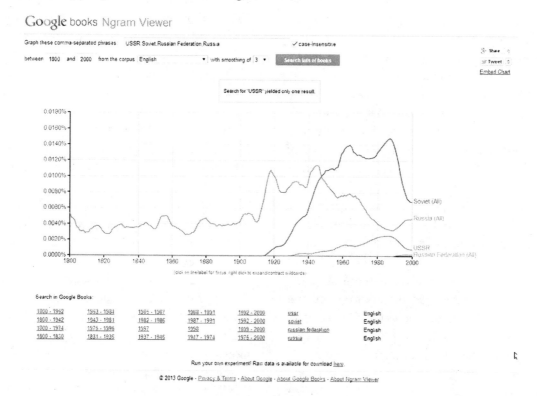

Figure 23. Multiple China references search in Ngram Viewer

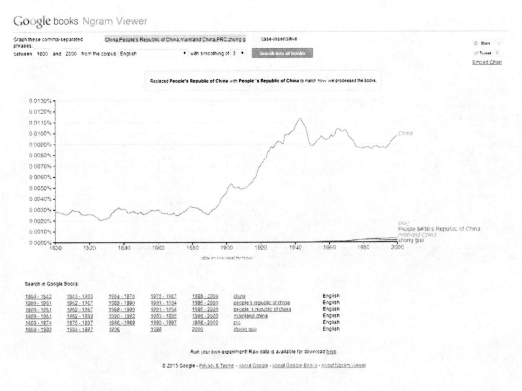

Figure 24. Wade-Giles and pinyin comparative on Ngram Viewer (1800 – 2000)

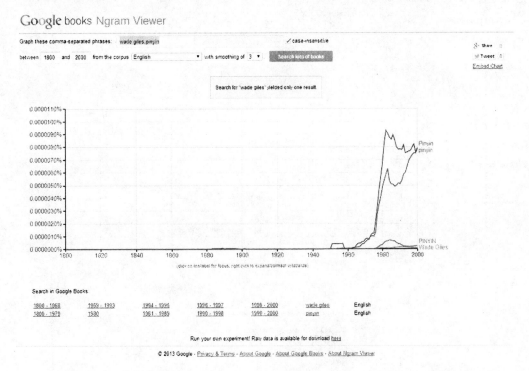

Figure 25. "Wade-Giles" and "pinyin" comparative on Ngram Viewer (1940 – 2000)

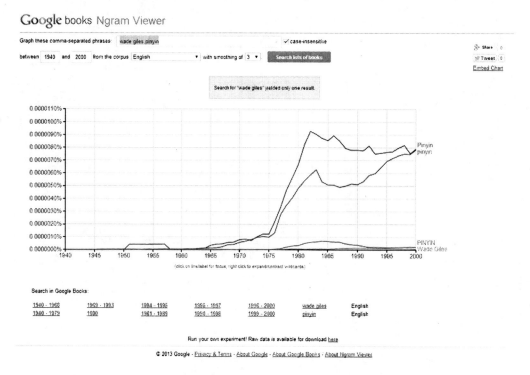

Figure 26. "google" search on Ngram Viewer

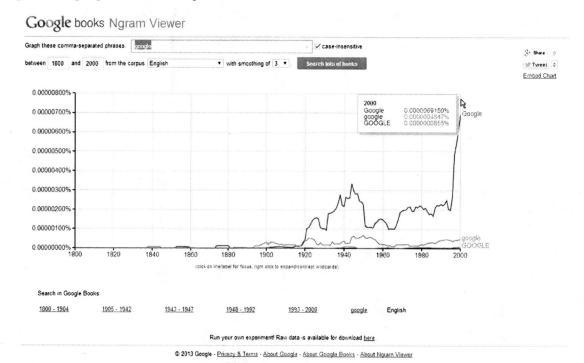

Figure 27. "Burma, Myanmar" comparative search on Ngram Viewer

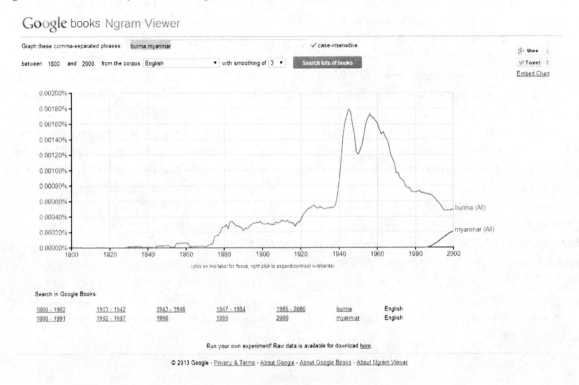

Figure 28. "Saigon" and "Ho Chi Minh City" comparative search on Ngram Viewer

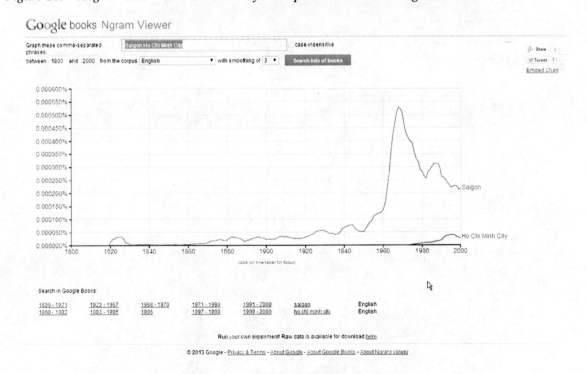

with the first three words referring to the same phenomena but the fourth to a different phenomena online. It is of interest that the "Dark Web" only registered one result.

A search for the text frequencies of "WWII, World War II, second world war" identifies which of the terms is most popular.

A case-sensitive text frequency count for "HIV-AIDS, human immunodeficiency virus, aids" offers a way to differentiate the disease from the general verb "aids."

A text frequency count of "Grateful Dead, grateful dead" shows a spike in 1907 in reference to a first edition book title using those words and then a rise again in use linked to the well-known band. The data extractions show something of the problem of disambiguation.

A search for "war" shows spikes at the times of both world wars.

A text frequency search for inherently contrastive terms "war" and "peace" shows some light mirroring in terms of spikes, but one term clearly dominates.

Synonyms, such as "Mount Everest, Sagarmatha, Chomolungma," may show their relative popularity in the public mind.

In terms of "CBRN," which stands for "chemical," "biological," "radiological," and "nuclear," concerns, a search on the Ngram Viewer found the top mentions of these words were both "chemical" and "nuclear" but likely over a range of contexts.

A comparison and contrast of contenders for the "7 wonders of the world" were searched in Figure 37.

Health events may be explored through the Google Books Ngram Viewer as well. Figure 38 compares the occurrences of "avian flu" and "swine flu."

Figure 29. Invisible, Deep, Hidden, and Dark Web search on Ngram Viewer

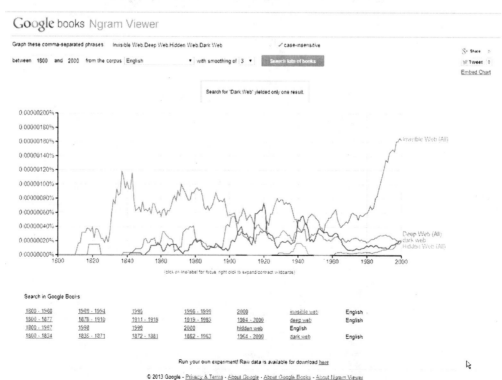

Figure 30. "WWII, World War 2, second world war" comparative search on Ngram Viewer

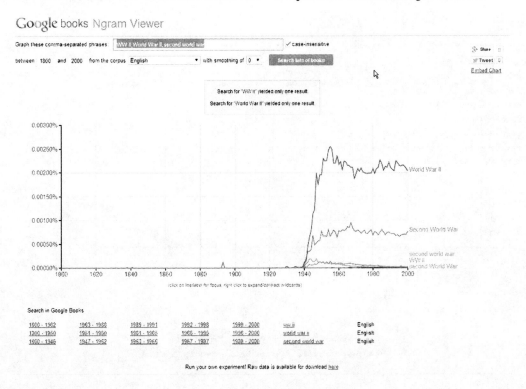

Figure 31. "HIV-AIDS, human immunodeficiency virus, aids" search on Ngram Viewer

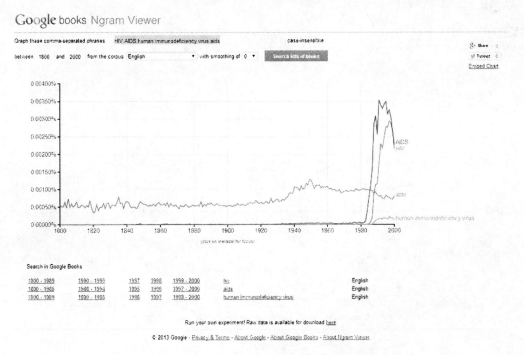

Figure 32. "Grateful Dead, grateful dead" search on Ngram Viewer

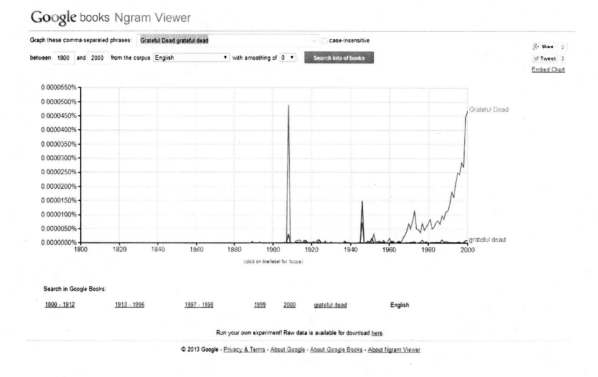

Figure 33. "war" search on Ngram Viewer

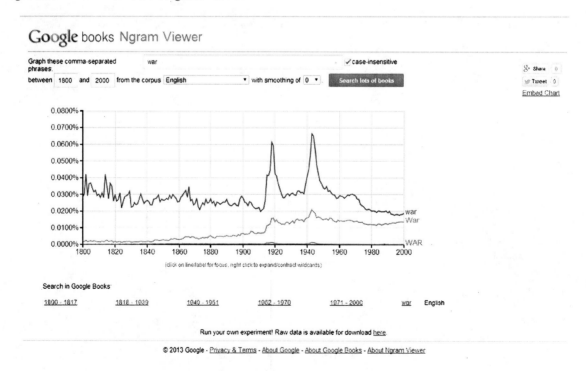

Figure 34. "war" and "peace" contrastive search on Ngram Viewer

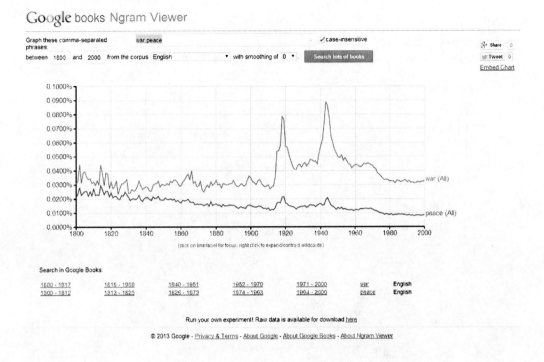

Figure 35. "Mount Everest, Sagarmatha, Chomolungma" search on Ngram Viewer

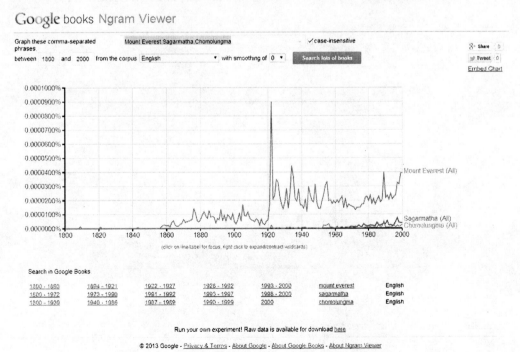

Figure 36. CBRN (chemical, biological, radiological, and nuclear) search on Ngram Viewer

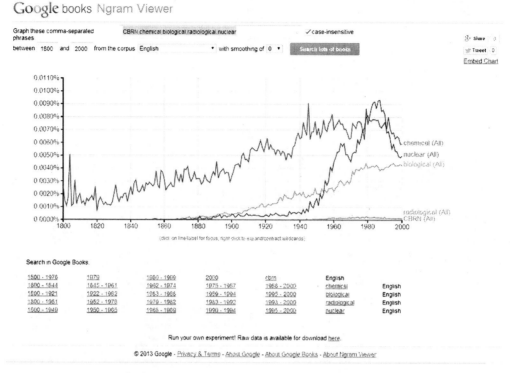

Figure 37. Some contenders for the "7 wonders of the world" searched on Ngram Viewer

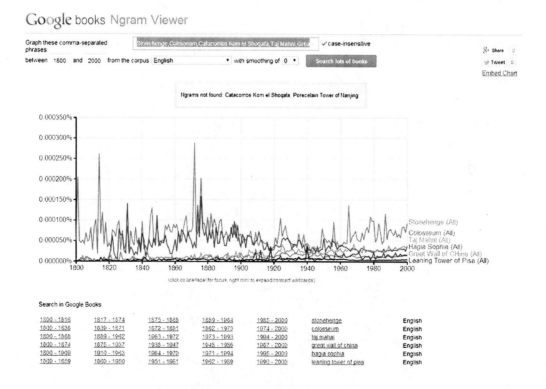

Figure 38. "avian flu" and "swine flu" comparative on Ngram Viewer

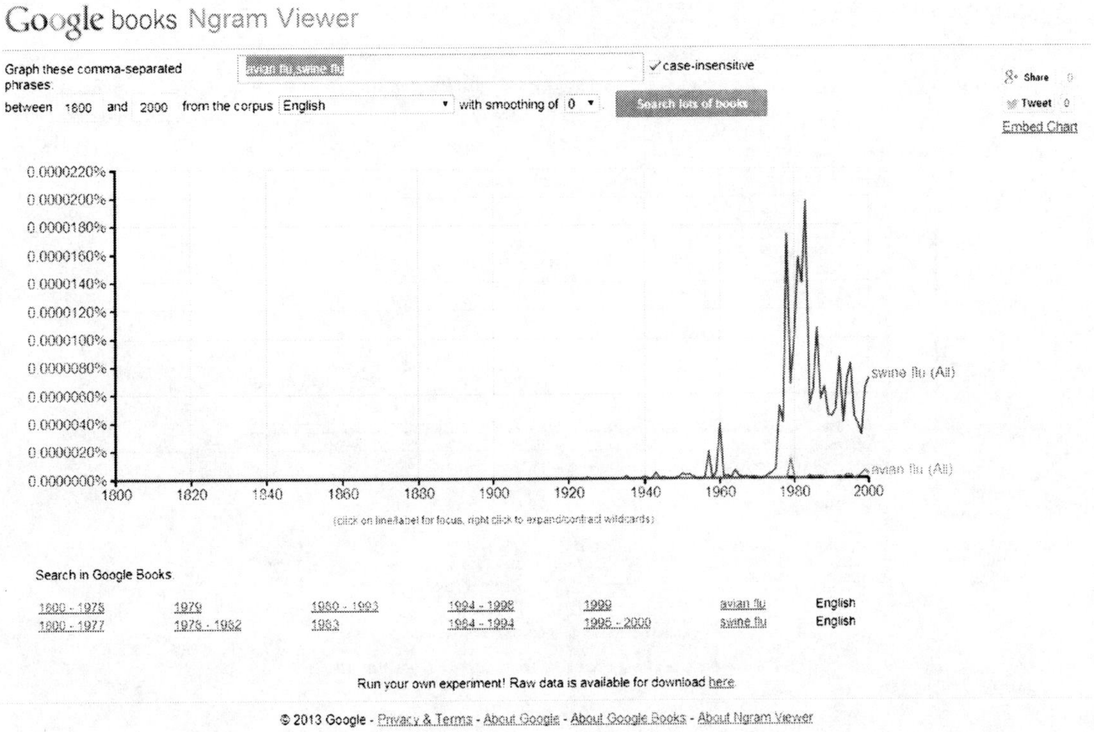

The three traditional news broadcasting companies are compared in Figure 39, but the addition of Cable News Network (CNN), a major competitor in Figure 40, adds contrastive value. The latter graph shows the changing popularity of news networks over time.

Figure 41, "Electronic communications methods search on Ngram Viewer," may be read as suggesting the popularity of some types of electronic communications over others, leading up to the year 2000.

Figure 42, "Selected artists of the 20ᵗʰ century search on Ngram Viewer," involves a listing of 20ᵗʰ century artists, with the towering figure of Picasso outranking the mentions of the other artists.

SOME ADVANCED GOOGLE BOOKS NGRAM VIEWER QUERYING

The affordances for advanced Ngram Viewer querying through inflections, wildcard extractions, parts-of-speech tagging, and case insensitivity may enable a wider range of knowledge.

One common example of a wildcard search involves "United States of *" to extract the 10 most common placeholder words in lieu of the asterisk.

Figure 44, "'Cyber*' wildcard search on Ngram Viewer," shows that there are a range of cyber issues, such as cyber café, cyber space, cyber crime, cyber terrorism, cyber attacks, cyber threats, cyber security, and others.

Figure 39. Three traditional news broadcasting companies in the U.S. market search on Ngram Viewer

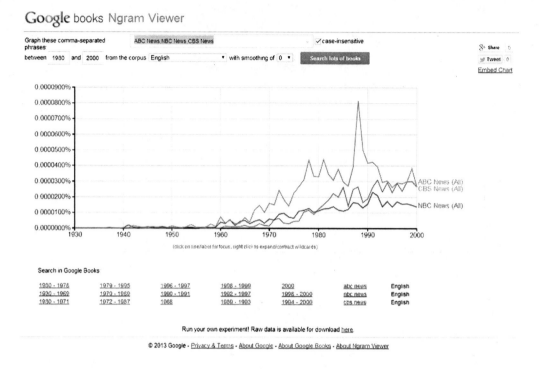

Figure 40. Three traditional news broadcasting companies in the U.S. market with CNN added search on Ngram Viewer

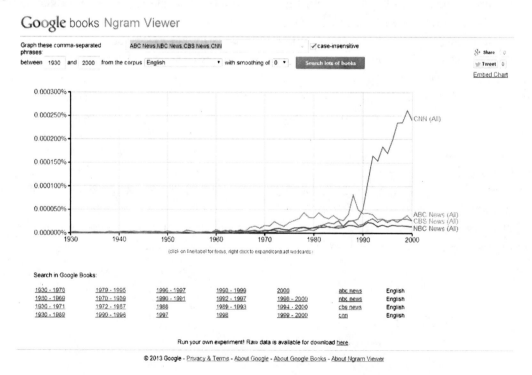

Figure 41. Electronic communications methods search on Ngram Viewer

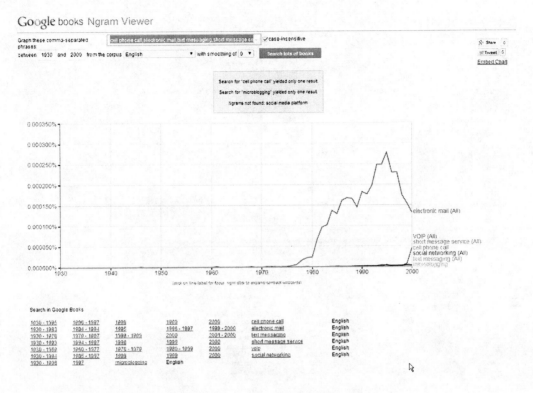

Figure 42. Selected artists of the 20th century search on Ngram Viewer

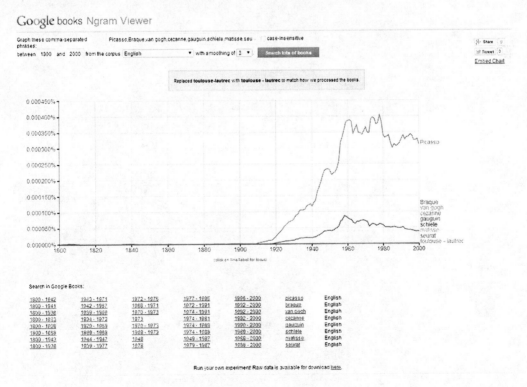

*Figure 43. "United States of *" wildcard search on Ngram Viewer*

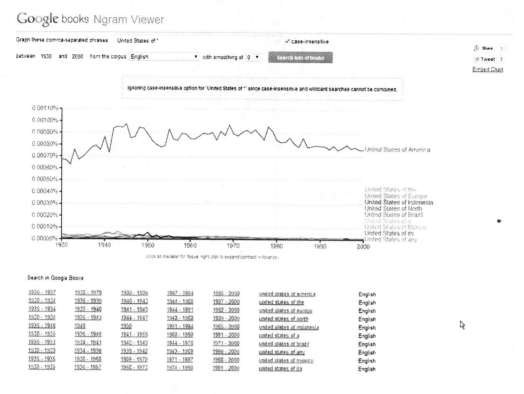

*Figure 44. "Cyber *" wildcard search on Ngram Viewer*

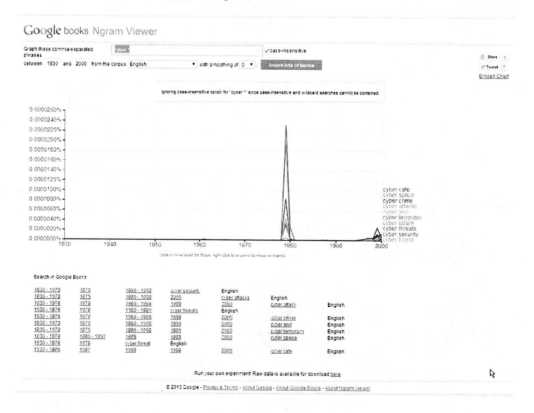

Figure 45, "'Boeing *' wildcard search on Ngram Viewer," shows some valuable insights about the context for the mentions of Boeing over a large part of the 20th century.

Depending on the placement of the wildcard asterisk (such as in front of the target term), the data extraction may identify a range of prepositions, articles, and possibly less useful terms. This may be seen in Figure 46, "'* espionage' wildcard search on Ngram Viewer." (It may help to have a stop words list here to omit some of these more common terms in lieu of those words with more meaning.)

The same challenge with extracting meaningful descriptive information occurs in the "*Dubai" wildcard search. It helps to use knowledge of language syntax and mechanics for the crawls.

Here, in Figure 48, "skunkworks" is disambiguated with a wildcard search for words following the use of this term.

In Figure 49, the term "* hijacking" is used for the data extraction.

Figure 50 shows a wildcard frequency count line graph for "* flu epidemic".

To gauge the size of the frequency of "cyber" without any connection to "attack," the minus feature may be used to create a different sort of composition on Ngram Viewer. Any of the variations (+, -, /, *, and:).

Finally, to conduct comparisons across different corpuses, it is important to apply the given syntax for the Ngram Viewer. A crawl was done searching for the occurrences of "police" in the eng_2012 dataset and then the Hebrew term for

*Figure 45. "Boeing *" wildcard search on Ngram Viewer*

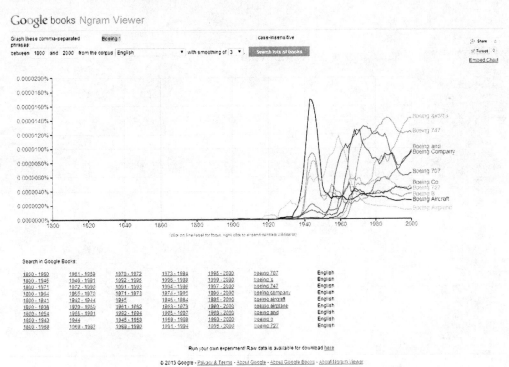

Figure 46. " espionage" wildcard search on Ngram Viewer*

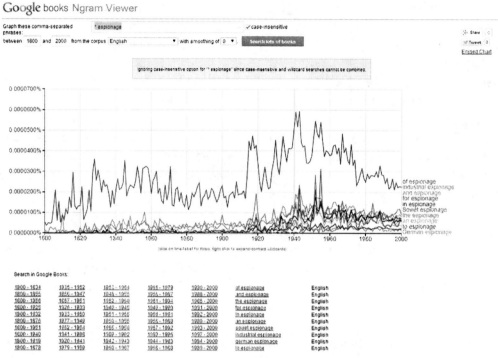

Figure 47. " Dubai" wildcard search on Ngram Viewer*

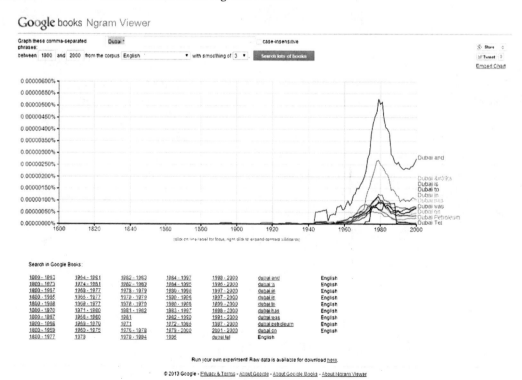

*Figure 48. "Skunkworks *" wildcard search on Ngram Viewer*

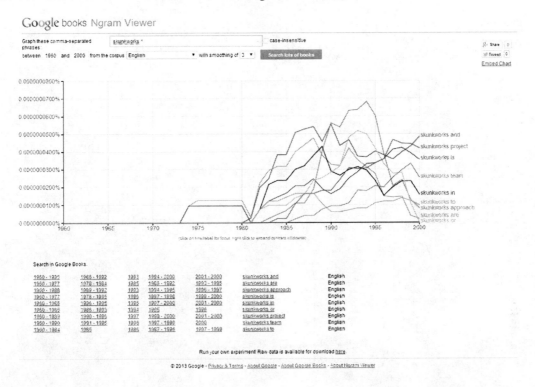

Figure 49. " hijacking" wildcard search on Ngram Viewer*

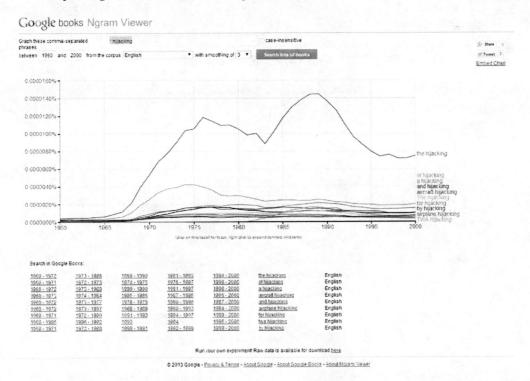

Figure 50. "*flu epidemic" wildcard search on Ngram Viewer

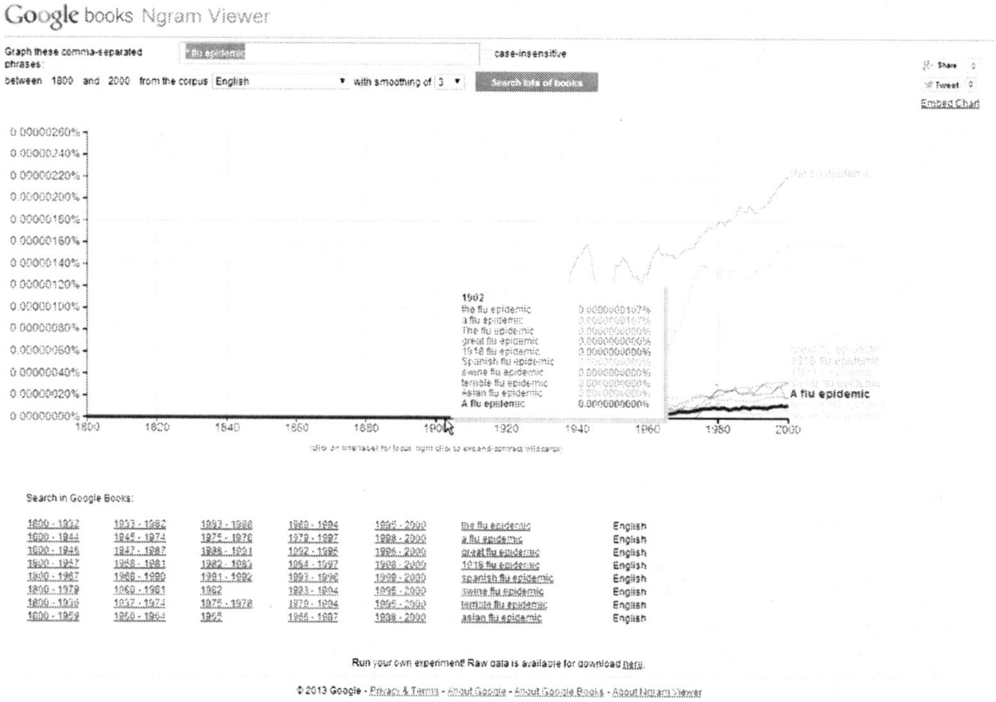

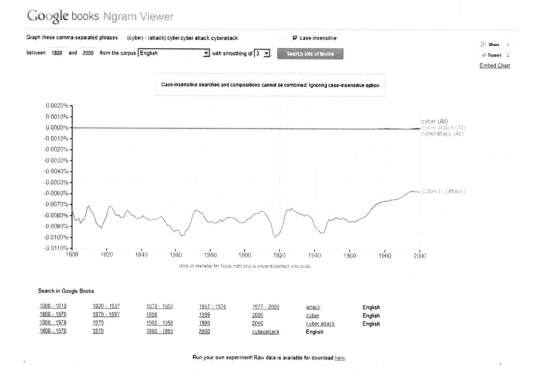

Figure 51. "(cyber) – (attack), cyber, cyberattack, cyberattack" search on Ngram Viewer

police in the heb_2012 dataset. The query read: police:eng_2012, הרטשמ:heb_2012. These are limited datasets limited to a recent year.

It may help to note that the various datasets need to be referred to by shorthand, such as the following: fre_2012, eng_2012, eng_us_2012, heb_2012, spa_2012, rus_2012, ita_2012, and chi_sim_2012, for example.

The sampler above was drawn from a wide range of topics without any particular theme in order to explore the effects of such range on the software tool and related text corpuses. The topics in general tend to be drawn from the humanities.

Discussion

The Google Books Ngram Viewer offers another way that books can be made relevant and informational for people today. It offers ways to answer research questions and to offer exploratory value. The word frequency counts may be used to complement a wide range of research—both historical and

present-day—and they may be used as stand-alone observations. While the tool is very simple to use (in both the basic and advanced levels), it does take some training into how to query the data for valuable insights. Then, too, researchers need to be careful about what may be assertable, so that they do not go beyond the available information (from this deconstructed data-reduced shadow dataset, which is essentially aggregate metadata extrapolated from language content). Data visualizations may be prone to the encapsulation of complexity and severe data reduction—which may lead to misreadings of the underlying information. The skills used in plumbing these depths will likely carry over to other queries of corpuses (of text, speech, or other data).

The tool itself enables a variety of functionalities with its range of query methods. Extracting insights though will require no small amount of skill. Being able to use the multilingual aspects of the tool will be a value-added approach as well. This tool offers insights to researchers who can

Figure 52. Corpus comparisons using "police:eng_2012, הרטשמ:heb_2012" in Ngram Viewer

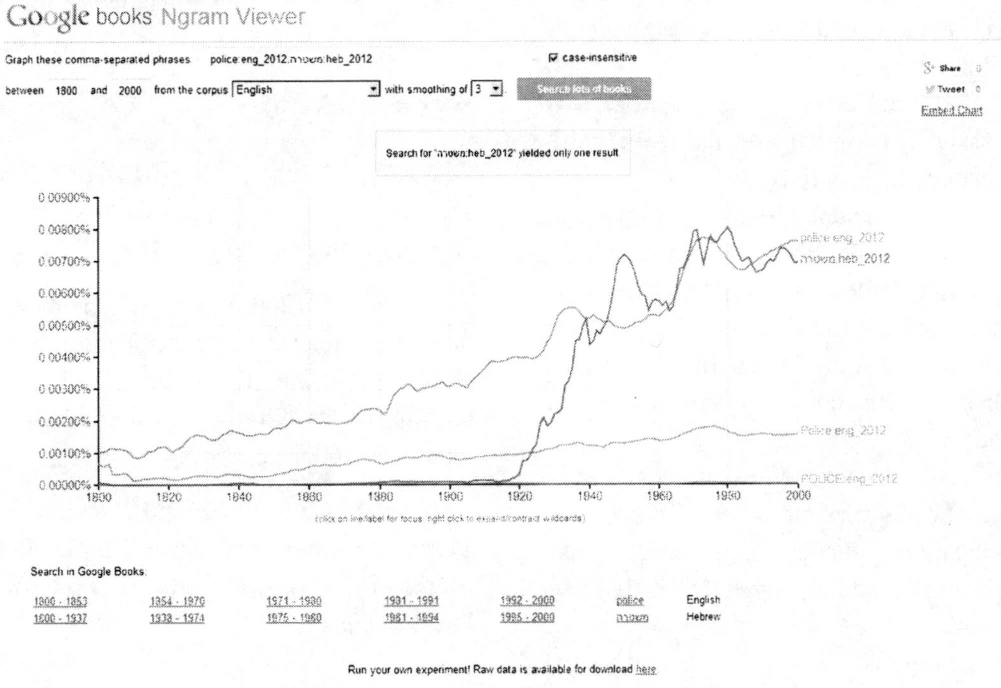

bring deep external knowledge to the data. After all, the isolated data has to be recontextualized (reconstituted, so to speak) to be valuable. What is knowable from the tool? An early answer to this may be summarized in the following questions:

- When did particular ideas first appear (the year of a term's first mention)? What does this say about the related ideas? How do ideas proliferate over time? How did these ideas evolve in use over time? When did the ideas sunset?
- What may be understood of certain individuals, events, periods, or genres based on the books being written in a particular time?
- If the ideas spiked in popularity over time, what real-world circumstances could account for those spikes?
- When did particular people first appear in the text corpus? What does this say about their influence?
- How does language evolve over time? What trends may be observable?
- What words do not appear that one would expect should appear in the literature corpus? What would this suggest about the world at the time?
- What cultural or linguistic questions may be asked by comparing results between different available corpuses?
- What is not captured here in this representation of the public mind? Theoretically, what is outside this dataset? In practice, what is outside this dataset?
- How may the data from this dataset be checked with other sources and other processes?
- As this dataset becomes more complete with the digitization of more books and publications, what additional insights may be drawn? And how may these insights be drawn?

Future Research

There is broad potential for fresh applications of the Google Books Ngram Viewer, which has after all only been in public use since late 2010. In terms of future research, there are many possible applications across a range of domains. Certainly, there are likely very clever applications of the tool in terms of formulating queries and extracting understandings.

CONCLUSION

The purpose of this chapter was to generally summarize some of the simpler applications of the Google Books Ngram Viewer as a tool to complement qualitative, quantitative, mixed methods research, and multimethods research. This chapter showed a powerful tool that enables free and open access to a shadow dataset from the Google Books project.

As new works are added to the text corpuses, and new methods are developed, this approach of probing big data in the literature stands to benefit human understandings in a range of fields.

REFERENCES

Aiden, E., & Michel, J.-B. (2013). *Uncharted: Big Data as a Lens on Human Culture*. New York: Riverhead Books, Penguin Books.

Anderson, C. (2008). The end of theory: The data deluge makes the scientific method obsolete. *Wired Magazine.* Retrieved March 18, 2014, at http://www.wired.com/science/discoveries/magazine/16-07/pb_theory

Barlow, J. (2011). *Google's Ngram Viewer. Berglund Center for Internet Studies.* Retrieved March 18, 2014, at http://bcis.pacificu.edu/interface/?p=379

Culturomics. (2014, Jan. 11). *Wikipedia*. Retrieved March 18, 2014, at http://en.wikipedia.org/wiki/Culturomics

Denbo, S., & Fraistat, N. (2011). Diggable data, scalable reading and new humanities scholarship. In *Proceedings of 2011 Second International Conference on Culture and Computing*. doi:10.1109/Culture-Computing.2011.49

Diller, H.-J. (2013). Culturomics and genre: *Wrath* and *anger* in the 17th century. In *Proceedings of the 2012 Symposium on New Approaches in English Historical Lexis* (pp. 54 – 65). Academic Press.

Gibbs, F. W., & Cohen, D. J. (2011). A conversation with data: Prospecting Victorian words and ideas. *Victorian Studies*, *54*(1), 69–77. doi:10.2979/victorianstudies.54.1.69

Gooding, P. (2013). Mass digitization and the garbage dump: The conflicting needs of quantitative and qualitative methods. *Literary and Linguistic Computing*, *28*(3), 425–431. doi:10.1093/llc/fqs054

Google Books Ngram Viewer. (2014). *About Ngram Viewer*. Retrieved March 20, 2014, at https://books.google.com/ngrams/info

Greenfield, P. M. (2013). The changing psychology of culture from 1800 through 2000. *Psychological Science*, *24*(9), 1722–1731. doi:10.1177/0956797613479387 PMID:23925305

Hassanpour, N. (2013). Tracking the semantics of politics: A case for online data research in political science. In *Proceedings of Symposium: Technology, Data, and Politics* (pp. 299 – 306). doi:10.1017/S1049096513000280

Hayes, B. (2014). Bit lit. *American Scientist*. Retrieved March 18, 2014, at http://www.americanscientist.org/issues/num2/bit-lit/2

Klein, D. B. (2013). *Cultural trends as seen in ngrams: Karl Polanyi with a Hayekian twist* (Working Paper No. 13-10). George Mason University, Department of Economics.

Lin, Y., Michel, J.-B., Lieberman, Aiden, E.L., Orwant, J., Brockman, W., & Petrov, S. (2012). Syntactic annotations for the Google Books Ngram Corpus. *In Proceedings of the 50th Annual Meeting of the Association for Computational Lingusitics*. Jeju, Korea: ACL.

Mayer-Schönberger, V., & Cukier, K. (2013). *Big Data: A Revolution that Will Transform How We Live, Work, and Think*. Boston: Houghton Mifflin Harcourt.

Michel, J.-B., Shen, Y.K., Aiden, A.P., Veres, A., Gray, M.K., Brockman, W., … Aiden, E.L. (2010). Quantitative Analysis of Culture Using Millions of Digitized Books. *Science*.

O'Malley, M. (2010, Dec. 21). Ngramattic. *The Aporetic*.

Percival, R. V. (2011). China's Green Leap Forward. *Vermont Journal of Environmental Law*, *12*, 633 – 657. Retrieved Mar. 17, 2014, at http://digitalcommons.law.umaryland.edu/cgi/viewcontent.cgi?article=2144&context=fac_pubs

Roivainen, E. (2014). Changes in word usage frequency may hamper intergenerational comparisons of vocabulary skills: An ngram analysis of Wordsum, WAIS, and WISC test items. *Journal of Psychoeducational Assessment*, *32*(1), 83–87. doi:10.1177/0734282913485542

Twenge, J. M., Campbell, W. K., & Gentile, B. (2012). Changes in pronoun use in American books and the rise in individualism, 1960–2008. *Journal of Cross-Cultural Psychology*, *44*(3), 406–415. doi:10.1177/0022022112455100

Westland, J. C. (2011). Affective data acquisition technologies in survey research. *Information Technology Management*, *12*(4), 387–408. doi:10.1007/s10799-011-0110-9

Zimmer, B. (2013, Oct. 17). Google's Ngram Viewer goes wild. *The Atlantic*. Retrieved from http://www.theatlantic.com/technology/archive/2013/10/googles-ngram-viewer-goes-wild/280601/

ADDITIONAL READING

Aiden, E., & Michel, J.-B. (2013). *Uncharted: Big Data as a Lens on Human Culture*. New York: Riverhead Books, Penguin Books.

Mayer-Schönberger, V., & Cukier, K. (2013). *Big Data: A Revolution that Will Transform How We Live, Work, and Think*. Boston: Houghton Mifflin Harcourt.

KEY TERMS AND DEFINITIONS

Bar Graph: A two-dimensional diagram (with an x and a y axis) and rectangular bars indicating measure, amount, frequency, or degree.

Bibliometrics: The application of statistical methods and quantitative analysis of academic so.

Big Data: A catch-all term indicating an N of all or a large dataset of information (such as with millions of records).

Cloud Service: A software service delivered remotely through the Internet or Web.

Culturomics: The study of cultural trends through quantitative analysis of digitized texts or text corpuses.

Data Reduction: The condensing and simplification of information through summaries and other systematic analytical work.

Data Visualization: The communication of information in a diagram, chart, illustration, or other drawing.

Datafication: The making of digital information machine-readable and machine-analyzable.

Deconstruction: The taking apart of a work to its component parts.

Digital Humanities: The use of digitized information and computational analysis to enhance studies in the humanities.

Digitization: Transcoding analog information into digital format.

Empirics: Observation and experimentation.

Google Books Ngram Viewer: A cloud-based text-frequency counting research tool available at https://books.google.com/ngrams.

Gram: A unit of alphanumeric text in a contiguous sequence.

Granularity: The level of specificity of units in a certain system (high granularity implies specific details; low granularity suggests coarser details).

Large-Scale Digital Initiatives (LSDIs): Endeavors that involve the digitization of information (such as books) and the application of big data analyses to these resources.

Metadata: Data about data.

N-Gram: A contiguous sequence of items such as words and phrases; alphanumeric text units in sequence; strings of letters and numbers (or ideograms or characters, depending on the language).

Parse: To analyze, to break a sentence down to its constituent parts by syntax.

Petabyte (PB): 10^{15} bytes of digital information.

Shadowing Data: The anonymizing and de-identification of data in order to allow some of the informational value in the original dataset while filtering out other information that may enable mis-used of the data (as regards privacy infringement, malicious use, or other unintended uses).

Smoothing: The integration of data points into a more integrated line by averaging the values of nearby data points into the value for a particular point (particularly in data visualization image processing).

Text Corpus: A collection of texts.

Token: A single element, an instance of a type of logic.

Word Frequency Count: An analytical approach which involves machine-counting of the number of times a term (or sequence of terms) appears.

Chapter 21

Expressing Data, Space, and Time with Tableau Public™:
Harnessing Open Data to Enhance Visual Learning through Interactive Maps and Dashboards

Shalin Hai-Jew
Kansas State University, USA

ABSTRACT

Virtually every subject area depicted in a learning object could conceivably involve a space-time element. Theoretically, every event may be mapped geospatially, and in time, these spatialized event maps may be overlaid with combined data (locations of particular natural and human-made objects, demographics, and other phenomena) to enable the identification and analysis of time-space patterns and interrelationships. They enable hypothesis formations, hunches, and the asking and answering of important research questions. The ability to integrate time-space insights into research work is enhanced by the wide availability of multiple new sources of free geospatial data: open data from governments and organizations (as part of Gov 2.0), locative information from social media platforms (as part of Web 2.0), and self-created geospatial datasets from multiple sources. The resulting maps and data visualizations, imbued with a time context and the potential sequencing of maps over time, enable fresh insights and increased understandings. In addition to the wide availability of validated geospatial data, Tableau Public is a free and open cloud-based tool that enables the mapping of various data sets for visualizations that are pushed out onto a public gallery for public consumption. The interactive dashboard enables users to explore the data and discover insights and patterns. Tableau Public is a tool that enables enhanced visual- and interaction-based knowing, through interactive Web-friendly maps, panel charts, and data dashboards. With virtually zero computational or hosting costs (for the user), Tableau Public enables the integration of geospatial mapping and analysis stands to benefit research work, data exploration and discovery and analysis, and learning.

DOI: 10.4018/978-1-4666-6493-7.ch021

INTRODUCTION

In the age of "big data" and "open data," the broad public has access to more information than they have ever had historically. Some of this data has been released to the public domain through open government endeavors (Gov 2.0). Others have been shared as part of the "digital exhaust" (or "data exhaust") of Web 2.0, or the social age of the Web (with APIs enabling access to a range of social media platforms, social networking sites, microblogging sites, wikis, blogs, and other platforms). Another source of datasets comes from academia, with a range of sites that host downloadable datasets as part of the formal publication process. Beyond these prior open-access and / or open-source datasets, there are also propriety ones released by for-profit companies as part of their public service and public relations outreaches. Much data are collected by sensor networks in physical spaces and robots on the Internet and Web. The popularity of mobile devices, navigation systems, and software applications that track location data means that there are publicly available datasets of geo-spatial or locative information. Much of this data, though, cannot be understood coherently without running them through data analysis and visualization tools—to identify patterns and anomalies, as well as create data-based maps, graphs, and charts. If "big data" is going to have direct relevance to the general public, they have to be "big data"-literate: they have to be able to understand and query big data. Concomitant with the "democratization of data" are some tools that enable data processing and visualization. One leading free online tool, Tableau Public, the free public version of a professional enterprise suite (Tableau Professional), serves as a gateway to such data analysis and visualization. This chapter provides a light overview of the software tool and its possible use in multimedia presentations to enhance discovery learning.

The dynamically generated visualizations themselves are almost invariably multivariate and multi-dimensional, with labeled data in a variety of accessible visualizations; these may include multiple pages of related visualizations. While these visualizations may be complex, there are others that may be created for other purposes than research and discovery; some data visualizations are whimsical and attention-getting (to capture attention and encourage awareness of the data).

The public edition of Tableau Public provides a gigabyte of storage for each registered user. There is no "save" for the visualizations except through publishing out the data visualizations on the Tableau Public Gallery, which makes all visualizations publicly viewable in an infographics and data visualization gallery, along with the downloads of related datasets. The panel charts are zoomable and pan-able; they enable data filtering (with responsive dynamic revisualizations). This gallery is of particular use if public awareness is part desired outcomes. Such maps and data visualizations have been used in an emerging class of digital narratives, used by journalists and other storytellers (Segel & Heer, 2010) in computational journalism, or journalism which relies on in-depth data processing to tell "data stories" or "narrative visualizations". Such presentations meld data, statistics, design, information technology, and storytelling, for a broad audience. As such, these visualizations appear also as parts of commercial sites based around business, real estate, and others. They are used as online conversation starters in a variety of contexts.

Contents may be authored in Windows machines only, but the dashboards and data visualizations are viewable on Windows and Mac machines without any plug-ins required (just browsers with JavaScript enabled). The makers of this tool use the tagline, "Data In. Brilliance Out," to express their objectives for the tool. As a tool for multimedia presentations, Tableau Public enables rich and interactive data visualizations to broaden the perceptual (visual) and cognitive (symbolic reasoning, textual, and kinesthetic) learning channels to understand data. Tableau Public is a free tool (albeit a cloud and a hosted solution) that enables the uploading of complex data (in .xl and .txt formats) for intuitive presentations on the Web. Such interactive depictions offer accessible ways of understanding interrelationships and potential trends over time, and provide some initial predictive analytics.

REVIEW OF THE LITERATURE

The phenomena of Web 2.0 (or the Social Web) and Gov 2.0 (social e-government) have meant that there is wide availability of datasets linked to social media platforms and open government geospatial datasets, among others. Social media platform data tend to be self-organizing and dynamic data based on people's lifestyles and activities; these involve the mapping of social networks based on people's electronic communications through social networking sites, microblogging sites, blog sites, wiki sites, and so on. The latter involve a mix of more static (less dynamically changeable) data about citizen demographics, business records, economics, national security, law enforcement, nature management, weather, and other aspects. As with various types of data, such sets may be combined to highlight particular issues of interest as long as there is a column of unique identifiers that can help researchers match records (such as record based on physical space).

Where the finesse of researchers comes in is in knowing what may be asserted from the mapped data and relating that to their research. Indeed, geospatial mapping in academic works may not require specialist training in some cases; often it may involve common-sense mapping informed by researchers' specialist topical focus. The assumptions of mapping such data are simple: that physical location may be relevant and interesting to represent certain phenomena. [The physical world is mapped, and all that is needed in most datasets to tie records to physical locations is a column with location data (whether latitude and longitude, ZIP codes, cities, counties, states, provinces, and countries, or other indicators). The quality of the location data enables various levels of specificity in terms of three-dimensional physical space. Some data are so precise that it can locate a smart mobile device to within inches of its actual location. With phenomena and data related to locations, other knowledge of those locations may be brought into play.] Map visualizations are often used for sharing the results of the research for specialist audiences as well as the broader public. Visualizations may make geo-spatial understandings more broadly accessible. They may reduce complexity. Variables themselves may be visually depicted (often as multi-faceted glyphs or semantic icons) to represent some of the differences in data. By convention, information about variables are communicated through "position, size, shape and, more recently, movement" to convey interrelationships and patterns (Manovich, 2011, p. 36).

Error and Data

Researchers in most fields have intensive training on the numerous ways that error may be introduced into data. While data visualizations enable the asking of certain types of data questions, and the unpacking and exploration of complex data, they may also be misleading. This risk of errors is a critical issue throughout the data collection and analysis pipeline. Figure 1 shows that error may be introduced at virtually every phase of the process.

Figure 1, "Critical Junctures for the Introduction of Error in Data Collection and Analysis," provides a general data collection and analysis sequence with the following semi-linear (occasionally recursive) steps:

1. Theorizing/mental modeling,
2. Research design,
3. Data collection methods/data collection tools (technologies and instrumentation) / data sourcing and provenance,

Figure 1. Critical junctures for the introduction of error in data collection and analysis

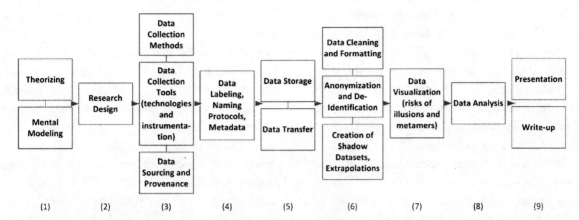

4. Data labeling, naming protocols, metadata,
5. Data storage/data transfer,
6. Data cleaning and formatting/anonymization and de-identification / creation of shadow datasets, extrapolations,
7. Data visualization (risks of illusions and metamers),
8. Data analysis, and
9. Presentation/write-up.

Errors are any distortions that may affect the accuracy of understandings; they may be intentional or unintentional. In theorizing or mental modeling, the analyst may apply an inaccurate conceptualization over the information, which may then be viewed inaccurately given cognitive dissonance and biases. The research design may introduce error into the data by introducing systematic (measurement) or sampling (non-random) errors. The way those data are collected, the technologies and instrumentation used in their collection, and the selected data sourcing and provenance may introduce error: the methods and tools have to align with the research context and what the researchers need to know, the data sources have to be solid, and all tools should be precisely created, tested, calibrated, and applied. The labeling of the data and the application of metadata may introduce error by allowing imprecision and inaccuracy. How the data are stored and transferred

may introduce error if it is not done securely (to ensure data validation and reliability). The work of data cleaning and formatting may introduce error through mishandling and mislabeling; the anonymization and de-identificaiton of data for attaining research standards may involve critical lossiness of information. Data visualization may introduce error with data reduction or simplification, which reduces the ability to discriminate between the finer points or nuances of given data. Data visualizations are summaries of the underlying data; they encapsulate complexity within their own simplicity. Those who consume visualizations themselves without understandings of the underlying data and their provenance and treatment can be misled and may experience false confidence about the knowability of the data and their level of knowledge of that data. (To elaborate, the data from a theoretical model, a thought experiment, or computational experiment should have difference resonance than from-world empirical data or scientific research.) Data analysis involves some of the classic errors of analysts—of data insufficiency, premature interpretive commitment, confusing noise (non-information or "static") for signal (false positive or a Type I error or a failure to reject a true null hypothesis), or insensitivity to signal (false negative or a Type 2 error or a failure to reject a false null hypothesis). Certainly, there are many other potential errors beyond the general ones mentioned here. There are unique challenges with accurate data for the respective research types and fields / domains. With complexity and high dimensional data, there are still other challenges. Clearly, it makes the best sense to get the error rates down in the first before the work is actually done, but in some cases, corrections may be applied afterwards. The discussions of that are beyond the purview of this chapter though.

While these steps are identified as junctures when error may be introduced, these are also the same junctures at which errors may be corrected for and headed off. Any time that information is handled, it may be handled in a way that is thorough, ethical, accurate, and constructive.

TABLEAU PUBLIC: THE TOOL

The underlying software for Tableau Public was created as part of a doctoral project out of Stanford University known as the Polaris project ("Polaris interactive database visualization") by Chris Stolte in 2002. The tool would enable basic users to create visualizations from data even without database experiences. One researcher explains:

Starting out in 2003 as an output of a PhD project called Polaris, an interface for the exploration of multidimensional databases that extends the Pivot Table interface to directly generate a rich, expressive set of graphical displays" (Stolte, et al. 2008), it became commercialized as Tableau later that year. In 2010, the free version, Tableau Public was released. Tableau Public requires a client to be downloaded and installed, and also requires an internet connection to function. Rather than accepting a specific data structure for a specific plot type, Tableau accepts an entire database, and allows the user to explore the variables in the data via a variety of potential plots.(Oh, 2013, p. 5)

The commercial product was released in 2003. The public version, Tableau Public, launched in February 2010, requires users to register with Tableau Software, Inc. and then download the Tableau Public desktop client. With this client, users are able to upload various types of datasets into the tool for manipulation and data visualizations. A range of data types from various heterogeneous sources may also be integrated, including from Google Analytics, Cloudera Hadoop, Google BigQuery, Microsoft SQL server, Oracle, and Teradata. There are also ways to extract data from various data mart servers. The data may be files, datacubes (three- or higher dimensional data expressed through an array of values), databases, data marts, and others (Morton, Balazinska, Grossman, Kosara, Mackinlay, & Halevy, 2012, p. 1). Tableau Public enables limited "data blending"—when a primary data source is combined with a secondary data source through "join keys," and duplicate records are excised from the visualization. Tableau Public has an intuitive graphical user interface (GUI) for data ingestion (importation or upload). In the drop-down menu for ways to connect to data, the file types enabled included Tableau data extract files, Microsoft Access, Microsoft Excel, and various text files (such as in comma or vertical bar-separated formats).

A variety of data visualizations may be created from the data. To use the tool's nomenclature (which draws in part from common terms), users may draw text tables, heat maps, highlight tables, symbol maps, filled maps, pie charts, horizontal bars, stacked bars, side-by-side bars, treemaps, circle views, side-by-side circles, continuous lines, dual lines, area charts (continuous and discrete), dual combination, scatterplots, histograms, box-and-whisker plots, Gantt charts, bullet graphs, and packed bubbles. Tableau Public has a built-in wizard that automatically detects data types and suggests appropriate data visualizations and chart types based on the selected variables. If additional data are needed for a full visualization, the "Show Me" tool will suggest what to add to the mix. Selected textual labels may be applied to each of the data points, individual records, or nodes. Gradations of data may be indicated by color, size, locations, and other indicators.

The end user license agreement ("EULA") for Tableau Public's software is described on their site. It delimits the uses of the "media elements" and visualizations created from the tool and disallows for-profit use. It reads: "For the avoidance of doubt, you may not sell, license or distribute copies of the Media Elements by themselves or as part of any collection or product. All Media Elements are provided 'AS IS', and Tableau makes no warranties, express or implied of any kind with respect to such Media Elements."

Users may publish out their interactive worksheets, dashboards, and panel charts (with the related dataset offered as a downloadable file) on the public Web gallery (located at https://www.tableausoftware.com/public/gallery) for anyone with any of the major Web browsers to view and interact with the data. Users may also use links or embed code to share their information through websites, blogs, wikis, and emails. In terms of interactivity, users may filter contents, visually explore the data, attain details of individual records, acquire data from different data sources, and even download the originating dataset(s). Users may also interact in the Community around Tableau Public (located at https://www.tableausoftware.com/public/community). The hosts of the site select a "Viz of the Day" to highlight notable data visualizations. The tool itself is the free and public version of Tableau Software's Desktop Business Intelligence / Business Analysis tool. The tool is Javascript-based. At present, the tool enables up to a million records, but big data is expected to present large challenges for data visualization (Morton, Balazinska, Grossman, & Mackinlay, 2014). If the host machine lacks sufficient processing power, that could also limit the capabilities of the Tableau Public desktop client (at which point a pop-up window indicates the limitation or the system hangs and crashes).

CREATING DATA VISUALIZATIONS WITH TABLEAU PUBLIC

To provide a sense of this tool, Tableau Public 8.1 was used to create some visualizations from real-world data. Figure 2, "Tableau Public Graphical User Interface for the Desktop Client" provides a sense of the simplicity of the desktop client interface.

Once the source for the data has been selected, users enter the main workspace. Figure 3, "Tableau Public Tool Highlights: A Brief and Basic Overview" shows some of the main features of the workspace of the desktop client. The tool uses dropdown menus and drag-and-drop features to simplify the data creation experience.

Once the visualizations are finalized, they may then be published out in a static format (such as through screenshots) or in a dynamic format (such as through a website).

An overview of this closer-in process is conceptualized in Figure 4, "The Work Pipeline in Tableau Public's Public Edition (One Conceptualization)." This process begins at the point of verifying the provenance of the data and acquiring select data, whether from open-source repositories or proprietary or self-created sources. It helps to know if the data provider has credibility in the field. It also helps to read the fine print about the data. For example, one dataset explored (but not depicted) as part of the work for this chapter included interpolated data (the construction of new data points from known data points); in other words, the data was not exact empirical data but a processed approximation based on other empirical data. (It is possible to start the pipeline earlier with a research question or need to discover particular information.) Once the data are selected, they may be integrated for mixed data sets or cleaned

Figure 2. Tableau public graphical user interface for the desktop client

for more effective analysis. The data are then ingested into Tableau Public and processed for various types of visualizations (maps and graphs) and dashboards. Additional labeling and annotation may be done. Finally, the visualizations and datasets may be shared out on the public web gallery (through an enforced sharing based on the free tool), or screenshots may be taken for static mapping. Clearly, the data analysis could also lead to further datasets and additional analysis.

SOME REAL-WORLD EXAMPLES

Understanding a tool requires putting it through the paces of the actual work. To this end, five real-world examples have been created. Example 1, "Visualizing Consumer Complaints about

Financial Products and Services" uses a dataset with over 200,000 records. Example 2, "Visualizing Hospital Acquired Infections (HAIs) in Hospitals in New York State" focuses on issues of nosocomial infections. Example 3, "Popular Baby Names: Beginning 2007" offers county-level information of popular baby names in the United States. Example 4, "Aviation Accidents Data from the NTSB (from 1982 - 2014)" offers insights about when flights are at the most risky. All four of the prior examples involve data from open-source datasets and created by various government agencies (with access through the Data.gov site). Finally, Example 5 "President Barack Obama's Tweets and Political Issues" uses an original dataset extracted from the Twitter microblogging site (using NCapture of NVivo) to show integration of an original researcher-created dataset.

Figure 3. Tableau public tool highlights: A brief and basic overview

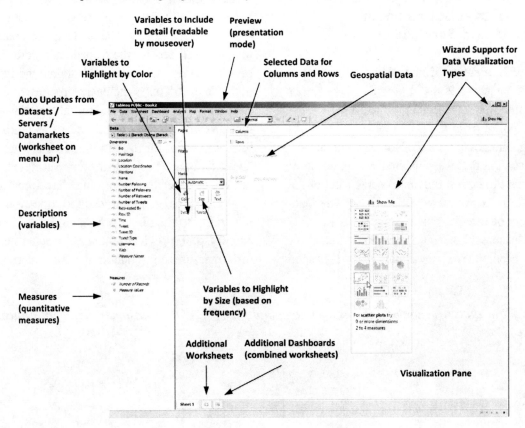

Figure 4. The work pipeline in Tableau Public's public edition (one conceptualization)

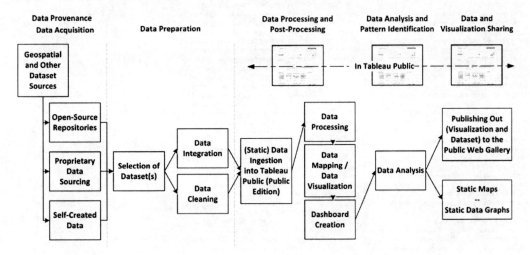

Example 1: Visualizing Consumer Complaints about Financial Products and Services

To provide a sense of how this process might work, a dataset of 208,474 records of consumer complaints about financial products and services was accessed from the Data.gov site (at https://catalog.data.gov/dataset/consumer-complaint-database). The data was collected by the Consumer Financial Protection Bureau. A screenshot of the raw dataset is available in Figure 5, "The Data Structure of the Consumer Complaints Records of the Consumer Financial Protection Bureau." As may be seen, the first row of data (Row 1) has the names of each of the columns of data which follow. Below, in each of the cells are various data. The first column (the one on the furthest left) contains unique identifiers for the respective record. Each row following the first one contains one record in the dataset. This is the basic structure of many common worksheets and data tables. Any data ingested into Tableau Public needs to be in this format in order for the machine to know how to "read" the data. The data in the worksheets or tables are read as either dimension data (descriptive data) or as measures (quantitative data). Location data may fall into the dimension category (such as a country, state, province, county, ZIP code, etc.), or in the measures one (quantitative expression), such

Figure 5. The data structure of the consumer complaints records of the Consumer Financial Protection Bureau

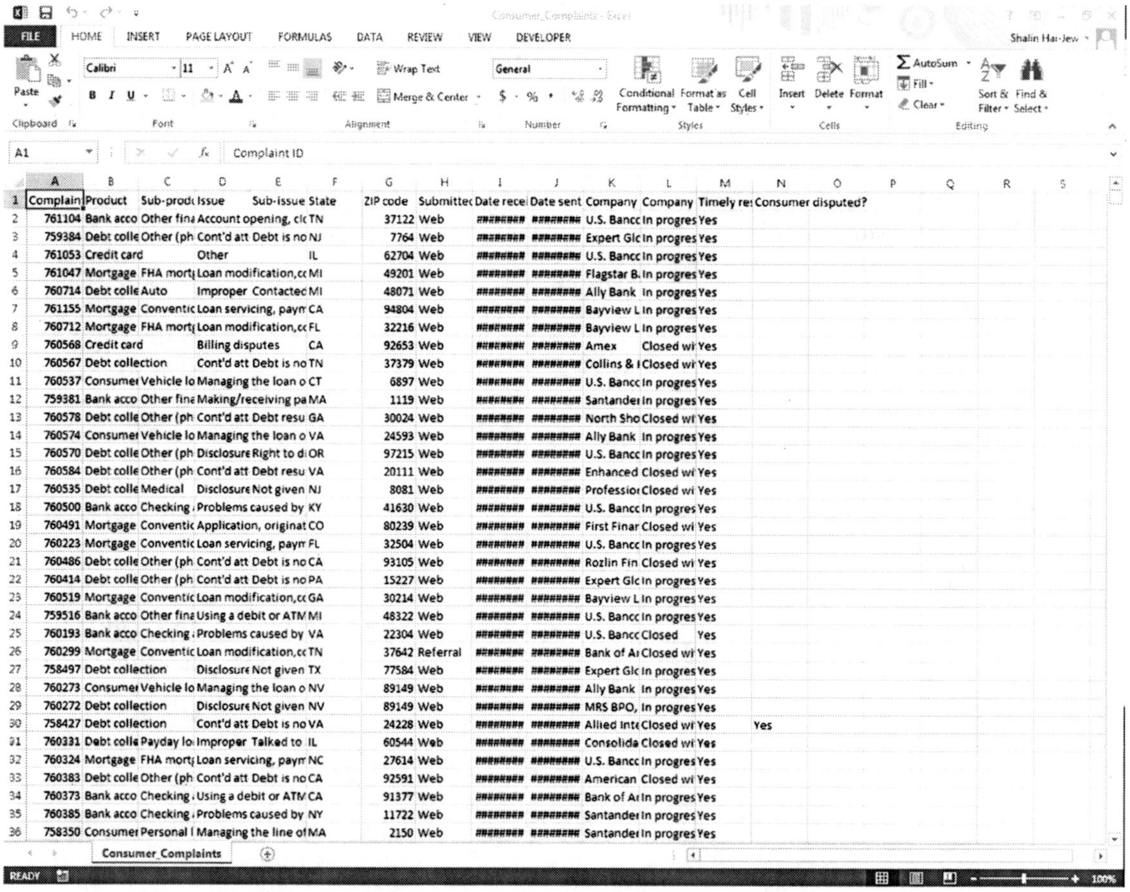

	A	B	C	D	E	F	G	H	I	J	K	L	M	N
1	Complain	Product	Sub-prod	Issue	Sub-issue	State	ZIP code	Submitte	Date recei	Date sent	Company	Company	Timely re	Consumer disputed?
2	761104	Bank acco	Other fin	Account opening, clc		TN	37122	Web	########	########	U.S. Bancc	In progres	Yes	
3	759384	Debt colle	Other (ph	Cont'd att	Debt is no	NJ	7764	Web	########	########	Expert Glc	In progres	Yes	
4	761053	Credit card		Other		IL	62704	Web	########	########	U.S. Bancc	In progres	Yes	
5	761047	Mortgage	FHA mort	Loan modification,cc		MI	49201	Web	########	########	Flagstar B.	In progres	Yes	
6	760714	Debt colle	Auto	Improper	Contacted	MI	48071	Web	########	########	Ally Bank	In progres	Yes	
7	761155	Mortgage	Conventic	Loan servicing, paym		CA	94804	Web	########	########	Bayview L	In progres	Yes	
8	760712	Mortgage	FHA mort	Loan modification,cc		FL	32216	Web	########	########	Bayview L	In progres	Yes	
9	760568	Credit card		Billing disputes		CA	92653	Web	########	########	Amex	Closed wi	Yes	
10	760567	Debt collection		Cont'd att	Debt is no	TN	37379	Web	########	########	Collins & I	Closed wi	Yes	
11	760537	Consumer	Vehicle lo	Managing the loan o		CT	6897	Web	########	########	U.S. Bancc	In progres	Yes	
12	759381	Bank acco	Other fin	Making/receiving pa		MA	1119	Web	########	########	Santander	In progres	Yes	
13	760578	Debt colle	Other (ph	Cont'd att	Debt resu	GA	30024	Web	########	########	North Sho	Closed wi	Yes	
14	760574	Consumer	Vehicle lo	Managing the loan o		VA	24593	Web	########	########	Ally Bank	In progres	Yes	
15	760570	Debt colle	Other (ph	Disclosure	Right to di	OR	97215	Web	########	########	U.S. Bancc	In progres	Yes	
16	760584	Debt colle	Other (ph	Cont'd att	Debt resu	VA	20111	Web	########	########	Enhanced	Closed wi	Yes	
17	760535	Debt colle	Medical	Disclosure	Not given	NJ	8081	Web	########	########	Professio	Closed wi	Yes	
18	760500	Bank acco	Checking	Problems caused by		KY	41630	Web	########	########	U.S. Bancc	In progres	Yes	
19	760491	Mortgage	Conventic	Application, originat		CO	80239	Web	########	########	First Finar	Closed wi	Yes	
20	760223	Mortgage	Conventic	Loan servicing, paym		FL	32504	Web	########	########	U.S. Bancc	In progres	Yes	
21	760486	Debt colle	Other (ph	Cont'd att	Debt is no	CA	93105	Web	########	########	Rozlin Fin	Closed wi	Yes	
22	760414	Debt colle	Other (ph	Cont'd att	Debt is no	PA	15227	Web	########	########	Expert Glc	In progres	Yes	
23	760519	Mortgage	Conventic	Loan modification,cc		GA	30214	Web	########	########	Bayview L	In progres	Yes	
24	759516	Bank acco	Other fin	Using a debit or ATM		MI	48322	Web	########	########	U.S. Bancc	In progres	Yes	
25	760193	Bank acco	Checking	Problems caused by		VA	22304	Web	########	########	U.S. Bancc	Closed	Yes	
26	760299	Mortgage	Conventic	Loan modification,cc		TN	37642	Referral	########	########	Bank of A	Closed wi	Yes	
27	758497	Debt collection		Disclosure	Not given	TX	77584	Web	########	########	Expert Glc	In progres	Yes	
28	760273	Consumer	Vehicle lo	Managing the loan o		NV	89149	Web	########	########	Ally Bank	In progres	Yes	
29	760272	Debt collection		Disclosure	Not given	NV	89149	Web	########	########	MRS BPO,	In progres	Yes	
30	758427	Debt collection		Cont'd att	Debt is no	VA	24228	Web	########	########	Allied Inte	Closed wi	Yes	Yes
31	760331	Debt colle	Payday lo	Improper	Talked to	IL	60544	Web	########	########	Consolida	Closed wi	Yes	
32	760324	Mortgage	FHA mort	Loan servicing, paym		NC	27614	Web	########	########	U.S. Bancc	In progres	Yes	
33	760383	Debt colle	Other (ph	Cont'd att	Debt is no	CA	92591	Web	########	########	American	Closed wi	Yes	
34	760373	Bank acco	Checking	Using a debit or ATM		CA	91377	Web	########	########	Bank of A	In progres	Yes	
35	760385	Bank acco	Checking	Problems caused by		NY	11722	Web	########	########	Santander	In progres	Yes	
36	758350	Consumer	Personal l	Managing the line of		MA	2150	Web	########	########	Santander	In progres	Yes	

as in terms of (generated) latitude and longitude. (Where this data structure knowledge is especially important is in realizing that various open-data datasets may download as a zipped folder full of additional folders with data tables, PDF figures, data declarations and overviews files, topics and resources, and even various other data file types).

More particularly, for this consumer complaints dataset, the names of the fields in the first row read as follows: 1A= Complaint ID, 1B=Product, 1C=Subproduct, and so forth. This dataset also includes by state information per both the columns F and G (State and then ZIP code). This dataset shows some of the complaints in progress...so this is not finalized data. In Tableau Public, the user begins through trial-and-error learning by moving

the elements from the dimensions or measures spaces onto the main visualization pane into the Columns or Rows text windows and elsewhere in the workspace to see what visualizations may be created. It helps to start simple and not overload the visualization with too many variables.

The workspace simulates what users may experience as they mouseover (place the cursor over) certain parts of the data visualization. The mouseover action brings up the selected "Detail" of each of the records represented by the particular node. (The screen capture tool did not enable the capture of the dynamic pop-up of the detail window). In Figure 6, the mouseover-triggered pop-up window showed the name of the Company, the Complaint ID, the Issue, the Product, the Sub-

Figure 6. A dashboard of consumer complaints records of the consumer financial protection bureau (created in Tableau Public)

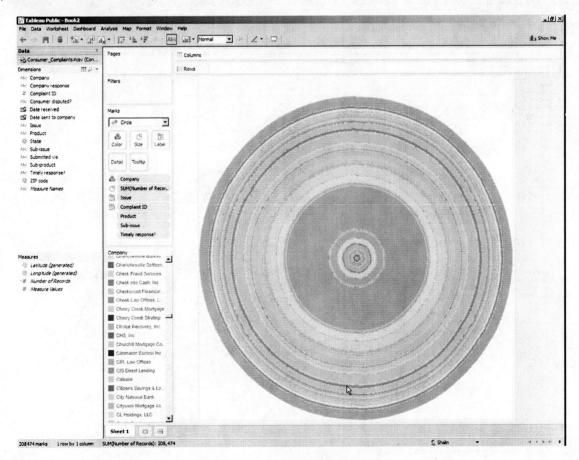

Issue, whether there was a Timely Response, and the Number of Records related to that issue. The "packed bubble" visualization looks more like a "tree trunk" diagram. Here, the "rings" of the virtual tree trunk contain the alphabetized names of the various financial institutions beginning with A's in the middle and Z's on the outside.

Another view of the data may involve a geospatial map to give a sense of proximity between these various types of financial complaints and to see if there is a deep clustering of such cases (such as on the two coasts where such financial firms may be clustered). A Filled Map (a chloropleth map that would show frequency of complaints by state through intensity of color) may have been made with the same information. (Such mapping of numerical data to space may make the information more accessible to some—who may innately understand data plotted on a map than tables of quantitative data). The tool itself is not drawing any maps (digital cartography) but is rather placing the data on pre-existing map templates; additional overlays of spatialized data may be applied to the map visualizations.

All the variables do not have to be used per se, and the user drawing the graphs may select to portray only some of the available information. So how well did the various financial institutions deal with resolving consumer complaints? Figure 7, "A Back-end Worksheet of Resolution Measures for Financial Complaints (created in Tableau Public)" shows a table with data pullouts to show the

Figure 7. A back-end worksheet showing a macro view of financial products that are the focus of consumer complaints overlaid on a symbol map (created in Tableau Public)

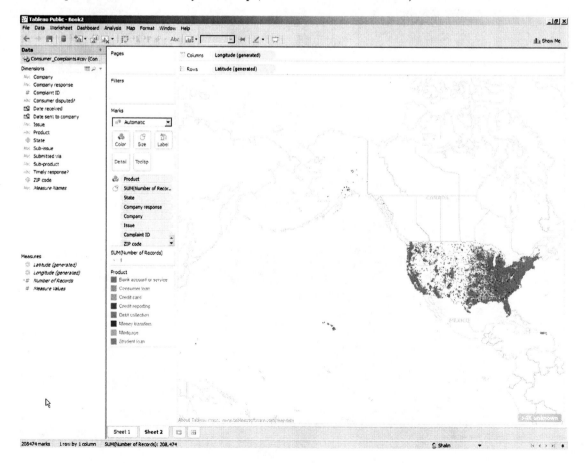

speed of the response and the type of resolution. Multiple visualizations were then created from one dataset, and certainly, many dozens more may be extracted to answer particular data questions. Data visualizations are often created to answer targeted questions made of the data.

Example 2: Visualizing Hospital Acquired Infections (HAIs) in Hospitals in New York State

This second example involves information from the New York State Department of Health (NYS-DOH), with 7,600 records of hospital-acquired (nosocomial) infections from 2008 - 2012. A description on the dataset reads: "This includes central line-associated blood stream infections in intensive care units; surgical site infections following colon, hip replacement/revision, and coronary artery bypass graft; and Clostridium difficile infections." This dataset, like many others, is in process—with a post-release audit and a revised file forthcoming a year after the original dataset was made public. (Strong analyses often work backwards and forwards in time. There is not a fixity of understanding or a closing of a case if there is any potential for new understandings.) This set was downloaded at https://catalog.data.gov/dataset/hospital-acquired-infections-beginning-2008.

A note with the dataset reads: "Because of the complicated nature of the risk-adjustment methodology used to produce the HAI rates, the advice of a statistician is recommended before at-

Figure 8. A back-end worksheet of resolution measures for financial complaints (created in Tableau Public)

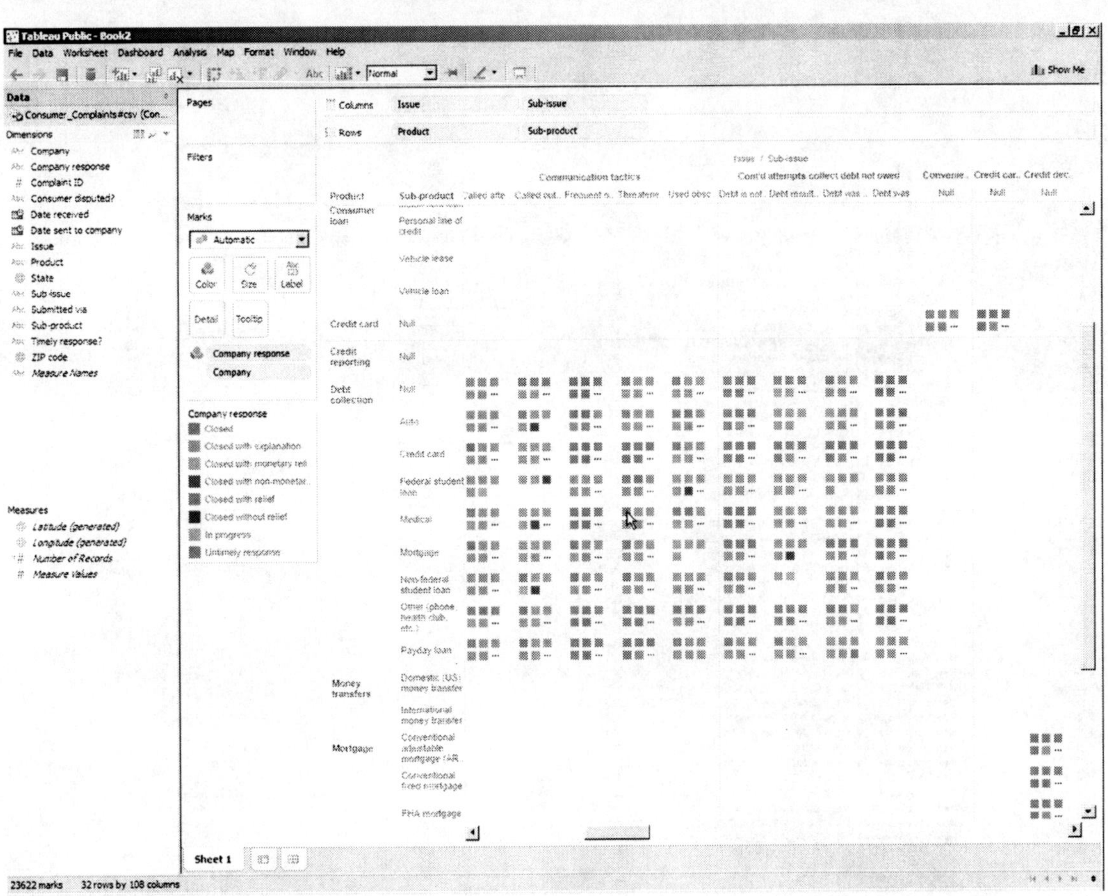

tempting to manipulate the data. Hospital-specific risk-adjusted rates cannot simply be combined." It seems advisable to consult with both statisticians and professionals in the field before making assertions about any data. (The general assumption in this chapter is that researchers are themselves experts in their respective fields and so know how to expertly engage the given information.)

Figure 9 shows a screenshot of the dataset. Generally, it is a good idea to keep the dataset open for observations while interacting with Tableau Public—so there are clear understandings of what types of information each of the columns contain and what the various variables mean, given the wide variance in data labeling, their brevity, and original nomenclature. Figure 9, "Hospital-acquired infections from New York Hospitals dataset (2008 - 2012)" shows a data visualization from the dataset that highlights the types of procedures that most commonly involved HAI by year. Below the first visualization is another view of the same data albeit with one particular hospital highlighted to see what its main HAIs were in each of the covered years.

Another way to view this data is by how many cases of HAIs exist for the particular hospitals. A packed bubble visualization may show frequency, with the largest bubbles those with the most frequencies of HAIs during the time period captured by the dataset. This preliminary visualization may be viewed in Figure 11. A packed bubble visualization of New York hospitals and their relative

Figure 9. Data structure of hospital-acquired infections (HAI) from New York hospitals dataset (2008 - 2012)

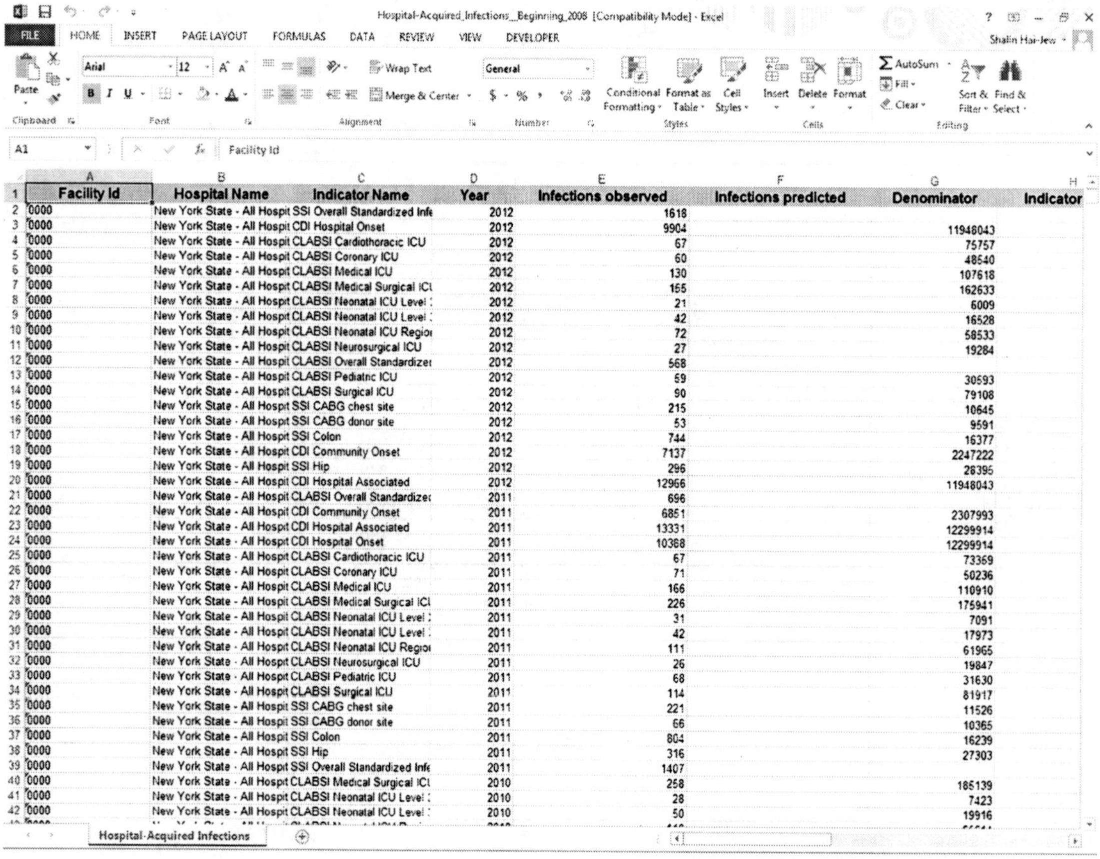

	Facility Id	Hospital Name	Indicator Name	Year	Infections observed	Infections predicted	Denominator	Indicator
2	0000	New York State - All Hospit	SSI Overall Standardized Infe	2012	1618			
3	0000	New York State - All Hospit	CDI Hospital Onset	2012	9904		11948043	
4	0000	New York State - All Hospit	CLABSI Cardiothoracic ICU	2012	67		75757	
5	0000	New York State - All Hospit	CLABSI Coronary ICU	2012	60		48540	
6	0000	New York State - All Hospit	CLABSI Medical ICU	2012	130		107618	
7	0000	New York State - All Hospit	CLABSI Medical Surgical ICU	2012	155		162633	
8	0000	New York State - All Hospit	CLABSI Neonatal ICU Level :	2012	21		6009	
9	0000	New York State - All Hospit	CLABSI Neonatal ICU Level :	2012	42		16528	
10	0000	New York State - All Hospit	CLABSI Neonatal ICU Regio	2012	72		58533	
11	0000	New York State - All Hospit	CLABSI Neurosurgical ICU	2012	27		19284	
12	0000	New York State - All Hospit	CLABSI Overall Standardize	2012	568			
13	0000	New York State - All Hospit	CLABSI Pediatric ICU	2012	59		30593	
14	0000	New York State - All Hospit	CLABSI Surgical ICU	2012	90		79108	
15	0000	New York State - All Hospit	SSI CABG chest site	2012	215		10645	
16	0000	New York State - All Hospit	SSI CABG donor site	2012	53		9591	
17	0000	New York State - All Hospit	SSI Colon	2012	744		16377	
18	0000	New York State - All Hospit	CDI Community Onset	2012	7137		2247222	
19	0000	New York State - All Hospit	SSI Hip	2012	296		28395	
20	0000	New York State - All Hospit	CDI Hospital Associated	2012	12966		11948043	
21	0000	New York State - All Hospit	CLABSI Overall Standardize	2011	696			
22	0000	New York State - All Hospit	CDI Community Onset	2011	6851		2307993	
23	0000	New York State - All Hospit	CDI Hospital Associated	2011	13331		12299914	
24	0000	New York State - All Hospit	CDI Hospital Onset	2011	10368		12299914	
25	0000	New York State - All Hospit	CLABSI Cardiothoracic ICU	2011	67		73369	
26	0000	New York State - All Hospit	CLABSI Coronary ICU	2011	71		50236	
27	0000	New York State - All Hospit	CLABSI Medical ICU	2011	166		110910	
28	0000	New York State - All Hospit	CLABSI Medical Surgical ICI	2011	226		175941	
29	0000	New York State - All Hospit	CLABSI Neonatal ICU Level :	2011	31		7091	
30	0000	New York State - All Hospit	CLABSI Neonatal ICU Level :	2011	42		17973	
31	0000	New York State - All Hospit	CLABSI Neonatal ICU Regio	2011	111		61965	
32	0000	New York State - All Hospit	CLABSI Neurosurgical ICU	2011	26		19847	
33	0000	New York State - All Hospit	CLABSI Pediatric ICU	2011	68		31630	
34	0000	New York State - All Hospit	CLABSI Surgical ICU	2011	114		81917	
35	0000	New York State - All Hospit	SSI CABG chest site	2011	221		11526	
36	0000	New York State - All Hospit	SSI CABG donor site	2011	66		10365	
37	0000	New York State - All Hospit	SSI Colon	2011	804		16239	
38	0000	New York State - All Hospit	SSI Hip	2011	316		27303	
39	0000	New York State - All Hospit	SSI Overall Standardized Infe	2011	1407			
40	0000	New York State - All Hospit	CLABSI Medical Surgical ICU	2010	258		185139	
41	0000	New York State - All Hospit	CLABSI Neonatal ICU Level :	2010	28		7423	
42	0000	New York State - All Hospit	CLABSI Neonatal ICU Level :	2010	50		19916	

Figure 10. Filtering in the hospital acquired infections from New York hospitals dataset (2008 - 2012)

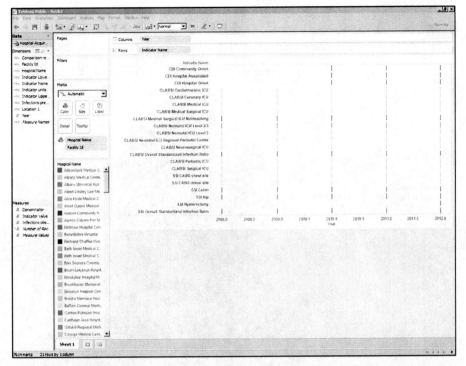

Cumulative Hospital-Acquired Infection Data by Type and Year (with Color-Coding Based on Facilities)

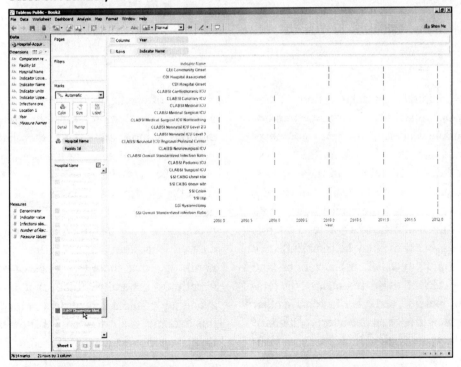

One Hospital Selected in the Left Menu Bar with a Resulting Change in the Main Data Visualization Pane (in the Design Back-end of Tableau Public)

Figure 11. A packed bubble visualization of New York hospitals and their relative frequency of hospital acquired infections (2008 - 2012)

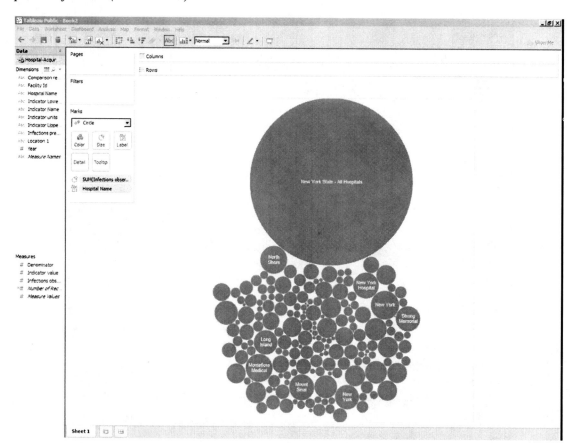

frequency of hospital acquired infections (2008 - 2012). This tool apparently requires a certain size before the bubble is labeled; however, a mouseover of the various bubbles will call up the hospital name and other details related to those related records. This packed bubbles visualization enables a rough-cut impression of the main hospitals with nosocomial infection concerns—at least relative to each other—but these may be issues affected by size of hospital, types of specializations (and the risks of HAI with those treatments), the relative health of patients, and other factors. In other words, there should not be naïve interpretations of the data or the visualization. In this sense, a visu-

alization offers the opportunity to create hunches and lightly-held impressions but not harder conclusions without more data. Such hunches may inform further research or lines of inquiry.

Another visualization from the HAI dataset from the New York Department of Health is to get an overview of the trendline data of which procedures were the most high-risk across the dataset. Trendline data refer to time-varying (temporal) data that show frequency of occurrences over time—generally without data smoothing (no averaging of the adjacent data points). As such, this data may show tendencies and changes over time; they show sequentiality. From the visualiza-

Figure 12. A trendline visualization of hospital acquired infections from New York hospitals dataset (2008 - 2012)

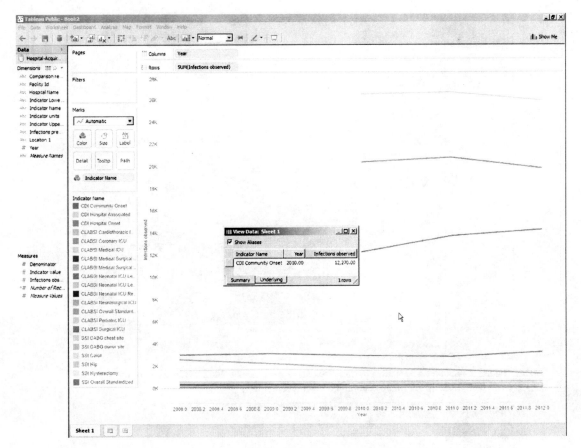

tion, it's clear that some paths start later because of a lack of information for some prior years... or the possibility of non-existence of the issue in prior years.

Example 3: Popular Baby Names: Beginning 2007

This third example involves a dataset from the U.S. Department of Health and Human Services. This set involves the most popular baby names in various counties or boroughs (based on birth certificates)...beginning in 2007 and running through 2012. An explanation came with the dataset: "The frequency of the Baby Name is listed,

if there are: 5 or more of the same baby name in a county outside of NYC; or 10 or more of the same baby name in a NYC borough." The data was downloaded from https://catalog.data.gov/dataset/baby-names-beginning-2007.

A dashboard is a mix of worksheets, with the visualizations, legends, filters, text labels, and other elements. When deployed on the Web (through the Tableau Public gallery), these are interactive and often informative. Figure 14, "An Interactive Dashboard with both Space (County) and Time Represented in First-Name Popularity in Birth Certificates in New York State" provides a back-end view of just such a dashboard, this one including both a sense of space and time.

Figure 13. The most popular baby names in New York state (by county or borough) from 2007 – 2012 (Trendline Visualization)

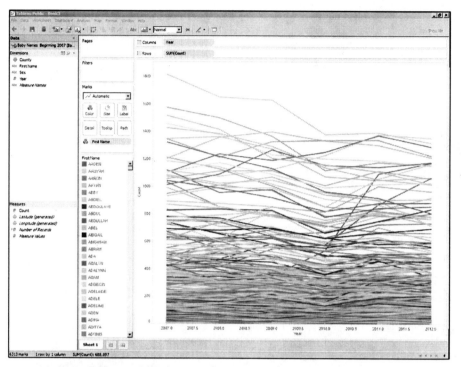

The Most Popular Baby Names in New York State from 2007 – 2012 based on Birth Certificates (with trendlines indicated by color and a legend to the left)

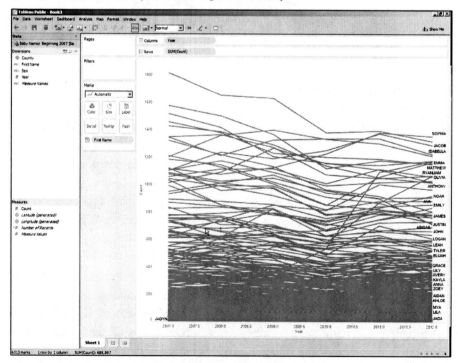

The Most Popular Baby Names in New York State from 2007 – 2012 based on Birth Certificates (with trendlines indicated by label and a name listing to the right)

Figure 14. An interactive dashboard with both space (county) and time represented in first-name popularity in birth certificates in New York State

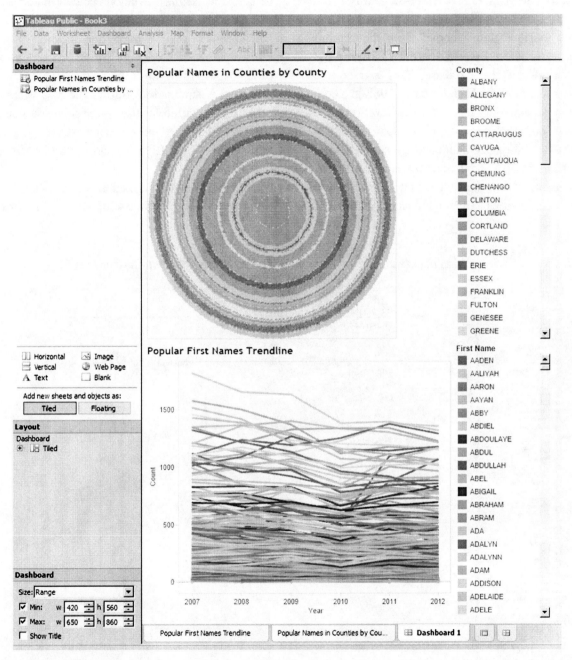

Example 4: Aviation Accidents Data from the NTSB (from 1982 -2014)

The fourth example comes from the National Transportation Safety Board (NTSB) and its aviation accident database. This extract from their records list accidents since 1982 in a common separated values (CSV) or text format. A descriptor that came with the data read: "The NTSB aviation accident database contains information about civil aviation accidents and selected incidents within the United States, its territories and possessions, and in international waters."

The dataset was downloaded from http://catalog. data.gov/dataset/ntsb-aviation-accident-database-extract-of-aviation-accident-records-since-1982-.

In terms of civil aviation, one question of interest for investigators is in which broad phases of an airplane's flight do most accidents occur? This data visualization follows the taxi, standing, takeoff, climb, cruise, go-around, descent, approach, landing, maneuvering, standing, and other phases of a flight (in no particular order listed here).

Another view of this data may be the distribution of accidents and incidents across the world

Figure 15. Civil aviation accidents dataset from the NTSB aviation accident database (1982 – 2014)

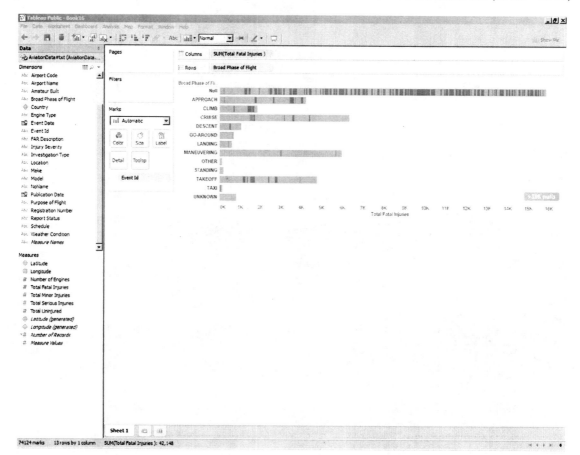

by location, as is shown in Figure 16, "Back-end view of geographical spread of Civil aviation Accidents and Incidents (from the NTSB aviation accident database) (1982 – 2014)".

Those interacting with this information may filter out particular data in order to enhance the focus. Are there certain locales where more of one type of incident happens than another? If so, why would that possibly be?

Example 5: President Barack Obama's Tweets and Political Issues

Finally, the last example involved a self-created dataset of U.S. President Barack Obama's Tweets from his @BarackObama Twitter account (https://twitter.com/BarackObama). The capture of this dataset was achieved with NCapture of NVivo 10. The target site mentioned 11,500 Tweets (a

Figure 16. Back-end view of geographical spread of civil aviation accidents and incidents (from the NTSB aviation accident database) (1982 – 2014)

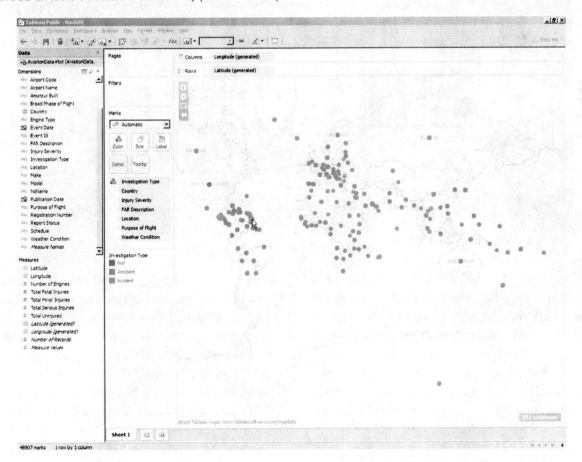

Figure 17. The landing page for the @BarackObama Twitter account

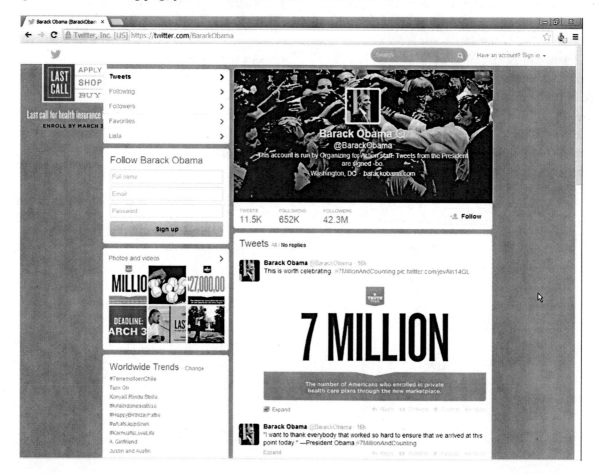

rounded-up number), with 652,000 accounts following (being followed by the @BarackObama account), and 42.3 million followers. The capture of the Tweet stream dataset included re-tweets, with 3,229 microblogging messages captured.

Figure 20, "A Packed Bubbles Chart of Tweets (orange) and Subset of Re-Tweets with Hashtags Available on Mouseover" shows a predominance of fresh Tweets with a smaller set of retweets.

To gain a sense of some of the topics being Tweeted about, Figure 21, "A Packed Bubbles Chart of Topics (based on Hashtags) @BarackObama on Twitter" shows dominant issues as recur-

rent terms. The size of the bubble here is based on the number of Tweets (represented as individual records). While Tableau Public could not create a geographical dimension, given the sparseness of such geo data (and a lack of consistent method for indicating geospatial information on Twitter), NVivo could. Figure 22, "A Geographical Map of Tweets @BarackObama from the NVivo Tool" represents this NVivo-created map extrapolated from the @BarackObama tweets and re-tweets.

Some data extraction tools that are used to extract data from social media platforms may have built-in data structures that are not necessarily

Figure 18. Export of the @BarackObama NCapture Tweet dataset from NVivo 10

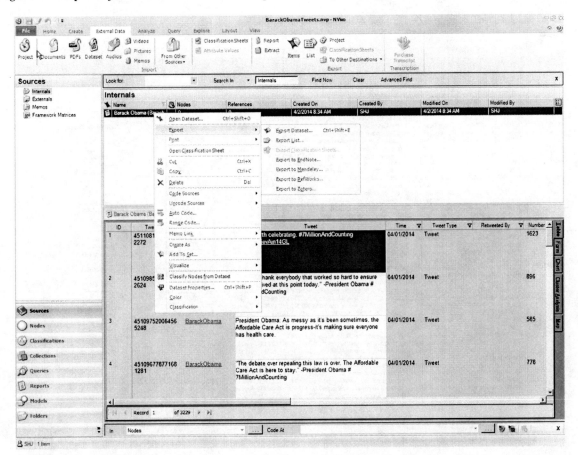

conducive to data visualizations in Tableau Public. As an example, the open-source and freeware tool NodeXL (Network Overview, Discovery, and Exploration for Excel) enables extracting social network data from various social media platforms and their visualization based on a number of popular layout algorithms, but the datasets extracted are not easily readable by Tableau Public (without some human intervention). .

Discussion

The uses of data visualizations in a multimedia presentation may enhance user understanding of particular concepts or relationships or phenomena. The foregrounding of some information will necessarily "background" other information. While some data are brought to the fore, others are obscured. There are almost always trade-offs.

The users of the data visualizations will also approach that information with varying skill levels and sophistication; they will have different purposes in using that data. Depending on how they use their attentional resources, those referring to a particular visualization may have varying degrees of understanding of the provenance of the data and then how that those are transformed into a diagram, chart, map, or dashboard. Some data consumers

Figure 19. The extracted NCapture Tweet dataset (as an Excel file) from @BarackObama on Twitter

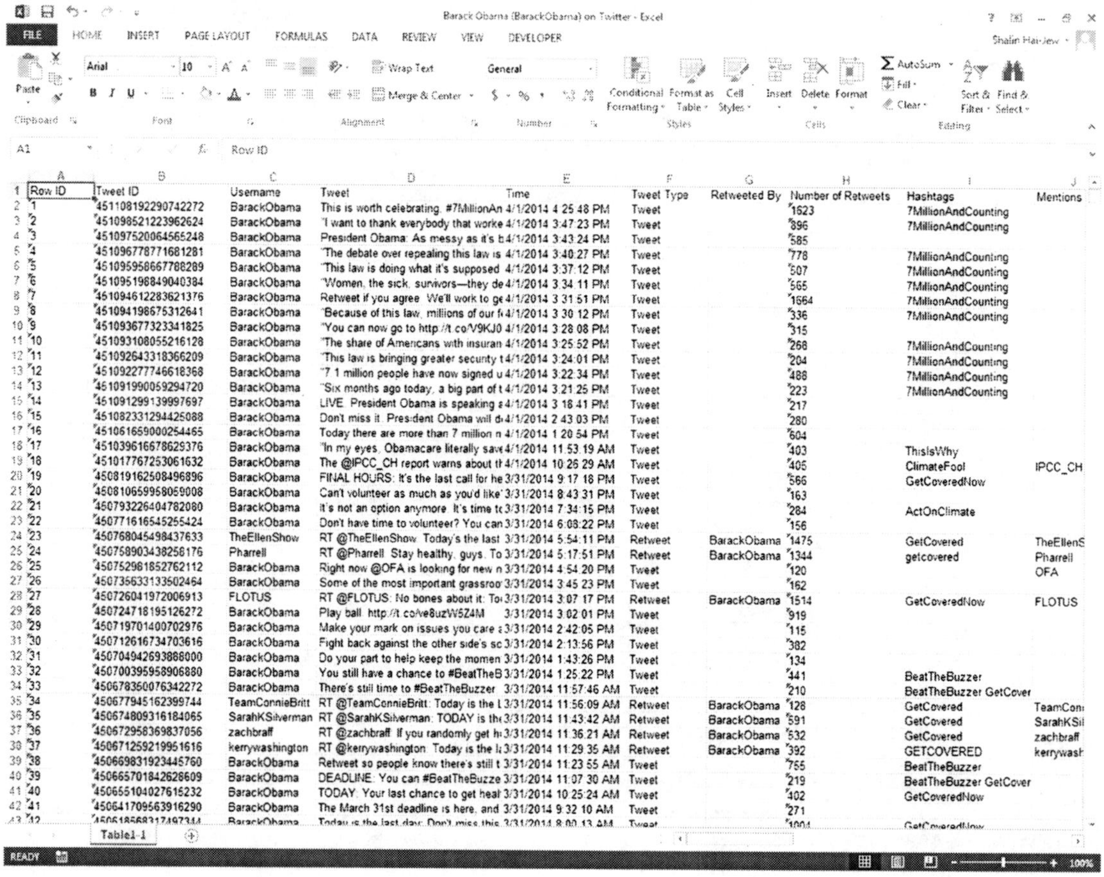

will just view a visualization in its resting state while others will interact with the data and explore the informational depths and implications. To meet the needs of a variety of potential users, those who would design such Tableau Public datasets, worksheets, and dashboards would do well to gain a lot of experiences in the work before going live. Every visualization should be as accurate as possible and as accessible and machine-readable as possible. The data visualizations should be conducive to use by both those with the more popular "naïve" common-sense geography (and understanding of data) and those with higher-level knowledge of the topic. The level of uncertainty inherent in

data should be defined and communicated. (After all, data is an "isolate" and abstraction from the real world. It should never be seen to map to the world with full fidelity, for example.) All data and their visualizations should be explained and contextualized.

Those who are uninterested in going public with their data visualizations may stop short of going live. They may create the visualizations for internal use only. They may take screenshots of the findings. They may maintain their own datasets…and also directions for how to achieve the visualization for analysis…but not output any "save-able" finalized file form Tableau Public.

Figure 20. A packed bubbles chart of Tweets (orange) and subset of Re-Tweets with hashtags Available on Mouseover

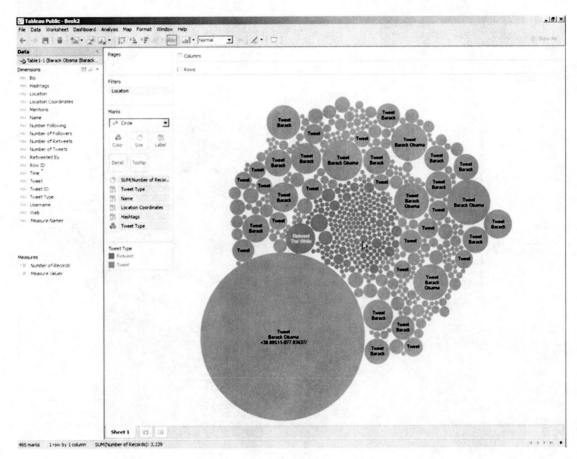

Screenshots, as static portrayals of the dashboards, may be taken for other purposes as well—such as report-writing, presentations, or publications.

Delimitations of the Software Tool

Tableau Public, as the free version, is limited by the types of data sources it may access. It is limited by the computational limits of the host machine where the desktop client is downloaded. While there are some claims that the software itself is relatively easy to use (and it does have plenty of wizard supports and help documentation, and it offers plenty of drag-and-drop features and does not require command line work), the complexity in using this tool comes from striving to create coherence with the datasets. Another limit is the inability to edit hard-baked features in the tool. Also, the two-dimensional visualizations are fairly standard; as such, a wide range of other possible ways of representing the data are not included here, including 3D, fractal, word clouds, and other methods. Currently, there are no included data animations in Tableau Public (to indicate changes over time).

Figure 21. A packed bubbles chart of topics (based on hashtags) @BarackObama on Twitter

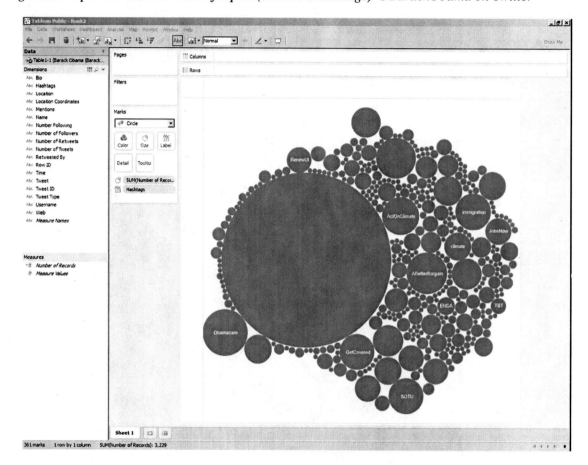

FUTURE RESEARCH DIRECTIONS

The potential directions for further research are many. Certainly, the research literature would benefit from research on different applications of the Tableau Public tool (and especially of the professional version). As the tool's functionalities evolve, unique applications of a range of visualization types and analytical approaches would benefit the work. More may be written about the development and evolution of this software tool. Research on how to contextualize data visualizations with the proper lead-up and lead-away information would be beneficial—particularly in regards to creating the proper explanatory depth.

CONCLUSION

This chapter has offered a simple introduction to Tableau Public and some of its functionalities with the visualizations of real-world datasets from open sources and social media platforms. It has addressed the potential for error in the data collection and analysis work stream. It has shown how Tableau Public may introduce the broad public to analyze and visualize data at minimal computational expense. This work suggests that the broader public may access this free tool to build their sense of data literacy and geospatial understandings (spatial cognition). Specialists and experts may use this tool to mine data, enhance

Figure 22. A geographical map of Tweets @BarackObama from the NVivo Tool

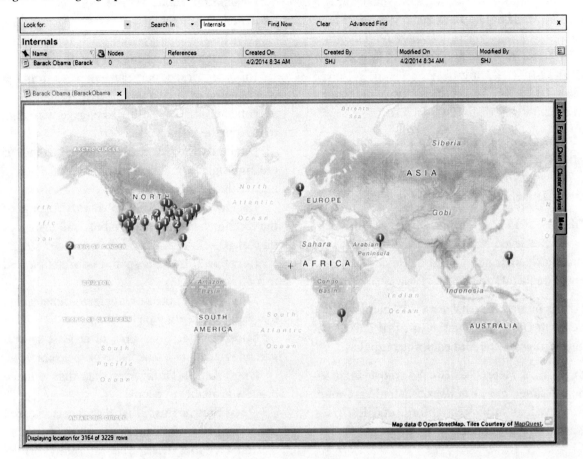

analysis, improve decision-making, and communicate data visually in multimedia presentations and websites.

While Tableau Public may serve as a powerful data visualization resource, it is a strong "gateway" tool to its own professional version and also to other types of data visualization tools: geospatial data analysis and visualization in ArcGIS; large-scale data animations through Gapminder World, Google Motion Charts; network depictions in NodeXL or UCINET; and others. Suffice it to say that there is expected to be ever-more open data released to the public and evolving ways of analyzing and visualizing data. Tableau Public offers a fine point-of-entry to start experimenting with data sets and making them coherent and understandable through interactive data visualizations in Web-friendly panel charts.

REFERENCES

Manovich, L. (2011). What is visualization. *Visual Studies*, 26(1), 36–49. doi:10.1080/147258 6X.2011.548488

Morton, K., Balazinska, M., Grossman, D., Kosara, R., Mackinlay, J., & Halevy, A. (2012). *A measurement study of two web-based collaborative visual analytics systems* (Technical Report UW-CSE-12-08-01). Univ. of Washington. Retrieved Mar. 10, 2014, at ftp://ftp.cs.washington.edu/tr/2012/08/UW-CSE-12-08-01.PDF

Morton, K., Balazinska, M., Grossman, D., & Mackinlay, J. (2014). *Support the data enthusiast: Challenges for next-generation data-analysis systems*. Hangzhou, China: Very Large Data Bases.

Oh, J. (2013). *Literature review—Graphical tools*. Retrieved Mar. 10, 2014, at https://www.stat.auckland.ac.nz/~joh024/LitReviews/LitReview_GraphicalTools.pdf

Polaris interactive database visualization. (n.d.). *Stanford University*. Retrieved April 3, 2014, at http://graphics.stanford.edu/projects/polaris/

Segel, E., & Heer, J. (2010). *Narrative visualization: Telling stories with data*. Stanford Vis Group. Retrieved at http://vis.stanford.edu/files/2010-Narrative-InfoVis.pdf

KEY TERMS AND DEFINITIONS

Cartography: The science of drawing maps.

Dashboard: A data panel of data visualizations and other information, a panel chart.

Data Blending: Connecting and mixing data from different sources for a new mixed dataset.

Data Mining: The exploration of data to exploit for informational value (through pattern and relationship identification).

Data Visualization: A diagram or image that represents data.

Dimension: A particular feature of a data point or entity.

Geolocation: Tracking an entity to a physical location through digital information processing.

Geospatial Data: Information related to a particular geographic position.

Glyph: A visual symbol often representing multiple angles or measures or details.

Infographics: A portmanteau word from the combination of "information" and "graphic".

Interaction: The ability to engage with data to change the visualization.

Interpolation: A mathematical method of creating data points within a range of discrete and defined data points.

Legend (Map): An explanatory listing of the meanings behind the symbols and distances on a map.

Locative Data: Geospatial information tied to a physical space.

Map: A two-dimensional or three-dimensional diagram representing physical space.

Multivariate: Consisting of at least several variables (that are quantifiable or measurable).

Open-Access Data: Raw data that is made broadly available to people.

Open-Source Data: Raw data that is released under free licensure (to promote universal access).

Self-Organization: The internally driven evolution and growth of an electronic community through local-level decisions by its members (without external influences); an emergent social organizational phenomena.

Spatiality: Relating to physical space.

Visualization: The representation of data as an image or diagram or map.

Wayfinding: A method of defining a path to a desired location.

Web Gallery: An online space which showcases digital objects and examples.

Wizard: A feature within software tools that guide users through the use of the tool (to simplify the experience).

ZIP Code: Zone Improvement Plan (ZIP) code.

Compilation of References

Zalta, E. N. (Ed.). (2003). Stanford encyclopedia of philosophy. Academic Press.

Abbot, A. (1988). Transcending general linear reality. *Sociological Theory*, *6*(2), 169–186. doi:10.2307/202114

Abbot, A. (1990). Conceptions of time and events in social science methods: Causal and narrative approaches. *Historical Methods*, *23*(4), 140–150. doi:10.1080/01615440.1990.10594204

Abbot, A. (1992). From causes to events: Notes on narrative positivism. *Sociological Methods & Research*, *20*(4), 428–455. doi:10.1177/0049124192020004002

Abbott, A. (2004). *Methods of Discovery: Heuristics for the Social Sciences*. New York: W.W. Norton & Company.

Abell, P. (2004). Narrative explanation: An alternative to variable-centered explanation? *Annual Review of Sociology*, *30*(1), 287–310. doi:10.1146/annurev.soc.29.010202.100113

Adam, F., & Fitzgerald, B. (2000). The Status of the IS Field:Historical Perspective and Practical Orientation. *Information Research*, *5*(4), 13.

Adams, J., Rodham, K., & Gavin, J. (2005). Investigating the "self" in deliberate self-harm. *Qualitative Health Research*, *15*(10), 1293–1309. doi:10.1177/1049732305281761 PMID:16263913

AERA. (2009). *Definition of scientifically based research*. Retrieved from http://aera.net/opportunities/?id=6790

Agarwal, A., Xie, B., Vovsha, I., Rambow, O., & Passonneau, R. (2011). Sentiment analysis of Twitter data. In *Proceedings of the Workshop on Language in Social Media*. Portland, OR: Association for Computational Linguistics.

Aguilar, A., Boerema, C., & Harrison, J. (2010). Meanings attributed by older adults to computer use. *Journal of Occupational Science*, *17*(1), 27–33. doi:10.1080/14427591.2010.9686669

Ahern, N. R. (2005). Using the Internet to conduct research. *Nurse Researcher*, *13*(2), 55–69. doi:10.7748/nr2005.10.13.2.55.c5968 PMID:16416980

Aiden, E., & Michel, J.-B. (2013). *Uncharted: Big data as a lens on human culture*. New York: Riverhead Books, Penguin.

Aiken, M., & Hage, J. (1972). *Organizational Permeability, Boundary Spanners and Organizational Structure*. New Orleans, LA: American Sociological Association.

Al-ahmad, W., Al-fagih, K., & Khanfar, K. (2009). A Taxonomy of an IT Project Failure: Root Causes. *Management Review*, *5*(1), 93–104.

Alasuutari, P. (1996). Theorizing in Qualitative Research: A Cultural Studies Perspective. *Qualitative Inquiry*, *2*(4), 371–384. doi:10.1177/107780049600200401

All time most popular tags. (2014, Jan. 4). *Flickr*. Retrieved at http://www.flickr.com/photos/tags/

Allen, E., & Lofferda, A. S. (2006). Ideas@work: Pushing response to an ethics survey. *Strategic Communication Management, 10*(3), 7.

Almuhimedi, H., Wilson, S., Liu, B., Sadeh, N., & Acquisti, A. (2013). Tweets are forever: A large-scale quantitative analysis of deleted Tweets. In *Proceedings of CSC@ '13*. San Antonio, TX: CSC. doi:10.1145/2441776.2441878

Altheide, D., & Johnson, J. M. C. (1998). Criteria for assessing interpretive validity in qualitative research. In N. K. Denzin, & Y. S. Lincoln (Eds.), *Collecting and interpreting qualitative materials*. Thousand Oaks, CA: Sage.

Altman, Y., Ozbilgin, M., & Wilson, E. (2008). *'Living Spirituality in the Workplace - the Cel Way - a Study on Organisational Effectiveness Ad Well-Being at Work: Cel as a Case-Study.' U004-0108-HG, Centre for Excellence in Leadership*. Barcelona: CEL.

Ames, M., & Naaman, M. (2007). Why we tag: Motivations for annotation in mobile and online media. In *Proceedings of CHI 2007*. San Jose, CA: ACM.

Anastas, P. T., & Zimmerman, J. B. (2006). The Twelve Principles of Green Engineering as a Foundation for Sustainability. In M. A. Abraham (Ed.), *Sustainability Science and Engineering: Defining Principles* (pp. 11–32). New York: Elsevier B.V. doi:10.1016/S1871-2711(06)80009-7

Anderson, C. (2008). The end of theory: The data deluge makes the scientific method obsolete. *Wired Magazine*. Retrieved March 18, 2014, at http://www.wired.com/science/discoveries/magazine/16-07/pb_theory

Andre, P., Bernstein, M. S., & Luther, K. (2012). Who gives a Tweet? Evaluating microblog content value. In *Proceedings of CSCW 12*. Seattle, WA: Association of Computing Machinery. doi:10.1145/2145204.2145277

Annells, M. (1996). GTM: Philosophical Perspectives, Paradigms of Inquiry, and Postmodernism. *Qualitative Health Research, 6*(3), 379–393. doi:10.1177/104973239600600306

Ardon, S., Bagchi, A., Mahanti, A., Ruhela, A., Seth, A., Tripathy, R. M., & Triukose, S. (2013). Spatio-temporal and events based analysis of topic popularity in Twitter. In *Proceedings of CIKM '13*. San Francisco, CA: Association of Computing Machinery. doi:10.1145/2505515.2505525

Aristotle, . (1941). *The basic words of Aristotle* (R. McKeon, Ed.). New York: Random House.

Armstrong, C. P., & Sambamurthy, V. (1999). Information Technology Assimilation in Firms: The Influence of Senior Leadership and IT-transformation. *Information Systems Research, 10*(4), 304–327. doi:10.1287/isre.10.4.304

Armstrong, D. A. (2011). Students' perceptions of online learning and instructional tools: A qualitative study of undergraduate students' use of online tools. *TOJET: The Turkish Online Journal of Educational Technology, 10*(3), 222–226.

Ashmos, D. P., & Dunchon, D. (2000). Spirituality at Work: A Conceptualization and Measure. *Journal of Management Inquiry, 9*(2), 134–145. doi:10.1177/105649260092008

Atkinson, J. M., & Heritage, J. (1984). *Structures of social action: Studies in conversation analysis*. Cambridge, UK: Cambridge University Press.

Australian Bureau of Statistics. (2008). Year Book Australia. Commonwealth of Australia.

Avison, D., Gregor, S., & Wilson, D. (2006). Managerial IT unconsciousness. *Communications of the ACM, 49*(7), 88–93. doi:10.1145/1139922.1139923

Avison, D., Jones, J., Powell, P., & Wilson, D. (2004). Using and validating the strategic alignment model. *The Journal of Strategic Information Systems, 13*(3), 223–246. doi:10.1016/j.jsis.2004.08.002

Babbie, E. (1992). *The practice of social research*. Belmont, CA: Wadsworth.

Baccarini, D., Salm, G., & Love, P. E. D. (2004). Management of risks in information technology projects. *Industrial Management & Data Systems, 104*(4), 286–295. doi:10.1108/02635570410530702

Bailey, J. (2008). First steps in qualitative data analysis: Transcribing. *Family Practice, 25*(2), 127–131. doi:10.1093/fampra/cmn003 PMID:18304975

Balajti, L., Darago, L., Adany, R., & Kosa, K. (2010). College Students' Response Rate to an Incentivized Combination of Postal and Web-Based Health Survey. *Evaluation & the Health Professions, 33*(2), 164-176.

Ball, P. (2004). *Critical Mass: How One Thing Leads to Another*. New York: Farrar, Straus and Giroux.

Bal, M. (1985). *Narratology: Introduction to the theory of narrative*. Toronto: University of Toronto Press.

Barbour, R. (2007). *Doing focus groups*. London: Sage.

Bar-Cohen, Y. (2005). *Biomimetics: biologically inspired technologies*. CRC Press.

Barki, H., Rivard, S., & Talbot, J. (1993). Toward an Assessment of Software Development Risk. *Development*, *10*(2), 203–225.

Barlow, J. (2011). *Google's Ngram Viewer. Berglund Center for Internet Studies*. Retrieved March 18, 2014, at http://bcis.pacificu.edu/interface/?p=379

Barone, T., & Eisner, E. (2006). Arts-based educational research. In J. Green, G. Camilli, & P. Elmore (Eds.), *Handbook of Complementary Methods in Education Research* (pp. 93–107). New York: Lawrence Erlbaum.

Barone, T., & Eisner, E. W. (2012). *Arts-based research*. Thousand Oaks, CA: Sage.

Barratt, J. (2010). A focus group study of the use of video-recorded stimulated objective structured clinical examinations in nurse practitioner education. *Nurse Education in Practice*, *10*(3), 170–175. doi:10.1016/j.nepr.2009.06.004 PMID:20202909

Bartel, C. A., & Garud, R. (2004). The role of narratives in sustaining organizational transition. *Organization Science*, *20*(1), 107–117. doi:10.1287/orsc.1080.0372

Barton, D., & Lee, C. K. M. (2012). Redefining vernacular literacies in the Age of Web 2.0. *Applied Linguistics*, *33*(3), 282–298. doi:10.1093/applin/ams009

Bartunek, J. (1984). Changing interpretive schemes and organizational restructuring: The example of a religious order. *Administrative Science Quarterly*, *29*(3), 355–372. doi:10.2307/2393029

Bauman, R. (1984). *Verbal art as performance*. Prospect Heights, IL: Waveland Press. (Original work published 1977)

Baym, N. K. (2006). Interpersonal life online. In L. A. Lievrouw, & S. Livingstone (Eds.), *The handbook of new media* (pp. 35–54). London: Sage.

Beaudoin, J. (2007, October). Flickr image tagging: Patterns made visible. *Bulletin of the American Society for Information Science and Technology*, 26–29.

Bekkering, E., & Shim, J. P. (2006). i2i trust in videoconferencing. *Communications of the ACM*, *49*(7), 103–107. doi:10.1145/1139922.1139925

Belanger, F. (2012). Theorizing in Information Systems Research Using Focus Groups. *Australasian Journal of Information Systems*, *17*(2), 109–135.

Belk, R. W. (1988). Possessions and the extended self. *The Journal of Consumer Research*, *15*(2), 139–168. doi:10.1086/209154

Benbasat, I., Goldstein, D. K., & Mead, M. (1987). The Case Research Strategy in Studies of IS. *Management Information Systems Quarterly*, *11*(3), 369–386. doi:10.2307/248684

Bendix, R. (1984). Rationalism and Historicism in the Social Sciences, Force, Fate, and Freedom. Berkeley, CA: University of California Press.

Benefiel, M. (2003). Mapping the terrain of spirituality in organizations research. *Journal of Organizational Change Management*, *16*(4), 367–377. doi:10.1108/09534810310484136

Benefiel, M. (2005). The second half of the journey: Spiritual leadership for organizational transformation. *The Leadership Quarterly*, *16*(5), 723–747. doi:10.1016/j.leaqua.2005.07.005

Bennett, L. (2012). Music fandom online: R.E.M. fans in pursuit of the ultimate first listen. *New Media & Society*, *14*(5), 748–763. doi:10.1177/1461444811422895

Berg, B. L. (2001). *Qualitative research methods for the social sciences* (4th ed.). Needham Heights, MA: Allyn & Bacon.

Berg, B. L., & Lune, H. (2012). *Qualitative Research Methods for the Social Sciences* (8th ed.). Boston: Pearson Publishers.

Berger, P., & Luckman, T. (1967). *The Social Construction of reality.* New York: Doubleday.

Berg, M. (2001). Implementing information systems in health care organizations: Myths and challenges. *International Journal of Medical Informatics, 64*(2-3), 143–156. doi:10.1016/S1386-5056(01)00200-3 PMID:11734382

Bermingham, A., & Smeaton, A. (2010). Classifying sentiment in microblogs: Is brevity an advantage? In *Proceedings of CIKM '10.* Toronto, Canada: Association of Computing Machinery.

Bernal, D. D. (2002). Critical Race Theory, Latino Critical Theory, and Critical Raced-Gendered Epistemologies: Recognizing Students of Color as Holders and Creators of Knowledge. *Qualitative Inquiry, 8*(1), 105–126. doi:10.1177/107780040200800107

Bernard, H. R. (1988). *Research methods in cultural anthropology.* New Berry Park, CA: Sage.

Bernhardt, B. A., Zayac, C., & Pyeritz, R. E. (2011). Why is genetic screening for autosomal dominant disorders underused in families? The case of hereditary hemorrhagic telangiectasia. *Genetics in Medicine, 13*(9), 812–820. doi:10.1097/GIM.0b013e31821d2e6d PMID:21637104

Bertolucci, J. (2005, September). Net phones grow up. *PC World,* 103-106.

Bertrand, C., & Bourdeau, L. (2010). Research interviews by Skype: A new data collection method. In *Proceedings of the 9th European Conference on Research Methodology for Business and Management Studies,* (pp. 70-79). Madrid: IE Business School. Retrieved from http://books.google.co.uk/books?id=8mTywIN8EXkC&printsec=frontcover#v=onepage&q&f=false

Bharadwaj, A., El Sawy, O. A., Pavlou, P. A., & Venkatraman, N. (2013). Visions and Voices on Emerging Challenges in Digital Business Strategy. *Management Information Systems Quarterly, 37*(2), 633–661.

Bhattacharya, K. (2005). *Border Crossings and Imagined Nations: A case study of socio-cultural negotiations of two female Indian graduate students in the U.S.* (Ph.D. Dissertation). University of Georgia, Athens, GA.

Bilalić, M., McLeod, P., & Gobet, F. (2008). Why good thoughts block better ones: The mechanism of the pernicious Eistellung (set) effect. *Cognition, 108*(3), 652–661. doi:10.1016/j.cognition.2008.05.005 PMID:18565505

Bird, C. M. (2005). How I Stopped Dreading and Learned to Love Transcription. *Qualitative Inquiry, 11*(2), 226–248. doi:10.1177/1077800404273413

Blaikie, N. (2007). *Approaches to Social Enquiry.* Cambridge, MA: Polity Press.

Blasius, J., & Brandt, M. (2010). Representativeness in Online Survey through Stratified Samples. *Bulletin de Methodologie Sociologique, 107*(1), 5–21. doi:10.1177/0759106310369964

Blonk, H. (2003). Writing Case Studies in Information Systems Research. *Journal of Information Technology, 18*(1), 45–52. doi:10.1080/0268396031000077440

Bloor, M., Frankland, J., Thomas, M., & Robson, K. (2001). *Focus groups in social research.* London, UK: Sage.

Blue Bird Jernigan, V., & Lorig, K. (2011). The Internet diabetes self-management workshop for American Indians and Alaska natives. *Health Promotion Practice, 12*(2), 261–270. doi:10.1177/1524839909335178 PMID:20534807

Blumer, H. (1969). *Symbolic interactionism: Perspective and method.* Prentice Hall.

Boczkowski, P. J. (1999). Mutual shaping of users and technologies in a national virtual community. *Journal of Communication, 49*(Spring), 86–108. doi:10.1111/j.1460-2466.1999.tb02795.x

Boddy, D., Boonstra, A., & Kennedy, G. (2009). Managing Information Systems: Strategy and Organisation (Third Edit., p. 312). Harlow: Prentide Hall.

Boellstorff, T. (2008). *Coming of age in Second Life: An anthropologist explores the virtually human.* Princeton, NJ: University Press.

Boellstorff, T., Nardi, B., Pearce, C., & Taylor, T. L. (2012). *Ethnography and virtual worlds: A handbook of method.* Princeton, NJ: Princeton University Press.

Boman, A., Povlsen, L., Dahlborg-Lyckhage, E., Hanas, R., & Borup, I. (2013). Fathers' encounter of support from paediatric diabetes team; the tension between general recommendations and personal experience. *Health & Social Care in the Community, 21*(3), 263–270. doi:10.1111/hsc.12013 PMID:23190009

Boshoff, K., Atlant, E., & May, E. (2005). Occupational therapy managers' perceptions of challenges faced in early intervention service delivery in South Australia. *Australian Occupational Therapy Journal, 52*(3), 232–242. doi:10.1111/j.1440-1630.2005.00495.x

Boudreau, R. (2003). *Boudreau Burnout Questionnaire (Bbq).* Retrieved 23rd May 2008, from http://www.cma.ca

Bourgeois, J., Pugmire, L., Stevenson, K., Swanson, N., & Swanson, B. (2006). *The Delphi Method: A qualitative means to a better future.* Retrieved August 13, 2013, from http://www.freequality.org/documents/knowledge/Delphimethod.pdf

Bové, P. (1990). Discourse. In F. Lentricchia, & T. Mclaughlin (Eds.), *Critical terms for literary study* (pp. 50–65). Chicago: University of Chicago Press.

Bower, J. L. (1997). Process research on strategic decisions: A personal perspective. In V. Papadakis, & P. Barwiese (Eds.), *Strategic decisions* (pp. 17–33). Dordrecht, The Netherlands: Kluwer Academic Publishers. doi:10.1007/978-1-4615-6195-8_2

Bowling, A. (2009). *Research Methods in Health: Investigating health and health services* (3rd ed.). London: Open University Press.

Bowman, W. A. (1996). Maximum ground level concentrations with downwash: The urban stability mode. *Journal of the Air & Waste Management Association, 46*(7), 615–620. doi:10.1080/10473289.1996.10467495

Brabazon, A., & O'Neill, M. (2006). *Biologically inspired algorithms for financial modelling.* Berlin: Springer.

Bracey, G. (2009). *The Bracey report on the condition of public education.* Boulder, CO: Education and the Public Interest Center & Education Policy Research Unit.

Bramlett Mayer, A., & Harrison, J. A. (2012). The use of online focus groups to design an online food safety education intervention. *Journal of Food Science Education, 11*(4), 47–51. doi:10.1111/j.1541-4329.2012.00145.x

Brenner, J. (2013). *Pew internet: Mobile.* Retrieved January 3, 2014, from http://pewinternet.org/Commentary/2012/February/Pew-Internet-Mobile.aspx

Brenner, J. (2013, Dec. 31). *Pew Internet: Social Networking (full detail).* Pew Internet & American Life Project. Retrieved Jan. 15, 2014, at http://pewinternet.org/Commentary/2012/March/Pew-Internet-Social-Networking-full-detail.aspx

Brewer, J., & Hunter, A. (1989). *Multimethod research: A synthesis of styles.* Newbury Park, CA: Sage.

Brooke, C. & S. Parker. (2009). Researching Spirituality and Meaning in the Workplace. *The Electronic Journal of Business Research Methods, 7*(1), 1-10.

Brooks, F. P. (1987). No silver bullet: Essence and accidents of software engineering. *IEEE Computer, 20*(4), 10–19. doi:10.1109/MC.1987.1663532

Brown, J.S. (2000, March/April). Growing up digital: How the web changes work, education, and the ways people learn. *Change Magazine,* 11-20.

Brown, A. D. (1998). Narrative, politics and legitimacy in an IT implementation. *Journal of Management Studies, 35*(1), 35–58. doi:10.1111/1467-6486.00083

Brown, D. (2002). Going digital and staying qualitative: Some alternative strategies for digitizing the qualitative research process. *Forum Qualitative Sozial Forschung, 3*(2), 69.

Brown, J. S., & Duguid, P. (1991). Organizational Learning and Communities-of-Practice: Toward a Unified View of Working, Learning and Innovation. *Organization Science, 2*(1), 40–57. doi:10.1287/orsc.2.1.40

Brown, M. H. (1990). Defining stories in organizations. *Communication Yearbook, 13*, 162–190.

Bruening, J. E., & Dixon, M. A. (2007). Work-family conflict in coaching II: Managing role conflict. *Journal of Sport Management, 21*, 471–496.

Bryant, A. (2002). Re-Grounding GT. *Journal of Information Technology Theory and Application, 4*(1), 25–42.

Bryant, A. (2003). "A Constructive/ist Response to Glaser" Forum Qualitative Sozialforschung/Forum: Qualitative. *Social Research, 4*(1).

Bryant, A. (2009). "GT and Pragmatism: The Curious Case of Anselm Strauss" Forum Qualitative Sozialforschung/ Forum: Qualitative. *Social Research, 10*(3).

Bryman, A. (2004). *Social research methods* (2nd ed.). Oxford, UK: Oxford University Press.

Bryman, A., & Hardy, M. (Eds.). (2004). *Handbook of data analysis*. London: Sage.

Burbules, N. C. (2004). Rethinking the virtual. *E-learning, 1*(2), 162–183. doi:10.2304/elea.2004.1.2.2

Burch, T. K. (2001). Longituinal Research in Social Science: Some theoretical Challenges. *Canadian Studies in Population, 28*(2), 263–283.

Burgess, S. (2010). The Use of Focus Groups in Information Systems Research. *International Journal of Interdisciplinary Social Sciences, 5*(2), 57–68.

Burke, L. A., & James, K. E. (2006). Using online surveys for primary research data collection: Lessons from the field. *International Journal of Innovation and Learning, 3*(1), 16–30. doi:10.1504/IJIL.2006.008177

Burnett, K., Bonnici, L. J., Miksa, S. D., & Kim, J. (2007). Frequency, intensity and topicality in online learning: An exploration of the interaction dimensions that contribute to student satisfaction in online learning. *Journal of Education for Library and Information Science, 48*(1), 21–35.

Burrell, G., & Morgan, G. (1979). *Sociological Paradigms and Organisational Analysis*. London: Heinemann.

Burton, L. J., & Bruening, J. E. (2003). Technology and method intersect in the online focus group. *Quest, 55*(4), 315–327. doi:10.1080/00336297.2003.10491807

Bush, M., Lederer, A. L., Li, X., Palmisano, J., & Rao, S. (2009). The alignment of information systems with organizational objectives and strategies in health care. *International Journal of Medical Informatics, 78*(7), 446–456. doi:10.1016/j.ijmedinf.2009.02.004 PMID:19307148

Caldarelli, G., Marchetti, R., & Pietronero, L. (2000). The fractal properties of internet. *Europhysics Letters*, 1 – 6.

Cameron, K., Salazar, L., Bernhardt, J., Burgess-Whitman, N., Wingood, G., & DiClemente, R. (2005). Adolescents' experience with sex on the web: Results from online focus groups. *Journal of Adolescence, 28*(4), 535–540. doi:10.1016/j.adolescence.2004.10.006 PMID:16022887

Campbell, B., Kay, R., & Avison, D. (2005). Strategic Alignment: A Practitioner's Perspective. *Journal of Enterprise Information Management, 18*(6), 653–664. doi:10.1108/17410390510628364

Cannella, G. S., & Lincoln, Y. S. (2004). Dangerous discourses II: Comprehending and countering the redeployment of discourses (and resources) in the generation of liberatory inquiry. *Qualitative Inquiry, 10*(2), 165–174. doi:10.1177/1077800404262988

Cantrell, M. A., & Lupinacci, P. (2007). Methodological issues in online data collection. *Journal of Advanced Nursing, 60*(5), 544–549. doi:10.1111/j.1365-2648.2007.04448.x PMID:17973718

Cao, J., Crews, J. M., Lin, M., Deokar, A. V., Burgoon, J. K., & Nunamaker, J. F. Jr. (2006). Interactions between System Evaluation and Theory Testing: A Demonstration of the Power of a Multifaceted Approach to Information Systems Research. *Journal of Management Information Systems, 22*(4), 207–235. doi:10.2753/MIS0742-1222220408

Carcary, M. (2009). The Resrarch Audit Trail - Enhancing Trustworthiness in Qualitative Inquiry. *The Electronic Journal of Business Research Methods, 7*(1), 11–24.

Carley, K. M., Pfeffer, J., Liu, H., Morstatter, F., & Goolsby, R. (2013). Near real time assessment of social media using geo-temporal network analytics. In *Proceedings of IEEE/ACM International Conference on Advances in Social Networks Analysis and Mining*. Niagara, Canada: IEEE/ACM. doi:10.1145/2492517.2492561

Carlile, P. (2004). Transferring, Translating, and Transforming: An Integrative Framework for Managing Knowledge across Boundaries. *Organization Science, 15*(5), 555–568. doi:10.1287/orsc.1040.0094

Carroll, J. M., & Swatman, P. A. (2000). Structured-case: A methodological framework for building theory in information systems research. *European Journal of Information Systems, 9*(4), 235–242. doi:10.1057/palgrave.ejis.3000374

Cassell, J., & Tversky, D. (2005). The language of online intercultural community formation. *Journal of Computer-Mediated Communication, 10*(2).

Cha, M., Benevenuto, F., Ahn, Y.-Y., & Gummadi, K. P. (2012). Delayed information cascades in Flickr: Measurement, analysis, and modeling. *Computer Networks, 56*(3), 1066–1076. doi:10.1016/j.comnet.2011.10.020

Chan, S., Satosh, S., & Yamana, H. (2011). Increase the image search results by using Flickr tags. In *Proceedings of the DEIM Forum C1-3*. DEIM.

Chandler, A. D. (1962). *Strategy and Structure: Chapters in the history of the American industrial enterprise.* Cambridge, MA: MIT Press.

Chang, S.-J., van Witteloostuijn, A., & Eden, L. (2010). From the Editors: Common method variance in international business research. Journal of Inernational Business Studies, 41, 178-184. doi:10.1057/jibs.2009.88

Chang, V., & Guetl, C. (2007) Distance education ecosystems (ELES). In *Proceedings of the Inaugural Conference on Digital Ecosystems and Technologies*. IEEE.

Chan, Y. E., & Reich, B. H. (2007). IT alignment: An annotated bibliography. *Journal of Information Technology, 22*(4), 316–396. doi:10.1057/palgrave.jit.2000111

Chapman, D. S., & Rowe, P. M. (2001). The impact of videoconference technology, interview structure, and interviewer gender on interviewer evaluations in the employment interview: A field experiment. *Journal of Occupational and Organizational Psychology, 74*(3), 279–298. doi:10.1348/096317901167361

Chapman, D. S., Uggerslev, K. L., & Webster, J. (2003). Applicant reactions to face-to-face and technology-mediated interviews: A field investigation. *The Journal of Applied Psychology, 88*(5), 944–953. doi:10.1037/0021-9010.88.5.944 PMID:14516254

Charmaz, K. (2000). *GT: Objectivist and Constructivist Methods. In Handbook of Qualitative Research* (pp. 509–535). Thousand Oaks, CA: Sage.

Charmaz, K. (2006). *Coding in grounded theory practice. In Constructing Grounded Theory: A Practical Guide through Qualitative Analysis* (pp. 42–73). Thousand Oaks, CA: Sage.

Charmaz, K. (2006). *Constructing GT - A Practical Guide through Qualitative Analysis*. London: Sage.

Charmaz, K. (2008). *Constructing grounded theory: A practical guide through qualitative analysis*. Thousand Oaks, CA: Sage Publications, Inc.

Chase, L., & Alvarez, J. (2000). Internet research: The role of the focus group. *Library & Information Science Research, 22*(4), 357–369. doi:10.1016/S0740-8188(00)00050-5

Chen, M. (2002). *Leveraging the asymmetric sensitivity of eye contact for videoconference*. Paper presented at the Special Interest Group on Computer-Human Interaction Conference on Human factors in Computing Systems. Minneapolis, MN. doi:10.1145/503384.503386

Chen, T., Lu, D., Kan, M.-Y., & Cui, P. (2013). Understanding and classifying image Tweets. In *Proceedings of MM'13*. Barcelona, Spain: Association of Computing Machinery. doi:10.1145/2502081.2502203

Chen, D. Q., Mocker, M., Preston, D. S., & Teubner, A. (2010). Information Systems Strategy: Reconceptualization, Measurement and Implications. *Management Information Systems Quarterly, 34*(2), 233–259.

Chen, R. S., Sun, C. M., Helms, M. M., & Jih, W. J. K. (2008). Aligning information technology and business strategy with a dynamic capabilities perspective: A longitudinal study of a Taiwanese Semiconductor Company. *International Journal of Information Management, 28*, 366–378. doi:10.1016/j.ijinfomgt.2008.01.015

Chen, W., & Hirschheim, R. (2004). A Paradigmatic and Methodological Examination of IS Research from 1991 to 2001. *IS Journal, 14*(3), 197–235.

Chesney, T., Coyne, I., Logan, B., & Madden, N. (2009). Griefing in Virtual Worlds: Causes, Casualties, and Coping Strategies. *Information Systems Journal, 19*(6), 525–548. doi:10.1111/j.1365-2575.2009.00330.x

Choi, C. J., Kim, S. W., & Kim, J. B. (2010). Globalizing Business Ethics Research and the Ethical Need. *Journal of Business Ethics, 94*(2), 299–306. doi:10.1007/s10551-009-0258-y

Cho, J., & Trent, A. (2006). Validity in qualitative research revisited. *Qualitative Research, 6*(3), 319–340. doi:10.1177/1468794106065006

Christian, L. M., Dillman, D. A., & Smyth, J. D. (2007). Helping respondents get it right the first time: The influence of words, symbols, and graphics in web surveys. *Public Opinion Quarterly, 71*(1), 113–125. doi:10.1093/poq/nfl039

Chua, W. F. (1986). Radical Developments in Accounting thought. *Accounting Review, 61*(4), 601–632.

Chung, C. J., & Reynolds, R. G. (1996, February). A Testbed for Solving Optimization Problems Using Cultural Algorithms. In Evolutionary programming (pp. 225-236). Academic Press.

Church, P. E. (1949). Dilution of Waste stack gases in the atmosphere. *Industrial & Engineering Chemistry, 41*(12), 2753–2756. doi:10.1021/ie50480a022

Clegg, C., Axtell, C., Damodaran, L., Farbey, B., Hull, R., & Lloyd-Jones, R. et al. (1997). Information technology: A study of performance and the role of human and organizational factors. *Ergonomics, 40*(9), 851–871. doi:10.1080/001401397187694

Clerc, M. (2006). *Particle swarm optimization* (Vol. 243). London: ISTE. doi:10.1002/9780470612163

Cliggett, L. (2013). Qualitative data archiving in the digital age: Strategies for data preservation and sharing. *Qualitative Report, 18*(1), 1–11. Retrieved from http://www.nova.edu/ssss/QR/QR18/cliggett1.pdf

Cochocki, A., & Unbehauen, R. (1993). *Neural networks for optimization and signal processing*. John Wiley & Sons, Inc.

Coello Coello, C. A., & Becerra, R. L. (2004). Efficient evolutionary optimization through the use of a cultural algorithm. *Engineering Optimization, 36*(2), 219–236. doi:10.1080/03052150410001647966

Coello, C. A. C., & Cortés, N. C. (2002, September). An approach to solve multiobjective optimization problems based on an artificial immune system. In *Proceedings of 1st International Conference on Artificial Immune Systems (ICARIS)*. University of Kent at Canterbury.

Coello, C. A. C., & Cortés, N. C. (2005). Solving multiobjective optimization problems using an artificial immune system. *Genetic Programming and Evolvable Machines, 6*(2), 163–190. doi:10.1007/s10710-005-6164-x

Coffey, A., Holbrook, B., & Atkinson, P. (1996). Qualitative data analysis: Technologies and representations. *Sociological Research Online, 1*(1). doi:10.5153/sro.1

Cohen, J. (1988). *Statistical power analysis for the behavioral sciences*. New York: Routledge.

Cole, S. T. (2005). Comparing Mail and Web-Based Survey Distribution Methods: Results of Surveys to Leisure Travel Retailers. *Journal of Travel Research, 43*(4), 422–430. doi:10.1177/0047287505274655

Conway, J. M., & Lance, C. E. (2010). What Reviewers Should Expect from Authors Regarding Common Method Bias in Organizational Research. *Journal of Business and Psychology*, 25(3), 325–334. doi:10.1007/s10869-010-9181-6

Cook, R. I. (2000). *How Complex Systems Fail* (pp. 1–5).

Cooksey, R. W. (2007). Illustrating Statistical Procedures for Business, Behavioural & Social Science Research. Prahan, Australia: Tilde University Press.

Couper, M. P., M. W. Traugott & M. J. Lamias. (2001). Web Survey Design and Administration. *Public Opinion Quarterly, 65*(2), 230-253.

Couper, M. P. (2000). Web Surveys: A Review of Issues and Approaches. *Public Opinion Quarterly*, 64(4), 464–494. doi:10.1086/318641 PMID:11171027

Couper, M. P., Tourangeao, R., & Kenyon, K. (2004). Picture This! Exploring Visual Effects in Web Surveys. *Public Opinion Quarterly*, 68(2), 255–266. doi:10.1093/poq/nfh013

Couper, M. P., Tourangeau, R., Conrad, F. G., & Crawford, S. D. (2004). What they see is what we get: Response options for web surveys. *Social Science Computer Review*, 22(1), 111–127. doi:10.1177/0894439303256555

Couper, M. P., Traugott, M. W., & Lamias, M. J. (2001). Web survey design and administration. *Public Opinion Quarterly*, 65(2), 230–253. doi:10.1086/322199 PMID:11420757

Coutu, L. (2000). Communication codes of rationality and spirituality in the discourse of and about Robert S. McNamara's "In retrospect". *Research on Language and Social Interaction*, 33(2), 179–211. doi:10.1207/S15327973RLSI3302_3

Cox, A. M. (2008). *Flickr: A case study of Web 2.0. In Proceedings: New Information Perspectives.* Emerald Group Publishing Limited. Doi:10.1108/00012530810908210

Coyle, I. T. (1997). Sampling in Qualitative Research: Purposeful and Theoretical Sampling: Merging or Clear Boundaries? *Journal of Advanced Nursing, 26*(3), 623–630. doi:10.1046/j.1365-2648.1997.t01-25-00999.x PMID:9378886

Crawford, S. D., Couper, M. P., & Lamias, M. J. (2001). Web Surveys: Perceptions of Burden. *Social Science Computer Review*, 19(2), 146–162. doi:10.1177/089443930101900202

Creswell, J. W. (1994). *Research Design: Qualitative and Quantitative Approaches.* Thousand Oaks, CA: Sage.

Creswell, J. W. (2007). *Qualitative inquiry and research design: Choosing among five approaches* (2nd ed.). Thousand Oaks, CA: Sage Publications.

Creswell, J. W. (2013). *Qualitative Inquiry and Research Design: Choosing Among Five Approaches* (3rd ed.). Thousand Oaks, CA: Sage Publications, Inc..

Creswell, J. W., & Plano Clark, V. L. (2007). *Designing and conducting mixed methods research.* Thousand Oaks, CA: Sage Publications, Inc.

Croix, W. (2007). *Adult learners and new traditions in higher education.* Retrieved from http://www.worldwidelearn.com/education-advisor/indepth/adult-learners-online.php

Cross, R., Rice, R. E., & Parker, A. (2001). Information Seeking in Social Context: Structural Influences and Receipt of Information Benefits. *IEEE Transactions on Systems, Man, and Cybernetics*, 31(4), 438–448. doi:10.1109/5326.983927

Crotty, M. (1998). *The foundations of social research: Meaning and perspective in the research process.* Thousand Oaks, CA: Sage Publications.

Crotty, M. (2003). *The Foundations of social Research.* London: Sage.

Crump, B., & Logan, K. (2008). A Framework for Mixed Stakeholders and Mixed Methods. *The Electronic Journal of Business Research Methods*, 6(1), 21–28.

Cuhls, K., Blind, K., & Grupp, H. (Eds.). (1998). Delphi '98 Umfrage: Zukunft nachgefragt: Studie zur globalen Entwicklung von Wissenschaft und Technik. Karlsruhe.

Cuhls, K., Blind, K., & Grupp, H. (2002). *Innovations for our Future. Delphi '98: New Foresight on Science and Technology.* Heidelberg: Physica. doi:10.1007/978-3-642-57472-6

Culturomics. (2014, Jan. 11). *Wikipedia*. Retrieved March 18, 2014, at http://en.wikipedia.org/wiki/Culturomics

Czarniawska, B. (1997). *Narrating the organization: Dramas of institutional identity*. Chicago, IL: University of Chicago Press.

Czarniawska, B. (1998). *A narrative approach to organizational studies*. Thousand Oaks, CA: Sage.

Daft, R., Lengel, R. H., & Trevino, L. K. (1987). Message Equivocality, Mode Selection, and Manager Performance: Implications for IS. *Management Information Systems Quarterly*, *11*(3), 355–366. doi:10.2307/248682

Danet, B., Rudenberg-Wright, L., & Rosenbaum-Tamari, Y. (1997). Hmmm... Where's that smoke coming from? Writing, play, and performance on Internet relay chat. *Journal of Computer-Mediated Communication*, *2*(4).

Danielson, P. (2010). Designing a machine to learn about the ethics of robotics: The N-reasons platform. *Ethics and Information Technology*, *12*(3), 251–261. doi:10.1007/s10676-009-9214-x

Darke, P., Shanks, G., & Broadbent, M. (1998). Successfully completing case study research: Combining rigour, relevance and pragmatism. *Information Systems Journal*, *8*(4), 273–289. doi:10.1046/j.1365-2575.1998.00040.x

DasGupta, D. (1999). *An overview of artificial immune systems and their applications* (pp. 3–21). Springer. doi:10.1007/978-3-642-59901-9

Data use through visualizations and narratives. (2013). *Statewide Longitudinal Data Systems Spotlight, 5*. Retrieved from http://nces.ed.gov/programs/SLDS

Datta, L. (1994). Paradigm Wars: A Basis for Peaceful Coexistence and Beyond. In C. S. Reichardt, & S. F. Rallis (Eds.), *The Qualitative-Quantitative Debate: New Perspectives* (pp. 53–70). San Francisco, CA: Jossey-Bass. doi:10.1002/ev.1668

Dattilo, J., Estrella, G., Estrella, L. J., Light, J., McNaughton, D., & Seabury, M. (2008). "I have chosen to live life abundantly": Perceptions of leisure by adults who use augmentative and alternative communication. *Augmentative and Alternative Communication*, *24*(1), 16–28. doi:10.1080/07434610701390558 PMID:18938755

Davidov, E., & Depner, F. (2009). Testing for measurement equivalence of human values across online and paper-and-pencil surveys. *Quality & Quantity*. doi:10.1007/s11135-11009-19297-11139

Davidson, J., & di Gregorio, S. (2011). Qualitative research and technology: In the midst of a revolution. In N. K. Denzin, & Y. S. Lincoln (Eds.), *The Sage handbook of qualitative research* (4th ed., pp. 627–643). Thousand Oaks, CA: Sage.

De Castro, L. N., & von Zuben, F. J. (Eds.). (2005). *Recent developments in biologically inspired computing*. IGI Global.

De Jong, I., Reinders-Messelink, H., Janssen, W., Poelma, M., van Wijk, I., & van der Sluis, C. K. (2012). Mixed feelings of children and adolescents with congenital below-elbow deficiency: An online focus group study. *PLoS ONE*, *7*(6), e37099. doi:10.1371/journal.pone.0037099 PMID:22715362

de Laat, P. B. (2005). Trusting virtual trust. *Ethics and Information Technology*, *7*(3), 167–180. doi:10.1007/s10676-006-0002-6

De Wit, B., & Meyer, R. (2002). *Strategy: Process, Content, Context - An International Perspective* (2nd ed.). London: Thomson Learning.

De Wit, B., & Meyer, R. (2005). *Strategy synthesis: Resolving strategy paradoxes to create competitive advantage* (2nd ed.). London: Thomson Learning.

Deakin, H., & Wakefield, K. (2013). Skype interviewing: Reflections of two PhD researchers. *Qualitative Research*. DOI: .10.1177/1468794113488126

Deb, K. (2001). Multi-objective optimization. *Multi-Objective Optimization using Evolutionary Algorithms*, 13-46.

DeLone, W. H., & McLean, E. R. (1992). Information systems success: The quest for the dependent variable. *Information Systems Research*, *3*(1), 60–95. doi:10.1287/isre.3.1.60

Dempsey, B., & McDonagh, J. (2014). Integrating Process Inquiry and the Case Method in the Study of IS Failure. In *Proceedings of the UKAIS, 2014*.

Denbo, S., & Fraistat, N. (2011). Diggable data, scalable reading and new humanities scholarship. In *Proceedings of 2011 Second International Conference on Culture and Computing*. doi:10.1109/Culture-Computing.2011.49

Deng, L., Xu, B., Zhang, L., Han, Y., Zhou, B., & Zou, P. (2013). Tracking the evolution of public concerns in social media. In *Proceedings of ICIMCS'13*. Huangshan, ChinaL ICIMCS. doi:10.1145/2499788.2499826

Denscombe, M. (2008). Communities of Practice: A Research Paradigm for the Mixed Methods Approach. *Journal of Mixed Methods Research*, 2(3), 270–283. doi:10.1177/1558689808316807

Denzin, N. K. (1978). *The research act: A theoretical introduction to sociological methods*. New York: McGraw-Hill.

Denzin, N. K., & Lincoln, Y. S. (1998). The fifth moment. In N. K. Denzin, & Y. S. Lincoln (Eds.), *The Landscape of Qualitative Research Theories and Issues* (p. 465). Thousand Oaks, CA: Sage Publications Inc..

Denzin, N. K., & Lincoln, Y. S. (2005). *The Sage handbook of qualitative research* (3rd ed.). Thousand Oaks, CA: Sage.

Denzin, N. K., & Lincoln, Y. S. (Eds.). (2003). *The Landscape of Qualitative Research: Theories and Issues*. Thousand Oaks, CA: Sage Publications, Inc..

Denzin, N., & Lincoln, Y. (1994). *The handbook of qualitative research in education*. Newbury Park, CA: Sage.

DeSanctis, G., & Poole, M. S. (1994). Capturing the complexity in advanced technology use: Adaptive structuration theory. *Organization Science*, 5(2), 121–147. doi:10.1287/orsc.5.2.121

Deutskens, E., Ruyter, K., & Wetzels, M. (2006). An Assessment of Equivalence Between Online and Mail Surveys in Service Research. *Journal of Service Research*, 8(4), 346–355. doi:10.1177/1094670506286323

Dey, I. (1999). *Grounding GT: Guidelines for Qualitative Inquiry*. San Diego, CA: Academic Press.

DiCicco-Bloom, B., & Crabtree, B. F. (2006). The qualitative research interview. *Medical Education*, 40(4), 314–321. doi:10.1111/j.1365-2929.2006.02418.x PMID:16573666

Dickinger, A., Arami, M., & Meyer, D. (2008). The Role of Perceived Enjoyment and Social Norm in the Adoption of Technology with Network Externalities. *European Journal of Information Systems*, 17(1), 1, 4–11. doi:10.1057/palgrave.ejis.3000726

Diller, H.-J. (2013). Culturomics and genre: *Wrath* and *anger* in the 17th century. In *Proceedings of the 2012 Symposium on New Approaches in English Historical Lexis* (pp. 54 – 65). Academic Press.

Dillman, D. A., & Bowker, D. K. (2001). The web questionnaire challenge to survey methodologies. In U. D. Reips & M. Bosnjak (Eds.), Dimensions of Internet Science (pp. 159-177). Papst: Lengerich.

Dillman, D. A. (2000). *Mail and Internet Surveys. The Tailored Design Method*. New York: Wiley.

Dillman, D. A. (2007). *Mail and Internet Surveys "The Tailored Design Method" 2007 update with new internet, visual and mixed-mode guide* (2nd ed.). Hoboken, NJ: John Wiley & Sons Inc..

Dilworth, K., Tao, M., Shapiro, S., & Timmings, C. (2013). Making health promotion evidence-informed: An organizational priority. *Health Promotion Practice*, 14(1), 139–145. doi:10.1177/1524839912461274 PMID:23099658

Dimond, J., Fiesler, C., DiSalvo, B., Pelc, J., & Bruckman, A. (n.d.). *Qualitative data collective technologies: A comparison of instant messaging, email, and phone*. Retrieved March, 2014 from http://jilldimond.com/wp-content/uploads/2010/10/group115-dimond.pdf

Dixon, J. E., & Byrne, R. M. J. (2011). 'If only' counterfactual thoughts about exceptional actions. *Memory & Cognition*, 39(7), 1317–1331. doi:10.3758/s13421-011-0101-4 PMID:21547605

Dixon, M. A., & Bruening, J. E. (2007). Work-family conflict in coaching I: A top-down perspective. *Journal of Sport Management*, 21, 377–406.

Donath, J. S. (1999). Identity and deception in the virtual community. In M. Smith, & P. Kollock (Eds.), *Communities in cyberspace* (pp. 29–59). New York: Routledge.

Dong, B., Qinghua, Z., Jie, Y., Haifei, L., & Mu, Q. (2009). *A distance education ecosystem based on cloud computing infrastructure.* Paper presented at the 9th IEEE International Conference on Advanced Learning Technologies. Riga, Latvia.

Doolin, B. (1993). Alternative views of case research in information systems. *Information Systems Research, 3*(2), 21–29.

Dorigo, M. (Ed.). (2006). *Ant Colony Optimization and Swarm Intelligence:5th International Workshop, (Vol. 4150).* Springer-Verlag New York Incorporated.

Dorigo, M., & Birattari, M. (2010). Ant colony optimization. In Encyclopedia of Machine Learning (pp. 36-39). Springer US.

Dorigo, M., & Di Caro, G. (1999). Ant colony optimization: a new meta-heuristic. In *Proceedings of Evolutionary Computation, (Vol. 2).* IEEE.

Dorigo, M. (2007). Ant colony optimization. *Scholarpedia, 2*(3), 1461. doi:10.4249/scholarpedia.1461

Douglas, D. (2003). Inductive Theory Generation: A Grounded Approach to Business Inquiry. *Electronic Journal of Business Research Methods, 2*(1), 47–54.

Dowling, S. (n.d.). Online asynchronous and face-to-face interviewing: Comparing methods for exploring women's experiences of breastfeeding long term. In J. Salmons (Ed.), *Cases in Online Interview Research* (pp. 277–296). London: Sage.

Drevin, L. (2008). Making sense of information systems failures by using narrative analysis methods. In *Proceeding of the 13th and 14th CPTS Working Conference 2008.* CPTS.

Drnevich, P. L., & Croson, D. C. (2013). Information Technology and Business-level Strategy: Toward an Integrated Theoretical Perspective. *Management Information Systems Quarterly, 37*(2), 483–509.

Du Bois, J. W. (1991). Transcription design principles for spoken discourse research. *Pragmatics, 1*(1), 71–106.

Dube, L., & Pare, G. (2003). Rigor in information systems positivist case research: Current practices, trends, and recommendations. *Management Information Systems Quarterly, 27*(4), 597–636.

Duchon, D. & D. A. Plowman. (2005). 'Nurturing the Spirit at Work: Impact on Work Unit Performance.' *The Leadership Quarterly, 16*(5), 807-833.

Duffy, M. E. (2002). Methodological issues in web-based research. *Journal of Nursing Scholarship, 34*(10), 83–88. doi:10.1111/j.1547-5069.2002.00083.x PMID:11901974

Duggleby, W. (2000). What about focus group interaction data? *Qualitative Health Research, 15*(6), 832–840. doi:10.1177/1049732304273916 PMID:15961879

Earl, M. J. (1989). *Management Strategies for Information Technology.* Upper Saddle River, NJ: Prentice Hall.

Earl, M. J. (2000). Perspectives - Are CIOs Obsolete? *Harvard Business Review, 78*(2), 60.

Easton, G., Easton, A., & Belch, M. (2003). An experimental investigation of electronic focus groups. *Information & Management, 40*(8), 717–727. doi:10.1016/S0378-7206(02)00098-8

Edgerly, L. (2011). Difference and political legitimacy: Speakers' construction of ''citizen'' and ''refugee'' personae in talk about Hurricane Katrina. *Western Journal of Communication, 75*(3), 304–322. doi:10.1080/10570314.2011.571653

Edwards, D. (1997). *Discourse and cognition.* London: Sage.

Edwards, D., & Potter, J. (1993). Language and causation: A discursive action model of description and attribution. *Psychological Review, 100*(1), 23–41. doi:10.1037/0033-295X.100.1.23

Eidlin, F. (2006). *Ideal Types and the Problem of Reification.* Philadelphia, PA: American Political Science Association.

Eisenhardt, K. M. (1989). Building theories from case study research. *Academy of Management Review, 14*(4), 532–550.

Eleta, I., & Golbeck, J. (2012). *A study of multilingual social tagging of art images: Cultural bridges and diversity. In Proceedings of CSCW '12* (pp. 696–704). Seattle, WA: Association of Computing Machinery. doi:10.1145/2145204.2145310

Emerson, R. M., Fretz, R. I., & Shaw, L. L. (1995). *Writing ethnographic fieldnotes*. Chicago, IL: The University of Chicago Press. doi:10.7208/chicago/9780226206851.001.0001

Ess, C., & the Association of Internet Researchers Ethics Working Committee. (2002). *Ethical decision-making and Internet research: Recommendations from the aoir ethics working committee*. Retrieved from http://aoir.org/reports/ethics.pdf

Eto, H. (2003). The suitability of technology forecasting/foresight methods for decision systems and strategy, A Japanese view. *Technological Forecasting and Social Change*, *70*(3), 231–249. doi:10.1016/S0040-1625(02)00194-4

Evans, A., Elford, J., & Wiggins, D. (2010). Using the internet for qualitative research in psychology. In C. Willig, & W. Stainton-Rogers (Eds.), *The Sage Handbook for Qualitative Research* (pp. 315–334). London: Sage.

Eveleens, J. L., & Verhoef, C. (2010). The Rise and Fall of the Chaos Report Figures. *IEEE Software*, *27*(1), 30–36. doi:10.1109/MS.2009.154

Eynon, R., Fry, J., & Schroeder, R. (2008). The ethics of Internet research. In N. Fielding, R. M. Lee, & G. Blank (Eds.), *The SAGE handbook of online research methods* (pp. 23–41). Thousand Oaks, CA: Sage. doi:10.4135/9780857020055.n2

Fambrough, M., & Comerford, S. (2006). The Changing Epistemological Assumptions of Group Theory. *The Journal of Applied Behavioral Science*, *42*(3), 330–349. doi:10.1177/0021886306286445

Farinha, C., & da Silva, M. (2009) Focus Groups for Eliciting Requirements in Information Systems Development. In *Proceedings of UK Academy for Information Systems Conference*. Academic Press.

Fassinger, R., & Morrow, S. L. (2013). Toward Best Practices in Quantitative, Qualitative, and Mixed-Method Research: A Social Justice Perspective. *Journal for Social Action in Counseling and Psychology*, *5*(2), 69–83.

Fassnacht, C., & Woods, D. (2005). *Transana v2.0x* [Computer software]. Retrieved from http://www.transana.org

Feig, B. (1989). How to run a focus group. *American Demographics*, *11*(December), 36–37.

Fenlason, K. J., & Suckow-Zimberg, K. (2006). Online surveys. Critical issues in using the web to conduct surveys. In A. I. Kraut (Ed.), *Getting Action from Organizational Surveys* (pp. 183–212). San Francisco: Jossey-Bass.

Fenton, C., & Langley, A. (2011). Strategy as Practice and the Narrative Turn. *Organization Studies*, *32*(9), 1171–1196. doi:10.1177/0170840611410838

Ferlie, E., Ashburner, L., Fitzgerald, L., & Pettigrew, A. M. (1996). *The New Public Management in Action*. Oxford: Oxford University Press. doi:10.1093/acprof:oso/9780198289029.001.0001

Ferlie, E., & Mcnulty, T. (1997). Going to Market ”: Changing Patterns in the Organisation and Character of Process Research. *Scandinavian Journal of Management*, *13*(4), 367–387. doi:10.1016/S0956-5221(97)00024-9

Fernandez, W. (2004). *The GTM and Case Study Data in IS Research: Issues and Design*. Paper presented at the 2nd Biennial IS Foundations Workshop. Canberra, Australia.

Ferreira, J., & Collins, J. F. (1979). The Changing Role of the MIS Executive. *Datamation*, *25*(13), 25.

Feuer, M. J., Towne, L., & Shavelson, R. J. (2002). Scientific Culture and Educational Research. *Educational Researcher*, *31*(8), 4–14. doi:10.3102/0013189X031008004

Field, A. (2005). *Discovering statistics using SPSS for windows: Advanced techniques for beginners* (2nd ed.). Thousand Oaks, CA: SAGE Publications, Inc.

Fielding, N. (2008). The role of computer-assisted qualitative data analysis: Impact on emergent methods in qualitative research. In S. Hesse-Biber, & P. Leavy (Eds.), *Handbook of emergent methods* (pp. 655–673). New York: The Guilford Press.

Fielding, N., & Lee, R. M. (2008). Qualitative e-social science/cyber-research. In N. Fielding, R. M. Lee, & G. Blank (Eds.), *The Sage handbook of online research methods* (pp. 491–506). Thousand Oaks, CA: Sage Publications. doi:10.4135/9780857020055.n26

Fine, C. (2006). *A Mind of its Own: How your Brain Distorts and Deceives*. New York: W.W. Norton & Company.

Fine, G. A. (1993). The sad demise, mysterious disappearance, and glorious triumph of symbolic interactionism. *Annual Review of Sociology*, *19*(1), 61–87. doi:10.1146/annurev.so.19.080193.000425

Finke, E. H., McNaughton, D. B., & Drager, K. D. R. (2009). "All children can and should have the opportunity to learn": General education teachers' perspectives on including children with autism spectrum disorder who require AAC. *Augmentative and Alternative Communication*, *25*(2), 110–122. doi:10.1080/07434610902886206 PMID:19444682

Flickr. (2013, Dec. 1). *Wikipedia*. Retrieved Dec. 9, 2013, at http://en.wikipedia.org/wiki/Flickr

Flick, U. (2002). *An Introduction to Qualitative Research*. London: Sage.

Flick, U. (2006). *An introduction to qualitative research*. Thousand Oaks, CA: Sage Publications.

Flowers, S. (1996). *Software Failure: Management Failure*. Chichester: John Wiley & Sons.

Ford, P. J. (2001). A further analysis of the ethics of representation in virtual reality: Multi-user environments. *Ethics and Information Technology*, *3*(3), 113–121. doi:10.1023/A:1011846009390

Fornaciari, C. J., & Lund-Dean, K. (2001). Making the quantum leap Lessons from physics on studying spirituality and religion in organizations. *Journal of Organizational Change Management*, *14*(4), 335–351. doi:10.1108/EUM0000000005547

Fortune, J., & Peters, G. (2005). *Information Systems Achieving Success by Avoiding Failure* (p. 220). Chichester: John Wiley & Sons.

Fournier, S. (1998). Consumers and their brands: Developing relationship theory in consumer research. *The Journal of Consumer Research*, *24*(4), 343–373. doi:10.1086/209515

Fowles, J. (1978). *Handbook of futures research*. Greenwood Press.

Fox, F. E., Morris, M., & Rumsey, N. (2007). Doing synchronous online focus groups with young people: Methodological reflections. *Qualitative Health Research*, *17*(4), 539–547. doi:10.1177/1049732306298754 PMID:17416707

Fox, F. E., Rumsey, N., & Morris, M. (2007). "Ur skin is the thing that everyone sees and you cant change it!": Exploring the appearance-related concerns of young people with psoriasis. *Developmental Neurorehabilitation*, *10*(2), 133–141. doi:10.1080/13638490701217594 PMID:17687986

Fram, S. M. (2013). The constant comparative analysis method outside of grounded theory. *Qualitative Report*, *18*(1), 1–25. Retrieved from http://www.nova.edu/ssss/QR/QR18/fram1.pdf

Freeman, M., deMarrais, K., Preissle, J., Roulston, K., & St. Pierre, E. A. (2007). Standards of Evidence in Qualitative Research: An Incitement to Discourse. *Educational Researcher*, *36*(1), 25–32. doi:10.3102/0013189X06298009

Frey, L. R., Botan, C. H., & Kreps, G. L. (2000). *Investigating communication: An introduction to research methods* (2nd ed.). Boston, MA: Allyn and Bacon.

Fricker, R. D. J., & Schonlau, M. (2002). Advantages and Disadvantages of Internet Research Surveys. Evidence from the Literature. *Field Methods*, *14*(4), 347–367. doi:10.1177/152582202237725

Frielick, S. (2004). Beyond constructivism: An ecological approach to distance education: Beyond the comfort zone. In *Proceedings of the 21st ASCILITE Conference* (pp. 328-332). ASCILITE. Retrieved August 13, 2013, from http://www.ascilite.org.au/conferences/perth04/procs/frielick.html

Friese, S. (2012). *Qualitative data analysis with ATLAS.ti*. Sage.

Gaiser, T. (2008). Online focus groups. In N. Fielding, R. M. Lee, & G. Blank (Eds.), *The SAGE handbook of online research methods* (pp. 290–306). Thousand Oaks, CA: Sage. doi:10.4135/9780857020055.n16

Gaiser, T. J. (1997). Conducting on-line focus group: A methodological discussion. *Social Science Computer Review*, *15*(2), 135–144. doi:10.1177/089443939701500202

Galimberti, C., Ignazi, S., Vercesi, P., & Riva, G. (2001). Communication and cooperation in networked environments: An experimental analysis. *Cyberpsychology & Behavior, 4*(1), 131–146. doi:10.1089/10949310151088514 PMID:11709902

Galliers, R. D. (2004). Reflecting on Information Systems Strategizing. In C. Avgerou, C. Ciborra, & F. Land (Eds.), *The Social Study of Information and Communication Technology: Innovation, Actors, and Contexts* (pp. 231–262). Oxford, UK: Oxford University Press.

Galliers, R. D. (2007). *Strategizing for Agility: Confronting IS Inflexibility in Dynamic Environments. In Agile IS: Conceptualization, Construction, and Management* (pp. 1–15). London: Elsevier.

Galup, S. D., Klein, G., & Jiang, J. J. (2008). The Impacts of Job Characteristics on Employee Satisfaction: A Comparison between Permanent and Temporary Employees. *Journal of Computer Information Systems, 48*(4), 58–68.

Garde-Hansen, J., & Calvert, B. (2007). Developing a research culture in the undergraduate curriculum. *Active Learning in Higher Education, 8*(2), 105–116. doi:10.1177/1469787407077984

Garrett, B. M., & Cutting, R. (2012). Using social media to promote international student partnerships. *Nurse Education in Practice, 12*(6), 340–345. doi:10.1016/j.nepr.2012.04.003 PMID:22595660

Gasson, S. (2004). *Rigor in GT Research: An Interpretive Perspective on Generating Theory from Qualitative Field Studies. In The Handbook of IS Research*. Hershey, PA: Idea Group Publishing.

Gastner, M. T., & Newman, M. E. J. (2006). The spatial structure of networks. *The European Physical Journal B, 49*(2), 247–252. doi:10.1140/epjb/e2006-00046-8

Gawande, A. (2009). *The Checklist Manifesto: How to Get Things Right*. New York: Metropolitan Books.

Geiger, J. (2009). *The Third Man Factor: Surviving the Impossible*. New York: Weinstein Books.

Geletkanycz, M. A., & Hambrick, D. (1997). The External Ties of Top Executives: Implications for Strategic Choice and Performance. *Administrative Science Quarterly, 42*(4), 654–681. doi:10.2307/2393653

Gendron, Y., Suddaby, R., & Lam, H. (2006). An examination of the ethical commitment of professional accountants to auditor independence. *Journal of Business Ethics, 64*(2), 169–193. doi:10.1007/s10551-005-3095-7

Gersick, C. J. (1991). Revolutionary change theories: A multilevel exploration of the punctuated equilibrium paradigm. *Academy of Management Review, 16*(1), 10–36.

Gerstein, J. (2014). *How to create and use infographics in educational settings*. Retrieved from http://www.scoop.it/t/infographics-in-educational-settings

Giacalone, R. A., & Jurkiewicz, C. L. (2003). *Handbook of Workplace Spirituality and Organizational Performance*. Armonk, NY: M.E. Sharpe.

Gibbons, D. E. (2004). Network structure and innovation ambiguity effects on diffusion in dynamic organizational fields. *Academy of Management Journal, 47*(6), 938–951. doi:10.2307/20159633

Gibbs, G. R., Friese, S., & Mangabeira, W. C. (2002). The use of new technology in qualitative research. *Forum: Qualitative Social Research, 3*(2), Art. 8.

Gibbs, F. W., & Cohen, D. J. (2011). A conversation with data: Prospecting Victorian words and ideas. *Victorian Studies, 54*(1), 69–77. doi:10.2979/victorianstudies.54.1.69

Gilbert, L. (2002). Going the Distance: "Closeness" in Qualitative Data Alaysis Software. *International Journal of Social Research Methodology, 5*(3), 215–228. doi:10.1080/13645570210146276

Giroux, H. (2003). Public pedagogy and the politics of resistance: Notes on a critical theory of educational struggle. *Educational Philosophy and Theory, 35*(1), 6–16. doi:10.1111/1469-5812.00002

Glaser, B. G. (1978). *Theoretical Sensitivity: Advances in the Methodology of GT*. Mill Valley, CA: Sociology Press.

Glaser, B. G. (1992). *Emergence Vs Forcing: Basics of GT Analysis*. Mill Valley, CA: Sociology Press.

Glaser, B. G. (1998). *Doing GT: Issues and Discussions*. Mill Valley, CA: Sociology Press.

Glaser, B. G. (2001). *The GT Perspective: Conceptualization Contrasted with Description*. Mill Valley, CA: Sociology Press.

Glaser, B. G. (2002). Conceptualization: On Theory and Theorizing using GT. *International Journal of Qualitative Methods*, *1*(2), 1–31.

Glaser, B. G. (2003). *The Grounded Theory Perspective II: Description's Remodeling of Grounded Theory Methodology*. Mill Valley: Sociology Press.

Glaser, B. G. (2005). *The GT Perspective III: Theoretical Coding. Mill Valley*, CA: Sociology Press.

Glaser, B. G., & Strauss, A. L. (1967). *The Discovery of GT: Strategies for Qualitative Research*. New York: Aldine de Guiter.

Goby, V. P. (2011). Psychological underpinnings of intrafamilial computer-mediated communication: A preliminary exploration of CMC uptake with parents and siblings. *Cyberpsychology, Behavior, and Social Networking*, *14*(6), 365–370. doi:10.1089/cyber.2010.0289 PMID:21114409

Goffman, E. (1959). *The presentation of self in everyday life*. New York, NY: Anchor Books.

Goldberg, D. E., & Holland, J. H. (1988). Genetic algorithms and machine learning. *Machine Learning*, *3*(2), 95–99. doi:10.1023/A:1022602019183

Goldfinch, S. (2007). Pessimism, computer failure, and information systems development in the public sector. *Public Administration Review*, *67*(5), 917–929. doi:10.1111/j.1540-6210.2007.00778.x

Goldsmith, J. R., & Friberg, L. T. (1976). Effects of air pollution on human health, Air Pollution. In A. C. Stern (Ed.), *The Effects of Air Pollution* (3rd ed., Vol. 2, pp. 457–610). New York, NY: Academic Press.

Goleman, D. (2006). *Social Intelligence: The New Science of Human Relationships*. New York: Bantam Books.

Goodfellow, R., & Lamy, M. N. (Eds.). (2009). *Learning cultures in online education*. London: Continuum.

Gooding, P. (2013). Mass digitization and the garbage dump: The conflicting needs of quantitative and qualitative methods. *Literary and Linguistic Computing*, *28*(3), 425–431. doi:10.1093/llc/fqs054

Google Books Ngram Viewer. (2014). *About Ngram Viewer*. Retrieved March 20, 2014, at https://books.google.com/ngrams/info

Gordon, T., Holland, J., & Lahelma, E. (2001). Ethnographic research in educational settings. In P. Atkinson, A. Coffey, S. Delamont, J. Lofland, & L. Lofland (Eds.), *Handbook of ethnography* (pp. 188–203). London: Sage. doi:10.4135/9781848608337.n13

Gorski, P. C. (2005). *The digital divide. In Multicultural education and the internet* (pp. 21–62). Boston: McGraw-Hill Education.

Gotterbarn, D. (1991). Computer Ethics: Responsibility Regained, National Forum. *The Phi Beta Kappa Journal*, *71*, 26-31.

Gottschalk, P. (2002). The Chief Information Officer: A Study of Managerial Roles in Norway. In *Proceedings of 35th Annual Hawaii International Conference on System Sciences*. IEEE. doi:10.1109/HICSS.2002.994350

Gottschalk, P. (1999). Strategic Management of IS/IT functions: The Role of the CIO in Norwegian Organisations. *International Journal of Information Management*, *19*(5), 389–399. doi:10.1016/S0268-4012(99)00034-1

Gottschalk, P. (2000). IS Leadership Roles: An Empirical Study of Information Technology Managers. *Journal of Global Information Management*, *8*(4), 43–52. doi:10.4018/jgim.2000100104

Goulding, C. (1999). GT: Some Reflections on Paradigm. In Procedures and Misconceptions. University of Wolverhampton.

Goulding, C. (1998). GT: The Missing Methodology on the Interpretivist Agenda. *Qualitative Market Research: An International Journal*, *1*(1), 50–57. doi:10.1108/13522759810197587

Goulding, C. (2002). *GT: A Practical Guide for Management, Business and Market Researchers*. London: Sage.

Grace, J.H., Zhao, D., & boyd, d. (2010). Microblogging: What and how can we learn from it?. In *Proceedings of CHI 2010*. Association of Computing Machinery.

Graffigna, G., & Bosio, A. C. (2006). The influence of setting on findings produced in qualitative health research: A comparison between face-to-face and online discussion groups about HIV/AIDS. *International Journal of Qualitative Methods, 5*(3), 1–16.

Grava-Gubins, I., & Scott, S. (2008). Effects of various methodological strategies: Survey response rates among Canadian physicians and physicians-in-training. *Canadian Family Physician Medecin de Famille Canadien, 54*(October), 1424–1430. PMID:18854472

Greaney, M. L., Less, F. D., White, A. A., Dayton, S. F., Riebe, D., & Blissmer, B. et al. (2009). College students' barriers and enablers for healthful weight management: A qualitative study. *Journal of Nutrition Education and Behavior, 41*(4), 281–286. doi:10.1016/j.jneb.2008.04.354 PMID:19508934

Greenberg, R. (2013). The history of VOIP. *The Digest*. Retrieved December 18, 2013, from http://www.thedigest.com/blog/the-history-of-voip

Greene, J. C. (2008). Is mixed methods social inquiry a distinctive methodology? *Journal of Mixed Methods Research, 2*(7), 17. doi:10.1177/1558689807309969

Greener, I. (2011). *Designing Social Research: A Guide for th bewildered*. London: SAGE Publications Ltd..

Greenfield, P. M. (2013). The changing psychology of culture from 1800 through 2000. *Psychological Science, 24*(9), 1722–1731. doi:10.1177/0956797613479387 PMID:23925305

Greenlaw, C., & Brown-Welty, S. (2009). A Comparison of Web-Based and Paper-Based Survey Methods: Testing Assumptions of Survey Mode and Response Cost. *Evaluation Review, 33*(5), 464–480. doi:10.1177/0193841X09340214 PMID:19605623

Greenspan, A. (2013). *The Map and the Territory: Risk, Human Nature, and the Future of Forecasting*. New York: The Penguin Press.

Gregor, S. (2006). The nature of theory in information systems. *Management Information Systems Quarterly, 30*(3), 611–642.

Griffiths, R. F. (1994). Errors in the use of the Briggs parameterization for atmospheric dispersion coefficients. *Atmospheric Environment, 28*(17), 2861–2865. doi:10.1016/1352-2310(94)90086-8

Guba, E. G., & Lincoln, Y. S. (2005). Paradigmatic Controversies, Contradictions, and Emerging Confluences. In N. K. Denzin, & Y. S. Lincoln (Eds.), *The Sage Handbook of Qualitative Research* (3rd ed., pp. 191–215). Thousand Oaks, CA: Sage Publications.

Guba, E., & Lincoln, Y. S. (1994). *Competing Paradigms in Qualitative Research. In Handbook of Qualitative Research*. (pp. 105–117). Thousand Oaks, CA: Sage.

Guerra, P. H. C., Veloso, A., Meira, W., & Almeida, V. (2011). From bias to opinion: A transfer-learning approach to real-time sentiment analysis. In *Proceedings of KDD*. San Diego, CA: Association of Computing Machinery.

Guo, Z., & Sheffield, J. (2007). Critical Heuristics: A Contribution to Addressing the Vexed Question of So-Called Knowledge Management. *Systems Research and Behavioral Science, 24*(6), 613–626. doi:10.1002/sres.834

Häder, M., & Häder, S. (1995). Delphi und Kognitionspsychologie: Ein Zugang zur theoretischen Fundierung der Delphi-Methode. *ZUMA-Nachrichten, 37*(19), 12.

Halitsky, J. (1989). A jet plume model for short stacks. *Journal of the Air Pollution Control Association, 39*(6), 856–858.

Hambrick, D., & Mason, P. A. (1984). Upper Echelons: The Organization as a Reflection of its Top Managers. *Academy of Management Review, 9*(2), 193–206.

Hammersley, M. (2010). Reproducing or construction? Some questions about transcription in social research. *Qualitative Research, 10*(5), 553–569. doi:10.1177/1468794110375230

Handy, C. (1995). Trust and the Virtual Organization. *Harvard Business Review, 73*(3), 40–50.

Hanna, B., & De Nooy, J. (2004). Negotiating cross-cultural difference in electronic discussion. *Multilingua, 23*(3), 257–281. doi:10.1515/mult.2004.012

Hanna, B., & De Nooy, J. (2009). *Learning language and culture via public internet discussion forums.* Houndmills, UK: Palgrave MacMillan. doi:10.1057/9780230235823

Hanna, P. (2012). Using internet technologies (such as Skype) as a research medium: A research note. *Qualitative Research, 2*(2), 239–242. doi:10.1177/1468794111426607

Hanna, R. C., Weinberg, B., Dant, R. P., & Berger, P. D. (2005). Do internet-based surveys increase personal self-disclosure? *Journal of Database Marketing and Customer Strategy Management, 12*(4), 342–356. doi:10.1057/palgrave.dbm.3240270

Hanna, S. R., Briggs, G. A., & Kosker, R. P. (1982). *Handbook on Atmospheric Diffusion.* NTIS. doi:10.2172/5591108

Hansen, D. L., Schneiderman, B., & Smith, M. A. (2011). *Analyzing Social Media Networks with NodeXL: Insights from a Connected World.* Burlington, MA: Elsevier.

Hansen, S. S. (2013). Exploring real-brand meanings and goods in virtual-world social interaction: Enhanced rewards, rarity, and realism. *Journal of Marketing Management, 29*(13-14), 1443–1461. doi:10.1080/0267257X.2013.821151

Harris, J. B., Mishra, P., & Koehler, M. (2009). Teachers' technological pedagogical content knowledge and learning activity types: Curriculum-based technology integration reframed. *Journal of Research on Technology in Education, 41*(4), 393–416. doi:10.1080/15391523.2009.10782536

Hart, T. (2011). Speech codes theory as a framework for analyzing communication in online educational settings. In S. Kelsey, & K. St.Amant (Eds.), *Computer mediated communication: Issues and approaches in education.* Hershey, PA: IGI Global. doi:10.4018/978-1-61350-077-4.ch012

Hassanpour, N. (2013). Tracking the semantics of politics: A case for online data research in political science. In *Proceedings of Symposium: Technology, Data, and Politics* (pp. 299–306). doi:10.1017/S1049096513000280

Hayes, B. (2014). Bit lit. *American Scientist.* Retrieved March 18, 2014, at http://www.americanscientist.org/issues/num2/bit-lit/2

Healey, B., (2007). Drop Downs and Scroll Mice: The Effect of Response Option Format and Input Mechanism Employed on Data Quality in Web Surveys. *Social Science Computer Review, 25*(1), 111-128.

Heath, C., & Health, D. (2007). *Made to Stick: Why Some Ideas Survive and Others Die.* New York: Random House.

Heath, H. (2006). Exploring the Influences and Use of the Literature during a GT Study. *Journal of Research in Nursing, 11*(6), 519–528. doi:10.1177/1744987106069338

Hendrickson, C., Conway-Schempf, N., Lave, L., & McMichael, F. (1999). *Introduction to Green Design.* Green Design Initiative, Carnegie Mellon University. Retrieved May 5, 2012 from http://gdi.ce.cmu.edu/gd/education/gdeintro.pdf

Hennig-Thurau, T., Gwinner, K. P., Walsh, G., & Gremler, D. D. (2004). Electronic word-of-mouth via consumer-opinion platforms: What motivates consumers to articulate themselves on the Internet? *Journal of Interactive Marketing, 18*(1), 38–52. doi:10.1002/dir.10073

Henshaw, M. (2012). *The Red Cell: Fact and Fiction.* Spycast. International Spy Museum. Retrieved Dec. 28, 2013, at http://www.spymuseum.org/multimedia/spycast/episode/the-red-cell-fact-and-fiction/

Herbert, W. (2010). *On Second Thought: Outsmarting your Mind's Hard-Wired Habits.* New York: Crown Books.

Herman, D., Phelan, J., Rabinowitz, P. J., Richardson, B., & Warhol, R. (2012). *Narrative Theory - Core concepts and Critical debates.* Columbus, Ohio: Ohio State University Press.

Hermanowicz, J. (2002). The great interview: 25 strategies for studying people in bed. *Qualitative Sociology*, *25*(4), 479–500. doi:10.1023/A:1021062932081

Hernandez, I., & Preston, J. L. (2013). Disfluency disrupts the confirmation bias. FlashReport. *Journal of Experimental Social Psychology*, *49*(1), 178–182. doi:10.1016/j.jesp.2012.08.010

Herriman, N. (2010). The great rumor mill: Gossip, mass media, and the ninja fear. *The Journal of Asian Studies*, *69*(3), 723–748. doi:10.1017/S0021911810001488

Hess-Biber, S., & Johnson, R. B. (2013). Coming at things differently: Future directions of possible engagement with mixed methods research. *Journal of Mixed Methods Research*. Retrieved March, 2014 from http://mmr.sagepub.com/content/7/2/103.full.pdf+html

Hesse-Biber, S., & Griffin, A. J. (2013). Internet-mediated technologies and mixed methods research: Problems and prospects. *Journal of Mixed Methods Research*, *7*(1), 43–61. doi:10.1177/1558689812451791

Heuer, R. J., Jr. (1999). *Psychology of Intelligence Analysis*. Center for the Study of Intelligence. CIA. Retrieved Aug. 30, 2013, at https://www.cia.gov/library/center-for-the-study-of-intelligence/csi-publications/books-and-monographs/psychology-of-intelligence-analysis/PsychofIntelNew.pdf

Hewitt, J. P. (2003). Symbols, objects, and meanings. In L. T. Reynolds, & N. J. Herman-Kinney (Eds.), *Handbook of symbolic interactionism*. Walnut Creek, CA: AltaMira Press.

Hewson, C. M., Yule, P., Laurent, D., & Vogel, C. M. (2003). *Internet research methods: A practical guide for the social and behavioral sciences*. London, UK: Sage.

Hewson, C., & Laurent, D. (2008). Research design and tools for Internet research. In N. Fielding, R. M. Lee, & G. Blank (Eds.), *The SAGE handbook of online research methods* (pp. 58–78). Thousand Oaks, CA: Sage. doi:10.4135/9780857020055.n4

Hey, T., Tansley, S., & Tolle, K. (2009). *The fourth paradigm: Data-intensive scientific discovery*. Redmond, WA: Microsoft.

Hickey, G. (1997). The Use of Literature in GT. *Nursing Times Research*, *2*(5), 371–378. doi:10.1177/174498719700200510

Hiemstra, R. (2002). Uses and benefits of journal writing. *New Directions for Adult and Continuing Learning*, *2001*(90), 19 – 26. Retrieved on Aug. 9, 2013, at http://onlinelibrary.wiley.com/doi/10.1002/ace.17/abstract

Hillier, L., Mitchell, K., & Ybarra, M. (2012). The Internet as a safety net: Findings from a series of online focus groups with LGB and non-LGB young people in the United States. *Journal of LGBT Youth*, *9*(3), 225–246. doi:10.1080/19361653.2012.684642

Hine, C. (2000). *Virtual ethnography*. London: Sage.

Hine, C. (2008). Virtual ethnography: Modes, varieties, affordances. In N. G. Fielding, & R. M. Lee (Eds.), *Sage handbook of online research methods* (pp. 257–270). Los Angeles, CA: Sage. doi:10.4135/9780857020055.n14

Hinings, C. R. (1997). Reflections on processual research. *Scandinavian Journal of Management*, *13*(4), 493–503. doi:10.1016/S0956-5221(97)00023-7

Hirschheim, R., & Klein, H. (1992). Paradigmatic Influences on IS Development Methodologies: Evolution and Conceptual Advances. *Advances in Computers*, *34*, 293–392. doi:10.1016/S0065-2458(08)60328-9

Hirschheim, R., & Newman, M. (1987). Symbolism and Information Systems Development: Myth, Metaphor and Magic. *Information Systems Research*, *2*(1), 29–62. doi:10.1287/isre.2.1.29

Hoffman, E. S., Caniglia, J., Knott, L., & Evitts, T. A. (2009). In their own words: Good mathematics teachers in the era of NCLB. *Mathematics Teacher*, *10*(6), 468–473.

Hofmeyr, S. A., & Forrest, S. (2000). Architecture for an artificial immune system. *Evolutionary Computation*, *8*(4), 443–473. doi:10.1162/106365600568257 PMID:11130924

Hofstede, G. (2001). *Culture's Consequences: Comparing values, behaviours, institutions, and organisations across nations*. Thousand Oaks, CA: Sage Publications.

Hogan, W. R., Cooper, G. F., Wagner, M. M., & Wallstrom, G. L. (2005). An inverted Gaussian Plume Model for estimating the location and amount of Release of airborne agents from downwind atmospheric concentrations. RODS Technical Report. Pittsburgh, PA: Real time Outbreak and Disease Surveillance Laboratory, University of Pittsburgh.

Holler, M., Tam, S., Castro, H., & Benson, R. (1989, June). An electrically trainable artificial neural network (etann) with 10240' floating gate'synapses. In *Proceedings of Neural Networks*, (pp. 191-196). IEEE.

Holt, A. (2010). Using telephones for narrative interviewing: A research note. *Qualitative Research*, *10*(1), 113–121. doi:10.1177/1468794109348686

Horvath, K., Danilenko, G., Williams, M., Simoni, J., Rivet Amico, K., Oakes, J. M., & Rosser, S. (2012). Technology use and reasons to participate in social networking health websites among people living with HIV in the US. *AIDS and Behavior*, *16*(4), 900–910. doi:10.1007/s10461-012-0164-7 PMID:22350832

Hotho, A. (2010). Data mining on folksonomies. *Intelligent Information Access*, *301*, 57–82. doi:10.1007/978-3-642-14000-6_4

House, E. R. (1994). Integrating the Quantitative and Qualitative. In C. S. Reichardt, & S. F. Rallis (Eds.), *The Qualitative-quantitative Debate: New Perspectives* (pp. 13–22). San Francisco, CA: Jossey-Bass.

Hu, X., Tang, L., Tang, J., & Liu, H. (2013). Exploiting social relations for sentiment analysis in microblogging. In *Proceedings of WSDM '13*. Rome, Italy: Association of Computing Machinery. doi:10.1145/2433396.2433465

Huang, H. H., Hsu, J., & Ku, C.-Y. (2012). Understanding the role of computer-mediated counter-argument in countering confirmation bias. *Decision Support Systems*, *53*(3), 438–447. doi:10.1016/j.dss.2012.03.009

Huff, A. (1990). *Mapping Strategic Thought*. Chichester, UK: Wiley.

Hughes, J., & Lang, K. R. (2004). Issues in online focus groups: Lessons learned from an empirical study of peer-to-peer filesharing system users. *Electronic Journal of Business Research Methods*, *2*(2), 95–110.

Hughes, J., & Wood-Harper, A. T. (2000). An Empirical Model of the IS Development Process: A Case Study of an Automotive Manufacturer. *Accounting Forum*, *24*(4), 391–406. doi:10.1111/1467-6303.00048

Humble, Á. M. (2012). Qualitative data analysis software: A call for understanding, detail, intentionality, and thoughtfulness. *Journal of Family Theory & Review*, *4*(2), 122–137. doi:10.1111/j.1756-2589.2012.00125.x

Hutcheon, L. (1987). Beginning to theorize postmodernism. *Textual Practice*, *1*(1), 10–31.

Hymes, D. (1962). The ethnography of speaking. In T. Gladwin, & W. C. Sturevant (Eds.), *Anthropology and human behavior* (pp. 13–53). Washington, DC: Anthropological Society of Washington.

Hymes, D. (1972). Models of the interaction of language and social life. In J. J. Gumperz, & D. Hymes (Eds.), *Directions in sociolinguistics: The ethnography of communication* (pp. 35–71). New York, NY: Holt, Rinehart and Winston.

Hymes, D. (1977). Qualitative/quantitative research methodologies in education: A linguistic perspective. *Anthropology & Education Quarterly*, *8*(3), 165–176. doi:10.1525/aeq.1977.8.3.05x1511c

Hyvari, I. (2006). Success of projects in different organizational conditions. *Project Management Journal*, *37*(4), 31–42.

Ibarra, H. (1993). Personal Networks of Women and Minorities in Management: A Conceptual Framework. *Academy of Management Review*, *18*(1), 56–87.

Ibarra, H., & Hunter, M. G. (2007). How Leaders Create and Use Networks. *Harvard Business Review*, *85*(1), 40–47. PMID:17286073

Iivari, J., Hirschheim, R., & Klein, H. (1998). A Paradigmatic Analysis Contrasting IS Development Approaches and Methodologies. *IS Research*, *9*(2), 164–193.

Im, E., & Chee, W. (2004). Issues in Internet survey research among cancer patients. *Cancer Nursing*, *27*(1), 34–44. doi:10.1097/00002820-200401000-00005 PMID:15108950

Innis, H. A. (1964). *The Bias of Communication*. Toronto: University of Toronto Press.

Innis, H. A. (1972). *Empire and Communications*. Toronto: University of Toronto Press.

Innovation. (1982). *Webster's New World Dictionary* (2nd college ed.). Webster's.

Issa, T. (2009). *Ethical Mindsets, Aesthetics and Spirituality: A Mixed-Methods Approach Analysis of the Australian Services Sector*. Retrieved from http://espace.library.curtin.edu.au/R/?func=dbin-jump-full&object_id=131986&local_base=GEN01-ERA02

Issa, T., Issa, T., & Chang, V. (2011). *Green IT and sustainable development strategies: An Australian experience*. Paper presented at the 12th International Conference of the Society for Global Business & Economic Development. Singapore.

Ives, B., & Learmonth, G. P. (1984). The Information System as a Competitive Weapon. *Communications of the ACM, 27*(12), 1193–1201. doi:10.1145/2135.2137

Ives, B., & Olson, M. H. (1981). Manager or Technician? The Nature of the IS Manager's job. *Management Information Systems Quarterly, 5*(4), 49–63. doi:10.2307/249327

Jackson, M. H. (1997). Assessing the structure of communication on the World Wide Web.[Wiley Library.]. *Journal of Computer-Mediated Communication, 3*(1). doi:10.1111/j.1083-6101.1997.tb00063.x

Jankowicz, A. D. (1995). *Business research projects*. London: International Thomson Business Press. doi:10.1007/978-1-4899-3386-7

Jefferson, G. (2004). Glossary of transcript symbols with an introduction. In G. H. Lerner (Ed.), *Conversation analysis: Studies from the First Generation* (pp. 13–31). Amsterdam: John Benjamins. doi:10.1075/pbns.125.02jef

Jenkins, H. (2006). *Convergence culture: Where old and new media collide*. New York: New York University Press.

Jeong, H. J., Kim, E. H., Suh, K. S., Hwang, W. T., Han, M. H., & Lee, H. K. (2005). Determination of the source rate released into the environment from a nuclear power plant. *Radiation Protection Dosimetry, 113*(3), 308–313. doi:10.1093/rpd/nch460 PMID:15687109

Jhuang, H., Serre, T., Wolf, L., & Poggio, T. (2007, October). A biologically inspired system for action recognition. In *Proceedings of Computer Vision,* (pp. 1-8). IEEE. doi:10.1109/ICCV.2007.4408988

Jick, T. D. (1979). Mixing Qualitative and Quantitative Methods: Triangulation in Action. *Administrative Science Quarterly, 24*(4), 602–611. doi:10.2307/2392366

Jin, X., & Reynolds, R. G. (1999). Using knowledge-based evolutionary computation to solve nonlinear constraint optimization problems: a cultural algorithm approach. In *Proceedings of Evolutionary Computation,* (Vol. 3). IEEE.

Johansson, F. (2012). *The Click Moment: Seizing Opportunity in an Unpredictable World*. New York: Portfolio / Penguin.

Johnson, B. R., & Onwuegbuzie, A. J. (2004). Mixed Methods Research: A Research Paradigm Whose Time Has Come. *Educational Researcher, 33*(7), 14–26. doi:10.3102/0013189X033007014

Johnson, G. M. (2012). The ecology of interactive learning environments: Situating traditional theory. *Interactive Learning Environments*. doi:10.1080/10494820.2011.649768

Johnson, J. D., & Tuttle, F. (1989). Problems in intercultural research. In W. Gudykunst, & M. Asante (Eds.), *Handbook of international and intercultural communication* (pp. 461–483). Newbury Park, CA: Sage.

Johnson, R. B., Onwuegbuzie, A. J., & Turner, L. A. (2007). Toward a definition of mixed methods research. *Journal of Mixed Methods Research, 1*(2), 112–133. doi:10.1177/1558689806298224

Jones, K. (2008). *Creating a Learning Ecosystem – Why Blended Learning is Now Inadequate*. Retrieved August 13, 2013, from http://engagedlearning.net/post/creating-a-learning-ecosystem-why-blended-learning-is-now-inadequate/

Jones, V. (2004). *Race is a verb: An effective history of young adults subjected to racial violence*. (Dissertation). Athens, GA.

Justinia, T. (2009). *Implementing large-scale healthcare information systems: The technological, managerial and behavioural issues.* (PhD Dissertation). Swansea University, Swansea, UK.

Justinia, T. (2014). *Implementing large-scale healthcare information systems: The technological, managerial and behavioural issues.* Scholars-Press.

Kahneman, D. (2011). *Thinking Fast and Slow.* New York: Farrar, Straus and Giroux.

Kanstrup, A. M. (2002). Picture the practice – Using photography to explore use of technology within teachers work practices. *Forum: Qualitative Social Research.* Retrieved March, 2014 from http://www.qualitative-research.net/index.php/fqs/article/view/856

Kaplan, B., & Duchon, D. (1988). Combining Qualitative Methods in IS Research: A Case Study. *Management Information Systems Quarterly, 12*(4), 571–586. doi:10.2307/249133

Kaplan, B., & Maxwell, J. (2005). Qualitative research methods for evaluating computer information systems. In *Evaluating the Organizational Impact of Healthcare Information Systems* (pp. 30–55). Springer. doi:10.1007/0-387-30329-4_2

Kaplowitz, M. D., Hadlock, T. D., & Levine, R. (2004). A comparison of web and mail survey response rates. *Public Opinion Quarterly, 68*(1), 94–101. doi:10.1093/poq/nfh006

Kappelman, L., McKeeman, R., & Zhang, L. (2006). Early Warning Signs of IT Project Failure: The Dominant Dozen. *Information Systems Management, 23*(4), 31–36. doi:10.1201/1078.10580530/46352.23.4.20060901/95110.4

Karahanna, E., & Preston, D. S. (2013). The Effect of Social Capital of the Relationship Between the CIO and Top Management Team on Firm Performance. *Journal of Management Information Systems, 30*(1), 15–55. doi:10.2753/MIS0742-1222300101

Katz, D., & Kahn, R. (1966). *The Social Psychology of Organizations.* New York: John Wiley & Sons.

Kazmer, M. M., & Xie, B. (2008). Qualitative interviewing in internet studies: Playing with the media, playing with the method. *Information Communication and Society, 11*(2), 257–278. doi:10.1080/13691180801946333

Keating, E. (2001). The ethnography of communication. In P. Atkinson, A. Coffey, S. Delamont, J. Lofland, & L. Lofland (Eds.), *Handbook of ethnography* (pp. 285–300). London: Sage. doi:10.4135/9781848608337.n20

Keating, E., & Mirus, G. (2003). American Sign Language in virtual space: Interactions between deaf users of computer-mediated video communication and the impact of technology on language practices. *Language in Society, 32*(05), 693–714. doi:10.1017/S0047404503325047

Keen, P. G. W. (1981). Information systems and organizational change. *Communications of the ACM, 24*(1), 24–33. doi:10.1145/358527.358543

Keil, M. (1995). Pulling the plug: Software project management and the problem of project escalation. *Management Information Systems Quarterly, 19*(4), 421–447. doi:10.2307/249627

Kelley, D. L. (1999). *Measurement made accessible: A research approach using qualitative, quantitative, and quality improvement methods.* London: Sage.

Kendall, J. (1999). Axial Coding and the GT Controversy. *Western Journal of Nursing Research, 21*(6), 743–757. doi:10.1177/01939459922044162 PMID:11512211

Kendall, L. (2002). *Hanging out in the virtual pub: Masculinities and relationships online.* Berkeley, CA: University of California Press.

Kennedy, J. (2010). Particle swarm optimization. In *Encyclopedia of Machine Learning* (pp. 760-766). Springer US.

Kenny, A. J. (2005). Interactions in cyberspace: An online focus group. *Journal of Advanced Nursing, 49*(4), 414–422. doi:10.1111/j.1365-2648.2004.03305.x PMID:15701156

Kenny, A. J., & Duckett, S. (2005). An online study of Australian enrolled nurse convention. *Journal of Advanced Nursing, 49*(4), 423–431. doi:10.1111/j.1365-2648.2004.03306.x PMID:15701157

Kieman, N. E., M. Kieman, M. A. Oyler & C. Gilles. (2005). Is a Web Survey as Effective as a Mail Survey? A Field Experiment among Computer Users. *American Journal of Evaluation, 26*(2), 245-252.

Kimbler, J., Moore, D., Maitland-Schladen, M., Sowers, B., & Snyder, M. (2013). *Emerging technology tools for qualitative data collection.* Nova Southeastern University. Retrieved March 2014 from http://www.nova.edu/ssss/QR/TQR2013/Kimbler_etal_TQRHandout.pdf

King, A. (2010). 'Membership matters': Applying membership categorization analysis (MCA) to qualitative data using computer-assisted qualitative data analysis (CAQDAS) software. *International Journal of Social Research Methodology, 13*(1), 1–16. doi:10.1080/13645570802576575

Klaus, T., & Blanton, J. (2010). User Resistance Determinants and the Psychological Contract in Enterprise System Implementations. *European Journal of Information Systems, 19*(6), 625–636. doi:10.1057/ejis.2010.39

Kleftodimos, A., & Evangelidis, G. (2013). An overview of Web mining in education. In *Proceedings of PCI 2013.* Thessaloniki, Greece: PCI. doi:10.1145/2491845.2491863

Klein, D. B. (2013). *Cultural trends as seen in ngrams: Karl Polanyi with a Hayekian twist* (Working Paper No. 13-10). George Mason University, Department of Economics.

Klein, E. E., Tellefsen, T., & Herskovitz, P. J. (2007). The use of group support systems in focus groups: Information technology meets qualitative research. *Computers in Human Behavior, 23*(5), 2113–2132. doi:10.1016/j.chb.2006.02.007

Klein, H., & Myers, M. D. (1999). A Set of Principles for Conducting and Evaluating Interpretive Field Studies in IS. *Management Information Systems Quarterly, 23*(1), 67–93. doi:10.2307/249410

Klein, J. (2002). Issues surrounding the use of Internet for data collection. *American Journal of Occupational Health, 56*(3), 340–343. doi:10.5014/ajot.56.3.340 PMID:12058524

Klofstad, C. A., S. Boulianne & D. Basson. (2008). Matching the Message to the Medium: Results from an Experiment on Internet Survey Email Contacts. *Social Science Computer Review, 26*(4), 498-509.

Kluge, S. (2000). "Empirically Grounded Construction of Types and Typologies in Qualitative Research." Forum Qualitative Sozialforschung/Forum: Qualitative. *Social Research, 1*(1).

Koch, S. C., & Zumbach, J. (2002). The use of video analysis software in behavior observation research: Interaction patterns in task-orientation small groups. *Forum: Qualitative Social Research.* Retrieved March, 2014 from http://www.qualitative-research.net/index.php/fqs/article/view/857

Kock, N. (2004). The psychobiological model: Toward a new theory of computer-mediated communication based on Darwinian evolution. *Organization Science, 15*(3), 327–348. doi:10.1287/orsc.1040.0071

Kock, N. (2005). Media richness or media naturalness? The evolution of our biological communication apparatus and its influence on our behavior toward e-communication tools. *IEEE Transactions on Professional Communication, 48*(2), 117–130. doi:10.1109/TPC.2005.849649

Koehler, M. J., & Mishra, P. (2008). *Handbook of technological pedagogical content knowledge (TPCK) for educators.* New York: Routledge.

Koehler, M. J., & Mishra, P. (2009). What is technological pedagogical content knowledge? *Contemporary Issues in Technology & Teacher Education, 9*(1), 11.

Koehn, D. (2003). The nature of and conditions for online trust. *Journal of Business Ethics, 43*(1/2), 3–19. doi:10.1023/A:1022950813386

Komito, L. (1998). The Net as a foraging society: Flexible Communities. *The Information Society, 14*(2), 97–106. doi:10.1080/019722498128908

Körner, C., Kern, R., Grahsl, H.-P., & Strohmaier, M. (2010). Of categorizers and describers: An evaluation of quantitative measures for tagging motivation. In *Proceedings of HT'10.* Toronto, Canada: Association of Computing Machinery.

Korzenny, F. (1978). A theory of electronic propinquity: Mediated communication in organizations. *Communication Research, 5*(1), 3–24. doi:10.1177/009365027800500101

Kozinets, R. (2009). *Netnography: Doing ethnographic research online.* London: Sage Publications Ltd.

Krasnova, H., Spiekermann, S., Koroleva, K., & Hildebrand, T. (2010). Online Social Networks: Why We Disclose. *Journal of Information Technology*, 25(2), 109–125. doi:10.1057/jit.2010.6

Krauss, R., & Fussell, S. (1990). *Mutual Knowledge and Communicative Effectiveness. In Intellectual Teamwork: The Social and Technological Bases of Cooperative Work* (pp. 114–144). Hillside, NJ: Erlbaum.

Krenz, C., & Sax, G. (1986). What Quantitative Research Is and Why It Doesn't Work. *The American Behavioral Scientist*, 30(1), 58–69. doi:10.1177/000276486030001007

Krestel, R. (2011). Recommendation on the Social Web: Diversification and personalization. In *Web Science—Investigating the future of information and communication*. Retrieved from http://detect.uni-koblenz.de/slides/detect11_pres.pdf

Krueger, R. (2000). *Focus groups: A practical guide for applied research* (3rd ed.). Thousand Oaks, CA: Sage. doi:10.1037/10518-189

Krueger, R. A., & Casey, M. A. (2009). *Focus Groups: A Practical Guide for Applied Research*. Thousand Oaks, CA: Sage.

Kunegis, J., & Preusse, J. (2012). Fairness on the web: Alternatives to the power law. In *Proceedings of WebSci 2012*. Evanston, IL: WebSci.

Ladson-Billings, G. (2009). *The dreamkeepers: Successful teachers of African American children*. San Francisco, CA: Josey-Bass.

Lagan, B., Sinclair, M., & Kernohan, G. (2011). What is the impact of the Internet on decision-making in pregnancy? A global study. *Birth Issues in Perinatal Care*, 38(4), 336–345. doi:10.1111/j.1523-536X.2011.00488.x PMID:22112334

Lai, T.-L., & Land, S. M. (2009). Supporting reflection in online learning environments. In M. Orey, et al. (Eds.), Educational Media and Technology Yearbook (pp. 141–154). DOI 9. doi:10.1007/978-0-387-09675-9

Lakeman, R. (1997). Using the Internet for data collection in nursing research. *Computers in Nursing*, 15(5), 269–275. PMID:9329228

Lamb, S. (2000). *White Saris and Sweet Mangoes*. Los Angeles, CA: University of California Press.

Langley, A. (1999). Strategies for theorizing from process data. *Academy of Management Review*, 24, 691–710.

Langley, A. (2009). Studying Processes In and Around Organizations. In D. Buchanan, & A. Bryman (Eds.), *Sage Handbook of Organisational Research Methods* (Vol. 2008, p. 776). Sage Publications.

Langley, A., & Tsoukas, H. (2010). Introducing Perspectives on Process Organization Studies. In *Process, sensemaking & organizing*. Oxford University Press. doi:10.1093/acprof:oso/9780199594566.003.0001

Lanier, J. (2013). *Who Owns the Future?* New York: Simon & Schuster.

Lapadat, J. C., & Lindsay, A. C. (1999). Transcription in research and practice: From standardization of technique to interpretive positionings. *Qualitative Inquiry*, 5(1), 64–86. doi:10.1177/107780049900500104

Lather, P. (1991). *Getting smart: Feminist research pedagogy with/in the postmodern*. New York: Routledge.

Lather, P. (1993). Fertile obsession: Validity after poststructuralism. *The Sociological Quarterly*, 34(4), 673–693. doi:10.1111/j.1533-8525.1993.tb00112.x

Lather, P. (1996). Troubling clarity: The politics of accessible language. *Harvard Educational Review*, 66(3), 525–545.

Lather, P. (2004). This IS Your Father's Paradigm: Government Intrusion and the Case of Qualitative Research in Education. *Qualitative Inquiry*, 10(1), 15–34. doi:10.1177/1077800403256154

Lather, P. (2008). (Post)Feminist methodology: Getting lost or a scientificity we can bear to learn from. *International Review of Qualitative Research*, 1(1), 55–64.

Le Rouge, C., & Niederman, F. (2006). Information Systems and Health Care Xi: Public Health Knowledge Management Architecture Design: A Case Study. *Communications of the Association for Information Systems*, 18, 2–54.

Lebow, R.N. (2009). Counterfactuals, history and fiction. *Historical Social Research / Historiche Sozialforschung, 34*(2), 57 – 73.

LeCompte, M. D., & Preissle, J. (1993). Analysis and interpretation of qualitative data. In Ethnography and qualitative research design in educational research (2nd ed., pp. 234-278). San Diego, CA: Academic Press, Inc.

Lee, C. K., & Kwon, S. (2008). A Cognitive Map-Driven Avatar Design Recommendation DSS and Its Empirical Validity. *Decision Support Systems, 45*(3), 461–472. doi:10.1016/j.dss.2007.06.008

Leech, L., & Onwuegbuzie, A. J. (2007). An Array of Qualitative Data Analysis Tools: A Call for Data Analysis Triangulation. *School Psychology Quarterly, 22*(4), 557–584. doi:10.1037/1045-3830.22.4.557

Lee, R. M., Fielding, N., & Blank, G. (2008). The Internet as a research medium: An editorial introduction to *The SAGE handbook of online research methods*. In N. Fielding, R. M. Lee, & G. Blank (Eds.), *The SAGE handbook of online research methods* (pp. 3–20). Thousand Oaks, CA: Sage. doi:10.4135/9780857020055.n1

Lee, T. (1999). *Using qualitative methods in organizational research*. Thousand Oaks, CA: Sage.

Lehdonvirta, V., Wilska, T.-A., & Johnson, M. (2009). Virtual consumerism: Case habbo hotel. *Information Communication and Society, 12*(7), 1059–1079. doi:10.1080/13691180802587813

Lei, X. R. B. W. (2002). Artificial Immune System: Principle, Models, Analysis and Perspectives. *Chinese Journal of Computers, 12*.

Leibnitz, K., Wakamiya, N., & Murata, M. (2006). Biologically inspired self-adaptive multi-path routing in overlay networks. *Communications of the ACM, 49*(3), 62–67. doi:10.1145/1118178.1118203

Lester, J. N. (2012). A discourse analysis of parents' talk around their children's autism labels. *Disability Studies Quarterly, 32*(4), Art. 1.

Lester, J. N., & Paulus, T. M. (2012). Performative acts of autism. *Discourse & Society, 12*(3), 259–273. doi:10.1177/0957926511433457

Lester, J. N., & Paulus, T. M. (2014). "That teacher takes everything badly": Discursively reframing non-normative behaviors in therapy sessions. *International Journal of Qualitative Studies in Education, 27*(5), 641-666.

Liamputtong, P. (2011). *Focus group methodology: Principles and practice*. Thousand Oaks, CA: Sage.

Liljedahl, P. (2007). Persona-based journaling: Striving for authenticity in representing the problem-solving process. *International Journal of Science and Mathematics Education, 5*(4), 661–680. doi:10.1007/s10763-007-9092-9

Lim, J. H., Stratopoulos, C., & Wirjanto, T. S. (2013). Sustainability of a Firm's Reputation for Information Technology Capability: The Role of Senior IT Executives. *Journal of Management Information Systems, 30*(1), 57–95. doi:10.2753/MIS0742-1222300102

Lim, S., Warner, S., Dixon, M., Berg, B., Kim, C., & Newhouse-Bailey, M. (2011). Sport participation across national contexts: A multilevel investigation of individual and systemic influences on adult sport participation. *European Sport Management Quarterly, 11*(3), 197–224. doi:10.1080/16184742.2011.579993

Lin, Y., Michel, J.-B., Lieberman, Aiden, E.L., Orwant, J., Brockman, W., & Petrov, S. (2012). Syntactic annotations for the Google Books Ngram Corpus. *In Proceedings of the 50th Annual Meeting of the Association for Computational Lingusitics*. Jeju, Korea: ACL.

Lin, Y-R., Sundaram, H., De Choudhury, M., & Kelliher, A. (2012). Discovering multirelational structure in social media streams. *ACM Transactions in Multimedia Computing, Communications and Applications, 8*(1), 4:1 – 4:28.

Lincoln, E. S., & Guba, E. A. (1985). *Naturalistic Enquiry* (p. 416). Beverly Hills: Sage Publications.

Lincoln, Y. S., & Guba, E. (2000). *Paradigmatic Controversies, Contradictions, and Emerging Confluences. In The Handbook of Qualitative Research* (pp. 54–76). Beverly Hills, CA: Sage.

Lincoln, Y. S., & Guba, E. G. (1985). *Naturalistic Inquiry.* Newbury Park, CA: Sage.

Lincoln, Y. S., & Guba, E. G. (2000). Paradigmatic Controversies, Contradictions, and Emerging Confluences. In N. K. Denzin, & Y. S. Lincoln (Eds.), *Handbook of Qualitative Research* (pp. 163–188). Thousand Oaks, CA: Sage Publications.

Lincoln, Y. S., Lynham, S. A., & Guba, E. G. (2011). Paradigmatic controversies, contradictions, and emerging confluences, revisited. In N. K. Denzin, & Y. S. Lincoln (Eds.), *The Sage handbook of qualitative research* (pp. 97–128). Thousand Oaks, CA.

Lindlof, T. R., & Taylor, B. C. (2002). *Qualitative communication research methods* (2nd ed.). Thousand Oaks, CA: Sage.

Linstone, H. A., & Turoff, M. (Eds.). (2002). The Delphi method - Techniques and applications. Reading, MA: Addison-Wesley.

Liu, C. (2007). Teaching Tip Web Survey Design in ASP. Net 2.0: A Simple Task with One Line of Code. *Journal of Information Systems Education, 18*(1), 11–14.

Lloyd, J. W., & Larsen, E. R. (2001). Veterinary practice management: Teaching needs as viewed by consultants and teachers. *Journal of Veterinary Medical Education, 28*(1), 16–21. doi:10.3138/jvme.28.1.16 PMID:11548770

Locke, K. (2001). *GT in Management Research.* London: Sage.

Loewenstein, G. (2005). Hot-cold empathy gaps and medical decision-making. *Health Psychology, 24*(4), 549–556. doi:10.1037/0278-6133.24.4.S49 PMID:16045419

Lonikila, M. (1995). Grounded theory as an emerging paradigm for computer-assisted qualitative data analysis. In U. Kelle (Ed.), *Computer-aided qualitative data analysis* (pp. 41–51). London: Sage.

Loomba, A. (1998/2002). *Colonialism/Postcolonialism.* London: Routledge.

Lorince, J., & Todd, P. M. (2013). Can simple social copying heuristics explain tag popularity in a collaborative tagging system? In *Proceedings of WEbSCi '13.* Paris, France: Association of Computing Machinery. doi:10.1145/2464464.2464516

Lucas, I. (2012). Phenomenological Approaches to Ethics and Information Technology. In *The Stanford Encyclopedia of Philosophy* (Summer 2011 ed.). Available at http://plato.stanford.edu/archives/sum2011/entries/ethics-it-phenomenology/

Lucas, J. C. Jr, Agarwal, R., Clemons, E. K., & El Sawy, O. A. (2013). Impactful Research on Transformational Information Technology: An Opportunity to Inform New Audiences. *Management Information Systems Quarterly, 37*(2), 371–382.

Ludlow, P., & Wallace, M. (2007). *The Second Life Herald: The virtual tabloid that witnessed the dawn of the metaverse.* Cambridge, MA: MIT Press.

Luftman, J., & Ben-Zvi, T. (2010). Key Issues for IT Executives 2010: Judicious IT Investments Continue Post-Recession. *MIS Quarterly Executive, 9*(4), 263–273.

Lund-Dean, K., Fornaciari, C., & McGee, J. (2003). Research in spirituality, religion, and work: Walking the line between relevance and legitimacy. *Journal of Organizational Change Management, 16*(4), 378–395. doi:10.1108/09534810310484145

Lusher, D. & Ackland, R. (2009). A relational hyperlink analysis of an online social movement. *Journal of Social Structure.*

Luzón, M. J. (2013). 'This is an erroneous argument': Conflict in academic blog discussions. *Discourse. Context and Media, 2*(2), 111–119. doi:10.1016/j.dcm.2013.04.005

Lyytinen, K., & Herscheim, R. (1987). *Information system failures - a survey and classification of the literature. New York.* New York, NY, USA: Oxford University Press, Inc.

Lyytinen, K., & Robey, D. (1999). Learning failure in information systems development. *Information Systems Journal, 9*(2), 85–101. doi:10.1046/j.1365-2575.1999.00051.x

MacKay, C., McKee, S., & Mulholland, A. J. (2006). Diffusion and convection of gaseous and fine particulate from a chimney. *IMA Journal of Applied Mathematics*, *71*(5), 670–691. doi:10.1093/imamat/hxl016

MacLure, M. (2007). Clarity bordering on stupidity: Where's the quality in systematic review? In B. Somekh & T. A. Schwandt (Eds.), Knowledge production: Research work in interesting times (pp. 45-70). Abdingdon, UK: Routledge.

MacMillan, K. (2005). More than just coding? Evaluating CAQDAS in a discourse analysis of news texts. *Forum Qualitative Sozial Forschung*, *6*(3), 25.

Maier, J. L., Rainer, R. K., & Snyder, C. A. (1997). Environmental Scanning for Information Technology: An Empirical Investigation. *Journal of Management IS*, *14*(2), 177–200.

Maimbo, H. (2003). *Designing a Case Study Protocol for Application in IS research* (pp. 1281–1292). PACIS.

Malhotra, A., & Majchrzak, A. (2004). Enabling Knowledge Creation in Far-flung Teams: Best Practices for IT Support and Knowledge Sharing. *Journal of Knowledge Management*, *8*(4), 75–88. doi:10.1108/13673270410548496

Manfreda, K. L., Batagelj, Z., & Vehovar, V. (2002, April). Design of Web Questionnaires: Three Basic Experiments. *Journal of Computer-Mediated Communication*, *7*, 3. Retrieved from http://jcmc.indiana.edu/vol7/issue3/vehovar.html

Mann, C., & Stewart, F. (2000). *Internet communication and qualitative research: A handbook for researching online*. London: Sage.

Manning, P. (2008). Barista rants about stupid customers at Starbucks: What imaginary conversations can teach us about real ones. *Language & Communication*, *28*(2), 101–126. doi:10.1016/j.langcom.2008.02.004

Manovich, L. (2011). What is visualization. *Visual Studies*, *26*(1), 36–49. doi:10.1080/1472586X.2011.548488

Mantymaki, M., & Salo, J. (2011). Teenagers in social virtual worlds: Continuous use and purchasing behavior in Habbo Hotel. *Computers in Human Behavior*, *27*(6), 2088–2097. doi:10.1016/j.chb.2011.06.003

Marchland, D. A., & Hykes, A. (2006, December). Designed to Fail: Why IT-enabled Business Projects Underacheive and What To Do About Them. *Tomorrows Challenges*, 1–4.

Markham, A. N., & Buchanan, E. (2012). *Ethical decision-making and internet research 2.0: Recommendations from the aoir ethics working committee*. Retrieved from http://www.aoir.org/reports/ethics2.pdf

Markham, A. N. (1998). *Life online: Researching real experience in virtual space*. Walnut Creek, CA: AltaMira.

Markus, M. L., & Robey, D. (1988). Information technology and organizational change: Causal structure in theory and research. *Management Science*, *34*(5), 583–598. doi:10.1287/mnsc.34.5.583

Marshall, C., & Rossman, G. B. (2006). *Designing qualitative research* (4th ed.). Thousand Oaks, CA: Sage Publications.

Martin, J. (2008). Consuming code: Use-value, exchange-value, and the role of virtual goods in Second Life. *Journal of Virtual Worlds Research*, *1*(2). Retrieved from http://journals.tdl.org/jvwr/index.php/jvwr/article/view/300

Martinez-Jerez, F. A. (2014). Rewriting the Playbook for Corporate Partnerships. *MIT Sloan Management Review*, *55*(2), 63–70.

Martin, P. Y., & Turner, B. A. (1986). GT and Organisational Research. *The Journal of Applied Behavioral Science*, *22*(2), 141–157. doi:10.1177/002188638602200207

Mason, J. (2002). *The Challenge of Qualitative Research*. London: Sage.

Matavire, R., & Brown, I. (2013). Profiling GT Approaches in IS Research. *European Journal of IS*, *22*, 119–129.

Mathews-Perez, A. (2013). *Speak, review, change, repeat: An analysis of discourse surrounding dilemmas At admission, review and dismissal meetings*. (Dissertation). Texas A & M University, Corpus Christi, TX.

Mathison, S. (1998). Why Triangulate ? *Educational Researcher*, *17*(2), 13–17.

Matthews, J., & Cramer, E. P. (2008). Using technology to enhance qualitative research with hidden populations. *Qualitative Report*, *13*(2), 301–315.

Max, H., & Ray, T. (2006). Skype: The definitive guide. Indianapolis, IN: Que.

May, C. (1998). The preparation and analysis of qualitative interview data. In R. B. & W. C. (Eds.), Research and development in clinical nursing practice. London: Whurr. doi:10.1002/9780470699270.ch5

Mayer-Schönberger, V., & Cukier, K. (2013). Big Data: A Revolution that will Transform How we Live, Work, and Think. Boston: Houghton Mifflin Harcourt.

Mayer-Schönberger, V., & Cukier, K. (2013). *Big Data: A Revolution that Will Transform How We Live, Work, and Think*. Boston: Houghton Mifflin Harcourt.

McBurney, D. H., & White, T. L. (2007). *Research Methods* (7th ed.). Thomson Learning.

McCalla, G. (2004). The ecological approach to the design of distance education environments: Purpose-based capture and use of information about learners. *Journal of Interactive Media in Education, 2004* (7), 1-23

McCoyd, J. L. M., & Kerson, T. S. (2006). Conducting intensive interviews using email: A serendipitous comparative opportunity. *Qualitative Social Work: Research and Practice, 5*(3), 389–406. doi:10.1177/1473325006067367

McCracken, G. (1988a). *Culture and consumption*. Bloomington, IN: Indiana University Press.

McCracken, G. (1988b). *The long interview* (Vol. 13). Newbury Park, CA: Sage. doi:10.4135/9781412986229

McDermott, R. P., Gospodinoff, K., & Aron, J. (1978). Criteria for an ethnographically adequate description of concerted activities and their contexts. *Semiotica, 24*(3/4), 245–275.

McDonagh, J. (2001). Not for the faint hearted: Social and organisational challenges in IT-enabled change. *Organization Development Journal, 19*(1), 11–20.

McDonald, M. L., & Westphal, J. D. (2003). Getting by with the Advice of their Friends: CEO's Advice Networks and Firms' Strategic Responses to Poor Performance. *Administrative Science Quarterly, 48*(1), 1–32. doi:10.2307/3556617

McFarlan, F. W. (1984). Information Technology Changes the Way you Compete. *Harvard Business Review, 62*(3), 98–103.

McIntyre, J. (2005). Part 2: Critical Systemic Praxis to Address Fixed and Fluid Identity of Politics at the Local, National and International Level. *Systemic Practice and Action Research, 18*(3), 223–259. doi:10.1007/s11213-005-4813-x

McLean, E., & Soden, J. (1977). *Strategic Planning for MIS*. New York: John Wiley & Sons.

McLellan, E., MacQueen, K. M., & Neidig, J. L. (2003). Beyond the qualitative interview: Data preparation and transcription. *Field Methods, 15*(1), 63–84. doi:10.1177/1525822X02239573

McLuhan, M. (1962). *The Gutenberg Galaxy: The Making of Typographic Man*. Toronto: University of Toronto Press.

McLuhan, M. (1964). *Understanding Media: The Extensions of Man*. New York, NY: McGraw-Hill.

Meho, L. I. (2006). E-mail interviewing in qualitative research: A methodological discussion. *Journal of the American Society for Information Science and Technology, 57*(10), 1284–1295. doi:10.1002/asi.20416

Melia, K. (1996). Rediscovering Glaser. *Qualitative Health Research, 6*(3), 368–378. doi:10.1177/104973239600600305

Merritt, A. C., Effron, D. A., & Monin, B. (2010). Moral self-licensing: When being good frees us to be bad. *Social and Personality Psychology Compass, 4/5*(5), 344–357. doi:10.1111/j.1751-9004.2010.00263.x

Merton, R. K. (1987). Three fragments from a sociologist's notebooks: Establishing the phenomenon, specified ignorance, and strategic research methods. *Annual Review of Sociology, 13*(1), 1–28. doi:10.1146/annurev.so.13.080187.000245

Meyrowitz, J. (1994). Medium Theory. In D. Crowley, & D. Mitchell (Eds.), *Communication Theory Today* (pp. 50–77). Stanford, CA: Stanford University Press.

Michaels, C. F., & Carello, C. (1981). *Direct Perception.* Englewood Cliffs, NJ: Prentice-Hall, Inc.

Michel, J.-B., Shen, Y.K., Aiden, A.P., Veres, A., Gray, M.K., Brockman, W., ... Aiden, E.L. (2010). Quantitative Analysis of Culture Using Millions of Digitized Books. *Science.*

Michelson, M., & Macskassy, S. A. (2010). *Discovering users' topics of interest on Twitter: A first look. In Proceedings of AND '10* (pp. 73–79). Toronto, Canada: Association of Computing Machinery.

Mika, P. (2007). Evaluation of web-based social network extraction. In *Mika's Social Networks and the Semantic Web.* New York: Springer Link.

Miles, M. B., & Huberman, A. M. (1984). *Qualitative Data Analysis - A Sourcebook of New Methods.* Thousand Oaks, CA: Sage Publications.

Miles, M. B., & Huberman, A. M. (1994). *An expanded Sourcebook: Qualitative Data Analysis* (2nd ed.). London: Sage.

Miles, M. B., & Huberman, A. M. (1994). *Qualitative Data Analysis.* London: Sage Publications.

Miles, M. B., Huberman, A. M., & Saldaña, J. (2014). *Qualitative Data Analysis: A Methods Sourcebook* (3rd ed.). Washington, DC: Sage.

Miles, R. E., Snow, C. C., & Pfeffer, J. (1974). Organization-Environment: Concepts and Issues. *Industrial Relations, 13*(3), 244–264. doi:10.1111/j.1468-232X.1974. tb00581.x

Miller, D., & Friesen, P. (1982). The longitudinal analysis of organizations: A methodological perspective. *Management Science, 28*(9), 1013–1034. doi:10.1287/ mnsc.28.9.1013

Miller, D., & Slater, D. (2001). *The Internet: An ethnographic approach.* Oxford, UK: Berg.

Miller, T. W., & Walkowski, J. (2004). *Qualitative research online.* Milton Keynes, UK: Research Publisher LLC.

Mills, J., Bonner, A., & Francis, K. (2006). The development of Constructivist GT. *International Journal of Qualitative Methods, 5*(1), 1–10.

Mingers, J. (1997). Multi-Paradigm Methodology. In J. Mingers, & A. Gill (Eds.), *Multimethodology: Theory and Practice of Combining Management Science Methodologies* (pp. 1–20). Chichester, UK: Wiley.

Mingers, J. (2001). Combining IS Research Methods: Towards a Pluralist Methodology. *Information Systems Research, 12*(3), 240–259. doi:10.1287/isre.12.3.240.9709

Mingers, J., Mutch, A., & Willcocks, L. (2013). Critical Realism in Information Systems Research. *Management Information Systems Quarterly, 37*(3), 795–802.

Mintzberg, H. (1973). *The Nature of Managerial Work.* New York: McGraw-Hill.

Mintzberg, H. (1979). An Emerging Strategy of Direct Research. *Administrative Science Quarterly, 24*(4), 582–589. doi:10.2307/2392364

Mitchell, M. (2009). *Complexity: A Guided Tour.* Oxford, UK: Oxford University Press.

Mitroff, I. I., & Turoff, M. (2002). Philosophical and Methodological Foundations of Delphi. In H. A. Linstone, & M. Turoff (Eds.), *The Delphi Method - Techniques and Applications.* Reading, MA: Addison-Wesley Educational Publishers Inc.

Mohr, L. (1982). *Explaining organizational behavior.* San Francisco, CA: Jossey-Bass.

Mohr, L. B. (1982). *Explaining Organisational Behavior: The Limits and Possibilities of Theory and Research.* San Francisco, CA: Jossey-Bass.

Monolescu, D., & Schifter, C. (1999). Online focus group: A tool to evaluate online students' course experience. *The Internet and Higher Education, 2*(2-3), 171–176. doi:10.1016/S1096-7516(00)00018-X

Moor, J. H. (1985). What Is Computer Ethics? *Metaphilosophy, 16*(4), 266–275. doi:10.1111/j.1467-9973.1985. tb00173.x

Morgan, D. L. (1997). *Focus Groups as Qualitative Research.* Newbury Park, CA: Sage Publications.

Morgan, D. L., & Scannell, A. U. (1998). *Planning Focus Groups.* London: Sage. doi:10.4135/9781483328171

Morse, J. M., & Niehaus, L. (2009). Mixed method design: Principles and procedures. In J. M. Morse (Ed.), Developing qualitative inquiry (Vol. 4). Walnut Creek, CA: Left Coast Press

Morse, J. M., & Niehaus, L. (2009). *Mixed Method Design: Principles and Procedures*. Walnut Creek, CA: Left Coast Press Inc..

Morton, K., Balazinska, M., Grossman, D., & Mackinlay, J. (2014). *Support the data enthusiast: Challenges for next-generation data-analysis systems*. Hangzhou, China: Very Large Data Bases.

Morton, K., Balazinska, M., Grossman, D., Kosara, R., Mackinlay, J., & Halevy, A. (2012). *A measurement study of two web-based collaborative visual analytics systems* (Technical Report UW-CSE-12-08-01). Univ. of Washington. Retrieved Mar. 10, 2014, at ftp://ftp.cs.washington.edu/tr/2012/08/UW-CSE-12-08-01.PDF

Muhr, T. (2004). User's manual for ATLAS.ti 5.0. Berlin: ATLAS.ti Scientific Software Development GmbH.

Murray, P. J. (1997). Using focus groups in qualitative research. *Qualitative Health Research, 7*(4), 542–549. doi:10.1177/104973239700700408

Murthy, D. (2008). Digital ethnography: An examination of the use of new technologies for social research. *Sociology, 42*(5), 837–855. doi:10.1177/0038038508094565

Myers, M., & Liu, F. (2009). *What Does The Best IS Research Look Like? An Analysis Of The AIS Basket Of Top Journals*. Paper presented at the Pacific Asia Conference on Information Systems (PACIS). Tokyo, Japan.

Myers, M., & Avison, D. (2002). *Qualitative Research Information System*. London: SAGE.

Nagpal, R. (2002, July). Programmable self-assembly using biologically-inspired multiagent control. In *Proceedings of the First International Joint Conference on Autonomous Agents and Multiagent Systems: Part 1* (pp. 418-425). ACM. doi:10.1145/544838.544839

Nasr, M., & Ouf, S. (2011). An Ecosystem in distance education Using Cloud Computing as platform and Web2.0. *The Research Bulletin of Jordan ACM, II*(1), 134–140.

NCH Software. (2014). *NCH Software*. Retrieved April 2014, 2014, from http://www.nch.com.au/scribe/

NDTV. (n.d.). *Japan: Earthquake triggers oil refinery fire*. Retrieved from http://www.ndtv.com

Nehls, K. (2013). Methodological considerations of email interviews. In Advancing Research Methods with New Media Technologies (pp. 303-315). New York: IGI-Global Publishing.

Nelson, R. R. (2007). IT project management: Infamous failures, classic mistakes, and best practices. *MIS Quarterly Executive, 6*(2).

Neuman, W. L. (2000). *Social research methods: Qualitative and quantitative approaches*. Boston: Allyn and Bacon.

Newell, R., & Burnard, P. (2006). *Research for Evidence-Based Practice in Healthcare*. Oxford, UK: Wiley-Blackwell.

Newman, M., & Robey, D. (1992). A Social Process Model of User-Analyst Relationships. *Management Information Systems Quarterly, 16*(2), 249–267. doi:10.2307/249578

NFC Forum. (2014). *What Is NFC?*. Retrieved from http://nfc-forum.org/what-is-nfc/

Nicholas, D. B., Lach, L., King, G., & Scott, M. et al. (2010). Contrasting Internet and face-to-face focus groups for children with chronic health conditions: Outcomes and participant experiences. *International Journal of Qualitative Methods, 9*(1), 105–121.

Nielsen, J. (2009). *Discount Usability: 20 Years*. Retrieved from http://www.nngroup.com/articles/discount-usability-20-years/

Nielsen, M. (2012). *Reinventing Discovery: The New Era of Networked Science*. Princeton, NJ: Princeton University Press.

Nissenbaum, H. (2001). Securing Trust Online: Wisdom or Oxymoron? *Boston University Law Review, 81*(3), 635–664.

Noble, G. I. (2002). *Managing Synergetic Momentum: A GT of the Management of Public-Private Partnerships*. University of Wollongong.

Northcote, M. T. (2012). Selecting Criteria to Evaluate Qualitative Research. In *Education Papers and Journal Articles,* 99-110. Retrieved from http://research.avondale.edu.au/edu_papers/38

O'Connor, M. K., Netting, F. E., & Thomas, M. L. (2008). Grounded Theory: Managing the Challenge for Those Facing Institutional Review Board Oversight. *Qualitative Inquiry, 14*(1), 28–45. doi:10.1177/1077800407308907

O'Grady, L., Wathen, C. N., Charnaw-Burger, J., Betel, L., Shachak, A., & Luke, R. et al. (2012). The use of tags and tag clouds to discern credible content in online health message forums. *International Journal of Medical Informatics, 81*(1), 36–44. doi:10.1016/j.ijmedinf.2011.10.001

O'hEocha, C., Wang, X., & Conboy, K.O'hEocha C. (2012). The Use of Focus Groups in Complex and Pressurised IS Studies and Evaluation Using Klein & Myers Principles for Interpretive Research. *Information Systems Journal, 22*(3), 235–256. doi:10.1111/j.1365-2575.2011.00387.x

O'Malley, M. (2010, Dec. 21). Ngramattic. *The Aporetic.*

O'Reilly, M. (2004). *"Disabling essentialism" accountability in family therapy: Issues of disability, complaints and child abuse.* (Unpublished doctoral dissertation). Loughborough University.

O'Brien, J. (1999). Writing in the body: Gender (re)production in online interaction. In M. Smith, & P. Kollock (Eds.), *Communities in cyberspace* (pp. 76–106). New York: Routledge.

Ochs, E. (1979). Transcription as theory. In E. Ochs, & B. Schieffelin (Eds.), *Developmental pragmatics* (pp. 43–72). New York: Academic Press.

O'Connor, H., Madge, C., Shaw, R., & Wellens, J. (2008). Internet-based interviewing. In N. G. Fielding, & R. M. Lee (Eds.), *Sage handbook of online research methods* (pp. 271–289). Los Angeles, CA: Sage. doi:10.4135/9780857020055.n15

Odum, E. P., & Barrett, G. W. (2005). *Fundamentals of Ecology.* Thomson Brooks.

Oh, J. (2013). *Literature review—Graphical tools.* Retrieved Mar. 10, 2014, at https://www.stat.auckland.ac.nz/~joh024/LitReviews/LitReview_GraphicalTools.pdf

Oringderff, J. (2004). "My Way": Piloting an online focus group. *International Journal of Qualitative Methods, 3*(3). Article 5. Retrieved December 28, 2013 from http://www.ualberta.ca/~iiqm/backissues/3_3/html/oringderff.html

Orlikowski, W. J. (1993). CASE Tools as Organizational Change: Investigating Incremental and Radical changes in Systems Development. *Management Information Systems Quarterly, 17*(3), 309–340. doi:10.2307/249774

Orlikowski, W. J. (2000). Using technology and constituting structures: A practice lens for studying technology in organizations. *Organization Science, 11*(4), 404–428. doi:10.1287/orsc.11.4.404.14600

Orlikowski, W. J., & Robey, D. (1991). Information Technology and the Structuring of Organizations. *Information Systems Research, 2*(2), 143–169. doi:10.1287/isre.2.2.143

Ormiston, M. E., & Wong, E. M. (2013). License to ill: The effects of corporate social responsibility and CEO moral identity on corporate social irresponsibility. *Personnel Psychology, 66*(4), 861–898. doi:10.1111/peps.12029

Otondo, R. F., Pearson, A. W., Pearson, R. A., Shaw, J. C., & Shim, J. P. (2009). Managerial Problem-Solving in the Adoption of Radio Frequency Identification Technologies. *European Journal of Information Systems, 18*(6), 553–569. doi:10.1057/ejis.2009.39

Özdenizci, B., Aydin, M., Coşkun, V., & Ok, K. (2010) NFC Research Framework: A Literature Review and Future Research Directions. In *Proceedings of 14th IBIMA Conference.* IBIMA.

Padgett, D. (2008). *Qualitative methods in social work research.* Los Angeles, CA: Sage Publications.

Paltoglou, G. & Thelwall, M. (2012). Twitter, MySpace, Digg: Unsupervised sentiment analysis in social media. *ACM Transactions on Intelligent Systems and Technology, 3*(4), 66:1–66:19. DOI: .10.1145/2337542.2337551

Palys, T., & Atchison, C. (2012). Qualitative research in the digital era: Obstacles and opportunities. *International Journal of Qualitative Methods*, *11*(4), 352–367.

Pandit, N. (1996). The Creation of Theory: A Recent Application of the GTM. *Qualitative Report*, *2*(4).

Pan, G., Hackney, R., & Pan, S. L. (2008). Information Systems implementation failure: Insights from prism. *International Journal of Information Management*, *28*(4), 259–269. doi:10.1016/j.ijinfomgt.2007.07.001

Pan, S. L., & Tan, B. (2011). Demystifying case research: A structured–pragmatic–situational (SPS) approach to conducting case studies. *Information and Organization*, *21*(3), 161–176. doi:10.1016/j.infoandorg.2011.07.001

Pare, G. (2004). Investigating information systems with positivist case study research. *Communications of the Association for Information Systems*, *13*(1), 233–264.

Pariser, E. (2011). *The Filter Bubble: What the Internet is Hiding from You*. New York: The Penguin Press.

Park, H. W. (2003). Hyperlink network analysis: A new method for the study of social structure on the Web. *Connections*, *25*(1), 49–61.

Parry, M. (2014). How the humanities compute in the classroom. *The Chronicle of Higher Education*. Retrieved from http://chronicle.com/article/How-the-Humanities-Compute-in/143809/?cid=wc&utm_source=wc&utm_medium=en

Parry, K. W. (1998). Grounded theory and social process: A new direction for leadership research. *The Leadership Quarterly*, *9*(1), 85–105. doi:10.1016/S1048-9843(98)90043-1

Parry, R. (2010). Video-based Conversation Analysis. In I. Bourgeault, R. Dingwall, & R. d. Vries (Eds.), *The SAGE Handbook of Qualitative Methods in Health Research* (pp. 373–396). London: Sage. doi:10.4135/9781446268247.n20

Pasquill, F. (1961). The Estimation of the Dispersion of Windborne Material. *The Meteorological Magazine*, *90*(1063), 33–49.

Pasquill, F. (1974). *Atmospheric Diffusion* (2nd ed.). New York, NY: Halsted Press, John Wiley & Sons.

Pata, K. (2012). *Modeling open education learning ecosystem*. Retrieved August 13, 2013, from http://tihane.wordpress.com/2012/05/08/modelling-digital-learning-ecosystem/

Patterson, D. W. (1998). *Artificial neural networks: theory and applications*. Prentice Hall PTR.

Patton. (2002). *Qualitative research and evaluation methods* (3rd ed.). Newbury Park, CA: Sage.

Paulus, T. & Lester, J. (September 2013). *Using ATLAS. ti for a conversation/discourse analysis study of blogging in an educational context*. Paper presented at ATLAS.ti User Conference 2013: Fostering Dialog on Qualitative Methods. Berlin, Germany.

Paulus, T. M., Lester, J. N., & Britt, G. (2013). Constructing "false hopes and fears": A discourse analysis of introductory qualitative research texts. *Qualitative Inquiry*, *19*(9), 637–649. doi:10.1177/1077800413500929

Paulus, T., Lester, J. N., & Dempster, P. (2014). *Digital tools for qualitative research*. London, UK: SAGE.

Pawlowski, S., & Robey, D. (2004). Bridging User Organisations: Knowledge Brokering and the Work of Information Technology Professionals. *Management Information Systems Quarterly*, *28*(4), 645–672.

Peacock, S., Robertson, A., Williams, S., & Clausen, M. (2009). The role of learning technologists in supporting e-research. *ALT-J*, *17*(2), 115–129. doi:10.1080/09687760903033041

Pentland, A. (2014). *Social Physics: How Good Ideas Spread—The Lessons from a New Science*. New York: The Penguin Press.

Pentland, B. (1999). Building process theory with narrative: From description to explanation. *Academy of Management Review*, *24*, 711–724.

Pentland, B. T., & Feldman, M. S. (2007). Narrative Networks: Patterns of Technology and Organization. *Organization Science*, *18*(5), 781–882. doi:10.1287/orsc.1070.0283

Pepper, S. C. (1942). *World Hypothesis*. Berkeley, CA: University of California Press.

Percival, R. V. (2011). China's Green Leap Forward. *Vermont Journal of Environmental Law, 12*, 633 – 657. Retrieved Mar. 17, 2014, at http://digitalcommons.law.umaryland.edu/cgi/viewcontent.cgi?article=2144&context=fac_pubs

Perfilieva, I., & Močkoř, J. (1999). *Mathematical principles of fuzzy logic*. Springer.

Peshkin, A. (1988). In search of subjectivity- One's own. *Educational Researcher, 17*(7), 17–22.

Peters, M. (1998). *Naming the multiple: Poststructuralism and education*. Westport, CT: Bergin & Garvey.

Peterson, M. F. (1998). Embedded organizational events: The units of process in organizational science. *Organization Science, 9*(1), 16–33. doi:10.1287/orsc.9.1.16

Petter, S., DeLone, W., & McLean, E. R. (2013). Information Systems Success: The Quest for the Independent Variables. *Journal of Management Information Systems, 29*(4), 7–61. doi:10.2753/MIS0742-1222290401

Pettigrew, A. M., & Webb, D. (1996). *Espoused business strategy and structure changes in the U.K. and German insurance industries* Paper presented at the Paper presented to the All Academy Symposium on the evolution of New Organisation Forms for the Information Age. Cincinnati, OH.

Pettigrew, A. M. (1973). *The Politics of Organizational Decision Making*. London, Assen: Tavistock/Van Gorcum.

Pettigrew, A. M. (1979). On studying organizational cultures. *Administrative Science Quarterly, 24*(4), 570–581. doi:10.2307/2392363

Pettigrew, A. M. (1985). Context and action in the transformation of the firm. *Journal of Management Studies, 24*(6), 649–670. doi:10.1111/j.1467-6486.1987.tb00467.x

Pettigrew, A. M. (1990). Longitudinal field research on change: Theory and practice. *Organization Science, 1*(3), 267–292. doi:10.1287/orsc.1.3.267

Pettigrew, A. M. (1992). The character and significance of strategy process research. *Strategic Management Journal, 13*(S2), 5–16. doi:10.1002/smj.4250130903

Pettigrew, A. M. (1997). What is a Processual Analysis? *Scandinavian Journal of Management, 13*(4), 337–348. doi:10.1016/S0956-5221(97)00020-1

Pettigrew, A. M. (2012). JMS Context and Action in the Transformation of the Firm. *Journal of Management Studies, 49*(7), 1304–1328. doi:10.1111/j.1467-6486.2012.01054.x

Pettigrew, A. M., Ferlie, E., & McKee, L. (1992). *Shaping Strategic Change: Making Change in Large Organizations, the Case of the NHS*. London: Sage.

Pettigrew, A. M., & McNulty, T. (1995). Power and Influence in and around the Boardroom. *Human Relations, 48*(8), 845–873. doi:10.1177/001872679504800802

Pettigrew, A. M., & Whipp, R. (1991). *Managing Change for Competitive Success*. Oxford, UK: Basil Blackwell.

Pettigrew, A. M., & Whipp, R. (1993). Managing the twin processes of competition and change: The role of intangible assets. In P. L. Lorange, B. Chakravarthy, J. Roos, & A. Van de Ven (Eds.), *Implementing strategic processes: Change, Learning, and Co-operation* (pp. 3–42). Cambridge, MA: Blackwell Business.

Peytchev, A., Couper, M. P., McCabe, S. E., & Crawford, S. D. (2006). Web Survey Design. *Public Opinion Quarterly, 70*(4), 596–607. doi:10.1093/poq/nfl028

Peytchev, A., & Crawford, S. D. (2005). A Typology of Real-Time Validations in Web-Based Surveys. *Social Science Computer Review, 23*(2), 235–249. doi:10.1177/0894439304273272

Philipsen, G. (1975). Speaking 'like a man' in Teamsterville: Culture patterns of role enactment in an urban neighborhood. *The Quarterly Journal of Speech, 61*(1), 13–23. doi:10.1080/00335637509383264

Philipsen, G. (1992). *Speaking culturally: Explorations in social communication*. Albany, NY: State University of New York Press.

Philipsen, G. (1997). A theory of speech codes. In G. Philipsen, & T. L. Albrecht (Eds.), *Developing communication theories* (pp. 119–156). New York, NY: State University of New York Press.

Philipsen, G., & Coutu, L. M. (2005). The ethnography of speaking. In K. L. Fitch, & R. E. Sanders (Eds.), *Handbook of language and social interaction* (pp. 355–379). Mahwah, NJ: Lawrence Erlbaum Associates.

Philipsen, G., Coutu, L. M., & Covarrubias, P. (2005). Speech codes theory: Restatement, revisions, and response to criticisms. In W. Gudykunst (Ed.), *Theorizing about intercultural communication* (pp. 55–68). Thousand Oaks, CA: Sage.

Pierce, C. S. (1955). Philosophical writings of Pierce. In J. Buchler (Ed.). *New York*: Dover.

Pierre, E. A. S. (2013). *Post Qualitative Research: The Critique and the Coming After.* Paper presented at the Ninth International Congress of Qualitative Inquiry. Champaign/Urbana, IL.

Pierre, E. A. S. (2013). The appearance of data. *Cultural Studies, Critical Methodologies, 13*(4), 223-227.

Pierre, E. A. S., & Jackson, A. (in press). Introduction: Qualitative data analysis after coding. *Qualitative Inquiry.*

Pittenger, A. L., Starner, C., Thompson, K., & Gleason, P. B. (2010). Pharmacy students' views of managed care pharmacy and PBMs: Should there be more exposure to managed care in the pharmacy curriculum? *Journal of Managed Care Pharmacy, 16*(5), 346–354. PMID:20518587

Plano-Clark, V. L., & Creswell, J. W. (Eds.). (2008). *The Mixed Methods Reader* (Vol. 1). Thousand Oaks, CA: Sage Publications.

Ployhart, R. E., & Vandenberg, R. J. (2010). Longitudinal Research: The Theory, Design, and Analysis of Change. *Journal of Management, 36*(1), 94–121. doi:10.1177/0149206309352110

Polaris interactive database visualization. (n.d.). *Stanford University.* Retrieved April 3, 2014, at http://graphics.stanford.edu/projects/polaris/

Poli, R., Kennedy, J., & Blackwell, T. (2007). Particle swarm optimization. *Swarm Intelligence, 1*(1), 33–57. doi:10.1007/s11721-007-0002-0

Pollack, K. M. (2013). *Unthinkable: Iran, the Bomb, and American Strategy.* New York: Simon & Schuster.

Polson, E. (2013). A gateway to the global city: Mobile place-making practices by expats. *New Media & Society.* doi:10.1177/1461444813510135

Pomfret, M. P., & Medford, J. L. (2007). Affective domain: Journaling. In R.J. Seidel, K.C. Perencevich, & A.L. Kett (Eds.), *From Principles of Learning to Strategies for Instruction with Workbook.* Springer. Retrieved Aug. 7, 2013, at http://link.springer.com/content/pdf/10.1007%2F978-0-387-71086-0_12.pdf

Poole, M. S., Van de Ven, A. H., Dooley, K., & Holmes, M. E. (2000). *Organizational change and innovation processes: Theory and methods for research.* New York: Oxford University Press.

Popescu, A., & Grefenstette, G. (2010). Image tagging and search—A gender oriented study. In Proceedings of WSM '10. Firenze, Italy: WSM.

Popkewitz, T. S. (2004). Is the National Research Council Committee's Report on Scientific Research in Education Scientific? On Trusting the Manifesto. *Qualitative Inquiry, 10*(1), 62–78. doi:10.1177/1077800403259493

Porter, S. R. & M. E. Whitcomb. (2005). E-Mail Subject Lines and Their Effect on Web Survey Viewing and Response. *Social Science Computer Review, 23*(3), 380-387.

Porter, M. E., & Millar, V. E. (1985). How Information gives you Competitive Advantage. *Harvard Business Review, 63*(4), 149–160.

Potter, J., & Hepburn, A. (2008). Discursive constructionism. In J. A. Holstein & J. F. Gubrium (Eds.), Handbook of constructionist research (pp. 275-293). New York: Guildford.

Potter, J. (2004). Discourse analysis. In M. A. Hardy, & A. Bryman (Eds.), *Handbook of Data Analysis* (pp. 607–624). London: Sage. doi:10.4135/9781848608184.n27

Potter, J., & Wetherell, M. (1987). *Discourse and social psychology.* London: Sage.

Powell, R. A., & Single, H. M. (1996). Focus groups. *International Journal for Quality in Health Care, 8*(5), 499–504. doi:10.1093/intqhc/8.5.499 PMID:9117204

Pozzebon, M. (2004). The influence of a structurationist view on strategic management research. *Journal of Management Studies, 41*(2), 247–272. doi:10.1111/j.1467-6486.2004.00431.x

Pratt, M. G. (2008). Fitting Oval Pegs Into Round Holes: Tensions in Evaluating and Publishing Qualitative Rearearch in Top-Tier North American Journals. *Organizational Research Methods, 11*(3), 481–509. doi:10.1177/1094428107303349

Pratt, M., & Rafaeli, A. (1997). Organizational Dress as a Symbol of Multilayered Social Identities. *Academy of Management Journal, 40*(4), 862–898. doi:10.2307/256951

Prensky, M. (2007). *How to teach with technology: Keeping both teachers and students comfortable in an era of exponential change. In Emerging technologies for learning* (Vol. 2, pp. 40–46). Covington, UK: Becta.

Preston, D. S., Chen, D., & Leidner, D. E. (2008). Examining the Antecedents and Consequences of CIO Strategic Decision-Making Authority: An Empirical Study. *Decision Sciences, 39*(4), 605–638. doi:10.1111/j.1540-5915.2008.00206.x

Preston, D. S., Karahanna, E., & Rowe, F. (2006). Development of Shared Understanding between the Chief Information Officer and Top Management Team in US and French Organizations: A Cross-Cultural Comparison. *IEEE Transactions on Engineering Management, 53*(2), 191–206. doi:10.1109/TEM.2006.872244

Prus, R. (1996). *Symbolic interactionism and ethnographic research.* Albany, NY: State University of New York Press.

Puchta, C., & Potter, J. (2004). *Focus Group Practice.* London: Sage.

Qiu, L., Lin, H., Ramsay, J., & Yang, F. (2012). You are what you tweet: Personality expression and perception on Twitter. *Journal of Research in Personality, 46*(6), 710–718. doi:10.1016/j.jrp.2012.08.008

Qualtrics. (2013). *Qualtrics Website.* Retrieved 23rd November 2013, from http://qualtrics.com

Radeke, F. (2010). How To Rigorously Develop Process Theory Using Case Research. In Proceedings of ECIS 2010 (pp. 1–12). ECIS.

Ramiller, N. C., & Pentland, B. T. (2009). Management Implications in Information Systems Research: The Untold Story. *Journal of the Association for Information Systems, 10*(6), 474–494.

Rapley, T. (2007). *Doing conversation, discourse and document analysis.* London: Sage.

Razikin, K., Goh, D. H-L., Chua, A.Y.K., & Lee, C.S. (2008). Can social tags help you find what you want? In *Proceedings of ECDL 2008* (LNCS) (pp. 50 – 61). Berlin: Springer.

Reave, L. (2005). Spiritual Values and Practices Related to Leadership Effectiveness. *The Leadership Quarterly, 16*(5), 655–687. doi:10.1016/j.leaqua.2005.07.003

Reichardt, C. S., & Rallis, S. F. (1994). Qualitative and Quantitative Inquiries are not Incompatible: A Call for a New Partnership. In C. S. Reichardt, & S. F. Rallis (Eds.), *The Qualitative-Quantitative Debate: New Perspectives* (pp. 85–92). San Francisco, CA: Jossey-Bass. doi:10.1002/ev.1670

Reich, B. H., & Benbasat, I. (1996). Measuring the Linkage Between Business and Information Technology Objectives. *Management Information Systems Quarterly, 20*(1), 55–81. doi:10.2307/249542

Reich, B. H., & Benbasat, I. (2000). Factors that Influence the Social Dimension of Alignment between Business and Information Technology Objectives. *Management Information Systems Quarterly, 24*(1), 81–113. doi:10.2307/3250980

Reich, B. H., & Kaarst-Brown, M. L. (2003). Creating Social and Intellectual Capital through IT Career Transitions. *The Journal of Strategic Information Systems, 12*(2), 91–109. doi:10.1016/S0963-8687(03)00017-9

Reid, D. J., & Reid, F. J. M. (2005). Online focus groups: An in-depth comparison of computer-mediated and conventional focus group discussions. *International Journal of Market Research, 47*(2), 131–162.

Reinharz, S. (1992). *Feminist methods in social research.* New York, NY: Oxford University Press.

Rescher, N. (1996). *Process metaphysics: An introduction to process philosophy*. Albany, NY: SUNY Press.

Reyna, J. (2011). Digital Teaching and Learning Ecosystem (DTLE): A Theoretical Approach for Online Learning Environments. In *Proceedings ASCILITE 2011*. Hobart, Australia: Concise Paper. Retrieved August 13, 2013, from http://www.ascilite.org.au/conferences/hobart11/downloads/papers/Reyna-concise.pdf

Reynolds, R. G., & Sverdlik, W. (1994, June). Problem solving using cultural algorithms. In *Proceedings of Evolutionary Computation*, (pp. 645-650). IEEE.

Reynolds, R. G. (1994, February). An introduction to cultural algorithms. In *Proceedings of the third annual conference on evolutionary programming* (pp. 131-139). World Scientific.

Rheingold, H. (1993). *The virtual community: Homesteading on the electronic frontier*. Reading, MA: Addison-Wesley.

Richards, L., & Morse, J. M. (2007). *Read me first for a user's guide to qualitative methods* (2nd ed.). Thousand Oaks, CA: Sage Publications Inc.

Richardson, A. (2002). *Ecology of Learning and the Role of Distance education in the Learning Environment*. Sun Microsystems Global Summit.

Richards, T. J., & Richards, L. (1994). *Using Computers in Qualitative Research. In Handbook of Qualitative Research*. Thousand Oaks, CA: Sage Publications.

Ridenour, C. S., & Newman, I. (2008). *Mixed Methods Research: Exploring the Interactive Continuum*. Carbondale, IL: Southern Illinois University Press.

Riesch, H., Oltra, C., Lis, A., Upham, P., & Pol, M. (2013). Internet-based public debate of CCS: Lessons from online focus groups in Poland and Spain. *Energy Policy*, *56*, 693–702. doi:10.1016/j.enpol.2013.01.029

Rieser, C. J. (2004). *Biologically inspired cognitive radio engine model utilizing distributed genetic algorithms for secure and robust wireless communications and networking*. (Doctoral dissertation). Virginia Polytechnic Institute and State University, Blacksburg, VA.

Rimmon-Kenan, S. (1983). *Narrative fiction: Contemporary poetics*. London: Routledge. doi:10.4324/9780203426111

Ritson, M., & Elliott, R. (1999). The social uses of advertising: An ethnographic study of adolescent advertising audiences. *The Journal of Consumer Research*, *26*(3), 260–277. doi:10.1086/209562

Roberts, J. (2000). From Know-How to Show-How? Questionioning the Role of Information and Communication Technologies in Knowledge Transfer. *Technology Analysis and Strategic Management*, *12*(4), 429–443. doi:10.1080/713698499

Roberts, K. A., & Wilson, R. W. (2002). ICT and the research process: Issues around the compatibility of technology with qualitative data analysis. *Forum Qualitative Sozialforschung/Forum: Qualitative, Social Research*, *3*(2), 15.

Robu, V., Halpin, H., & Shepherd, H. (2009). Emergence of consensus and shared vocabularies in collaborative tagging systems. *ACM Transactions on the Web*, *2*(4), 14:1 – 14:34.

Rodrigues, E. M., & Milic-Frayling, N. (2011). Flickr: Linking people, photos, and tags. In *Analyzing Social Media Networks with NodeXL: Insights from a Connected World*. Burlington, MA: Elsevier. doi:10.1016/B978-0-12-382229-1.00013-8

Roivainen, E. (2014). Changes in word usage frequency may hamper intergenerational comparisons of vocabulary skills: An ngram analysis of Wordsum, WAIS, and WISC test items. *Journal of Psychoeducational Assessment*, *32*(1), 83–87. doi:10.1177/0734282913485542

Romm, N. R. A. (2006). The Social Significance of Churchman's Epistemological Position. In J. P. Van Gigch, & J. McIntyre-Mills (Eds.), *Resucing the Enlightnment from Itself Critical and Systemic Implications for Democracy* (pp. 68–92). Springer. doi:10.1007/0-387-27589-4_6

Rose, G. (2007). *Visual methodologies: An introduction to the interpretation of visual materials* (2nd ed.). Thousand Oaks, CA: Sage Publications.

Ross, D. (1949). *Aristotle*. London: Methuen.

Rossi, P. H. (1994). The War between the Quals and the Quants: Is a Lasting Peace Possible? In C. S. Reichardt, & S. F. Rallis (Eds.), *The Qualitative-Quantitative Debate: New Perspectives* (pp. 23–36). San Francisco, CA: Jossey-Bass. doi:10.1002/ev.1665

Rotman, D., & Golbeck, J. (2011). YouTube: Contrasting patterns of content, interaction, and prominence. In *Analyzing Social Media Networks with NodeXL: Insights from a Connected World*. Burlington, MA: Elsevier. doi:10.1016/B978-0-12-382229-1.00014-X

Roveri, N., Falini, G., Sidoti, M. C., Tampieri, A., Landi, E., Sandri, M., & Parma, B. (2003). Biologically inspired growth of hydroxyapatite nanocrystals inside self-assembled collagen fibers. *Materials Science and Engineering C, 23*(3), 441–446. doi:10.1016/S0928-4931(02)00318-1

Rowe, M. P., Pugh, E. N. Jr, Tyo, J. S., & Engheta, N. (1995). Polarization-difference imaging: A biologically inspired technique for observation through scattering media. *Optics Letters, 20*(6), 608–610. doi:10.1364/OL.20.000608 PMID:19859271

Rowlands, B. H. (2005). Grounded in Practice: Using Interpretive Research to Build Theory. *Journal of Business Research Methodology, 3*(1), 81–92.

Roy, A. & P. D Berger. (2005). E-Mail and Mixed Mode Database Surveys Revisited: Exploratory Analyses of Factors Affecting Response Rates. *Journal of Database Marketing and Customer Strategy Management, 12*(2), 153-171.

Ruch, P., Geissbuhler, A., Gobeill, J., Lisacek, F., Tbahriti, I., Veuthey, A. L., & Aronson, A. R. (2007). Using discourse analysis to improve text categorization in MEDLINE. *Studies in Health Technology and Informatics, 129*(Pt 1), 710–715. PMID:17911809

Runeson, P., & Höst, M. (2009). Guidelines for Conducting and Reporting Case Study Research in Software Engineering. *Empirical Software Engineering, 14*(2), 131–164. doi:10.1007/s10664-008-9102-8

Sacks, H. (1984). Everyday activities as sociological phenomena. In J. M. Atkinson, & J. Heritage (Eds.), *Structures of social action: Studies in conversation analysis* (pp. 411–429). Cambridge, UK: Cambridge University Press.

Sacks, H. (1992). *Lectures on Conversation*. Oxford, UK: Blackwell.

Saldaña, J. (2014). Blue-collar qualitative research: A rant. *Qualitative Inquiry*. doi:10.1177/1077800413513739

Saldaña, J. (2003). Dramatizing data: A primer. *Qualitative Inquiry, 9*(2), 218–236. doi:10.1177/1077800402250932

Saldaña, J. (2009/2013). *The Coding Manual for Qualitative Researchers* (2nd ed.). Thousand Oaks, CA: Sage.

Saldaña, J. (Ed.). (2005). *Ethnodrama: An anthology of reality theatre* (Vol. 5). Walnut Creek, CA: AltaMira Press.

Salmons, J. (2010). *Online interviews in real time*. Thousand Oaks, CA: Sage.

Salmons, J. (2011). *Cases in online interview research*. Thousand Oaks, CA: Sage.

Sambamurthy, V., Bharadwaj, A., & Grover, V. (2003). Shaping Agility through Digital Options: Reconceptualizing the Role of Information Technology in Contemporary Firms. *Management Information Systems Quarterly, 27*(2), 237–263.

Sandler, R. (2012). *Nanotechnology: The Social and Ethical Issues*. Woodrow Wilson International Center for Scholars. Available at http://www.nanotechproject.org/process/assets/files/7060/nano_pen16_final.pdf

Sandstrom, K., Martin, D. D., & Fine, G. A. (2006). *Symbols, selves and social reality*. Los Angeles, CA: Roxbury Publishing Company.

Sarangi, S. (2010). Practicing Discourse Analysis in Healthcare Settings. In I. Bourgeault, R. Dingwall, & R. d. Vries (Eds.), *The SAGE Handbook of Qualitative Methods in Health Research* (pp. 397–416). London: Sage. doi:10.4135/9781446268247.n21

Sarantakos, S. (2005). *Social Research*. London: Palgrave Macmillan.

Sarle, W. S. (1994). *Neural networks and statistical models*. Academic Press.

Sauer, C. (1993). In D. E. Avison, & G. Fitzgerald (Eds.), *Why Information systems fail: A Case Study Approach* (p. 359). Henley-on-Thames: Alfred Waller Ltd.

Sauer, C. (1999). Deciding the future for IS failures: not the choice you might think. In *Re-thinking Management Information Systems* (pp. 279–309). Oxford: Oxford University Press.

Saunders, M., Lewis, P., & Thornhill, A. (2003). *Research Methods for Business Students*. London: Prentice Hall.

Saville-Troike, M. (1982). *The ethnography of communication: An introduction*. Baltimore, MD: University Park Press.

Sawant, N., Datta, R., Li, J., & Wang, J. Z. (2010). *Quest for relevant tags using local interaction networks and visual content. In Proceedings of MIR '10*. Philadelphia, PA: Association of Computing Machinery.

Saxenian, A. (1996). Regional advantage: Culture and competition in silicon valley and route 128. Cambridge, MA: Harvard University Press.

Schau, H. J., & Gilly, M. C. (2003). We are what we post? Self-presentation in personal web space. *The Journal of Consumer Research, 30*(3), 385–404. doi:10.1086/378616

Scheele, D. S. (2002). Reality Construction as a Product of Delphi Interaction. In H. A. Linstone, & M. Turoff (Eds.), *The Delphi Method - Techniques and Applications*. Reading, MA: Addison-Wesley Educational Publishers Inc.

Schifanella, R., Barrat, A., Cattuto, C., Markines, B., & Menczer, F. (2010). Folks in folksonomies: social link prediction from shared metadata. In *Proceedings of the third ACM International Conference on Web Search and Data Mining*, (pp. 271–280). ACM. doi:10.1145/1718487.1718521

Schmidt, R. C., Lyytinen, K., Keil, M., & Cule, P. (2001). Identifying software project risks: An international Delphi Study. *Journal of Management Information Systems, 17*(4), 5–36.

Schmitz Weiss, A., & de Macedo Higgins Joyce, V. (2009). Compressed dimensions in digital media occupations: Journalists in transformation. *Journalism, 10*(5), 587–603. doi:10.1177/1464884909106534

Schneider, S. J., Kerwin, J., Frechtling, J., & Vivari, B. (2002). Characteristics of the discussion in the online and face-to-face focus groups. *Social Science Computer Review, 20*(1), 31–42. doi:10.1177/089443930202000104

Schofield, J. W. (2002). Increasing the Generalisability of Qualitative Research. In A. M. Huberman, & M. B. Miles (Eds.), *The qualitative researcher's companion*. Thousand Oaks, CA: Sage Publications.

Schwandt, T. A. (2007). *The sage dictionary of qualitative inquiry* (3rd ed.). Los Angeles, CA: SAGE Publications.

Schwartz, T. (2014, Jan. 17). In praise of depth. *The New York Times.*

Scott-Morton, M. S. (1991). *The Corporation of the 1990s: Informational technology and organizational transformation*. New York: Oxford Press.

Seale, C. (2000). Using computers to analyse qualitative data. In D. Silverman (Ed.), *Doing qualitative research: A practical handbook* (pp. 154–174). London, UK: Sage.

Secrist, C., Lise de Koeyer, H. B., & Fogel, A. (2002). Combining digital video technology and narrative methods for understanding infant development. *Forum: Qualitative Social Research*. Retrieved March, 2014 from http://www.qualitative-research.net/index.php/fqs/article/view/863/1874

Sedgwick, M., & Spiers, J. (2009). The use of video-conferencing as a medium for the qualitative interview. *International Journal of Qualitative Methods, 8*(1), 1–11.

Segel, E., & Heer, J. (2010). *Narrative visualization: Telling stories with data*. Stanford Vis Group. Retrieved at http://vis.stanford.edu/files/2010-Narrative-InfoVis.pdf

Seinfeld, J. H. (1986). *Atmospheric Chemistry and Physics of Air Pollution*. New York: J. Wiley.

Serrano, M.A., Maguitman, A., Boguñá, M., Fortunato, S., & Vespignani, A. (2007). Decoding the structure of the WWW: A comparative analysis of web crawls. *ACM Transactions on the Web, 1*(2), 10:1 – 10:25.

Shamma, D. A., Kennedy, L., & Churchill, E. F. (2012). Watching and talking: Media content as social nexus. In *Proceedings of ICMR '12*. Hong Kong, China: Association of Computing Machinery.

Shavelson, R. J., & Towne, L. (2002). *Scientific research in education*. Washington, DC: National Academy Press.

Shaw, T., & Jarvenpaa, S. (1997). Process Models in Information Systems. In A. S. Lee, L. J. Leibenau, & J. I. De Gross (Eds.), *Information Systems and Qualitative Research1* (pp. 70–100). London: Chapman and Hall. doi:10.1007/978-0-387-35309-8_6

Shenton, A. (2004). Strategies for Ensuring Trustworthiness in Qualitative Research Projects. *Education for Information, 22*, 63–75.

Shore, J., Brooks, E., Savin, D., Manson, S., & Libby, A. (2007). An economic evaluation of telehealth data collection with rural populations. *Psychiatric Services (Washington, D.C.), 58*(6), 830–835. doi:10.1176/appi.ps.58.6.830 PMID:17535944

Short, J., Williams, E., & Christie, B. (1976). *The Social Psychology of Telecommunications*. New York, NY: John Wiley & Sons.

Sieck, W. R., Merkle, E. C., & Van Zandt, T. (2007). Option fixation: A cognitive contributor to overconfidence. *Organizational Behavior and Human Decision Processes, 103*(1), 68–83. doi:10.1016/j.obhdp.2006.11.001

Silva, L., & Hirschheim, R. (2007). Fighting Against Windmills: Strategic Information Systems and Organizational Deep Structures. *Management Information Systems Quarterly, 31*(2), 327–354.

Silverman, D. (2001). *Interpreting qualitative data: methods for analysing talk, text and interaction* (2nd ed.). London: Sage.

Silverman, D. (2005). *Doing qualitative research* (2nd ed.). London: Sage.

Silverman, D. (Ed.). (2006). *Qualitative research: theory, method and practice*. London: Sage.

Silver, N. (2012). *The Signal and the Noise: Why so Many Predictions Fail—but Some Don't*. New York: The Penguin Press.

Simons, J. (2008). Tag-elese or the language of tags. *The Fibreculture Journal, 12*. Retrieved from http://twelve.fibreculturejournal.org/fcj-083-tag-elese-or-the-language-of-tags/

Sinclair, A. (2009). Provocative pedagogies in e-Learning: Making the invisible visible. *International Journal of Teaching and Learning in Higher Education, 21*(2), 197–209.

Singh, A., Taneja, A., & Mangalaraj, G. (2009). Creating Online Surveys: Some Wisdom from the Trenches Tutorial. *IEEE Transactions on Professional Communication, 52*(2), 197–212. doi:10.1109/TPC.2009.2017986

Skype grows FY revenues 20%, reaches 663 million users. (2011). Retrieved April 8, 2014, from http://www.telecompaper.com/news/skype-grows-fy-revenues-20-reaches-663-mln-users--790254

Slade, D. H. (Ed.). (1986). *Meteorology and Atomic Energy*. Washington, DC: Atomic Energy Commission, Air Resources Laboratories, Research Laboratories, Environmental Science Services Administration, U.S Department of Commerce.

Slavin, R. E. (2007). *Educational research: In an age of accountability*. Boston: Pearson Education, Inc.

Smaltz, D. H., Sambamurthy, V., & Agarwal, R. (2006). The Antecedents of CIO Role Effectiveness in Organizations: An Empirical Study in the Healthcare Sector. *IEEE Transactions on Engineering Management, 53*(2), 207–222. doi:10.1109/TEM.2006.872248

Sminia, H. (2009). Process research in strategy formation: Theory, methodology and relevance. *International Journal of Management Reviews, 11*(1), 97–125. doi:10.1111/j.1468-2370.2008.00253.x

Smith, N. J. (2010). *Third arm, gateway drug, or just a toy? Inductively driven mixed methods study on the use of mobile learning technologies in higher education*. (Dissertation). Texas A&M University, Corpus Christi, TX.

Smith, H. A., & McKeen, J. D. (2007). Developments in Practice Xxiv: Information Management: The Nexus of Business and IT. *Communications of the Association for Information Systems, 19*, 34–46.

Smith, H. J., Milberg, S. J., & Burke, S. J. (1996). Information Privacy: Measuring Individuals' Concerns About Organizational Practices. *Management Information Systems Quarterly, 20*(2), 2. doi:10.2307/249477

Smith, L. T. (1999/2012). *Decolonizing methodologies: Research and indigenous peoples* (2nd ed.). London, UK: Zed Books.

Smith, V. (2001). Ethnographies of work and the work of ethnographers. In P. Atkinson, A. Coffey, S. Delamont, J. Lofland, & L. Lofland (Eds.), *Handbook of ethnography* (pp. 220–233). London: Sage. doi:10.4135/9781848608337.n15

Sobreperez, P. (2008). Using Plenary Focus Groups in Information Systems Research: More than a Collection of Interviews. *The Electronic Journal of Business Research Methods, 6*(2), 181–188.

Solomon, M. (1983). The role of products as social stimuli: A symbolic interactionism perspective. *The Journal of Consumer Research, 10*(3), 319–328. doi:10.1086/208971

Sousanis, N. (2014). *Stories, MLA, & Microsoft*. Retrieved from http://www.spinweaveandcut.blogspot.com/

Spellman, B. A., & Mandel, D. R. (1999, August). When possibility informs reality: Counterfactual thinking as a cue to causality. *Current Directions in Psychological Science, 8*(4), 120–123. doi:10.1111/1467-8721.00028

Spiers, J. A. (2004). Tech tips: Using video management/analysis technology in qualitative research. *International Journal of Qualitative Methods, 3*(1), Article 5. Retrieved March, 2014 from http://www.ualberta.ca/~iiqm/backissues/3_1/pdf/spiersvideo.pdf

Spiggle, S. (1994). Analysis and Interpretation of Qualitative Data in Consumer Research. *The Journal of Consumer Research, 21*(3), 491–503. doi:10.1086/209413

Spradley, J. P. (1980). *Step seven: Making a taxonomic analysis. In Participant Observation* (pp. 112–116). Wadsworth Thomson Learning.

St. Pierre, E. A. (2011). *Data analysis after coding in qualitative research*. Paper presented at the Seventh International Congress of Qualitative Inquiry. Champaign/Urbana, IL.

St. Pierre, E. A. (2013). The appearance of data. *Cultural Studies, Critical Methodologies, 13*(4), 223-227. doi:10.1177/1532708613487862

St. Pierre, E. A. (2000). Poststructural feminism in education: An overview. *International Journal of Qualitative Studies in Education, 13*(5), 4677–5150. doi:10.1080/09518390050156422

St. Pierre, E. A. (2002). "Science" rejects postmodernism. *Educational Researcher, 31*(8), 25–27. doi:10.3102/0013189X031008025

St. Pierre, E. A., & Pillow, W. S. (2000). *Working the ruins: feminist poststructural theory and methods in education.* New York: Routledge.

Stadler, F. (2001). The Vienna Circle (C. Nielsen, J. Golb, S. Schmidt & T. Ernst, Trans.). Vienna, Austria: Springer-Verlag/Wien.

Stahl, B. C. (2007). ETHICS, Morality and Critique: An Essay on Enid Mumford's Socio-Technical Approach. *Journal of the Association for Information Systems, 8*(9), 479-490.

Stahl, B., Tremblay, M., & LeRouge, C. (2011). Focus Groups and Critical Social IS Research: How the Choice of Method Can Promote Emancipation of Respondents and Researchers. *European Journal of Information Systems, 20*(4), 378–394. doi:10.1057/ejis.2011.21

Stephens, C. S. (1991). *A Structured Observation of Five Chief Information Officers: The Nature of Information Technology Managerial Work.* Auburn University.

Sterne, J. (1999). Thinking the Internet: Cultural studies versus the millenium. In S. Jones (Ed.), *Doing Internet research: Critical issues and methods for examining the Net* (pp. 257–288). Thousand Oaks, CA: Sage. doi:10.4135/9781452231471.n13

Stern, P. N. (1994). *Eroding GT. Critical Issues in Qualitative Research Methods. J. Morse* (pp. 212–223). Thousand Oaks, CA: Sage.

Stevens, R., & Casillas, A. (2006). *Artificial neural networks. In Automated Scoring of Complex Tasks in Computer Based Testing: An Introduction* (pp. 259–312). Mahwah, NJ: Lawrence Erlbaum.

Stewart, D. W., & Shamdasani, P. N. (1990). *Focus groups: Theory and practice*. Sage Publications Inc.

Stewart, K., & Williams, M. (2005). Researching online populations: The use of online focus groups in social research. *Qualitative Research*, 5(4), 395–416. doi:10.1177/1468794105056916

Stone, A. R. (1995). *The war of desire and technology at the close of the mechanical age*. Cambridge, MA: The MIT Press.

Strati, A. & P. G. de Montoux. (2002). Introduction: Organizing Aesthetics. *Human Relations, 55*(7), 755-766.

Strauss, A. L., & Corbin, J. (1994). *GTMology: An Overview. In Handbook of Qualitative Research* (pp. 273–285). Thousand Oaks, CA: Sage.

Strauss, A., & Corbin, J. (1990). *Basics of qualitative research: Grounded theory procedures and techniques*. Newbury Park, CA: Sage.

Strauss, A., & Corbin, J. (1990). Open coding. In A. Strauss, & J. Corbin (Eds.), *Basics of qualitative research: Grounded theory procedures and techniques* (2nd ed., pp. 101–121). Thousand Oaks, CA: Sage.

Strauss, A., & Corbin, J. (1998). *Basics of qualitative research: Techniques and procedures for developing grounded theory* (2nd ed.). Thousand Oaks, CA: Sage Publications.

Strohmaier, M., Körner, C., & Kern, R. (2012). Understanding why users tag: A survey of tagging motivation literature and results from an empirical study. *Web Semantics: Science, Services, and Agents on the World Wide Web, 17*, 1–11. doi:10.1016/j.websem.2012.09.003

Stvilia, B., Jöorgensen, C., & Wu, S. (2012). Establishing the value of socially-created metadata to image indexing. *Library & Information Science Research, 34*(2), 99–109. doi:10.1016/j.lisr.2011.07.011

Suchanek, F. M., Vojnović, M., & Gunawardena, D. (2008). *Social tags: Meaning and suggestions. In Proceedings of CIKM '08*. Napa Valley, CA: Association of Computing Machinery. doi:10.1145/1458082.1458114

Sun, A. & Bhowmick, S.S. (2009, Oct. 23). Image tag clarity: In search of visual-representative tags for social images. In *Proceedings of WSIM*. Beijing, China: Association of Computing Machinery (ACM).

Sutton, R., & Staw, B. M. (1995). ASQ Forum What Theory is Not. *Administrative Science Quarterly, 40*(3), 371–384. doi:10.2307/2393788

Sutton, S. G., Khazanchi, D., Hampton, C., & Arnold, V. (2008). Risk Analysis in Extended Enterprise Environments: Identification of Critical Risk Factors in B2b E-Commerce Relationships. *Journal of the Association for Information Systems, 9*(4), 151–174.

Sztompka, P. (1991). *Society in Action: The Theory of Social Becoming*. Chicago, IL: University of Chicago Press.

Sztompka, P. (1993). *The Sociology of Social Change*. Oxford, UK: Blackwell.

Takeda, P. (2006). *An Eye at the Top of the World: The Terrifying Legacy of the Cold War's Most Daring Operation*. New York: Avalon Publishing Group.

Taleb, N. N. (2010). *The Black Swan: The Impact of the Highly Improbable* (2nd ed.). New York: Random House.

Taleb, N. N. (2012). *Antifragile: Things that Gain from Disorder*. New York: Random House.

Tarafdar, M., & Qrunfleh, S. (2009). IT-Business Alignment: A Two-Level Analysis. *Information Systems Management, 26*(4), 338–349. doi:10.1080/10580530903245705

Tashakkori, A., & Teddlie, C. (Eds.). (2010). *Sage handbook of mixed methods in social & behavioral research*. Thousand Oaks, CA: Sage Publications Inc.

Tasler, N. (2008). *The Impulse Factor: Why Some of Us Play it Safe and Others Risk it All*. New York: Fireside, Simon & Schuster Publishers.

Tateosian, L. G. (2005). *Characterizing Aesthetic Visualizations*. North Carolina State University.

Tates, K., Zwaanswijk, M., Otten, R., & van Dulmen, S. et al. (2009). Online focus groups as a tool to collect data in hard-to-include populations: Examples from paediatric oncology. *BMC Medical Research Methodology, 9*(15). Available from http://www.biomedcentral.com/1471-2288/9/15 PMID:19257883

Taylor, S. (2001). Locating and conducting discourse analytic research. In M. Wetherell, S. Taylor, & S. J. Yates (Eds.), *Discourse as data: A guide for analysis* (pp. 5–48). London: Sage.

Taylor, T. L. (2006). *Play between worlds: Exploring online game culture*. Cambridge, MA: The MIT Press.

Teddlie, C., & Tashakkori, A. (2003). Major Issues and Controversies in the Use of Mixed Methods in the Social and Behavioral Sciences. In A. Tashakkori, & C. Teddlie (Eds.), *Handbook of Mixed Methods in Social and Behavioral Research* (pp. 3–50). Thousand Oaks, CA: Sage Publications.

Teddlie, C., & Tashakkori, A. (2009). *Foundations of Mixed Methods Research*. Thousand Oaks, CA: Sage Publications.

Templeton, J. F. (1994). *The focus group: A strategic guide to organizing, conducting and analyzing the focus group interview*. New York: McGraw-Hill Professional Publishing.

ten Have, P. (1991). User Routines for Computer Assisted Conversation Analysis. *The Discourse Analysis Research Group Newsletter, 7*(3), 3-9.

ten Have, P. (1998). *Doing conversation analysis: A practical guide*. London: Sage.

Terrell, S. R. (2011). Face-to-face in writing: My first attempt at conducting a text-based online focus group. *Qualitative Report, 16*(1), 2860291.

Tesch, R. (1991). *Software for Qualitative researchers: Analysis Needs and Program Capabilities. In Using Computers in Qualitative Research*. London: Sage.

Tetlock, P. E., & Belkin, A. (1996). Counterfactual thought experiments in world politics: Logical, methodological, and psychological perspectives. Princeton, NJ: Princeton University Press.

Thomas, C. (2004). How is disability understood? An examination of sociological approaches. *Disability & Society, 19*(6), 569–583. doi:10.1080/0968759042000252506

Thomas, C., Wootten, A., & Robinson, P. (2013). The experiences of gay and bisexual men diagnosed with prostate cancer: Results from an online focus group. *European Journal of Cancer Care, 22*(4), 522–529. doi:10.1111/ecc.12058 PMID:23730947

Thorngate, W. (1976). Possible limits on a science of social behaviour. In J. H. Strickland, F. E. Aboud, & K. J. Gergen (Eds.), *Social psychology in transition*. New York: Plenum. doi:10.1007/978-1-4615-8765-1_9

Tilley, S. A. (2003). "Challenging" Research Practices: Turning a Critical Lens on the Work of Transcription. *Qualitative Inquiry, 9*(5), 750–773. doi:10.1177/1077800403255296

Timmis, J., & Neal, M. (2001). A resource limited artificial immune system for data analysis. *Knowledge-Based Systems, 14*(3), 121–130. doi:10.1016/S0950-7051(01)00088-0

Timmis, J., Neal, M., & Hunt, J. (2000). An artificial immune system for data analysis. *Bio Systems, 55*(1), 143–150. doi:10.1016/S0303-2647(99)00092-1 PMID:10745118

Tisselli, E. (2010). Thinkflickrthink: A case study on strategic tagging. *Communications of the ACM, 53*(8), 141–145. doi:10.1145/1787234.1787270

Tobin, G., & Begley, C. (2004). Methodological Rigour within a Qualitative Framework. *Journal of Advanced Nursing, 48*(4), 388–396. doi:10.1111/j.1365-2648.2004.03207.x PMID:15500533

Trauth, E. M. (2001). *The Choice of Qualitative Methods in IS Research. In Qualitative Research in IS: Issues and Trends* (pp. 1–19). London: Idea Group Publishing.

Tremblay, C. M., Hevner, A. R., & Berndt, D. J. (2010). Focus Groups for Artifact Refinement and Evaluation in Design Research. *Communications of the Association for Information Systems, 26*, 27.

Trivers, R. (2011). *The Folly of Fools: The Logic of Deceit and Self-Deception in Human Life*. New York: Basic Books.

Trochim, W., Marcus, S. E., Mâsse, L. C., Moser, R. P., & Weld, P. (2008). The Evaluation of Large Research Initiatives: A Participatory Integrative Mixed-Methods Approach. *The American Journal of Evaluation, 29*(1), 1, 8–28. doi:10.1177/1098214007309280

Tsoukas, H. (2005). *Complex knowledge: Studies in organizational epistemology*. Oxford, UK: Oxford University Press.

Tsoukas, H., & Chia, R. (2002). On organizational becoming: Rethinking organizational change. *Organization Science, 13*(5), 567–582. doi:10.1287/orsc.13.5.567.7810

Tsur, O., & Rappoport, A. (2012). What's in a hashtag? Content based prediction of the spread of ideas in microblogging communities. In *Proceedings of WSDM '12*. Seattle, WA: Association of Computing Machinery.

Tuchman, G. (2009). *Wannabe U: Inside the Corporate University*. Chicago: University of Chicago Press. doi:10.7208/chicago/9780226815282.001.0001

Tucker, P. (2014). *The Naked Future: What Happens in a World that Anticipates Your Every Move?* New York: Current, Penguin-Random House.

Turkle, S. (1995). *Life on the screen: Identity in the age of the Internet*. New York: Simon & Schuster.

Turner, B. (1981). Some practical aspects of Qualitative Data Analysis: One way of Organising the Cognitive Processes Associated with the Generation of GT. *Quality & Quantity, 15*(3), 225–247. doi:10.1007/BF00164639

Turner, D. B. (1979). Atmospheric Dispersion Modeling. *Journal of the Air Pollution Control Association, 29*(5), 502–519. doi:10.1080/00022470.1979.10470821

Turner, D. B. (1994). *Workbook of Atmospheric Dispersion Estimates: An Introduction to Dispersion Modeling* (2nd ed.). Boca Raton, FL: Lewis Publishers.

Turner, D. B., Bender, L. W., Pierce, T. E., & Petersen, W. B. (1989). Air Quality Simulation Models from EPA. *Environmental Software, 4*(2), 52–61. doi:10.1016/0266-9838(89)90031-2

Tushman, M. L., & Scanlan, T. (1981). Boundary Spanning Individuals: Their Role in Information Transfer and Their Antecedents. *Academy of Management Journal, 24*(2), 289–305. doi:10.2307/255842

Tushman, M., & Romanelli, E. (1985). Organizational evolution: A metamorphis model of convergence and reorientation. In B. Staw, & L. Cummings (Eds.), *Research in organizational behavior* (pp. 171–222). Greenwich, CT: JAI Press.

Twenge, J. M., Campbell, W. K., & Gentile, B. (2012). Changes in pronoun use in American books and the rise in individualism, 1960–2008. *Journal of Cross-Cultural Psychology, 44*(3), 406–415. doi:10.1177/0022022112455100

Uden, L., & Damiani, E. (2007). The future of distance education: distance education ecosystem. In *Proceedings of Inaugural IEEE International Conference on Digital Ecosystems and Technologies*, (pp. 113-117). IEEE.

Ulrich, W. (1987). Critical heuristics of social systems design. *European Journal of Operational Research, 31*(3), 276–283. doi:10.1016/0377-2217(87)90036-1

Ulrich, W. (2001). The quest for competence in systemic research and practice. *Systems Research and Behavioral Science, 18*(1), 3–28. doi:10.1002/sres.366

Underhill, C., & Olmsted, M. G. (2003). An experimental comparison of computer-mediated and face-to-face focus groups. *Social Science Computer Review, 21*(4), 506–512. doi:10.1177/0894439303256541

United States Chemical Safety Board. (n.d.). Retrieved from http://www.csb.gov

Urquhart, C. (2001). *An Encounter with GT: Tackling the Practical and Philosophical Issues. In Qualitative Research in IS: Issues and Trends* (pp. 104–140). London: Idea Group Publishing.

Urquhart, C., & Fernandez, W. (2013). Using GT Methid in IS: The researcher as a Blank Slate and Other Myths. *Journal of Information Technology*, 28, 224–236. doi:10.1057/jit.2012.34

Urquhart, C., Lehmann, H., & Myers, M. D. (2010). Putting the "Theory" back into GT: Guidelines for GT Studies in IS. *IS Journal*, 20, 357–381.

Vakali, A. (2012). Evolving social data mining and affective analysis methodologies, framework and applications. In *Proceedings of IDEAS 12*. Prague, Czech Republic: Association of Computing Machinery. doi:10.1145/2351476.2351477

Van de Ven, A. H. (1992). Suggestions for studying strategy process: A research note. *Strategic Management Journal*, 13(S1), 169–188. doi:10.1002/smj.4250131013

Van de Ven, A. H., & Huber, G. P. (1990). Longitudinal field research methods for studying processes of organizational change. *Organization Science*, 1(3), 213–219. doi:10.1287/orsc.1.3.213

Van de Ven, A. H., & Poole, M. S. (2002). Field Research Methods. In A. C. Baum (Ed.), *Companion to Organizations* (pp. 867–888). Oxford: Blackwell Publishers.

Van de Ven, A. H., & Poole, M. S. (2005). Alternative Approaches for Studying Organizational Change. *Organization Studies*, 26(9), 1377–1404. doi:10.1177/0170840605056907

Van der Heijden, H., & Sørensen, L. S. (2003). *Measuring attitudes towards mobile information services: An empirical validation of the HED/UT scale*. Paper presented at the European Conference on Information Systems (ECIS). Naples, Italy.

Van Dijck, J'. (2007). *Mediated memories in the digital age*. Stanford, CA: Stanford University Press.

Van Laere, O., Schockaert, S., & Dhoedt, B. (2013). Georeferencing Flickr resources based on textual metadata. *Information Sciences*, 238, 52–74. doi:10.1016/j.ins.2013.02.045

Van Zwol, R. (2007). Flickr: Who is looking? In *Proceedings of the IEEE/WIC/ACM International Conference on Web Intelligence*. (pp. 184–190). IEEE. DOI doi:10.1109/WI.2007.22

Vandic, D., van Dam, J.-W., Fransincar, F., & Hogenboom, F. (2011). A semantic clustering-based approach for searching and browsing tag spaces. In *Proceedings of SAC'11*. TaiChung, Taiwan: SAC. doi:10.1145/1982185.1982538

Varki, A., & Brower, D. (2013). *Denial: Self-Deception, False Beliefs, and the Origins of the Human Mind*. New York: Hachette Book Group.

Vasluian, E., de Jong, I., Janssen, W., Poelma, M., van Wijk, I., Reinders-Messelink, H. A., & van der Sluis, C. K. (2013). Opinions of youngsters with congenital below-elbow deficiency, and those of their parents and professionals concerning prosthetic use and rehabilitation treatment. *PLoS ONE*, 8(6), e67101. doi:10.1371/journal.pone.0067101 PMID:23826203

Venkatesh, V., Brown, S. A., & Bala, H. (2013). Bridging the Qualitative-Quantitative Divide: Guidelines for Conducting Mixed Methods Research in Information Systems. *Management Information Systems Quarterly*, 37(1), 21–54.

Venkatraman, N. (2000). Five Steps to a Dot-Com Strategy: How to find your footing on the Web. *MIT Sloan Management Review*, 41(3), 15–28.

Venter, G., & Sobieszczanski-Sobieski, J. (2003). Particle swarm optimization. *AIAA Journal*, 41(8), 1583–1589. doi:10.2514/2.2111

Vose, M. D. (1999). *The simple genetic algorithm: foundations and theory* (Vol. 12). The MIT Press.

Walker, D. (2013). The Internet as a medium for health services research. Part 2. *Nurse Researcher*, 20(5), 33–37. doi:10.7748/nr2013.05.20.5.33.e295 PMID:23687847

Wallace, L., Keil, M., & Rai, A. (2004). How Software Project Risk Affects Project Performance: An Investigation of the Dimensions of Risk and an Exploratory Model. *Decision Sciences*, 35(2), 289–321. doi:10.1111/j.00117315.2004.02059.x

Walsham, G. (1995a). Interpretive case studies in IS research: Nature and method. *European Journal of Information Systems*, 4(2), 74–81. doi:10.1057/ejis.1995.9

Walsham, G. (1995b). The Emergence of Interpretivism in IS Research. *Information Systems Research*, 6(4), 376–394. doi:10.1287/isre.6.4.376

Walsham, G. (2006). Doing interpretive research. *European Journal of Information Systems, 15*(3), 320–330. doi:10.1057/palgrave.ejis.3000589

Walsh, J. R., White, A. A., & Greaney, M. L. (2009). Using focus groups to identify factors affecting healthy weight maintenance in college men. *Nutrition Research (New York, N.Y.), 29*(6), 371–378. doi:10.1016/j.nutres.2009.04.002 PMID:19628102

Wang Y, Lo H-P, & Yang, Y (2004). An Integrated Framework for Service Quality, Customer Value, Satisfaction: Evidence from China's Telecommunication Industry. *Information Systems Frontiers, 6*(4), 325.

Wang, L., & Fu, K. (2008). *Artificial neural networks.* John Wiley & Sons, Inc.

Ward, J., & Peppard, J. (2002). *Strategic Planning for Information Systems* (3rd ed.). Chichester, UK: John Wiley and Sons.

Watson, R. T. (1990). Influences on the IS Manager's Perceptions of Key Issues: Information Scanning and the Relationship with the CEO. *Management Information Systems Quarterly, 14*(2), 217–231. doi:10.2307/248780

Webb, C. (1999). Analysing qualitative data: Computerized and other approaches. *Journal of Advanced Nursing, 29*(2), 323–330. doi:10.1046/j.1365-2648.1999.00892.x PMID:10197931

Weber, M. (1949). *The Methodology of the Social Sciences.* New York: Free Press.

Weber, M. (1962). *Basic Concepts in Sociology.* New York: The Citadel Press.

Weber, R. (2004). The Retoric of Positivism versus Interpretivism: A Personal View. *Management Information Systems Quarterly, 28*(1), 3–12.

Weggeman, M., I. Lammers & H. Akkermans. (2007). Aesthetics from a Design Perspective. *Journal of Organizational Change Management, 20*(3), 346-358.

Weick, K. (1979). *The social psychology of organizing.* Reading, MA: Addison-Wesley.

Weidong, X., & Lee, G. (2005). Complexity of Information Systems Development Projects: Conceptualization and Measurement Development. *Journal of Management Information Systems, 22*(1), 45–83.

Weinmann, T., Thomas, S., Brilmayer, S., Henrich, S., & Radon, K. (2012). Testing Skype as an interview method in epidemiologic research: Response and feasibility. *International Journal of Public Health, 57*(6), 959–961. doi:10.1007/s00038-012-0404-7 PMID:22945842

Weinstein, M. (2008). *TAMS analyzer.* Retrieved from http://tamsys.sourceforge.net/

Wellin, C., & Fine, G. A. (2001). Ethnography as work: Career socialization, settings and problems. In P. Atkinson, A. Coffey, S. Delamont, J. Lofland, & L. Lofland (Eds.), *Handbook of ethnography* (pp. 323–338). London: Sage. doi:10.4135/9781848608337.n22

Wenger, E. (1998). Communities of Practice: Learning as a Social System. *Systems Thinker*, 1-10. Retrieved from www.co-i-l/coil/knowledge-garden/cop/ss.shtml

Wenger, E., & Snyder, W. M. (2000). Communities of Practice: The Organizational Frontier. *Harvard Business Review, 78*(1), 139–145. PMID:11184968

Werner, O., & Schoepfle, G. M. (1987). Systematic Fieldwork. In *Foundations of Ethnography and Interviewing (vol. 1).* Thousand Oaks, CA: Sage.

Westland, J. C. (2011). Affective data acquisition technologies in survey research. *Information Technology Management, 12*(4), 387–408. doi:10.1007/s10799-011-0110-9

Westman, S., & Freund, L. (2010). Information interaction in 140 characters or less: Genres on Twitter. In *Proceedings of IIiX 2010.* New Brunswick, NJ: Association of Computing Machinery.

Wharton, C. M., Hampl, J. S., Hall, R., & Winham, D. M. (2003). PCs or paper-and-pencil: Online surveys for data collection. *Journal of the American Dietetic Association, 103*(11), 1458–1459. doi:10.1016/j.jada.2003.09.004 PMID:14626248

What 5 tech experts expect in 2014. (2014). *The Chronicle of Higher Education*. Retrieved from http://chronicle.com/article/What-5-Tech-Experts-Expect-in/143829/?cid=wc&utm_source=wc&utm_medium=en

Whetten, D. A. (2006). Albert and Whetten Revisited: Strengthening the Concept of Organizational Identity. *Journal of Management Inquiry*, *15*(3), 219–234. doi:10.1177/1056492606291200

Whitcomb, M. E., & Porter, S. R. (2004). E-Mail Contacts: A Test of Complex Graphical Designs in Survey Research. *Social Science Computer Review, 22*(3), 370-376.

White, H. (1981). The value of narrativity in the representation of reality. In W. J. T. Mitchell (Ed.), *On Narrative* (pp. 1–24). Chicago, IL: University of Chicago Press.

Whitley, D. (1994). A genetic algorithm tutorial. *Statistics and Computing*, *4*(2), 65–85. doi:10.1007/BF00175354

Whittemore, R., Chase, S. K., & Mandle, C. L. (2001). Validity in qualitative research. *Qualitative Health Research*, *11*(4), 522–537. doi:10.1177/104973201129119299 PMID:11521609

Wickens, C. D. (2002). Multiple resources and performance prediction. *Theoretical Issues in Ergonomics Science*, *3*(2), 159–177. doi:10.1080/14639220210123806

Wilcox, H. (2011). *Press Release: 1 in 5 Smartphones will have NFC by 2014, Spurred by Recent Breakthroughs: New Juniper Research Report*. Retrieved from http://www.juniperresearch.com/viewpressrelease.php?pr=239

Wilkerson, J. M., Iantaffi, A., Smolenski, D., Brady, S., Horvath, K., Grey, J., & Rosser, S. (2012). The SEM risk behavior (SRB) model: A new conceptual model of how pornography influences the sexual intentions and HIV risk behavior of MSM. *Sexual and Relationship Therapy*, *27*(3), 217–230. doi:10.1080/14681994.2012.734605 PMID:23185126

Williams, F., Rice, R. E., & Rogers, E. M. (1988). *Research methods and the new media*. New York: Free Press.

Williamson, D. A. (2007). *Kids and teens online: Virtual worlds open new universe*. Retrieved from http://www.emarketer.com/Reports/All/Emarketer_2000437.aspx?src=report1_home

Williams, S., Clausen, M., Robertson, A., Peacock, S., & McPherson, K. (2012). Methodological reflections on the use of asynchronous online focus groups in health research. *International Journal of Qualitative Methods*, *11*(4), 368–383.

Williams, S., & Reid, M. (2012). 'It's like there are two people in my head': A phenomenological exploration of anorexia nervosa and its relationship to the self. *Psychology & Health*, *27*(7), 798–815. doi:10.1080/08870446.2011.595488 PMID:21736500

Wilson, M., & Howcroft, D. (2002). Re-conceptualising failure : Social shaping meets IS research. *Fortune*, *11*, 236–250.

Wilson, V. (2011). Research Methods: Design, Methods, Case Study...oh my! *Evidence Based Library and Information Practice*, *6*(3), 90–93.

Winzenburg, S. (2011). How Skype is changing the interview process. *The Chronicle of Higher Education*. Retrieved April 15, 2012, from http://chronicle.com/article/How-Skype-Is-Changing-the/126529/

Wolcott, H. F. (1999). *Ethnography: A way of seeing*. Walnut Creek, CA: AltaMira Press.

Wolfe, A. (2013). Alan Greenspan: What Went Wrong. *Wall Street Journal*, Retrieved October 18, 2013, from http://online.wsj.com/news/articles/SB10001424052702304410204579139900796324772

Wolfinbarger, M., & Gilly, M. C. (2003). eTailQ: Dimensionalizing, measuring and predicting etail quality. *Journal of Retailing*, *79*(3), 183–198. doi:10.1016/S0022-4359(03)00034-4

Wood, L. A., & Kroger, R. O. (2000). *Doing discourse analysis: Methods for studying action in talk and text*. Thousand Oaks, CA: Sage.

Woodson, A. (2007, March 29). MTV to pimp "Ride" online. *Reuters*. Retrieved from http://www.reuters.com/article/industryNews/idUSN2933239120070330

Wouters, H., van Geffen, E., Baas-Thijssen, M., Krol-Warmerdam, E., Stiggelbout, A. M., & Belitser, S. et al. (2013). Disentangling breast cancer patients' perceptions and experiences with regard to endocrine therapy: Nature and relevance for non-adherence. *The Breast*, *22*(5), 661–666. doi:10.1016/j.breast.2013.05.005 PMID:23770134

Wu, R., Rossos, P., Quan, S., Reeves, S., Lo, V., Wong, B., et al. (2011). *Works citing "an evaluation of the use of smartphones to communicate between clinicians: A mixed-methods study"*. Paper presented at the World Congress on Social Media, Mobile Apps, Internet/Web 2.0. Retrieved March 2014 from http://www.jmir.org/article/citations/1655

Yang, L., Sun, T., Zhang, M., & Meik, Q. (2012). We know what @you #tag: Does the dual role affect hashtag adoption?. In *Proceedings of WWW'12*. Lyon, France: Association of Computing Machinery.

Yang, X., & Zheng, J. (2009). Artificial neural networks. Handbook of Research on Geoinformatics, 122.

Yang, D.-J., Chiu, J.-Z., & Chen, Y.-K. (2011). Examining the social influence on college students for playing online games: Gender differences and implications. *TOJET: The Turkish Online Journal of Educational Technology*, *10*(3), 115–122.

Yee, N., & Bailenson, J. (2007). The proteus effect: The effect of transformed self-representation on behavior. *Human Communication Research*, *33*(3), 271–290. doi:10.1111/j.1468-2958.2007.00299.x

Yee, R. (2008). *Pro-Web 2.0 Mashups: Remixing Data and Web Services*. New York: Springer-Verlag.

Yeo, K. T. (2002). Critical failure factors in information system projects. *International Journal of Project Management*, *20*(3), 241–246. doi:10.1016/S0263-7863(01)00075-8

Yin, R. K. (2009). Case Study Research Design and Methods (4th ed.). Sage Publications.

Yin, R. K. (2003). *Applications of case study research* (2nd ed.). Thousand Oaks, CA: Sage.

Young, S. D., & Jaganath, D. (2012). Using social networking technologies for mixed methods HIV prevention research. *Journal of Mobile Technology in Medicine*. Retrieved from http://www.journalmtm.com/2012/using-social-networking-technologies-for-mixed-methods-hiv-prevention-research/

Yu, J., Taverner, N., & Madden, K. (2011). Young people's views on sharing health-related stories on the Internet. *Health & Social Care in the Community*, *19*(3), 326–334. doi:10.1111/j.1365-2524.2010.00987.x PMID:21288270

Zachry, M. (2000). The ecology of an online education site in professional communication. In Technology and Teamwork, (pp. 433-442). IEEE.

Zadeh, L. A. (1965). Fuzzy sets. *Information and Control*, *8*(3), 338–353. doi:10.1016/S0019-9958(65)90241-X

Zhang, W., & Kramarae, C. (2012). Are Chinese women turning sharp-tongued? *Discourse & Society*, *23*(6), 749–770. doi:10.1177/0957926512455376

Zickuhr, K., & Smith, A. (2012). *Digital differences*. Pew Internet & American Life Project. Retrieved April 30, 2012, from http://pewinternet.org/Reports/2012/Digital-differences.aspx

Zimmer, B. (2013, Oct. 17). Google's Ngram Viewer goes wild. *The Atlantic*. Retrieved from http://www.theatlantic.com/technology/archive/2013/10/googles-ngram-viewer-goes-wild/280601/

About the Contributors

Shalin Hai-Jew is an instructional designer at Kansas State University, where she works on a range of instructional design projects for online learning. She has recently been using Network Overview, Discovery, and Exploration for Excel (NodeXL), Maltego Radium/Tungsten, and NVivo 10 for various projects and research. She has BAs in English and Psychology, and an MA in Creative Writing from the University of Washington; she has an EdD in Educational Leadership (with a focus on public administration) from Seattle University (2005), where she was a Morford Scholar. She has edited several technical books and authored a number of articles and chapters. Most recently, she presented a session at the Sloan-C/MERLOT 7th Annual International Symposium on Emerging Technologies for Online Learning. She teaches part-time through WashingtonOnline. Based on current work, she is interested in electronic social network analysis, network science, and agent-based modeling. Currently, Dr. Hai-Jew is editing texts on digital presentations. She was born in Huntsville, Alabama.

* * *

Kakali Bhattacharya is an Associate Professor at Kansas State University. She holds a PhD from University of Georgia in Educational Psychology. Specifically, her program of study was in Research, Evaluation, Measurement, and Statistics with a specialization in Qualitative Inquiry. Her scholarly interests include, but are not limited to, race, class, gender issues in higher education, technology-integrated learning and social spaces, de/colonizing epistemologies and methodologies, transnationalism, and qualitatively driven mixed methods approaches. She is a widely published author with her articles and book chapters appearing in venues with national and international visibility. She has published in journals such as *Qualitative Inquiry, International Review of Qualitative Research, Technology, Humanities, Education, and Narrative, Cultural Studies <=> Critical Methodologies, The Qualitative Report,* and *Electronic Journal of Science Education,* to name a few. Her refereed book chapters have appeared in publications such as *Higher Education: Handbook of Theory and Research, Academic Knowledge Construction and Multimodal Curriculum Development, Qualitative Inquiry as Global Endeavor,* and *Arts-Based Research in Education: Foundations for Practice.* Additionally, Kakali Bhattacharya is a certified trainer of NVivo, has extensive program evaluation experience, and is a trained instructional designer from Southern Illinois University at Carbondale, Illinois. She has been the recipient of numerous awards and honors, including being an invited keynote speaker for Southern Connecticut State University, an Outstanding Islander award and an ELITE's Outstanding Faculty Award, from Texas A&M University, Corpus Christi, and the Dean's Award for Outstanding Research and Scholarship, from the College of Education at University of Memphis. She is quite active and visible in various national and international organizations, such as

American Educational Research Association and International Congress of Qualitative Inquiry. Recently, Kakali Bhattacharya has developed an interest in contemplative pedagogy and practices and how such approaches inform inspired teaching, learning, research, and leadership. This interest of hers intersects with several arts-based approaches she has taken to inform her research methodology, data analysis, and data representation. She has been invited by the American Educational Research Association to lead a mini course with her colleague Patricia Leavy on "Arts-Based Research: Pedagogy and Practices" for their annual meeting in 2014.

Eamonn Caffrey holds a BSc and MA in Business and Information Technology (IT). He was awarded a PhD by the University of Dublin. His doctoral thesis focused on roles of middle managers in aligning business and IT strategies in public organizations. He has extensive experience working with multinational corporations and small-medium enterprises, both in Ireland and internationally. Current interests include research, teaching, consulting, writing and publishing. Research foci are concerned with strategic IT alignment and business performance; corporate-level issues in relation to strategy and technology; and facilitating management teams to develop and execute IT strategy. This includes maximizing business value from IT investment, building an IT resource capability, and strengthening managerial strategic capability. Teaching interests can include strategy and technology; strategic management; digital business strategy; and organization and management. In terms of scientific conduct, process research is central to his work.

Tianxing Cai is a researcher in the Dan. F Smith Department of Chemical Engineering, Lamar University. Dr. Cai specializes in the research fields of modeling, simulation and optimization for industrial operation, process safety and environment protection. His major research is the development of optimization models (Linear Programming, Quadratic Constraint Programming, Nonlinear Programming, Mixed Integer Programming, Relaxed Mixed Integer Programming, Mixed Integer Quadratic Constraint Programming, Mixed Integer Nonlinear Programming, Relaxed Mixed Integer Quadratic Constraint Programming) to realize the synthesis of energy and water systems, manufacturing planning and scheduling and plant wide optimization. Besides that, he also involves the software application of Aspen, HYSYS, ProII, MATLAB, and gPROMS to conduct simulation and optimization for the process design, environment impact reduction, and safety assessment.

Brian Davis is Adjunct Professor of Information Systems at Trinity College Dublin, Ireland, where he lectures on both the Full-time and Part-time MBA courses. Previously, he has taught at other colleges in Ireland, including the Dublin Business School and the Irish Management Institute. He holds the Professional Exams of the British Computer Society, an MBA from Dublin City University and a PhD in Management Information Systems from Trinity College, Dublin. In addition, he operates as a management consultant specialising in the Utility and Financial Services sectors. His research, teaching and consulting focus on the management of large-scale change programs operating across complex systems of organisations, involving change enabled by modern technological systems. Prior to working with Trinity College, he spent almost two decades in industry, operating in a number of senior IT related management roles, including acting as Group CIO for ESB, Ireland's national electricity utility. In between researching, teaching, and consulting he devotes himself to his family and sporting interests including soccer and athletics. His professional Web page is available at http://www.tcd.ie/business/mba/structure/part-time/faculty/.

Brian Dempsey has over 30 years of experience in the Information and Communications Technology (ICT) sector in the areas of engineering, IT strategy, IT systems design and development, programme management, product design and development, enterprise sales management and business development, business transformation and change management, and related ICT consultancy services. He has been involved in the development of IT strategy for a large telecommunications organisation in Ireland and has provided consultancy services in the area of e-government in Africa. He has been involved in the design and development of a number of enterprise systems, including customised billing systems, enterprise IT architectures, network management systems, and intelligent network platforms, including state of the art IP infrastructure with value added services. He has been responsible for programme managing the rollout of a large number of integrated enterprise networks for a range of clients. He has also been involved in business development and sales management in the ICT industry for a number of years, and has led a number of business development and enterprise sales initiatives in highly competitive markets. During this time, he has also provided consultancy services in the areas of organisation transformation, new product development, business development strategy, and professional sales development. He currently specialises in the areas of business and technical strategy, systems integration planning and management, procurement and vendor management, project and programme management, business development and sales strategy, and related transformation programmes. He holds a BSc (Computer Science) and MA from Trinity College Dublin, and an MBA from the Open University. He is currently studying for a PhD at Trinity College Dublin, specialising in the role of senior management in large scale IT initiatives. His thesis is due for submission in September 2014.

Gulsun Eby is a professor in Distance Education at the College of Open Education of Anadolu University. Dr. Eby undertook graduate studies at Anadolu University, Turkey (MA Educational Technology) and the University of Cincinnati, USA (EdD Curriculum & Instruction), and also has worked a post-doctoral fellow at the College of Education at New Mexico State University, USA (2001-2002). Dr. Eby earned her BS degree in Computer Engineering from the College of Informatics Technologies and Engineering of Hoca Ahmet Yesevi International Turk-Kazakhstani University in the year 2012-2013. In addition, she is currently a graduate student in the Department of Computer and Instructional Technologies. Dr. Eby has over 27 years of experience in focusing on the egalitarian and ecological aspects of distance education; finding new answers, viewpoints, and explanations to online communication problems through critical pedagogy; and improving learner critical thinking skills through project-based online learning. She continues to manage and provide pedagogical support for distance learning programs.

M. Banu Gundogan is an instructor in Computer Education and Instructional Technology Department of Middle East Technical University. As an Industrial Design graduate, she started her career working on hands on science exhibits and managed Turkey's first science centre, Feza Gürsey Science Centre project in Ankara. Working on the development, implementation and management of instructional design projects regarding interactive science education, she has developed "bilimce" (science language) project and managed science school-science camp projects. While transferring "bilimce" activities to the Web, she started studying distance education and is continuing her studies focusing on the ecology and sustainability issues regarding open and distance learning.

Mohanad Halaweh is an Assistant Professor in the College of Information Technology (CIT) at the University of Dubai (UD). Before joining UD in 2009, he taught in De Montfort University, UK. Dr. Halaweh is very active in research. He has published more than 20 articles at international journals and conferences such as the *Journal of Information Technology Theory and Application* (ranked A in the ABDC rating list), *Journal of Information Technology Management, Journal of Information Systems and Technology Management, Electronic Journal of Information Systems in Developing Countries*, and many others. He has also published and participated in many international conferences in Information Systems (IS) field such as ICIS, AMCIS, and ACIS; a top-tier conferences in IS research (ranked A according to the ERA rating). He received a Best Paper Award presented at 8th International Multidisciplinary Conference on e-Commerce and e-Government, October 2008, Poland. He also received the Excellence Research Award for the college of IT for 2011/2012 academic year. He is the founding Editor-in-Chief for the *International Journal of Qualitative Information Systems Research*. He also served as a program committee member and reviewer for several international journals and conferences, and acted as external examiner for PhD thesis. He also supervised MS theses. Dr Halaweh taught several courses in college of IT such as management information systems, programming, Web design, human computer interface, and systems analysis and design. His research focus is on e-commerce, security and privacy issues in e-commerce, IT acceptance and adoption, business value of IT, IT/IS Impact, and IS research methods.

Sara Steffes Hansen, PhD (University of Wisconsin), MBA (University of Colorado – Denver), is an assistant professor of strategic communication in the Department of Journalism at the University of Wisconsin Oshkosh. She teaches advertising, public relations, and new media courses for the Department of Journalism and the College of Business' Interactive Web Management degree. Her research focuses on strategic communication in interactive media, with emphasis on consumer engagement with marketing campaigns via social media. Her research has appeared in several journals and books, including *Journal of Marketing Communications, Journal of Interactive Advertising,* and *Journal of Marketing Management.* She previously worked as a manager, director, and consultant in public relations and marketing for Fortune 500 and high-tech companies, including Kinder Morgan, Inc., CIBER, Inc., and J.D. Edwards (now part of Oracle Corp.).

Tabitha Hart is an Assistant Professor in the Department of Communication Studies at San Jose State University. She has a PhD in Communication from the University of Washington, an MA in Communication Studies from California State University Sacramento, and a BA in Communication from the University of California San Diego. Her research foci are applied strategic communication in online and offline organizational environments, cultural communication, and customer service communication. Her most recent research deals with intercultural (United States-China) service communication in a virtual language-learning community. One of her favorite past projects was analyzing baristas' perceptions of the appropriateness and effectiveness of the customer service protocols used at Starbucks cafes in Berlin, Germany. She currently directs her department's internship program and is developing a study abroad opportunity to take American college students to Berlin. You can learn more about her work by visiting http://tabithahart.net/.

Theodora Issa is an award winning Senior Lecturer at the Curtin Business School, Curtin University, Australia. Her research interests include teaching and learning, ethical mindsets, spirituality, aesthetic judgment, ethical-global mindsets, cloud computing, sustainable development, business strategy, social media and Church history and Syriac Genocide. Theodora is a member of the Central Committee of the World Council of Churches (WCC), and in July 2014 has been appointed a member of the Education and Ecumenical Formation (EEF) of the WCC representing the Syriac Orthodox Patriarchate. Theodora is a member in several academic bodies, such as the Australian and New Zealand Academy of Management (ANZAM), American Academy of Management (AOM). Theodora has several publications in peer-reviewed journals and books. Theodora has co-authored and co-edited books on moral issues, ethics and corporate social responsibility. Theodora authored and co-authored book chapters on spirituality, ethical mindsets, and the influence of Christianity on society and ethical practices, a Syriac (Aramaic) perspective. Theodora co-authored, and co-edited books on Moral Issues, Ethics and Growth and Corporate Social Responsibility and Empowerment. Theodora acts as a reviewer to conference papers and peer-reviewed journal articles for different journals as such Journal of Business Ethics, AOM and ANZAM conferences. Theodora is currently working on a new book on ethical mindsets. Theodora is a co-editor of the weekly bulletin THE LIGHT (NOOHRO) since 1995.

Taghreed Justinia is an Assistant Professor of Health Informatics having obtained a PhD in Health Informatics and an MSc in Healthcare Management from Swansea University, UK where she is also Honorary Lecturer. She is Regional Director Information Technology Services and Health Informatics at King Saud bin Abdulaziz University for Health Sciences (KSAU-HS) in Saudi Arabia. Dr. Justinia's work background and experience are in the IT Executive Management and Health Informatics fields, and she has led several IT transformation projects throughout her career. She has a special interest in IT leadership, organisational behaviour, medical informatics, change management, and the socio-technical aspects of technological change. This is in addition to her academic role in undergraduate and post-graduate programs teaching Health Informatics, Leadership/Management and Research courses. She is also a devout qualitative researcher and has developed an original qualitative data analysis framework.

Jessica Nina Lester is an Assistant Professor in Inquiry Methodology at Indiana University and holds a PhD in Educational Psychology and Research. She teaches research methods courses, including a course focused on the use of digital tools in qualitative research. She has published journal articles in the areas of qualitative methodologies, disability studies, discourse studies, and refugee studies. She recently co-edited a book focused on performance ethnography and schooling practices and co-authored a book focused on digital tools and qualitative research.

Joe McDonagh is an Associate Professor of Business at the School of Business, Trinity College Dublin, Ireland where he also serves as Director of Doctoral Studies. He teaches at Trinity College, the Irish Management Institute and a number of international business schools. He holds a BSc in Computer Science and MA from the University of Dublin, an MBS in Management and Information Systems from the National University of Ireland, and a PhD in Organization Development and Change from the University of Warwick. He also holds CITP and FBCS qualifications. His research, teaching and consulting focus on the process of leading large-scale change across complex systems of organisations, particularly change enabled by modern technological systems. He has extensive international experience and advises executive and technology leaders in governments and large corporations on the effective integration of both organisational and technological change. Some recent government assignments include Ireland, United Kingdom, United States of America, and the United Nations while corporate assignments include large private sector organisations. He is a regular conference speaker and contributor to the media whilst also publishing widely on the dynamics of large-scale change. Research output has appeared in a wide range of conference papers, book chapters, journal articles, and government reports. Specific journals include *Administration*, *Irish Journal of Management*, *Organization Development Journal*, *Public Administration Quarterly*, and *Strategic Change*. Prior to joining Trinity College, he spent almost two decades in industry in a number of management and consulting roles with Continental, Imperial Chemical Industries, Philips, and Price Waterhouse. In between researching, teaching, and consulting he devotes himself to hiking, biking and fundraising for Dublin's homeless. He lives in Dublin with his wife, Majella, and two sons, Colin and Sean.

Kimberly Nehls has served as the Executive Director of the Association for the Study of Higher Education (ASHE) since 2008. Additionally, Kim teaches classes for both the educational psychology and higher education programs at UNLV. Kim enjoys conducting research on fundraising for colleges and universities, as well as student engagement through social media. Kim earned a PhD in higher education administration and a Master's degree in communication from UNLV and bachelor's degrees in political science and speech communication from University of Illinois.

Oksana Parylo received her MS in Curriculum and Instruction from the Southern Illinois University Carbondale, USA, and an interdisciplinary qualitative studies certificate and a PhD in Educational Administration and Policy from the University of Georgia, Athens, USA. While working for five years on her PhD, Oksana was a research and teaching assistant at the University of Georgia. During this time, she was a part of a research team working on several research projects on educational leadership. Dr. Parylo's doctoral research focused on preparation, professional development, instructional supervision, coaching, and evaluation of teachers and leaders. Dr. Parylo received several awards and recognitions including the Fulbright scholarship (2005-2007) and the 2011-2012 Global Supplementary Grant from the Open Society Foundations and Scholarship Programs (New York, NY). From January 2013, Dr. Parylo is a research associate in the Methodology of Educational Sciences Research Group at KU Leuven - Katholieke Universiteit Leuven, Belgium. Her current research interests include qualitative meta-synthesis and qualitative and mixed methodologies. Dr. Parylo's career goals include methodological inquiry into research methods used in the humanities and social sciences. In particular, she is interested in examining various ways of combining different research frameworks to achieve the most comprehensive results.

David Pick is an Associate Professor in Management at Curtin University. He gained his in PhD in 2002. Recent research interests include exploring theoretical and methodological issues in Management and Organization studies and undertaking empirical research into public sector management, paying particular attention to the effects of change. He has been published in *The Journal of Business Ethics, Society and Business Review,* and *Higher Education Quarterly*. He also has recent papers at *The Academy of Management Conference* and *The British Academy of Management Conference.*

Holly A. Schneider is a PhD candidate in the Department of Educational Psychology and Higher Education at the University of Nevada, Las Vegas. She also serves as a graduate assistant for the Association for the Study of Higher Education. Her research focuses on doctoral students' perceptions of mattering to advisers, first-generation graduate student experiences, and technology in qualitative research. Holly holds a bachelor's degree in Kinesiology from California State University, San Bernardino, an MS in Sport Pedagogy from the University of Nevada, Las Vegas, and anticipates graduating with her PhD in Higher Education from the University of Nevada, Las Vegas in the 2014-2015 academic year.

Brandy D. Smith, PhD, is a post-doctoral scholar for the Association for the Study of Higher Education. Her research focuses on the use of technology in qualitative research, the diffusion of change within higher education systems, and service culture within higher education. Brandy holds a bachelor's degree in business management, an MBA, and a PhD in higher educational leadership from the University of Nevada, Las Vegas.

Nancy J. Smith, EdD, joined the Department of Educational Leadership Curriculum and Instruction at Texas A&M University – Corpus Christi in the Fall 2013 as qualitative research methodologist. She holds an EdD in Educational Leadership from Texas A&M University – Corpus Christi and an MA in Learning Technology from Pepperdine University. Dr. Smith holds a Colorado Professional Teaching License and has recently worked with the TAMUCC ELITE Graduate Program assisting doctoral students in completion of their writing process in qualitative dissertations. Her interest in learning technologies began in the mid-90s, and in 2001, she was awarded a research grant from Palm, Inc. and became a Palm Education Pioneer. In 2002, she received training from the Bill and Melinda Gates Foundation in adult learning and teacher training and became an LEA and trainer for the Intel Teach to the Future project, through which she trained over 300 teachers in effective integration of classroom technology. Before coming to Corpus Christi, she was a facilitator of the K-12 gifted and talented program and middle school technology for the Montrose County School District in Montrose, Colorado. She was active in the NASA Student Involvement Program, the University of Colorado's Science Explorers, and the Denver Museum of Natural History's Meteorite Tracking project; through these partnerships, her students won numerous awards and recognitions from NASA for their innovative earth and space science research projects. She has taught graduate research courses and technology innovation face-to-face and online. Dr. Smith's research interests are in technology integration, gifted and exceptional learners, qualitative and inductively driven mixed methods, and doctoral student retention and achievement. One of her favorite things about Texas A&M University – Corpus Christi is the beautiful island campus and the feral cat population, which the university supports through TNR.

T. Volkan Yuzer, Ph.D, is a professor in Distance Education at the College of Open Education, Anadolu University. He undertook graduate studies at Anadolu University, Turkey. His research interests are new communication technologies, synchronous, asynchronous and interactive communications and transformative learning milieus in distance and online education. He has over seventeen years experience in exploring additional distance learning media and providing communication and technological support for distance learning programs as well as developing online learning courses. He has participated in projects related to distance learning, online synchronous learning, and virtual classroom. He has been teaching courses in distance learning, communication and information technologies.

638

Index

CPSIA information can be obtained at www.ICGtesting.com
Printed in the USA
BVOW06*0527281014

372292BV00006B/59/P